THE

MISCELLANEOUS WORKS

OF

THE RIGHT HONOURABLE

SIR JAMES MACKINTOSH

THREE VOLUMES,

COMPLETE IN ONE

PHILADELPHIA:
A. HART, LATE CAREY & HART,
No. 126 CHESTNUT STREET.
1850.

Printed by T. K. & P. G. Collins.

ADVERTISEMENT TO THE LONDON EDITION,

BY THE EDITOR.

These Volumes* contain whatever (with the exception of his History of England) is believed to be of the most value in the writings of Sir James Mackintosh. Something of method, it will be observed, has been attempted in their arrangement by commencing with what is more purely Philosophical, and proceeding through Literature to Politics; each of those heads being generally, though not quite precisely, referable to each volume respectively. With such selection would naturally have terminated his responsibility; but in committing again to the press matter originally for the most part hastily printed, the Editor has assumed—as the lesser of two evils—a larger exercise of discretion in the revision of the text than he could have wished to have felt had been imposed upon him. Instead, therefore, of continually arresting the eye of the reader by a notification of almost mechanical alterations, he has to premise here that where inaccuracies and redundancies of expression were obvious, these have been throughout corrected and retrenched. A few transpositions of the text have also been made;—as where, by the detachment of the eleventh chapter of what the present Editor, on its original publication allowed to be called, perhaps too largely, the "History of the Revolution of 1688," a stricter chronological order has been observed, at the same time that the residue—losing thereby much of its fragmentary character—may now, it is hoped, fairly claim to be all that is assumed in its new designation. Of the contributions to periodical publications, such portions only find place here as partake most largely of the character of completeness. Some extended quotations, appearing for the most part as notes on former occasions, have been omitted, with a view to brevity, on the present; while, in addition to a general verification of the Author's references, a few explanatory notes have been appended, wherever apparently needful, by the Editor.

R. J. MACKINTOSH.

---

* The Miscellaneous Works of the Right Honourable Sir James Mackintosh, 3 vols. 8vo., London: Longman, Brown, Green, and Longman, 1846.

CONTENTS.

ON THE

PHILOSOPHICAL GENIUS

OF

LORD BACON AND MR. LOCKE.*

"History," says Lord Bacon, "is Natural, Civil or Ecclesiastical, or Literary; whereof of the three first I allow as extant, *the fourth I note as deficient*. For no man hath propounded to himself the general state of learning, to be described and represented from age to age, as many have done the works of Nature, and the State civil and ecclesiastical; without which the history of the world seemeth to me to be as the statue of Polyphemus with his eye out; that part being wanting which doth most show the spirit and life of the person. And yet I am not ignorant, that in divers particular sciences, as of the jurisconsults, the mathematicians, the rhetoricians, the philosophers, there are set down some small memorials of the schools,—of authors of books; so likewise some barren relations touching the invention of arts or usages. But a just story of learning, containing the antiquities and originals of knowledges, and their sects, their inventions, their traditions, their divers administrations and managings, their oppositions, decays, depressions, oblivions, removes, with the causes and occasions of them, and all other events concerning learning throughout the ages of the world, I may truly affirm to be wanting. The use and end of which work I do not so much design for curiosity, or satisfaction of those who are lovers of learning, but chiefly for a more serious and grave purpose, which is this, in few words, '*that it will make learned men wise in the use and administration of learning.*'"†

Though there are passages in the writings of Lord Bacon more splendid than the above, few, probably, better display the union of all the qualities which characterized his philosophical genius. He has in general inspired a fervour of admiration which vents itself in indiscriminate praise, and is very adverse to a calm examination of the character of his understanding, which was very peculiar, and on that account described with more than ordinary imperfection, by that unfortunately vague and weak part of language which attempts to distinguish the varieties of mental superiority. To this cause it may be ascribed, that perhaps no great man has been either more ignorantly censured, or more uninstructively commended. It is easy to describe his transcendent merit in general terms of commendation; for some of his great qualities lie on the surface of his writings. But that in which he most excelled all other men, was the range and compass of his intellectual view and the power of contemplating many and distant objects together without indistinctness or confusion, which he himself has called the "discursive" or "comprehensive" understanding. This wide ranging intellect was illuminated by the brightest Fancy that ever contented itself with the office of only ministering to Reason: and from this singular relation of the two grand faculties of man, it has resulted, that his philosophy, though illustrated still more than adorned by the utmost splendour of imagery, continues still subject to the undivided supremacy of Intellect. In the midst of all the prodigality of an imagination which, had it been independent, would have been poetical, his opinions remained severely rational.

It is not so easy to conceive, or at least to describe, other equally essential elements of his greatness, and conditions of his success. His is probably a single instance of a mind which, in philosophizing, always reaches the point of elevation whence the whole prospect is commanded, without ever rising to such a distance as to lose a distinct perception of every part of it.* It is perhaps not less singu-

---

* These remarks are extracted from the Edinburgh Review, vol. xxvii. p. 180; vol. xxxvi. p. 229.—Ed.

† Advancement of Learning, book ii.

* He himself who alone was qualified, has described the genius of his philosophy both in respect to the degree and manner in which he rose from particulars to generals: "Axiomata infima non multum ab experientiâ nudâ discrepant. Suprema vero illa et generalissima (quæ habentur) notionalia sunt et abstracta, et nil habent solidi. At media sunt axiomata illa vera, et solida, et viva, in quibus humanæ res et fortunæ sitæ sunt, et supra hæc quoque, *tandem* ipsa illa generalissima, talia scilicet quæ non abstracta sint, sed per hæc media verè limitantur."—Novum Organum, lib. i. aphoris. 104.

lar, that his philosophy should be founded at once on disregard for the authority of men, and on reverence for the boundaries prescribed by Nature to human inquiry; that he who thought so little of what man had done, hoped so highly of what he could do; that so daring an innovator in science should be so wholly exempt from the love of singularity or paradox; and that the same man who renounced imaginary provinces in the empire of science, and withdrew its landmarks within the limits of experience, should also exhort posterity to push their conquests to its utmost verge, with a boldness which will be fully justified only by the discoveries of ages from which we are yet far distant.

No man ever united a more poetical style to a less poetical philosophy. One great end of his discipline is to prevent mysticism and fanaticism from obstructing the pursuit of truth. With a less brilliant fancy, he would have had a mind less qualified for philosophical inquiry. His fancy gave him that power of illustrative metaphor, by which he seemed to have invented again the part of language which respects philosophy; and it rendered new truths more distinctly visible even to his own eye, in their bright clothing of imagery. Without it, he must, like others, have been driven to the fabrication of uncouth technical terms, which repel the mind, either by vulgarity or pedantry, instead of gently leading it to novelties in science, through agreeable analogies with objects already familiar. A considerable portion doubtless of the courage with which he undertook the reformation of philosophy, was caught from the general spirit of his extraordinary age, when the mind of Europe was yet agitated by the joy and pride of emancipation from long bondage. The beautiful mythology, and the poetical history of the ancient world,—not yet become trivial or pedantic,—appeared before his eyes in all their freshness and lustre. To the general reader they were then a discovery as recent as the world disclosed by Columbus. The ancient literature, on which his imagination looked back for illustration, had then as much the charm of novelty as that rising philosophy through which his reason dared to look onward to some of the last periods in its unceasing and resistless course.

In order to form a just estimate of this wonderful person, it is essential to fix steadily in our minds, what he was not,—what he did not do,—and what he professed neither to be, nor to do. He was not what is called a metaphysician: his plans for the improvement of science were not inferred by abstract reasoning from any of those primary principles to which the philosophers of Greece struggled to fasten their systems. Hence he has been treated as empirical and superficial by those who take to themselves the exclusive name of profound speculators. He was not, on the other hand, a mathematician, an astronomer, a physiologist, a chemist. He was not eminently conversant with the particular truths of any of those sciences which existed in his time. For this reason, he was underrated even by men themselves of the highest merit, and by some who had acquired the most just reputation, by adding new facts to the stock of certain knowledge. It is not therefore very surprising to find, that Harvey, "though the friend as well as physician of Bacon, though he esteemed him much for his wit and style, would not allow him to be a great philosopher;" but said to Aubrey, "He writes philosophy like a Lord Chancellor,"—"in derision,"—as the honest biographer thinks fit expressly to add. On the same ground, though in a manner not so agreeable to the nature of his own claims on reputation, Mr. Hume has decided, that Bacon was not so great a man as Galileo, because he was not so great an astronomer. The same sort of injustice to his memory has been more often committed than avowed, by professors of the exact and the experimental sciences, who are accustomed to regard, as the sole test of service to Knowledge, a palpable addition to her store. It is very true that he made no discoveries: but his life was employed in teaching the method by which discoveries are made. This distinction was early observed by that ingenious poet and amiable man, on whom we, by our unmerited neglect, have taken too severe a revenge, for the exaggerated praises bestowed on him by our ancestors:—

"Bacon, like Moses, led us forth at last,
The barren wilderness he past,
Did on the very border stand
Of the blest promised land;
And from the mountain top of his exalted wit,
Saw it himself, and showed us it."*

The writings of Bacon do not even abound with remarks so capable of being separated from the mass of previous knowledge and reflection, that they can be called new. This at least is very far from their greatest distinction: and where such remarks occur, they are presented more often as examples of his general method, than as important on their own separate account. In physics, which presented the principal field for discovery, and which owe all that they are, or can be, to his method and spirit, the experiments and observations which he either made or registered, form the least valuable part of his writings, and have furnished some cultivators of that science with an opportunity for an ungrateful triumph over his mistakes. The scattered remarks, on the other hand, of a moral nature, where absolute novelty is precluded by the nature of the subject, manifest most strongly both the superior force and the original bent of his understanding. We more properly contrast than compare the experiments in the Natural History, with the moral and political observations which enrich the Advancement of Learning, the speeches, the letters, the History of Henry VII., and, above all, the Essays, a book which, though it has been praised with equal

* Cowley, Ode to the Royal Society.

fervour by Voltaire, Johnson and Burke, has never been characterized with such exact justice and such exquisite felicity of expression, as in the discourse of Mr. Stewart.* It will serve still more distinctly to mark the natural tendency of his mind, to observe that his moral and political reflections relate to these practical subjects, considered in their most practical point of view; and that he has seldom or never attempted to reduce to theory the infinite particulars of that "civil knowledge," which, as he himself tells us, is, "of all others, most immersed in matter, and hardliest reduced to axiom."

His mind, indeed, was formed and exercised in the affairs of the world: his genius was eminently civil. His understanding was peculiarly fitted for questions of legislation and of policy; though his character was not an instrument well qualified to execute the dictates of his reason. The same civil wisdom which distinguishes his judgments on human affairs, may also be traced through his reformation of philosophy. It is a practical judgment applied to science. What he effected was reform in the maxims of state, —a reform which had always before been unsuccessfully pursued in the republic of letters. It is not derived from metaphysical reasoning, nor from scientific detail, but from a species of intellectual prudence, which, on the practical ground of failure and disappointment in the prevalent modes of pursuing knowledge, builds the necessity of alteration, and inculcates the advantage of administering the sciences on other principles. It is an error to represent him either as imputing fallacy to the syllogistic method, or as professing his principle of induction to be a discovery. The rules and forms of argument will always form an important part of the art of logic; and the method of induction, which is the art of discovery, was so far from being unknown to Aristotle, that it was often faithfully pursued by that great observer. What Bacon aimed at, he accomplished; which was, not to discover new principles, but to excite a new spirit, and to render observation and experiment the predominant characteristics of philosophy. It is for this reason that Bacon could not have been the author of a system or the founder of a sect. He did not deliver opinions; he taught modes of philosophizing. His early immersion in civil affairs fitted him for this species of scientific reformation. His political course, though in itself unhappy, probably conduced to the success, and certainly influenced the character, of the contemplative part of his life. Had it not been for his active habits, it is likely that the pedantry and quaintness of his age would have still more deeply corrupted his significant and majestic style. The force of the illustrations which he takes from his experience of ordinary life, is often as remarkable as the beauty of those which he so happily borrows from his study of antiquity. But if we have caught the leading principle of his intellectual character, we must attribute effects still deeper and more extensive, to his familiarity with the active world. It guarded him against vain subtlety, and against all speculation that was either visionary or fruitless. It preserved him from the reigning prejudices of contemplative men, and from undue preference to particular parts of knowledge. If he had been exclusively bred in the cloister or the schools, he might not have had courage enough to reform their abuses. It seems necessary that he should have been so placed as to look on science in the free spirit of an intelligent spectator. Without the pride of professors, or the bigotry of their followers, he surveyed from the world the studies which reigned in the schools; and, trying them by their fruits, he saw that they were barren, and therefore pronounced that they were unsound. He himself seems, indeed, to have indicated as clearly as modesty would allow, in a case that concerned himself, and where he departed from an universal and almost natural sentiment, that he regarded scholastic seclusion, then more unsocial and rigorous than it now can be, as a hindrance in the pursuit of knowledge. In one of the noblest passages of his writings, the conclusion "of the Interpretation of Nature," he tells us, "That there is no composition of estate or society, nor order or quality of persons, which have not some point of contrariety towards true knowledge; that monarchies incline wits to profit and pleasure; commonwealths to glory and vanity; universities to sophistry and affectation; cloisters to fables and unprofitable subtlety; study at large to variety; and that it is hard to say whether mixture of contemplations with an active life, or retiring wholly to contemplations, do disable or hinder the mind more."

But, though he was thus free from the prejudices of a science, a school or a sect, other prejudices of a lower nature, and belonging only to the inferior class of those who conduct civil affairs, have been ascribed to him by encomiasts as well as by opponents. He has been said to consider the great end of science to be the increase of the outward accommodations and enjoyments of human life: we cannot see any foundation for this charge. In labouring, indeed, to correct the direction of study, and to withdraw it from these unprofitable subtleties, it was neces-

* "Under the same head of Ethics, may be mentioned the small volume to which he has given the title of 'Essays,'—the best known and most popular of all his works. It is also one of those where the superiority of his genius appears to the greatest advantage; *the novelty and depth of his reflections often receiving a strong relief from the triteness of the subject.* It may be read from beginning to end in a few hours; and yet, after the twentieth perusal, one seldom fails to remark in it something unobserved before. This, indeed, is a characteristic of all Bacon's writings, and is only to be accounted for *by the inexhaustible aliment they furnish to our own thoughts, and the sympathetic activity they impart to our torpid faculties.*" Encyclopædia Britannica, vol. i. p. 36.

sary to attract it powerfully towards outward acts and works. He no doubt duly valued "the dignity of this end, the endowment of man's life with new commodities;" and he strikingly observes, that the most poetical people of the world had admitted the inventors of the useful and manual arts among the highest beings in their beautiful mythology. Had he lived to the age of Watt and Davy, he would not have been of the vulgar and contracted mind of those who cease to admire grand exertions of intellect, because they are useful to mankind: but he would certainly have considered their great works rather as tests of the progress of knowledge than as parts of its highest end. His important questions to the doctors of his time were:—"Is truth ever barren? Are we the richer by one poor invention, by reason of all the learning that hath been these many hundred years?" His judgment, we may also hear from himself:—"Francis Bacon thought in this manner. The knowledge whereof the world is now possessed, especially that of nature, extendeth not to *magnitude and certainty of works.*" He found knowledge barren; he left it fertile. He did not underrate the utility of particular inventions; but it is evident that he valued them most, as being themselves among the highest exertions of superior intellect,—as being monuments of the progress of knowledge,—as being the bands of that alliance between action and speculation, wherefrom spring an appeal to experience and utility, checking the proneness of the philosopher to extreme refinements; while teaching men to revere, and exciting them to pursue science by these splendid proofs of its beneficial power. Had he seen the change in this respect, which, produced chiefly in his own country by the spirit of his philosophy, has made some degree of science almost necessary to the subsistence and fortune of large bodies of men, he would assuredly have regarded it as an additional security for the future growth of the human understanding. He taught, as he tells us, the means, not of the "amplification of the power of one man over his country, nor of the amplification of the power of that country over other nations; but the amplification of the power and kingdom of mankind over the world,"—"a restitution of man to the sovereignty of nature,"*—"and the enlarging the bounds of human empire to the effecting all things possible."†—From the enlargement of reason, he did not separate the growth of virtue, for he thought that "truth and goodness were one, differing but as the seal and the print; for truth prints goodness."‡

As civil history teaches statesmen to profit by the faults of their predecessors, he proposes that the history of philosophy should teach, by example, "learned men to become wise in the administration of learning." Early immersed in civil affairs, and deeply imbued with their spirit, his mind in this place contemplates science only through the analogy of government, and considers principles of philosophizing as the easiest maxims of policy for the guidance of reason. It seems also, that in describing the objects of a history of philosophy, and the utility to be derived from it, he discloses the principle of his own exertions in behalf of knowledge;—whereby a reform in its method and maxims, justified by the experience of their injurious effects, is conducted with a judgment analogous to that civil prudence which guides a wise lawgiver. If (as may not improperly be concluded from this passage) the reformation of science was suggested to Lord Bacon, by a review of the history of philosophy, it must be owned, that his outline of that history has a very important relation to the general character of his philosophical genius. The smallest circumstances attendant on that outline serve to illustrate the powers and habits of thought which distinguished its author. It is an example of his faculty of anticipating, —not insulated facts or single discoveries,—but (what from its complexity and refinement seem much more to defy the power of prophecy) the tendencies of study, and the modes of thinking, which were to prevail in distant generations, that the parts which he had chosen to unfold or enforce in the Latin versions, are those which a thinker of the present age would deem both most excellent and most arduous in a history of philosophy; —"the causes of literary revolutions; the study of contemporary writers, not merely as the most authentic sources of information, but as enabling the historian to preserve in his own description the peculiar colour of every age, and to recall its literary genius from the dead." This outline has the uncommon distinction of being at once original and complete. In this province, Bacon had no forerunner; and the most successful follower will be he, who most faithfully observes his precepts.

Here, as in every province of knowledge, he concludes his review of the performances and prospects of the human understanding, by considering their subservience to the grand purpose of improving the condition, the faculties, and the nature of man, without which indeed science would be no more than a beautiful ornament, and literature would rank no higher than a liberal amusement. Yet it must be acknowledged, that he rather perceived than felt the connexion of Truth and Good. Whether he lived too early to have sufficient experience of the moral benefit of civilization, or his mind had early acquired too exclusive an interest in science, to look frequently beyond its advancement; or whether the infirmities and calamities of his life had blighted his feelings, and turned away his eyes from the active world;—to whatever cause we may ascribe the defect, certain it is, that his works want one excellence

* Of the Interpretation of Nature.
† New Atlantis.
‡ Advancement of Learning, book i.

of the highest kind, which they would have possessed if he had habitually represented the advancement of knowledge as the most effectual means of realizing the hopes of Benevolence for the human race.

The character of Mr. Locke's writings cannot be well understood, without considering the circumstances of the writer. Educated among the English Dissenters, during the short period of their political ascendency, he early imbibed the deep piety and ardent spirit of liberty which actuated that body of men; and he probably imbibed also, in their schools, the disposition to metaphysical inquiries which has every where accompanied the Calvinistic theology. Sects, founded on the right of private judgment, naturally tend to purify themselves from intolerance, and in time learn to respect, in others, the freedom of thought, to the exercise of which they owe their own existence. By the Independent divines who were his instructors, our philosopher was taught those principles of religious liberty which they were the first to disclose to the world.* When free inquiry led him to milder dogmas, he retained the severe morality which was their honourable singularity, and which continues to distinguish their successors in those communities which have abandoned their rigorous opinions. His professional pursuits afterwards engaged him in the study of the physical sciences, at the moment when the spirit of experiment and observation was in its youthful fervour, and when a repugnance to scholastic subtleties was the ruling passion of the scientific world. At a more mature age, he was admitted into the society of great wits and ambitious politicians. During the remainder of his life, he was often a man of business, and always a man of the world, without much undisturbed leisure, and probably with that abated relish for merely abstract speculation, which is the inevitable result of converse with society and experience in affairs. But his political connexions agreeing with his early bias, made him a zealous advocate of liberty in opinion and in government; and he gradually limited his zeal and activity to the illustration of such general principles as are the guardians of these great interests of human society.

Almost all his writings (even his Essay itself) were occasional, and intended directly to counteract the enemies of reason and freedom in his own age. The first Letter on Toleration, the most original perhaps of his works, was composed in Holland, in a retirement where he was forced to conceal himself from the tyranny which pursued him into a foreign land; and it was published in England, in the year of the Revolution, to vindicate the Toleration Act, of which he lamented the imperfection.*

His Treatise on Government is composed of three parts, of different character, and very unequal merit. The confutation of Sir Robert Filmer, with which it opens, has long lost all interest, and is now to be considered as an instance of the hard fate of a philosopher who is compelled to engage in a conflict with those ignoble antagonists who acquire a momentary importance by the defence of pernicious falsehoods. The same slavish absurdities have indeed been at various times revived: but they never have assumed, and probably never will again assume, the form in which they were exhibited by Filmer. Mr. Locke's general principles of government were adopted by him, probably without much examination, as the doctrine which had for ages prevailed in the schools of Europe, and which afforded an obvious and adequate justification of a resistance to oppression. He delivers them as he found them, without even appearing to have made them his own by new modifications. The opinion, that the right of the magistrate to obedience is founded in the original delegation of power by the people to the government, is at least as old as the writings of Thomas Aquinas:† and in the beginning of the seventeenth century, it was regarded as the common doctrine of all the divines, jurists and philosophers, who had at that time examined the moral foundation of political authority.‡ It then prevailed indeed so universally,

* Orme's Memoirs of Dr. Owen, pp. 99—110. In this very able volume, it is clearly proved that the Independents were the first teachers of religious liberty. The industrious, ingenious, and tolerant writer, is unjust to Jeremy Taylor, who had no share (as Mr. Orme supposes) in the persecuting councils of Charles II. It is an important fact in the history of Toleration, that Dr. Owen, the Independent, was Dean of Christchurch in 1651, when Locke was admitted a member of that College, "*under a fanatical tutor*," as Antony Wood says.

* "We have need," says he, "of more generous remedies than have yet been used in our distempers. It is neither declarations of indulgence, nor acts of comprehension such as have yet been practised or projected amongst us, that can do the work among us. Absolute liberty, just and true liberty, equal and impartial liberty, is the thing that we stand in need of. Now, though this has indeed been much talked of, I doubt it has not been much understood,—I am sure not at all practised, either by our governors towards the people in general, or by any dissenting parties of the people towards one another." How far are we, at this moment [1821], from adopting these admirable principles! and with what absurd confidence do the enemies of religious liberty appeal to the authority of Mr. Locke for continuing those restrictions on conscience which he so deeply lamented!

† "Non cujuslibet ratio facit legem, sed multitudinis, aut *principis, vicem multitudinis gerentis.*" —Summa Theologiæ, pars i. quæst 90.

‡ "Opinionem jam factam communem omnium Scholasticorum." Antonio de Dominis, De Republicâ Ecclesiasticâ, lib. vi. cap. 2. Antonio de Dominis, Archbishop of Spalato in Dalmatia, having imbibed the free spirit of Father Paul, inclined towards Protestantism, or at least towards such reciprocal concessions as might reunite the churches of the West. During Sir Henry Wotton's remarkable embassy at Venice, he was persuaded to go to England, where he was made Dean of Windsor. Finding, perhaps, the Protest-

that it was assumed by Hobbes as the basis of his system of universal servitude. The divine right of kingly government was a principle very little known, till it was inculcated in the writings of English court divines after the accession of the Stuarts. The purpose of Mr. Locke's work did not lead him to inquire more anxiously into the solidity of these universally received principles; nor were there at the time any circumstances, in the condition of the country, which could suggest to his mind the necessity of qualifying their application. His object, as he says himself, was "to establish the throne of our great Restorer, our present King William; to make good his title in the consent of the people, which, being the only one of all lawful governments, he has more fully and clearly than any prince in Christendom; and to justify to the world the people of England, whose love of their just and natural rights, with their resolution to preserve them, saved the nation when it was on the very brink of slavery and ruin." It was essential to his purpose to be exact in his more particular observations: that part of his work is, accordingly, remarkable for general caution, and every where bears marks of his own considerate mind. By calling William "a Restorer," he clearly points out the characteristic principle of the Revolution; and sufficiently shows that he did not consider it as intended to introduce novelties, but to defend or recover the ancient laws and liberties of the kingdom. In enumerating cases which justify resistance, he confines himself, almost as cautiously as the Bill of Rights, to the grievances actually suffered under the late reign: and where he distinguishes between a dissolution of government and a dissolution of society, it is manifestly his object to guard against those inferences which would have rendered the Revolution a source of anarchy, instead of being the parent of order and security. In one instance only, that of taxation, where he may be thought to have introduced subtle and doubtful speculations into a matter altogether practical, his purpose was to discover an immovable foundation for that ancient principle of rendering the government dependent on the representatives of the people for pecuniary supply, which first established the English Constitution; which improved and strengthened it in a course of ages; and which, at the Revolution, finally triumphed over the conspiracy of the Stuart princes. If he be ever mistaken in his premises, his conclusions at least are, in this part of his work, equally just, generous, and prudent. Whatever charge of haste or inaccuracy may be brought against his abstract principles, he thoroughly weighs, and maturely considers the practical results. Those who consider his moderate plan of Parliamentary Reform as at variance with his theory of government, may perceive, even in this repugnance, whether real or apparent, a new indication of those dispositions which exposed him rather to the reproach of being an inconsistent reasoner, than to that of being a dangerous politician. In such works, however, the nature of the subject has, in some degree, obliged most men of sense to treat it with considerable regard to consequences; though there are memorable and unfortunate examples of an opposite tendency.

The metaphysical object of the Essay on Human Understanding, therefore, illustrates the natural bent of the author's genius more forcibly than those writings which are connected with the business and interests of men. The reasonable admirers of Mr. Locke would have pardoned Mr. Stewart, if he had pronounced more decisively, that the first book of that work is inferior to the others; and we have satisfactory proof that it was so considered by the author himself, who, in the abridgment of the Essay which he published in Leclerc's Review, omits it altogether, as intended only to obviate the prejudices of some philosophers against the more important contents of his work.* It must be owned, that the very terms "innate ideas" and "innate principles," together with the division of the latter into "speculative and practical," are not only vague, but equivocal; that they are capable of different senses; and that they are not always employed in the same sense throughout this discussion. Nay, it will be found very difficult, after the most careful perusal of Mr. Locke's first book, to state the question in dispute clearly and shortly, in language so strictly philosophical as to be free from any hypothesis. As the antagonists chiefly contemplated by Mr. Locke were the followers of Descartes, perhaps the only proposition for which he must necessarily be held to contend was, that the mind has no ideas which do not *arise* from impressions on the senses, or from reflections on our own thoughts and feelings. But it is certain, that he sometimes appears to contend for much more than this proposition; that he has generally been understood in a larger sense; and that, thus interpreted, his doctrine is not irreconcilable to those philosophical systems with which it has been supposed to be most at variance.

These general remarks may be illustrated by a reference to some of those ideas which are more general and important, and seem

ants more inflexible than he expected, he returned to Rome, possibly with the hope of more success in that quarter. But, though he publicly abjured his errors, he was soon, in consequence of some free language in conversation, thrown into a dungeon, where he died. His own writings are forgotten; but mankind are indebted to him for the admirable history of the Council of Trent by Father Paul, of which he brought the MSS. with him to London.

* "J'ai taché d'abord de prouver que notre esprit est au commencement ce qu'on appelle un *tabula rasa*, c'est-à-dire, sans idées et sans connoissances. Mais comme ce n'a été que pour détruire les préjugés de quelques philosophes, j'ai cru que dans ce petit abrégé de mes principes, je devois passer toutes les disputes préliminaires qui composent le livre premier." Bibliothèque Universelle, Janv. 1688

more dark than any others;—perhaps only because we seek in them for what is not to be found in any of the most simple elements of human knowledge. The nature of our notion of space, and more especially of that of time, seems to form one of the mysteries of our intellectual being. Neither of these notions can be conceived separately. Nothing outward can be conceived without space; for it is space which gives *out*ness to objects, or renders them capable of being conceived as outward. Nothing can be conceived to exist, without conceiving some time in which it exists. Thought and feeling may be conceived, without at the same time conceiving space; but no operation of mind can be recalled which does not suggest the conception of a portion of time, in which such mental operation is performed. Both these ideas are so clear that they cannot be illustrated, and so simple that they cannot be defined: nor indeed is it possible, by the use of any words, to advance a single step towards rendering them more, or otherwise intelligible than the lessons of Nature have already made them. The metaphysician knows no more of either than the rustic. If we confine ourselves merely to a statement of the facts which we discover by experience concerning these ideas, we shall find them reducible, as has just been intimated, to the following;—namely, that they are simple; that neither space nor time can be conceived without some other conception; that the idea of space always attends that of every outward object; and that the idea of time enters into every idea which the mind of man is capable of forming. Time cannot be conceived separately from something else; nor can any thing else be conceived separately from time. If we are asked whether the idea of time be innate, the only proper answer consists in the statement of the fact, that it never arises in the human mind otherwise than as the concomitant of some other perception; and that thus understood, it is not innate, since it is always directly or indirectly occasioned by some action on the senses. Various modes of expressing these facts have been adopted by different philosophers, according to the variety of their technical language. By Kant, space is said to be the *form* of our perceptive faculty, as applied to outward objects; and time is called the *form* of the same faculty, as it regards our mental operations: by Mr. Stewart, these ideas are considered "as *suggested to the understanding*"* by sensation or reflection, though, according to him, "the mind is not directly and immediately *furnished*" with such ideas, either by sensation or reflection: and, by a late eminent metaphysician,† they were regarded as *perceptions*, in the nature of those arising from the senses, of which the one is attendant on the idea of every outward object, and the other concomitant with the consciousness of every mental operation. Each of these modes of expression has its own advantages. The first mode brings forward the universality and necessity of these two notions; the second most strongly marks the distinction between them and the fluctuating perceptions naturally referred to the senses; while the last has the opposite merit of presenting to us that incapacity of being analyzed, in which they agree with all other simple ideas. On the other hand, each of them (perhaps from the inherent imperfection of language) seems to insinuate more than the mere results of experience. The technical terms introduced by Kant have the appearance of an attempt to explain what, by the writer's own principles, is incapable of explanation; Mr. Wedgwood may be charged with giving the same name to mental phenomena, which coincide in nothing but simplicity; and Mr. Stewart seems to us to have opposed two modes of expression to each other, which, when they are thoroughly analyzed, represent one and the same fact.

* Philosophical Essays, essay i. chap. 2.

† Mr. Thomas Wedgwood; see Life of Mackintosh, vol. i. p. 289.

Leibnitz thought that Locke's admission of "ideas of reflection" furnished a ground for negotiating a reconciliation between his system and the opinions of those who, in the etymological sense of the word, are more metaphysical; and it may very well be doubted, whether the ideas of Locke much differed from the "innate ideas" of Descartes, especially as the latter philosopher explained the term, when he found himself pressed by acute objectors. "I never said or thought," says Descartes, "that the mind needs innate ideas, which are something different from its own faculty of thinking; but, as I observed certain thoughts to be in my mind, which neither proceeded from outward objects, nor were determined by my will, but merely from my own faculty of thinking, I called these 'innate ideas,' to distinguish them from such as are either adventitious (*i. e.* from without), or compounded by our imagination. I call them innate, in the same sense in which generosity is innate in some families, gout and stone in others; because the children of such families come into the world with a disposition to such virtue, or to such maladies."* In a letter to Mersenne,† he says, "by the word 'idea,' I understand all that can be in our thoughts, and I distinguish three sorts of ideas;—*adventitious*, like the common idea of the sun; *framed by the mind*, such as that which astronomical reasoning gives us of the sun; and *innate*,

* This remarkable passage of Descartes is to be found in a French translation of the preface and notes to the Principia Philosophiæ, probably by himself.—(Lettres de Descartes, vol. i. lett. 99.) It is justly observed by one of his most acute antagonists, that Descartes does not steadily adhere to this sense of the word "innate," but varies it in the exigencies of controversy, so as to give it at each moment the import which best suits the nature of the objection with which he has then to contend.—Huet, Censura Philosophiæ Cartesianæ, p. 93.

† Lettres, vol. ii. lett. 54.

as the idea of God, mind, body, a triangle, and generally all those which represent true, immutable, and eternal essences." It must be owned, that, however nearly the first of these representations may approach to Mr. Locke's ideas of reflection, the second deviates from them very widely, and is not easily reconcilable with the first. The comparison of these two sentences, strongly impeaches the steadiness and consistency of Descartes in the fundamental principles of his system.

A principle in science is a proposition from which many other propositions may be inferred. That principles, taken in this sense of propositions, are part of the original structure or furniture of the human mind, is an assertion so unreasonable, that perhaps no philosopher has avowedly, or at least permanently, adopted it. But it is not to be forgotten, that there must be certain general laws of perception, or ultimate facts respecting that province of mind, beyond which human knowledge cannot reach. Such facts bound our researches in every part of knowledge, and the ascertainment of them is the utmost possible attainment of Science. Beyond them there is nothing, or at least nothing discoverable by us. These observations, however universally acknowledged when they are stated, are often hid from the view of the system-builder when he is employed in rearing his airy edifice. There is a common disposition to exempt the philosophy of the human understanding from the dominion of that irresistible necessity which confines all other knowledge within the limits of experience ;—arising probably from a vague notion that the science, without which the principles of no other are intelligible, ought to be able to discover the foundation even of its own principles. Hence the question among the German metaphysicians, "What makes experience possible?" Hence the very general indisposition among metaphysicians to acquiesce in any mere fact as the result of their inquiries, and to make vain exertions in pursuit of an explanation of it, without recollecting that the explanation must always consist of another fact, which must either equally require another explanation, or be equally independent of it. There is a sort of sullen reluctance to be satisfied with ultimate facts, which has kept its ground in the theory of the human mind long after it has been banished from all other sciences. Philosophers are, in this province, often led to waste their strength in attempts to find out what supports the foundation; and, in these efforts to prove first principles, they inevitably find that their proof must contain an assumption of the thing to be proved, and that their argument must return to the point from which it set out.

Mental philosophy can consist of nothing but facts; and it is at least as vain to inquire into the cause of thought, as into the cause of attraction. What the number and nature of the ultimate facts respecting mind may be, is a question which can only be determined by experience: and it is of the utmost importance not to allow their arbitrary multiplication, which enables some individuals to impose on us their own erroneous or uncertain speculations as the fundamental principles of human knowledge. No general criterion has hitherto been offered, by which these last principles may be distinguished from all other propositions. Perhaps a practical standard of some convenience would be, *that all reasoners should be required to admit every principle of which the denial renders reasoning impossible.* This is only to require that a man should admit, in general terms, those principles which he must assume in every particular argument, and which he has assumed in every argument which he has employed against their existence. It is, in other words, to require that a disputant shall not contradict himself; for every argument against the fundamental laws of thought absolutely assumes their existence in the premises, while it totally denies it in the conclusion.

Whether it be among the ultimate facts in human nature, that the mind is disposed or determined to assent to some propositions, and to reject others, when they are first submitted to its judgment, without inferring their truth or falsehood from any process of reasoning, is manifestly as much a question of mere experience as any other which relates to our mental constitution. It is certain that such inherent inclinations may be conceived, without supposing the ideas of which the propositions are composed to be, in any sense, 'innate'; if, indeed, that unfortunate word be capable of being reduced by definition to any fixed meaning. "Innate," says Lord Shaftesbury, "is the word Mr. Locke poorly plays with: the right word, though less used, is connate. The question is not about the time when the ideas enter the mind, but, *whether the constitution of man be such*, as at some time or other (no matter when), the ideas will not necessarily spring up in him." These are the words of Lord Shaftesbury in his Letters, which, not being printed in any edition of the Characteristics, are less known than they ought to be; though, in them, the fine genius and generous principles of the writer are less hid by occasional affectation of style, than in any other of his writings.*

The above observations apply with still greater force to what Mr. Locke calls "practical principles." Here, indeed, he contradicts himself; for, having built one of his chief arguments against other speculative or practical principles, on what he thinks the incapacity of the majority of mankind to entertain those very abstract ideas, of which these principles, if innate, would imply the presence in every mind, he very inconsistent-

* Dr. Lee, an antagonist of Mr. Locke, has stated the question of innate ideas more fully than Shaftesbury, or even Leibnitz: he has also anticipated some of the reasonings of Buffier and Reid.—Lee's Notes on Locke, folio, London, 1702.

ly admits the existence of one innate practical principle,—"a desire of happiness, and an aversion to misery,"* without considering that happiness and misery are also abstract terms, which excite very indistinct conceptions in the minds of "a great part of mankind." It would be easy also to show, if this were a proper place, that the desire of happiness, so far from being an innate, is not even an original principle; that it presupposes the existence of all those particular appetites and desires of which the gratification is pleasure, and also the exercise of that deliberate reason which habitually examines how far each gratification, in all its consequences, increases or diminishes that sum of enjoyment which constitutes happiness. If that subject could be now fully treated, it would appear that this error of Mr. Locke, or another equally great, that we have only one practical principle,—the desire of pleasure,—is the root of most false theories of morals; and that it is also the source of many mistaken speculations on the important subjects of government and education, which at this moment mislead the friends of human improvement, and strengthen the arms of its enemies. But morals fell only incidentally under the consideration of Mr. Locke; and his errors on that greatest of all sciences were the prevalent opinions of his age, which cannot be justly called the principles of Hobbes, though that extraordinary man had alone the boldness to exhibit these principles in connexion with their odious but strictly logical consequences.

The exaggerations of this first book, however, afford a new proof of the author's steady regard to the highest interests of mankind. He justly considered the free exercise of reason as the highest of these, and that on the security of which all the others depend. The circumstances of his life rendered it a long warfare against the enemies of freedom in philosophising, freedom in worship, and freedom from every political restraint which necessity did not justify. In his noble zeal for liberty of thought, he dreaded the tendency of a doctrine which might "gradually prepare mankind to swallow that for an innate principle which may serve his purpose who teacheth them."† He may well be excused, if, in the ardour of his generous conflict, he sometimes carried beyond the bounds of calm and neutral reason his repugnance to doctrines which, as they were then generally explained, he justly regarded as capable of being employed to shelter absurdity from detection, to stop the progress of free inquiry, and to subject the general reason to the authority of a few individuals. Every error of Mr. Locke in speculation may be traced to the influence of some virtue;—at least every error except some of the erroneous opinions generally received in his age, which, with a sort of passive acquiescence, he suffered to retain their place in his mind.

It is with the second book that the Essay on the Human Understanding properly begins; and this book is the first considerable contribution in modern times towards the experimental* philosophy of the human mind. The road was pointed out by Bacon; and, by excluding the fallacious analogies of thought to outward appearance, Descartes may be said to have marked out the limits of the proper field of inquiry. But, before Locke, there was no example in intellectual philosophy of an ample enumeration of facts, collected and arranged for the express purpose of legitimate generalization. He himself tells us, that his purpose was, "*in a plain historical method, to give an account* of the ways by which our understanding comes to attain those notions of things we have." In more modern phraseology, this would be called an attempt to ascertain, by observation, the most general facts relating to the origin of human knowledge. There is something in the plainness, and even homeliness of Locke's language, which strongly indicates his very clear conception, that experience must be his sole guide, and his unwillingness, by the use of scholastic language, to imitate the example of those who make a show of explaining facts, while in reality they only "darken counsel by words without knowledge." He is content to collect the laws of thought, as he would have collected those of any other object of physical knowledge, from observation alone. He seldom embarrasses himself with physiological hypothesis,† or wastes his strength on those

* Essay on Human Understanding, book i. chap. 3. § 3.

† Chap. 4. § 24.

* This word "experimental," has the defect of not appearing to comprehend the knowledge which flows from *observation*, as well as that which is obtained by *experiment*. The German word "empirical," is applied to all the information which experience affords; but it is in our language degraded by another application. I therefore must use "experimental" in a larger sense than its etymology warrants.

† A stronger proof can hardly be required than the following sentence, of his freedom from physiological prejudice. "This laying up of our ideas in the repository of the memory, signifies no more but this, that the mind has the power in many cases to revive perceptions, with another perception annexed to them, that it has had them before." The same chapter is remarkable for the exquisite, and almost poetical beauty, of some of its illustrations. "Ideas quickly fade, and often vanish quite out of the understanding, leaving no more footsteps or remaining characters of themselves than shadows do flying over a field of corn." —"The ideas, as well as children of our youth, often die before us, and our minds represent to us those tombs to which we are approaching; where, though the brass and marble remain, yet the inscriptions are effaced by time, and the imagery moulders away. Pictures drawn in our minds are laid in fading colours, and, unless sometimes refreshed, vanish and disappear,"—book ii. chap. 10. This pathetic language must have been inspired by experience; and, though Locke could not have been more than fifty-six when he wrote these sentences, it is too well known that the first decays of memory may be painfully felt long before they can be detected by the keenest observer.

insoluble problems which were then called metaphysical. Though, in the execution of his plan, there are many and great defects, the conception of it is entirely conformable to the Verulamian method of induction, which, even after the fullest enumeration of particulars, requires a cautious examination of each subordinate class of phenomena, before we attempt, through a very slowly ascending series of generalizations, to soar to comprehensive laws. "Philosophy," as Mr. Playfair excellently renders Bacon, "has either taken much from a few things, or too little from a great many; and in both cases has too narrow a basis to be of much duration or utility." Or, to use the very words of the Master himself—"We shall then have reason to hope well of the sciences, when we rise by continued steps from particulars to inferior axioms, and then to the middle, and only at last to the most general.* It is not so much by an appeal to experience (for some degree of that appeal is universal), as by the mode of conducting it, that the followers of Bacon are distinguished from the framers of hypotheses." It is one thing to borrow from experience just enough to make a supposition plausible; it is quite another to take from it all that is necessary to be the foundation of just theory.

In this respect perhaps, more than in any other, the philosophical writings of Locke are contradistinguished from those of Hobbes. The latter saw, with astonishing rapidity of intuition some of the simplest and most general facts which may be observed in the operations of the understanding; and perhaps no man ever possessed the same faculty of conveying his abstract speculations in language of such clearness, precision, and force, as to engrave them on the mind of the reader. But he did not wait to examine whether there might not be other facts equally general relating to the intellectual powers; and he therefore "took too little from a great many things." He fell into the double error of hastily applying his general laws to the most complicated processes of thought, without considering whether these general laws were not themselves limited by other not less comprehensive laws, and without trying to discover how they were connected with particulars, by a scale of intermediate and secondary laws. This mode of philosophising was well suited to the dogmatic confidence and dictatorial tone which belonged to the character of the philosopher of Malmsbury, and which enabled him to brave the obloquy attendant on singular and obnoxious opinions. "The plain historical method," on the other hand, chosen by Mr. Locke, produced the natural fruits of caution and modesty; taught him to distrust hasty and singular conclusions; disposed him, on fit occasions, to entertain a mitigated scepticism; and taught him also the rare courage to make an ingenuous avowal of ignorance. This contrast is one of our reasons for doubting whether Locke be much indebted to Hobbes for his speculations; and certainly the mere coincidence of the opinions of two metaphysicians is slender evidence, in any case, that either of them has borrowed his opinions from the other. Where the premises are different, and they have reached the same conclusion by different roads, such a coincidence is scarcely any evidence at all. Locke and Hobbes agree chiefly on those points in which, except the Cartesians, all the speculators of their age were also agreed. They differ on the most momentous questions,—the sources of knowledge,—the power of abstraction,—the nature of the will; on the two last of which subjects, Locke, by his very failures themselves, evinces a strong repugnance to the doctrines of Hobbes. They differ not only in all their premises, and many of their conclusions, but in their manner of philosophising itself. Locke had no prejudice which could lead him to imbibe doctrines from the enemy of liberty and religion. His style, with all its faults, is that of a man who thinks for himself; and an original style is not usually the vehicle of borrowed opinions.

Few books have contributed more than Mr. Locke's Essay to rectify prejudice; to undermine established errors; to diffuse a just mode of thinking; to excite a fearless spirit of inquiry, and yet to contain it within the boundaries which Nature has prescribed to the human understanding. An amendment of the general habits of thought is, in most parts of knowledge, an object as important as even the discovery of new truths; though it is not so palpable, nor in its nature so capable of being estimated by superficial observers. In the mental and moral world, which scarcely admits of any thing which can be called discovery, the correction of the intellectual habits is probably the greatest service which can be rendered to Science. In this respect, the merit of Locke is unrivalled. His writings have diffused throughout the civilized world, the love of civil liberty and the spirit of toleration and charity in religious differences, with the disposition to reject whatever is obscure, fantastic, or hypothetical in speculation,—to reduce verbal disputes to their proper value,—to abandon problems which admit of no solution,—to distrust whatever cannot clearly be expressed,—to render theory the simple expression of facts,—and to prefer those studies which most directly contribute to human happiness. If Bacon first discovered the rules by which knowledge is improved, Locke has most contributed to make mankind at large observe them. He has done most, though often by remedies of silent and almost insensible operation, to cure those mental distempers which obstructed the adoption of these rules; and has thus led to that general diffusion of a healthful and vigorous understanding, which is at once the greatest of all improvements, and the

* Novum Organum, lib. i. § civ.

instrument by which all other progress must be accomplished. He has left to posterity the instructive example of a prudent reformer, and of a philosophy temperate as well as liberal, which spares the feelings of the good, and avoids direct hostility with obstinate and formidable prejudice. These benefits are very slightly counterbalanced by some political doctrines liable to misapplication, and by the scepticism of some of his ingenious followers;—an inconvenience to which every philosophical school is exposed, which does not steadily limit its theory to a mere exposition of experience. If Locke made few discoveries, Socrates made none: yet both did more for the improvement of the understanding, and not less for the progress of knowledge, than the authors of the most brilliant discoveries. Mr. Locke will ever be regarded as one of the great ornaments of the English nation; and the most distant posterity will speak of him in the language addressed to him by the poet—

"O Decus Angliacæ certè, O Lux altera gentis!"*

* Gray, De Principiis Cogitandi.

A DISCOURSE

ON THE

LAW OF NATURE AND NATIONS.*

Before I begin a course of lectures on a science of great extent and importance, I think it my duty to lay before the public the reasons which have induced me to undertake such a labour, as well as a short account of the nature and objects of the course which I propose to deliver. I have always been unwilling to waste in unprofitable inactivity that leisure which the first years of my profession usually allow, and which diligent men, even with moderate talents, might often employ in a manner neither discreditable to themselves, nor wholly useless to others. Desirous that my own leisure should not be consumed in sloth, I anxiously looked about for some way of filling it up, which might enable me according to the measure of my humble abilities, to contribute somewhat to the stock of general usefulness. I had long been convinced that public lectures, which have been used in most ages and countries to teach the elements of almost every part of learning, were the most convenient mode in which these elements could be taught;—that they were the best adapted for the important purposes of awakening the attention of the student, of abridging his labours, of guiding his inquiries, of relieving the tediousness of private study, and of impressing on his recollection the principles of a science. I saw no reason why the law of England should be less adapted to this mode of instruction, or less likely to benefit by it, than any other part of knowledge. A learned gentleman, however, had already occupied that ground,* and will, I doubt not, persevere in the useful labour which he has undertaken. On his province it was far from my wish to intrude. It appeared to me that a course of lectures on another science closely connected with all liberal professional studies, and which had long been the subject of my own reading and reflection, might not only prove a most useful introduction to the law of England, but might also become an interesting part of general study, and an important branch of the education of those who were not destined for the profession of the law. I was confirmed in my opinion by the assent and approbation of men, whose names, if it were becoming to mention them on so slight an occasion, would add authority to truth, and furnish some excuse even for error. Encouraged by their approbation, I resolved without delay to commence the undertaking, of which I shall now proceed to give some account; without interrupting the progress of my discourse by anticipating or answering the remarks of those who may, perhaps, sneer at me for a departure from the usual course of my profession, because I am desirous of employing in a rational and useful pursuit that leisure, of which the same men would have required no account, if it had been wasted on trifles, or even abused in dissipation.

The science which teaches the rights and duties of men and of states, has, in modern times, been called "the law of nature and nations." Under this comprehensive title

* This discourse was the preliminary one of a course of lectures delivered in the hall of Lincoln's Inn during the spring of the year 1799. From the state of the original MSS. notes of these lectures, in the possession of the editor, it would seem that the lecturer had trusted, with the exception of a few passages prepared *in extenso*, to his powerful memory for all the aid that was required beyond what mere *catchwords* could supply.—Ed.

* See "A Syllabus of Lectures on the Law of England, to be delivered in Lincoln's Inn Hall by M. Nolen, Esq."

are included the rules of morality, as they prescribe the conduct of private men towards each other in all the various relations of human life; as they regulate both the obedience of citizens to the laws, and the authority of the magistrate in framing laws, and administering government; and as they modify the intercourse of independent commonwealths in peace, and prescribe limits to their hostility in war. This important science comprehends only that part of private ethics which is capable of being reduced to fixed and general rules. It considers only those general principles of jurisprudence and politics which the wisdom of the lawgiver adapts to the peculiar situation of his own country, and which the skill of the statesman applies to the more fluctuating and infinitely varying circumstances which affect its immediate welfare and safety. "For there are in nature certain fountains of justice whence all civil laws are derived, but as streams; and like as waters do take tinctures and tastes from the soils through which they run, so do civil laws vary according to the regions and governments where they are planted, though they proceed from the same fountains."*

On the great questions of morality, of politics, and of municipal law, it is the object of this science to deliver only those fundamental truths of which the particular application is as extensive as the whole private and public conduct of men;—to discover those "fountains of justice," without pursuing the "streams" through the endless variety of their course. But another part of the subject is to be treated with greater fulness and minuteness of application; namely, that important branch of it which professes to regulate the relations and intercourse of states, and more especially, (both on account of their greater perfection and their more immediate reference to use), the regulations of that intercourse as they are modified by the usages of the civilized nations of Christendom. Here this science no longer rests on general principles. That province of it which we now call the "law of nations," has, in many of its parts, acquired among European ones much of the precision and certainty of positive law; and the particulars of that law are chiefly to be found in the works of those writers who have treated the science of which I now speak. It is because they have classed (in a manner which seems peculiar to modern times) the duties of individuals with those of nations, and established their obligation on similar grounds, that the whole science has been called, "the law of nature and nations."

Whether this appellation be the happiest that could have been chosen for the science, and by what steps it came to be adopted among our modern moralists and lawyers,* are inquiries, perhaps, of more curiosity than use, and ones which, if they deserve any where to be deeply pursued, will be pursued with more propriety in a full examination of the subject than within the short limits of an introductory discourse. Names are, however, in a great measure arbitrary; but the distribution of knowledge into its parts, though it may often perhaps be varied with little disadvantage, yet certainly depends upon some fixed principles. The modern method of considering individual and national morality as the subjects of the same science, seems to me as convenient and reasonable an arrangement as can be adopted. The same rules of morality which hold together men in families, and which form families into commonwealths, also link together these commonwealths as members of the great society of mankind. Commonwealths, as well as private men, are liable to injury, and capable of benefit, from each other; it is, therefore, their interest, as well as their duty, to reverence, to practise, and to enforce those rules of justice which control and restrain injury,—which regulate and augment benefit,—which, even in their present imperfect observance, preserve civilized states in a tolerable condition of security from wrong, and which, if they could be generally obeyed, would establish, and permanently maintain, the well-being of the universal commonwealth of the human race. It is therefore with justice, that one part of this science has been called "the natural law of *individuals*," and the other "the natural law of *states*;" and it is too obvious to require observation,† that the application of both these laws, of the former as much as of the latter, is modified and varied by customs,

* Advancement of Learning, book ii. I have not been deterred by some petty incongruity of metaphor from quoting this noble sentence. Mr. Hume had, perhaps, this sentence in his recollection, when he wrote a remarkable passage of his works. See his Essays, vol. ii. p. 352.

* The learned reader is aware that the "jus naturæ" and "jus gentium" of the Roman lawyers are phrases of very different import from the modern phrases, "law of nature" and "law of nations." "Jus naturale," says Ulpian, "est quod natura omnia animalia docuit." "Quod naturalis ratio inter omnes homines constituit, id apud omnes peræque custoditur; vocaturque jus gentium." But they sometimes neglect this subtle distinction—"Jure naturali quod appellatur jus gentium." "Jus feciale" was the Roman term for our law of nations. "Belli quidem æquitas sanctissimè populi Rom. feciali jure perscripta est." De Officiis, lib. i. cap. ii. Our learned civilian Zouch has accordingly entitled his work, "De Jure Feciali, sive de Jure inter Gentes." The Chancellor D'Aguesseau, probably without knowing the work of Zouch, suggested that this law should be called, "Droit entre les Gens" (Œuvres, vol. ii. p. 337), in which he has been followed by a late ingenious writer, Mr. Bentham, (Introduction to the Principles of Morals and Legislation, p. 324.) Perhaps these learned writers do employ a phrase which expresses the subject of this law with more accuracy than our common language; but I doubt whether innovations in the terms of science always repay us by their superior precision for the uncertainty and confusion which the change occasions.

† This remark is suggested by an objection of Vattel, which is more specious than solid. See his Preliminaries, § 6.

conventions, character, and situation. With a view to these principles, the writers on general jurisprudence have considered states as moral persons; a mode of expression which has been called a fiction of law, but which may be regarded with more propriety as a bold metaphor, used to convey the important truth, that nations, though they acknowledge no common superior, and neither can, nor ought, to be subjected to human punishment, are yet under the same obligations mutually to practise honesty and humanity, which would have bound individuals,—if the latter could be conceived ever to have subsisted without the protecting restraints of government, and if they were not compelled to the discharge of their duty by the just authority of magistrates, and by the wholesome terrors of the laws. With the same views this law has been styled, and (notwithstanding the objections of some writers to the vagueness of the language) appears to have been styled with great propriety, "the law of nature." It may with sufficient correctness, or at least by an easy metaphor, be called a "law," inasmuch as it is a supreme, invariable, and uncontrollable rule of conduct to all men, the violation of which is avenged by natural punishments, necessarily flowing from the constitution of things, and as fixed and inevitable as the order of nature. It is "the law of nature," because its general precepts are essentially adapted to promote the happiness of man, as long as he remains a being of the same nature with which he is at present endowed, or, in other words, as long as he continues to be man, in all the variety of times, places, and circumstances, in which he has been known, or can be imagined to exist; because it is discoverable by natural reason, and suitable to our natural constitution; and because its fitness and wisdom are founded on the general nature of human beings, and not on any of those temporary and accidental situations in which they may be placed. It is with still more propriety, and indeed with the highest strictness, and the most perfect accuracy, considered as a law, when, according to those just and magnificent views which philosophy and religion open to us of the government of the world, it is received and reverenced as the sacred code, promulgated by the great Legislator of the Universe for the guidance of His creatures to happiness;—guarded and enforced, as our own experience may inform us, by the penal sanctions of shame, of remorse, of infamy, and of misery; and still farther enforced by the reasonable expectation of yet more awful penalties in a future and more permanent state of existence. It is the contemplation of the law of nature under this full, mature, and perfect idea of its high origin and transcendent dignity, that called forth the enthusiasm of the greatest men, and the greatest writers of ancient and modern times, in those sublime descriptions, in which they have exhausted all the powers of language, and surpassed all the other exertions, even of their own eloquence, in the display of its beauty and majesty. It is of this law that Cicero has spoken in so many parts of his writings, not only with all the splendour and copiousness of eloquence, but with the sensibility of a man of virtue, and with the gravity and comprehension of a philosopher.* It is of this law that Hooker speaks in so sublime a strain:—"Of Law, no less can be said, than that her seat is the bosom of God, her voice the harmony of the world; all things in heaven and earth do her homage, the very least as feeling her care, the greatest as not exempted from her power; both angels and men, and creatures of what condition soever, though each in different sort and manner, yet all with uniform consent admiring her as the mother of their peace and joy."†

Let not those who, to use the language of the same Hooker, "talk of truth," without "ever sounding the depth from whence it springeth," hastily take it for granted, that these great masters of eloquence and reason were led astray by the specious delusions of mysticism, from the sober consideration of the true grounds of morality in the nature, necessities, and interests of man. They studied and taught the principles of morals; but they thought it still more necessary, and more wise,—a much nobler task, and more becoming a true philosopher, to inspire men with a love and reverence for virtue.‡ They were not contented with elementary speculations: they examined the foundations of our duty; but they felt and cherished a most natural, a most seemly, a most rational enthusiasm, when they contemplated the majestic edifice which is reared on these solid foundations. They devoted the highest exertions of their minds to spread that beneficent enthusiasm among men. They consecrated as a homage to Virtue the most perfect

* "Est quidem vera lex recta ratio, naturæ congruens, diffusa in omnes, constans, sempiterna; quæ vocet ad officium jubendo, vetando à fraude deterreat, quæ tamen neque probos frustra jubet aut vetat, neque improbos jubendo aut vetando movet. Huic legi neque obrogari fas est, neque derogari ex hac aliquid licet, neque tota abrogari potest. Nec verò aut per senatum aut per populum solvi hac lege possumus: neque est quærendus explanator aut interpres ejus alius. Nec erit alia lex Romæ, alia Athenis, alia nunc, alia posthac; sed et omnes gentes et omni tempore una lex et sempiterna, et immutabilis continebit; unusque erit communis quasi magister et imperator omnium Deus, ille legis hujus inventor, disceptator, lator: cui qui non parebit *ipse se fugiet et naturam hominis aspernabitur*, atque hoc ipso luet maximas pœnas, etiamsi cætera supplicia, quæ putantur, effugerit."—De Repub. lib. iii. cap. 22.

† Ecclesiastical Polity, book i. in the conclusion.

‡ "Age verò urbibus constitutis, ut fidem colere et justitiam retinere discerent, et aliis parere suâ voluntate consuescerent, ac non modò labores excipiendos communis commodi causâ, sed etiam vitam amittendam existimarent; qui tandem fieri potuit, nisi homines ea, quæ ratione invenissent, eloquentiâ persuadere potuissent?"—De Invent. Rhet. lib. i. cap. 2.

fruits of their genius. If these grand sentiments of "the good and fair" have sometimes prevented them from delivering the principles of ethics with the nakedness and dryness of science, at least we must own that they have chosen the better part,—that they have preferred virtuous feeling to moral theory, and practical benefit to speculative exactness. Perhaps these wise men may have supposed that the minute dissection and anatomy of Virtue might, to the ill-judging eye, weaken the charm of her beauty.

It is not for me to attempt a theme which has perhaps been exhausted by these great writers. I am indeed much less called upon to display the worth and usefulness of the law of nations, than to vindicate myself from presumption in attempting a subject which has been already handled by so many masters. For the purpose of that vindication it will be necessary to sketch a very short and slight account (for such in this place it must unavoidably be) of the progress and present state of the science, and of that succession of able writers who have gradually brought it to its present perfection.

We have no Greek or Roman treatise remaining on the law of nations. From the title of one of the lost works of Aristotle, it appears that he composed a treatise on the laws of war,* which, if we had the good fortune to possess it, would doubtless have amply satisfied our curiosity, and would have taught us both the practice of the ancient nations and the opinions of their moralists, with that depth and precision which distinguish the other works of that great philosopher. We can now only imperfectly collect that practice and those opinions from various passages which are scattered over the writings of philosophers, historians, poets, and orators. When the time shall arrive for a more full consideration of the state of the government and manners of the ancient world, I shall be able, perhaps, to offer satisfactory reasons why these enlightened nations did not separate from the general province of ethics that part of morality which regulates the intercourse of states, and erect it into an independent science. It would require a long discussion to unfold the various causes which united the modern nations of Europe into a closer society,—which linked them together by the firmest bands of mutual dependence, and which thus, in process of time, gave to the law that regulated their intercourse, greater importance, higher improvement, and more binding force. Among these causes, we may enumerate a common extraction, a common religion, similar manners, institutions, and languages; in earlier ages the authority of the See of Rome, and the extravagant claims of the imperial crown; in latter times the connexions of trade, the jealousy of power, the refinement of civilization, the cultivation of science, and, above all, that general mildness of character and manners which arose from the combined and progressive influence of chivalry, of commerce, of learning and of religion. Nor must we omit the similarity of those political institutions which, in every country that had been overrun by the Gothic conquerors, bore discernible marks (which the revolutions of succeeding ages had obscured, but not obliterated) of the rude but bold and noble outline of liberty that was originally sketched by the hand of these generous barbarians. These and many other causes conspired to unite the nations of Europe in a more intimate connexion and a more constant intercourse, and, of consequence, made the regulation of their intercourse more necessary, and the law that was to govern it more important. In proportion as they approached to the condition of provinces of the same empire, it became almost as essential that Europe should have a precise and comprehensive code of the law of nations, as that each country should have a system of municipal law. The labours of the learned, accordingly, began to be directed to this subject in the sixteenth century, soon after the revival of learning, and after that regular distribution of power and territory which has subsisted, with little variation, until our times. The critical examination of these early writers would, perhaps, not be very interesting in an extensive work, and it would be unpardonable in a short discourse. It is sufficient to observe that they were all more or less shackled by the barbarous philosophy of the schools, and that they were impeded in their progress by a timorous deference for the inferior and technical parts of the Roman law, without raising their views to the comprehensive principles which will for ever inspire mankind with veneration for that grand monument of human wisdom. It was only, indeed, in the sixteenth century that the Roman law was first studied and understood as a science connected with Roman history and literature, and illustrated by men whom Ulpian and Papinian would not have disdained to acknowledge as their successors.* Among the writers of that age we may perceive the ineffectual attempts, the partial advances, the occasional streaks of light which always precede great discoveries, and works that are to instruct posterity.

The reduction of the law of nations to a system was reserved for Grotius. It was by the advice of Lord Bacon and Peiresc that he undertook this arduous task. He produced a work which we now, indeed, justly deem imperfect, but which is perhaps the most complete that the world has yet owed, at so early a stage in the progress of any science, to the

* Δικαιώματα τῶν πολέμων.

* Cujacius, Brissonius, Hottomannus, &c., &c. —See Gravina Origines Juris Civilis (Lips. 1737), pp. 132—138. Leibnitz, a great mathematician as well as philosopher, declares that he knows nothing which approaches so near to the method and precision of Geometry as the Roman law.—Op. vol. iv. p. 254.

genius and learning of one man. So great is the uncertainty of posthumous reputation, and so liable is the fame even of the greatest men to be obscured by those new fashions of thinking and writing which succeed each other so rapidly among polished nations, that Grotius, who filled so large a space in the eye of his contemporaries, is now perhaps known to some of my readers only by name. Yet if we fairly estimate both his endowments and his virtues, we may justly consider him as one of the most memorable men who have done honour to modern times. He combined the discharge of the most important duties of active and public life with the attainment of that exact and various learning which is generally the portion only of the recluse student. He was distinguished as an advocate and a magistrate, and he composed the most valuable works on the law of his own country; he was almost equally celebrated as an historian, a scholar, a poet, and a divine;—a disinterested statesman, a philosophical lawyer, a patriot who united moderation with firmness, and a theologian who was taught candour by his learning. Unmerited exile did not damp his patriotism; the bitterness of controversy did not extinguish his charity. The sagacity of his numerous and fierce adversaries could not discover a blot on his character; and in the midst of all the hard trials and galling provocations of a turbulent political life, he never once deserted his friends when they were unfortunate, nor insulted his enemies when they were weak. In times of the most furious civil and religious faction he preserved his name unspotted, and he knew how to reconcile fidelity to his own party, with moderation towards his opponents.

Such was the man who was destined to give a new form to the law of nations, or rather to create a science, of which only rude sketches and undigested materials were scattered over the writings of those who had gone before him. By tracing the laws of his country to their principles, he was led to the contemplation of the law of nature, which he justly considered as the parent of all municipal law.* Few works were more celebrated than that of Grotius in his own days, and in the age which succeeded. It has, however, been the fashion of the last half-century to depreciate his work as a shapeless compilation, in which reason lies buried under a mass of authorities and quotations. This fashion originated among French wits and declaimers, and it has been, I know not for what reason, adopted, though with far greater moderation and decency, by some respectable writers among ourselves. As to those who first used this language, the most candid supposition that we can make with respect to them is, that they never read the work; for, if they had not been deterred from the perusal of it by such a formidable display of Greek characters, they must soon have discovered that Grotius never quotes on any subject till he has first appealed to some principles, and often, in my humble opinion, though not always, to the soundest and most rational principles.

But another sort of answer is due to some of those* who have criticised Grotius, and that answer might be given in the words of Grotius himself.† He was not of such a stupid and servile cast of mind, as to quote the opinions of poets or orators, of historians and philosophers, as those of judges, from whose decision there was no appeal. He quotes them, as he tells us himself, as witnesses whose conspiring testimony, mightily strengthened and confirmed by their discordance on almost every other subject, is a conclusive proof of the unanimity of the whole human race on the great rules of duty and the fundamental principles of morals. On such matters, poets and orators are the most unexceptionable of all witnesses; for they address themselves to the general feelings and sympathies of mankind; they are neither warped by system, nor perverted by sophistry; they can attain none of their objects, they can neither please nor persuade, if they dwell on moral sentiments not in unison with those of their readers. No system of moral philosophy can surely disregard the general feelings of human nature and the according judgment of all ages and nations. But where are these feelings and that judgment recorded and preserved? In those very writings which Grotius is gravely blamed for having quoted. The usages and laws of nations, the events of history, the opinions of philosophers, the sentiments of orators and poets, as well as the observation of common life, are, in truth, the materials out of which the science of morality is formed; and those who neglect them are justly chargeable with a vain attempt to philosophise without regard to fact and experience,—the sole foundation of all true philosophy.

If this were merely an objection of taste, I should be willing to allow that Grotius has indeed poured forth his learning with a profusion that sometimes rather encumbers than adorns his work, and which is not always necessary to the illustration of his subject. Yet, even in making that concession, I should rather yield to the taste of others than speak from my own feelings. I own that such richness and splendour of literature have a powerful charm for me. They fill my mind with an endless variety of delightful recollections and associations. They relieve the understanding in its progress through a vast science, by calling up the memory of great men and of interesting events. By this means we see the truths of morality clothed with all the eloquence,—not that could be produced by the powers of one man,—but that could be bestowed on them by the col-

* "Proavia juris civilis." De Jure Belli ac Pacis, proleg. § xvi.

* Dr. Paley, Principles of Moral and Political Philosophy, pref. pp. xiv. xv.

† De Jure Belli, proleg. § 40.

lective genius of the world. Even Virtue and Wisdom themselves acquire new majesty in my eyes, when I thus see all the great masters of thinking and writing called together, as it were, from all times and countries, to do them homage, and to appear in their train.

But this is no place for discussions of taste, and I am very ready to own that mine may be corrupted. The work of Grotius is liable to a more serious objection, though I do not recollect that it has ever been made. His method is inconvenient and unscientific: he has inverted the natural order. That natural order undoubtedly dictates, that we should first search for the original principles of the science in human nature; then apply them to the regulation of the conduct of individuals; and lastly, employ them for the decision of those difficult and complicated questions that arise with respect to the intercourse of nations. But Grotius has chosen the reverse of this method. He begins with the consideration of the states of peace and war, and he examines original principles only occasionally and incidentally, as they grow out of the questions which he is called upon to decide. It is a necessary consequence of this disorderly method,—which exhibts the elements of the science in the form of scattered digressions, that he seldom employs sufficient discussion on these fundamental truths, and never in the place where such a discussion would be most instructive to the reader.

This defect in the plan of Grotius was perceived and supplied by Puffendorff, who restored natural law to that superiority which belonged to it, and, with great propriety, treated the law of nations as only one main branch of the parent stock. Without the genius of his master, and with very inferior learning, he has yet treated this subject with sound sense, with clear method, with extensive and accurate knowledge, and with a copiousness of detail sometimes indeed tedious, but always instructive and satisfactory. His work will be always studied by those who spare no labour to acquire a deep knowledge of the subject; but it will, in our times, I fear, be oftener found on the shelf than on the desk of the general student. In the time of Mr. Locke it was considered as the manual of those who were intended for active life; but in the present age, I believe it will be found that men of business are too much occupied,—men of letters are too fastidious, and men of the world too indolent, for the study or even the perusal of such works. Far be it from me to derogate from the real and great merit of so useful a writer as Puffendorff. His treatise is a mine in which all his successors must dig. I only presume to suggest, that a book so prolix, and so utterly void of all the attractions of composition, is likely to repel many readers who are interested in its subject, and who might perhaps be disposed to acquire some knowledge of the principles of public law.

Many other circumstances might be mentioned, which conspire to prove that neither of the great works of which I have spoken, has superseded the necessity of a new attempt to lay before the public a system of the law of nations. The language of Science is so completely changed since both these works were written, that whoever was now to employ their terms in his moral reasonings would be almost unintelligible to some of his hearers or readers,—and to some among them, too, who are neither ill qualified, nor ill disposed, to study such subjects with considerable advantage to themselves. The learned, indeed, well know how little novelty or variety is to be found in scientific disputes. The same truths and the same errors have been repeated from age to age, with little variation but in the language; and novelty of expression is often mistaken by the ignorant for substantial discovery. Perhaps, too, very nearly the same portion of genius and judgment has been exerted in most of the various forms under which science has been cultivated at different periods of history. The superiority of those writers who continue to be read, perhaps often consists chiefly in taste, in prudence, in a happy choice of subject, in a favourable moment, in an agreeable style, in the good fortune of a prevalent language, or in other advantages which are either accidental, or are the result rather of the secondary, than of the highest, faculties of the mind. But these reflections, while they moderate the pride of invention, and dispel the extravagant conceit of superior illumination, yet serve to prove the use, and indeed the necessity, of composing, from time to time, new systems of science adapted to the opinions and language of each succeeding period. Every age must be taught in its own language. If a man were now to begin a discourse on ethics with an account of the "moral entities" of Puffendorff,* he would speak an unknown tongue.

It is not, however, alone as a mere translation of former writers into modern language that a new system of public law seems likely to be useful. The age in which we live possesses many advantages which are peculiarly favourable to such an undertaking. Since the composition of the great works of Grotius and Puffendorff, a more modest, simple, and intelligible philosophy has been introduced into the schools; which has indeed been grossly abused by sophists, but which, from the time of Locke, has been cultivated and improved by a succession of disciples worthy of their illustrious master. We are thus enabled to discuss with precision, and to explain with clearness, the principles of the science of human nature,

* I do not mean to impeach the soundness of any part of Puffendorff's reasoning founded on moral entities: it may be explained in a manner consistent with the most just philosophy. He used, as every writer must do, the scientific language of his own time. I only assert that, to those who are unacquainted with ancient systems, his philosophical vocabulary is obsolete and unintelligible.

which are in themselves on a level with the capacity of every man of good sense, and which only appeared to be abstruse from the unprofitable subtleties with which they were loaded, and the barbarous jargon in which they were expressed. The deepest doctrines of morality have since that time been treated in the perspicuous and popular style, and with some degree of the beauty and eloquence of the ancient moralists. That philosophy on which are founded the principles of our duty, if it has not become more certain (for morality admits no discoveries), is at least less "harsh and crabbed," less obscure and haughty in its language, and less forbidding and disgusting in its appearance, than in the days of our ancestors. If this progress of leaning towards popularity has engendered (as it must be owned that it has) a multitude of superficial and most mischievous sciolists, the antidote must come from the same quarter with the disease: popular reason can alone correct popular sophistry.

Nor is this the only advantage which a writer of the present age would possess over the celebrated jurists of the last century. Since that time vast additions have been made to the stock of our knowledge of human nature. Many dark periods of history have since been explored: many hitherto unknown regions of the globe have been visited and described by travellers and navigators not less intelligent than intrepid. We may be said to stand at the confluence of the greatest number of streams of knowledge flowing from the most distant sources that ever met at one point. We are not confined, as the learned of the last age generally were, to the history of those renowned nations who are our masters in literature. We can bring before us man in a lower and more abject condition than any in which he was ever before seen. The records have been partly opened to us of those mighty empires of Asia* where the beginnings of civilization are lost in the darkness of an unfathomable antiquity. We can make human society pass in review before our mind, from the brutal and helpless barbarism of Terra del Fuego, and the mild and voluptuous savages of Otaheite, to the tame, but ancient and immovable civilization of China, which bestows its own arts on every successive race of conquerors,—to the meek and servile natives of Hindostan, who preserve their ingenuity, their skill, and their science, through a long series of ages, under the yoke of foreign tyrants,—and to the gross and incorrigible rudeness of the Ottomans, incapable of improvement, and extinguishing the remains of civilization among their unhappy subjects, once the most ingenious nations of the earth. We can examine almost every imaginable variety in the character, manners, opinions, feelings, prejudices, and institutions of mankind, into which they can be thrown, either by the rudeness of barbarism, or by the capricious corruptions of refinement, or by those innumerable combinations of circumstances, which, both in these opposite conditions, and in all the intermediate stages between them, influence or direct the course of human affairs. History, if I may be allowed the expression, is now a vast museum, in which specimens of every variety of human nature may be studied. From these great accessions to knowledge, lawgivers and statesmen, but, above all, moralists and political philosophers, may reap the most important instruction. They may plainly discover in all the useful and beautiful variety of governments and institutions, and under all the fantastic multitude of usages and rites which have prevailed among men, the same fundamental, comprehensive truths, the sacred master-principles which are the guardians of human society, recognised and revered (with few and slight exceptions) by every nation upon earth, and uniformly taught (with still fewer exceptions) by a succession of wise men from the first dawn of speculation to the present moment. The exceptions, few as they are, will, on more reflection, be found rather apparent than real. If we could raise ourselves to that height from which we ought to survey so vast a subject, these exceptions would altogether vanish; the brutality of a handful of savages would disappear in the immense prospect of human nature, and the murmurs of a few licentious sophists would not ascend to break the general harmony. This consent of mankind in first principles, and this endless variety in their application, which is one among many valuable truths which we may collect from our present extensive acquaintance with the history of man, is itself of vast importance. Much of the majesty and authority of virtue is derived from their consent, and almost the whole of practical wisdom is founded on their variety.

What former age could have supplied facts for such a work as that of Montesquieu? He indeed has been, perhaps justly, charged with abusing this advantage, by the undistinguishing adoption of the narratives of travellers of very different degrees of accuracy and veracity. But if we reluctantly confess the justness of this objection; if we are compelled to own that he exaggerates the influence of climate,—that he ascribes too much to the foresight and forming skill

* I cannot prevail on myself to pass over this subject without paying my humble tribute to the memory of Sir William Jones, who has laboured so successfully in Oriental literature; whose fine genius, pure taste, unwearied industry, unrivalled and almost prodigious variety of acquirements,—not to speak of his amiable manners, and spotless integrity,—must fill every one who cultivates or admires letters with reverence, tinged with a melancholy which the recollection of his recent death is so well adapted to inspire. I hope I shall be pardoned if I add my applause to the genius and learning of Mr. Maurice, who treads in the steps of his illustrious friend, and who has bewailed his death in a strain of genuine and beautiful poetry, not unworthy of happier periods of our English literature.

of legislators, and far too little to time and circumstances, in the growth of political constitutions,—that the substantial character and essential differences of governments are often lost and confounded in his technical language and arrangement,—that he often bends the free and irregular outline of nature to the imposing but fallacious geometrical regularity of system,—that he has chosen a style of affected abruptness, sententiousness, and vivacity, ill suited to the gravity of his subject;—after all these concessions (for his fame is large enough to spare many concessions), the Spirit of Laws will still remain not only one of the most solid and durable monuments of the powers of the human mind, but a striking evidence of the inestimable advantages which political philosophy may receive from a wide survey of all the various conditions of human society.

In the present century a slow and silent, but very substantial, mitigation has taken place in the practice of war; and in proportion as that mitigated practice has received the sanction of time, it is raised from the rank of mere usage, and becomes part of the law of nations. Whoever will compare our present modes of warfare with the system of Grotius* will clearly discern the immense improvements which have taken place in that respect since the publication of his work, during a period, perhaps in every point of view the happiest to be found in the history of the world. In the same period many important points of public law have been the subject of contest both by argument and by arms, of which we find either no mention, or very obscure traces, in the history of preceding times.

There are other circumstances to which I allude with hesitation and reluctance, though it must be owned that they afford to a writer of this age some degree of unfortunate and deplorable advantage over his predecessors. Recent events have accumulated more terrible practical instruction on every subject of politics than could have been in other times acquired by the experience of ages. Men's wit sharpened by their passions has penetrated to the bottom of almost all political questions. Even the fundamental rules of morality themselves have, for the first time, unfortunately for mankind, become the subject of doubt and discussion. I shall consider it as my duty to abstain from all mention of these awful events, and of these fatal controversies. But the mind of that man must indeed be incurious and indocile, who has either overlooked all these things, or reaped no instruction from the contemplation of them.

From these reflections it appears, that, since the composition of those two great works on the law of nature and nations which continue to be the classical and standard works on that subject, we have gained both more convenient instruments of reasoning and more extensive materials for science,—that the code of war has been enlarged and improved,—that new questions have been practically decided,—and that new controversies have arisen regarding the intercourse of independent states, and the first principles of morality and civil government.

Some readers may, however, think that in these observations which I offer, to excuse the presumption of my own attempt, I have omitted the mention of later writers, to whom some part of the remarks is not justly applicable. But, perhaps, further consideration will acquit me in the judgment of such readers. Writers on particular questions of public law are not within the scope of my observations. They have furnished the most valuable materials; but I speak only of a system. To the large work of Wolffius, the observations which I have made on Puffendorff as a book for general use, will surely apply with tenfold force. His abridger, Vattel, deserves, indeed, considerable praise: he is a very ingenious, clear, elegant, and useful writer. But he only considers one part of this extensive subject,—namely, the law of nations, strictly so called; and I cannot help thinking, that, even in this department of the science, he has adopted some doubtful and dangerous principles,—not to mention his constant deficiency in that fulness of example and illustration, which so much embellishes and strengthens reason. It is hardly necessary to take any notice of the text-book of Heineccius, the best writer of elementary books with whom I am acquainted on any subject. Burlamaqui is an author of superior merit; but he confines himself too much to the general principles of morality and politics, to require much observation from me in this place. The same reason will excuse me for passing over in silence the works of many philosophers and moralists, to whom, in the course of my proposed lectures, I shall owe and confess the greatest obligations; and it might perhaps deliver me from the necessity of speaking of the work of Dr. Paley, if I were not desirous of this public opportunity of professing my gratitude for the instruction and pleasure which I have received from that excellent writer, who possesses, in so eminent a degree, those invaluable qualities of a moralist,—good sense, caution, sobriety, and perpetual reference to convenience and practice; and who certainly is thought less original than he really is, merely because his taste and modesty have led him to disdain the ostentation of novelty, and because he generally employs more art to blend his own arguments with the body of received opinions (so as that they are scarce to be distinguished), than other men in the pursuit of a transient popularity, have exerted to disguise the most miserable commonplaces in the shape of paradox.

No writer since the time of Grotius, of Puffendorff, and of Wolf, has combined an investigation of the principles of natural and public law, with a full application of these

* Especially those chapters of the third book, entitled, "Temperamentum circa Captivos," &c.

principles to particular cases; and in these circumstances, I trust, it will not be deemed extravagant presumption in me to hope that I shall be able to exhibit a view of this science, which shall, at least, be more intelligible and attractive to students, than the learned treatises of these celebrated men. I shall now proceed to state the general plan and subjects of the lectures in which I am to make this attempt.

I. The being whose actions the law of nature professes to regulate, is man. It is on the knowledge of his nature that the science of his duty must be founded.* It is impossible to approach the threshold of moral philosophy without a previous examination of the faculties and habits of the human mind. Let no reader be repelled from this examination by the odious and terrible name of "metaphysics;" for it is, in truth, nothing more than the employment of good sense, in observing our own thoughts, feelings, and actions; and when the facts which are thus observed are expressed, as they ought to be, in plain language, it is, perhaps, above all other sciences, most on a level with the capacity and information of the generality of thinking men. When it is thus expressed, it requires no previous qualification, but a sound judgment perfectly to comprehend it; and those who wrap it up in a technical and mysterious jargon, always give us strong reason to suspect that they are not philosophers, but impostors. Whoever thoroughly understands such a science, must be able to teach it plainly to all men of common sense. The proposed course will therefore open with a very short, and, I hope, a very simple and intelligible account of the powers and operations of the human mind. By this plain statement of facts, it will not be difficult to decide many celebrated, though frivolous and merely verbal, controversies, which have long amused the leisure of the schools, and which owe both their fame and their existence to the ambiguous obscurity of scholastic language. It will, for example, only require an appeal to every man's experience, that we often act purely from a regard to the happiness of others, and are therefore social beings; and it is not necessary to be a consummate judge of the deceptions of language, to despise the sophistical trifler, who tells us, that, because we experience a gratification in our benevolent actions, we are therefore exclusively and uniformly selfish. A correct examination of facts will lead us to discover that quality which is common to all virtuous actions, and which distinguishes them from those which are vicious and criminal. But we shall see that it is necessary for man to be governed, not by his own transient and hasty opinion upon the tendency of every particular action, but by those fixed and unalterable rules, which are the joint result of the impartial judgment, the natural feelings, and the embodied experience of mankind. The authority of these rules is, indeed, founded only on their tendency to promote private and public welfare; but the morality of actions will appear solely to consist in their correspondence with the rule. By the help of this obvious distinction we shall vindicate a just theory, which, far from being modern, is, in fact, as ancient as philosophy, both from plausible objections, and from the odious imputation of supporting those absurd and monstrous systems which have been built upon it. Beneficial tendency is the foundation of rules, and the criterion by which habits and sentiments are to be tried: but it is neither the immediate standard, nor can it ever be the principal motive of action. An action to be completely virtuous, must accord with moral rules, and must flow from our natural feelings and affections, moderated, matured, and improved into steady habits of right conduct.* Without, however, dwelling longer on subjects which cannot be clearly stated, unless they are fully unfolded, I content myself with observing, that it shall be my object, in this preliminary, but most important, part of the course, to lay the foundations of morality so deeply in human nature, as to satisfy the coldest inquirer; and, at the same time, to vindicate the paramount authority of the rules of our duty, at all times, and in all places, over all opinions of interest and speculations of benefit, so extensively, so universally, and so inviolably, as may well justify the grandest and the most apparently extravagant effusions of moral enthusiasm. If, notwithstanding all my endeavours to deliver these doctrines with the utmost simplicity, any of my auditors should still reproach me for introducing such abstruse matters, I must shelter myself behind the authority of the wisest of men. "If they (the ancient moralists), before they had come to the popular and received notions of virtue and vice, had staid a little longer upon the inquiry concerning *the roots of good and evil*, they had given, in my opinion, a great light to that which followed; and especially if they had consulted with nature, they had made their doctrines less prolix, and more profound."† What Lord Bacon desired for the mere gratification of scientific curiosity, the welfare of mankind now imperiously demands. Shallow systems of metaphysics have given birth to a brood of abominable and pestilential paradoxes, which nothing but a more profound philosophy can destroy. However we may, perhaps, lament the necessity of discussions which may shake the habitual reverence of some men for those rules which it is the chief interest of all men to practise, we have now no choice left. We must either dispute, or abandon the ground. Undistinguishing and unmerited invectives

* "Natura enim juris explicanda est nobis, eaque ab hominis repetenda naturâ."—De Leg. lib. i. c. 5.

* "Est autem virtus nihil aliud, quam in se perfecta atque ad summum perducta natura." Ibid. lib. i. c. 8.

† Advancement of Learning, book ii.

against philosophy will only harden sophists and their disciples in the insolent conceit, that they are in possession of an undisputed superiority of reason; and that their antagonists have no arms to employ against them, but those of popular declamation. Let us not for a moment even appear to suppose, that philosophical truth and human happiness are so irreconcilably at variance. I cannot express my opinion on this subject so well as in the words of a most valuable, though generally neglected writer: "The science of abstruse learning, when completely attained, is like Achilles' spear, that healed the wounds it had made before; so this knowledge serves to repair the damage itself had occasioned, and this perhaps is all that it is good for; it casts no additional light upon the paths of life, but disperses the clouds with which it had overspread them before; it advances not the traveller one step in his journey, but conducts him back again to the spot from whence he wandered. Thus the land of philosophy consists partly of an open champaign country, passable by every common understanding, and partly of a range of woods, traversable only by the speculative, and where they too frequently delight to amuse themselves. Since then we shall be obliged to make incursions into this latter track, and shall probably find it a region of obscurity, danger, and difficulty, it behooves us to use our utmost endeavours for enlightening and smoothing the way before us."* We shall, however, remain in the forest only long enough to visit the fountains of those streams which flow from it, and which water and fertilise the cultivated region of morals, to become acquainted with the modes of warfare practised by its savage inhabitants, and to learn the means of guarding our fair and fruitful land against their desolating incursions. I shall hasten from speculations, to which I am naturally, perhaps, but too prone, and proceed to the more profitable consideration of our practical duty.

The first and most simple part of ethics is that which regards the duties of private men towards each other, when they are considered apart from the sanction of positive laws. I say *apart* from that sanction, not *antecedent* to it; for though we *separate* private from political duties for the sake of greater clearness and order in reasoning, yet we are not to be so deluded by this mere arrangement of convenience as to suppose that human society ever has subsisted, or ever could subsist, without being protected by government, and bound together by laws. All these relative duties of private life have been so copiously and beautifully treated by the moralists of antiquity, that few men will now choose to follow them, who are not actuated by the wild ambition of equalling Aristotle in precision, or rivalling Cicero in eloquence. They have been also admirably treated by modern moralists, among whom it would be gross injustice not to number many of the preachers of the Christian religion, whose peculiar character is that spirit of universal charity, which is the living principle of all our social duties. For it was long ago said, with great truth, by Lord Bacon, "that there never was any philosophy, religion, or other discipline, which did so plainly and highly exalt that good which is communicative, and depress the good which is private and particular, as the Christian faith."* The appropriate praise of this religion is not so much that it has taught new duties, as that it breathes a milder and more benevolent spirit over the whole extent of morals.

On a subject which has been so exhausted, I should naturally have contented myself with the most slight and general survey, if some fundamental principles had not of late been brought into question, which, in all former times, have been deemed too evident to require the support of argument, and almost too sacred to admit the liberty of discussion. I shall here endeavour to strengthen some parts of the fortifications of morality which have hitherto been neglected, because no man had ever been hardy enough to attack them. Almost all the relative duties of human life will be found more immediately, or more remotely, to arise out of the two great institutions of property and marriage. They constitute, preserve, and improve society. Upon their gradual improvement depends the progressive civilization of mankind; on them rests the whole order of civil life. We are told by Horace, that the first efforts of lawgivers to civilize men consisted in strengthening and regulating these institutions, and fencing them round with rigorous penal laws.

"Oppida cœperunt munire, et ponere leges,
Ne quis fur esset, neu latro, neu quis adulter."†

A celebrated ancient orator,‡ of whose poems we have but a few fragments remaining, has well described the progressive order in which human society is gradually led to its highest improvements under the guardianship of those laws which secure property and regulate marriage.

"Et leges sanctas docuit, et chara jugavit
Corpora conjugiis; et magnas condidit urbes."

These two great institutions convert the selfish as well as the social passions of our nature into the firmest bands of a peaceable and orderly intercourse; they change the sources of discord into principles of quiet; they discipline the most ungovernable, they refine the grossest, and they exalt the most sordid propensities; so that they become the perpetual fountain of all that strengthens, and preserves, and adorns society: they sustain the individual, and they perpetuate the race. Around these institutions all our social duties will be found at various distances to range themselves; some more near, obviously

* Light of Nature, vol.i. pref. p. xxxiii.

* Advancement of Learning, book ii.
† Sermon. lib. i. Serm. iii. 105.
‡ C. Licinius Calvus.

essential to the good order of human life; others more remote, and of which the necessity is not at first view so apparent; and some so distant, that their importance has been sometimes doubted, though upon more mature consideration they will be found to be outposts and advanced guards of these fundamental principles,—that man should securely enjoy the fruits of his labour, and that the society of the sexes should be so wisely ordered, as to make it a school of the kind affections, and a fit nursery for the commonwealth.

The subject of property is of great extent. It will be necessary to establish the foundation of the rights of acquisition, alienation, and transmission, not in imaginary contracts or a pretended state of nature, but in their subserviency to the subsistence and well-being of mankind. It will not only be curious, but useful, to trace the history of property from the first loose and transient occupancy of the savage, through all the modifications which it has at different times received, to that comprehensive, subtle, and anxiously minute code of property which is the last result of the most refined civilization.

I shall observe the same order in considering the society of the sexes, as it is regulated by the institution of marriage.* I shall endeavour to lay open those unalterable principles of general interest on which that institution rests; and if I entertain a hope that on this subject I may be able to add something to what our masters in morality have taught us, I trust, that the reader will bear in mind, as an excuse for my presumption, that *they* were not likely to employ much argument where they did not foresee the possibility of doubt. I shall also consider the history† of marriage, and trace it through all the forms which it has assumed, to that descent and happy permanency of union, which has, perhaps above all other causes, contributed to the quiet of society, and the refinement of manners in modern times. Among many other inquiries which this subject will suggest, I shall be led more particularly to examine the natural station and duties of the female sex, their condition among different nations, its improvement in Europe, and the bounds which nature herself has prescribed to the progress of that improvement; beyond which every pretended advance will be a real degradation.

Having established the principles of private duty, I shall proceed to consider man under the important relation of subject and sovereign, or, in other words, of citizen and magistrate. The duties which arise from this relation I shall endeavour to establish, not upon supposed compacts, which are altogether chimerical, which must be admitted to be false in fact, and which, if they are to be considered as fictions, will be found to serve no purpose of just reasoning, and to be equally the foundation of a system of universal despotism in Hobbes, and of universal anarchy in Rousseau; but on the solid basis of general convenience. Men cannot subsist without society and mutual aid; they can neither maintain social intercourse nor receive aid from each other without the protection of government; and they cannot enjoy that protection without submitting to the restraints which a just goverment imposes. This plain argument establishes the duty of obedience on the part of the citizens, and the duty of protection on that of magistrates, on the same foundation with that of every other moral duty; and it shows, with sufficient evidence, that these duties are reciprocal;—the only rational end for which the fiction of a contract should have been invented. I shall not encumber my reasoning by any speculations on the origin of government,—a question on which so much reason has been wasted in modern times; but which the ancients* in a higher spirit of philosophy have never once mooted. If our principles be just, our origin of government must have been coeval with that of mankind; and as no tribe has ever been discovered so brutish as to be without some government, and yet so enlightened as to establish a government by common consent, it is surely unnecessary to employ any serious argument in the confutation of the doctrine that is inconsistent with reason, and unsupported by experience. But though all inquiries into the origin of government be chimerical, yet the history of its progress is curious and useful. The various stages through which it passed from savage independence, which implies every man's power of injuring his neighbour, to legal liberty, which consists in every man's security against wrong; the manner in which a family expands into a tribe, and tribes coalesce into a

* See on this subject an incomparable fragment of the first book of Cicero's Economics, which is too long for insertion here, but which, if it be closely examined, may perhaps dispel the illusion of those gentlemen, who have so strangely taken it for granted that Cicero was incapable of exact reasoning.

† This progress is traced with great accuracy in some beautiful lines of Lucretius:—

—— Mulier, conjuncta viro, concessit in unum;
Castaque privatæ Veneris connubia læta
Cognita sunt, prolemque ex se vidêre creatam;
Tum genus humanum primum mollescere cœpit.
——————— puerique parentum
Blanditiis facile ingenium fregere superbum.
Tunc et amicitiam cœperunt jungere, habentes
Finitimi inter se, nec lædere, nec violare;
Et pueros commendârunt, muliebreque sæclum,
Vocibus et gestu; cum balbè significarent,
Imbecillorum esse æquum miserier omni.

De Rerum Nat. lib. v.

* The introduction to the first book of Aristotle's Politics is the best demonstration of the necessity of political society to the well-being, and indeed to the very being, of man, with which I am acquainted. Having shown the circumstances which render man necessarily a social being, he justly concludes, "Καὶ ὅτι ἄνθρωπος φύσει πολιτικὸν ζῶον." The same scheme of philosophy is admirably pursued in the short, but invaluable fragment of the sixth book of Polybius, which describes the history and revolutions of government.

nation,—in which public justice is gradually engrafted on private revenge, and temporary submission ripened into habitual obedience; form a most important and extensive subject of inquiry, which comprehends all the improvements of mankind in police, in judicature, and in legislation.

I have already given the reader to understand that the description of liberty which seems to me the most comprehensive, is that of *security against wrong*. Liberty is therefore the object of all government. Men are more free under every government, even the most imperfect, than they would be if it were possible for them to exist without any government at all: they are more secure from wrong, more undisturbed in the exercise of their natural powers, and therefore more free, even in the most obvious and grossest sense of the word, than if they were altogether unprotected against injury from each other. But as general security is enjoyed in very different degrees under different governments, those which guard it most perfectly, are by the way of eminence called "free." Such governments attain most completely the end which is common to all government. A free constitution of government and a good constitution of government are therefore different expressions for the same idea.

Another material distinction, however, soon presents itself. In most civilized states the subject is tolerably protected against gross injustice from his fellows by impartial laws, which it is the manifest interest of the sovereign to enforce: but some commonwealths are so happy as to be founded on a principle of much more refined and provident wisdom. The subjects of such commonwealths are guarded not only against the injustice of each other, but (as far as human prudence can contrive) against oppression from the magistrate. Such states, like all other extraordinary examples of public or private excellence and happiness, are thinly scattered over the different ages and countries of the world. In them the will of the sovereign is limited with so exact a measure, that his protecting authority is not weakened. Such a combination of skill and fortune is not often to be expected, and indeed never can arise, but from the constant though gradual exertions of wisdom and virtue, to improve a long succession of most favourable circumstances. There is, indeed, scarce any society so wretched as to be destitute of some sort of weak provision against the injustice of their governors. Religious institutions, favourite prejudices, national manners, have in different countries, with unequal degrees of force, checked or mitigated the exercise of supreme power. The privileges of a powerful nobility, of opulent mercantile communities, of great judicial corporations, have in some monarchies approached more near to a control on the sovereign. Means have been devised with more or less wisdom to temper the despotism of an aristocracy over their subjects, and in democracies to protect the minority against the majority, and the whole people against the tyranny of demagogues. But in these unmixed forms of government, as the right of legislation is vested in one individual or in one order, it is obvious that the legislative power may shake off all the restraints which the laws have imposed on it. All such governments, therefore, tend towards despotism, and the securities which they admit against misgovernment are extremely feeble and precarious. The best security which human wisdom can devise, seems to be the distribution of political authority among different individuals and bodies, with separate interests, and separate characters, corresponding to the variety of classes of which civil society is composed,—each interested to guard their own order from oppression by the rest,—each also interested to prevent any of the others from seizing on exclusive, and therefore despotic power; and all having a common interest to co-operate in carrying on the ordinary and necessary administration of government. If there were not an interest to resist each other in extraordinary cases, there would not be liberty: if there were not an interest to co-operate in the ordinary course of affairs, there could be no government. The object of such wise institutions, which make selfishness of governors a security against their injustice, is to protect men against wrong both from their rulers and their fellows. Such governments are, with justice, peculiarly and emphatically called "free;" and in ascribing that liberty to the skilful combination of mutual dependance and mutual check, I feel my own conviction greatly strengthened by calling to mind, that in this opinion I agree with all the wise men who have ever deeply considered the principles of politics;—with Aristotle and Polybius, with Cicero and Tacitus, with Bacon and Machiavel, with Montesquieu and Hume.* It is impossible in such a cursory sketch as the present, even to allude to a very small part of those philosophical principles, poli-

* To the weight of these great names let me add the opinion of two illustrious men of the present age, as both their opinions are combined by one of them in the following passages: "He (Mr. Fox) always thought any of the simple unbalanced governments bad; simple monarchy, simple aristocracy, simple democracy; he held them all imperfect or vicious, all were bad by themselves; the composition alone was good. These had been always his principles, in which he agreed with his friend, Mr. Burke."—Speech on the Army Estimates, 9th Feb. 1790. In speaking of both these illustrious men, whose names I here join, as they will be joined in fame by posterity, which will forget their temporary differences in the recollection of their genius and their friendship, I do not entertain the vain imagination that I can add to their glory by any thing that I can say. But it is a gratification to me to give utterance to my feelings; to express the profound veneration with which I am filled for the memory of the one, and the warm affection which I cherish for the other, whom no one ever heard in public without admiration, or knew in private life without loving.

tical reasonings, and historical facts, which are necessary for the illustration of this momentous subject. In a full discussion of it I shall be obliged to examine the general frame of the most celebrated governments of ancient and modern times, and especially of those which have been most renowned for their freedom. The result of such an examination will be, that no institution so detestable as an absolutely unbalanced government, perhaps ever existed; that the simple governments are mere creatures of the imagination of theorists, who have transformed names used for convenience of arrangement into real politics; that, as constitutions of government approach more nearly to that unmixed and uncontrolled simplicity they become despotic, and as they recede farther from that simplicity they become free.

By the constitution of a state, I mean "the body of those written and unwritten fundamental laws which regulate the most important rights of the higher magistrates, and the most essential privileges* of the subjects." Such a body of political laws must in all countries arise out of the character and situation of a people; they must grow with its progress, be adapted to its peculiarities, change with its changes, and be incorporated with its habits. Human wisdom cannot form such a constitution by one act, for human wisdom cannot create the materials of which it is composed. The attempt, always ineffectual, to change by violence the ancient habits of men, and the established order of society, so as to fit them for an absolutely new scheme of government, flows from the most presumptuous ignorance, requires the support of the most ferocious tyranny, and leads to consequences which its authors can never foresee,—generally, indeed, to institutions the most opposite to those of which they profess to seek the establishment.† But human wisdom indefatigably employed in remedying abuses, and in seizing favourable opportunities of improving that order of society which arises from causes over which we have little control, after the reforms and amendments of a series of ages, has sometimes, though very rarely, shown itself capable of building up a free constitution, which is "the growth of time and nature, rather than the work of human invention."* Such a constitution can only be formed by the wise imitation of "the great innovater Time, which, indeed, innovateth greatly, but quietly, and by degrees scarce to be perceived."† Without descending to the puerile ostentation of panegyric, on that of which all mankind confess the excellence, I may observe, with truth and soberness, that a free government not only establishes a universal security against wrong, but that it also cherishes all the noblest powers of the human mind; that it tends to banish both the mean and the ferocious vices; that it improves the national character to which it is adapted, and out of which it grows; that its whole administration is a practical school of honesty and humanity; and that there the social affections, expanded into public spirit, gain a wider sphere, and a more active spring.

I shall conclude what I have to offer on government, by an account of the constitution of England. I shall endeavour to trace the progress of that constitution by the light of history, of laws, and of records, from the earliest times to the present age; and to show how the general principles of liberty, originally common to it with the other Gothic monarchies of Europe, but in other countries lost or obscured, were in this more fortunate island preserved, matured, and adapted to the progress of civilization. I shall attempt to exhibit this most complicated machine, as our history and our laws show it in action; and not as some celebrated writers have most imperfectly represented it, who have torn out a few of its more simple springs, and putting them together, miscal them the British constitution. So prevalent, indeed, have these imperfect representations hitherto been, that I will venture to affirm, there is scarcely any subject which has been less treated as it deserved than the government of England. Philosophers of great and merited reputation‡ have told us that it consisted of certain portions of monarchy, aristocracy, and democracy,—names which are, in truth, very little applicable, and which, if they were, would as little give an idea of this government, as an account of the weight of bone, of flesh, and of blood in a human body, would be a picture of a living man. Nothing but a patient and minute investigation of the

* Privilege, in Roman jurisprudence, means the *exemption* of one individual from the operation of a law. Political privileges, in the sense in which I employ the terms, mean those rights of the subjects of a free state, which are deemed so essential to the well-being of the commonwealth, that they are *excepted* from the ordinary discretion of the magistrate, and guarded by the same fundamental laws which secure his authority.

† See an admirable passage on this subject in Dr. Smith's Theory of Moral Sentiments (vol. ii. pp. 101—112), in which the true doctrine of reformation is laid down with singular ability by that eloquent and philosophical writer. See also Mr. Burke's Speech on Economical Reform; and Sir M. Hale on the Amendment of Laws, in the Collection of my learned and most excellent friend, Mr. Hargrave, p. 248.

* Pour former un gouvernement modéré, il faut combiner les puissances, les régler, les tempérer, les faire agir; donner pour ainsi dire un lest à l'une, pour la mettre en état de résister à une autre; c'est un chef-d'œuvre de législation que le hasard fait rarement, et que rarement on laisse faire à la prudence. Un gouvernement despotique au contraire saute, pour ainsi dire, aux yeux; il est uniforme partout: comme il ne faut que des passions pour l'établir, tout le monde est bon pour cela.—Montesquieu, De l'Esprit de Loix, liv. v. c. 14.

† Bacon, Essay xxiv. (Of Innovations.)

‡ The reader will perceive that I allude to Montesquieu, whom I never name without reverence, though I shall presume, with humility, to criticise his account of a government which he only saw at a distance.

practice of the government in all its parts, and through its whole history, can give us just notions on this important subject. If a lawyer, without a philosophical spirit, be unequal to the examination of this great work of liberty and wisdom, still more unequal is a philosopher without practical, legal, and historical knowledge; for the first may want skill, but the second wants materials. The observations of Lord Bacon on political writers in general, are most applicable to those who have given us systematic descriptions of the English constitution. "All those who have written of governments have written as philosophers, or as lawyers, *and none as statesmen*. As for the philosophers, they make imaginary laws for imaginary commonwealths, and their discourses are as the stars, which give little light because they are so high."—"Hæc cognitio ad viros civiles proprie pertinet," as he tells us in another part of his writings; but unfortunately no experienced philosophical British statesman has yet devoted his leisure to a delineation of the constitution, which such a statesman alone can practically and perfectly know.

In the discussion of this great subject, and in all reasonings on the principles of politics, I shall labour, above all things, to avoid that which appears to me to have been the constant source of political error:—I mean the attempt to give an air of system, of simplicity, and of rigorous demonstration, to subjects which do not admit it. The only means by which this could be done, was by referring to a few simple causes, what, in truth, arose from immense and intricate combinations, and successions of causes. The consequence was very obvious. The system of the theorist, disencumbered from all regard to the real nature of things, easily assumed an air of speciousness: it required little dexterity, to make his arguments appear conclusive. But all men agreed that it was utterly inapplicable to human affairs. The theorist railed at the folly of the world, instead of confessing his own; and the man of practice unjustly blamed Philosophy, instead of condemning the sophist. The causes which the politician has to consider are, above all others, multiplied, mutable, minute, subtile, and, if I may so speak, evanescent, —perpetually changing their form, and varying their combinations,—losing their nature, while they keep their name,—exhibiting the most different consequences in the endless variety of men and nations on whom they operate,—in one degree of strength producing the most signal benefit, and, under a slight variation of circumstances, the most tremendous mischiefs. They admit indeed of being reduced to theory; but to a theory formed on the most extensive views, of the most comprehensive and flexible principles, to embrace all their varieties, and to fit all their rapid transmigrations,—a theory, of which the most fundamental maxim is, distrust in itself, and deference for practical prudence. Only two writers of former times have, as far as I know, observed this general defect of political reasoners; but these two are the greatest philosophers who have ever appeared in the world. The first of them is Aristotle, who, in a passage of his politics, to which I cannot at this moment turn, plainly condemns the pursuit of a delusive geometrical accuracy in moral reasonings as the constant source of the grossest error. The second is Lord Bacon, who tells us, with that authority of conscious wisdom which belongs to him, and with that power of richly adorning Truth from the wardrobe of Genius which he possessed above *almost* all men, "Civil knowledge is conversant about a subject which, above all others, is most immersed in matter, and hardliest reduced to axiom."†

I shall next endeavour to lay open the general principles of civil and criminal laws. On this subject I may with some confidence hope that I shall be enabled to philosophise with better materials by my acquaintance with the laws of my own country, which it is the business of my life to practise, and of which the study has by habit become my favourite pursuit.

The first principles of jurisprudence are simple maxims of Reason, of which the observance is immediately discovered by experience to be essential to the security of men's rights, and which pervade the laws of all countries. An account of the gradual application of these original principles, first to more simple, and afterwards to more complicated cases, forms both the history and the theory of law. Such an historical account of the progress of men, in reducing justice to an applicable and practical system, will enable us to trace that chain, in which so many breaks and interruptions are perceived by superficial observers, but which in truth inseparably, though with many dark and hidden windings, links together the security of life and property with the most minute and apparently frivolous formalities of legal proceeding. We shall perceive that no human foresight is sufficient to establish such a system at once, and that, if it were so established, the occurrence of unforeseen cases would shortly altogether change it; that there is but one way of forming a civil code, either consistent with common sense, or that has ever been practised in any country,—namely, that of gradually building up the law in proportion as the facts arise which it is to regulate. We shall learn to appre-

* Probably book iii. cap. 11.—Ed.

† This principle is expressed by a writer of a very different character from these two great philosophers,—a writer, "qu'on n'appellera plus philosophe, mais qu'on appellera le plus éloquent des sophistes," with great force, and, as his manner is, with some exaggeration. "Il n'y a point de principes abstraits dans la politique. C'est une science des calculs, des combinaisons, et des exceptions, selon les lieux, les tems, et les circonstances."—Lettre de Rousseau au Marquis de Mirabeau. The second proposition is true; but the first is not a just inference from it.

ciate the merit of vulgar objections against the subtilty and complexity of laws. We shall estimate the good sense and the gratitude of those who reproach lawyers for employing all the powers of their mind to discover subtle distinctions for the prevention of justice;* and we shall at once perceive that laws ought to be neither more simple nor more complex than the state of society which they are to govern, but that they ought exactly to correspond to it. Of the two faults, however, the excess of simplicity would certainly be the greatest; for laws, more complex than are necessary, would only produce embarrassment; whereas laws more simple than the affairs which they regulate would occasion a defeat of Justice. More understanding has perhaps been in this manner exerted to fix the rules of life than in any other science;† and it is certainly the most honourable occupation of the understanding, because it is the most immediately subservient to general safety and comfort. There is not so noble a spectacle as that which is displayed in the progress of jurisprudence; where we may contemplate the cautious and unwearied exertions of a succession of wise men, through a long course of ages, withdrawing every case as it arises from the dangerous power of discretion, and subjecting it to inflexible rules,—extending the dominion of justice and reason, and gradually contracting, within the narrowest possible limits, the domain of brutal force and of arbitrary will. This subject has been treated with such dignity by a writer who is admired by all mankind for his eloquence, but who is, if possible, still more admired by all competent judges for his philosophy,—a writer, of whom I may justly say, that he was "gravissimus et dicendi et intelligendi auctor et magister,"—that I cannot refuse myself the gratification of quoting his words:—"The science of jurisprudence, the pride of the human intellect, which, with all its defects, redundancies, and errors, is the collected reason of ages combining the principles of original justice with the infinite variety of human concerns."‡

I shall exemplify the progress of law, and illustrate those principles of Universal Justice on which it is founded, by a comparative review of the two greatest civil codes that have been hitherto formed,—those of Rome and of England,§—of their agreements and disagreements, both in general provisions, and in some of the most important parts of their minute practice. In this part of the course, which I mean to pursue with such detail as to give a view of both codes, that may perhaps be sufficient for the purposes of the general student, I hope to convince him that the laws of civilized nations, particularly those of his own, are a subject most worthy of scientific curiosity; that principle and system run through them even to the minutest particular, as really, though not so apparently, as in other sciences, and applied to purposes more important than those of any other science. Will it be presumptuous to express a hope, that such an inquiry may not be altogether a useless introduction to that larger and more detailed study of the law of England, which is the duty of those who are to profess and practise that law?

In considering the important subject of criminal law it will be my duty to found, on a regard to the general safety, the right of the magistrate to inflict punishments, even the most severe, if that safety cannot be effectually protected by the example of inferior punishments. It will be a more agreeable part of my office to explain the temperaments which Wisdom, as well as Humanity, prescribes in the exercise of that harsh right, unfortunately so essential to the preservation of human society. I shall collate the penal codes of different nations, and gather together the most accurate statement of the result of experience with respect to the efficacy of lenient and severe punishments; and I shall endeavour to ascertain the principles on which must be founded both the proportion and the appropriation of penalties to crimes. As to the law of criminal proceeding, my labour will be very easy; for on that subject an English lawyer, if he were to delineate the model of perfection, would find that, with few exceptions, he had transcribed the institutions of his own country.

The next great division of the subject is the "law of nations," strictly and properly so called. I have already hinted at the general principles on which this law is founded. They, like all the principles of natural jurisprudence, have been more happily cultivated, and more generally obeyed, in some ages and countries than in others; and, like them, are susceptible of great variety in their application, from the character and usage of nations. I shall consider these principles in the gradation of those which are necessary to any tolerable intercourse between nations, of those which are essential to all well-regulated and mutually ad-

* "The casuistical subtilties are not perhaps greater than the subtilties of lawyers; but the latter are innocent, and even necessary."—Hume, Essays, vol. ii. p. 558.

† "Law," said Dr. Johnson, "is the science in which the greatest powers of the understanding are applied to the greatest number of facts." Nobody, who is acquainted with the variety and multiplicity of the subjects of jurisprudence, and with the prodigious powers of discrimination employed upon them, can doubt the truth of this observation.

‡ Burke, Works, vol. iii. p. 134.

§ On the intimate connection of these two codes, let us hear the words of Lord Holt, whose name never can be pronounced without veneration, as long as wisdom and integrity are revered among men:—"Inasmuch as the laws of all nations are doubtless raised out of the ruins of the civil law, as all governments are sprung out of the ruins of the Roman empire, it must be owned that the principles of our law are borrowed from the civil law, therefore grounded upon the same reason in many things."—12 Mod. Rep. 482.

vantageous intercourse, and of those which are highly conducive to the preservation of a mild and friendly intercourse between civilized states. Of the first class, every understanding acknowledges the necessity, and some traces of a faint reverence for them are discovered even among the most barbarous tribes; of the second, every well-informed man perceives the important use, and they have generally been respected by all polished nations; of the third, the great benefit may be read in the history of modern Europe, where alone they have been carried to their full perfection. In unfolding the first and second class of principles, I shall naturally be led to give an account of that law of nations, which, in greater or less perfection, regulated the intercourse of savages, of the Asiatic empires, and of the ancient republics. The third brings me to the consideration of the law of nations, as it is now acknowledged in Christendom. From the great extent of the subject, and the particularity to which, for reasons already given, I must here descend, it is impossible for me, within my moderate compass, to give even an outline of this part of the coursè. It comprehends, as every reader will perceive, the principles of national independence, the intercourse of nations in peace, the privileges of ambassadors and inferior ministers, the commerce of private subjects, the grounds of just war, the mutual duties of belligerent and neutral powers, the limits of lawful hostility, the rights of conquest, the faith to be observed in warfare, the force of an armistice,—of safe conducts and passports, the nature and obligation of alliances, the means of negotiation, and the authority and interpretation of treaties of peace. All these, and many other most important and complicated subjects, with all the variety of moral reasoning, and historical examples which is necessary to illustrate them, must be fully examined in that part of the lectures, in which I shall endeavour to put together a tolerably complete practical system of the law of nations, as it has for the last two centuries been recognised in Europe.

"Le droit des gens est naturellement fondé sur ce principe, que les diverses nations doivent se faire, dans la paix le plus de bien, et dans la guerre le moins de mal, qu'il est possible, sans nuire à leurs véritables intérêts. L'objet de la guerre c'est la victoire; celui de la victoire la conquête; celui de la conquête la conservation. De ce principe et du précédent, doivent dériver toutes les loix qui forment le droit des gens. Toutes les nations ont un droit des gens; et les Iroquois même, qui mangent leurs prisonniers, en ont un. Ils envoient et reçoivent des embassades; ils connoissent les droits de la guerre et de la paix: le mal est que ce droit des gens n'est pas fondé sur les vrais principes."*

As an important supplement to the practical system of our modern law of nations, or rather as a necessary part of it, I shall conclude with a survey of the diplomatic and conventional law of Europe, and of the treaties which have materially affected the distribution of power and territory among the European states,—the circumstances which gave rise to them, the changes which they effected, and the principles which they introduced into the public code of the Christian commonwealth. In ancient times the knowledge of this conventional law was thought one of the greatest praises that could be bestowed on a name loaded with all the honours that eminence in the arts of peace and war can confer: "Equidem existimo judices, cùm in omni genere ac varietate artium, etiam illarum, quæ sine summo otio non facilè discuntur, Cn. Pompeius excellat, singularem quandam laudem ejus et præstabilem esse scientiam, in fœderibus, pactionibus, conditionibus, populorum, regum, exterarum nationum: in universo denique belli jure ac pacis."* Information on this subject is scattered over an immense variety of voluminous compilations, not accessible to every one, and of which the perusal can be agreeable only to a very few. Yet so much of these treaties has been embodied into the general law of Europe, that no man can be master of it who is not acquainted with them. The knowledge of them is necessary to negotiators and statesmen; it may sometimes be important to private men in various situations in which they may be placed; it is useful to all men who wish either to be acquainted with modern history, or to form a sound judgment on political measures. I shall endeavour to give such an abstract of it as may be sufficient for some, and a convenient guide for others in the farther progress of their studies. The treaties which I shall more particularly consider, will be those of Westphalia, of Oliva, of the Pyrenees, of Breda, of Nimeguen, of Ryswick, of Utrecht, of Aix-la-Chapelle, of Paris (1763), and of Versailles (1783). I shall shortly explain the other treaties, of which the stipulations are either alluded to, confirmed, or abrogated in those which I consider at length. I shall subjoin an account of the diplomatic intercourse of the European powers with the Ottoman Porte, and with other princes and states who are without the pale of our ordinary federal law; together with a view of the most important treaties of commerce, their principles, and their consequences.

As an useful appendix to a practical treatise on the law of nations, some account will be given of those tribunals which in different countries of Europe decide controversies arising out of that law; of their constitution, of the extent of their authority, and of their modes of proceeding; more especially of those courts which are peculiarly appointed for that purpose by the laws of Great Britain.

Though the course, of which I have sketched the outline, may seem to comprehend so

* De l'Esprit des Loix, liv. i. c. 3.

* Cic. Orat. pro L. Corn. Balbo, c. vi.

great a variety of miscellaneous subjects, yet they are all in truth closely and inseparably interwoven. The duties of men, of subjects, of princes, of lawgivers, of magistrates, and of states, are all parts of one consistent system of universal morality. Between the most abstract and elementary maxim of moral philosophy, and the most complicated controversies of civil or public law, there subsists a connection which it will be the main object of these lectures to trace. The principle of justice, deeply rooted in the nature and interest of man, pervades the whole system, and is discoverable in every part of it, even to its minutest ramification in a legal formality, or in the construction of an article in a treaty.

I know not whether a philosopher ought to confess, that in his inquiries after truth he is biassed by any consideration,—even by the love of virtue. But I, who conceive that a real philosopher ought to regard truth itself chiefly on account of its subserviency to the happiness of mankind, am not ashamed to confess, that I shall feel a great consolation at the conclusion of these lectures, if, by a wide survey and an exact examination of the conditions and relations of human nature, I shall have confirmed but one individual in the conviction, that justice is the permanent interest of all men, and of all commonwealths. To discover one new link of that eternal chain by which the Author of the universe has bound together the happiness and the duty of His creatures, and indissolubly fastened their interests to each other, would fill my heart with more pleasure than all the fame with which the most ingenious paradox ever crowned the most eloquent sophist. I shall conclude this Discourse in the noble language of two great orators and philosophers, who have, in a few words, stated the substance, the object, and the result of all morality, and politics, and law. "Nihil est quod adhuc de republicâ putem dictum, et quo possim longius progredi, nisi sit confirmatum, non modo falsum esse illud, sine injuriâ non posse, sed hoc verissimum, sine summâ justitiâ rempublicam geri nullo modo posse."* "Justice is itself the great standing policy of civil society, and any eminent departure from it, under any circumstances, lies under the suspicion of being no policy at all."†

* Cic De Repub. lib. ii.

† Burke, Works, vol. iii. p. 207.

LIFE OF SIR THOMAS MORE.

Aristotle and Bacon, the greatest philosophers of the ancient and the modern world, agree in representing poetry as being of a more excellent nature than history. Agreeably to the predominance of mere understanding in Aristotle's mind, he alleges as his cause of preference that poetry regards general truth, or conformity to universal nature; while history is conversant only with a confined and accidental truth, dependent on time, place, and circumstance. The ground assigned by Bacon is such as naturally issued from that fusion of imagination with reason, which constitutes his philosophical genius. Poetry is ranked more highly by him, because the poet presents us with a pure excellence and an unmingled grandeur, not to be found in the coarse realities of life or of history; but which the mind of man, although not destined to reach, is framed to contemplate with delight.

The general difference between biography and history is obvious. There have been many men in every age whose lives are full of interest and instruction; but who, having never taken a part in public affairs, are altogether excluded from the province of the historian: there have been also, probably, equal numbers who have influenced the fortune of nations in peace or in war, of the peculiarities of whose character we have no information; and who, for the purposes of the biographer, may be said to have had no private life. These are extreme cases: but there are other men, whose manners and acts are equally well known, whose individual lives are deeply interesting, whose characteristic qualities are peculiarly striking, who have taken an important share in events connected with the most extraordinary revolutions of human affairs, and whose biography becomes more difficult from that combination and intermixture of private with public occurrences, which render it instructive and interesting. The variety and splendour of the lives of such men render it often difficult to distinguish the portion of them which ought to be admitted into history, from that which should be reserved for biography. Generally speaking, these two parts are so distinct and unlike, that they cannot be confounded without much injury to both;—as when the biographer hides the portrait of the individual by a crowded and confined picture of events, or when the historian allows unconnected narratives of the lives of men to break the thread of history. The historian contemplates only the surface of human nature, adorned and disguised (as when actors perform brilliant parts before a great audience), in the midst of so many dazzling circumstances, that it is hard to estimate the intrinsic worth of individuals, —and impossible, in an historical relation, to exhibit the secret springs of their conduct.

The biographer endeavours to follow the hero and the statesman, from the field, the council, or the senate, to his private dwelling, where, in the midst of domestic ease, or of social pleasure, he throws aside the robe and the mask, becomes again a man instead of an actor, and, in spite of himself, often betrays those frailties and singularities which are visible in the countenance and voice, the gesture and manner, of every one when he is not playing a part. It is particularly difficult to observe the distinction in the case of Sir Thomas More, because he was so perfectly natural a man that he carried his amiable peculiarities into the gravest deliberations of state, and the most solemn acts of law. Perhaps nothing more can be universally laid down, than that the biographer never ought to introduce public events, except in as far as they are absolutely necessary to the illustration of character, and that the historian should rarely digress into biographical particulars, except in as far as they contribute to the clearness of his narrative of political occurrences.

Sir Thomas More was born in Milk Street, in the city of London, in the year 1480, three years before the death of Edward IV. His family was respectable,—no mean advantage at that time. His father, Sir John More, who was born about 1440, was entitled by his descent to use an armorial bearing,—a privilege guarded strictly and jealously as the badge of those who then began to be called gentry, and who, though separated from the lords of parliament by political rights, yet formed with them in the order of society one body, corresponding to those called noble in the other countries of Europe. Though the political power of the barons was on the wane, the social position of the united body of nobility and gentry retained its dignity.* Sir John More was one of the justices of the court of King's Bench to the end of his long life; and, according to his son's account, well performed the peaceable duties of civil life, being gentle in his deportment, blameless, meek and merciful, an equitable judge, and an upright man.†

Sir Thomas More received the first rudiments of his education at St. Anthony's school, in Thread-needle Street, under Nicholas Hart: for the daybreak of letters was now so bright, that the reputation of schools was carefully noted, and schoolmasters began to be held in some part of the estimation which they merit. Here, however, his studies were confined to Latin; the cultivation of Greek, which contains the sources and models of Roman literature, being yet far from having descended to the level of the best among the schools. It was the custom of that age that young gentlemen should pass part of their boyhood in the house and service of their superiors, where they might profit by listening to the conversation of men of experience, and gradually acquire the manners of the world. It was not deemed derogatory from youths of rank,—it was rather thought a beneficial expedient for inuring them to stern discipline and implicit obedience, that they should be trained, during this noviciate, in humble and even menial offices. A young gentleman thought himself no more lowered by serving as a page in the family of a great peer or prelate, than a Courtenay or a Howard considered it as a degradation to be the huntsman or the cupbearer of a Tudor.

More was fortunate in the character of his master: when his school studies were thought to be finished, about his fifteenth year, he was placed in the house of Cardinal Morton, archbishop of Canterbury. This prelate, who was born in 1410, was originally an eminent civilian, canonist, and a practiser of note in the ecclesiastical courts. He had been a Lancastrian, and the fidelity with which he adhered to Henry VI., till that unfortunate prince's death, recommended him to the confidence and patronage of Edward IV. He negotiated the marriage with the princess Elizabeth, which reconciled (with whatever confusion of titles) the conflicting pretensions of York and Lancaster, and raised Henry Tudor to the throne. By these services, and by his long experience in affairs, he continued to be prime minister till his death, which happened in 1500, at the advanced age of ninety.* Even at the time of More's entry into his household, the old cardinal, though then fourscore and five years, was pleased with the extraordinary promise of the sharp and lively boy; as aged persons sometimes, as it were, catch a glimpse of the pleasure of youth, by entering for a moment into its feelings. More broke into the rude dramas performed at the cardinal's Christmas festivities, to which he was too young to be invited, and often invented at the moment speeches for himself, "which made the lookers-on more sport than all the players beside." The cardinal, much delighting in his wit and towardness, would often say of him unto the nobles that dined with him,—"This child here waiting at the table, whosoever shall live to see it, will

* "In Sir Thomas More's epitaph, he describes himself as 'born of no noble family, but of an honest stock,' (or in the words of the original, familiâ non celebri, sed honestâ natus,) a true translation, as we here take *nobility* and *noble;* for none under a baron, except he be of the privy council, doth challenge it; and in this sense he meant it; but as the Latin word *nobilis* is taken in other countries for gentrie, it was otherwise. Sir John More bare arms from his birth; and though we cannot certainly tell who were his ancestors, they must needs be gentlemen."—Life of More (commonly reputed to be) by Thomas More, his great grandson, pp. 3, 4. This book will be cited henceforward as "More."

† "Homo civilis, innocens, mitis, integer."—Epitaph

* Dodd's Church History, vol. i. p. 141. The Roman Catholics, now restored to their just rank in society, have no longer an excuse for not continuing this useful work. [This has been accordingly done since this note was written, by the Rev. M. A. Tierney.—Ed.]

prove a marvellous man."* More, in his historical work, thus commemorates this early friend, not without a sidelong glance at the acts of a courtier:—"He was a man of great natural wit, very well learned, honourable in behaviour, lacking in no wise to win favour."† In Utopia he praises the cardinal more lavishly, and with no restraint from the severe justice of history. It was in Morton's house that he was probably first known to Colet, dean of St. Paul's, the founder of St. Paul's school, and one of the most eminent restorers of ancient literature in England; who was wont to say, that "there was but one wit in England, and that was young Thomas More."‡

More went to Oxford in 1497, where he appears to have had apartments in St. Mary's Hall, but to have carried on his studies at Canterbury College,§ on the spot where Wolsey afterwards reared the magnificent edifice of Christchurch. At that university he found a sort of civil war waged between the partisans of Greek literature, who were then innovators in education and suspected of heresy, if not of infidelity, on the one hand; and on the other side the larger body, comprehending the aged, the powerful, and the celebrated, who were content to be no wiser than their forefathers. The younger followers of the latter faction affected the ridiculous denomination of Trojans, and assumed the names of Priam, Hector, Paris, and Æneas, to denote their hostility to the Greeks. The puerile pedantry of these coxcombs had the good effect of awakening the zeal of More for his Grecian masters, and of inducing him to withstand the barbarism which would exclude the noblest productions of the human mind from the education of English youth. He expostulated with the university in a letter addressed to the whole body, reproaching them with the better example of Cambridge, where the gates were thrown open to the higher classics of Greece, as freely as to their Roman imitators.‖ The established clergy even then, though Luther had not yet alarmed them, strangers as they were to the new learning, affected to contemn that of which they were ignorant, and could not endure the prospect of a rising generation more learned than themselves. Their whole education was Latin, and their instruction was limited to Roman and canon law, to theology, and school philosophy. They dreaded the downfal of the authority of the Vulgate from the study of Greek and Hebrew. But the course of things was irresistible. The scholastic system was now on the verge of general disregard, and the perusal of the greatest Roman writers turned all eyes towards the Grecian masters. What man of high capacity, and of ambition becoming his faculties, could read Cicero without a desire to comprehend Demosthenes and Plato? What youth desirous of excellence but would rise from the study of the Georgics and the Æneid, with a wish to be acquainted with Hesiod and Apollonius, with Pindar, and above all with Homer? These studies were then pursued, not with the dull languor and cold formality with which the indolent, incapable, incurious majority of boys obey the prescribed rules of an old establishment, but with the enthusiastic admiration with which the superior few feel an earnest of their own higher powers, in the delight which arises in their minds at the contemplation of new beauty, and of excellence unimagined before.

More found several of the restorers of Grecian literature at Oxford, who had been the scholars of the exiled Greeks in Italy;—Grocyn, the first professor of Greek in the university; Linacre, the accomplished founder of the college of physicians; and William Latimer, of whom we know little more than what we collect from the general testimony borne by his most eminent contemporaries to his learning and virtue. Grocyn, the first of the English restorers, was a late learner, being in the forty-eighth year of his age when he went, in 1488, to Italy, where the fountains of ancient learning were once more opened. After having studied under Politian, and learnt Greek from Chalcondylas, one of the lettered emigrants who educated the teachers of the western nations, he returned to Oxford, where he taught that language to More, to Linacre, and to Erasmus. Linacre followed the example of Grocyn in visiting Italy, and profiting by the instructions of Chalcondylas. Colet spent four years in the same country, and in the like studies. William Latimer repaired at a mature age to Padua, in quest of that knowledge which was not to be acquired at home. He was afterwards chosen to be tutor to Reginald Pole, the King's cousin; and Erasmus, by attributing to him "maidenly modesty," leaves in one word an agreeable impression of the character of a man chosen for his scholarship to be Linacre's colleague in a projected translation of Aristotle, and solicited by the latter for aid in his edition of the New Testament.*

At Oxford More became known to a man far more extraordinary than any of these scholars. Erasmus had been invited to England by Lord Mountjoy, who had been his pupil at Paris, and continued to be his friend during life. He resided at Oxford during a great part of 1497; and having returned to Paris in 1498, spent the latter portion of the same year at the university of Oxford, where he again had an opportunity of pouring his zeal for Greek study into the mind of More. Their friendship, though formed at an age of considerable disparity,—Erasmus being then

* Roper's Life of Sir T. More, edited by Singer. This book will be cited henceforward as "Roper."

† History of Richard III.

‡ More, p. 25.

§ Athenæ Oxonienses, vol. i. p. 79.

‖ See this Letter in the Appendix to the second volume of Jortin's Life of Erasmus.

* For Latimer, see Dodd, Church History, vol. i. p. 219.: for Grocyn, Ibid. p. 227: for Colet and Linacre, all biographical compilations.

thirty and More only seventeen,—lasted throughout the whole of their lives. Erasmus had acquired only the rudiments of Greek at the age most suited to the acquisition of languages, and was now completing his knowledge on that subject at a period of mature manhood, which he jestingly compares with the age at which the elder Cato commenced his Grecian studies.* Though Erasmus himself seems to have been much excited towards Greek learning by the example of the English scholars, yet the cultivation of classical literature was then so small a part of the employment or amusement of life, that William Latimer, one of the most eminent of these scholars, to whom Erasmus applied for aid in his edition of the Greek Testament, declared that he had not read a page of Greek or Latin for nine years,† that he had almost forgotten his ancient literature, and that Greek books were scarcely procurable in England. Sir John More, inflexibly adhering to the old education, and dreading that the allurements of literature might seduce his son from law, discouraged the pursuit of Greek, and at the same time reduced the allowance of Thomas to the level of the most frugal life;—a parsimony for which the son was afterwards, though not then, thankful, as having taught him good husbandry, and preserved him from dissipation.

At the university, or soon after leaving it, young More composed the greater part of his English verses; which are not such as, from their intrinsic merit, in a more advanced state of our language and literature, would be deserving of particular attention. But as the poems of a contemporary of Skelton, they may merit more consideration. Our language was still neglected, or confined chiefly to the vulgar uses of life. Its force, its compass, and its capacity of harmony, were untried: for though Chaucer had shone brightly for a season, the century which followed was dark and wintry. No master genius had impregnated the nation with poetical sensibility. In these inauspicious circumstances, the composition of poems, especially if they manifest a sense of harmony, and some adaptation of the sound to the subject, indicates a delight in poetry, and a proneness to that beautiful art, which in such an age is a more than ordinary token of a capacity for it. The experience of all ages, however it may be accounted for, shows that the mind, when melted into tenderness, or exalted by the contemplation of grandeur, vents its feelings in language suited to a state of excitement, and delights in distinguishing its diction from common speech by some species of measure and modulation, which combines the gratification of the ear with that of the fancy and the heart. The secret connection between a poetical ear and a poetical soul is touched by the most sublime of poets, who consoled himself in his blindness by the remembrance of those who, under the like calamity,

> ——Feed on thoughts that voluntary move
> Harmonious numbers.

We may be excused for throwing a glance over the compositions of a writer, who is represented a century after his death, by Ben Jonson, as one of the models of English literature. More's poem on the death of Elizabeth, the wife of Henry VII., and his merry jest How a Serjeant would play the Friar, may be considered as fair samples of his pensive and sportive vein. The superiority of the latter shows his natural disposition to pleasantry. There is a sort of dancing mirth in the metre which seems to warrant the observation above hazarded, that in a rude period the structure of verse may be regarded as some presumption of a genius for poetry. In a refined age, indeed, all the circumstances are different: the frame-work of metrical composition is known to all the world; it may be taught by rule, and acquired mechanically; the greatest facility of versification may exist without a spark of genius. Even then, however, the secrets of the art of versification are chiefly revealed to a chosen few by their poetical sensibility; so that sufficient remains of the original tie still continue to attest its primitive origin. It is remarkable, that the most poetical of the poems is written in Latin: it is a poem addressed to a lady, with whom he had been in love when he was sixteen years old, and she fourteen; and it turns chiefly on the pleasing reflection that his affectionate remembrance restored to her the beauty, of which twenty-five years seemed to others to have robbed her.*

When More had completed his time at Oxford, he applied himself to the study of the law, which was to be the occupation of his life. He first studied at New Inn, and afterwards at Lincoln's Inn.† The societies of lawyers having purchased some *inns*, or noblemen's residences, in London, were hence called "inns of court." It was not then a metaphor to call them an university; they had professors of law; they conferred the characters of barrister and serjeant, analogous to the degrees of bachelor, master, and doctor, bestowed by the universities; and every man, before he became a barrister, was subjected to examination, and obliged

* "Delibavimus et olim has literas, sed summis duntaxat labiis; at nuper paulo altius ingressi, videmus id quod sæpenumero apud gravissimos auctores legimus,—Latinam eruditionem, quamvis impendiosam, citra Græcismum mancam esse ac dimidiatam. Apud nos enim rivuli vix quidam sunt, et lacunulæ lutulentæ; apud illos fontes purissimi et flumina aurum volventia."—Opera. Lug. Bat. 1703. vol. iii. p. 63.

† Ibid. vol. iii. p. 293.

* "Gratulatur quod eam repererit incolumem quam olim fermè puer amaverat."—Not. in Poem. It does not seem reconcilable with dates, that his lady could have been the younger sister of Jane Colt. Vide *infrà*.

† Inn was successively applied, like the French word *hotel*, first to the town mansion of a great man, and afterwards to a house where all mankind were entertained for money.

to defend a thesis. More was appointed reader at Furnival's Inn, where he delivered lectures for three years. The English law had already grown into a science, formed by a process of generalisation from usages and decisions, with less help from the Roman law than the jurisprudence of any other country, though not with that total independence of it which English lawyers in former times considered as a subject of boast: it was rather formed as the law of Rome itself had been formed, than adopted from that noble system. When More began to lecture on English law, it was by no means in a disorderly and neglected state. The ecclesiastical lawyers, whose arguments and determinations were its earliest materials, were well prepared, by the logic and philosophy of their masters the Schoolmen, for those exact and even subtle distinctions which the precision of the rules of jurisprudence eminently required. In the reigns of the Lancastrian princes, Littleton had reduced the law to an elementary treatise, distinguished by a clear method and an elegant conciseness. Fortescue had during the same time compared the governments of England and France with the eye of a philosophical observer. Brooke and Fitzherbert had compiled digests of the law, which they called (it might be thought, from their size, ironically) "Abridgments." The latter composed a treatise, still very curious, on "writs;" that is, on those commands (formerly from the king) which constitute essential parts of every legal proceeding. Other writings on jurisprudence occupied the printing presses of London in the earliest stage* of their existence. More delivered lectures also at St. Lawrence's church in the Old Jewry, on the work of St. Augustine, De Civitate Dei, that is, on the divine government of the moral world; which must seem to readers who look at ancient times through modern habits, a very singular occupation for a young lawyer. But the clergy were then the chief depositaries of knowledge, and were the sole canonists and civilians, as they had once been the only lawyers.† Religion, morals, and law, were then taught together without due distinction between them, to the injury and confusion of them all. To these lectures, we are told by the affectionate biographer, "there resorted Doctor Grocyn, an excellent cunning man, and all the chief learned of the city of London."‡ More, in his lectures, however, did not so much discuss "the points of divinity as the precepts of moral philosophy and history, wherewith these books are replenished."§ The effect of the deep study of the first was, perhaps, however, to embitter his polemical writings, and somewhat to sour that naturally sweet temper, which was so deeply felt by his companions, that Erasmus scarcely ever concludes a letter to him without epithets more indicative of the most tender affection than of the calm feelings of friendship.*

The tenderness of More's nature combined with the instructions and habits of his education to predispose him to piety. As he lived in the neighbourhood of the great Carthusian monastery, called the "Charterhouse," for some years, he manifested a predilection for monastic life, and is said to have practised some of those austerities and self-inflictions which prevail among the gloomier and sterner orders. A pure mind in that age often sought to extinguish some of the inferior impulses of human nature, instead of employing them for their appointed purpose,—that of animating the domestic affections, and sweetening the most important duties of life. He soon learnt, however, by self-examination, his unfitness for the priesthood, and relinquished his project of taking orders, in words which should have warned his church against the imposition of unnatural self-denial on vast multitudes and successive generations of men.†

The same affectionate disposition which had driven him towards the visions, and, strange as it may seem, to the austerities of the monks, now sought a more natural channel. "He resorted to the house of one Maister Colt, a gentleman of Essex, who had often invited him thither; having three daughters, whose honest conversation and virtuous education provoked him there especially to set his affection. And albeit his mind most served him to the second daughter, for that he thought her the fairest and best favoured, yet when he considered that it would be both great grief, and some shame also, to the eldest, to see her younger sister preferred before her in marriage, he then of a certain pity framed his fancy toward her, and soon after married her, neverthemore discontinuing his study of the law at Lincoln's Inn."‡ His more remote descendant adds, that Mr. Colt "proffered unto him the choice of any of his daughters; and that More, out of a kind of compassion, settled his fancy on the eldest."§ Erasmus gives a turn to More's marriage with Jane Colt, which is too ingenious to be probable:—"He wedded a very young girl of respectable family, but who had hitherto lived in the country with her parents and sisters, and was so uneducated, that he could mould her to his own tastes and manners. He caused her to be instructed in letters; and she became a very skilful musician, which peculiarly pleased him."‖

The plain matter of fact seems to have been, that in an age when marriage chiefly depended upon a bargain between parents,

* Doctor and Student (by St. Germain) and Diversité des Courtes were both printed by Rastell in 1534.

† *Nullus causidicus nisi clericus.*

‡ Roper, p. 5. § More, p. 44.

* "Suavissime More." "Charissime More." "Mellitissime More."

† "Maluit maritus esse castus quam sacerdos impurus." Erasmus, Op. vol. iii. p. 475.

‡ Roper, p. 6. § More, p. 30.

‖ Erasmus, Op. vol. iii. p. 475.

on which sons were little consulted, and daughters not at all, More, emerging at twenty-one from the toil of acquiring Greek, and the voluntary self-torture of Carthusian mystics, was delighted at his first entry among pleasing young women, of whom the least attractive might, in these circumstances, have touched him; and that his slight preference for the second easily yielded to a good-natured reluctance to mortify the elder. Most young ladies in Essex, in the beginning of the sixteenth century, must have required some tuition to appear in London among scholars and courtiers, who were at that time more mingled than it is now usual for them to be. It is impossible to ascertain the precise shade of feeling which the biographers intended to denote by the words "pity" and "compassion," for the use of which they are charged with a want of gallantry or delicacy by modern writers; although neither of these terms, when the context is at the same time read, seems unhappily employed to signify the natural refinement, which shrinks from humbling the harmless self-complacency of an innocent girl.

The marriage proved so happy, that nothing was to be regretted in it but the shortness of the union, in consequence of the early death of Jane Colt, who left a son and three daughters; of whom Margaret, the eldest, inherited the features, the form, and the genius of her father, and requited his fond partiality by a daughterly love, which endured to the end.

In no long time* after the death of Jane Colt, he married Alice Middleton, a widow, seven years older than himself, and not handsome;—rather, for the care of his family, and the management of his house, than as a companion and a friend. He treated her, and indeed all females, except his daughter Margaret, as better qualified to relish a jest, than to take a part in more serious conversation; and in their presence gave an unbounded scope to his natural inclination towards pleasantry. He even indulged himself in a Latin play of words on her want of youth and beauty, calling her "nec bella nec puella."† "She was of good years, of no good favour or complexion, nor very rich, and by disposition near and worldly. It was reported that he wooed her for a friend of his; but she answering that he might speed if he spoke for himself, he married her with the consent of his friend, yielding to her that which perhaps he never would have done of his own accord. Indeed, her favour could not have bewitched, or scarce moved, any man to love her; but yet she proved a kind and careful mother-in-law to his children." Erasmus, who was often an inmate in the family, speaks of her as "a keen and watchful manager, with whom More lived on terms of as much respect and kindness as if she had been fair and young." Such is the happy power of a loving disposition, which overflows on companions, though their attractions or deserts should be slender. "No husband," continues Erasmus, "ever gained so much obedience from a wife by authority and severity, as More won by gentleness and pleasantry. Though verging on old age, and not of a yielding temper, he prevailed on her to take lessons on the lute, the cithara, the viol, the monochord, and the flute, which she daily practised to him. With the same gentleness he ruled his whole family, so that it was without broils or quarrels. He composed all differences, and never parted with any one on terms of unkindness. The house was fated to the peculiar felicity that those who dwelt in it were always raised to a higher fortune; and that no spot ever fell on the good name of its happy inhabitants." The course of More's domestic life is minutely described by eye-witnesses. "His custom was daily (besides his private prayers with his children) to say the seven psalms, the litany, and the suffrages following; so was his guise with his wife, children, and household, nightly before he went to bed, to go to his chapel, and there on his knees ordinarily to say certain psalms and collects with them."* "With him," says Erasmus, "you might imagine yourself in the academy of Plato. But I should do injustice to his house by comparing it to the academy of Plato, where numbers, and geometrical figures, and sometimes moral virtues, were the subjects of discussion; it would be more just to call it a school and exercise of the Christian religion. All its inhabitants, male or female, applied their leisure to liberal studies and profitable reading, although piety was their first care. No wrangling, no angry word, was heard in it; no one was idle: every one did his duty with alacrity, and not without a temperate cheerfulness."† Erasmus had not the sensibility of More; he was more prone to smile than to sigh at the concerns of men: but he was touched by the remembrance of these domestic solemnities in the household of his friend. He manifests an agreeable emotion at the recollection of these scenes in daily life, which tended to hallow the natural authority of parents, to bestow a sort of dignity on humble occupation, to raise menial offices to the rank of virtues, and to spread peace and cultivate kindness among those who had shared, and were soon again to share, the same modest rites, in gently breathing around them a spirit of meek equality, which rather humbled the pride of the great than disquieted the spirits of the lowly. More himself justly speaks of the hourly interchange of the smaller acts of kindness which flow from the charities of domestic life, as having a claim on his time as strong as the occupations which seemed

* "In a few months," says Erasmus, Op. vol. iii. p. 475.:—"within two or three years," according to his great grandson.—More, p. 32.

† Erasmus, vol. iii. p. 475.

* Roper, p. 25.

† Op. vol. iii. p. 1812.

to others so much more serious and important. "While," says he, "in pleading, in hearing, in deciding causes or composing differences, in waiting on some men about business, and on others out of respect, the greatest part of the day is spent on other men's affairs, the remainder of it must be given to my family at home; so that I can reserve no part of it to myself, that is, to study. I must talk with my wife, and chat with my children, and I have somewhat to say to my servants; for all these things I reckon as a part of my business, except a man will resolve to be a stranger at home; and with whomsoever either nature, chance, or choice, has engaged a man in any commerce, he must endeavour to make himself as acceptable to those about him as he can."*

His occupations now necessarily employed a large portion of his time. His professional practice became so considerable, that about the accession of Henry VIII., in 1509, with his legal office in the city of London, it produced 400*l.* a year, probably equivalent to an annual income of 5000*l.* in the present day. Though it be not easy to determine the exact period of the occurrences of his life, from his establishment in London to his acceptance of political office, the beginning of Henry VIII.'s reign may be considered as the time of his highest eminence at the bar. About this time a ship belonging to the Pope, or claimed by his Holiness on behalf of some of his subjects, happened to come to Southampton, where she was seized as a forfeiture,—probably as what is called a droit of the crown, or a droit of the admiralty,—though under what circumstances, or on what grounds we know not. The papal minister made suit to the King that the case might be argued for the Pope by learned counsel in a public place, and in presence of the minister himself, who was a distinguished civilian. None was found so well qualified to be of counsel for him as More, who could report in Latin all the arguments to his client, and who argued so learnedly on the Pope's side, that he succeeded in obtaining an order for the restitution of the vessel detained.

It has been already intimated, that about the same time he had been appointed to a judicial office in the city of London, which is described by his son-in-law as "that of one of the under-sheriffs." Roper, who was himself for many years an officer of the court of King's Bench, gives the name of the office correctly; but does not describe its nature and importance so truly as Erasmus, who tells his correspondent that More passed several years in the city of London as a judge in civil causes. "This office," he says, "though not laborious, for the court sits only on the forenoon of every Thursday, is accounted very honourable. No judge of that court ever went through more causes; none decided them more uprightly; often remitting the fees to which he was entitled from the suitors. His deportment in this capacity endeared him extremely to his fellow-citizens."* The under-sheriff was then apparently judge of the sheriff's court, which, being the county court for London and Middlesex, was, at that time, a station of honour and advantage.† For the county courts in general, and indeed all the ancient subordinate jurisdictions of the common law, had not yet been superseded by that concentration of authority in the hands of the superior courts at Westminster, which contributed indeed to the purity and dignity of the judicial character, as well as to the uniformity and the improvement of the administration of law,—but which cannot be said to have served in the same degree to promote a speedy and cheap redress of the wrongs suffered by those suitors to whom cost and delay are most grievous. More's office, in that state of the jurisdiction, might therefore have possessed the importance which his contemporaries ascribed to it; although the denomination of it would not make such an impression on modern ears. It is apparent, that either as a considerable source of his income, or as an honourable token of public confidence, this office was valued by More; since he informs Erasmus, in 1516, that he had declined a handsome pension offered to him by the king on his return from Flanders, and that he believed he should always decline it; because either it would oblige him to resign his office in the city, which he preferred to a better, or if he retained it, in case of a controversy of the city with the king for their privileges, he might be deemed by his fellow-citizens to be disabled by dependence on the crown from sincerely and faithfully maintaining their rights.‡ This last reasoning is also interesting, as the first intimation of the necessity of a city law-officer being independent of the crown, and of the legal resistance of the corporation of London to a Tudor king. It paved the way for those happier times in which the great city had the honour to number the Holts and the Denmans among her legal advisers.§

* Dedication of Utopia to Peter Giles, (Burnet's translation,) 1684.

* Erasmus, Op. vol. iii. p. 476.

† "In urbe suâ pro shyrevo dixit."—Epitaph.

‡ Erasmus, Op. vol. iii. p. 220.

§ From communications obtained for me from the records of the City, I am enabled to ascertain some particulars of the nature of More's appointment, which have occasioned a difference of opinion. On the 8th of May, 1514, it was agreed by the common council, "that, Thomas More, gentleman, one of the under-sheriffs of London, should occupy his office and chamber by a sufficient deputy, during his absence as the king's ambassador in Flanders." It appears from several entries in the same records, from 1496 to 1502 inclusive, that the under-sheriff was annually elected, or rather confirmed; for the practice was not to remove him without his own application or some serious fault. For six years of Henry's reign, Edward Dudley was one of the under-sheriffs; a circumstance which renders the superior importance of the office at that time probable. Thomas Marowe, the author of works on law esteemed in his time, though not published, appears also in the above records as under-sheriff.

More is the first person in our history distinguished by the faculty of public speaking. A remarkable occasion on which it was successfully employed in parliament against a lavish grant of money to the crown is thus recorded by his son-in-law as follows:—"In the latter time of king Henry VII. he was made a burgess of the parliament, wherein was demanded by the king about three fifteenths for the marriage of his eldest daughter, that then should be the Scottish queen. At the last debating whereof he made such arguments and reasons there against, that the king's demands were thereby clean overthrown; so that one of the king's privy chamber, named maister Tyler, being present thereat, brought word to the king out of the parliament house, that a beardless boy had disappointed all his purpose. Whereupon the king, conceiving great indignation towards him, could not be satisfied until he had some way revenged it. And forasmuch as he, nothing having, could nothing lose, his grace devised a causeless quarrel against his father; keeping him in the Tower till he had made him to pay 100*l.* fine," (probably on a charge of having infringed some obsolete penal law). "Shortly after, it fortuned that Sir T. More, coming in a suit to Dr. Fox, bishop of Winchester, one of the king's privy council, the bishop called him aside, and, pretending great favour towards him, promised that if he would be ruled by him he would not fail into the king's favour again to restore him; meaning, as it was afterwards conjectured, to cause him thereby to confess his offences against the king, whereby his highness might, with the better colour, have occasion to revenge his displeasure against him. But when he came from the bishop he fell into communication with one maister Whitforde, his familiar friend, then chaplain to that bishop, and showed him what the bishop had said, praying for his advice. Whitforde prayed him by the passion of God not to follow the counsel; for my lord, to serve the king's turn, will not stick to agree to his own father's death. So Sir Thomas More returned to the bishop no more; and had not the king died soon after, he was determined to have gone over sea."* That the advice of Whitforde was wise, appeared from a circumstance which occurred nearly ten years after, which exhibits a new feature in the character of the King and of his bishops. When Dudley was sacrificed to popular resentment, under Henry VIII., and when he was on his way to execution, he met Sir Thomas, to whom he said,—"Oh More, More! God was your good friend, that you did not ask the king forgiveness, as manie would have had you do; for if you had done so, *perhaps you should have been in the like case with us now.*"*

It was natural that the restorer of political eloquence, which had slumbered for a long series of ages,† should also be the earliest of the parliamentary champions of liberty. But it is lamentable that we have so little information respecting the oratorical powers which alone could have armed him for the noble conflict. He may be said to hold the same station among us, which is assigned by Cicero, in his dialogue On the Celebrated Orators of Rome, to Cato the censor, whose consulship was only about ninety years prior to his own. His answer, as Speaker of the House of Commons, to Wolsey, of which more will be said presently, is admirable for its promptitude, quickness, seasonableness, and caution, combined with dignity and spirit. It unites presence of mind and adaptation to the person and circumstances, with address and management seldom surpassed. If the tone be more submissive than suits modern ears, it is yet remarkable for that ingenious refinement which for an instant shows a glimpse of the sword generally hidden under robes of state. "His eloquent tongue," says Erasmus, "so well seconds his fertile invention, that no one speaks better when suddenly called forth. His attention never languishes; his mind is always before his words; his memory has all its stock so turned into ready money, that, without hesitation or delay, it gives out whatever the time and the case may require. His acuteness in dispute is unrivalled, and he often perplexes the most renowned theologians when he enters their province."‡ Though much of this encomium may be applicable rather to private conversation than to public debate, and though this presence of mind may refer altogether to promptitude of repartee, and comparatively little to that readiness of reply, of which his experience must have been limited; it is still obvious that the great critic has ascribed to his friend the higher part of those mental qualities, which, when justly balanced and perfectly trained, constitute a great orator.

As if it had been the lot of More to open all the paths through the wilds of our old English speech, he is to be considered also as our earliest prose writer, and as the first Englishman who wrote the history of his country in its present language. The historical fragment§ commands belief by simplicity, and by abstinence from too confident affirmation. It betrays some negligence about minute particulars, which is not displeasing as a symptom of the absence of eagerness to enforce a narrative. The composition has an ease and a rotundity (which gratify the ear without awakening the sus-

* Roper, p. 7. There seems to be some forgetfulness of dates in the latter part of this passage, which has been copied by succeeding writers. Margaret, it is well known, was married in 1503; the debate was not, therefore, later than that year: but Henry VII. lived till 1509.

* More, p. 38.

† "Postquam pugnatum est apud Actium, magna illa ingenia cessere."—Tacitus, Hist. lib. i. cap. 1.

‡ Erasmus, Op. vol. iii. p. 476.

§ History of Richard III.

picion of art) of which there was no model in any preceding writer of English prose.

In comparing the prose of More with the modern style, we must distinguish the words from the composition. A very small part of his vocabulary has been superannuated; the number of terms which require any explanation is inconsiderable: and in that respect the stability of the language is remarkable. He is, indeed, in his words, more English than the great writers of a century after him, who loaded their native tongue with expressions of Greek or Latin derivation. Cicero, speaking of "old Cato," seems almost to describe More. "His style is rather antiquated; he has some words displeasing to our ears, but which were then in familiar use. Change those terms, which he could not, you will then prefer no speaker to Cato."*

But in the combination and arrangement of words, in ordinary phraseology and common habits of composition, he differs more widely from the style that has now been prevalent among us for nearly two centuries. His diction seems a continued experiment to discover the forms into which the language naturally runs. In that attempt he has frequently failed. Fortunate accident, or more varied experiment in aftertimes, led to the adoption of other combinations, which could scarcely have succeeded, if they had not been more consonant to the spirit of the language, and more agreeable to the ear and the feelings of the people. The structure of his sentences is frequently not that which the English language has finally adopted: the language of his countrymen has decided, without appeal, against the composition of the father of English prose.

The speeches contained in his fragment, like many of those in the ancient historians, were probably substantially real, but brightened by ornament, and improved in composition. It could, indeed, scarcely be otherwise: for the history was written in 1513,† and the death of Edward IV., with which it opens, occurred in 1483; while Cardinal Morton, who became prime minister two years after that event, appears to have taken young More into his household about the year 1493. There is, therefore, little scope, in so short a time, for much falsification, by tradition, of the arguments and topics really employed. These speeches have the merit of being accommodated to the circumstances, and of being of a tendency to dispose those to whom they were addressed to promote the object of the speaker; and this merit, rare in similar compositions, shows that More had been taught, by the practice of speaking in contests where objects the most important are the prize of the victor, that eloquence is the art of persuasion, and that the end of the orator is not the display of his talents, but dominion over the minds of his hearers. The dying speech, in which Edward exhorts the two parties of his friends to harmony, is a grave appeal to their prudence, as well as an affecting address from a father and a king to their public feelings. The surmises thrown out by Richard against the Widvilles are short, dark, and well adapted to awaken suspicion and alarm. The insinuations against the Queen, and the threats of danger to the lords themselves from leaving the person of the Duke of York in the hands of that princess, in Richard's speech to the Privy Council, before the Archbishop of York was sent to Westminster to demand the surrender of the boy, are admirable specimens of the address and art of crafty ambition. Generally speaking, the speeches have little of the vague common-place of rhetoricians and declaimers; and the time is not wasted in parade. In the case, indeed, of the dispute between the Archbishop and the Queen, about taking the Duke of York out of his mother's care, and from the Sanctuary at Westminster, there is more ingenious argument than the scene allows; and the mind rejects logical refinements, of which the use, on such an occasion, is quite irreconcilable to dramatic verisimilitude. The Duke of Buckingham alleged in council, that sanctuary could be claimed only against danger; and that the royal infant had neither wisdom to desire sanctuary, nor the malicious intention in his acts without which he could not require it. To this notable paradox, which amounted to an affirmation that no certainly innocent person could ever claim protection from a sanctuary, when it was carried to the Queen, she answered readily, that if she could be in sanctuary, it followed that her child, who was her ward, was included in her protection, as much as her servants, who were, without contradiction, allowed to be.

The Latin epigrams of More, a small volume which it required two years to carry though the press at Basle, are mostly translations from the Anthologia, which were rather made known to Europe by the fame of the writer, than calculated to increase it. They contain, however, some decisive proofs that he always entertained the opinions respecting the dependence of all government on the consent of the people, to which he professed his adherence almost in his dying moments. Latin versification was not in that early period successfully attempted in any Transalpine country. The rules of prosody, or at least the laws of metrical composition, were not yet sufficiently studied for such attempts. His Latinity was of the same school with that of his friend Erasmus; which was, indeed, common to the first generation of scholars after the revival of classical study. Finding Latin a sort of general

* De Clar. Orat. cap. 17.

† Holinshed, vol. iii. p. 360. Holinshed called More's work "unfinished." That it was meant to extend to the death of Richard III. seems probable from the following sentence:—"But, forasmuch as this duke's (the Duke of Gloucester) demeanour ministereth in effect all the whole matter whereof this book shall entreat, it is therefore convenient to show you, as we farther go, what manner of man this was that could find in his heart such mischief to conceive."—p. 361.

language employed by men of letters in their conversation and correspondence, they continued the use of it in the mixed and corrupted state to which such an application had necessarily reduced it: they began, indeed, to purify it from some grosser corruptions; but they built their style upon the foundation of this colloquial dialect, with no rigorous observation of the good usage of the Roman language. Writings of business, of pleasantry, of familiar intercourse, could never have been composed in pure Latinity; which was still more inconsistent with new manners, institutions, and opinions, and with discoveries and inventions added to those which were transmitted by antiquity. Erasmus, who is the master and model of this system of composition, admirably shows how much had been gained by loosening the fetters of a dead speech, and acquiring in its stead the nature, ease, variety, and vivacity of a spoken and living tongue. The course of circumstances, however, determined that this language should not subsist, or at least flourish, for much more than a century. It was assailed on one side by the purely classical, whom Erasmus, in derision, calls "Ciceronians;" and when it was sufficiently emasculated by dread of their censure, it was finally overwhelmed by the rise of a national literature in every European language.

More exemplified the abundance and flexibility of the Erasmian Latinity in Utopia, with which this short view of all his writings, except those of controversy, may be fitly concluded. The idea of the work had been suggested by some of the dialogues of Plato, who speaks of vast territories, formerly cultivated and peopled, but afterwards, by some convulsion of nature, covered by the Atlantic Ocean. These Egyptian traditions, or legends, harmonised admirably with that discovery of a new continent by Columbus, which had roused the admiration of Europe about twenty years before the composition of Utopia. This was the name of an island feigned to have been discovered by a supposed companion of Amerigo Vespucci, who is made to tell the wondrous tale of its condition to More, at Antwerp, in 1514: and in it was the seat of the Platonic conception of an imaginary commonwealth. All the names which he invented for men or places* were intimations of their being unreal, and were, perhaps, by treating with raillery his own notions, intended to silence gainsayers. The first book, which is preliminary, is naturally and ingeniously opened by a conversation, in which Raphael Hythloday, the Utopian traveller, describes his visit to England; where, as much as in other countries, he found all proposals for improvement encountered by the remark, that,—"Such things pleased our ancestors, and it were well for us if we could but match them; as if it were a great mischief that any should be found wiser than his ancestors." "I met," he goes on to say, "these proud, morose, and absurd judgments, particularly once when dining with Cardinal Morton at London." "There happened to be at table an English lawyer, who run out into high commendation of the severe execution of justice upon thieves, who were then hanged so fast that there were sometimes twenty hanging upon one gibbet, and added, 'that he could not wonder enough how it came to pass that there were so many thieves left robbing in all places.'" Raphael answered, "that it was because the punishment of death was neither just in itself, nor good for the public; for as the severity was too great, so the remedy was not effectual. You, as well as other nations, like bad schoolmasters, chastise their scholars because they have not the skill to teach them." Raphael afterwards more specially ascribed the gangs of banditti who, after the suppression of Perkin Warbeck's Cornish revolt, infested England, to two causes; of which the first was the frequent disbanding of the idle and armed retainers of the nobles, who, when from necessity let loose from their masters, were too proud for industry, and had no resource but rapine; and the second was the conversion of much corn field into pasture for sheep, because the latter had become more profitable,—by which base motives many landholders were tempted to expel their tenants and destroy the food of man. Raphael suggested the substitution of hard labour for death; for which he quoted the example of the Romans, and of an imaginary community in Persia. "The lawyer answered, 'that it could never be so settled in England, without endangering the whole nation by it:' he shook his head, and made some grimaces, and then held his peace, and all the company seemed to be of his mind. But the cardinal said, 'It is not easy to say whether this plan would succeed or not, since no trial has been made of it; but it might be tried on thieves condemned to death, and adopted if found to answer; and vagabonds might be treated in the same way.' When the cardinal had said this, they all fell to commend the motion, though

---

* The following specimen of Utopian etymologies may amuse some readers:—

Utopia - - οὐτόπος - nowhere.
Achorians - ἀ-χῶρος - of no country
Alemians - - ἀ-δῆμος - of no people.

Anyder (a river) ἀ-ὕδωρ - waterless.
Amaurot (a city) ἀ-μαῦρος dark,
Hythloday - δαίω-ὕθλος - a learner of trifles, &c.

{ The invisible city is on the river waterless. }

Some are intentionally unmeaning, and others are taken from little known language in order to perplex pedants. Joseph Scaliger represents Utopia as a word not formed according to the analogy which regulates the formation of Greek words.

they had despised it when it came from me. They more particularly commended that concerning the vagabonds, because it had been added by him." *

From some parts of the above extracts it is apparent that More, instead of having anticipated the economical doctrines of Adam Smith, as some modern writers have fancied, was thoroughly imbued with the prejudices of his contemporaries against the inclosure of commons, and the extension of pasture. It is, however, observable, that he is perfectly consistent with himself, and follows his principles through all their legitimate consequences, though they may end in doctrines of very startling sound. Considering separate property as always productive of unequal distribution of the fruits of labour, and regarding that inequality of fortune as the source of bodily suffering to those who labour, and of mental depravation to those who are not compelled to toil for subsistence, Hythloday is made to say, that, "as long as there is any property, and while money is the standard of all other things, he cannot expect that a nation can be governed either justly or happily."† More himself objects to Hythloday: "It seems to me that men cannot live conveniently where all things are common. How can there be any plenty where every man will excuse himself from labouring? for as the hope of gain does not excite him, so the confidence that he has in other men's industry may make him slothful. And if people come to be pinched with want, and yet cannot dispose of any thing as their own, what can follow but perpetual sedition and bloodshed; especially when the reverence and authority due to magistrates fall to the ground; for I cannot imagine how they can be kept among those that are in all things equal to one another." These remarks do in reality contain the germs of unanswerable objections to all those projects of a community of goods, which suppose the moral character of the majority of mankind to continue, at the moment of their adoption, such as it has been heretofore in the most favourable instances. If, indeed, it be proposed only on the supposition, that by the influence of laws, or by the agency of any other cause, mankind in general are rendered more honest, more benevolent, more disinterested than they have hitherto been, it is evident that they will, in the same proportion, approach to a practice more near the principle of an equality and a community of all advantages. The hints of an answer to Plato, thrown out by More, are so decisive, that it is not easy to see how he left this speck on his romance, unless we may be allowed to suspect that the speculation was in part suggested as a convenient cover for that biting satire on the sordid and rapacious government of Henry VII., which occupies a considerable portion of Hythloday's first discourse. It may also be supposed that More, not anxious to save visionary reformers from a few light blows in an attack aimed at corrupt and tyrannical statesmen, thinks it suitable to his imaginary personage, and conducive to the liveliness of his fiction, to represent the traveller in Utopia as touched by one of the most alluring and delusive of political chimeras.

In Utopia, farm-houses were built over the whole country, to which inhabitants were sent in rotation from the fifty-four cities. Every family had forty men and women, besides two slaves; a master and mistress preside over every family; and over thirty families a magistrate. Every year twenty of the family return to town, being two years in the country; so that all acquire some knowledge of agriculture, and the land is never left in the hands of persons quite unacquainted with country labours. When they want any thing in the country which it doth not produce, they fetch it from the city without carrying any thing in exchange: the magistrates take care to see it given to them. The people of the towns carry their commodities to the market place, where they are taken away by those who need them. The chief business of the magistrates is to take care that no man may live idle, and that every one should labour in his trade for six hours of every twenty-four;—a portion of time, which, according to Hythloday, was sufficient for an abundant supply of all the necessaries and moderate accommodations of the community; and which is not inadequate where all labour, and none apply extreme labour to the production of superfluities to gratify a few,—where there are no idle priests or idle rich men,—and where women of all sorts perform their light allotment of labour. To women all domestic offices which did not degrade or displease were assigned. Unhappily, however, the iniquitous and unrighteous expedient was devised, of releasing the better order of females from offensive and noisome occupations; by throwing them upon slaves. Their citizens were forbidden to be butchers, "because they think that pity and good-nature, which are among the best of those affections that are born within us, are much impaired by the butchering of animals;"—a striking representation, indeed, of the depraving effects of cruelty to animals, but abused for the iniquitous and cruel purpose of training inferiors to barbarous habits, in order to preserve for their masters the exclusive benefit of a discipline of humanity. Slaves, too, were employed in hunting, which was deemed too frivolous and barbarous an amusement for citizens. "They look upon hunting as one of the basest parts of a butcher's business, for they account it more decent to kill beasts for the sustenance of mankind, than to take pleasure in seeing a weak, harmless, and fearful hare torn in pieces by a strong, fierce, and cruel dog." An excess of population

*Burnet's translation, p. 13, *et seq.*

† Burnet's translation, p. 57. Happening to write where I have no access to the original, I use Burnet's translation. There can be no doubt of Burnet's learning or fidelity.

was remedied by planting colonies; a defect, by the recall of the necessary number of former colonists; irregularities of distribution, by transferring the superfluous members of one township to supply the vacancies in another. They did not enslave their prisoners, nor the children of their own slaves. In those maladies where there is no hope of cure or alleviation, it was customary for the Utopian priests to advise the patient voluntarily to shorten his useless and burthensome life by opium or some equally easy means. In cases of suicide, without permission of the priests and the senate, the party is excluded from the honours of a decent funeral. They allow divorce in cases of adultery, and incorrigible perverseness. Slavery is the general punishment of the highest crime. They have few laws, and no lawyers. "Utopus, the founder of the state, made a law that every man might be of what religion he pleased, and might endeavour to draw others to it by force of argument and by amicable and modest ways; but those who used reproaches or violence in their attempts were to be condemned to banishment or slavery." The following passage is so remarkable, and has hitherto been so little considered in the history of toleration, that I shall insert it at length:—"This law was made by Utopus, not only for preserving the public peace, which, he said, suffered much by daily contentions and irreconcilable heat in these matters, but because he thought the interest of religion itself required it. As for those who so far depart from the dignity of human nature as to think that our souls died with our bodies, or that the world was governed by chance without a wise and over-ruling Providence, the Utopians never raise them to honours or offices, nor employ them in any public trust, but despise them as men of base and sordid minds; yet they do not punish such men, because they lay it down as a ground, that a man cannot make himself believe any thing he pleases: nor do they drive any to dissemble their thoughts; so that men are not tempted to lie or disguise their opinions among them, which, being a sort of fraud, is abhorred by the Utopians:"—a beautiful and conclusive reason, which, when it was used for the first time, as it probably was in Utopia, must have been drawn from so deep a sense of the value of sincerity as of itself to prove that he who thus employed it was sincere. "These unbelievers are not allowed to argue before the common people; but they are suffered and even encouraged to dispute in private with their priests and other grave men, being confident that they will be cured of these mad opinions by having reason laid before them."

It may be doubted whether some extravagancies in other parts of Utopia were not introduced to cover such passages as the above, by enabling the writer to call the whole a mere sport of wit, and thus exempt him from the perilous responsibility of having maintained such doctrines seriously. In other cases he seems diffidently to propose opinions to which he was in some measure inclined, but in the course of his statement to have warmed himself into an indignation against the vices and corruptions of Europe, which vents itself in eloquent invectives not unworthy of Gulliver. He makes Hythloday at last declare,—"As I hope for mercy, I can have no other notion of all the other governments that I see or know, but that they are a conspiracy of the richer sort, who, on pretence of managing the public, do only pursue their private ends." The true notion of Utopia is, however, that it intimates a variety of doctrines, and exhibits a multiplicity of projects, which the writer regards with almost every possible degree of approbation and shade of assent; from the frontiers of serious and entire belief, through gradations of descending plausibility, where the lowest are scarcely more than the exercises of ingenuity, and to which some wild paradoxes are appended, either as a vehicle, or as an easy means (if necessary) of disavowing the serious intention of the whole of this Platonic fiction.

It must be owned, that though one class of More's successors was more susceptible of judicious admiration of the beauties of Plato and Cicero than his less perfectly formed taste could be, and though another division of them had acquired a knowledge of the words of the Greek language, and perception of their force and distinctions, for the attainment of which More came too early into the world, yet none would have been so heartily welcomed by the masters of the Lyceum and the Academy, as qualified to take a part in the discussion of those grave and lofty themes which were freely agitated in these early nurseries of human reason.

The date of the publication of Utopia would mark, probably, also the happiest period of its author's life. He had now acquired an income equivalent to four or five thousand pounds sterling of our present money, by his own independent industry and well-earned character. He had leisure for the cultivation of literature, for correspondence with his friend Erasmus, for keeping up an intercourse with European men of letters, who had already placed him in their first class, and for the composition of works, from which, unaware of the rapid changes which were to ensue, he probably promised himself more fame, or at least more popularity, than they have procured for him. His affections and his temper continued to insure the happiness of his home, even when his son with a wife, three daughters with their husbands, and a proportionable number of grandchildren, dwelt under his patriarchal roof.

At the same period, the general progress of European literature, and the cheerful prospects of improved education and diffused knowledge, had filled the minds of More and Erasmus with delight. The expectation of an age of pacific improvement seems to have prevailed among studious men in the twenty years which elapsed between the migration of classical learning across the Alps, and the rise of the religious dissensions stirred up by the preaching of Luther. "I foresee," says Bishop Tunstall, writing to Erasmus, "that our posterity will rival the ancients in every sort of study; and if they be not ungrateful, they will pay the greatest thanks to those who have revived these studies. Go on, and deserve well of posterity, who will never suffer the name of Erasmus to perish."* Erasmus, himself, two years after, expresses the same hopes, which, with unwonted courtesy, he chooses to found on the literary character of the conversation in the palace of Henry VIII.:—"The world is recovering the use of its senses, like one awakened from the deepest sleep; and yet there are some who cling to their old ignorance with their hands and feet, and will not suffer themselves to be torn from it."† To Wolsey, he speaks in still more sanguine language, mixed with the like personal compliment:—"I see another golden age arising, if other rulers be animated by your spirit. Nor will posterity be ungrateful. This new felicity, obtained for the world by you, will be commemorated in immortal monuments by Grecian and Roman eloquence."‡ Though the judgment of posterity in favour of kings and cardinals is thus confidently foretold, the writers do not the less betray their hope of a better age, which will bestow the highest honours on the promoters of knowledge. A better age was, in truth, to come; but the time and circumstances of its appearance did not correspond to their sanguine hopes. An age of iron was to precede, in which the turbulence of reformation and the obstinacy of establishment were to meet in long and bloody contest.

When the storm seemed ready to break out, Erasmus thought it his duty to incur the obloquy which always attends mediatorial counsels. "You know the character of the Germans, who are more easily led than driven. Great danger may arise, if the native ferocity of that people be exasperated by untimely severities. We see the pertinacity of Bohemia and the neighbouring provinces. A bloody policy has been tried without success. Other remedies must be employed. The hatred of Rome is fixed in the minds of many nations, chiefly from the rumours believed of the dissolute manners of that city, and from the immoralities of the representatives of the supreme pontiff abroad." The uncharitableness, the turbulence, the hatred, the bloodshed, which followed the preaching of Luther, closed the bright visions of the two illustrious friends, who agreed in an ardent love of peace, though not without a difference in the shades and modifications of their pacific temper, arising from some dissimilarity of original character. The tender heart of More clung more strongly to the religion of his youth; while Erasmus more anxiously apprehended the disturbance of his tastes and pursuits. The last betrays in some of his writings a temper, which might lead us to doubt, whether he considered the portion of truth which was within reach of his friend as equivalent to the evils attendant on the search.

* Erasmi Opera, vol. iii. p. 267.

† Ibid. p. 321.

‡ Ibid. p. 591. To this theory neither of the parties about to contend could have assented; but it is not on that account the less likely to be in a great measure true.

The public life of More may be said to have begun in the summer of 1514,* with a mission to Bruges, in which Tunstall, then Master of the Rolls, and afterwards Bishop of Durham, was his colleague, and of which the object was to settle some particulars relating to the commercial intercourse of England with the Netherlands. He was consoled for a detention, unexpectedly long, by the company of Tunstall, whom he describes† as one not only fraught with all learning, and severe in his life and morals, but inferior to no man as a delightful companion. On this mission he became acquainted with several of the friends of Erasmus in Flanders, where he evidently saw a progress in the accommodations and ornaments of life, to which he had been hitherto a stranger. With Peter Giles of Antwerp, to whom he intrusted the publication of Utopia by a prefatory dedication, he continued to be closely connected during the lives of both. In the year following, he was again sent to the Netherlands on a like mission; the intricate relations of traffic between the two countries having given rise to a succession of disputes, in which the determination of one case generally produced new complaints.

In the beginning of 1516 More was made a privy-councillor; and from that time may be dated the final surrender of his own tastes for domestic life, and his predilections for studious leisure, to the flattering importunities of Henry VIII. "He had resolved," says Erasmus, "to be content with his private station; but having gone on more than one mission abroad, the King, not discouraged by the unusual refusal of a pension, did not rest till he had drawn More into the palace. For why should I not say '*drawn*,' since no man ever laboured with more industry for admission to a court, than More to avoid it? The King would scarcely ever suffer the philosopher to quit him. For if serious affairs were to be considered, who could give more prudent counsel? or if the King's mind was to be relaxed by cheerful conversation, where could there be a more facetious companion?"‡ Roper, who was an eye-witness of these circumstances, relates them with an agreeable simplicity. "So from time to time was he by the King advanced, continuing in his singular favour and trusty service for twenty years. A good

* Records of the Common Council of London.

† In a letter to Erasmus, 30th April, 1516.

‡ Erasmus, Op. vol. iii. p. 476.

part thereof used the King, upon holidays, when he had done his own devotion, to send for him; and there, sometimes in matters of astronomy, geometry, divinity, and such other faculties, and sometimes on his worldly affairs, to converse with him. And other whiles in the night would he have him up into the leads, there to consider with him the diversities, courses, motions, and operations of the stars and planets. And because he was of a pleasant disposition, it pleased the King and Queen, *after the council had supped* at the time of their own (*i. e.* the royal) supper, to call for him to be merry with them." What Roper adds could not have been discovered by a less near observer, and would scarcely be credited upon less authority: "When them he perceived so much in his talk to delight, that he could not once in a month get leave to go home to his wife and children (whose company he most desired), he, much misliking this restraint on his liberty, began thereupon somewhat to dissemble his nature, and so by little and little from his former mirth to disuse himself, that he was of them from thenceforth, at such seasons, no more so ordinarily sent for."* To his retirement at Chelsea, however, the King followed him. "He used of a particular love to come of a sudden to Chelsea, and leaning on his shoulder, to talk with him of secret counsel in his garden, yea, and to dine with him upon no inviting."† The taste for More's conversation, and the eagerness for his company thus displayed, would be creditable to the King, if his behaviour in after time had not converted them inte the strongest proofs of utter depravity. Even in Henry's favour there was somewhat tyrannical; and his very friendship was dictatorial and self-willed. It was reserved for him afterwards to exhibit the singular, and perhaps solitary, example of a man unsoftened by the recollection of a communion of counsels, of studies, of amusements, of social pleasures with such a companion. In the moments of Henry's partiality, the sagacity of More was not so utterly blinded by his good-nature, that he did not in some degree penetrate into the true character of these caresses from a beast of prey. "When I saw the King," says his son-in-law, "walking with him for an hour, holding his arm about his neck, I rejoiced, and said to Sir Thomas, how happy he was whom the King had so familiarly entertained, as I had never seen him do to any one before, except Cardinal Wolsey. 'I thank our Lord, son,' said he, 'I find his grace my very good lord indeed, and I believe he doth as singularly favour me as any other subject within this realm: howbeit, son Roper, I may tell thee, I have no cause to be proud thereof; for if my head would win him a castle in France, when there was war between us, it should not fail to go.' "‡

An edition of Utopia had been printed incorrectly, perhaps clandestinely, at Paris; but, in 1518, Erasmus' friend and printer, Froben, brought out a correct one at Basle, the publication of which had been retarded by the expectation of a preface from Budæus, the restorer of Greek learning in France, and probably the most critical scholar in that province of literature on the north of the Alps. The book was received with loud applause by the scholars of France and Germany. Erasmus in confidence observed to an intimate friend, that the second book having been written before the first, had occasioned some disorder and inequality of style; but he particularly praised its novelty and originality, and its keen satire on the vices and absurdities of Europe.

So important was the office of under-sheriff then held to be, that More did not resign it till the 23d of July, 1519,* though he had in the intermediate time served the public in stations of trust and honour. In 1521 he was knighted, and raised to the office of treasurer of the exchequer,† a station in some respects the same with that of chancellor of the exchequer, who at present is on his appointment designated by the additional name of under-treasurer. It is a minute but somewhat remarkable, stroke in the picture of manners, that the honour of knighthood should be spoken of by Erasmus, if not as of superior dignity to so important an office, at least as observably adding to its consequence.

From 1517 to 1522, More was employed at various times at Bruges, in missions like his first to the Flemish government, or at Calais in watching and conciliating Francis I., with whom Henry and Wolsey long thought it convenient to keep up friendly appearances. To trace the date of More's reluctant journeys in the course of the uninteresting attempts of politicians on both sides to gain or dupe each other, would be vain, without some outline of the negotiations in which he was employed, and repulsive to most readers, even if the inquiry promised a better chance of a successful result.—Wolsey appears to have occasionally ap-

---

* Roper, p. 12. † More, p. 49.

‡ Roper, pp. 21, 22. Compare this insight into Henry's character with a declaration *post* of an opposite nature, though borrowed also from castles and towns, made by Charles V. when he heard of More's murder.

* Records of the city of London.

† Est quod Moro gratuleris; nam Rex *hunc nec ambientem nec flagitantem* munere magnifico honestavit, addito salario nequaquam penitendo: est enim principi suo à thesauris. . . Nec hoc contentus, equitis aurati dignitatem adjecit.—Erasmus, Op. vol. iii. p. 378.

"Then died Master Weston, treasurer of the exchequer, whose office the King, *of his own accord, without any asking, freely* gave unto Sir Thomas More."—Roper, 13.

The minute verbal coincidences which often occur between Erasmus and Roper, cannot be explained otherwise than by the probable supposition, that copies or originals of the correspondence between More and Erasmus were preserved by Roper after the death of the former.

pointed commissioners to conduct his own affairs, as well as those of his master, at Calais. At this place they could receive instructions from London with the greatest rapidity, and it was easy to manage negotiations, and to shift them speedily, with Brussels and Paris; with the additional advantage, that it might be somewhat easier to conceal from each one in turn of those jealous courts the secret dealings of his employers with the other, than if the despatches had been sent directly from London to the place of their destination. Of this commission More was once at least an unwilling member. Erasmus, in a letter to Peter Giles on the 15th of November, 1518, says, "More is still at Calais, of which he is heartily tired. He lives with great expense, and is engaged in business most odious to him. Such are the rewards reserved by kings for their favourites."* Two years afterwards, More writes more bitterly to Erasmus, of his own residence and occupations. "I approve your determination never to be involved in the busy trifling of princes; from which, as you love me, you must wish that I were extricated. You cannot imagine how painfully I feel myself plunged in them, for nothing can be more odious to me than this legation. I am here banished to a petty sea-port, of which the air and the earth are equally disagreeable to me. Abhorrent as I am by nature from strife, even when it is profitable, as at home, you may judge how wearisome it is here where it is attended by loss."†—On one of his missions,—that of the summer of 1519—More had harboured hopes of being consoled by seeing Erasmus at Calais, for all the tiresome pageantry, selfish scuffles, and paltry frauds, which he was to witness at the congress of kings,‡ where he could find little to alter those splenetic views of courts, which his disappointed benevolence breathed in Utopia. Wolsey twice visited Calais during the residence of More, who appears to have then had a weight in council, and a place in the royal favour, second only to those of the cardinal.

In 1523,§ a parliament was held in the middle of April, at Westminster, in which More took a part so honourable to his memory, that though it has been already mentioned when touching on his eloquence, it cannot be so shortly passed over here, because it was one of those signal acts of his life which bears on it the stamp of his character. Sir John, his father, in spite of very advanced age, had been named at the beginning of this parliament one of "the triers of petitions from Gascony,"—an office of which the duties had become nominal, but which still retained its ancient dignity; while of the House of Commons, Sir Thomas himself was chosen to be the speaker. He excused himself, as usual, on the ground of alleged disability; but his excuse was justly pronounced to be inadmissible. The Journals of Parliament are lost, or at least have not been printed; and the Rolls exhibit only a short account of what occurred, which is necessarily an unsatisfactory substitute for the deficient Journals. But as the matter personally concerns Sir Thomas More, and as the account of it given by his son-in-law, then an inmate in his house, agrees with the abridgment of the Rolls, as far as the latter goes, it has been thought proper in this place to insert the very words of Roper's narrative. It may be reasonably conjectured that the speeches of More were copied from his manuscript by his pious son-in-law."*—"Sith I perceive, most redoubted sovereign, that it standeth not with your pleasure to reform this election, and cause it to be changed, but have, by the mouth of the most reverend father in God the legate, your highness's chancellor, thereunto given your most royal assent, and have of your benignity determined far above that I may bear for this office to repute me meet, rather than that you should seem to impute unto your commons that they had unmeetly chosen, I am ready obediently to conform myself to the accomplishment of your highness's pleasure and commandment. In most humble wise I beseech your majesty, that I may make to you two lowly petitions;—the one privately concerning myself, the other the whole assembly of your commons' house. For myself, most gracious sovereign, that if it mishap me in any thing hereafter, that is, on the behalf of your commons in your high presence to be declared, to mistake my message, and in lack of good utterance by my mishearsal to prevent or impair their prudent instructions, that it may then like your most noble majesty to give me leave to repair again unto the commons' house, and to confer with them and take their advice what things I shall on their behalf utter and speak before your royal grace.

"Mine other humble request, most excellent prince, is this: forasmuch as there be of your commons here by your high commandment assembled for your parliament, a great number of which are after the accustomed manner appointed in the commons' house to heal and advise of the common affairs among themselves apart; and albeit, most dear liege lord, that according to *your most prudent advice*, by your honourable writs every where declared, there hath been

* Op. vol. ii. p. 357.
† Op. vol. iii. p. 589.
‡ Ibid. From the dates of the following letters of Erasmus, it appears that the hopes of More were disappointed.
§ 14 Henry VIII.

* This conjecture is almost raised above that name by what precedes. "Sir Thomas More made an oration, not now extant, to the king's highness, for his discharge from the speakership, whereunto when the king would not consent, the speaker spoke to his grace in the form following."—It cannot be doubted, without injustice to the honest and amiable biographer, that he would have his readers to understand that the original of the speeches, which actually follow, were *extant* in his hands.

as due diligence used in sending up to your highness's court of parliament the most discreet persons out of every quarter that men could esteem meet thereunto; whereby it is not to be doubted but that there is a very substantial assembly of right wise, meet, and politique persons: yet, most victorious prince, sith among so many wise men, neither is every man wise alike, nor among so many alike well witted, every man well spoken; and it often happeth that as much folly is uttered with painted polish speech, so many boisterous and rude in language give right substantial counsel; and sith also in matters of great importance, the mind is often so occupied in the matter, that a man rather studieth what to say than how; by reason whereof the wisest man and best spoken in a whole country fortuneth, when his mind is fervent in the matter, somewhat to speak in such wise as he would afterwards wish to have been uttered otherwise, and yet no worse will had when he spake it than he had when he would so gladly change it; therefore, most gracious sovereign, considering that in your high court of parliament is nothing treated but matter of weight and importance concerning your realm, and your own royal estate, it could not fail to put to silence from the giving of their advice and counsel many of your discreet commons, to the great hindrance of your common affairs, unless every one of your commons were utterly discharged from all doubt and fear how any thing that it should happen them to speak, should happen of your highness to be taken. And in this point, though your well-known and proved benignity putteth every man in good hope; yet such is the weight of the matter, such is the reverend dread that the timorous hearts of your natural subjects conceive towards your highness, our most redoubted king and undoubted sovereign, that they cannot in this point find themselves satisfied, except your gracious bounty therein declared put away the scruple of their timorous minds, and put them out of doubt. It may therefore like your most abundant grace to give to all your commons here assembled your most gracious licence and pardon freely, without doubt of your dreadful displeasure, every man to discharge his conscience, and boldly in every thing incident among us to declare his advice; and whatsoever happeneth any man to say, that it may like your noble majesty, of your inestimable goodness, to take all in good part, interpreting every man's words, how uncunningly soever they may be couched, to proceed yet of good zeal towards the profit of your realm, and honour of your royal person; and the prosperous estate and preservation whereof, most excellent sovereign, is the thing which we all, your majesty's humble loving subjects, according to the most bounden duty of our natural allegiance, most highly desire and pray for."

This speech, the substance of which is in the Rolls denominated "the protest," is conformable to former usage, and the model of speeches made since that time in the like circumstances. What follows is more singular, and not easily reconciled with the intimate connection then subsisting between the speaker and the government, especially with the cardinal:—

"At this parliament Cardinal Wolsey found himself much aggrieved with the burgesses thereof; for that nothing was so soon done or spoken therein, but that it was immediately blown abroad in every alehouse. It fortuned at that parliament a very great subsidy to be demanded, which the cardinal, fearing would not pass the commons' house, determined, for the furtherance thereof, to be there present himself. Before where coming, after long debating there, whether it was better but with a few of his lords, as the most opinion of the house was, or with his whole train royally to receive him; 'Masters,' quoth sir Thomas More, 'forasmuch as my lord cardinal lately, ye wot well, laid to our charge the lightness of our tongues for things uttered out of this house, it shall not in my mind be amiss to receive him with all his pomp, with his maces, his pillars, his poll-axes, his hat, and great seal too; to the intent, that if he find the like fault with us hereafter, we may be the bolder from ourselves to lay the blame on those whom his grace bringeth here with him.' Whereunto the house wholly agreeing, he was received accordingly. Where after he had by a solemn oration, by many reasons, proved how necessary it was the demand then moved to be granted, and farther showed that less would not serve to maintain the prince's purpose; he seeing the company sitting still silent, and thereunto nothing answering, and, contrary to his expectation, showing in themselves towards his request no towardness of inclination, said to them, 'Masters, you have many wise and learned men amongst you, and sith I am from the king's own person sent hitherto unto you, to the preservation of yourselves and of all the realm, I think it meet you give me some reasonable answer.' Whereat every man holding his peace, then began to speak to one Master Marney, afterwards lord Marney; 'How say you,' quoth he, 'Master Marney?' who making him no answer neither, he severally asked the same question of divers others, accounted the wisest of the company; to whom, when none of them all would give so much as one word, being agreed before, as the custom was, to give answer by their speaker; 'Masters,' quoth the cardinal, 'unless it be the manner of your house, as of likelihood it is, by the mouth of your speaker, whom you have chosen for trusty and wise (as indeed he is), in such cases to utter your minds, here is, without doubt, a marvellously obstinate silence:' and thereupon he required answer of Mr. Speaker; who first reverently, on his knees, excusing the silence of the house, abashed at the presence of so noble a personage, able to amaze the wisest and best learned in a realm, and then, by many probable arguments, proving that for them to make answer was neither expedient nor agreeable with the ancient liberty of the house, in conclusion for himself, showed, that though they had all with their voices trusted him, yet except every one of them could put into his own head their several wits, he alone in so weighty a matter was unmeet to make his grace answer. Whereupon the cardinal, displeased with Sir Thomas More, that had not in this parliament in all things satisfied his desire, suddenly arose and departed." *

This passage deserves attention as a specimen of the mild independence and quiet steadiness of More's character, and also as a proof how he perceived the strength which the commons had gained by the power of the purse, which was daily and silently growing, and which could be disturbed only by such an unseasonable show of an immature authority as might too soon have roused the crown to resistance. It is one among many instances of the progress of the influence of parliaments in the midst of their apparently indiscriminate submission, and it affords a pregnant proof that we must not estimate the spirit of our forefathers by the humility of their demeanour.

The reader will observe how nearly the example of More was followed by a succeeding speaker, comparatively of no distinction, but in circumstances far more memorable, in the answer of Lenthall to Charles I., when that unfortunate prince came to the House of Commons to arrest the five members of that assembly, who had incurred his displeasure.

There is another point from which these early reports of parliamentary speeches may be viewed, and from which it is curious to consider them. They belong to that critical moment in the history of our language when it was forming a prose style,—a written diction adapted to grave and important occasions. In the passage just quoted, there are about twenty words and phrases (some of them, it is true, used more than once) which would not now be employed. Some of them are shades, such as "lowly," where we say "humble;" "company," for "a house of parliament;" "simpleness," for "simplicity," with a deeper tinge of folly than the single word now ever has; "right," then used as a general sign of the superlative, where we say "very," or "most;" "reverend," for "reverent," or "reverential." "If it mishap me," if it should so happen, " to mishap in me," "it often happeth," are instances of the employment of the verb "hap" for happen, or of a conjugation of the former, which has fallen into irrecoverable disuse. A phrase was then so frequent as to become, indeed, the established mode of commencing an address to a superior, in which the old usage was, "It may like," or "It may please your Majesty," where modern language absolutely requires us to say, "May it please," by a slight inversion of the words retained, but with the exclusion of the word "like" in that combination. "Let" is used for "hinder," as is still the case in some public forms, and in the excellent version of the Scriptures. "Well witted" is a happy phrase lost to the language except on familiar occasions with a smile, or by a master in the art of combining words. Perhaps "enable me," for "give me by your countenance the ability which I have not," is the only phrase which savours of awkwardness or of harsh effect in the excellent speaker. The whole passage is a remarkable example of the almost imperceptible differences which mark various stages in the progress of a language. In several of the above instances we see a sort of contest for admission into the language between two phrases extremely similar, and yet a victory which excluded one of them as rigidly as if the distinction had been very wide. Every case where subsequent usage has altered or rejected words and phrases must be regarded as a sort of national verdict, which is necessarily followed by their disfranchisement. They have no longer any claim on the English language, other than that which may be possessed by all alien suppliants for naturalization. Such examples should warn a writer, desirous to be lastingly read, of the danger which attends new words, or very new acceptations of those which are established, or even of attempts to revive those which are altogether superannuated. They show in the clearest light that the learned and the vulgar parts of language, being those which are most liable to change, are unfit materials for a durable style; and they teach us to look to those words which form the far larger portion of ancient as well as of modern language,—that "well of English undefiled," which has been happily resorted to from More to Cowper, as being proved by the unimpeachable evidence of that long usage to fit the rest of our speech more perfectly, and to flow more easily, clearly, and sweetly, in our composition.

Erasmus tells us that Wolsey rather feared than liked More. When the short session of parliament was closed, Wolsey, in his gallery of Whitehall, said to More, "I wish to God you had been at Rome, Mr. More, when I made you speaker."—"Your Grace not offended, so would I too, my lord," replied Sir Thomas; "for then should I have seen the place I long have desired to visit."* More turned the conversation by saying that he liked this gallery better than the cardinal's at Hampton Court. But the latter secretly brooded over his revenge, which he afterwards tried to gratify by banishing More, under the name of an ambassador to Spain. He tried to effect his purpose by magnifying the learning and wisdom of More, his peculiar fitness for a conciliatory adjustment of

* Roper, pp. 13—21.

* Roper, p. 20.

the difficult matters which were at issue between the King and his kinsman the Emperor. The King suggested this proposal to More, who, considering the unsuitableness of the Spanish climate to his constitution, and perhaps suspecting Wolsey of sinister purposes, earnestly besought Henry not to send his faithful servant to his grave. The King, who also suspected Wolsey of being actuated by jealousy, answered, "It is not our meaning, Mr. More, to do you any hurt; but to do you good we should be glad; we shall therefore employ you otherwise."* More could boast that he had never asked the King the value of a penny for himself, when on the 25th of December, 1525,† the King appointed him chancellor of the duchy of Lancaster, as successor of Sir Anthony Wingfield—an office of dignity and profit, which he continued to hold for nearly three years.

In the summer of 1527, Wolsey went on his magnificent embassy to France, in which More and other officers of state were joined with him. On this occasion the main, though secret object of Henry was to pave the way for a divorce from Queen Catharine, with a view to a marriage with Anne Boleyn, a young beauty who had been bred at the French court, where her father, Sir Thomas Boleyn, created Earl of Wiltshire, had been repeatedly ambassador.

On their journey to the coast, Wolsey sounded Archbishop Wareham and Bishop Fisher on the important secret with which he was intrusted. Wareham, an estimable and amiable prelate, appears to have intimated that his opinion was favourable to Henry's pursuit of a divorce.‡ Fisher, bishop of Rochester, an aged and upright man, promised Wolsey that he would do or say nothing in the matter, nor in any way counsel the Queen, except what stood with Henry's pleasure; "for," said he, "though she be queen of this realm, yet he acknowledgeth you to be his sovereign lord:"§ as if the rank or authority of the parties had any concern with the duty of honestly giving counsel where it is given at all. The overbearing deportment of Wolsey probably overawed both these good prelates: he understood them in the manner most suitable to his purpose; and, confident that he should by some means finally gain them, he probably coloured very highly their language in his communication to Henry, whom he had himself just before displeased by unexpected scruples.

It was generally believed by their contemporaries that More and Fisher had corrected the manuscript of Henry's answer to Luther; while it is certain that the propensity of the King to theological discussions constituted one of the links of his intimacy with the former. As More's writings against the Lutherans were of great note in his own time, and as they were probably those of his works on which he exerted the most acuteness, and employed most knowledge, it would be wrong to omit all mention of them in an estimate of his mind, or as proofs of his disposition. They contain many anecdotes which throw considerable light on our ecclesiastical history during the first prosecution of the Protestants, or, as they were then called, Lutherans, under the old statutes against Lollards, during the period which extended from 1520 to 1532; and they do not seem to have been enough examined with that view by the historians of the Church.

Legal responsibility, in a well-constituted commonwealth, reaches to all the avowed advisers of the government, and to all those whose concurrence is necessary to the validity of its commands: but moral responsibility is usually or chiefly confined to the actual authors of each particular measure. It is true, that when a government has attained a state of more than usual regularity, the feelings of mankind become so well adapted to it, that men are held to be even morally responsible for sanctioning, by a base continuance in office, the bad policy which may be known not to originate with themselves. These refinements were, however, unknown in the reign of Henry VIII. The administration was then carried on under the personal direction of the monarch, who generally admitted one confidential servant only into his most secret counsels; and all the other ministers, whatever their rank might be, commonly confined their attention to the business of their own offices, or to the execution of special commands intrusted to them. This system was probably carried to its utmost height under so self-willed a prince as Henry, and by so domineering a minister as Wolsey. Although there can be no doubt that More, as a privy-councillor, attended and co-operated at the examination of the unfortunate Lutherans, his conduct in that respect was regarded by his contemporaries as little more than the enforcement of orders which he could not lawfully decline to obey. The opinion that a minister who disapproves measures which he cannot control is bound to resign his office, is of very modern

* More, p. 53. with a small variation.

† Such is the information which I have received from the records in the Tower. The accurate writer of the article on More, in the Biographia Britannica, is perplexed by finding Sir Thomas More, chancellor of the duchy, as one of the negotiators of a treaty in August, 1526, which seems to the writer in the Biographia to bring down the death of Wingfield to near that time; he being on all sides acknowledged to be More's immediate predecessor. But there is no difficulty, unless we needlessly assume that the negotiation with which Wingfield was concerned related to the same treaty which More concluded. On the contrary, the first appears to have been a treaty with Spain; the last a treaty with France.

‡ State Papers, Hen. VIII. vol. i. p. 196. Wolsey's words are,—"He expressly affirmed, that however displeasantly the queen took this matter, yet the truth and judgment of the law must take place. I have instructed him how he shall order himself if the queen shall demand his counsel, which he promises me to follow."

§ State Papers, Hen. VIII. vol. i. p. 168.

origin, and still not universally entertained, especially if fidelity to a party be not called in to its aid. In the time of Henry, he was not thought even entitled to resign. The fact of More's attendance, indeed, appears in his controversial writings, especially by his answer to Tyndal. It is not equitable to treat him as effectively and morally, as well as legally, answerable for measures of state, till the removal of Wolsey, and the delivery of the great seal into his own hands. The injustice of considering these transactions in any other light appears from the circumstance, that though he was joined with Wolsey in the splendid embassy to France in 1527, there is no reason to suppose that More was intrusted with the secret and main purpose of the embassy,—that of facilitating a divorce and a second marriage. His responsibility, in its most important and only practical part, must be contracted to the short time which extends from the 25th of October, 1529, when he was appointed chancellor, to the 16th of May, 1532, when he was removed from his office, not much more than two years and a half.* Even after confining it to these narrow limits, it must be remembered, that he found the system of persecution established, and its machinery in a state of activity. The prelates, like most other prelates in Europe, did their part in convicting the Protestants of Lollardy in the spiritual courts, which were the competent tribunals for trying that offence. Our means of determining what executions for Lollardy (if any) took place when More had a decisive ascendant in the royal councils, are very imperfect. If it were certain that he was the adviser of such executions, it would only follow that he executed one part of the criminal law, without approving it, as succeeding judges have certainly done in cases of fraud and theft;—where they no more approved the punishment of death than the author of Utopia might have done in its application to heresy. If the progress of civilization be not checked, we seem not far from the period when such capital punishments will appear as little consistent with humanity, and indeed with justice, as the burning of heretics now appears to us. More himself deprecates an appeal to his writings and those of his friend Erasmus, innocently intended by themselves, but abused by incendiaries to inflame the fury of the ignorant multitude.† "Men," says he (alluding evidently to Utopia), "cannot almost now speak of such things insomuch as in play, but that such evil hearers were a great deal the worse." "I would not now translate the Moria of Erasmus,—even some works that I myself have written ere this, into English, albeit there be none harm therein." It is evident that the two philosophers deeply felt the injustice of citing against them, as a proof of inconsistency, that they departed from the pleasantries, the gay dreams,—at most the fond speculations, of their early days, when they saw these harmless visions turned into weapons of destruction in the blood-stained hands of the boors of Saxony, and of the ferocious fanatics of Munster. The virtuous love of peace might be more prevalent in More; the Epicurean desire of personal ease predominated more in Erasmus: but both were, doubtless from commendable or excusable causes, incensed against those odious disciples, who now, "with no friendly voice," invoked their authority against themselves.

If, however, we examine the question on the grounds of positive testimony, it is impossible to appeal to a witness of more weight than Erasmus. "It is," said he, "a sufficient proof of his clemency, that while he was chancellor no man was put to death for these pestilent dogmas, while so many have suffered capital punishment for them in France, in Germany, and in the Netherlands."* The only charges against him on this subject, which are adverted to by himself, relate to minor severities; but as these may be marks of more cruelty than the infliction of death, let us listen on this subject to the words of the merciful and righteous man:† "Divers of them have said that of such as were in my house when I was chancellor, I used to examine them with torments, causing them to be bound to a tree in my garden, and there piteously beaten. Except their sure keeping, I never did else cause any such thing to be done unto any of the heretics in all my life, except only twain: one was a child and a servant of mine in mine own house, whom his father, ere he came to me, had nursed up in such matters, and set him to attend upon George Jay. This Jay did teach the child his ungracious heresy against the blessed sacrament of the altar; which heresy this child in my house began to teach another child. And upon that point I caused a servant of mine to strip him like a child before mine household, for amendment of himself and ensample of others." "Another was one who, after he had fallen into these frantic heresies, soon fell into plain open frensy: albeit that he had been in Bedlam, and afterwards by beating and correction gathered his remembrance;‡ being therefore set at liberty, his old frensies fell again into his head. Being informed of his relapse, I caused him to be taken by the constables and bounden to a tree in the street before the whole town, and there striped him till he waxed weary. Verily, God be thanked, I hear no harm of him now. And of all who ever came in my hand for heresy, as help me God, else had never any of them any stripe or stroke given them, *so much as a fillip in the forehead.*"§

* Records in the Tower.

† More's answer to Tyndal, part i. p. 128.—(Printed by John Rastell, 1532.)

* Op. vol. iii. p. 1811.

† More's Apology, chap. 36.

‡ Such was then the mode of curing insanity!

§ Apology, chap. 36.

This statement, so minute, so capable of easy confutation, if in any part false, was made public after his fall from power, when he was surrounded by enemies, and could have no friends but the generous. It relates circumstances of public notoriety, or at least so known to all his own household (from which it appears that Protestant servants were not excluded), which it would have been rather a proof of insanity than of imprudence to have alleged in his defence, if they had not been indisputably and confessedly true. Wherever he touches this subject, there is a quietness and a circumstantiality, which are among the least equivocal marks of a man who adheres to the temper most favourable to the truth, because he is conscious that the truth is favourable to him.* Without relying, therefore, on the character of More for probity and veracity (which it is derogatory to him to employ for such a purpose), the evidence of his humanity having prevailed over his opinion decisively outweighs the little positive testimony produced against him. The charge against More rests originally on Fox alone, from whom it is copied by Burnet, and with considerable hesitation by Strype. But the honest martyrologist writes too inaccurately to be a weighty witness in this case; for he tells us that Firth was put to death in June 1533, and yet imputes it to More, who had resigned his office a year before. In the case of James Baynham, he only says that the accused was chained to two posts for two nights in More's house, at some unspecified distance of time before his execution.

Burnet, in mentioning the extreme toleration taught in Utopia, truly observes, that if More had died at the time of its publication, "he would have been reckoned among those who only wanted a fit opportunity of declaring themselves openly for a reformation."† The same sincere and upright writer was too zealous for an historian, when he added:—"When More was raised to the chief post in the ministry, he became a persecutor even to blood, and defiled those hands which were never polluted with bribes." In excuse for the total silence of the honest bishop respecting the opposite testimony of More himself (of whom Burnet speaks even then with reverence), the reader must be reminded that the third volume of the History of the Reformation was written in the old age of the Bishop of Salisbury, thirty years after those more laborious researches, which attended the composition of the two former volumes, and under the influence of those animosities against the Roman Catholic Church, which the conspiracy of Queen Anne's last ministers against the Revolution had revived with more than their youthful vigour. It must be owned that he from the commencement acquiesced too lightly in the allegations of Fox; and it is certain, that if the fact, however deplorable, had been better proved, yet in that age it would not have warranted such asperity of condemnation.*

The date of the work in which More denies the charge, and challenges his accusers to produce their proofs, would have aroused the attention of Burnet if he had read it. This book, entitled "The Apology of Sir Thomas More," was written in 1533, "after he had given over the office of lord chancellor," and when he was in daily expectation of being committed to the Tower. Defenceless and obnoxious as he then was, no man was hardy enough to dispute his truth. Fox was the first who, thirty years afterwards, ventured to oppose it in a vague statement, which we know to be in some respects inaccurate; and on this slender authority alone has rested such an imputation on the veracity of the most sincere of men. Whoever reads the Apology will perceive, from the melancholy ingenuousness with which he speaks of the growing unpopularity of his religion in the court and country, that he could not have hoped to escape exposure, if it had been then possible to question his declaration.†

On the whole, then, More must not only be absolved; but when we consider that his administration occurred during a hot paroxysm of persecution,—that intolerance was the creed of his age,—that he himself, in his days of compliance and ambition, had been drawn over to it as a theory,—that he was filled with alarm and horror by the excesses of the heretical insurgents in Germany, we must pronounce him, by his abstinence from any practical share in it, to have given stronger proofs than any other man, of a repugnance to that execrable practice, founded

* There is a remarkable instance of this observation in More's Dialogue, book iii. chap. xvi., where he tells, with some prolixity, the story of Richard Dunn, who was found dead, and hanging in the Lollard's Tower. The only part taken by More in this affair was his share as a privy councillor in the inquiry, whether Dunn hanged himself, or was murdered and then hanged up by the Bishop of London's chancellor. The evidence to prove that the death could not be suicide, was as absurd as the story of the bishop's chancellor was improbable. He was afterwards, however, convicted by a jury, but pardoned, it should seem rightly, by the King.

† History of the Reformation (Lond. 1820), vol. iii. part i. p. 45.

* The change of opinion in Erasmus, and the less remarkable change of More in the same respect, is somewhat excused by the excesses and disorders which followed the Reformation. "To believe," says Bayle, "that the church required reformation, and to approve a particular manner of reforming it, are two very different things. To blame the opponents of reformation, and to disapprove the conduct of the reformers, are two things very compatible. A man may then imitate Erasmus, without being an apostate or a traitor."—Dictionary, art. Castellan. These are positions too reasonable to be practically believed, at the time when their adoption would be most useful.

† In the Apology, More states that four-tenths of the people were unable to read;—probably an overrated estimate of the number of readers.

on the unshaken basis of his natural humanity.

The fourth book of the Dialogue* exhibits a lively picture of the horror with which the excesses of the Reformers had filled the mind of this good man, whose justice and even humanity were disturbed, so far at least as to betray him into a bitterness of language and harshness of opinion foreign from his general temper. The events themselves are, it must be owned, sufficient to provoke the meekest,—to appal the firmest of men. "The temporal lords," he tells us, "were glad to hear the cry against the clergy; the people were glad to hear it against the clergy and the lords too. They rebelled first against an abbot, and after against a bishop, wherewith the temporal lords had good game and sport, and dissembled the matter, gaping after the lands of the spirituality, till they had almost played, as Æsop telleth of the dog, which, to snatch at the shadow of the cheese in the water, let fall and lost the cheese which he bare in his mouth. The uplandish Lutherans set upon the temporal lords: they slew 70,000 Lutherans in one summer, and subdued the remnant in that part of Almayne into a right miserable servitude. Of this sect was the great part† of those ungracious people which of late entered Rome with the Duke of Bourbon." The description of the horrible crimes perpetrated on that occasion is so disgusting in some of its particulars, as to be unfit for the decency of historical narrative. One specimen will suffice, which, considering the constant intercourse between England and Rome, is not unlikely to have been related to More by an eye-witness:—"Some took children and bound them to torches, and brought them gradually nearer to the fire to be roasted, while the fathers and mothers were looking on, and then began to speak of a price for the sparing of the children; asking first 100 ducats, then fifty, then forty, then at last offered to take twain: after they had taken the last ducat from the father, then would they let the child roast to death." This wickedness (More contended) was the fruit of Luther's doctrine of predestination; "for what good deed can a man study or labour to do, who believeth Luther, that he hath no free will of his own."‡ "If the world were not near an end, and the fervour of devotion almost quenched, it could never have come to pass that so many people should fall to the following of so beastly a sect." He urges at very great length, and with great ability, the tendency of belief in destiny to overthrow morality; and represents it as an opinion of which, on account of its incompatibility with the order of society, the civil magistrate may lawfully punish the promulgation; little aware how decisively experience was about to confute such reasoning, however specious, by the examples of nations, who, though their whole religion was founded on predestination, were, nevertheless, the most moral portion of mankind.* "The fear," says More, "of outrages and mischiefs to follow upon such heresies, with the proof that men have had in some countries thereof, have been the cause that princes and people have been constrained to punish heresies by a terrible death; whereas else more easy ways had been taken with them. If the heretics had never begun with violence, good Christian people had peradventure used less violence against them: while they forbare violence, there was little violence done unto them. 'By my soul,' quoth your friend,† 'I would all the world were agreed to take violence and compulsion away.' 'And sooth,' said I, 'if it were so, yet would God be too strong for his enemies.'" In answer, he faintly attempts to distinguish the case of Pagans, who may be tolerated, in order to induce them to tolerate Christians, from that of heretics, from which no such advantage was to be obtained in exchange;—a distinction, however, which disappeared as soon as the supposed heretics acquired supreme power. At last, however, he concludes with a sentence which sufficiently intimates the inclination of his judgment, and shows that his ancient opinions still prevailed in the midst of fear and abhorrence. "And yet, as I said in the beginning, never were they by any temporal punishment of their bodies any thing sharply handled till they began to be violent themselves." It is evident that his mind misgave him when he appeared to assent to intolerance as a principle; for otherwise there was no reason for repeatedly relying on the defence of society against aggression as its justification. His silence, however, respecting the notorious fact, that Luther strained every nerve to suppress the German insurgents, can never be excused by the sophistry which ascribes to all reformers the evil done by those who abuse their names. It was too much to say that Luther should not have uttered what he believed to be sacred and necessary truth, because evil-doers took occasion from it to screen their bad deeds. This controversial artifice, however grossly unjust, is yet so plausible and popular, that perhaps no polemic ever had virtue enough to resist the temptation of employing it. What other controversialist can be named, who, having the power to crush antagonists whom he viewed as the disturbers of the quiet of his own declining age,—the destroyers of all the hopes which he had cherished for mankind, contented himself with severity of language (for which he humbly excuses himself in his

* Dialogue of Sir Thomas More, touching the pestilent sect of Luther, composed and published when he was chancellor of the duchy of Lancaster, "but newly *oversene* by the said Sir T. More, chancellor of England," 1530.

† A violent exaggeration.

‡ Dialogue, book iv. chap. 8.

* Switzerland, Holland, Scotland, English puritans, New England, French Huguenots, &c.

† This wish is put into the mouth of the adverse speaker in the Dialogue.

Apology—in some measure a dying work), and with one instance of unfair inference against opponents who were too zealous to be merciful.

In the autumn of 1529, More, on his return from Cambray, where he had been once more joined in commission with his friend Tunstall as ambassador to the emperor, paid a visit to the court, then at Woodstock. A letter written from thence to his wife, on occasion of a mishap at home, is here inserted as affording a little glimpse into the management of his most homely concerns, and especially as a specimen of his regard for a deserving woman, who was, probably, too "coarsely kind" even to have inspired him with tenderness.*

"Mistress Alyce, in my most harty will, I recomend me to you. And whereas I am enfourmed by my son Heron of the loss of our barnes and our neighbours also, w[t] all the corne that was therein, albeit (saving God's pleasure) it is gret pitie of so much good corne lost, yet sith it hath liked hym to send us such a chance, we must saie bounden, not only to be content, but also to be glad of his visitation. He sent us all that we have lost: and sith he hath by such a chance taken it away againe, his pleasure be fulfilled. Let us never grudge thereat, but take it in good worth, and hartely thank him, as well for adversitie, as for prosperitie. And par adventure we have more cause to thank him for our losse, than for our winning: for his wisedom better seeth what is good for us then we do ourselves. Therefore I pray you be of good cheere, and take all the howsold with you to church, and there thank God both for that he hath given us, and for that he has left us, which if it please hym, he can increase when he will. And if it please him to leave us yet lesse, at hys pleasure be it. I praye you to make some good ensearche what my poor neighbours have loste, and bidde them take no thought therefore, and if I shold not leave myself a spone, there shall no poore neighbour of mine bere no losse by any chance happened in my house. I pray you be with my children and household mery in God. And devise somewhat with your friends, what way wer best to take, for provision to be made for corne for our household and for sede thys yere coming, if ye thinke it good that we keepe the ground still in our handes. And whether ye think it good y[t] we so shall do or not, yet I think it were not best sodenlye thus to leave it all up, and to put away our folk of our farme, till we have somewhat advised us thereon. Howbeit if we have more nowe than ye shall neede, and which can get the other maisters, ye may then discharge us of them. But I would not that any man wer sodenly sent away he wote nere wether. At my coming hither, I perceived none other, but that I shold tary still with the kinges grace. But now I shall (I think), because of this chance, get leave this next weke to come home and se you; and then shall we further devise together uppon all thinges, what order shall be best to take: and thus as hartely fare you well with all our children as you can wishe. At Woodstok the thirde daye of Septembre, by the hand of

"Your loving husband,

"THOMAS MORE, Knight."

A new scene now opened on More, of whose private life the above simple letter enables us to form no inadequate or unpleasing estimate. On the 25th of October 1529, sixteen days after the commencement of the prosecution against Wolsey, the King, by delivering the great seal to him at Greenwich, constituted him lord chancellor,—the highest dignity of the state and of the law, and which had previously been generally held by ecclesiastics.* A very summary account of the nature of this high office, may perhaps prevent some confusion respecting it among those who know it only in its present state. The office of chancellor was known to all the European governments, who borrowed it, like many other institutions, from the usage of the vanquished Romans. In those of England and France, which most resembled each other, and whose history is most familiar and most interesting to us,† the chancellor, whose office had been a conspicuous dignity under the Lower Empire, was originally a secretary who derived a great part of his consequence from the trust of holding the king's seal, the substitute for subscription under illiterate monarchs, and the stamp of legal authority in more cultivated times. From his constant access to the king, he acquired every where some authority in the cases which were the frequent subject of complaint to the crown. In France he became a minister of state with a peculiar superintendence over courts of justice, and some remains of a special jurisdiction, which continued till the downfal of the French monarchy. In the English chancellor were gradually united the characters of a legal magistrate and a political adviser; and since that time the office has been confined to lawyers in eminent practice. He has been presumed to have a due reverence for the law, as well as a familiar acquaintance with it; and his presence and weight in the counsels of a free commonwealth have been regarded as links which bind the state to the law.

One of the earliest branches of the chancellor's duties seems, by slow degrees, to have enlarged his jurisdiction to the extent

* In More's metrical inscription for his own monument, we find a just but long, and somewhat laboured, commendation of Alice, which in tenderness is outweighed by one word applied to the long-departed companion of his youth.

"Chara Thomæ jacet hic Joanna uxorcula Mori."

* Thorpe, in 1371, and Knivet, in 1372, seem to be the last exceptions.

† Ducange and Spelman, *voce* Cancellarius, who give us the series of Chancellors in both countries.

which it reached in modern times.* From the chancery issued those writs which first put the machinery of law in motion in every case where legal redress existed. In that court new writs were framed, when it was fit to adapt the proceedings to the circumstances of a new case. When a case arose in which it appeared that the course and order of the common law could hardly be adapted, by any variation in the forms of procedure, to the demands of justice, the complaint was laid by the chancellor, before the king, who commanded it to be considered in council,—a practice which, by degrees, led to a reference to that magistrate by himself. To facilitate an equitable determination in such complaints, the writ was devised called the writ of "*subpœnâ*," commanding the person complained of to appear before the chancellor, and to answer the complaint. The essential words of a petition for this writ, which in process of time has become of so great importance, were in the reign of Richard III. as follows: "Please it therefore, your lordship,—considering that your orator has no remedy by course of the common law,—to grant a writ *subpœnâ*, commanding T. Coke to appear in chancery, at a certain day, and upon a certain pain to be limited by you, and then to do what by this court shall be thought reasonable and according to conscience." The form had not been materially different in the earliest instances, which appear to have occurred from 1380 to 1400. It would seem that this device was not first employed, as has been hitherto supposed,† to enforce the observance of the duties of trustees who held lands, but for cases of an extremely different nature, where the failure of justice in the ordinary courts might ensue, not from any defect in the common law, but from the power of turbulent barons, who, in their acts of outrage and lawless violence, bade defiance to all ordinary jurisdiction. In some of the earliest cases we find a statement of the age and poverty of the complainant, and of the power, and even learning, of the supposed wrongdoer;—topics addressed to compassion, or at most to equity in a very loose and popular sense of the word, which throw light on the original nature of this high jurisdiction.‡ It is apparent, from the earliest cases in the reign of Richard II., that the occasional relief proceeding from mixed feelings of pity and of regard to substantial justice, not effectually aided by law, or overpowered by tyrannical violence, had then grown into a regular system, and was subject to rules resembling those of legal jurisdiction. At first sight it may appear difficult to conceive how ecclesiastics could have moulded into a regular form this anomalous branch of jurisprudence. But many of the ecclesiastical order,—originally the only lawyers,—were eminently skilled in the civil and canon law, which had attained an order and precision unknown to the digests of barbarous usages then attempted in France and England. The ecclesiastical chancellors of those countries introduced into their courts a course of proceeding very similar to that adopted by other European nations, who all owned the authority of the canon law, and were enlightened by the wisdom of the Roman code. The proceedings in chancery, lately recovered from oblivion, show the system to have been in regular activity about a century and a half before the chancellorship of Sir Thomas More,—the first common lawyer who held the great seal since the Chancellor had laid any foundations (known to us) of his equitable jurisdiction. The course of education, and even of negotiation in that age, conferred on Moore, who was the most distinguished of the practisers of the common law, the learning and ability of a civilian and a canonist.

Of his administration, from the 25th of October 1529, to the 16th of May 1532, four hundred bills and answers are still preserved, which afford an average of about a hundred and sixty suits annually. Though this average may by no means adequately represent the whole occupations of a court which had many other duties to perform, it supplies us with some means of comparing the extent of its business under him with the number of similar proceedings in succeeding times. The whole amount of bills and answers in the reign of James I. was thirty-two thousand. How far the number may have differed at different parts of that reign, the unarranged state of the records does not yet enable us to ascertain. But supposing it, by a rough estimate, to have continued the same, the annual average of bills and answers during the four years of Lord Bacon's administration was fourteen hundred and sixty-one, being an increase of nearly ten-fold in somewhat less than a century. Though cases connected with the progress of the jurisdiction and the character of the chancellor must have somewhat contributed to this remarkable increase, yet it must be ascribed principally to the extraordinary impulse given to

* "Non facile est digito monstrare quibus gradibus, sed conjecturam accipe."—Spelman, *voce* Cancellarius.

† Blackstone, book iii. chap. 4.

‡ Calendars of Proceedings in Chancery, temp. Eliz. London, 1827. Of ten of these suits which occurred in the last ten years of the fourteenth century, one complains of ouster from land by violence; another, of exclusion from a benefice, by a writ obtained from the king under false suggestions; a third, for the seizure of a freeman, under pretext of being a slave (or nief); a fourth, for being disturbed in the enjoyment of land by a trespasser, abetted by the sheriff; a fifth for imprisonment on a false allegation of debt. No case is extant prior to the first year of Henry V., which relates to the trust of lands, which eminent writers have represented as the original object of this jurisdiction. In the reign of Henry VI. there is a bill against certain Wycliffites for outrages done to the plaintiff, Robert Burton, chanter of the cathedral of Lincoln, on account of his zeal as an inquisitor in the diocese of Lincoln, to convict and punish heretics.

daring enterprise and national wealth by the splendid administration of Elizabeth, which multiplied alike the occasions of litigation and the means of carrying it on.* In a century and a half after, when equitable jurisdiction was completed in its foundations and most necessary parts by Lord Chancellor Nottingham, the yearly average of suits was, during his tenure of the great seal, about sixteen hundred.† Under Lord Hardwicke, the chancellor of most professional celebrity, the yearly average of bills and answers appears to have been about two thousand; probably in part because more questions had been finally determined, and partly also because the delays were so aggravated by the multiplicity of business, that parties aggrieved chose rather to submit to wrong than to be ruined in pursuit of right. This last mischief arose in a great measure from the variety of affairs added to the original duties of the judge, of which the principal were bankruptcy and parliamentary appeals. Both these causes continued to act with increasing force; so that, in spite of a vast increase of the property and dealings of the kingdom, the average number of bills and answers was considerably less from 1800 to 1802 than it had been from 1745 to 1754.‡

It must not be supposed that men trained in any system of jurisprudence, as were the ecclesiastical chancellors, could have been indifferent to the inconvenience and vexation which necessarily harass the holders of a merely arbitrary power. Not having a law, they were a law unto themselves; and every chancellor who contributed by a determination to establish a principle, became instrumental in circumscribing the power of his successor. Selden is, indeed, represented to have said, "that equity is according to the conscience of him who is chancellor; which is as uncertain as if we made the chancellor's foot the standard for the measure which we call a foot."§ But this was spoken in the looseness of table-talk, and under the influence of the prejudices then prevalent among common lawyers against equitable jurisdiction. Still, perhaps, in his time what he said might be true enough for a smart saying: but in process of years a system of rules has been established which has constantly tended to limit the originally discretionary powers of the chancery. Equity, in the acceptation in which that word is used in English jurisprudence, is no longer to be confounded with that *moral equity* which generally corrects the unjust operation of law, and with which it seems to have been synonymous in the days of Selden and Bacon. It is a part of law formed from usages and determinations which sometimes differ from what is called "common law" in its subjects, but chiefly varies from it in its modes of proof, of trial, and of relief; it is a jurisdiction so irregularly formed, and often so little dependent on general principles, that it can hardly be defined or made intelligible otherwise than by a minute enumeration of the matters cognisable by it.*

It will be seen from the above that Sir Thomas More's duties differed very widely from the various exertions of labour and intellect required from a modern chancellor. At the utmost he did not hear more than two hundred cases and arguments yearly, including those of every description. No authentic account of any case tried before him, if any such be extant, has been yet brought to light. No law book alludes to any part of his judgments or reasonings. Nothing of this higher part of his judicial life is preserved, which can warrant us in believing more than that it must have displayed his never-failing integrity, reason, learning, and eloquence.

The particulars of his instalment are not unworthy of being specified as a proof of the reverence for his endowments and excellences professed by the King and entertained by the public, to whose judgment the ministers of Henry seemed virtually to appeal, with an assurance that the King's appointment would be ratified by the general voice. "He was led between the Dukes of Norfolk and Suffolk up Westminster Hall to the Stone Chamber, and there they honourably placed him in the high judgment-seat of chancellor;"† (for the chancellor was, by his office, the president of that terrible tribunal.) "The Duke of Norfolk, premier peer and lord high treasurer of England," continues the biographer, "by the command of the king, spoke thus *unto the people there with great applause and joy gathered together*:—

"'The King's majesty (which, I pray God, may prove happie and fortunate to the whole realme of England) hath raised to the most high dignitie of chancellourship Sir Thomas More, a man for his extraordinarie worth and sufficiencie well knowne to himself and the whole realme, for no other cause or earthlie respect, but for that he hath plainely perceaved all the gifts of nature and grace to be heaped upon him, which either the people could desire, or himself wish, for the discharge of so great an office. For the admirable wisedome, integritie, and innocencie, joyned with most pleasant facilitie of witt, that this man is endowed withall, have been sufficiently knowen to all Englishmen from his youth, and for these manie yeares also to

* From a letter of Lord Bacon (Lords' Journals, 20th March, 1680,) it appears that he made two thousand decrees and orders in a year; so that in his time the bills and answers amounted to about two-thirds of the whole business.

† The numbers have been obligingly supplied by the gentlemen of the Record Office in the Tower.

‡ Account of Proceedings in Parliament relative to the Court of Chancery. By C. P. Cooper, Esq. (Lond. 1828,) p. 102, &c.—A work equally remarkable for knowledge and acuteness.

§ Table Talk, (Edinb. 1809,) p. 55.

* Blackstone, book iii. chap. 27. Lord Hardwicke's Letter to Lord Kames, 30th June, 1757.—Lord Woodhouselee's Life of Lord Kames, vol. i. p. 237.

† More, pp. 156, 163.

the King's majestie himself. This hath the King abundantly found in manie and weightie affayres, which he hath happily dispatched both at home and abroad, in divers offices which he hath born, in most honourable embassages which he hath undergone, and in his daily counsell and advises upon all other occasions. He hath perceaved no man in his realme to be more wise in deliberating, more sincere in opening to him what he thought, nor more eloquent to adorne the matter which he uttered. Wherefore, because he saw in him such excellent endowments, and that of his especiall care he hath a particular desire that his kingdome and people might be governed with all equitie and justice, integritie and wisedome, he of his owne most gracious disposition hath created this singular man lord chancellor; that, by his laudable performance of this office, his people may enjoy peace and justice; and honour also and fame may redounde to the whole kingdome. It may perhaps seem to manie a strange and unusuall matter, that this dignitie should be bestowed upon a layman, none of the nobilitie, and one that hath wife and children; because heretofore none but singular learned prelates, or men of greatest nobilitie, have possessed this place; but what is wanting in these respects, the admirable vertues, the matchless guifts of witt and wisedome of this man, doth most plentifully recompence the same. For the King's majestie hath not regarded how great, but what a man he was; he hath not cast his eyes upon the nobilitie of his bloud, but on the worth of his person; he hath respected his sufficiencie, not his profession; finally, he would show by this his choyce, that he hath some rare subjects amongst the rowe of gentlemen and laymen, who deserve to manage the highest offices of the realme, which bishops and noblemen think they only can deserve. The rarer therefore it was, so much both himself held it to be the more excellent, and to his people he thought it would be the more gratefull. Wherefore, receave this your chancellour with joyful acclamations, at whose hands you may expect all happinesse and content.'

"Sir Thomas More, according to his wonted modestie, was somewhat abashed at this the duke's speech, in that it sounded so much to his praise, but recollecting himself as that place and time would give him leave, he answered in this sorte:—'Although, most noble duke, and you right honourable lords, and worshipfull gentlemen, I knowe all these things, which the King's majestie, it seemeth, hath bene pleased should be spoken of me at this time and place, and your grace hath with most eloquent wordes thus amplifyed, are as far from me, as I could wish with all my hart they were in me for the better performance of so great a charge; and although this your speach hath caused in me greater feare than I can well express in words: yet this incomparable favour of my dread soueraigne, by which he showeth how well, yea how highly he conceaveth of my weakenesse, having commanded that my meanesse should be so greatly commended, cannot be but most acceptable unto me; and I cannot choose but give your most noble grace exceeding thankes, that what his majestie hath willed you briefly to utter, you, of the abundance of your love unto me, have in a large and eloquent oration dilated. As for myself, I can take it no otherwise, but that his majestie's incomparable favour towards me, the good will and incredible propension of his royall minde (wherewith he has these manie yeares favoured me continually) hath alone without anie desert of mine at all, caused both this my new honour, and these your undeserved commendations of me. For who am I, or what is the house of my father, that the King's highnesse should heape upon me by such a perpetuall streame of affection, these so high honours? I am farre lesse then anie the meanest of his benefitts bestowed on me; how can I then thinke myself worthie or fitt for this so peerlesse dignitie? I have bene drawen by force, as the King's majestie often professeth, to his highnesse's service, to be a courtier; but to take this dignitie upon me, is most of all against my will; yet such is his highnesse's benignitie, such is his bountie, that he highly esteemeth the small dutiefulnesse of his meanest subjects, and seeketh still magnificently to recompence his servants; not only such as deserve well, but even such as have but a desire to deserve well at his hands, in which number I have alwaies wished myself to be reckoned, because I cannot challenge myself to be one of the former; which being so, you may all perceave with me how great a burden is layde upon my backe, in that I must strive in some sorte with my diligence and dutie to corresponde with his royall benevolence, and to be answerable to that great expectation, which he and you seeme to have of me; wherefore those so high praises are by me so much more grievous unto me, by how much more I know the greater charge I have to render myself worthie of, and the fewer means I have to make them goode. This weight is hardly suitable to my weake shoulders; this honour is not correspondent to my poore desert; it is a burden, not a glorie; a care, not a dignitie; the one therefore I must beare as manfully as I can, and discharge the other with as much dexteritie as I shall be able. The earnest desire which I have alwaies had and doe now acknowledge myself to have, to satisfye by all meanes I can possible, the most ample benefitts of his highnesse, will greatly excite and ayde me to the diligent performance of all, which I trust also I shall be more able to doe, if I finde all your good wills and wishes both favourable unto me, and conformable to his royall munificence: because my serious endeavours to doe well, joyned with your favourable acceptance, will easily procure that whatsoever is performed by me, though it be in itself but small, yet will it seeme great and praiseworthie; for those things are alwaies atchieved happily, which are accepted willingly; and those succeede fortunately, which are receaved by others courteously. As you therefore doe hope for great matters, and the best at my hands, so though I dare not promise anie such, yet do I promise truly and affectionately to performe the best I shall be able.'

"When Sir Thomas More had spoken these wordes, turning his face to the high judgment seate of the chancerie, he proceeded in this manner:—'But when I looke upon this seate, when I thinke how greate and what kinde of personages have possessed this place before me, when I call to minde who he was that sate in it last of all—a man of what singular wisdome, of what notable experience, what a prosperous and favourable fortune he had for a great space, and how at the last he had a most grevious fall, and dyed inglorious—I have cause enough by my predecessor's example to think honour but slipperie, and this dignitie not so grateful to me as it may seeme to others; for both is it a hard matter to follow with like paces or praises, a man of such admirable witt, prudence, authoritie, and splendour, to whome I may seeme but as the lighting of a candle, when the sun is downe; and also the sudden and unexpected fall of so great a man as he was doth terribly putt me in minde that this honour ought not to please me too much, nor the lustre of this glistering seate dazel mine eyes. Wherefore I ascende this seate as a place full of labour and danger, voyde of all solide and true honour; the which by how much the higher it is, by so much greater fall I am to feare, as well in respect of the verie nature of the thing it selfe, as because I am warned by this late fearfull example. And truly I might even now at this verie just entrance stumble, yea faynte, but that his majestie's most singular favour towardes me, and all your good wills, which your joyfull countenance doth testifye in this most honorable assemblie, doth somewhat recreate and refresh me; otherwise this seate would be no more pleasing to me, than that sword was to Damocles, which hung over his head, tyed only by a hayre of a horse's tale, when he had store of delicate fare before him, seated in the chair of state of Denis the tirant of Sicilie; this therefore shall be always fresh in my minde, this will I have still before mine eies, that this seate will be honorable, famous, and full of glorie unto me, if I shall with care and diligence, fidelitie and wisedome, endeavour to doe my dutie, and shall persuade myself, that the enjoying thereof may be but short and uncertaine; the one whereof my labour ought to performe; the other my predecessor's example may easily teach me. All which being so, you may easily perceave what great pleasure I take in this high dignitie, or in this most noble duke's praising of me.'

"All the world took notice now of sir Thomas's dignitie, whereof Erasmus writeth to John Fabius, bishop of Vienna, thus:—'Concerning the new increase of honour lately happened to Thomas More, I should easily make you believe it, if I should show you the letters of many famous men, rejoicing with much alacritie, and congratulating the King, the realme, himself, and also me, for More's honor, in being made lord chancellour of England.'"

At the period of the son's promotion, Sir John More who was nearly of the age of ninety, was the most ancient judge of the King's Bench. "What a grateful spectacle was it," says their descendant, "to see the son ask the blessing of the father every day upon his knees before he sat upon his own seat?"* Even in a more unceremonious age, the simple character of More would have protected these daily rites of filial reverence from that suspicion of affectation, which could alone destroy their charm. But at that time it must have borrowed its chief power from the conspicuous excellence of the father and son. For if inward worth had then borne any proportion to the grave and reverend ceremonial of the age, we might be well warranted in regarding our forefathers as a race of superior beings.

The contrast which the humble and affable More afforded to the haughty cardinal, astonished and delighted the suitors. No application could be made to Wolsey, which did not pass through many hands; and no man could apply, whose fingers were not tipped with gold: but More sat daily in an open hall, that he might receive in person the petitions of the poor. If any reader should blame his conduct in this respect, as a breach of an ancient and venerable precept,—"Ye shall do no unrighteousness *in judgment;* thou shalt not respect the person of the poor, nor honour the person of the mighty; but in *righteousness* shalt thou *judge* thy neighbour,"† let it be remembered, that there still clung to the equitable jurisdiction some remains of that precarious and eleemosynary nature from which it originally sprung; which, in the eyes of the compassionate chancellor, might warrant more preference for the helpless poor than could be justified in proceedings more rigorously legal.

Courts of law were jealous then, as since, of the power assumed by chancellors to issue *injunctions* to parties to desist from doing certain acts which they were by law entitled to do, until the court of chancery should determine whether the exercise of the legal right would not work injustice. There are many instances in which irreparable wrong may be committed, before a right can be ascertained, in the ordinary course of proceedings. In such cases it is the province of the Chancellor to take care that affairs shall continue in their actual condition until the questions in dispute be determined. A considerable outcry against this necessary, though invidious authority, was raised at the

* More, p. 163.

† Leviticus, chap. xix. v. 15.

commencement of More's chancellorship. He silenced this clamour with his wonted prudence and meekness. Having caused one of the six clerks to make out a list of the injunctions issued by him, or pending before him, he invited all the judges to dinner. He laid the list before them; and explained the circumstances of each case so satisfactorily, that they all confessed that in the like case they would have done no less. Nay, he offered to desist from the jurisdiction, if they would undertake to contain the law within the boundaries of righteousness, which he thought they ought in conscience to do. The judges declined to make the attempt; on which he observed privately to Roper, that he saw they trusted to their influence for obtaining verdicts which would shift the responsibility from them to the juries. "Wherefore," said he, "I am constrained to abide the adventure of their blame."

Dauncey, one of his sons-in-law, alleged that under Wolsey "even the door-keepers got great gains," and was so perverted by the venality there practised that he expostulated with More for his churlish integrity. The chancellor said, that if "his father, whom he reverenced dearly, were on the one side, and the devil, whom he hated with all his might, on the other, the devil should have his right." He is represented by his descendant, as softening his answer by promising minor advantages, such as priority of hearing, and recommendation of arbitration, where the case of a friend was bad. The biographer, however, not being a lawyer, might have misunderstood the conversation, which had to pass through more than one generation before the tradition reached him; or the words may have been a hasty effusion of good nature, uttered only to qualify the roughness of his honesty. If he had been called on to perform these promises, his head and heart would have recoiled alike from breaches of equality which he would have felt to be altogether dishonest. When Heron, another of his sons-in-law, relied on the bad practices of the times, so far as to entreat a favourable judgment in a cause of his own, More, though the most affectionate of fathers, immediately undeceived him by an adverse decree. This act of common justice is made an object of panegyric by the biographer, as if it were then deemed an extraordinary instance of virtue; a deplorable symptom of that corrupt state of general opinion, which, half a century later, contributed to betray into ignominious vices the wisest of men, and the most illustrious of chancellors,—if the latter distinction be not rather due to the virtue of a More or a Somers.

He is said to have despatched the causes before him so speedily, that, on asking for the next, he was told that none remained; which is boastfully contrasted by Mr. More, his descendant, with the arrear of a thousand in the time of that gentleman, who lived in the reign of Charles I.; though we have already seen that this difference may be referred to other causes, and therefore that the fact, if true, proves no more than his exemplary diligence and merited reputation.

The scrupulous and delicate integrity of More (for so it must be called in speaking of that age) was more clearly shown after his resignation, than it could have been during his continuance in office. One Parnell complained of him for a decree obtained by his adversary Vaughan, whose wife had bribed the chancellor by a gilt cup. More surprised the counsel at first, by owning that he received the cup as a new year's gift. Lord Wiltshire, a zealous Protestant, indecently, but prematurely, exulted: "Did I not tell you, my lords," said he, "that you would find this matter true?" "But, my lords," replied More, "hear the other part of my tale." He then told them that, "having drank to her of wine with which his butler had filled the cup, and she having pledged him, he restored it to her, and would listen to no refusal." When Mrs. Croker, for whom he had made a decree against Lord Arundel, came to him to request his acceptance of a pair of gloves, in which were contained 40*l.* in angels, he told her, with a smile, that it were ill manners to refuse a lady's present; but though he should keep the gloves, he must return the gold, which he enforced her to receive. Gresham, a suitor, sent him a present of a gilt cup, of which the fashion pleased him: More accepted it; but would not do so till Gresham received from him another cup of greater value, but of which the form and workmanship were less suitable to the Chancellor. It would be an indignity to the memory of such a man to quote these facts as proofs of his probity; but they may be mentioned as specimens of the simple and unforced honesty of one who rejected improper offers with all the ease and pleasantry of common courtesy.

Henry, in bestowing the great seal on More, hoped to dispose his chancellor to lend his authority to the projects of divorce and second marriage, which were now agitating the King's mind, and were the main objects of his policy.* Arthur, the eldest son of Henry VII., having married Catharine, the daughter of Ferdinand and Isabella, sovereigns of Castile and Arragon, and dying very shortly after his nuptials, Henry had obtained a dispensation from Pope Julius II. to enable the princess to marry her brother-in-law, afterwards Henry VIII.; and in this last-mentioned union, of which the Princess Mary was the only remaining fruit, the parties had lived sixteen years in apparent harmony. But in the year 1527, arose a concurrence of events, which tried and established the virtue of More, and revealed to the world the depravity of his master. Henry had been touched by the charms of Anne Boleyn, a beautiful young lady, in her twenty-

*"Thomas Morus, doctrinâ et probitate spectabilis vir, cancellarius in Wolsæi locum constituitur. *Neutiquam Regis causæ æquior.*"—Thuanus, Historia sui Temporis, lib. ii. c. 16.

second year, the daughter of Sir Thomas Boleyn, Earl of Wiltshire, who had lately returned from the court of France, where her youth had been spent. At the same moment it became the policy of Francis I. to loosen all the ties which joined the King of England to the Emperor. When the Bishop of Tarbes, his ambassador in England, found, on his arrival in London, the growing distaste of Henry for his inoffensive and exemplary wife, he promoted the King's inclination towards divorce, and suggested a marriage with Margaret Duchess of Alençon, the beautiful and graceful sister of Francis I.*

At this period Henry for the first time professed to harbour conscientious doubts whether the dispensation of Julius II. could suspend the obligation of the divine prohibition pronounced against such a marriage as his in the Levitical law.† The court of Rome did not dare to contend that the dispensation could reach the case if the prohibition were part of the universal law of God. Henry, on the other side, could not consistently question its validity, if he considered the precept as belonging to merely positive law. To this question, therefore, the dispute was confined, though both parties shrunk from an explicit and precise avowal of their main ground. The most reasonable solution that it was a local and temporary law, forming a part of the Hebrew code, might seem at first sight to destroy its authority altogether. But if either party had been candid, this prohibition, adopted by all Christendom, might be justified by that general usage, in a case where it was not remarkably at variance with reason or the public welfare. But such a doctrine would have lowered the ground of the Papal authority too much to be acceptable to Rome, and yet, on the other hand, rested it on too unexceptionable a foundation to suit the case of Henry. False allegations of facts in the preamble of the bull were alleged on the same side; but they were inconclusive. The principal arguments in the King's favour were, that no precedents of such a dispensation seem to have been produced; and that if the Levitical prohibitions do not continue in force under the Gospel, there is no prohibition against incestuous marriages in the system of the New Testament. It was a disadvantage to the Church of Rome in the controversy, that being driven from the low ground by its supposed tendency to degrade the subject, and deterred from the high ground by the fear of the reproach of daring usurpation, the inevitable consequence was confusion and fluctuation respecting the first principles on which the question was to be determined.

To pursue this subject through the long negotiations and discussions which it occasioned during six years, would be to lead us far from our subject. Clement VII. (*Medici*) had been originally inclined to favour the suit* of Henry, according to the usual policy of the Roman Court, which sought plausible pretexts for facilitating the divorce of kings, whose matrimonial connections might be represented as involving the quiet of nations. The sack of Rome, however, and his own captivity left him full of fear of the Emperor's power and displeasure; it is even said that Charles V., who had discovered the secret designs of the English court, had extorted from the Pope, before his release, a promise that no attempt would be made to dishonour an Austrian princess by acceding to the divorce.† The Pope, unwilling to provoke Henry, his powerful and generous protector, instructed Campeggio to attempt, at first, a reconciliation between the King and Queen; secondly, if that failed, to endeavour to persuade her that she ought to acquiesce in her husband's desires, by entering into a cloister —(a proposition which seems to show a readiness in the Roman court to waive their theological difficulties); and thirdly, if neither of these attempts were successful, to spin out the negotiation to the greatest length, in order to profit by the favourable incidents which time might bring forth. The impatience of the King and the honest indignation of the Queen defeated these arts of Italian policy; while the resistance of Anne Boleyn to the irregular gratification of the King's desires,—without the belief of which it is impossible to conceive the motives for his perseverance in the pursuit of an unequal marriage,—opposed another impediment to the counsels and contrivances of Clement, which must have surprised and perplexed a Florentine pontiff. The proceedings, however, terminated in the sentence pronounced by Cranmer annulling the marriage, the espousal of Anne Boleyn by the King, and the rejection of the Papal jurisdiction by the kingdom, which still, however, adhered to the doctrines of the Roman Catholic Church.

The situation of More during a great part of these memorable events was embarrassing. The great offices to which he had been raised by the King, the personal favour hitherto constantly shown to him, and the

* "Margarita Francisci soror, spectatæ formæ et venustatis fœmina, Carolo Alenconio duce marito paulo ante mortuo, vidua permanserat. Ea destinata uxor Henrico: missique Wolsæus et Bigerronum Præsul qui de dissolvendo matrimonio cum Gallo agerent. Ut Caletum appulit, Wolsæus mandatum à rege contrarium accipit, rescivitque per amicos Henricum non tam Galli affinitatem quam insanum amorem, quo Annam Bolenam prosequebatur, explere velle."—Ibid. No trace of the latter part appears in the State Papers just (1831) published.

† Leviticus, chap. xx. v. 22. But see Deuteronomy, chap. xxv. v. 5. The latter text, which allows an exception in the case of a brother's wife being left childless, may be thought to strengthen the prohibition in all cases not excepted. It may seem applicable to the precise case of Henry. But the application of that text is impossible; for it contains an injunction, of which the breach is chastised by a disgraceful punishment.

* Pallavicino, lib. ii. c. 15. † Ibid.

natural tendency of his gentle and quiet disposition, combined to disincline him to resistance against the wishes of his friendly master. On the other hand, his growing dread and horror of heresy, with its train of disorders; his belief that universal anarchy would be the inevitable result of religious dissension, and the operation of seven years' controversy on behalf of the Catholic Church, in heating his mind on all subjects involving the extent of her authority, made him recoil from designs which were visibly tending towards disunion with the Roman pontiff,—the centre of Catholic union, and the supreme magistrate of the ecclesiastical commonwealth. Though his opinions relating to the Papal authority were of a moderate and liberal nature, he at least respected it as an ancient and venerable control on licentious opinions, of which the prevailing heresies attested the value and the necessity. Though he might have been better pleased with another determination by the supreme pontiff, it did not follow that he should contribute to weaken the holy See, assailed as it was on every side, by taking an active part in resistance to the final decision of a lawful authority. Obedience to the supreme head of the Church in a case which ultimately related only to discipline, appeared peculiarly incumbent on all professed Catholics. But however sincere the zeal of More for the Catholic religion and his support of the legitimate supremacy of the Roman See undoubtedly were, he was surely influenced at the same time by the humane feelings of his just and generous nature, which engaged his heart to espouse the cause of a blameless and wronged princess, driven from the throne and the bed of a tyrannical husband. Though he reasoned the case as a divine and a canonist, he must have felt it as a man; and honest feeling must have glowed beneath the subtleties and formalities of doubtful and sometimes frivolous disputations. It was probably often the chief cause of conduct for which other reasons might be sincerely alleged.

In steering his course through the intrigues and passions of the court, it is very observable that More most warily retired from every opposition but that which Conscience absolutely required: he shunned unnecessary disobedience as much as unconscientious compliance. If he had been influenced solely by prudential considerations, he could not have more cautiously shunned every needless opposition; but in that case he would not have gone so far. He displayed, at the time of which we now speak, that very peculiar excellence of his character, which, as it showed his submission to be the fruit of sense of duty, gave dignity to that which in others is apt to seem, and to be slavish. His anxiety had increased with the approach to maturity of the King's projects of divorce and second marriage. Some anecdotes of this period are preserved by the affectionate and descriptive pen of Margaret Roper's husband, which, as he evidently reports in the chancellor's language, it would be unpardonable to relate in any other words than those of the venerable man himself. Roper, indeed, like another Plutarch, consults the unrestrained freedom of his story by a disregard of dates, which, however agreeable to a general reader, is sometimes unsatisfactory to a searcher after accuracy. Yet his office in a court of law, where there is the strongest inducement to ascertain truth, and the largest experience of the means most effectual for that purpose, might have taught him the extreme importance of time as well as place in estimating the bearing and weight of testimony.

"On a time walking with me along the Thames' side at Chelsea, he said unto me, 'Now would to our Lord, son Roper, upon condition that three things were well established in Christendom, I were put into a sack, and were presently cast into the Thames.' —'What great things be those, sir?' quoth I, 'that should move you so to wish.'—'In faith, son, they be these,' said he. 'The *first* is, that whereas the most part of Christian princes be at mortal war, they were all at universal peace. The *second*, that where the church of Christ is at present sore afflicted with many errors and heresies, it were well settled in perfect uniformity of religion. The *third*, that as the matter of the King's marriage is now come in question, it were, to the glory of God and quietness of all parties, brought to a good conclusion.' "* On another occasion,† "before the matrimony was brought in question, when I, in talk with Sir Thomas More (of a certain joy), commended unto him the happy estate of this realm, that had so catholic a prince, so grave and sound a nobility, and so loving, obedient subjects, agreeing in one faith. 'Truth it is, indeed, son Roper; and yet I pray God, as high as we sit upon the mountains, treading heretics under our feet like ants, live not the day that we gladly would wish to be at league and composition with them, to let them have their churches, so that they would be contented to let us have ours quietly.' I answered, 'By my troth, it is very desperately spoken.' He, perceiving me to be in a *fume*, said merrily,—'Well, well, son Roper, it shall not be so.' Whom," concludes Roper, in sixteen years and more, being in his house, conversant with him, I never could perceive him as much as once in a fume." Doubtless More was somewhat disquieted by the reflection, that some of those who now appealed to the freedom of his youthful philosophy against himself would speedily begin to abuse such doctrines by turning them against the peace which he loved,—that some of the spoilers of Rome

* The description of the period appears to suit the year 1529, before the peace of Cambray and the recall of the legate Campeggio.

† Probably in the beginning of 1527, after the promotion of More to be chancellor of the duchy of Lancaster.

might exhibit the like scenes of rapine and blood in the city which was his birth-place and his dwelling-place: yet, even then, the placid mien, which had stood the test of every petty annoyance for sixteen years, was unruffled by alarms for the impending fate of his country and of his religion.

Henry used every means of procuring an opinion favourable to his wishes from his chancellor, who, however, excused himself as unmeet for such matters, having never professed the study of divinity. But the King "*sorely*" pressed him,* and never ceased urging him until he had promised to give his consent, at least, to examine the question, conjointly with his friend Tunstall and other learned divines. This examination over, More, with his wonted ingenuity and gentleness, conveyed the result to his master. "To be plain with your grace, neither your bishops, wise and virtuous though they be, nor myself, nor any other of your council, by reason of your manifold benefits bestowed on us, are meet counsellors for your grace herein. If you mind to understand the truth, consult St. Jerome, St. Augustin, and other holy doctors of the Greek and Latin churches, who will not be inclined to deceive you by respect of their own worldly commodity, or by fear of your princely displeasure."† Though the King did not like what "was disagreeable to his desires, yet the language of More was so wisely tempered, that for the present he took it in good part, and oftentimes had conferences with the chancellor thereon." The native meekness of More was probably more effectual than all the arts by which courtiers ingratiate themselves, or insinuate unpalatable counsel. Shortly after, the King again moved him to weigh and consider the great matter: the chancellor fell down on his knees, and reminding Henry of his own words on delivering the great seal, which were,—"First look upon God, and after God upon me," added, that nothing had ever so pained him as that he was not able to serve him in that matter, without a breach of that original injunction. The King said he was content to continue his favour, and never with that matter molest his conscience afterwards; but when the progress towards the marriage was so far advanced that the chancellor saw how soon his active co-operation must be required, he made suit to his "singular dear friend," the Duke of Norfolk, to procure his discharge from office. The duke, often solicited by More, then obtained, by importunate suit, a clear discharge for the chancellor; and upon the repairing to the King, to resign the great seal into his hands, Henry received him with thanks and praise for his worthy service, and assured him, that in any suit that should either concern his honour or appertain unto his profit, he would show himself a good and gracious master to his faithful servant. He then further directed Norfolk, when he installed his successor, to declare publicly, "that his majesty had with pain yielded to the prayers of Sir Thomas More, by the removal of such a magistrate."*

* Roper, p. 32. † Ibid. p. 48.

At the time of his resignation More asserted, and circumstances, without reference to his character, demonstrate the truth of his assertion, that his whole income, independent of grants from the crown, did not amount to more than 50*l.* yearly. This was not more than an eighth part of his gains at the bar and his judicial salary from the city of London taken together;—so great was the proportion in which his fortune had declined during eighteen years of employment in offices of such trust, advantage, and honour.† In this situation the clergy voted, as a testimonial of their gratitude to him, the sum of 5000*l.*, which, according to the rate of interest at that time, would have yielded him 500*l.* a year, being ten times the yearly sum which he could then call his own. But good and honourable as he knew their messengers, of whom Tunstall was one, to be, he declared, "*that he would rather cast their money into the sea than take it*;"—not speaking from a boastful pride, most foreign from his nature, but shrinking with a sort of instinctive delicacy from the touch of money, even before he considered how much the acceptance of the gift might impair his usefulness.

His resources were of a nobler nature. The simplicity of his tastes, and the moderation of his indulgences rendered retrenchment a task so easy to himself, as to be scarcely perceptible in his personal habits. His fool or jester, then a necessary part of a great man's establishment, he gave to the lord mayor for the time being. His first care was to provide for his attendants, by placing his gentlemen and yeomen with peers and prelates, and his eight watermen in the service of his successor Sir T. Audley, to whom he gave his great barge,—one of the most indispensable appendages of his office in an age when carriages were unknown. His sorrows were for separation from those whom he loved. He called together his children and grandchildren, who had hitherto lived in peace and love under his patriarchal roof, and, lamenting that he could not, as he was wont, and as he gladly would, bear out the whole charges of them all himself, continue living together as they were wont, he prayed them to give him their counsel on this trying occasion. When he saw them silent, and unwilling to risk their opinion, he gave them his, seasoned with his natural gaiety, and containing some strokes illustrative of the state of society at that time:—"I have been brought up," quoth he, "at Oxford, at an inn of chancery, at Lincoln's Inn, and also in the king's court, from the lowest degree to the highest, and yet I have at present left me little above 100*l.* a year" (including the king's

* "Honorificè jussit rex de me testatum reddere quod ægrè ad preces meas me demiserit."—More to Erasmus.

† Apology, chap. x.

grants;) "so that now if we like to live together we must be content to be contributaries together; but we must not fall to the lowest fare first:—we will begin with Lincoln's Inn diet, where many right worshipful and of good years do live full well; which, if we find not ourselves the first year able to maintain, then will we the next year go one step to New Inn fare: if that year exceed our ability, we will the next year descend to Oxford fare, where many grave, learned, and ancient fathers are continually conversant. If our ability stretch not to maintain either, then may we yet with bags and wallets go a begging together, and hoping for charity at every man's door, to sing *Salve regina;* and so still keep company and be merry together."* On the Sunday following his resignation, he stood at the door of his wife's pew in the church, where one of his dismissed gentlemen had been used to stand, and making a low obeisance to Alice as she entered, said to her with perfect gravity,—"Madam, my lord is gone." He who for seventeen years had not raised his voice in displeasure, could not be expected to sacrifice the gratification of his innocent merriment to the heaviest blows of fortune.

Nor did he at fit times fail to prepare his beloved children for those more cruel strokes which he began to foresee. Discoursing with them, he enlarged on the happiness of suffering for the love of God, the loss of goods, of liberty, of lands, of life. He would further say unto them, "that if he might perceive his wife and children would encourage him to die in a good cause, it should so comfort him, that for very joy, it would make him run merrily to death."

It must be owned that Henry felt the weight of this great man's opinion, and tried every possible means to obtain at least the appearance of his spontaneous approbation. Tunstall and other prelates were commanded to desire his attendance at the coronation of Anne at Westminster. They wrote a letter to persuade him to comply, and accompanied it with the needful present of 20*l.* to buy a court dress. Such overtures he had foreseen; for he said some time before to Roper, when he first heard of that marriage, "God grant, son Roper, that these matters within a while be not confirmed with oaths!" He accordingly answered his friends the bishops well:—"Take heed, my lords: by procuring your lordships to be present at the coronation, they will next ask you to preach for the setting forth thereof; and finally to write books to all the world in defence thereof."

Another opportunity soon presented itself for trying to subdue the obstinacy of More, whom a man of violent nature might believe to be fearful, because he was peaceful. Elizabeth Barton, called "the holy maid of Kent," who had been, for a considerable number of years, afflicted by convulsive maladies, felt her morbid susceptibility so excited by Henry's profane defiance of the Catholic Church, and his cruel desertion of Catharine, his faithful wife, that her pious and humane feelings led her to represent, and probably to believe, herself to be visited by a divine revelation of those punishments which the King was about to draw down on himself and on the kingdom. In the universal opinion of the sixteenth century, such interpositions were considered as still occurring. The neighbours and visiters of the unfortunate young woman believed her ravings to be prophecies, and the contortions of her body to be those of a frame heaving and struggling under the awful agitations of divine inspiration, and confirmed that conviction of a mission from God, for which she was predisposed by her own pious benevolence, combined with the general error of the age. Both Fisher and More appear not to have altogether disbelieved her pretensions: More expressly declared, that he durst not and would not be bold in judging her miracles.* In the beginning of her prophecies, the latter had been commanded by the King to inquire into her case; and he made a report to Henry, who agreed with him in considering the whole of her miraculous pretensions as frivolous, and deserving no farther regard. But in 1532, several monks† so magnified her performances to More that he was prevailed on to see her; but refused to hear her speak about the King, saying to her, in general terms, that he had no desire to pry into the concerns of others. Pursuant, as it is said, to a sentence by or in the Star Chamber, she stood in the pillory at Paul's Cross, acknowledging herself to be guilty of the imposture of claiming inspiration, and saying that she was tempted to this fraud by the instigation of the devil. Considering the circumstances of the case, and the character of the parties, it is far more probable that the ministers should have obtained a false confession from her hopes of saving her life, than that a simple woman should have contrived and carried on, for many years, a system of complicated and elaborate imposture. It would not be inconsistent with this aquittal, to allow that, in the course of her self-delusion, she should have been induced, by some ecclesiastics of the tottering Church, to take an active part in these pious frauds, which there is too much reason to believe that persons of unfeigned religion have been often so far misguided by enthusiastic zeal, as to perpetrate or to patronize. But whatever were the motives or the extent of the "holy maid's" confession, it availed her nothing; for in the session of parliament which met in January, 1534, she and her ecclesiastical prompters were attainted of high treason, and adjudged to suffer death as traitors. Fisher, bishop of Rochester, and others, were attainted of misprision, or concealment of treason, for which they were adjudged to forfeiture

* Roper, pp. 51, 52.

* Letter to Cromwell, probably written in the end of 1532.

† Of whom some were afterwards executed.

and imprisonment during the King's pleasure.* The "holy maid," with her spiritual guides, suffered death at Tyburn on the 21st of April, she confirming her former confession, but laying her crime to the charge of her companions, if we may implicitly believe the historians of the victorious party.†

Fisher and his supposed accomplices in misprision remained in prison according to their attainder. Of More the statute makes no mention; but it contains a provision, which, when it is combined with other circumstances to be presently related, appears to have been added to the bill for the purpose of providing for his safety. By this provision, the King's majesty, at the humble suit of his well beloved wife Queen Anne, pardons all persons not expressly by name attainted by the statute, for all misprision and concealments relating to the false and feigned miracles and prophecies of Elizabeth Barton, on or before the 20th day of October, 1533. Now we are told by Roper,‡ "that Sir Thomas More's name was originally inserted in the bill," the King supposing that this bill would "to Sir Thomas More be so troublous and terrible, that it would force him to relent and condescend to his request; wherein his grace was much deceived." More was personally to have been received to make answer in his own defence: but the King, not liking that, sent the Archbishop of Canterbury, the Chancellor, the Duke of Norfolk, and Cromwell, to attempt his conversion. Audley reminded More of the King's special favour and many benefits: More admitted them; but modestly added, that his highness had most graciously declared that on this matter he should be molested no more. When in the end they saw that no persuasion could move him, they then said, "that the King's highness had given them in commandment, if they could by no gentleness win him, in the King's name with ingratitude to charge him, that never was servant to his master so villainous,§ nor subject to his prince so traitorous as he." They even reproached him for having either written in the name of his master, or betrayed his sovereign into writing, the book against Luther, which had so deeply pledged Henry to the support of Papal pretensions. To these upbraidings he calmly answered:—"The terrors are arguments for children, and not for me. As to the fact, the King knoweth, that after the book was finished by his highness's appointment, or the consent of the maker, I was only a sorter out and placer of the principal matters therein contained." He added, that he had warned the King of the prudence of "touching the pope's authority more slenderly, and that he had reminded Henry of the statutes of *premunire*," whereby "a good part of the pope's pastoral care was pared away;" and that impetuous monarch had answered, "We are so much bounden unto the See of Rome, that we cannot do too much honour unto it." On More's return to Chelsea from his interview with these lords, Roper said to him:—"I hope all is well, since you are so merry?"—"It is so, indeed," said More, "I thank God."—"Are you, then, out of the parliament bill?" said Roper.—"By my troth, I never remembered it; but," said More, "I will tell thee why I was so merry; because I had given the devil a foul fall, and that with those lords I had gone so far, as without great shame I can never go back again." This frank avowal of the power of temptation, and this simple joy at having at the hazard of life escaped from the farther seductions of the court, bestows a greatness on these few and familiar words which scarcely belongs to any other of the sayings of man.

Henry, incensed at the failure of wheedling and threatening measures, broke out into violent declarations of his resolution to include More in the attainder, and said that he should be personally present to insure the passing of the bill. Lord Audley and his colleagues on their knees besought their master to forbear, lest by an overthrow in his own presence, he might be contemned by his own subjects, and dishonoured throughout Christendom for ever;—adding, that they doubted not that they should find a more meet occasion "to serve his turn;" for that in this case of the nun he was so clearly innocent, that men deemed him far worthier of praise than of reproof. Henry was compelled to yield.* Such was the power of defenceless virtue over the slender remains of independence among slavish peers, and over the lingering remnants of common humanity which might still be mingled with a cooler policy in the bosoms of subservient politicians. One of the worst of that race, Thomas Cromwell, on meeting Roper in the Parliament House next day after the King assented to the prayer of his ministers, told him to tell More that he was put out of the bill. Roper sent a messenger to Margaret Roper, who hastened to her beloved father with the tidings. More answered her, with his usual gaiety and fondness, "In faith, Megg, what is put off is not given up."†

---

* 25 H. viii. c. 12.

† Such as Hall and Holinshed. ‡ p. 62.

§ Like a *slave* or a *villain*. The word in the mouth of these gentlemen appears to have been in a state of transition, about the middle point between the original sense of "like a slave," and its modern acceptation of mean or malignant offenders. What proof is not supplied by this single fact in the history of the language of the masters, of their conviction, that the slavery maintained by them doomed the slaves to depravity!

* The House of Lords addressed the King, praying him to declare whether it would be agreeable to his pleasure that Sir Thomas More and others should not be heard in their own defence before "the lords in the royal senate called the *Stere* Chamber." Nothing more appears on the Journals relating to this matter. Lords' Journals, 6th March, 1533. The Journals prove the narrative of Roper, from which the text is composed, to be as accurate as it is beautiful.

† He spoke to her in his conversational Latin,—"*Quod differtur non aufertur.*"

Soon after, the Duke of Norfolk said to him,—"By the mass! Master More, it is perilous striving with princes; the anger of a prince brings death."—"Is that all, my lord? then the difference between you and me is but this,—*that I shall die to-day, and you to-morrow*." No life in Plutarch is more full of happy sayings and striking retorts than that of More; but the terseness and liveliness of his are justly overlooked in the contemplation of that union of perfect simplicity with moral grandeur, which, perhaps, no other human being has so uniformly reached.

By a tyrannical edict, miscalled "a law," in the same session of 1533–4, it was made high treason, after the 1st of May, 1534, by writing, print, deed or act, to do or to procure, or cause to be done or procured, any thing to the prejudice, slander, disturbance, or derogation of the King's lawful matrimony with Queen Anne. If the same offences should be committed by words, they were to be only misprision. The same act enjoined all persons to take an oath to maintain *its whole contents;* and an obstinate refusal to make oath was subjected to the penalties of misprision. No form of oath was enacted, but on the 30th of March,* 1534, which was the day of closing the session, the Chancellor Audley, when the commons were at the bar, but when they could neither deliberate nor assent, read the King's letters patent, containing one, and appointing the Archbishop of Canterbury, the Chancellor, the Dukes of Norfolk and Suffolk, to be commissioners for administering it.

More was summoned to appear before these commissioners at Lambeth, on Monday the 13th of April. On other occasions he had used, at his departure from his wife and children, whom he tenderly loved, to have them brought to his boat, and there to kiss them, and bid them all farewell. At this time he would suffer none of them to follow him forth of the gate, but pulled the wicket after him, and shut them all from him, and with Roper and four servants took boat towards Lambeth. He sat for a while; but at last, his mind being lightened and relieved by those high principles to which with him every low consideration yielded, whispered:—"Son Roper! I thank our Lord, the field is won."—"As I conjectured," says Roper, "it was for that his love to God conquered his carnal affections." What follows is from an account of his conduct during the subsequent examination at Lambeth sent to his darling child, Margaret Roper. After having read the statute and the form of the oath, he declared his readiness to swear that he would maintain and defend the order of succession to the crown as established by parliament. He disclaimed all censure of those who had imposed, or on those who had taken, the oath, but declared it to be impossible that he could swear to the whole contents of it, without offending against his own conscience; adding, that if they doubted whether his refusal proceeded from pure scruple of conscience or from his own phantasies, he was willing to satisfy their doubts by oath. The commissioners urged that he was the first who refused it; they showed him the subscriptions of all the lords and commons who had sworn; and they held out the King's sure displeasure against him should he be the single recusant. When he was called on a second time, they charged him with obstinacy for not mentioning any special part of the oath which wounded his conscience. He answered, that if he were to open his reasons for refusal farther, he should exasperate the King still more: he offered, however, to assign them if the lords would procure the King's assurance that the avowal of the grounds of his defence should not be considered as offensive to the King, nor prove dangerous to himself. The commissioners answered that such assurances would be no defence against a legal charge: he offered, however, to trust himself to the King's honour. Cranmer took some advantage of More's candour, urging that, as he had disclaimed all blame of those who had sworn, it was evident that he thought it only doubtful whether the oath was unlawful; and desired him to consider whether the obligation to obey the King was not absolutely certain. More was struck with the subtilty of this reasoning, which took him by surprise,—but not convinced of its solidity: notwithstanding his surprise, he seems to have almost touched upon the true answer, that as the oath contained a profession of opinion,—such, for example, as the lawfulness of the King's marriage, on which men might differ,—it might be declined by some and taken by others with equal honesty. Cromwell, whom More believed to favour him, loudly swore that he would rather see his only son had lost his head than that More had thus refused the oath; he it was who bore the answer to the King, the Chancellor Audley distinctly enjoining him to state very clearly More's willingness to swear to the succession. "Surely," said More, "as to swearing to the succession, I see no peril." Cromwell was not a good man; but the gentle virtue of More subdued even the bad. To his own house More never more returned, being on the same day committed to the custody of the Abbot of Westminster, in which he continued four days; and at the end of that time, on Friday the 17th, he was conveyed to the Tower.*

* Lords' Journals, vol. i. p. 82.

* Roper tells us that the King, who had intended to desist from his importunities, was exasperated by Queen Anne's clamour to tender the oath at Lambeth; but he detested that unhappy lady, whose marriage was the occasion of More's ruin: and though Roper was an unimpeachable witness relating to Sir Thomas' conversation, he is of less weight as to what passed in the interior of the palace. The ministers might have told such a story to excuse themselves to Roper: Anne could have had no opportunity of contradiction.

Soon after the commencement of the session, which began on the 3d of November following,* an act was passed which ratified, and professed to recite, the form of oath promulgated on the day of the prorogation; and enacted that the oath therein recited should be *reputed* to be the very oath intended by the former act;† though there were, in fact, some substantial and important interpolations in the latter act;—such as the words "most dear and entirely beloved, lawful wife, Queen Anne," which tended to render that form still less acceptable than before, to the scrupulous consciences of More and Fisher. Before the end of the same session two statutes‡ were passed attainting More and Fisher of misprision of treason, and specifying the punishment to be imprisonment of body and loss of goods. By that which relates to More, the King's grants of land to him in 1523 and 1525 are resumed; it is also therein recited that he refused the oath since the 1st of May of 1534, with an intent to sow sedition; and he is reproached for having demeaned himself in other respects ungratefully and unkindly to the King, his benefactor.

That this statement of the legislative measures which preceded it is necessary to a consideration of the legality of More's trial, which must be owned to be a part of its justice, will appear in its proper place. In the mean time, the few preparatory incidents which occurred during thirteen months' imprisonment, must be briefly related. His wife Alice, though an excellent housewife, yet in her visits to the Tower handled his misfortunes and his scruples too roughly. "Like an ignorant, and somewhat worldly, woman, she bluntly said to him,—'How can a man taken for wise, like you, play the fool in this close filthy prison, when you might be abroad at your liberty, if you would but do as the bishops have done?'" She enlarged on his fair house at Chelsea—"his library, gallery, garden, and orchard, together with the company of his wife and children." He bore with kindness in its most unpleasing form, and answered her cheerfully after his manner, which was to blend religious feeling with quaintness and liveliness:—"Is not this house as nigh heaven as mine own?" She answered him in what then appears to have been a homely exclamation of contempt,§ "*Tilly valle, tilly valle.*"‖ He treated her harsh language as a wholesome exercise for his patience, and replied with equal mildness, though with more gravity, "Why should I joy in my gay house, when, if I should rise from the grave in seven years, I should not fail to find some one there who would bid me to go out of doors, for it was none of mine?" It was not thus that his Margaret Roper conversed or corresponded with him during his confinement. A short note written to her a little while after his conmitment, with a coal (his only pen and ink) begins, "Mine own good daughter," and is closed in the following fond and pious words:—"Written with a coal, by your tender loving father, who in his poor prayers forgetteth none of you, nor your babes, nor your good husband, nor your father's shrewd wife neither." Shortly after, mistaking the sense of a letter from her, which he thought advised him to compliance, he wrote a rebuke of her supposed purpose with the utmost vehemence of affection, and the deepest regard to her judgment!—"I hear many terrible things towards me; but they all never touched me, never so near, nor were they so grievous unto me as to see you, my well beloved child, in such a piteous and vehement manner, labour to persuade me to a thing whereof I have of pure necessity, for respect unto myne own soul, so often given you so precise an answer before. The matters that move my conscience I have sundry times shown you, that I will disclose them to no one."* Margaret's reply was worthy of herself: she acquiesces in his "faithful and delectable letter, the faithful messenger of his virtuous mind," and almost rejoices in his victory over all earthborn cares;—concluding thus:—"Your own most loving obedient daughter and bedeswoman,† Margaret Roper, who desireth above all worldly things to be in John Wood's‡ stede to do you some service." After some time pity prevailed so far that she obtained the King's licence to resort to her father in the Tower. On her first visit, after gratefully performing their accustomed devotions, his first care was to soothe her afflicted heart by the assurance that he saw no cause to reckon himself in worse case there than in his own house. On another occasion he asked her how Queen Anne did? "In faith, father," said she, "never better."—"Never better, Megg!" quoth he; "alas! Megg, it pitieth me to remember into what misery, poor soul, she shall shortly come." Various attempts continued still to be made to cajole him; partly, perhaps, with the hope that his intercourse with the beloved Margaret might have softened him. Cromwell told him that the King was still his good master, and did not wish to press his conscience. The lords commissioners went twice to the Tower to tender the oath to him: but neither he nor Fisher would advance farther than their original declaration of perfect willingness to maintain the settlement of the crown, which, being a matter purely political, was within the undisputed competence of parliament. They refused to include in their oath any other matter on account of scruples of conscience, which they forbore to particularise, lest they might thereby furnish their enemies with a

* 26 H. VIII. c. 2.
† 25 Id. c. 22. § 9. Compare Lords' Journals, vol. i. p. 82.
‡ 26 H. VIII. c. 22, 23.
§ Roper, p. 78.
‖ Nares' Glossary, London, 1822.

* English Works, vol. i. p. 1430.
† His waiting-man, Ibid. p. 1431. Bedesman—one who prays for another.
‡ Roper, p. 72.

pretext for representing their defence as a new crime. A statement of their real ground of objection,—that it would be insincere in them to declare upon oath, that they believed the King's marriage with Anne to be lawful,—might, in defending themselves against a charge of misprision of treason, have exposed them to the penalties of high treason.

Two difficulties occurred in reconciling the destruction of the victim with any form or colour of law. The first of them consisted in the circumstance that the naked act of refusing the oath was, even by the late statute, punishable only as a misprision; and though concealment of treason was never expressly declared to be only a misprision till the statute to that effect was passed under Philip and Mary,*—chiefly perhaps occasioned by the case of More,—yet it seemed strange thus to prosecute him for the refusal, as an act of treason, after it had been positively made punishable as a misprision by a general statute, and after a special act of attainder for misprision had been passed against him. Both these enactments were, on the supposition of the refusal being indictable for treason, absolutely useless, and such as tended to make More believe that he was safe as long as he remained silent. The second has been already intimated, that he had yet said nothing which could be tortured into a semblance of those acts derogatory to the King's marriage, which had been made treason. To conquer this last difficulty, Sir Robin Rich, the solicitor-general, undertook the infamous task of betraying More into some declaration, in a confidential conversation, and under pretext of familiar friendship, which might be pretended to be treasonable. What the success of this flagitious attempt was, the reader will see in the account of More's trial. It appears from a letter of Margaret Roper, apparently written sometime in the winter, that his persecutors now tried another expedient for vanquishing his constancy, by restraining him from attending church; and she adds, "from the company of my good mother and his poor children."† More, in his answer, expresses his wonted affection in very familiar, but in most significant language:—"If I were to declare in writing how much pleasure your daughterly loving letters gave me, a peck of coals would not suffice to make the pens." So confident was he of his innocence, and so safe did he deem himself on the side of law, that "he believed some new causeless suspicion, founded upon some secret sinister information," had risen up against him.‡

On the 2d or 3d of May, 1535, More informed his dear daughter of a visit from Cromwell, attended by the attorney and solicitor-general, and certain civilians, at which Cromwell had urged to him the statute which made the King head of the Church, and required an answer on that subject; and that he had replied:—"I am the King's true faithful subject, and daily bedesman: I say no harm, and do no harm; and if this be not enough to keep a man alive, in good faith I long not to live." This ineffectual attempt was followed by another visit from Cranmer, the Chancellor, the Duke of Suffolk, the Earl of Wiltshire, and Cromwell, who, after much argument, tendered an oath, by which he was to promise to make answers to questions which they might put;* and on his decisive refusal, Cromwell gave him to understand that, agreeably to the language at the former conference, "his grace would follow the course of his laws towards such as he should find obstinate." Cranmer, who too generally complied with evil counsels, but nearly always laboured to prevent their execution, wrote a persuasive letter to Cromwell, earnestly praying the King to be content with More and Fisher's proffered engagement to maintain the succession, which would render the whole nation unanimous on the practical part of that great subject.

On the 6th of the same month, almost immediately after the defeat of every attempt to practise on his firmness, More was brought to trial at Westminster; and it will scarcely be doubted, that no such culprit stood at any European bar for a thousand years. It is rather from caution than from necessity that the ages of Roman domination are excluded from the comparison. It does not seem that in any moral respect Socrates himself could claim a superiority. It is lamentable that the records of the proceedings against such a man should be scanty. We do not certainly know the specific offence of which he was convicted. There does not seem, however, to be much doubt that the prosecution was under the act "for the establishment of the king's succession," passed in the session of 1533-4,† which made it high treason "to do any thing to the prejudice, slander, disturbance, or derogation of the lawful marriage" between Henry and Anne. Almost any act, done or declined, might be forced within the undefined limits of such vague terms. In this case the prosecutors probably represented his refusal to answer certain questions which, according to them, must have related to the marriage, his observations at his last examination, and especially his conversation with Rich, as overt acts of that treason, inasmuch as it must have been known by him that his conduct on these occasions tended to create a general doubt of the legitimacy of the marriage.

To the first alleged instance of his resistance to the King, which consisted in his original judgment against the marriage, he answered in a manner which rendered reply impossible; "that it could never be treason for one of the King's advisers to give him

* 1 & 2 Phil. and Mar. c. 10.
† English Works, vol. i. p. 1446.
‡ Ibid. p. 1447.

* English Works, vol. i. p. 1452.
† 25 H. VIII. c. 22.

honest advice." On the like refusal respecting the King's headship of the Church, he answered that "no man could be punished for silence." The attorney-general said, that the prisoner's silence was "malicious:"—More justly answered, that "he had a right to be silent where his language was likely to be injuriously misconstrued." Respecting his letters to Bishop Fisher, they were burnt, and no evidence was offered of their contents, which he solemnly declared to have no relation to the charges. And as to the last charge, that he had called the Act of Settlement "a two-edged sword, which would destroy his soul if he complied with it, and his body if he refused," it was answered by him, that "he supposed the reason of his refusal to be equally good, whether the question led to an offence against his conscience, or to the necessity of criminating himself."

Cromwell had before told him, that though he was suffering perpetual imprisonment for the misprision, that punishment did not release him from his allegiance, and that he was amenable to the law for treason;—overlooking the essential circumstances, that the facts laid as treason were the same on which the attainder for misprision was founded. Even if this were not a strictly maintainable objection in technical law, it certainly showed the flagrant injustice of the whole proceeding.

The evidence, however, of any such strong circumstances attendant on the refusal as could raise it into an act of treason must have seemed defective; for the prosecutors were reduced to the necessity of examining Rich, one of their own number, to prove circumstances of which he could have had no knowledge, without the foulest treachery on his part. He said, that he had gone to More as a friend, and had asked him, if an act of parliament had made him, Rich, king, would not he, More, acknowledge him. More had said, "Yes, sir, that I would?"—"If they declared me pope, would you acknowledge me?"—"In the first case, I have no doubt about temporal governments; but suppose the parliament should make a law that God should not be God, would you then, Mr. Rich, say that God should not be God?"—"No," says Rich, "no parliament could make such a law." Rich went on to swear, that More had added, "No more could the parliament make the King the supreme head of the Church." More denied the latter part of Rich's evidence altogether; which is, indeed, inconsistent with the whole tenor of his language: he was then compelled to expose the profligacy of Rich's character. "I am," he said, "more sorry for your perjury, than for mine own peril. Neither I, nor any man, ever took you to be a person of such credit as I could communicate with on such matters. We dwelt near in one parish, and you were always esteemed very light of your tongue, and not of any commendable fame. Can it be likely to your lordships that I should so unadvisedly overshoot myself, as to trust Mr. Rich with what I have concealed from the King, or any of his noble and grave counsellors?" The credit of Rich was so deeply wounded, that he was compelled to call Sir Richard Southwell and Mr. Palmer, who were present at the conversation, to prop his tottering evidence. They made a paltry excuse, by alleging that they were so occupied in removing More's books, that they did not listen to the words of this extraordinary conversation.

The jury,* in spite of all these circumstances, returned a verdict of "guilty." Chancellor Audley, who was at the head of the commission, of which Spelman and Fitzherbert, eminent lawyers, were members, was about to pronounce judgment, when he was interrupted by More, who claimed the usual privilege of being heard to show that judgment should not be passed. More urged, that he had so much ground for his scruples as at least to exempt his refusal from the imputation of disaffection, or of what the law deems to be malice. The chancellor asked him once more how his scruples could balance the weight of the parliament, people, and Church of England?—a topic which had been used against him at every interview and conference since he was brought prisoner to Lambeth. The appeal to weight of authority influencing Conscience was, however, singularly unfortunate. More answered, as he had always done, "Nine out of ten of Christians now in the world think with me; nearly all the learned doctors and holy fathers who are already dead, agree with me; and therefore I think myself not bound to conform my conscience to the councell of one realm against the general consent of all Christendom." Chief Justice Fitzjames concurred in the sufficiency of the indictment; which, after the verdict of the jury, was the only matter before the court.

The chancellor then pronounced the savage sentence which the law then directed in cases of treason. More, having no longer any measures to keep, openly declared, that after seven years' study, "he could find no colour for holding that a layman could be head of the Church." The commissioners once more offered him a favourable audience for any matter which he had to propose.—"More have I not to say, my lords," he replied, "but that as St. Paul held the clothes of those who stoned Stephen to death, and as they are both now saints in heaven, and shall continue there friends for ever; so I verily trust, and shall therefore right heartily pray, that though your lordships have now here on earth been judges to my condemnation, we may, nevertheless, hereafter cheer-

---

* Sir T. Palmer, Sir T. Bent, G. Lovell, esquire, Thomas Burbage, esquire, and G. Chamber, Edward Stockmore, William Brown, Jasper Leake, Thomas Bellington, John Parnell, Richard Bellamy, and G. Stoakes, gentlemen, were the jury.

fully meet in heaven, in everlasting salvation."*

Sir W. Kingston, "his very dear friend," constable of the Tower, as, with tears running down his cheeks, he conducted him from Westminster, condoled with his prisoner, who endeavoured to assuage the sorrow of his friend by the consolations of religion. The same gentleman said afterwards to Roper,—"I was ashamed of myself when I found my heart so feeble, and his so strong." Margaret Roper, his good angel, watched for his landing at the Tower wharf. "After his blessing upon her knees reverently received, without care of herself, pressing in the midst of the throng, and the guards that were about him with halberts and bills, she hastily ran to him, and openly, in sight of them all, embraced and kissed him. He gave her again his fatherly blessing. After separation she, all ravished with the entire love of her dear father, suddenly turned back again, ran to him as before, took him about the neck, and divers times kissed him most lovingly,—a sight which made many of the beholders weep and mourn."† Thus tender was the heart of the admirable woman who had at the same time the greatness of soul to strengthen her father's fortitude, by disclaiming the advice for which he, having mistaken her meaning, had meekly rebuked her,—to prefer life to right.

On the 14th of June, More was once more examined by four civilians in the Tower. "He was asked, first, whether he would obey the King as supreme head of the Church of England on earth immediately under Christ? to which he said, that he could make no answer: secondly, whether he would consent to the King's marriage with Queen Anne, and affirm the marriage with the lady Catharine to have been unlawful? to which he answered that he did never speak nor meddle against the same: and, thirdly, whether he was not bound to answer the said question, and to recognise the headship as aforesaid? to which he said, that he could make no answer."‡ It is evident that these interrogatories, into which some terms peculiarly objectionable to More were now for the first time inserted, were contrived for the sole purpose of reducing the illustrious victim to the option of uttering a lie, or of suffering death. The conspirators against him might, perhaps, have had a faint idea that they had at length broken his spirit; and if he persisted, they might have hoped that he could be represented as bringing destruction on himself by his own obstinacy. Such, however, was his calm and well-ordered mind, that he said and did nothing to provoke his fate. Had he given affirmative answers, he would have sworn falsely: he was the martyr of veracity; he perished only because he was sincere.

On Monday, the 5th of July, he wrote a farewell letter to Margaret Roper, with his usual materials of coal. It contained blessings on all his children by name, with a kind remembrance even to one of Margaret's maids. Adverting to their last interview, on the quay, he says,—"I never liked your manner towards me better than when you kissed me last; for I love when daughterly love and dear charity have no leisure to look to worldly courtesy."

Early the next morning Sir Thomas Pope, "his singular good friend," came to him with a message from the King and council, to say that he should die before nine o'clock of the same morning. "The King's pleasure," said Pope, "is that you shall not use many words."—"I did purpose," answered More, "to have spoken somewhat, but I will conform myself to the King's commandment, and I beseech you to obtain from him that my daughter Margaret may be present at my burial."—"The King is already content that your wife, children, and other friends shall be present thereat." The lieutenant brought him to the scaffold, which was so weak that it was ready to fall; on which he said, merrily, "Master lieutenant, I pray you see me safe up, and for my coming down let me shift for myself." When he laid his head on the block he desired the executioner to wait till he had removed his beard, "for that had never offended his highness,"—ere the axe fell.

He has been censured by some for such levities at the moment of death. These are censorious cavils, which would not be worthy of an allusion if they had not occasioned some sentences of as noble reflection, and beautiful composition, as the English language contains. "The innocent mirth, which had been so conspicuous in his life, did not forsake him to the last. His death was of a piece with his life; there was nothing in it new, forced, or affected. He did not look upon the severing his head from his body as a circumstance which ought to produce any change in the disposition of his mind; and as he died in a fixed and settled hope of immortality, he thought any unusual degree of sorrow and concern improper."*

According to the barbarous practice of laws which vainly struggle to carry their cruelty beyond the grave, the head of Sir Thomas More was placed on London bridge. His darling daughter, Margaret, had the courage to procure it to be taken down, that she might exercise her affection by continuing to look on a relic so dear; and carrying her love beyond the grave, she desired that it might be buried with her when she died.† The remains of this precious relic are said to have been since observed, lying on what had once been her bosom. The male descendants of this admirable woman appear to have been soon extinct: her descendants through females are probably numerous.‡

* Roper, p. 90. † Ibid. p. 90. ‡ Ibid. p. 92.

* Spectator, No. 349.

† She survived her father about nine years.

‡ One of them, Mr. James Hinton Baverstock, inserted his noble pedigree from Margaret, in

She resembled her father in mind, in manner, in the features and expression of her countenance, and in her form and gait. Her learning was celebrated throughout Christendom. It is seldom that literature wears a more agreeable aspect than when it becomes a bond of union between such a father and such a daughter.

Sir Thomas More's eldest son, John, married Anne Cresacre, the heiress of an estate, still held by his posterity through females, at Barnborough, near Doncaster,* where the mansion of the Mores still subsists. The last male desendant was Thomas More, a Jesuit, who was principal of the college of Jesuits at Bruges, and died at Bath in 1795, having survived his famous order, and, according to the appearances of that time, his ancient religion;—as if the family of More were one of the many ties which may be traced, through the interval of two centuries and a half, between the revolutions of religion and those of government.

The letters and narratives of Erasmus diffused the story of his friend's fate throughout Europe. Cardinal Pole bewailed it with elegance and feeling. It filled Italy, then the most cultivated portion of Europe, with horror. Paulo Jovio called Henry "a Phalaris," though we shall in vain look in the story of Phalaris, or of any other real or legendary tyrant, for a victim worthy of being compared to More. The English ministers throughout Europe were regarded with averted eyes as the agents of a monster. At Venice, Henry, after this deed, was deemed capable of any crimes: he was believed there to have murdered Catharine, and to be about to murder his daughter Mary.† The Catholic zeal of Spain, and the resentment of the Spanish people against the oppression of Catharine, quickened their sympathy with More, and aggravated their detestation of Henry. Mason, the envoy at Valladolid, thought every pure Latin phrase too weak for More, and describes him by one as contrary to the rules of that language as "thrice greatest"‡ would be to those of ours. When intelligence of his death was brought to the Emperor Charles V., he sent for Sir T. Elliot, the English ambassador, and said to him, "My lord ambassador, we understand that the king your master has put his wise counsellor Sir Thomas More to death." Elliot, abashed, made answer that he understood nothing thereof. "Well," said the Emperor, "it is too true; and this we will say, that, if we had been master of such a servant, we should rather have lost the best city in our dominions than have lost such a worthy counsellor;"—"which matter," says Roper, in the concluding words of his beautiful narrative, "was by Sir T. Elliot told to myself, *my wife*, to Mr. Clement and his wife, and to Mr. Heywood and his wife."*

Of all men nearly perfect, Sir Thomas More had, perhaps, the clearest marks of individual character. His peculiarities, though distinguishing him from all others, were yet withheld from growing into moral faults. It is not enough to say of him that he was unaffected, that he was natural, that he was simple; so the larger part of truly great men have been. But there is something homespun in More which is common to him with scarcely any other, and which gives to all his faculties and qualities the appearance of being the native growth of the soil. The homeliness of his pleasantry purifies it from show. He walks on the scaffold clad only in his household goodness. The unrefined benignity with which he ruled his patriarchal dwelling at Chelsea enabled him to look on the axe without being disturbed by feeling hatred for the tyrant. This quality bound together his genius and learning, his eloquence and fame, with his homely and daily duties,—bestowing a genuineness on all his good qualities, a dignity on the most ordinary offices of life, and an accessible familiarity on the virtues of a hero and a martyr, which silences every suspicion that his excellencies were magnified. He thus simply performed great acts, and uttered great thoughts, because they were familiar to his great soul. The charm of this inborn and homebred character seems as if it would have been taken off by polish. It is this household character which relieves our notion of him from vagueness, and divests perfection of that generality and coldness to which the attempt to paint a perfect man is so liable.

It will naturally, and very strongly, excite the regret of the good in every age, that the life of this best of men should have been in the power of one who has been rarely surpassed in wickedness. But the execrable Henry was the means of drawing forth the magnanimity, the fortitude, and the meekness of More. Had Henry been a just and merciful monarch, we should not have known the degree of excellence to which human nature is capable of ascending. Catholics ought to see in More, that mildness and candour are the true ornaments of all modes of faith. Protestants ought to be taught humility and charity from this instance of the wisest and best of men falling into, what they deem, the most fatal errors. All men, in the fierce contests of contending factions, should, from such an example, learn the wisdom to fear lest in their most hated antagonist they may strike down a Sir Thomas More: for assuredly virtue is not so narrow as to be confined to any party; and we have in the

1819, in a copy of More's English Works, at this moment before me.

* Hunter's South Yorkshire, vol. i. pp. 374, 375.

† Ellis' Original Letters, 2d series, lett. cxvii.

‡ Ibid. lett. cx. "Ter maximus ille Morus."

* Instead of Heywood, perhaps we ought to read "Heron?" In that case the three daughters of Sir Thomas More would be present: Mrs. Roper was the eldest, Mrs. Clement the second, and Cecilia Heron the youngest.

case of More a signal example that the nearest approach to perfect excellence does not exempt men from mistakes which we may justly deem mischievous. It is a pregnant proof, that we should beware of hating men for their opinions, or of adopting their doctrines because we love and venerate their virtues.

APPENDIX.

A.

Some particulars in the life of Sir Thomas More I am obliged to leave to more fortunate inquirers. They are, indeed, very minute; but they may appear to others worthy of being ascertained, as they appeared to me, from their connection with the life of a wise and good man.

The records of the Privy Council are preserved only since 1540, so that we do not exactly know the date of his admission into that body. The time when he was knighted (then a matter of some moment) is not known. As the whole of his life passed during the great chasm in writs for election, and returns of members of parliament, from 1477 to 1542, the places for which he sat, and the year of his early opposition to a subsidy, are unascertained;—notwithstanding the obliging exertion of the gentlemen employed in the repositories at the Tower, and in the Rolls' chapel. We know that he was speaker of the House of Commons in 1523 and 1524.* Browne Willis owns his inability to fix the place which he represented;† but he conjectured it to have been "either Middlesex, where he resided, or Lancaster, of which duchy he was chancellor." But that laborious and useful writer would not have mentioned the latter branch of his alternative, nor probably the former, if he had known that More was not Chancellor of the Duchy till two years after his speakership.

B.

An anecdote in More's chancellorship is connected with an English phrase, of which the origin is not quite satisfactorily explained. An attorney in his court, named Tubb, gave an account in court of a cause in which he was concerned, which the Chancellor (who with all his gentleness loved a joke) thought so rambling and incoherent, that he said at the end of Tubb's speech, "This is a tale of a tub;" plainly showing that the phrase was then familiarly known. The learned Mr. Douce has informed a friend of mine, that in Sebastian Munster's Cosmography, there is a cut of a ship, to which a whale was coming too close for her safety, and of the sailors throwing a tub to the whale, evidently to play with. The practice of throwing a tub or barrel to a large fish, to divert the animal from gambols dangerous to a vessel, is also mentioned in an old prose translation of The Ship of Fools. These passages satisfactorily explain the common phrase of throwing a tub to a whale; but they do not account for leaving out the whale, and introducing the new word "tale." The transition from the first phrase to the second is a considerable stride. It is not, at least, *directly* explained by Mr. Douce's citations; and no explanation of it has hitherto occurred which can be supported by proof. It may be thought probable that, in process of time, some nautical wag compared a rambling story, which he suspected of being lengthened and confused, in order to turn his thoughts from a direction not convenient to the story-teller, with the tub which he and his shipmates were wont to throw out to divert the whale from striking the bark, and perhaps said, "This tale is, like our tub to the whale." The comparison might have become popular; and it might gradually have been shortened into "a tale of a tub."

* Rolls of Parliament in Lords' Journals, vol. i.
† Notitia Parliamentaria, vol. iii. p. 112.

C.

EXTRACTS FROM THE RECORDS OF THE CITY OF LONDON RELATING TO THE APPOINTMENT OF SIR THOMAS MORE TO BE UNDER-SHERIFF OF LONDON, AND SOME APPOINTMENTS OF HIS IMMEDIATE PREDECESSORS AND OF HIS SUCCESSOR.

(A. D. 1496. 27th September.)

"Commune consilium tentum die Martij Vicesimo Septimo die Septembr̃ Anno Regni Regis Henr̃ Septimi duo decimo.

"In isto Comūn Consilio Thomas Sall et Thomas Marowe confirmati sunt in Subvic̃ Civitati : London p anno sequent, &c."

(1497.)

"Comūne Consiliū tent die Lune xxv[to] die Sept̃ anno Regni Reg̃s Henr̃ vii. xiij°.

"Isto die Thomas Marowe et Ed[s] Dudley confirmat̃ sunt in Sub Vic̃ Sit[s] London p anno seqū."

(1498 & 1501.)

Similar entries of the confirmation of Thomas Marowe and Edward Dudley are made in the 14th, 15th, 16th, and 17th Henry VII., and at a court of aldermen, held on the

(1502.)

17th Nov. 18 Henry 7. the following entry appears:—

"Ad hanc Cur̃ Thomas Marowe uñs sub vicecomitū sponte resignat offim̃ suū."

And at a Common Council held on the same day, is entered—

"In isto Communi Consilio Radūs adye Gentilman elec̃t est in unū Subvic̃ Civitats London loco Thomẽ Marwe Gentilman qui illud officiū sponte resignavit, capiend̃ feod̃ consuet̃."

"Cōē Consiliū tent die Martis iij° die Septembris anno Regni Reg[s] Henrici Octavi Secundo.

"Eodm̃ die Thom̃s More Gent elec̃t est in unū Subvic̃ Civitats London loc̃ Ric̃ Broke Gent qui nup elec̃t fuit in Recordator London."

"Martis viij die Maii 6th Henry 8.
"Court of Aldermen.

"Yt ys agreed that Thomas More Gent oon of Undersheryfes of London which shall go oṽ the Kings Ambasset̃ in to ffaunders shall occupie his Rowme and office by his sufficient Depute untyll his cūmyng home ageyn"

"Martis xj die Marcii 7 Henry VIIIth
"Court of Aldermen.

"Ye shall sweare that ye shall kepe the Secrets of this Courte and not to disclose eny thing ther spoken for the cõen welthe of this citie that myght hurt eny ꝑsone or brother of the seyd courte onles yt be spoken to his brothr or to other which in his conscience and discreĉon shall thynk yt to be for the cõen welthe of this citie.

So help you God."

"Jovis xiij die Marcii 7 Henry 8.
"Court of Aldermen.

"Itm̃ ad ista Cur̃ Thomas More and Wills̃ Shelley Subvicecs Cits London jur̃ sunt ad articlm supdcm̃ spect xj die marcii."

"Ven̄is 23 July, 10 Henry 8.
Court of Aldermen.

"Ad istam Cur̃ Thomas More Gent un Subvic̃ Cits in Compur̃ Pulletr London libẽ et sponte Surr̃ et resign̄ officm̄ pdc̄m in̄ manū Maioris et Aldrōr."

"Coie Consiliu tent̃ die Ven̄is xxiij die Julii anno regni regis Henrici Octavi decimo."

"Isto die Johes Pakyngton Gent admissus est in unū subvic̃ Civitats London loco Thome More qui spont et libẽ resignavit Officiū illud in Man̄ Maioris aldrōr et Cōis consilii. Et jur est &c."

A REFUTATION OF THE CLAIM ON BEHALF OF KING CHARLES I. TO THE AUTHORSHIP OF THE ΕἸΚῺΝ ΒΑΣΙΛΙΚΉ.*

A succession of problems or puzzles in the literary and political history of modern times has occasionally occupied some ingenious writers, and amused many idle readers. Those who think nothing useful which does not yield some palpable and direct advantage, have, indeed, scornfully rejected such inquiries as frivolous and useless. But their disdain has not repressed such discussions: and it is fortunate that it has not done so. Amusement is itself an advantage. The vigour which the understanding derives from exercise on every subject is a great advantage. If there is to be any utility in history, the latter must be accurate,—which it never will be, unless there be a solicitude to ascertain the truth even of its minutest parts. History is read with pleasure, and with moral effect, only as far as it engages our feelings in the merit or demerit, in the fame or fortune, of historical personages. The breathless anxiety with which the obscure and conflicting evidence on a trial at law is watched by the bystander is but a variety of the same feeling which prompts the reader to examine the proofs against Mary, Queen of Scots, with as deep an interest as if she were alive, and were now on *her* trial. And it is wisely ordered that it should be so: for our condition would not, upon the whole, be bettered by our feeling less strongly about each other's concerns.

The question "Who wrote Icôn Basilikè?" seemed more than once to be finally determined. Before the publication of the private letters of Bishop Gauden, the majority of historical inquirers had pronounced it spurious; and the only writers of great acuteness who maintained its genuineness—Warburton and Hume—spoke in a tone which rather indicated an anxious desire that others should believe, than a firm belief in their own minds. It is perhaps the only matter on which the former ever expressed himself with diffidence; and the case must indeed have seemed doubtful, which compelled the most dogmatical and arrogant of disputants to adopt a language almost sceptical. The successive publications of those letters in Maty's Review, in the third volume of the Clarendon Papers, and lastly, but most decisively, by Mr. Todd, seemed to have closed the dispute.

The main questions on which the whole dispute hinges are, Whether the acts and words of Lord Clarendon, of Lord Bristol, of Bishop Morley, of Charles II., and James II., do not amount to a distinct acknowledgment of Gauden's authorship? and, Whether an admission of that claim *by these persons* be not a conclusive evidence of its truth? If these questions can be answered affirmatively, the other parts of the case will not require very long consideration.

The Icôn Basilikè was intended to produce a favourable effect during the King's

* Contributed to the Edinburgh Review (vol. xliv. p. 1.) as a review of "Who wrote Εἰκὼν Βασιλική?" by Christopher Wordsworth, D. D., Master of Trinity College, Cambridge. London, 1824.—Ed.

trial; but its publication was retarded till some days after his death, by the jealous and rigorous precautions of the ruling powers. The impression made on the public by a work which purported to convey the pious and eloquent language of a dying King, could not fail to be very considerable; and, though its genuineness was from the beginning doubted or disbelieved by some,* it would have been wonderful and unnatural, if unbounded faith in it had not become one of the fundamental articles of a Royalist's creed.† Though much stress, therefore, is laid by Dr. Wordsworth on passages in anonymous pamphlets published before the Restoration, we can regard these as really no more than instances of the belief which must then have only prevailed among that great majority of Royalists who had no peculiar reasons for doubt. Opinion, even when it was impartial, of the genuineness of a writing given before its authenticity was seriously questioned, and when the attention of those who gave the opinion was not strongly drawn to the subject, must be classed in the lowest species of historical evidence. One witness who bears testimony to a forgery, when the edge of his discernment is sharpened by an existing dispute, outweighs many whose language only indicates a passive acquiescence in the unexamined sentiments of their own party. It is obvious, indeed, that such testimonies must be of exceedingly little value; for every imposture, in any degree successful, *must* be able to appeal to them. Without them, no question on such a subject could ever be raised; since it would be idle to expose the spuriousness of what no one appeared to think authentic.

Dr. Gauden, a divine of considerable talents, but of a temporizing and interested character, was, at the beginning of the Civil War, chaplain to the Earl of Warwick, a Presbyterian leader. In November 1640, after the close imprisonment of Lord Strafford, he preached a sermon before the House of Commons, so agreeable to that assembly, that it is said they presented him with a silver tankard,—a token of their esteem which (if the story be true) may seem to be the stronger for its singularity and unseemliness.‡ This discourse seems to have contained a warm invective against the ecclesiastical policy of the Court; and it was preached not only at a most critical time, but on the solemn occasion of the sacrament being first taken by the whole House. As a reward for so conspicuous a service to the Parliamentary cause, he soon after received the valuable living of Bocking in Essex, which he held through all the succeeding changes of government,—forbearing, of necessity, to use the Liturgy, and complying with all the conditions which the law then required from the beneficed clergy. It has been disputed whether he took the Covenant, though his own evasive answers imply that he had: but it is certain that he published a Protest* against the trial of the King in 1648, though that never could have pretended to the same merit with the solemn Declaration of the whole Presbyterian clergy of London against the same proceeding, which, however, did not save them at the Restoration.

At the moment of the Restoration of Charles II., he appears, therefore, to have had as little *public* claim on the favour of that prince as any clergyman who had conformed to the ecclesiastical principles of the Parliament and the Protectorate; and he was, accordingly, long after called by a zealous Royalist "the false Apostate!"† Bishoprics were indeed offered to Baxter, who refused, and to Reynolds, who accepted, a mitre; but if they had not been, as they were, men venerable for every virtue, they were the acknowledged leaders of the Presbyterians, whose example might have much effect in disposing that powerful body to conformity. No such benefit could be hoped from the preferment of Gauden: and that his public character must have rendered him rather the object of disfavour than of patronage to the Court at this critical and jealous period, will be obvious to those who are conversant with one small, but not insignificant circumstance. The Presbyterian party is well known to have predominated in the Convention Parliament, especially when it first assembled; and it was the policy of the whole assembly to give a Presbyterian, or moderate and mediatorial colour, to their collective proceedings. On the 25th April 1660, they chose Mr. Calamy, Dr. Gauden, and Mr. Baxter, to preach before them, on the fast which they then appointed to be held,—thus placing Gauden between two eminent divines of the Presbyterian persuasion, on an occasion when they appear studiously to have avoided the appointment of an Episcopalian. It is evident that Gauden was then thought nearer in principle to Baxter than to Juxon. He was sufficiently a Presbyterian in party to make him no favourite with the Court: yet he was not so decided a Presbyterian in opinion as to have the influence among his brethren which could make him worth so high a price as a mitre. They who dispute his claim to be the writer of the Icôn, will be the last to ascribe his preferment to transcendent abilities: he is not mentioned as having ever shown kindness to Royalists; there is no trace of his correspondence with the exiled Court; he

* Milton, Goodwyn, Lilly, &c.

† See Wagstaffe's Vindication of King Charles, pp. 77—79. London, 1711.

‡ The Journals say nothing of the tankard, which was probably the gift of some zealous members, but bear, "That the thanks of this house be given to Mr. *Gaudy* and Mr. Morley for their sermons last Sunday, and that they be desired, if they please, to print the same." Vol. ii. p. 40.

* The Religious and Loyal Protestation of John Gauden, &c. London, 1648.

† Kennet, Register, p. 773.

contributed nothing to the recall of the King; nor indeed had he the power of performing such atoning services.

Let the reader then suppose himself to be acquainted only with the above circumstances, and let him pause to consider whether, in the summer of 1660, there could be many clergymen of the Established Church who had fewer and more scanty pretensions to a bishopric than Gauden: yet he was appointed Bishop of Exeter on the 3d of November following. He received, in a few months, 20,000*l.* in fines for the renewal of leases;* and yet he had scarcely arrived at his episcopal palace when, on the 21st of December, he wrote a letter to the Lord Chancellor Clarendon,† bitterly complaining of the "distress," "infelicity," and "horror" of such a bishopric!—"a hard fate which" (he reminds the Chancellor) "he had before deprecated."—— "I make this complaint," (he adds,) "to your Lordship, because you chiefly put me on this adventure. Your Lordship commanded mee to trust in your favour for an honourable maintenance and some such additional support as might supply the defects of the bishopric." * * * "*Nor am I so unconscious to the service I have done to the Church and to his Majesty's family, as to beare with patience such a ruine most undeservedly put upon mee. Are these the effects of his liberall expressions, who told mee I might have what I would desire?* * * * Yf your Lordship will not concern yourselfe in my affaire, I must make my last complaint to the King." In five days after (26th December 1660) he wrote another long letter, less angry and more melancholy, to the same great person, which contains the following remarkable sentence:—"*Dr. Morly once offered mee my option, upon account of some service which he thought I had done extraordinary for the Church and the Royall Family, of which he told mee your Lordship was informed.* This made mee modestly secure of your Lordship's favour; though I found your Lordship would never owne your consciousnes to mee, as if it would have given mee too much confidence of a proportionable expectation. * * * I knew your Lordship knew my service and merit to be no way inferior to the best of *your friends, or enemyes.*"‡

In these two letters,—more covertly in the first, more openly in the second,—Gauden apprises Lord Clarendon, that Dr. Morly (who was Clarendon's most intimate friend) had acknowledged *some extraordinary service* done by Gauden to the Royal Family, which had been made known to the Chancellor; though that nobleman had avoided a direct acknowledgment of it to the bishop before he left London. Gauden appears soon after to have written to Sir E. Nicholas, Secretary of State, a letter of so peculiar a character as to have been read by the King; for an answer was sent to him by Nicholas, dated on the 19th January 1661, in which the following sentence deserves attention:—"As for your owne particular, he desires you not to be discouraged at the poverty of your bishoprick at present; and if that answer not the expectation of what was promised you, *His Majesty will take you so particularly into his care, that he bids me assure you, that you shall have no cause to remember Bocking.*"* These remarkable words by no means imply that Gauden did not then believe that the nature of his "extraordinary service" had been before known to the King. They evidently show his letter to have consisted of a complaint of the poverty of his bishopric, with an intelligible allusion to this service, probably expressed with more caution and reserve than in his addresses to the Chancellor. What was really then first made known to the King was not his merits, but his poverty. On the 21st January, the importunate prelate again addressed to Clarendon a letter, explicitly stating the nature of his services, probably rendered necessary in his opinion by the continued silence of Clarendon, who did not answer his applications till the 13th March. From this letter the following extract is inserted:—

"All I desire is an augment of 500*l.* per annum, y[t] if cannot bee at present had in a commendam; yet possible the King's favor to me will not grudg mee this pension out of the first fruits and tenths of this diocesse; till I bee removed or otherwayes provided for: Nor will y[r] Lordship startle at this motion, or wave the presenting of it to hys Majesty, yf you please to consider the pretensions I may have *beyond any of my calling*, not as to merit, but *duty performed to the Royall Family.* True, I once presumed y[r] Lordship had fully known that *arcanam*, for soe Dr. Morley told mee, at the King's first coming; when he assured mee the greatnes of that service was such, that I might have any preferment I desired. This consciousnes of your Lordship (as I supposed) and Dr. Morley, made mee confident my affaires would bee carried on to some proportion of what I had done, and he thought deserved. Hence my silence of it to your Lordship: as to the King and Duke of York, whom before I came away I acquainted with it, when I saw myself not so much considered in my present disposition as I did hope I should have beene, what trace their Royall goodnes hath of it is best expressed by themselves; nor do I doubt but I shall, by your Lordship's favor, find the fruits as to somthing extraordinary, since the service was soe: not as to *what was known to the world under my name*, in order to vindicate the Crowne and the Church, *but what goes under the late blessed King's name*, 'the εἰκὼν or portraiture of hys Majesty in hys solitudes and sufferings.' This book and figure was wholy and only my invention, making and designe; in order to vindicate the King's wisdome, honor and piety. My wife indeed was conscious to it, and had an hand in disguising the letters of that copy which I sent to the King in the ile of Wight, by favor of the late Marquise of Hartford, which was delivered to the King by the now Bishop of Winchester:† hys Majesty graciously accepted, owned, and adopted it as hys sense and

* Biographia Britannica, article "Gauden."
† Wordsworth, Documentary Supplement, p. 9.
‡ Ibid. pp. 11—13.

* Wordsworth, Documentary Supplement, p. 14.
† Duppa.

genius; not only with great approbation, but admiration. Hee kept it with hym; and though hys cruel murtherers went on to perfect hys martyrdome, yet God preserved and prospered this book to revive hys honor, and redeeme hys Majesty's name from that grave of contempt and abhorrence or infamy, in which they aymed to bury hym. When it came out, just upon the King's death; Good God! what shame, rage and despite, filled hys murtherers! What comfort hys friends! How many enemyes did it convert! How many hearts did it mollify and melt! What devotions it raysed to hys posterity, as children of such a father! What preparations it made in all men's minds for this happy restauration, and which I hope shall not prove my affliction! In a word, it was an army, and did vanquish more than any sword could. My Lord, every good subject conceived hopes of restauration; meditated reveng and separation. Your Lordship and all good subjects with hys Majesty enjoy the reeall and now ripe fruites of that plant. O let not mee wither! who was the author, and ventured wife, children, estate, liberty, life, and all but my soule, in so great an atchievement, which hath filled England and all the world with the glory of it. I did lately present my fayth in it to the Duke of York, and by hym to the King; both of them were pleased to give mee credit, and owne it as a rare service in those horrors of times. True, I played this best card in my hand something too late; else I might have sped as well as Dr. Reynolds and some others; but I did not lay it as a ground of ambition, nor use it as a ladder. *Thinking myselfe secure in the just valew of Dr. Morely, who I was sure knew it, and told mee your Lordship did soe too;** who, I believe, intended mee somthing at least competent, though lesse convenient, in this preferment. All that I desire is, that your Lordship would make that good, which I think you designed; and which I am confident the King will not deny mee, agreeable to hys royall munificence, which promiseth extraordinary rewards to extraordinary services: Certainly this service is such, for the matter, manner, timing and efficacy, as was never exceeded, nor will ever be equalled, yf I may credit the judgment of the best and wisest men that have read it; and I know your Lordship, who is soe great a master of wisdome and eloquence, cannot but esteeme the author of that peice; and accordingly, make mee to see those effects which may assure mee that my loyalty, paines, care, hazard and silence, are accepted by the King and Royall Family, to which your Lordship's is now grafted."

The Bishop wrote three letters more to Clarendon,—on the 25th January, 20th February, and 6th of March respectively, to which on the 13th of the last month the Chancellor sent a reply containing the following sentence:—*The particular which you often renewed, I do confesse was imparted to me*† *under secrecy, and of which I did not take myself to be at liberty to take notice; and truly when it ceases to be a secrett, I know nobody will be gladd of it but Mr. Milton; I have very often wished I had never been trusted with it.*

It is proper here to remark, that all the letters of Gauden are still extant, endorsed by Lord Clarendon, or by his eldest son. In the course of three months, then, it appears that Gauden, with unusual importunity and confidence, with complaints which were disguised reproaches, and sometimes with an approach to menaces, asserted his claim to be richly rewarded, as the author of the Icôn. He affirms that it was sent to the King by the Duke of Somerset, who died about a month before his first letter, and delivered to his Majesty by Dr. Duppa, Bishop of Winchester, who was still alive. He adds, that he had acquainted Charles II. with the secret through the Duke of York, that Morley, then Bishop of Worcester, had informed Clarendon of it, and that Morley himself had declared the value of the service to be such, as to entitle Gauden to choose his own preferment. Gauden thus enabled Clarendon to convict him of falsehood,—if his tale was untrue,—in three or four circumstances, differing indeed in their importance as to the main question, but equally material to his own veracity. A single word from Duppa would have overwhelmed him with infamy. How easy was it for the Chancellor to ascertain whether the information had been given to the King and his brother! Morley was his bosom-friend, and the spiritual director of his daughter, Anne Duchess of York. How many other persons might have been quietly sounded by the numerous confidential agents of a great minister, on a transaction which had occurred only twelve years before! To suppose that a statesman, then at the zenith of his greatness, could not discover the truth on this subject, without a noise like that of a judicial inquiry, would betray a singular ignorance of affairs. Did Clarendon relinquish, without a struggle, his belief in a book, which had doubtless touched his feelings when he read it as the work of his Royal Master? Even curiosity might have led Charles II., when receiving the blessing of Duppa on his deathbed, to ask him a short confidential question. To how many chances of detection did Gauden expose himself? How nearly impossible is it that the King, the Duke, the Chancellor, and Morley should have abstained from the safest means of inquiry, and, in opposition to their former opinions and prejudices, yielded at once to Gauden's assertion.

The previous belief of the Royalist party in the Icôn very much magnifies the improbability of such suppositions. The truth might have been discovered by the parties appealed to, and conveyed to the audacious pretender, without any scandal. There was no need of any public exposure: a private intimation of the falsehood of one material circumstance must have silenced Gauden. But what, on the contrary, is the answer of Lord Clarendon? Let any reader consider the above cited sentence of his letter, and determine for himself whether it does not express such an unhesitating assent to the claim as could only have flowed from inquiry and evidence. By confessing that the

* It is not to be inferred from this and the like passages, that Gauden doubted the previous communication of Morley to Clarendon: he uses such language as a reproach to the Chancellor for his silence.

† Evidently by Morley.

secret was imparted to him, he admits the other material part of Gauden's statement, that the information came through Morley. Gauden, if his story was true, chose the persons to whom he imparted it both prudently and fairly. He dealt with it as a secret of which the disclosure would injure the Royal cause; and he therefore confined his communications to the King's sons and the Chancellor, who could not be indisposed to his cause by it, and whose knowledge of it was necessary to justify his own legitimate claims. Had it been false, no choice could have been more unfortunate. He appealed to those who, for aught he knew, might have in their possession the means of instantly demonstrating that he was guilty of a falsehood so imprudent and perilous, that nothing parallel to it has ever been hazarded by a man of sound mind. How could Gauden know that the King did not possess his father's MS., and that Royston the printer was not ready to prove that he had received it from Charles I., through hands totally unconnected with Gauden? How great must have been the risk if we suppose, with Dr. Wordsworth, and Mr. Wagstaffe, that more than one copy of the MS. existed, and that parts of it had been seen by many! It is without any reason that Dr. Wordsworth and others represent the *secrecy* of Gauden's communications to Clarendon as a circumstance of suspicion; for he was surely bound, by that sinister honour which prevails in the least moral confederacies, to make no needless disclosures on this delicate subject.

Clarendon's letter is a declaration that he was *converted* from his former opinion about the author of the Icôn: that of Sir E. Nicholas is a declaration to the same purport on his own part, and on that of the King. The confession of Clarendon is more important, from being apparently wrung from him, after the lapse of a considerable time; in the former part of which he evaded acknowledgment in conversation, while in the latter part he incurred the blame of incivility, by delaying to answer letters,—making his admission at last in the hurried manner of an unwilling witness. The decisive words, however, were at length extorted from him, "*When it ceases to be a secret, I know nobody will be glad of it, but Mr. Milton.*" Wagstaffe argues this question as if Gauden's letters were to be considered as a man's assertions in his own cause; without appearing ever to have observed that they are not offered as proof of the facts which they affirm, but as a claim which circumstances show to have been recognized by the adverse party.

The course of another year did not abate the solicitations of Gauden. In the end of 1661 and beginning of 1662, the infirmities of Duppa promised a speedy vacancy in the great bishopric of Winchester, to which Gauden did not fail to urge his pretensions with undiminished confidence, in a letter to the Chancellor (28th December), in a letter to the Duke of York (17th January), and in a memorial to the King, without a date, but written on the same occasion. The two letters allude to the particulars of former communications. The memorial, as the nature of such a paper required, is fuller and more minute: it is expressly founded on "a private service," for the reality of which it again appeals to the declarations of Morley, to the evidence of Duppa, ("who," says Gauden, "encouraged me in that great work,") still alive, and visited on his sick-bed by the King, and to the testimony of the Duke of Somerset.* It also shows that Gauden had applied to the King for Winchester as soon as it should become vacant, about or before the time of his appointment to Exeter.

On the 19th of March, 1662, Gauden was complimented at Court as the author of the Icôn, by George Digby, second Earl of Bristol, a nobleman of fine genius and brilliant accomplishments, but remarkable for his inconstancy in political and religious opinion. The bond of connection between them seems to have been their common principles of toleration, which Bristol was solicitous to obtain for the Catholics, whom he had secretly joined, and which Gauden was willing to grant, not only to the Old Nonconformists, but to the more obnoxious Quakers. On the day following Gauden writes a letter, in which it is supposed that "the Grand Arcanum" had been disclosed to Bristol "by the King or the Royal Duke." In six days after he writes again, on the death of Duppa, to urge his claim to Winchester. This third letter is more important. He observes, with justice, that he could not expect "any extraordinary instance of his Majesty's favour on account of his signal service only, because that might put the world on a dangerous curiosity, if he had been in other respects unconspicuous;" but he adds, in effect, that his public services would be a sufficient reason or pretext for the great preferment to which he aspired. He appeals to a new witness on the subject of the Icôn,—Dr. Shel-

* Doc. Sup. p. 30. We have no positive proof that these two letters were sent, or the memorial delivered. It seems (Ibid. p. 27) that there are marks of the letters having been sealed and broken open; and it is said to be singular that such letters should be found among the papers of him who wrote them. But as the early history of these papers is unknown, it is impossible to expect an explanation of every fact. A collector might have found them elsewhere, and added them to the Gauden papers. An anxious writer might have broken open two important letters, in which he was fearful that some expression was indiscreet, and afterwards sent corrected duplicates, without material variation. Gauden might have received information respecting the disposal of Winchester and Worcester, or about the state of parties at Court, before the letters were dispatched, which would render them then unseasonable. What is evident is, that they were written with an intention to send them,—that they coincide with his previous statements,—and that *the determination not to send them was not occasioned by any doubts entertained by the Chancellor of his veracity; for such doubts would have prevented his preferment to the bishopric of Worcester*,—one of the most coveted dignities of the Church.

don, then Bishop of London;—thus, once more, if his story were untrue, almost wantonly adding to the chance of easy, immediate, and private detection. His danger would have, indeed, been already enhanced by the disclosure of the secret to Lord Bristol, who was very intimately acquainted with Charles I., and among whose good qualities discretion and circumspection cannot be numbered. The belief of Bristol must also be considered as a proof that Gauden continued to be believed by the King and the Duke, from whom Bristol's information proceeded. A friendly correspondence, between the Bishop and the Earl, continued till near the death of the former, in the autumn of 1662.

In the mean time, the Chancellor gave a still more decisive proof of his continued conviction of the justice of Gauden's pretensions, by his translation in May to Worcester. The Chancellor's personal ascendant over the King was perhaps already somewhat impaired; but his power was still unshaken; and he was assuredly the effective as well as formal adviser of the Crown on ecclesiastical promotions. It would be the grossest injustice to the memory of Lord Clarendon to believe, that if, after two years' opportunity for inquiry, any serious doubts of Gauden's veracity had remained in his mind, he would have still farther honoured and exalted the contriver of a falsehood, devised for mercenary purposes, to rob an unhappy and beloved Sovereign of that power which, by his writings, he still exercised over the generous feelings of men. It cannot be doubted, and ought not to be forgotten, that a false claim to the Icôn is a crime of a far deeper dye than the publication of it under the false appearance of a work of the King. To publish such a book in order to save the King's life, was an offence, attended by circumstances of much extenuation, in one who believed, or perhaps knew, that it substantially contained the King's sentiments, and who deeply deprecated the proceedings of the army and of the remnant of the House of Commons against him. But to usurp the reputation of the work so long after the death of the Royal Author, for sheer lucre, is an act of baseness perhaps without a parallel. That Clarendon should wish to leave the more venial deception undisturbed, and even shrink from such refusals as might lead to its discovery, is not far beyond the limits which good men may overstep in very diffiult situations: but that he should have rewarded the most odious of impostors by a second bishopric, would place him far lower than a just adversary would desire. If these considerations seem of such moment at this distant time, what must have been their force in the years 1660 and 1662, in the minds of Clarendon, and Somerset, and Duppa, and Morley, and Sheldon! It would have been easy to avoid the elevation of Gauden to Worcester: he had himself opened the way for offering him a pension; and the Chancellor might have answered almost in Gauden's own words, that farther preferment might lead to perilous inquiry. Clarendon, in 1662, must either have doubted who was the author of the Icôn, or believed the claim of Gauden, or adhered to his original opinion. If he believed it to be the work of the King, he could not have been so unfaithful to his memory as to raise such an impostor to a second bishopric: if he believed it to be the production of Gauden, he might have thought it an excusable policy to recompense a pious fraud, and to silence the possessor of a dangerous secret: if he had doubts, they would have prompted him to investigation, which, conducted by him, and relating to transactions so recent, must have terminated in certain knowledge.

Charles II. is well known, at the famous conference between the Episcopalians and Presbyterians, when the Icôn was quoted as his father's, to have said, "All that is in that book is not gospel." Knowing, as we now do, that Gauden's claim was preferred to him in 1660, this answer must be understood to have been a familiar way of expressing his scepticism about its authenticity. In this view of it, it coincides with his declaration to Lord Anglesea twelve years after; and it is natural indeed to suppose, that his opinion was that of those whom he then most trusted on such matters, of whom Clarendon was certainly one. To suppose, with some late writers, that he and his brother looked with favour and pleasure on an attempt to weaken the general interest in the character of their father, merely because the Icôn is friendly to the Church of England, is a wanton act of injustice to them. Charles II. was neither a bigot, nor without regard to his kindred; the family affections of James were his best qualities,—though by a peculiar perverseness of fortune, they proved the source of his sharpest pangs.

But to return to Lord Clarendon, who survived Gauden twelve years, and who, almost to the last day of his life, was employed in the composition of an historical work, originally undertaken at the desire of Charles I., and avowed, with honest partiality to be destined for the vindication of his character and cause. This great work, not intended for publication in the age of the writer, was not actually published till thirty years after his death, and even then not without the suppression of important passages, which it seems the public was not yet likely to receive in a proper temper. Now, neither in the original edition, nor in any of the recently restored passages,* is there any allusion to the supposed work of the King. No reason of temporary policy can account for this extraordinary silence. However the statesman might be excused for the momentary sacrifice of truth to quiet, the historian could have no temptation to make the sacrifice perpetual. Had he believed that his Royal Master was the writer of the only book ever written by a dying monarch on his own misfortunes, it would have been unjust as an historian, treacherous as a

* In the Oxford Edition of 1826.

friend, and unfeeling as a man, to have passed over in silence such a memorable and affecting circumstance. Merely as a fact, his narrative was defective without it. But it was a fact of a very touching and interesting nature, on which his genius would have expatiated with affectionate delight. No later historian of the Royal party has failed to dwell on it. How should he then whom it must have most affected be silent, unless his pen had been stopped by the knowledge of the truth? He had even personal inducements to explain it, at least in those more private memoirs of his administration, which form part of what is called his "Life." Had he believed in the genuineness of the Icôn, it would have been natural for him in these memoirs to have reconciled that belief with the successive preferments of the impostor. He had good reason to believe that the claims of Gauden would one day reach the public; he had himself, in his remarkable letter of March 13th, 1661, spoken of such a disclosure as likely. This very acknowledgment contained in that letter, which he knew to be in the possession of Gauden's family, increased the probability. It was scarcely possible that such papers should for ever elude the search of curiosity, of historical justice, or of party spirit. But besides these probabilities, Clarendon, a few months before his death, "*had learned that ill people endeavoured to persuade the King that his father was not the author of the book that goes by his name.*" This information was conveyed to him from Bishop Morley through Lord Cornbury, who went to visit his father in France in May 1674. On hearing these words, Clarendon exclaimed, 'Good God! I thought *the Marquis of Hertford had satisfied the King in that matter.*'* By this message Clarendon was therefore warned, that the claim of Gauden was on its way to the public,—that it was already assented to by the Royal Family themselves, and was likely at last to appear with the support of the most formidable authorities. What could he now conclude but that, if undetected and unrefuted, or, still more, if uncontradicted in a history destined to vindicate the King, the claim would be considered by posterity as established by his silence? Clarendon's language on this occasion also strengthens very much another part of the evidence; for it proves, beyond all doubt, that the authorship of the Icôn *had been discussed by the King with the Duke of Somerset before that nobleman's death in October* 1660,—a fact nearly conclusive of the whole question. Had the Duke assured the King that his father was the author, what a conclusive answer was ready to Gauden, who asserted that the first had been the bearer of the manuscript of the Icôn from Gauden to Charles I.! As there had been such a communication between the King and the Duke of Somerset, it is altogether incredible that Clarendon should not have recurred to the same pure source of information. The only admissible meaning of Clarendon's words is, that "*Lord Hertford* (afterwards Duke of Somerset) *had satisfied the King*" of the impropriety of speaking on the subject. We must otherwise suppose that the King and Clarendon had been "satisfied," or perfectly convinced, that Charles was the writer of the Icôn;—a supposition which would convert the silence of the Chancellor and the levity of the Monarch into heinous offences. The message of Morley to Clarendon demonstrates that they had previous conversation on the subject. The answer shows that both parties knew of information having been given by Somerset to the King, before Gauden's nomination to Exeter: but Gauden had at that time appealed, in his letters, both to Morley and Somerset as his witness. That Clarendon therefore knew all that Morley and Somerset could tell, is no longer matter of inference, but is established by the positive testimony of the two survivors in 1674. Wagstaffe did not perceive the consequences of the letter which he published, because he had not seen the whole correspondence of Gauden. But it is much less easy to understand, how those who have compared the letters of Gauden with the messages between Clarendon and Morley, should not have discovered the irresistible inference which arises from the comparison.

The silence of Lord Clarendon, as an historian, is the strongest moral evidence that he believed the pretensions of Bishop Gauden: and his opinion on the question must be held to include the testimony in point of fact, and the judgment in point of opinion, of all those men whom he had easy opportunities and strong inducements to consult. It may be added, that however Henry Earl of Clarendon chose to express himself, (his language is not free from an air of mental reservation), neither he nor his brother Lord Rochester, when they published their father's history in 1702, thought fit, in their preface, to attempt any explanation of his silence respecting the Icôn, though their attention must have been called to that subject by the controversy respecting it which had been carried on a few years before with great zeal and activity. Their silence becomes the more remarkable, from the strong interest taken by Lord Clarendon in the controversy. He wrote two letters on it to Wagstaffe, in 1694 and 1699; he was one of the few persons present at the select consecration of Wagstaffe as a nonjuring bishop, in 1693: yet there is no allusion to the Icôn in the preface to his father's history, published in 1702.

It cannot be pretended that the final silence of Clarendon is agreeable to the rigorous rules of historical morality: it is no doubt an infirmity which impairs his credit as an historian. But it is a light and venial fault compared with that which must be laid to his charge, if we suppose, that, with a conviction

* The first letter of the second Earl of Clarendon to Wagstaffe in 1694, about twenty years after the event, has not, as far as we know, been published. We know only the extracts in Wagstaffe. The second letter written in 1699 is printed entire in Wagstaffe's Defence, p. 37.

of the genuineness of the Icôn, and with such testimony in support of it as the evidence of Somerset and Morley,—to say nothing of others,—he should not have made a single effort, in a work destined for posterity, to guard from the hands of the impostor the most sacred property of his unfortunate master. The partiality of Clarendon to Charles I. has never been severely blamed; his silence in his history, if he believed Gauden, would only be a new instance of that partiality: but the same silence, if he believed the King to be the author, would be fatal to his character as an historian and a man.

The knowledge of Gauden's secret was obtained by Clarendon as a minister; and he might deem his duty with respect to secrets of state still to be so far in force, as at least to excuse him from disturbing one of the favourite opinions of his party, and for not disclosing what he thought could gratify none but regicides and agitators. Even this excuse, on the opposite supposition, he wanted. That Charles was the author of the Icôn (if true) was no state secret, but the prevalent and public opinion. He might have collected full proofs of its truth, in private conversation with his friends. He had only to state such proof, and to lament the necessity which made him once act as if the truth were otherwise, rather than excite a controversy with an unprincipled enemy, dangerous to a new government, and injurious to the interests of monarchy. His mere testimony would have done infinitely more for the King's authorship, than all the volumes which have been written to maintain it:—even that testimony is withheld. If the Icôn be Gauden's, the silence of Clarendon is a vice to which he had strong temptations: if it be the King's, it is a crime without a motive. Those who are willing to ascribe the lesser fault to the historian, must determine against the authenticity of the Icôn.

That good men, of whom Lord Clarendon was one, were, at the period of the Restoration, ready to use expedients of very dubious morality to conceal secrets dangerous to the Royal cause, will appear from a fact, which seems to have escaped the notice of the general historians of England. It is uncertain, and not worth inquiring, when Charles II. threw over his doubts and vices that slight and thin vesture of Catholicism, which he drew a little closer round him at the sight of death:* but we know with certainty, that, in the beginning of the year 1659, the Duke of Ormonde accidentally discovered the conversion, by finding him on his knees at mass in a church at Brussels. Ormonde, after it was more satisfactorily proved to him, by communication with Henry Bennett and Lord Bristol,† imparted the secret in England to Clarendon and Southampton, who agreed with him in the necessity of preventing the enemies of monarchy, or the friends of Popery, from promulgating this fatal secret. Accordingly, the "*Act for the better security of his Majesty's person and government*"* provided, that to affirm the King to be a Papist, should be punishable by "disability to hold any office or promotion, civil, military, or ecclesiastical, besides being liable to such *other* punishments as by common or statute law might be inflicted."

As soon as we take our stand on the ground, that the acquiescence of all the Royalists in the council and court of Charles II., and the final silence of Clarendon in his history, on a matter so much within his province, and so interesting to his feelings, are irreconcilable with the supposition, that they believed the Icôn to be the work of the King, all the other circumstances on both sides not only dwindle into insignificance, but assume a different colour. Thus, the general credit of the book among Royalists before the Restoration serves to show, that the evidence which changed the opinion of Clarendon and his friends must have been very strong,—probably far stronger than what we now possess; the firmer we suppose the previous conviction to have been, the more probable it becomes, that the proofs then discovered were of a more direct nature than those which remain. Let it be very especially observed, that those who decided the question practically in 1660 were within twelve years of the fact; while fifty years had passed before the greater part of the traditional and hearsay stories, ranged on the opposite side, were brought together by Wagstaffe.

Let us consider, for example, the effect of the proceedings of 1660, upon the evidence of the witnesses who speak of the Icôn as having been actually taken from the King at Naseby, and afterwards restored to him by the conquerors. Two of the best known are the Earl of Manchester and Mr. Prynne. Eales, a physician at Welwyn in Hertfordshire, certifies, in 1699, that some years before the Restoration (*i. e.* about 1656), he heard Lord Manchester declare, that the MS. of the Icôn was taken at Naseby, and that he had seen it in the King's own hand.† Jones, at the distance of fifty years, says that he *had heard* from Colonel Stroud that Stroud *had heard* from Prynne in 1649, that he, by order of Parliament, had read the MS. of the Icôn taken at Naseby.‡ Now it is certain that Manchester was taken into favour, and Prynne was patronised at the Restoration. If this were so, how came matters, of which they spoke so publicly, to remain unknown to Clarendon and Southampton? Had the MS. Icôn been intrusted to Prynne by Parliament, or even by a committee, its existence must have been known to a body mnch too large to allow the supposition of secrecy. The application of the same remark disposes of the mob of second-hand witnesses. The very number of the witnesses increases the incredibility that

* His formal reconciliation probably took place at Cologne in 1658, under the direction of Dr. Peter Talbot, Catholic Archbishop of Armagh.

† Carte, Life of Ormonde, vol. ii. pp. 254—256.

* 13 Car. 2. st. 1.

† "Who wrote," &c. p. 93. Wagstaffe's Vindication, p. 19.

‡ Ibid. p. 80.

their testimony could have escaped notice in 1660. Huntingdon, a Major in Cromwell's regiment, who abandoned the Parliamentary cause, is a more direct witness. In the year 1679, he informed Dugdale that he had procured the MS. Icôn taken at Naseby to be restored to the King at Hampton,—that it was *written* by Sir E. Walker, but *interlined* by the King, who wrote all the devotions. In 1681, Dugdale published The Short View, in which is the same story, with the variation, "that it was written with the King's own hand;"—a statement which, in the summary language of a general narrative, can hardly be said to vary materially from the former. Now, Major Huntingdon had particularly attracted the notice of Clarendon: he is mentioned in the history with commendation.* He tendered his services to the King before the Restoration;† and, what is most important of all to our present purpose, his testimony regarding the conduct of Berkeley and Ashburnham, in the journey from Hampton Court, is expressly mentioned by the historian as being, in 1660, thought worthy of being weighed even against that of Somerset and Southampton.‡ When we thus trace a direct communication between him and the minister, and when we remember that it took place at the very time of the claim of Gauden, and that it related to events contemporary with the supposed recovery of the Icôn, it is scarcely necessary to ask, whether Clarendon would not have sounded him on that subject, and whether Huntingdon would not then have boasted of such a personal service to the late King. It would be contrary to common sense not to presume that something then passed on that subject, and that, if Huntingdon's account at that time coincided with his subsequent story, it could not have been rejected, unless it was outweighed by contrary evidence.§ He must have been thought either a deceiver or deceived: for the more candid of these suppositions there was abundant scope. It is known that one MS. (*not the Icôn*) *written* by Sir Edward Walker and *corrected* by the King, was taken with the King's correspondence at Naseby, and restored to him by Fairfax through an officer at Hampton Court.‖ This was an account of the military transactions in the Civil War, written by Walker, and published in his Historical Discourses long after. It was natural that the King should be pleased at the recovery of this manuscript, which he soon after sent from Hampton Court to Lord Clarendon in Jersey, as a "contribution" towards his History. How easily Huntingdon, an old soldier little versed in manuscripts, might, thirty years afterwards, have confounded these memorials with the Icôn! A few prayers in the King's handwriting might have formed a part of the papers restored. So slight and probable are the only suppositions necessary to save the veracity of Huntingdon, and to destroy the value of his evidence.

Sir Thomas Herbert, who wrote his Memoirs thirty years after the event, in the seventy-third year of his age, when, as he told Antony Wood, "he was grown old, and not in such a capacity as he could wish to publish it," found a copy of the Icôn among the books which Charles I. left to him, and thought "the handwriting was the King's." Sir Philip Warwick states Herbert's testimony (probably from a conversation more full than the Memoirs) to be, that "he saw the MS. in the King's hand, as he believes; but it was in a running character, *and not in that which the King usually wrote*."* Now, more than one copy of the Icôn might have been sent to Charles; they might have been written with some resemblances to his handwriting; but assuredly the original MS. would not have been loosely left to Herbert, while works on general subjects were bequeathed to the King's children. It is equally certain that this was not the MS. from which the Icôn was published a few days afterwards; and, above all, it is clear that information from Herbert† would naturally be sought, and would have been easily procured, in 1660. The ministers of that time perhaps examined the MS.; or if it could not be produced, they might have asked why it was not preserved,—a question to which, on the supposition of its being written by the King, it seems now impossible to imagine a satisfactory answer. The same observations are applicable to the story of Levett, a page, who said that he had seen the King writing the Icôn, and had read several chapters of it,—but more forcibly, from his being less likely to be intrusted, and more liable to confusion and misrecollection;—to say nothing of our ignorance of his character for veracity, and of the interval of forty-two years which had passed before his attestation on this subject.

The Naseby copy being the only fragment of positive evidence in support of the King's authorship, one more observation on it may be excused. If the Parliamentary leaders thought the Icôn so dangerous to their cause, and so likely to make an impression favourable to the King, how came they to restore it so easily to its author, whom they had

* Vol. v. p. 484. † Ibid. vol. vii. p. 432.

‡ Ibid. vol. v. p. 495.

§ Dr. Wordsworth admits, that if Clarendon had consulted Duppa, Juxon, Sheldon, Morley, Kendal, Barwick, Legge, Herbert, &c. &c.; nay, if he had consulted only Morley alone, he must have been *satisfied*,—(Dr. Wordsworth, of course, says for the King.) Now, it is certain, from the message of Morley to Clarendon in 1674, that previous discussion had taken place between them. Does not this single fact decide the question on Dr. Wordsworth's own admission?

‖ Clarendon, vol. v. p. 476; and Warburton's note.

* Memoirs, p. 69. How much this coincides with Gauden's account, that his wife had disguised the writing of the copy sent to the Isle of Wight.

† He was made a baronet at the Restoration, for his personal services to Charles I.

deeply injured by the publication of his private letters? The advocates of the King charge this publication on them, as an act of gross indelicacy, and at the same time ascribe to them, in the restoration of the Icôn, a singular instance of somewhat wanton generosity.

It may be a question whether lawyers are justified in altogether rejecting hearsay evidence; but it never can be supposed, in its best state, to be other than secondary. When it passes through many hands,—when it is given after a long time,—when it is to be found almost solely in one party,—when it relates to a subject which deeply interests their feelings, we may confidently place it at the very bottom of the scale; and without being able either to disprove many particular stories, or to ascertain the proportion in which each of them is influenced by unconscious exaggeration, inflamed zeal, intentional falsehood, inaccurate observation, confused recollection, or eager credulity, we may safely treat the far greater part as the natural produce of these grand causes of human delusion. Among the evidence first collected by Wagstaffe, one story fortunately refers to authorities still in our possession. Hearne, a servant of Sir Philip Warwick, declared that he had heard his master and one Oudart often say that they had transcribed the Icôn from a copy in Charles' handwriting.* Sir Philip Warwick (who is thus said to have copied the Icôn from the King's MS.) has himself positively told us, "*I cannot say I know that he wrote the Icôn which goes under his name*;† and Oudart was secretary to Sir Edward Nicholas, whose letter to Gauden, virtually acknowledging his claim, has been already quoted!

Two persons appear to have been privy to the composition of the Icôn by Gauden,—his wife, and Walker his curate. Mrs. Gauden, immediately after her husband's death, applied to Lord Bristol for favour, on the ground of her knowledge of the secret; adding, that the bishop was prevented only by death from writing to him,—surely to the same effect. Nine years afterwards she sent to one of her sons the papers on this subject, to be used "if there be a good occasion to make it manifest," among which was an epitome "drawn out by the hand of him that did hope to have made a fortune by it."‡ This is followed by her narrative of the whole transactions, on which two short remarks will suffice. It coincides with Gauden's letters, in the most material particulars, in appeals to the same eminent persons said to be privy to the secret, who might and must have been consulted after such appeal: it proves also her firm persuasion that her husband had been ungratefully requited, and that her family had still pretensions founded on his services, which these papers might one day enable them to assert with more effect.

Walker, the curate, tells us that he had a hand in the business all along. He wrote his book, it is true, forty-five years after the events: but this circumstance, which so deeply affects the testimony of men who speak of words spoken in conversation, and reaching them through three or four hands, rather explains the inaccuracies, than lessens the substantial weight, of one who speaks of his own acts, on the most, and perhaps only, remarkable occasion of his life. There are two facts in Walker's account which seem to be decisive;—namely, that Gauden told him, about the time of the fabrication, that the MS. was sent by the Duke of Somerset to the King, and that two chapters of it were added by Bishop Duppa. To both these witnesses Gauden appealed at the Restoration, and Mrs. Gauden after his death. These communications were somewhat indiscreet; but, if false, what temptation had Gauden at that time to invent them, and to communicate them to his curate? They were new means of detecting his imposture. But the declaration of Gauden, that the book and figure was wholly and solely my "invention, making, and design," is quoted with premature triumph, as if it were incompatible with the composition of two chapters by Duppa;*—as if the contribution of a few pages to a volume could affect the authorship of the man who had planned the whole, and executed all the rest. That he mentioned the particular contribution of Duppa at the time to Walker, and only appealed in general to the same prelate in his applications to Clarendon and the King, is a variation, but no inconsistency.

Walker early represented the coincidence of some peculiar phrases in the devotions of the Icôn with Gauden's phraseology, as an important fact in the case. That argument has recently been presented with much more force by Mr. Todd, whose catalogues of coincidences between the Icôn and the avowed writings of Gauden is certainly entitled to serious consideration.† They are not all of equal importance, but some of the phrases are certainly very peculiar. It seems very unlikely that Charles should have copied peculiar phrases from the not very conspicuous writings of Gauden's early life; and it is almost equally improbable that Gauden, in his later writings, when he is said to have been eager to reap the fruits of his imposture, should not have carefully shunned those modes of expression which were peculiar to the Icôn. To the list of Mr. Todd, a very curious addition has been made by Mr. Benjamin Bright, a discerning and liberal collector, from a manuscript volume of prayers by Gauden,‡ which is of more value than the other coincidences, inasmuch as it corroborates the testimony of Walker, who said that he "met with expressions in the devotional parts of the Icôn very frequently used

---

* Who wrote, &c. p. 138. † Memoirs, p. 68.
‡ Doc. Sup. pp. 42, 48.

* Who wrote, &c. p. 156.
† Letter to the Archbishop of Canterbury, pp. 51—76.
‡ Ibid. Appendix, No. 1.

by Dr. Gauden in his prayers!" Without laying great stress on these resemblances, they are certainly of more weight than the general arguments founded either on the inferiority of Gauden's talents, (which Dr. Wordsworth candidly abandons,) or on the impure and unostentatious character of his style, which have little weight, unless we suppose him to have had no power of varying his manner when speaking in the person of another man.

Conclusions from internal evidence have so often been contradicted by experience, that prudent inquirers seldom rely on them when there are any other means of forming a judgment. But in such cases as the present, internal evidence does not so much depend on the discussion of words, or the dissection of sentences, as on the impression made by the whole composition, on minds long accustomed to estimate and compare the writings of different men in various circumstances. A single individual can do little more than describe that impression; and he must leave it to be determined by experience, how far it agrees with the impressions made on the minds of the majority of other men of similar qualifications. To us it seems, as it did to Archbishop Herring, that the Icôn is greatly more like the work of a priest than a king. It has more of dissertation than effusion. It has more regular division and systematic order than agree with the habits of the King. The choice and arrangement of words show a degree of care and neatness which are seldom attained but by a practised writer. The views of men and affairs, too, are rather those of a bystander than an actor. They are chiefly reflections, sometimes in themselves obvious, but often ingeniously turned, such as the surface of events would suggest to a spectator not too deeply interested. It betrays none of those strong feelings which the most vigilant regard to gravity and dignity could not have uniformly banished from the composition of an actor and a sufferer. It has no allusion to facts not accessible to any moderately informed man; though the King must have (sometimes rightly) thought that his superior knowledge of affairs would enable him to correct vulgar mistakes. If it be really the private effusion of a man's thoughts on himself and his own affairs, it would be the only writing of that sort in the world in which it is impossible to select a trace of peculiarities and weaknesses,—of partialities and dislikes,—of secret opinions, —of favourite idioms, and habitual familiarities of expression: every thing is *impersonal*. The book consists entirely of generalities; while real writings of this sort never fail to be characterised by those minute and circumstantial touches, which parties deeply interested cannot, if they would, avoid. It is also very observable, that the Icôn dwells little on facts, where a mistake might so easily betray its not being the King's, and expatiates in reasoning and reflection, of which it is impossible to try the genuineness by any palpable test. The absence of every allusion to those secrets of which it would be very hard for the King himself wholly to conceal his knowledge, seems, indeed, to indicate the hand of a writer who was afraid of venturing on ground where his ignorance might expose him to irretrievable blunders. Perhaps also the want of all the smaller strokes of character betrays a timid and faltering forger, who, though he ventured to commit a pious fraud, shrunk from an irreverent imitation of the Royal feelings, and was willing, after the great purpose was served, so to soften the imposture, as to leave his retreat open, and to retain the means, in case of positive detection, of representing the book to have been published as what might be put into the King's mouth, rather than as what was actually spoken by him.

The section which relates to the civil war in Ireland not only exemplifies the above remarks, but closely connects the question respecting the Icôn with the character of Charles for sincerity. It certainly was not more unlawful for him to seek the aid of the Irish Catholics, than it was for his opponents to call in the succour of the Scotch Presbyterians. The Parliament procured the assistance of the Scotch army, by the imposition of the Covenant in England; and the King might, on the like principle, purchase the help of the Irish, by promising to tolerate, and even establish, the Catholic religion in Ireland. Warburton justly observes, that the King was free from blame in his negotiations with the Irish, "as a politician, and king, and governor of his people; but the necessity of his affairs obliging him at the same time to play the Protestant saint and confessor, there was found much disagreement between his professions and declarations, and actions in this matter."* As long as the disagreement was confined to official declarations and to acts of state, it must be owned that it is extenuated by the practice of politicians, and by the consideration, that the concealment of negotiations, which is a lawful end, can very often be obtained by no other means than a disavowal of them. The rigid moralist may regret this excuse, though it be founded on that high public convenience to which Warburton gives the name of "necessity." But all mankind will allow, that the express or implied denial of real negotiations in a private work,—a picture of the writer's mind, professing to come from the Man and not from the King, mixed with solemn appeals and fervid prayers to the Deity, is a far blacker and more aggravated instance of insincerity. It is not, therefore, an act of judicious regard to the memory of Charles to ascribe to him the composition of the twelfth section of the Icôn. The impression manifestly aimed at in that section is, that the imputation of a private connexion with the Irish revolters

* Clarendon, vol. vii. p. 591.

was a mere calumny; and in the only paragraph which approaches to particulars, it expressly confines his intercourse with them to the negotiation for a time through Ormonde, and declares that his only object was to save "the poor Protestants of Ireland from their desperate enemies." In the section which relates to the publication of his letters, when the Parliament had explicitly charged him with clandestine negotiations, nothing is added on the subject. The general protestations of innocence, not very specifically applied even to the first instigation of the revolt, are left in that indefinite state in which the careless reader may be led to apply them to all subsequent transactions, which are skilfully,—not to say artfully,—passed over in silence. Now it is certain that the Earl of Glamorgan, a Catholic himself, was authorised by Charles to negotiate with the Catholics in 1645, independently of Ormonde, and with powers, into the nature of which the Lord Lieutenant thought himself bound not curiously to pry. It is, also, certain that, in the spring of that year, Glamorgan concluded a secret treaty with the Catholic assembly at Kilkenny, by which,—besides the repeal of penalties or disabilities,—all the churches and Church property in Ireland occupied by the Catholics since the revolt, were continued and secured to them;* while they, on their parts, engaged to send ten thousand troops to the King's assistance in England. Some correspondence on this subject was captured at sea, and some was seized in Ireland: both portions were immediately published by the Parliament, which compelled the King to imprison and disavow Glamorgan.† It is clear that these were measures of policy, merely intended to conceal the truth:‡ and the King, if he was the writer of the Icôn, must have deliberately left on the minds of the readers of that book an opinion, of his connexion with the Irish Catholics, which he knew to be false. On the other hand it is to be observed, that Gauden could not have known the secret of the Irish negotiations, and that he would naturally avoid a subject of which he was ignorant, and confine himself to a general disavowal of the instigation of the revolt. The silence of the Icôn on this subject, if written by Gauden, would be neither more wonderful nor more blamable than that of Clarendon, who, though he was of necessity acquainted with the negotiations of Glamorgan, does not suffer an allusion to the true state of them to escape him, either in the History, or in that apology for Ormonde's administration, which he calls "A Short View of the State of Ireland." Let it not be said, either by Charles' mistaken friends, or by his undistinguishing enemies, that he incurs the same blame for suffering an omission calculated to deceive to remain in the Icôn of Gauden, as if he had himself written the book. If the manuscript were sent to him by Gauden in September 1648, he may have intended to direct an explanation of the Irish negotiations to be inserted in it;—he may not have finally determined on the immediate publication. At all events, it would be cruel to require that he should have critically examined, and deliberately weighed, every part of a manuscript, which he could only occasionally snatch a moment to read in secret during the last four months of his life. In this troubled and dark period, divided between great negotiations, violent removals, and preparations for asserting his dignity,—if he could not preserve his life,—justice, as much as generosity requires that we should not hold him responsible for a negative offence, however important, in a manuscript which he had then only read. But if he was the author, none of these extenuations have any place: he must then have composed the work several years before his death; he was likely to have frequently examined it; he doubtless read it with fresh attention, after it was restored to him at Hampton Court; and he afterwards added several chapters to it. On that supposition, the fraudulent omission must have been a contrivance "aforethought" carried on for years, persisted in at the approach of death, and left, as the dying declaration of a pious monarch, in a state calculated to impose a falsehood upon posterity.*

* Birch, Inquiry, p. 68. The King's warrant, on 12th March, 1645, gives Glamorgan power "*to treat with the Roman Catholics upon necessity, wherein our Lieutenant cannot so well be seen.*"—p. 20.

† Harleian Miscellany, vol. iv. p. 494.

‡ See a curious letter published by Leland (History of Ireland, book v. chap. 7), which clearly proves that the blindness of Ormonde was voluntary, and that he was either trusted with the secret, or discovered it; and that the imprisonment of Glamorgan was, what the Parliament called it, "*a colourable commitment.*" Leland is one of those writers who deserve more reputation than they enjoy: he is not only an elegant writer, but, considering his time and country, singularly candid, unprejudiced, and independent.

* After sketching the above, we have been convinced, by a reperusal of the note of Mr. Laing on this subject (History of Scotland, vol. iii. p. 565), that if he had employed his great abilities as much in unfolding facts as in ascertaining them, nothing could have been written for the Icôn, or ought to have been written against it, since that decisive note. His merit, as a critical inquirer into history, an enlightened collector of materials, and a sagacious judge of evidence, has never been surpassed. If any man believes the innocence of Queen Mary, after an impartial and dispassionate perusal of Mr. Laing's examination of her case, the state of such a man's mind would be a subject worthy of much consideration by a philosophical observer of human nature. In spite of his ardent love of liberty, no man has yet presumed to charge him with the slightest sacrifice of historical integrity to his zeal. That he never perfectly attained the art of full, clear, and easy narrative was owing to the peculiar style of those writers who were popular in his youth, and may be mentioned as a remarkable instance of the disproportion of particular talents to a general vigour of mind.

DISSERTATION

ON THE PROGRESS OF

ETHICAL PHILOSOPHY,

CHIEFLY DURING THE

SEVENTEENTH AND EIGHTEENTH CENTURIES.

[ORIGINALLY PREFIXED TO THE SEVENTH EDITION OF THE ENCYCLOPÆDIA BRITANNICA.]

INTRODUCTION.

THE inadequacy of the words of ordinary language for the purposes of Philosophy, is an ancient and frequent complaint; of which the justness will be felt by all who consider the state to which some of the most important arts would be reduced, if the coarse tools of the common labourer were the only instruments to be employed in the most delicate operations of manual expertness. The watchmaker, the optician, and the surgeon, are provided with instruments which are fitted, by careful ingenuity, to second their skill; the philosopher alone is doomed to use the rudest tools for the most refined purposes. He must reason in words of which the looseness and vagueness are suitable, and even agreeable, in the usual intercourse of life, but which are almost as remote from the extreme exactness and precision required, not only in the conveyance, but in the search of truth, as the hammer and the axe would be unfit for the finest exertions of skilful handiwork: for it is not to be forgotten, that he must himself think in these gross words as unavoidably as he uses them in speaking to others. He is in this respect in a worse condition than an astronomer who looked at the heavens only with the naked eye, whose limited and partial observation, however it might lead to error, might not directly, and would not necessarily, deceive. He might be more justly compared to an arithmetician compelled to employ numerals not only cumbrous, but used so irregularly to denote different quantities, that they not only often deceive others, but himself.

The natural philosopher and mathematician have in some degree the privilege of framing their own terms of art; though that liberty is daily narrowed by the happy diffusion of these great branches of knowledge, which daily mixes their language with the general vocabulary of educated men. The cultivator of mental and moral philosophy can seldom do more than mend the faults of his words by definition;—a necessary, but very inadequate expedient, and one in a great measure defeated in practice by the unavoidably more frequent recurrence of the terms in their vague, than in their definite acceptation. The mind, to which such definition is faintly, and but occasionally, present, naturally suffers, in the ordinary state of attention, the scientific meaning to disappear from remembrance, and insensibly ascribes to the word a great part, if not the whole, of that popular sense which is so very much more familiar even to the most veteran speculator. The obstacles which stood in the way of Lucretius and Cicero, when they began to translate the subtile philosophy of Greece into their narrow and barren tongue, are always felt by the philosopher when he struggles to express, with the necessary discrimination, his abstruse reasonings in words which, though those of his own language, he must take from the mouths of those to whom his distinctions would be without meaning.

The moral philosopher is in this respect subject to peculiar difficulties. His statements and reasonings often call for nicer discriminations of language than those which are necessary in describing or discussing the purely intellectual part of human nature; but his freedom in the choice of words is more circumscribed. As he treats of matters on which all men are disposed to form a judgment, he can as rarely hazard glaring innovations in diction,—at least in an adult and mature language like ours,—as the orator or the poet. If he deviates from common use, he must atone for his deviation by hiding it, and can only give a new sense to an old word by so skilful a position of it as to render the new meaning so quickly understood that its novelty is scarcely perceived. Add to this, that in those most difficult inquiries for which the utmost coolness is not more than sufficient, he is often forced to use terms commonly connected with warm feeling, with high praise, with severe reproach;—which excite the passions of his readers when he most needs their calm attention and the undisturbed exercise of their impartial judgment. There is scarcely a neutral term left in Ethics; so quickly are such expressions enlisted on the side of Praise or Blame, by the address of contending passions. A true philosopher must not even desire that men should less love Virtue, or hate Vice, in order to fit them for a more unprejudiced judgment on his speculations.

There are, perhaps, not many occasions where the penury and laxity of language are more felt than in entering on the history of sciences where the first measure must be to mark out the boundary of the whole subject with some distinctness. But no exactness in these important operations can be approached without a new division of human knowledge, adapted to the present stage of its progress, and a reformation of all those barbarous, pedantic, unmeaning, and (what is worse) wrong-meaning names which continue to be applied to the greater part of its branches. Instances are needless where nearly all the appellations are faulty. The term "Metaphysics" affords a specimen of all the faults which the name of a science can combine. To those who know only their own language, it must, at their entrance on the study, convey no meaning: it points their attention to nothing. If they examine the language in which its parts are significant, they will be misled into the pernicious error of believing that it seeks something more than the interpretation of nature. It is only by examining the history of ancient philosophy that the probable origin of this name will be found, in its application, as the running title of several essays of Aristotle, placed in a collection of the manuscripts of that great philosopher, after his treatise on Physics. It has the greater fault of an unsteady and fluctuating signification;—denoting one class of objects in the seventeenth century, and another in the eighteenth;—even in the nineteenth not quite of the same import in the mouth of a German, as in that of a French or English philosopher; to say nothing of the farther objection that it continues to be a badge of undue pretension among some of the followers of the science, while it has become a name of reproach and derision among those who altogether decry it. The modern name of the very modern science called "Political Economy," though deliberately bestowed on it by its most eminent teachers, is perhaps a still more notable sample of the like faults. It might lead the ignorant to confine it to retrenchment in national expenditure; and a consideration of its etymology alone would lead us into the more mischievous error of believing it to teach, that national wealth is best promoted by the contrivance and interference of lawgivers, in opposition to its surest doctrine, and the one which it most justly boasts of having discovered and enforced.

It is easy to conceive an exhaustive analysis of human knowledge, and a consequent division of it into parts corresponding to all the classes of objects to which it relates:—a representation of that vast edifice, containing a picture of what is finished, a sketch of what is building, and even a conjectural outline of what, though required by completeness and convenience, as well as symmetry, is yet altogether untouched. A system of names might also be imagined derived from a few roots, indicating the objects of each part, and showing the relation of the parts to each other. An order and a language somewhat resembling those by which the objects of the sciences of Botany and Chemistry have, in the eighteenth century, been arranged and denoted, are doubtless capable of application to the sciences generally, when considered as parts of the system of knowledge. The attempts, however, which have hitherto been made to accomplish that analytical division of knowledge which must necessarily precede a new nomenclature of the sciences, have required so prodigious a superiority of genius in the single instance of approach to success by Bacon, as to discourage rivalship nearly as much as the frequent examples of failure in subsequent times could do. The nomenclature itself is attended with great difficulties, not indeed in its conception, but in its adoption and usefulness. In the Continental languages to the south of the Rhine, the practice of deriving the names of science from the Greek must be continued; which would render the new names for a while unintelligible to the majority of men. Even if successful in Germany, where a flexible and fertile language affords unbounded liberty of derivation and composition from native roots or elements, and where the newly derived and compounded words would thus be as clear to the mind, and almost as little startling to the ear of every man, as the oldest terms in the language, yet the whole nomenclature would be unintelligible to other nations. But, the intercommunity of the technical terms of science in Europe having been so far broken down by the Germans, the influence of their literature and philosophy is so rapidly increasing in the greater part of the Continent, that though a revolution in scientific nomenclature be probably yet far distant, the foundation of it may be considered as already prepared.

Although so great an undertaking must be reserved for a second Bacon and a future generation, it is necessary for the historian of any branch of knowledge to introduce his work by some account of the limits and contents of the sciences of which he is about to trace the progress; and though it will be found impossible to trace throughout this treatise a distinct line of demarcation, yet a general and imperfect sketch of the boundaries of the whole, and of the parts, of our present subject, may be a considerable help to the reader, as it has been a useful guide to the writer.

There is no distribution of the parts of knowledge more ancient than that of them into the physical and moral sciences, which seems liable to no other objection than that it does not exhaust the subject. Even this division, however, cannot be safely employed, without warning the reader that no science is entirely insulated, and that the principles of one are often only the conclusions and results of another. Every branch of knowledge has its root in the theory of the Understanding, from which even the mathematician must learn what can be known of his magnitude and his numbers; moral science is founded on that other,—hitherto unnamed,—part of the philosophy of human nature (to be constantly and vigilantly distinguished from *intellectual* philosophy), which contemplates the laws of sensibility, of emotion, of desire and aversion, of pleasure and pain, of happiness and misery; and on which arise the august and sacred landmarks that stand conspicuous along the frontier between Right and Wrong.

But however multiplied the connections of the moral and physical sciences are, it is not difficult to draw a general distinction between them. The purpose of the physical sciences throughout all their provinces, is to answer the question *What is?* They consist only of facts arranged according to their likeness, and expressed by general names given to every class of similar facts. The purpose of the moral sciences is to answer the question *What ought to be?* They aim at ascertaining the rules which *ought* to govern voluntary action, and to which those habitual dispositions of mind which are the source of voluntary actions *ought* to be adapted.

It is obvious that "will," "action," "habit," "disposition," are terms denoting facts in human nature, and that an explanation of them must be sought in mental philosophy, which, if knowledge be divided into physical and moral, must be placed among physical sciences, though it essentially differs from them all in having for its chief object those laws of thought which alone render any other sort of knowledge possible. But it is equally certain that the word "ought" introduces the mind into a new region, to which nothing physical corresponds. However philosophers may deal with this most important of words, it is instantly understood by all who do not attempt to define it. No civilized speech, perhaps no human language, is without correspondent terms. It would be as reasonable to deny that "space" and "greenness" are significant words, as to affirm that "ought," "right," "duty," "virtue," are sounds without meaning. It would be fatal to an ethical theory that it did not explain them, and that it did not comprehend all the conceptions and emotions which they call up. There never yet was a theory which did not attempt such an explanation.

SECTION I.

PRELIMINARY OBSERVATIONS.

THERE is no man who, in a case where he was a calm bystander, would not look with more satisfaction on acts of kindness than on acts of cruelty. No man, after the first excitement of his mind has subsided, ever whispered to himself with self-approbation and secret joy that he had been guilty of cruelty or baseness. Every criminal is strongly impelled to hide these qualities of his actions from himself, as he would do from others, by clothing his conduct in some disguise of duty, or of necessity. There is no tribe so rude as to be without a faint perception of a difference between Right and Wrong. There is no subject on which men of all ages and nations coincide in so many points as in the general rules of conduct, and in the qualities of the human character which deserve esteem. Even the grossest deviations from the general consent will appear, on close examination, to be not so much corruptions of moral feeling, as ignorance of facts; or errors with respect to the consequences of action; or cases in which the dissentient party is inconsistent with other parts of his own principles, which destroys the value of his dissent; or where each dissident is condemned by all the other dissidents, which immeasurably augments the majority against him. In the first three cases he may be convinced by argument that his moral judgment should be changed on principles which he recognises as just; and he can seldom, if ever, be condemned at the same time by the body of mankind who agree in their moral systems, and by those who on some other points dissent from that general code, without being also convicted of error by inconsistency with himself. The tribes who expose new-born infants, condemn those who abandon their decrepit parents to destruction: those who betray and murder strangers, are condemned by the rules of faith and humanity which they acknowledge in their intercourse with their countrymen. Mr. Hume, in a dialogue in which he ingeniously magnifies the moral heresies of two nations so polished as the Athenians and the French, has very satisfactorily resolved his own difficulties:—"In how many circumstances would an Athenian and a Frenchman of merit certainly resemble each other! —Humanity, fidelity, truth, justice, courage, temperance, constancy, dignity of mind." "The principles upon which men reason in Morals are always the same, though the conclusions which they draw are often very different."* He might have added, that almost every deviation which he imputes to each nation is at variance with some of the virtues justly esteemed by both, and that

* Philosophical Works, (Edinb. 1826,) vol. iv. pp. 420, 422.

the reciprocal condemnation of each other's errors which appears in his statement entitles us, on these points, to strike out the suffrages of both when collecting the general judgment of mankind. If we bear in mind that the question relates to the coincidence of all men in considering the same qualities as virtues, and not to the preference of one class of virtues by some, and of a different class by others, the exceptions from the agreement of mankind, in their system of practical morality, will be reduced to absolute insignificance; and we shall learn to view them as no more affecting the harmony of our moral faculties, than the resemblance of our limbs and features is affected by monstrous conformations, or by the unfortunate effects of accident and disease in a very few individuals.*

It is very remarkable, however, that though all men agree that there are acts which ought to be done, and acts which ought not to be done; though the far greater part of mankind agree in their list of virtues and duties, of vices and crimes; and though the whole race, as it advances in other improvements, is as evidently tending towards the moral system of the most civilized nations, as children in their growth tend to the opinions, as much as to the experience and strength, of adults; yet there are no questions in the circle of inquiry to which answers more various have been given than—How men have thus come to agree in the 'Rule of Life?' Whence arises their general reverence for it? and, What is meant by affirming that it ought to be inviolably observed? It is singular, that where we are most nearly agreed respecting rules, we should perhaps most widely differ as to the *causes* of our agreement, and as to the *reasons* which justify us for adhering to it. The discussion of these subjects composes what is usually called the "Theory of Morals" in a sense not in all respects coincident with what is usually considered as theory in other sciences. When we investigate the *causes* of our moral agreement, the term "theory" retains its ordinary scientific sense; but when we endeavour to ascertain the *reasons* of it, we rather employ the term as importing the theory of the rules of an art. In the first case, 'theory' denotes, as usual, the most general laws to which certain facts can be reduced; whereas in the second, it points out the efficacy of the observance, in practice, of certain rules, for producing the effects intended to be produced in the art. These reasons also may be reduced under the general sense by stating the question relating to them thus:—What are the causes why the observance of certain rules enables us to execute certain purposes? An account of the various answers attempted to be made to these inquiries, properly forms the history of Ethics.

The attentive reader may already perceive, that these momentous inquiries relate to at least two perfectly distinct subjects:—1. The nature of the distinction between Right and Wrong in human conduct, and 2. The nature of those feelings with which Right and Wrong are contemplated by human beings. The latter constitutes what has been called the '*Theory of Moral Sentiments*;' the former consists in an investigation into the *criterion of Morality in action*. Other most important questions arise in this province: but the two problems which have been just stated, and the essential distinction between them, must be clearly apprehended by all who are desirous of understanding the controversies which have prevailed on ethical subjects. The discrimination has seldom been made by moral philosophers; the difference between the two problems has never been uniformly observed by any of them: and it will appear, in the sequel, that they have been not rarely altogether confounded by very eminent men, to the destruction of all just conception and of all correct reasoning in this most important, and, perhaps, most difficult, of sciences.

It may therefore be allowable to deviate so far from historical order, as to illustrate the nature, and to prove the importance, of the distinction, by an example of the effects of neglecting it, taken from the recent works of justly celebrated writers; in which they discuss questions much agitated in the present age, and therefore probably now familiar to most readers of this Dissertation.

Dr. Paley represents the principle of a Moral Sense as being opposed to that of utility.* Now, it is evident that this representation is founded on a confusion of the two questions which have been started above. That we are endued with a Moral Sense, or, in other words, a faculty which immediately approves what is right, and condemns what is wrong, is only a statement of the feelings with which we contemplate actions. But

* "On convient le plus souvent de ces instincts de la conscience. La plus grande et la plus saine partie du genre humain leur rend témoignage. Les Orientaux, et les Grecs, et les Romains conviennent en cela; et il faudroit être aussi abruti que les sauvages Américains pour approuver leurs coutumes, pleines d'une cruauté qui passe même celle des bêtes. *Cependant ces mêmes sauvages sentent bien ce que c'est que la justice en d'autres occasions;* et quoique il n'y ait point de mauvaise pratique peut-être qui ne soit autorisée quelque part, il y en a peu pourtant qui ne soient condamnées le plus souvent, et par la plus grande partie des hommes."—Leibnitz, Œuvres Philosophiques, (Amst. et Leipz. 1765, 4to.) p. 49. There are some admirable observations on this subject in Hartley, especially in the development of the 49th Proposition:—" The rule of life drawn from the practice and opinions of mankind corrects and improves itself perpetually, till at last it determines entirely for virtue, and excludes all kinds and degrees of vice."—Observations on Man, vol. ii. p. 214.

* Principles of Moral and Political Philosophy. Compare book i. chap. v. with book ii. chap. vi.

to affirm that right actions are those which conduce to the well-being of mankind, is a proposition concerning the outward effects by which right actions themselves may be recognised. As these affirmations relate to different subjects, they cannot be opposed to each other, any more than the solidity of earth is inconsistent with the fluidity of water; and a very little reflection will show it to be easily conceivable that they may be both true. Man may be so constituted as instantaneously to approve certain actions without any reference to their consequences; and yet Reason may nevertheless discover, that a tendency to produce general happiness is the essential characteristic of such actions. Mr. Bentham also contrasts the principle of Utility with that of Sympathy, of which he considers the Moral Sense as being one of the forms.* It is needless to repeat, that propositions which affirm, or deny, anything of different subjects, cannot contradict each other. As these celebrated persons have thus inferred or implied the non-existence of a Moral Sense, from their opinion that the morality of actions depends upon their usefulness, so other philosophers of equal name have concluded, that the utility of actions cannot be the criterion of their morality, because a perception of that utility appears to them to form a faint and inconsiderable part of our Moral Sentiments,—if indeed it be at all discoverable in them.† These errors are the more remarkable, because the like confusion of perceptions with their objects, of emotions with their causes, or even the omission to mark the distinctions, would in every other subject be felt to be a most serious fault in philosophizing. If, for instance, an element were discovered to be common to all bodies which our taste perceives to be sweet, and to be found in no other bodies, it is apparent that this discovery, perhaps important in other respects, would neither affect our perception of sweetness, nor the pleasure which attends it. Both would continue to be what they have been since the existence of mankind. Every proposition concerning that element would relate to sweet bodies, and belong to the science of Chemistry; while every proposition respecting the perception or pleasure of sweetness would relate either to the body or mind of man, and accordingly belong either to the science of Physiology, or to that of Mental Philosophy. During the many ages which passed before the analysis of the sun's beams had proved them to be compounded of different colours, white objects were seen, and their whiteness was sometimes felt to be beautiful, in the very same manner as since that discovery. The qualities of light are the object of Optics; the nature of beauty can be ascertained only by each man's observation of his own mind; the changes in the living frame which succeed the refraction of light in the eye, and precede mental operation, will, if they are ever to be known by man, constitute a part of Physiology. But no proposition relating to one of these orders of phenomena can contradict or support a proposition concerning another order.

The analogy of this latter case will justify another preliminary observation. In the case of the pleasure derived from beauty, the question whether that pleasure be original, or derived, is of secondary importance. It has been often observed that the same properties which are admired as beautiful in the horse, contribute also to his safety and speed; and they who infer that the admiration of beauty was originally founded on the convenience of fleetness and firmness, if they at the same time hold that the idea of usefulness is gradually effaced, and that the admiration of a certain shape at length rises instantaneously, without reference to any purpose, may, with perfect consistency, regard a sense of beauty as an independent and universal principle of human nature. The laws of such a feeling of beauty are discoverable only by self-observation: those of the qualities which call it forth are ascertained by examination of the outward things which are called beautiful. But it is of the utmost importance to bear in mind, that he who contemplates the beautiful proportions of a horse, as the signs and proofs of security or quickness, and has in view these convenient qualities, is properly said to prefer the horse for his usefulness, not for his beauty; though he may choose him from the same outward appearance which pleases the admirer of the beautiful animal. He alone who derives immediate pleasure from the appearance itself, without reflection on any advantages which it may promise, is truly said to feel the beauty. The distinction, however, manifestly depends, not on the origin of the emotion, but on its object and nature when completely formed. Many of our most important perceptions through the eye are universally acknowledged to be acquired: but they are as general as the original perceptions of that organ; they arise as independently of our will, and human nature would be quite as imperfect without them. The case of an adult who did not immediately see the different distances of objects from his eye, would be thought by every one to be as great a deviation from the ordinary state of man, as if he were incapable of distinguishing the brightest sunshine from the darkest midnight. Acquired perceptions and sentiments may therefore be termed natural, as much as those which are more commonly so called, if they be as rarely found wanting. Ethical theories can never be satisfactorily discussed by those who do not constantly bear in mind, that the question

* Introduction to the Principles of Morality and Legislation, chap. ii.

† Smith, Theory of Moral Sentiments, part iv. Even Hume, in the third book of his Treatise of Human Nature, the most precise, perhaps, of his philosophical writings, uses the following as the title of one of the sections: "*Moral Distinctions, derived from a Moral Sense.*"

concerning the existence of a moral faculty in man, which immediately approves or disapproves, without reference to any farther object, is perfectly distinct, on the one hand, from that which inquires into the qualities of actions, thus approved or disapproved; and on the other, from an inquiry whether that faculty be derived from other parts of our mental frame, or be itself one of the ultimate constituent principles of human nature.

SECTION II.

RETROSPECT OF ANCIENT ETHICS.

Inquiries concerning the nature of Mind, the first principles of Knowledge, the origin and government of the world, appear to have been among the earliest objects which employed the understanding of civilized men. Fragments of such speculation are handed down from the legendary age of Greek philosophy. In the remaining monuments of that more ancient form of civilization which sprung up in Asia, we see clearly that the Braminical philosophers, in times perhaps before the dawn of Western history, had run round that dark and little circle of systems which an unquenchable thirst of knowledge has since urged both the speculators of ancient Greece and those of Christendom to retrace. The wall of adamant which bounds human inquiry in that direction has scarcely ever been discovered by any adventurer, until he has been roused by the shock which drove him back. It is otherwise with the theory of Morals. No controversy seems to have arisen regarding it in Greece till the rise and conflict of the Stoical and Epicurean schools; and the ethical disputes of the modern world originated with the writings of Hobbes about the middle of the seventeenth century. Perhaps the longer abstinence from debate on this subject may have sprung from reverence for Morality. Perhaps also, where the world were unanimous in their practical opinions, little need was felt of exact theory. The teachers of Morals were content with partial or secondary principles,—with the combination of principles not always reconcilable,—even with vague but specious phrases which in any degree explained or seemed to explain the Rules of the Art of Life, appearing, as these last did, at once too evident to need investigation, and too venerable to be approached by controversy.

Perhaps the subtile genius of Greece was in part withheld from indulging itself in ethical controversy by the influence of Socrates, who was much more a teacher of virtue than even a searcher after Truth—

> Whom, well inspired, the oracle pronounced
> Wisest of men.

It was doubtless because he chose that better part that he was thus spoken of by the man whose commendation is glory, and who, from the loftiest eminence of moral genius ever reached by a mortal, was perhaps alone worthy to place a new crown on the brow of the martyr of Virtue.

Aristippus indeed, a wit and a worldling, borrowed nothing from the conversations of Socrates but a few maxims for husbanding the enjoyments of sense. Antisthenes also, a hearer but not a follower, founded a school of parade and exaggeration, which caused his master to disown him by the ingenious rebuke,—"I see your vanity through your threadbare cloak."* The modest doubts of the most sober of moralists, and his indisposition to fruitless abstractions, were in process of time employed as the foundation of a systematic scepticism;—the most presumptuous, inapplicable, and inconsistent of all the results of human meditation. But though his lessons were thus distorted by the perverse ingenuity of some who heard him, the authority of his practical sense may be traced in the moral writings of those most celebrated philosophers who were directly or indirectly his disciples.

Plato, the most famous of his scholars, the most eloquent of Grecian writers, and the earliest moral philosopher whose writings have come down to us, employed his genius in the composition of dialogues, in which his master performed the principal part. These beautiful conversations would have lost their charm of verisimilitude, of dramatic vivacity, and of picturesque representation of character, if they had been subjected to the constraint of method. They necessarily presuppose much oral instruction. They frequently quote, and doubtless oftener allude to, the opinions of predecessors and contemporaries whose works have perished, and of whose doctrines only some fragments are preserved. In these circumstances, it must be difficult for the most learned and philosophical of his commentators to give a just representation of his doctrines, even if he really framed or adopted a system. The moral part of his works is more accessible.† The vein of thought which runs through them is always visible. The object is to inspire the love of Truth, of Wisdom, of Beauty, especially of Goodness—the highest Beauty, and of that Supreme and Eternal Mind, which contains all Truth and Wisdom, all Beauty and Goodness. By the love or delightful contemplation and pursuit of these transcendent aims for their own sake only, he represented the mind of man as raised from low and perishable objects, and prepared for those high destinies which are appointed for all those who are capable of enjoying them. The application to moral qualities of terms which denote outward beauty, though by him perhaps carried to excess, is

---

* Diog. Laert. lib. vi. Ælian, lib. ix. cap. 35.

† Heyse, Init. Phil. Plat. 1827;—a hitherto incomplete work of great perspicuity and elegance, in which we must excuse the partiality which belongs to a labour of love.

an illustrative metaphor, as well warranted by the poverty of language as any other employed to signify the acts or attributes of Mind.* The "beautiful" in his language denoted all that of which the mere contemplation is in itself delightful, without any admixture of organic pleasure, and without being regarded as the means of attaining any farther end. The feeling which belongs to it he called "love;" a word which, as comprehending complacency, benevolence, and affection, and reaching from the neighbourhood of the senses to the most sublime of human thoughts, is foreign to the colder and more exact language of our philosophy; but which, perhaps, then happily served to lure both the lovers of Poetry, and the votaries of Superstition, to the school of Truth and Goodness in the groves of the Academy. He enforced these lessons by an inexhaustible variety of just and beautiful illustrations,—sometimes striking from their familiarity, sometimes subduing by their grandeur; and his works are the storehouse from which moralists have from age to age borrowed the means of rendering moral instruction easier and more delightful. Virtue he represented as the harmony of the whole soul;—as a peace between all its principles and desires, assigning to each as much space as they can occupy, without encroaching on each other; —as a state of perfect health, in which every function was performed with ease, pleasure, and vigour;—as a well-ordered commonwealth, where the obedient passions executed with energy the laws and commands of Reason. The vicious mind presented the odious character, sometimes of discord, of war;—sometimes of disease;—always of passions warring with each other in eternal anarchy. Consistent with himself, and at peace with his fellows, the good man felt in the quiet of his conscience a foretaste of the approbation of God. "Oh, what ardent love would virtue inspire if she could be seen." "If the heart of a tyrant could be laid bare, we should see how it was cut and torn by its own evil passions and by an avenging conscience."†

Perhaps in every one of these illustrations, an eye trained in the history of Ethics may discover the germ of the whole or of a part of some subsequent theory. But to examine it thus would not be to look at it with the eye of Plato. His aim was as practical as that of Socrates. He employed every topic, without regard to its place in a system, or even always to its argumentative force, which could attract the small portion of the community then accessible to cultivation; who, it should not be forgotten, had no moral instructor but the Philosopher, unaided, if not thwarted, by the reigning superstition: for Religion had not then, besides her own discoveries, brought down the most awful and the most beautiful forms of Moral Truth to the humblest station in human society.*

Ethics retained her sober spirit in the hands of his great scholar and rival Aristotle, who, though he certainly surpassed all men in acute distinction, in subtile argument, in severe method, in the power of analyzing what is most compounded, and of reducing to simple principles the most various and unlike appearances, yet appears to be still more raised above his fellows by the prodigious faculty of laying aside these extraordinary endowments whenever his present purpose required it;—as in his History of Animals, in his treatises on philosophical criticism, and in his practical writings, political as well as moral. Contrasted as his genius was to that of Plato, not only by its logical and metaphysical attributes, but by the regard to experience and observation of Nature which, in him perhaps alone, accompanied them; (though the two may be considered as the original representatives of the two antagonist tendencies of philosophy—that which would ennoble man, and that which seeks rather to explain nature;) yet opposite as they are in other respects, the master and the scholar combine to guard the Rule of Life against the licentious irruptions of the Sophists.

In Ethics alone their systems differed more in words than in things.† That hap-

* The most probable etymology of "καλός" seems to be from καίω to burn. What burns commonly shines. "Schön," in German, which means beautiful, is derived from "scheinen," to shine. The word καλός was used for right, so early as the Homeric Poems. Ιλ. xvii. 19. In the philosophical age it became a technical term, with little other remains of the metaphorical sense than what the genius and art of a fine writer might sometimes rekindle. "Honestum" the term by which Cicero translates the "καλόν," being derived from outward honours, is a less happy metaphor. In our language, the terms, being from foreign roots, contribute nothing to illustrate the progress of thought.

† Let it not be forgotten, that for this terrible description, Socrates, to whom it is ascribed by Plato (Πολ. I.) is called "Præstantissimus sapientiæ," by a writer of the most masculine understanding, the least subject to be transported by enthusiasm.—Tac. Ann. lib. vi. cap. 6. "Quæ vulnera!" says Cicero, in alluding to the same passage.—De Off. lib. iii. cap. 21.

* There can hardly be a finer example of Plato's practical morals than his observations on the treatment of slaves. "Genuine humanity and real probity," says he, "are brought to the test, by the behaviour of a man to slaves, whom he may wrong with impunity." Διάδηλος γὰρ ὁ φύσει καὶ μὴ πλαστῶς σέβων τὴν δίκην, μισῶν δὲ ὄντως τὸ ἄδικον ἐν τούτοις τῶν ἀνθρώπων ἐν οἷς αὐτῷ ῥᾴδιον ἀδικεῖν,—Νομ. lib. vi. cap. 19. That Plato was considered as the fountain of ancient morals, would be sufficiently evident from Cicero alone: "Ex hoc igitur Platonis, quasi quodam sancto augustoque fonte, nostra omnis manabit oratio."—Tusc. Quæst. lib. v. cap. 12. Perhaps the sober Quintilian meant to mingle some censure with the highest praise: "Plato, qui eloquendi facultate divinâ quâdam et Homericâ, multum supra prosam orationem surgit." De Inst. Orat. lib. x. cap. 1.

† "Una et consentiensduobus vocabulis philosophiæ forma instituta est, Academicorum et Peripateticorum; qui rebus congruentes nominibus differebant."—Cic. Acad. Quæst. lib i. cap. 4. Βούλεται (Αριστοτελης) διττὸν εἶναι τὸν κατὰ φιλοσοφίαν

piness consisted in virtuous pleasure, chiefly dependent on the state of mind, but not unaffected by outward agents, was the doctrine of both. Both would with Socrates have called happiness "unrepented pleasure." Neither distinguished the two elements which they represented as constituting the Supreme Good from each other; partly, perhaps, from fear of appearing to separate them. Plato more habitually considered happiness as the natural fruit of Virtue; Aristotle oftener viewed Virtue as the means of attaining happiness. The celebrated doctrine of the Peripatetics, which placed all virtues in a medium between opposite vices, was probably suggested by the Platonic representation of its necessity to keep up harmony between the different parts of our nature. The perfection of a compound machine is attained where all its parts have the fullest scope for action. Where one is so far exerted as to repress others, there is a vice of excess: where any one has less activity than it might exert without disturbing others, there is a vice of defect. The point which all reach without collision with each other, is the mediocrity in which the Peripatetics placed Virtue.

It was not till near a century after the death of Plato that Ethics became the scene of philosophical contest between the adverse schools of Epicurus and Zeno; whose errors afford an instructive example, that in the formation of a theory, partial truth is equivalent to absolute falsehood. As the astronomer who left either the centripetal or the centrifugal force of the planets out of his view, would err as completely as he who excluded both, so the Epicureans and Stoics, who each confined themselves to real but not exclusive principles in Morals, departed as widely from the truth as if they had adopted no part of it. Every partial theory is indeed directly false, inasmuch as it ascribes to one or few causes what is produced by more. As the extreme opinions of one, if not of both, of these schools have been often revived with variations and refinements in modern times, and are still not without influence on ethical systems, it may be allowable to make some observations on this earliest of moral controversies.

"All other virtues," said Epicurus, "grow from prudence, which teaches that we cannot live pleasurably without living justly and virtuously, nor live justly and virtuously without living pleasurably."* The illustration of this sentence formed the whole moral discipline of Epicurus. To him we owe the general concurrence of reflecting men in succeeding times, in the important truth that men cannot be happy without a virtuous frame of mind and course of life; a truth of inestimable value, not peculiar to the Epicureans, but placed by their exaggerations in a stronger light;—a truth, it must be added, of less importance as a motive to right conduct than as completing Moral Theory, which, however, it is very far from solely constituting. With that truth the Epicureans blended another position, which indeed is contained in the first words of the above statement; namely, that because Virtue promotes happiness, every act of virtue must be done in order to promote the happiness of the agent. They and their modern followers tacitly assume, that the latter position is the consequence of the former; as if it were an inference from the necessity of food to life, that the fear of death should be substituted for the appetite of hunger as a motive for eating. "Friendship," says Epicurus, "is to be pursued by the wise man only for its usefulness, but he will begin; as he sows the field in order to reap."* It is obvious, that if these words be confined to outward benefits, they may be sometimes true, but never can be pertinent; for outward acts sometimes show kindness, but never compose it. If they be applied to kind feeling, they would indeed be pertinent, but they would be evidently and totally false; for it is most certain that no man acquires an affection merely from his belief that it would be agreeable or advantageous to feel it. Kindness cannot indeed be pursued on account of the pleasure which belongs to it; for man can no more know the pleasure till he has felt the affection, than he can form an idea of colour without the sense of sight. The moral character of Epicurus was excellent; no man more enjoyed the pleasure, or better performed the duties of friendship. The letter of his system was no more indulgent to vice than that of any other moralist.† Although, therefore, he has the merit of having more strongly inculcated the connection of Virtue with happiness, perhaps by the faulty excess of treating it as an exclusive principle; yet his doctrine was justly charged with indisposing the mind to those exalted and generous sentiments, without which no pure, elevated, bold, generous, or tender virtues can exist.‡

As Epicurus represented the *tendency* of Virtue, which is a most important truth in ethical theory, as the sole inducement to virtuous practice; so Zeno, in his disposition

---

λόγον· τὸν μὲν πρακτικόν, τὸν δὲ θεωρητικόν. καὶ τοῦ πρακτικοῦ, τόν τε ἠθικὸν καὶ πολιτικόν· τοῦ δὲ θεωρητικοῦ, τόν τε φυσικὸν, καὶ λογικὸν.—Diog. Laert. lib. v. § 28.

* Diog. Laert. lib. x. § 132.

* Τὴν φιλίαν διὰ τῆς χρείας.—Diog. Laert. lib. x. § 120. "Hic est locus," Gassendi confesses, "ob quem Epicurus non parum vexatur, quando nemo non reprehendit, parari amicitiam non sui, sed utilitatis gratiâ"

† It is due to him to observe, that he treated humanity towards slaves, as one of the characteristics of a wise man. Οὔτε κολάσειν οἰκέτας, ἐλεήσειν μέντοι, καὶ συγγνώμην τινὶ ἕξειν τῶν σπουδαίων.—Diog. Laert. lib. x. § 118. It is not unworthy of remark, that neither Plato nor Epicurus thought it necessary to abstain from these topics in a city full of slaves, many of whom were men not destitute of knowledge.

‡ "Nil generosum, nil magnificum sapit."—De Fin. lib. i. cap. 7.

towards the opposite extreme, was inclined to consider the moral sentiments, which are the motives of right conduct, as being the sole principles of moral science. The confusion was equally great in a philosophical view, but that of Epicurus was more fatal to interests of higher importance than those of Philosophy. Had the Stoics been content with affirming that Virtue is the source of all that part of our happiness which depends on ourselves, they would have taken a position from which it would have been impossible to drive them; they would have laid down a principle of as great comprehension in practice as their wider pretensions; a simple and incontrovertible truth, beyond which every thing is an object of mere curiosity to man. Our information, however, about the opinions of the more celebrated Stoics is very scanty. None of their own writings are preserved. We know little of them but from Cicero, the translator of Grecian philosophy, and from the Greek compilers of a later age; authorities which would be imperfect in the history of facts, but which are of far less value in the history of opinions, where a right conception often depends upon the minutest distinctions between words. We know that Zeno was more simple, and that Chrysippus, who was accounted the prop of the Stoic Porch, abounded more in subtile distinction and systematic spirit.* His power was attested as much by the antagonists whom he called forth, as by the scholars whom he formed. "Had there been no Chrysippus, there would have been no Carneades," was the saying of the latter philosopher himself; as it might have been said in the eighteenth century, "Had there been no Hume, there would have been no Kant and no Reid." Cleanthes, when one of his followers would pay court to him by laying vices to the charge of his most formidable opponent, Arcesilaus the academic, answered with a justice and candour unhappily too rare, "Silence,—do not malign him;—though he attacks Virtue by his arguments, he confirms its authority by his life." Arcesilaus, whether modestly or churlishly, replied, "I do not choose to be flattered." Cleanthes, with a superiority of repartee, as well as charity, replied, "Is it flattery to say that you speak one thing and do another?" It would be vain to expect that the fragments of the professors who lectured in the Stoic School for five hundred years, should be capable of being moulded into one consistent system; and we see that in Epictetus at least, the exaggeration of the sect was lowered to the level of Reason, by confining the sufficiency of Virtue to those cases only where happiness is attainable by our voluntary acts. It ought to be added, in extenuation of a noble error, that the power of habit and character to struggle against outward evils has been proved by experience to be in some instances so prodigious, that no man can presume to fix the utmost limit of its possible increase.

The attempt, however, of the Stoics to stretch the bounds of their system beyond the limits of Nature, doomed them to fluctuate between a wild fanaticism on the one hand, and, on the other, concessions which left their differences from other philosophers purely verbal. Many of their doctrines appear to be modifications of their original opinions, introduced as opposition became more formidable. In this manner they were driven to the necessity of admitting that the objects of our desires and appetites are worthy of preference, though they are denied to be constituents of happiness. It was thus that they were obliged to invent a double morality; one for mankind at large, from whom was expected no more than the *καθῆκον*,—which seems principally to have denoted acts of duty done from inferior or mixed motives; and the other (which they appear to have hoped from their ideal wise man) *κατόρθωμα*, or perfect observance of rectitude, —which consisted only in moral acts done from mere reverence for Morality, unaided by any feelings; all which (without the exception of pity) they classed among the enemies of Reason and the disturbers of the human soul. Thus did they shrink from their proudest paradoxes into verbal evasions. It is remarkable that men so acute did not perceive and acknowledge, that if pain were not an evil, cruelty would not be a vice; and that, if patience were of power to render torture indifferent, Virtue must expire in the moment of victory. There can be no more triumph, when there is no enemy left to conquer.*

The influence of men's opinions on the conduct of their lives is checked and modified by so many causes; it so much depends on the strength of conviction, on its habitual combination with feelings, on the concurrence or resistance of interest, passion, example, and sympathy,—that a wise man is not the most forward in attempting to determine the power of its single operation over human actions. In the case of an individual it becomes altogether uncertain. But when the experiment is made on a large scale, when it is long continued and varied in its circumstances, and especially when great bodies of men are for ages the subject of it, we cannot reasonably reject the consideration of the inferences to which it appears to lead. The Roman Patriciate, trained in the conquest and government of the civilized world, in spite of the tyrannical vices which sprung from that training, were raised by

* "Chrysippus, qui fulcire putatur porticum Stoicorum."—Acad. Quæst. lib. ii. cap. 24. Elsewhere (De Orat. lib. i. cap. 12.—De Fin. lib. iv. cap. 3.), "Acutissimus, sed in scribendo exilis et jejunus, scripsit rhetoricam seu potiùs obmutescendi artem;"—nearly as we should speak of a Schoolman.

* "Patience, sovereign o'er transmuted ill." But as soon as the ill was really "transmuted" into good, it is evident that there was no longer any scope left for the exercise of patience.

the greatness of their objects to an elevation of genius and character unmatched by any other aristocracy, ere the period when, after preserving their power by a long course of wise compromise with the people, they were betrayed by the army and the populace into the hands of a single tyrant of their own order—the most accomplished of usurpers, and, if Humanity and Justice could for a moment be silenced, one of the most illustrious of men. There is no scene in history so memorable as that in which Cæsar mastered a nobility of which Lucullus and Hortensius, Sulpicius and Catulus, Pompey and Cicero, Brutus and Cato were members. This renowned body had from the time of Scipio sought the Greek philosophy as an amusement or an ornament. Some few, "in thought more elevate," caught the love of Truth, and were ambitious of discovering a solid foundation for the Rule of Life. The influence of the Grecian systems was tried, during the five centuries between Carneades and Constantine, by their effect on a body of men of the utmost originality, energy, and variety of character, in their successive positions of rulers of the world, and of slaves under the best and under the worst of uncontrolled masters. If we had found this influence perfectly uniform, we should have justly suspected our own love of system of having in part bestowed that appearance on it. Had there been no trace of such an influence discoverable in so great an experiment, we must have acquiesced in the paradox, that opinion does not at all affect conduct. The result is the more satisfactory, because it appears to illustrate general tendency without excluding very remarkable exceptions. Though Cassius was an Epicurean, the true representative of that school was the accomplished, prudent, friendly, good-natured time-server Atticus, the pliant slave of every tyrant, who could kiss the hand of Antony, imbrued as it was in the blood of Cicero. The pure school of Plato sent forth Marcus Brutus, the signal humanity of whose life was both necessary and sufficient to prove that his daring breach of venerable rules flowed only from that dire necessity which left no other means of upholding the most sacred principles. The Roman orator, though in speculative questions he embraced that mitigated doubt which allowed most ease and freedom to his genius, yet in those moral writings where his heart was most deeply interested, followed the severest sect of Philosophy, and became almost a Stoic. If any conclusion may be hazarded from this trial of systems,—the greatest which History has recorded, we must not refuse our decided, though not undistinguishing, preference to that noble school which preserved great souls untainted at the court of dissolute and ferocious tyrants; which exalted the slave of one of Nero's courtiers to be a moral teacher of aftertimes;—which for the first, and hitherto for the only time, breathed philosophy and justice into those rules of law which govern the ordinary concerns of every man; and which, above all, has contributed, by the examples of Marcus Portius Cato and of Marcus Aurelius Antoninus, to raise the dignity of our species, to keep alive a more ardent love of Virtue, and a more awful sense of duty throughout all generations.*

The result of this short review of the practical philosophy of Greece seems to be, that though it was rich in rules for the conduct of life, and in exhibitions of the beauty of Virtue, and though it contains glimpses of just theory and fragments of perhaps every moral truth, yet it did not leave behind any precise and coherent system; unless we except that of Epicurus, who purchased consistency, method, and perspicuity too dearly by sacrificing Truth, and by narrowing and lowering his views of human nature, so as to enfeeble, if not extinguish, all the vigorous motives to arduous virtue. It is remarkable, that while of the eight professors who taught in the Porch, from Zeno to Posidonius, every one either softened or exaggerated the doctrines of his predecessor; and while the beautiful and reverend philosophy of Plato had, in his own Academy, degenerated into a scepticism which did not spare Morality itself, the system of Epicurus remained without change; and his disciples continued for ages to show personal honours to his memory, in a manner which may seem unaccountable among those who were taught to measure propriety by a calculation of palpable and outward usefulness. This steady adherence is in part doubtless attributable to the portion of truth which the doctrine contains; in some degree perhaps to the amiable and unboastful character of Epicurus; not a little, it may be, to the dishonour of deserting an unpopular cause; but probably most of all to that mental indolence which disposes the mind to rest in a simple system, comprehended at a glance, and easily falling in, both with ordinary maxims of discretion, and with the vulgar commonplaces of satire on human nature.† When all instruction was conveyed by lectures, and when one master taught the whole circle of the sciences in one school, it was natural that the attachment of pupils to a professor should be more devoted than when, as in

* Of all testimonies to the character of the Stoics, perhaps the most decisive is the speech of the vile sycophant Capito, in the mock impeachment of Thrasea Pætus, before a senate of slaves: "Ut quondam C. Cæsarem et M. Catonem, ita nunc te, Nero, et Thraseam, avida discordiarum civitas loquitur . . . . . Ista secta Tuberones et Favonios, veteri quoque reipublicæ ingrata nomina, genuit." —Tacit. Ann. lib. xvi. cap. 22. See Appendix, Note A.

† The progress of commonplace satire on sexes or professions, and (he might have added) on nations, has been exquisitely touched by Gray in his Remarks on Lydgate; a fragment containing passages as finely thought and written as any in English prose. General satire on mankind is still more absurd; for no invective can be so unreasonable as that which is founded on falling short of an ideal standard.

our times, he can teach only a small portion of a Knowledge spreading towards infinity, and even in his own little province finds a rival in every good writer who has treated the same subject. The superior attachment of the Epicureans to their master is not without some parallel among the followers of similar principles in our own age, who have also revived some part of that indifference to eloquence and poetry which may be imputed to the habit of contemplating all things in relation to happiness, and to (what seems its uniform effect) the egregious miscalculation which leaves a multitude of mental pleasures out of the account. It may be said, indeed, that the Epicurean doctrine has continued with little change to the present day; at least it is certain that no other ancient doctrine has proved so capable of being restored in the same form among the moderns: and it may be added, that Hobbes and Gassendi, as well as some of our own contemporaries, are as confident in their opinions, and as intolerant of scepticism, as the old Epicureans. The resemblance of modern to ancient opinions, concerning some of those questions upon which ethical controversy must always hinge, may be a sufficient excuse for a retrospect of the Greek morals, which, it is hoped, will simplify and shorten subsequent observation on those more recent disputes which form the proper subject of this discourse.

The genius of Greece fell with Liberty. The Grecian philosophy received its mortal wound in the contests between scepticism and dogmatism which occupied the Schools in the age of Cicero. The Sceptics could only perplex, and confute, and destroy. Their occupation was gone as soon as they succeeded. They had nothing to substitute for what they overthrew; and they rendered their own art of no further use. They were no more than venomous animals, who stung their victims to death, but also breathed their last into the wound.

A third age of Grecian literature indeed arose at Alexandria, under the Macedonian kings of Egypt; laudably distinguished by exposition, criticism, and imitation (sometimes abused for the purposes of literary forgery), and still more honoured by some learned and highly-cultivated poets, as well as by diligent cultivators of History and Science; among whom a few began, about the first preaching of Christianity, to turn their minds once more to that high Philosophy which seeks for the fundamental principles of human knowledge. Philo, a learned and philosophical Hebrew, one of the flourishing colony of his nation established in that city, endeavoured to reconcile the Platonic philosophy with the Mosaic Law and the Sacred Books of the Old Testament. About the end of the second century, when the Christians, Hebrews, Pagans, and various other sects of semi- or pseudo-Christian Gnostics appear to have studied in the same schools, the almost inevitable tendency of doctrines, however discordant, in such circumstances to amalgamate, produced its full effect under Ammonius Saccas, a celebrated professor, who, by selection from the Greek systems, the Hebrew books, and the Oriental religions, and by some concession to the rising spirit of Christianity, of which the Gnostics had set the example, composed a very mixed system, commonly designated as the Eclectic philosophy. The controversies between his contemporaries and followers, especially those of Clement and Origen, the victorious champions of Christianity, with Plotinus and Porphyry, who endeavoured to preserve Paganism by clothing it in a disguise of philosophical Theism, are, from the effects towards which they contributed, the most memorable in the history of human opinion.* But their connection with modern Ethics is too faint to warrant any observation in this place, on the imperfect and partial memorials of them which have reached us. The death of Boethius in the West, and the closing of the Athenian Schools by Justinian, may be considered as the last events in the history of ancient philosophy.†

SECTION III.

RETROSPECT OF SCHOLASTIC ETHICS.

An interval of a thousand years elapsed between the close of ancient and the rise of modern philosophy; the most unexplored, yet not the least instructive portion of the history of European opinion. In that period the sources of the institutions, the manners, and the characteristic distinctions of modern nations, have been traced by a series of philosophical inquirers from Montesquieu to Hallam; and there also, it may be added, more than among the Ancients, are the well-springs of our speculative doctrines and controversies. Far from being inactive, the human mind, during that period of exaggerated darkness, produced discoveries in Science, inventions in Art, and contrivances in Go-

* The change attempted by Julian, Porphyry, and their friends, by which Theism would have become the popular Religion, may be estimated by the memorable passage of Tacitus on the Theism of the Jews. In the midst of all the obloquy and opprobrium with which he loads that people, his tone suddenly rises, when he comes to contemplate them as the only nation who paid religious honours to the Supreme and Eternal Mind alone, and his style swells at the sight of so sublime and wonderful a scene. "Summum *illud* et æternum, neque mutabile, neque interiturum." Hist. lib. v. cap. 5.

† The punishment of death was inflicted on Pagans by a law of Constantius. "Volumus cunctos sacrificiis abstinere: si aliquid hujusmodi perpetraverint, gladio ultore sternantur." Cod. Just. lib. i. tit. xi. 'de Paganis.' From the authorities cited by Gibbon, (note, chap. xi.) as well as from some research, it should seem that the edict for the suppression of the Athenian schools was not admitted into the vast collection of laws enacted or systematized by Justinian.

vernment, some of which, perhaps, were rather favoured than hindered by the disorders of society, and by the twilight in which men and things were seen. Had Boethius, the last of the ancients, foreseen, that within four centuries of his death, in the province of Britain, then a prey to all the horrors of barbaric invasion, a chief of one of the fiercest tribes of barbarians* should translate into the jargon of his freebooters the work on The Consolations of Philosophy, of which the composition had soothed the cruel imprisonment of the philosophic Roman himself, he must, even amidst his sufferings, have derived some gratification from such an assurance of the recovery of mankind from ferocity and ignorance. But had he been allowed to revisit the earth in the middle of the sixteenth century, with what wonder and delight might he have contemplated the new and fairer order which was beginning to disclose its beauty, and to promise more than it revealed. He would have seen personal slavery nearly extinguished, and women, first released from Oriental imprisonment by the Greeks, and raised to a higher dignity among the Romans,† at length fast approaching to due equality;—two revolutions the most signal and beneficial since the dawn of civilization. He would have seen the discovery of gunpowder, which for ever guarded civilized society against barbarians, while it transferred military strength from the few to the many; of paper and printing, which rendered a second destruction of the repositories of knowledge impossible, as well as opened a way by which it was to be finally accessible to all mankind; of the compass, by means of which navigation had ascertained the form of the planet, and laid open a new continent, more extensive than his world. If he had turned to civil institutions, he might have learned that some nations had preserved an ancient, simple, and seemingly rude mode of legal proceeding, which threw into the hands of the majority of men a far larger share of judicial power, than was enjoyed by them in any ancient democracy. He would have seen everywhere the remains of that principle of representation, the glory of the Teutonic race, by which popular government, anciently imprisoned in cities, became capable of being strengthened by its extension over vast countries, to which experience cannot even now assign any limits; and which, in times still distant, was to exhibit, in the newly discovered Continent, a republican confederacy, likely to surpass the Macedonian and Roman empires in extent, greatness, and duration, but gloriously founded on the equal rights, not like them on the universal subjection, of mankind. In one respect, indeed, he might have lamented that the race of man had made a really retrograde movement; that they had lost the liberty of philosophizing; that the open exercise of their highest faculties was interdicted. But he might also have perceived that this giant evil had received a mortal wound from Luther, who in his warfare against Rome had struck a blow against all human authority, and unconsciously disclosed to mankind that they were entitled, or rather bound, to form and utter their own opinions, and that most certainly on whatever subjects are the most deeply interesting: for although this most fruitful of moral truths was not yet so released from its combination with the wars and passions of the age as to assume a distinct and visible form, its action was already discoverable in the divisions among the Reformers, and in the fears and struggles of civil and ecclesiastical oppressors. The Council of Trent, and the Courts of Paris, Madrid, and Rome, had before that time foreboded the emancipation of Reason.

Though the middle age be chiefly memorable as that in which the foundations of a new order of society were laid, uniting the stability of the Oriental system, without its inflexibility, to the activity of the Hellenic civilization, without its disorder and inconstancy; yet it is not unworthy of notice by us here, on account of the subterranean current which flows through it, from the speculations of ancient to those of modern times. That dark stream must be uncovered before the history of the European Understanding can be thoroughly comprehended. It was lawful for the emancipators of Reason in their first struggles to carry on mortal war against the Schoolmen. The necessity has long ceased; they are no longer dangerous; and it is now felt by philosophers that it is time to explore and estimate that vast portion of the history of Philosophy from which we have scornfully turned our eyes.* A few sentences only can be allotted to the subject in this place. In the very depths of the Middle Age, the darkness of Christendom was

* King Alfred.

† The steps of this important progress, as far as relates to Athens and Rome, are well remarked upon by one of the finest of the Roman writers. "Quem enim Romanorum pudet uxorem ducere in convivium? aut cujus materfamilias non primum locum tenet ædium, atque in celebritate versatur? quod multo fit aliter in Græciâ: nam neque in convivium adhibetur, nisi propinquorum; neque sedet nisi in interiore parte ædium, quæ *Gynæconitis* appellatur, quo nemo accedit, nisi propinquâ cognatione conjunctus." Corn. Nep. in Præfat.

* Tennemann, Geschichte der Philosophie. Cousin, Cours de Philosophie, Paris, 1828. My esteem for this last admirable writer encourages me to say, that the beauty of his diction has sometimes the same effect on his thoughts that a sunny haze produces on outward objects; and to submit to his serious consideration, whether the allurements of Schelling's system have not betrayed him into a too frequent forgetfulness that principles, equally adapted to all phenomena, furnish in speculation no possible test of their truth, and lead, in practice, to total indifference and inactivity respecting human affairs. I quote with pleasure an excellent observation from this work: "Le moyen âge n'est pas autre chose que la formation pénible, lente et sanglante, de tous les élémens de la civilisation moderne; je dis la formation, et non leur développement." (2nd Lecture, p. 27.)

faintly broken by a few thinly scattered lights. Even then, Moses Ben Maimon taught philosophy among the persecuted Hebrews, whose ancient schools had never perhaps been wholly interrupted; and a series of distinguished Mahometans, among whom two are known to us by the names of Avicenna and Averroes, translated the Peripatetic writings into their own language, expounded their doctrines in no servile spirit to their followers, and enabled the European Christians to make those versions of them from Arabic into Latin, which in the eleventh and twelfth centuries gave birth to the scholastic philosophy.

The Schoolmen were properly theologians, who employed philosophy only to define and support that system of Christian belief which they and their contemporaries had embraced. The founder of that theological system was Aurelius Augustinus* (called by us Augustin), bishop of Hippo, in the province of Africa; a man of great genius and ardent character, who adopted, at different periods of his life, the most various, but at all times the most decisive and systematic, as well as daring and extreme opinions. This extraordinary man became, after some struggles, the chief Doctor, and for ages almost the sole oracle, of the Latin church. It happened by a singular accident, that the Schoolmen of the twelfth century, who adopted his theology, instead of borrowing their defensive weapons from Plato, the favourite of their master, had recourse for the exposition and maintenance of their doctrines to the writings of Aristotle, the least pious of philosophical theists. The Augustinian doctrines of original sin, predestination, and grace, little known to the earlier Christian writers, who appear indeed to have adopted opposite and milder opinions, were espoused by Augustin himself in his old age; when, by a violent swing from his youthful Manicheism, which divided the sovereignty of the world between two adverse beings, he did not shrink, in his pious solicitude for tracing the power of God in all events, from presenting the most mysterious parts of the moral government of the Universe, in their darkest colours and their sternest shape, as articles of faith, the objects of the habitual meditation and practical assent of mankind. The principles of his rigorous system, though not with all their legitimate consequences, were taught in the schools; respectfully promulgated rather than much inculcated by the Western Church (for in the East these opinions seem to have been unknown); scarcely perhaps distinctly assented to by the majority of the clergy; and seldom heard of by laymen till the systematic genius and fervid eloquence of Calvin rendered them a popular creed in the most devout and moral portion of the Christian world. Anselm,† the Piedmontese Archbishop of Canterbury, was the earliest reviver of the Augustinian opinions. Aquinas* was their most redoubted champion. To them, however, the latter joined others of a different spirit. Faith, according to him, was a virtue, not in the sense in which it denotes the things believed, but in that in which it signifies the state of mind which leads to right Belief. Goodness he regarded as the moving principle of the Divine Government; Justice, as a modification of Goodness; and, with all his zeal to magnify the Sovereignity of God, he yet taught, that though God always wills what is just, nothing is just solely because He wills it. Scotus,† the most subtile of doctors, recoils from the Augustinian rigour, though he rather intimates than avows his doubts. He was assailed for his tendency towards the Pelagian or Anti-Augustinian doctrines by many opponents, of whom the most famous in his own time was Thomas Bradwardine,‡ Archbishop of Canterbury, formerly confessor of Edward III., whose defence of Predestination was among the most noted works of that age. He revived the principles of the ancient philosophers, who, from Plato to Marcus Aurelius, taught that error of judgment, being involuntary, is not the proper subject of moral disapprobation; which indeed is implied in Aquinas' account of Faith.§ But he appears to have been the first whose language inclined towards that most pernicious of moral heresies, which represents Morality to be founded on Will.‖

William of Ockham, the most justly celebrated of English Schoolmen, went so far beyond this inclination of his master, as to affirm, that "if God had commanded his creatures to hate Himself, the hatred of God would ever be the duty of man;"—a monstrous hyperbole, into which he was perhaps betrayed by his denial of the doctrine of general ideas, the pre-existence of which in the Eternal Intellect was commonly regarded as the foundation of the immutable nature of Morality. This doctrine of Ockham, which by necessary implication refuses moral attributes to the Deity, and contradicts the existence of a moral government, is practically

* See Note B. † Born, 1033; died, 1109.

* Born, 1224; died, 1274. See Note C.

† Born about 1265; died at Cologne (where his grave is still shown) in 1308. Whether he was a native of Dunston in Northumberland, or of Dunse in Berwickshire, or of Down in Ireland, was a question long and warmly contested, but which seems to be settled by his biographer, Luke Wadding, who quotes a passage of Scotus' Commentary on Aristotle's Metaphysics, where he illustrates his author thus: "As in the definition of St. Francis, or St. Patrick, man is necessarily presupposed." Scott. Op. i. 3. As Scotus was a Franciscan, the mention of St. Patrick seems to show that he was an Irishman. See Note D.

‡ Born about 1290; died 1349; the contemporary of Chaucer, and probably a fellow-student of Wicliffe and Roger Bacon. His principal work was entitled, 'De Causâ Dei contra Pelagium, et de Virtute Causarum, Libri tres.'

§ See Note E. ‖ See Note F.

equivalent to atheism.* As all devotional feelings have moral qualities for their sole object; as no being can inspire love or reverence otherwise than by those qualities which are naturally amiable or venerable, this doctrine would, if men were consistent, extinguish piety, or, in other words, annihilate Religion. Yet so astonishing are the contradictions of human nature, that this most impious of all opinions probably originated in a pious solicitude to magnify the Sovereignty of God, and to exalt His authority even above His own goodness. Hence we may understand its adoption by John Gerson, the oracle of the Council of Constance, and the great opponent of the spiritual monarchy of the Pope,—a pious mystic, who placed religion in devout feeling.† In further explanation, it may be added, that Gerson was of the sect of the Nominalists, of which Ockham was the founder, and that he was the more ready to follow his master, because they both courageously maintained the independence of the State on the Church, and the authority of the Church over the Pope. The general opinion of the schools was, however, that of Aquinas, who, from the native soundness of his own understanding, as well as from the excellent example of Aristotle, was averse from all rash and extreme dogmas on questions which had any relation, however distant, to the duties of life.

It is very remarkable, though hitherto unobserved, that Aquinas anticipated those controversies respecting perfect disinterestedness in the religious affections which occupied the most illustrious members of his communion‡ four hundred years after his death; and that he discussed the like question respecting the other affections of human nature with a fulness and clearness, an exactness of distinction, and a justness of determination, scarcely surpassed by the most acute of modern philosophers.§ It ought to be added, that, according to the most natural and reasonable construction of his words, he allowed to the Church a control only over spiritual concerns, and recognised the supremacy of the civil powers in all temporal affairs.‖

It has already been stated that the scholastic system was a collection of dialectical subtilties, contrived for the support of the corrupted Christianity of that age, by a succession of divines, whose extraordinary powers of distinction and reasoning were morbidly enlarged in the long meditation of the Cloister, by the exclusion of every other pursuit, and the consequent palsy of every other faculty;—who were cut off from all the materials on which the mind can operate, and doomed for ever to toil in defence of what they must never dare to examine;—to whom their age and their condition denied the means of acquiring literature, of observing Nature, or of studying mankind. The few in whom any portion of imagination and sensibility survived this discipline, retired from the noise of debate, to the contemplation of pure and beautiful visions. They were called Mystics. The greater part, driven back on themselves, had no better employment than to weave cobwebs out of the terms of art which they had vainly, though ingeniously, multiplied. The institution of clerical celibacy, originating in an enthusiastic pursuit of Purity, promoted by a mistake in moral prudence, which aimed at raising religious teachers in the esteem of their fellows, and at concentrating their whole minds on professional duties, at last encouraged by the ambitious policy of the See of Rome, which was desirous of detaching them from all ties but her own, had the effect of shutting up all the avenues which Providence has opened for the entrance of social affection and virtuous feeling into the human heart. Though this institution perhaps prevented Knowledge from becoming once more the exclusive inheritance of a sacerdotal caste; though the rise of innumerable laymen, of the lowest condition, to the highest dignities of the Church, was the grand democratical principle of the Middle Age, and one of the most powerful agents in impelling mankind towards a better order; yet celibacy must be considered as one of the peculiar infelicities of these secluded philosophers; not only as it abridged their happiness, nor even solely, though chiefly, as it excluded them from the school in which the heart is humanized, but also (an inferior consideration, but more pertinent to our present purpose) because the extinction of these moral feelings was as much a subtraction from the moralist's store of facts and means of knowledge, as the loss of sight or of touch could prove to those of the naturalist.

Neither let it be thought that to have been destitute of Letters was to them no more than a want of an ornament and a curtailment of gratification. Every poem, every history, every oration, every picture, every statue, is an experiment on human feeling,—the grand object of investigation by the moralist. Every work of genius in every department of ingenious Art and polite Literature, in proportion to the extent and duration of its sway over the Spirits of men, is a repository of ethical facts, of which the moral philosopher cannot be deprived by his own insensibility, or by the iniquity of the

* A passage to this effect, from Ockham, with nearly the same remark, has, since the text was written, been discovered on a reperusal of Cudworth's Immutable Morality, p. 10.

† "Remitto ad quod Occam de hâc materiâ in Lib. Sentent. dicit, in quâ explicatione si rudis judicetur, nescio quid appellabitur subtilitas."—De Vitâ Spirit. Op. iii. 14.

‡ Bossuet and Fenelon.

§ See Aquinas.—"Utrum Deus sit super omnia diligendus ex caritate."—"Utrum in dilectione Dei possit haberi respectus ad aliquam mercedem."—Opera, ix. 322, 325. Some illustrations of this memorable anticipation, which has escaped the research even of the industrious Tenneman, will be found in the Note G.

‖ See Note H.

times, without being robbed of the most precious instruments and invaluable materials of his science. Moreover, Letters, which are closer to human feeling than Science can ever be, have another influence on the sentiments with which the sciences are viewed, on the activity with which they are pursued, on the safety with which they are preserved, and even on the mode and spirit in which they are cultivated: they are the channels by which ethical science has a constant intercourse with general feeling. As the arts called useful maintain the popular honour of physical knowledge, so polite Letters allure the world into the neighbourhood of the sciences of Mind and of Morals. Whenever the agreeable vehicles of Literature do not convey their doctrines to the public, they are liable to be interrupted by the dispersion of a handful of recluse doctors, and the overthrow of their barren and unlamented seminaries. Nor is this all: these sciences themselves suffer as much when they are thus released from the curb of common sense and natural feeling, as the public loses by the want of those aids to right practice which moral knowledge in its sound state is qualified to afford. The necessity of being intelligible, at least to all persons who join superior understanding to habits of reflection, and who are themselves in constant communication with the far wider circle of intelligent and judicious men, which slowly but surely forms general opinion, is the only effectual check on the natural proneness of metaphysical speculations to degenerate into gaudy dreams, or a mere war of words. The disputants who are set free from the wholesome check of sense and feeling, generally carry their dogmatism so far as to rouse the sceptic, who from time to time is provoked to look into the flimsiness of their cobwebs, and rushes in with his besom to sweep them, and their systems, into oblivion. It is true, that Literature, which thus draws forth Moral Science from the schools into the world, and recalls her from thorny distinctions to her natural alliance with the intellect and sentiments of mankind, may, in ages and nations otherwise situated, produce the contrary evil of rendering Ethics shallow, declamatory, and inconsistent. Europe at this moment affords, in different countries, specimens of these opposite and alike-mischievous extremes. But we are now concerned only with the temptations and errors of the scholastic age.

We ought not so much to wonder at the mistakes of men so situated, as that they, without the restraints of the general understanding, and with the clogs of system and establishment, should in so many instances have opened questions untouched by the more unfettered Ancients, and veins of speculation since mistakenly supposed to have been first explored in more modern times. Scarcely any metaphysical controversy agitated among recent philosophers was unknown to the Schoolmen, unless we except that which relates to Liberty and Necessity, and this would be an exception of doubtful propriety; for the disposition to it is clearly discoverable in the disputes of the Thomists and Scotists respecting the Augustinian and Pelagian doctrines,* although they were restrained from the avowal of legitimate consequences on either side by the theological authority which both parties acknowledged. The Scotists steadily affirmed the blamelessness of erroneous opinion; a principle which is the only effectual security for conscientious inquiry, for mutual kindness, and for public quiet. The controversy between the Nominalists and Realists, treated by some modern writers as an example of barbarous wrangling, was in truth an anticipation of that modern dispute which still divides metaphysicians,—Whether the human mind can form general ideas, or Whether the words which are supposed to convey such ideas be not terms, representing only a number of particular perceptions?—questions so far from frivolous, that they deeply concern both the nature of reasoning and the structure of language; on which Hobbes, Berkeley, Hume, Stewart, and Tooke, have followed the Nominalist; and Descartes, Locke, Reid, and Kant have, with various modifications and some inconsistencies, adopted the doctrine of the Realists.† With the Schoolmen appears to have originated the form, though not the substance, of the celebrated maxim, which, whether true or false, is pregnant with systems,—"There is nothing in the Understanding which was not before in the Senses." Ockham‡ the Nominalist first denied the Peripatetic doctrine of the existence of certain species (since the time of Descartes called "ideas") as the direct objects of perception and thought, interposed between the mind and outward objects; the modern opposition to which by Dr. Reid has been supposed to justify the allotment of so high a station to that respectable philosopher. He taught also that we know nothing of Mind but its acts, of which we are conscious. More inclination towards an independent philosophy is to be traced among the Schoolmen than might be expected from their circumstances. Those who follow two guides will sometimes choose for themselves, and may prefer the subordinate one on some occasions. Aristotle rivalled the Church; and the Church herself safely allowed consider-

* See Note I.

† Locke speaks on this subject inconsistently; Reid calls himself a conceptualist; Kant uses terms so different, that he ought perhaps to be considered as of neither party. Leibnitz, varying in some measure from the general spirit of his speculations, warmly panegyrizes the Nominalists: "Secta Nominalium, omnium inter scholasticos profundissima, et hodiernæ reformatæ philosophandi rationi congruentissima."—Op. iv. 59.

‡ "Maximi vir ingenii, et eruditionis pro illo ævo summæ, Wilhelmus Occam, Anglus." Ib. 60. The writings of Ockham, which are very rare, I have never seen. I owe my knowledge of them to Tennemann, who however quotes the words of Ockham, and of his disciple Biel.

able latitude to the philosophical reasonings of those who were only heard or read in colleges or cloisters, on condition that they neither impugned her authority, nor dissented from her worship, nor departed from the language of her creeds. The Nominalists were a freethinking sect, who, notwithstanding their defence of kings against the Court of Rome, were persecuted by the civil power. It should not be forgotten that Luther was a Nominalist.*

If not more remarkable, it is more pertinent to our purpose, that the ethical system of the Schoolmen, or, to speak more properly, of Aquinas, as the Moral Master of Christendom for three centuries, was in its practical part so excellent as to leave little need of extensive changé, with the inevitable exception of the connection of his religious opinions with his precepts and counsels. His Rule of Life is neither lax nor impracticable. His grounds of duty are solely laid in the nature of man, and in the well-being of society. Such an intruder as Subtilty seldom strays into his moral instructions. With a most imperfect knowledge of the Peripatetic writings, he came near the Great Master, by abstaining, in practical philosophy, from the unsuitable exercise of that faculty of distinction, in which he would probably have shown that he was little inferior to Aristotle, if he had been equally unrestrained. His very frequent coincidence with modern moralists is doubtless to be ascribed chiefly to the nature of the subject; but in part also to that unbroken succession of teachers and writers, which preserved the observations contained in what had been long the text-book of the European Schools, after the books themselves had been for ages banished and forgotten. The praises bestowed on Aquinas by every one of the few great men who appear to have examined his writings since the downfal of his power, among whom may be mentioned Erasmus, Grotius, and Leibnitz, are chiefly, though not solely, referable to his ethical works.†

Though the Schoolmen had thus anticipated many modern controversies of a properly metaphysical sort, they left untouched most of those questions of ethical theory which were unknown to, or neglected by, the Ancients. They do not appear to have discriminated between the nature of moral sentiments, and the criterion of moral acts; to have considered to what faculty of our mind moral approbation is referable; or to have inquired whether our Moral Faculty, whatever it may be, is implanted or acquired. Those who measure only by palpable results, have very consistently regarded the metaphysical and theological controversies of the Schools as a mere waste of intellectual power. But the contemplation of the athletic vigour and versatile skill manifested by the European understanding, at the moment when it emerged from this tedious and rugged discipline, leads, if not to approbation, yet to more qualified censure. What might have been the result of a different combination of circumstances, is an inquiry which, on a large scale, is beyond human power. We may, however, venture to say that no abstract science, unconnected with Religion, is likely to be respected in a barbarous age; and we may be allowed to doubt whether any knowledge dependent directly on experience and applicable to immediate practice, would have so trained the European mind as to qualify it for that series of inventions, and discoveries, and institutions, which begins with the sixteenth century, and of which no end can now be foreseen but the extinction of the race of man.

The fifteenth century was occupied by the disputes of the Realists with the Nominalists, in which the scholastic doctrine expired. After its close no Schoolman of note appeared. The sixteenth may be considered as the age of transition from the scholastic to the modern philosophy. The former, indeed, retained possession of the Universities, and was long after distinguished by all the ensigns of authority. But the mines were already prepared: the revolution in Opinion had commenced. The moral writings of the preceding times had generally been commentaries on that part of the Summa Theologiæ of Aquinas which relates to Ethics. Though these still continued to be published, yet the most remarkable moralists of the sixteenth century indicated the approach of other modes of thinking, by the adoption of the more independent titles of "Treatises on Justice" and "Law." These titles were suggested, and the spirit, contents, and style of the writings themselves were materially affected by the improved cultivation of the Roman law, by the renewed study of ancient literature, and by the revival of various systems of Greek philosophy, now studied in the original, which at once mitigated and rivalled the scholastic doctors, and while they rendered philosophy more free, re-opened its communications with society and affairs. The speculative theology which had arisen under the French governments of Paris and London in the twelfth century, which flourished in the thirteenth in Italy in the hands of Aquinas, which was advanced in the British Islands by Scotus and Ockham in the fourteenth, was, in the sixteenth, with unabated acuteness, but with a clearness and elegance unknown before the restoration of Letters, cultivated by Spain, in that age the most powerful and magnificent of the European nations.

Many of these writers treated the law of war and the practice of hostilities in a juridical form.* Francis Victoria, who began to

* "In Martini Lutheri scriptis prioribus amor Nominalium satis elucet, donec procedente tempore erga omnes monachos æqualiter affectus esse cœpit."—Leibnitz, Opp. iv. 60.

† See especially the excellent Preface of Leibnitz to Nizolius, § 37.—Ib. 59.

* Many of the separate dissertations, on points of this nature, are contained in the immense collec-

teach at Valladolid in 1525, is said to have first expounded the doctrines of the Schools in the language of the age of Leo the Tenth. Dominic Soto,* a Dominican, the confessor of Charles V., and the oracle of the Council of Trent, to whom that assembly were indebted for much of the precision and even elegance for which their doctrinal decrees are not unjustly commended, dedicated his Treatise on Justice and Law to Don Carlos, in terms of praise which, used by a writer who is said to have declined the high dignities of the Church, led us to hope that he was unacquainted with the brutish vices of that wretched prince. It is a concise and not inelegant compound of the Scholastic Ethics, which continued to be of considerable authority for more than a century.† Both he and his master Victoria deserve to be had in everlasting remembrance, for the part which they took on behalf of the natives of America and of Africa, against the rapacity and cruelty of the Spaniards. Victoria pronounced war against the Americans for their vices, or for their paganism, to be unjust.‡ Soto was the authority chiefly consulted by Charles V., on occasion of the conference held before him at Valladolid, in 1542, between Sepulveda, an advocate of the Spanish colonists, and Las Casas, the champion of the unhappy Americans, of which the result was a very imperfect edict of reformation in 1543. This, though it contained little more than a recognition of the principle of justice, almost excited a rebellion in Mexico. Sepulveda, a scholar and a reasoner, advanced many maxims which were specious and in themselves reasonable, but which practically tended to defeat even the scanty and almost illusive reform which ensued. Las Casas was a passionate missionary, whose zeal, kindled by the long and near contemplation of cruelty, prompted him to exaggerations of fact and argument;§ yet, with all its errors, it afforded the only hope of preserving the natives of America from extirpation. The opinion of Soto could not fail to be conformable to his excellent principle, that "there can be no difference between Christians and pagans, for the law of nations is equal to all nations."* To Soto belongs the signal honour of being the first writer who condemned the African slave-trade. "It is affirmed," says he, "that the unhappy Ethiopians are by fraud or force carried away and sold as slaves. If this is true, neither those who have taken them, nor those who purchased them, nor those who hold them in bondage, can ever have a quiet conscience till they emancipate them, even if no compensation should be obtained."† As the work which contains this memorable condemnation of man-stealing and slavery was the substance of lectures for many years delivered at Salamanca, Philosophy and Religion appear, by the hand of their faithful minister, to have thus smitten the monsters in their earliest infancy. It is hard for any man of the present age to conceive the praise which is due to the excellent monks who courageously asserted the rights of those whom they never saw, against the prejudices of their order, the supposed interest of their religion, the ambition of their government, the avarice and pride of their countrymen, and the prevalent opinions of their time.

Francis Suarez,‡ a Jesuit, whose voluminous works amount to twenty-four volumes in folio, closes the list of writers of his class. His work on Laws and on God the Lawgiver, may be added to the above treatise of Soto, as exhibiting the most accessible and perspicuous abridgment of the theological philosophy in its latest form. Grotius, who, though he was the most upright and candid of men, could not have praised a Spanish Jesuit beyond his deserts, calls Suarez the most acute of philosophers and divines.§ On a practical matter, which may be naturally mentioned here, though in strict method it belongs to another subject, the merit of Suarez is conspicuous. He first saw that international law was composed not only of the simple principles of justice applied to the intercourse between states, but of those usages, long observed in that intercourse by the European race, which have since been more exactly distinguished as the consuetudinary law acknowledged by the Christian nations of Europe and America.‖ On

tion entitled "Tractatus Tractatuum," published at Venice in 1584, under the patronage of the Roman See. There are three De Bello; one by Lupus of Segovia, when Francis I. was prisoner in Spain; another, more celebrated, by Francis Arias, who, on the 11th June, 1532, discussed before the College of Cardinals the legitimacy of a war by the Emperor against the Pope. There are two De Pace; and others De Potestate Regiâ, De Pœnâ Mortis, &c. The most ancient and scholastic is that of J. de Lignano of Milan, De Bello. The above writers are mentioned in the prolegomena to Grotius, De Jure Belli. Pietro Belloni, Counsellor of the Duke of Savoy (De Re Militari), treats his subject with the minuteness of a Judge-Advocate, and has more modern examples, chiefly Italian, than Grotius.

* Born, 1494; died, 1560.—Antonii Bib. Hisp. Nov. The opinion of the extent of Soto's knowledge entertained by his contemporaries is expressed in a jingle, *Qui scit Sotum scit totum.*

† See Note K.

‡ "Indis non debere auferri imperium, ideo quia sunt peccatores, vel ideo quia non sunt Christiani," were the words of Victoria.

§ See Note L.

* "Neque discrepantia (ut reor) est inter Christianos et infideles, quoniam jus gentium cunctis gentibus æquale est."

† De Just. et Jure, lib. iv. quæst. ii. art. 2.

‡ Born, 1538; died, 1617.

§ "Tantæ subtilitatis philosophum et theologum, ut vix quemquam habeat parem."—Grotii Epist. apud Anton. Bib. Hisp. Nov.

‖ "Nunquam enim civitates sunt sibi tam sufficientes quin indigeant mutuo juvamine et societate, interdum ad majorem utilitatem, interdum ob necessitatem moralem. Hâc igitur ratione indigent aliquo jure quo dirigantur et recte ordinentur in hoc genere societatis. Et quamvis magnâ ex parte hoc fiat per rationem naturalem, non

this important point his views are more clear than those of his contemporary Alberico Gentili.* It must even be owned, that the succeeding intimation of the same general doctrine by Grotius is somewhat more dark,—perhaps from his excessive pursuit of concise diction.†

SECTION IV.

MODERN ETHICS.

GROTIUS—HOBBES.

The introduction to the great work of Grotius,‡ composed in the first years of his exile, and published at Paris in 1625, contains the most clear and authentic statement of the general principles of Morals prevalent in Christendom after the close of the Schools, and before the writings of Hobbes had given rise to those ethical controversies which more peculiarly belong to modern times. That he may lay down the fundamental principles of Ethics, he introduces Carneades on the stage as denying altogether the reality of moral distinctions; teaching that law and morality are contrived by powerful men for their own interest; that they vary in different countries, and change in successive ages; that there can be no natural law, since Nature leads men as well as other animals to prefer their own interest to every other object; that, therefore, there is either no justice, or if there be, it is another name for the height of folly, inasmuch as it is a fond attempt to persuade a human being to injure himself for the unnatural purpose of benefitting his fellow-men.§ To this Grotius answered, that even inferior animals, under the powerful, though transient, impulse of parental love, prefer their young to their own safety or life; that gleams of compassion, and, he might have added, of gratitude and indignation, appear in the human infant long before the age of moral discipline; that man at the period of maturity is a social animal, who delights in the society of his fellow-creatures for its own sake, independently of the help and accommodation which it yields; that he is a reasonable being, capable of framing and pursuing general rules of conduct, of which he discerns that the observance contributes to a regular, quiet, and happy intercourse between all the members of the community; and that from these considerations all the precepts of Morality, and all the commands and prohibitions of just Law, may be derived by impartial Reason. "And these principles," says the pious philosopher, "would have their weight, even if it were to be granted (which could not be conceded without the highest impiety) that there is no God, or that He exercises no moral government over human affairs."*—"Natural law is the dictate of right Reason, pronouncing that there is in some actions a moral obligation, and in other actions a moral deformity, arising from their respective suitableness or repugnance to the reasonable and social nature; and that consequently such acts are either forbidden or enjoined by God, the Author of Nature.—Actions which are the subject of this exertion of Reason, are in themselves lawful or unlawful, and are therefore, as such, necessarily commanded or prohibited by God."

Such was the state of opinion respecting the first principles of the moral sciences, when, after an imprisonment of a thousand years in the Cloister, they began once more to hold intercourse with the general understanding of mankind. It will be seen in the laxity and confusion, as well as in the prudence and purity of this exposition, that some part of the method and precision of the Schools was lost with their endless subtilties and their barbarous language. It is manifest that the latter paragraph is a proposition,—not, what it affects to be, a definition; that as a proposition it contains too many terms very necessary to be defined; that the purpose of the excellent writer is not so much to lay down a first principle of Morals, as to exert his unmatched power of saying much in few words, in order to assemble within the smallest compass the most weighty inducements, and the most effectual persuasions to well-doing.

This was the condition in which ethical theory was found by Hobbes, with whom the present Dissertation should have commenced, if it had been possible to state modern controversies in a satisfactory manner, without a retrospect of the revolutions in Opinion from which they in some measure flowed.

HOBBES.†

Thomas Hobbes of Malmesbury may be numbered among those eminent persons born

---

tamen sufficienter et immediatè quoad omnia, *ideoque specialia jura poterant usu earundem gentium introduci.*"—De Leg., lib. ii. cap. ii.

* Born in the March of Ancona, 1550; died at London, 1608.

† De Jur. Bell., lib. i. cap. i. § 14.

‡ Prolegomena. His letter to Vossius, of 1st August, 1625, determines the exact period of the publication of this famous work.—Epist. 74.

§ The same commonplace paradoxes were retailed by the Sophists, whom Socrates is introduced as chastising in the Dialogues of Plato. They were common enough to be put by the Historian into the mouth of an ambassador in a public speech. Ἀνδρὶ δὲ τυράννῳ ἢ πόλει ἀρχὴν ἐχούσῃ οὐδὲν ἄλογον ὅ τι ξυμφέρον. Thucyd. lib. vi. cap. 85.

* "Et hæc quidem locum aliquem haberent, etiamsi daretur (quod sine summo scelere dari nequit) non esse Deum, aut non curari ab eo negotia humana."—Proleg. 11. And in another place, "Jus naturale est dictatum rectæ rationis, indicans actui alicui, ex ejus convenientia aut disconvenientia cum ipsa natura rationali et sociali, inesse moralem turpitudinem aut necessitatem, moralem, ac consequenter ab auctore naturæ Deo talem actum aut vetari aut præcipi." "Actus de quibus tale exstat dictatum, debiti sunt aut illiciti per se, atque ideo a Deo necessario præcepti aut vetiti intelliguntur."—De Jur. Bell. lib. i. cap. i. § 10.

† Born, 1588; died 1679.

in the latter half of the sixteenth century, who gave a new character to European philosophy, in the succeeding age.* He was one of the late writers and late learners. It was not till he was nearly thirty that he supplied the defects of his early education, by classical studies so successfully prosecuted, that he wrote well in the Latin then used by his scientific contemporaries; and made such proficiency in Greek as, in his earliest work, the Translation of Thucydides, published when he was forty, to afford a specimen of a version still valued for its remarkable fidelity, though written with a stiffness and constraint very opposite to the masterly facility of his original compositions. It was after forty that he learned the first rudiments of Geometry (so miserably defective was his education); but yielding to the paradoxical disposition apt to infect those who begin to learn after the natural age of commencement, he exposed himself, by absurd controversies with the masters of a Science which looks down with scorn on the sophist. A considerable portion of his mature age was passed on the Continent, where he travelled as tutor to two successive Earls of Devonshire;—a family with whom he seems to have passed near half a century of his long life. In France his reputation, founded at that time solely on personal intercourse, became so great, that his observations on the meditations of Descartes were published in the works of that philosopher, together with those of Gassendi and Arnauld.† It was about his sixtieth year that he began to publish those philosophical writings which contain his peculiar opinions;—which set the understanding of Europe into general motion, and stirred up controversies among metaphysicians and moralists, not even yet determined. At the age of eighty-seven he had the boldness to publish metrical versions of the Iliad and Odyssey, which the greatness of his name, and the singularity of the undertaking, still render objects of curiosity, if not of criticism.

He owed his influence to various causes; at the head of which may be placed that genius for system, which, though it cramps the growth of Knowledge,‡ perhaps finally atones for that mischief, by the zeal and activity which it rouses among followers and opponents, who discover truth by accident, when in pursuit of weapons for their warfare. A system which attempts a task so hard as that of subjecting vast provinces of human knowledge to one or two principles, if it presents some striking instances of conformity to superficial appearances, is sure to delight the framer, and, for a time, to subdue and captivate the student too entirely for sober reflection and rigorous examination. The evil does not, indeed, very frequently recur. Perhaps Aristotle, Hobbes, and Kant, are the only persons who united in the highest degree the great faculties of comprehension and discrimination which compose the *Genius of System*. Of the three, Aristotle alone could throw it off where it was glaringly unsuitable; and it is deserving of observation, that the reign of system seems, from these examples, progressively to shorten in proportion as Reason is cultivated and Knowledge advances. But, in the first instance, consistency passes for Truth. When principles in some instances have proved sufficient to give an unexpected explanation of facts, the delighted reader is content to accept as true all other deductions from the principles. Specious premises being assumed to be true, nothing more can be required than logical inference. Mathematical forms pass current as the equivalent of mathematical certainty. The unwary admirer is satisfied with the completeness and symmetry of the plan of his house,—unmindful of the need of examining the firmness of the foundation, and the soundness of the materials. The system-maker, like the conqueror, long dazzles and overawes the world; but when their sway is past, the vulgar herd, unable to measure their astonishing faculties, take revenge by trampling on fallen greatness.

The dogmatism of Hobbes was, however unjustly, one of the sources of his fame. The founders of systems deliver their novelties with the undoubting spirit of discoverers; and their followers are apt to be dogmatical, because they can see nothing beyond their own ground. It might seem incredible, if it were not established by the experience of all ages, that those who differ most from the opinions of their fellow-men are most confident of the truth of their own. But it commonly requires an overweening conceit of the superiority of a man's own judgment, to make him espouse very singular notions; and when he has once embraced them, they are endeared to him by the hostility of those whom he contemns as the prejudiced vulgar. The temper of Hobbes must have been originally haughty. The advanced age at which he published his obnoxious opinions,

* Bacon, Descartes, Hobbes, and Grotius. The writings of the first are still as delightful and wonderful as they ever were, and his authority will have no end. Descartes forms an era in the history of Metaphysics, of Physics, of Mathematics. The controversies excited by Grotius have long ceased, but the powerful influence of his works will be doubted by those only who are unacquainted with the disputes of the seventeenth century.

† The prevalence of freethinking under Louis XIII., to a far greater degree than it was avowed, appears not only from the complaints of Mersenne and of Grotius, but from the disclosures of Guy Patin; who, in his Letters, describes his own conversations with Gassendi and Naude, so as to leave no doubt of their opinions.

‡ "Another error," says the Master of Wisdom, "is the over-early and peremptory reduction of knowledge into arts and methods, from which time commonly receives small augmentation."—Advancement of Learning, book i. "Method," says he, "carrying a show of total and perfect knowledge, has a tendency to generate acquiescence." What pregnant words!

rendered him more impatient of the acrimonious opposition which they necessarily provoked; until at length a strong sense of the injustice of the punishment impending over his head, for the publication of what he believed to be truth, co-operated with the peevishness and timidity of his years, to render him the most imperious and morose of dogmatists. His dogmatism has indeed one quality more offensive than that of most others. Propositions the most adverse to the opinions of mankind, and the most abhorrent from their feelings, are introduced into the course of his argument with mathematical coldness. He presents them as demonstrated conclusions, without deigning to explain to his fellow-creatures how they all happened to believe the opposite absurdities, and without even the compliment of once observing how widely his discoveries were at variance with the most ancient and universal judgments of the human understanding. The same quality in Spinoza indicates a recluse's ignorance of the world. In Hobbes it is the arrogance of a man who knows mankind and despises them.

A permanent foundation of his fame remains in his admirable style, which seems to be the very perfection of didactic language. Short, clear, precise, pithy, his language never has more than one meaning, which it never requires a second thought to find. By the help of his exact method, it takes so firm a hold on the mind, that it will not allow attention to slacken. His little tract on Human Nature has scarcely an ambiguous or a needless word. He has so great a power of always choosing the most significant term, that he never is reduced to the poor expedient of using many in its stead. He had so thoroughly studied the genius of the language, and knew so well how to steer between pedantry and vulgarity, that two centuries have not superannuated probably more than a dozen of his words. His expressions are so luminous, that he is clear without the help of illustration. Perhaps no writer of any age or nation, on subjects so abstruse, has manifested an equal power of engraving his thoughts on the mind of his readers. He seems never to have taken a word for ornament or pleasure; and he deals with eloquence and poetry as the natural philosopher who explains the mechanism of children's toys, or deigns to contrive them. Yet his style so stimulates attention, that it never tires; and, to those who are acquainted with the subject, appears to have as much spirit as can be safely blended with Reason. He compresses his thoughts so unaffectedly, and yet so tersely, as to produce occasionally maxims which excite the same agreeable surprise with wit, and have become a sort of philosophical proverbs;—the success of which he partly owed to the suitableness of such forms of expression to his dictatorial nature. His words have such an appearance of springing from his thoughts, as to impress on the reader a strong opinion of his originality, and indeed to prove that he was not conscious of borrowing: though conversation with Gassendi must have influenced his mind; and it is hard to believe that his coincidence with Ockham should have been purely accidental, on points so important as the denial of general ideas, the reference of moral distinctions to superior power, and the absolute thraldom of Religion under the civil power, which he seems to have thought necessary, to maintain that independence of the State on the Church with which Ockham had been contented.

His philosophical writings might be read without reminding any one that the author was more than an intellectual machine. They never betray a feeling except that insupportable arrogance which looks down on his fellow-men as a lower species of beings; whose almost unanimous hostility is so far from shaking the firmness of his conviction, or even ruffling the calmness of his contempt, that it appears too petty a circumstance to require explanation, or even to merit notice. Let it not be forgotten, that part of his renown depends on the application of his admirable powers to expound Truth when he meets it. This great merit is conspicuous in that part of his treatise of Human Nature which relates to the percipient and reasoning faculties. It is also very remarkable in many of his *secondary* principles on the subject of Government and Law, which, while the *first* principles are false and dangerous, are as admirable for truth as for his accustomed and unrivalled propriety of expression.* In many of these observations he even shows a disposition to soften his paradoxes, and to conform to the common sense of mankind.†

It was with perfect truth observed by my excellent friend Mr. Stewart, that "the ethical principles of Hobbes are completely interwoven with his political system."‡ He might have said, that the whole of Hobbes' system, moral, religious, and in part philosophical, depended on his political scheme; not indeed logically, as conclusions depend upon premises, but (if the word may be excused) *psychologically*, as the formation of one opinion may be influenced by a disposition to adapt it to others previously cherished. The Translation of Thucydides, as he him-

* See De Corpore Politico, Part i. chap. ii. iii. iv. and Leviathan, Part i. chap. xiv. xv. for remarks of this sort, full of sagacity.

† "The laws of Nature are *immutable and eternal;* for injustice, ingratitude, arrogance, pride, iniquity, acception of persons, and the rest, can never be made lawful. For it can never be that war shall preserve life, and peace destroy it."—*Leviathan*, Part i. chap. xv.—See also Part ii. chap. xxvi. xxviii. on Laws, and on Punishments.

‡ See Encyc. Brit. i. 42. The political state of England is indeed said by himself to have occasioned his first philosophical publication.

Nascitur interea scelus execrabile belli.
. . . . Horreo spectans,
Meque ad dilectam confero Lutetiam,
Postque duos annos edo De Cive Libellum.

self boasts, was published to show the evils of popular government.* Men he represented as being originally equal, and having an equal right to all things, but as being taught by Reason to sacrifice this right for the advantages of peace, and to submit to a common authority, which can preserve quiet, only by being the sole depositary of force, and must therefore be absolute and unlimited. The supreme authority cannot be sufficient for its purpose, unless it be wielded by a single hand; nor even then, unless his absolute power extends over Religion, which may prompt men to discord by the fear of an evil greater than death. The perfect state of a community, according to him, is where Law prescribes the religion and morality of the people, and where the will of an absolute sovereign is the sole fountain of law. Hooker had inculcated the simple truth, that "to live by one man's will is the cause of many men's misery:"—Hobbes embraced the daring paradox, that to live by one man's will is the only means of all men's happiness. Having thus rendered Religion the slave of every human tyrant, it was an unavoidable consequence, that he should be disposed to lower her character, and lessen her power over men; that he should regard atheism as the most effectual instrument of preventing rebellion,—at least that species of rebellion which prevailed in his time, and had excited his alarms. The formidable alliance of Religion with Liberty haunted his mind, and urged him to the bold attempt of rooting out both these mighty principles; which, when combined with interests and passions, when debased by impure support, and provoked by unjust resistance, have indeed the power of fearfully agitating society; but which are, nevertheless, in their own nature, and as far as they are unmixed and undisturbed, the parents of Justice, of Order, of Peace, as well as the sources of those hopes, and of those glorious aspirations after higher excellence, which encourage and exalt the Soul in its passage through misery and depravity. A Hobbist is the only consistent persecutor; for he alone considers himself as bound, by whatever conscience he has remaining, to conform to the religion of the sovereign. He claims from others no more than he is himself ready to yield to any master;† while the religionist who persecutes a member of another communion, exacts the sacrifice of conscience and sincerity, though professing that rather than make it himself, he is prepared to die.

REMARKS.

The fundamental errors on which the ethical system of Hobbes is built are not peculiar to him; though he has stated them with a bolder precision, and placed them in a more conspicuous station in the van of his main force, than any other of those who have either frankly avowed, or tacitly assumed, them, from the beginning of speculation to the present moment. They may be shortly stated as follows:

1. The first and most inveterate of these errors is, that he does not distinguish *thought* from *feeling*, or rather that he in express words confounds them. The mere *perception* of an object, according to him, differs from the *pleasure* or *pain* which that perception may occasion, no otherwise than as they affect different organs of the bodily frame. The action of the mind in perceiving or conceiving an object is precisely the same with that of feeling the agreeable or disagreeable.* The necessary result of this original confusion is, to extend the laws of the intellectual part of our nature over that other part of it, (hitherto without any adequate name,) which feels, and desires, and loves, and hopes, and wills. In consequence of this long confusion, or want of distinction, it has happened that, while the simplest act of the merely intellectual part has many names (such as "sensation," "perception," "impression," &c.), the correspondent act of the other not less important portion of man is not denoted by a technical term in philosophical systems; nor by a convenient word in common language. "Sensation" has another more com-

---

* The conference between the ministers from Athens and the Melean chiefs, in the 5th book, and the speech of Euphemus in the 6th book of that historian, exhibit an undisguised *Hobbism*, which was very dramatically put into the mouth of Athenian statesmen at a time when, as we learn from Plato and Aristophanes, it was preached by the Sophists.

† Spinoza adopted precisely the same first principle with Hobbes, that all men have a natural right to all things.—Tract. Theol. Pol. cap. ii. § 3. He even avows the absurd and detestable maxim, that states are not bound to observe their treaties longer than the interest or danger which first formed the treaties continues. But on the internal constitution of states he embraces opposite opinions. Servitutis *enim, non pacis, interest omnem potestatem ad unum transferre.*—(Ibid. cap. vi. § 4.) Limited monarchy he considers as the only tolerable example of that species of government. An aristocracy nearly approaching to the Dutch system during the suspension of the Stadtholdership, he seems to prefer. He speaks favourably of democracy, but the chapter on that subject is left unfinished. "Nulla plane templa urbium sumptibus ædificanda, nec jura de opinionibus statuenda." He was the first republican atheist of modern times, and probably the earliest irreligious opponent of an ecclesiastical establishment.

* This doctrine is explained in his tract on Human Nature, c. vii. "*Conception* is a motion in some internal substance of the head, which proceeding to the heart, where it helpeth the motion there, is called *pleasure;* when it weakeneth or hindereth the motion, it is called *pain.*" The same matter is handled more cursorily, agreeably to the practical purpose of the work, in Leviathan, part i. chap. vi. These passages are here referred to as proofs of the statement in the text. With the materialism of it we have here no concern. If the multiplied suppositions were granted, we should not advance one step towards understanding what they profess to explain. The first four words are as unmeaning as if one were to say that greenness is very loud. It is obvious that many motions which promote the motion of the heart are extremely painful.

mon sense; "Emotion" is too warm for a generic term; "Feeling" has some degree of the same fault, besides its liability to confusion with the sense of touch; "Pleasure" and "Pain" represent only two properties of this act, which render its repetition the object of desire or aversion;—which last states of mind presuppose the act. Of these words, "Emotion" seems to be the least objectionable, since it has no absolute double meaning, and does not require so much vigilance in the choice of the accompanying words as would be necessary if we were to prefer "Feeling;" which, however, being a more familiar word, may, with due caution, be also sometimes employed. Every man who attends to the state of his own mind will acknowledge, that these words, "Emotion" and "Feeling," thus used, are perfectly simple, and as incapable of further explanation by words as sight and hearing; which may, indeed, be rendered into synonymous words, but never can be defined by any more simple or more clear. Reflection will in like manner teach that perception, reasoning, and judgment may be conceived to exist without being followed by emotion. Some men hear music without gratification: one may distinguish a taste without being pleased or displeased by it; or at least the relish or disrelish is often so slight, without lessening the distinctness of the sapid qualities, that the distinction of it from the perception cannot be doubted.

The multiplicity of errors which have flowed into moral science from this original confusion is very great. They have spread over many schools of philosophy; and many of them are prevalent to this day. Hence the laws of the Understanding have been applied to the Affections; virtuous feelings have been considered as just reasonings; evil passions have been represented as mistaken judgments; and it has been laid down as a principle, that the Will always follows the last decision of the Practical Intellect.*

2. By this great error, Hobbes was led to represent all the variety of the desires of men, as being only so many instances of objects deliberately and solely pursued; because they were the means, and at the time perceived to be so, of directly or indirectly procuring organic gratification to the individual.† The human passions are described as if they reasoned accurately, deliberated coolly, and calculated exactly. It is assumed that, in performing these operations, there is and can be no act of life in which a man does not bring distinctly before his eyes the pleasure which is to accrue to himself from the act. From this single and simple principle, all human conduct may, according to him, be explained and even foretold. The true laws of this part of our nature (so totally different from those of the percipient part) were, by this grand mistake, entirely withdrawn from notice. Simple as the observation is, it seems to have escaped not only Hobbes, but many, perhaps most, philosophers, that our desires seek a great diversity of objects; that the attainment of these objects is indeed followed by, or rather called "Pleasure;" but that it could not be so, if the objects had not been previously desired. Many besides him have really represented *self* as the ultimate object of every action; but none ever so hardily thrust forward the selfish system in its harshest and coarsest shape. The mastery which he shows over other metaphysical subjects, forsakes him on this. He does not scruple, for the sake of this system, to distort facts of which all men are conscious, and to do violence to the language in which the result of their uniform experience is conveyed. "Acknowledgment of power is called Honour."* His explanations are frequently sufficient confutations of the doctrine which required them. "Pity is the imagination of future calamity to ourselves, proceeding from the sense (observation) of another man's calamity." "Laughter is occasioned by sudden glory in our eminence, or in comparison with the infirmity of others." Every man who ever wept or laughed, may determine whether this be a true account of the state of his mind on either occasion. "Love is a conception of his need of the one person desired;"— a definition of Love, which, as it excludes kindness, might perfectly well comprehend the hunger of a cannibal, provided that it were not too ravenous to exclude choice. "Goodwill, or charity, which containeth the natural affection of parents to their children, consists in a man's conception that he is able not only to accomplish his own desires, but to assist other men in theirs:" from which it follows, as the pride of power is felt in destroying as well as in saving men, that cruelty and kindness are the same passion.† Such were the expedients to which a man of the highest class of understanding was driven, in order to evade the admission of the simple and evident truth, that there are in our nature perfectly disinterested passions, which seek the well-being of others as their object and end, without looking beyond it to self, or pleasure, or happiness. A proposition, from which such a man could attempt to escape only by such means, may be strongly presumed to be true.

3. Hobbes having thus struck the affections out of his map of human nature, and having totally misunderstood (as will appear

* "Voluntas semper sequitur ultimum judicium intellectûs practici."—[See Spinozæ Cog. Met. pars. ii. cap. 12. Ed.]

† See the passages before quoted.

* Human Nature, chap. viii. The ridiculous explanation of the admiration of personal beauty, "as a sign of power generative," shows the difficulties to which this extraordinary man was reduced by a false system.

† Ibid. chap. ix. I forbear to quote the passage on Platonic love, which immediately follows: but, considering Hobbes' blameless and honourable character, that passage is perhaps the most remarkable instance of the shifts to which his selfish system reduced him.

in a succeeding part of this Dissertation) the nature even of the appetites, it is no wonder that we should find in it not a trace of the moral sentiments. Moral Good* he considers merely as consisting in the signs of a power to produce pleasure; and repentance is no more than regret at having missed the way: so that, according to this system, a disinterested approbation of, and reverence for Virtue, are no more possible than disinterested affections towards our fellow-creatures. There is no sense of duty, no compunction for our own offences, no indignation against the crimes of others,—unless they affect our own safety;—no secret cheerfulness shed over the heart by the practice of well-doing. From his philosophical writings it would be impossible to conclude that there are in man a set of emotions, desires, and aversions, of which the sole and final objects are the voluntary actions and habitual dispositions of himself and of all other voluntary agents; which are properly called "moral sentiments;" and which, though they vary more in degree, and depend more on cultivation, than some other parts of human nature, are as seldom as most of them found to be entirely wanting.

4. A theory of Man which comprehends in its explanations neither the social affections, nor the moral sentiments, must be owned to be sufficiently defective. It is a consequence, or rather a modification of it, that Hobbes should constantly represent the deliberate regard to personal advantage, as the only possible motive of human action; and that he should altogether disdain to avail himself of those refinements of the selfish scheme which allow the pleasures of benevolence and of morality, themselves, to be a most important part of that interest which reasonable beings pursue.

5. Lastly, though Hobbes does in effect acknowledge the necessity of Morals to society, and the general coincidence of individual with public interest—truths so palpable that they have never been excluded from any ethical system, he betrays his utter want of moral sensibility by the coarse and odious form in which he has presented the first of these great principles; and his view of both leads him most strongly to support that common and pernicious error of moral reasoners, that a perception of the tendency of good actions to preserve the being and promote the well-being of the community, and a sense of the dependence of our own happiness upon the general security, either are essential constituents of our moral feelings, or are ordinarily mingled with the most effectual motives to right conduct.

The court of Charles II. were equally pleased with Hobbes' poignant brevity, and his low estimate of human motives. His ethical epigrams became the current coin of profligate wits. Sheffield, Duke of Buckinghamshire, who represented the class still more perfectly in his morals than in his faculties, has expressed their opinion in verses, of which one line is good enough to be quoted:

"Fame bears no fruit till the vain planter dies."

Dryden speaks of the "philosopher and *poet* (for such is the condescending term employed) of Malmesbury," as resembling Lucretius in haughtiness. But Lucretius, though he held many of the opinions of Hobbes, had the sensibility as well as genius of a poet. His dogmatism is full of enthusiasm; and his philosophical theory of society discovers occasionally as much tenderness as can be shown without reference to individuals. He was a Hobbist in only half his nature.

The moral and political system of Hobbes was a palace of ice, transparent, exactly proportioned, majestic, admired by the unwary as a delightful dwelling; but gradually undermined by the central warmth of human feeling, before it was thawed into muddy water by the sunshine of true Philosophy.

When Leibnitz, in the beginning of the eighteenth century, reviewed the moral writers of modern times, his penetrating eye saw only two who were capable of reducing Morals and Jurisprudence to a science. "So great an enterprise," says he, "might have been executed by the deep-searching genius of Hobbes, if he had not set out from evil principles; or by the judgment and learning of the incomparable Grotius, if his powers had not been scattered over many subjects, and his mind distracted by the cares of an agitated life."* Perhaps in this estimate, admiration of the various and excellent qualities of Grotius may have overrated his purely philosophical powers, great as they unquestionably were. Certainly the failure of Hobbes was owing to no inferiority in strength of intellect. Probably his fundamental errors may be imputed, in part, to the faintness of his moral sensibilities, insufficient to make him familiar with those sentiments and affections which can be known only by being felt;—a faintness perfectly compatible with his irreproachable life, but which obstructed, and at last obliterated, the only channel through which the most important materials of ethical science enter into the mind.

Against Hobbes, says Warburton, the whole Church militant took up arms. The answers to the Leviathan would form a library. But the far greater part would have followed the fate of all controversial pamphlets. Sir Robert Filmer was jealous of any rival theory of servitude: Harrington defended Liberty, and Clarendon the Church, against

* Which he calls the "pulchrum," for want, as he says, of an English word to express it.—Leviathan, part. i. c. vi.

* "Et tale aliquid potuisset, vel ab incomparabilis Grotii judicio et doctrina, vel à profundo Hobbii ingenio præstari; nisi illum multa distraxissent; hic verò prava constituisset principia." Leib. Op. iv. pars. iii. 276.

a common enemy. His philosophical antagonists were, Cumberland, Cudworth, Shaftesbury, Clarke, Butler, and Hutcheson. Though the last four writers cannot be considered as properly polemics, their labours were excited, and their doctrines modified, by the stroke from a vigorous arm which seemed to shake Ethics to its foundation. They lead us far into the eighteenth century; and their works, occasioned by the doctrines of Hobbes, sowed the seed of the ethical writings of Hume, Smith, Price, Kant, and Stewart; in a less degree, also, of those of Tucker and Paley:—not to mention Mandeville, the buffoon and sophister of the alehouse, or Helvetius, an ingenious but flimsy writer, the low and loose Moralist of the vain, the selfish, and the sensual.

SECTION V.

CONTROVERSIES CONCERNING THE MORAL FACULTIES AND THE SOCIAL AFFECTIONS.

CUMBERLAND—CUDWORTH—CLARKE—SHAFTESBURY—BOSSUET—FENELON—LEIBNITZ—MALEBRANCHE—EDWARDS—BUFFIER.

Dr. Richard Cumberland,* raised to the See of Peterborough after the Revolution of 1688, was the only professed answerer of Hobbes. His work On the Laws of Nature still retains a place on the shelf, though not often on the desk. The philosophical epigrams of Hobbes form a contrast to the verbose, prolix, and languid diction of his answerer. The forms of scholastic argument serve more to encumber his style, than to insure his exactness. But he has substantial merits. He justly observes, that all men can only be said to have had originally a right to all things, in a sense in which "right" has the same meaning with "power." He shows that Hobbes is at variance with himself, inasmuch as the dictates of Right Reason, which, by his own statement, teach men for their own safety to forego the exercise of that right, and which he calls "laws of Nature," are coeval with it; and that mankind perceive the moral limits of their power as clearly and as soon as they are conscious of its existence. He enlarges the intimations of Grotius on the social feelings, which prompt men to the pleasures of pacific intercourse, as certainly as the apprehension of danger and of destruction urges them to avoid hostility. The fundamental principle of his system of Ethics is, that "the greatest benevolence of every rational agent to all others is the happiest state of each individual, as well as of the whole."† The happiness accruing to each man from the observance and cultivation of benevolence, he considers as appended to it by the Supreme Ruler; through which He sanctions it as His law, and reveals it to the mind of every reasonable creature. From this principle he deduces the rules of Morality, which he calls the "laws of Nature." The surest, or rather the only mark that they are the commandments of God, is, that their observance promotes the happiness of man: for that reason alone could they be imposed by that Being whose essence is Love. As our moral faculties must to us be the measure of all moral excellence, he infers that the moral attributes of the Divinity must in their nature be only a transcendent degree of those qualities which we most approve, love, and revere, in those moral agents with whom we are familiar.* He had a momentary glimpse of the possibility that some human actions might be performed with a view to the happiness of others, without any consideration of the pleasure reflected back on ourselves.† But it is too faint and transient to be worthy of observation, otherwise than as a new proof how often great truths must flit before the Understanding, before they can be firmly and finally held in its grasp. His only attempt to explain the nature of the Moral Faculty, is the substitution of Practical Reason (a phrase of the Schoolmen, since become celebrated from its renewal by Kant) for Right Reason;‡ and his definition of the first, as that which points out the ends and means of action. Throughout his whole reasoning, he adheres to the accustomed confusion of the equality which renders actions virtuous, with the sentiments excited in us by the contemplation of them. His language on the identity of general and individual interest is extremely vague; though it be, as he says, the foundation-stone of the Temple of Concord among men.

It is little wonderful that Cumberland should not have disembroiled this ancient and established confusion, since Leibnitz himself, in a passage where he reviews the theories of Morals which had gone before him, has done his utmost to perpetuate it. "It is a question," says the latter, "whether the preservation of human society be the first principle of the law of Nature. This our author denies, in opposition to Grotius, who laid down sociability to be so;—to Hobbes, who ascribed that character to mutual fear; and to Cumberland, who held that it was mutual benevolence; which are all three only different names for the safety and wel-

---

* Born, 1632; died, 1718.

† De Leg. Nat. chap. i. § 12, first published in London, 1672, and then so popular as to be reprinted at Lubeck in 1683.

* Ibid. cap. v. § 19. † Ibid. cap. ii. § 20.

‡ "Whoever determines his Judgment and his Will by Right Reason, must agree with all others who judge according to Right Reason in the same matter."—Ibid. cap. ii. § 8. This is in one sense only a particular instance of the identical proposition, that two things which agree with a third thing must agree with each other in that, in which they agree with the third. But the difficulty entirely consists in the particular third thing here introduced, namely, "Right Reason," the nature of which not one step is made to explain. The position is curious, as coinciding with "the universal categorical imperative," adopted as a first principle by Kant.

fare of society."* Here the great philosopher considered benevolence or fear, two feelings of the human mind, to be the first principles of the law of Nature, in the same sense in which the tendency of certain actions to the well-being of the community may be so regarded. The confusion, however, was then common to him with many, as it even now is with most. The comprehensive view was his own. He perceived the close resemblance of these various, and even conflicting opinions, in that important point of view in which they relate to the effects of moral and immoral actions on the general interest. The tendency of Virtue to preserve amicable intercourse was enforced by Grotius; its tendency to prevent injury was dwelt on by Hobbes; its tendency to promote an interchange of benefits was inculcated by Cumberland.

CUDWORTH.†

Cudworth, one of the eminent men educated or promoted in the English Universities during the Puritan rule, was one of the most distinguished of the Latitudinarian, or Arminian, party who came forth at the Restoration, with a love of Liberty imbibed from their Calvinistic masters, as well as from the writings of antiquity, yet tempered by the experience of their own agitated age; and with a spirit of religious toleration more impartial and mature, though less systematic and professedly comprehensive, than that of the Independents, the first sect who preached that doctrine. Taught by the errors of their time, they considered Religion as consisting, not in vain efforts to explain unsearchable mysteries, but in purity of heart exalted by pious feelings, manifested by virtuous conduct.‡ The government of the Church was placed in their hands by the Revolution, and their influence was long felt among its rulers and luminaries. The first generation of their scholars turned their attention too much from the cultivation of the heart to the mere government of outward action: and in succeeding times the tolerant spirit, not natural to an establishment, was with difficulty kept up by a government whose existence depended on discouraging intolerant pretensions. No sooner had the first sketch of the Hobbian philosophy* been privately circulated at Paris, than Cudworth seized the earliest opportunity of sounding the alarm against the most justly odious of the modes of thinking which it cultivates, or forms of expression which it would introduce;†—the prelude to a war which occupied the remaining forty years of his life. The Intellectual System, his great production, is directed against the atheistical opinions of Hobbes: it touches ethical questions but occasionally and incidentally. It is a work of stupendous erudition, of much more acuteness than at first appears, of frequent mastery over diction and illustration on subjects where it is most rare; and it is distinguished, perhaps beyond any other volume of controversy, by that best proof of the deepest conviction of the truth of a man's principles, a fearless statement of the most formidable objections to them;—a fairness rarely practised but by him who is conscious of his power to answer them. In all his writings, it must be owned, that his learning obscures his reasonings, and seems even to repress his powerful intellect. It is an unfortunate effect of the redundant fulness of his mind, that it overflows in endless digressions, which break the chain of argument, and turn aside the thoughts of the reader from the main object. He was educated before usage had limited the naturalization of new words from the learned languages; before the failure of those great men, from Bacon to Milton, who laboured to follow a Latin order in their sentences, and the success of those men of inferior powers, from Cowley to Addison, who were content with the order, as well as the words, of pure and elegant conversation, had, as it were, by a double series of experiments, ascertained that the involutions and inversions of the ancient languages are seldom reconcilable with the genius of ours; and that they are, unless skilfully, as well as sparingly introduced, at variance with the natural beauties of our prose composition. His mind was more that of an ancient than of a modern philosopher. He often indulged in that sort of amalgamation of fancy with speculation, the delight of the Alexandrian doctors, with whom he was most familiarly conversant; and the Intellectual System, both in thought and expression, has an old and foreign air, not unlike a translation from the work of a later Platonist. Large ethical works of this eminent writer are extant in manuscript in the British Museum.‡ One

* Leib. Op. pars. iii. 271. The unnamed work which occasioned these remarks (perhaps one of Thomasius) appeared in 1699. How long after this Leibnitz's Dissertation was written, does not appear.

† Born 1617; died, 1688.

‡ See the the beautiful account of them by Burnet, (Hist. of His own Time, i. 321. Oxford, 1823) who was himself one of the most distinguished of this excellent body; with whom may be classed, notwithstanding some shades of doctrinal difference, his early master, Leighton, Bishop of Dunblane, a beautiful writer, and one of the best of men. The earliest account of them is in a curious contemporary pamphlet, entitled, "An Account of the new Sect of Latitude-men at Cambridge," republished in the collection of tracts, entitled "Phœnix Britannicus." Jeremy Taylor deserves the highest, and perhaps the earliest place among them: but Cudworth's excellent sermon before the House of Commons (31st March 1647) in the year of the publication of Taylor's Liberty of Prophesying, may be compared even to Taylor in charity, piety, and the most liberal toleration.

* De Cive, 1642.

† "Dantur boni et mali rationes æternæ et indispensabiles." Thesis for the degree of B. D. at Cambridge in 1664.—Birch's Life of Cudworth, prefixed to his edition of the Intellectual System, (Lond. 1743.) i. 7.

‡ A curious account of the history of these MSS. by Dr. Kippis, is to be found in the Biographia Britannica, iv. 549.

posthumous volume on Morals was published by Dr. Chandler, Bishop of Durham, entitled "A Treatise concerning Eternal and Immutable Morality."* But there is the more reason to regret (as far as relates to the history of Opinion) that the larger treatises are still unpublished, because the above volume is not so much an ethical treatise as an introduction to one: Protagoras of old, and Hobbes then alive, having concluded that Right and Wrong were unreal, because they were not perceived by the senses, and because all human knowledge consists only in such perception, Cudworth endeavours to refute them, by disproving that part of their premises which forms the last-stated proposition. The mind has many conceptions (*νοηματα*) which are not cognizable by the senses; and though they are occasioned by sensible objects, yet they cannot be formed but by a faculty superior to sense. The conceptions of Justice and Duty he places among them. The distinction of Right from Wrong is discerned by Reason; and as soon as these words are defined, it becomes evident that it would be a contradiction in terms to affirm that any power, human or Divine, could change their nature; or, in other words, make the same act to be just and unjust at the same time. They have existed eternally in the only mode in which truths can be said to be eternal, in the Eternal Mind; and they are indestructible and unchangeable like that Supreme Intelligence.† Whatever judgment may be formed of this reasoning, it is manifest that it relates merely to the philosophy of the *Understanding*, and does not attempt any explanation of What constitutes the very essence of Morality,—its relation to the *Will*. That we perceive a distinction between Right and Wrong, as much as between a triangle and a square, is indeed true; and may possibly lead to an explanation of the reason why men should adhere to the one and avoid the other. But it is not that reason. A command or a precept is not a proposition: it cannot be said that either is true or false. Cudworth, as well as many who succeeded him, confounded the mere apprehension by the Understanding that Right is different from Wrong, with the practical authority of these important conceptions, exercised over voluntary actions, in a totally distinct province of the human soul.

* 8vo. Lond. 1731.

† "There are many objects of our mind which we can neither see, hear, feel, smell, nor taste, and which did never enter into it by any sense; and therefore we can have no sensible pictures or ideas of them, drawn by the pencil of that inward limner, or painter, which borrows all his colours from sense, which we call 'Fancy:' and if we reflect on our own cogitations of these things, we shall sensibly perceive that they are not *phantastical*, but *noematical:* as, for example, justice, equity, duty and obligation, cogitation, opinion, intellection, volition, memory, verity, falsity, cause, effect, genus, species, nullity, contingency, possibility, impossibility, and innumerable others." —Ibid. 140. We have here an anticipation of Kant.

Though his life was devoted to the assertion of Divine Providence, and though his philosophy was imbued with the religious spirit of Platonism,* yet he had placed Christianity too purely in the love of God and Man to be considered as having much regard for those controversies about rights and opinions with which zealots disturb the world. They represented him as having fallen into the same heresy with Milton and with Clarke;† and some of them even charged him with atheism, for no other reason than that he was not afraid to state the atheistic difficulties in their fullest force. As blind anger heaps inconsistent accusations on each other, they called him at least "an Arian, a Socinian, or a Deist."‡ The courtiers of Charles II., who were delighted with every part of Hobbes but his integrity, did their utmost to decry his antagonist. They turned the railing of the bigots into a sarcasm against Religion; as we learn from him who represented them with unfortunate fidelity. "He has raised," says Dryden, "such strong objections against the being of God, that many think he has not answered them;"—"the common fate," as Lord Shaftesbury tells us, "of those who dare to appear fair authors."§ He had, indeed, earned the hatred of some theologians, better than they could know from the writings published during his life; for in his posthumous work he classes with the ancient atheists those of his contemporaries, (whom he forbears to name,) who held "that God may command what is contrary to moral rules; that He has no inclination to the good of His creatures; that He may justly doom an innocent being to eternal torments; and that whatever God does will, for that reason is just, because He wills it."‖

It is an interesting incident in the life of a philosopher, that Cudworth's daughter, Lady Masham, had the honour to nurse the infirmities and to watch the last breath of Mr. Locke, who was opposed to her father in speculative philosophy, but who heartily

* *Ευσέβει, ω τέκνον, ὁ γαρ ευσέβων ἄχρως Χριστιανίζει.*—(Motto affixed to the sermon above mentioned.)

† The following doctrine is ascribed to Cudworth by Nelson, a man of good understanding and great worth: "Dr. Cudworth maintained that the Father, absolutely speaking, is the only Supreme God; the Son and Spirit being God only by his concurrence with them, and their subordination and subjection to him."—Life of Bull, 339.

‡ Turner's discourse on the Messiah, 335.

§ Moralists, part ii. § 3.

‖ Etern. and Immut. Mor. 11. He quotes Ockham as having formerly maintained the same monstrous positions. To many, if not to most of these opinions or expressions, ancient and modern, reservations are adjoined, which render them *literally* reconcilable with practical Morals. But the dangerous abuse to which the incautious language of ethical theories is liable, is well illustrated by the anecdote related in Plutarch's Life of Alexander, of the sycophant Anaxarchas consoling that monarch for the murder of Clitus, by assuring him that every act of a ruler must be just. *Πᾶν το πραχθεν ὑπο του κρατοῦντος δίκαιον.*—Op. i. 639.

agreed with him in the love of Truth, Liberty, and Virtue.

CLARKE.*

Connected with Cudworth by principle, though separated by some interval of time, was Dr. Samuel Clarke, a man eminent at once as a divine, a mathematician, a metaphysical philosopher, and a philologer; who, as the interpreter of Homer and Cæsar, the scholar of Newton, and the antagonist of Leibnitz, approved himself not unworthy of correspondence with the highest order of human Spirits. Roused by the prevalence of the doctrines of Spinoza and Hobbes, he endeavoured to demonstrate the Being and Attributes of God, from a few axioms and definitions, in the manner of Geometry. In this attempt, with all his powers of argument, it must be owned that he is compelled sometimes tacitly to assume what the laws of reasoning required him to prove; and that, on the whole, his failure may be regarded as a proof that such a mode of argument is beyond the faculties of man.† Justly considering the Moral Attributes of the Deity as what alone render him the object of Religion, and to us constitutes the difference between Theism and atheism, he laboured with the utmost zeal to place the distinctions of Right and Wrong on a more solid foundation, and to explain the conformity of Morality to Reason, in a manner calculated to give a precise and scientific signification to that phraseology which all philosophers had, for so many ages, been content to employ, without thinking themselves obliged to define.

It is one of the most rarely successful efforts of the human mind, to place the understanding at the point from which a philosopher takes the views that compose his system, to recollect constantly his purposes, to adopt for a moment his previous opinions and prepossessions, to think in his words and to see with his eyes;—especially when the writer widely dissents from the system which he attempts to describe, and after a general change in the modes of thinking and in the use of terms. Every part of the present Dissertation requires such an excuse; but perhaps it may be more necessary in a case like that of Clarke, where the alterations in both respects have been so insensible, and in some respects appear so limited, that they may escape attention, than after those total revolutions in doctrine, where the necessity of not measuring other times by our own standard must be apparent to the most undistinguishing.

The sum of his moral doctrine may be stated as follows. Man can conceive nothing without at the same time conceiving its relations to other things. He must ascribe the same law of perception to every being to whom he ascribes thought. He cannot therefore doubt that all the relations of all things to all must have always been present to the Eternal Mind. The relations in this sense are eternal, however recent the things may be between whom they subsist. The whole of these relations constitute Truth: the knowledge of them is Omniscience. These eternal *different* relations of things involve a consequent eternal *fitness* or *unfitness* in the application of things, one to another; with a regard to which, the will of God always chooses, and which ought likewise to determine the wills of all subordinate rational beings. These eternal differences make it fit and reasonable for the creatures so to act; they cause it to be their duty, or lay an *obligation* on them so to do, separate from the will of God,* and antecedent to any prospect of advantage or reward.† Nay, wilful wickedness is the same absurdity and insolence in Morals, as it would be in natural things to pretend to alter the relations of numbers, or to take away the properties of mathematical figures.‡ "Morality," says one of his most ingenious scholars, "is the practice of reason."§

Clarke, like Cudworth, considered such a scheme as the only security against Hobbism, and probably also against the Calvinistic theology, from which they were almost as averse. Not content, with Cumberland, to attack Hobbes on ground which was in part his own, they thought it necessary to build on entirely new foundations. Clarke more especially, instead of substituting social and generous feeling for the selfish appetites, endeavoured to bestow on Morality the highest dignity, by thus deriving it from Reason. He made it more than disinterested; for he placed its seat in a region where interest never enters, and passion never disturbs. By ranking her principles with the first truths of Science, he seemed to render them pure and impartial, infallible and unchangeable. It might be excusable to regret the failure of so noble an attempt, if the indulgence of such regrets did not betray an unworthy apprehension that the same excellent ends could only be attained by such frail

* Born, 1675; died, 1729.

† This admirable person had so much candour as in effect to own his failure, and to recur to those other arguments in support of this great truth, which have in all ages satisfied the most elevated minds. In Proposition viii. (Being and Attributes of God, 47.) which affirms that the first cause *must* be "intelligent" (wherein, as he truly states, "lies the main question between us and the atheists"), he owns, that the proposition cannot be demonstrated strictly and properly *à priori.* —See Note M.

* "Those who found all moral obligation on the will of God must recur to the same thing, only they do not explain how the nature and will of God is good and just."—Being and Attributes of God, Proposition xii.

† Evidence of Natural and Revealed Religion, p. 4. Lond. 1724.

‡ Ibid. p. 42.

§ Lowman on the Unity and Perfections of God, p. 29. Lond. 1737

means; and that the dictates of the most severe reason would not finally prove reconcilable with the majesty of Virtue.

REMARKS.

The adoption of mathematical forms and terms was, in England, a prevalent fashion among writers on moral subjects during a large part of the eighteenth century. The ambition of mathematical certainty, on matters concerning which it is not given to man to reach it, is a frailty from which the disciple of Newton ought in reason to have been withheld, but to which he was naturally tempted by the example of his master. Nothing but the extreme difficulty of detaching assent from forms of expression to which it has been long wedded, can explain the fact, that the incautious expressions above cited, into which Clarke was hurried by his moral sensibility, did not awaken him to a sense of the error into which he had fallen. As soon as he had said that "a wicked act was as absurd as an attempt to take away the properties of a figure," he ought to have seen that principles which led logically to such a conclusion were untrue. As it is an impossibility to make three and three cease to be six, it ought, on his principles, to be impossible to do a wicked act. To act without regard to the relations of things,—as if a man were to choose fire for cooling, or ice for heating,—would be the part either of a lunatic or an idiot. The murderer who poisons by arsenic, acts agreeably to his knowledge of the power of that substance to kill, which is a relation between two things; as much as the physician who employs an emetic after the poison, acts upon his belief of the tendency of that remedy to preserve life, which is another relation between two things. All men who seek a good or bad end by good or bad means, must alike conform their conduct to some relation between their actions as means and their object as an end. All the relations of inanimate things to each other are undoubtedly observed as much by the criminal as by the man of virtue.

It is therefore singular that Dr. Clarke suffered himself to be misled into the representation, that Virtue is a conformity with the relations of things universally, Vice a universal disregard of them, by the certain, but here insufficient truth, that the former necessarily implied a regard to *certain particular relations*, which were always disregarded by those who chose the latter. The distinction between Right and Wrong can, therefore, no longer depend on relations as such, but on a particular class of relations. And it seems evident that no relations are to be considered, except those in which a living, intelligent, and voluntary agent is one of the beings related. His acts may relate to a law, as either observing or infringing it; they may relate to his own moral sentiments and those of his fellows, as they are the objects of approbation or disapprobation; they may relate to his own welfare, by increasing or abating it; they may relate to the well-being of other sentient beings, by contributing to promote or obstruct it: but in all these, and in all supposable cases, the inquiry of the moral philosopher must be, not whether there be a relation, but what the relation is; whether it be that of obedience to law, or agreeableness to moral feeling, or suitableness to prudence, or coincidence with benevolence. The term "relation" itself, on which Dr. Clarke's system rests, being common to Right and Wrong, must be struck out of the reasoning. He himself incidentally drops intimations which are at variance with his system. "The Deity," he tells us, "acts according to the eternal relations of things, in order to the welfare of the whole Universe;" and subordinate moral agents ought to be governed by the same rules, "for the good of the public."* No one can fail to observe that a new element is here introduced, —the well-being of communities of men, and the general happiness of the world,—which supersedes the consideration of abstract relations and fitnesses.

There are other views of this system, however, of a more general nature, and of much more importance, because they extend in a considerable degree to all systems which found moral distinctions or sentiments, solely or ultimately, upon Reason. A little reflection will discover an extraordinary vacuity in this system. Supposing it were allowed that it satisfactorily accounts for moral judgments, there is still an important part of our moral sentiments which it passes by without an attempt to explain them. Whence, on this scheme, the pleasure or pain with which we review our own actions or survey those of others? What is the nature of remorse? Why do we feel shame? Whence is indignation against injustice? These are surely no exercise of Reason. Nor is the assent of Reason to any other class of propositions followed or accompanied by emotions of this nature, by any approaching them, or indeed necessarily by any emotion at all. It is a fatal objection to a moral theory that it contains no means of explaining the most conspicuous, if not the most essential, parts of moral approbation and disapprobation.

But to rise to a more general consideration: Perception and Emotion are states of mind perfectly distinct, and an emotion of pleasure or pain differs much more from a mere perception, than the perceptions of one sense do from those of another. The perceptions of all the senses have some qualities in common. But an emotion has not necessarily anything in common with a perception, but that they are both states of mind. We perceive exactly the same qualities in the taste of coffee when we may dislike it, as afterwards when we come to like it. In other words, the perception remains the same when the sensation of pain is

* Evid. of Nat. and Rev. Rel. p. 4.

changed into the opposite sensation of pleasure. The like change may occur in every case where pleasure or pain (in such instances called "sensations"), enter the mind with perceptions through the eye or the ear. The prospect or the sound which was disagreeable may become agreeable, without any alteration in our idea of the objects. We can easily imagine a percipient and thinking being without a capacity of receiving pleasure or pain. Such a being might perceive what we do; if we could conceive him to reason, he might reason justly; and if he were to judge at all, there seems no reason why he should not judge truly. But what could induce such a being to *will* or to *act?* It seems evident that his existence could only be a state of passive contemplation. Reason, as Reason, can never be a motive to action. It is only when we superadd to such a being sensibility, or the capacity of emotion or sentiment, or (what in corporeal cases is called sensation) of desire and aversion, that we introduce him into the world of action. We then clearly discern that, when the conclusion of a process of reasoning presents to his mind an object of desire, or the means of obtaining it, a motive of action begins to operate, and Reason may then, but not till then, have a powerful though indirect influence on conduct. Let any argument to dissuade a man from immorality be employed, and the issue of it will always appear to be an appeal to a feeling. You prove that drunkenness will probably ruin health: no position founded on experience is more certain; most persons with whom you reason must be as much convinced of it as you are. But your hope of success depends on the drunkard's fear of ill health; and he may always silence your argument by telling you that he loves wine more than he dreads sickness. You speak in vain of the infamy of an act to one who disregards the opinion of others, or of its imprudence to a man of little feeling for his own future condition. You may truly, but vainly tell of the pleasures of friendship to one who has little affection. If you display the delights of liberality to a miser, he may always shut your mouth by answering, "The spendthrift may prefer such pleasures; I love money more." If you even appeal to a man's conscience, he may answer you that you have clearly proved the immorality of the act, and that he himself knew it before; but that now when you had renewed and freshened his conviction, he was obliged to own that his love of Virtue, even aided by the fear of dishonour, remorse, and punishment, was not so powerful as the desire which hurried him into vice.

Nor is it otherwise, however confusion of ideas may cause it to be so deemed, with that calm regard to the welfare of the agent, to which philosophers have so grossly misapplied the hardly intelligible appellation of "self-love." The general tendency of right conduct to permanent well-being is indeed one of the most evident of all truths. But the success of persuasives or dissuasives addressed to it, must always be directly proportioned, not to the clearness with which the truth is discerned, but to the strength of the principle addressed, in the mind of the individual, and to the degree in which he is accustomed to keep an eye on its dictates. A strange prejudice prevails, which ascribes to what is called "self-love" an invariable superiority over all the other motives of human action. If it were to be called by a more fit name, such as "foresight," "prudence," or, what seems most exactly to describe its nature, "a sympathy with the future feelings of the agent," it would appear to every observer to be one very often too languid and inactive, always of late appearance, and sometimes so faint as to be scarcely perceptible. Almost every human passion in its turn prevails over self-love.

It is thus apparent that the influence of Reason on the Will is indirect, and arises only from its being one of the channels by which the objects of desire or aversion are brought near to these springs of voluntary action. It is only one of these channels. There are many other modes of presenting to the mind the proper objects of the emotions which it is intended to excite, whether of a calmer or of a more active nature; so that they may influence conduct more powerfully than when they reach the Will through the channel of conviction. The distinction between conviction and persuasion would indeed be otherwise without a meaning; to teach the mind would be the same thing as to move it; and eloquence would be nothing but logic, although the greater part of the power of the former is displayed in the direct excitement of feeling;—on condition, indeed (for reasons foreign to our present purpose), that the orator shall never appear to give counsel inconsistent with the duty or the lasting welfare of those whom he would persuade. In like manner it is to be observed, that though reasoning be one of the instruments of education, yet education is not a process of reasoning, but a wise disposal of all the circumstances which influence character, and of the means of producing those habitual dispositions which insure well-doing, of which reasoning is but one. Very similar observations are applicable to the great arts of legislation and government; which are here only alluded to as forming a strong illustration of the present argument.

The abused extension of the term "Reason" to the moral faculties, one of the predominant errors of ancient and modern times, has arisen from causes which it is not difficult to discover. Reason does in truth perform a great part in every case of moral sentiment. To Reason often belong the preliminaries of the act; to Reason altogether belongs the choice of the means of execution. The operations of Reason, in both cases, are comparatively slow and lasting; they are capable of being distinctly recalled by memory. The emotion which intervenes between the previous and the succeeding exertions of Reason is often faint, generally transient, and scarcely ever capable of being reproduced by an effort of the mind. Hence the name of Reason is applied to this mixed state of mind; more especially when the feeling, being of a cold and general nature, and scarcely ruffling the surface of the soul,—such as that of prudence and of ordinary kindness and propriety,—almost passes unnoticed, and is irretrievably forgotten. Hence the mind is, in such conditions, said by moralists to act from *reason*, in contradistinction to its more excited and disturbed state, when it is said to act from *passion*. The calmness of Reason gives to the whole compound the appearance of unmixed reason. The illusion is further promoted by a mode of expression used in most languages. A man is said to act reasonably, when his conduct is such as may be reasonably expected. Amidst the disorders of a vicious mind, it is difficult to form a reasonable conjecture concerning future conduct; but the quiet and well-ordered state of Virtue renders the probable acts of her fortunate votaries the object of very rational expectation.

As far as it is not presumptuous to attempt a distinction between modes of thinking foreign to the mind which makes the attempt, and modes of expression scarcely translatable into the only technical language in which that mind is wont to think, it seems that the systems of Cudworth and Clarke, though they appear very similar, are in reality different in some important points of view. The former, a Platonist, sets out from those "Ideas" (a word, in this acceptation of it, which has no corresponding term in English), the eternal models of created things, which, as the Athenian master taught, pre-existed in the Everlasting Intellect, and, of right, rule the will of every inferior mind. The illustrious scholar of Newton, with a manner of thinking more natural to his age and school, considered primarily the very relations of things themselves;—conceived indeed by the Eternal Mind, but which, if such inadequate language may be pardoned, are the law of Its will, as well as the model of Its works.*

EARL OF SHAFTESBURY.†

Lord Shaftesbury, the author of the Characteristics, was the grandson of Sir Antony Ashley Cooper, created Earl of Shaftesbury, one of the master spirits of the English nation, whose vices, the bitter fruits of the insecurity of a troublous time succeeded by the corrupting habits of an inconstant, venal, and profligate court, have led an ungrateful posterity to overlook his wisdom and disinterested perseverance, in obtaining for his country the unspeakable benefits of the Habeas Corpus act. The fortune of the Characteristics has been singular. For a time the work was admired more undistinguishingly than its literary character warrants. In the succeeding period it was justly criticised, but too severely condemned. Of late, more unjustly than in either of the former cases, it has been generally neglected. It seemed to have the power of changing the temper of its critics. It provoked the amiable Berkeley to a harshness equally unwonted and unwarranted;* while it softened the rugged Warburton so far as to dispose the fierce, yet not altogether ungenerous, polemic to praise an enemy in the very heat of conflict.†

Leibnitz, the most celebrated of Continental philosophers, warmly applauded the Characteristics, and, (what was a more certain proof, of admiration) though at an advanced age, criticised that work minutely.‡ Le Clerc, who had assisted the studies of the author, contributed to spread its reputation by his Journal, then the most popular in Europe. Locke is said to have aided in his education, probably rather by counsel than by tuition. The author had indeed been driven from the regular studies of his country by the insults with which he was loaded at Winchester school, when he was only twelve years old, immediately after the death of his grandfather;§—

* Mr. Wollaston's system, that morality consisted in acting according to truth, seems to coincide with that of Dr. Clarke. The murder of Cicero by Popilius Lenas, was, according to him, a practical falsehood; for Cicero had been his benefactor, and Popilius acted as if that were untrue. If the truth spoken of be that gratitude is due for benefits, the reasoning is evidently a circle. If *any truth* be meant, indifferently, it is plain that the assassin acted in perfect conformity to several certain truths;—such as the malignity of Antony, the ingratitude and venality of Popilius, and the probable impunity of his crime, when law was suspended, and good men without power.

† Born, 1671; died, 1713.

* See Minute Philosopher, Dialogue iii.; but especially his Theory of Vision Vindicated, Lond. 1733 (not republished in the quarto edition of his works), where this most excellent man sinks for a moment to the level of a railing polemic.

† It is remarkable that the most impure passages of Warburton's composition are those in which he lets loose his controversial zeal, and that he is a fine writer principally where he writes from generous feeling. "Of all the virtues which were so much in this noble writer's heart, and in his writings, there was not one he more revered than the love of public liberty.... The noble author of the Characteristics had many excellent qualities, both as a man and a writer: he was temperate, chaste, honest, and a lover of his country. In his writings he has shown how much he has imbibed the deep sense, and how naturally he could copy the gracious manner of Plato.—(Dedication to the Freethinkers, prefixed to the Divine Legation.) He, however, soon relapses, but not without excuse; for he thought himself vindicating the memory of Locke.

‡ Op. iii. 39—56.

§ [With regard to this story, authorised as it is, the Editor cannot help, on behalf of his own "nursing mother," throwing out some suspicion that the Chancellor's politics must have been made use of somewhat as a scapegoat; else the nature of boys was at that time more excitable touching their schoolmates' grandfathers than it is now. There is a rule traditionally observed in College, "that no boy has a right to think till he

a choice of time which seemed not so much to indicate anger against the faults of a great man, as triumph over the principles of liberty, which seemed at that time to have fallen for ever. He gave a genuine proof of respect for freedom of thought, by preventing the expulsion, from Holland, of Bayle, (from whom he differs in every moral, political, and, it may be truly added, religious opinion) when, it must be owned, the right of asylum was, in strict justice, forfeited by the secret services which the philosopher had rendered to the enemy of Holland and of Europe. In the small part of his short life which premature infirmities allowed him to apply to public affairs, he co-operated zealously with the friends of freedom; but, as became a moral philosopher, he supported, even against them, a law to allow those who were accused of treason to make their defence by counsel, although the parties first to benefit from this act of imperfect justice were persons conspired together to assassinate King William, and to re-enslave their country. On that occasion it is well known with what admirable quickness he took advantage of the embarrassment which seized him, when he rose to address the House of Commons. "If I," said he, "who rise only to give my opinion on this bill, am so confounded that I cannot say what I intended, what must the condition of that man be, who, without assistance is pleading for his own life!" Lord Shaftesbury was the friend of Lord Somers; and the tribute paid to his personal character by Warburton, who knew many of his contemporaries and some of his friends, may be considered as evidence of its excellence.

His fine genius and generous spirit shine through his writings; but their lustre is often dimmed by peculiarities, and, it must be said, by affectations, which, originating in local, temporary, or even personal circumstances, are particularly fatal to the permanence of fame. There is often a charm in the egotism of an artless writer, or of an actor in great scenes: but other laws are imposed on the literary artist. Lord Shaftsbury, instead of hiding himself behind his work, stands forward with too frequent marks of self-complacency, as a nobleman of polished manners, with a mind adorned by the fine arts, and instructed by ancient philosophy; shrinking with a somewhat effeminate fastidiousness from the clamour and prejudices of the multitude, whom he neither deigns to conciliate, nor puts forth his strength to subdue. The enmity of the majority of churchmen to the government established at the Revolution, was calculated to fill his mind with angry feelings; which overflowed too often, if not upon Christianity itself, yet upon representations of it, closely intertwined with those religious feelings to which, in other forms, his own philosophy ascribes surpassing worth. His small, and occasional writings, of which the main fault is the want of an object or a plan, have many passages remarkable for the utmost beauty and harmony of language. Had he imbibed the simplicity, as well as copied the expression and cadence, of the greater ancients, he would have done more justice to his genius; and his works, like theirs, would have been preserved by that first-mentioned quality, without which but a very few writings, of whatever mental power, have long survived their writers. Grace belongs only to natural movements; and Lord Shaftesbury, notwithstanding the frequent beauty of his thoughts and language, has rarely attained it. He is unfortunately prone to pleasantry, which is obstinately averse from constraint, and which he had no interest in raising to be the test of truth. His affectation of liveliness as a man of the world, tempts him sometimes to overstep the indistinct boundaries which separate familiarity from vulgarity. Of his two more considerable writings, The Moralists, on which he evidently most valued himself, and which is spoken of by Leibnitz with enthusiasm, is by no means the happiest.—Yet perhaps there is scarcely any composition in our language more lofty in its moral and religious sentiments, and more exquisitely elegant and musical in its diction, than the Platonic representation of the scale of beauty and love, in the speech to Palemon, near the close of the first part.* Many passages might be quoted, which in some measure justify the enthusiasm of the septuagenarian geometer. Yet it is not to be concealed that, as a whole, it is heavy and languid. It is a modern antique. The dialogues of Plato are often very lively representations of conversations which might take place daily at a great university, full, like Athens, of rival professors and eager disciples, between men of various character, and great fame as well as ability. Socrates runs through them all. His great abilities, his still more venerable virtues, his cruel fate, especially when joined to his very characteristic peculiarities,—to his grave humour, to his homely sense, to his assumed humility, to the honest slyness with which he ensnared the Sophists, and to the intrepidity with which he dragged them to justice, gave unity and dramatic interest to these dialogues as a whole. But Lord Shaftesbury's dialogue is between fictitious personages, and in a tone at utter variance with English conversation. He had great power of thought and command over words; but he had no talent for inventing character and bestowing life on it.

The inquiry concerning Virtue† is nearly exempt from the faulty peculiarities of the author; the method is perfect, the reasoning just, the style precise and clear. The writer has no purpose but that of honestly proving his principles; he himself altogether disappears; and he is intent only on earnestly en-

has forty juniors;" upon which rock the cock-boat of the embryo metaphysician might have foundered.]

* § 3. † Characteristics, treatise iv.

forcing what he truly, conscientiously, and reasonably believes. Hence the charm of simplicity is revived in this production, which is unquestionably entitled to a place in the first rank of English tracts on moral philosophy. The point in which it becomes especially pertinent to the subject of this Dissertation is, that it contains more intimations of an original and important nature on the theory of Ethics than perhaps any preceding work of modern times.* It is true that they are often but intimations, cursory, and appearing almost to be casual; so that many of them have escaped the notice of most readers, and even writers on these subjects.—That the consequences of some of them are even yet not unfolded, must be owned to be a proof that they are inadequately stated; and may be regarded as a presumption that the author did not closely examine the bearings of his own positions. Among the most important of these suggestions is, the existence of dispositions in man, by which he takes pleasure in the well-being of others, without any further view;—a doctrine, however, to all the consequences of which he has not been faithful in his other writings.† Another is, that goodness consists in the prevalence of love for the system of which we are a part, over the passions pointing to our individual welfare,—a proposition which somewhat confounds the motives of right acts with their tendency, and seems to favour the melting of all particular affections into general benevolence, because the tendency of these affections is to general good. The next, and certainly the most original, as well as important, is, that there are certain affections of the mind which, being contemplated by the mind itself through what he calls "a reflex sense," become the objects of love, or the contrary, according to their nature. So approved and loved, they constitute *virtue* or *merit*, as distinguished from mere *goodness*, of which there are traces in animals who do not appear to *reflect* on the state of their own minds, and who seem, therefore, destitute of what he elsewhere calls "a moral sense." These statements are, it is true, far too short and vague. He nowhere inquires into the origin of the reflex sense: what is a much more material defect, he makes no attempt to ascertain in what state of mind it consists. We discover only by implication, and by the use of the term "sense," that he searches for the fountain of moral sentiments, not in mere reason, where Cudworth and Clarke had vainly sought for it, but in the heart, whence the main branch of them assuredly flows. It should never be forgotten, that we owe to these hints the reception, into ethical theory, of a moral sense; which, whatever may be thought of its origin, or in whatever words it may be described, must always retain its place in such theory as a main principle of our moral nature.

His demonstration of the utility of Virtue to the individual, far surpasses all other attempts of the same nature; being founded, not on a calculation of outward advantages or inconveniences, alike uncertain, precarious, and degrading, but on the unshaken foundation of the delight, which is of the very essence of social affection and virtuous sentiment; on the dreadful agony inflicted by all malevolent passions upon every soul that harbours the hellish inmates; on the all-important truth, that to love is to be happy, and to hate is to be miserable,—that affection is its own reward, and ill-will its own punishment; or, as it has been more simply and more affectingly, as well as with more sacred authority, taught, that "to give is more blessed than to receive," and that to love one another is the sum of all human virtue.

The relation of Religion to Morality, as far as it can be discovered by human reason, was never more justly or more beautifully stated. If he represents the mere hope of reward and dread of punishment as selfish, and therefore inferior motives to virtue and piety, he distinctly owns their efficacy in reclaiming from vice, in rousing from lethargy, and in guarding a feeble penitence; in all which he coincides with illustrious and zealous Christian writers. "If by the hope of reward be understood the love and desire of virtuous enjoyment, or of the very practice and exercise of virtue in another life; an expectation or hope of this kind is so far from being derogatory from virtue, that it is an evidence of our loving it the more sincerely and *for its own sake*."*

* I am not without suspicion that I have overlooked the claims of Dr. Henry More, who, notwithstanding some uncouthness of language, seems to have given the first intimations of a distinct moral faculty, which he calls "the Boniform Faculty:" a phrase against which an outcry would now be raised as German. Happiness, according to him, consists in a constant satisfaction, *ἐν τῷ ἀγαθοειδεῖ τῆς ψυχῆς*.—Enchiridion Ethicum, lib. i. cap. ii.

† "It is the height of wisdom no doubt to be rightly selfish."—Charact. i. 121. The observation seems to be taken from what Aristotle says of *Φιλαυτία*: *Τὸν μὲν ἀγαθὸν δεῖ φίλαυτον εἶναι*.—Ethics, lib. ix. c. viii. The chapter is admirable, and the assertion of Aristotle is very capable of a good sense.

* Inquiry, book i. part iii. § 3. So Jeremy Taylor; "He that is grown in grace pursues virtue purely and simply for its own interest. When persons come to that height of grace, and love God for himself, that is but heaven in another sense."—(Sermon on Growth in Grace.) So before him the once celebrated Mr. John Smith of Cambridge: "The happiness which good men shall partake is not distinct from their godlike nature. Happiness and holiness are but two several notions of one thing. Hell is rather a nature than a place, and heaven cannot be so well defined by any thing *without* us, as by something *within* us."—(Select Discourses, 2d edit. Cambridge, 1673.) In accordance with these old authorities is the recent language of a most ingenious as well as benevolent and pious writer. "The *holiness* of heaven is still more attractive to the Christian than its *happiness*. The desire of doing that which is right for its own sake is a part of his desire after

FENELON.*—BOSSUET.†

As the last question, though strictly speaking theological, is yet in truth dependent on the more general question, which relates to the reality of disinterested affections in human nature, it seems not foreign from the present purpose to give a short account of a dispute on the subject in France, between two of the most eminent persons of their time; namely, the controversy between Fenelon and Bossuet, concerning the possibility of men being influenced by the pure and disinterested love of God. Never were two great men more unlike. Fenelon in his writings exhibits more of the qualities which predispose to religious feelings, than any other equally conspicuous person; a mind so pure as steadily to contemplate supreme excellence; a heart capable of being touched and affected by the contemplation; a gentle and modest spirit, not elated by the privilege, but seeing clearer its own want of worth as it came nearer to such brightness, and disposed to treat with compassionate forbearance those errors in others, of which it felt a humbling consciousness. Bossuet was rather a great minister in the ecclesiastical commonwealth; employing knowledge, eloquence, argument, the energy of his character, the influence, and even the authority of his station, to vanquish opponents, to extirpate revolters, and sometimes with a patrician firmness, to withstand the dictatorial encroachment of the Roman Pontiff on the spiritual aristocracy of France. Fenelon had been appointed tutor to the Duke of Burgundy. He had all the qualities which fit a man to be the preceptor of a prince, and which most disable him to get or to keep the office. Even birth, and urbanity, and accomplishment, and vivacity, were an insufficient atonement for his genius and virtue. Louis XIV. distrusted so fine a spirit, and appears to have early suspected, that a fancy moved by such benevolence might imagine examples for his grandson which the world would consider as a satire on his own reign. Madame de Maintenon, indeed, favoured him; but he was generally believed to have forfeited her good graces by discouraging her projects for at least a nearer approach to a seat on the throne. He offended her too by obeying her commands, in laying before her an account of her faults, and some of those of her royal husband, which was probably the more painfully felt for its mildness, justice, and refined observation.* An opportunity for driving such an intruder from a court presented itself somewhat strangely, in the form of a subtile controversy on one of the most abstruse questions of metaphysical theology. Molinos, a Spanish priest, reviving and perhaps exaggerating the maxims of the ancient Mystics, had recently taught, that Christian perfection consisted in the pure love of God, without hope of reward or fear of punishment. This offence he expiated by seven years' imprisonment in the dungeons of the Roman Inquisition. His opinions were embraced by Madame Guyon, a pious French lady of strong feeling and active imagination, who appears to have expressed them in a hyperbolical language, not infrequent in devotional exercises, especially in those of otherwise amiable persons of her sex and character. In the fervour of her zeal, she disregarded the usages of the world and the decorum imposed on females. She left her family, took a part in public conferences, and assumed an independence scarcely reconcilable with the more ordinary and more pleasing virtues of women. Her pious effusions were examined with the rigour which might be excusable if exercised on theological propositions. She was falsely charged by Harlay, the dissolute Archbishop of Paris, with personal licentiousness. For these crimes she was dragged from convent to convent, imprisoned for years in the Bastile, and, as an act of mercy, confined during the latter years of her life to a provincial town, as a prison at large. A piety thus pure and disinterested could not fail to please Fenelon. He published a work in justification of Madame Guyon's character, and in explanation of the degree in which he agreed with her. Bossuet, the oracle and champion of the Church, took up arms against him. It would be painful to suppose that a man of such great powers was actuated by mean jealousy; and it is needless. The union of zeal for opinion with the pride of authority, is apt to give sternness to the administration of controversial bishops; to say nothing of the haughty and inflexible character of Bossuet himself. He could not brook the independence of him who was hitherto so docile a scholar and so gentle a friend. He was jealous of novelties, and dreaded a fervour of piety likely to be ungovernable, and productive of movements of which no man could foresee the issue. It must be allowed that he had reason to be displeased with the indiscretion and turbulence of the innovators, and might apprehend that, in preaching motives to virtue and religion which he

heaven."—(Unconditional Freeness of the Gospel, by T. Erskine, Esq. Edinb. 1828, p. 32, 33.) See also the Appendix to Ward's Life of Henry More, Lond. 1710, pp. 247—271. This account of that ingenious and amiable philosopher contains an interesting view of his opinions, and many beautiful passages of his writings, but unfortunately very few particulars of the man. His letters on Disinterested Piety (see the Appendix to Mr Ward's work), his boundless charity, his zeal for the utmost toleration, and his hope of general improvement from "a pacific and perspicacious posterity," place him high in the small number of true philosophers who, in their estimate of men, value dispositions more than opinions, and in their search for good, more often look forward than backward.

* Born, 1651; died, 1715.

† Born, 1627; died, 1704.

* Bausset, Histoire de Fénelon, i. 252.

thought unattainable, the coarser but surer foundations of common morality might be loosened. A controversy ensued, in which he employed the utmost violence of polemical or factious contest. Fenelon replied with brilliant success, and submitted his book to the judgment of Rome. After a long examination, the commission of ten Cardinals appointed to examine it were equally divided, and he seemed in consequence about to be acquitted. But Bossuet had in the mean time easily gained Louis XIV. Madame de Maintenon betrayed Fenelon's confidential correspondence; and he was banished to his diocese, and deprived of his pensions and official apartments in the palace. Louis XIV. regarded the slightest differences from the authorities of the French church as rebellion against himself. Though endowed with much natural good sense, he was too grossly ignorant to be made to comprehend one of the terms of the question in dispute. He did not, however, scruple to urge the Pope to the condemnation of Fenelon. Innocent XII. (Pignatelli,) an aged and pacific Pontiff, was desirous of avoiding such harsh measures. He said that "the archbishop of Cambray might have erred from excess in the love of God, but the bishop of Meaux had sinned by a defect of the love of his neighbour."* But he was compelled to condemn a series of propositions, of which the first was, "There is an habitual state of love to God, which is pure from every motive of personal interest, and in which neither the fear of punishment nor the hope of reward has any part."† Fenelon read the bull which condemned him in his own cathedral, and professed as humble a submission as the lowest of his flock. In some of the writings of his advanced years, which have been recently published, we observe with regret that, when wearied out by his exile, ambitious to regain a place at court through the Jesuits, or prejudiced against the Calvinising doctrines of the Jansenists, the strongest anti-papal party among Catholics, or somewhat detached from a cause of which his great antagonist had been the victorious leader, he made concessions to the absolute monarchy of Rome, which did not become a luminary of the Gallican church.‡

Bossuet, in his writings on this occasion, besides tradition and authorities, relied mainly on the supposed principle of philosophy, that man must desire his own happiness, and cannot desire anything else, otherwise than as a means towards it; which renders the controversy an incident in the history of Ethics. It is immediately connected with the preceding part of this Dissertation, by the almost literal coincidence between Bossuet's foremost objection to the disinterested piety contended for by Fenelon, and the fundamental position of a very ingenious and once noted divine of the English church, in his attack on the disinterested affections, believed by Shaftesbury to be a part of human nature.*

* Bausset, Histoire de Fénelon, ii. 220, note.

† Œuvres de Bossuet, viii. 308.—(Liege, 1767.)

‡ De Summi Pontificis Auctoritate Dissertatio.

LEIBNITZ.†

There is a singular contrast between the form of Leibnitz's writings and the character of his mind. The latter was systematical, even to excess. It was the vice of his prodigious intellect, on every subject of science where it was not bound by geometrical chains, to confine his view to those most general principles, so well called by Bacon "merely notional," which render it, indeed, easy to build a system, but only because they may be alike adapted to every state of appearances, and become thereby really inapplicable to any. Though his genius was thus naturally turned to system, his writings were, generally, occasional and miscellaneous. The fragments of his doctrines are scattered in reviews; or over a voluminous literary correspondence; or in the prefaces and introductions to those compilations to which this great philosopher was obliged by his situation to descend. This defective and disorderly mode of publication arose partly from the conflicts between business and study, inevitable in his course of life; but probably yet more from the nature of his system, which while it widely deviates from the most general principles of former philosophers, is ready to embrace their particular doctrines under its own generalities, and thus to reconcile them to each other, as well as to accommodate itself to popular or established opinions, and compromise with them, according to his favourite and oft-repeated maxim, "that most received doctrines are capable of a good sense;"‡ by which last words our philosopher meant a sense reconcilable with his own principles. Partial and occasional exhibitions of these principles

* "Hæc est natura voluntatis humanæ, ut et beatitudinem, et ea quorum necessaria connexio cum beatitudine clare intelligitur, *necessario* appetat... Nullus est actus ad quem revera non impellimur motivo beatitudinis, explicite vel *implicite;*" meaning by the latter that it may be concealed from ourselves, as he says, *for a short time*, by a nearer object.—Œuvres de Bossuet, viii. 80. "The only motive by which individuals *can* be induced to the practice of virtue, *must* be the feeling or the prospect of private happiness."—Brown's Essays on the Characteristics, p. 159. Lond. 1752. It must, however, be owned, that the selfishness of the Warburtonian is more rigid; making no provision for the object of one's own happiness slipping out of view for a moment. It is due to the very ingenious author of this forgotten book to add, that it is full of praise of his adversary, which, though just, was in the answerer generous; and that it contains an assertion of the *unbounded* right of public discussion, unusual even at the tolerant period of its appearance.

† Born, 1646; died, 1716.

‡ "Nouveaux Essais sur l'Entendement Humain," liv. i. chap. ii. These Essays, which form the greater part of the publication entitled "Œuvres Philosophiques," edited by Raspe, Amst. et Leipz. 1765, are not included in Dutens' edition of Leibnitz's works.

suited better that constant negotiation with opinions, establishments, and prejudices, to which extreme generalities are well adapted, than would have a full and methodical statement of the whole at once. It is the lot of every philosopher who attempts to make his principles extremely flexible, that they become like those tools which bend so easily as to penetrate nothing. Yet his manner of publication perhaps led him to those wide intuitions, as comprehensive as those of Bacon, of which he expressed the result as briefly and pithily as Hobbes. The fragment which contains his ethical principles is the preface to a collection of documents illustrative of international law, published at Hanover in 1693* to which he often referred as his standard afterwards, especially when he speaks of Lord Shaftesbury, or of the controversy between the two great theologians of France. "Right," says he, "is moral power; obligation, moral necessity. By "moral" I understand what with a good man prevails as much as if it were physical. A good man is he who loves all men as far as reason allows. Justice is the benevolence of a wise man. To love is to be pleased with the happiness of another; or, in other words, to convert the happiness of another into a part of one's own. Hence is explained the possibility of a disinterested love. When we are pleased with the happiness of any being, his happiness becomes one of our enjoyments. Wisdom is the science of happiness."†

REMARKS.

It is apparent from the above passage, that Leibnitz had touched the truth on the subject of disinterested affection; and that he was more near clinging to it than any modern philosopher, except Lord Shaftesbury. It is evident, however, from the latter part of it, that, like Shaftesbury, he shrunk from his own just conception; under the influence of that most ancient and far-spread prejudice of the schools, which assumed that such an abstraction as "Happiness" could be the object of love, and that the desire of so faint, distant, and refined an object, was the first principle of all moral nature, and that of it every other desire was only a modification or a fruit. Both he and Shaftesbury, however, when they relapsed into the selfish system, embraced it in its most refined form; considering the benevolent affections as valuable parts of our own happiness, not in consequence of any of their effects or extrinsic advantages, but of that intrinsic delightfulness which was inherent in their very essence. But Leibnitz considered this refined pleasure as the object in the view of the benevolent man; an absurdity, or rather a contradiction, which, at least in the Inquiry concerning Virtue, Shaftesbury avoids. It will be seen from Leibnitz's limitation, taken together with his definition of Wisdom, that he regarded the distinction of the moral sentiments from the social affections, and the just subordination of the latter, as entirely founded on the tendency of general happiness to increase that of the agent, not merely as being real, but as being present to the agent's mind when he acts. In a subsequent passage he lowers his tone not a little. "As for the sacrifice of life, or the endurance of the greatest pain for others, these things are rather generously enjoined than solidly demonstrated by philosophers. For honour, glory, and self-congratulation, to which they appeal under the name of Virtue, are indeed mental pleasures, and of a high degree, but not to all, nor outweighing every bitterness of suffering; since all cannot imagine them with equal vivacity, and that power is little possessed by those whom neither education, nor situation, nor the doctrines of Religion or Philosophy, have taught to value mental gratifications."* He concludes very truly, that Morality is completed by a belief of moral government. But the Inquiry concerning Virtue, had reached that conclusion by a better road. It entirely escaped his sagacity, as it has that of nearly all other moralists, that the coincidence of Morality with well-understood interest in our outward actions, is very far from being the most important part of the question; for these actions flow from habitual dispositions, from affections and sensibilities, which determine their nature. There may be, and there are many immoral acts, which, in the sense in which words are commonly used, are advantageous to the actor. But the whole sagacity and ingenuity of the world may be safely challenged to point out a case in which virtuous dispositions, habits, and feelings, are not conducive in the highest degree to the happiness of the individual; or to maintain that he is not the happiest, whose moral sentiments and affections are such as to prevent the possibility of any unlawful advantage being presented to his mind. It would indeed have been impossible to prove to Regulus that it was his interest to return to a death of torture in Africa. But what, if the proof had been easy? The most thorough conviction on such a point would not have enabled him to set this example, if he had not been supported by his own integrity and generosity, by love of his country, and reverence for his pledged faith. What could the conviction add to that greatness of soul, and to these glorious attributes? With such virtues he could not act otherwise than he did. Would a father affectionately interested in a son's happiness, of very lukewarm feelings of morality, but of good sense enough to weigh gratifications and sufferings exactly, be really desirous that his son should have these virtues in a less degree than Regulus,

* Codex Juris Gentium Diplomaticus.—Hanov. 1695.

† See Note N

* See Note N

merely because they might expose him to the fate which Regulus chose? On the coldest calculation he would surely perceive, that the high and glowing feelings of such a mind during life altogether throw into shade a few hours of agony in leaving it. And, if he himself were so unfortunate that no more generous sentiment arose in his mind to silence such calculations, would it not be a reproach to his understanding not to discover, that, though in one case out of millions such a character might lead a Regulus to torture, yet, in the common course of nature, it is the source not only of happiness in life, but of quiet and honour in death? A case so extreme as that of Regulus will not perplex us, if we bear in mind, that though we cannot prove the *act* of heroic virtue to be conducive to the interest of the hero, yet we may perceive at once, that nothing is so conducive to his interest as to have a mind so formed that it could not shrink from it, but must rather embrace it with gladness and triumph. Men of vigorous health are said sometimes to suffer most in a pestilence. No man was ever so absurd as for that reason to wish that he were more infirm. The distemper might return once in a century: if he were then alive, he might escape it; and even if he fell, the balance of advantage would be in most cases greatly on the side of robust health. In estimating beforehand the value of a strong bodily frame, a man of sense would throw the small chance of a rare and short evil entirely out of the account. So must the coldest and most selfish moral calculator, who, if he be sagacious and exact, must pronounce, that the inconveniences to which a man may be sometimes exposed by a pure and sound mind, are no reasons for regretting that we do not escape them by possessing minds more enfeebled and distempered. Other occasions will call our attention, in the sequel, to this important part of the subject; but the great name of Leibnitz seemed to require that his degrading statement should not be cited without warning the reader against its egregious fallacy.

MALEBRANCHE.*

This ingenious philosopher and beautiful writer is the only celebrated Cartesian who has professedly handled the theory of Morals.† His theory has in some points of view a conformity to the doctrine of Clarke; while in others it has given occasion to his English follower Norris‡ to say, that if the Quakers understood their own opinion of the illumination of all men, they would explain it on the principles of Malebranche. "There is," says he, "one parent virtue, the universal virtue, the virtue which renders us just and perfect, the virtue which will one day render us happy. It is the only virtue. It is the love of the universal order, as it eternally existed in the Divine Reason, where every created reason contemplates it. This order is composed of practical as well as speculative truth. Reason perceives the moral superiority of one being over another, as immediately as the equality of the radii of the same circle. The relative perfection of beings is that part of the immovable order to which men must conform their minds and their conduct. The love of order is the whole of virtue, and conformity to order constitutes the morality of actions." It is not difficult to discover, that in spite of the singular skill employed in weaving this web, it answers no other purpose than that of hiding the whole difficulty. The love of universal order, says Malebranche, requires that we should value an animal more than a stone, because it is more valuable; and love God infinitely more than man, because he is infinitely better. But without *presupposing* the reality of moral distinctions, and the power of moral feelings,—the two points to be proved, how can either of these propositions be evident or even intelligible? To say that a love of the Eternal Order will produce the love and practice of every virtue, is an assertion untenable, unless we take Morality for granted, and useless, if we do. In his work on Morals, all the incidental and secondary remarks are equally well considered and well expressed. The manner in which he applied his principle to the particulars of human duty is excellent. He is perhaps the first philosopher who has precisely laid down and rigidly adhered to the great principle, *that Virtue consists in pure intentions and dispositions of mind*, without which, actions, however conformable to rules, are not truly moral;—a truth of the highest importance, which, in the theological form, may be said to have been the main principle of the first Protestant Reformers. The ground of piety, according to him, is the conformity of the attributes of God to those moral qualities which we irresistibly love and revere.* "Sovereign princes," says he, "have no right to use their authority without reason. Even God has no such miserable right."† His distinction between a religious society and an established church, and his assertion of the right of the temporal power alone to employ coercion, are worthy of notice, as instances in which a Catholic, at once philosophical and orthodox, could thus speak, not only of the nature of God, but of the rights of the Church.

* Born, 1638; died, 1715.

† Traité de Morale. Rotterdam, 1684.

‡ Author of the Theory of the Ideal World, who well copied, though he did not equal, the clearness and choice of expression which belonged to his master.

* "Il faut aimer l'Etre infiniment parfait, et non pas un fantôme épouvantable, un Dieu injuste, absolu, puissant, mais sans bonté et sans sagesse. S'il y avoit un tel Dieu, le vrai Dieu nous défendroit de l'adorer et de l'aimer. Il y a peut-être plus de danger d'offenser Dieu lorsqu'on lui donne une forme si horrible, que de mépriser son fantôme."—Traité de Morale, chap. viii.

† Ibid. chap. xxii.

JONATHAN EDWARDS.*

This remarkable man, the metaphysician of America, was formed among the Calvinists of New England, when their stern doctrine retained its rigorous authority.† His power of subtile argument, perhaps unmatched, certainly unsurpassed among men, was joined, as in some of the ancient Mystics, with a character which raised his piety to fervour. He embraced their doctrine, probably without knowing it to be theirs. "True religion," says he, "in a great measure consists in holy affections. A love of divine things, for the beauty and sweetness of their moral excellency, is the spring of all holy affections."‡ Had he suffered this noble principle to take the right road to all its fair consequences, he would have entirely concurred with Plato, with Shaftesbury, and Malebranche, in devotion to "the first good, first perfect, and first fair." But he thought it necessary afterwards to limit his doctrine to his own persuasion, by denying that such moral excellence could be discovered in divine things by those Christians who did not take the same view as he did of their religion. All others, and some who hold his doctrines with a more enlarged spirit, may adopt his principle without any limitation. His ethical theory is contained in his Dissertation on the Nature of True Virtue; and in another, On God's chief End in the Creation, published in London thirty years after his death. True virtue, according to him, consists in benevolence, or love to "being in general," which he afterwards limits to "intelligent being," though "sentient" would have involved a more reasonable limitation. This good-will is felt towards a particular being, first in proportion to his degree of existence, (for, says he, "that which is great has more existence, and is farther from nothing, than that which is little;") and secondly, *in proportion to the degree in which that particular being feels benevolence to others.* Thus God, having infinitely more existence and benevolence than man, ought to be infinitely more loved; and for the same reason, God must love himself infinitely more than he does all other beings.§ He can act only from regard to Himself, and His end in creation can only be to manifest His whole nature, which is called acting for His own glory.

As far as Edwards confines himself to created beings, and while his theory is perfectly intelligible, it coincides with that of universal benevolence, hereafter to be considered. The term "being" is a mere encumbrance, which serves indeed to give it a mysterious outside, but brings with it from the schools nothing except their obscurity. He was betrayed into it, by the cloak which it threw over his really unmeaning assertion or assumption, that there are *degrees of existence;* without which that part of his system which relates to the Deity would have appeared to be as baseless as it really is. When we try such a phrase by applying it to matters within the sphere of our experience, we see that it means nothing but *degrees* of certain faculties and powers. But the very application of the term "being" to all things, shows that the least perfect has as much being as the most perfect; or rather that there can be no difference, so far as that word is concerned, between two things to which it is alike applicable. The justness of the compound proportion on which human virtue is made to depend, is capable of being tried by an easy test. If we suppose the greatest of evil spirits to have a hundred times the bad passions of Marcus Aurelius, and at the same time a hundred times his faculties, or, in Edwards' language, a hundred times his quantity of "being," it follows from this moral theory, that we ought to esteem and love the devil exactly in the same degree as we esteem and love Marcus Aurelius.

The chief circumstance which justifies so much being said on the last two writers, is their concurrence in a point towards which ethical philosophy had been slowly approaching from the time of the controversies raised up by Hobbes. They both indicate the increase of this tendency, by introducing an element into their theory, foreign from those cold systems of ethical abstraction, with which they continued in other respects to have much in common. Malebranche makes virtue consist in the love of "order," Edwards in the love of "being." In this language we perceive a step beyond the representation of Clarke, which made it a conformity to the relations of things; but a step which cannot be made without passing into a new province;—without confessing, by the use of the word "love," that not only perception and reason, but emotion and sentiment, are among the fundamental principles of Morals. They still, however, were so wedded to scholastic prejudice, as to choose two of the most aerial abstractions which can be introduced into argument,—"being" and "order,"—to be the objects of those strong active feelings which were to govern the human mind.

BUFFIER.*

The same strange disposition to fix on abstractions as the objects of our primitive feelings, and the end sought by our warmest desires, manifests itself in the ingenious writer with whom this part of the Disserta-

* Born in 1703, at Windsor in Connecticut; died in 1758, at Princeton in New Jersey.

† See Note O.

‡ On Religious Affections, pp. 4, 187.

§ The coincidence of Malebranche with this part of Edwards, is remarkable. Speaking of the Supreme Being, he says, "Il s'aime invinciblement." He adds another more startling expression, "Certainement Dieu ne peut agir que pour lui-même: il n'a point d'autre motif que son amour propre."—Traité de Morale, chap. xvii.

* Born, 1661; died, 1737.

tion closes, under a form of less dignity than that which it assumes in the hands of Malebranche and Clarke. Buffier, the only Jesuit whose name has a place in the history of abstract philosophy, has no peculiar opinions which would have required any mention of him as a moralist, were it not for the just reputation of his Treatise on First Truths, with which Dr. Reid so remarkably, though unaware of its existence, coincides, even in the misapplication of so practical a term as "common sense" to denote the faculty which recognises the truth of first principles. His philosophical writings* are remarkable for that perfect clearness of expression, which, since the great examples of Descartes and Pascal, has been so generally diffused, as to have become one of the enviable peculiarities of French philosophical style, and almost of the French language. His ethical doctrine is that most commonly received among philosophers, from Aristotle to Paley and Bentham: "I desire to be happy; but as I live with other men, I cannot be happy without consulting their happiness:" a proposition perfectly true indeed, but far too narrow; as inferring, that in the most benevolent acts a man must pursue only his own interest, from the fact that the practice of benevolence does increase his happiness, and that because a virtuous mind is likely to be the happiest, our observation of that property of Virtue is the cause of our love and reverence for it.

* Cours de Sciences. Paris, 1732.

SECTION VI.

FOUNDATIONS OF A MORE JUST THEORY OF ETHICS.

BUTLER—HUTCHESON—BERKELEY—HUME—SMITH—PRICE—HARTLEY—TUCKER—PALEY—BENTHAM—STEWART—BROWN.

From the beginning of ethical controversy to the eighteenth century, it thus appears, that the care of the individual for himself, and his regard for the things which regard self, were thought to form the first, and, in the opinion of most, the earliest of all principles which prompt men and other animals to activity; that nearly all philosophers regarded the appetites and desires, which look only to self-gratification, as modifications of this primary principle of self-love; and that a very numerous body considered even the social affections themselves as nothing more than the produce of a more latent and subtile operation of the desire of interest, and the pursuit of pleasure. It is true that they often spoke otherwise; but it was rather from the looseness and fluctuation of their language, than from distrust in their doctrine. It is true, also, that perhaps all represented the gratifications of Virtue as more unmingled, more secure, more frequent, and more lasting, than other pleasures; without which they could neither have retained a hold on the assent of mankind, nor reconciled the principles of their systems with the testimony of their hearts. We have seen how some began to be roused from a lazy acquiescence in this ancient hypothesis, by the monstrous consequences which Hobbes had legitimately deduced from it. A few, of pure minds and great intellect, laboured to render Morality disinterested, by tracing it to Reason as its source; without considering that Reason, elevated indeed far above interest, is also separated by an impassable gulf, from feeling, affection, and passion. At length it was perceived by more than one, that through whatever length of reasoning the mind may pass in its advances towards action, there is placed at the end of any avenue through which it can advance, some principle wholly unlike mere Reason,—some *emotion* or *sentiment* which must be touched, before the springs of Will and Action can be set in motion. Had Lord Shaftesbury steadily adhered to his own principles,—had Leibnitz not recoiled from his statement, the truth might have been regarded as promulged, though not unfolded. The writings of both prove, at least to us, enlightened as we are by what followed, that they were skilful in sounding, and that their lead had touched the bottom. But it was reserved for another moral philosopher to determine this hitherto unfathomed depth.*

BUTLER.†

Butler, who was the son of a Presbyterian trader, early gave such promise, as to induce his father to fit him, by a proper education, for being a minister of that persuasion. He was educated at one of their seminaries under Mr. Jones of Gloucester, where Secker, afterwards Archbishop of Canterbury was his fellow-student. Though many of the dissenters had then begun to relinquish Calvinism, the uniform effect of that doctrine, in disposing its adherents to metaphysical speculation, long survived the opinions which caused it, and cannot be doubted to have influenced the mind of Butler. When a student at the academy at Gloucester, he wrote

* The doctrine of the Stoics is thus put by Cicero into the mouth of Cato: "Placet his, inquit, quorum ratio mihi probatur, simul atque natum sit animal (hinc enim est ordiendum), ipsum sibi conciliari et commendari ad se conservandum, et ad suum statum, et ad ea, quæ conservantia sunt ejus status, diligenda; alienari autem ab interitu, iisque rebus quæ interitum videantur afferre. Id ita esse sic probant, quod, antequam voluptas aut dolor attigerit, salutaria appetant parvi, aspernenturque contraria: quod non fieret, nisi statum suum diligerent, interitum timerent: fieri autem non posset, ut appeterent aliquid, nisi sensum haberent sui, eoque se et sua diligerent. Ex quo intelligi debet, principium ductum esse a se diligendi sui."—De Fin. lib. iii. cap. v. We are told that *diligendo* is the reading of an ancient MS. Perhaps the omission of "a" would be the easiest and most reasonable emendation. The above passage is perhaps the fullest and plainest statement of the doctrines prevalent till the time of Butler.

† Born, 1692; died, 1752.

private letters to Dr. Clarke on his celebrated Demonstration, suggesting objections which were really insuperable, and which are marked by an acuteness which neither himself nor any other ever surpassed. Clarke, whose heart was as well schooled as his head, published the letters, with his own answers, in the next edition of his work, and, by his good offices with his friend and follower, Sir Joseph Jekyll, obtained for the young philosopher an early opportunity of making his abilities and opinions known, by the appointment of preacher at the Chapel of the Master of the Rolls. He was afterwards raised to one of the highest seats on the episcopal bench, through the philosophical taste of Queen Caroline, and her influence over the mind of her husband, which continued long after her death. "He was wafted," says Horace Walpole, "to the See of Durham, on a cloud of Metaphysics."* Even in the fourteenth year of his widowhood, George II. was desirous of inserting the name of the Queen's metaphysical favourite in the Regency Bill of 1751.

His great work on the Analogy of Religion to the Course of Nature, though only a commentary on the singularly original and pregnent passage of Origen,† which is so honestly prefixed to it as a motto, is, notwithstanding, the most original and profound work extant in any language on the philosophy of religion. It is entirely beyond our present scope. His ethical discussions are contained in those deep and sometimes dark dissertations which he preached at the Chapel of the Rolls, and afterwards published under the name of "Sermons," while he was yet fresh from the schools, and full of that courage with which youth often delights to exercise its strength in abstract reasoning, and to push its faculties into the recesses of abstruse speculation. But his youth was that of a sober and mature mind, early taught by Nature to discern the boundaries of Knowledge, and to abstain from fruitless efforts to reach inaccessible ground. In these Sermons,‡ he has taught truths more capable of being exactly distinguished from the doctrines of his predecessors. more satisfactorily established, more comprehensively applied to particulars, more rationally connected with each other, and therefore more worthy of the name of "discovery," than any with which we are acquainted;—if we ought not, with some hesitation, to except the first steps of the Grecian philosophers towards a theory of Morals. It is a peculiar hardship, that the extreme ambiguity of language, an obstacle which it is one of the chief merits of an ethical philosopher to vanquish, is one of the circumstances which prevent men from seeing the justice of applying to him so ambitious a term as "discoverer." He owed more to Lord Shaftesbury than to all other writers besides. He is just and generous towards that philosopher; yet, whoever carefully compares their writings, will without difficulty distinguish the two builders, and the larger as well as more regular and laboured part of the edifice, which is the work of Butler.

Mankind have various principles of action, some leading directly to the good of the individual, some immediately to the good of the community. But the former are not instances of self-love, or of any form of it; for self-love is the desire of a man's own happiness, whereas the object of an appetite or passion is some outward thing. Self-love seeks things as means of happiness; the private appetites seek things, not as means, but as ends. A man eats from hunger, and drinks from thirst; and though he knows that these acts are necessary to life, that knowledge is not the motive of his conduct. No gratification can indeed be imagined without a previous desire. If all the particular desires did not exist independently, self-love would have no object to employ itself about; for there would in that case be no happiness, which, by the very supposition of the opponents, is made up of the gratifications of various desires. No pursuit could be selfish or interested, if there were not satisfactions to be gained by appetites which seek their own outward objects without regard to self. These satisfactions in the mass compose what is called a man's interest.

In contending, therefore, that the benevolent affections are disinterested, no more is claimed for them than must be granted to mere animal appetites and to malevolent passions. Each of these principles alike seeks its own object, for the sake simply of obtaining it. Pleasure is the result of the attainment, but no separate part of the aim of the agent. The desire that another person may be gratified, seeks that outward object alone, according to the general course of human desire. Resentment is as disinterested as gratitude or pity, but not more so. Hunger or thirst may be, as much as the purest benevolence, at variance with self-love. A regard to our own general happiness is not a vice, but in itself an excellent quality. It were well if it prevailed more generally over craving and short-sighted appetites. The weakness of the social affections, and the strength of the private desires, properly constitute selfishness; a vice utterly at variance with the happiness of him who harbours it, and as such, condemned by self-love. There are as few who attain the greatest satisfaction to themselves, as who do the greatest good to others. It is absurd to say with some, that the pleasure of benevolence is selfish because it is felt by self. Understanding and reasoning are acts of self, for

* Memoirs of Geo. II., i. 129.

† "Ejus (analogia) vis est; ut id quod dubium est ad aliquid simile de quo non quæritur, referat; ut incerta certis probet."

‡ See Sermons i. ii. iii. On Human Nature; v. On Compassion; viii. On Resentment; ix. On Forgiveness; xi. and xii. On the Love of Our Neighbour; and xiii. On the Love of God; together with the excellent Preface.

no man can think by proxy; but no one ever called them *selfish*. Why? Evidently because they do not *regard* self. Precisely the same reason applies to benevolence. Such an argument is a gross confusion of "self," as it is a *subject* of feeling or thought, with "self" considered as the *object* of either. It is no more just to refer the private appetites to self-love because they commonly promote happiness, than it would be to refer them to self-hatred in those frequent cases where their gratification obstructs it.

But, besides the private or public desires, and besides the calm regard to our own general welfare, there is a principle in man, in its nature supreme over all others. This natural supremacy belongs to the faculty which surveys, approves, or disapproves the several affections of our minds and actions of our lives. As self-love is superior to the private passions, so Conscience is superior to the whole of man. Passion implies nothing but an inclination to follow an object, and in that respect passions differ only in force: but no notion can be formed of the principle of reflection, or Conscience, which does not comprehend judgment, direction, superintendency; authority over all other principles of action is a constituent part of the idea of it, and cannot be separated from it. Had it strength as it has right, it would govern the world. The passions would have their power, but according to their nature, which is to be subject to Conscience. Hence we may understand the purpose at which the ancients, perhaps confusedly, aimed when they laid it down "that Virtue consisted in following Nature." It is neither easy, nor, for the main object of the moralist, important, to render the doctrines of the ancients by modern language. If Butler returns to this phrase too often, it was rather from the remains of undistinguishing reverence for antiquity, than because he could deem its employment important to his own opinions.

The tie which holds together Religion and Morality is, in the system of Butler, somewhat different from the common representations of it, but not less close. Conscience, or the faculty of approving or disapproving, necessarily constitutes the bond of union. Setting out from the belief of Theism, and combining it, as he had entitled himself to do, with the reality of Conscience, he could not avoid discovering that the being who possessed the highest moral qualities, is the object of the highest moral affections. He contemplates the Deity through the moral nature of man. In the case of a being who is to be perfectly loved, "goodness must be the simple actuating principle within him, this being the moral quality which is the immediate object of love." "The highest, the adequate object of this affection, is perfect goodness, which, therefore, we are to love with all our heart, with all our soul, and with all our strength." "We should refer ourselves implicitly to him, and cast ourselves entirely upon him. The whole attention of life should be to obey his commands."* Moral distinctions are thus presupposed before a step can be made towards Religion: Virtue leads to piety; God is to be loved, because goodness is the object of love; and it is only after the mind rises through human morality to divine perfection, that all the virtues and duties are seen to hang from the throne of God.†

REMARKS.

There do not appear to be any *errors* in the ethical principles of Butler: the following remarks are intended to point out some *defects* in his scheme. And even that attempt is made with the unfeigned humility of one who rejoices in an opportunity of doing justice to that part of the writings of a great philosopher which has not been so clearly understood nor so justly estimated by the generality as his other works.

1. It is a considerable defect, though perhaps unavoidable in a sermon, that he omits all inquiry into the nature and origin of the private appetites, which first appear in human nature. It is implied, but it is not expressed in his reasonings, that there is a time before the child can be called selfish, any more than social, when these appetites seem as it were separately to pursue their distinct objects, and that this is long antecedent to that state of mind in which their gratification is regarded as forming the mass called "happiness." It is hence that they are likened to instincts distinct as these latter subsequently become.‡

2. Butler shows admirably well, that unless there were principles of action independent of self, there could be no pleasures and no happiness for self-love to watch over. A step farther would have led him to perceive that self-love is altogether a secondary formation, the result of the joint operation of Reason and habit upon the primary principles. It could not have existed without presupposing original appetites and organic gratifications. Had he considered this part of the subject, he would have strengthened his case by showing that self-love is as truly a derived principle, not only as any of the social affections, but as any of the most confessedly acquired passions. It would appear clear, that as self-love is not divested of its self-regarding character by considering it as acquired, so the social affections do not lose any part of their disinterested character, if they be considered as formed from simpler elements. Nothing would more tend to root out the old prejudice which treats a regard

* Sermon xiii.—"On the Love of God."

† "The part in which I think I have done most service is that in which I have endeavoured to slip in a foundation under Butler's doctrine of the supremacy of Conscience, which he left baseless."—Sir James Mackintosh to Professor Napier.—Ed.

‡ The very able work ascribed to Mr. Hazlitt, entitled "Essay on the Principles of Human Action," Lond. 1805, contains original views on this subject.

to self as analogous to a self-evident principle, than the proof that self-love is itself formed from certain original elements, and that a living being long subsists before its appearance.*

3. It must be owned that those parts of Butler's discourses which relate to the social affections are more satisfactory than those which handle the question concerning the moral sentiments. It is not that the real existence of the latter is not as well made out as that of the former. In both cases he occupies the unassailable ground of an appeal to consciousness. All men (even the worst), feel that they have a conscience and disinterested affections. But he betrays a sense of the greater vagueness of his notions on this subject: he falters as he approaches it. He makes no attempt to determine in what state of mind the action of Conscience consists. He does not venture steadily to denote it by a name; he fluctuates between different appellations, and multiplies the metaphors of authority and command, without a simple exposition of that mental operation which these metaphors should only have illustrated. It commands other principles: but the question recurs, Why, or How?

Some of his own hints and some fainter intimations of Shaftesbury, might have led him to what appears to be the true solution, which, perhaps from its extreme simplicity, has escaped him and his successors. The truth seems to be, that the moral sentiments in their mature state, are *a class of feelings which have no other object but the mental dispositions leading to voluntary action, and the voluntary actions which flow from these dispositions.* We are pleased with some dispositions and actions, and displeased with others, in ourselves and our fellows. We desire to cultivate the dispositions and to perform the actions, which we contemplate with satisfaction. These objects, like all those of human appetite or desire, are sought for their own sake. The peculiarity of these desires is, that their gratification *requires the use of no means*; nothing (unless it be a volition) is interposed between the desire and the voluntary act. It is impossible, therefore, that these passions should undergo any change by transfer from being the end to being the means, as is the case with other practical principles. On the other hand, as soon as they are fixed on these ends, they cannot regard any further object. When another passion prevails over them, the end of the moral faculty is converted into a means of gratification. But volitions and actions are not themselves the end or last object in view, of any other desire or aversion. Nothing stands between the moral sentiments and their object; they are, as it were, in contact with the Will. It is this sort of mental position, if the expression may be pardoned, that explains or seems to explain those characteristic properties which true philosophers ascribe to them, and which all reflecting men feel to belong to them. Being the only desires, aversions, sentiments, or emotions which regard dispositions and actions, they necessarily extend to the *whole* character and conduct. Among motives to action, they alone are justly considered as *universal*. They may and do stand between any other practical principle and its object, while it is absolutely impossible that another shall intercept their connexion with the Will. Be it observed, that though many passions prevail over them, no other can act beyond its own appointed and limited sphere; and that such prevalence itself, leaving the natural order disturbed in no other part of the mind, is perceived to be a disorder, whenever seen in another, and felt to be so by the very mind disordered, when the disorder subsides. Conscience may forbid the Will to contribute to the gratification of a desire: no desire ever forbids the Will to obey Conscience.

This result of the peculiar relation of Conscience to the Will, justifies those metaphorical expressions which ascribe to it "authority" and the right of "universal command." It is *immutable*; for, by the law which regulates all feelings, it must rest on *action*, which is its object, and beyond which it cannot look; and as it employs no *means*, it never can be transferred to nearer objects, in the way in which he who first desires an object as a means of gratification, may come to seek it as his end. Another remarkable peculiarity is bestowed on the moral feelings by the nature of their object. As the objects of all other desires are outward, the satisfaction of them may be frustrated by outward causes: the moral sentiments may always be gratified, because voluntary actions and moral dispositions spring from within. No external circumstance affects them;—hence their *independence*. As the moral sentiment needs *no means*, and the desire is instantaneously followed by the volition, it seems to be either that which first suggests the relation between *command* and *obedience*, or at least that which affords the simplest instance of it. It is therefore with the most rigorous precision that authority and universality are ascribed to them. Their only unfortunate property is their too frequent weakness; but it is apparent that it is from that circumstance alone that their failure arises. Thus considered, the language of Butler concerning Conscience, that, "had it strength, as it has right, it would govern the world," which may seem to be only an effusion of generous feeling, proves to be a just statement of the nature and action of the highest of human faculties. The union of universality, immutability, and independence, with direct action on the Will, which distinguishes the Moral Sense from every other part of our practical nature, renders it scarcely metaphorical language to ascribe to

* Compare this statement with the Stoical doctrine explained by Cicero in the book De Finibus, quoted above, of which it is the direct opposite.

it unbounded sovereignty and awful authority over the whole of the world within;—shows that attributes, well denoted by terms significant of command and control, are, in fact, inseparable from it, or rather constitute its very essence; and justifies those ancient moralists who represent it as alone securing, if not forming the moral liberty of man. When afterwards the religious principle is evolved, Conscience is clothed with the sublime character of representing the divine purity and majesty in the human soul. Its title is not impaired by any number of defeats; for every defeat necessarily disposes the disinterested and dispassionate by-stander to wish that its force were strengthened: and though it may be doubted whether, consistently with the present constitution of human nature, it could be so invigorated as to be the only motive to action, yet every such by-stander rejoices at all accessions to its force; and would own, that man becomes happier, more excellent, more estimable, more venerable, in proportion as it acquires a power of banishing malevolent passions, of strongly curbing all the private appetites, and of influencing and guiding the benevolent affections themselves.

Let it be carefully considered whether the same observations could be made with truth, or with plausibility, on any other part or element of the nature of man. They are entirely independent of the question, whether Conscience be an inherent, or an acquired principle. If it be inherent, that circumstance is, according to the common modes of thinking, a sufficient proof of its title to veneration. But if provision be made in the constitution and circumstances of all men, for uniformly producing it, by processes similar to those which produce other acquired sentiments, may not our reverence be augmented by admiration of that Supreme Wisdom which, in such mental contrivances, yet more brightly than in the lower world of matter, accomplishes mighty purposes by instruments so simple? Should these speculations be thought to have any solidity by those who are accustomed to such subjects, it would be easy to unfold and apply them so fully, that they may be thoroughly apprehended by every intelligent person.

4. The most palpable defect of Butler's scheme is, that it affords no answer to the question, "What is the distinguishing quality common to all right actions?" If it were answered, "Their criterion is, that they are approved and commanded by Conscience," the answerer would find that he was involved in a vicious circle; for Conscience itself could be no otherwise defined than as the faculty which approves and commands right actions.

There are few circumstances more remarkable than the small number of Butler's followers in Ethics; and it is perhaps still more observable, that his opinions were not so much rejected as overlooked. It is an instance of the importance of style. No thinker so great was ever so bad a writer. Indeed, the ingenious apologies which have been lately attempted for this defect, amount to no more than that his power of thought was too much for his skill in language. How general must the reception have been of truths so certain and momentous as those contained in Butler's discourses,—with how much more clearness must they have appeared to his own great understanding, if he had possessed the strength and distinctness with which Hobbes enforces odious falsehood, or the unspeakable charm of that transparent diction which clothed the unfruitful paradoxes of Berkeley!

HUTCHESON.*

This ingenious writer began to try his own strength by private letters, written in his early youth to Dr. Clarke, the metaphysical patriarch of his time; on whom young philosophers seem to have considered themselves as possessing a claim, which he had too much goodness to reject. His correspondence with Hutcheson is lost; but we may judge of its spirit by his answers to Butler, and by one to Mr. Henry Home,† afterwards Lord Kames, then a young adventurer in the prevalent speculations. Nearly at the same period with Butler's first publication,‡ the writings of Hutcheson began to show coincidences with him, indicative of the tendency of moral theory to assume a new form, by virtue of an impulse received from Shaftesbury, and quickened to greater activity by the adverse system of Clarke. Lord Molesworth, the friend of Shaftesbury, patronised Hutcheson, and even criticised his manuscript; and though a Presbyterian, he was befriended by King, Archbishop of Dublin, himself a metaphysician; and aided by Mr. Synge, afterwards also a bishop, to whom speculations somewhat similar to his own had occurred.

Butler and Hutcheson coincided in the two important positions, that disinterested affections, and a distinct moral faculty, are essential parts of human nature. Hutcheson is a chaste and simple writer, who imbibed the opinions, without the literary faults of his master, Shaftesbury. He has a clearness of expression, and fulness of illustration, which are wanting in Butler. But he is inferior to both these writers in the appearance at least of originality, and to Butler especially in that

* Born in Ireland, 1694; died at Glasgow, 1747.

† Woodhouselee's Life of Lord Kames, vol. i. Append. No. 3.

‡ The first edition of Butler's Sermons was published in 1726, in which year also appeared the second edition of Hutcheson's Inquiry into Beauty and Virtue. The Sermons had been preached some years before, though there is no likelihood that the contents could have reached a young teacher at Dublin. The place of Hutcheson's birth is not mentioned in any account known to me. Ireland may be truly said to be "*incuriosa suorum.*"

philosophical courage which, when it discovers the fountains of truth and falsehood, leaves others to follow the streams. He states as strongly as Butler, that "the same cause which determines us to pursue happiness for ourselves, determines us both to esteem and benevolence on their proper occasions—even the very frame of our nature."* It is in vain, as he justly observes, for the patrons of a refined selfishness to pretend that we pursue the happiness of others for the sake of the pleasure which we derive from it; since it is apparent that there could be no such pleasure if there had been no previous affection. "Had we no affection distinct from self-love, nothing could raise a desire of the happiness of others, but when viewed as a mean of our own."† He seems to have been the first who entertained just notions of the formation of the secondary desires, which had been overlooked by Butler. "There must arise, in consequence of our original desires, *secondary* desires of every thing useful to gratify the primary desire. Thus, as soon as we apprehend the use of wealth, or power, to gratify our original desires, we also *desire* them. From their universality as means arises the general prevalence of these desires of wealth and power."‡ Proceeding farther in his zeal against the selfish system than Lord Shaftesbury, who seems ultimately to rest the reasonableness of benevolence on its subserviency to the happiness of the individual, he represents the moral faculty to be, as well as self-love and benevolence, a calm general impulse, which may and does impel a good man to sacrifice not only happiness, but even life itself, to Virtue.

As Mr. Locke had spoken of "an internal sensation;" Lord Shaftesbury once or twice of "a reflex sense," and once of "a moral sense;" Hutcheson, who had a steadier, if not a clearer view of the nature of Conscience than Butler, calls it "a moral sense;" a name which quickly became popular, and continues to be a part of philosophical language. By "sense" he understood a capacity of receiving ideas, together with pleasures and pains, from a class of objects: the term "moral" was used to describe the particular class in question. It implied only that Conscience was a separate element in our nature, and that it was not a state or act of the Understanding. According to him, it also implied that it was an original and implanted principle; but every other part of his theory might be embraced by those who hold it to be derivative.

The object of moral approbation, according to him, is general benevolence; and he carries this generous error so far as to deny that prudence, as long as it regards ourselves, can be morally approved;—an assertion contradicted by every man's feelings, and to which we owe the Dissertation on the Nature of Virtue, which Butler annexed to his Analogy. By proving that all virtuous actions produce general good, he fancied that he had proved the necessity of regarding the general good in every act of virtue;—an instance of that confusion of the theory of moral sentiments with the criterion of moral actions, against which the reader was warned at the opening of this Dissertation, as fatal to ethical philosophy. He is chargeable, like Butler, with a vicious circle, in describing virtuous acts as those which are approved by the moral sense, while he at the same time describes the moral sense as the faculty which perceives and feels the morality of actions.

Hutcheson was the father of the modern school of speculative philosophy in Scotland; for though in the beginning of the sixteenth century the Scotch are said to have been known throughout Europe by their unmeasured passion for dialectical subtilties,* and though this metaphysical taste was nourished by the controversies which followed the Reformation, yet it languished, with every other intellectual taste and talent, from the Restoration,—first silenced by civil disorders, and afterwards repressed by an exemplary, but unlettered clergy,—till the philosophy of Shaftesbury was brought by Hutcheson from Ireland. We are told by the writer of his Life (a fine piece of philosophical biography) that "he had a remarkable degree of rational enthusiasm for learning, liberty, Religion, Virtue, and human happiness;"† that he taught in public with persuasive eloquence; that his instructive conversation was at once lively and modest; and that he united pure manners with a kind disposition. What wonder that such a man should have spread the love of Knowledge and Virtue around him, and should have rekindled in his adopted country a relish for the sciences which he cultivated! To him may also be ascribed that proneness to multiply ultimate and original principles in human nature, which characterized the Scottish school till the second extinction of a passion for meta-

* Inquiry, p. 152.

† Essay on the Passions, p. 17.

‡ Ibid. p. 8.

* The character given of the Scotch by the famous and unfortunate Servetus (edition of Ptolemy. 1533,) is in many respects curious: "Gallis amicissimi, Anglorumque regi maximê infesti.*** Subita ingenia, et in ultionem prona, ferociaque.*** In bello fortes; inediæ, vigiliæ, algoris patientissimi; decenti formâ sed cultu negligentiori; invidi naturâ, et cæterorum mortalium contemptores; ostentant *plus nimio nobilitatem suam, et in summâ etiam egestate suum genus ad regiam stirpem referunt; nec non dialecticis argutiis sibi blandiuntur.*" "Subita ingenia" is an expression equivalent to the "Præfervidum Scotorum ingenium" of Buchanan. Churchill almost agrees in words with Servetus:

"Whose lineage springs
From great and glorious, though forgotten kings."

The strong antipathy of the late King George III. to what he called "Scotch Metaphysics," proves the permanency of the last part of the national character.

† Life by Dr. Leechman, prefixed to the System of Moral Philosophy.

physical speculation in Scotland. A careful perusal of the writings of this now little studied philosopher will satisfy the well-qualified reader, that Dr. Adam Smith's ethical speculations are not so unsuggested as they are beautiful.

BERKELEY.*

This great metaphysician was so little a moralist, that it requires the attraction of his name to excuse its introduction here. His Theory of Vision contains a great discovery in mental philosophy. His immaterialism is chiefly valuable as a touchstone of metaphysical sagacity; showing those to be altogether without it, who, like Johnson and Beattie, believed that his speculations were sceptical, that they implied any distrust in the senses, or that they had the smallest tendency to disturb reasoning or alter conduct. Ancient learning, exact science, polished society, modern literature, and the fine arts, contributed to adorn and enrich the mind of this accomplished man. All his contemporaries agreed with the satirist in ascribing

> "To Berkeley every virtue under heaven."†

Adverse factions and hostile wits concurred only in loving, admiring, and contributing to advance him. The severe sense of Swift endured his visions; the modest Addison endeavoured to reconcile Clarke to his ambitious speculations. His character converted the satire of Pope into fervid praise; even the discerning, fastidious, and turbulent Atterbury said, after an interview with him, "So much understanding, so much knowledge, so much innocence, and such humility, I did not think had been the portion of any but angels, till I saw this gentleman."‡ Lord Bathurst told me, that the members of the Scriblerus Club being met at his house at dinner, they agreed to rally Berkeley, who was also his guest, on his scheme at Bermudas. Berkeley, having listened to the many lively things they had to say, begged to be heard in his turn, and displayed his plan with such an astonishing and animating force of eloquence and enthusiasm, that they were struck dumb, and after some pause, rose all up together, with earnestness exclaiming, 'Let us set out with him immediately.'"§ It was when thus beloved and celebrated that he conceived, at the age of forty-five, the design of devoting his life to reclaim and convert the natives of North America; and he employed as much influence and solicitation as common men do for their most prized objects, in obtaining leave to resign his dignities and revenues, to quit his accomplished and affectionate friends, and to bury himself in what must have seemed an intellectual desert. After four years' residence at Newport, in Rhode Island, he was compelled, by the refusal of government to furnish him with funds for his College, to forego his work of heroic, or rather godlike benevolence; though not without some consoling forethought of the fortune of the country where he had sojourned.

> Westward the course of empire takes its way,
> The first four acts already past,
> A fifth shall close the drama with the day,
> TIME'S NOBLEST OFFSPRING IS ITS LAST.

Thus disappointed in his ambition of keeping a school for savage children, at a salary of a hundred pounds by the year, he was received, on his return, with open arms by the philosophical queen, at whose metaphysical parties he made one with Sherlock, who, as well as Smalridge, was his supporter, and with Hoadley, who, following Clarke, was his antagonist. By her influence, he was made bishop of Cloyne. It is one of his highest boasts, that though of English extraction, he was a true Irishman, and the first eminent Protestant, after the unhappy contest at the Revolution, who avowed his love for all his countrymen. He asked, "Whether their habitations and furniture were not more sordid than those of the savage Americans?"* "Whether a scheme for the welfare of this nation should not take in the whole inhabitants?" and "Whether it was a vain attempt, to project the flourishing of our Protestant gentry, exclusive of the bulk of the natives?"† He proceeds to promote the reformation suggested in this pregnant question by a series of Queries, intimating with the utmost skill and address, every reason that proves the necessity, and the safety, and the wisest mode of adopting his suggestion. He contributed, by a truly Christian address to the Roman Catholics of his diocese, to their perfect quiet during the rebellion of 1745; and soon after published a letter to the clergy of that persuasion, beseeching them to inculcate industry among their flocks, for which he received their thanks. He tells them that it was a saying among the negro slaves, "if negro were not negro, Irishman would be negro." It is difficult to read these proofs of benevolence and foresight without emotion, at the moment when, after a lapse of near a century, his suggestions have been at length, at the close of a struggle of twenty-five years, adopted, by the admission of the whole Irish nation to the privileges of the British constitution.‡ The patriotism of Berkeley was not, like that of Swift, tainted by disappointed ambition, nor was it, like Swift's, confined to a colony of English Protestants. Perhaps the Querist contains more hints, then original, and still unapplied in legislation and political economy, than are to be found in any other equal space. From the writings of his advanced years, when he chose a medical tract§ to be the vehicle of his philosophical

* Born near Thomastown, in Ireland, 1684; died at Oxford, 1753.
† Epilogue to Pope's Satires, dialogue 2.
‡ Duncombe's Letters, pp. 106, 107.
§ Wharton on Pope, i. 199.

* See his Querist, 358; published in 1735.
† Ibid., 255. ‡ April, 1829.
§ Siris, or Reflections on Tar Water.

reflections, though it cannot be said that he relinquished his early opinions, it is at least apparent that his mind had received a new bent, and was habitually turned from reasoning towards contemplation. His immaterialism indeed modestly appears, but only to purify and elevate our thoughts, and to fix them on Mind, the paramount and primeval principle of all things. "Perhaps," says he, "the truth about innate ideas may be, that there are properly no ideas, or passive objects, in the mind but what are derived from sense, but that there are also, besides these, her own acts and operations,—such are notions;" a statement which seems once more to admit *general conceptions*, and which might have served, as well as the parallel passage of Leibnitz, as the basis of the modern philosophy of Germany. From these compositions of his old age, he appears then to have recurred with fondness to Plato and the later Platonists; writers from whose mere reasonings an intellect so acute could hardly hope for an argumentative satisfaction of all its difficulties, and whom he probably rather studied as a means of inuring his mind to objects beyond the "visible diurnal sphere," and of attaching it, through frequent meditation, to that perfect and transcendent goodness to which his moral feelings always pointed, and which they incessantly strove to grasp. His mind, enlarging as it rose, at length receives every theist, however imperfect his belief, to a communion in its philosophic piety. "Truth," he beautifully concludes, "is the cry of all, but the game of a few. Certainly, where it is the chief passion, it does not give way to vulgar cares, nor is it contented with a little ardour in the early time of life; active perhaps to pursue, but not so fit to weigh and revise. He that would make a real progress in knowledge, must dedicate his age as well as youth, the later growth as well as first fruits, at the altar of Truth." So did Berkeley, and such were almost his latest words.

His general principles of Ethics may be shortly stated in his own words:—"As God is a being of infinite goodness, His end is the good of His creatures. The general well-being of all men of all nations, of all ages of the world, is that which He designs should be procured by the concurring actions of each individual." Having stated that this end can be pursued only in one of two ways,—either by computing the consequences of each action, or by obeying rules which generally tend to happiness,—and having shown the first to be impossible, he rightly infers, "that the end to which God requires the concurrence of human actions, must be carried on by the observation of certain determinate and universal rules, or moral precepts, which in their own nature have a necessary tendency to promote the well-being of mankind, taking in all nations and ages, from the beginning to the end of the world."* A romance, of which a journey to an Utopia, in the centre of Africa, forms the chief part, called "The Adventures of Signor Gaudentio di Lucca," has been commonly ascribed to him; probably on no other ground than its union of pleasing invention with benevolence and elegance.* Of the exquisite grace and beauty of his diction, no man accustomed to English composition can need to be informed. His works are, beyond dispute, the finest models of philosophical style since Cicero. Perhaps they surpass those of the orator, in the wonderful art by which the fullest light is thrown on the most minute and evanescent parts of the most subtile of human conceptions. Perhaps, also, he surpassed Cicero in the charm of simplicity, a quality eminently found in Irish writers before the end of the eighteenth century;—conspicuous in the masculine severity of Swift, in the Platonic fancy of Berkeley, in the native tenderness and elegance of Goldsmith, and not withholding its attractions from Hutcheson and Leland, writers of classical taste, though of inferior power. The two Irish philosophers of the eighteenth century may be said to have co-operated in calling forth the metaphysical genius of Scotland; for, though Hutcheson spread the taste for, and furnished the principles of such speculations, yet Berkeley undoubtedly produced the scepticism of Hume, which stimulated the instinctive school to activity, and was thought incapable of confutation, otherwise than by their doctrines.

* Sermon in Trinity College chapel, on Passive Obedience, 1712.

* See Gentleman's Magazine for January, 1777.

DAVID HUME.†

The life of Mr. Hume, written by himself, is remarkable above most, if not all writings of that sort, for hitting the degree of interest between coldness and egotism which becomes a modest man in speaking of his private history. Few writers, whose opinions were so obnoxious, have more perfectly escaped every personal imputation. Very few men of so calm a character have been so warmly beloved. That he approached to the character of a perfectly good and wise man, is an affectionate exaggeration, for which his friend Dr. Smith, in the first moments of his sorrow, may well be excused.‡ But such a praise can never be earned without passing through either of the extremes of fortune,—without standing the test of temptations, dangers, and sacrifices. It may be said with truth, that the private character of Mr. Hume exhibited all the virtues which a man of reputable station, under a mild government, in the quiet times of a civilized country, has often the opportunity to practise. He showed no want of the qualities which fit men for more severe trials. Though others had warmer affections, no man was a

† Born at Edinburgh, 1711; died there, 1776.

‡ Dr. Smith's Letter to Mr. Strahan, annexed to the Life of Hume.

kinder relation, a more unwearied friend, or more free from meanness and malice. His character was so simple, that he did not even affect modesty; but neither his friendships nor his deportment were changed by a fame which filled all Europe. His good nature, his plain manners, and his active kindness, procured him in Paris the enviable name of "*the good David*," from a society not so alive to goodness, as without reason to place it at the head of the qualities of a celebrated man.* His whole character is faithfully and touchingly represented in the story of La Roche,† where Mr. Mackenzie, without concealing Mr. Hume's opinions, brings him into contact with scenes of tender piety, and yet preserves the interest inspired by genuine and unalloyed, though moderated, feelings and affections. The amiable and venerable patriarch of Scottish literature,—opposed, as he was to the opinions of the philosopher on whom he has composed his best panegyric,—tells us that he read his manuscript to Dr. Smith, "who declared that he did not find a syllable to object to, but added, with his characteristic absence of mind, that he was surprised he had never heard of the anecdote before."‡ So lively was the delineation, thus sanctioned by the most natural of all testimonies. Mr. Mackenzie indulges his own religious feelings by modestly intimating, that Dr. Smith's answer seemed to justify the last words of the tale, "that there were moments when the philosopher recalled to his mind the venerable figure of the good La Roche, and wished that he had never doubted." To those who are strangers to the seductions of paradox, to the intoxication of fame, and to the bewitchment of prohibited opinions, it must be unaccountable, that he who revered benevolence should, without apparent regret, cease to see it on the throne of the Universe. It is a matter of wonder that his habitual esteem for every fragment and shadow of moral excellence should not lead him to envy those who contemplated its perfection in that living and paternal character which gives it a power over the human heart.

On the other hand, if we had no experience of the power of opposite opinions in producing irreconcilable animosities, we might have hoped that those who retained such high privileges, would have looked with more compassion than dislike on a virtuous man who had lost them. In such cases it is too little remembered, that repugnance to hypocrisy and impatience of long concealment, are the qualities of the best formed minds, and that, if the publication of some doctrines proves often painful and mischievous, the habitual suppression of opinion is injurious to Reason, and very dangerous to sincerity. Practical questions thus arise, so difficult and perplexing that their determination generally depends on the boldness or timidity of the individual,—on his tenderness for the feelings of the good, or his greater reverence for the free exercise of reason. The time is not yet come when the noble maxim of Plato, "that every soul is *unwillingly* deprived of truth," will be practically and heartily applied by men to the honest opponents who differ from them most widely.

It was in his twenty-seventh year that Mr. Hume published at London the Treatise of Human Nature, the first systematic attack on all the principles of knowledge and belief, and the most formidable, if universal scepticism could ever be more than a mere exercise of ingenuity.* This memorable work was reviewed in a Journal of that time,† in a criticism not distinguished by ability, which affects to represent the style of a very clear writer as unintelligible,—sometimes from a purpose to insult, but oftener from sheer dulness,—which is unaccountably silent respecting the consequences of a sceptical system, but which concludes with the following prophecy so much at variance with the general tone of the article, that it would seem to be added by a different hand. "It bears incontestable marks of a great capacity, of a soaring genius, but young, and not yet thoroughly practised. Time and use may ripen these qualities in the author, and we shall probably have reason to consider this, compared with his later productions, in the same light as we view the Juvenile works of Milton or the first manner of Raphael."

The great speculator did not in this work amuse himself, like Bayle, with dialectical exercises, which only inspire a disposition towards doubt, by showing in detail the uncertainty of most opinions. He aimed at proving, not that nothing was known, but that nothing could be known,—from the structure of the Understanding to demonstrate that we are doomed for ever to dwell in absolute and universal ignorance. It is true that such a system of universal scepticism never can be more than an intellectual amusement, an exercise of subtilty, of which the only use is to check dogmatism, but which perhaps oftener provokes and produces that much more common evil. As those dictates of experience which regulate

* See Note P. † Mirror, Nos. 42, 43, 44.
‡ Mackenzie's Life of John Home, p. 21.

* Sextus, a physician of the empirical, *i. e.* anti-theoretical school, who lived at Alexandria in the reign of Antoninus Pius, has preserved the reasonings of the ancient Sceptics as they were to be found in their most improved state, in the writings of Ænesidemus, a Cretan, who was a professor in the same city, soon after the reduction of Egypt into a Roman province. The greater part of the grounds of doubt are very shallow and popular: there are, among them, intimations of the argument against a necessary connection of causes with effects, afterwards better presented by Glanville in his Scepsis Scientifici.—See Note Q.

† The Works of the Learned for Nov. and Dec. 1739, pp. 353—404. This review is attributed by some (Chalmer's Biogr. Dict., *voce* Hume) to Warburton, but certainly without foundation.

conduct must be the objects of belief, all objections which attack them in common with the principles of reasoning, must be utterly ineffectual. Whatever attacks every principle of belief can destroy none. As long as the foundations of Knowledge are allowed to remain on the same level (be it called of certainty or uncertainty), with the maxims of life, the whole system of human conviction must continue undisturbed. When the sceptic boasts of having involved the results of experience and the elements of Geometry in the same ruin with the doctrines of Religion and the principles of Philosophy, he may be answered, that no dogmatist ever claimed more than the same degree of certainty for these various convictions and opinions, and that his scepticism, therefore, leaves them in the relative condition in which it found them. No man knew better or owned more frankly than Mr. Hume, that to this answer there is no serious reply. Universal scepticism involves a contradiction in terms: *it is a belief that there can be no belief*. It is an attempt of the mind to act without its structure, and by other laws than those to which its nature has subjected its operations. To reason without assenting to the principles on which reasoning is founded, is not unlike an effort to feel without nerves, or to move without muscles. No man can be allowed to be an opponent in reasoning, who does not set out with admitting all the principles, without the admission of which it is impossible to reason.* It is indeed a puerile, nay, in the eye of Wisdom, a childish play, to attempt either to establish or to confute principles by argument, which every step of that argument must presuppose. The only difference between the two cases is, that he who tries to prove them can do so only by first taking them for granted, and that he who attempts to impugn them falls at the very first step into a contradiction from which he never can rise.

It must, however, be allowed, that universal scepticism has practical consequences of a very mischievous nature. This is because its *universality* is not steadily kept in view, and constantly borne in mind. If it were, the above short and plain remark would be an effectual antidote to the poison. But in practice, it is an armoury from which weapons are taken to be employed against *some* opinions, while it is hidden from notice that the same weapon would equally cut down every other conviction. It is thus that Mr. Hume's theory of causation is used as an answer to arguments for the existence of the Deity, without warning the reader that it would equally lead him not to expect that the sun will rise to-morrow. It must also be added, that those who are early accustomed to dispute first principles are never likely to acquire, in a sufficient degree, that earnestness and that sincerity, that strong love of Truth, and that conscientious solicitude for the formation of just opinions, which are not the least virtues of men, but of which the cultivation is the more especial duty of all who call themselves philosophers.*

It is not an uninteresting fact that Mr. Hume, having been introduced by Lord Kames (then Mr. Henry Home) to Dr. Butler, sent a copy of his Treatise to that philosopher at the moment of his preferment to the bishopric of Durham; and that the perusal of it did not deter the philosophic prelate from "everywhere recommending Mr. Hume's Moral and Political Essays,"† published two years afterwards;—essays which it would indeed have been unworthy of such a man not to have liberally commended; for they, and those which followed them, whatever may be thought of the contents of some of them, must be ever regarded as the best models in any language, of the short but full, of the clear and agreeable, though deep discussion of difficult questions.

Mr. Hume considered his Inquiry concerning the Principles of Morals as the best of his writings. It is very creditable to his character, that he should have looked back with most complacency on a tract the least distinguished by originality, and the least tainted by paradox, among his philosophical works; but deserving of all commendation for the elegant perspicuity of the style, and the novelty of illustration and inference with which he unfolded to general readers a doctrine too simple, too certain, and too important, to remain till his time undiscovered among philosophers. His diction has, indeed, neither the grace of Berkeley, nor the strength of Hobbes; but it is without the verbosity of the former, or the rugged sternness of the latter. His manner is more lively, more easy, more ingratiating, and, if the word may be so applied, more amusing, than that of any other metaphysical writer.‡ He knew himself too

* This maxim, which contains a sufficient answer to all universal scepticism, or, in other words, to all scepticism properly so called, is significantly conveyed in the quaint title of an old and rare book, entitled, "Scivi; sive Sceptices et Scepticorum a Jure Disputationis Exclusio," by Thomas White, the metaphysician of the English Catholics in modern times. "Fortunately," says the illustrious sceptic himself, "since Reason is incapable of dispelling these clouds, Nature herself suffices for that purpose, and cures me of this philosophical delirium."—Treat. of Hum. Nat., i. 467; almost in the sublime and immortal words of Pascal: "La Raison confond les dogmatistes, et la Nature les sceptiques."

* It would be an act of injustice to those readers who are not acquainted with that valuable volume entitled, "Essays on the Formation of Opinions," not to refer them to it as enforcing that neglected part of morality. To it may be added, a masterly article in the Westminster Review, vi. 1, occasioned by the Essays.

† Woodhouselee's Life of Kames, i. 86. 104.

‡ These commendations are so far from being at variance with the remarks of the late most ingenious Dr. Thomas Brown, on Mr. Hume's "mode of writing," (Inquiry into the Relation of Cause and Effect, 3d ed. p. 327,) that they may rather be regarded as descriptive of those excellencies of

well to be, as Dr. Johnson asserted, an imitator of Voltaire; who, as it were, embodied in his own person all the wit and quickness and versatile ingenuity of a people which surpasses other nations in these brilliant qualities. If he must be supposed to have had an eye on any French writer, it would be a more plausible guess, that he sometimes copied, with a temperate hand, the unexpected thoughts and familiar expressions of Fontenelle. Though he carefully weeded his writings in their successive editions, yet they still contain Scotticisms and Gallicisms enough to employ the successors of such critics as those who exulted over the Patavinity of the Roman historian. His own great and modest mind would have been satisfied with the praise which cannot be withheld from him, that there is no writer in our language who, through long works, is more agreeable; and it is no derogation from him, that, as a Scotsman, he did not reach those native and secret beauties, characteristical of a language, which are never attained, in elaborate composition, but by a very small number of those who familiarly converse in it from infancy. The Inquiry affords perhaps the best specimen of his style. In substance, its chief merit is the proof, from an abundant enumeration of particulars, that all the qualities and actions of the mind which are generally approved by mankind agree in the circumstance of being useful to society. In the proof (scarcely necessary), that benevolent affections and actions have that tendency, he asserts the real existence of these affections with unusual warmth; and he well abridges some of the most forcible arguments of Butler,* whom it is remarkable that he does not mention. To show the importance of his principle, he very unnecessarily distinguishes the comprehensive duty of justice from other parts of Morality, as an artificial virtue, for which our respect is solely derived from notions of utility. If all things were in such plenty that there could never be a want, or if men were so benevolent as to provide for the wants of others as much as for their own, there would, says he, in neither case be any justice, because there would be no need for it. But it is evident that the same reasoning is applicable to every good affection and right action. None of them could exist if there were no scope for their exercise. If there were no suffering, there could be no pity and no relief; if there were no offences, there could be no placability: if there were no crimes, there could be no mercy. Temperance, prudence, patience, magnanimity, are qualties of which the value depends on the evils by which they are respectively exercised.†

With regard to purity of manners, it must be owned that Mr. Hume, though he controverts no rule, yet treats vice with too much indulgence. It was his general disposition to distrust those virtues which are liable to exaggeration, and may be easily counterfeited. The ascetic pursuit of purity, and hypocritical pretences to patriotism, had too much withdrawn the respect of his equally calm and sincere nature from these excellent virtues; more especially as severity in both these respects was often at apparent variance with affection, which can neither be long assumed, nor ever overvalued. Yet it was singular that he who, in his essay on Polygamy and Divorce,* had so well shown the connection of domestic ties with the outward order of society, should not have perceived their deeper and closer relation to all the social feelings of human nature. It cannot be enough regretted, that, in an inquiry written with a very moral purpose, his habit of making truth attractive, by throwing over her the dress of paradox, should have given him for a moment the appearance of weighing the mere amusements of society and conversation against domestic fidelity, which is the preserver of domestic affection, the source of parental fondness and filial regard, and, indirectly, of all the kindness which exists between human beings. That families are schools where the infant heart learns to love, and that pure manners are the cement which alone holds these schools together, are truths so certain, that it is wonderful he should not have betrayed a stronger sense of their importance. No one could so well have proved that all the virtues of that class, in their various orders and degrees, minister to the benevolent affections; and that every act which separates the senses from the affections tends, in some degree, to deprive kindness of its natural auxiliary, and to lessen its prevalence in the world. It did not require his sagacity to discover that the gentlest and tenderest feelings flourish only under the stern guardianship of these severe virtues. Perhaps his philosophy was

---

which the excess produced the faults of Mr. Hume, as a mere searcher and teacher, justly, though perhaps severely, animadverted on by Dr. Brown.

* Inquiry, § ii. part. i., especially the concluding paragraphs; those which precede being more his own.

† "Si nobis, cum ex hac vita migraverimus, in beatorum insulis, ut fabulæ ferunt, immortale ævum degere liceret, quid opus esset eloquentia, cum judicia nulla fierent? aut ipsis etiam virtutibus? Nec enim fortitudine indigeremus, nullo proposito aut labore aut periculo; *nec justitia, cum esset nihil quod appeteretur alieni;* nec temperantia, quæ regeret eas quæ nullæ essent libidines: ne prudentia quidem egeremus, nullo proposito delectu bonorum et malorum. Una igitur essemus beati cognitione rerum et scientia."—Frag. Cic. Hortens. apud Augustine de Trinitate. Cicero is more extensive, and therefore more consistent than Hume; but his enumeration errs both by excess and defect. He supposes Knowledge to render beings happy in this imaginary state, without stooping to inquire how. He omits a virtue which might well exist in it, though we cannot conceive its formation in such a state—the delight in each other's well-being; and he omits a conceivable though unknown vice, that of unmixed ill-will, which would render such a state a hell to the wretch who harboured the malevolence.

* Essays and Treatises, vol. i.

loosened, though his life was uncorrupted, by that universal and undistinguishing profligacy which prevailed on the Continent, from the regency of the Duke of Orleans to the French Revolution; the most dissolute period of European history, at least since the Roman emperors.* At Rome, indeed, the connection of licentiousness with cruelty, which, though scarcely traceable in individuals, is generally very observable in large masses, bore a fearful testimony to the value of austere purity. The alliance of these remote vices seemed to be broken in the time of Mr. Hume. Pleasure, in a more improved state of society, seemed to return to her more natural union with kindness and tenderness, as well as with refinement and politeness. Had he lived fourteen years longer, however, he would have seen, that the virtues which guard the natural seminaries of the affections are their only true and lasting friends. He would also then have seen (the demand of well-informed men for the improvement of civil institutions,—and that of all classes growing in intelligence, to be delivered from a degrading inferiority, and to be admitted to a share of political power proportioned to their new importance, having been feebly, yet violently resisted by those ruling castes who neither knew how to yield, nor how to withstand,) how speedily the sudden demolition of the barriers (imperfect as they were) of law and government, led to popular excesses, desolating wars, and a military dictatorship, which for a long time threatened to defeat the reformation, and to disappoint the hopes of mankind. This tremendous conflagration threw a fearful light on the ferocity which lies hid under the arts and pleasures of corrupted nations; as earthquakes and volcanoes disclose the rocks which compose the deeper parts of our planet, beneath a fertile and flowery surface. A part of this dreadful result may be ascribed, not improbably, to that relaxation of domestic ties, which is unhappily natural to the populace of all vast capitals, and was at that time countenanced and aggravated by the example of their superiors. Another part doubtless arose from the barbarising power of absolute government, or, in other words, of injustice in high places. A narration of those events attests, as strongly as Roman history, though in a somewhat different manner, the humanising efficacy of the family virtues, by the consequences of the want of them in the higher classes, whose profuse and ostentatious sensuality inspired the labouring and suffering portion of mankind with contempt, disgust, envy, and hatred.

The Inquiry is disfigured by another speck of more frivolous paradox. It consists in the attempt to give the name of Virtue to qualities of the *Understanding;* and it would not have deserved the single remark about to be made on it, had it been the paradox of an inferior man. He has altogether omitted the circumstance on which depends the difference of our sentiments regarding moral and intellectual qualities. We *admire* intellectual excellence, but we bestow no *moral approbation* on it. Such approbation has no tendency directly to increase it, because it is not voluntary. We cultivate our natural disposition to esteem and love benevolence and justice, because these moral sentiments, and the expression of them, directly and materially dispose others, as well as ourselves, to cultivate these two virtues. We cultivate a natural anger against oppression, which guards ourselves against the practice of that vice, and because the manifestation of it deters others from its exercise. The first rude resentment of a child is against every instrument of hurt: we confine it to intentional hurt, when we are taught by experience that it prevents only that species of hurt; and at last it is still further limited to *wrong* done to ourselves or others, and in that case becomes a purely moral sentiment. We morally approve industry, desire of knowledge, love of Truth, and all the habits by which the Understanding is strengthened and rectified, because their formation is subject to the Will;* but we do not feel moral anger against folly or ignorance, because they are involuntary. No one but the religious persecutor,—a mischievous and overgrown child, wreaks his vengeance on involuntary, inevitable, compulsory acts or states of the Understanding, which are no more affected by blame than the stone which the foolish child beats for hurting him. Reasonable men apply to every thing which they wish to move, the agent which is capable of moving it;—force to outward substances, arguments to the Understanding, and blame, together with all other motives, whether moral or personal, to the Will alone. It is as absurd to entertain an abhorrence of intellectual inferiority or error, however extensive or mischievous, as it would be to cherish a warm indignation against earthquakes or hurricanes. It is singular that a philosopher who needed the most liberal toleration should, by representing states of the Understanding as moral or immoral, have offered the most philosophical apology for persecution.

That general utility constitutes a uniform ground of moral distinctions, is a part of Mr. Hume's ethical theory which never can be impugned, until some example can be produced of a virtue generally pernicious, or of a vice generally beneficial. The religious philosopher who, with Butler, holds that benevolence must be the actuating principle of the Divine mind, will, with Berkeley, maintain that pure benevolence can prescribe no rules of human conduct but such as are beneficial to men; thus bestowing on the theory of *moral distinctions* the certainty of demonstration in the eyes of all who believe in God

* See Note R.

* "In hâc quæstione primas tenet Voluntas, *quâ*, ut ait Augustinus, *peccatur, et recte vivitur.*"—Erasmus, Diatribe adversus Lutherum.

The other question of moral philosophy which relates to the theory of *moral approbation*, has been by no means so distinctly and satisfactorily handled by Mr. Hume. His general doctrine is, that an interest in the well-being of others, implanted by nature, which he calls "sympathy" in his Treatise of Human Nature, and much less happily "benevolence" in his subsequent Inquiry,* prompts us to be pleased with all generally beneficial actions. In this respect his doctrine nearly resembles that of Hutcheson. He does not trace his principle through the variety of forms which our moral sentiments assume: there are very important parts of them, of which it affords no solution. For example, though he truly represents our approbation, in others, of qualities useful to the individual, as a proof of benevolence, he makes no attempt to explain our moral approbation of such virtues as temperance and fortitude in ourselves. He entirely overlooks that consciousness of the rightful supremacy of the Moral Faculty over every other principle of human action, without an explanation of which, ethical theory is wanting in one of its vital organs.

Notwithstanding these considerable defects, his proof from induction of the beneficial tendency of Virtue, his conclusive arguments for human disinterestedness, and his decisive observations on the respective provinces of Reason and Sentiment in Morals, concur in ranking the Inquiry with the ethical treatises of the highest merit in our language,—with Shaftesbury's Inquiry concerning Virtue, Butler's Sermons, and Smith's Theory of Moral Sentiments.

ADAM SMITH.†

The great name of Adam Smith rests upon the Inquiry into the Nature and Causes of the Wealth of Nations; perhaps the only book which produced an immediate, general, and irrevocable change in some of the most important parts of the legislation of all civilized states. The works of Grotius, of Locke, and of Montesquieu, which bear a resemblance to it in character, and had no inconsiderable analogy to it in the extent of their popular influence, were productive only of a general amendment, not so conspicuous in particular instances, as discoverable, after a time, in the improved condition of human affairs. The work of Smith, as it touched those matters which may be numbered, and measured, and weighed, bore more visible and palpable fruit. In a few years it began to alter laws and treaties, and has made its way, throughout the convulsions of revolution and conquest, to a due ascendant over the minds of men, with far less than the average of those obstructions of prejudice and clamour, which ordinarily choke the channels through which truth flows into practice.‡ The most eminent of those who have since cultivated and improved the science will be the foremost to address their immortal master,

..... Tenebris tantis tam clarum extollere lumen
Qui primus potuisti, inlustrans commoda vitæ,
Te sequor !*

In a science more difficult, because both ascending to more simple general principles, and running down through more minute applications, though the success of Smith has been less complete, his genius is not less conspicuous. Perhaps there is no ethical work since Cicero's Offices, of which an abridgment enables the reader so inadequately to estimate the merit, as the Theory of Moral Sentiments. This is not chiefly owing to the beauty of diction, as in the case of Cicero; but to the variety of explanations of life and manners which embellish the book often more than they illuminate the theory. Yet, on the other hand, it must be owned that, for purely philosophical purposes, few books more need abridgment; for the most careful reader frequently loses sight of principles buried under illustrations. The naturally copious and flowing style of the author is generally redundant; and the repetition of certain formularies of the system is, in the later editions, so frequent as to be wearisome, and sometimes ludicrous. Perhaps Smith and Hobbes may be considered as forming the two extremes of good style in our philosophy; the first of graceful fulness falling into flaccidity; while the masterly concision of the second is oftener carried forward into dictatorial dryness. Hume and Berkeley, though they are nearer the extreme of abundance,† are probably the least distant from perfection.

That mankind are so constituted as to sympathize with each other's feelings, and to feel pleasure in the accordance of these feelings, are the only facts required by Dr. Smith; and they certainly must be granted to him. To adopt the feelings of another, is to *approve* them. When the sentiments of another are such as would be excited in us by the same objects, we approve them as *morally proper*. To obtain this accordance, it becomes necessary for him who enjoys, or suffers, to lower the expression of his feeling to the point to which the by-stander can raise his fellow-feelings; on this attempt are founded all the high virtues of self-denial and self-command: and it is equally necessary for the by-stander to raise his sympathy as near as he can to the level of the original feeling. In all unsocial passions, such as anger, we have a *divided sympathy* between him who feels them, and those who are the objects of them. Hence the propriety of extremely moderating them. Pure malice is always to be concealed or

* Essays and Treatises, vol. ii.
† Born, 1723; died, 1790. ‡ See Note S.

* Lucret. lib. iii.
† This remark is chiefly applicable to Hume's Essays. His Treatise of Human Nature is more Hobbian in its general tenor, though it has Ciceronian passages.

disguised, because *all sympathy* is arrayed against it. In the private passions, where there is only a *simple sympathy*,—that with the original passion,—the expression has more liberty. The benevolent affections, where there is a *double sympathy*,—with those who feel them, and those who are their objects,—are the most agreeable, and may be indulged with the least apprehension of finding no echo in other breasts. Sympathy with the gratitude of those who are benefited by good actions, prompts us to consider them as deserving of reward, and forms the *sense of merit;* as fellow-feeling with the resentment of those who are injured by crimes leads us to look on them as worthy of punishment, and constitutes the *sense of demerit*. These sentiments require not only beneficial actions, but benevolent motives; being compounded, in the case of merit, of a direct sympathy with the good disposition of the benefactor, and an indirect sympathy with the persons benefited; in the opposite case, with precisely opposite sympathies. He who does an act of wrong to another to gratify his own passions, must not expect that the spectators, who have none of his undue partiality to his own interest, will enter into his feelings. In such a case, he knows that they will pity the person wronged, and be full of indignation against him. When he is cooled, he adopts the sentiments of others on his own crime, feels shame at the impropriety of his former passion, pity for those who have suffered by him, and a dread of punishment from general and just resentment. Such are the constituent parts of remorse.

Our moral sentiments respecting *ourselves* arise from those which others feel concerning us. We feel a self-approbation whenever we believe that the general feeling of mankind coincides with that state of mind in which we ourselves were at a given time. "We suppose ourselves the spectators of our own behaviour, and endeavour to imagine what effect it would in this light produce in us." We must view our own conduct with the eyes of others before we can judge it. The sense of duty arises from putting ourselves in the place of others, and adopting their sentiments respecting our own conduct. In utter solitude there could have been no self-approbation. The rules of Morality are a summary of those sentiments; and often beneficially stand in their stead when the self-delusions of passion would otherwise hide from us the non-conformity of our state of mind with that which, in the circumstances, can be entered into and approved by impartial by-standers. It is hence that we learn to raise our mind above local or temporary clamour, and to fix our eyes on the surest indications of the general and lasting sentiments of human nature. "When we approve of any character or action, our sentiments are derived from four sources: *first*, we sympathize with the motives of the agent; *secondly*, we enter into the gratitude of those who have been benefited by his actions; *thirdly*, we observe that his conduct has been agreeable to the general rules by which those two sympathies generally act; and, *last of all*, when we consider such actions as forming part of a system of behaviour which tends to promote the happiness either of the individual or of society, they appear to derive a beauty from this utility, not unlike that which we ascribe to any well-contrived machine."*

REMARKS.

That Smith is the first who has drawn the attention of philosophers to one of the most curious and important parts of human nature,—who has looked closely and steadily into the workings of Sympathy, its sudden action and re-action, its instantaneous conflicts and its emotions, its minute play and varied illusions, is sufficient to place him high among the cultivators of mental philosophy. He is very original in applications and explanations; though, for his principle, he is somewhat indebted to Butler, more to Hutcheson, and most of all to Hume. These writers, except Hume in his original work, had derived sympathy, or a great part of it, from benevolence:† Smith, with deeper insight, inverted the order. The great part performed by various sympathies in moral approbation was first unfolded by him; and besides its intrinsic importance, it strengthened the proofs against those theories which ascribe that great function to Reason.—Another great merit of the theory of "sympathy" is, that it brings into the strongest light that most important characteristic of the moral sentiments which consist in their being the only principles leading to action, and dependent on emotion or sensibility, with respect to the objects of which, it is not only possible but natural for all mankind to agree.‡

The main defects of this theory seem to be the following.

1. Though it is not to be condemned for declining inquiry into the origin of our fellow-feeling, which, being one of the most certain of all facts, might well be assumed as ultimate in speculations of this nature, it is evident that the circumstances to which some speculators ascribe the formation of sympathy at least contribute to strengthen or impair, to contract or expand it. It will appear, more conveniently, in the next article, that the theory of "sympathy" has suffered from the omission of these circumstances. For the present, it is enough to observe how much our compassion for various

* Theory of Moral Sentiments, Edinb. 1801, ii. 304.

† There is some confusion regarding this point in Butler's first sermon on Compassion.

‡ The feelings of beauty, grandeur, and whatever else is comprehended under the name of Taste, form no exception, for *they do not lead to action*, but terminate in delightful contemplation; which constitutes the essential distinction between them and the moral sentiments, to which, in some points of view, they may doubtless be likened.

sorts of animals, and our fellow-feeling with various races of men, are proportioned to the resemblance which they bear to ourselves, to the frequency of our intercourse with them, and to other causes which, in the opinion of some, afford evidence that sympathy itself is dependent on a more general law.

2. Had Smith extended his view beyond the mere play of sympathy itself, and taken into account all its preliminaries, and accompaniments, and consequences, it seems improbable that he would have fallen into the great error of representing the sympathies in their primitive state, without undergoing any transformation, as continuing exclusively to constitute the moral sentiments. He is not content with teaching that they are the roots out of which these sentiments grow, the stocks on which they are grafted, the elements of which they are compounded; —doctrines to which nothing could be objected but their unlimited extent. He tacitly assumes, that if a sympathy in the beginning caused or formed a moral approbation, so it must ever continue to do. He proceeds like a geologist who should tell us that the body of this planet had always been in the same state, shutting his eyes to transition states, and secondary formations; or like a chemist who should inform us that no compound substance can possess new qualities entirely different from those which belong to its materials. His acquiescence in this old and still general error is the more remarkable, because Mr. Hume's beautiful Dissertation on the Passions* had just before opened a striking view of some of the compositions and decompositions which render the mind of a formed man as different from its original state, as the organization of a complete animal is from the condition of the first dim speck of vitality. It is from this oversight (ill supplied by moral rules,—a loose stone in his building) that he has exposed himself to objections founded on experience, to which it is impossible to attempt any answer. For it is certain that in many, nay in most cases of moral approbation, the adult man approves the action or disposition merely *as right*, and with a distinct consciousness that no process of sympathy intervenes between the approval and its object. It is certain that an unbiassed person would call it *moral approbation*, only as far as it excluded the interposition of any reflection between the conscience and the mental state approved. Upon the supposition of an unchanged state of our active principles, it would follow that sympathy never had any share in the greater part of them. Had he admitted the sympathies to be only elements entering into the formation of Conscience, their disappearance, or their appearance only as auxiliaries, after the mind is mature, would have been no more an objection to his system, than the conversion of a substance from a transitional to a permanent state is a perplexity to the geologist. It would perfectly resemble the destruction of qualities, which is the ordinary effect of chemical composition.

3. The same error has involved him in another difficulty perhaps still more fatal. The sympathies have nothing more of an *imperative* character than any other emotions. They attract or repel like other feelings, according to their intensity. If, then, the sympathies continue in mature minds to constitute the whole of Conscience, it becomes utterly impossible to explain the character of command and supremacy, which is attested by the unanimous voice of mankind to belong to that faculty, and to form its essential distinction. Had he adopted the other representation, it would be possible to conceive, perhaps easy to explain, that Conscience should possess a quality which belonged to none of its elements.

4. It is to this representation that Smith's theory owes that unhappy appearance of rendering the rule of our conduct dependent on the notions and passions of those who surround us, of which the utmost efforts of the most refined ingenuity have not been able to divest it. This objection, or topic, is often ignorantly urged; the answers are frequently solid; but to most men they must always appear to be an ingenious and intricate contrivance of cycles and epicycles, which perplex the mind too much to satisfy it, and seem devised to evade difficulties which cannot be solved. All theories which treat Conscience as built up by circumstances inevitably acting on all human minds, are, indeed, liable to somewhat of the same misconception; unless they place in the strongest light (what Smith's theory excludes) the total destruction of the scaffolding, which was necessary only to the erection of the building, after the mind is adult and mature, and warn the hastiest reader, that it then rests on its own foundation alone.

5. The constant reference of our own dispositions and actions to the point of view from which they are estimated by others, seems to be rather an excellent expedient for preserving our impartiality, than a fundamental principle of Ethics. But impartiality, which is no more than a removal of some hinderance to right judgment, supplies no materials for its exercise, and no rule, or even principle, for its guidance. It nearly coincides with the Christian precept of "doing unto others as we would they should do unto us;"—an admirable practical maxim, but, as Leibnitz has said truly, intended only as a correction of self-partiality.

6. Lastly, this ingenious system renders all morality *relative*, by referring it to the pleasure of an agreement of our feelings with those of others,—by confining itself entirely to the question of moral approbation, and by providing no place for the consideration of that quality which distinguishes all good from all bad actions;—a defect which will appear in the sequel to be more

* Essays and Treatises, vol. ii.

immediately fatal to a theorist of the *sentimental*, than to one of the *intellectual* school. Smith shrinks from considering utility in that light, as soon as it presents itself, or very strangely ascribes its power over our moral feelings to admiration of the mere adaptation of means to ends, (which might surely be as well felt for the production of wide-spread misery, by a consistent system of wicked conduct,)—instead of ascribing it to benevolence, with Hutcheson and Hume, or to an extension of that very sympathy which is his own first principle.

RICHARD PRICE.*

About the same time with the celebrated work of Smith, but with a popular reception very different, Dr. Richard Price, an excellent and eminent non-conformist minister, published A Review of the Principal Questions in Morals;†—an attempt to revive the intellectual theory of moral obligation, which seemed to have fallen under the attacks of Butler, Hutcheson, and Hume, and before that of Smith. It attracted little observation at first; but being afterwards countenanced by the Scottish school, it may seem to deserve some notice, at a moment when the kindred speculations of the German metaphysicians have effected an establishment in France, and are no longer unknown in England.

The Understanding itself is, according to Price, an independent source of simple ideas. "The various kinds of agreement and disagreement between our ideas, spoken of by Locke, are so many new simple ideas." "This is true of our ideas of proportion, of our ideas of identity and diversity, existence, connection, cause and effect, power, possibility, and of our ideas of right and wrong." "The first relates to quantity, the last to actions, the rest to all things." "Like all other simple ideas, they are undefinable."

It is needless to pursue this theory farther, till an answer be given to the observation made before, that as no perception or judgment, or other unmixed act of Understanding, merely as such, and without the agency of some intermediate *emotion*, can affect the Will, the account given by Dr. Price of perceptions or judgments respecting moral subjects, does not advance one step towards the explanation of the authority of Conscience over the Will, which is the matter to be explained. Indeed, this respectable writer felt the difficulty so much as to allow, "that in contemplating the acts of moral agents, we have both a perception of the understanding and a feeling of the heart." He even admits, that it would have been highly pernicious to us if our reason had been left without such support. But he has not shown how, on such a supposition, we could have acted on a mere opinion; nor has he given any proof that what he calls "support" is not, in truth, the whole of what directly produces the conformity of voluntary acts to Morality.*

* Born, 1723; died, 1791.

† The third edition was published at London in 1787.

DAVID HARTLEY.†

The work of Dr. Hartley, entitled "Observations on Man,"‡ is distinguished by an uncommon union of originality with modesty, in unfolding a simple and fruitful principle of human nature. It is disfigured by the absurd affectation of mathematical forms then prevalent; and it is encumbered and deformed by a mass of physiological speculations,—groundless, or at best uncertain, and wholly foreign from its proper purpose, —which repel the inquirer into mental philosophy from its perusal, and lessen the respect of the physiologist for the author's judgment. It is an unfortunate example of the disposition predominent among undistinguishing theorists to class together all the appearances which are observed at the same time, and in the immediate neighbourhood of each other. At that period, chemical phenomena were referred to mechanical principles; vegetable and animal life were subjected to mechanical or chemical laws: and while some physiologists§ ascribed the vital functions of the Understanding, the greater part of metaphysicians were disposed, with a grosser confusion, to derive the intellectual operations from bodily causes. The error in the latter case, though less immediately perceptible, is deeper and more fundamental than in the other; since it overlooks the primordial and perpetual distinction between *the being which thinks* and *the thing which is thought of*,—not to be lost sight of, by the mind's eye, even for a twinkling, without involving all nature in darkness and confusion. Hartley and Condillac,‖ who, much about the same time, but seemingly without any knowledge of each other's speculations,¶ began in a very similar mode to

* The following sentences will illustrate the text, and are in truth applicable to all moral theories on merely intellectual principles: "Reason alone, did we possess it in a higher degree, would answer all the ends of the passions. Thus there would be no need of parental affection, were all parents sufficiently acquainted with the reasons for taking upon them the guidance and support of those whom Nature has placed under their care, *and were they virtuous enough to be always determined by those reasons*."—Review, p. 121. A very slight consideration will show, that without the last words the preceding part would be utterly false, and with them it is utterly insignificant.

† Born, 1705; died, 1757.

‡ London, 1749.

§ Among them was G. E. Stahl, born, 1660; died, 1734;—a German physician and chemist of deserved eminence.

‖ Born, 1715; died, 1780.

¶ Traité sur l'Origine des Connoissances Humaines, 1746; Traité des Systèmes, 1749; Traité des Sensations, 1754. Foreign books were then little and slowly known in England. Hartley's reading, except on theology, seems confined to the physical and mathematical sciences: and his whole

simplify, but also to mutilate the system of Locke, stopped short of what is called "materialism," which consummates the confusion, but touched the threshold. Thither, it must be owned, their philosophy pointed, and thither their followers proceeded. Hartley and Bonnet,* still more than Condillac, suffered themselves, like most of their contemporaries, to overlook the important truth, that all the changes in the organs which can be likened to other material phenomena, are nothing more than *antecedents and prerequisites of perception*, bearing not the faintest likeness to it,—as much *outward* in relation to the thinking principle, as if they occurred in any other part of matter; and that the entire comprehension of those changes, if it were attained, would not bring us a step nearer to the nature of thought. They who would have been the first to exclaim against the mistake of a sound for a colour, fell into the more unspeakable error of confounding the perception of objects, as outward, with the consciousness of our own mental operations. Locke's doctrine, that "reflection" was a separate source of ideas, left room for this greatest of all distinctions; though with much unhappiness of expression, and with no little variance from the course of his own speculations. Hartley, Condillac, and Bonnet, in hewing away this seeming deformity from the system of their master, unwittingly struck off the part of the building which, however unsightly, gave it the power of yielding some shelter and guard to truths, of which the exclusion rendered it utterly untenable. They became consistent Nominalists; in reference to whose controversy Locke expresses himself with confusion and contradiction: but on this subject they added nothing to what had been taught by Hobbes and Berkeley. Both Hartley and Condillac† have the merit of having been unseduced by the temptations either of scepticism, or of useless idealism; which, even if Berkeley and Hume could have been unknown to them, must have been within sight. Both agree in referring all the intellectual operations to the "association of ideas," and in representing that association as reducible to the single law, "that ideas which enter the mind at the same time, acquire a tendency to call up each other, which is in direct proportion to the frequency of their having entered together." In this important part of their doctrine they seem, whether unconsciously or otherwise, to have only repeated, and very much expanded, the opinion of Hobbes.* In its simplicity it is more agreeable than the system of Mr. Hume, who admitted five independent laws of association; and it is in comprehension far superior to the views of the same subject by Mr. Locke, whose ill-chosen name still retains its place in our nomenclature, but who only appeals to the principle as explaining some fancies and whimsies of the human mind. The capital fault of Hartley is that of a rash generalization, which may prove imperfect, and which is at least premature. All attempts to explain instinct by this principle have hitherto been unavailing: many of the most important processes of reasoning have not hitherto been accounted for by it.† It would appear by a close examination, that even this theory, simple as it appears, *presupposes* many facts relating to the mind, of which its authors do not seem to have suspected the existence. How many ultimate facts of that nature, for example, are contained and involved in Aristotle's celebrated comparison of the mind in its first state to a sheet of unwritten paper!‡ The texture of the paper, even its colour, the sort of instrument fit to act on it, its capacity to receive and to retain impressions, all its differences, from steel on the one hand to water on the other, certainly presuppose some facts, and may imply many, without a distinct statement of which, the nature of writing could not be explained to a person wholly ignorant of it. How many more, as well as greater laws, may be necessary to enable mind to perceive outward objects! If the power of perception may be thus dependent, why may not what is called the "association of ideas," the attraction between thoughts, the power of one to suggest another, be affected by mental laws hitherto unexplored, perhaps unobserved?

But, to return from this digression into the intellectual part of man, it becomes proper to say, that the difference between Hartley and Condillac, and the immeasurable superiority of the former, are chiefly to be found in the application which Hartley first made of the law of association to that other unnamed portion of our nature with which Morality more immediately deals;—that which feels pain and pleasure,—is influenced by appetites and loathings, by desires and aversions, by affections and repugnances. Condillac's Treatise on Sensation, published five years after the work of Hartley, repro-

manner of thinking and writing is so different from that of Condillac, that there is not the least reason to suppose the work of the one to have been known to the other. The work of Hartley, as we learn from the sketch of his life by his son, prefixed to the edition of 1791, was begun in 1730, and finished in 1746.

* Born, 1720; died, 1793.

† The following note of Condillac will show how much he differed from Hartley in his mode of considering the Newtonian hypothesis of vibrations, and how far he was in that respect superior to him. "Je suppose ici et ailleurs que les perceptions de l'âme ont pour cause physique l'ébranlement des fibres du cerveau; *non que je regarde cette hypothèse comme démontrée, mais parcequ'elle est la plus commode pour expliquer ma pensée.*"—Œuvres de Condillac, Paris, 1798, i. 60.

* Human Nature, chap. iv. v. vi. For more ancient statements, see Note T.

† "Ce que les logiciens ont dit des raisonnements dans bien des volumes, me paroit entièrement superflu, et de nul usage."—Condillac, i. 115; an assertion of which the gross absurdity will be apparent to the readers of Dr. Whateley's Treatise on Logic, one of the most important works of the present age.

‡ See Note U.

duces the doctrine of Hobbes, with its root, namely, that love and hope are but transformed "sensations,"* (by which he means perceptions of the senses,) and its wide-spread branches, consisting in desires and passions, which are only modifications of self-love. "The words 'goodness' and 'beauty,'" says he, almost in the very words of Hobbes, "express those qualities of things by which they contribute to our pleasure."† In the whole of his philosophical works, we find no trace of any desire produced by association, of any disinterested principle, or indeed of any distinction between the percipient and what, perhaps, we may venture to call the *emotive* or the *pathematic* part of human nature, for the present, until some more convenient and agreeable name shall be hit on by some luckier or more skilful adventurer.

To the ingenuous, humble, and anxiously conscientious character of Hartley himself, we owe the knowledge that, about the year 1730, he was informed that the Rev. Mr. Gay of Sidney-Sussex College, Cambridge, then living in the west of England, asserted the possibility of deducing all our intellectual pleasures and pains from association; that this led him (Hartley) to consider the power of association; and that about that time Mr. Gay published his sentiments on this matter in a dissertation prefixed to Bishop Law's Translation of King's Origin of Evil.‡ No writer deserves the praise of abundant fairness more than Hartley in this avowal. The dissertation of which he speaks is mentioned by no philosopher but himself. It suggested nothing apparently to any other reader. The general texture of it is that of homespun selfishness. The writer had the merit to see and to own that Hutcheson had established as a fact the reality of moral sentiments and disinterested affections. He blames, perhaps justly, that most ingenious man,§ for assuming that these sentiments and affections are implanted, and partake of the nature of instincts. The object of his dissertation is to reconcile the mental appearances described by Hutcheson with the first principle of the selfish system, that "the true principle of all our actions is our own happiness." Moral feelings and social affections are, according to him, "resolvable into reason, pointing out our private happiness; and *whenever this end is not perceived*, they are to be accounted for from the association of ideas." Even in the single passage in which he shows a glimpse of the truth, he begins with confusion, advances with hesitation, and after holding in his grasp for an instant the principle which sheds so strong a light around it, suddenly drops it from his hand. Instead of receiving the statements of Hutcheson (his silence relating to Butler is unaccountable) as enlargements of the science of man, he deals with them merely as difficulties to be reconciled with the received system of universal selfishness. In the conclusion of his fourth section, he well exemplifies the power of association in forming the love of money, of fame, of power, &c.; but he still treats these effects of association as aberrations and infirmities, the fruits of our forgetfulness and shortsightedness, and not at all as the great process employed to sow and rear the most important principles of a social and moral nature.

This precious mine may therefore be truly said to have been opened by Hartley; for he who did such superabundant justice to the hints of Gay, would assuredly not have withheld the like tribute from Hutcheson, had he observed the happy expression of "secondary passions," which ought to have led that philosopher himself farther than he ventured to advance. The extraordinary value of this part of Hartley's system has been hidden by various causes, which have also enabled writers, who have borrowed from it, to decry it. The influence of his medical habits renders many of his examples displeasing, and sometimes disgusting. He has none of that knowledge of the world, of that familiarity with Literature, of that delicate perception of the beauties of Nature and Art, which not only supply the most agreeable illustrations of mental philosophy, but afford the most obvious and striking instances of its happy application to subjects generally interesting. His particular applications of the general law are often mistaken, and are seldom more than brief notes and hasty suggestions;—the germs of theories which, while some might adopt them without detection, others might discover without being aware that they were anticipated.—To which it may be added, that in spite of the imposing forms of Geometry, the work is not really distinguished by good method, or even uniform adherence to that which had been chosen. His style is entitled to no praise but that of clearness, and a simplicity of diction, through which is visible a singu-

* Condillac, iii. 21; more especially Traité des Sensations, part ii. chap. vi. "Its love for outward objects is only an effect of love for itself."

† Traité des Sensations, part iv. chap. iii.

‡ Hartley's preface to the Observations on Man. The word "intellectual" is too narrow. Even "mental" would be of very doubtful propriety. The theory in its full extent requires a word such as "inorganic" (if no better can be discovered), extending to all gratification, not distinctly referred to some specific organ, or at least to some assignable part of the bodily frame.

§ It has not been mentioned in its proper place, that Hutcheson appears nowhere to greater advantage than in some letters on the Fable of the Bees, published when he was very young, at Dublin, with the signature of "Hibernicus." "Private vices—public benefits," says he, "may signify any one of these five distinct propositions: 1st. They are in themselves public benefits; or, 2d. They naturally produce public happiness; or, 3d. They may be made to produce it; or, 4th. They may naturally flow from it; or, 5th. At least they may probably flow from it in our infirm nature." See a small volume containing Thoughts on Laughter, and Remarks on the Fable of the Bees, Glasgow, 1758, in which these letters are republished.

lar simplicity of mind. No book perhaps exists which, with so few of the common allurements, comes at last so much to please by the picture it presents of the writer's character,—a character which kept him pure from the pursuit, often from the consciousness of novelty, and rendered him a discoverer in spite of his own modesty. In those singular passages in which, amidst the profound internal tranquillity of all the European nations, he foretells approaching convulsions, to be followed by the overthrow of states and Churches, his quiet and gentle spirit, elsewhere almost ready to inculcate passive obedience for the sake of peace, is supported under its awful forebodings by the hope of that general progress in virtue and happiness which he saw through the preparatory confusion. A meek piety, inclining towards mysticism, and sometimes indulging in visions which borrow a lustre from his fervid benevolence, was beautifully, and perhaps singularly, blended in him with zeal for the most unbounded freedom of inquiry, flowing both from his own conscientious belief and his unmingled love of Truth. Whoever can so far subdue his repugnance to petty or secondary faults as to bestow a careful perusal on the work, must be unfortunate if he does not see, feel, and own, that the writer was a great philosopher and a good man.

To those who thus study the work, it will be apparent that Hartley, like other philosophers, either overlooked or failed explicitly to announce that distinction between perception and emotion, without which no system of mental philosophy is complete.—Hence arose the partial and incomplete view of Truth conveyed by the use of the phrase "association of ideas." If the word "association," which rather indicates the connection between ~~separate things than the perfect~~ combination and fusion which occur in many operations of the mind, must, notwithstanding its inadequacy, still be retained, the phrase ought at least to be "association" of thoughts *with emotions*, as well as *with each other*. With that enlargement an objection to the Hartleian doctrine would have been avoided, and its originality, as well as superiority over that of Condillac, would have appeared indisputable. The examples of avarice and other factitious passions are very well chosen; first, because few will be found to suppose that they are original principles of human nature;* secondly, because the process by which they are generated, being subsequent to the age of attention and recollection, may be brought home to the understanding of all men; and, thirdly, because they afford the most striking instance of secondary passions, which not only become independent of the primary principles from which they are derived, but hostile to them, and so superior in strength as to be capable of overpowering their parents. As soon as the mind becomes familiar with the frequent case of the man who first pursued money to purchase pleasure, but at last, when he becomes a miser, loves his hoard better than all that it could purchase, and sacrifices all pleasures for its increase, we are prepared to admit that, by a like process, the affections, when they are fixed on the happiness of others as their ultimate object, without any reflection on self, may not only be perfectly detached from self-regard or private desires, but may subdue these and every other antagonist passion which can stand in their way. As the miser loves money for its own sake, so may the benevolent man delight in the well-being of his fellows. His good-will becomes as disinterested as if it had been implanted and underived. The like process applied to what is called "self-love," or the desire of permanent well-being, clearly explains the mode in which that principle is gradually formed from the separate appetites, without whose previous existence no notion of well-being could be obtained.—In like manner, sympathy, perhaps itself the result of a transfer of our own personal feelings by association to other sentient beings, and of a subsequent transfer of their feelings to our own minds, engenders the various social affections, which at last generate in most minds some regard to the well-being of our country, of mankind, of all creatures capable of pleasure. Rational Self-love controls and guides those far keener self-regarding passions of which it is the child, in the same manner as general benevolence balan~~ces and~~ governs the variety of much warmer social affections from which it springs. It is an ancient and obstinate error of philosophers to represent these two calm principles as being the source of the impelling passions and affections, instead of being among the last results of them. Each of them exercises a sort of authority in its sphere; but the dominion of neither is co-existent with the whole nature of man. Though they have the power to quicken and check, they are both too feeble to impel; and if the primary principles were extinguished, they would both perish from want of nourishment. If indeed all appetites and desires were destroyed, no subject would exist on which either of these general principles could act.

The affections, desires, and emotions, having for their ultimate object the dispositions and actions of voluntary agents, which alone, from the nature of their object, are co-extensive with the whole of our active nature, are, according to the same philosophy, necessarily formed in every human mind by the transfer of feeling which is effected by the principle of Association. Gratitude, pity, resentment, and shame, seem to

* A very ingenious man, Lord Kames, whose works had a great effect in rousing the mind of his contemporaries and countrymen, has indeed fancied that there is "a hoarding instinct" in man and other animals. But such conclusions are not so much objects of confutation, as ludicrous proofs of the absurdity of the premises which lead to them.

be the simplest, the most active, and the most uniform elements in their composition. It is easy to perceive how the complacency inspired by a benefit may be transferred to a benefactor,—thence to all beneficent beings and acts. The well-chosen instance of the nurse familiarly exemplifies the manner in which the child transfers his complacency from the gratification of his senses to the cause of it, and thus learns an affection for her who is the source of his enjoyment.—With this simple process concur, in the case of a tender nurse, and far more of a mother, a thousand acts of relief and endearment, the complacency that results from which is fixed on the person from whom they flow, and in some degree extended by association to all who resemble that person. So much of the pleasure of early life depends on others, that the like process is almost constantly repeated. Hence the origin of benevolence may be understood, and the disposition to approve all benevolent, and disapprove all malevolent acts. Hence also the same approbation and disapprobation are extended to all acts which we clearly perceive to promote or obstruct the happiness of men. When the complacency is expressed in action, benevolence may be said to be transformed into a part of Conscience. The rise of sympathy may probably be explained by the process of association, which transfers the feelings of others to ourselves, and ascribes our own feelings to others,—at first, and in some degree always, in proportion as the resemblance of ourselves to others is complete. The likeness in the outward signs of emotion is one of the widest channels in this commerce of hearts. Pity thereby becomes one of the grand sources of benevolence, and perhaps contributes more largely than gratitude: it is indeed one of the first motives to the conferring of those benefits which inspire grateful affection.—Sympathy with the sufferer, therefore, is also transformed into a real sentiment, directly approving benevolent actions and dispositions, and more remotely, all actions that promote happiness. The anger of the sufferer, first against all causes of pain, afterwards against all intentional agents who produce it, and finally against all those in whom the infliction of pain proceeds from a mischievous disposition, when it is communicated to others by sympathy, and is so far purified by gradual separation from selfish and individual interest as to be equally felt against all wrong-doers,—whether the wrong be done against ourselves, our friends, or our enemies,—is the root out of which springs that which is commonly and well called a "sense of justice"—the most indispensable, perhaps, of all the component parts of the moral faculties.

This is the main guard against Wrong. It relates to that portion of Morality where many of the outward acts are capable of being reduced under certain rules, of which the violations, wherever the rule is sufficiently precise, and the mischief sufficiently great, may be guarded against by the terror of punishment. In the observation of the rules of justice consists *duty;* breaches of them we denominate "*crimes.*" An abhorrence of crimes, especially of those which indicate the absence of benevolence, as well as of regard for justice, is strongly felt; because well-framed penal laws, being the lasting declaration of the moral indignation of many generations of mankind, as long as they remain in unison with the sentiments of the age and country for which they are destined, exceedingly strengthen the same feeling in every individual; and this they do wherever the laws do not so much deviate from the habitual feelings of the multitude as to produce a struggle between law and sentiment, in which it is hard to say on which side success is most deplorable. A man who performs his duties may be esteemed, but is not admired; because it requires no more than ordinary virtue to act well where it is shameful and dangerous to do otherwise. The righteousness of those who act solely from such inferior motives, is little better than that "of the Scribes and Pharisees." Those only are just in the eye of the moralist who act justly from a constant disposition to render to every man his own.* Acts of kindness, of generosity, of pity, of placability, of humanity, when they are long continued, can hardly fail mainly to flow from the pure fountain of an excellent nature. They are not reducible to rules; and the attempt to enforce them by punishment would destroy them. They are *virtues,* of which the essence consists in a good disposition of mind.

As we gradually transfer our desire from praise to praiseworthiness, this principle also is adopted into consciousness. On the other hand, when we are led by association to feel a painful contempt for those feelings and actions of our past self which we despise in others, there is developed in our hearts another element of that moral sense. It is a remarkable instance of the power of the law of Association, that the contempt or abhorrence which we feel for the bad actions of others may be transferred by it, in any degree of strength, to our own past actions of the like kind: and as the hatred of bad actions is transferred to the agent, the same transfer may occur in our own case in a manner perfectly similar to that of which we are conscious in our feelings towards our fellow-creatures. There are many causes which render it generally feebler; but it is perfectly evident that it requires no more than a sufficient strength of moral feeling to make it equal; and that the most apparently hyperbolical language used by peni-

* "Justitia est constans et perpetua voluntas suum cuique tribuendi:" an excellent definition in the mouth of the Stoical moralists, from whom it is borrowed, but altogether misplaced by the Roman jurists in a body of laws which deal only with outward acts in their relation to the order and interests of society.

tents, in describing their remorse, may be justified by the principle of Association.

At this step in our progress, it is proper to observe, that a most important consideration has escaped Hartley, as well as every other philosopher.* The language of all mankind implies that the Moral Faculty, whatever it may be, and from what origin soever it may spring, is intelligibly and properly spoken of as ONE. It is as common in mind, as in matter, for a compound to have properties not to be found in any of its constituent parts. The truth of this proposition is as certain in the human feelings as in any material combination. It is therefore easily to be understood, that originally separate feelings may be so perfectly blended by a process performed in each mind, that they can no longer be disjoined from each other, but must always co-operate, and thus reach the only union which we can conceive. The sentiment of moral approbation, formed by association out of antecedent affections, may become so perfectly independent of them, that we are no longer conscious of the means by which it was formed, and never can in practice repeat, though we may in theory perceive, the process by which it was generated. It is in that mature and sound state of our nature that our emotions at the view of Right and Wrong are ascribed to Conscience. But why, it may be asked, do these feelings, rather than others, run into each other, and constitute Conscience? The answer seems to be what has already been intimated in the observations on Butler. The affinity between these feelings consists in this, that while all other feelings relate to outward objects, they alone contemplate exclusively the *dispositions and actions of voluntary agents*. When they are completely transferred from objects, and even persons, to dispositions and actions, they are fitted, by the perfect coincidence of their *aim*, for combining to form that one faculty which is directed only to *that* aim.

The words "Duty" and "Virtue," and the word "ought," which most perfectly denotes duty, but is also connected with Virtue, in every well-constituted mind, in this state become the fit language of the acquired, perhaps, but universally and necessarily acquired, faculty of Conscience. Some account of its peculiar nature has been attempted in the remarks on Butler; for a further one a fitter occasion will occur hereafter. Some light may however now be thrown on the subject by a short statement of the hitherto unobserved distinction between the moral sentiments and another class of feelings with which they have some qualities in common. The "pleasures" (so called) of imagination appear, at least in most cases, to originate in association: but it is not till the original cause of the gratification is obliterated from the mind, that they acquire their proper character. Order and proportion may be at first chosen for their convenience: it is not until they are admired for their own sake that they become objects of taste. Though all the proportions for which a horse is valued may be indications of speed, safety, strength, and health, it is not the less true that they only can be said to admire the animal for his beauty, who leave such considerations out of the account while they admire. The pleasure of contemplation in these particulars of Nature and Art becomes universal and immediate, being entirely detached from all regard to individual beings. It contemplates neither use nor interest. In this important particular the pleasures of imagination agree with the moral sentiments: hence the application of the same language to both in ancient and modern times;—hence also it arises that they may contemplate the very same qualities and objects. There is certainly much beauty in the softer virtues,—much grandeur in the soul of a hero or a martyr: but the essential distinction still remains; the purest moral taste contemplates these qualities only with *quiescent* delight or reverence; it has no further view; it points towards no action. Conscience, on the contrary, containing in it a pleasure in the prospect of doing right, and an ardent desire to act well, having for its sole object the dispositions and acts of voluntary agents, is not, like moral taste, satisfied with passive contemplation, but constantly tends to act on the will and conduct of the man. Moral taste may aid it, may be absorbed into it, and usually contributes its part to the formation of the moral faculty; but it is distinct from that faculty, and may be disproportioned to it. Conscience, being by its nature confined to mental dispositions and voluntary acts, is of necessity excluded from the ordinary consideration of all things antecedent to these dispositions. The circumstances from which such states of mind may arise, are most important objects of consideration for the Understanding; but they are without the sphere of Conscience, which never ascends beyond the heart of the man. It is thus that in the eye of Conscience man becomes amenable to its authority for all his inclinations as well as deeds; that some of them are approved, loved, and revered; and that all the outward effects of disesteem, contempt, or moral anger, are felt to be the just lot of others.

But, to return to Hartley, from this perhaps intrusive statement of what does not properly belong to him: he represents all the social affections of gratitude, veneration, and love, inspired by the virtues of our fellow-men, as capable of being transferred by association to the transcendent and unmingled goodness of the Ruler of the world, and thus to give rise to piety, to which he gives the name of "the theopathetic affection." This principle, like all the former in the mental series, is gradually detached from the trunk on which it grew: it takes separate root, and may altogether overshadow

* See *suprà*, section on Butler.

the parent stock. As such a Being cannot be conceived without the most perfect and constant reference to His goodness, so piety may not only become a part of Conscience, but its governing and animating principle, which, after long lending its own energy and authority to every other, is at last described by our philosopher as swallowing up all of them in order to perform the same functions more infallibly.

In every stage of this progress we are taught by Dr. Hartley that a new product appears, which becomes perfectly distinct from the elements which formed it, which may be utterly dissimilar to them, and may attain any degree of vigour, however superior to theirs. Thus the objects of the private desires disappear when we are employed in the pursuit of our lasting welfare; that which was first sought only as a means, may come to be pursued as an end, and preferred to the original end; the good opinion of our fellows becomes more valued than the benefits for which it was at first courted; a man is ready to sacrifice his life for him who has shown generosity, even to others; and persons otherwise of common character are capable of cheerfully marching in a forlorn hope, or of almost instinctively leaping into the sea to save the life of an entire stranger. These last acts, often of almost unconscious virtue, so familiar to the soldier and the sailor, so unaccountable on certain systems of philosophy, often occur without a thought of applause and reward;—too quickly for the thought of the latter, too obscurely for the hope of the former; and they are of such a nature that no man could be impelled to them by the mere expectation of either.

The gratitude, sympathy, resentment, and shame, which are the principal constituent parts of the Moral Sense, thus lose their separate agency, and constitute an entirely new faculty, co-extensive with all the dispositions and actions of voluntary agents; though some of them are more predominant in particular cases of moral sentiment than others, and though the aid of all continues to be necessary in their original character, as subordinate but distinct motives of action. Nothing more evidently points out the distinction of the Hartleian system from all systems called "selfish,"—not to say its superiority in respect to disinterestedness over all moral systems before Butler and Hutcheson,—than that excellent part of it which relates to the "rule of life." The various principles of human action rise in value according to the order in which they spring up after each other. We can then only be in a state of as much enjoyment as we are evidently capable of attaining, when we prefer interest to the original gratifications; honour to interest; the pleasures of imagination to those of sense; the dictates of Conscience to pleasure, interest, and reputation; the well-being of fellow-creatures to our own indulgences; in a word, when we pursue moral good and social happiness chiefly and for their own sake. "With self-interest," says Hartley, somewhat inaccurately in language, "man must begin. He may end in self-annihilation. Theopathy, or piety, although the last result of the purified and exalted sentiments, may at length swallow up every other principle, and absorb the whole man." Even if this last doctrine should be an exaggeration unsuited to our present condition, it will the more strongly illustrate the compatibility, or rather the necessary connection, of this theory with the existence and power of perfectly disinterested principles of human action.

It is needless to remark on the *secondary* and *auxiliary* causes which contribute to the formation of moral sentiment;—education, imitation, general opinion, laws, and government. They all presuppose the Moral Faculty: in an improved state of society they contribute powerfully to strengthen it, and on some occasions they enfeeble, distort, and maim it; but in all cases they must themselves be tried by the test of an ethical standard. The value of this doctrine will not be essentially affected by supposing a greater number of original principles than those assumed by Dr. Hartley. The principle of Association applies as much to a greater as to a smaller number. It is a quality common to it with all theories, that the more simplicity it reaches consistently with truth, the more perfect it becomes. Causes are not to be multiplied without necessity. If by a considerable multiplication of primary desires the law of Association were lowered nearly to the level of an auxiliary agent, the philosophy of human nature would still be under indelible obligations to the philosopher who, by his fortunate error, rendered the importance of that great principle obvious and conspicuous.

ABRAHAM TUCKER.*

It has been the remarkable fortune of this writer to have been more prized and more disregarded by the cultivators of moral speculation, than perhaps any other philosopher.† He had many of the qualities which might be expected in an affluent country gentleman, living in a privacy undisturbed by political zeal, and with a leisure unbroken by the calls of a profession, at a time when England had not entirely renounced her old taste for metaphysical speculation. He was naturally endowed; not indeed with more than or-

* Born, 1705; died, 1774.

† "I have found in this writer more original thinking and observation upon the several subjects that he has taken in hand than in any other,—not to say than in all others put together. His talent also for illustration is unrivalled."—Paley, Preface to Moral and Political Philosophy. See the excellent preface to an abridgment, by Mr. Haslitt, of Tucker's work, published in London in 1807. May I venture to refer also to my own Discourse on the Law of Nature and Nations, London, 1799? Mr. Stewart treats Tucker and Hartley with unwonted harshness.

dinary acuteness or sensibility, nor with a high degree of reach and range of mind, but with a singular capacity for careful observation and original reflection, and with a fancy perhaps unmatched in producing various and happy illustration. The most observable of his moral qualities appear to have been prudence and cheerfulness, good-nature and easy temper. The influence of his situation and character is visible in his writings. Indulging his own tastes and fancies, like most English squires of his time, he became, like many of them, a sort of humourist. Hence much of his originality and independence; hence the boldness with which he openly employs illustrations from homely objects. He wrote to please himself more than the public. He had too little regard for readers, either to sacrifice his sincerity to them, or to curb his own prolixity, repetition, and egotism, from the fear of fatiguing them. Hence he became as loose, as rambling, and as much an egotist as Montaigne; but not so agreeably so, notwithstanding a considerable resemblance of genius; because he wrote on subjects where disorder and egotism are unseasonable, and for readers whom they disturb instead of amusing. His prolixity at last so increased itself, when his work became long, that repetition in the latter parts partly arose from forgetfulness of the former; and though his freedom from slavish deference to general opinion is very commendable, it must be owned, that his want of a wholesome fear of the public renders the perusal of a work which is extremely interesting, and even amusing in most of its parts, on the whole a laborious task. He was by early education a believer in Christianity, if not by natural character religious. His calm good sense and accommodating temper led him rather to explain established doctrines in a manner agreeable to his philosophy, than to assail them. Hence he was represented as a time-server by freethinkers, and as a heretic by the orthodox.* Living in a country where the secure tranquillity flowing from the Revolution was gradually drawing forth all mental activity towards practical pursuits and outward objects, he hastened from the rudiments of mental and moral philosophy, to those branches of it which touch the business of men.† Had he recast without changing his thoughts,—had he detached those ethical observations for which he had so peculiar a vocation, from the disputes of his country and his day, he might have thrown many of his chapters into their proper form of essays, and these might have been compared, though not likened, to those of Hume. But the country gentleman, philosophic as he was, had too much fondness for his own humours to engage in a course of drudgery and deference. It may, however, be confidently added, on the authority of all those who have fairly made the experiment, that whoever, unfettered by a previous system, undertakes the labour necessary to discover and relish the high excellences of this metaphysical Montaigne, will find his toil lightened as he proceeds, by a growing indulgence, if not partiality, for the foibles of the humourist, and at last rewarded, in a greater degree perhaps than by any other writer on mixed and applied philosophy, by being led to commanding stations and new points of view, whence the mind of a moralist can hardly fail to catch some fresh prospects of Nature and duty.

It is in mixed, not in pure philosophy, that his superiority consists. In the part of his work which relates to the Intellect, he has adopted much from Hartley, hiding but aggravating the offence by a change of technical terms; and he was ungrateful enough to countenance the vulgar sneer which involves the mental analysis of that philosopher in the ridicule to which his physiological hypothesis is liable.* Thus, for the Hartleian term "association" he substitutes that of "translation," when adopting the same theory of the principles which move the mind to action. In the practical and applicable part of that inquiry he indeed far surpasses Hartley; and it is little to add, that he unspeakably exceeds that bare and naked thinker in the useful as well as admirable faculty of illustration. In the strictly theoretical part his exposition is considerably fuller; but the defect of his genius becomes conspicuous when he handles a very general principle. The very term "translation" ought to have kept up in his mind a steady conviction that the secondary motives to action become as independent, and seek their own objects as exclusively, as the primary principles. His own examples are rich in proofs of this important truth. But there is a slippery descent in the theory of human nature, by which he, like most of his forerunners, slid unawares into Selfishness. He was not preserved from this fall by seeing that all the deliberate principles which have self for their object are themselves of *secondary formation;* and he was led into the general error by the notion that pleasure, or, as he calls it, "satisfaction," was the original and

* This disposition to compromise and accommodation, which is discoverable in Paley, was carried to its utmost length by Mr. Hey, a man of much acuteness, Professor of Divinity at Cambridge.

† Perhaps no philosopher ever stated more justly, more naturally, or more modestly than Tucker, the ruling maxim of his life. "My thoughts," says he, "have taken a turn from my earliest youth towards searching into the foundations and measures of Right and Wrong; my love for retirement has furnished me with continual leisure; and the exercise of my reason has been my daily employment."

* Light of Nature, vol. ii. chap. xviii., of which the conclusion may be pointed out as a specimen of unmatched fruitfulness, vivacity, and felicity of illustration. The admirable sense of the conclusion of chap. xxv. seems to have suggested Paley's good chapter on Happiness. The alteration of Plato's comparison of Reason to a charioteer, and the passions to the horses, in chap. xxvi., is of characteristic and transcendent excellence.

sole object of all appetites and desires;—confounding this with the true, but very different proposition, that the attainment of all the objects of appetite and desire is productive of pleasure. He did not see that, without presupposing desires, the word "pleasure" would have no signification; and that the representations by which he was seduced would leave only *one appetite* or *desire* in human nature. He had no adequate and constant conception, that the translation of desire from being the end to be the means occasioned the formation of a new passion, which is perfectly distinct from, and altogether independent of, the original desire. Too frequently (for he was neither obstinate nor uniform in error) he considered these translations as accidental defects in human nature, not as the appointed means of supplying it with its variety of active principles. He was too apt to speak as if the selfish elements were not destroyed in the new combination, but remained still capable of being recalled, when convenient, like the links in a chain of reasoning, which we pass over from forgetfulness, or for brevity. Take him all in all, however, the neglect of his writings is the strongest proof of the disinclination of the English nation, for the last half century, to metaphysical philosophy.*

WILLIAM PALEY.†

This excellent writer, who, after Clarke and Butler, ought to be ranked among the brightest ornaments of the English Church in the eighteenth century, is, in the history of philosophy, naturally placed after Tucker, to whom, with praiseworthy liberality, he owns his extensive obligations. It is a mistake to suppose that he owed his system to Hume,—a thinker too refined, and a writer perhaps too elegant, to have naturally attracted him. A coincidence in the principle of Utility, common to both with so many other philosophers, affords no sufficient ground for the supposition. Had he been habitually influenced by Mr. Hume, who has translated so many of the dark and crabbed passages of Butler into his own transparent and beautiful language, it is not possible to suppose that such a mind as that of Paley would have fallen into those principles of gross selfishness of which Mr. Hume is a uniform and zealous antagonist.

The natural frame of Paley's understanding fitted it more for business and the world than for philosophy; and he accordingly enjoyed with considerable relish the few opportunities which the latter part of his life afforded of taking a part in the affairs of his county as a magistrate. Penetration and shrewdness, firmness and coolness, a vein of pleasantry, fruitful though somewhat unrefined, with an original homeliness and significancy of expression, were perhaps more remarkable in his conversation than the restraints of authorship and profession allowed them to be in his writings. Grateful remembrance brings this assemblage of qualities with unfaded colours before the mind at the present moment, after the long interval of twenty-eight years. His taste for the common business and ordinary amusements of life fortunately gave a zest to the company which his neighbours chanced to yield, without rendering him insensible to the pleasures of intercourse with more enlightened society. The practical bent of his nature is visible in the language of his writings, which, on practical matters, is as precise as the nature of the subject requires, but, in his rare and reluctant efforts to rise to first principles, become indeterminate and unsatisfactory; though no man's composition was more free from the impediments which hinder a man's meaning from being quickly and clearly seen. He seldom distinguishes more exactly than is required for palpable and direct usefulness. He possessed that chastised acuteness of discrimination, exercised on the affairs of men, and habitually looking to a purpose beyond the mere increase of knowledge, which forms the character of a lawyer's understanding, and which is apt to render a mere lawyer too subtile for the management of affairs, and yet too gross for the pursuit of general truth. His style is as near perfection in its kind as any in our language. Perhaps no words were ever more expressive and illustrative than those in which he represents the art of life to be that of rightly "setting our habits."

The most original and ingenious of his writings is the Horæ Paulinæ. The Evidences of Christianity are formed out of an admirable translation of Butler's Analogy, and a most skilful abridgment of Lardner's Credibility of the Gospel History. He may be said to have thus given value to two works, of which the first was scarcely intelligible to the majority of those who were most desirous of profiting by it; while the second soon wearies out the larger part of readers, though the more patient few have almost always been gradually won over to feel pleasure in a display of knowledge, probity, charity, and meekness, unmatched by any other avowed advocate in a case deeply interesting his warmest feelings. His

* Much of Tucker's chapter on Pleasure, and of Paley's on Happiness (both of which are invaluable), is contained in the passage of the Traveller, of which the following couplet expresses the main object:

"Unknown to them when sensual pleasures cloy,
To fill the languid pause with finer joy."

"An honest man," says Hume, (Inquiry concerning Morals, § ix.) "has the frequent satisfaction of seeing knaves betrayed by their own maxims." "I used often to laugh at your honest simple neighbour Flamborough, and one way or another generally cheated him once a year: yet still the honest man went forward without suspicion, and grew rich, while I still continued tricksy and cunning, and was poor, without the consolation of being honest."—Vicar of Wakefield, chap. xxvi.

† Born, 1743; died, 1805.

Natural Theology is the wonderful work of a man who, after sixty, had studied Anatomy in order to write it; and it could only have been surpassed by one who, to great originality of conception and clearness of exposition, adds the advantage of a high place in the first class of physiologists.*

It would be unreasonable here to say much of a work which is in the hands of so many as his Moral and Political Philosophy. A very few remarks on one or two parts of it may be sufficient to estimate his value as a moralist, and to show his defects as a metaphysician. His general account of Virtue may indeed be chosen for both purposes. The manner in which he deduces the necessary tendency of all virtuous actions to promote general happiness, from the goodness of the Divine Lawgiver, (though the principle be not, as has already more than once appeared, peculiar to him, but rather common to most religious philosophers,) is characterised by a clearness and vigour which have never been surpassed. It is indeed nearly, if not entirely, an identical proposition, that a Being of unmixed benevolence will prescribe those laws only to His creatures which contribute to their well-being. When we are convinced that a course of conduct is generally beneficial to all men, we cannot help considering it as acceptable to a benevolent Deity. The usefulness of actions is the mark set on them by the Supreme Legislator, by which reasonable beings discover it to be His will that such actions should be done. In this apparently unanswerable deduction it is partly admitted, and universally implied, that the principles of Right and Wrong may be treated apart from the manifestation of them in the Scriptures. If it were otherwise, how could men of perfectly different religions deal or reason with each other on moral subjects? How could they regard rights and duties as subsisting between them? To what common principles could they appeal in their differences? Even the Polytheists themselves, those worshippers of

> Gods partial, changeful, passionate, unjust,
> Whose attributes are rage, revenge, or lust,†

by a happy inconsistency are compelled, however irregularly and imperfectly, to ascribe some general enforcement of the moral code to their divinities. If there were no foundation for Morality antecedent to the Revealed Religion, we should want that important test of the conformity of a revelation to pure morality, by which its claim to a divine origin is to be tried. The internal evidence of Religion necessarily presupposes such a standard. The Christian contrasts the precepts of the Koran with the pure and benevolent morality of the Gospel. The Mahometan claims, with justice, a superiority over the Hindoo, inasmuch as the Musselman religion inculcates the moral perfection of one Supreme Ruler of the world. The ceremonial and exclusive character of Judaism has ever been regarded as an indication that it was intended to pave the way for an universal religion, a morality seated in the heart, and a worship of sublime simplicity. These discussions would be impossible, unless Morality were previously proved or granted to exist. Though the science of Ethics is thus far independent, it by no means follows that there is any equality, or that there may not be the utmost inequality, in the moral tendency of religious systems. The most ample scope is still left for the zeal and activity of those who seek to spread important truth. But it is absolutely essential to ethical science that it should contain principles, the authority of which must be recognised by men of every conceivable variety of religious opinion.

The peculiarities of Paley's mind are discoverable in the comparison, or rather contrast, between the practical chapter on Happiness, and the philosophical portion of the chapter on Virtue. "Virtue is the doing good to mankind, in obedience to the will of God, and for the sake of everlasting happiness."* It is not perhaps very important to observe, that these words, which he offers as a "definition," ought in propriety to have been called a "proposition;" but it is much more necessary to say that they contain a false account of Virtue. According to this doctrine, every action not done *for the sake* of the agent's happiness is vicious. Now, it is plain, that an act cannot be said to be done for the sake of any thing which is not present to the mind of the agent at the moment of action: it is a contradiction in terms to affirm that a man acts for the sake of any object, of which, however it may be the necessary consequence of his act, he is not at the time fully aware. The *unfelt* consequences of his act can no more influence his will than its *unknown* consequences. Nay, further, a man is only with any propriety said to act for the sake of his chief object; nor can he with entire correctness be said to act for the sake of any thing but his sole object. So that it is a necessary consequence of Paley's proposition, that every act which flows from generosity or benevolence is a vice;—so also is every act of obedience to the will of God, if it arises from any motive but a desire of the reward which He will bestow. Any act of obedience influenced by gratitude, and affection, and veneration towards Supreme Benevolence and Perfection, is so far imperfect; and if it arises solely from these motives it becomes a vice. It must be owned, that this excellent and most enlightened man has laid the foundations of Religion and Virtue in a more intense and exclusive selfishness than was avowed by the Catholic enemies of Fenelon, when

* See Animal Mechanics, by Mr. Charles Bell, published by the Society for the diffusion of Useful Knowledge.

† Essay on Man, Ep. iii.

* Book i. chap. vii.

they persecuted him for his doctrine of a pure and disinterested love of God.

In another province, of a very subordinate kind, the disposition of Paley to limit his principles to his own time and country, and to look at them merely as far as they are calculated to amend prevalent vices and errors, betrayed him into narrow and false views. His chapter on what he calls the "Law of Honour" is unjust, even in its own small sphere, because it supposes Honour to *allow* what it *does not forbid;* though the truth be, that the vices enumerated by him are only not *forbidden* by Honour, because they are not within its jurisdiction. He considers it as "a system of rules constructed by people of fashion;"—a confused and transient mode of expression, which may be understood with difficulty by our posterity, and which cannot now be exactly rendered perhaps in any other language. The subject, however, thus narrowed and lowered, is neither unimportant in practice, nor unworthy of the consideration of the moral philosopher. Though all mankind honour Virtue and despise Vice, the degree of respect or contempt is often far from being proportioned to the place which virtues and vices occupy in a just system of Ethics. Wherever higher honour is bestowed on one moral quality than on others of equal or greater moral value, *what is called a "point of honour" may be said to exist.* It is singular that so shrewd an observer as Paley should not have observed a law of honour far more permanent than that which attracted his notice, in the feelings of Europe respecting the conduct of men and women. Cowardice is not so immoral as cruelty, nor indeed so detestable; but it is more despicable and disgraceful: the female point of honour forbids indeed a great vice, but one not so great as many others by which it is not violated. It is easy enough to see, that where we are strongly prompted to a virtue by a natural impulse, we love the man who is constantly actuated by the amiable sentiment; but we do not consider that which is done without difficulty as requiring or deserving admiration and distinction. The kind affections are their own rich reward, and they are the object of affection to others. To encourage kindness by praise would be to insult it, and to encourage hypocrisy. It is for the conquest of fear, it would be still more for the conquest of resentment,—if that were not, wherever it is real, the cessation of a state of mental agony,—that the applause of mankind is reserved. Observations of a similar nature will easily occur to every reader respecting the point of honour in the other sex. The conquest of natural frailties, especially in a case of far more importance to mankind than is at first sight obvious, is well distinguished as an object of honour, and the contrary vice is punished by shame. Honour is not wasted on those who abstain from acts which are punished by the law. These acts may be avoided without a pure motive. Wherever a virtue is easily cultivable by good men; wherever it is by nature attended by delight; wherever its outward observance is so necessary to society as to be enforced by punishment, it is not the proper object of honour. Honour and shame, therefore, may be reasonably dispensed, without being strictly proportioned to the intrinsic morality of actions, if the inequality of their distribution contributes to the general equipoise of the whole moral system. A wide disproportion, however, or indeed any disproportion not justifiable on moral grounds, would be a depravation of the moral principle. Duelling is among us a disputed case, though the improvement of manners has rendered it so much more infrequent, that it is likely in time to lose its support from opinion. Those who excuse individuals for yielding to a false point of honour, as in the suicides of the Greeks and Romans, may consistently blame the faulty principle, and rejoice in its destruction. The shame fixed on a Hindoo widow of rank who voluntarily survives her husband, is regarded by all other nations with horror.

There is room for great praise and some blame in other parts of Paley's work. His political opinions were those generally adopted by moderate Whigs in his own age. His language on the Revolution of 1688 may be very advantageously compared, both in precision and in generous boldness,* to that of Blackstone,—a great master of classical and harmonious composition, but a feeble reasoner and a confused thinker, whose writings are not exempt from the charge of slavishness.

It cannot be denied that Paley was sometimes rather a lax moralist, especially on public duties. It is a sin which easily besets men of strong good sense, little enthusiasm, and much experience. They are naturally led to lower their precepts to the level of their expectations. They see that higher pretensions often produce less good,—to say nothing of the hypocrisy, extravagance, and turbulence, which they may be said to foster. As those who claim more from men often gain less, it is natural for more sober and milder casuists to present a more accessible Virtue to their followers. It was thus that the Jesuits began, till, strongly tempted by their perilous station as the moral guides of the powerful, some of them by degrees fell into that absolute licentiousness for which all, not without injustice, have

* "*Government may be too secure.* The greatest tyrants have been those whose titles were the most unquestioned. Whenever, therefore, the opinion of right becomes too predominant and superstitious, *it is abated by breaking the custom.* Thus the Revolution broke the custom of succession, and thereby moderated, both in the prince and in the people, those lofty notions of hereditary right, which in the one were become a continual incentive to tyranny, and disposed the other to invite servitude, by undue compliances and dangerous concessions."—Book vi. chap. 2.

been cruelly immortalized by Pascal. Indulgence, which is a great virtue in judgment concerning the actions of others, is too apt, when blended in the same system with the precepts of Morality, to be received as a licence for our own offences. Accommodation, without which society would be painful, and arduous affairs would become impracticable, is more safely imbibed from temper and experience, than taught in early and systematic instruction. The middle region between laxity and rigour is hard to be defined; and it is still harder steadily to remain within its boundaries. Whatever may be thought of Paley's observations on political influence and ecclesiastical subscription to tests, as temperaments and mitigations which may preserve us from harsh judgment, they are assuredly not well qualified to form a part of that discipline which ought to breathe into the opening souls of youth, at the critical period of the formation of character, those inestimable virtues of sincerity, of integrity, of independence, which will even guide them *more safely* through life than will mere prudence; while they provide an inward fountain of pure delight, immeasurably more abundant than all the outward sources of precarious and perishable pleasure.

JEREMY BENTHAM.*

The general scheme of this Dissertation would be a sufficient reason for omitting the name of a living writer. The devoted attachment and invincible repugnance which an impartial estimate of Mr. Bentham has to encounter on either side, are a strong inducement not to deviate from that scheme in his case. But the most brief sketch of ethical controversy in England would be imperfect without it; and perhaps the utter hopelessness of finding any expedient for satisfying his followers, or softening his opponents, may enable a writer to look steadily and solely at what he believes to be the dictates of Truth and Justice. He who has spoken of former philosophers with unreserved freedom, ought perhaps to subject his courage and honesty to the severest test by an attempt to characterize such a contemporary. Should the very few who are at once enlightened and unbiassed be of opinion that his firmness and equity have stood this trial, they will be the more disposed to trust his fairness where the exercise of that quality may have been more easy.

The disciples of Mr. Bentham are more like the hearers of an Athenian philosopher than the pupils of a modern professor, or the cool proselytes of a modern writer. They are in general men of competent age, of superior understanding, who voluntarily embrace the laborious study of useful and noble sciences; who derive their opinions, not so much from the cold perusal of his writings, as from familiar converse with a master from whose lips these opinions are recommended by simplicity, disinterestedness, originality, and vivacity,—aided rather than impeded by foibles not unamiable,—enforced of late by the growing authority of years and of fame, and at all times strengthened by that undoubting reliance on his own judgment which mightily increases the ascendant of such a man over those who approach him. As he and they deserve the credit of braving vulgar prejudices, so they must be content to incur the imputation of falling into the neighbouring vices of seeking distinction by singularity,—of clinging to opinions, because they are obnoxious,—of wantonly wounding the most respectable feelings of mankind,—of regarding an immense display of method and nomenclature as a sure token of a corresponding increase of knowledge,—and of considering themselves as a chosen few, whom an initiation into the most secret mysteries of Philosophy entitles to look down with pity, if not contempt, on the profane multitude. Viewed with aversion or dread by the public, they become more bound to each other and to their master; while they are provoked into the use of language which more and more exasperates opposition to them. A hermit in the greatest of cities, seeing only his disciples, and indignant that systems of government and law which he believes to be perfect, are disregarded at once by the many and the powerful, Mr. Bentham has at length been betrayed into the most unphilosophical hypothesis, that all the ruling bodies who guide the community have conspired to stifle and defeat his discoveries. He is too little acquainted with doubts to believe the honest doubts of others, and he is too angry to make allowance for their prejudices and habits. He has embraced the most extreme party in practical politics;—manifesting more dislike and contempt towards those who are moderate supporters of popular principles than towards their most inflexible opponents. To the unpopularity of his philosophical and political doctrines, he has added the more general and lasting obloquy due to the unseemly treatment of doctrines and principles which, if there were no other motives for reverential deference, ought, from a regard to the feelings of the best men, to be approached with decorum and respect.

Fifty-three years have passed since the publication of Mr. Bentham's first work, A Fragment on Government,—a considerable octavo volume, employed in the examination of a short paragraph of Blackstone, unmatched in acute hypercriticism, but conducted with a severity which leads to an unjust estimate of the writer criticised, till the like experiment be repeated on other writings. It was a waste of extraordinary power to employ it in pointing out flaws and patches in the robe occasionally stolen from the philosophical schools, which hung loosely, and not unbecomingly, on the elegant commentator. This volume, and especially the preface,

* Born, 1748; died, 1832.—Ed.

abounds in fine, original, and just observation; it contains the germs of most of his subsequent productions, and it is an early example of that disregard for the method, proportions, and occasion of a writing which, with all common readers, deeply affects its power of interesting or instructing. Two years after, he published a most excellent tract on the Hard Labour Bill, which, concurring with the spirit excited by Howard's inquiries, laid the foundation of just reasoning on reformatory punishment. The Letters on Usury,* are perhaps the best specimen of the exhaustive discussion of a moral or political question, leaving no objection, however feeble, unanswered, and no difficulty, however small, unexplained;—remarkable also, as they are, for the clearness and spirit of the style, for the full exposition which suits them to all intelligent readers, and for the tender and skilful hand with which prejudice is touched. The urbanity of the apology for projectors, addressed to Dr. Smith, whose temper and manner the author seems for a time to have imbibed, is admirable.

The Introduction to the Principles of Morals and Politics, printed before the Letters, but published after them, was the first sketch of his system, and is still the only account of it by himself. The great merit of this work, and of his other writings in relation to Jurisprudence properly so called, is not within our present scope. To the Roman jurists belongs the praise of having alloted a separate portion of their Digest to the signification of the words of the most frequent use in law and legal discussion.† Mr. Bentham not only first perceived and taught the great value of an introductory section, composed of the definitions of general terms, as subservient to brevity and precision in every part of a code; but he also discovered the unspeakable importance of natural arrangement in Jurisprudence, by rendering the mere place of a proposed law in such an arrangement a short and easy test of the fitness of the proposal.*

But here he does not distinguish between the value of arrangement as scaffolding, and the inferior convenience of its being the very frame-work of the structure. He, indeed, is much more remarkable for laying down desirable rules for the determination of rights, and the punishment of wrongs, in general, than for weighing the various circumstances which require them to be modified in different countries and times, in order to render them either more useful, more easily introduced, more generally respected, or more certainly executed. The art of legislation consists in thus applying the principles of Jurisprudence to the situation, wants, interests, feelings, opinions, and habits, of each distinct community at any given time. It bears the same relation to Jurisprudence which the mechanical arts bear to pure Mathematics. Many of these considerations serve to show, that the sudden establishment of new codes can seldom be practicable or effectual for their purpose; and that reformations, though founded on the principles of Jurisprudence, ought to be not only adapted to the peculiar interests of a people, but engrafted on their previous usages, and brought into harmony with those national dispositions on which the execution of laws depends.† The Romans, under Justinian, adopted at least the true principle, if they did not apply it with sufficient freedom and boldness. They considered the multitude of occasional laws, and the still greater mass of usages, opinions, and determinations, as the materials of legislation, not precluding, but demanding a systematic arrangement of the whole by the supreme authority. Had the arrangement

* They were addressed to Mr. George Wilson, who retired from the English bar to his own country, and died at Edinburgh in 1816;—an early friend of Mr. Bentham, and afterwards an intimate one of Lord Ellenborough, of Sir Vicary Gibbs, and of all the most eminent of his professional contemporaries. The rectitude of judgment, purity of heart, elevation of honour, the sternness only in integrity, the scorn of baseness, and indulgence towards weakness, which were joined in him with a gravity exclusive neither of feeling nor of pleasantry, contributed still more than his abilities and attainments of various sorts, to a moral authority with his friends, and in his profession, which few men more amply possessed, or more usefully exercised. The same character, somewhat softened, and the same influence, distinguished his closest friend, the late Mr. Lens. Both were inflexible and incorruptible friends of civil and religious liberty, and both knew how to reconcile the warmest zeal for that sacred cause, with a charity towards their opponents, which partisans, often more violent than steady, treated as lukewarm. The present writer hopes that the good-natured reader will excuse him for having thus, perhaps unseasonably, bestowed heartfelt commendation on those who were above the pursuit of praise, and the remembrance of whose good opinion and good-will help to support him under a deep sense of faults and vices.

† Digest, lib. i. tit. 16. De Verborum Significatione.

* See a beautiful article on Codification, in the Edinburg Review, vol. xxix. p. 217. It need no longer be concealed that it was contributed by Sir Samuel Romilly. The steadiness with which he held the balance in weighing the merits of his friend against his unfortunate defects, is an example of his union of the most commanding moral principle with a sensibility so warm, that, if it had been released from that stern authority, it would not so long have endured the coarseness and roughness of human concerns. From the tenderness of his feelings, and from an anger never roused but by cruelty and baseness, as much as from his genius and his pure taste, sprung that original and characteristic eloquence, which was the hope of the afflicted as well as the terror of the oppressor. If his oratory had not flowed so largely from this moral source, which years do not dry up, he would not perhaps have been the only example of an orator who, after the age of sixty, daily increased in polish, in vigour, and in splendour.

† An excellent medium between those who absolutely require new codes, and those who obstinately adhere to ancient usages, has been pointed out by M. Meyer, in his most justly celebrated work, Esprit, &c. des Institutions Judiciares des Principaux Pays de l'Europe, La Haye, 1819, tome i. Introduction, p. 8.

been more scientific, had there been a bolder examination and a more free reform of many particular branches, a model would have been offered for liberal imitation by modern lawgivers. It cannot be denied, without injustice and ingratitude, that Mr. Bentham has done more than any other writer to rouse the spirit of juridical reformation, which is now gradually examining every part of law, and which, when further progress is facilitated by digesting the present laws, will doubtless proceed to the improvement of all. Greater praise it is given to few to earn: it ought to satisfy him for the disappointment of hopes which were not reasonable, that Russia should receive a code from him, or that North America could be brought to renounce the variety of her laws and institutions, on the single authority of a foreign philosopher, whose opinions had not worked their way, either into legislation or into general reception, in his own country. It ought also to dispose his followers to do fuller justice to the Romillys and Broughams, without whose prudence and energy, as well as reason and eloquence, the best plans of reformation must have continued a dead letter;—for whose sake it might have been fit to reconsider the obloquy heaped on their profession, and to show more general indulgence to all those whose chief offence seems to consist in their doubts whether sudden changes, almost always imposed by violence on a community, be the surest road to lasting improvement.

It is unfortunate that ethical theory, with which we are now chiefly concerned, is not the province in which Mr. Bentham has reached the most desirable distinction. It may be remarked, both in ancient and in modern times, that whatever modifications prudent followers may introduce into the system of an innovator, the principles of the master continue to mould the habitual dispositions, and to influence the practical tendency of the school. Mr. Bentham preaches the principle of Utility with the zeal of a discoverer. Occupied more in reflection than in reading, he knew not, or forgot, how often it had been the basis, and how generally an essential part, of all moral systems.* That in which he really differs from others, is in the Necessity which he teaches, and the example which he sets, of constantly bringing that principle before us. This peculiarity appears to us to be his radical error. In an attempt, of which the constitution of human nature forbids the success, he seems to us to have been led into fundamental errors in moral theory, and to have given to his practical doctrine a dangerous direction.

The confusion of *moral approbation* with the *moral qualities* which are its objects, common to Mr. Bentham with many other philosophers, is much more uniform and prominent in him than in most others. This general error, already mentioned at the opening of this Dissertation, has led him more than others to assume, that because the principle of Utility forms a necessary part of every moral theory, it ought therefore to be the chief motive of human conduct. Now it is evident that this assumption, rather tacitly than avowedly made, is wholly gratuitous. No practical conclusion can be deduced from the principle, but that we ought to cultivate those habitual dispositions which are the most effectual motives to useful actions. But before a regard to our own interest, or a desire to promote the welfare of men in general, be allowed to be the exclusive, or even the chief regulators of human conduct, it must be shown that they are the most effectual motives to such useful actions: it is demonstrated by experience that they are not. It is even owned by the most ingenious writers of Mr. Bentham's school, that desires which are pointed to general and distant objects, although they have their proper place and their due value, are commonly very faint and ineffectual inducements to action. A theory founded on Utility, therefore, requires that we should cultivate, as excitements to practice, those other habitual dispositions which we know by experience to be generally the source of actions beneficial to ourselves and our fellows;—habits of feeling productive of habits of virtuous conduct, and in their turn strengthened by the re-action of these last. What is the result of experience on the choice of the objects of moral culture? Beyond all dispute, that we should labour to attain that state of mind in which all the social affections are felt with the utmost warmth, giving birth to more comprehensive benevolence, but not supplanted by it;—when the Moral Sentiments most strongly approve what is right and good, without being perplexed by a calculation of consequences, though not incapable of being gradually rectified by Reason, whenever they are decisively proved by experience not to correspond in some of their parts to the universal and perpetual effects of conduct. It is a false representation of human nature to affirm that "courage" is only "prudence."* They coincide in their effects, and it is always prudent to be courageous: but a man who fights *because* he thinks it more hazardous to yield, is not brave. He does not become brave till he feels cowardice to be base and painful, and till he is no longer in need of any aid from prudence. Even if it were the *interest* of every man to be bold, it is clear that so cold a considera-

* See Note V.

* Mill, Analysis of the Human Mind, vol. ii. p. 237. It would be unjust not to say that this book, partly perhaps from a larger adoption of the principles of Hartley, holds out fairer opportunities of negotiation with natural feelings and the doctrines of former philosophers, than any other production of the same school. But this very assertion about courage clearly shows at least a forgetfulness that courage, even if it were the offspring of prudence, would not for that reason be a species of it.

tion cannot prevail over the fear of danger. Where it seems to do so, it must be the unseen power either of the fear of shame, or of some other powerful passion, to which it lends its name. It was long ago with striking justice observed by Aristotle, that he who abstains from present gratification, under a distinct apprehension of its painful consequences, is only *prudent*, and that he must acquire a disrelish for excess on its own account, before he deserves the name of a temperate man. It is only when the means are firmly and unalterably converted into ends, that the process of forming the mind is completed. Courage may then seek, instead of avoiding danger: Temperance may prefer abstemiousness to indulgence: Prudence itself may choose an orderly government of conduct, according to certain rules, without regard to the degree in which it promotes welfare. Benevolence must desire the happiness of others, to the exclusion of the consideration how far it is connected with that of the benevolent agent; and those alone can be accounted just who obey the dictates of Justice from having thoroughly learned an habitual veneration for her strict rules and for her larger precepts. In that complete state the mind possesses no power of dissolving the combinations of thought and feeling which impel it to action. Nothing in this argument turns on the difference between implanted and acquired principles. As no man can cease, by any act of his, to *see* distance, though the power of seeing it be universally acknowledged to be an acquisition, so no man has the power to extinguish the affections and the moral sentiments, (however much they may be thought to be acquired,) any more than that of eradicating the bodily appetites. The best writers of Mr. Bentham's school overlook the indissolubility of these associations, and appear not to bear in mind that their strength and rapid action constitute the perfect state of a moral agent.

The pursuit of our own general welfare, or of that of mankind at large, though from their vagueness and coldness they are unfit habitual motives and unsafe ordinary guides of conduct, yet perform functions of essential importance in the moral system. The former, which we call "self-love," preserves the balance of all the active principles which regard ourselves ultimately, and contributes to subject them to the authority of the moral principles.* The latter, which is general benevolence, regulates in like manner the equipoise of the narrower affections,—quickens the languid, and checks the encroaching,—borrows strength from pity, and even from indignation,—receives some compensation, as it enlarges, in the addition of beauty and grandeur, for the weakness which arises from dispersion,—enables us to look on all men as brethren, and overflows on every sentient being. The general interest of mankind, in truth, almost solely affects us through the affections of benevolence and sympathy; for the coincidence of general with individual interest,—even where it is certain,—is too dimly seen to produce any emotion which can impel to, or restrain from action. As a general truth, its value consists in its completing the triumph of Morality, by demonstrating the absolute impossibility of forming any theory of human nature which does not preserve the superiority of Virtue over Vice; —a great, though not a directly practical advantage.

The followers of Mr. Bentham have carried to an unusual extent the prevalent fault of the more modern advocates of Utility, who have dwelt so exclusively on the outward advantages of Virtue as to have lost sight of the delight which is a part of virtuous feeling, and of the beneficial influence of good actions upon the frame of the mind. "Benevolence towards others," says Mr. Mill, "produces a return of benevolence from them." The fact is true, and ought to be stated: but how unimportant is it in comparison with that which is passed over in silence,—the pleasure of the affection itself, which, if it could become lasting and intense, would convert the heart into a heaven! No one who has ever felt kindness, if he could accurately recall his feelings, could hesitate about their infinite superiority. The cause of the general neglect of this consideration is, that it is only when a gratification is something distinct from a state of mind, that we can easily learn to consider it as a pleasure. Hence the great error respecting the affections, where the *inherent* delight is not duly estimated, on account of that very peculiarity of its being a part of a state of mind which renders it unspeakably more valuable as independent of every thing without. The social affections are the only principles of human nature which have no direct pains: to have any of these desires is to be in a state of happiness. The malevolent passions have properly no pleasures; for that attainment of their purpose which is improperly so called, consists only in healing or assuaging the torture which envy, jealousy, and malice, inflict on the malignant mind. It might with as much propriety be said that the toothache and the stone have pleasures, because their removal is followed by an agreeable feeling. These bodily disorders, indeed, are often cured by the process which removes the sufferings; but the mental distempers of envy and revenge are nourished by every act of odious indulgence which for a moment suspends their pain.

The same observation is applicable to every virtuous disposition, though not so obviously as to the benevolent affections. That a brave man is, on the whole, far less exposed to danger than a coward, is not the chief advantage of a courageous temper. Great dangers are rare; but the constant absence of such painful and mortifying sensations as those of fear, and the steady con-

* See Note W.

sciousness of superiority to what subdues ordinary men, are a perpetual source of inward enjoyment. No man who has ever been visited by a gleam of magnanimity, can place any outward advantage of fortitude in comparison with the feeling of being always able fearlessly to defend a righteous cause.* Even humility, in spite of first appearances, is a remarkable example:—though it has of late been unwarrantably used to signify that painful consciousness of inferiority which is the first stage of envy.† It is a term consecrated in Christian Ethics to denote that disposition which, by inclining towards a modest estimate of our qualities, corrects the prevalent tendency of human nature to overvalue our merits and to overrate our claims. What can be a less doubtful, or a much more considerable blessing than this constant sedative, which soothes and composes the irritable passions of vanity and pride? What is more conducive to lasting peace of mind than the consciousness of proficiency in that most delicate species of equity which, in the secret tribunal of Conscience, labours to be impartial in the comparison of ourselves with others? What can so perfectly assure us of the purity of our Moral Sense, as the habit of contemplating, not that excellence which we have reached, but that which is still to be pursued,‡—of not considering how far we may outrun others, but how far we are from the goal?

Virtue has often outward advantages, and always inward delights: but the last, though constant, strong, inaccessible and inviolable, are not easily considered by the common observer as apart from the form with which they are blended. They are so subtile and evanescent as to escape the distinct contemplation of all but the very few who meditate on the acts of the mind. The outward advantages, on the other hand,—cold, uncertain, dependent and precarious as they are,—yet stand out to the sense and to the memory, may be as it were handled and counted, and are perfectly on a level with the general apprehension. Hence they have become the almost exclusive theme of all moralists who profess to follow Reason. There is room for suspecting that a very general illusion prevails on this subject. Probably the smallest part of the pleasure of Virtue, because it is the most palpable, has become the sign and mental representative of the whole: the outward and visible sign suggests only insensibly the inward and mental delight. Those who are prone to display chiefly the external benefits of magnanimity and kindness, would speak with far less fervour, and perhaps less confidence, if their feelings were not unconsciously affected by the mental state which is overlooked in their statements. But when they speak of what is *without*, they feel what was *within*, and their words excite the same feeling in others.

Is it not probable that much of our love of praise may be thus ascribed to humane and sociable pleasure in the sympathy of others with us? Praise is the symbol which represents sympathy, and which the mind insensibly substitutes for it in recollection and in language. Does not the desire of posthumous fame, in like manner, manifest an ambition for the fellow-feeling of our race, when it is perfectly unproductive of any advantage to ourselves? In this point of view, it may be considered as the passion the very existence of which proves the mighty power of disinterested desire. Every other pleasure from sympathy is derived from contemporaries: the love of fame alone seeks the sympathy of unborn generations, and stretches the chain which binds the race of man together, to an extent to which Hope sets no bounds. There is a noble, even if unconscious union of Morality with genius in the mind of him who sympathizes with the masters who lived twenty centuries before him, in order that he may learn to command the sympathies of the countless generations who are to come.

In the most familiar, as well as in the highest instances, it would seem, that the inmost thoughts and sentiments of men are more pure than their language. Those who speak of "a regard to character," if they be serious, generally infuse into that word, unawares, a large portion of that sense in which it denotes the frame of the mind. Those who speak of "honour" very often mean a more refined and delicate sort of conscience, which ought to render the more educated classes of society alive to such smaller wrongs as the laborious and the ignorant can scarcely feel. What heart does not warm at the noble exclamation of the ancient poet: "Who is pleased by false honour, or frightened by lying infamy, but he who is false and depraved!"* Every uncorrupted mind feels unmerited praise as a bitter reproach, and regards a consciousness of demerit as a drop of poison in the cup of honour. How different is the applause which truly delights us all, a proof that the consciences of others are in harmony with our own! "What," says Cicero, "is glory but the concurring praise of the good, the unbought approbation of those who judge aright of excellent Virtue!"† A far greater

* According to Cicero's definition of fortitude, "Virtus pugnans pro æquitate." The remains of the original sense of "virtus," manhood, give a beauty and force to these expressions, which cannot be preserved in our language. The Greek "ἀρετή," and the German "tugend," originally denoted "strength," afterwards "courage," and at last "virtue." But the happy derivation of "virtus" from "vir" gives an energy to the phrase of Cicero, which illustrates the use of etymology in the hands of a skilful writer.

† Anal. Hum. Mind, vol. ii. p. 222.

‡ For a description of vanity, by a great orator, see the Rev. R. Hall's Sermon on Modern Infidelity.

* Horat. Epistol. lib. i. 16.

† Probably quoted memoriter from De Fin. lib. iv. cap. 23.—Ed.

than Cicero rises from the purest praise of man, to more sublime contemplations.

Fame is no plant that grows on mortal soil,
But lives and spreads aloft, by those pure eyes
And perfect witness of all-judging Jove.*

Those who have most earnestly inculcated the doctrine of Utility have given another notable example of the very vulgar prejudice which treats the unseen as insignificant. Tucker is the only one of them who occasionally considers that most important effect of human conduct which consists in its action on the frame of the mind, by fitting its faculties and sensibilities for their appointed purpose. A razor or a penknife would well enough cut cloth or meat; but if they were often so used, they would be entirely spoiled. The same sort of observation is much more strongly applicable to habitual dispositions, which, if they be spoiled, we have no certain means of replacing or mending. Whatever act, therefore, discomposes the moral machinery of Mind, is more injurious to the welfare of the agent than most disasters from without can be: for the latter are commonly limited and temporary; the evil of the former spreads through the whole of life. Health of mind, as well as of body, is not only productive in itself of a greater amount of enjoyment than arises from other sources, but is the only condition of our frame in which we are capable of receiving pleasure from without. Hence it appears how incredibly absurd it is to prefer, on grounds of calculation, a present interest to the preservation of those mental habits on which our well-being depends. When they are most moral, they may often prevent us from obtaining advantages: but it would be as absurd to desire to lower them for that reason, as it would be to weaken the body, lest its strength should render it more liable to contagious disorders of rare occurrence.

It is, on the other hand, impossible to combine the benefit of the general habit with the advantages of occasional deviation; for every such deviation either produces remorse, or weakens the habit, and prepares the way for its gradual destruction. He who obtains a fortune by the undetected forgery of a will, may indeed be honest in his other acts; but if he had such a scorn of fraud before as he must himself allow to be generally useful, he must suffer a severe punishment from contrition; and he will be haunted with the fears of one who has lost his own security for his good conduct. In all cases, if they be well examined, his loss by the distemper of his mental frame will outweigh the profits of his vice.

By repeating the like observation on similar occasions, it will be manifest that the infirmity of recollection, aggravated by the defects of language, gives an appearance of more selfishness to man than truly belongs to his nature; and that the effect of active agents upon the habitual state of mind,—one of the considerations to which the epithet "sentimental" has of late been applied in derision,—is really among the most serious and reasonable objects of Moral Philosophy. When the internal pleasures and pains which *accompany* good and bad feelings, or rather form a part of them, and the internal advantages and disadvantages which *follow* good and bad actions, are sufficiently considered, the comparative importance of *outward consequences* will be more and more narrow; so that the Stoical philosopher may be thought almost excusable for rejecting it altogether, were it not an almost indispensably necessary consideration for those in whom right habits of feeling are not sufficiently strong. They alone are happy, or even truly virtuous, who have little need of it.

The later moralists who adopt the principle of Utility, have so *misplaced* it, that in their hands it has as great a tendency as any theoretical error can have, to lessen the intrinsic pleasure of Virtue, and to unfit our habitual feelings for being the most effectual inducements to good conduct. This is the natural tendency of a discipline which brings Utility too closely and frequently into contact with action. By this habit, in its best state, an essentially weaker motive is gradually substituted for others which must always be of more force. The frequent appeal to Utility as the standard of action tends to introduce an uncertainty with respect to the conduct of other men, which would render all intercourse with them insupportable. It affords also so fair a disguise for selfish and malignant passions, as often to hide their nature from him who is their prey. Some taint of these mean and evil principles will at least spread itself, and a venomous animation, not its own, will be given to the cold desire of Utility. Moralists who take an active part in those affairs which often call out unamiable passions, ought to guard with peculiar watchfulness against such self-delusions. The sin that must most easily beset them, is that of sliding from general to particular consequences,—that of trying single actions, instead of dispositions, habits, and rules, by the standard of Utility,—that of authorizing too great a latitude for discretion and policy in moral conduct,—that of readily allowing exceptions to the most important rules,—that of too lenient a censure of the use of doubtful means, when the end seems to them good,—and that of believing unphilosophically, as well as dangerously, that there can be any measure or scheme so useful to the world as the existence of men who would not do a base thing for any public advantage. It was said of Andrew Fletcher, "that he would lose his life to *serve* his country, but would not do a base thing to *save* it." Let those preachers of Utility who suppose that such a man sacrifices *ends* to *means*, consider whether the scorn of baseness be not akin to the contempt of danger,

* Lycidas, l. 78.

and whether a nation composed of such men would not be invincible. But theoretical principles are counteracted by a thousand causes, which confine their mischief as well as circumscribe their benefits. Men are never so good or so bad as their opinions. All that can be with reason apprehended is, that these last may always produce some part of their natural evil, and that the mischief will be greatest among the many who seek excuses for their passions. Aristippus found in the Socratic representation of the union of virtue and happiness a pretext for sensuality; and many Epicureans became voluptuaries in spite of the example of their master,—easily dropping by degrees the limitations by which he guarded his doctrines. In proportion as a man accustoms himself to be influenced by the utility of particular acts, without regard to rules, he approaches to the casuistry of the Jesuits, and to the practical maxims of Cæsar Borgia.

Injury on this, as on other occasions, has been suffered by Ethics, from their close affinity to Jurisprudence. The true and eminent merit of Mr. Bentham is that of a reformer of Jurisprudence: he is only a moralist with a view to being a jurist; and he sometimes becomes for a few hurried moments a metaphysician with a view to laying the foundation of both the moral sciences. Both he and his followers have treated Ethics too *juridically*: they do not seem to be aware, or at least they do not bear constantly in mind, that there is an essential difference in the subjects of these two sciences.

The object of law is the prevention of actions injurious to the community: it considers the dispositions from which they flow only *indirectly*, to ascertain the likelihood of their recurrence, and thus to determine the necessity and the means of preventing them. The *direct* object of Ethics is only mental disposition: it considers actions *indirectly* as the signs by which such dispositions are manifested. If it were possible for the mere moralist to see that a moral and amiable temper was the mental source of a bad action, he could not cease to approve and love the temper, as we sometimes presume to suppose may be true of the judgments of the Searcher of Hearts. Religion necessarily coincides with Morality in this respect; and it is the peculiar distinction of Christianity that it places the seat of Virtue in the heart. Law and Ethics are necessarily so much blended, that in many intricate combinations the distinction becomes obscure: but in all strong cases the difference is evident. Thus, law punishes the most sincerely repentant; but wherever the soul of the penitent can be thought to be thoroughly purified, Religion and Morality receive him with open arms.

It is needless, after these remarks, to observe, that those whose habitual contemplation is directed to the rules of action, are likely to underrate the importance of feeling and disposition;—an error of very unfortunate consequences, since the far greater part of human actions flow from these neglected sources; while the law interposes only in cases which may be called exceptions, which are now rare, and ought to be less frequent.

The coincidence of Mr. Bentham's school with the ancient Epicureans in the disregard of the pleasures of taste and of the arts dependent on imagination, is a proof both of the inevitable adherence of much of the popular sense of the words "interest" and "pleasure," to the same words in their philosophical acceptation, and of the pernicious influence of narrowing Utility to mere visible and tangible objects, to the exclusion of those which form the larger part of human enjoyment.

The mechanical philosophers who, under Descartes and Gassendi, began to reform Physics in the seventeenth century, attempted to explain all the appearances of nature by an immediate reference to the figure of particles of matter impelling each other in various directions, and with unequal force, but in all other points alike. The communication of motion by impulse they conceived to be perfectly simple and intelligible. It never occurred to them, that the movement of one ball when another is driven against it, is a fact of which no explanation can be given which will amount to more than a statement of its constant occurrence. That no body can act where it is not, appeared to them as self-evident as that the whole is equal to all the parts. By this axiom they understood that no body moves another without touching it. They did not perceive, that it was only self-evident where it means that no body can act *where it has not the power of acting*; and that if it be understood more largely, it is a mere assumption of the proposition on which their whole system rested. Sir Isaac Newton reformed Physics, not by simplifying that science, but by rendering it much more complicated. He introduced into it the force of attraction, of which he ascertained many laws, but which even he did not dare to represent as being as intelligible, and as conceivably ultimate as impulsion itself. It was necessary for Laplace to introduce intermediate laws, and to calculate disturbing forces, before the phenomena of the heavenly bodies could be reconciled even to Newton's more complex theory. In the present state of physical and chemical knowledge, a man who should attempt to refer all the immense variety of facts to the simple impulse of the Cartesians, would have no chance of serious confutation. The number of laws augments with the progress of knowledge.

The speculations of the followers of Mr. Bentham are not unlike the unsuccessful attempt of the Cartesians. Mr. Mill, for example, derives the whole theory of Government* from the single fact, that every man pursues his interest when he knows it; which he assumes to be a sort of self-evi-

* Encyc. Brit., article "Government."

dent practical principle,—if such a phrase be not contradictory. That a man's pursuing the interest of another, or indeed any other object in nature, is just as *conceivable* as that he should pursue his own interest, is a proposition which seems never to have occurred to this acute and ingenious writer. Nothing, however, can be more certain than its truth, if the term "interest" be employed in its proper sense of general well-being, which is the only acceptation in which it can serve the purpose of his arguments. If, indeed, the term be employed to denote the gratification of a predominant desire, his proposition is self-evident, but wholly unserviceable in his argument; for it is clear that individuals and multitudes often desire what they know to be most inconsistent with their general welfare. A nation, as much as an individual, and sometimes more, may not only mistake its interest, but, perceiving it clearly, may prefer the gratification of a strong passion to it.* The whole fabric of his political reasoning seems to be overthrown by this single observation; and instead of attempting to explain the immense variety of political facts by the simple principle of a contest of interests, we are reduced to the necessity of once more referring them to that variety of passions, habits, opinions, and prejudices, which we discover only by experience. Mr. Mill's essay on Education† affords another example of the inconvenience of leaping at once from the most general laws, to a multiplicity of minute appearances. Having assumed, or at least inferred from insufficient premises, that the intellectual and moral character is entirely formed by circumstances, he proceeds, in the latter part of the essay, as if it were a necessary consequence of that doctrine that we might easily acquire the power of combining and directing circumstances in such a manner as to produce the best possible character. Without disputing, for the present, the theoretical proposition, let us consider what would be the reasonableness of similar expectations in a more easily intelligible case. The general theory of the winds is pretty well understood; we know that they proceed from the rushing of air from those portions of the atmosphere which are more condensed, into those which are more rarefied: but how great a chasm is there between that simple law and the great variety of facts which experience exhibits! The constant winds between the tropics are large and regular enough to be in some measure capable of explanation: but who can tell why, in variable climates, the wind blows to-day from the east, to-morrow from the west? Who can foretell what its shifting and variations are to be? Who can account for a tempest on one day, and a calm on another? Even if we could foretell the irregular and infinite variations, how far might we not still be from the power of combining and guiding their causes? No man but the lunatic in the story of Rasselas ever dreamt that he could command the weather. The difficulty plainly consists in the multiplicity and minuteness of the circumstances which act on the atmosphere: are those which influence the formation of the human character likely to be less minute and multiplied?

The style of Mr. Bentham underwent a more remarkable revolution than perhaps befell that of any other writer. In his early works, it was clear, free, spirited, often and seasonably eloquent: many passages of his later writings retain the inimitable stamp of genius; but he seems to have been oppressed by the vastness of his projected works,—to have thought that he had no longer more than leisure to preserve the heads of them,—to have been impelled by a fruitful mind to new plans before he had completed the old. In this state of things, he gradually ceased to use words for conveying his thoughts to others, but merely employed them as a sort of short-hand to preserve his meaning for his own purpose. It was no wonder that his language should thus become obscure and repulsive. Though many of his technical terms are in themselves exact and pithy, yet the overflow of his vast nomenclature was enough to darken his whole diction.

It was at this critical period that the arrangement and translation of his manuscripts were undertaken by M. Dumont, a generous disciple, who devoted a genius formed for original and lasting works, to diffuse the principles, and promote the fame of his master. He whose pen Mirabeau did not disdain to borrow,—who, in the same school with Romilly, had studiously pursued the grace as well as the force of composition, was perfectly qualified to strip of its uncouthness a philosophy which he understood and admired. As he wrote in a general language, he propagated its doctrines throughout Europe, where they were beneficial to Jurisprudence, but perhaps injurious to the cause of reformation in Government. That they became more popular abroad than at home, is partly to be ascribed to the taste and skill of M. Dumont; partly to that tendency towards free speculation and bold reform which was more prevalent among nations newly freed, or impatiently aspiring to freedom, than in a people such as ours, long satisfied with their government, but not yet aware of the imperfections and abuses in their laws;—to the amendment of which last a cautious consideration of Mr. Bentham's works will undoubtedly most materially contribute.

DUGALD STEWART.*

Manifold are the discouragements rising up at every step in that part of this Disserta-

* The same mode of reasoning has been adopted by the writer of a late criticism, on Mr. Mill's Essay. See Edinburgh Review, vol. xlix. p. 159.

† Encyc. Brit., article "Education."

* Born, 1753; died, 1828.

tion which extends to very recent times. No sooner does the writer escape from the angry disputes of the living, than he may feel his mind clouded by the name of a departed friend. But there are happily men whose fame is brightened by free discussion, and to whose memory an appearance of belief that they needed tender treatment would be a grosser injury than it could suffer from a respectable antagonist.

Dugald Stewart was the son of Dr. Matthew Stewart, Professor of Mathematics in the University of Edinburgh,—a station immediately before filled by Maclaurin, on the recommendation of Newton. Hence the poet* spoke of "the philosophic sire and son." He was educated at Edinburgh, and he heard the lectures of Reid at Glasgow. He was early associated with his father in the duties of the mathematical professorship; and during the absence of Dr. Adam Ferguson as secretary to the commissioners sent to conclude a peace with North America, he occupied the chair of Moral Philosophy. He was appointed to the professorship on the resignation of Ferguson,—not the least distinguished among the modern moralists inclined to the Stoical school.

This office, filled in immediate succession by Ferguson, Stewart, and Brown, received a lustre from their names, which it owed in no degree to its modest exterior or its limited advantages; and was rendered by them the highest dignity, in the humble, but not obscure, establishments of Scottish literature. The lectures of Mr. Stewart, for a quarter of a century, rendered it famous through every country where the light of reason was allowed to penetrate. Perhaps few men ever lived, who poured into the breasts of youth a more fervid and yet reasonable love of liberty, of truth, and of virtue. How many are still alive, in different countries, and in every rank to which education reaches, who, if they accurately examined their own minds and lives, would not ascribe much of whatever goodness and happiness they possess, to the early impressions of his gentle and persuasive eloquence! He lived to see his disciples distinguished among the lights and ornaments of the council and the senate.† He had the consolation, to be sure, that no words of his promoted the growth of an impure taste, of an exclusive prejudice, or of a malevolent passion. Without derogation from his writings, it may be said that his disciples were among his best works. He, indeed, who may justly be said to have cultivated an extent of mind which would otherwise have lain barren, and to have contributed to raise virtuous dispositions where the natural growth might have been useless or noxious, is not less a benefactor of mankind, and may *indirectly* be a larger contributor to knowledge, than the author of great works, or even the discoverer of important truths. The system of conveying scientific instruction to a large audience by lectures, from which the English universities have in a great measure departed, renders his qualities as a lecturer a most important part of his merit in a Scottish university which still adheres to the general method of European education. Probably no modern ever exceeded him in that species of eloquence which springs from sensibility to literary beauty and moral excellence,—which neither obscures science by prodigal ornament, nor disturbs the serenity of patient attention,—but though it rather calms and soothes the feelings, yet exalts the genius, and insensibly inspires a reasonable enthusiasm for whatever is good and fair.

He embraced the philosophy of Dr. Reid, a patient, modest, and deep thinker,* who,

---

* Burns.

† As an example of Mr. Stewart's school may be mentioned Francis Horner, a favourite pupil, and, till his last moment, an affectionate friend. The short life of this excellent person is worthy of serious contemplation, by those more especially, who, in circumstances like his, enter on the slippery path of public affairs. Without the aids of birth or fortune, in an assembly where aristocratical propensities prevail,—by his understanding, industry, pure taste, and useful information,—still more by modest independence, by steadiness and sincerity, joined to moderation,—by the stamp of unbending integrity, and by the conscientious considerateness which breathed through his well-chosen language, he raised himself, at the early age of thirty-six, to a *moral authority* which, without these qualities, no brilliancy of talents or power of reasoning could have acquired. No eminent speaker in Parliament owed so much of his success to his moral character. His high place was therefore honourable to his audience and to his country. Regret for his death was expressed with touching unanimity from every part of a divided assembly, unused to manifestations of sensibility, abhorrent from theatrical display, and whose tribute on such an occasion derived its peculiar value from their general coldness and sluggishness. The tears of those to whom he was unknown were shed over him; and at the head of those by whom he was "praised, wept, and honoured," was one, whose commendation would have been more enhanced in the eye of Mr. Horner, by his discernment and veracity, than by the signal proof of the concurrence of all orders, as well as parties, which was afforded by the name of Howard.

* Those who may doubt the justice of this description will do well to weigh the words of the most competent of judges, who, though candid and even indulgent, was not prodigal of praise. "It is certainly very rare that a piece so *deeply philosophical* is wrote with so much spirit, and affords so much entertainment to the reader. Whenever I enter into your ideas, no man appears to express himself with greater perspicuty. Your style is so correct and so good English, that I found not any thing worth the remarking. I beg my compliments to my friendly adversaries Dr. Campbell and Dr. Gerard, and also to Dr. Gregory, whom I suspect to be of the same disposition, though he has not openly declared himself such."—Letter from Mr. Hume to Dr. Reid: Stewart's Biographical Memoirs, p. 417. The latter part of the above sentences (written after a perusal of Dr. Reid's Inquiry, but before its publication) sufficiently shows, that Mr. Hume felt no displeasure against Reid and Campbell, undoubtedly his most formidable antagonist, however he might resent the language of Dr. Beattie, an amiable man, an elegant and tender poet, and a good writer on

in his first work (Inquiry into the Human Mind), deserves a commendation more descriptive of a philosopher than that bestowed upon him by Professor Cousin,—of having made "a vigorous protest against scepticism on behalf of common sense." Reid's observations on Suggestion, on natural signs, on the connection between what he calls "sensation" and "perception," though perhaps suggested by Berkeley (whose idealism he had once adopted), are marked by the genuine spirit of original observation. As there are too many who seem more wise than they are, so it was the more uncommon fault with Reid to appear less a philosopher than he really was. Indeed his temporary adoption of Berkeleianism is a proof of an unprejudiced and acute mind. Perhaps no man ever rose finally above the seductions of that simple and ingenious system, who had not sometimes tried their full effect by surrendering his whole mind to them.

But it is never with entire impunity that philosophers borrow vague and inappropriate terms from vulgar use. Never did any man afford a stronger instance of this danger than Reid, in his two most unfortunate terms, "common sense" and "instinct." Common sense is that average portion of understanding, possessed by most men, which, as it is nearly always applied to conduct, has acquired an almost exclusively practical sense. Instinct is the habitual power of producing effects like contrivances of Reason, yet so far beyond the intelligence and experience of the agent, as to be utterly inexplicable by reference to them. No man, if he had been in search of improper words, could have discovered any more unfit than these two, for denoting that *law*, or *state*, or *faculty* of Mind, which compels us to acknowledge certain simple and very abstract truths, not being identical propositions, to lie at the foundation of all reasoning, and to be the necessary ground of all belief.

Long after the death of Dr. Reid, his philosophy was taught at Paris by M. Royer Collard,* who on the restoration of free debate, became the most philosophical orator of his nation, and now† fills, with impartiality and dignity, the chair of the Chamber of Deputies. His ingenious and eloquent scholar, Professor Cousin, dissatisfied with what he calls "the sage and timid" doctrines of Edinburgh, which he considered as only a vigorous protest, on behalf of common sense, against the scepticism of Hume, sought in Germany for a philosophy of "such a masculine and brilliant character as might command the attention of Europe, and be able to struggle with success on a great theatre, against the genius of the adverse school."* It may be questioned whether he found in Kant more than the same *vigorous protest*, under a more systematic form, with an immense nomenclature, and constituting a philosophical edifice of equal symmetry and vastness. The preference of the more boastful system, over a philosophy thus chiefly blamed for its modest pretensions, does not seem to be entirely justified by its permanent authority even in the country which gave it birth; where, however powerful its influence still continues to be, its doctrines do not appear to have now many supporters. Indeed, the accomplished professor himself has rapidly shot through Kantianism, and now appears to rest or to stop at the doctrines of Schelling and Hegel, at a point so high, that it is hard to descry from it any distinction between objects,—even that indispensable distinction between *reality* and *illusion*. As the works of Reid, and those of Kant, otherwise so different, appear to be simultaneous efforts of the conservative power of philosophy to expel the mortal poison of scepticism, so the exertions of M. Royer Collard and M. Cousin, however at variance in metaphysical principles, seem to have been chiefly roused by the desire of delivering Ethics from that fatal touch of personal, and, indeed, gross interest, which the science had received in France at the hands of the followers of Condillac,—especially Helvetius, St. Lambert, and Cabanis. The success of these attempts to render speculative philosophy once more popular in the country of Descartes, has already been considerable. The French youth, whose desire of knowledge and love of liberty afford an auspicious promise of the succeeding age, have eagerly received doctrines, of which the moral part is so much more agreeable to their liberal spirit, than is the Selfish theory, generated in the stagnation of a corrupt, cruel, and dissolute tyranny.

These agreeable prospects bring us easily back to our subject; for though the restoration of speculative philosophy in the country of Descartes is due to the precise statement and vigorous logic of M. Royer Collard, the modifications introduced by him into the doctrine of Reid coincide with those of Mr. Stewart, and would have appeared to agree more exactly, if the forms of the French philosopher had not been more dialectical, and the composition of Mr. Stewart had retained less of that oratorical character, which belonged to a justly celebrated speaker. Amidst excellencies of the highest order, the writings of the latter, it must be confessed, leave some room for criticism. He took precautions against offence to the feelings of his contemporaries, more anxiously and frequently than the impatient searcher for truth may deem necessary. For the sake of promoting the favourable reception of philosophy

miscellaneous literature in prose, but who, in his Essay on Truth,—(an unfair appeal to the multitude of philosophical questions) indulged himself in the personalities and invectives of a popular pamphleteer.

* Fragments of his lectures have been recently published in a French translation of Dr. Reid, by M. Jonffroy: Œuvres Completes de Thomas Reid, vol iv. Paris, 1828.

† 1831.—Ed.

* Cours de Philosophie, par M. Cousin, leçon xii. Paris, 1828

itself, he studies, perhaps too visibly, to avoid whatever might raise up prejudices against it. His gratitude and native modesty dictated a superabundant care in softening and excusing his dissent from those who had been his own instructors, or who were the objects of general reverence. Exposed by his station, both to the assaults of political prejudice, and to the religious animosities of a country where a few sceptics attacked the slumbering zeal of a Calvinistic people, it would have been wonderful if he had not betrayed more weariness than would have been necessary or becoming in a very different position. The fulness of his literature seduced him too much into multiplied illustrations. Too many of the expedients happily used to allure the young may unnecessarily swell his volumes. Perhaps a successive publication in separate parts made him more voluminous than he would have been if the whole had been at once before his eyes. A peculiar susceptibility and delicacy of taste produced forms of expression, in themselves extremely beautiful, but of which the habitual use is not easily reconcilable with the condensation desirable in works necessarily so extensive. If, however, it must be owned that the caution incident to his temper, his feelings, his philosophy, and his station, has somewhat lengthened his composition, it is not less true, that some of the same circumstances have contributed towards those peculiar beauties which place him at the head of the most adorned writers on philosophy in our language.

Few writers rise with more grace from a plain groundwork, to the passages which require greater animation or embellishment. He gives to narrative, according to the precept of Bacon, the colour of the time, by a selection of happy expressions from original writers. Among the secret arts by which he diffuses elegance over his diction, may be remarked the skill which, by deepening or brightening a shade in a secondary term, and by opening partial or preparatory glimpses of a thought to be afterwards unfolded, unobservedly heightens the import of a word, and gives it a new meaning, without any offence against old use. It is in this manner that philosophical originality may be reconciled to purity and stability of speech, and that we may avoid new terms, which are the easy resource of the unskilful or the indolent, and often a characteristic mark of writers who love their language too little to feel its peculiar excellencies, or to study the art of calling forth its powers.

He reminds us not unfrequently of the character given by Cicero to one of his contemporaries, "who expressed refined and abstruse thought in soft and transparent diction." His writings are a proof that the mild sentiments have their eloquence as well as the vehement passions. It would be difficult to name works in which so much refined philosophy is joined with so fine a fancy,—so much elegant literature, with such a delicate perception of the distinguishing excellencies of great writers, and with an estimate in general so just of the services rendered to Knowledge by a succession of philosophers. They are pervaded by a philosophical benevolence, which keeps up the ardour of his genius, without disturbing the serenity of his mind,—which is felt equally in the generosity of his praise, and in the tenderness of his censure. It is still more sensible in the general tone with which he relates the successful progress of the human understanding, among many formidable enemies. Those readers are not to be envied who limit their admiration to particular parts, or to excellencies merely literary, without being warmed by the glow of that honest triumph in the advancement of Knowledge, and of that assured faith in the final prevalence of Truth and Justice, which breathe through every page of them, and give the unity and dignity of a moral purpose to the whole of these classical works.

In quoting poetical passages, some of which throw much light on our mental operations, if he sometimes prized the moral common-places of Thomson and the speculative fancy of Akenside more highly than the higher poetry of their betters, it was not to be wondered at that the metaphysician and the moralist should sometimes prevail over the lover of poetry. His natural sensibility was perhaps occasionally cramped by the cold criticism of an unpoetical age; and some of his remarks may be thought to indicate a more constant and exclusive regard to diction than is agreeable to a generation which has been trained by tremendous events to a passion for daring inventions, and to an irregular enthusiasm, impatient of minute elegancies and refinements. Many of those beauties which his generous criticism delighted to magnify in the works of his contemporaries, have already faded under the scorching rays of a fiercer sun.

Mr. Stewart employed more skill in contriving, and more care in concealing his very important reforms of Reid's doctrines, than others exert to maintain their claims to originality. Had his well-chosen language of "laws of human thought or belief" been at first adopted in that school, instead of "instinct" and "common sense," it would have escaped much of the reproach (which Dr. Reid himself did not merit) of shallowness and popularity. Expressions so exact, employed in the opening, could not have failed to influence the whole system, and to have given it, not only in the general estimation, but in the minds of its framers, a more scientific complexion. In those parts of Mr. Stewart's speculations in which he farthest departed from his general principles, he seems sometimes, as it were, to be suddenly driven back by what he unconsciously shrinks from as ungrateful apostasy, and to be desirous of making amends to his master, by more harshness, than is otherwise natural to him towards the writers whom he has insensibly approached. Hence perhaps the unwonted severity of his language towards Tucker and Hartley. It is thus at the very time when he largely adopts the principle of Association in his excellent Essay on the Beautiful,* that he treats most rigidly the latter of these writers, to whom, though neither the discoverer nor the sole advocate of that principle, it surely owes the greatest illustration and support.

In matters of far other importance, causes perhaps somewhat similar may have led to the like mistake. When he absolutely contradicts Dr. Reid, by truly stating that "it is more philosophical to resolve the power of habit into the association of ideas, than to resolve the association of ideas into habit,"† he, in the sequel of the same volume,‡ refuses to go farther than to own, that "the theory of Hartley concerning the origin of our affections, and of the Moral Sense, is a most *ingenious refinement on the Selfish system*, and that by means of it the force of many of the common reasonings against that system is *eluded*;" though he somewhat inconsistently allows, that "active principles which, arising from circumstances in which all the situations of mankind must agree, are therefore common to the whole species, at whatever period of life they may appear, are to be regarded as a part of human nature, no less than the instinct of suction, in the same manner as the acquired perception of distance, by the eye, is to be ranked among the perceptive powers of man, no less than the original perceptions of the other senses."§ In another place also he makes a remark on mere beauty, which might have led him to a more just conclusion respecting the theory of the origin of the affections and the Moral Sense: "It is scarcely necessary for me to observe, that, in those instances where association operates in heightening" (or he might have said creates) "the pleasure we receive from sight, the pleasing emotion continues still to appear, to our consciousness, simple and uncompounded."¶ To this remark he might have added, that until all the separate pleasures be melted into one,—as long as any of them are discerned and felt as distinct from each other,—the associations are incomplete, and the qualities which gratify are not called by the name of "beauty." In like manner, as has been repeatedly observed, it is only when all the separate feelings, pleasurable and painful, excited by the contemplation of voluntary action, are lost in the general sentiments of approbation or disapprobation,—when these general feelings retain no trace of the various emotions which originally attended different actions,—when they are held in a state of perfect fusion by the habitual use of the words used in every language to denote them, that Conscience can be said to exist, or that we can be considered as endowed with a moral nature. The theory which thus ascribes the uniform formation of the Moral Faculty to universal and paramount laws, is not a refinement of the Selfish system, nor is it any modification of that hypothesis. The partisans of Selfishness maintain, that in acts of Will the agent must have a view to the pleasure or happiness which he hopes to reap from it: the philosophers who regard the social affections and the Moral Sentiments as formed by a process of association, on the other hand, contend that these affections and sentiments must work themselves clear from every particle of *self-regard*, before they deserve the names of benevolence and of Conscience. In the actual state of human motives the two systems are not to be likened, but to be contrasted to each other. It is remarkable that Mr. Stewart, who admits the "question respecting the *origin* of the affections to be rather curious than important,"* should have held a directly contrary opinion respecting the Moral Sense,† to which these words, in his sense of them, seem to be equally applicable. His meaning in the former affirmation is, that if the affections be *acquired*, yet they are justly called *natural*; and if their *origin* be personal, yet their nature may and does *become* disinterested. What circumstance distinguishes the former from the latter case? With respect to the origin of the affections, it must not be overlooked that his language is somewhat contradictory. For if the theory on that subject from which he dissents were merely "a refinement on the Selfish system," its truth or falsehood could not be represented as subordinate; since the controversy would continue to relate to the existence of disinterested motives of human conduct.‡ It may also be observed, that he uniformly represents his opponents as deriving the affections from 'self-love,' which, in its proper sense, is not the source to which they refer even avarice, and which is itself derived from other antecedent principles, some of which are inherent, and some acquired. If the object of this theory of the rise of the most important feelings of human nature were, as our philosopher supposes, "to *elude* objections against the Selfish system," it would be at best worthless.

* Philosophical Essays, part ii. essay i., especially chap. vi. The condensation, if not omission, of the discussion of the theories of Buffier, Reynolds, Burke, and Price, in this essay, would have lessened that temporary appearance which is unsuitable to a scientific work.

† Elements of the Philosophy of the Human Mind (1792, 4to.), vol. i. p. 281.

‡ Ibid. p. 383. § Ibid. p. 385.

¶ Philosophical Essays, part ii. essay i. chap. xi.

* Outlines of Moral Philosophy, p. 93.

† Outlines, p. 117. "This is the most important question that can be stated with respect to the theory of Morals."

‡ In the Philosophy of the Active and Moral Powers of Man (vol. i. p. 164.), Mr. Stewart has done more manifest injustice to the Hartleian theory, by calling it "a doctrine *fundamentally the same with the Selfish system*," and especially by representing Hartley, who ought to be rather classed with Butler and Hume, as agreeing with Gay, Tucker, and Paley.

Its positive merits are several. It affirms the actual disinterestedness of human motives, as strongly as Butler himself. The explanation of the mental law, by which benevolence and Conscience are formed habitually, when it is contemplated deeply, impresses on the mind the truth that they not only *are* but *must be* disinterested. It confirms, as it were, the testimony of consciousness, by exhibiting to the Understanding the means employed to insure the production of disinterestedness. It affords the only effectual answer to the prejudice against the disinterested theory, from the multiplication of ultimate facts and implanted principles, which, under all its other forms, it seems to require. No room is left for this prejudice by a representation of disinterestedness, which *ultimately* traces its formation to principles almost as simple as those of Hobbes himself. Lastly, every step in just generalization is an advance in philosophy. No one has yet shown, either that Man is not actually disinterested, or that he may not have been destined to become so by such a process as has been described: the cause to which the effects are ascribed is a real agent, which seems adequate to the appearance; and if future observation should be found to require that the theory shall be confined within narrower limits, such a limitation will not destroy its value.

The acquiescence of Mr. Stewart in Dr. Reid's general representation of our mental constitution, led him to indulge more freely the natural bent of his understanding, by applying it to theories of character and manners, of life and literature, of taste and the arts, rather than to the consideration of those more simple principles which rule over human nature under every form. His chief work, as he frankly owns, is indeed rather a collection of such theories, pointing toward the common end of throwing light on the structure and functions of the mind, than a systematic treatise, such as might be expected from the title of "Elements." It is in essays of this kind that he has most surpassed other cultivators of mental philosophy. His remarks on the effects of casual associations may be quoted as a specimen of the most original and just thoughts, conveyed in the best manner.* In this beautiful passage, he proceeds from their power of confusing speculation to that of disturbing experience and of misleading practice, and ends with their extraordinary effect in bestowing on trivial, and even ludicrous circumstances, some portion of the dignity and sanctity of those sublime principles with which they are associated. The style, at first only clear, afterwards admitting the ornaments of a calm and grave elegance, and at last rising to as high a strain as Philosophy will endure, (all the parts, various as their nature is, being held together by an invisible thread of gentle transition,) affords a specimen of adaptation of manner to matter which it will be hard to match in any other philosophical writing. Another very fine remark, which seems to be as original as it is just, may be quoted as a sample of those beauties with which his writings abound. "The apparent coldness and selfishness of mankind may be traced, in a great measure, to a want of attention and a want of imagination. In the case of those misfortunes which happen to ourselves or our near connections, neither of these powers is necessary to make us acquainted with our situation. But without an uncommon degree of both, it is impossible for any man to comprehend completely the situation of his neighbour, or to have an idea of the greater part of the distress which exists in the world. If we feel more for ourselves than for others, in the former case the facts are more fully before us than they can be in the latter."* Yet several parts of his writings afford the most satisfactory proof, that his abstinence from what is commonly called metaphysical speculation, arose from no inability to pursue it with signal success. As examples, his observations on "general terms," and on "causation," may be appealed to with perfect confidence. In the first two dissertations of the volume bearing the title "Philosophical Essays," he with equal boldness and acuteness grapples with the most extensive and abstruse questions of mental philosophy, and points out both the sources and the uttermost boundaries of human knowledge with a Verulamean hand. In another part of his writings, he calls what are usually denominated first principles of experience, "fundamental laws of human belief, or primary elements of human reason;"† which last form of expression has so close a resemblance to the language of Kant, that it should have protected the latter from the imputation of writing jargon.

The excellent volume entitled "Outlines of Moral Philosophy," though composed only as a text-book for the use of his hearers, is one of the most decisive proofs that he was perfectly qualified to unite precision with ease, to be brief with the utmost clearness, and to write with becoming elegance in a style where the meaning is not overladen by ornaments. This volume contains his properly ethical theory,‡ which is much expanded, but not substantially altered, in his Philosophy of the Active and Moral Powers, —a work almost posthumous, and composed under circumstances which give it a deeper interest than can be inspired by any desert in science. Though, with his usual modesty, he manifests an anxiety to fasten his ethical theory to the kindred speculations of other philosophers of the "Intellectual school," especially to those of Cudworth,—recently clothed in more modern phraseology by Price,—yet he still shows that independence and originality which all his aversion from parade could not entirely conceal. "Right,"

* Elem. Philos. Hum. Mind, vol. i. pp. 340—352.

* Ibid. vol. i. p. 502. † Ibid. vol. ii. p. 57.
‡ pp. 76—148.

"duty," "virtue," "moral obligation," and the like or the opposite forms of expression, represent, according to him, certain thoughts, which arise necessarily and instantaneously in the mind, (or in the Reason, if we take that word in the large sense in which it denotes all that is not emotive) at the contemplation of actions, and which are utterly incapable of all resolution, and consequently of all explanation, and which can be known only by being experienced. These "thoughts" or "ideas," by whatever name they may be called, are followed,—as inexplicably as inevitably,—by pleasurable and painful emotions, which suggest the conception of *moral beauty*;—a quality of human actions distinct from their *adherence to, or deviation from rectitude*, though generally coinciding with it. The question which a reflecting reader will here put is, whether any purpose is served by the introduction of the intermediate mental process between the particular thoughts and the moral emotions? How would the view be darkened or confused, or indeed in any degree changed, by withdrawing that process, or erasing the words which attempt to express it? No advocate of the intellectual origin of the Moral Faculty has yet stated a case in which a mere operation of Reason or Judgment, unattended by emotion, could, consistently with the universal opinion of mankind, as it is exhibited by the structure of language, be said to have the nature or to produce the effects of Conscience. Such an example would be equivalent to an *experimentum crucis* on the side of that celebrated theory. The failure to produce it, after long challenge, is at least a presumption against it, nearly approaching to that sort of decisively discriminative experiment. It would be vain to restate what has already been too often repeated, that all the objections to the Selfish philosophy turn upon the actual nature, not upon the original source, of our principles of action, and that it is by a confusion of these very distinct questions alone that the confutation of Hobbes can be made apparently to involve Hartley. Mr. Stewart appears, like most other metaphysicians, to have blended the inquiry into the nature of our Moral Sentiments with that other which only seeks a criterion to distinguish moral from immoral habits of feeling and action; for he considers the appearance of the Moral Sentiments at an early age, before the general tendency of actions can be ascertained, as a decisive objection to the origin of these sentiments in Association,—an objection which assumes that, if utility be the criterion of Morality, associations with utility must be the mode by which the Moral Sentiments are formed: but this no skilful advocate of the theory of Association will ever allow. That the main, if not sole object of Conscience is to govern our voluntary exertions, is manifest: but how could it perform this great function if it did not impel the Will? and how could it have the latter effect as a mere act of Reason, or, indeed, in any respect otherwise than as it is made up of emotions? Judgment and Reason are therefore preparatory to Conscience,—not properly a part of it. The assertion that the exclusion of Reason reduces Virtue to be a relative quality, is another instance of the confusion of the two questions in moral theory; for though a fitness to excite approbation may be only a relation of objects to our susceptibility, yet the proposition that all virtuous actions are beneficial, is a proposition as absolute as any other within the range of our understanding.

A delicate state of health, and an ardent desire to devote himself exclusively to study and composition, induced Mr. Stewart, while in the full blaze of his reputation as a lecturer, to retire, in 1810, from the labour of public instruction. This retirement, as he himself describes it, was that of a quiet but active life. Three quarto and two octavo volumes, besides the magnificent Dissertation prefixed to the Encyclopædia Britannica, were among its happy fruits. This Dissertation is, perhaps, the most profusely ornamented of any of his compositions;—a peculiarity which must in part have arisen from a principle of taste, which regarded decoration as more suitable to the history of philosophy than to philosophy itself. But the memorable instances of Cicero, of Milton, and still more those of Dryden and Burke, seem to show that there is some natural tendency in the fire of genius to burn more brightly, or to blaze more fiercely, in the evening than in the morning of human life. Probably the materials which long experience supplies to the imagination, the boldness with which a more established reputation arms the mind, and the silence of the low but formidable rivals of the higher principles, may concur in producing this unexpected and little observed effect.

It was in the last years of his life, when suffering under the effects of a severe attack of palsy, with which he had been afflicted in 1822, that Mr. Stewart most plentifully reaped the fruits of long virtue and a well-ordered mind. Happily for him, his own cultivation and exercise of every kindly affection had laid up a store of that domestic consolation which none who deserve it ever want, and for the loss of which, nothing beyond the threshold can make amends. The same philosophy which he had cultivated from his youth upward, employed his dying hand; aspirations after higher and brighter scenes of excellence, always blended with his elevated morality, became more earnest and deeper as worldly passions died away, and earthly objects vanished from his sight.

THOMAS BROWN.*

A writer, as he advances in life, ought to speak with diffidence of systems which he has only begun to consider with care after

* Born, 1778; died, 1820.

the age in which it becomes hard for his thoughts to flow into new channels. A reader cannot be said practically to understand a theory, till he has acquired the power of thinking, at least for a short time, with the theorist. Even a hearer, with all the helps of voice in the instructor, and of countenance from him and from fellow-hearers, finds it difficult to perform this necessary process, without either being betrayed into hasty and undistinguishing assent, or falling while he is in pursuit of an impartial estimate of opinions, into an indifference about their truth. I have felt this difficulty in reconsidering old opinions: but it is perhaps more needful to own its power, and to warn the reader against its effects, in the case of a philosopher well known to me, and with whom common friendships stood in the stead of much personal intercourse, as a cement of kindness. I very early read Brown's Observations on the Zoonomia of Dr. Darwin,—the perhaps unmatched work of a boy in the eighteenth year of his age.* His first tract on Causation appeared to me to be the finest model of discussion in mental philosophy since Berkeley and Hume,—with this superiority over the latter, that its aim is that of a philosopher who seeks to enlarge knowledge,—not that of sceptic, who—even the most illustrious—has no better end than that of displaying his powers in confounding and darkening truth,—and the happiest efforts of whose scepticism cannot be more leniently described than as brilliant fits of mental debauchery.† From a diligent perusal of his succeeding works at the time of their publication, I was prevented by pursuits and duties of a very different nature. These causes, together with ill health and growing occupation, hindered me from reading his Lectures with due attention, till it has now become a duty to consider with care that part of them which relates to Ethics.

Dr. Brown was born of one of those families of ministers in the Scottish Church, who, after a generation or two of a humble life spent in piety and usefulness, with no more than needful knowledge, have more than once sent forth a man of genius from their cool and quiet shade, to make his fellows wiser or better by tongue or pen, by head or hand. Even the scanty endowments and constant residence of that Church, by keeping her ministers far from the objects which awaken turbulent passions and disperse the understanding on many pursuits, affords some of the leisure and calm of monastic life, without the exclusion of the charities of family and kindred. It may be well doubted whether this undissipated retirement, which during the eighteenth century was very general in Scotland, did not make full amends for the loss of curious and ornamental knowledge, by its tendency to qualify men for professional duty; with its opportunities for the cultivation of the reason for the many, and for high meditation, and concentration of thought on worthy objects for the few who have capacity for such exertions.* An authentic account of the early exercises of Brown's mind is preserved by his biographer,† from which it appears that at the age of nineteen he took a part with others (some of whom became the most memorable men of their time), in the foundation of a private society in Edinburgh, under the name of "the Academy of Physics."‡

The character of Dr. Brown is very attractive, as an example of one in whom the utmost tenderness of affection, and the indulgence of a flowery fancy, were not repressed by the highest cultivation, and by

* Welsh's Life of Brown, p. 43;—a pleasingly affectionate work, full of analytical spirit and metaphysical reading,—of such merit, in short, that I could wish to have found in it no phrenology. Objections *a priori* in a case dependent on facts are, indeed, inadmissible: even the allowance of presumptions of that nature would open so wide a door for prejudices, that at most they can be considered only as maxims of logical prudence, which fortify the watchfulness of the individual. The fatal objection to phrenology seems to me to be, that what is new in it, or peculiar to it, has no approach to an adequate foundation in experience.

† "Bayle, a writer who, pervading human nature at his ease, struck into the province of paradox, as an exercise for the unwearied vigour of his mind; who, with a soul superior to the sharpest attacks of fortune, and a heart practised to the best philosophy, had not enough of real greatness to overcome that last foible of superior minds, the temptation of honour, which the academic exercise of wit is conceived to bring to its professor." So says Warburton (Divine Legation, book i. sect. 4), speaking of Bayle, but perhaps in part excusing himself, in a noble strain, of which it would have been more agreeable to find the repetition than the contrast in his language towards Hume.

* See Sir H. Moncreiff's Life of the Reverend Dr. Erskine.

† Welsh's Life of Brown, p. 77, and App. p. 498.

‡ A part of the first day's minutes is here borrowed from Mr. Welsh:—"7th January, 1797.—Present, Mr. Erskine, President,—Mr. Brougham, Mr. Reddie, Mr. Brown, Mr. Birbeck, Mr. Leyden," &c. who were afterwards joined by Lord Webb Seymour, Messrs. Horner, Jeffrey, Sidney Smith, &c. Mr. Erskine, who thus appears at the head of so remarkable an association, and whom diffidence and untoward circumstances have hitherto withheld from the full manifestation of his powers, continued to be the bosom friend of Brown to the last. He has shown the constancy of his friendship for others by converting all his invaluable preparations for a translation of Sultan Baber's Commentaries, (perhaps the best, certainly the most European work of modern Eastern prose) into the means of completing the imperfect attempt of Leyden, with a regard equally generous to the fame of his early friend, and to the comfort of that friend's surviving relations. The review of Baber's Commentaries, by M. Silvestre de Sacy, in the Journal des Savans for May and June 1829, is perhaps one of the best specimens extant of the value of literary commendation when it is bestowed with conscientious calmness, and without a suspicion of bias, by one of the greatest orientalists, in a case where he pronounces every thing to have been done by Mr. Erskine "which could have been performed by the most learned and the most scrupulously conscientious of editors and translators."

a perhaps excessive refinement of intellect. His mind soared and roamed through every region of philosophy and poetry; but his untravelled heart clung to the hearth of his father, to the children who shared it with him, and after them, first to the other partners of his childish sports, and then almost solely to those companions of his youthful studies who continued to be the friends of his life. Speculation seemed to keep his kindness at home. It is observable, that though sparkling with fancy, he does not seem to have been deeply or durably touched by those affections which are lighted at its torch, or at least tinged with its colours. His heart sought little abroad, but contentedly dwelt in his family and in his study. He was one of those men of genius who repaid the tender care of a mother by rocking the cradle of her reposing age. He ended a life spent in searching for truth, and exercising love, by desiring that he should be buried in his native parish, with his "dear father and mother." Some of his delightful qualities were perhaps hidden from the casual observer in general society, by the want of that perfect simplicity of manner which is doubtless their natural representative. Manner is a better mark of the state of a mind, than those large and deliberate actions which form what is called conduct; it is the constant and insensible transpiration of character. In serious acts a man may display himself; in the thousand nameless acts which compose manner, the mind betrays its habitual bent. But manner is then only an index of disposition, when it is that of men who live at ease in the intimate familiarity of friends and equals. It may be diverted from simplicity by causes which do not reach so deep as the character;—by bad models, or by a restless and wearisome anxiety to shine, arising from many circumstances,—none of which are probably more common than the unseasonable exertions of a recluse student in society, and the unfortunate attempts of some others, to take by violence the admiration of those with whom they do not associate with ease. The association with unlike or superior companions which least distorts manners, is that which takes place with those classes whose secure dignity generally renders their own manners easy,—with whom the art of pleasing or of not displeasing each other in society is a serious concern,—who have leisure enough to discover the positive and negative parts of the smaller moralities, and who, being trained to a watchful eye on what is ludicrous, apply the lash of ridicule to affectation, the most ridiculous of faults. The busy in every department of life are too respectably occupied to form these manners: they are the frivolous work of polished idleness; and perhaps their most serious value consists in the war which they wage against affectation,—though even there they betray their origin in punishing it, not as a deviation from nature. but as a badge of vulgarity.

The prose of Dr. Brown is brilliant to excess: it must not be denied that its beauty is sometimes womanly,—that it too often melts down precision into elegance,—that it buries the main idea under a load of illustration, of which every part is expanded and adorned with such visible labour, as to withdraw the mind from attention to the thoughts which it professes to introduce more easily into the understanding. It is darkened by excessive brightness; it loses ease and liveliness by over-dress; and, in the midst of its luscious sweetness, we wish for the striking and homely illustrations of Tucker, and for the pithy and sinewy sense of Paley;—either of whom, by a single short metaphor from a familiar, perhaps a low object, could at one blow set the two worlds of Reason and Fancy in movement.

It would be unjust to censure severely the declamatory parts of his Lectures: they are excusable in the first warmth of composition; they might even be justifiable allurements in attracting young hearers to abstruse speculations. Had he lived, he would probably have taken his thoughts out of the declamatory forms of spoken address, and given to them the appearance, as well as the reality, of deep and subtile discussion. The habits, indeed, of so successful a lecturer, and the natural luxuriance of his mind, could not fail to have somewhat affected all his compositions; but though he might still have fallen short of simplicity, he certainly would have avoided much of the diffusion, and even common-place, which hang heavily on original and brilliant thoughts: for it must be owned, that though, as a thinker, he is unusually original, yet when he falls among the declaimers, he is infected by their common-places. In like manner, he would assuredly have shortened, or left out, many of the poetical quotations which he loved to recite, and which hearers even beyond youth hear with delight. There are two very different sorts of passages of poetry to be found in works on philosophy, which are as far asunder from each other in value as in matter. A philosopher will admit some of those wonderful lines or words which bring to light the infinite varieties of character, the furious bursts or wily workings of passion, the winding approaches of temptation, the slippery path to depravity, the beauty of tenderness, and the grandeur of what is awful and holy in Man. In every such quotation, the moral philosopher, if he be successful, uses the best materials of his science; for what are they but the results of experiment and observation on the human heart, performed by artists of far other skill and power than his? They are facts which could have only been ascertained by Homer, by Dante, by Shakspeare, by Cervantes, by Milton. Every year of admiration since the unknown period when the Iliad first gave delight, has extorted new proofs of the justness of the picture of human nature, from the responding hearts of the admirers. Every strong feeling which these masters have excited, is a successful repetition of their original experiment, and a continually growing evidence of the greatness of their discoveries. Quotations of this nature may be the most satisfactory, as well as the most delightful, proofs of philosophical positions. Others of inferior merit are not to be interdicted: a pointed maxim, especially when familiar, pleases, and is recollected. I cannot entirely conquer my passion for the Roman and Stoical declamation of some passages in Lucan and Akenside: but quotations from those who have written on philosophy in verse, or, in other words, from those who generally are inferior philosophers, and voluntarily deliver their doctrines in the most disadvantageous form, seem to be unreasonable. It is agreeable, no doubt, to the philosopher, and still more to the youthful student, to meet his abstruse ideas clothed in the sonorous verse of Akenside; the surprise of the unexpected union of verse with science is a very lawful enjoyment: but such slight and momentary pleasures, though they may tempt the writer to display them, do not excuse a vain effort to obtrude them on the sympathy of the searcher after truth in after-times. It is peculiarly unlucky that Dr. Brown should have sought supposed ornament from the moral common-places of Thomson, rather than from that illustration of philosophy which is really to be found in his picturesque strokes.

Much more need not be said of Dr. Brown's own poetry,—somewhat voluminous as it is,—than that it indicates fancy and feeling, and rises at least to the rank of an elegant accomplishment. It may seem a paradox, but it appears to me that he is really most poetical in those poems and passages which have the *most properly metaphysical* character. For every varied form of life and nature, when it is habitually contemplated, may inspire feeling; and the just representation of these feelings may be poetical. Dr. Brown observed Man, and his wider world, with the eye of a metaphysician; and the dark results of such contemplations, when he reviewed them, often filled his soul with feelings which, being both grand and melancholy, were truly poetical. Unfortunately, however, few readers can be touched with fellow-feelings. He sings to few, and must be content with sometimes moving a string in the soul of the lonely visionary, who, in the day-dreams of youth, has felt as well as meditated on the mysteries of nature. His heart has produced charming passages in all his poems; but, generally speaking, they are only beautiful works of art and imitation. The choice of Akenside as a favourite and a model may, without derogation from that writer, be considered as no proof of a poetically formed mind.* There is more poetry in many single lines of Cowper than in volumes of sonorous verses such as Akenside's. Philosophical poetry is very different from versified philosophy: the former is the highest exertion of genius; the latter cannot be be ranked above the slighter amusements of ingenuity. Dr. Brown's poetry was, it must be owned, composed either of imitations, which, with some exceptions, may be produced and read without feeling, or of effusions of such feelings only as meet a rare and faint echo in the human breast.

A few words only can here be bestowed on the intellectual part of his philosophy. It is an open revolt against the authority of Reid; and, by a curious concurrence, he began to lecture nearly at the moment when the doctrines of that philosopher came to be taught with applause in France. Mr. Stewart had dissented from the language of Reid, and had widely departed from his opinions on several secondary theories: Dr. Brown rejected them entirely. He very justly considered the claim of Reid to the merit of detecting the universal delusion which had betrayed philosophers into the belief that ideas which were the sole objects of knowledge had a separate existence, as a proof of his having mistaken their illustrative language for a metaphysical opinion;* but he does not do justice to the service which Reid really rendered to mental science, by keeping the attention of all future speculators in a state of more constant watchfulness against the transient influence of such an illusion. His choice of the term "feeling"† to denote the operations which we usually refer to the Understanding, is evidently too wide a departure from its ordinary use, to have any probability of general adoption. No definition can strip so familiar a word of the thoughts and emotions which have so long accompanied it, so as to fit it for a technical term of the highest abstraction. If we can be said to have a feeling "of the equality of the angle of forty-five to half the angle of ninety degrees,"‡ we may call Geometry and Arithmetic sciences of "feeling." He has very forcibly stated the necessity of assuming "*the primary universal intuitions of direct belief*," which, in their nature, are incapable of all proof. They seem to be accurately described as notions which cannot be conceived separately, but without which nothing can be conceived. They are not only necessary to reasoning and to belief, but to thought itself. It is equally impossible to prove or to disprove them. He has very justly blamed the school of Reid for "an extravagant and ridiculous" multiplication of those principles which he truly represents as inconsistent with sound philosophy. To philosophize is indeed nothing more than to simplify securely.§

* His accomplished friend Mr. Erskine confesses that Brown's poems "are not written in the language of plain and gross emotion. The string touched is too delicate for general sympathy. They are in an unknown tongue to one half" (he might have said nineteen twentieths) "of the reading part of the community."—Welsh's Life of Brown, p. 431.

* Brown's Lectures, vol. ii. pp. 1—49.

† Ibid. vol. i. p. 220. ‡ Ibid. vol. i. p. 222.

§ Dr. Brown always expresses himself best

The substitution of "suggestion" for the former phrase of "association of ideas," would hardly deserve notice in so cursory a view, if it had not led him to a serious misconception of the doctrines and deserts of other philosophers. The fault of the latter phrase is rather in the narrowness of the last than in the inadequacy of the first word. 'Association' presents the fact in the light of a *relation* between two mental acts: 'suggestion' denotes rather the *power* of the one to call up the other. But whether we say that the sight of ashes 'suggests' fire, or that the ideas of fire and ashes are 'associated,' we mean to convey the same fact, and, in both cases, an exact thinker means to accompany the fact with no hypothesis. Dr. Brown has supposed the word "association" as intended to affirm that there is some "intermediate process"* between the original succession of the mental acts and the power which they acquired therefrom of calling up each other. This is quite as much to raise up imaginary antagonists for the honour of conquering them, as he justly reprehends Dr. Reid for doing in the treatment of preceding philosophers. He falls into another more important and unaccountable error, in representing his own reduction of Mr. Hume's principles of association (—resemblance, contrariety, causation, contiguity in time or place) to the one principle of contiguity, as a discovery of his own, by which his theory is distinguished from "the universal opinion of philosophers."† Nothing but too exclusive a consideration of the doctrines of the Scottish school could have led him to speak thus of what was hinted by Aristotle, distinctly laid down by Hobbes, and fully unfolded both by Hartley and Condillac. He has, however, extremely enlarged the proof and the illustration of this law of mind, by the exercise of "a more subtile analysis" and the disclosure of "a finer species of proximity."‡ As he has thus aided and confirmed, though he did not discover, the general law, so he has rendered a new and very important service to mental science, by drawing attention to what he properly calls "secondary laws of Suggestion"§ or Association, which modify the action of the general law, and must be distinctly considered, in order to explain its connection with the phenomena. The enumeration and exposition are instructive, and the example is worthy of commendation. For it is in this lower region of the science that most remains to be discovered; it is that which rests most on observation, and least tempts to controversy: it is by improvements in this part of our knowledge that the foundations are secured, and the whole building so repaired as to rest steadily on them. The distinction of common language between the head and the heart, which, as we have seen, is so often overlooked or misapplied by metaphysicians, is, in the system of Brown, signified by the terms "mental states" and "emotions." It is unlucky that no single word could be found for the former, and that the addition of the generic term "feeling" should disturb its easy comprehension, when it is applied more naturally.

In our more proper province Brown followed Butler (who appears to have been chiefly known to him through the writings of Mr. Stewart), in his theory of the social affections. Their disinterestedness is enforced by the arguments of both these philosophers, as well as by those of Hutcheson.* It is observable, however, that Brown applies the principle of Suggestion, or Association, boldly to this part of human nature, and seems inclined to refer to it even Sympathy itself.† It is hard to understand how, with such a disposition on the subject of a principle so generally thought ultimate as Sympathy, he should, inconsistently with himself, follow Mr. Stewart in representing the theory which derives the affections from Association as "a modification of the Selfish system."‡ He mistakes that theory when he states, that it derives the affections from our experience that our own interest is connected with that of others; since, in truth, it considers our regard to our own interest as formed from the same original pleasures by association, which, by the like process, may and do *directly* generate affections towards others, without passing through the channel of regard to our general happiness. But, says he, this is only an hypothesis, since the formation of these affections is acknowledged to belong to a time of which there is no remembrance;§—an objection fatal to every theory of any mental functions,—subversive, for example, of Berkeley's discovery of acquired visual perception, and most strangely inconsistent in the mouth of a philosopher whose numerous simplifications of mental theory are and must be founded on occurrences which precede experience. It is in all other cases, and it must be in this, sufficient that the principle of the theory is really existing,—that it explains the appearances,—that its supposed action *resembles* what we know to be its action in those similar cases of which we have direct experience. Lastly, he in express words admits that, according to the theory to which he objects, we have affections which are at present disin-

where he is short and familiar. "An hypothesis is nothing more than a reason for making one experiment or observation rather than another."—Lectures, vol. i. p. 170. In 1812, as the present writer observed to him that Reid and Hume differed more in words than in opinion, he answered, "Yes, Reid bawled out, we must believe an outward world, but added in a whisper, we can give no reason for our belief: Hume cries out, we can give no reason for such a notion, and whispers, I own we cannot get rid of it."

* Brown's Lectures, vol. ii. pp. 335—347.

† Ibid. vol. ii. p. 349. ‡ Ibid. vol. ii. p. 218.

§ Ibid. vol. ii. p. 270.

* Brown's Lectures, vol. iii. p. 248.

† Ibid. vol. iv. p. 82. ‡ Ibid. vol. iii. p. 282.

§ Ibid. vol. iv. p. 87.

terested.* Is it not a direct contradiction in terms to call such a theory "a modification of the Selfish system?" His language in the sequel clearly indicates a distrust of his own statement, and a suspicion that he is not only inconsistent with himself, but altogether mistaken.†

As we enter farther into the territory of Ethics, we at length discover a distinction, originating with Brown, the neglect of which by preceding speculators we have more than once lamented as productive of obscurity and confusion. "The moral affections," says he, "which I consider at present, I consider rather physiologically" (or, as he elsewhere better expresses it, "psychologically") "than ethically, *as parts of our mental constitution*, not as involving the *fulfilment or violation of duties*."‡ He immediately, however, loses sight of this distinction, and reasons inconsistently with it, instead of following its proper consequences in his analysis of Conscience. Perhaps, indeed, (for the words are capable of more than one sense) he meant to distinguish the virtuous affections from those sentiments which have Morality exclusively in view, rather than to distinguish the theory of Moral Sentiment from the attempt to ascertain the characteristic quality of right action. Friendship is conformable in its dictates to Morality; but it may, and does exist, without any view to it: he who feels the affections, and performs the duties of friendship, is the object of that distinct emotion which is called "moral approbation."

It is on the subject of Conscience that, in imitation of Mr. Stewart, and with the arguments of that philosopher, he makes his chief stand against the theory which considers the formation of that master faculty itself as probably referable to the necessary and universal operation of those laws of human nature to which he himself ascribes almost every other state of mind. On both sides of this question the supremacy of Conscience is alike held to be venerable and absolute. Once more, be it remembered, that the question is purely philosophical, and is only whether, from the impossibility of explaining its formation by more general laws, we are reduced to the necessity of considering it as an original fact in human nature, of which no further account can be given. Let it, however, be also remembered, that we are not driven to this supposition by the mere circumstance, that no satisfactory explanation has yet appeared; for there are many analogies in an unexplained state of mind to states already explained, which may justify us in believing that the explanation requires only more accurate observation, and more patient meditation, to be brought to that completeness which it probably will attain.

* Brown's Lectures, vol. iv. p. 87.
† Ibid. vol. iv. pp. 94—97.
‡ Ibid. vol. iii. p. 281.

SECTION VII.

GENERAL REMARKS.

The oft-repeated warning with which the foregoing section concluded being again premised, it remains that we should offer a few observations, which naturally occur on the consideration of Dr. Brown's argument in support of the proposition, that moral approbation is not only in its mature state independent of, and superior to, any other principle of human nature (regarding which there is no dispute), but that its origin is altogether inexplicable, and that its existence is an ultimate fact in mental science. Though these observations are immediately occasioned by the writings of Brown, they are yet, in the main, of a general nature, and might have been made without reference to any particular writer.

The term "suggestion," which might be inoffensive in describing merely intellectual associations, becomes peculiarly unsuitable when it is applied to those combinations of thought with emotion, and to those unions of feeling, which compose the emotive nature of Man. Its common sense of a sign *recalling* the thing signified, always embroils the new sense vainly forced upon it. No one can help owning, that if it were consistently pursued, so as that we were to speak of "suggesting a feeling" or "passion," the language would be universally thought absurd. To "suggest love" or "hatred" is a mode of expression so manifestly incongruous, that most readers would choose to understand it as suggesting reflections on the subject of these passages. "Suggest" would not commonly be understood as synonymous with "revive" or "rekindle." Defects of the same sort may indeed be found in the parallel phrases of most, if not all, philosophers; and all of them proceed from the erroneous but prevalent notion, that the law of Association produces only such a close union of a thought and a feeling, as gives one the power of reviving the other;—the truth being that it forms them into a new compound, in which the properties of the component parts are no longer discoverable, and which may itself become a substantive principle of human nature. They supposed the condition, produced by the power of that law, to resemble that of material substances in a state of mechanical separation; whereas in reality it may be better likened to a chemical combination of the same substances, from which a totally new product arises. Their language involves a confusion of the question which relates to the *origin* of the principles of human activity, with the other and far more important question which relates to their *nature;* and as soon as this distinction is hidden, the theorist is either betrayed into the Selfish system by a desire of clearness and simplicity, or tempted to the needless multiplication of ultimate facts by mistaken anxiety for what he supposes to be the guards of our social and moral nature. The defect is common to Brown with his predecessors, but in him it is less excusable; for he saw the truth and recoiled from it. It is the main defect of the term "association" itself, that it does not, till after long use, convey the notion of a perfect union, but rather leads to that of a combination which may be dissolved, if not at pleasure, at least with the help of care and exertion; which is utterly and dangerously false in the important cases where such unions are considered as constituting the most essential principles of human nature. Men can no more dissolve these unions than they can disuse their habit of judging of distance by the eye, and often by the ear. But "suggestion" implies, that what suggests is separate from what is suggested, and consequently negatives that unity in an active principle which the whole analogy of nature, as well as our own direct consciousness, shows to be perfectly compatible with its origin in composition.

Large concessions are, in the first place, to be remarked, which must be stated, because they very much narrow the matter in dispute. Those who, before Brown, contended against "beneficial tendency" as the standard of Morality, have either shut their eyes on the connection of Virtue with general utility, or carelessly and obscurely allowed, without further remark, a connection which is at least one of the most remarkable and important of ethical facts. He acts more boldly, and avowedly discusses "the relation of Virtue to Utility." He was compelled by that discussion to make those concessions which so much abridge this controversy. "Utility and Virtue are so related, that there is perhaps no action generally felt to be virtuous, which it would not be beneficial that all men in similar circumstances should imitate."* "In every case of benefit or injury willingly done, there arise certain emotions of moral approbation or disapprobation."† "The intentional produce of evil, as pure evil, is always hated, and that of good, as pure good, always loved."‡ All virtuous acts are thus admitted to be universally beneficial; Morality and the general benefit are acknowledged always to coincide. It is hard to say, then, why they should not be reciprocally tests of each other, though in a very different way;—the virtuous feelings, fitted as they are by immediate appearance, by quick and powerful action, to be sufficient tests of Morality in the moment of action, and for all practical purposes; while the consideration of tendency of those acts to contribute to general happiness, a more obscure and slowly discoverable quality, should be applied in general reasoning, as a test of the sentiments and dispositions themselves. In cases where such last-mentioned test has been applied, no proof has been attempted that it has ever deceived those who used it in the proper place. It has uniformly served to justify our moral constitution, and to show how reasonable it is for us to be guided in action by our higher feelings. At all events it should be, but has not been considered, that from these concessions alone it follows, that beneficial tendency is at least one constant property of Virtue. Is not this, in effect, an admission that beneficial tendency does distinguish virtuous acts and dispositions from those which we call vicious? If the criterion be incomplete or delusive, let its faults be specified, and let some other quality be pointed out, which, either singly or in combination with beneficial tendency, may more perfectly indicate the distinction. But let us not be assailed by arguments which leave untouched its value as a test, and are in truth directed only against its fitness as an *immediate* incentive and guide to right action. To those who contend for its use in the latter character, it must be left to defend, if they can, so untenable a position: but all others must regard as pure sophistry the use of arguments against it as a test, which really show nothing more than its acknowledged unfitness to be a motive.

When voluntary benefit and voluntary injury are pointed out as the main, if not the sole objects of moral approbation, and disapprobation,—when we are told truly, that the production of good, as good, is always loved, and that of evil, as such, always hated, can we require a more clear, short, and unanswerable proof, that beneficial tendency is an essential quality of Virtue? It is indeed an evidently necessary consequence of this statement, that if benevolence be amiable in itself, our affection for it must increase with its extent, and that no man can be in a perfectly right state of mind, who, if he consider general happiness at all, is not ready to acknowledge that a good man must regard it as being in its own nature the most desirable of all objects, however the constitution and circumstances of human nature may render it unfit or impossible to pursue it *directly* as the object of life. It is at the same time apparent that no such man can consider any habitual disposition, clearly discerned to be in its whole result at variance with general happiness, as not unworthy of being cultivated, or as not fit to be rooted out. It is manifest that, if it were otherwise, he would cease to be benevolent. As soon as we conceive the sublime idea of a Being who not only foresees, but commands, all the consequences of the actions of all voluntary agents, this scheme of reasoning appears far more clear. In such a case, if our moral sentiments remain the same, they compel us to

* Lectures, vol. iv. p. 45. The unphilosophical word "perhaps" must be struck out of the proposition, unless the whole be considered as a mere conjecture; it limits no affirmation, but destroys it, by converting it into a guess. See the like concession, vol. iv. p. 33, with some words interlarded, which betray a sort of reluctance and fluctuation, indicative of the difficulty with which Brown struggled to withhold his assent from truths which he unreasonably dreaded.

† Ibid. vol. iii. p. 567.

‡ Ibid. vol. iii. p. 621.

attribute His whole government of the world to benevolence. The consequence is as necessary as in any process of reason; for if our moral nature be supposed, it will appear self-evident, that it is as much impossible for us to love and revere such a Being, if we ascribe to Him a mixed or imperfect benevolence, as to believe the most positive contradiction in terms. Now, as Religion consists in that love and reverence, it is evident that it cannot subsist without a belief in benevolence as the sole principle of divine government. It is nothing to tell us that this is not a process of reasoning, or, to speak more exactly, that the first propositions are assumed. The first propositions in every discussion relating to intellectual operations must likewise be assumed. Conscience is not Reason, but it is not less an essential part of human nature. Principles which are essential to all its operations are as much entitled to immediate and implicit assent, as those principles which stand in the same relation to the reasoning faculties. The laws prescribed by a benevolent Being to His creatures must necessarily be founded on the principle of promoting their happiness. It would be singular indeed, if the proofs of the goodness of God, legible in every part of Nature, should not, above all others, be most discoverable and conspicuous in the beneficial tendency of His moral laws.

But we are asked, if tendency to general welfare be the standard of Virtue, why is it not always present to the contemplation of every man who does or prefers a virtuous action? Must not Utility be in that case "the felt essence of Virtue?"* Why are other ends, besides general happiness, fit to be morally pursued?

These questions, which are all founded on that confusion of the theory of *actions* with the theory of *sentiments*, against which the reader was so early warned,† might be dismissed with no more than a reference to that distinction, from the forgetfulness of which they have arisen. By those advocates of the principle of Utility, indeed, who hold it to be a necessary part of their system, that some glimpse at least of tendency to personal or general well-being is an essential part of the motives which render an action virtuous, these questions cannot be satisfactorily answered. Against such they are arguments of irresistible force; but against the doctrine itself, rightly understood and justly bounded, they are altogether powerless. The reason why there may, and must be many ends morally more fit to be pursued in practice than general happiness, is plainly to be found in the limited capacity of Man. A perfectly good Being, who foresees and commands all the consequences of action, cannot indeed be conceived by us to have any other end in view than general well-being. Why evil exists under that perfect government, is a question towards the solution of which the human understanding can scarcely advance a single step. But all who hold the evil to exist only for good, and own their inability to explain why or how, are perfectly exempt from any charge of inconsistency in their obedience to the dictates of their moral nature. The measure of the faculties of Man renders it absolutely necessary for him to have many other practical ends; the pursuit of all of which is moral, when it actually tends to general happiness, though that last end never entered into the contemplation of the agent. It is impossible for us to calculate the effects of a single action, any more than the chances of a single life. But let it not be hastily concluded, that the calculation of consequences is impossible in moral subjects. To calculate the general tendency of every sort of human action, is a possible, easy, and common operation. The general good effects of temperance, prudence, fortitude, justice, benevolence, gratitude, veracity, fidelity, of the affections of kindred, and of love for our country, are the subjects of calculations which, taken as generalities, are absolutely unerring. They are founded on a larger and firmer basis of more uniform experience, than any of those ordinary calculations which govern prudent men in the whole business of life. An appeal to these daily and familiar transactions furnishes at once a decisive answer, both to those advocates of Utility who represent the consideration of it as a necessary ingredient in virtuous motives, as well as moral approbation, and to those opponents who turn the unwarrantable inferences of unskilful advocates into proofs of the absurdity into which the doctrine leads.

The cultivation of all the habitual sentiments from which the various classes of virtuous actions flow, the constant practice of such actions, the strict observance of rules in all that province of Ethics which can be subjected to rules, the watchful care of all the outworks of every part of duty, and of that descending series of useful habits which, being securities to Virtue, become themselves virtues,—are so many ends which it is absolutely necessary for man to pursue and to seek for their own sake. "I saw D'Alembert," says a very late writer, "congratulate a young man very coldly, who brought him a solution of a problem. The young man said, 'I have done this in order to have a seat in the Academy.' 'Sir,' answered D'Alembert, 'with such dispositions you never will earn one. Science must be loved for its own sake, and not for the advantage to be derived. No other principle will enable a man to make progress in the sciences.'"* It is singular that D'Alembert should not perceive the extensive application of this truth to the whole nature of Man. No man can make progress in a virtue who does not seek it for its own sake. No man is a

* Lectures, vol. iv. p. 38.

† See *suprà*, p. 97.

* Mémoires de Montlosier, vol. i. p. 50.

friend, a lover of his country, a kind father, a dutiful son, who does not consider the cultivation of affection and the performance of duty in all these cases, respectively, as incumbent on him for their own sake, and not for the advantage to be derived from them. Whoever serves another with a view of advantage to himself is universally acknowledged not to act from affection. But the more immediate application of this truth to our purpose is, that in the case of those virtues which are the means of cultivating and preserving other virtues, it is necessary to acquire love and reverence for the secondary virtues for their own sake, without which they never will be effectual means of sheltering and strengthening those intrinsically higher qualities to which they are appointed to minister. Every moral act must be considered as an end, and men must banish from their practice the regard to the most naturally subordinate duty as a means. Those who are perplexed by the supposition that secondary virtues, making up by the *extent* of their beneficial tendency for what in each particular instance they may want in *magnitude*, may become of as great importance as the primary virtues themselves, would do well to consider a parallel though very homely case. A house is useful for many purposes: many of these purposes are in themselves, for the time, more important than shelter. The destruction of the house may, nevertheless, become a greater evil than the defeat of several of these purposes, because it is permanently convenient, and indeed necessary to the execution of most of them. A floor is made for warmth, for dryness,—to support tables, chairs, beds, and all the household implements which contribute to accommodation and to pleasure. The floor is valuable only as a means; but, as the only means by which many ends are attained, it may be much more valuable than some of them. The table might be, and generally is, of more valuable timber than the floor; but the workman who should for that reason take more pains in making the table strong, than the floor secure, would not long be employed by customers of common sense.

The connection of that part of Morality which regulates the intercourse of the sexes with benevolence, affords the most striking instance of the very great importance which may belong to a virtue, in itself secondary, but on which the general cultivation of the highest virtues permanently depends. Delicacy and modesty may be thought chiefly worthy of cultivation, because they guard purity; but they must be loved for their own sake, without which they cannot flourish. Purity is the sole school of domestic fidelity, and domestic fidelity is the only nursery of the affections between parents and children, from children towards each other, and, through these affections, of all the kindness which renders the world habitable. At each step in the progress, the appropriate end must be loved for its own sake; and it is easy to see how the only means of sowing the seeds of benevolence, in all its forms, may become of far greater importance than many of the modifications and exertions even of benevolence itself. To those who will consider this subject, it will not long seem strange that the sweetest and most gentle affections grow up only under the apparently cold and dark shadow of stern duty. The obligation is strengthened, not weakened, by the consideration that it arises from human imperfection; which only proves it to be founded on the nature of man. It is enough that the pursuit of all these separate ends leads to general well-being, the promotion of which is the final purpose of the Creation.

The last and most specious argument against beneficial tendency, even as a test, is conveyed in the question, Why moral approbation is not bestowed on every thing beneficial, instead of being confined, as it confessedly is, to voluntary acts? It may plausibly be said, that the establishment of the beneficial tendency of all those voluntary acts which are the objects of moral approbation, is not sufficient;—since, if such tendency be the standard, it ought to follow, that whatever is useful should also be morally approved. To answer, as has before been done,* that experience gradually limits moral approbation and disapprobation to voluntary acts, by teaching us that they influence the Will, but are wholly wasted if they be applied to any other object,—though the fact be true, and contributes somewhat to the result,—is certainly not enough. It is at best a partial solution. Perhaps, on reconsideration, it is entitled only to a secondary place. To seek a foundation for universal, ardent, early, and immediate feelings, in processes of an intellectual nature, has, since the origin of philosophy, been the grand error of ethical inquirers into human nature. To seek for such a foundation in Association,—an early and insensible process, which confessedly mingles itself with the composition of our first and simplest feelings, and which is common to both parts of our nature, is not liable to the same animadversion. If Conscience be uniformly produced by the regular and harmonious co-operation of many processes of association, the objection is in reality a challenge to produce a complete theory of it, founded on that principle, by exhibiting such a full account of all these processes as may satisfactorily explain why it proceeds thus far and no farther. This would be a very arduous attempt, and perhaps it may be premature. But something may be more modestly tried towards an *outline*, which, though it may leave many particulars unexplained, may justify a reasonable expectation that they are not incapable of explanation, and may even now assign such reasons for the limitation of approbation

* See *suprà*, *p.* 142.

to voluntary acts, as may convert the objection derived from that fact into a corroboration of the doctrines to which it has been opposed as an insurmountable difficulty. Such an attempt will naturally lead to the close of the present Dissertation. The attempt has indeed been already made,* but not without great apprehensions on the part of the author that he has not been clear enough, especially in those parts which appeared to himself to owe most to his own reflection. He will now endeavour, at the expense of some repetition, to be more satisfactory.

There must be primary pleasures, pains, and even appetites, which arise from no prior state of mind, and which, if explained at all, can be derived only from bodily organization; for if there were not, there could be no secondary desires. What the number of the underived principles may be, is a question to which the answers of philosophers have been extremely various, and of which the consideration is not necessary to our present purpose. The rules of philosophizing, however, require that causes should not be multiplied without necessity. Of two explanations, therefore, which give an equally satisfactory account of appearances, that theory is manifestly to be preferred which supposes the smaller number of ultimate and inexplicable principles. This maxim, it is true, is subject to three indispensable conditions:—1st, That the principles employed in the explanation should be known really to exist; in which consists the main distinction between hypothesis and theory. Gravity is a principle universally known to exist; ether and a nervous fluid are mere suppositions.—2dly, That these principles should be known to produce effects *like* those which are ascribed to them in the theory. This is a further distinction between hypothesis and theory; for there are an infinite number of degrees of *likeness*, from the faint resemblances which have led some to fancy that the functions of the nerves depend on electricity, to the remarkable coincidences between the appearances of projectiles on earth, and the movements of the heavenly bodies, which constitutes the Newtonian system,—a theory now perfect, though exclusively founded on analogy, and in which one of the classes of phenomena brought together by it is not the subject of direct experience.—3dly, That it should correspond, if not with all the facts to be explained, at least with so great a majority of them as to render it highly probable that means will in time be found of reconciling it to all. It is only on this ground that the Newtonian system justly claimed the title of a legitimate theory during that long period when it was unable to explain many celestial appearances, before the labours of a century, and the genius of Laplace, at length completed it by adapting it to all the phenomena. A theory may be just before it is complete.

In the application of these canons to the theory which derives most of the principles of human action from the transfer of a small number of pleasures, perhaps organic ones, by the law of Association to a vast variety of new objects, it cannot be denied, 1st, That it satisfies the first of the above conditions, inasmuch as Association is *really* one of the laws of human nature; 2dly, That it also satisfies the second, for Association certainly produces effects *like* those which are referred to it by this theory;—otherwise there would be no secondary desires, no acquired relishes and dislikes,—facts universally acknowledged, which are, and can be explained only by the principle called by Hobbes "Mental Discourse,"—by Locke, Hume, Hartley, Condillac, and the majority of speculators, as well as in common speech, "Association,"—by Tucker, "Translation," —and by Brown, "Suggestion." The facts generally referred to the principle *resemble* those facts which are claimed for it by the theory in this important particular, that in both cases equally, pleasure becomes attached to perfectly new things,—so that the derivative desires become perfectly independent of the primary. The great dissimilarity of these two classes of passions has been supposed to consist in this, that the former always regards the interest of the individual, while the latter regards the welfare of others. The philosophical world has been almost entirely divided into two sects,—the partisans of Selfishness, comprising mostly all the predecessors of Butler, and the greater part of his successors, and the advocates of Benevolence, who have generally contended that the reality of Disinterestedness depends on its being a *primary principle*. Enough has been said by Butler against the more fatal heresy of Selfishness: something also has already been said against the error of the advocates of Disinterestedness, in the progress of this attempt to develope ethical truths historically, in the order in which inquiry and controversy brought them out with increasing brightness. The analogy of the material world is indeed faint, and often delusive; yet we dare not utterly reject that on which the whole technical language of mental and moral science is necessarily grounded. The whole creation teems with instances where the most powerful agents and the most lasting bodies are the acknowledged results of the composition, sometimes of a few, often of many elements. These compounds often in their turn become the elements of other substances; and it is with them that we are conversant chiefly in the pursuits of knowledge, and solely in the concerns of life. No man ever fancied, that because they were compounds, they were therefore less *real*. It is impossible to confound them with any of the separate elements which contribute towards their formation. But a much more close resemblance

* See *supra* p. 149, *et seq.*

presents itself: every secondary desire, or acquired relish, involves in it a transfer of pleasure to something which was before indifferent or disagreeable. Is the new pleasure the less real for being acquired? Is it not often preferred to the original enjoyment? Are not many of the secondary pleasures indestructible? Do not many of them survive primary appetites? Lastly, the important principle of regard to our own general welfare, which disposes us to prefer it to immediate pleasure (unfortunately called "Self-love,"—as if, in any intelligible sense of the term "love," it were possible for a man to love himself), is perfectly intelligible, if its origin be ascribed to Association, but utterly incomprehensible, if it be considered as prior to the appetites and desires, which alone furnish it with materials. As happiness consists of satisfactions, Self-love presupposes appetites and desires which are to be satisfied. If the order of time were important, the affections are formed at an earlier period than many self-regarding passions, and they always precede the formation of Self-love.

Many of the later advocates of the Disinterested system, though recoiling from an apparent approach to the Selfishness into which the purest of their antagonists had occasionally fallen, were gradually obliged to make concessions to the Derivative system, though clogged with the contradictory assertion, that it was only a refinement of Selfishness: and we have seen that Brown, the last and not the least in genius of them, has nearly abandoned the greater, though not indeed the most important, part of the territory in dispute, and scarcely contends for any underived principle but the Moral Faculty. This being the state of opinion among the very small number in Great Britain who still preserve some remains of a taste for such speculations, it is needless here to trace the application of the law of Association to the formation of the secondary desires, whether private or social. For our present purposes, the explanation of their origin may be assumed to be satisfactory. In what follows, it must, however, be steadily borne in mind, that this concession involves an admission that the pleasure derived from low objects may be transferred to the most pure,—that from a part of a self-regarding appetite such a pleasure may become a portion of a perfectly disinterested desire,—and that the disinterested nature and absolute independence of the latter are not in the slightest degree impaired by the consideration, that it is formed by one of those grand mental processes to which the formation of the other habitual states of the human mind have been, with great probability, ascribed.

When the social affections are thus formed, they are naturally followed in every instance by the will to do whatever can promote their object. Compassion excites a voluntary determination to do whatever relieves the person pitied: the like process must occur in every case of gratitude, generosity, and affection. Nothing so uniformly follows the kind disposition as the act of Will, because it is the only means by which the benevolent desire can be gratified. The result of what Brown justly calls "a finer analysis," shows a mental contiguity of the affection to the volition to be much closer than appears on a coarser examination of this part of our nature. No wonder, then, that the strongest association, the most active power of reciprocal suggestion, should subsist between them. As all the affections are delightful, so the volitions,—voluntary acts which are the only means of their gratification,—become agreeable objects of contemplation to the mind. The habitual disposition to perform them is felt in ourselves, and observed in others, with satisfaction. As these feelings become more lively, the absence of them may be viewed in ourselves with a pain,—in others with an alienation capable of indefinite increase. They become entirely independent sentiments,—still, however, receiving constant supplies of nourishment from their parent affections,—which, in well-balanced minds, reciprocally strengthen each other;—unlike the unkind passions, which are constantly engaged in the most angry conflicts of civil war. In this state we desire to experience the *beneficient volitions*, to cultivate a disposition towards them, and to do every correspondent voluntary act: they are for their own sake the objects of desire. They thus constitute a large portion of those emotions, desires, and affections, which regard certain dispositions of the mind, and determinations of the Will as their sole and ultimate end. These are what are called the "Moral Sense," the "Moral Sentiments," or best, though most simply, by the ancient name of Conscience,—which has the merit, in our language, of being applied to no other purpose,—which peculiarly marks the strong working of these feelings on conduct,—and which, from its solemn and sacred character, is well adapted to denote the venerable authority of the highest principle of human nature.

Nor is this all: it has already been seen that not only sympathy with the sufferer, but indignation against the wrong-doer, contributes a large and important share towards the moral feelings. We are angry at those who disappoint our wish for the happiness of others; we make the resentment of the innocent person wronged our own: our moderate anger approves all well-proportioned punishment of the wrong-doer. We hence approve those dispositions and actions of voluntary agents which promote such suitable punishment, and disapprove those which hinder its infliction, or destroy its effect; at the head of which may be placed that excess of punishment beyond the average feelings of good men which turns the indignation of the calm by-stander against the culprit into pity. In this state, when anger is duly moderated,—when it is proportioned to the wrong,—when it is detached from personal considerations,—*when dispositions and actions are its ultimate objects*, it becomes a sense of justice, and is so purified as to be fitted to be a new element of Conscience. There is no part of Morality which is so *directly* aided by a conviction of the necessity of its observance to the general interest, as Justice. The connection between them is discoverable by the most common understanding. All public deliberations profess the public welfare to be their object; all laws propose it as their end. This calm principle of public utility serves to mediate between the sometimes repugnant feelings which arise in the punishment of criminals, by repressing undue pity on one hand, and reducing resentment to its proper level on the other. Hence the unspeakable importance of criminal laws as a part of the moral education of mankind. Whenever they carefully conform to the Moral Sentiments of the age and country,—when they are withheld from approaching the limits within which the disapprobation of good men would confine punishment, they contribute in the highest degree to increase the ignominy of crimes, to make men recoil from the first suggestions of criminality, and to nourish and mature the sense of justice, which lends new vigour to the conscience with which it has been united.

Other contributary streams present themselves: qualities which are necessary to Virtue, but may be subservient to Vice, may, independently of that excellence, or of that defect, be in themselves admirable: courage, energy, decision, are of this nature. In their wild state they are often savage and destructive: when they are tamed by the society of the affections, and trained up in obedience to the Moral Faculty, they become virtues of the highest order, and, by their name of "magnanimity," proclaim the general sense of mankind that they are the characteristic qualities of a great soul. They retain whatever was admirable in their unreclaimed state, together with all that they borrow from their new associate and their high ruler. Their nature, it must be owned, is prone to evil; but this propensity does not hinder them from being rendered capable of being ministers of good, when in a state where the gentler virtues require to be vigorously guarded against the attacks of daring depravity. It is thus that the strength of the well-educated elephant is sometimes employed in vanquishing the fierceness of the tiger, and sometimes used as a means of defence against the shock of his brethren of the same species. The delightful contemplation, however, of these qualities, when purely applied, becomes one of the sentiments of which the dispositions and actions of voluntary agents are the direct and final object. By this resemblance they are associated with the other moral principles, and with them contribute to form Conscience, which, as the master faculty of the soul, levies such large contributions on every province of human nature.

It is important, in this point of view, to consider also the moral approbation which is undoubtedly bestowed *on those dispositions and actions of voluntary agents* which terminate in their own satisfaction, security, and well-being. They have been called "duties to ourselves," as absurdly as a regard to our own greatest happiness is called "self-love." But it cannot be reasonably doubted, that intemperance, improvidence, timidity,—even when considered only in relation to the individual,—are not only regretted as imprudent, but blamed as morally wrong. It was excellently observed by Aristotle, that a man is not commended as *temperate*, so long as it costs him efforts of *self-denial* to persevere in the practice of temperance, but only when *he prefers that virtue for its own sake*. He is not meek, nor brave, as long as the most vigorous self-command is necessary to bridle his anger or his fear. On the same principle, he may be judicious or prudent, but he is not benevolent, if he confers benefits with a view to his own greatest happiness. In like manner, it is ascertained by experience, that all the masters of science and of art,—that all those who have successfully pursued Truth and Knowledge, love them for their own sake, without regard to the generally imaginary dower of interest, or even to the dazzling crown which Fame may place on their heads.* But it may still be reasonably asked, why these useful qualities are morally improved, and how they become capable of being combined with those public and disinterested sentiments which principally constitute Conscience? The answer is, because they are entirely conversant with volitions and voluntary actions, and in that respect resemble the other constituents of Conscience, with which they are thereby fitted to mingle and coalesce. Like those other principles, they may be detached from what is personal and outward, and fixed on the dispositions and actions, which are the only means of promoting their ends. The sequence of these principles and acts of Will becomes so frequent, that the association between both may be as firm as in the for-

* See the Pursuit of Knowledge under Difficulties, a discourse forming the first part of the third volume of the Library of Entertaining Knowledge, London, 1829. The author of this essay, for it can be no other than Mr. Brougham, will by others be placed at the head of those who, in the midst of arduous employments, and surrounded by all the allurements of society, yet find leisure for exerting the unwearied vigour of their minds in every mode of rendering permanent service to the human species; more especially in spreading a love of knowledge, and diffusing useful truth among all classes of men. These voluntary occupations deserve our attention still less as examples of prodigious power than as proofs of an intimate conviction, which binds them by unity of purpose with his public duties, that (to use the almost dying words of an excellent person) "man can neither be happy without virtue, nor actively virtuous without liberty, nor securely free without rational knowledge."—Close of Sir W. Jones' last Discourse to the Asiatic Society of Calcutta.

mer cases. All those sentiments of which the final object is a state of the Will, become thus intimately and inseparably blended; and of that perfect state of solution (if such words may be allowed) the result is Conscience—the judge and arbiter of human conduct—which, though it does not supersede *ordinary motives* of virtuous feelings and habits (equally the ordinary motives of good actions), yet exercises a lawful authority even over them, and ought to blend with them. Whatsoever actions and dispositions are approved by Conscience acquire the name of virtues or duties: they are pronounced to deserve commendation; and we are justly considered as under a moral *obligation* to practise the actions and cultivate the dispositions.

The coalition of the private and public feelings is very remarkable in two points of view, from which it seems hitherto to have been scarcely observed. 1st. It illustrates very forcibly all that has been here offered to prove, that the peculiar character of the Moral Sentiments consists in their *exclusive reference to states of Will*, and that every feeling which has that quality, when it is purified from all admixture with different objects, becomes capable of being absorbed into Conscience, and of being assimilated to it, so as to become a part of it. For no feelings can be more unlike each other in their object, than the private and the social; and yet, as both employ voluntary actions as their sole immediate means, both may be transferred by association to states of the Will, in which case they are transmuted into moral sentiments. No example of the coalition of feelings in their general nature less widely asunder, could afford so much support to this position. 2d. By raising qualities useful to ourselves to the rank of virtues, it throws a strong light on the relation of Virtue to individual interest; very much as Justice illustrates the relation of Morality to general interest. The coincidence of Morality with individual interest is an important truth in Ethics: it is most manifest in that part of the science which we are now considering. A calm regard to our general interest is indeed a faint and infrequent motive to action. Its chief advantage is, that it is regular, and that its movements may be calculated. In deliberate conduct it may often be relied on, though perhaps never safely without knowledge of the whole temper and character of the agent. But in moral reasoning at least, the fore-named coincidence is of unspeakable advantage. If there be a miserable man who has cold affections, a weak sense of justice, dim perceptions of right and wrong, and faint feelings of them,—if, still more wretched, his heart be constantly torn and devoured by malevolent passions—the vultures of the soul, we have one resource still left, even in cases so dreadful. Even *he* still retains a human principle, to which we can speak: he must own that he has some wish for his own lasting welfare. We can prove to him that his state of mind is inconsistent with it. It may be impossible indeed to show, that while his disposition continues the same, he can derive any enjoyment from the practice of virtue: but it may be most clearly shown, that every advance in the amendment of that disposition is a step towards even temporal happiness. If he do not amend his character, we may compel him to own that he is at variance with himself and offends against a principle of which even *he* must recognise the reasonableness.

The formation of Conscience from so many elements, and especially from the combination of elements so unlike as the private desires and the social affections, early contributes to give it the appearance of that simplicity and independence which in its mature state really distinguish it. It becomes, from these circumstances, more difficult to distinguish its separate principles; and it is impossible to exhibit them in separate action. The affinity of these various passions to each other, which consists in their having no object but *states of the Will*, is the only common property which strikes the mind. Hence the facility with which the general terms, first probably limited to the relations between ourselves and others, are gradually extended to all voluntary acts and dispositions. Prudence and temperance become the objects of moral approbation. When imprudence is immediately disapproved by the by-stander, without deliberate consideration of its consequences, it is not only displeasing, as being pernicious, but is blamed as *wrong*, though with a censure so much inferior to that bestowed on inhumanity and injustice, as may justify those writers who use the milder term *'improper.'* At length, when the general words come to signify the objects of moral approbation, and the reverse, they denote merely the power to excite feelings, which are as independent as if they were underived, and which coalesce the more perfectly, because they are detached from objects so various and unlike as to render their return to their primitive state very difficult.

The question,* Why we do not morally approve the useful qualities of actions which are altogether *involuntary*? may now be shortly and satisfactorily answered:—because Conscience is in perpetual contact, as it were, with all the dispositions and actions of *voluntary* agents, and is by that means indissolubly associated with them exclusively. It has a direct action on the Will, and a constant mental contiguity to it. It has no such mental contiguity to involuntary changes. It has never perhaps been observed, that an operation of the conscience precedes all acts deliberate enough to be in the highest sense voluntary and does so as much when it is defeated as when it prevails. In either case the association is repeated. It extends to the whole of the ac-

* See *suprà*, p. 178.

tive man. All passions have a definite outward object to which they tend, and a limited sphere within which they act. But Conscience has no object but a state of Will; and as an act of Will is the sole means of gratifying any passion, Conscience is co-extensive with the whole man, and without encroachment curbs or aids every feeling,—even within the peculiar province of that feeling itself. As Will is the universal means, Conscience, which regards Will, must be a universal principle. As nothing is interposed between Conscience and the Will when the mind is in its healthy state, the dictate of Conscience is followed by the determination of the Will, with a promptitude and exactness which very naturally is likened to the obedience of an inferior to the lawful commands of those whom he deems to be rightfully placed over him. It therefore seems clear, that on the theory which has been attempted, moral approbation must be limited to voluntary operations, and Conscience must be universal, independent, and commanding.

One remaining difficulty may perhaps be objected to the general doctrines of this Dissertation, though it does not appear at any time to have been urged against other modifications of the same principle. "If moral approbation," it may be said, "involve no perception of beneficial tendency, whence arises the coincidence between that principle and the Moral Sentiments?" It may seem at first sight, that such a theory rests the foundation of Morals upon a coincidence altogether mysterious, and apparently capricious and fantastic. Waiving all other answers, let us at once proceed to that which seems conclusive. It is true that Conscience rarely contemplates so distant an object as the welfare of all sentient beings;—but to what point is every one of its elements directed? What, for instance, is the aim of all the social affections?—Nothing but the production of larger or smaller masses of happiness among those of our fellow-creatures who are the objects of these affections. In every case these affections promote happiness, as far as their foresight and their power extend. What can be more conducive, or even necessary, to the being and well-being of society, than the rules of justice? Are not the angry passions themselves, as far as they are ministers of Morality, employed in removing hindrances to the welfare of ourselves and others, and so in indirectly promoting it? The private passions terminate indeed in the happiness of the individual, which, however, is a part of general happiness, and the part over which we have most power. Every principle of which Conscience is composed has some portion of happiness for its object: to that point they all converge. General happiness is not indeed one of the natural objects of Conscience, because our voluntary acts are not felt and perceived to affect it. But how small a step is left for Reason! It only casts up the items of the account. It has only to discover that the acts of those who labour to promote separate portions of happiness must increase the amount of the whole. It may be truly said, that if observation and experience did not clearly ascertain that beneficial tendency is the constant attendant and mark of all virtuous dispositions and actions, the same great truth would be revealed to us by the voice of Conscience. The coincidence, instead of being arbitrary, arises necessarily from the laws of human nature, and the circumstances in which mankind are placed. We perform and approve virtuous actions, partly because Conscience regards them as right, partly because we are prompted to them by good affections. All these affections contribute towards general well-being, though it is not necessary, nor would it be fit, that the agent should be distracted by the contemplation of that vast and remote object.

The various relations of Conscience to Religion we have already been led to consider on the principles of Butler, of Berkeley, of Paley, and especially of Hartley, who was brought by his own piety to contemplate as the last and highest stage of virtue and happiness, a sort of self-annihilation, which, however unsuitable to the present condition of mankind, yet places in the strongest light the disinterested character of the system, of which it is a conceivable, though perhaps not attainable, result. The completeness and rigour acquired by Conscience, when all its dictates are revered as the commands of a perfectly wise and good Being, are so obvious, that they cannot be questioned by any reasonable man, however extensive his incredulity may be. It is thus that she can add the warmth of an affection to the inflexibility of principle and habit. It is true that, in examining the evidence of the divine original of a religious system, in estimating an imperfect religion, or in comparing the demerits of religions of human origin, hers must be the standard chiefly applied: but it follows with equal clearness, that those who have the happiness to find satisfaction and repose in divine revelation are bound to consider all those precepts for the government of the Will, delivered by her, which are manifestly universal, as the rules to which all their feelings and actions should conform. The true distinction between Conscience and a taste for moral beauty has already been pointed out;*—a distinction which, notwithstanding its simplicity, has been unobserved by philosophers, perhaps on account of the frequent co-operation and intermixture of the two feelings. Most speculators have either denied the existence of the taste, or kept it out of view in their theory, or exalted it to the place which is rightfully filled only by Conscience. Yet it is perfectly obvious that, like all the other feelings called "pleasures of imagination," it terminates in delightful contemplation, while the Moral

* See *suprà*, p. 151.

Faculty always aims exclusively at voluntary action. Nothing can more clearly show that this last quality is the characteristic of Conscience, than its being thus found to distinguish that faculty from the sentiments which most nearly resemble it, most frequently attend it, and are most easily blended with it.

Some attempt has now been made to develope the fundamental principles of Ethical theory, in that historical order in which meditation and discussion brought them successively into a clearer light. That attempt, as far as it regards Great Britain, is at least chronologically complete. The spirit of bold speculation, conspicuous among the English of the seventeenth century, languished after the earlier part of the eighteenth, and seems, from the time of Hutcheson, to have passed into Scotland, where it produced Hume, the greatest of sceptics, and Smith, the most eloquent of modern moralists; besides giving rise to that sober, modest, perhaps timid philosophy which is commonly called Scotch, and which has the singular merit of having first strongly and largely inculcated the absolute necessity of admitting certain principles as the foundation of all reasoning, and the indispensable conditions of thought itself. In the eye of the moralist all the philosophers of Scotland,—Hume and Smith as much as Reid, Campbell, and Stewart,—have also the merit of having avoided the Selfish system, and of having, under whatever variety of representation, alike maintained the disinterested nature of the social affections and the supreme authority of the Moral Sentiments. Brown reared the standard of revolt against the masters of the Scottish School, and in reality still more than in words, adopted those very doctrines against which his predecessors, after their war against scepticism, uniformly combated. The law of Association, though expressed in other language, became the nearly universal principle of his system; and perhaps it would have been absolutely universal, if he had not been restrained rather by respectful feelings than by cogent reasons. With him the love of speculative philosophy, as a pursuit, appears to have expired in Scotland. There are some symptoms, yet however very faint, of the revival of a taste for it among the English youth: while in France instruction in it has been received with approbation from M. Royer Collard, the scholar of Stewart more than of Reid, and with enthusiasm from his pupil and successor M. Cousin, who has clothed the doctrines of the Schools of Germany in an unwonted eloquence, which always adorns, but sometimes disguises them.

The history of political philosophy, even if its extent and subdivisions were better defined, would manifestly have occupied another dissertation, at least equal in length to the present. The most valuable parts of it belong to civil history. It has too much of the spirit of faction and turbulence infused into it to be easily combined with the calmer history of the progress of Science, or even with that of the revolutions of speculation. In no age of the world were its principles so interwoven with political events, and so deeply imbued with the passions and divisions excited by them, as in the eighteenth century.

It was at one time the purpose, or rather perhaps the hope, of the writer, to close this discourse by an account of the Ethical systems which have prevailed in Germany during the last half century;—which, maintaining the same spirit amidst great changes of technical language, and even of speculative principle, have now exclusive possession of Europe to the north of the Rhine,—have been welcomed by the French youth with open arms,—have roused in some measure the languishing genius of Italy, but are still little known, and unjustly estimated by the mere English reader. He found himself, however, soon reduced to the necessity of either being superficial, and by consequence uninstructive, or of devoting to that subject a far longer time than he can now spare, and a much larger space than the limits of this work would probably allow. The majority of readers will, indeed, be more disposed to require an excuse for the extent of what has been done, than for the relinquishment of projected additions. All readers must agree that this is peculiarly a subject on which it is better to be silent than to say too little.

A very few observations, however, on the German philosophy, as far as relates to its ethical bearings and influence, may perhaps be pardoned. These remarks are not so much intended to be applied to the moral doctrines of that school, considered in themselves, as to those apparent defects in the prevailing systems of Ethics throughout Europe, which seem to have suggested the necessity of their adoption. Kant has himself acknowledged that his whole theory of the percipient and intellectual faculty was intended to protect the first principles of human knowledge against the assaults of Hume. In like manner, his Ethical system is evidently framed for the purpose of guarding certain principles, either directly governing, or powerfully affecting practice, which seemed to him to have been placed on unsafe foundations by their advocates, and which were involved in perplexity and confusion, especially by those who adapted the results of various and sometimes contradictory systems to the taste of multitudes,—more eager to know than prepared to be taught. To the theoretical Reason the former superadded the Practical Reason, which had peculiar laws and principles of its own, from which all the rules of Morals may be deduced. The Practical Reason cannot be conceived without these laws; therefore they are *inherent*. It perceives them to be *necessary* and *universal*. Hence, by a process not altogether dissimilar, at least in its gross results, to that which was employed for the like purpose by Cudworth and Clarke, by Price, and in some degree by Stewart, he raises the social affections, and still more the Moral Sentiments, above the sphere of enjoyment, and beyond that series of enjoyments which is called happiness. The performance of duty, not the pursuit of happiness, is in this system the chief end of man. By the same intuition we discover that Virtue deserves happiness; and as this desert is not uniformly so requited in the present state of existence, it compels us to believe a moral government of the world, and a future state of existence, in which all the conditions of the Practical Reason will be realized;—truths, of which, in the opinion of Kant, the argumentative proofs were at least very defective, but of which the revelations of the Practical Reason afforded a more conclusive demonstration than any process of reasoning could supply. The Understanding, he owned, saw nothing in the connection of motive with volition different from what it discovered in every other uniform sequence of a cause and an effect. But as the moral law delivered by the Practical Reason issues peremptory and inflexible commands, the power of always obeying them is implied in their very nature. All individual objects, all outward things, must indeed be viewed in the relation of cause and effect: these last are necessary conditions of all reasoning. But the acts of the faculty which *wills*, of which we are immediately conscious, belong to another province of mind, and are not subject to these laws of the Theoretical Reason. The mere intellect must still regard them as necessarily connected; but the Practical Reason distinguishes its own *liberty* from the *necessity* of nature, conceives volition without at the same time conceiving an antecedent to it, and regards all moral beings as the original authors of their own actions.

Even those who are unacquainted with this complicated and comprehensive system, will at once see the slightness of the above sketch: those who understand it, will own that so brief an outline could not be otherwise than slight. It will, however, be sufficient for the present purpose, if it render what follows intelligible.

With respect to what is called the "Practical Reason," the Kantian system varies from ours, in treating it as having more resemblance to the intellectual powers than to sentiment and emotion:—enough has already been said on that question. At the next step, however, the difference seems to resolve itself into a misunderstanding. The character and dignity of the human race surely depend, not on the state in which they are born, but on that which they are all destined to attain, or to approach. No man would hesitate in assenting to this observation, when applied to the intellectual faculties. Thus, the human infant comes into the world imbecile and ignorant; but a vast majority acquire some vigour of reason and extent of knowledge. Strictly, the human infant is born neither selfish nor social; but a far greater part acquire some provident regard to their own welfare, and a number, probably not much smaller, feel some sparks of affection towards others. On our principles, therefore, as much as on those of Kant, human nature is capable of disinterested sentiments. For we too allow and contend that our Moral Faculty is a *necessary* part of human nature,—that it *universally* exists in human beings,—and that we cannot conceive any moral agents without qualities which are either like, or produce the like effects. It is necessarily regarded by us as co-extensive with human, and even with moral nature. In what other sense can *universality* be predicated of any proposition not identical? Why should it be tacitly assumed that all these great characteristics of Conscience should necessarily presuppose its being unformed and underived? What contradiction is there between them and the theory of regular and uniform formation?

In this instance it would seem that a general assent to truth is chiefly, if not solely, obstructed by an inveterate prejudice, arising from the mode in which the questions relating to the affections and the Moral Faculty have been discussed among ethical philosophers. Generally speaking, those who contend that these parts of the mind are acquired, have also held that they are, in their perfect state, no more than modifications of self-love. On the other hand, philosophers "of purer fire," who felt that Conscience is sovereign, and that affection is disinterested, have too hastily fancied that their ground was untenable, without contending that these qualities were inherent or innate, and absolutely underived from any other properties of Mind. If a choice were necessary between these two systems as masses of opinion, without any freedom of discrimination and selection, I should unquestionably embrace that doctrine which places in the clearest light the reality of benevolence and the authority of the Moral Faculty. But it is surely easy to apply a test which may be applied to our conceptions as effectually as a decisive experiment is applied to material substances. Does not he who, whatever he may think of the origin of these parts of human nature, believes that *actually* Conscience is supreme, and affection terminates in its direct object, retain all that for which the partisans of the underived principles value and cling to their system? "But they are made," these philosophers may say, "by this class of our antagonists, to rest on insecure foundations: unless they are underived, we can see no reason for regarding them as independent." In answer, it may be asked, how is connection between these two qualities established? It is really assumed. It finds its way easily into the mind under the protection of another coincidence, which is of a totally different nature. The great majority of those specu lators who have represented the moral and social feelings as acquired, have also considered them as being mere modifications of self-love, and sometimes as being casually formed and easily eradicated, like local and temporary prejudices. But when the nature of our feelings is thoroughly explored, is it not evident that this coincidence is the result of superficial confusion? The better moralists observed accurately, and reasoned justly, on the province of the Moral Sense and the feelings in the formed and mature man: they reasoned mistakenly on the origin of these principles. But the Epicureans were by no means right, even on the latter question; and they were totally wrong on the other, and far more momentous, part of the subject: their error is more extensive, and infinitely more injurious. But what should now hinder an inquirer after truth from embracing, but amending their doctrine where it is partially true, and adopting without any change the just description of the most important principles of human nature which we owe to their more enlightened as well as more generous antagonists?

Though unwilling to abandon the arguments by which, from the earliest times, the existence of the Supreme and Eternal Mind has been established, we, as well as the German philosophers, are entitled to call in the help of our moral nature to lighten the burden of those tremendous difficulties which cloud His moral government. The moral nature is an actual part of man, as much on our scheme as on theirs.

Even the celebrated questions of Liberty and Necessity may perhaps be rendered somewhat less perplexing, if we firmly bear in mind that peculiar relation of Conscience to the Will which we have attempted to illustrate. It is impossible for Reason to consider occurrences otherwise than as bound together by the connection of cause and effect; and in this circumstance consists the strength of the Necessitarian system. But Conscience, which is equally a constituent part of the mind, has other laws. It is composed of *emotions and desires, which contemplate only those dispositions which depend on the Will.* Now, it is the nature of an emotion to withdraw the mind from the contemplation of every idea but that of the object which excites it: while every desire exclusively looks at the object which it seeks. Every attempt to enlarge the mental vision alters the state of mind, weakens the emotion, or dissipates the desire, and tends to extinguish both. If a man, while he was pleased with the smell of a rose, were to reflect on the chemical combinations from which it arose, the condition of his mind would be changed from an enjoyment of the senses to an exertion of the Understanding. If, in the view of a beautiful scene, a man were suddenly to turn his thoughts to the disposition of water, vegetables, and earths, on which its appearance depended, he might enlarge his knowledge of Geology, but he must lose the pleasure of the prospect. The anatomy and analysis of the flesh and blood of a beautiful woman necessarily suspend admiration and affection. Many analogies here present themselves. When life is in danger either in a storm or a battle, it is certain that less fear is felt by the commander or the pilot, and even by the private soldier actively engaged, or the common seaman laboriously occupied, than by those who are exposed to the peril, but not employed in the means of guarding against it. The reason is not that the one class believe the danger to be less: they are likely in many instances to perceive it more clearly. But having acquired a habit of instantly turning their thoughts to means of counteracting the danger, their minds are thrown into a state which excludes the ascendency of fear.—Mental fortitude entirely depends on this habit. The timid horseman is haunted by the fear of a fall: the bold and skilful thinks only about the best way of curbing or supporting his horse. Even when all means of avoiding danger are in both cases evidently unavailable, the brave man still owes to his fortunate habit that he does not suffer the agony of the coward. Many cases have been known where fortitude has reached such strength that the faculties, instead of being confounded by danger, are never raised to their highest activity by a less violent stimulant. The distinction between such men and the coward does not depend on difference of opinion about the reality or extent of the danger, but on a state of mind which renders it more or less accessible to fear. Though it must be owned that the Moral Sentiments are very different from any other human faculty, yet the above observations seem to be in a great measure applicable to every state of mind. The emotions and desires which compose Conscience, while they occupy the mind, must exclude all contemplation of the cause in which the object of these feelings may have originated. To their eye the *voluntary* dispositions and actions, their sole object, must appear to be the first link of a chain; in the view of Conscience these have no foreign origin, and her view, constantly associated as she is with *all volitions*, becomes habitual. Being always possessed of some, and capable of intense warmth, it predominates over the habits of thinking of those few who are employed in the analysis of mental occupations.

The reader who has in any degree been inclined to adopt the explanations attempted above, of the imperative character of Conscience, may be disposed also to believe that they afford some foundation for that conviction of the existence of a power to obey its commands, which (it ought to be granted to the German philosophers) is irresistibly suggested by the commanding tone of all its dictates. If such an explanation should be thought worthy of consideration, it must be very carefully distinguished from that illusive sense by which some writers have laboured to reconcile the feeling of liberty with the reality of necessity.* In this case there is no illusion; nothing is required but the admission, that every faculty observes its own laws, and that when the action of the one fills the mind, that of every other is suspended. The ear cannot see, nor can the eye hear: why then should not the greater powers of Reason and Conscience have different habitual modes of contemplating voluntary actions? How strongly do experience and analogy seem to require the arrangement of motive and volition under the class of causes and effects! With what irresistible power, on the other hand, do all our moral sentiments remove extrinsic agency from view, and concentrate all feeling in the agent himself! The one manner of thinking may predominate among the speculative few in their short moments of abstraction; the other will be that of all other men, and of the speculator himself when he is called upon to act, or when his feelings are powerfully excited by the amiable or odious dispositions of his fellow-men. In these workings of various faculties there is nothing that can be accurately described as contrariety of opinion. An intellectual state, and a feeling, never can be contrary to each other: they are too utterly incapable of comparison to be the subject of contrast; they are agents of a perfectly different nature, acting in different spheres. A feeling can no more be called true or false, than a demonstration, considered simply in itself, can be said to be agreeable or disagreeable. It is true, indeed, that in consequence of the association of all mental acts with each other, emotions and desires may occasion habitual errors of judgment: but liability to error belongs to every exercise of human reason; it arises from a multitude of causes; it constitutes, therefore, no difficulty peculiar to the case before us. Neither truth nor falsehood can be predicated of the perceptions of the senses, but they lead to false opinions. An object seen through different mediums may by the inexperienced be thought to be no longer the same. All men long concluded falsely, from what they saw, that the earth was stationary, and the sun in perpetual motion around it: the greater part of mankind still adopt the same error. Newton and Laplace used the same language with the ignorant, and conformed,—if we may not say to their opinion,—at least to their habits of thinking on all ordinary occasions, and during the far greater part of their lives. Nor is this all: the language which represents various states of mind is very vague. The word which denotes a compound state is often taken from its *principal* fact,—from that which is most conspicuous, most easily called to mind, most warmly felt, or most frequently recurring. It is sometimes borrowed from a separate, but, as it were, neighbouring condition of mind. The grand distinction between thought and feeling is so little observed, that we are peculiarly liable to confusion on this subject.—Perhaps when we use language which indicates an opinion concerning the acts of the Will, we may mean little more than to express strongly and warmly the moral sentiments which voluntary acts alone call up. It would argue disrespect for the human understanding, vainly employed for so many centuries in reconciling contradictory opinions, to propose such suggestions without peculiar diffidence; but before they are altogether rejected, it may be well to consider, whether the constant success of the advocates of Necessity on one ground, and of the partisans of Free Will on another, does not seem to indicate that the two parties contemplate the subject from different points of view, that neither habitually sees more than one side of it, and that they look at it through the medium of different states of mind.

It should be remembered that these hints of a possible reconciliation between seemingly repugnant opinions are proposed, not as perfect analogies, but to lead men's minds into the inquiry, whether that which certainly befalls the mind, in many cases on a small scale, may not, under circumstances favourable to its development, occur with greater magnitude and more important consequences. The coward and brave man, as has been stated, act differently at the approach of danger, because it produces exertion in the one, and fear in the other. But very brave men must, by force of the term, be few: they have little aid in their highest acts, therefore, from fellow-feeling. They are often too obscure for the hope of praise; and they have seldom been trained to cultivate courage as a virtue. The very reverse occurs in the different view taken by the Understanding and by Conscience, of the nature of voluntary actions. The conscientious view must, in some degree, present itself to all mankind; it is therefore unspeakably strengthened by general sympathy. All men respect themselves for being habitually guided by it: it is the object of general commendation; and moral discipline has no other aim but its cultivation. Whoever does not feel more pain from his crimes than from his misfortunes, is looked on with general aversion. And when it is considered that a Being of perfect wisdom and goodness estimates us according to the degree in which Conscience governs our voluntary acts, it is surely no wonder that, in this most important discrepancy between the great faculties of our nature, we should consider the best habitual disposition to be that which the coldest Reason shows us to be most conducive to well-doing and well-being.

On every other point, at least, it would seem that, without the multiplied suppositions and immense apparatus of the German school, the authority of Morality may be vindicated, the disinterestedness of human

* Lord Kames, in his Essays on Morality and Natural Religion, and in his Sketches of the History of Man.

nature asserted, the first principles of knowledge secured, and the hopes and consolations of mankind preserved. Ages may yet be necessary to give to ethical theory all the forms and language of a science, and to apply it to the multiplied and complicated facts and rules which are within its province. In the mean time, if the opinions here unfolded, or intimated, shall be proved to be at variance with the reality of social affections, and with the feeling of moral distinction, the author of this Dissertation will be the first to relinquish a theory which will then show itself inadequate to explain the most indisputable, as well as by far the most important, parts of human nature. If it shall be shown to lower the character of Man, to cloud his hopes, or to impair his sense of duty, he will be grateful to those who may point out his error, and deliver him from the poignant regret of adopting opinions which lead to consequences so pernicious.

NOTES AND ILLUSTRATIONS.

NOTE A. page 103.

THE remarks of Cicero on the Stoicism of Cato are perhaps the most perfect specimen of that refined raillery which attains the object of the orator without general injustice to the person whose authority is for the moment to be abated:—

"Accessit his tot doctrina non moderata, nec mitis, sed, ut mihi videtur, paulo asperior et durior quam aut veritas aut natura patiatur." After an enumeration of the Stoical paradoxes, he adds: "Hæc homo ingeniosissimus, M. Cato, auctoribus eruditissimis inductus, arripuit; neque disputandi causa, ut magna pars, sed ita vivendi...Nostri autem isti (fatebor enim, Cato, me quoque in adolescentia diffisum ingenio meo quæsisse adjumenta doctrinæ) nostri, inquam, illi a Platone atque Aristotele moderati homines et temperati aiunt apud sapientem valere aliquando gratiam; viri boni esse misereri; . . . omnes virtutes mediocritate quadam esse moderatas. Hos ad magistros si qua te fortuna, Cato, cum ista natura detulisset, non tu quidem vir melior esses, nec fortior, nec temperantior, nec justior (neque enim esse potes), sed paulo ad lenitatem propensior."—*Pro Murena.*—Cap. xxix.—xxxi.

NOTE B. page 106.

The greater part of the following extract from Grotius' History of the Netherlands is inserted as the best abridgment of the ancient history of these still subsisting controversies known in our time. I extract also the introduction as a model of the manner in which an historian may state a religious dispute which has influenced political affairs; but far more because it is an unparalleled example of equity and forbearance in the narrative of a contest of which the historian was himself a victim:—

"Habuit hic annus (1608) haud spernendi quoque mali semina, vix ut arma desierant, exorto publicæ religionis dissidio, latentibus initiis, sed ut paulatim in majus erumperet. Lugduni sacras literas docebant viri eruditione præstantes Gomarus et Arminius; quorum ille æternâ Dei lege fixum memorabat, cui hominum salus destinaretur, quis in exitium tenderet; inde alios ad pietatem trahi, et tractos custodiri ne elabantur; relinqui alios communi humanitatis vitio et suis criminibus involutos: hic vero contrà integrum judicem, sed eundem optimum patrem, id reorum fecisse discrimen, ut peccandi pertæsis fiduciamque in Christum reponentibus veniam ac vitam daret, contumacibus pœnam; Deoque gratum, ut omnes resipiscant, ac meliora edocti retineant; sed cogi neminem. Accusabantque invicem; Arminius Gomarum, quod peccandi causas Deo ascriberet, ac fati persuasione teneret immobiles animos; Gomarus Arminium, quod longius ipsis Romanensium scitis hominem arrogantiâ impleret, *nec pateretur soli Deo acceptam ferri, rem maximam, bonam mentem.* Constat his queis cura legere veterum libros, antiquos Christianorum tribuisse hominum voluntati vim liberam, tam in acceptandâ, quam in retinendâ disciplinâ; unde sua præmiis ac suppliciis æquitas. Neque iidem tamen omisere cuncta divinam ad bonitatem referre, cujus munere salutare semen ad nos pervenisset, ac cujus singulari auxilio pericula nostra indigerent. Primus omnium Augustinus, ex quo ipsi cum Pelagio et eum secutis certamen (*nam antè aliter et ipse senseret*), acer disputandi, ita libertatis vocem relinquere, ut ei decreta quædam Dei præponeret, quæ vim ipsam destruere viderentur. At per Græciam quidem Asiamque retenta vetus illa ac simplicior sententia. Per Occidentem magnum Augustini nomen multos traxit in consensum, repertis tamen per Galliam et alibi qui se opponerent, posterioribus sæculis, cum schola non alio magis quam Augustino doctore uteretur, quis ipsi sensus, quis dexter pugnare visa conciliandi modus, diu inter Francisci et Dominici familiam disputato, doctissimi Jesuitarum, cum exactiori subtilitate nodum solvere laborassent, Romæ accusati ægrè damnationem effugere. At Protestantium princeps, Lutherus, egressus monasterio quod Augustini ut nomen, ita sensus sequebatur, parte Augustini arreptâ, id quod is reliquerat, libertatis nomen, cœpit exscindere; quod tam grave Erasmo visum, ut cum cætera ipsius aut probaret aut silentio transmitteret, hic objiciat sese: cujus argumentis motus Philippus Melanchthon, Lutheri adjutor, quæ prius scripserat immutavit, auctorque fuit Luthero, quod multi volunt, certe quod constat Lutheranis, deserendi decreta rigida et conditionem respuentia; sic tamen ut libertatis vocabulum quam rem magis perhorrescerent. At in alterâ Protestantium parte dux Calvinus, primis Lutheri dictis in hac controversiâ inhærescens, novis ea fulsit præsidiis, *addiditque intactum Augustino, veram ac salutarem fidem rem esse perpetuam et amitti nesciam:* cujus proinde qui sibi essent conscii, eos æternæ felicitatis jam nunc certos esse, quos interim in crimina, quantumvis gravia, prolabi posse non diffitebatur. Auxit sententiæ rigorem Genevæ Beza, per Germaniam Zanchius, Ursinus, Piscator, sæpe eo usque provecti, ut, quod alii anxiè vitaverant, apertius nonnunquam traderent, etiam peccandi necessitatem a primâ causâ pendere: quæ ampla Lutheranis criminandi materia."—Lib. xvii. p. 552.

Note C. page 106.

The Calvinism, or rather Augustinianism, of Aquinas is placed beyond all doubt by the following passages: "Prædestinatio est causa gratiæ et gloriæ."—Opera, (Paris, 1664.) vol. vii. p. 356. "Numerus prædestinatorum certus est."—p. 363. "Præscientia meritorum nullo modo est causa prædestinationis divinæ." — p. 370. "Liberum arbitrium est facultas quâ bonum eligitur, gratiâ assistente, vel malum, eâdem desistente."—vol. viii. p. 222. "Deus inclinat ad bonum administrando virtutem agendi et monendo ad bonum. Sed ad malum dicitur inclinare in quantum gratiam non præbet, per quam aliquis a malo retraheretur."—p. 364. On the other side: "Accipitur fides pro eo quo creditur, et est virtus, et pro eo quod creditur, et non est virtus. Fides quâ creditur, si cum caritate sit, virtus est."—vol. ix. p. 236. "Divina bonitas est primum principium communicationis totius quam Deus creaturis largitur." "Quamvis omne quod Deus vult justum sit, non tamen ex hoc justum dicitur quod Deus illud vult."—p. 697.

Note D. page 106.

The Augustinian doctrine is, with some hesitation and reluctance, acquiesced in by Scotus, in that milder form which ascribes election to an express decree, and considers the rest of mankind as only left to the deserved penalties of their transgressions. "In hujus quæstionis solutione mallem alios audire quam docere."—Opera, Lugd. 1639. vol. v. p. 1329. This modesty and prudence is foreign to the dogmatical genius of a Schoolman; and these qualities are still more apparent in the very remarkable language which he applies to the tremendous doctrine of reprobation. "Eorum autem non miseretur (scil. Deus) *quibus gratiam non præbendam esse æquitate occultissimâ et ab humanis sensibus remotissimâ judicat*."—p. 1329. In the commentary on Scotus which follows, it appears that his acute disciple Ockham disputed very freely against the opinions of his master. "*Mala fieri bonum est*" is a startling paradox, quoted by Scotus from Augustin.—p. 1381. It appears that Ockham saw no difference between election and reprobation, and considered those who embraced only the former as at variance with themselves.—p. 1313. Scotus, at great length, contends that our thoughts (consequently our opinions) are not subject to the will.—vol. vi. pp. 1054—1056. One step more would have led him to acknowledge that all erroneous judgment is involuntary, and therefore inculpable and unpunishable, however pernicious. His attempt to reconcile foreknowledge with contingency (vol. v. pp. 1300—1327), is a remarkable example of the power of human subtlety to keep up the appearance of a struggle where it is impossible to make one real effort. But the most dangerous of all the deviations of Scotus from the system of Aquinas is, that he opened the way to the opinion that the distinction of right and wrong depends on the mere will of the Eternal Mind. The absolute power of the Deity, according to him, extends to all but contradictions. His regular power (*ordinata*) is exercised conformably to an order established by himself: "si placet voluntati, sub quâ libera est, recta est lex."—p. 1368, *et seq.*

Note E. page 106.

Ἀλλα μὴν ψυχήν γε ἴσμεν ἄκουσαν πᾶσαν πᾶν ἀγνοοῦσαν. Plat. Op. (Bipont. 1781.) vol. ii. p. 224. —*Πᾶσαν ἀκουσιον ἀμαθίαν εἱναι.*—p. 227. Plato is quoted on this subject by Marcus Aurelius, in a manner which shows, if there had been any doubt, the meaning to be, that all *error* is involuntary. *Πᾶσα ψυχὴ ἄκουσα στερεῖται τῆς ἀληθείας, ὥς λέγει Πλάτων.* Every mind is unwillingly led from truth.—Epict. Dissert. lib. i. cap. xxviii. Augustin closes the long line of ancient testimony to the involuntary character of error: "Quis est qui velit decipi? Fallere nolunt boni; falli autem nec boni volunt nec mali."—Sermo de Verbo.

Note F. page 106.

From a long, able, and instructive dissertation by the commentator on Scotus, it appears that this immoral dogma was propounded in terms more bold and startling by Ockham, who openly affirmed, that "moral evil was only evil because it was prohibited."—Ochamus, qui putat quod nihil posset esse malum sine voluntate prohibitiva Dei, hancque voluntatem esse liberam; sic ut posset eam non habere, et consequenter ut posset fieri quod nulla prorsus essent mala."—Scot. Op. vol. vii. p. 859. But, says the commentator, "Dico primo legem naturalem non consistere in jussione ullâ quæ sit actus voluntatis Dei. Hæc est communissima theologorum sententia."—p. 858. And indeed the reason urged against Ockham completely justifies this approach to unanimity. "For," he asks, "why is it right to obey the will of God? Is it because our moral faculties perceive it to be right? But they equally perceive and feel the authority of all the primary principles of morality; and if this answer be made, it is obvious that those who make it do in effect admit the independence of moral distinctions on the will of God." "If God," said Ockham, "had commanded his creatures to hate himself, hatred of God would have been praiseworthy."—Domin. Soto de Justitiâ et Jure, lib. ii. quæst. 3. "*Utrum præcepta Decalogi sint dispensabilia;*"—a book dedicated to Don Carlos, the son of Phillip II. Suarez, the last scholastic philosopher, rejected the Ockhamical doctrine, but allowed will to be a *part* of the foundation of Morality. "Voluntas Dei non est *tota* ratio bonitatis aut malitiæ.—De Legibus, (Lond. 1679.) p. 71. As the great majority of the Schoolmen supported their opinion of this subject by the consideration of eternal and immutable ideas of right and wrong in the Divine Intellect, it was natural that the Nominalists, of whom Ockham was the founder, who rejected all general ideas, should also have rejected those moral distinctions which were then supposed to originate in such ideas. Gerson was a celebrated Nominalist; and he was the more disposed to follow the opinions of his master because they agreed in maintaining the independence of the State on the Church, and the superiority of the Church over the Pope.

Note G. page 107.

It must be premised that *Charitas* among the ancient divines corresponded with Ἐρως of the Platonists, and with the *φιλία* of later philosophers, as comprehending the love of all that is loveworthy in the Creator or his creatures. It is the theological virtue of charity, and corresponds with no term in use among modern moralists. "Cum objectum amoris sit bonum, dupliciter potest aliquis tendere in bonum alicujus rei; uno modo, quod bonum *illius rei ad alterum referat*, sicut amat quis vinum in quantum dulcedinem vini peroptat; et hic amor vocatur a quibusdam amor concupiscentiæ. *Amor autem iste non terminatur ad rem quæ dicitur amari, sed reflectitur ad rem illam cui optatur bonum illius rei.* Alio modo amor fortior in bonum alicujus rei, *ita quod ad rem ipsam terminatur;* et hic est amor benevolentiæ. Quâ bonum nostrum in Deo perfectum est, sicut in causâ universali bonorum; ideo bonum in ipso esse magis naturaliter complacet quam in nobis ipsis: et ideo etiam amore amicitiæ naturaliter Deus ab homine plus seipso diligitur." The above quotations from Aquinas will probably be sufficient for those who are acquainted with these questions, and they will certainly be thought too large by those who are not. In the next question he inquires, whether in the love of God there can be any view to reward. He appears to consider himself as bound by authority to answer in the affirmative; and he employs much ingenuity in reconciling a certain expectation of reward with the disinterested character ascribed by him to piety in common with all the affections which terminate in other beings. "*Nihil aliud est merces nostra quam perfrui Deo.* Ergo charitas non solum non excludit, sed etiam facit habere oculum ad mercedem." In this answer he seems to have anticipated the representations of Jeremy Taylor (Sermon on Growth in Grace), of Lord Shaftesbury (Inquiry concerning Virtue, book i. part iii. sect. 3), of Mr. T. Erskine (Freeness of the Gospel, Edin. 1828), and more especially of Mr. John Smith (Discourses, Lond. 1660). No extracts could convey a just conception of the observations which follow, unless they were accompanied by a longer examination of the technical language of the Schoolmen than would be warranted on this occasion. It is clear that he distinguishes well the affection of piety from the happy fruits, which, as he cautiously expresses it, "are in the nature of a reward;"—just as the consideration of the pleasures and advantages of friendship may enter into the affection and strengthen it, though they are not its objects, and never could inspire such a feeling. It seems to me also that he had a dimmer view of another doctrine, by which we are taught, that though our own happiness be not the end which we pursue in loving others, yet it may be the final cause of the insertion of disinterested affections into the nature of man. "Ponere mercedem aliquam finem amoris ex parte amati, est contra rationem amicitiæ. Sed ponere mercedem esse finem amoris ex parte amantis, non tamen ultimam, prout scilicet ipse amor est quædam operatio amantis, non est contra rationem amicitiæ. Possum operationem amoris amare propter aliquid aliud, salvâ amicitiâ. *Potest habeas charitatem habere oculum ad mercedem, uti ponat beatitudinem creatam finem amoris, non autem finem amati.*" Upon the last words my interpretation chiefly depends. The immediately preceding sentence must be owned to have been founded on a distinction between viewing the good fruits of our own affections as enhancing their intrinsic pleasures, and feeling love for another on account of the advantage to be derived from him; which last is inconceivable.

NOTE H. p. 107.

"Potestas spiritualis et secularis utraque deducitur a potestate divinâ; ideo in tantum secularis est sub spirituali, in quantum est a Deo supposita; scilicet, in his quæ ad salutem animæ pertinent. In his autem quæ ad bonum civile spectant, est magis obediendum potestati seculari; sicut illud Matthæi, 'Reddite quæ sunt Cæsaris Cæsari.'" What follows is more doubtful. "... Nisi *forte* potestati spirituali etiam potestas secularis conjungatur, ut in Papa, qui utriusque potestatis apicem tenet."—Op. vol. viii. p. 435. Here, says the French editor, it may be doubted whether Aquinas means the Pope's temporal power in his own dominions, or a secular authority indirectly extending over all for the sake of religion. My reasons for adopting the more rational construction are shortly these:—1. The text of Matthew is so plain an assertion of the independence of both powers, that it would be the height of extravagance to quote it as an *authority* for the dependence of the state. At most it could only be represented as *reconcilable* with such a dependence in one case. 2. The word '*forte*' seems manifestly to refer to the territorial sovereignty acquired by the Popes. If they have a general power in secular affairs, it must be because it is necessary to their spiritual authority; and in that case to call it fortuitous would be to ascribe to it an adjunct destructive of its nature. 3. His former reasoning on the same question seems to be decisive. The power of the Pope over bishops, he says, is not founded merely in his superior nature, but in their authority being altogether derived from his, as the proconsular power from the imperial. Therefore he infers that this case is not analagous to the relation between the civil and spiritual power, which are alike derived from God. 4. Had an Italian monk of the twelfth century really intended to affirm the Pope's temporal authority, he probably would have laid it down in terms more explicit and more acceptable at Rome. Hesitation and ambiguity are here indications of unbelief. Mere veneration for the apostolical See might present a more precise determination against it, as it caused the quotation which follows, respecting the primacy of Peter.—A mere abridgment of these very curious passages might excite a suspicion that I had tinctured Aquinas unconsciously with a colour of my own opinions. Extracts are very difficult, from the scholastic method of stating objections and answers, as well as from the mixture of theological authorities with philosophical reasons.

NOTE I. page 108.

The debates in the first assembly of the Council of Trent (A. D. 1546) between the Dominicans who adhered to Aquinas, and the Franciscans who followed Scotus on Original Sin, Justification, and Grace, are to be found in Fra Paolo (Istoria del Concilio Tridentino, lib. ii.) They show how much metaphysical controversy is hid in a theological form; how many disputes of our times are of no very ancient origin, and how strongly the whole Western Church, through all the divisions into which it has been separated, has manifested the same unwillingness to avow the Augustinian system, and the same fear of contradicting it. To his admirably clear and short statement of these abstruse controversies, must be added that of his accomplished opponent Cardinal Pallavicino (Istoria, &c. lib. vii. et viii.), who shows still more evidently the strength of the Augustinian party, and the disposition of the Council to tolerate opinions almost Lutheran, if not accompanied by revolt from the Church. A little more compromising disposition in the Reformers might have betrayed reason to a prolonged thraldom. We must esteem Erasmus and Melanchthon, but we should reserve our gratitude for Luther and Calvin. The Scotists maintained their doctrine of merit of congruity, waived by the Council, and soon after condemned by the Church of England; by which they meant that they who had good dispositions always received the Divine grace, not indeed as a reward of which they were worthy, but as aid which they were fit and willing to receive. The Franciscans denied that belief was in the power of man. "I Francescani lo negavano seguendo Scoto, qual vuole che siccome dalle dimostrazioni per necessità nasce la scienza, cosdallè persuasioni nasca la fede; e ch' essa è nell' intelletto, il quale è agente naturale, e mosso naturalmente dall' oggetto. Allegavano l' esperienza, che nessuno può credere quello che vuole, ma quello che gli par vero."—Fra. Paolo, Istoria, &c. (Helmstadt, 1763, 4to.), vol. i. p. 193. Cardinal Sforza Pallavicino, a learned and very able Jesuit, was appointed, according to his own account, in 1651, many years after the death of Fra Paolo, to write a true history of the Council of Trent, as a corrective of the misrepresentations of the celebrated Venetian. Algernon Sidney, who knew this court historian at Rome, and who may be believed when he speaks well of a Jesuit and a cardinal, commends the work in a letter to his father, Lord

Leicester. At the end of Pallavicino's work is a list of three hundred and sixty errors in matters of fact, which the Papal party pretended to have detected in the independent historian, whom they charge with heresy or infidelity, and in either case, with hypocrisy.

NOTE K. page 110.

"Hoc tempòre, Ferdinando et Isabella regnantibus, in academiâ Salmantinâ jacta sunt robustioris theologiæ semina; ingentis enim famæ vir Franciscus de Victoria, non tam lucubrationibus editis, quamvis hæc non magnæ molis aut magni pretii sint, sed doctissimorum theologorum educatione, quamdiu fuerit sacræ scientiæ honos inter mortales, vehementer laudabitur."—Antonio, Bibliotheca Hispanica Nova, (Madrid, 1783,) in præf. "Si ad morum instructores respicias, Sotus iterum nominabitur."—*Ibid.*

NOTE L. page 110.

The title of the published account of the conference at Valladolid is, "The controversy between the Bishop of Chiapa and Dr. Sepulveda; in which the Doctor contended that the conquest of the Indies from the natives was lawful, and the Bishop maintained that it was unlawful, tyrannical, and unjust, in the presence of many theologians, lawyers, and other learned men assembled by his Majesty."-Bibl. Hisp. Nova, tom. i. p. 192.

Las Casas died in 1566, in the 92d year of his age; Sepulveda died in 1571, in his 82d year. Sepulveda was the scholar of Pomponatius, and a friend of Erasmus, Cardinal Pole, Aldus Manutius, &c. In his book "De Justis Belli Causis contra Indos suscepti," he contended only that the king ought justly "ad ditionem Indos, non herilem sed regiam et civilem, lege belli redigere." —Antonio, *voce* Sepulveda, Bibl. Hisp. Nova, tom. i. p. 703. But this smooth and specious language concealed poison. Had it entirely prevailed, the cruel consequence of the defeat of the advocate of the oppressed would alone have remained; the limitations and softenings employed by their opponent to obtain success would have been speedily disregarded and forgotten. Covarruvias, another eminent Jurist, was sent by Philip II. to the Council of Trent, at its renewal in 1560, and, with Cardinal Buoncampagni, drew up the decrees of reformation. Francis Sanchez, the father of philosophical grammar, published his Minerva at Salamanca in 1587;—so active was the cultivation of philosophy in Spain in the age of Cervantes.

NOTE M. page 120.

"Alors en repassant dans mon esprit les diverses opinions qui m'avoient tour-à-tour entrainé depuis ma naissance, je vis que bien qu'aucune d'elles ne fût assez évidente pour produire immédiatement la conviction, elles avoient divers degrés de vraisemblance, et que l'assentiment intérieur s'y prétoit ou s'y refusoit à différentes mesures. Sur cette première observation, comparant entr'elles toutes ces différentes idées dans le silence des préjugés, je trouvai que la première, et la plus commune, étoit aussi la plus simple et la plus raisonnable; et qu'il ne lui manquoit, pour réunir tous les suffrages, que d'avoir été proposée la dernière. Imaginez tous vos philosophes anciens et modernes, ayant d'abord épuisé leur bizarres systèmes de forces, de chances, de fatalité, de nécessité, d'atomes, de monde animé, de matière vivante, de matérialisme de toute espèce; et après eux tous l'illustre Clarke, éclairant le monde, annonçant enfin l'Etre des êtres, et le dispensateur des choses. Avec quelle universelle admiration, avec quel applaudissement unanime n'eût point été reçu ce nouveau systême si grand, si consolant, si sublime, si propre à élever l'âme, à donner une base à la vertu, et en même tems si frappant, si lumineux, si simple, et, ce me semble, offrant moins de choses incompréhensibles à l'esprit humain, qu'il n'en trouve d'absurdes en tout autre système! Je me disois, les objections insolubles sont communes à tous, parceque l'esprit de l'homme est trop borné pour les résoudre; elles ne prouvent donc rien contre aucun par préférence: mais quelle différence entre les preuves directes!"—Rousseau. Œuvres, tome ix. p. 25.

NOTE N. page 128.

"Est autem *jus* quædam potentia moralis, et *obligatio* necessitas moralis. *Moralem* autem intelligo, quæ apud virum bonum æquipollet naturali: Nam ut præclarè jurisconsultus Romanus ait, *quæ contra bonos mores sunt, ea nec facere nos posse credendum est. Vir bonus* autem est, qui amat omnes, quantum ratio permittit. *Justitiam* igitur, quæ virtus est hujus affectus rectrix, quem Φιλανθρωπίαν Græci vocant, commodissimè, ni fallor, definiemus caritatem sapientis, hoc est, sequentem sapientiæ dictata. Itaque, quod *Carneades* dixisse fertur, justitiam esse summam stultitiam, quia alienis utilitatibus consuli jubeat, neglectis propriis, ex ignoratâ ejus definitione natum est. *Caritas* est benevolentia universalis, et *benevolentia* amandi sive diligendi habitus. *Amare* autem sive diligere est felicitate alterius delectari, vel, quod eodem redit, felicitatem alienam adsciscere in suam. Unde difficilis nodus solvitur, magni etiam in Theologia momenti, quomodo amor non mercenarius detur, qui sit a spe metuque et omni utilitatis respectu separatus: scilicet, quorum utilitas delectat, eorum felicitas nostram ingreditur; nam quæ delectant, per se expetuntur. Et uti pulchrorum contemplatio ipsa jucunda est, pictaque tabula *Raphaelis* intelligentem afficit, étsi nullos census ferat, adeo ut in oculis deliciisque feratur, quodam simulacro amoris; ita quum res pulchra simul etiam felicitatis est capax, transit affectus in verum amorem. Superat autem *divinus amor* alios amores, quos Deus cum maximo successu amare potest, quando Deo simul et felicius nihil est, et nihil pulchrius felicitateque dignius intelligi potest. Et quum idem sit potentiæ sapientiæque summæ, felicitas ejus non tantum ingreditur nostram (si sapimus, id est, ipsum amamus), sed et facit. Quia autem sapientia caritatem dirigere debet, hujus quoque definitione opus erit. Arbitror autem notioni hominum optimè satisfieri, si *sapientiam* nihil aliud esse dicamus, quam ipsam scientiam felicitatis."—Leibnitii Opera, vol. iv. pars iii. p. 294. "Et jus quidem merum sive strictum nascitur ex principio servandæ pacis; æquitas sive caritas ad majus aliquid contendit, ut, dum quisque alteri prodest, quantum potest, felicitatem suam augeat in aliena; et, ut verbo dicam, jus strictum miseriam vitat, jus superius ad felicitatem tendit, sed qualis in hanc mortalitatem cadit. Quod verò ipsam vitam, et quicquid hanc vitam expetendam facit, magno commodo alieno posthabere debeamus, ita ut maximos etiam dolores in aliorum gratiam perferre oporteat; magis pulchre præcipitur a philosophis quàm solidè demonstratur. Nam decus et gloriam, et animi sui virtute gaudentis sensum, ad quæ sub honestatis nomine provocant, cogitationis sive mentis bona esse constat, magna quidem, sed non omnibus, nec omni malorum acerbitati prævalitura, quando non omnes æquè imaginando afficiuntur; præsertim quos neque educatio liberalis, neque consuetudo vivendi ingenua, vel vitæ sectæve disciplina ad honoris æstimationem, vel animi bona sentienda assuefecit. Ut verò universali demonstrationi conficiatur, omne honestum esse utile, et omne turpe damnosum, assumenda est immortalitas animæ, et rector universi Deus. Ita fit, ut omnes in civitate perfectissima vivere intelligamur, sub monarcha, qui nec ob sapientiam falli, nec ob potentiam vitari potest; idemque tam amabilis est, ut felicitas sit tali domino servire. Huic igitur qui animam impendit, Christo docente, eam lucratur. Hujus potentia providentiaque efficitur, ut omne jus in factum transeat, ut nemo lædatur nisi a se ipso, ut nihil rectè gestum sine præmio sit, nullum peccatum sine pœna."—p. 296.

Note O. page 130.

The writer of this Discourse was led, on a former occasion, by a generally prevalent notion, to confound the theological doctrine of Predestination with the philosophical opinion which supposes the determination of the Will to be, like other events, produced by adequate causes. (See a criticism on Mr. Stewart's Dissertation, Edinb. Review, vol. xxxvi. p. 225.) More careful reflection has corrected a confusion common to him with most writers on the subject. What is called "Sublapsarian Calvinism," which was the doctrine of the most eminent men, including Augustin and Calvin himself, ascribed to God, and to man before the Fall, what is called "free-will," which they even own still to exist in all the ordinary acts of life, though it be lost with respect to religious morality. The decree of election, on this scheme, arises from God's foreknowledge that man was to fall, and that all men became thereby with justice liable to eternal punishment. The election of some to salvation was an act of Divine goodness, and the preterition of the rest was an exercise of holiness and justice. This Sublapsarian predestination is evidently irreconcilable with the doctrine of Necessity, which considers free-will, or volitions not caused by motives, as absolutely inconsistent with the definition of an intelligent being,—which is, that he acts from a motive, or, in other words, with a purpose. The Supralapsarian scheme, which represents the Fall itself as fore-ordained, may indeed be built on necessitarian principles. But on that scheme original sin seems wholly to lose that importance which the former system gives it as a revolution in the state of the world, requiring an interposition of Divine power to remedy a part of its fatal effects. It becomes no more than the first link in the chain of predestined offences. Yet both Catholic and Protestant predestinarians have borrowed the arguments and distinctions of philosophical necessitarians. One of the propositions of Jansenius, condemned by the bull of Innocent X. in 1653, is, that "to merit or demerit in a state of lapsed nature, it is not necessary that there should be in man a liberty free from necessity; it is sufficient that there be a liberty free from constraint."—Dupin, Histoire de l'Eglise en abrégé, livre iv. chap. viii. Luther, in his once famous treatise De Servo Arbitrio against Erasmus (printed in 1526), expresses himself as follows: "Hic est fidei summus gradus, credere illum esse clementem qui tam paucos salvat, tam multos damnat; credere justum qui suâ voluntate nos necessario damnabiles facit, ut videatur, ut Erasmus refert, delectari cruciatibus miserorum, et odio potius quam amore dignus." (My copy of this stern and abusive book is not paged.) In another passage, he states the distinction between co-action and necessity as familiar a hundred and thirty years before it was proposed by Hobbes, or condemned in the Jansenists. "Necessario dico, non coactè, sed, ut illi dicunt, necessitate immutabilitatis, non coactionis; hoc est, homo, cum vocat Spiritus Dei, non quidem violentiâ, velut raptus obtorto collo, nolens facit malum, quemadmodum fur aut latro nolens ad pœnam ducitur, sed sponte et liberâ voluntate facit." He uses also the illustration of Hobbes, from the difference between a stream *forced* out of its course, and *freely* flowing in its channel.

[The following is the whole of the passage in the Edinburgh Review, referred to above: the reader, while bearing in mind the modification of opinion there announced, may still find sufficient interest in the general statement of the argument to justify its admission here.—Ed.]

". . . It would be inexcusable to revive the mention of such a controversy as that which relates to Liberty and Necessity, for any other purpose than to inculcate mutual candour, and to censure the introduction of invidious topics. If there were any hope of terminating that endless and fruitless controversy, the most promising expedient would be a general agreement to banish the technical terms hitherto employed on both sides from philosophy, and to limit ourselves rigorously to a statement of those facts in which all men agree, expressed in language perfectly purified from all tincture of system. The agreement in facts would then probably be found to be much more extensive than is often suspected by either party. Experience is, and indeed must be, equally appealed to by both. All mankind feel and own, that their actions are at least very much affected by their situation, their opinions, their feelings, and their habits; yet no man would deserve the compliment of confutation, who seriously professed to doubt the distinction between right and wrong, the reasonableness of moral approbation and disapprobation, the propriety of praising and censuring voluntary actions, and the justice of rewarding or punishing them according to their intention and tendency. No reasonable person, in whatever terms he may express himself concerning the Will, has ever meant to deny that man has powers and faculties which justify the moral judgments of the human race. Every advocate of Free Will admits the fact of the influence of motives, from which the Necessarian infers the truth of his opinion. Every Necessarian must also admit those attributes of moral and responsible agency, for the sake of which the advocate of Liberty considers his own doctrine as of such unspeakable importance. Both parties ought equally to own, that the matter in dispute is a question of fact relating to the mind, which must be ultimately decided by its own consciousness. The Necessarian is even bound to admit, that no speculation is tenable on this subject, which is not reconcilable to the general opinions of mankind, and which does not afford a satisfactory explanation of that part of common language which at first sight appears to be most at variance with it.

"After the actual antecedents of volition had been thus admitted by one party, and its moral consequences by another, the subject of contention would be reduced to the question,—What is the state of the mind in the interval which passes between motive and action? or, to speak with still more strict propriety, By what words is that state of the mind most accurately described? If this habit of thinking could be steadily and long preserved, so evanescent a subject of dispute might perhaps in the end disappear, and the contending parties might at length discover that they had been only looking at opposite sides of the same truth. But the terms "Liberty" and "Necessity" embroil the controversy, inflame the temper of disputants, and involve them in clouds of angry zeal, which render them incapable not only of perceiving their numerous and important coincidences, but even of clearly discerning the single point in which they differ. Every generous sentiment, and every hostile passion of human nature, have for ages been connected with these two words. They are the badges of the oldest, the widest, and the most obstinate warfare waged by metaphysicians.—Whoever refuses to try the experiment of renouncing them, at least for a time, can neither be a peace-maker nor a friend of dispassionate discussion; and, if he stickles for mere words, he may be justly suspected of being almost aware that he is contending for nothing but words.

"But if projects of perpetual peace should be as Utopian in the schools as in the world, it is the more necessary to condemn the use of weapons which exasperate animosity, without contributing to decide the contest. Of this nature, in our opinion, are the imputations of irreligion and immorality which have for ages been thrown on those divines and philosophers who have espoused Necessarian opinions. Mr. Stewart, though he anxiously acquits individuals of evil intention, has too much lent the weight of his respectable opinion to these useless and inflammatory charges. We are at a loss to conceive how he could imagine that there is the slightest connection between the doctrine of Necessity and the system of Spinoza. That the world is governed by a Supreme Mind, which is invariably influenced by the dictates of its own wisdom and goodness, seems to be the very essence of theism; and no man who substantially dissents from that proposition, can deserve the name of a pure theist. But this is precisely the reverse of the doctrine of Spinoza, which, in spite of all its ingenious disguises, undoubtedly denies the supremacy of mind. This objection, however, has already been answered, not only by the pious and profound Jonathan Edwards (Inquiry, part iv. chap. 7.), an avowed Necessarian, but by Mr. Locke, (whose opinions, however, about this question are not very distinct,) and even by Dr. Clarke himself, the ablest and most celebrated of the advocates of liberty. (Demonstration of the Being and Attributes of God.)

"The charge of immoral tendency, however, deserves more serious consideration, as it has been repeatedly enforced by Mr. Stewart, and brought forward also by Dr. Copplestone.* (Discourses, Lond. 1821),—the only writer of our time who has equally distinguished himself in paths so distant from each other as classical literature, political economy, and metaphysical philosophy. His general candour and temperance give weight to his accusation; and it is likely to be conveyed to posterity by a volume, which is one of the best models of philosophical style that our age has produced,—a Sermon of Archbishop King, republished by Mr. Whately,† an ingenious and learned member of Oriel College. The Sermons of Dr. Copplestone do indeed directly relate to theology; but, in this case, it is impossible to separate that subject from philosophy. Necessity is a philosophical opinion relating to the human will: Predestination is a theological doctrine, concerning the moral government of the world. But since the writings of Leibnitz and Jonathan Edwards, all supporters of Predestination endeavour to show its reasonableness by the arguments of the Necessarian. It is possible, and indeed very common, to hold the doctrines of Necessity, without adopting many of the dogmas which the Calvinist connects with it: but it is not possible to make any argumentative defence of Calvinism, which is not founded on the principle of Necessity. The moral consequences of both (whatever they may be) must be the same; and both opinions are, accordingly, represented by their opponents as tending, in a manner very similar, to weaken the motives to virtuous action.

"There is no topic which requires such strong grounds to justify its admission into controversy, as that of moral consequences; for, besides its incurable tendency to inflame the angry passions, and to excite obloquy against individuals, which renders it a practical restraint on free inquiry, the employment of it in dispute seems to betray apprehensions derogatory from the dignity of Morals, and not consonant either to the dictates of Reason or to the lessons of experience. The rules of Morality are too deeply rooted in human nature, to be shaken by every veering breath of metaphysical theory. Our Moral Sentiments spring from no theory: they are as general as any part of our nature; the causes which generate, or unfold and nourish them, lie deep in the unalterable interests of society, and in those primitive feelings of the human heart which no circumstance can eradicate. The experience of all ages teaches, that these deep-rooted principles are far less affected than is commonly supposed, by the revolutions of philosophical opinion, which scarcely penetrate beyond the surface of human nature. Exceptions there doubtless are: the most speculative opinions are not pretended to be absolutely indifferent in their moral tendency; and it is needless to make an express exception of those opinions which directly relate to practice, and which may have a considerable moral effect. But, in general, the power of the moral feelings, and the feebleness of speculative opinions, are among the most striking phenomena in the history of mankind. What teacher, either philosophical or religious, has ever been successful in spreading his doctrines, who did not reconcile them to our moral sentiments, and even recommend them by pretensions to a purer and more severe morality? Wherever there is a seeming, or a real repugnance between speculative opinions and moral rules, the speculator has always been compelled to devise some compromise which, with whatever sacrifice of consistency, may appease the alarmed conscience of mankind. The favour of a few is too often earned by flattering their vicious passions; but no immoral system ever acquired popularity. Wherever there is a contest, the speculations yield, and the principles prevail. The victory is equally decisive, whether the obnoxious doctrine be renounced, or so modified as no longer to dispute the legitimate authority of Conscience.

"Nature has provided other guards for Virtue against the revolt of sophistry and the inconstancy of opinion. The whole system of morality is of great extent, and comprehends a variety of principles and sentiments,—of duties and virtues. Wherever new and singular speculation has been at first sight thought to weaken some of the motives of moral activity, it has almost uniformly been found, by longer experience, that the same speculation itself makes amends, by strengthening other inducements to right conduct. There is thus a principle of compensation in the opinions, as in the circumstances of man; which, though not sufficient to level distinction and to exclude preference, has yet such power, that it ought to appease our alarms, and to soften our controversies. A moral nature assimilates every speculation which it does not reject. If these general reasonings be just, with what increased force do they prove the innocence of error, in a case where, as there seems to be no possibility of difference about facts, the mistake of either party must be little more than verbal!

"We have much more ample experience respecting the practical tendency of religious than of philosophical opinions. The latter were formerly confined to the schools, and are still limited to persons of some education. They are generally kept apart from our passions and our business, and are entertained, as Cicero said of the Stoical paradoxes, "more as a subject of dispute than as a rule of life." Religious opinions, on the contrary, are spread over ages and nations; they are felt perhaps most strongly by the more numerous classes of mankind; wherever they are sincerely entertained, they must be regarded as the most serious of all concerns; they are often incorporated with the warmest passions of which the human heart is capable; and, in this state, from their eminently social and sympathetic nature,

* Afterwards Bishop of Llandaff.—Ed.

† Afterwards Archbishop of Dublin.—Ed.

they are capable of becoming the ruling principle of action in vast multitudes. Let us therefore appeal to experience, on the moral influence of Necessarian opinions in their theological form. By doing so, we shall have an opportunity of contemplating the principle in its most active state, operating upon the greatest masses, and for the longest time. Predestination, or doctrines much inclining towards it, have, on the whole, prevailed in the Christian churches of the West since the days of Augustine and Aquinas. Who were the first formidable opponents of these doctrines in the Church of Rome? The Jesuits—the contrivers of courtly casuistry, and the founders of lax morality. Who, in the same Church, inclined to the stern theology of Augustine? The Jansenists—the teachers and the models of austere morals. What are we to think of the morality of Calvinistic nations, especially of the most numerous classes of them, who seem, beyond all other men, to be most zealously attached to their religion, and most deeply penetrated with its spirit? Here, if any where, we have a practical and a decisive test of the moral influence of a belief in Necessarian opinions. In Protestant Switzerland, in Holland, in Scotland, among the English Nonconformists, and the Protestants of the north of Ireland, in the New England States, Calvinism long was the prevalent faith, and is probably still the faith of a considerable majority. Their moral education was at least completed, and their collective character formed, during the prevalence of Calvinistic opinions. Yet where are communities to be found of a more pure and active virtue? Perhaps these, and other very striking facts, might justify speculations of a somewhat singular nature, and even authorize a retort upon our respectable antagonists. But we have no such purpose. It is sufficient for us to do what in us lies to mitigate the acrimony of controversy, to teach disputants on both sides to respect the sacred neutrality of Morals, and to show that the provident and parental care of Nature has sufficiently provided for the permanent security of the principles of Virtue.

"If we were to amuse ourselves in remarks on the practical tendency of opinions, we might with some plausibility contend, that there was a tendency in infidelity to produce Toryism. In England alone, we might appeal to the examples of Hobbes, Bolingbroke, Hume, and Gibbon; and to the opposite cases of Milton, Locke, Addison, Clarke, and even Newton himself; for the last of these great men was also a Whig. The only remarkable example which now occurs to us of a zealous believer who was a bigoted Tory, is that of Dr. Johnson; and we may balance against him the whole, or the greater part of the life of his illustrious friend, Mr. Burke. We would not, however, rest much on observations founded on so small an experience, that the facts may arise from causes wholly independent of the opinion. But another unnoticed coincidence may serve as an introduction to a few observations on the scepticism of the eighteenth century.

"The three most celebrated sceptics of modern times have been zealous partisans of high authority in government. It would be rash to infer, from the remarkable examples of this coincidence, in Montaigne, Bayle, and Hume, that there is a natural connection between scepticism and Toryism; or, even, if there were a tendency to such a connection, that it might not be counteracted by more powerful circumstances, or by stronger principles of human nature. It is more worth while, therefore, to consider the particulars in the history of these three eminent persons, which may have strengthened or created this propensity.

"Montaigne, who was methodical in nothing, does not indeed profess systematic scepticism. He was a freethinker who loosened the ground about received opinions, and indulged his humour in arguing on both sides of most questions. But the sceptical tendency of his writings is evident; and there is perhaps nowhere to be found a more vigorous attack on popular innovations, than in the latter part of the 22d Essay of his first book. But there is no need of any general speculations to account for the repugnance to change, felt by a man who was wearied and exasperated by the horrors of forty years' civil war.

"The case of Bayle is more remarkable. Though banished from France as a Protestant, he published, without his name, a tract, entitled, "Advice to the Refugees," in the year 1690, which could be considered in no other light than that of an apology for Louis XIV., an attack on the Protestant cause, and a severe invective against his companions in exile. He declares, in this unavowed work, for absolute power and passive obedience, and inveighs, with an intemperance scarcely ever found in his avowed writings, against "the execrable doctrines of Buchanan," and the "pretended sovereignty of the people," without sparing even the just and glorious Revolution, which had at that moment preserved the constitution of England, the Protestant religion, and the independence of Europe. It is no wonder therefore, that he was considered as a partisan of France, and a traitor to the Protestant cause; nor can we much blame King William for regarding him as an object of jealous policy. Many years after, he was represented to Lord Sunderland as an enemy of the Allies, and a detractor of their great captain, the Duke of Marlborough. The generous friendship of the illustrious author of the Characteristics,—the opponent of Bayle on almost every question of philosophy, government, and, we may add, religion,—preserved him, on that occasion, from the sad necessity of seeking a new place of refuge in the very year of his death. The vexations which Bayle underwent in Holland from the Calvinist ministers, and his long warfare against their leader Jurieu, who was a zealous assertor of popular opinions, may have given this bias to his mind, and disposed him to "fly from petty tyrants to the throne." His love of paradox may have had its share; for passive obedience was considered as a most obnoxious paradox in the schools and societies of the oppressed Calvinists. His enemies, however, did not fail to impute his conduct to a design of paying his court to Louis XIV., and to the hope of being received with open arms in France;—motives which seem to be at variance both with the general integrity of his life, and with his favourite passion for the free indulgence of philosophical speculation. The scepticism of Bayle must, however, be distinguished from that of Hume. The former of these celebrated writers examined many questions in succession, and laboured to show that doubt was, on all of them, the result of examination. His, therefore, is a sort of inductive scepticism, in which general doubt was an inference from numerous examples of uncertainty in particular cases. It is a kind of appeal to experience, whether so many failures in the search of truth ought not to deter wise men from continuing the pursuit. Content with proving, or seeming to himself to prove, that we have not attained certainty, he does not attempt to prove that we *cannot* reach it.

"The doctrine of Mr. Hume, on the other hand, is not that we have not reached truth, but that we never can reach it. It is an absolute and universal system of scepticism, professing to be derived from the very structure of the Understanding, which, if any man could seriously believe it, would render it impossible for him to form an opinion upon any subject,—to give the faintest assent to any proposition,—to ascribe any meaning to the words 'truth' and 'falsehood,'—to believe, to inquire, or to reason, and, on the very same ground, to disbelieve, to dissent, or to doubt,—to adhere to his own principle of universal doubt, and lastly, if he be consistent with himself, even to *think*. It is not easy to believe that speculations so shadowy, which never can pretend to be more than the amusements of idle ingenuity, should have any influence on the opinions of men of great understanding, concerning the most important concerns of human life. But perhaps it may be reasonable to allow, that the same character which disposes men to scepticism, may dispose them also to acquiesce in considerable abuses, and even oppressions, rather than to seek redress in forcible resistance. Men of such a character have misgivings in every enterprise; their acuteness is exercised in devising objections,—in discovering difficulties,—in foreseeing obstacles; they hope little from human wisdom and virtue, and are rather secretly prone to that indolence and indifference which forbade the Epicurean sage to hazard his quiet for the doubtful interests of a contemptible race. They do not lend a credulous ear to the Utopian projector; they doubt whether the evils of change will be so little, or the benefits of reform so great, as the sanguine reformer foretells that they will be. The sceptical temper of Mr. Hume may have thus insensibly moulded his political opinions. But causes still more obvious and powerful had probably much more share in rendering him so zealous a partisan of regal power. In his youth, the Presbyterians, to whose enmity his opinions exposed him, were the zealous and only friends of civil liberty in Scotland; and the close connection of liberty with Calvinism, made both more odious to him. The gentry in most parts of Scotland, except in the west, were then Jacobites; and his early education was probably among that party. The prejudices which he perhaps imbibed in France against the literature of England, extended to her institutions; and in the state of English opinion, when his history was published, if he sought distinction by paradox, he could not so effectually have obtained his object by the most startling of his metaphysical dogmas, as by his doubts of the genius of Shakespeare, and the virtue of Hampden."

Note P. page 139.

Though some parts of the substance of the following letter have already appeared in various forms, perhaps the account of Mr. Hume's illness, in the words of his friend and physician Dr. Cullen, will be acceptable to many readers. I owe it to the kindness of Mrs. Baillie, who had the goodness to copy it from the original, in the collection of her late learned and excellent husband, Dr. Baillie. Some portion of what has been formerly published I do not think it necessary to reprint.

From Dr. Cullen to Dr. Hunter.

"My Dear Friend,—I was favoured with yours by Mr. Halket on Sunday, and have answered some part of it by a gentleman whom I was otherwise obliged to write by; but as I was not certain how soon that might come to your hand, I did not answer your postscript; in doing which, if I can oblige you, a part of the merit must be that of the information being early, and I therefore give it you as soon as I possibly could. You desire an account of Mr. Hume's last days, and I give it you with some pleasure; for though I could not look upon him in his illness without much concern, yet the tranquillity and pleasantry which he constantly discovered did even then give me satisfaction, and, now that the curtain is dropped, allows me to indulge the less allayed reflection. He was truly an example *des grands hommes qui sont morts en plaisantant*. . . . For many weeks before his death he was very sensible of his gradual decay; and his answer to inquiries after his health was, several times, that he was going as fast as his enemies could wish, and as easily as his friends could desire. He was not, however, without a frequent recurrence of pain and uneasiness; but he passed most part of the day in his drawing-room, admitted the visits of his friends, and, with his usual spirit, conversed with them upon literature, politics, or whatever else was accidentally started. In conversation he seemed to be perfectly at ease, and to the last abounded with that pleasantry, and those curious and entertaining anecdotes, which ever distinguished him. This, however, I always considered rather as an effort to be agreeable; and he at length acknowledged that it became too much for his strength. For a few days before his death, he became more averse to receive visits; speaking became more and more difficult for him, and for twelve hours before his death his speech failed altogether. His senses and judgment did not fail till the last hour of his life. He constantly discovered a strong sensibility to the attention and care of his friends; and, amidst great uneasiness and langour, never betrayed any peevishness or impatience. This is a general account of his last days; but a particular fact or two may perhaps convey to you a still better idea of them.

* * * *

"About a fortnight before his death, he added a codicil to his will, in which he fully discovered his attention to his friends, as well as his own pleasantry. What little wine he himself drank was generally port, a wine for which his friend the poet [John Home] had ever declared the strongest aversion. David bequeaths to his friend John one bottle of port; and, upon condition of his drinking this even at two down-sittings, bestows upon him twelve dozen of his best claret. He pleasantly adds, that this subject of wine was the only one upon which they had ever differed. In the codicil there are several other strokes of raillery and pleasantry, highly expressive of the cheerfulness which he then enjoyed. He even turned his attention to some of the simple amusements with which he had been formerly pleased. In the neighbourhood of his brother's house in Berwickshire is a brook, by which the access in time of floods is frequently interrupted. Mr. Hume bequeaths 100*l*. for building a bridge over this brook, but upon the express condition that none of the stones for that purpose shall be taken from a quarry in the neighbourhood, which forms part of a romantic scene in which, in his earlier days, Mr. Hume took particular delight:—otherwise the money to go to the poor of the parish.

"These are a few particulars which may perhaps appear trifling; but to me no particulars seem trifling that relate to so great a man. It is perhaps from trifles that we can best distinguish the tranquillity and cheerfulness of the philosopher, at a time when the most part of mankind are under disquiet, anxiety, and sometimes even horror. . . . I had gone so far when I was called to the country; and I have returned only so long before the post as to say, that I am most affectionately yours,

"William Cullen.

"*Edinburgh, 17th September*, 1776."

Note Q. page 139.

Pyrrho was charged with carrying his scepticism so far as not to avoid a carriage if it was driven against him. Ænesidemus, the most famous of ancient sceptics, with great probability vindicates the more ancient doubter from such lunacy, of which indeed his having lived to the age of ninety seems sufficient to acquit him. Αἰνεσίδημος δέ φησι φιλοσοφεῖν μὲν αὐτὸν κατὰ τὸν τῆς ἐποχῆς λόγον, μὴ μέντοι γε ἀπροοράτως ἕκαστα πράττειν.—

Diogenes Laertius, lib. ix. sect. 62. Brief and imperfect as our accounts of ancient scepticism are, it does appear that their reasoning on the subject of causation had some resemblance to that of Mr. Hume. Ἀναιροῦσι δὲ τὸ αἴτιον ὧδε· τὸ αἴτιον τῶν πρός τί ἐστι, πρὸς γὰρ τῷ αἰτιατῷ ἐστι· τὰ δὲ πρός τι ἐπινοεῖται μόνον ὑπάρχει δὲ οὔ· καὶ τὸ αἴτιον οὖν ἐπινοοῖτο ἂν μόνον.—Ibid. sec. 97. It is perhaps impossible to translate the important technical expression τὰ πρός τι. It comprehends two or more things as related to each other; both the relative and correlative being taken together as such. Fire considered as having the power of burning wood is τὸ πρός τι. The words of Laertius may therefore be nearly rendered into the language of modern philosophy as follows: "Causation they take away thus:—A cause is so only in relation to an effect. What is relative is only conceived, but does not exist. Therefore cause is a mere conception." The first attempt to prove the necessity of belief in a Divine revelation, by demonstrating that natural reason leads to universal scepticism, was made by Algazel, a professor at Bagdad, in the beginning of the twelfth century of our era; whose work entitled the "Destruction of the Philosopher" is known to us only by the answer of Averroes, called "Destruction of the Destruction." He denied a necessary connection between cause and effect; for of two separate things, the affirmation of the existence of one does not necessarily contain the affirmation of the existence of the other; and the same may be said of denial. It is curious enough that this argument was more especially pointed against those Arabian philosophers who, from the necessary connection of causes and effects, reasoned against the possibility of miracles;—thus anticipating one doctrine of Mr. Hume, to impugn another.—Tennemann, Geschichte der Philosophie, vol. viii. p. 387. The same attempt was made by the learned but unphilosophical Huet, bishop of Avranches.—(Quæstiones Alnetanæ, Caen, 1690, and Traité de la Foiblesse de l'Esprit Humain, Amsterdam, 1723.) A similar motive urged Berkeley to his attack on Fluxions. The attempt of Huet has been lately renewed by the Abbé Lamennais, in his treatise on Religious Indifference;—a fine writer whose apparent reasonings amount to little more than well-varied assertions, and well-disguised assumptions of the points to be proved. To build religion upon scepticism is the most extravagant of all attempts; for it destroys the proofs of a divine mission, and leaves no natural means of distinguishing between revelation and imposture. The Abbé Lamennais represents authority as the sole ground of belief. Why? If any reason can be given, the proposition must be false; if none, it is obviously a mere groundless assertion.

Note R. page 142.

Casanova, a Venetian doomed to solitary imprisonment in the dungeons at Venice in 1755, thus speaks of the only books which for a time he was allowed to read. The title of the first was "La Cité Mystique de Sœur Marie de Jesus, appellée d'Agrada." "J'y lus tout ce que peut enfanter l'imagination exaltée d'une vierge Espagnole extravagamment dévote, cloitrée, mélancholique, ayant des directeurs de conscience, ignorans, faux, et dévots. Amoureuse et amie très intime de la Sainte Vierge, elle avait reçu ordre de Dieu même d'écrire la vie de sa divine mère. Les instructions nécessaires lui avaient été fournies par le Saint Esprit. Elle commençoit la vie de Marie, non pas du jour de sa naissance, mais du moment de son immaculée conception dans le sein de sa mère Anne. Après avoir narré en détail tout ce que sa divine héroïne fit les neuf mois qu'elle a passé dans le sein maternel, elle nous apprend qu'à l'âge de trois ans elle balayoit la maison, aidée par neuf cents domestiques, tous anges, commandés par leur propre Prince Michel. Ce qui frappe dans ce livre est l'assurance que tout est dit de bonne foi. Ce sont les visions d'un esprit sublime, qui, sans aucune ombre d'orgueil, ivre de Dieu, croit ne révéler que ce que l'Esprit Saint lui inspire."—Mémoires de Casanova (Leipsic, 1827), vol. iv. p. 343. A week's confinement to this volume produced such an effect on Casanova, an unbeliever and a debauchee, but who was then enfeebled by melancholy, bad air, and bad food, that his sleep was haunted, and his waking hours disturbed by its horrible visions. Many years after, passing through Agrada in Old Castile, he charmed the old priest of that village by speaking of the biographer of the virgin. The priest showed him all the spots which were consecrated by her presence, and bitterly lamented that the Court of Rome had refused to canonize her. It is the natural reflection of Casanova that the book was well qualified to turn a solitary prisoner mad, or to make a man at large an atheist. It ought not to be forgotten, that the inquisitors of state at Venice, who proscribed this book, were probably of the latter persuasion. It is a striking instance of the infatuation of those who, in their eagerness to rivet the bigotry of the ignorant, use means which infallibly tend to spread utter unbelief among the educated. The book is a disgusting, but in its general outline seemingly faithful, picture of the dissolute manners spread over the Continent of Europe in the middle of the eighteenth century.

Note S. page 143.

"The Treatise on the Law of War and Peace, the Essay on Human Understanding, the Spirit of Laws, and the Inquiry into the Causes of the Wealth of Nations, are the works which have most directly influenced the general opinion of Europe during the two last centuries. They are also the most conspicuous landmarks in the progress of the sciences to which they relate. It is remarkable that the defects of all these great works are very similar. The leading notions of none of them can, in the strictest sense, be said to be original, though Locke and Smith in that respect surpass their illustrious rivals. All of them employ great care in ascertaining those laws which are immediately deduced from experience, or directly applicable to practice; but apply metaphysical and abstract principles with considerable negligence. Not one pursues the order of science, beginning with first elements, and advancing to more and more complicated conclusions; though Locke is perhaps less defective in method than the rest. All admit digressions which, though often intrinsically excellent, distract attention and break the chain of thought. Not one of them is happy in the choice, or constant in the use, of technical terms; and in none do we find much of that rigorous precision which is the first beauty of philosophical language. Grotius and Montesquieu were imitators of Tacitus,—the first with more gravity, the second with more vivacity; but both were tempted to forsake the simple diction of science, in pursuit of the poignant brevity which that great historian has carried to a vicious excess. Locke and Smith chose an easy, clear, and free, but somewhat loose and verbose style,—more concise in Locke,—more elegant in Smith,—in both exempt from pedantry, but not void of ambiguity and repetition. Perhaps all these apparent defects contributed in some degree to the specific usefulness of these great works; and, by rendering their contents more accessible and acceptable to the majority of readers, have more completely blended their principles with the common opinions of mankind."—Edinburgh Review, vol. xxxvi. p. 244. [This is a further extract from the article alluded to at p. 192. -Ed.]

Notes T—U. p. 147.

Δεῖ δ' οὕτως, ὥσπερ ἐν γραμματείῳ ᾧ μηδὲν ὑπάρχει ἐντελεχείᾳ γεγραμμένον· ὅσπερ συμβαίνει ἐπὶ τοῦ νοῦ.—Aristotle. "De Animâ," Opera, (Paris, 1639) tome ii. p. 50. A little before, in the same treatise, appears a great part of the substance of the famous maxim, *Nil est in intellectu quod non prius fuit in sensu.* Ἡδὲ φαντασία κίνησίς τις δόκει εἶναι, καὶ οὐκ ἄνευ αἰσθήσεως γίγνεσθαι.—Ibid. p. 47. In the tract on Memory and Reminiscence we find his enumeration of the principles of association. Διὰ καὶ τὸ ἐφεξῆς θηρεύομεν, νοησοῦντες ἀπὸ τοῦ νῦν ἢ ἄλλου τινὸς, καὶ ἀφ' ὁμοίου ἢ ἐναντίου, ἢ τοῦ σύνεγγυς.—Ibid. p. 86. If the latter word be applied to time as well as space, and considered as comprehending causation, the enumeration will coincide with that of Hume. The term θηρεύω is as significant as if it had been chosen by Hobbes. But it is to be observed, that these principles are applied only to explain memory.

Something has been said on the subject, and something on the present writer, by Mr. Coleridge, in his unfortunately unfinished work called "Biographia Literaria," chap. v., which seems to justify, if not to require, a few remarks. That learned gentleman seems to have been guilty of an oversight in quoting as a distinct work the "Parva Naturalia," which is the collective name given by the scholastic translators to those treatises of Aristotle which form the second volume of Duval's edition of his works, published at Paris in 1639. I have already acknowledged the striking resemblance of Mr. Hume's principles of association to those of Aristotle. In answer, however, to a remark of Mr. Coleridge, I must add, that the manuscript of a part of the Aquinas which I bought many years ago (on the faith of a bookseller's catalogue) as being written by Mr. Hume, was not a copy of the Commentary on the "Parva Naturalia," but of Aquinas' own "Secunda Secundæ;" and that, on examination, it proves not to be the handwriting of Mr. Hume, and to contain nothing written by him. It is certain that, in the passages immediately preceding the quotation, Aristotle explains recollection as depending on a general law,—that the idea of an object will remind us of the objects which immediately preceded or followed when originally perceived. But what Mr. Coleridge has not told us is, that the Stagyrite confines the application of this law *exclusively to the phenomena of recollection alone*, without any glimpse of a more general operation extending to all connections of thought and feeling,—a wonderful proof, indeed, even so limited, of the sagacity of the great philosopher, but which for many ages continued barren of further consequences. The illustrations of Aquinas throw light on the original doctrine, and show that it was unenlarged in his time. "When we recollect Socrates, the thought of Plato occurs 'as like him.' When we remember Hector, the thought of Achilles occurs 'as contrary.' The idea of a father is followed by that of a son 'as near.'"—Opera, vol. i. pars ii. p. 62. *et seq.* Those of Ludovicus Vives, as quoted by Mr. Coleridge, extend no farther. But if Mr. Coleridge will compare the parts of Hobbes on Human Nature which relate to this subject, with those which explain general terms, he will perceive that the philosopher of Malmesbury builds on these two foundations a general theory of the human understanding, of which reasoning is only a particular case. In consequence of the assertion of Mr. Coleridge, that Hobbes was anticipated by Descartes in his excellent and interesting discourse on Method, I have twice reperused the latter's work in quest of this remarkable anticipation, though, as I thought, well acquainted by my old studies with the writings of that great philosopher. My labour has, however, been vain: I have discovered no trace of that or of any similar speculation. My edition is in Latin by Elzevir, at Amsterdam, in 1650, the year of Descartes' death. I am obliged, therefore, to conjecture, that Mr. Coleridge, having mislaid his references, has, by mistake, quoted the discourse on Method, instead of another work; which would affect his inference from the priority of Descartes to Hobbes. It is not to be denied, that the opinion of Aristotle, repeated by so many commentators, may have found its way into the mind of Hobbes, and also of Hume; though neither might be aware of its source, or even conscious that it was not originally his own. Yet the very narrow view of Association taken by Locke, his apparently treating it as a novelty, and the silence of common books respecting it, afford a presumption that the Peripatetic doctrine was so little known, that it might have escaped the notice of these philosophers;—one of whom boasted that he was unread, while the other is not liable to the suspicion of unacknowledged borrowing.

To Mr. Coleridge, who distrusts his own power of building a bridge by which his ideas may pass into a mind so differently trained as mine, I venture to suggest, with that sense of his genius which no circumstance has hindered me from seizing every fit occasion to manifest, that more of my early years were employed in contemplations of an abstract nature, than of those of the majority of his readers,—that there are not, even now, many of them less likely to be repelled from doctrines by singularity or uncouthness; or many more willing to allow that every system has caught an advantageous glimpse of some side or corner of the truth; or many more desirous of exhibiting this dispersion of the fragments of wisdom by attempts to translate the doctrine of one school into the language of another; or many who when they cannot discover a reason for an opinion, consider it more important to discover the causes of its adoption by the philosopher;—believing, as I do, that one of the most arduous and useful offices of mental philosophy is to explore the subtile illusions which enable great minds to satisfy themselves by mere words, before they deceive others by payment in the same counterfeit coin. My habits, together with the natural influence of my age and avocations, lead me to suspect that in speculative philosophy I am nearer to indifference than to an exclusive spirit. I hope that it can neither be thought presumptuous nor offensive in me to doubt, whether the circumstance of its being found difficult to convey a metaphysical doctrine to a person who, at one part of his life, made such studies his chief pursuit, may not imply either error in the opinion, or defect in the mode of communication.

Note V. page 159.

A very late writer, who seems to speak for Mr. Bentham with authority, tells us that "the first time the phrase of 'the principle of utility' was brought decidedly into notice, was in the 'Essays,' by David Hume, published about the year 1742. In that work it is *mentioned* as the *name* of a principle which *might* be made the foundation of a system of morals, in *opposition to a system then in vogue, which was founded on what was called the 'moral sense.'* The ideas, however, there attached to it, are *vague*, and *defective in practical application.*"—Westminster Review, vol. xi. p. 258. If these few sentences were scrutinised with the severity and minuteness of Bentham's Fragment on Government, they would be found to contain almost as many misremembrances as assertions. The principle of Utility is not "*mentioned,*" but fully discussed, in Mr. Hume's discourse. It is seldom spoken of by "*name.*" Instead of charging the statements of it with "*vagueness*," it would be more just to admire the precision which it combines with beauty. Instead of being "*defective in practical application*," perhaps the desire of rendering it popular has crowded it with examples and illustrations taken from life. To the assertion that "*it was opposed to the moral sense*," no reply can be needful but the following words extracted from the discourse itself: "I am apt to suspect that reason and *sentiment* concur in almost all moral determinations and conclusions. *The final sentence which pronounces characters and actions amiable or odious, probably depends on some internal sense or feeling, which nature has made universal in the whole species.*"—Inquiry concerning the Principles of Morals, sect. i. The phrase "made universal," which is here used instead of the more obvious and common word "implanted," shows the anxious and perfect precision of language, by which a philosopher avoids the needless decision of a controversy not at the moment before him.

[Dr. Whewell puts the case against the present *mis*-denomination assumed by the disciples of Mr. Bentham thus neatly:—"If the word from which Deontology is derived had borrowed its meaning from the notion of utility alone, it is not likely that it would have become more intelligible by being translated out of Latin into Greek. But the term 'Deontology' expresses moral science (and expresses it well), precisely because it signifies *the science of duty*, and contains no reference to Utility. Mackintosh, who held that τὸ δέον,—what men *ought* to do—was the fundamental notion of morality, might very probably have termed the science "Deontology." The system of which Mr. Bentham is the representative,—that of those who make morality dependent on the production of happiness,—has long been designated in Germany by the term '*Eudemonism*,' derived from the Greek word for happiness (εὐδαιμονία). If we were to adopt this term we should have to oppose the Deontological to the Eudemonist school; and we must necessarily place those who hold a peculiar moral faculty,—Butler, Stewart, Brown, and Mackintosh,—in the former, and those who are usually called Utilitarian philosophers in the latter class."—Preface to this Dissertation, 8vo, Edinburg, 1837. Ed.]

Note W. page 160.

A writer of consummate ability, who has failed in little but the respect due to the abilities and character of his opponents, has given too much countenance to the abuse and confusion of language exemplified in the well-known verse of Pope,

> Modes of self-love the Passions we may call.

"We know," says he, "no universal proposition respecting human nature which is true but one,—that men always act from self-interest."—Edinburgh Review, vol. xlix. p. 185. It is manifest from the sequel, that the writer is not the dupe of the confusion; but many of his readers may be so. If, indeed, the word 'self-interest' could with propriety be used for the gratification of every prevalent desire, he has clearly shown that this change in the signification of terms would be of no advantage to the doctrine which he controverts. It would make as many sorts of self-interest as there are appetites, and it is irreconcilably at variance with the system of association embraced by Mr. Mill. To the word 'self-love' Hartley properly assigns two significations: — 1. gross self-love, which consists in the pursuit of the greatest pleasures, from all those desires which look to individual gratification; or, 2. refined self-love, which seeks the greatest pleasure which can arise from all the desires of human nature,—the latter of which is an invaluable, though inferior principle. The admirable writer whose language has occasioned this illustration,—who at an early age has mastered every species of composition, — will doubtless hold fast to simplicity, which survives all the fashions of deviation from it, and which a man of a genius so fertile has few temptations to forsake.

AN ACCOUNT

OF

THE PARTITION OF POLAND.*

Little more than fifty years have passed since Poland occupied a high place among the Powers of Europe. Her natural means of wealth and force were inferior to those of few states of the second order. The surface of the country exceeded that of France; and the number of its inhabitants was estimated at fourteen millions,—a population probably exceeding that of the British Islands, or of the Spanish Peninsula, at that time. The climate was nowhere unfriendly to health, or unfavourable to labour; the soil was fertile, the produce redundant: a large portion of the country, still uncleared, afforded ample scope for agricultural enterprise. Great rivers afforded easy means of opening an internal navigation from the Baltic to the Mediterranean. In addition to these natural advantages, there were many of those circumstances in the history and situation of Poland which render a people fond and proud of their country, and foster that national spirit which is the most effectual instrument either of defence or aggrandisement. Till the middle of the seventeenth century, she had been the predominating power of the North. With Hungary, and the maritime

* From the Edinburgh Review, vol. xxxvii., p. 463.

strength of Venice, she had formed the eastern defence of Christendom against the Turkish tyrants of Greece; and, on the north-east, she had been long its sole barrier against the more obscure barbarians of Muscovy. A nation which thus constituted a part of the vanguard of civilization, necessarily became martial, and gained all the renown in arms which could be acquired before war had become a science. The wars of the Poles, irregular, romantic, full of personal adventure, depending on individual courage and peculiar character, proceeding little from the policy of Cabinets, but deeply imbued by those sentiments of chivalry which may pervade a nation, chequered by extraordinary vicissitudes, and carried on against barbarous enemies in remote and wild provinces, were calculated to leave a deep impression on the feelings of the people, and to give every man the liveliest interest in the glories and dangers of his country. Whatever renders the members of a community more like each other, and unlike their neighbours, usually strengthens the bonds of attachment between them. The Poles were the only representatives of the Sarmatian race in the assembly of civilized nations. Their language and their national literature—those great sources of sympathy and objects of national pride—were cultivated with no small success. They contributed, in one instance, signally to the progress of science; and they took no ignoble part in those classical studies which composed the common literature of Europe. They were bound to their country by the peculiarities of its institutions and usages,—perhaps, also, by those dangerous privileges, and by that tumultuary independence which rendered their condition as much above that of the slaves of an absolute monarchy, as it was below the lot of those who inherit the blessings of legal and moral freedom. They had once another singularity, of which they might justly have been proud, if they had not abandoned it in times which ought to have been more enlightened. Soon after the Reformation, they had set the first example of that true religious liberty which equally admits the members of all sects to the privileges, the offices, and dignities of the commonwealth. For nearly a century they had afforded a secure asylum to those obnoxious sects of Anabaptists and Unitarians, whom all other states excluded from toleration; and the Hebrew nation, proscribed every where else, found a second country, with protection for their learned and religious establishments, in this hospitable and tolerant land. A body, amounting to about half a million, professing the equality of gentlemen amidst the utmost extremes of affluence and poverty, forming at once the legislature and the army, or rather constituting the commonwealth, were reproached, perhaps justly, with the parade, dissipation, and levity, which generally characterise the masters of slaves: but their faculties were roused by ambition; they felt the dignity of conscious independence; and they joined to the brilliant valour of their ancestors, an uncommon proportion of the accomplishments and manners of a polished age. Even in the days of her decline, Poland had still a part allotted to her in the European system. By her mere situation, without any activity on her own part, she in some measure prevented the collision, and preserved the balance, of the three greatest military powers of the Continent. She constituted an essential member of the federative system of France; and, by her vicinity to Turkey, and influence on the commerce of the Baltic, directly affected the general interest of Europe. Her preservation was one of the few parts of continental policy in which both France and England were concerned; and all Governments dreaded the aggrandisement of her neighbours. In these circumstances, it might have been thought that the dismemberment of the territory of a numerous, brave, ancient, and renowned people, passionately devoted to their native land, without colour of right or pretext of defence, in a period of profound peace, in defiance of the law of nations, and of the common interest of all states, was an event not much more probable, than that it should have been swallowed up by a convulsion of nature. Before that dismemberment, nations, though exposed to the evils of war and the chance of conquest, in peace placed some reliance on each other's faith. The crime has, however, been triumphantly consummated. The principle of the balance of power has perished in the Partition of Poland.

The succession to the crown of Poland appears, in ancient times, to have been governed by that rude combination of inheritance and election which originally prevailed in most European monarchies, where there was a general inclination to respect hereditary claims, and even the occasional elections were confined to the members of the reigning family. Had not the male heirs of the House of Jagellon been extinct, or had the rule of female succession been introduced, it is probable that the Polish monarchy would have become strictly hereditary. The inconveniences of the elective principle were chiefly felt in the admission of powerful foreign princes as candidates for the crown: but that form of government proved rather injurious to the independence, than to the internal peace of the country. More than a century, indeed, elapsed before the mischief was felt. In spite of the ascendant acquired by Sweden in the affairs of the North, Poland still maintained her high rank. Her last great exertion, when John Sobieski, in 1683, drove the Turks from the gates of Vienna, was worthy of her ancient character as the guardian of Christendom.

His death, in 1696, first showed that the admission of such competition might lead to the introduction of foreign influence, and even arms. The contest which then occurred between the Prince of Conti and Augustus, Elector of Saxony, had been decided in favour of the latter by his own army, and by Russian influence, when Charles XII., before he had reached the age of twenty, having already compelled Denmark to submit, and defeated a great Russian army, entered Warsaw in triumph, deposed him as an usurper raised to the royal dignity by foreign force, and obliged him, by express treaty, to renounce his pretensions to the crown. Charles was doubtless impelled to these measures by the insolence of a youthful conqueror, and by resentment against the Elector; but he was also influenced by those rude conceptions of justice, sometimes degenerating into cruelty, which were blended with his irregular ambition. He had the generosity, however, to spare the territory of the republic, and the good sense to propose the son of the great Sobieski to fill the vacant throne;—a proposal which, had it been successful, might have banished foreign factions, by gradually conferring on a Polish family an hereditary claim to the crown. But the Saxons, foreseeing such a measure, carried away young Sobieski a prisoner. Charles then bestowed it on Stanislaus Leczinski, a Polish gentleman of worth and talent, but destitute of the genius and boldness which the public dangers required, and by the example of a second king enthroned by a foreign army, struck another blow at the independence of Poland. The treaty of Alt-Ranstadt was soon after annulled by the battle of Pultowa; and Augustus, renewing the pretensions which he had solemnly renounced, returned triumphantly to Warsaw. The ascendant of the Czar was for a moment suspended by the treaty of Pruth, in 1711, where the Turks compelled Peter to swear that he would withdraw his troops from Poland, and never to interfere in its internal affairs; but as soon as the Porte were engaged in a war with Austria, he marched an army into it; and the first example of a compromise between the King and the Diet, under the mediation of a Russian ambassador, and surrounded by Russian troops, was exhibited in 1717.

The death of Augustus, in 1733, had nearly occasioned a general war throughout Europe. The interest of Stanislaus, the deposed king, was espoused by France, partly perhaps because Louis XV. had married his daughter, but chiefly because the cause of the new Elector of Saxony, who was his competitor, was supported by Austria, the ally of England, and by Russia, then closely connected with Austria. The court of Petersburgh then set up the fatal pretext of a guarantee of the Polish constitution, founded on the transactions of 1717. A guarantee of the territories and rights of one independent state against others, is perfectly compatible with justice: but a guarantee of the institutions of a people against themselves, is but another name for its dependence on the foreign power which enforces it. In pursuance of this pretence, the country was invaded by sixty thousand Russians, who ravaged with fire and sword every district which opposed their progress; and a handful of gentlemen, some of them in chains, whom they brought together in a forest near Warsaw, were compelled to elect Augustus III.

Henceforward Russia treated Poland as a vassal. She indeed disappeared from the European system,—was the subject of wars and negotiations, but no longer a party engaged in them. Under Augustus III., she was almost as much without government at home as without influence abroad, slumbering for thirty years in a state of pacific anarchy, which is almost without example in history. The Diets were regularly assembled, conformably to the laws; but each one was dissolved, without adopting a single measure of legislation or government. This extraordinary suspension of public authority arose from the privilege which each nuncio possessed, of stopping any public measure, by declaring his dissent from it, in the well known form of the *Liberum Veto*. To give a satisfactory account of the origin and progress of this anomalous privilege, would probably require more industrious and critical research than were applied to the subject when Polish antiquaries and lawyers existed.* The absolute negative enjoyed by each member seems to have arisen from the principle, that the nuncios were not representatives, but ministers; that their power was limited by the imperative instructions of the provinces; that the constitution was rather a confederacy than a commonwealth; and that the Diet was not so much a deliberative assembly, as a meeting of delegates, whose whole duty consisted in declaring the determination of their respective constituents. Of such a state of things, unanimity seemed the natural consequence. But, as the sovereign power was really vested in the gentry, they were authorised, by the law, to interfere in public affairs, in a manner most inconvenient and hazardous, though rendered in some measure necessary by the unreasonable institution of unanimity. This interference was effected by that species of legal insurrection called a "confederation," in which any number of gentlemen subscribing the alliance bound themselves to pursue, by force of arms, its avowed object, either of defending the country, or preserving the laws, or maintaining the privileges of any class of citizens. It was equally lawful for another body to associate themselves against the former; and the war between them was legitimate. In these confederations, the sovereign power released itself from the restraint of unanimity; and in order to obtain that liberty, the Diet sometimes resolved itself into a confederation, and lost little by being obliged to rely on the zeal of voluntary

* The information on this subject in Lengnich (Jus Publicum Poloniæ) is vague and unsatisfactory.

adherents, rather than on the legal obedience of citizens.

On the death of Augustus III., it pleased the Empress Catharine to appoint Stanislaus Poniatowski, a discarded lover, to the vacant throne,—a man who possessed many of the qualities and accomplishments which are attractive in private life; but who, when he was exposed to the tests of elevated station and public danger, proved to be utterly void of all dignity and energy. Several circumstances in the state of Europe enabled her to bestow the crown on him without resistance from foreign powers. France was unwilling to expose herself so early to the hazard of a new war, and was farther restrained by her recent alliance with Austria; and the unexpected death of the Elector of Saxony deprived the Courts of Versailles and Vienna of the competitor whom they could have supported with most hope of success against the influence of the Czarina. Frederic II., abandoned, or (as he himself with reason thought) betrayed by England,* found himself, at the general peace, without an ally, exposed to the deserved resentment of Austria, and no longer with any hope of aid from France, which had become the friend of his natural enemy. In this situation, he thought it necessary to court the friendship of Catharine, and in the beginning of the year 1764, concluded a defensive alliance with her, the stipulations of which with respect to Poland were, that they were to oppose every attempt either to make that crown hereditary or to strengthen the royal power; that they were to unite in securing the election of Stanislaus; and that they were to protect the Dissidents of the Greek and Protestant communions, who, since the year 1717, had been deprived of that equal admissibility to public office which was bestowed on them by the liberality of the ancient laws. The first of these stipulations was intended to perpetuate the confusions of Poland, and to insure her dependence on her neighbours; while the last would afford a specious pretext for constant interference. In a declaration delivered at Warsaw, Catharine asserted, "that she did nothing but in virtue of the right of vicinage, acknowledged by all nations;"† and, on another occasion, observed, "that justice and humanity were the sole rules of her conduct; and that her virtues alone had placed her on the throne:"‡ while Frederic declared, that "he should constantly labour to defend the states of the republic in their integrity;" and Maria Theresa, a sovereign celebrated for piety and justice, assured the Polish Government of "her resolution to maintain the republic in all her rights, prerogatives, and possessions." Catharine again, when Poland, for the first time, acknowledged her title of Empress of all the Russias, granted to the republic a solemn guarantee of all its possessions!*

Though abandoned by their allies and distracted by divisions, the Poles made a gallant stand against the appointment of the discarded lover of a foreign princess to be their King. One party, at the head of which was the illustrious house of Czartorinski, by supporting the influence of Russia, and the election of Stanislaus, hoped to obtain the power of reforming the constitution, of abolishing the veto, and giving due strength to the crown. The other, more generous though less enlightened, spurned at foreign interference, and made the most vigorous efforts to assert independence, but were unhappily averse to reforms of the constitution, wedded to ancient abuses, and resolutely determined to exclude their fellow-citizens of different religions from equal privileges. The leaders of the latter party were General Branicki, a veteran of Roman dignity and intrepidity, and Prince Radzivil, a youth of almost regal revenue and dignity, who, by a singular combination of valour and generosity with violence and wildness, exhibited a striking picture of a Sarmatian grandee. The events which passed in the interregnum, as they are related by Rulhière, form one of the most interesting parts of modern history. The variety of character, the elevation of mind, and the vigour of talent exhibited in the fatal struggle which then began, afford a memorable proof of the superiority of the worst aristocracy over the best administered absolute monarchy. The most turbulent aristocracy, with all its disorders and insecurity, must contain a certain number of men who respect themselves, and who have some scope for the free exercise of genius and virtue.

In spite of all the efforts of generous patriotism, the Diet, surrounded by a Russian army, were compelled to elect Stanislaus. The Princes Czartorinski expected to reign under the name of their nephew. They had carried through their reforms so dexterously as to be almost unobserved; but Catharine had too deep an interest in the anarchy of Poland not to watch over its preservation. She availed herself of the prejudices of the party most adverse to her, and obliged the Diet to abrogate the reforms. Her ambassadors were her viceroys. Keyserling, a crafty and smooth German jurist, Saldern, a desperate adventurer, banished from Holstein for forgery, and Repnin, a haughty and brutal Muscovite, were selected, perhaps from the variety of their character, to suit the fluctuating circumstances of the country: but all of them spoke in that tone of authority which has ever since continued to distinguish Russian diplomacy. Prince Czartorinski was

* Mémoires de Frederic II. 1763—1775. Introduction. Frederick charges the new Administration of Geo. III., not with breach of treaty in making peace without him, but with secretly offering to regain Silesia for Maria Theresa, and with labouring to embroil Peter III. with Prussia.

† Rulhière, Histoire de l'Anarchie de Pologne, vol. ii. p. 41.

‡ Ibid. p. 151.

* Ferrand, Histoire des trois Demembrements de la Pologne (Paris, 1820), p. 1.

desirous not to be present in the Diet when his measures were repealed; but Repnin told him, that if he was not, his palaces should be burnt, and his estates laid waste. Understanding this system of Muscovite canvass, he submitted to the humiliation of proposing to abrogate those reformations which he thought essential to the existence of the republic.

In September of the same year, the Russian and Prussian ministers presented notes in favour of the Dissidents,* and afterwards urged the claims of that body more fully to the Diet of 1766, when they were seconded with honest intentions, though perhaps with a doubtful right of interference, by Great Britain, Denmark, and Sweden, as parties to, or as guarantees of, the Treaty of Oliva, the foundation of the political system of the north of Europe. The Diet, influenced by the unnatural union of an intolerant spirit with a generous indignation against foreign interference, rejected all these solicitations, though undoubtedly agreeable to the principle of the treaty, and though some of them proceeded from powers which could not be suspected of unfriendly intentions. The Dissidents were unhappily prevailed upon to enter into confederations for the recovery of their ancient rights, and thus furnished a pretext for the armed interference of Russia. Catharine now affected to espouse the cause of the Republicans, who had resisted the election of Stanislaus. A general confederation of malcontents was formed under the auspices of Prince Radzivil at Radom, but surrounded by Russian troops, and subject to the orders of the brutal Repnin. This capricious barbarian used his power with such insolence as soon to provoke general resistance. He prepared measures for assembling a more subservient Diet by the utmost excesses of military violence at the elections, and by threats of banishment to Siberia held out to every one whose opposition he dreaded.

This Diet, which met on the 4th of October, 1767, showed at first strong symptoms of independence,† but was at length intimidated; and Repnin obtained its consent to a treaty‡ stipulating for the equal admission of all religious sectaries to civil offices, containing a reciprocal guarantee "of *the integrity of the territories of both powers in the most solemn and sacred manner*," confirming the constitution of Poland, especially the fatal law of unanimity, with a few alterations recently made by the Diet, and placing this "constitution, with the government, liberty, and rights of Poland, under the guarantee of her Imperial Majesty, who most solemnly promises to preserve the republic for ever entire." Thus, again, under the pretence of enforcing religious liberty, were the disorder and feebleness of Poland perpetuated; and by the principle of the foreign guarantee was her independence destroyed. Frederick II., an accomplice in these crimes, describes their immediate effect with the truth and coolness of an unconcerned spectator. "So many acts of sovereignty," says he, "exercised by a foreign power on the territory of the republic, at length excited universal indignation: the offensive measures were not softened by the arrogance of Prince Repnin: enthusiasm seized the minds of all, and the grandees availed themselves of the fanaticism of their followers and serfs, to throw off a yoke which had become insupportable." In this temper of the nation, the Diet rose on the 6th of March following, and with it expired the Confederation of Radom, which furnished the second example, within five years, of a Polish party so blind to experience as to become the dupes of Russia.

* Martens, Recueil de Traités, vol. i. p. 340.
† Rulhière, vol. ii. pp. 466. 470.
‡ Martens, vol. iv. p. 582.

Another confederation was immediately formed at Bar, in Podolia, for the preservation of religion and liberty,* which, in a moment, spread over the whole kingdom. The Russian officers hesitated for a moment whether they could take a part in this intestine war. Repnin, by pronouncing the word "Siberia," compelled those members of the Senate who were at Warsaw to claim the aid of Russia, notwithstanding the dissent of the Czartorinskis and their friends, who protested against that inglorious and ruinous determination. The war that followed presented, on the part of Russia, a series of acts of treachery, falsehood, rapacity, and cruelty, not unworthy of Cæsar Borgia. The resistance of the Poles, an undisciplined and almost unarmed people, betrayed by their King and Senate, in a country without fastnesses or fortifications, and in which the enemy had already established themselves at every important point, forms one of the most glorious, though the most unfortunate, of the struggles of mankind for their rights. The council of the confederation established themselves at Eperies, within the frontier of Hungary, with the connivance and secret favour of Austria. Some French officers, and aid in money from Versailles and Constantinople, added something to their strength, and more to their credit. Repnin entered into a negotiation with them, and proposed an armistice, till he could procure reinforcements. Old Pulaski, the first leader of the confederation, objected:—"There is no word," said he, "in the Russian language for honour." Repnin, as soon as he was reinforced, laughed at the armistice, fell upon the confederates, and laid waste the lands of all true Poles with fire and sword. The Cossacks brought to his house at Warsaw, Polish gentlemen tied to the tails of their horses, and dragged in this manner along the ground.† A Russian colonel, named Drewitz, seems to have surpassed all his comrades in ferocity. Not content with massacring the gentlemen to whom quarter had

* See their Manifesto, Martens, vol. i. p. 456.
† Rulhière, vol. iii. p. 55.

been given, he inflicted on them the punishments invented in Russia for slaves; sometimes tying them to trees as a mark for his soldiers to fire at; sometimes scorching certain parts of their skin, so as to represent the national dress of Poland; sometimes dispersing them over the provinces, after he had cut off their hands, arms, noses, or ears, as living examples of the punishment to be suffered by those who should love their country.* It is remarkable, that this ferocious monster, then the hero of the Muscovite army, was deficient in the common quality of military courage. Peter had not civilized the Russians; that was an undertaking beyond his genius, and inconsistent with his ferocious character: he had only armed a barbarous people with the arts of civilized war.

But no valour could have enabled the Confederates of Bar to resist the power of Russia for four years, if they had not been seconded by certain important changes in the political system of Europe, which at first raised a powerful diversion in their favour, but at length proved the immediate cause of the dismemberment of their country. These changes may be dated from the alliance of France with Austria in 1756, and still more certainly from the peace of 1762. On the day on which the Duke de Choiseul signed the preliminaries of peace at Fontainebleau, he entered into a secret convention with Spain, by which it was agreed, that the war should be renewed against England in eight years,—a time which was thought sufficient to repair the exhausted strength of the two Bourbon monarchies.† The hostility of the French Minister to England was at that time extreme. "If I was master," said he, "we should act towards England as Spain did to the Moors. If we really adopted that system, England would, in thirty years, be reduced and destroyed."‡ Soon after, however, his vigilance was directed to other quarters by projects which threatened to deprive France of her accustomed and due influence in the North and East of Europe. He was incensed with Catharine for not resuming the alliance with Austria, and the war which had been abruptly suspended by the caprice of her unfortunate husband. She, on the other hand, soon after she was seated on the throne, had formed one of those vast and apparently chimerical plans to which absolute power and immense territory have familiarised the minds of Russian sovereigns. She laboured to counteract the influence of France, which she considered as the chief obstacle to her ambition, on all the frontiers of her empire, in Sweden, Poland, and Turkey, by the formation of a great alliance of the North, to consist of England, Prussia, Sweden, Denmark, and Poland,—Russia being of course the head of the league.* Choiseul exerted himself in every quarter to defeat this project, or rather to be revenged on Catharine for attempts which were already defeated by their own extravagance. In Sweden his plan for reducing the Russian influence was successfully resisted; but the revolution accomplished by Gustavus III. in 1772, re-established the French ascendant in that kingdom. The Count de Vergennes, ambassador at Constantinople, opened the eyes of the Sultan to the ambitious projects of Catharine in Sweden, in Poland, and in the Crimea, and held out the strongest assurances of powerful aid, which, had Choiseul remained in power, would probably have been carried into effect. By all these means, Vergennes persuaded the Porte to declare war against Russia on the 30th of October, 1768.†

The Confederates of Bar, who had established themselves in the neighbourhood of the Turkish, as well as of the Austrian provinces, now received open assistance from the Turks. The Russian arms were fully occupied in the Turkish war; a Russian fleet entered the Mediterranean; and the agents of the Court of St. Petersburgh excited a revolt among the Greeks, whom they afterwards treacherously and cruelly abandoned to the vengeance of their Turkish tyrants. These events suspended the fate of Poland. French officers of distinguished merit and gallantry guided the valour of the undisciplined Confederates: Austria seemed to countenance, if not openly to support them. Supplies and reinforcements from France passed openly through Vienna into Poland; and Maria Theresa herself publicly declared, that there was no principle or honour in that country, but among the Confederates. But the Turkish war, which had raised up an important ally for the struggling Poles, was in the end destined to be the cause of their destruction.

The course of events had brought the Russian armies into the neighbourhood of the Austrian dominions, and began to fill the Court of Vienna with apprehensions for the security of Hungary. Frederic had no desire that his ally should become stronger; while both the great powers of Germany were averse to the extension of the Russian territories at the expense of Turkey. Frederic was restrained from opposing it forcibly by his treaty with Catharine, who continued to be his sole ally; but Kaunitz, who ruled the councils at Vienna, still adhered to the French alliance, seconding the French negotiations

* Rulhière, vol. iii. p. 124.

† Ferrand, vol. i. p. 76. The failure of this perfidious project is to be ascribed to the decline of Choiseul's influence. The affair of the Falkland Islands was a fragment of the design.

‡ Despatch from M. de Choiseul to M. D'Ossun at Madrid, 5th April. Flassan. Histoire de la Diplomatie Française, vol. vi. p. 466. About *thirty years* afterwards, the French monarchy was destroyed!

* Rulhière, vol. ii. p. 310. Ferrand, vol. i. p. 75.

† Flassan, vol. iii. p. 83. Vergennes was immediately recalled, notwithstanding this success, for having lowered (*deconsiderê*) himself by marrying the daughter of a physician. He brought back with him the three millions which had been remitted to him to bribe the Divan. Catharine called him "*Mustapha's Prompter.*"

at Constantinople. Even so late as the month of July, 1771, he entered into a secret treaty with Turkey, by which Austria bound herself to recover from Russia, by negotiation or by force, all the conquests made by the latter from the Porte. But there is reason to think that Kaunitz, distrusting the power and the inclination of France under the feeble government of Louis XV., and still less disposed to rely on the councils of Versailles after the downfal of Choiseul in December, 1770, though he did not wish to dissolve the alliance, was desirous of loosening its ties, and became gradually disposed to adopt any expedient against the danger of Russian aggrandisement, which might relieve him from the necessity of engaging in a war, in which his chief confidence must necessarily have rested on so weak a stay as the French Government. Maria Theresa still entertained a rooted aversion for Frederic, whom she never forgave for robbing her of Silesia; and openly professed her abhorrence of the vices and crimes of Catharine, whom she never spoke of but in a tone of disgust, as "*that woman.*" Her son Joseph, however, affected to admire, and, as far as he had power, to imitate the King of Prussia; and in spite of his mother's repugnance, found means to begin a personal intercourse with him. Their first interview occurred at Neiss, in Silesia, in August, 1769, where they entered into a secret engagement to prevent the Russians from retaining Moldavia and Wallachia. In September, 1770, a second took place at Neustadt in Moravia, where the principal subject seems also to have been the means of staying the progress of Russian conquest, and where despatches were received from Constantinople, desiring the mediation of both Courts in the negotiations for peace.* But these interviews, though lessening mutual jealousies, do not appear to have directly influenced their system respecting Poland.† The mediation, however, then solicited, ultimately gave rise to that fatal proposition.

* Mémoires de Frederic II.

† It was at one time believed, that the project of Partition was first suggested to Joseph by Frederic at Neustadt, if not at Neiss. Goertz's papers (Mémoires et Actes Authentiques relatifs aux Negotiations qui ont précédées le Partage de la Pologne, Weimar, 1810) demonstrate the contrary. These papers are supported by Viomenil (Lettres), by the testimony of Prince Henry, by Rulhière, and by the narrative of Frederic. Dohm (Denkwürdigkeiten meiner Zeit) and Schoell (Histoire Abrégée des Traités des Paix) have also shown the impossibility of this supposition. Mr. Coxe (History of the House of Austria, vol. iii. p. 499) has indeed adopted it, and endeavours to support it by the declarations of Hertzberg to himself: but when he examines the above authorities, the greater part of which have appeared since his work, he will probably be satisfied that he must have misunderstood the Prussian minister; and he may perhaps follow the example of the excellent abbreviator Koch, who, in the last edition of his useful work, has altered that part of his narrative which ascribed the first plan of partition to Frederic.

Frederic had proposed a plan for the pacification of Poland, on condition of reasonable terms being made with the Confederates, and of the Dissidents being induced to moderate their demands. Austria had assented to this plan, and was willing that Russia should make an honourable peace, but insisted on the restitution of Moldavia and Wallachia, and declared, that if her mediation were slighted, she must at length yield to the instances of France, and take an active part for Poland and Turkey. These declarations Frederic communicated to the Court of Petersburgh;* and they alone seem sufficient to demonstrate that no plan of partition was then contemplated by that monarch. To these communications Catharine answered, in a confidential letter to the King, by a plan of peace, in which she insisted on the independence of the Crimea, the acquisition of a Greek island, and of a pretended independence for Moldavia and Wallachia, which should make her the mistress of these provinces. She spoke of Austria with great distrust and alienation; but, on the other hand, intimated her readiness to enter into a closer intimacy with that Court, if it were possible to disengage her from her present absurd system, and to make her enter into their views; by which means Germany would be restored to its natural state, and the House of Austria would be diverted, *by other prospects*, from those views on his Majesty's possessions, which her present connections kept up.† This correspondence continued during January and February, 1771; Frederic objecting, in very friendly language, to the Russian demands, and Catharine adhering to them.‡ In January, Panin notified to the Court of Vienna his mistress' acceptance of the good offices of Austria towards the pacification, though she declined a formal mediation. This despatch is chiefly remarkable for a declaration,§ "*that the Empress had adopted, as an invariable maxim, never to desire any aggrandisement of her states.*" When the Empress communicated her plan of peace to Kaunitz in May, that minister declared that his Court could not propose conditions of peace, which must be attended with ruin to the Porte, and with great danger to the Austrian monarchy.

In the summer of the year 1770, Maria Theresa had caused her troops to take possession of the county of Zipps, a district anciently appertaining to Hungary, but which had been enjoyed by Poland for about three hundred and sixty years, under a mortgage made by Sigismond, king of Hungary, on the strange condition that if it was not redeemed by a fixed time, it could only be so by payment of as many times the original sum as there had years elapsed since the appointed

* Frederic to Count Solms, his Minister at Petersburgh, 12th Sept. and 13th Oct. 1770. Goertz, pp. 100—105.

† Ibid. pp. 107. 128. The French alliance is evidently meant.

‡ Ibid. pp. 129—146.

§ Ibid. p. 9.

term. So unceremonious an adjudication to herself of this territory, in defiance of such an ancient possession, naturally produced a remonstrance even from the timid Stanislaus, which, however, she coolly overruled. In the critical state of Poland, it was impossible that such a measure should not excite observation; and an occasion soon occurred, when it seems to have contributed to produce the most important effects.

Frederic, embarrassed and alarmed by the difficulties of the pacification, resolved to send his brother Henry to Petersburgh, with no other instructions than to employ all his talents and address in bringing Catharine to such a temper as might preserve Prussia from a new war. Henry arrived in that capital on the 9th December; and it seems now to be certain, that the first open proposal of a dismemberment of Poland arose in his conversations with the Empress, and appeared to be suggested by the difficulty of making peace on such terms as would be adequate to the successes of Russia, without endangering the safety of her neighbours.* It would be difficult to guess who first spoke out in a conversation about such a matter between two persons of great adroitness, and who were, doubtless, both equally anxious to throw the blame on each other. Unscrupulous as both were, they were not so utterly shameless that each party would not use the utmost address to bring the dishonest plan out of the mouth of the other. A look, a smile, a hint, or a question were sufficiently intelligible. The best accounts agree, that in speaking of the entrance of the Austrian troops into Poland, and of a report that they had occupied the fortress of Czentokow, Catharine smiling, and casting down her eyes, said to Henry, "It seems that in Poland you have only to *stoop and take*;" that he seized on the expression; and that she then, resuming an air of indifference, turned the conversation to other subjects. At another time, speaking of the subsidy which Frederic paid to her by treaty, she said, "I fear he will be weary of this burden, and will leave me. I wish I could secure him by some equivalent advantage." "Nothing," replied Henry, "will be more easy. You have only to give him some territory to which he has pretensions, and which will facilitate the communication between his dominions." Catharine, without appearing to understand a remark, the meaning of which could not be mistaken, adroitly rejoined, "that she would willingly consent, if the balance of Europe was not disturbed; and that she wished for nothing."† In a conversation with Baron Saldern on the terms of peace, Henry suggested that a plan must be contrived which would detach Austria from Turkey, and by which the three powers would gain. "Very well," replied the former, "provided that it is not at the expense of Poland;"—"as if," said Henry afterwards, when he told the story, "there were any other country about which such plans could be formed." Catharine, in one of the conferences in which she said to the Prince, "I will frighten Turkey and flatter England; it is your business to gain Austria, that she may lull France to sleep," became so eager, that she dipped her finger into ink, and drew with it the lines of partition on a map of Poland which lay before them. "The Empress," says Frederic, "indignant that any other troops than her own should give law to Poland, said to Prince Henry, that if the Court of Vienna wished to dismember Poland, the other neighbours had a right to do as much."* Henry said that there were no other means of preventing a general war;—"*Pour prévenir ce malheur il n'y a qu'un moyen,—de mettre trois têtes dans un bonnet; et cela ne peut pas se faire qu'aux depens d'un quart.*" It is hard to settle the order and time of these fragments of conversation, which, in a more or less imperfect state, have found their way to the public. The probability seems to be, that Henry, who was not inferior in address, and who represented the weaker party, would avoid the first proposal in a case where, if it was rejected, the attempt might prove fatal to the objects of his mission. However that may be, it cannot be doubted that before he left Petersburg on the 30th of January, 1771, Catharine and he had agreed on the general outline to be proposed to his brother.

On his return to Berlin, he accordingly disclosed it to the King, who received it at first with displeasure, and even with indignation, as either an extravagant chimera, or a snare held out to him by his artful and dangerous ally. For twenty-four hours this anger lasted. It is natural to believe that a ray of conscience shot across so great a mind, during one honest day; or, if then too deeply tainted by habitual king-craft for sentiments worthy of his native superiority, that he shrunk for a moment from disgrace, and felt a transient, but bitter, foretaste of the lasting execration of mankind. On the next day, however, he embraced his brother, as if inspired, and declared that he was a second time the saviour of the monarchy.† He was still, however, not without apprehensions from the inconstant councils of a despotic government, influenced by so many various sorts of favourites, as that of Russia. Orlow, who still held the office of Catharine's lover, was desirous of continuing the war. Panin desired peace, but opposed the Partition, which he probably

* Rulhière, vol. iv. p. 209.
† Ferrand, vol. i. p. 140.

* Mémoires. This account is very much confirmed by the well-informed writer who has prefixed his Recollections to the Letters of Viomenil, who probably was General Grimouard. His account is from Prince Henry, who told it to him at Paris in 1788, calling the news of the Austrian proceedings in Poland, and Catharine's observations on it, *a fortunate accident, which suggested the plan of partition.*
† Ferrand, vol. i. p. 149.

considered as the division of a Russian province. But the great body of lovers and courtiers who had been enriched by grants of forfeited estates in Poland, were favourable to a project which would secure their former booty, and, by exciting civil war, lead to new and richer forfeitures. The Czernitcheffs were supposed not to confine their hopes to confiscation, but to aspire to a principality to be formed out of the ruins of the republic. It appears that Frederic, in his correspondence with Catharine, urged, perhaps sincerely, his apprehension of general censure: her reply was,—"I take all the blame upon myself."*

The consent of the Court of Vienna, however, was still to be obtained; where the most formidable and insuperable obstacles were still to be expected in the French alliance, in resentment towards Prussia, and in the conscientious character of Maria Theresa. Prince Henry, on the day of his return to Berlin, in a conversation with Van Swieten the Austrian minister, assured him, on the part of Catharine, "that if Austria would favour her negotiations with Turkey, she would consent to a considerable augmentation of the Austrian territory." On Van Swieten asking "where?" Henry replied, "You know as well as I do what your Court might take, and what it is in the power of Russia and Prussia to cede to her." The cautious minister was silent; but it was impossible that he should either have mistaken the meaning of Henry, or have failed to impart such a declaration to his Court.† As soon as the Court of Petersburgh had vanquished the scruples or fears of Frederic, they required that he should sound that of Vienna, which he immediately did through Van Swieten.‡ The state of parties there was such, that Kaunitz thought it necessary to give an ambiguous answer. That celebrated coxcomb, who had grown old in the ceremonial of courts and the intrigues of cabinets, and of whom we are told that the death of his dearest friend never shortened his toilet nor retarded his dinner, still felt some regard to the treaty with France, which was his own work; and was divided between his habitual submission to the Empress Queen and the court which he paid to the young Emperor. It was a difficult task to minister to the ambition of Joseph, without alarming the conscience of Maria Theresa. That Princess had, since the death of her husband, "passed several hours of every day in a funeral apartment, adorned by crucifixes and death's heads, and by a portrait of the late Emperor, painted when he had breathed his last, and by a picture of herself, as it was supposed she would appear, when the paleness and cold of death should take from her countenance the remains of that beauty which made her one of the finest women of her age."* Had it been possible, in any case, to rely on the influence of the conscience of a sovereign over measures of state, it might be supposed that a princess, occupied in the practice of religious austerities, and in the exercise of domestic affections, advanced in years, loving peace, beloved by her subjects, respected in other countries, professing remorse for the bloodshed which her wars had occasioned, and with her children about to ascend the greatest thrones of Europe, would not have tarnished her name by cooperating with one monarch whom she detested, and another whom she scorned and disdained, in the most faithless and shameless measures which had ever dishonoured the Christian world. Unhappily, she was destined to be a signal example of the insecurity of such a reliance. But she could not instantly yield; and Kaunitz was obliged to temporize. On the one hand, he sent Prince Lobkowitz on an embassy to Petersburgh, where no minister of rank had of late represented Austria; while, on the other, he continued his negotiation for a defensive alliance with Turkey. After having first duly notified to Frederic that his Court disapproved the impracticable projects of Partition, and was ready to withdraw their troops from the district which they had occupied in virtue of an ancient claim,† he soon after proposed neutrality to him, in the event of a war between Austria and Russia. Frederic answered, that he was bound by treaty to support Russia; but intimated that Russia might probably recede from her demand of Moldavia and Wallachia. Both parts of the answer seemed to have produced the expected effect on Kaunitz, who now saw his country placed between a formidable war and a profitable peace. Even then, probably, if he could have hoped for effectual aid from France, he might have chosen the road of honour. But the fall of the Duc de Choiseul, and the pusillanimous rather than pacific policy of his successors, destroyed all hope of French succour, and disposed Kaunitz to receive more favourably the advances of the Courts of Berlin and Petersburgh. He seems to have employed the time, from June to October, in surmounting the repugnance of his Court to the new system.

The first certain evidence of a favourable disposition at Vienna towards the plan of the

* This fact was communicated by Sabatier, the French resident at Petersburgh, to his Court in a despatch of the 11th February, 1774. (Ferrand, vol. i. p. 152.) It transpired at that time, on occasion of an angry correspondence between the two Sovereigns, in which the King reproached the Empress with having desired the Partition, and quoted the letter in which she had offered to take on herself the whole blame.

† Ferrand, vol. i. p. 149.

‡ Mémoires de Frederic II. The King does not give the dates of this communication. It probably was in April, 1771.

* Rulhière, vol. iv. p. 167.

† The want of dates in the King of Prussia's narrative is the more unfortunate, because the Count de Goertz has not published the papers relating to the negotiations between Austria and Prussia,—an omission which must be owned to be somewhat suspicious.

two Powers, is in a despatch of Prince Galitzin at Vienna to Count Panin, on the 25th of October,* in which he gives an account of a conversation with Kaunitz on the day before. The manner of the Austrian minister was more gracious and cordial than formerly; and, after the usual discussions about the difficulties of the terms of peace, Galitzin at last asked him—"What equivalent do you propose for all that you refuse to allow us? It seems to me that there can be none." Kaunitz, suddenly assuming an air of cheerfulness, pressed his hand, and said "Sir, since you point out the road, I will tell you, —but in such strict confidence, that it must be kept a profound secret at your Court; for if it were to transpire and be known even to the ally and friend of Russia, my Court would solemnly retract and disavow this communication." He then proposed a moderate plan of peace, but added, that the Court of Vienna could not use its good offices to cause it to be adopted, unless the Court of Petersburgh would give the most positive assurances that she would not subject Poland to dismemberment for her own advantage, or for that of any other; provided always, that their Imperial Majesties were to retain the county of Zipps, but to evacuate every other part of the Polish territory which the Austrian troops might have occupied. Galitzin observed, that the occupation of Zipps had much the air of a dismemberment. This Kaunitz denied; but said, that his Court would co-operate with Russia in forcing the Poles to put an end to their dissensions. The former observed, that the plan of pacification showed the perfect disinterestedness of her Imperial Majesty towards Poland, and that no idea of dismemberment had ever entered into her mind, or into that of her ministers. "I am happy," said Kaunitz, "to hear you say so." Panin, in his answer, on the 16th of December,† to Galitzin, seems to have perfectly well understood the extraordinary artifice of the Austrian minister. "The Court of Vienna," says he, "claims the thirteen towns, and disclaims dismemberment: but there is no state which does not keep claims open against its neighbours, and the right to enforce them when there is an opportunity; and there is none which does not feel the necessity of the balance of power to secure the possession of each. To be sincere, we must not conceal that Russia is also in a condition to produce well-grounded claims against Poland, and that we can with confidence say the same of our ally the King of Prussia; and if the Court of Vienna finds it expedient to enter into measures with us and our ally to compare and arrange our claims, we are ready to agree." The fears of Kaunitz for the union of France and England were unhappily needless. These great Powers, alike deserters of the rights of nations, and betrayers of the liberties of Europe, saw the crime consummated without stretching forth an arm to prevent it.

In the midst of the conspiracy, a magnificent embassy from France arrived at Vienna early in January, 1772.* At the head of it was the Prince de Rohan, then appointed to grace the embassy by his high birth; while the business continued to be in the hands of M. Durand, a diplomatist of experience and ability. Contrary to all reasonable expectation, the young prince discovered the secret which had escaped the sagacity of the veteran minister. Durand, completely duped by Kaunitz, warned Rohan to hint no suspicions of Austria in his despatches to Versailles. About the end of February, Rohan received information of the treachery of the Austrian court so secretly,† that he was almost obliged to represent it as a discovery made by his own penetration. He complained to Kaunitz, that no assistance was given to the Polish confederates, who had at that moment brilliantly distinguished themselves by the capture of the Castle of Cracow. Kaunitz assured him, that "the Empress Queen never would suffer the balance of power to be disturbed by a dismemberment which would give too much preponderance to neighbouring and rival Courts." The ambassador suspected the intentions that lurked beneath this equivocal and perfidious answer, and communicated them to his Court, in a despatch on the 2d of March, giving an account of the conference. But the Duc d'Aiguillon, either deceived, or unwilling to appear so, rebuked the Prince for his officiousness, observing, that "the ambassador's conjectures being incompatible with the positive assurances of the Court of Vienna, constantly repeated by Count Mercy, the ambassador at Paris, and with the promises recently made to M. Durand, the thread which could only deceive must be quitted." In a private letter to M. d'Aiguillon, to be shown only to the King, referring to a private audience with the Empress, he says:—"I have indeed seen Maria Theresa weep over the misfortunes of oppressed Poland; but that Princess, practised in the art of concealing her designs, has tears at command. With one hand she lifts her handkerchief to her eyes to wipe away tears; with the other she wields the sword for the Partition of Poland."‡

* Goertz, p. 75. † Ibid. p. 153.

* Mémoires de l'Abbé Georgel, vol. i. p. 219.

† The Abbé Georgel ascribes the detection to his master the ambassador; but it is more probably ascribed by M. Shoell (Histoire de Traités, vol. xiv. p. 76,) to a young native of Strasburg, named Barth, the second secretary of the French Legation, who, by his knowledge of German, and intimacy with persons in inferior office, detected the project, but required the ambassador to conceal it even from Georgel. Schoell quotes a passage of a letter from Barth to a friend at Strasburg, which puts his early knowledge of it beyond dispute.

‡ Georgel, vol. i. p. 264. The letter produced some remarkable effects. Madame du Barri got possession of it, and read the above passage aloud at one of her supper parties. An enemy of Rohan,

In February and March, 1772, the three Powers exchanged declarations, binding themselves to adhere to the principle of equality in the Partition. In August following, the treaties of dismemberment were executed at Petersburgh; and in September, the demands and determinations of the combined Courts were made known at Warsaw. It is needless to characterize papers which have been universally regarded as carried to the extremity of human injustice and effrontery. An undisputed possession of centuries, a succession of treaties, to which all the European states were either parties or guarantees,—nay, the recent, solemn, and repeated engagements of the three Governments themselves, were considered as forming no title of dominion. In answer, the Empress Queen and the King of Prussia appealed to some pretensions of their predecessors in the thirteenth century: the Empress of Russia alleged only the evils suffered by neighbouring states from the anarchy of Poland.* The remonstrances of the Polish Government, and their appeals to all those states who were bound to protect them as guarantees of the Treaty of Olivia, were equally vain. When the Austrian ambassador announced the Partition at Versailles, the old King said, "If the other man (Choiseul) had been here, this would not have happened."† But in truth, both France and Great Britain had, at that time, lost all influence in the affairs of Europe:—France, from the imbecility of her Government, and partly, in the case of Poland, from reliance on the Court of Vienna; Great Britain, in consequence of her own treachery to Prussia, but in a still greater degree from the unpopularity of her Government at home, and the approaches of a revolt in the noblest part of her colonies. Had there been a spark of spirit, or a ray of wise policy in the councils of England and France, they would have been immediately followed by all the secondary powers whose very existence depended on the general reverence for justice.

The Poles made a gallant stand. The Government was compelled to call a Diet; and the three Powers insisted on its unanimity in the most trivial act. In spite, however, of every species of corruption and violence, the Diet, surrounded as it was by foreign bayonets, gave powers to deputies to negotiate with the three Powers, by a majority of only one; and it was not till September, 1773, that it was compelled to cede, by a pretended treaty, some of her finest provinces, with nearly five millions of her population. The conspirators were resolved to deprive the remains of the Polish nation of all hope of re-establishing a vigorous government, or attaining domestic tranquillity; and the Liberum Veto, the elective monarchy, and all the other institutions which tended to perpetuate disorder, were again imposed.

Maria Theresa had the merit of confessing her fault. On the 19th of February, 1775, when M. de Breteuil, the ambassador of Louis XVI., had his first audience, after some embarrassed remarks on the subject of Poland, she at length exclaimed, in a tone of sorrow, "I know, Sir, that I have brought a deep stain on my reign, by what has been done in Poland; but I am sure that I should be forgiven, if it could be known what repugnance I had to it, and how many circumstances combined against my principles."* The guilt of the three parties to the Partition was very unequal. Frederic, the weakest, had most to apprehend, both from a rupture with his ally, and from the accidents of a general war; while, on the other hand, some enlargement seemed requisite to the defence of his dominions. The House of Austria entered late and reluctantly into the conspiracy, which she probably might have escaped, if France had been under a more vigorous Government. Catharine was the great criminal. She had for eight years oppressed, betrayed, and ravaged Poland,—had imposed on her King,—had prevented all reformation of the government,—had fomented divisions among the nobility,—in a word, had created and maintained that anarchy, which she at length used as a pretence for the dismemberment. Her vast empire needed no accession of territory for defence, or, it might have been hoped, even for ambition. Yet, by her insatiable avidity, was occasioned the

who was present, immediately told the Dauphiness of this attack on her mother. The young Princess was naturally incensed at such language, especially as she had been given to understand that the letter was written to Madame du Barri. She became the irreconcilable enemy of the Prince, afterwards Cardinal de Rohan, who, in hopes of conquering her hostility, engaged in the strange adventure of the Diamond Necklace, one of the secondary agents in promoting the French Revolution, and not the least considerable source of the popular prejudices against the Queen.

* Martens, vol. i. p. 461.

† It has been said that Austria did not accede to the Partition till France had refused to co-operate against it. Of this M. de Segur tells us, that he was assured by Kaunitz, Cobentzel, and Vergennes. The only circumstance which approaches to a confirmation of his statement is, that there are traces in Ferrand of secret intimations conveyed by D'Aiguillon to Frederic, that there was no likelihood of France proceeding to extremities in favour of Poland. This clandestine treachery is, however, very different from a public refusal. It has, on the other hand, been stated (Coxe, vol. ii. p. 516.) that the Duc d'Aiguillon proposed to Lord Rochfort, that an English or French fleet should be sent to the Baltic to prevent the dismemberment. But such a proposal, if it occurred at all, must have related to transactions long antecedent to the Partition, and to the administration of D'Aiguillon, for Lord Rochfort was recalled from the French embassy in 1768, to be made Secretary of State, on the resignation of Lord Shelburne. Neither can the application have been to him as Secretary of State; for France was not in his department. It is to be regretted that Mr. Coxe should, in the same place, have quoted a writer so discredited as the Abbé Soulavie (Mémoires de Louis XVI.), from whom he quotes a memorial, without doubt altogether imaginary, of D'Aiguillon to Louis XV.

* Flassan. vol. vii. p. 125.

pretended necessity for the Partition. To prevent her from acquiring the Crimea, Moldavia, and Wallachia, the Courts of Vienna and Berlin agreed to allow her to commit an equivalent robbery on Poland. Whoever first proposed it, Catharine was the real cause and author of the whole monstrous transaction; and, should any historian,—dazzled by the splendour of her reign, or more excusably seduced by her genius, her love of letters, her efforts in legislation, and her real services to her subjects,—labour to palliate this great offence, he will only share her infamy in the vain attempt to extenuate her guilt.

The defects of the Polish government probably contributed to the loss of independence most directly by their influence on the military system. The body of the gentry retaining the power of the sword, as well as the authority of the state in their own hands, were too jealous of the Crown to strengthen the regular army; though even that body was more in the power of the great officers named by the Diet, than in that of the King. They continued to serve on horseback as in ancient times, and to regard the *Pospolite*, or general armament of the gentry, as the impenetrable bulwark of the commonwealth. Nor, indeed, unless they had armed their slaves, would it have been possible to have established a formidable native infantry. Their armed force was adequate to the short irruptions or sudden enterprises of ancient war; but a body of noble cavalry was altogether incapable of the discipline, which is of the essence of modern armies; and their military system was irreconcilable with the acquisition of the science of war. In war alone, the Polish nobility were barbarians; while war was the only part of civilization which the Russians had obtained. In one country, the sovereign nobility of half a million durst neither arm their slaves, nor trust a mercenary army: in the other, the Czar naturally employed a standing army, recruited, without fear, from the enslaved peasantry. To these military conscription was a reward, and the station of a private soldier a preferment; and they were fitted by their previous condition to be rendered, by military discipline, the most patient and obedient of soldiers,—without enterprise, but without fear, and equally inaccessible to discontent and attachment, passive and almost insensible members of the great military machine. There are many circumstances in the institutions and destiny of a people, which seem to arise from original peculiarities of national character, of which it is often impossible to explain the origin, or even to show the nature. Denmark and Sweden are countries situated in the same region of the globe, inhabited by nations of the same descent, language, and religion, and very similar in their manners, their ancient institutions, and modern civilization: yet he would be a bold speculator who should attempt to account for the talent, fame, turbulence, and revolutions of the former; and for the quiet prosperity and obscure mediocrity, which have formed the character of the latter.

There is no political doctrine more false or more pernicious than that which represents vices in its internal government as an extenuation of unjust aggression against a country, and a consolation to mankind for the destruction of its independence. As no government is without great faults, such a doctrine multiplies the grounds of war, gives an unbounded scope to ambition, and furnishes benevolent pretexts for every sort of rapine. However bad the government of Poland may have been, its bad qualities do not in the least degree abate the evil consequence of the Partition, in weakening, by its example, the security of all other nations. An act of robbery on the hoards of a worthless miser, though they be bestowed on the needy and the deserving, does not the less shake the common basis of property. The greater number of nations live under governments which are indisputably bad; but it is a less evil that they should continue in that state, than that they should be gathered under a single conqueror, even with a chance of improvement in their internal administration. Conquest and extensive empire are among the greatest evils, and the division of mankind into independent communities is among the greatest advantages, which fall to the lot of men. The multiplication of such communities increases the reciprocal control of opinion, strengthens the principles of generous rivalship, makes every man love his own ancient and separate country with a warmer affection, brings nearer to all mankind the objects of noble ambition, and adds to the incentives to which we owe works of genius and acts of virtue. There are some peculiarities in the condition of every civilized country which are peculiarly favourable to some talents or good qualities. To destroy the independence of a people, is to annihilate a great assemblage of intellectual and moral qualities, forming the character of a nation, and distinguishing it from other communities, which no human skill can bring together. As long as national spirit exists, there is always reason to hope that it will work real reformation: when it is destroyed, though better forms may be imposed by a conqueror, there is no farther hope of those only valuable reformations which represent the sentiments, and issue from the heart of a people. The barons at Runnymede continued to be the masters of slaves; but the noble principles of the charter shortly began to release these slaves from bondage. Those who conquered at Marathon and Platæa were the masters of slaves; yet, by the defeat of Eastern tyrants, they preserved knowledge, liberty, and civilization itself, and contributed to that progress of the human mind which will one day banish slavery from the world. Had the people of Scotland been conquered by Edward II. or by Henry VIII., a common observer would have seen nothing in the event but that a race of turbulent barbarians was reduced to subjection by a more civilized state.

After this first Partition was completed in 1776, Poland was suffered for sixteen years to enjoy an interval of more undisturbed tranquillity than it had known for a century. Russian armies ceased to vex it: the dispositions of other foreign powers became more favourable. Frederic II. now entered on that honourable portion of his reign, in which he made a just war for the defence of the integrity of Bavaria, and of the independence of Germany. Still attempts were not wanting to seduce him into new enterprises against Poland. When, in the year 1782, reports were current that Potemkin was to be made King of Poland, that haughty and profligate barbarian told the Count de Goertz, then Prussian ambassador at Petersburgh, that he despised the Polish nation too much to be ambitious of reigning over them.* He desired the ambassador to communicate to his master a plan for a new Partition, observing "that the first was only child's play, and that if they had taken all, the outcry would not have been greater." Every man who feels for the dignity of human nature, will rejoice that the illustrious monarch firmly rejected the proposal. Potemkin read over his refusal three times before he could believe his eyes, and at length exclaimed, in language very common among certain politicians, "I never could have believed that King Frederic was capable of *romantic* ideas."† As soon as Frederic returned to counsels worthy of himself, he became unfit for the purposes of the Empress, who, in 1780, refused to renew her alliance with him, and found more suitable instruments in the restless character, and shallow understanding, of Joseph II., whose unprincipled ambition was now released from the restraint which his mother's scruples had imposed on it. The project of re-establishing an Eastern empire now occupied the Court of Petersburgh, and a portion of the spoils of Turkey was a sufficient lure to Joseph. The state of Europe tended daily more and more to restore some degree of independence to the remains of Poland. Though France, her most ancient and constant ally, was then absorbed in the approach of those tremendous convulsions which have for more than thirty years agitated Europe, other Powers now adopted a policy, the influence of which was favourable to the Poles. Prussia, as she receded from Russia, became gradually connected with England, Holland, and Sweden; and her honest policy in the case of Bavaria placed her at the head of all the independent members of the Germanic Confederacy. Turkey declared war against Russia. The Austrian Government was disturbed by the discontent and revolts which the precipitate innovations of Joseph had excited in various provinces of the monarchy. A formidable combination against the power of Russia was in time formed. In the treaty between Prussia and the Porte, concluded at Constantinople in January, 1790, the contracting parties bound themselves to endeavour to obtain from Austria the restitution of those Polish provinces, to which she had given the name of Galicia.*

During the progress of these auspicious changes, the Poles began to entertain the hope that they might at length be suffered to reform their institutions, to provide for their own quiet and safety, and to adopt that policy which might one day enable them to resume their ancient station among European nations. From 1778 to 1788, no great measures had been adopted, but no tumults disturbed the country; while reasonable opinions made some progress, and a national spirit was slowly reviving. The nobility patiently listened to plans for the establishment of a productive revenue and a regular army; a disposition to renounce their dangerous right of electing a king made perceptible advances; and the fatal law of unanimity had been so branded as an instrument of Russian policy, that in the Diets of these ten years, no nuncio was found bold enough to employ his negative. At the breaking out of the Turkish war, the Poles ventured to refuse not only an alliance offered by Catharine, but even permission to her to raise a body of cavalry in the territories of the republic.†

In the midst of these excellent symptoms of public sense and temper, a Diet assembled at Warsaw in October, 1788, from whom the restoration of the republic was hoped, and by whom it would have been accomplished, if their prudent and honest measures had not been defeated by one of the blackest acts of treachery recorded in the annals of mankind. Perhaps the four years which followed present more signal examples than any other part of history,—of patience, moderation, wisdom, and integrity, in a popular assembly,—of spirit and unanimity among a turbulent people,—of inveterate malignity in an old oppressor,—and of the most execrable perfidy in a pretended friend. The Diet applied itself with the utmost diligence and caution to reform the state, watching the progress of popular opinion, and proposing no reformation till the public seemed ripe for its reception. While the spirit of the French Revolution was every where prevalent, these reformers had the courageous prudence to avoid whatever was visionary in its principles, or violent in their execution. They refused the powerful but perilous aid of the enthusiasm which it excited

* Dohm, vol. ii. p. 45.

† It was about this time that Goertz gave an account of the Court of Russia to the Prince Royal of Prussia, who was about to visit Petersbugh, of which the following passage is a curious specimen:—"Le Prince Bariatinski est reconnu scélérat, et même comme tel employé encore de tems en tems."—Dohm, vol. ii. p. 32.

* Schoell, vol. xiv. p. 473.

† Ferrand, vol. ii. p. 336.

long before its excesses and atrocities had rendered it odious. They were content to be reproached by their friends for the slowness of their reformatory measures; and to be despised for the limited extent of these by many of those generous minds who then aspired to bestow a new and more perfect liberty on mankind. After having taken measures for the re-establishment of the finances and the army, they employed the greater part of the year 1789 in the discussion of constitutional reforms.* A committee appointed in September, before the conclusion of the year, made a report which contained an outline of the most necessary alterations. No immediate decision was made on these propositions; but the sense of the Diet was, in the course of repeated discussions, more decisively manifested. It was resolved, without a division, that the Elector of Saxony should be named successor to the crown; which determination,—the prelude to the establishment of hereditary monarchy,—was confirmed by the Dietines, or electoral assemblies. The elective franchise, formerly exercised by all the nobility, was limited to landed proprietors. Many other fundamental principles of a new constitution were perfectly understood to be generally approved, though they were not formally established. In the mean time, as the Diets were biennial, the assembly approached to the close of its legal duration; and as it was deemed dangerous to intrust the work of reformation to an entirely new one, and equally so to establish the precedent of an existence prolonged beyond the legal period, an expedient was accordingly adopted, not indeed sanctioned by law, but founded in constitutional principles, the success of which afforded a signal proof of the unanimity of the Polish nation. New writs were issued to all the Dietines requiring them to choose the same number of nuncios as usual. These elections proceeded regularly; and the new members being received by the old, formed with them a double Diet. Almost all the Dietines instructed their new representatives to vote for hereditary monarchy, and declared their approbation of the past conduct of the Diet.

On the 16th of December, 1790, this double Diet assembled with a more direct, deliberate, formal, and complete authority, from the great majority of the freemen, to reform the abuses of the government, than perhaps any other representative assembly in Europe ever possessed. They declared the pretended guarantee of Russia in 1776 to be "null, an invasion of national independence, incompatible with the natural rights of every civilized society, and with the political privileges of every free nation."* They felt the necessity of incorporating, in one law, all the reforms which had passed, and all those which had received the unequivocal sanction of public approbation. The state of foreign affairs, as well as the general voice at home, loudly called for the immediate adoption of such a measure; and the new Constitution was presented to the Diet on the 3d of May following,† after being read and received the night before with unanimous and enthusiastic applause by far the greater part of the members of both Houses, at the palace of Prince Radzivil. Only twelve dissentient voices opposed it in the Diet. Never were debates and votes more free: these men, the most hateful of apostates, were neither attacked, nor threatened, nor insulted. The people, on this great and sacred occasion, seemed to have lost all the levity and turbulence of their character, and to have already learnt those virtues which are usually the slow fruit of that liberty which they were then only about to plant.

This constitution confirmed the rights of the Established Church, together with religious liberty, as dictated by the charity which religion inculcates and inspires. It established an hereditary monarchy in the Electoral House of Saxony; reserving to the nation the right of choosing a new race of Kings, in case of the extinction of that family. The executive power was vested in the King, whose ministers were responsible for its exercise. The Legislature was divided into two Houses,—the Senate and the House of Nuncios, with respect to whom the ancient constitutional language and forms were preserved. The necessity of unanimity was taken away, and, with it, those dangerous remedies of confederation and confederate Diets which it had rendered necessary. Each considerable town received new rights, with a restoration of all their ancient privileges. The burgesses recovered the right of electing their own magistrates. All their property within their towns were declared to be inheritable and inviolable. They were empowered to acquire land in Poland, as they always had done in Lithuania. All the offices of the state, the law, the church, and the army, were thrown open to them. The larger towns were empowered to send deputies to the Diet, with a right to vote on all

* Schoell, vol. xiv. p. 117. On the 12th of October, 1788, the King of Prussia had offered, by Buckholz, his minister at Warsaw, to guarantee the integrity of the Polish territory.—Ferrand, vol. ii. p. 452. On the 19th of November, he advises them not to be diverted from "ameliorating their form of government;" and declares, "that he will guarantee their independence without mixing in their internal affairs, or restraining the liberty of their discussions, which, on the contrary, he will guarantee."—Ibid. p. 457. The negotiations of Prince Czartorinski at Berlin, and the other notes of Buckholz, seconded by Mr. Hailes, the English minister, agree entirely in language and principles with the passages which have been cited.

* Ferrand, vol. iii. p. 55. The absence of dates in this writer obliges us to fix the time of this decree by conjecture.

† The particular events of the 3d of May are related fully by Ferrand, and shortly in the Annual Register of 1791,—a valuable narrative, though not without considerable mistakes.

local and commercial subjects, and to speak on all questions whatsoever. All these deputies became noble, as did every officer of the rank of captain, and every lawyer who filled the humblest office of magistracy, and every burgess who acquired a property in land, paying 5*l.* of yearly taxes. Two hundred burgesses were ennobled at the moment, and a provision was made for ennobling thirty at every future Diet. Industry was perfectly unfettered. Immunity from arrest till after conviction was extended to the burgesses;—the extension of which most inconvenient privilege was well adapted to raise traders to a level with the gentry. The same object was promoted by a provision, that no nobleman, by becoming a merchant, a shopkeeper, or artisan, should forfeit his privileges, or be deemed to derogate from his rank. Numerous paths to nobility were thus thrown open; and every art was employed to make the ascent easy. The wisdom and liberality of the Polish gentry, if they had not been defeated by flagitious enemies, would, by a single act of legislation, have accomplished that fusion of the various orders of society, which it has required the most propitious circumstances, in a long course of ages, to effect, in the freest and most happy of the European nations. Having thus communicated political privileges to hitherto disregarded freemen, the new constitution extended to all serfs the full protection of law, which before was enjoyed only by those of the royal demesnes; while it facilitated and encouraged voluntary manumission, by ratifying all contracts relating to it,—the first step to be taken in every country towards the accomplishment of the highest of all the objects of human legislation.

The course of this glorious revolution was not dishonoured by popular tumult, by sanguinary excesses, or by political executions. So far did the excellent Diet carry its wise regard to the sacredness of property, that, though it was in urgent need of financial resources, it postponed, till after the death of present incumbents, the application to the relief of the state of the income of those ecclesiastical offices which were no longer deemed necessary. History will one day do justice to that illustrious body, and hold out to posterity their work, as the perfect model of a most arduous reformation.

The storm which demolished this noble edifice came from abroad. On the 29th of March, of the preceding year, a treaty of alliance had been concluded at Warsaw between the King of Prussia and the Republic, containing, among others, the following stipulation:—"If any foreign Power, in virtue of any preceding acts and stipulations whatsoever, should claim the right of interfering in the internal affairs of the republic of Poland, at what time or in what manner soever, his Majesty the King of Prussia will first employ his good offices to prevent hostilities in consequence of such pretension; but, if his good offices should be ineffectual, and that hostilities against Poland should ensue, his Majesty the King of Prussia, considering such an event as a case provided for in this treaty, will assist the republic according to the tenor of the fourth article of the present treaty."* The aid here referred to was, on the part of Prussia, twenty-two thousand or thirty thousand men, or, in case of necessity, all its disposable force. The undisputed purpose of the article had been to guard Poland against an interference in her affairs by Russia, under pretence of the guarantee of the Polish constitution in 1775.

Though the King of Prussia had, after the conclusion of the treaty, urgently pressed the Diet for the cession of the cities of Dantzick and Thorn, his claim had been afterwards withdrawn and disavowed. On the 13th of May, in the present year, Goltz, then Prussian Chargé d'Affaires at Warsaw, in a conference with the Deputation of the Diet for Foreign Affairs, said, "that he had received orders from his Prussian Majesty to express to them his satisfaction at the happy revolution which had at length given to Poland a wise and regular constitution."† On the 23d of May, in his answer to the letter of Stanislaus, announcing the adoption of the constitution, the same Prince, after applauding the establishment of hereditary monarchy in the House of Saxony, (which, it must be particularly borne in mind, was a positive breach of the constitution guaranteed by Russia in 1775,) proceeds to say, "I congratulate myself on having contributed to the liberty and independence of Poland; and my most agreeable care will be, to preserve and strengthen the ties which unite us." On the 21st of June, the Prussian minister, on occasion of alarm expressed by the Poles that the peace with Turkey might prove dangerous to them, declares, that if such dangers were to arise, "the king of Prussia, faithful to all his obligations, will have it particularly at heart to fulfil those which were last year contracted by him." If there was any reliance in the faith of treaties, or on the honour of kings, Poland might have confidently hoped, that, if she was attacked by Russia, in virtue of the guarantee of 1775, her independence and her constitution would be defended by the whole force of the Prussian monarchy.

The remaining part of the year 1791 passed in quiet, but not without apprehension. On the 9th of January, 1792, Catharine concluded a peace with Turkey at Jassy; and being thus delivered from all foreign enemies, began once more to manifest intentions of interfering in the affairs of Poland. Emboldened by the removal of Herztberg from the councils of Prussia, and by the death of the Emperor Leopold, a prince of experience and

---

* Martens, vol. iii. pp. 161—165.

† Ferrand, vol. iii. p. 121. See the letter of the King of Prussia to Goltz, expressing his admiration and applause of the new constitution. Segur, vol. iii. p. 252.

prudence, she resolved to avail herself of the disposition then arising in all European Governments, to sacrifice every other object to a preparation for a contest with the principles of the French Revolution. A small number of Polish nobles furnished her with that very slender pretext, with which she was always content. Their chiefs were Rzewuski, who, in 1768, had been exiled to Siberia, and Felix Potocki, a member of a potent and illustrious family, which was inviolably attached to the cause of the republic. These unnatural apostates deserting their long-suffering country at the moment when, for the first time, hope dawned on her, were received by Catharine with the honours due from her to aggravated treason in the persons of the Confederates of Targowitz. On the 18th of May the Russian minister at Warsaw declared, that the Empress, "called on by many distinguished Poles who had confederated against the pretended constitution of 1791, would, in virtue of her guarantee, march an army into Poland to restore the liberties of the republic." The hope, meantime, of help from Prussia was speedily and cruelly deceived. Lucchesini, the Prussian minister at Warsaw, in an evasive answer to a communication made to him respecting the preparations for defence against Russia, said coldly, "that his master received the communication as a proof of the esteem of the King and Republic of Poland; but that he could take no cognisance of the affairs which occupied the Diet." On Stanislaus himself claiming his aid, Frederic on the 8th of June answered:—"In considering the new constitution which the republic adopted, without my knowledge and without my concurrence, I never thought of supporting or protecting it." So signal a breach of faith is not to be found in the modern history of great states. It resembles rather the vulgar frauds and low artifices, which, under the name of "reason of state," made up the policy of the petty tyrants of Italy in the fourteenth century.

Assured of the connivance of Prussia, Catharine now poured an immense army into Poland, along the whole line of frontier, from the Baltic to the neighbourhood of the Euxine. But the spirit of the Polish nation was unbroken. A series of brilliant actions occupied the summer of 1792, in which the Polish army, under Poniatowski and Kosciusko, alternately victorious and vanquished, gave equal proofs of unavailing gallantry.

Meantime Stanislaus, who had remained in his capital, willing to be duped by the Russian and Prussian ambassadors, whom he still suffered to continue there, made a vain attempt to disarm the anger of the Empress, by proposing that her grandson Constantine should be the stock of the new constitutional dynasty; to which she haughtily replied, that he must re-establish the old constitution, and accede to the Confederation of Targowitz;—"perhaps," says M. Ferrand, "because a throne acquired without guilt or perfidy might have few attractions for her."* Having on the 4th of July published a proclamation, declaring "that he would not survive his country," on the 22d of the same month, as soon as he received the commands of Catharine, this dastard prince declared his accession to the Confederation of Targowitz, and thus threw the legal authority of the republic into the hands of that band of conspirators. The gallant army, over whom the Diet had intrusted their unworthy King with absolute authority, were now compelled, by his treacherous orders, to lay down their arms amidst the tears of their countrymen, and the insolent exultation of their barbarous enemies.† The traitors of Targowitz were, for a moment, permitted by Russia to rule over the country which they had betrayed, to prosecute the persons and lay waste the property of all good citizens, and to re-establish every ancient abuse.

Such was the unhappy state of Poland during the remainder of the year 1792, a period which will be always memorable for the invasion of France by a German army, their ignominious retreat, the eruption of the French forces into Germany and Flanders, the dreadful scenes which passed in the interior of France, and the apprehension professed by all Governments of the progress of the opinions to which these events were ascribed. The Empress of Russia, among the rest, professed the utmost abhorrence of the French Revolution, made war against it by the most vehement manifestoes, stimulated every other power to resist it, but never contributed a battalion or a ship to the confederacy against it. Frederic-William also plunged headlong into the coalition against the advice of his wisest counsellors.‡ At the moment of the Duke of Brunswick's entry into France, in July,—if we may believe M. Ferrand, himself a zealous royalist, who had evidently more than ordinary means of information,—the ministers of the principal European powers met at Luxemburg, provided with various projects for new arrangements of territory, in the event which they

* Ferrand, vol. iii. p. 217.

† A curious passage of De Thou shows the apprehension early entertained of the Russian power. "Livonis prudentè et reipublicæ Christianæ utili consilio navigatio illuc interdicta fuerat, ne commercio nostrorum Barbari varias artes ipsis ignotas, et quæ ad rem navalem et militarem pertinent, edocerentur. Sic enim eximistabant Moscos, qui maximam Septentrionis partem tenerent, Narvæ condito emporio, et constructo armamentario, non solum in Livoniam, sed etiam in Germaniam effuso exercitu penetraturos."—Lib. xxxix. cap. 8.

‡ Prince Henry and Count Hertzberg, who agree perhaps in nothing else.—Vie du Prince Henri, p. 297. In the same place, we have a very curious extract from a letter of Prince Henry, of the 1st of November, 1792, in which he says, that "every year of war will make the conditions of peace worse for the Allies." Henry was not a Democrat, nor even a Whig. His opinions were confirmed by all the èvents of the first war, and are certainly not contradicted by occurrences towards the close of a second war, twenty years afterwards, and in totally new circumstances.

thought inevitable, of the success of the invasion. The Austrian ministers betrayed the intention of their Court, to renew its attempt to compel the Elector of Bavaria to exchange his dominions for the Low Countries; which, by the dissolution of their treaties with France, they deemed themselves entitled again to propose. The King of Prussia, on this alarming disclosure, showed symptoms of an inclination to abandon an enterprise, which many other circumstances combined to prove was impracticable, at least with the number of troops with which he had presumptuously undertaken it. These dangerous projects of the Court of Vienna made him also feel the necessity of a closer connection with Russia; and in an interview with the Austrian and Russian ministers at Verdun, he gave them to understand, that Prussia could not continue the war without being assured of an indemnity. Russia eagerly adopted a suggestion which engaged Prussia more completely in her Polish schemes; and Austria willingly listened to a proposal which would furnish a precedent and a justification for similar enlargements of her own dominions: while both the Imperial Courts declared, that they would acquiesce in the occupation of another portion of Poland by the Prussian armies.*

Whether in consequence of the supposed agreement at Verdun or not, the fact at least is certain, that Frederic-William returned from his French disgraces to seek consolation in the plunder of Poland. Nothing is more characteristic of a monarch without ability, without knowledge, without resolution, whose life had been divided between gross libertinism and abject superstition, than that, after flying before the armies of a powerful nation, he should instantly proceed to attack an oppressed, and, as he thought, defenceless people. In January, 1793, he entered Poland; and, while Russia was charging the Poles with the extreme of royalism, he chose the very opposite pretext, that they propagated anarchical principles, and had established Jacobin clubs. Even the criminal Confederates of Targowitz were indignant at these falsehoods, and remonstrated, at Berlin and Petersburgh, against the entry of the Prussian troops. But the complaints of such apostates against the natural results of their own crimes were heard with contempt. The Empress of Russia, in a Declaration of the 9th of April, informed the world that, acting in concert with Prussia, and with the consent of Austria, the only means of controlling the Jacobinism of Poland was "by confining it within more narrow limits, and by giving it proportions which better suited an intermediate power." The King of Prussia, accordingly, seized Great Poland; and the Russian army occupied all the other provinces of the republic. It was easy, therefore, for Catharine to determine the extent of her new robbery.

In order, however, to give it some shadow of legality, the King was compelled to call a Diet, from which every one was excluded who was not a partisan of Russia, and an accomplice of the Confederates of Targowitz. The unhappy assembly met at Grodno in June; and, in spite of its bad composition, showed still many sparks of Polish spirit. Sievers, the Russian ambassador, a man apparently worthy of his mission, had recourse to threats, insults, brutal violence, military imprisonment, arbitrary exile, and every other species of outrage and intimidation which, for near thirty years, had constituted the whole system of Russia towards the Polish legislature. In one note, he tells them that, unless they proceed more rapidly, "he shall be under the painful necessity of removing all incendiaries, disturbers of the public peace, and partisans of the 3d of May, from the Diet."* In another, he apprises them, that he must consider any longer delay "as a declaration of hostility; in which case, the lands, possessions, and dwellings of the malcontent members, must be subject to military execution." "If the King adheres to the Opposition, the military execution must extend to his demesnes, the pay of the Russian troops will be stopped, and they will live at the expense of the unhappy peasants."† Grodno was surrounded by Russian troops; loaded cannon were pointed at the palace of the King and the hall of the Diet; four nuncios were carried away prisoners by violence in the night; and all the members were threatened with Siberia. In these circumstances, the captive Diet was compelled, in July and September, to sign two treaties with Russia and Prussia, stipulating such cessions as the plunderers were pleased to dictate, and containing a repetition of the same insulting mockery which had closed every former act of rapine,—a guarantee of the remaining possessions of the republic.‡ It had the consolation of being allowed to perform one act of justice,—that of depriving the leaders of the Confederation of Targowitz, Felix Potocki, Rzewuski, and Braneki, of the great offices which they dishonoured. It may hereafter be discovered, whether it be actually true that Alsace and Lorraine were to have been the compensation to Austria for forbearing to claim her share of the spoils of Poland at this period of the second Partition. It is already well known that the allied army refused to receive the surrender of Strasburgh in the name of Louis XVII., and that Valenciennes and Condé were taken in the name of Austria.

In the beginning of 1794, a young officer named Madalinski, who had kept together, at the disbanding of the army, eighty gentlemen, gradually increased his adherents, till they amounted to a force of about four thousand men, and began to harass the Russian

* Ferrand, vol. iii. pp. 252—255

* Ferrand, vol. iii. p. 369. † Ibid. p. 372.
‡ Martens, vol. v. pp. 162. 202.

posts. The people of Cracow expelled the Russian garrison; and, on the night of the 28th of March, the heroic Kosciusko, at the head of a small body of adherents, entered that city, and undertook its government and defence. Endowed with civil as well as military talents, he established order among the insurgents, and caused the legitimate constitution to be solemnly proclaimed in the cathedral, where it was once more hailed with genuine enthusiasm. He proclaimed a national confederation, and sent copies of his manifesto to Petersburgh, Berlin, and Vienna; treating the two first courts with deserved severity, but speaking amicably of the third, whose territory he enjoined his army to respect. These marks of friendship, the Austrian resident at Warsaw publicly disclaimed, imputing to Kosciusko and his friends "the monstrous principles of the French Convention;"—a language which plainly showed that the Court of Vienna, which had only consented to the last Partition, was willing to share in the next. Kosciusko was daily reinforced; and on the 17th of April rose on the Russian garrison of Warsaw, and compelled Igelstrom the commander, after an obstinate resistance of thirty-six hours, to evacuate the city with a loss of two thousand men wounded. The citizens of the capital, the whole body of a proud nobility, and all the friends of their country throughout Poland, submitted to the temporary dictatorship of Kosciusko, a private gentleman only recently known to the public, and without any influence but the reputation of his virtue. Order and tranquillity generally prevailed; some of the burghers, perhaps excited by the agents of Russia, complained to Kosciusko of the inadequacy of their privileges. But this excellent chief, instead of courting popularity, repressed an attempt which might lead to dangerous divisions. Soon after, more criminal excesses for the first time dishonoured the Polish revolution, but served to shed a brighter lustre on the humanity and intrepidity of Kosciusko. The papers of the Russian embassy laid open proofs of the venality of many of the Poles who had betrayed their country. The populace of Warsaw, impatient of the slow forms of law, apprehensive of the lenient spirit which prevailed among the revolutionary leaders, and instigated by the incendiaries, who are always ready to flatter the passions of a multitude, put to death eight of these persons, and, by their clamours, extorted from the tribunal a precipitate trial and execution of a somewhat smaller number. Kosciusko did not content himself with reprobating these atrocities. Though surrounded by danger, attacked by the most formidable enemies, betrayed by his own Government, and abandoned by all Europe, he flew from his camp to the capital, brought the ringleaders of the massacre to justice, and caused them to be immediately executed. We learn, from very respectable authority, that during all the perils of his short administration, he persuaded the nobility to take measures for a more rapid enfranchisement of the peasantry, than the cautious policy of the Diet had hazarded.*

Harassed by the advance of Austrian, Prussian, and Russian armies, Kosciusko concentrated the greater part of his army around Warsaw, against which Frederic-William advanced at the head of forty thousand disciplined troops. With an irregular force of twelve thousand he made an obstinate resistance for several hours on the 8th of June, and retired to his entrenched camp before the city. The Prussians having taken possession of Cracow, summoned the capital to surrender, under pain of all the horrors of an assault. After two months employed in vain attempts to reduce it, the King of Prussia was compelled, by an insurrection in his lately acquired Polish province, to retire with precipitation and disgrace. But in the mean time, the Russians were advancing, in spite of the gallant resistance of General Count Joseph Sierakowski, one of the most faithful friends of his country; and on the 4th of October, Kosciusko, with only eighteen thousand men, thought it necessary to hazard a battle at Macciowice, to prevent the junction of the two Russian divisions of Suwarrow and Fersen. Success was long and valiantly contested. According to some narrations, the enthusiasm of the Poles would have prevailed, but for the treachery or incapacity of Count Poninski.† Kosciusko, after the most admirable exertions of judgment and courage, fell, covered with wounds; and the Polish army fled. The Russians and Cossacks were melted at the sight of their gallant enemy, who lay insensible on the field. When he opened his eyes, and learnt the full extent of the disaster, he vainly implored the enemy to put an end to his sufferings. The Russian officers, moved with admiration and compassion, treated him with tenderness, and sent him, with due respect, a prisoner of war to Petersburgh, where Catharine threw him into a dungeon; from which he was released by Paul on his succession, perhaps partly from hatred to his mother, and partly from one of those paroxysms of transient generosity, of which that brutal lunatic was not incapable.

From that moment the farther defence of Poland became hopeless. Suwarrow advanced to the capital, and stimulated his army to the assault of the great suburb of Praga, by the barbarous promise of a license to pillage for forty-eight hours. A dreadful contest ensued on the 4th of November, in which the inhabitants performed prodigies of useless valour, making a stand in every street, and almost at every house. All the hor-

* Segur, Règne de Frederic-Guillaume II., tome iii. p. 169. These important measures are not mentioned in any other narration which I have read.

† Segur, vol. iii. p. 171.

rors of war, which the most civilized armies practised on such occasions, were here seen with tenfold violence. No age or sex, or condition, was spared; the murder of children forming a sort of barbarous sport for the assailants. The most unspeakable outrages were offered to the living and the dead. The mere infliction of death was an act of mercy. The streets streamed with blood. Eighteen thousand human carcasses were carried away after the massacre had ceased. Many were burnt to death in the flames which consumed the town. Multitudes were driven by the bayonet into the Vistula. A great body of fugitives perished by the fall of the great bridge over which they fled. These tremendous scenes closed the resistance of Poland, and completed the triumph of her oppressors. The Russian army entered Warsaw on the 9th of November, 1794. Stanislaus was suffered to amuse himself with the formalities of royalty for some months longer, till, in obedience to the order of Catharine, he abdicated on the 25th of November, 1795,—a day which, being the anniversary of his coronation, seemed to be chosen to complete his humiliation. Quarrels about the division of the booty retarded the complete execution of the formal and final Partition, till the beginning of the next year.

Thus fell the Polish people, after a wise and virtuous attempt to establish liberty, and a heroic struggle to defend it, by the flagitious wickedness of Russia, by the foul treachery of Prussia, by the unprincipled accession of Austria, and by the short-sighted, as well as mean-spirited, acquiescence of all the other nations of Europe. Till the first Partition, the right of every people to its own soil had been universally regarded as the guardian principle of European independence. But in the case of Poland, a nation was robbed of its ancient territory without the pretence of any wrong which could justify war, and without even those forms of war which could bestow on the acquisition the name of conquest. It is a cruel and bitter aggravation of this calamity, that the crime was perpetrated, under the pretence of the wise and just principle of maintaining the balance of power;—as if that principle had any value but its tendency to *prevent* such crimes;—as if an equal division of the booty bore any resemblance to a joint exertion to prevent the robbery. In the case of private highwaymen and pirates, a fair division of the booty tends, no doubt, to the harmony of the gang and the safety of its members, but renders them more formidable to the honest and peaceable part of mankind.*

For about eleven years the name of Poland was erased from the map of Europe. By the Treaty of Tilsit, in 1807, the Prussian part of that unfortunate country was restored to as much independence as could then be enjoyed, under the name of the Grand Duchy of Warsaw; and this revived state received a considerable enlargement in 1809, by the treaty of Shoenbrunn, at the expense of Austria.

When Napoleon opened the decisive campaign of 1812, in what he called in his proclamations "the Second Polish War," he published a Declaration, addressed to the Poles, in which he announced that Poland would be greater than she had been under Stanislaus, and that the Archduke, who then governed Wurtsburg, was to be their sovereign; and when on the 12th of July in that year, Wybicki, at the head of a deputation of the Diet, told him, at Wilna, with truth, "The interest of your empire requires the re-establishment of Poland; the honour of France is interested in it,"—he replied, "that he had done all that duty to his subjects allowed him to restore their country; that he would second their exertions; and that he authorized them to take up arms, every where but in the Austrian provinces, of which he had guaranteed the integrity, and which he should not suffer to be disturbed." In his answer,—too cold and guarded to inspire enthusiasm,—he promised even less than he had acquired the the power of performing; for, by the secret articles of his treaty with Austria, concluded in March, provision had been made for an exchange of the Illyrian provinces (which he had retained at his own disposal) for such a part of Austrian Poland as would be equivalent to them.* What his real designs respecting Poland were, it is not easy to conjecture. That he was desirous of re-establishing its independence, and that he looked forward to such an event as the result of his success, cannot be doubted. But he had probably grown too much of a politician and an emperor, to trust, or to love that national feeling and popular enthusiasm to which he had owed the splendid victories of his youth. He was now rather willing to owe every thing to his policy and his army. Had he thrown away the scabbard in this just cause,—had he solemnly pledged himself to the restoration of Poland,—had he obtained the exchange of Galicia for Dalmatia, instead of secretly providing for it,—had he considered Polish independence, not merely as the consequence of victory, but as one of the most powerful means of securing it,—had he, in short, retained some part of his early faith in the attachment of nations, instead of relying exclusively on the mechanism of armies, perhaps the success of that memorable campaign might have been more equally balanced. Seventy thousand Poles were then fighting under his banners.† Forty thousand are supposed to have fallen in the French armies from the destruction of Poland to the

* The sentiments of wise men on the first Partition are admirably stated in the Annual Register of 1772, in the Introduction to the History of Europe, which could scarcely have been written by any man but Mr. Burke.

* Schöell, vol. x. p. 129. † Ibid. p. 139.

battle of Waterloo.* There are few instances of the affection of men for their country more touching than that of these gallant Poles, who, in voluntary exile, amidst every privation, without the hope of fame, and when all the world had become their enemies, daily sacrificed themselves in the battles of a foreign nation, in the faint hope of its one day delivering their own from bondage. Kosciusko had originally encouraged his countrymen to devote themselves to this chance; but when he was himself offered a command in 1807, this perfect hero refused to quit his humble retreat, unless Napoleon would pledge himself for the restoration of Poland.

When Alexander entered France in 1814, as the avowed patron of liberal institutions, Kosciusko addressed a letter to him,† in which he makes three requests,—that the Emperor would grant an universal amnesty, a free constitution, resembling, as nearly as possible, that of England, with means of general education, and, after the expiration of ten years, an emancipation of the peasants. It is but justice to Alexander to add, that when Kosciusko died, in 1817, after a public and private life, worthy of the scholar of Washington, the Emperor, on whom the Congress of Vienna had then bestowed the greater part of the duchy of Warsaw, with the title of King of Poland, allowed his Polish subjects to pay due honours to the last of their heroes; and that Prince Jablonowski was sent to attend his remains from Switzerland to Cracow, there to be interred in the only spot of the Polish territory which is now not dishonoured by a foreign master. He might have paid a still more acceptable tribute to his memory, by executing his pure intentions, and acceding to his disinterested prayers.

The Partition of Poland was the model of all those acts of rapine which have been committed by monarchs or republicans during the wars excited by the French Revolution. No single cause has contributed so much to alienate mankind from ancient institutions, and loosen their respect for established governments. When monarchs show so signal a disregard to immemorial possession and legal right, it is in vain for them to hope that subjects will not copy the precedent. The law of nations is a code without tribunals, without ministers, and without arms, which rests only on a general opinion of its usefulness, and on the influence of that opinion in the councils of states, and most of all, perhaps, on a habitual reverence, produced by the constant appeal to its rules even by those who did not observe them, and strengthened by the elaborate artifice to which the proudest tyrants deigned to submit, in their attempts to elude an authority which they did not dare to dispute. One signal triumph over such an authority was sufficient to destroy its power. Philip II. and Louis XIV. had often violated the law of nations; but the spoilers of Poland overthrew it.

* Julien, Notice Biographique sur Kosciusko.

† Published in M. Julien's interesting little work.

SKETCH

OF

THE ADMINISTRATION AND FALL

OF

STRUENSEE.*

On the arrival of Charles VII. of Sweden, at Altona, in need of a physician,—an attendant whom his prematurely broken constitution made peculiarly essential to him even at the age of nineteen,—Struensee, the son of a Lutheran bishop in Holstein, had just begun to practise medicine, after having been for some time employed as the editor of a newspaper in that city. He was now appointed physician to the King, at the moment when he was projecting a professional establishment at Malaga, or a voyage to India, which his imagination, excited by the perusal of the elder travellers, had covered with "barbaric pearl and gold." He was now twenty-nine years old, and appears to have been recommended to the royal favour by an agreeable exterior, pleasing manners, and some slight talents and superficial knowledge, with the subserviency indispensable in a favourite, and the power of amusing his listless and exhausted master. His name

* From the Edinburgh Review, vol. xliv. p. 366.—Ed.

appears in the publications of the time as "Doctor Struensee," among the attendants of his Danish Majesty in England; and he received, in that character, the honorary degree of Doctor of Medicine from the University of Oxford.

Like all other minions, his ascent was rapid, or rather his flight to the pinnacle of power was instantaneous; for the passion of an absolute prince on such occasions knows no bounds, and brooks no delay. Immediately after the King's return to Copenhagen, Struensee was appointed a Cabinet Minister. While his brother was made a counsellor of justice, he appointed Brandt, another adventurer, to superintend the palace and the imbecile King; and intrusted Rantzau, a disgraced Danish minister, who had been his colleague in the editorship of the Altona Journal, with the conduct of foreign affairs. He and his friend Brandt were created Earls. Stolk, his predecessor in favour, had fomented and kept up an animosity between the King and Queen: Struensee (unhappily for himself as well as for her) gained the confidence of the Queen, by restoring her to the good graces of her husband. Caroline Matilda, sister of George III., who then had the misfortune to be Queen of Denmark, is described by Falkenskiold* as the handsomest woman of the Court, as of a mild and reserved character, and as one who was well qualified to enjoy and impart happiness, if it had been her lot to be united to an endurable husband. Brandt seems to have been a weak coxcomb, and Rantzau a turbulent and ungrateful intriguer.

The only foreign business which Struensee found pending on his entrance into office, was a negotiation with Russia, concerning the pretensions of that formidable competitor to a part of Holstein, which Denmark had unjustly acquired fifty years before. Peter III., the head of the house of Holstein, was proud of his German ancestry, and ambitious of recovering their ancient dominions. After his murder, Catharine claimed these possessions, as nominal Regent of Holstein, during the minority of her son. The last act of Bernstorff's administration had been a very prudent accommodation, in which Russia agreed to relinquish her claims on Holstein, in consideration of the cession to her by Denmark of the small principality of Oldenburg, the very ancient partimony of the Danish Royal Family. Rantzau, who in his exile had had some quarrel with the Russian Government, prevailed on the inexperienced Struensee to delay the execution of this politic convention, and aimed at establishing the influence of France and Sweden at Copenhagen instead of that of Russia, which was then supported by England. He even entertained the chimerical project of driving the Empress from Petersburgh. Falkenskiold, who had been sent on a mission to Petersburgh, endeavoured, after his return, to disabuse Struensee, and to show him the ruinous tendency of such rash counsels, proposing to him even to recall Bernstorff, to facilitate the good understanding which could hardly be re-restored as long as Counts Osten and Rantzau, the avowed enemies of Russia, were in power. Struensee, like most of those who must be led by others, was exceedingly fearful of being thought to be so. When Falkenskiold warned him against yielding to Rantzau, his plans were shaken: but when the same weapon was turned against Falkenskiold, Struensee returned to his obstinacy. Even after Rantzau had become his declared enemy, he adhered to the plans of that intriguer, lest he should be suspected of yielding to Falkenskiold. Wherever there were only two roads, it was easy to lead Struensee, by exciting his fear of being led by the opposite party.

Struensee's measures of internal policy appear to have been generally well-meant, but often ill-judged. Some of his reforms were in themselves excellent: but he showed, on the whole, a meddling and restless spirit, impatient of the necessary delay, often employed in petty change, choosing wrong means, braving prejudices that might have been softened, and offending interests that might have been conciliated. He was a sort of inferior Joseph II.; like him, rather a servile copyist than an enlightened follower of Frederic II. His dissolution of the Guards (in itself a prudent measure of economy) turned a numerous body of volunteers into the service of his enemies. The removal of Bernstorff was a very blamable means of strengthening himself. The suppression of the Privy Council, the only feeble restraint on despotic power, was still more reprehensible in itself, and excited the just resentment of the Danish nobility. The repeal of a barbarous law, inflicting capital punishment on adultery, was easily misrepresented to the people as a mark of approbation of that vice.

Both Struensee and Brandt had embraced the infidelity at that time prevalent among men of the world, which consisted in little more than a careless transfer of implied faith from Luther to Voltaire. They had been acquainted with the leaders of the Philosophical party at Paris, and they introduced the

* General Falkenskiold was a Danish gentleman of respectable family, who, after having served in the French army during the Seven Years' War, and in the Russian army during the first war of Catharine II. against the Turks, was recalled to his country under the administration of Struensee, to take a part in the reform of the military establishment, and to conduct the negotiation at Petersburgh, respecting the claims of the Imperial family to the dutchy of Holstein. He was involved in the fall of Struensee, and was, without trial, doomed to imprisonment for life at Munkholm, a fortress situated on a rock opposite to Drontheim. After five years' imprisonment he was released, and permitted to live, first at Montpellier, and afterwards at Lausanne, at which last city (with the exception of one journey to Copenhagen) he past the latter part of his life, and where he died in September, 1820, in the eighty-third year of his age. He left his Memoirs for publication to his friend, M. Secretan, First Judge of the canton of Vaud.

conversation of their masters at Copenhagen. In the same school they were taught to see clearly enough the distempers of European society; but they were not taught (for their teachers did not know) which of these maladies were to be endured, which were to be palliated, and what were the remedies and regimen by which the remainder might, in due time, be effectually and yet safely removed. The dissolute manners of the Court contributed to their unpopularity; rather, perhaps, because the nobility resented the intrusion of upstarts into the sphere of their priviledged vice, than because there was any real increase of licentiousness.

It must not be forgotten that Struensee was the first minister of an absolute monarchy who abolished the torture; and that he patronized those excellent plans for the emancipation of the enslaved husbandmen, which were first conceived by Reverdil, a Swiss, and the adoption of which by the second Bernstorff has justly immortalized that statesman. He will be honoured by after ages for what offended the Lutheran clergy,—the free exercise of religious worship granted to Calvinists, to Moravians, and even to Catholics; for the Danish clergy were ambitious of retaining the right to persecute, not only long after it was impossible to exercise it, but even after they had lost the disposition to do so;—at first to overawe, afterwards to degrade non-conformists; in both stages, as a badge of the privileges and honour of an established church.

No part, however, of Struensee's private or public conduct can be justly considered as the cause of his downfall. His irreligion, his immoralities, his precipitate reforms, his parade of invidious favour, were only the instruments or pretexts by which his competitors for office were able to effect his destruction. Had he either purchased the good-will, or destroyed the power of his enemies at Court, he might long have governed Denmark, and perhaps have been gratefully remembered by posterity as a reformer of political abuses. He fell a victim to an intrigue for a change of ministers, which, under such a King, was really a struggle for the sceptre.

His last act of political imprudence illustrates both the character of his enemies, and the nature of absolute government. When he was appointed Secretary of the Cabinet, he was empowered to execute such orders as were very urgent, without the signature of the King, on condition, however, that they should be weekly laid before him, to be confirmed or annulled under his own hand. This liberty had been practised before his administration; and it was repeated in many thousand instances after his downfall. Under any monarchy, the substantial fault would have consisted rather in assuming an independence of his colleagues, than in encroaching on any royal power which was real or practicable. Under so wretched a pageant as the King of Denmark, Struensee showed his folly in obtaining, by a formal order, the power which he might easily have continued to execute without it. But this order was the signal of a clamour against him, as an usurper of royal prerogative. The Guards showed symptoms of mutiny: the garrison of the capital adopted their resentment. The populace became riotous. Rantzau, partly stimulated by revenge against Struensee, for having refused a protection to him against his creditors, being secretly favoured by Count Osten, found means of gaining over Guldberg, an ecclesiastic of obscure birth, full of professions of piety, the preceptor of the King's brother, who prevailed on that prince and the Queen-Dowager to engage in the design of subverting the Administration. Several of Struensee's friends warned him of his danger; but, whether from levity or magnanimity, he neglected their admonitions. Rantzau himself, either jealous of the ascendant acquired by Guldberg among the conspirators, or visited by some compunctious remembrances of friendship and gratitude, spoke to Falkenskiold confidentially of the prevalent rumours, and tendered his services for the preservation of his former friend. Falkenskiold distrusted the advances of Rantzau, and answered coldly, "Speak to Struensee:" Rantzau turned away, saying, "He will not listen to *me*."

Two days afterwards, on the 16th of January, 1772, there was a brilliant masked ball at Court, where the conspirators and their victims mingled in the festivities (as was observed by some foreign ministers present) with more than usual gaiety. At four o'clock in the morning, the Queen-Dowager, who was the King's step-mother, her son, and Count Rantzau, entered the King's bedchamber, compelled his valet to awaken him, and required him to sign an order to apprehend the Queen, the Counts Struensee and Brandt, who, with other conspirators, they pretended were then engaged in a plot to depose, if not to murder him. Christian is said to have hesitated, from fear or obstinacy,—perhaps from some remnant of humanity and moral restraint: but he soon yielded; and his verbal assent, or perhaps a silence produced by terror, was thought a sufficient warrant. Rantzau, with three officers, rushed with his sword drawn into the apartment of the Queen, compelled her to rise from her bed, and, in spite of her tears and threats, sent her, half-dressed, a prisoner to the fortress of Cronenbourg, together with her infant daughter Louisa, whom she was then suckling, and Lady Mostyn, an English lady who attended her. Struensee and Brandt were in the same night thrown into prison, and loaded with irons. On the next day, the King was paraded through the streets in a carriage drawn by eight milk-white horses, as if triumphing after a glorious victory over his enemies, in which he had saved his country: the city was illuminated. The preachers of the Established Church are charged by several concurring witnesses with inhuman and unchristian invectives from the pulpit against the Queen and the fallen ministers; the good, doubtless, believing too easily the tale of the victors, the base paying court to the dispensers of preferment, and the bigoted greedily swallowing the most incredible accusations against unbelievers. The populace, inflamed by these declamations, demolished or pillaged from sixty to a hundred houses.

The conspirators distributed among themselves the chief offices. The King was suffered to fall into his former nullity: the formality of his signature was dispensed with; and the affairs of the kingdom were conducted in his name, only till his son was of an age to assume the regency. Guldberg, under the modest title of "Secretary of the Cabinet," became Prime Minister. Rantzau was appointed a Privy Councillor; and Osten retained the department of Foreign Affairs: but it is consolatory to add, that, after a few months, both were discarded at the instance of the Court of Petersburgh, to complete the desired exchange of Holstein for Oldenburgh.

The object of the conspiracy being thus accomplished, the conquerors proceeded, as usual, to those judicial proceedings against the prisoners, which are intended formally to justify the violence of a victorious faction, but substantially aggravate its guilt. A commission was appointed to try the accused: its leading members were the chiefs of the conspiracy. Guldberg, one of them, had to determine, by the sentence which he pronounced, whether he was himself a rebel. General Eichstedt, the president, had personally arrested several of the prisoners, and was, by his judgment on Struensee, who had been his benefactor, to decide, that the criminality of that minister was of so deep a die as to cancel the obligations of gratitude. To secure his impartiality still more, he was appointed a minister, and promised the office of preceptor of the hereditary prince,—the permanence of which appointments must have partly depended on the general conviction that the prisoners were guilty.

The charges against Struensee and Brandt are dated on the 21st of April. The defence of Struensee was drawn up by his counsel on the 22d; that of Brandt was prepared on the 23d. Sentence was pronounced against both on the 23d. On the 27th, it was approved, and ordered to be executed by the King. On the 28th, after their right hands had been cut off on the scaffold, they were beheaded. For three months they had been closely and very cruelly imprisoned. The proceedings of the commission were secret: the prisoners were not confronted with each other; they heard no witnesses; they read no depositions; they did not appear to have seen any counsel till they had received the indictments. It is characteristic of this scene to add, that the King went to the Opera on the 25th, after signifying his approbation of the sentence; and that on the 27th, the day of its solemn confirmation, there was a masked ball at Court. On the day of the execution, the King again went to the Opera. The passion which prompts an absolute monarch to raise an unworthy favourite to honour, is still less disgusting than the levity and hardness with which, on the first alarm, he always abandons the same favourite to destruction. It may be observed, that the very persons who had represented the patronage of operas and masquerades as one of the offences of Struensee, were the same who thus unseasonably paraded their unhappy Sovereign through a succession of such amusements.

The Memoirs of Falkenskiold contain the written answers of Struensee to the preliminary questions of the commission, the substance of the charges against him, and the defence made by his counsel. The first were written on the 14th of April, when he was alone in a dungeon, with irons on his hands and feet, and an iron collar fastened to the wall round his neck. The Indictment is prefaced by a long declamatory invective against his general conduct and character, such as still dishonour the criminal proceedings of most nations, and from which England has probably been saved by the scholastic subtlety and dryness of her system of what is called "special pleading." Laying aside his supposed connection with the Queen, which is reserved for a few separate remarks, the charges are either perfectly frivolous, or sufficiently answered by his counsel, in a defence which he was allowed only one day to prepare, and which bears evident marks of being written with the fear of the victorious faction before the eyes of the feeble advocate. One is, that he caused the young Prince to be trained so hardily as to endanger his life; in answer to which, he refers to the judgment of physicians, appeals to the restored health of the young Prince, and observes, that even if he had been wrong, his fault could have been no more than an error of judgment. The truth is, that he was guilty of a ridiculous mimicry of the early education of Emile, at a time when all Europe was intoxicated by the writings of Rousseau. To the second charge, that he had issued, on the 21st of December preceding, unknown to the King, an order for the incorporation of the Foot Guards with the troops of the line, and on their refusal to obey, had, on the 24th, obtained an order from him for their reduction, he answered, that the draught of the order had been read and approved by the King on the 21st, signed and sealed by him on the 23d, and finally confirmed by the order for reducing the refractory Guards, as issued by his Majesty on the 24th; so that he could scarcely be said to have been even in form guilty of a two days' usurpation. It might have been added, that it was immediately fully pardoned by the royal confirmation; that Rantzau, and others of his enemies, had taken an active share in it; and that it was so recent, that the conspirators must have resolved on their measures before its occurrence. He was further charged with taking or granting exorbitant pensions; and he answered, seemingly with truth, that they were not higher than those of his predecessors. He was accused also of having falsified the public accounts; to which his answer is necessarily too detailed for our purpose, but appears to be satisfactory. Both these last offences, if they had been committed, could not have been treated as high treason in any country not wholly barbarous; and the evidence on which the latter and more precise of the charges rested, was a declaration of the imbecile and imprisoned King on an intricate matter of account reported to him by an agent of the enemies of the prisoner.

Thus stands the case of the unfortunate Struensee on all the charges but one, as it appears in the accusation which his enemies had such time and power to support, and on the defence made for him under such cruel disadvantages. That he was innocent of the political offences laid to his charge, is rendered highly probable by the Narrative of his Conversion, published soon after his execution by Dr. Munter, a divine of Copenhagen, appointed by the Danish Government to attend him;* a composition, which bears the strongest marks of the probity and sincerity of the writer, and is a perfect model of the manner in which a person, circumstanced like Struensee, ought to be treated by a kind and considerate minister of religion. Men of all opinions, who peruse this narrative, must own that it is impossible, with more tenderness, to touch the wounds of a sufferer, to reconcile the agitated penitent to himself, to present religion as the consoler, not as the disturber of his dying moments, gently to dispose him to try his own actions by a higher test of morality, to fill his mind with indulgent benevolence towards his fellow-men, and to exalt it to a reverential love of boundless perfection. Dr. Munter deserved the confidence of Struensee, and seems entirely to have won it. The unfortunate man freely owned his private licentiousness, his success in corrupting the principles of the victims of his desires, his rejection not only of religion, but also in theory, though not quite in feeling, of whatever ennobles and elevates the mind in morality, the imprudence and rashness by which he brought ruin on his friends, and plunged his parents in deep affliction, and the ignoble and impure motives of all his public actions, which, in the eye of reason, deprived them of that pretension to virtuous character, to which their outward appearance might seem to entitle them. He felt for his friends with unusual tenderness. Instead of undue concealment from Munter, he is, perhaps, chargeable with betraying to him secrets which were not exclusively his own: but he denies the truth of the political charges against him, —more especially those of peculation and falsification of accounts.

The charges against Brandt would be altogether unworthy of consideration, were it not for the light which one of them throws on the whole of this atrocious procedure. The main accusation against him was, that he had beaten, flogged, and scratched the sacred person of the King. His answer was, that the King, who had a passion for wrestling and boxing, had repeatedly challenged him to a match, and had severely beaten him five or six times; that he did not gratify his master's taste till after these provocations; that two of the witnesses against him, servants of the King, had indulged their master in the same sport; and that he received liberal gratifications, and continued to enjoy the royal favour for months after this pretended treason. The King inherited this perverse taste in amusements from his father, whose palace had been the theatre of the like kingly sports. It is impossible to entertain the least doubt of the truth of this defence: it affords a natural and probable explanation of a fact which would be otherwise incomprehensible.

A suit for divorce was commenced against the Queen, on the ground of criminal connection with Struensee, who was himself convicted of high treason for that connection. This unhappy princess had been sacrificed, at the age of seventeen, to the brutal caprices of a husband who, if he had been a private man, would have been deemed incapable of the deliberate consent which is essential to marriage. She had early suffered from his violence, though she so far complied with his fancies as to ride with him in male apparel,—an indecorum for which she had been sharply reprehended by her mother, the Princess-Dowager of Wales, in a short interview between them, during a visit which the latter had paid to her brother at Gotha, after an uninterrupted residence of thirty-four years in England. The King had suffered the Russian minister at Copenhagen to treat her with open rudeness; and had disgraced his favourite cousin, the Prince of Hesse, for taking her part. He had never treated her with common civility, till they were reconciled by Struensee, at that period of overflowing good-nature when that minister obtained the recall from banishment of the ungrateful Rantzau.

The evidence against her consisted of a number of circumstances (none of them incapable of an innocent explanation) sworn to by attendants, who had been employed as spies on her conduct. She owned that she had been guilty of much imprudence; but in her dying moments she declared to M. Roques, pastor of the French church at Zell, that she never had been unfaithful to her husband.* It is true, that her own signature affixed to a confession was alleged against her: but if General Falkenskiold was rightly informed (for he has every mark of honest intention), that signature proves nothing but

* Reprinted by the late learned and exemplary Mr. Rennell of Kensington. London, 1824.

* Communicated by him to M. Secretan on the 7th of March, 1780.

the malice and cruelty of her enemies. Schack, the counsellor sent to interrogate her at Cronenbourg, was received by her with indignation when he spoke to her of connection with Struensee. When he showed Struensee's confession to her, he artfully intimated that the fallen minister would be subjected to a very cruel death if he was found to have falsely criminated the Queen. "What!" she exclaimed, "do you believe that if I was to confirm this declaration, I should save the life of that unfortunate man?" Schack answered by a profound bow. The Queen took a pen, wrote the first syllable of her name, and fainted away. Schack completed the signature, and carried away the fatal document in triumph.

Struensee himself, however, had confessed his intercourse to the Commissioners. It is said that this confession was obtained by threats of torture, facilitated by some hope of life, and influenced by a knowledge that the proceeding against the Queen could not be carried beyond divorce. But his repeated and deliberate avowals to Dr. Munter do not (it must be owned) allow of such an explanation. Scarcely any supposition favourable to this unhappy princess remains, unless it should be thought likely, that as Dr. Munter's Narrative was published under the eye of her oppressors, they might have caused the confessions of Struensee to be inserted in it by their own agents, without the consent—perhaps without the knowledge—of Munter; whose subsequent life is so little known, that we cannot determine whether he ever had the means of exposing the falsification. It must be confessed, that internal evidence does not favour this hypothesis; for the passages of the Narrative, which contain the avowals of Struensee, have a striking appearance of genuineness. If Caroline betrayed her sufferings to Struensee,—if she was led to a dangerous familiarity with a pleasing young man who had rendered essential services to her,—if mixed motives of confidence, gratitude, disgust, and indignation, at last plunged her into an irretrievable fault, the reasonable and the virtuous will reserve their abhorrence for the conspirators who, for the purposes of their own ambition, punished her infirmity by ruin, endangered the succession to the crown, and disgraced their country in the eyes of Europe. It is difficult to contain the indignation which naturally arises from the reflection, that at this very time, and with a full knowledge of the fate of the Queen of Denmark, the Royal Marriage Act was passed in England, for the avowed purpose of preventing the only marriages of preference, which a princess, at least, has commonly the opportunity of forming. Of a monarch, who thought so much more of the pretended degradation of his brother than of the cruel misfortunes of his sister, less cannot be said than that he must have had more pride than tenderness. Even the capital punishment of Struensee, for such an offence will be justly condemned by all but English lawyers, who ought to be silenced by the consciousness that the same barbarous disproportion of a penalty to an offence is sanctioned in the like case by their own law.

Caroline Matilda died at Zell about three years after her imprisonment. The last tidings which reached the Princess-Dowager of Wales on her death-bed, was the imprisonment of this ill-fated daughter, which was announced to her in a letter dictated to the King of Denmark by his new masters, and subscribed with his own hand. Two days before her death, though in a state of agony, she herself wrote a letter to the nominal sovereign, exhorting him to be at least indulgent and lenient towards her daughter. After hearing the news from Copenhagen she scarcely swallowed any nourishment. The intelligence was said to have accelerated her death; but the dreadful malady* under which she suffered, neither needed the cooperation of sorrow, nor was of a nature to be much affected by it.

What effects were produced by the interference of the British Minister for the Queen?—How far the conspirators were influenced by fear of the resentment of King George III.?—and, In what degree that monarch himself may have acquiesced in the measures finally adopted towards his sister?—are questions which must be answered by the historian from other sources than those from which we reason on the present occasion. The only legal proceeding ever commenced against the Queen was a suit for a divorce, which was in form perfectly regular: for in all Protestant countries but England, the offended party is entitled to release from the bands of marriage by the ordinary tribunals. It is said that two legal questions were then agitated in Denmark, and "even occasioned great debates among the Commissioners:—1st. Whether the Queen, as a sovereign, could be legally tried by her subjects; and, 2dly, Whether, as a foreign princess, she was amenable to the law of Denmark?" But it is quite certain on general principles, (assuming that no Danish law had made their Queen a partaker of the sovereign power, or otherwise expressly exempted her from legal responsibility,) that however high in dignity and honour, she was still a subject; and that as such, she, as well as every other person wherever born, resident in Denmark, was, during her residence at least, amenable to the laws of that country.

It was certain that there was little probability of hostility from England. Engaged in a contest with the people at home, and dreading the approach of a civil war with America, Lord North was not driven from an inflexible adherence to his pacific system by the Partition of Poland itself. An address for the production of the diplomatic correspondence respecting the French conquest, or purchase of Corsica, was moved in the

* An affection of the throat which precluded the passage of all nourishment.—Ed.

House of Commons on the 17th of November, 1768, for the purpose of condemning that unprincipled transaction, and with a view indirectly to blame the supineness of the English ministers respecting it. The motion was negatived by a majority of 230 to 84, on the same ground as that on which the like motions respecting Naples and Spain were resisted in 1822 and 1823;—that such proposals were too little if war was intended, and too much if it was not. The weight of authority, however, did not coincide with the power of numbers. Mr. Greenville, the most experienced statesman, and Mr. Burke, the man of greatest genius and wisdom in the House, voted in the minority, and argued in support of the motion. 'Such,' said the latter, 'was the general zeal for the Corsican, that if the Ministers would withdraw the Proclamation issued by Lord Bute's Government, forbidding British subjects to assist the Corsican "rebels,"' (a measure similar to our Foreign Enlistment Act), 'private individuals would supply the brave insurgents with sufficient means of defence.' The young Duke of Devonshire, then at Florence, had sent 400*l.* to Corsica, and raised 2000*l.* more for the same purpose by a subscription among the English in Italy.* A Government which looked thus passively at such breaches of the system of Europe on occasions when the national feeling was favourable to a more generous, perhaps a more wise policy, would hardly have been diverted from its course by any indignities or outrages which a foreign Government could offer to an individual of however illustrious rank. Little, however, as the likelihood of armed interference by England was, the apprehension of it might have been sufficient to enable the more wary of the Danish conspirators to contain the rage of their most furious accomplices. The ability and spirit displayed by Sir Robert Murray Keith on behalf of the Queen was soon after rewarded by his promotion to the embassy at Vienna, always one of the highest places in English diplomacy. His vigorous remonstrances in some measure compensated for the timidity of his Government; and he powerfully aided the cautious policy of Count Osten, who moderated the passions of his colleagues, though giving the most specious colour to their acts in his official correspondence with foreign Powers.

Contemporary observers of enlarged minds considered these events in Denmark not so much as they affected individuals, or were connected with temporary policy, as in the higher light in which they indicated the character of nations, and betrayed the prevalence of dispositions inauspicious to the prospects of mankind. None of the unavowed writings of Mr. Burke, and perhaps few of his acknowledged ones, exhibit more visible marks of his hand than the History of Europe in the Annual Register of 1772, which opens with a philosophical and eloquent vindication of the policy which watched over the balance of power, and with a prophetic display of the evils which were to flow from the renunciation of that policy by France and England, in suffering the partition of Poland. The little transactions of Denmark, which were despised by many as a petty and obscure intrigue, and affected the majority only as a part of the romance or tragedy of real life, appeared to the philosophical statesman pregnant with melancholy instruction. "It has," says he, "been too hastily and too generally received as an opinion with the most eminent writers, and from them too carelessly received by the world, that the Northern nations, at all times and without exception, have been passionate admirers of liberty, and tenacious to an extreme of their rights. A little attention will show that this opinion ought to be received with many restrictions. Sweden and Denmark have, within little more than a century, given absolute demonstration to the contrary; and the vast nation of the Russes, who overspread so great a part of the North, have, at all times, so long as their name has been known, or their acts remembered by history, been incapable of any other than a despotic government. And notwithstanding the contempt in which we hold the Eastern nations, and the slavish disposition we attribute to them, it may be found, if we make a due allowance for the figurative style and manner of the Orientals, that the official papers, public acts, and speeches, at the Courts of Petersburgh, Copenhagen, and Stockholm, are in as unmanly a strain of servility and adulation as those of the most despotic of the Asiatic governments."

It was doubtless an error to class Russia with the Scandinavian nations, merely because they were both comprehended within the same parallels of latitude. The Russians differ from them in race,—a circumstance always to be considered, though more liable to be exaggerated or underrated, than any other which contributes to determine the character of nations. No Sarmatian people has ever been free. The Russians profess a religion, founded on the blindest submission of the understanding, which is, in their modern modification of it, directed to their temporal sovereign. They were for ages the slaves of Tartars; the larger part of their dominions is Asiatic; and they were, till lately, with justice, more regarded as an Eastern than as a Western nation. But the nations of Scandinavia were of that Teutonic race, who were the founders of civil liberty: they early embraced the Reformation, which ought to have taught them the duty of exercising reason freely on every subject: and their spirit has never been broken by a

* These particulars are not to be found in the printed debate, which copies the account of this discussion given in the Annual Register by Mr. Burke, written, like his other abstracts of Parliamentary proceedings, with the brevity and reserve, produced by his situation as one of the most important parties in the argument, and by the severe notions then prevalent on such publications.

foreign yoke. Writing in the year when despotism was established in Sweden, and its baneful effects so strikingly exhibited in Denmark, Mr. Burke may be excused for comparing these then unhappy countries with those vast regions of Asia which have been the immemorial seat of slavery. The revolution which we have been considering, shows the propriety of the parallel in all its parts. If it only proved that absolute power corrupts the tyrant, there are many too debased to dread it on that account. But it shows him at Copenhagen, as at Ispahan, reduced to personal insignificance, a pageant occasionally exhibited by his ministers, or a tool in their hands, compelled to do whatever suits their purpose, without power to save the life even of a minion, and without security, in cases of extreme violence, for his own. Nothing can more clearly prove that under absolute monarchy, good laws, if they could by a miracle be framed, must always prove utterly vain; that civil cannot exist without political liberty; and that the detestable distinction, lately attempted in this country by the advocates of intolerance,* between freedom and political power, never can be allowed in practice without, in the first instance, destroying all securities for good government, and very soon introducing every species of corruption and oppression.

The part of Mr. Burke's History, which we have quoted, is followed by a memorable passage which seems, in later times, to have escaped the notice both of his opponents and adherents, and was probably forgotten by himself. After speaking of the final victory of Louis XV. over the French Parliaments, of whom he says, "that their fate seems to be finally decided,† and the few remains of public liberty that were preserved in these illustrious bodies are now no more," he proceeds to general reflection on the condition and prospects of Europe. "In a word, if we seriously consider the mode of supporting great standing armies, which becomes daily more prevalent, it will appear evident, that nothing less than a convulsion that will shake the globe to its centre, can ever restore the European nations to that liberty by which they were once so much distinguished. The Western world was its seat until another more western was discovered: and that other will probably be its asylum when it is hunted down in every other part of the world. Happy it is that the worst of times may have one refuge left for humanity."

This passage is not so much a prophecy of the French Revolution, as a declaration that without a convulsion as deep and dreadful as that great event, the European nations had no chance of being restored to their ancient dignity and their natural rights. Had it been written after, or at least soon after the event, it might have been blamed as indicating too little indignation against guilt, and compassion for suffering. Even when considered as referring to the events of a distant futurity, it may be charged with a pernicious exaggeration, which seems to extenuate revolutionary horrors by representing them as inevitable, and by laying it down falsely that Wisdom and Virtue can find no other road to Liberty. It would, however, be very unjust to charge such a purpose on Mr. Burke, or indeed to impute such a tendency to his desponding anticipations. He certainly appears to have foreseen that the progress of despotism would at length provoke a general and fearful resistance, the event of which, with a wise scepticism, he does not dare to foretel; rather, however, as a fond, and therefore fearful, lover of European liberty, foreboding that she will be driven from her ancient seats, and leave the inhabitants of Europe to be numbered with Asiatic slaves. The fierceness of the struggle he clearly saw, and most distinctly predicts; for he knew that the most furious passions of human nature would be enlisted on both sides. He does not conclude, from this dreadful prospect, that the chance of liberty ought to be relinquished rather than expose a country to the probability or possibility of such a contest; but, on the contrary, very intelligibly declares by the melancholy tone in which he adverts to the expulsion of Liberty, that every evil is to be hazarded for her preservation. It would be well if his professed adherents would bear in mind, that such is the true doctrine of most of those whom they dread and revile as incendiaries. The friends of freedom only profess that those who have recourse to the only remaining means of preserving or acquiring liberty, are not morally responsible for the evils which may arise in an inevitable combat.

The Danish dominions continued to be administered in the name of Christian VII., for the long period of thirty-six years after the deposition of Struensee. The mental incapacity under which he always laboured, was not formally recognised till the association of his son, now King of Denmark, with him in the government. He did not cease to breathe till 1808, after a nominal reign of forty-three years, and an animal existence of near sixty. During the latter part of that period, the real rulers of the country were wise and honest men. It enjoyed a considerable interval of prosperity under the administration of Bernstorff, whose merit in forbearing to join the coalition against France in 1793, is greatly enhanced by his personal abhorrence of the Revolution. His adoption of Reverdil's measures of enfranchisement, sheds the purest glory on his name.

The fate of Denmark, after the ambition of Napoleon had penetrated into the North,—the iniquity with which she was stripped by Russia of Norway, for adherence to an al-

* This was written in 1826.—Ed.

† They were re-established four years afterwards: but as this arose, not from the spirit of the nation, but from the advisers of the young King, who had full power to grant or withhold their restoration, the want of foresight is rather apparent than substantial.

liance which Russia had compelled her to join, and as a compensation to Sweden for Finland, of which Sweden had been robbed by Russia, are events too familiarly known to be recounted here. She is now no more than a principality, whose arms are still surmounted by a royal crown. A free and popular government, under the same wise administration, might have arrested many of these calamities, and afforded a new proof that the attachment of a people to a government in which they have a palpable interest and a direct share, is the most secure foundation of defensive strength.

The political misfortunes of Denmark disprove the commonplace opinion, that all enslaved nations deserve their fate: for the moral and intellectual qualities of the Danes seem to qualify them for the firm and prudent exercise of the privileges of freemen. All those by whom they are well known, commend their courage, honesty, and industry. The information of the labouring classes has made a considerable progress since their enfranchisement. Their literature, like that of the Northern nations, has generally been dependent on that of Germany, with which country they are closely connected in language and religion. In the last half century, they have made persevering efforts to build up a national literature. The resistance of their fleet in 1801, has been the theme of many Danish poets; but we believe that they have been as unsuccessful in their bold competition with Campbell, as their mariners in their gallant contest with Nelson. However, a poor and somewhat secluded country, with a small and dispersed population, which has produced Tycho Brahe, Oehlenschlæger, and Thorwaldsen, must be owned to have contributed her full contingent to the intellectual greatness of Europe.

STATEMENT OF THE CASE

OF

DONNA MARIA DA GLORIA,

AS

A CLAIMANT TO THE CROWN OF PORTUGAL.*

Before the usurpation of Portugal by Philip II. of Spain in 1580, the Portuguese nation, though brilliantly distinguished in arts and arms, and as a commercial and maritime power, in some measure filling up the interval between the decline of Venice and the rise of Holland, had not yet taken a place in the political system of Europe. From the restoration of her independence under the House of Braganza in 1640, to the peace of Utrecht, Spain was her dangerous enemy, and France, the political opponent of Spain, was her natural protector. Her relation to France was reversed as soon as a Bourbon King was seated on the throne of Spain. From that moment the union of the two Bourbon monarchies gave her a neighbour far more formidable than the Austrian princes who had slumbered for near a century at the Escurial. It became absolutely necessary for her safety that she should strengthen herself against this constantly threatening danger by an alliance, which, being founded in a common and permanent interest, might be solid and durable. England, the political antagonist of France, whose safety would be endangered by every aggrandizement of the House of Bourbon, and who had the power of rapidly succouring Portugal, without the means of oppressing her independence, was evidently the only state from which friendship and aid, at once effectual, safe, and lasting, could be expected:—hence the alliance between England and Portugal, and the union, closer than can be created by written stipulations, between these two countries.

The peril, however, was suspended during forty years of the dissolute and unambitious government of Louis XV. till the year 1761, when, by the treaty known under the name of the 'Family Compact,' the Duc de Choiseul may be justly said (to borrow the language of Roman ambition) to have reduced Spain to the form of a province. A separate and secret convention was executed on the same day (15th of August), by which it was agreed, that if England did not make peace with France by the 1st of May, 1762, Spain should then declare war against the former power. The sixth article fully disclosed the magnitude of the danger which, from that moment to this, has hung over the head of Portugal. His Most Faithful Majesty was to be desired to accede to the convention; "it not being

* From the Edinburgh Review, vol. xlv. p. 202.—Ed.

just," in the judgment of these royal jurists, "that he should remain a tranquil spectator of the disputes of the two Courts with England, and continue to enrich the enemies of the two Sovereigns, by keeping his ports open to them." The King of Portugal refused to purchase a temporary exemption from attack by a surrender of his independence. The French and Spanish Ministers declared, "that the Portuguese alliance with England, though called '*defensive*,' became in reality *offensive*, from the situation of the Portuguese dominions, and from the nature of the English power."* A war ensued,—being probably the first ever waged against a country, on the avowed ground of its geographical position. It was terminated by the Treaty of Paris in 1763, without, however, any proposition on the part of France and Spain that Portugal should be cut away from the Continent, and towed into the neighbourhood of Madeira,—where perhaps she might re-enter on her right as an independent state to observe neutrality, and to provide for her security by defensive alliances. This most barefaced act of injustice might be passed over here in silence, if it did not so strongly illustrate the situation of Portugal, since Spain became a dependent ally of France; and if we could resist the temptation of the occasion to ask whether the authors of such a war were as much less ambitious than Napoleon, as they were beneath him in valour and genius.

In the American war, it does not appear that any attempt was made, *on principles of geography*, to compel Portugal to make war on England.† The example of the Family Compact, however, was not long barren. As soon as the French Republic had re-established the ascendant of France at Madrid, they determined to show that they inherited the principles as well as the sceptre of their monarchs. Portugal, now overpowered, was compelled to cede Olivenza to Spain, and to shut her ports on English ships.‡ Thus terminated the second war made against her to oblige her to renounce the only ally capable of assisting her, and constantly interested in her preservation. But these compulsory treaties were of little practical importance, being immediately followed by the Peace of Amiens. They only furnished a new proof that the insecurity of Portugal essentially arose from the dependence of Spain on France, and could not be lessened by any change in the government of the latter country.

When the war, or rather wars, against universal monarchy broke out, the Regent of Portugal declared the neutrality of his dominions.* For four years he was indulged in the exercise of this right of an independent prince, in spite of the geographical position of the kingdom. At the end of that period the 'geographical principle' was enforced against him more fully and vigorously than on the former instances of its application. The Portuguese monarchy was confiscated and partitioned in a secret convention between France and Spain, executed at Fontainebleau on the 27th of October, 1807, by which considerable parts of its continental territory were granted to the Prince of the Peace, and to the Spanish Princess, then called Queen of Etruria, in sovereignty, but as feudatories of the crown of Spain.† A French army under Junot marched against Portugal, and the Royal Family were compelled, in November following, to embark for Brazil; a measure which was strongly suggested by the constant insecurity to which European Portugal was doomed by the Family Compact, and which had been seriously entertained by the Government since the treaty of Badajoz.

The events which followed in the Spanish Peninsula are too memorable to be more than alluded to. Portugal was governed by a Regency nominated by the King. The people caught the generous spirit of the Spaniards, took up arms against the conquerors, and bravely aided the English army to expel them. The army, delivered from those unworthy leaders to whom the abuses of despotism had subjected them, took an ample share in the glorious march from Torres Vedras to Toulouse, which forms one of the most brilliant pages in history.

The King opened the ports of his American territories to all nations;—a measure in him of immediate necessity, but fraught with momentous consequences. He cemented his ancient relations with Great Britain (which geography no longer forbade) by new treaties; and he bestowed on Brazil a separate administration, with the title of a kingdom. The course of events in the spring of 1814 had been so rapid, that there was no minister in Europe authorized to represent the Court of Rio Janeiro at the Treaty of Paris: but so close was the alliance with England then deemed, that Lord Castlereagh took it upon him, on the part of Portugal, to stipulate for the restoration of French Guiana, which had been conquered by the Portuguese arms. At the Congress of Vienna in the following year, the Portuguese plenipotentiaries protested against the validity of this restoration, and required the retrocession of Olivenza, which had been wrested from them at Badajoz, in a war in which they had been the allies of England. The good offices of the European powers to obtain this last resto-

* Note of Don Joseph Torrero and Don Jacques O'Dun, Lisbon, 1st April, 1762.—Annual Register.

† Portugal did indeed accede to the Armed Neutrality; but it was not till the 15th of July, 1782, on the eve of a general peace.—Martens, Recueil de Traités, vol. ii. p. 208.

‡ By the Treaty between France and Spain of the 19th August, 1796.—Martens, vol. vi. p. 656.

* Treaties of Badajoz, 6th of June; of Madrid, 20th of September, 1801.—Martens, Supplément, vol. ii. pp. 340, 539.

† Schoëll, Histoire Abrégée des Traités de Paix, &c., vol. ix. p. 110.

ration were then solemnly promised, but have hitherto been in vain.

In 1816, John VI. refused to return to Lisbon, though a squadron under Sir John Beresford had been sent to convey him thither; partly because he was displeased at the disregard of his rights, shown by the Congress of Vienna; partly because the unpopularity of the Commercial Treaty had alienated him from England; but probably still more, because he was influenced by the visible growth of a Brazilian party which now aimed at independence. Henceforward, indeed, the separation manifestly approached. The Portuguese of Europe began to despair of seeing the seat of the monarchy at Lisbon; the Regency were without strength; all appointments were obtained from the distant Court of Rio Janeiro; men and money were drawn away for the Brazilian war on the Rio de la Plata; the army left behind was unpaid: in fine, all the materials of formidable discontent were heaped up in Portugal, when, in the beginning of 1820, the Spanish Revolution broke out. Six months elapsed without a spark having fallen in Portugal. Marshal Beresford went to Rio Janeiro to solicit the interference of the King: but that Prince made no effort to prevent the conflagration; and perhaps no precaution would then have been effectual.

In August, the garrison of Oporto declared for a revolution; and being joined on their march to the Capital by all the troops on their line, were received with open arms by the garrison of Lisbon. It was destined to bestow on Portugal a still more popular constitution than that of Spain. With what prudence or justice the measures of the popular leaders in the south of Europe were conceived or conducted, it is happily no part of our present business to inquire. Those who openly remonstrated against their errors when they seemed to be triumphant, are under no temptation to join the vulgar cry against the fallen. The people of Portugal, indeed, unless guided by a wise and vigorous Government, were destined by the very nature of things, in any political change made at that moment, to follow the course of Spain. The Regency of Lisbon, by the advice of a Portuguese Minister,* at once faithful to his Sovereign, and friendly to the liberty of his country, made an attempt to stem the torrent, by summoning an assembly of the Cortes. The attempt was too late; but it pointed to the only means of saving the monarchy.

The same Minister, on his arrival in Brazil, at the end of the year, advised the King to send his eldest son to Portugal as Viceroy, with a constitutional charter; recommending also the assembling of the most respectable Brazilians at Rio Janeiro, to consider of the improvements which seemed practicable in Brazil. But while these honest, and not unpromising counsels, were the objects of longer discussions than troublous times allow, a revolution broke out in Brazil, in the spring of 1821, the first professed object of which was, not the separation of that country, but the adoption of the Portuguese Constitution. It was acquiesced in by the King, and espoused with the warmth of youth, by his eldest son Don Pedro. But in April, the King, disquieted by the commotions which encompassed him, determined to return to Lisbon, and to leave the conduct of the American revolution to his son. Even on the voyage he was advised to stop at the Azores, as a place where he might negotiate with more independence: but he rejected this counsel; and on his arrival in the Tagus, on the 3d of July, nothing remained but a surrender at discretion. The revolutionary Cortes were as tenacious of the authority of the mother country, as the Royal Administration; and they accordingly recalled the Heir-apparent to Lisbon. But the spirit of independence arose among the Brazilians, who, encouraged by the example of the Spanish-Americans, presented addresses to the Prince, beseeching him not to yield to the demands of the Portuguese Assembly, who desired to make him a prisoner, as they had made his father; but, by assuming the crown of Brazil, to provide for his own safety, as well as for their liberty. In truth it is evident, that he neither could have continued in Brazil without acceding to the popular desire, nor could have then left it without insuring the destruction of monarchy in that country. He acquiesced therefore in the prayer of these flattering petitions: the independence of Brazil was proclaimed; and the Portuguese monarchy was finally dismembered.

In the summer of 1823, the advance of the French army into Spain, excited a revolt of the Portuguese Royalists. The infant Don Miguel, the King's second son, attracted notice, by appearing at the head of a battalion who declared against the Constitution; and the inconstant soldiery, equally ignorant of the object of their revolts against the King or the Cortes, were easily induced to overthrow the slight work of their own hands. Even in the moment of victory, however, John VI. solemnly promised a free government to the Portuguese nation.* A few weeks afterwards, he gave a more deliberate and decisive proof of what was then thought necessary for the security of the throne, and the well-being of the people, by a Royal Decree,† which, after pronouncing the nullity of the constitution of the Cortes, proceeds as follows:—"Conformably to my feelings, and the sincere promises of my Proclamations, and considering that the ancient fundamental laws of the monarchy cannot entirely answer my paternal purposes, without being accommodated to the present state of civilization, to the mutual relations

* Count Palmella.—Ed.

* Proclamations from Villa Francha of the 31st of May and 3d of June.

† Of the 18th of June.

of the different parts which compose the monarchy, and to the form of representative governments established in Europe, I have appointed a Junta to prepare the plan of a charter of the fundamental laws of the Portuguese monarchy, which shall be founded on the principles of public law, and open the way to a progressive reformation of the administration."

Count Palmella was appointed President of this Junta, composed of the most distinguished men in the kingdom. They completed their work in a few months; and presented to the King the plan of a Constitutional Charter, almost exactly the same with that granted in 1826 by Don Pedro. John VI. was favourable to it, considering it as an adaptation of the ancient fundamental laws to present circumstances. While the revolution was triumphant, the more reasonable Royalists regretted that no attempt had been made to avoid it by timely concession; and in the first moment of escape, the remains of the same feelings disposed the Court to concede something. But after a short interval of quiet, the possessors of authority relapsed into the ancient and fatal error of their kind,—that of placing their security in maintaining the unbounded power which had proved their ruin. A resistance to the form of the constitution, which grew up in the interior of the Court, was fostered by foreign influence, and after a struggle of some months, prevented the promulgation of the charter.

In April 1824, events occurred at Lisbon, on which we shall touch as lightly as possible. It is well known that part of the garrison of Lisbon surrounded the King's palace, and hindered the access of his servants to him; that some of his ministers were imprisoned; that the diplomatic body, including the Papal Nuncio, the French Ambassador, and the Russian as well as English Ministers, were the means of restoring him to some degree of liberty, which was however so imperfect and insecure, that, by the advice of the French Ambassador, the King took refuge on board an English ship of war lying in the Tagus, from whence he was at length able to assert his dignity and re-establish his authority. Over the part in these transactions, into which evil counsellors betrayed the inexperience of Don Miguel, it is peculiarly proper to throw a veil, in imitation of his father, who forgave these youthful faults as 'involuntary errors.' This proof of the unsettled state of the general opinion and feeling respecting the government, suggested the necessity of a conciliatory measure, which might in some measure compensate for the defeat of the Constitutional Charter in the preceding year. The Minister who, both in Europe and in America, had attempted to avert revolution by reform, was not wanting to his sovereign and his country at this crisis. Still counteracted by foreign influence, and opposed by a colleague who was a personal favourite of the King, he could not again propose the Charter, nor even obtain so good a substitute for it as he desired: but he had the merit of being always ready to do the best practicable. By his counsel, the King issued a Proclamation on the 4th of June, for restoring the ancient constitution of the Portuguese monarchy, with assurances that an assembly of the Cortes, or Three Estates of the Realm, should be speedily held with all their legal rights, and especially with the privilege of laying before the King, for his consideration, the heads of such measures as they might deem necessary for the public good. To that assembly was referred the consideration of the periodical meetings of succeeding Cortes, and 'the means of progressively ameliorating the administration of the state.' The proclamation treats this re-establishment of the ancient constitution as being substantially the same with the Constitutional Charter drawn up by the Junta in the preceding year; and it was accordingly followed by a Decree, dissolving that Junta, as having performed its office. Though these representations were not scrupulously true, yet when we come to see what the rights of the Cortes were in ancient times, the language of the Proclamation will not be found to deviate more widely into falsehood than is usual in the preambles of Acts of State. Had the time for the convocation of the Cortes been fixed, the restoration of the ancient constitution might, without much exaggeration, have been called the establishment of liberty. For this point the Marquis Palmella made a struggle: but the King thought that he had done enough, in granting such a pledge to the Constitutionalists, and was willing to soothe the Absolutists, by reserving to himself the choice of a time. On the next day he created a Junta, to prepare, 'without loss of time,' the regulations necessary 'for the convocation of the Cortes, and for the election of the members.' As a new proof of the growing conviction that a free constitution was necessary, and as a solemn promise that it should be established, the Declaration of the 4th of June is by no means inferior in force to its predecessors. Nay, in that light, it may be considered as deriving additional strength from those appearances of reserve and reluctance which distinguish it from the more ingenious, and really more politic Declarations of 1823. But its grand defect was of a practical nature, and consisted in the opportunity which indefinite delay affords, for evading the performance of a promise.

Immediately after the counter-revolution in 1823, John VI. had sent a mission to Rio Janeiro, requiring the submission of his son and his Brazilian subjects. But whatever might be the wishes of Don Pedro, he had no longer the power to transfer the allegiance of a people who had tasted independence,—who were full of the pride of their new acquisition,—who valued it as their only security against the old monopoly, and who may well be excused for thinking it more advantageous to name at home the officers of their own government, than to receive rulers and magistrates from the intrigues of courtiers at Lisbon. Don Pedro could not restore to Portugal her American empire; but he might easily lose Brazil in the attempt. A negotiation was opened at London, in the year 1825, under the mediation of Austria and England. The differences between the two branches of the House of Braganza were, it must be admitted, peculiarly untractable. Portugal was to surrender her sovereignty, or Brazil to resign her independence. Union, on equal terms, was equally objected to by both. It was evident that no amicable issue of such a negotiation was possible, which did not involve acquiescence in the separation; and the very act of undertaking the mediation, sufficiently evinced that this event was contemplated by the mediating Powers. The Portuguese minister in London, Count Villa-Real, presented projects which seemed to contain every concession short of independence: but the Brazilian deputies who, though not admitted to the conference, had an unofficial intercourse with the British Ministers, declared, as might be expected, that nothing short of independence could be listened to. It was agreed, therefore, that Sir Charles Stuart, who was then about to go to Rio Janeiro to negotiate a treaty between England and Brazil, should take Lisbon on his way, and endeavour to dispose the Portuguese Government to consent to a sacrifice which could no longer be avoided. He was formally permitted by his own Government to accept the office of Minister Plenipotentiary from Portugal to Brazil, if it should be proposed to him at Lisbon. Certainly no man could be more fitted for this delicate mediation, both by his extraordinary knowledge of the ancient constitution of Portugal, and by the general confidence which he had gained while a minister of the Regency during the latter years of the war. After a series of conferences with the Count de Porto Santo, Minister for Foreign Affairs, which continued from the 5th of April to the 23d of May, and in the course of which two points were considered as equally understood,—that John VI. should cede to Don Pedro the sovereignty of Brazil, and that Don Pedro should preserve his undisputed right as heir of Portugal,—he set sail for Rio Janeiro, furnished with full powers, as well as instructions, and more especially with Royal Letters-Patent of John VI., to be delivered on the conclusion of an amicable arrangement, containing the following important and decisive clause:—"And as the succession of the Imperial and Royal Crowns belongs to my beloved son Don Pedro, I do, by these Letters-Patent, cede and transfer to him the full exercise of sovereignty in the empire of Brazil, which is to be governed by him; nominating him Emperor of Brazil, and Prince Royal of Portugal and the Algarves."

A treaty was concluded on the 29th of August, by Sir Charles Stuart, recognising the independence and separation of Brazil; acknowledging the sovereignty of that country to be vested in Don Pedro; allowing the King of Portugal also to assume the Imperial title; binding the Emperor of Brazil to reject the offer of any Portuguese colony to be incorporated with his dominions; and containing some other stipulations usual in treaties of peace. It was ratified at Lisbon, on the 5th of November following, by Letters-Patent,* from which, at the risk of some repetition, it is necessary to extract two clauses, the decisive importance of which will be shortly seen. "I have ceded and transferred to my beloved son Don Pedro de Alcantara, heir and successor of these kingdoms, all my rights over that country, recognising its independence with the title of empire." "We recognise our said son Don Pedro de Alcantara, Prince of Portugal and the Algarves, as Emperor, and having the exercise of sovereignty in the whole empire."

The part of this proceeding which is intended to preserve the right of succession to the crown of Portugal to Don Pedro, is strictly conformable to diplomatic usage, and to the principles of the law of nations. Whatever relates to the cession of a claim is the proper subject of agreement between the parties, and is therefore inserted in the treaty. The King of Portugal, the former Sovereign of Brazil, cedes his rights or pretensions in *that* country to his son. He releases all his former subjects from their allegiance. He abandons those claims which alone could give him any colour or pretext for interfering in the internal affairs of that vast region. Nothing could have done this effectually, solemnly, and notoriously, but the express stipulation of a treaty. Had Don Pedro therefore been at the same time understood to renounce his right of succession to the crown of Portugal, an explicit stipulation in the treaty to that effect would have been necessary: for such a renunciation would have been the cession of a right. Had it even been understood, that the recognition of his authority as an independent monarch *implied* the abdication of his rights as heir-apparent to the Portuguese crown, it would have been consonant to the general tenor of the treaty, explicitly to recognise this abdication. The silence of the treaty is a proof that none of the parties to it considered these rights as taken away or impaired, by any previous or concomitant circumstance. Stipulations were necessary when the state of regal rights was to be altered; but they would be at least impertinent where it remained unchanged. Silence is in the latter case sufficient; since, where nothing is to be done, nothing needs be said. There is no stipulation in the treaty, by which Don Pedro acknowledges the sovereignty of his father in Portugal; because that sovereignty is left in the same condition in which it was

* Gazeta de Lisbon, of the 15th of November

before. For the very same reason the treaty has no article for the preservation of Don Pedro's right of succession to Portugal. Had Don Pedro required a stipulation in the treaty for the maintenance of these rights, he would have done an act which would have tended more to bring them into question, than to strengthen them. As they were rights which John VI. could not take away, it was fit and wise to treat them also as rights which no act of his could bestow or confirm.

But though a provision for the preservation of these rights in the treaty was needless, and would have been altogether misplaced, there were occasions on which the recognition of them was fit, and, as a matter of abundant caution, expedient. These occasions are accordingly not passed over. The King of Portugal styles Don Pedro the heir of Portugal, both in the first Letters-Patent, addressed to his Brazilian subjects, in which he recognises the independence of Brazil, and in the second, addressed to his Portuguese subjects, where he ratifies the treaty which definitively established that independence. Acknowledged to be the monarch, and for the time the lawgiver of Portugal, and necessarily in these acts, claiming the same authority in Brazil, he announces to the people of both countries that the right of his eldest son to inherit the crown was, in November 1825, inviolate, unimpaired, unquestioned.

The ratifications are, besides, a portion of the treaty; and when they are exchanged, they become as much articles of agreement between the parties, as any part of it which bears that name. The recognition repeated in this Ratification proceeded from John VI., and was accepted by Don Pedro. Nothing but express words could have taken away so important a right as that of succession to the crown: in this case, there are express words which recognise it. Though it has been shown that silence would have been sufficient, the same conclusion would unanswerably follow, if the premises were far more scanty. The law of nations has no established forms, a deviation from which is fatal to the validity of the trasactions to which they are appropriated. It admits no merely technical objections to conventions formed under its authority, and is bound by no positive rules in the interpretation of them. Wherever the intention of contracting parties is plain, it is the sole interpreter of a contract. Now, it is needless to say that, in the Treaty of Rio Janeiro, taken with the preceding and following Letters-Patent, the *manifest intention* of John VI. was not to impair, but to recognise the rights of his eldest son to the inheritance of Portugal.

On the 10th of March 1826, John VI. died at Lisbon. On his death-bed, however, he had made provision for the temporary administration of the government. By a Royal Decree, of the 6th,* he committed the government to his daughter, the Infanta Donna Isabella Maria, assisted by a council during his illness, or, in the event of his death, till "*the legitimate heir and successor to the crown* should make other provision in this respect." These words have no ambiguity. In every hereditary monarchy they must naturally, and almost necessarily, denote the eldest son of the King, when he leaves a son. It would, in such a case, require the strongest evidence to warrant the application of them to any other person. It is clear that the King must have had an individual in view, unless we adopt the most extravagant supposition that, as a dying bequest to his subjects, he meant to leave them a disputed succession and a civil war. Who could that individual be, but Don Pedro, his eldest son, whom, according to the ancient order of succession to the crown of Portugal, he had himself called "*heir and successor*," on the 13th of May and 5th of November preceding. Such, accordingly, was the conviction, and the correspondent conduct of all whose rights or interests were concerned. The Regency was immediately installed, and universally obeyed at home, as well as acknowledged, without hesitation or delay, by all the Powers of Europe. The Princess Regent acted in the name, and on the behalf of her brother, Don Pedro. It was impossible that the succession of any Prince to a throne could be more quiet and undisputed.

The Regency, without delay, notified the demise of the late King to their new Sovereign: and then the difficulties of that Prince's situation began to show themselves. Though the treaty had not weakened his hereditary right to Portugal, yet the main object of it was to provide, not only for the independence of Brazil, but for its "separation" from Portugal, which undoubtedly imported a separation of the crowns. Possessing the government of Brazil, and inheriting that of Portugal, he became bound by all the obligations of the treaty between the two states. Though he inherited the crown of Portugal by the laws of that country, yet he was disabled by treaty from *permanently* continuing to hold it with that of Brazil. But if, laying aside unprofitable subtilties, we consult only conscience and common sense, we shall soon discover that these rights and duties are not repugnant, but that, on the contrary, the legal right is the only means of performing the federal duty. The treaty did not expressly determine which of the two crowns Don Pedro was bound to renounce; it therefore left him to make an option between them. For the implied obligations of a contract extend only to those acts of the parties which are necessary to the attainment of its professed object. If he chose,—as he has chosen,—to retain the crown of Brazil, it could not, by reasonable implication, require an *instantaneous* abdication of that of Portugal; because such a limitation of time was not necessary, and might have been very injurious to the object.

* Gazeta de Lisbon, of the 7th of March.

It left the choice of time, manner, and conditions to himself, requiring only good faith, and interdicting nothing but fraudulent delay. Had he not (according to the principle of all hereditary monarchs) become King of Portugal at the instant of his father's demise, there would have been no person possessed of the legal and actual power in both countries necessary to carry the treaty of separation into effect. If the Portuguese had not acquiesced in his authority, they must have voluntarily chosen anarchy; for no one could have the power to discharge the duty imposed by treaty, or to provide for any of the important changes which it might occasion. The most remarkable example of this latter sort, was the order of succession. The separation of the two crowns rendered it absolutely impossible to preserve that order in both monarchies; for both being hereditary, the legal order required that both crowns should descend to the same person, the eldest son of Don Pedro—the very union which it was the main or sole purpose of the treaty to prevent. A breach in the order of succession became therefore inevitable, either in Portugal or Brazil. Necessity required the deviation. But the same necessity vested in Don Pedro, as a king and a father, the power of regulating in this respect, the rights of his family; and the permanent policy of monarchies required that he should carry the deviation no farther than the necessity.

As the nearer female would inherit before the more distant male, Don Miguel had no right which was immediately involved in the arrangement to be adopted. It is acknowledged, that the two daughters of John VI., married and domiciled in Spain, had lost their rights as members of the Royal Family. Neither the Queen, nor indeed any other person, had a legal title to the regency, which in Portugal, as in France and England, was a case omitted in the constitutional laws, and, as no Cortes had been assembled for a century, could only be provided for by the King, who, of necessity, was the temporary lawgiver. The only parties who could be directly affected by the allotment of the two crowns, were the children of Don Pedro, the eldest of whom was in her sixth year. The more every minute part of this case is considered, the more obvious and indisputable will appear to be the necessity, that Don Pedro should retain the powers of a King of Portugal, until he had employed them for the quiet and safety of both kingdoms, as far as these might be endangered by the separation. He held, and holds, that crown as a trustee for the execution of the treaty. To hold it after the trust is performed, would be usurpation: to renounce it before that period, would be treachery to the trust.

That Don Pedro should have chosen Brazil, must have always been foreseen; for his election was almost determined by his preceding conduct. He preferred Brazil, where he had been the founder of a state, to Portugal, where the most conspicuous measures of his life could be viewed with no more than reluctant acquiescence. The next question which arose was, whether the inevitable breach in the order of succession was to be made in Portugal or Brazil; or, in other words, of which of these two disjointed kingdoms, the Infant Don Sebastian should be the heir-apparent. The father made the same choice for his eldest son as for himself. As Don Sebastian preserved his right of succession in Brazil, *the principle of the least possible deviation from the legal order* required that the crown of Portugal should devolve on his sister Donna Maria, the next in succession of the Royal Family.

After this exposition of the rights and duties of Don Pedro, founded on the principles of public law, and on the obligations of treaty, and of the motives of policy which have influenced him in a case where he was left free to follow the dictates of his own judgment, let us consider very shortly what a conscientious ruler would, in such a case, deem necessary to secure to both portions of his subjects all the advantages of their new position. He would be desirous of softening the humiliation of one, of effacing the recent animosities between them, and of reviving their ancient friendship, by preserving every tie which reminded them of former union and common descent. He would therefore, even if he were impartial, desire that they should continue under the same Royal Family which had for centuries ruled both. He would labour, as far as the case allowed, to strengthen the connections of language, of traditions, of manners, and of religion, by the resemblance of laws and institutions. He would clearly see that his Brazilian subjects never could trust his fidelity to their limited monarchy, if he maintained an absolute government in Portugal; and that the Portuguese people would not long endure to be treated as slaves, while those whom they were not accustomed to regard as their superiors were thought worthy of the most popular constitution. However much a monarch was indifferent or adverse to liberty, these considerations would lose nothing of their political importance: for a single false step in this path might overthrow monarchy in Brazil, and either drive Portugal into a revolution, or seat a foreign army in her provinces, to prevent it. It is evident that popular institutions can alone preserve monarchy in Brazil from falling before the principles of republican America; and it will hardly be denied, that, though some have questioned the advantage of liberty, no people were ever so mean-spirited as not to be indignant at being thought unworthy of it, as a privilege. Viewing liberty with the same cold neutrality, a wise statesman would have thought it likely to give stability to a new government in Portugal, and to be received there as some consolation for loss of dominion. Portugal, like all the other countries between the Rhine and the Mediterranean, had been convulsed by conquest and revolution. Ambition and rapacity, fear and revenge, political fanaticism and religious bigotry,—all the ungovernable passions which such scenes excite, still agitated the minds of those who had been actors or victims of them. Experience has proved, that no expedient can effectually allay these deep-seated disorders, but the institution of a government in which all interests and opinions are represented,—which keeps up a perpetual negotiation between them,—which compels each in its turn to give up some part of its pretensions,—and which provides a safe field of contest in those cases where a treaty cannot be concluded. Of all the stages in the progress of human society, the period which succeeds the troubles of civil and foreign war is that which most requires this remedy: for it is that in which the minds of men are the most dissatisfied, the most active, and the most aspiring. The experiment has proved most eminently successful in the Netherlands, now beyond all doubt the best governed country of the Continent. It ought to be owned, that it has also in a great measure succeeded in France, Italy, and Spain. Of these countries we shall now say nothing but that, being occupied by foreign armies, they cannot be quoted. If any principle be now universally received in government, it seems to be, that the disorders of such a country must either be contained by foreign arms, or composed by a representative constitution.

But there were two circumstances which rendered the use of this latter remedy peculiarly advisable in Portugal. The first is, that it was so explicitly, repeatedly, and solemnly promised by John VI. In the second place, the establishment of a free constitution in Portugal, afforded an opportunity of sealing a definitive treaty of peace between the most discordant parties, by opening (after a due period of probation) to the Prince whom the Ultra-Royalist faction had placed in their front, a prospect of being one day raised to a higher station, under the system of liberty, than he could have expected to reach if both Portugal and Brazil had continued in slavery.*

It is unworthy of a statesman, or of a philosopher, to waste time in childishly regretting the faults of a Prince's personal character. The rulers of Portugal can neither create circumstances, nor form men according to their wishes. They must take men and things as they find them; and their wisdom will be shown, by turning both to the best account. The occasional occurrence of great personal faults in princes, is an inconvenience of hereditary monarchy, which a wise limitation of royal power may abate and mitigate. Elective governments are not altogether exempt from the same evils, besides being liable to others. All comparison of the two systems is, in the present case, a mere exercise of ingenuity: for it is apparent, that liberty has at this time no chance of establishment in Portugal, in any other form than that of a limited monarchy. The situation of Don Miguel renders it possible to form the constitution on an union between him, as the representative of the Ultra-Royalists, and a young Princess, whose rights will be incorporated with the establishment of liberty.

As soon as Don Pedro was informed of his father's death, he proceeded to the performance of the task which had devolved on him. He began, on the 20th of April, by granting a Constitutional Charter to Portugal. On the 26th, he confirmed the Regency appointed by his father, till the proclamation of the constitution. On the 2d of May he abdicated the crown in favour of his daughter, Donna Maria; on condition, however, "that the abdication should not be valid, and the Princess should not quit Brazil, until it be made officially known to him, that the constitution had been sworn to, according to his orders; and that the espousals of the Princess with Don Miguel should have been made, and the marriage concluded; and that the abdidation and cession should not take place if either of these two conditions should fail."* On the 26th of April, Letters-Patent, or writs of summons, had issued, addressed to each of those who were to form the House of Peers, of which the Duke de Cadaval was named President, and the Patriarch Elect of Lisbon Vice-President. A Decree had also been issued on the same day, commanding the Regency of Portugal to take the necessary measures for the immediate election of members of the other House, according to the tenor of the constitutional law.† When these laws and decrees were received at Lisbon, the Regency proceeded instantly to put them into execution; in consequence of which, the Constitution was proclaimed, the Regency installed, the elections commenced, and the Cortes were finally assembled at Lisbon on the 30th of October.

Whether the Emperor of Brazil had, by the laws of Portugal, the power to regulate the affairs of that kingdom, had hitherto given rise to no question. All parties within and without Portugal had treated his right of succession to his father in the throne of that kingdom as undisputed. But no sooner had he exercised that right, by the grant of a free constitution, than it was discovered by some Ultra-Royalists, that he had forfeited the right itself; that his power over Portugal was an usurpation, and his constitutional law an absolute nullity! Don Miguel, whose name was perpetually in the mouth of these writers, continued at Vienna. The Spanish Government and its officers breathed menace and invective. Foreign agency

* This was written in the month of December, 1826, before the plan for conciliating the two opposite political parties by means of a matrimonial alliance between Donna Maria and her uncle was abandoned.—Ed.

* Diario Fluminense, of the 20th of May.

† Ibid. 3d of May.

manifested itself in Portugal; and some bodies of troops, both on the northern and southern frontier, were excited to a sedition for slavery. "All foreigners," say the objectors," are, by the fundamental laws of Portugal, excluded from the succession to the crown. This law passed at the foundation of the monarchy, by the celebrated Cortes of Lamego, in 1143, was confirmed, strengthened, and enlarged by the Cortes of 1641; and under it, on the last occasion, the King of Spain was declared an usurper, and the House of Braganza were raised to the throne. Don Pedro had, by the treaty which recognised him as Emperor of Brazil, become a foreign sovereign, and was therefore, at the death of his father, disqualified from inheriting the crown of Portugal."

A few years after the establishment of the Normans in England, Henry, a Burgundian Prince, who served under the King of Castile in his wars against the Moors, obtained from that monarch, as a fief, the newly conquered territory between the rivers Douro and Minho. His son Alfonso threw off the superiority of Castile, and, after defeating the Moors at the great battle of Campo Ouriquez, in 1139, was declared King by the Pope, and acknowledged in that character by an assembly of the principal persons of the community, held at Lamego, in 1143, composed of bishops, nobles of the court, and, as it should seem, of procurators of the towns. The crown, after much altercation, was made hereditary, first in males and then in females; but on condition "that the female should always marry a man of Portugal, that the kingdom might not fall to foreigners; and that if she should marry a foreign prince, she should not be Queen;"—"*because we will that our kingdom shall go only to the Portuguese, who, by their bravery, have made us King without foreign aid.*" On being asked whether the King should pay tribute to the King of Leon, they all rose up, and, with naked swords uplifted, and answered, "Our King is independent; our arms have delivered us; the King who consents to such things shall die." The King, with his drawn sword in his hand, said, "If any one consent to such, let him die. If he should be my son, let him not reign."

The Cortes of 1641, renewing the laws of Lamego, determined that, according to these fundamental institutions, the Spanish Princes had been usurpers, and pronounced John, Duke of Braganza, who had already been seated on the throne by a revolt of the whole people, to be the rightful heir. This Prince, though he appears not to have had any pretensions as a male heir, yet seems to have been the representative of the eldest female who had not lost the right of succession by marriage to a foreigner; and, consequently, he was entitled to the crown, according to the order of succession established at Lamego. The Three Estates presented the Heads of laws to the King, praying that effectual means might be taken to enforce the exclusion of foreigners from the throne, according to the laws passed at Lamego. But as the Estates, according to the old constitution of Portugal, presented their Chapters severally to the King, it was possible that they might differ; and they did so, in some respects, on this important occasion,—not indeed as to the end, for which they were equally zealous, but as to the choice of the best means of securing its constant attainment. The answer of the King to the Ecclesiastical Estate was as follows:—"On this Chapter, for which I thank you, I have already answered to the Chapters of the States of the People and of the Nobles, in ordaining a law to be made in conformity to that ordained by Don John IV., with the declarations and modifications which shall be most conducive to the conservation and common good of the kingdom." Lawyers were accordingly appointed to draw up the law; but it is clear that the reserve of the King left him ample scope for the exercise of his own discretion, even if it had not been rendered necessary by the variation between the proposals of the three Orders, respecting the means of its execution. But, in order to give our opponents every advantage, as we literally adopt their version, so we shall suppose (for the sake of argument) the royal assent to have been given to the Chapter of the Nobles without alteration, and in all its specific provisions; it being that on which the Absolutists have chosen to place their chief reliance. The Chapter stands thus in their editions:—"The State of the Nobility prays your Majesty to enact a law, ordaining that the succession to the kingdom may never fall to a foreign Prince, nor to his children, though they may be the next to the last in possession; and that, in case the King of Portugal should be called to the succession of another crown, or of a greater empire, he be compelled to live always there; and that if he has two or more male children, the eldest son shall assume the reins in the foreign country, and the second in Portugal, and the latter shall be the only recognised heir and legitimate successor; and, in case there should be only one child to inherit these two kingdoms, these said kingdoms shall be divided between the children of the latter, in the order and form above mentioned. In case there shall be daughters only, the eldest shall succeed in this kingdom, with the declaration that she marry here with a native of the country, chosen and named by the Three Estates assembled in Cortes: should she marry without the consent of the States, she and her descendants shall be declared incapable, and be ousted of the succession; and the Three Estates shall be at liberty to choose a King from among the natives, if there be no male relation of the Royal Family to whom the succession should devolve."

Now the question is, whether Pedro IV. as the monarch of Brazil, a country separated from Portugal by treaty, became a foreign prince, in the sense intended by these ancient laws, and was thereby disabled from inheriting the crown of Portugal on the decease of John VI.?

This question is not to be decided by verbal chicane. The mischief provided against in these laws was twofold:—the supposed probability of mal-administration through the succession of a foreigner, ignorant of the country and not attached to it; and the loss of domestic government, if it fell by inheritance to the sovereign of another, especially a greater country. The intention of the lawgiver to guard against both these occurrences affords the only sure means of ascertaining the meaning of his words. But the present case has not even the slightest tendency to expose the country to either danger. Pedro IV. is a native Portuguese, presumed to have as much of the knowledge and feelings belonging to that character as any of his predecessors. The danger to Portuguese independence arises from the inheritance of the crown devolving *in perpetuity, and without qualification*, to a foreign sovereign. Such was the evil actually experienced under Philip II. King of Spain, and his two successors; and the most cursory glance over the law of 1641 shows that the Cortes had that case in view. Had the present resembled it in the important quality of a claim to unconditional inheritance, the authority would have been strong. But, instead of being annexed to a foreign dominion, Pedro IV. takes it only for the express purpose of effectually and perpetually disannexing his other territories from it;—a purpose which he immediately proceeds to carry into execution, by establishing a different line of succession for the crowns of both countries, and by an abdication, which is to take effect as soon as he has placed the new establishment in a state of security. The case provided against by the law is, that of permanent annexation to a foreign crown: the right exercised by Pedro IV. is, that of a guardian and administrator of the kingdom, during an operation which is necessary to secure it against such annexation. The whole transaction is conformable to the spirit of the two laws, and not repugnant to their letter.

That a *temporary administration* is perfectly consistent with these laws, is evident from the passage:—"If the King of Portugal should be called to the succession of another crown, and there should be only *one* child to inherit the two kingdoms, these said kingdoms shall be divided among the children of the latter"—meaning after his death, and if he should leave children. Here then is a case of *temporary administration* expressly provided for. The father is to rule *both* kingdoms, till there should be at least *two* children to render the division practicable. He becomes, for an uncertain, and possibly a long period, the provisional sovereign of both; merely because he is presumed to be the most proper regulator of territories which are to be divided between his posterity. Now, the principle of such an express exception is, by the rules of fair construction, applicable to every truly and evidently parallel case; and there is precisely the same reason for the tutelary power of Pedro IV. as there would be for that of a father, in the event contemplated by the law of 1641.

The effect of the Treaty of Rio Janeiro cannot be inconsistent with this temporary union. Even on the principle of our opponents, it must exist for a shorter or longer time. The Treaty did not deprive Pedro of his option between Portugal and Brazil: he must have possessed both crowns, when he was called upon to determine which of them he would lay down. But if it be acknowledged that a short but actual union is necessary, in order to effect the abdication, how can it be pretended that a longer union may not be equally justifiable, for the honest purpose of quiet and amicable separation?

The Treaty of Rio de Janeiro would have been *self-destructive*, if it had taken from Pedro the power of sovereignty in Portugal immediately on the death of his father: for in that case no authority would exist capable of carrying the Treaty into execution. It must have been left to civil war to determine who was to govern the kingdom; while, if we adopt the principle of Pedro's hereditary succession by law, together with his obligation by treaty to separate the kingdoms, the whole is consistent with itself, and every measure is quietly and regularly carried into effect.

To these considerations we must add the recognition of Pedro "as heir and successor" in the Ratification. Either John VI. had power to decide this question, or he had not. If he had not, the Treaty is null; for it is impossible to deny that the recognition is really a condition granted to Brazil, which is a security for its independence, and the breach of which would annul the whole contract. In that case, Portugal and Brazil are not legally separated. Pedro IV. cannot be called a "foreign prince;" and no law forbids him to reside in the American provinces of the Portuguese dominions. In that case also, exercising all the power of his immediate predecessors, his authority in Portugal becomes absolute; he may punish the Absolutists as rebels, according to their own principles; and it will be for them to show, that his rights, as supreme lawgiver, can be bounded by laws called 'fundamental.' But,—to take a more sober view,—can it be doubted, that, in a country where the monarch had exercised the whole legislative power for more than a century, his authoritative interpretation of the ancient laws, especially if it is part of a compact with another state, must be conclusive? By repeatedly declaring in the introduction to the Treaty, and in the Ratification of it, that Pedro IV. was "heir and successor" of Portugal, and that he was not divested of that character by the Treaty, which recognised him as Sovereign of Brazil, John VI. did most deliberately and solemnly determine, that his eldest son was *not* a "foreign prince" in the sense in which these words are used by the ancient laws. Such too seems to have been the sense of all parties, even of those the most bitterly adverse to Pedro IV., and most deeply interested in disputing his succession, till he granted a Constitutional Charter to the people of Portugal.

John VI., by his decree for the re-establishment of the ancient constitution of Portugal, had really abolished the absolute monarchy, and in its stead established a government, which, with all its inconveniences and defects, was founded on principles of liberty. For let it not be supposed that the ancient constitution of Portugal had become forgotten or unknown by disuse for centuries, like those legendary systems, under cover of which any novelty may be called a restoration. It was perfectly well known; it was long practised; and never legally abrogated. Indeed the same may be affirmed, with equal truth, of the ancient institutions of the other inhabitants of the Peninsula, who were among the oldest of free nations, but who have so fallen from their high estate as to be now publicly represented as delighting in their chains and glorying in their shame. In Portugal, however, the usurpation of absolute power was not much older than a century. We have already seen, that the Cortes of Lamego, the founders of the monarchy, proclaimed the right of the nation in a spirit as generous, and in a Latinity not much more barbarous, than that of the authors of Magna Charta about seventy years later.

The Infant Don Miguel has sworn to observe and maintain the constitution. In the act of his espousals he acknowledges the sovereignty of the young Queen, and describes himself as only her first subject. The mutinies of the Portuguese soldiers have ceased; but the conduct of the Court of Madrid still continues to keep up agitation and alarm: for no change was ever effected which did not excite discontent and turbulence enough to serve the purposes of a neighbour straining every nerve to vex and disturb a country. The submission of Don Miguel to his brother and sovereign are, we trust, sincere. He will observe his oath to maintain the constitution, and cheerfully take his place as the first subject of a limited monarchy. The station to which he is destined, and the influence which must long, and may always belong to it, form together a more attractive object of ambition than any thing which he could otherwise have hoped peaceably and lawfully to attain. No man of common prudence, whatever may be his political opinions, will advise the young Prince to put such desirable prospects to hazard. He will be told by all such counsellors of every party that he must now adapt himself to occurrences which he may learn to consider as fortunate; that loyalty to his brother and his country would now be his clearest interest, if they were not his highest duty; that he must forget all his enmities, renounce all his prejudices, and even sacrifice some of his partialities; and that he must leave full time to a great part of the people of Portugal to recover from those prepossessions and repugnances which they may have contracted.

CHARACTER

OF

CHARLES, FIRST MARQUIS CORNWALLIS.*

CHARLES, Marquis Cornwallis, the representative of a family of ancient distinction, and of no modern nobility, had embraced in early youth the profession of arms. The sentiments which have descended to us from ancient times have almost required the sacrifice of personal ease, and the exposure of personal safety, from those who inherit distinction. All the superiority conferred by society must either be earned by previous services, or at least justified by subsequent merit. The most arduous exertions are therefore imposed on those who enjoy advantages which they have not earned. Noblemen are required to devote themselves to danger for the safety of their fellow-citizens, and to spill their blood more readily than others in the public cause. Their choice is almost limited to that profession which derives its dignity from the contempt of danger and death, and which is preserved from mercenary contamination by the severe but noble renunciation of every reward except honour.

In the early stages of his life there were no remarkable events. His sober and well-regulated mind probably submitted to that industry which is the excellence of a subor

* This character formed the chief part of a discourse delivered at Bombay soon after the decease of Lord Cornwallis.

dinate station, and the basis of higher usefulness in a more elevated sphere. The brilliant irregularities which are the ambiguous distinctions of the youth of others found no place in his. He first appeared in the eye of the public during the unhappy civil war between Great Britain and her Colonies, which terminated in the division of the empire. His share in that contest was merely military: in that, as well as in every subsequent part of his life, he was happily free from those conflicts of faction in which the hatred of one portion of our fellow-citizens is insured by those acts which are necessary to purchase the transient and capricious attachment of the other. A soldier, more fortunate, deserves, and generally receives, the unanimous thanks of his country.

It would be improper here to follow him through all the vicissitudes of that eventful war. There is one circumstance, however, which forms too important a part of his character to be omitted,—he was unfortunate. But the moment of misfortune was, perhaps, the most honourable moment of his life. So unshaken was the respect felt, that calamity did not lower him in the eyes of that public which is so prone to estimate men merely by the effect of their councils. He was not received with those frowns which often undeservedly await the return of the unsuccessful general: his country welcomed him with as much honour as if fortune had attended his virtue, and his sovereign bestowed on him new marks of confidence and favour. This was a most signal triumph. Chance mingles with genius and science in the most renowned victories; but merit and well-earned reputation alone can preserve an unfortunate general from sinking in popular estimation.

In 1786 his public life became more connected with that part of the British Empire which we now inhabit. This choice was made under circumstances which greatly increased the honour. No man can recollect the situation of India at that period, or the opinions concerning it in Great Britain, without remembering the necessity, universally felt and acknowledged, for committing the government of our Asiatic territories to a person peculiarly and conspicuously distinguished for prudence, moderation, integrity, and humility. On these grounds he was undoubtedly selected; and it will not be disputed by any one acquainted with the history of India that his administration justified the choice.

Among the many wise and honest measures which did honour to his government, there are two which are of such importance that they cannot be passed over in silence. The first was, the establishment of a fixed land-rent throughout Bengal, instead of those annually varying, and often arbitrary, exactions to which the landholders of that great province had been for ages subject. This reformation, one of the greatest, perhaps, ever peaceably effected in an extensive and opulent country, has since been followed in the other British territories in the East; and it is the first certain example in India of a secure private property in land, which the extensive and undefined territorial claims of Indian Princes had, in former times, rendered a subject of great doubt and uncertainty. The other distinguishing measure of his government was that judicial system which was necessary to protect and secure the property thus ascertained, and the privileges thus bestowed. By the combined influence of these two great measures, he may confidently be said to have imparted to the subjects of Great Britain in the East a more perfect security of person and property, and a fuller measure of all the advantages of civil society, than had been enjoyed by the natives of India within the period of authentic history;—a portion of these inestimable benefits larger than appears to have been ever possessed by any people of Asia, and probably not much inferior to the share of many flourishing states of Europe in ancient and modern times. It has sometimes been objected to these arrangements, that the revenue of the sovereign was sacrificed to the comfort and prosperity of the subject. This would have been impossible: the interests of both are too closely and inseparably connected. The security of the subject will always enrich him; and his wealth will always overflow into the coffers of his sovereign. But if the objection were just in point of policy, it would be the highest tribute to the virtue of the governor. To sacrifice revenue to the well-being of a people is a blame of which Marcus Aurelius would have been proud!*

The war in which he was engaged during his Indian government it belongs to the historian to describe: in this place it is sufficient to say that it was founded in the just defence of an ally, that it was carried on with vigour, and closed with exemplary moderation.

In 1793 Lord Cornwallis returned to Europe, leaving behind him a greater and purer name than that of any foreigner who had ruled over India for centuries.

It is one of the most remarkable circumstances in the history of his life, that great

* The facility with which he applied his sound and strong understanding to subjects the most distant from those which usually employed it is proved in a very striking manner by a fact which ought not to be forgotten by those who wish to form an accurate estimate of this venerable nobleman. The Company's extensive investment from Bengal depended in a great measure on manufactures, which had fallen into such a state of decay as to be almost hopeless. The Court of Directors warmly recommended this very important part of their interest to Marquis Cornwallis. He applied his mind to the subject with that conscientious zeal which always distinguished him as a servant of the public. He became as familiarly acquainted with its most minute details as most of those who had made it the business of their lives; and he has the undisputed merit of having retrieved these manufactures from a condition in which they were thought desperate.

offices were scarcely ever bestowed on him in times when they could be mere marks of favour, or very desirable objects of pursuit; but that he was always called upon to undertake them in those seasons of difficulty when the acceptance became a severe and painful duty. One of these unhappy occcasions arose in the year 1798. A most dangerous rebellion had been suppressed in Ireland, without extinguishing the disaffection that threatened future rebellions. The prudence, the vigilance, the unspotted humanity, the inflexible moderation of Marquis Cornwallis, pointed him out as the most proper person to compose the dissensions of that generous and unfortunate people. He was accordingly chosen for that mission of benevolence, and he most amply justified the choice. Besides the applause of all good men and all lovers of their country, he received the still more unequivocal honour of the censure of violent, and the clamours of those whose ungovernable resentments he refused to gratify. He not only succeeded in allaying the animosities of a divided nation, but he was happy enough to be instrumental in a measure which, if it be followed by moderate and healing counsels, promises permanent quiet and prosperity: under his administration Ireland was united to Great Britain. A period was at length put to the long misgovernment and misfortunes of that noble island, and a new era of justice, happiness, and security opened for both the great members of the British Empire.

The times were too full of difficulty to suffer him long to enjoy the retirement which followed his Irish administration. A war, fortunate and brilliant in many of its separate operations, but unsuccessful in its grand objects, was closed by a treaty of peace, which at first was joyfully hailed by the feelings of the public, but which has since given rise to great diversity of judgment. It may be observed, without descending into political contests, that if the terms of the treaty* were necessarily not flattering to national pride, it was the more important to choose a negotiator who should inspire public confidence, and whose character might shield necessary concessions from unpopularity. Such was unquestionably the principle on which Lord Cornwallis was selected; and such (whatever judgment may be formed of the treaty) is the honourable testimony which it bears to his character.

The offices bestowed on him were not matters of grace: every preferment was a homage to his virtue. He was never invited to the luxuries of high station: he was always summoned to its most arduous and perilous duties. India once more needed, or was thought to need, the guardian care of him who had healed the wounds of conquest, and bestowed on her the blessings of equitable and paternal legislation. Whether the opinion held in England of the perils of our Eastern territories was correct or exaggerated, it is not for us in this place to inquire. It is enough to know that the alarm was great and extensive, and that the eyes of the nation were once more turned towards Lord Cornwallis. Whether the apprehensions were just or groundless, the tribute to his character was equal. He once more accepted the government of these extensive dominions, with a full knowledge of his danger, and with no obscure anticipation of the probability of his fate. He obeyed his sovereign, nobly declaring, "that if he could render service to his country, it was of small moment to him whether he died in India or in Europe;" and no doubt thoroughly convinced that it was far better to die in the discharge of great duties than to add a few feeble inactive years to life. Great Britain, divided on most public questions, was unanimous in her admiration of this signal sacrifice; and British India, however various might be the political opinions of her inhabitants, welcomed the Governor General with only one sentiment of personal gratitude and reverence.

Scarcely had he arrived when he felt the fatal influence of the climate which, with a clear view of its terrors, he had resolved to brave. But he neither yielded to the languor of disease, nor to the infirmity of age. With all the ardour of youth, he flew to the post where he was either to conclude an equitable peace, or, if that were refused, to prosecute necessary hostilities with rigour. His malady became more grievous, and for some time stopped his progress. On the slightest alleviation of his symptoms he resumed his journey, though little hope of recovery remained, with an inflexible resolution to employ what was left of life, in the performance of his duty to his country. He declared to his surrounding friends, "that he knew no reason to fear death; and that if he could remain in the world but a short time longer to complete the plans of public service in which he was engaged, he should then cheerfully resign his life to the Almighty Giver;"—a noble and memorable declaration, expressive of the union of every private, and civil, and religious excellence, in which the consciousness of a blameless and meritorious life is combined with the affectionate zeal of a dying patriot, and the meek submission of a pious Christian. But it pleased God, "whose ways are not as our ways," to withdraw him from this region of the universe before his honest wishes of usefulness could be accomplished, though doubtless not before the purposes of Providence were fulfilled. He expired at Gazeepore, in the province of Benares, on the 5th of October, 1805,—supported by the remembrance of his virtue, and by the sentiments of piety which had actuated his whole life.

His remains are interred on the spot where he died, on the banks of that famous river, which washes no country not either blessed by his government, or visited by his renown; and in the heart of that province so long the

* Of Amiens.

chosen seat of religion and learning in India, which under the influence of his beneficent system, and under the administration of good men whom he had chosen, had risen from a state of decline and confusion to one of prosperity probably unrivalled in the happiest times of its ancient princes. "His body is buried in peace, and his name liveth for evermore."

The Christian religion is no vain superstition, which divides the worship of God from the service of man. Every social duty is a Christian grace. Public and private virtue is considered by Christianity as the purest and most acceptable incense which can ascend before the Divine Throne. Political duties are a most momentous part of morality, and morality is the most momentous part of religion. When the political life of a great man has been guided by the rules of morality, and consecrated by the principles of religion, it may, and it ought to be commemorated, that the survivors may admire and attempt to copy, not only as men and citizens, but as Christians. It is due to the honour of Religion and Virtue,—it is fit for the confusion of the impious and the depraved, to show that these sacred principles are not to be hid in the darkness of humble life to lead the prejudiced and amuse the superstitious, but that they appear with their proper lustre at the head of councils, of armies, and of empires,—the supports of valour,—the sources of active and enlightened beneficence,—the companions of all real policy,—and the guides to solid and durable glory.

A distinction has been made in our times among statesmen, between Public and Private Virtue: they have been supposed to be separable. The neglect of every private obligation, has been supposed to be compatible with public virtue, and the violation of the most sacred public trust has been thought not inconsistent with private worth:—a deplorable distinction, the creature of corrupt sophistry, disavowed by Reason and Morals, and condemned by all the authority of Religion. No such disgraceful inconsistency, or flagrant hypocrisy, disgraced the character of the venerable person of whom I speak,—of whom we may, without suspicion of exaggeration, say, that he performed with equal strictness every office of public or private life; that his public virtue was not put on for parade, like a gaudy theatrical dress, but that it was the same integrity and benevolence which attended his most retired moments; that with a simple and modest character, alien to ostentation, and abhorrent from artifice,—with no pursuit of popularity, and no sacrifice to court favour,—by no other means than an universal reputation for good sense, humanity, and honesty, he gained universal confidence, and was summoned to the highest offices at every call of danger.

He has left us an useful example of the true dignity of these invaluable qualities, and has given us new reason to thank God that we are the natives of a country yet so uncorrupted as to prize them thus highly. He has left us an example of the pure statesman,—of a paternal governor,—of a warrior who loved peace,—of a hero without ambition,—of a conqueror who showed unfeigned moderation in the moment of victory,—and of a patriot who devoted himself to death for his country. May this example be as fruitful, as his memory will be immortal! May the last generations of Britain aspire to copy and rival so pure a model! And when the nations of India turn their eyes to his monument, rising amidst fields which his paternal care has restored to their ancient fertility, may they who have long suffered from the violence of those who are unjustly called 'Great,' at length learn to love and reverence the Good.

CHARACTER

OF THE

RIGHT HONOURABLE GEORGE CANNING.*

WITHOUT invidious comparison, it may be safely said that, from the circumstances in which he died, his death was more generally interesting among civilized nations than that of any other English statesman had ever been. It was an event in the internal history of every country. From Lima to Athens, every nation struggling for independence or existence, was filled by it with sorrow and dismay. The Miguelites of Portugal, the Apostolicals of Spain, the Jesuit faction in France, and the Divan of Constantinople,

* Contributed to the "Keepsake of 1828, under the title of "Sketch of a Fragment of the History of the Nineteenth Century," in which, as the Author announces in a notice prefixed to it, the temper of the future historian of the present times is affected.—ED.

raised a shout of joy at the fall of their dreaded enemy. He was regretted by all who, heated by no personal or party resentment, felt for genius struck down in the act of attempting to heal the revolutionary distemper, and to render future improvements pacific, on the principle since successfully adopted by more fortunate, though not more deserving, ministers,—that of an honest compromise between the interests and the opinions,—the prejudices and the demands, —of the supporters of establishments, and the followers of reformation.

* * * * *

The family of Mr. Canning, which for more than a century had filled honourable stations in Ireland, was a younger branch of an ancient one among the English gentry. His father, a man of letters, had been disinherited for an imprudent marriage; and the inheritance went to a younger brother, whose son was afterwards created Lord Garvagh. Mr. Canning was educated at Eton and Oxford, according to that exclusively classical system, which, whatever may be its defects, must be owned, when taken with its constant appendages, to be eminently favourable to the cultivation of sense and taste, as well as to the development of wit and spirit. From his boyhood he was the foremost among very distinguished contemporaries, and continued to be regarded as the best specimen, and the most brilliant representative, of that eminently national education. His youthful eye sparkled with quickness and arch pleasantry; and his countenance early betrayed that jealousy of his own dignity, and sensibility to suspected disregard, which were afterwards softened, but never quite subdued. Neither the habits of a great school, nor those of a popular assembly, were calculated to weaken his love of praise and passion for distinction: but, as he advanced in years, his fine countenance was ennobled by the expression of thought and feeling; he more pursued that lasting praise, which is not to be earned without praiseworthiness; and, if he continued to be a lover of fame, he also passionately loved the glory of his country. Even he who almost alone was entitled to look down on fame as 'that last infirmity of noble minds,' had not forgotten that it was—

> "The spur that the clear spirit doth raise,
> To scorn delights, and live laborious days."*

The natural bent of character is, perhaps, better ascertained from the undisturbed and unconscious play of the mind in the common intercourse of society, than from its movements under the power of strong interest or warm passions in public life. In social intercourse Mr. Canning was delightful. Happily for the true charm of his conversation he was too busy not to treat society as more fitted for relaxation than for display. It is but little to say, that he was neither disputatious, declamatory, nor sententious,—neither a dictator nor a jester. His manner was simple and unobtrusive; his language always quite familiar. If a higher thought stole from his mind, it came in its conversational undress. From this plain ground his pleasantry sprang with the happiest effect; and it was nearly exempt from that alloy of taunt and banter, which he sometimes mixed with more precious materials in public contest. He may be added to the list of those eminent persons who pleased most in their friendly circle. He had the agreeable quality of being more easily pleased in society than might have been expected from the keenness of his discernment, and the sensibility of his temper: still he was liable to be discomposed, or even silenced, by the presence of any one whom he did not like. His manner in company betrayed the political vexations or anxieties which preyed on his mind: nor could he conceal that sensitiveness to public attacks which their frequent recurrence wears out in most English politicians. These last foibles may be thought interesting as the remains of natural character, not destroyed by refined society and political affairs. He was assailed by some adversaries so ignoble as to wound him through his filial affection, which preserved its respectful character through the whole course of his advancement.

The ardent zeal for his memory, which appeared immediately after his death, attests the warmth of those domestic affections which seldom prevail where they are not mutual. To his touching epitaph on his son, parental love has given a charm which is wanting in his other verses. It was said of him, at one time, that no man had so little popularity and such affectionate friends; and the truth was certainly more sacrificed to point in the former than in the latter member of the contrast. Some of his friendships continued in spite of political differences (which, by rendering intercourse less unconstrained, often undermine friendship;) and others were remarkable for a warmth, constancy, and disinterestedness, which, though chiefly honourable to those who were capable of so pure a kindness, yet redound to the credit of him who was the object of it. No man is thus beloved who is not himself formed for friendship.

Notwithstanding his disregard for money, he was not tempted in youth by the example or the kindness of affluent friends much to overstep his little patrimony. He never afterwards sacrificed to parade or personal indulgence; though his occupations scarcely allowed him to think enough of his private affairs. Even from his moderate fortune, his bounty was often liberal to suitors to whom official relief could not be granted. By a sort of generosity still harder for him to practise, he endeavoured, in cases where the suffering was great, though the suit could not be granted, to satisfy the feelings of the suitor by a full explanation in writing of the causes which rendered compliance impracti-

* Lycidas.

cable. Wherever he took an interest, he showed it as much by delicacy to the feelings of those whom he served or relieved, as by substantial consideration for their claims;—a rare and most praiseworthy merit among men in power.

In proportion as the opinion of a people acquires influence over public affairs, the faculty of persuading men to support or oppose political measures acquires importance. The peculiar nature of Parliamentary debate contributes to render eminence in that province not so imperfect a test of political ability as it might appear to be. Recited speeches can seldom show more than powers of reasoning and imagination; which have little connection with a capacity for affairs. But the unforeseen events of debate, and the necessity of immediate answer in unpremeditated language, afford scope for the quickness, firmness, boldness, wariness, presence of mind, and address in the management of men, which are among the qualities most essential to a statesman. The most flourishing period of our Parliamentary eloquence extends for about half a century,—from the maturity of Lord Chatham's genius to the death of Mr. Fox. During the twenty years which succeeded, Mr. Canning was sometimes the leader, and always the greatest orator, of the party who supported the Administration; in which there were able men who supported, without rivalling him, against opponents also not thought by him inconsiderable. Of these last, one, at least, was felt by every hearer, and acknowledged in private by himself, to have always forced his faculties to their very uttermost stretch.*

Had he been a dry and meagre speaker, he would have been universally allowed to have been one of the greatest masters of argument; but his hearers were so dazzled by the splendour of his diction, that they did not perceive the acuteness and the occasionally excessive refinement of his reasoning; a consequence which, as it shows the injurious influence of a seductive fault, can with the less justness be overlooked in the estimate of his understanding. Ornament, it must be owned, when it only pleases or amuses, without disposing the audience to adopt the sentiments of the speaker, is an offence against the first law of public speaking; it obstructs instead of promoting its only reasonable purpose. But eloquence is a widely extended art, comprehending many sorts of excellence; in some of which ornamented diction is more liberally employed than in others; and in none of which the highest rank can be attained, without an extraordinary combination of mental powers. Among our own orators, Mr. Canning seems to have been the best model of the adorned style. The splendid and sublime descriptions of Mr. Burke,—his comprehensive and profound views of general principle,—though they must ever delight and instruct the reader, must be owned to have been digressions which diverted the mind of the hearer from the object on which the speaker ought to have kept it steadily fixed. Sheridan, a man of admirable sense, and matchless wit, laboured to follow Burke into the foreign regions of feeling and grandeur. The specimens preserved of his most celebrated speeches show too much of the exaggeration and excess to which those are peculiarly liable who seek by art and effort what nature has denied. By the constant part which Mr. Canning took in debate, he was called upon to show a knowledge which Sheridan did not possess, and a readiness which that accomplished man had no such means of strengthening and displaying. In some qualities of style, Mr. Canning surpassed Mr. Pitt. His diction was more various,—sometimes more simple,—more idiomatical, even in its more elevated parts. It sparkled with imagery, and was brightened by illustration; in both of which Mr. Pitt, for so great an orator, was defective.

No English speaker used the keen and brilliant weapon of wit so long, so often, or so effectively, as Mr. Canning. He gained more triumphs, and incurred more enmity, by it than by any other. Those whose importance depends much on birth and fortune are impatient of seeing their own artificial dignity, or that of their order, broken down by derision; and perhaps few men heartily forgive a successful jest against themselves, but those who are conscious of being unhurt by it. Mr. Canning often used this talent imprudently. In sudden flashes of wit, and in the playful description of men or things, he was often distinguished by that natural felicity which is the charm of pleasantry; to which the air of art and labour is more fatal than to any other talent. Sheridan was sometimes betrayed by an imitation of the dialogue of his master, Congreve, into a sort of laboured and finished jesting, so balanced and expanded, as sometimes to vie in tautology and monotony with the once applauded triads of Johnson; and which, even in its most happy passages, is more sure of commanding serious admiration than hearty laughter. It cannot be denied that Mr. Canning's taste was, in this respect, somewhat influenced by the example of his early friend. The exuberance of fancy and wit lessened the gravity of his general manner, and perhaps also indisposed the audience to feel his earnestness where it clearly showed itself. In that important quality he was inferior to Mr. Pitt,—

> "Deep on whose front engraven,
> Deliberation sat, and public care;"*

and no less inferior to Mr. Fox, whose fervid eloquence flowed from the love of his country, the scorn of baseness, and the hatred of cruelty, which were the ruling passions of his nature.

* Mr. (now Lord) Brougham is the person alluded to.—Ed.

* Paradise Lost, Book II.—Ed.

On the whole, it may be observed, that the range of Mr. Canning's powers as an orator was wider than that in which he usually exerted them. When mere statement only was allowable, no man of his age was more simple. When infirm health compelled him to be brief, no speaker could compress his matter with so little sacrifice of clearness, ease, and elegance. In his speech on Colonial Reformation, in 1823, he seemed to have brought down the philosophical principles and the moral sentiments of Mr. Burke to that precise level where they could be happily blended with a grave and dignified speech, intended as an introduction to a new system of legislation. As his oratorical faults were those of youthful genius, the progress of age seemed to purify his eloquence, and every year appeared to remove some speck which hid, or, at least, dimmed, a beauty. He daily rose to larger views, and made, perhaps, as near approaches to philosophical principles as the great difence between the objects of the philosopher and those of the orator will commonly allow.

Mr. Canning possessed, in a high degree, the outward advantages of an orator. His expressive countenance varied with the changes of his eloquence: his voice, flexible and articulate, had as much compass as his mode of speaking required. In the calm part of his speeches, his attitude and gesture might have been selected by a painter to represent grace rising towards dignity.

When the memorials of his own time,—the composition of which he is said never to have interrupted in his busiest moments,—are made known to the public, his abilities as a writer may be better estimated. His only known writings in prose are State Papers, which, when considered as the composition of a Minister for Foreign Affairs, in one of the most extraordinary periods of European history, are undoubtedly of no small importance. Such of these papers as were intended to be a direct appeal to the judgment of mankind combine so much precision, with such uniform circumspection and dignity, that they must ever be studied as models of that very difficult species of composition. His Instructions to ministers abroad, on occasions both perplexing and momentous, will be found to exhibit a rare union of comprehensive and elevated views, with singular ingenuity in devising means of execution; on which last faculty he sometimes relied perhaps more confidently than the short and dim foresight of man will warrant. "Great affairs," says Lord Bacon, "are commonly too coarse and stubborn to be worked upon by the fine edges and points of wit."* His papers in negotiation were occasionally somewhat too controversial in their tone: they were not near enough to the manner of an amicable conversation about a disputed point of business, in which a negotiator does not so much draw out his argument, as hint his own object, and sound the intention of his opponent. He sometimes seems to have pursued triumph more than advantage, and not to have remembered that to leave the opposite party satisfied with what he has got, and in good humour with himself, is not one of the least proofs of a negotiator's skill. Where the papers were intended ultimately to reach the public through Parliament, it might have been prudent to regard chiefly the final object; and when this excuse was wanting, much must be pardoned to the controversial habits of a Parliamentary life. It is hard for a debater to be a negotiator: the faculty of guiding public assemblies is very remote from the art of dealing with individuals.

Mr. Canning's power of writing verse may rather be classed with his accomplishments, than numbered among his high and noble faculties. It would have been a distinction for an inferior man. His verses were far above those of Cicero, of Burke, and of Bacon. The taste prevalent in his youth led him to feel more relish for sententious declaimers than is shared by lovers of the true poetry of imagination and sensibility. In some respects his poetical compositions were also influenced by his early intercourse with Mr. Sheridan, though he was restrained by his more familiar contemplation of classical models from the glittering conceits of that extraordinary man. Something of an artificial and composite diction is discernible in the English poems of those who have acquired reputation by Latin verse,—more especially since the pursuit of rigid purity has required so timid an imitation as not only to confine itself to the words, but to adopt none but the phrases of ancient poets. Of this effect Gray must be allowed to furnish an example.

Absolute silence about Mr. Canning's writings as a political satirist,—which were for their hour so popular,—might be imputed to undue timidity. In that character he yielded to General Fitzpatrick in arch stateliness and poignant raillery; to Mr. Moore in the gay prodigality with which he squanders his countless stores of wit; and to his own friend Mr. Frere in the richness of a native vein of original and fantastic drollery. In that ungenial province, where the brightest of laurels are apt very soon to fade, and where Dryden only boasts immortal lays, it is perhaps his best praise to record that there is no writing of his, which a man of honour might not have avowed as soon as the first heat of contest was past.

In some of the amusements or tasks of his boyhood there are passages which, without much help from fancy, might appear to contain allusions to his greatest measures of policy, as well as to the tenor of his life, and to the melancholy splendour which surrounded his death. In the concluding line of the first English verses written by him at

* It may be proper to remind the reader, that here the word "wit" is used in its ancient sense.

Eton, he expressed a wish, which has been singularly realised, that he might

"Live in a blaze, and in a blaze expire."

It is a striking coincidence, that the statesman, whose dying measure was to mature an alliance for the deliverance of Greece, should, when a boy, have written English verses on the slavery of that country; and that in his prize poem at Oxford, on the Pilgrimage to Mecca,—a composition as much applauded as a modern Latin poem can aspire to be—he should have as bitterly deplored the lot of other renowned countries, now groaning under the same barbarous yoke,—

"Nunc Satrapæ imperio et sævo subdita Turcæ."*

To conclude:—he was a man of fine and brilliant genius, of warm affections, of a high and generous spirit,—a statesman who, at home, converted most of his opponents into warm supporters; who, abroad, was the sole hope and trust of all who sought an orderly and legal liberty; and who was cut off in the midst of vigorous and splendid measures, which, if executed by himself, or with his own spirit, promised to place his name in the first class of rulers, among the founders of lasting peace, and the guardians of human improvement.

* Iter ad Meccam, Oxford, 1789.

PREFACE

TO A REPRINT OF

THE EDINDURGH REVIEW

OF 1755.*

It is generally known that two numbers of a Critical Journal were published at Edinburgh in the year 1755, under the title of the "Edinburgh Review." The following volume contains an exact reprint of that Review, now become so rare that it is not to be found in the libraries of some of the most curious collectors. To this reprint are added the names of the writers of the most important articles. Care has been taken to authenticate the list of names by reference to well-informed persons, and by comparison with copies in the possession of those who have derived their information from distinct and independent sources. If no part of it should be now corrected by those Scotchmen of letters still living, who may have known the fact from the writers themselves, we may regard this literary secret as finally discovered, with some gratification to the curious reader, and without either pain to the feelings, or wrong to the character of any one. There are few anonymous writers the discovery of whose names would be an object of curiosity after the lapse of sixty years: there are perhaps still fewer whose secret might be exposed to the public after that long period with perfect security to their reputation for equity and forbearance.

The mere circumstance that this volume contains the first printed writings of Adam Smith and Robertson, and the only known publication of Lord Chancellor Rosslyn, will probably be thought a sufficient reason for its present appearance.

Of the eight articles which appear to have been furnished by Dr. Robertson, six are on historical subjects. Written during the composition of the History of Scotland, they show evident marks of the wary understanding, the insight into character, the right judgment in affairs, and the union of the sober speculation of a philosopher with the practical prudence of a statesman, as well as the studied elegance and somewhat ceremonious stateliness of style which distinguish his more elaborate writings. He had already succeeded in guarding his diction against the words and phrases of the dialect which he habitually spoke;—an enterprise in which he had no forerunner, and of which the difficulty even now can only be estimated by a native of Scotland. The dread of inelegance in a language almost foreign kept him, as it has kept succeeding Scotch writers, at a distance from the familiar English, the perfect use of which can be acquired only by conversation from the earlist years. Two inaccurate expressions only are to be found in these early and hasty productions of this elegant writer. Instead of "individuals" he uses the Gallicism "particulars;" and for "enumeration" he employs "induction,"—a term properly applicable only with a view to the general inference which enumeration affords. In the review of the History of Peter the Great it is not uninteresting to find it remarked, that the violence and ferocity of that renowned barba-

* Published in 1816.—Ed.

rian perhaps partly fitted him to be the reformer of a barbarous people; as it was afterwards observed in the Histories of Scotland and of Charles V., that a milder and more refined character might have somewhat disqualified Luther and Knox for their great work. Two articles being on Scottish affairs were natural relaxations for the historian of Scotland. In that which relates to the Catalogue of Scottish Bishops we observe a subdued smile at the eagerness of the antiquary and the ecclesiastical partisan, qualified indeed by a just sense of the value of the collateral information which their toil may chance to throw up, but which he was too cautious and decorous to have hazarded in his avowed writings. That he reviewed Douglas' Account of North America was a fortunate circumstance, if we may suppose that the recollection might at a distant period have contributed to suggest the composition of the History of America. None of these writings could have justified any expectation of his historical fame; because they furnished no occasion for exerting the talent for narration,—the most difficult but the most necessary attainment for an historian, and one in which he has often equalled the greatest masters of his art. In perusing the two essays of a literary sort ascribed to him, it may seem that he has carried lenient and liberal criticism to an excess. His mercy to the vicious style of Hervey may have been in some measure the result of professional prudence: but it must be owned that he does not seem enough aware of the interval between Gray and Shenstone, and that he names versifiers now wholly forgotten. Had he and his associates, however, erred on the opposite extreme,—had they underrated and vilified works of genius, their fault would now appear much more offensive. To overrate somewhat the inferior degrees of real merit which are reached by contemporaries is indeed the natural disposition of superior minds, when they are neither degraded by jealousy nor inflamed by hostile prejudice. The faint and secondary beauties of contemporaries are aided by novelty; they are brought near enough to the attention by curiosity; and they are compared with their competitors of the same time instead of being tried by the test of likeness to the produce of all ages and nations. This goodnatured exaggeration encourages talent, and gives pleasure to readers as well as writers, without any permanent injury to the public taste. The light which seems brilliant only because it is near the eye, cannot reach the distant observer. Books which please for a year, which please for ten years, and which please for ever, gradually take their destined stations. There is little need of harsh criticism to forward this final justice. The very critic who has bestowed too prodigal praise, if he long survives his criticism, will survive also his harmless error. Robertson never ceased to admire Gray: but he lived long enough probably to forget the name of Jago.

In the contributions of Dr. Adam Smith it is easy to trace his general habits both of thinking and writing. Among the inferior excellencies of this great philosopher, it is not to be forgotten that in his full and flowing composition he manages the English language with a freer hand and with more native ease than any other Scottish writer. Robertson avoids Scotticisms: but Smith might be taken for an English writer not peculiarly idiomatical. It is not improbable that the early lectures of Hutcheson, an eloquent native of Ireland, and a residence at Oxford from the age of seventeen to that of twenty-four, may have aided Smith in the attainment of this more free and native style. It must however be owned, that his works, confined to subjects of science or speculation, do not afford the severest test of a writer's familiarity with a language. On such subjects it is comparatively easy, without any appearance of constraint or parade, to avoid the difficulties of idiomatical expression by the employment of general and technical terms. His review of Johnson's Dictionary is chiefly valuable as a proof that neither of these eminent persons was well qualified to write an English dictionary. The plan of Johnson and the specimens of Smith are alike faulty. At that period, indeed, neither the cultivation of our old literature, nor the study of the languages from which the English springs or to which it is related, nor the habit of observing the general structure of language, was so far advanced as to render it possible for this great work to approach perfection. His parallel between French and English writers* is equally just and ingenious, and betrays very little of that French taste in polite letters, especially in dramatic poetry to which Dr. Smith and his friend Mr. Hume were prone. The observations on the life of a savage, which when seen from a distance appears to be divided between Arcadian repose and chivalrous adventure, and by this union is the most alluring object of general curiosity and the natural scene of the golden age both of the legendary, and of the paradoxical sophist, are an example of those original speculations on the reciprocal influence of society and opinions which characterize the genius of Smith. The commendation of Rousseau's eloquent Dedication to the Republic of Geneva, for expressing "that *ardent* and *passionate esteem* which it becomes a good citizen to entertain for the government of his country and the character of his countrymen," is an instance of the seeming exaggeration of just principles, arising from the employment of the language of moral feeling, as that of ethical philosophy, which is very observable in the Theory of Moral Sentiments.

Though the contributions of Alexander Wedderburn, afterwards Earl of Rosslyn, afforded little scope for the display of mental superiority, it is not uninteresting to examine

* Letter to the Editor, at the end of the volume.

the first essays in composition of a man whose powers of reason and eloquence raised him to the highest dignity of the state. A Greek grammar and two law books were allotted to him as subjects of criticism. Humble as these subjects are, an attentive perusal will discover in his remarks on them a distinctness of conception and a terseness as well as precision of language which are by no means common qualities of writing. One error in the use of the future tense deserves notice only as it shows the difficulties which he had to surmount in acquiring what costs an Englishman no study. The praise bestowed in his Preface on Buchanan for an "undaunted spirit of liberty," is an instance of the change which sixty years have produced in political sentiment. Though that great writer was ranked among the enemies of monarchy,* the praise of him, especially in Scotland, was a mark of fidelity to a government which, though monarchical, was founded on the principles of the Revolution, and feared no danger but from the partisans of hereditary right. But the criticisms and the ingenious and judicious Preface show the early taste of a man who at the age of twenty-two withstands every temptation to unseasonable display. The love of letters, together with talents already conspicuous, had in the preceding year (1754) placed him in the chair at the first meeting of a literary society of which Hume and Smith were members. The same dignified sentiment attended him through a long life of activity and ambition, and shed a lustre over his declining years. It was respectably manifested by fidelity to the literary friends of his youth, and it gave him a disposition, perhaps somewhat excessive, to applaud every shadow of the like merit in others.

The other writers are only to be regarded as respectable auxiliaries in such an undertaking. Dr. Blair is an useful example, that a station among good writers may be attained by assiduity and good sense, with the help of an uncorrupted taste; while for the want of these qualities, it is often not reached by others whose powers of mind may be allied to genius.

The delicate task of reviewing the theological publications of Scotland was allotted to Mr. Jardine, one of the ministers of Edinburgh, whose performance of that duty would have required no particular notice, had it not contributed with other circumstances to bring the work to its sudden and unexpected close. At the very moment when Mr. Wedderburn (in his note at the end of the second number) had announced an intention to enlarge the plan, he and his colleagues were obliged to relinquish the work.

The temper of the people of Scotland was at that moment peculiarly jealous on every question that approached the boundaries of theology. A popular election of the parochial clergy had been restored with Presbytery by the Revolution. The rights of Patrons had been reimposed on the Scottish Church in the last years of Queen Anne, by Ministers who desired, if they did not meditate, the re-establishment of Episcopacy. But for thirty years afterwards this unpopular right was either disused by the Patrons or successfully resisted by the people. The zealous Presbyterians still retained the doctrine and spirit of the Covenanters; and their favourite preachers, bred up amidst the furious persecutions of Charles the Second, had rather learnt piety and fortitude than acquired that useful and ornamental learning which becomes their order in times of quiet. Some of them had separated from the Church on account of lay Patronage, among other marks of degeneracy. But besides these Seceders, the majority of the Established clergy were adverse to the law of Patronage, and disposed to connive at resistance to its execution. On the other hand, the more lettered and refined ministers of the Church, who had secretly relinquished many parts of the Calvinistic system,—from the unpopularity of their own opinions and modes of preaching, from their connection with the gentry who held the rights of Patronage, and from repugnance to the vulgar and illiterate ministers whom turbulent elections had brought into the Church,—became hostile to the interference of the people, and zealously laboured to enforce the execution of a law which had hitherto remained almost dormant. The Orthodox party maintained the rights of the people against a regulation imposed on them by their enemies; and the party which in matters of religion claimed the distinction of liberality and toleration, contended for the absolute authority of the civil magistrate to the destruction of a right which more than any other interested the conscience of the people of Scotland. At the head of this last party was Dr. Robertson, one of the contributors to the present volume, who about the time of its appearance was on the eve of effecting a revolution in the practice of the Church, by at length compelling the stubborn Presbyterians to submit to the authority of a law which they abhorred.

Another circumstance rendered the time very perilous for Scotch reviewers of ecclesiastical publications. The writings of Mr. Hume, the intimate friend of the leader of the tolerant clergy, very naturally excited the alarm of the Orthodox party, who, like their predecessors of the preceding age, were zealous for the rights of the people, but confined their charity within the pale of their own communion, and were much disposed to regard the impunity of heretics and infidels as a reproach to a Christian magistrate. In the year 1754 a complaint to the General Assembly against the philosophical writings of Mr. Hume and Lord Kames was with difficulty eluded by the friends of free discussion. The writers of the Review were aware of the danger to which they were exposed by

* He is usually placed with Languet and Althusen among the *Monarchomists*.

these circumstances. They kept the secret of their Review from Mr. Hume, the most intimate friend of some of them. They forbore to notice in it his History of the Stuarts, of which the first volume appeared at Edinburgh two months before the publication of the Review; though it is little to say that it was the most remarkable work which ever issued from the Scottish press.

They trusted that the moderation and well-known piety of Mr. Jardine would conduct them safely through the suspicion and jealousy of jarring parties. Nor does it in fact appear that any part of his criticisms is at variance with that enlightened reverence for religion which he was known to feel; but he was somewhat influenced by the ecclesiastical party to which he adhered. He seems to have thought that he might securely assail the opponents of Patronage through the sides of Erskine, Boston, and other popular preachers, who were either Seceders, or divines of the same school. He even ventured to use the weapon of ridicule against their extravagant metaphors, their wire-drawn allegories, their mean allusions, and to laugh at those who complained of "the connivance at Popery, the toleration of Prelacy, the pretended rights of Lay Patrons,—of heretical professors in the universities, and a lax clergy in possession of the churches," as the crying evils of the time.

This species of attack, at a moment when the religious feelings of the public were thus susceptible, appears to have excited general alarm. The Orthodox might blame the writings criticised without approving the tone assumed by the critic: the multitude were exasperated by the scorn with which their favourite writers were treated: and many who altogether disapproved these writings might consider ridicule as a weapon of doubtful propriety against language habitually employed to convey the religious and moral feelings of a nation. In these circumstances the authors of the Review did not think themselves bound to hazard their quiet, reputation, and interest, by perseverance in their attempt to improve the taste of their countrymen.

It will not be supposed that the remarks made above on the ecclesiastical parties in Scotland sixty years ago can have any reference to their political character at the present day. The principles of toleration now seem to prevail among the Scottish clergy more than among any other established church in Europe. A public act of the General Assembly may be considered as a renunciation of that hostility to the full toleration of Catholics which was for a long time the disgrace of the most liberal Protestants. The party called 'Orthodox' are purified from the intolerance which unhappily reigned among their predecessors, and have in general adopted those principles of religious liberty which the sincerely pious, when consistent with themselves, must be the foremost to maintain. Some of them also, even in these times, espouse those generous and sacred principles of civil liberty which distinguished the old Puritans, and which in spite of their faults entitle them to be ranked among the first benefactors of their country.*

* "The precious spark of liberty had been kindled and was preserved by the Puritans alone: and it was to this sect, whose principles appear so frivolous and habits so ridiculous, that the English owe the whole freedom of their constitution."—Hume, History of England, chap. xl. This testimony to the merits of the Puritans, from the mouth of their enemy, must be owned to be founded in exaggeration. But if we allow them to have materially contributed to the preservation of English liberty, we must acknowledge that the world owes more to the ancient Puritans than to any other sect or party among men.

ON THE

WRITINGS OF MACHIAVEL.*

LITERATURE, which lies much nearer to the feelings of mankind than science, has the most important effect on the sentiments with which the sciences are regarded, the activity with which they are pursued, and the mode in which they are cultivated. It is the instrument, in particular, by which ethical science is generally diffused. As the useful arts maintain the general honour of physical knowledge, so polite letters allure the world into the neighbourhood of the sciences of morals and of mind. Wherever the agreeable vehicle of literature does not convey their doctrines to the public, they remain as the occupation of a few recluses in the schools, with no root in the general feelings, and liable to be destroyed by the dispersion of a handful of doctors, and the destruction of their unlamented seminaries. Nor is this all:—polite literature is not only the true guardian of the moral sciences, and the sole instrument of spreading their benefits among men, but it becomes, from these

* From the Edinburgh Review, vol. xxvii. p. 207.—ED.

very circumstances, the regulator of their cultivation and their progress. As long as they are confined to a small number of men in scholastic retirement, there is no restraint upon their natural proneness to degenerate either into verbal subtilties or shadowy dreams. As long as speculation remained in the schools, all its followers were divided into mere dialecticians, or mystical visionaries, both alike unmindful of the real world, and disregarded by its inhabitants. The revival of literature produced a revolution at once in the state of society, and in the mode of philosophizing. It attracted readers from the common ranks of society, who were gradually led on from eloquence and poetry, to morals and philosophy. Philosophers and moralists, after an interval of almost a thousand years, during which they had spoken only to each other, once more discovered that they might address the great body of mankind, with the hope of fame and of usefulness. Intercourse with this great public, supplied new materials, and imposed new restraints: the feelings, the common sense, the ordinary affairs of men, presented themselves again to the moralist; and philosophers were compelled to speak in terms intelligible and agreeable to their new hearers. Before this period, little prose had been written in any modern language, except chronicles or romances. Boccacio had indeed acquired a classical rank, by compositions of the latter kind; and historical genius had risen in Froissart and Comines to a height which has not been equalled among the same nation in times of greater refinement. But Latin was still the language in which all subjects then deemed of higher dignity, and which occupied the life of the learned by profession, were treated. This system continued till the Reformation, which, by the employment of the living languages in public worship, gave them a dignity unknown before, and, by the versions of the Bible, and the practice of preaching and writing on theology and morals in the common tongues, did more for polishing modern literature, for diffusing knowledge, and for improving morality, than all the other events and discoveries of that active age.

Machiavel is the first still celebrated writer who discussed grave questions in a modern language. This peculiarity is the more worthy of notice, because he was not excited by the powerful stimulant of the Reformation. That event was probably regarded by him as a disturbance in a barbarous country, produced by the novelties of a vulgar monk, unworthy of the notice of a man wholly occupied with the affairs of Florence, and the hope of expelling strangers from Italy; and having reached, at the appearance of Luther, the last unhappy period of his agitated life.

The Prince is an account of the means by which tyrannical power is to be acquired and preserved: it is a theory of that class of phenomena in the history of mankind. It is essential to its purpose, therefore, that it should contain an enumeration and exposition of tyrannical arts; and, on that account, it may be viewed and used as a manual of such arts. A philosophical treatise on poisons, would in like manner determine the quantity of each poisonous substance capable of producing death, the circumstances favourable or adverse to its operation, and every other information essential to the purpose of the poisoner, though not intended for his use. But it is also plain, that the calm statement of tyrannical arts is the bitterest of all satires against them. The Prince must therefore have had this double aspect, though neither of the objects which they seem to indicate had been actually in the contemplation of the author. It may not be the object of the chemist to teach the means of exhibiting antidotes, any more than those of administering poisons; but his readers may employ his discoveries for both objects. Aristotle* had long before given a similar theory of tyranny, without the suspicion of an immoral intention. Nor was it any novelty in more recent times, among those who must have been the first teachers of Machiavel. The Schoolmen followed the footsteps of Aristotle too closely, to omit so striking a passage; and Aquinas explains it, in his commentary, like the rest, in the unsuspecting simplicity of his heart. To us accordingly, we confess, the plan of Machiavel seems, like those of former writers, to have been purely scientific; and so Lord Bacon seems to have understood him, where he thanks him for an exposition of immoral policy. In that singular passage, where the latter lays down the theory of the advancement of fortune (which, when compared with his life, so well illustrates the fitness of his understanding, and the unfitness of his character for the affairs of the world), he justifies his application of learning to such a subject, on a principle which extends to The Prince:—"that there be not any thing in being or action which should not be drawn and collected into contemplation and doctrine."

Great defects of character, we readily admit, are manifested by the writings of Machiavel: but if a man of so powerful a genius had shown a nature utterly depraved, it would have been a painful, and perhaps single, exception to the laws of human nature. And no depravity can be conceived greater than a deliberate intention to teach perfidy and cruelty. That a man who was a warm lover of his country, who bore cruel sufferings for her liberty, and who was beloved by the best of his countrymen,† should fall into such unparalleled wickedness, may be considered

* Politics, lib. v. c. iii.

† Among other proofs of the esteem in which he was held by those who knew his character, we may refer to the affectionate letters of Guicciardini, who, however independent his own opinions were, became, by his employment under the Popes of the House of Medici, the supporter of their authority, and consequently a political opponent of Machiavel, the most zealous of the Republicans.

as wholly incredible. No such depravity is consistent with the composition of the History of Florence. It is only by exciting moral sentiment, that the narrative of human actions can be rendered interesting. Divested of morality, they lose their whole dignity, and all their power over feeling. History would be thrown aside as disgusting, if it did not inspire the reader with pity for the sufferer,—with anger against the oppressor,—with anxiety for the triumph of right;—to say nothing of the admiration for genius, and valour, and energy, which, though it disturbs the justice of our historical judgments, partakes also of a moral nature. The author of The Prince, according to the common notion of its intention, could never have inspired these sentiments, of which he must have utterly emptied his own heart. To possess the power, however, of contemplating tyranny with scientific coldness, and of rendering it the mere subject of theory, must be owned to indicate a defect of moral sensibility. The happier nature, or fortune, of Aristotle, prompted him to manifest distinctly his detestation of the flagitious policy which he reduced to its principles.

As another subject of regret, not as an excuse for Machiavel, a distant approach to the same defect may be observed in Lord Bacon's History of Henry the Seventh; where we certainly find too little reprehension of falsehood and extortion, too cool a display of the expedients of cunning, sometimes dignified by the name of wisdom, and throughout, perhaps, too systematic a character given to the measures of that monarch, in order to exemplify, in him, a perfect model of kingcraft; pursuing safety and power by any means,—acting well in quiet times, because it was most expedient, but never restrained from convenient crimes. This History would have been as delightful as it is admirable, if he had felt the difference between wisdom and cunning as warmly in that work, as he has discerned it clearly in his philosophy.

Many historical speculators have indeed incurred some part of this fault. Enamoured of their own solution of the seeming contradictions of a character, they become indulgent to the character itself; and, when they have explained its vices, are disposed, unconsciously, to write as if they had excused them. A writer who has made a successful exertion to render an intricate character intelligible, who has brought his mind to so singular an attempt as a theory of villany, and has silenced his repugnance and indignation sufficiently for the purposes of rational examination, naturally exults in his victory over so many difficulties, delights in contemplating the creations of his own ingenuity, and the order which he seems to have introduced into the chaos of malignant passions, and may at length view his work with that complacency which diffuses clearness and calmness over the language in which he communicates his imagined discoveries.

It should also be remembered, that Machiavel lived in an age when the events of every day must have blunted his moral feelings, and wearied out his indignation. In so far as we acquit the intention of the writer, his work becomes a weightier evidence of the depravity which surrounded him. In this state of things, after the final disappointment of all his hopes, when Florence was subjected to tyrants, and Italy lay under the yoke of foreigners,—having undergone torture for the freedom of his country, and doomed to beggary in his old age, after a life of public service, it is not absolutely unnatural that he should have resolved to compose a theory of the tyranny under which he had fallen, and that he should have manifested his indignation against the cowardly slaves who had yielded to it, by a stern and cold description of its maxims.

His last chapter, in which he seems once more to breathe a free air, has a character totally different from all the preceding ones. His exhortation to the Medici to deliver Italy from foreigners, again speaks out his ancient feelings. Perhaps he might have thought it possible to pardon any means employed by an Italian usurper to expel the foreign masters of his country. This ray of hope might have supported him in delineating the means of usurpation; by doing which he might have had some faint expectation that he could entice the usurper to become a deliverer.—Knowing that the native governments were too base to defend Italy, and that all others were leagued to enslave her, he might, in his despair of all legitimate rulers, have hoped something for independence, and perhaps at last even for liberty, from the energy and genius of an illustrious tyrant.

From Petrarch, with some of whose pathetic verses Machiavel concludes, to Alfieri, the national feeling of Italy seems to have taken refuge in the minds of her writers. They write more tenderly of their country as it is more basely abandoned by their countrymen. Nowhere has so much been well said, or so little nobly done. While we blame the character of the nation, or lament the fortune which in some measure produced it, we must, in equity, excuse some irregularities in the indignation of men of genius, when they see the ingenious inhabitants of their beautiful and renowned country now apparently for ever robbed of that independence which is enjoyed by obscure and barbarous communities.

The dispute about the intention of The Prince has thrown into the shade the merit of the Discourses on Livy. The praise bestowed on them by Mr. Stewart* is scanty. that "they furnish lights to the school of Montesquieu" is surely inadequate commendation. They are the first attempts in a new science—the philosophy of history; and, as such, they form a brilliant point in the progress of reason. For this Lord Bacon com-

* In the Dissertation prefixed to the Encyclopædia Britannica.—Ed.

mends him:—"the form of writing which is the fittest for this variable argument of negotiation, is that which Machiavel chose wisely and aptly for government, namely, discourse upon histories or examples: for, knowledge drawn freshly, and in our view, out of particulars, findeth its way best to particulars again; and it hath much greater life on practice when the discourse attendeth upon the example, than when the example attendeth upon the discourse." It is observable, that the Florentine Secretary is the only modern writer who is named in that part of the Advancement of Learning which relates to civil knowledge. The apology of Albericus Gentilis for the morality of The Prince, has been often quoted, and is certainly weighty as a testimony, when we consider that the writer was born within twenty years of the death of Machiavel, and educated at no great distance from Florence. It is somewhat singular, that the context of this passage should never have been quoted:—"To the knowledge of history must be added that part of philosophy which treats of morals and politics; for this is the soul of history, which explains the causes of the actions and sayings of men, and of the events which befall them: and on this subject I am not afraid to name Nicholas Machiavel, as the most excellent of all writers, in his golden Observations on Livy. He is the writer whom I now seek, because he reads history not with the eyes of a grammarian, but with those of a philosopher."*

It is a just and refined observation of Mr. Hume, that the mere theory of Machiavel (to waive the more important consideration of morality) was perverted by the atrocities which, among the Italians, then passed under the name of 'policy.' The number of men who took a part in political measures in the republican governments of Italy, spread the taint of this pretended policy farther, and made it a more national quality than in the Transalpine monarchies. But neither the civil wars of France and England, nor the administrations of Henry the Seventh, Ferdinand and Louis the Eleventh (to say nothing of the succeeding religious wars), will allow us to consider it as peculiarly Italian. It arose from the circumstances of Europe in those times. In every age in which contests are long maintained by chiefs too strong, or bodies of men too numerous for the ordinary control of law, for power, or privileges, or possessions, or opinions to which they are ardently attached, the passions excited by such interests, heated by sympathy, and inflamed to madness by resistance, soon throw off moral restraint in the treatment of enemies. Retaliation, which deters individuals, provokes multitudes to new cruelty; and the atrocities which originated in the rage of ambition and fanaticism, are at length thought necessary for safety. Each party adopts the cruelties of the enemy, as we now adopt a new discovery in the art of war. The craft and violence thought necessary for existence are admitted into the established policy of such deplorable times.

But though this be the tendency of such circumstances in all times, it must be owned that these evils prevail among different nations, and in different ages, in a very unequal degree. Some part of these differences may depend on national peculiarities, which cannot be satisfactorily explained: but, in the greater part of them, experience is striking and uniform. Civil wars are comparatively regular and humane, under circumstances that may be pretty exactly defined;—among nations long accustomed to popular government, to free speakers and to free writers; familiar with all the boldness and turbulence of numerous assemblies; not afraid of examining any matter human or divine; where great numbers take an interest in the conduct of their superiors of every sort, watch it, and often censure it; where there is a public, and where that public boldly utters decisive opinions; where no impassable lines of demarcation destine the lower classes to eternal servitude, and the higher to envy and hatred and deep curses from their inferiors; where the administration of law is so purified by the participation and eye of the public, as to become a grand school of humanity and justice; and where, as the consequence of all, there is a general diffusion of the comforts of life, a general cultivation of reason, and a widely diffused feeling of equality and moral pride. The species seems to become gentler as all galling curbs are gradually disused. Quiet, or at least comparative order, is promoted by the absence of all the expedients once thought essential to preserve tranquillity. Compare Asia with Europe;—the extremes are there seen. But if all the immediate degrees be examined, it will be found that civil wars are milder, in proportion to the progress of the body of the people in importance and well-being. Compare the civil wars of the two Roses with those under Charles the First: compare these, again, with the humanity and wisdom of the Revolution of sixteen hundred and eighty-eight. Examine the civil war which led to the American Revolution: we there see anarchy without confusion, and governments abolished and established without spilling a drop of blood. Even the progress of civilization, when unattended by the blessings of civil liberty, produces many of the same effects. When Mr. Hume wrote the excellent observations quoted by Mr. Stewart, Europe had for more than a century been exempt from those general convulsions which try the moral character of nations, and ascertain their progress towards a more civilized state of mind. We have since been visited by one of the most tremendous of these tempests; and our minds are yet filled with the dreadful calamities, and the ambiguous and precarious benefits, which have sprung from it. The contemporaries

* De Legat. lib. iii. c. ix.

of such terrific scenes are seldom in a temper to contemplate them calmly: and yet, though the events of this age have disappointed the expectations of sanguine benevolence concerning the state of civilization in Europe, a dispassionate posterity will probably decide that it has stood the test of general commotions, and proved its progress by their comparative mildness. One period of frenzy has been, indeed, horribly distinguished, perhaps beyond any equal time in history, by popular massacres and judicial murders, among a people peculiarly susceptible of a momentary fanaticism. This has been followed by a war in which one party contended for universal dominion, and all the rest of Europe struggled for existence. But how soon did the ancient laws of war between European adversaries resume the ascendant, which had indeed been suspended more in form than in fact! How slight are the traces which the atrocities of faction and the manners of twenty years' invasion and conquest have left on the sentiments of Europe! On a review of the disturbed period of the French Revolution, the mind is struck by the disappearance of classes of crimes which have often attended such convulsions;—no charge of poison; few assassinations, properly so called; no case hitherto authenticated of secret execution! If any crimes of this nature can be proved, the truth of history requires that the proof should be produced. But those who assert them without proof must be considered as calumniating their age, and bringing into question the humanizing effects of order and good government.

REVIEW OF MR. GODWIN'S LIVES

OF

EDWARD AND JOHN PHILIPS, &c. &c.*

The public would have perhaps welcomed Mr. Godwin's reappearance as an author, most heartily, if he had chosen the part of a novelist. In that character his name is high, and his eminence undisputed. The time is long past since this would have been thought a slight, or even secondary praise. No addition of more unquestionable value has been made by the moderns, to the treasures of literature inherited from antiquity, than those fictions which paint the manners and character of the body of mankind, and affect the reader by the relation of misfortunes which may befall himself. The English nation would have more to lose than any other, by undervaluing this species of composition. Richardson has perhaps lost, though unjustly, a part of his popularity at home; but he still contributes to support the fame of his country abroad. The small blemishes of his diction are lost in translation; and the changes of English manners, and the occasional homeliness of some of his representations, are unfelt by foreigners. Fielding will for ever remain the delight of his country, and will always retain his place in the libraries of Europe, notwithstanding the unfortunate grossness,—the mark of an uncultivated taste,—which if not yet entirely excluded from conversation, has been for some time banished from our writings, where, during the best age of our national genius, it prevailed more than in those of any other polished nation. It is impossible in a Scottish journal, to omit Smollett, even if there had not been much better reasons for the mention of his name, than for the sake of observing, that he and Arbuthnot are sufficient to rescue Scotland from the imputation of wanting talent for pleasantry: though, it must be owned, we are grave people, happily educated under an austere system of morals; possessing, perhaps, some humour, in our peculiar dialect, but fearful of taking the liberty of jesting in a foreign language like the English; prone to abstruse speculation, to vehement dispute, to eagerness in the pursuit of business and ambition, and to all those intent occupations of mind which rather indispose it to unbend in easy playfulness.

Since the beautiful tales of Goldsmith and Mackenzie, the composition of novels has been almost left to women; and, in the distribution of literary labour, nothing seems more natural, than that, as soon as the talents of women are sufficiently cultivated, this task should be assigned to the sex which has most leisure for the delicate observation of manners, and whose importance depends on the sentiments which most usually checker common life with poetical incidents.

* From the Edinb. Rev. vol. xxv. p. 485.—Ed.

They have performed their part with such signal success, that the literary works of women, instead of receiving the humiliating praise of being gazed at as wonders and prodigies, have, for the first time, composed a considerable part of the reputation of an ingenious nation in a lettered age. It ought to be added, that their delicacy, co-operating with the progress of refinement, has contributed to efface from these important fictions the remains of barbarism which had disgraced the vigorous genius of our ancestors.

Mr. Godwin has preserved the place of men in this branch of literature. Caleb Williams is probably the finest novel produced by a man,—at least since the Vicar of Wakefield. The sentiments, if not the opinions, from which it arose, were transient. Local usages and institutions were the subjects of its satire, exaggerated beyond the usual privilege of that species of writing. Yet it has been translated into most languages; and it has appeared in various forms, on the theatres, not only in England, but of France and Germany. There is scarcely a Continental circulating library in which it is not one of the books which most quickly require to be replaced. Though written with a temporary purpose, it will be read with intense interest, and with a painful impatience for the issue, long after the circumstances which produced its original composition shall cease to be known to all but to those who are well read in history. There is scarcely a fiction in any language which it is so difficult to lay by. A young person of understanding and sensibility, not familiar with the history of its origin, nor forewarned of its connection with peculiar opinions, in whose hands it is now put for the first time, will peruse it with perhaps more ardent sympathy and trembling curiosity, than those who read it when their attention was divided, and their feelings disturbed by controversy and speculation. A building thrown up for a season, has become, by the skill of the builder, a durable edifice. It is a striking, but not a solitary example, of the purpose of the writer being swallowed up by the interest of the work, —of a man of ability intending to take part in the disputes of the moment, but led by the instinct of his talent to address himself to the permanent feelings of human nature. It must not, however, be denied, that the marks of temporary origin and peculiar opinion, are still the vulnerable part of the book. A fiction contrived to support an opinion is a vicious composition. Even a fiction contrived to enforce a maxim of conduct is not of the highest class. And though the vigorous powers of Mr. Godwin raised him above his own intention, still the marks of that intention ought to be effaced as marks of mortality; and nothing ought to remain in the book which will not always interest the reader. The passages which betray the metaphysician, more than the novelist, ought to be weeded out with more than ordinary care. The character of Falkland is a beautiful invention. That such a man could have become an assassin, is perhaps an improbability; and if such a crime be possible for a soul so elevated, it may be due to the dignity of human nature to throw a veil over so humiliating a possibility, except when we are compelled to expose it by its real occurrence. In a merely literary view, however, the improbability of this leading incident is more than compensated, by all those agitating and terrible scenes of which it is the parent: and if the colours had been delicately shaded, if all the steps in the long progress from chivalrous sentiment to assassination had been more patiently traced, and more distinctly brought into view, more might have been lost by weakening the contrast, than would have been gained by softening or removing the improbability. The character of Tyrrel, is a grosser exaggeration; and his conduct is such as neither our manners would produce, nor our laws tolerate. One or two monstrous examples of tyranny, nursed and armed by immense wealth, are no authority for fiction, which is a picture of general nature. The descriptive power of several parts of this novel is of the highest order. The landscape in the morning of Caleb's escape from prison, and a similar escape from a Spanish prison in St. Leon, are among the scenes of fiction which must the most frequently and vividly reappear in the imagination of a reader of sensibility. His disguises and escapes in London, though detailed at too great length, have a frightful reality, perhaps nowhere paralleled in our language, unless it be in some paintings of Daniel De Foe,* with whom it is distinction enough to bear comparison. There are several somewhat similar scenes in the Colonel Jack of that admirable writer, which, among his novels, is indeed only the second; but which could be second to none but Robinson Crusoe,—one of those very few books which are equally popular in every country of Europe, and which delight every reader from the philosopher to the child. Caleb Williams resembles the novels of De Foe, in the austerity with which it rejects the agency of women and the power of love.

It would be affectation to pass over in silence so remarkable a work as the Inquiry into Political Justice; but it is not the time to say much of it. The season of controversy is past, and the period of history is not yet arrived. Whatever may be its mistakes, which we shall be the last to underrate, it is certain that works in which errors equally dangerous are maintained with far less ingenuity, have obtained for their authors a conspicuous place in the philosophical history of the eighteenth century. But books, as well as men, are subject to what is called 'fortune.' The same circumstances which

* A great-grandson of Daniel De Foe, of the same name, is now a creditable tradesman in Hungerford Market in London. His manners give a favourable impression of his sense and morals. He is neither unconscious of his ancestor's fame, nor ostentatious of it.

favoured its sudden popularity, have since unduly depressed its reputation. Had it appeared in a metaphysical age, and in a period of tranquillity, it would have been discussed by philosophers, and might have excited acrimonious disputes; but these would have ended, after the correction of erroneous speculations, in assigning to the author that station to which his eminent talents had entitled him. It would soon have been acknowledged, that the author of one of the most deeply interesting fictions of his age, and of a treatise on metaphysical morals which excited general alarm, whatever else he might be, must be a person of vigorous and versatile powers. But the circumstances of the times, in spite of the author's intention, transmuted a philosophical treatise into a political pamphlet. It seemed to be thrown up by the vortex of the French Revolution, and it sunk accordingly as that whirlpool subsided; while by a perverse fortune, the honesty of the author's intentions contributed to the prejudice against his work. With the simplicity and good faith of a retired speculator, conscious of no object but the pursuit of truth, he followed his reasonings wherever they seemed to him to lead, without looking up to examine the array of sentiment and institution, as well as of interest and prejudice, which he was about to encounter. Intending no mischief, he considered no consequences; and, in the eye of the multitude, was transformed into an incendiary, only because he was an undesigning speculator. The ordinary clamour was excited against him: even the liberal sacrificed him to their character for liberality,—a fate not very uncommon for those who, in critical times, are supposed to go too far; and many of his own disciples, returning into the world, and, as usual, recoiling most violently from their visions, to the grossest worldly-mindedness, offered the fame of their master as an atonement for their own faults. For a time it required courage to brave the prejudice excited by his name. It may, even now perhaps, need some fortitude of a different kind to write, though in the most impartial temper, the small fragment of literary history which relates to it. The moment for doing full and exact justice will come.

All observation on the personal conduct of a writer, when that conduct is not of a public nature, is of dangerous example; and, when it leads to blame, is severely reprehensible. But it is but common justice to say, that there are few instances of more respectable conduct among writers, than is apparent in the subsequent works of Mr. Godwin. He calmly corrected what appeared to him to be his own mistakes; and he proved the perfect disinterestedness of his corrections, by adhering to opinions as obnoxious to the powerful as those which he relinquished. Untempted by the success of his scholars in paying their court to the dispensers of favour, he adhered to the old and rational principles of liberty,—violently shaken as these venerable principles had been, by the tempest which had beaten down the neighbouring erections of anarchy. He continued to seek independence and reputation, with that various success to which the fashions of literature subject professed writers; and to struggle with the difficulties incident to other modes of industry, for which his previous habits had not prepared him. He has thus, in our humble opinion, deserved the respect of all those, whatever may be their opinions, who still wish that some men in England may think for themselves, even at the risk of thinking wrong; but more especially of the friends of liberty, to whose cause he has courageously adhered.

The work before us, is a contribution to the literary history of the seventeenth century. It arose from that well-grounded reverence for the morality, as well as the genius, of Milton, which gives importance to every circumstance connected with him. After all that had been written about him, it appeared to Mr. Godwin, that there was still an unapproached point of view, from which Milton's character might be surveyed,—the history of those nephews to whom he had been a preceptor and a father. "It was accident," he tells us, "that first threw in my way two or three productions of these writers, that my literary acquaintance,* whom I consulted, had never heard of. Dr. Johnson had told me, that the pupils of Milton had given to the world 'only one genuine production.' Persons better informed than Dr. Johnson, could tell me perhaps of half a dozen. How great was my surprise, when I found my collection swelling to forty or fifty!" Chiefly from these publications, but from a considerable variety of little-known sources, he has collected, with singular industry, all the notices, generally incidental, concerning these two persons, which are scattered over the writings of their age.

Their lives are not only interesting as a fragment of the history of Milton, but curious as a specimen of the condition of professed authors in the seventeenth century. If they had been men of genius, or contemptible scribblers, they would not in either case have been fair specimens of their class. Dryden and Flecknoe are equally exceptions. The nephews of Milton belonged to that large body of literary men who are destined to minister to the general curiosity; to keep up the stock of public information; to compile, to abridge, to translate;—a body of importance in a great country, being necessary to maintain, though they cannot advance, its literature. The degree of good sense, good taste, and sound opinions diffused among this class of writers, is of no small moment to

* This plural use of 'acquaintance' is no doubt abundantly warranted by the example of Dryden, the highest authority in a case of diction, of any single English writer: but as the usage is divided, the convenience of distinguishing the plural from the singular at first sight seems to determine, that the preferable plural is "acquaintances."

the public reason and morals; and we know not where we should find so exact a representation of the literary life of two authors, of the period between the Restoration and the Revolution, as in this volume. The complaint, that the details are too multiplied and minute for the importance of the subject, will be ungracious in an age distinguished by a passion for bibliography, and a voracious appetite for anecdote. It cannot be denied, that great acuteness is shown in assembling and weighing all the very minute circumstances, from which their history must often be rather conjectured than inferred. It may appear singular, that we, in this speculative part of the island, should consider the digressions from the biography, and the passages of general speculation, as the part of the work which might, with the greatest advantage, be retrenched: but they are certainly episodes too large for the action, and have sometimes the air of openings of chapters in an intended history of England. These two faults, of digressions too expanded, and details too minute, are the principal defects of the volume; which, however, must be considered hereafter as a necessary part of all collections respecting the biography of Milton.

Edward and John Philips were the sons of Edward Philips of Shrewsbury, Secondary of the Crown Office in the Court of Chancery, by Anne, sister of John Milton. Edward was born in London in 1630, and John in 1631. To this sister the first original English verses of Milton were addressed,—which he composed before the age of seventeen,—to soothe her sorrow for the loss of an infant son. His first published verses were the Epitaph on Shakespeare. To perform the offices of domestic tenderness, and to render due honour to kindred genius, were the noble purposes by which he consecrated his poetical power at the opening of a life, every moment of which corresponded to this early promise. On his return from his travels, he found his nephews, by the death of their father, become orphans. He took them into his house, supporting and educating them; which he was enabled to do by the recompense which he received for the instruction of other pupils. And for this act of respectable industry, and generous affection, in thus remembering the humblest claims of prudence and kindness amidst the lofty ambition and sublime contemplations of his mature powers, he has been sneered at by a moralist, in a work which, being a system of our poetical biography, ought especially to have recommended this most moral example to the imitation of British youth.

John published very early a vindication of his uncle's Defence of the People of England. Both brothers, in a very few years, weary of the austere morals of the Republicans, quitted the party of Milton, and adopted the politics, with the wit and festivity, of the young Cavaliers: but the elder, a person of gentle disposition and amiable manners, more a man of letters than a politician, retained at least due reverence and gratitude for his benefactor, and is conjectured by Mr. Godwin, upon grounds that do not seem improbable, to have contributed to save his uncle at the Restoration. Twenty years after the death of Milton, the first Life of him was published by Edward Philips; upon which all succeeding narratives have been built. This Theatrum Poetarum will be always read with interest, as containing the opinions concerning poetry and poets, which he probably imbibed from Milton. This amiable writer died between 1694 and 1698.

John Philips, a coarse buffoon, and a vulgar debauchee, was, throughout life, chiefly a political pamphleteer, who turned with every change of fortune and breath of popular clamour, but on all sides preserved a consistency in violence, scurrility, and servility to his masters, whether they were the favourites of the Court, or the leaders of the rabble. Having cried out for the blood of his former friends at the Restoration, he insulted the memory of Milton, within two years of his death. He adhered to the cause of Charles II. till it became unpopular; and disgraced the then new name of Whig by associating with the atrocious Titus Oates. In his vindication of that execrable wretch, he adopts the maxim, "that the attestations of a hundred Catholics cannot be put in balance with the oath of one Protestant;"—which, if 'our own party' were substituted for 'Protestant,' and 'the opposite one' for 'Catholic,' may be regarded as the general principle of the jurisprudence of most triumphant factions. He was silenced, or driven to literary compilation, by those fatal events in 1683, which seemed to be the final triumph of the Court over public liberty. His servile voice, however, hailed the accession of James II. The Revolution produced a new turn of this weathercock; but, happily for the kingdom, no second Restoration gave occasion to another display of his inconstancy. In 1681 he had been the associate of Oates, and the tool of Shaftesbury: in 1685 he thus addresses James II. in doggerel scurrility:

> "Must the Faith's true Defender bleed to death,
> A sacrifice to Cooper's wrath?"

In 1695 he took a part in that vast mass of bad verse occasioned by the death of Queen Mary; and in 1697 he celebrated King William as Augustus Britannicus, in a poem on the Peace of Ryswick. From the Revolution to his death, about 1704, he was usefully employed as editor of the Monthly Mercury, a journal which was wholly, or principally, a translation from Le Mercure Historique, published at the Hague, by some of those ingenious and excellent Protestant refugees, whose writings contributed to excite all Europe against Louis XIV. Mr. Godwin at last, very naturally, relents a little towards him: he is unwilling to part on bad terms with one who has been so long a companion. All, however, that indulgent ingenuity can discover in his favour is, that he was an indefatigable writer; and that, during his last years, he rested, after so many vibrations, in the opinions of a constitutional Whig. But, in a man like John Philips, the latter circumstance is only one of the signs of the times, and proves no more than that the principles of English liberty were patronized by a government which owed to these principles its existence.

The above is a very slight sketch of the lives of these two persons, which Mr. Godwin, with equal patience and acuteness of research, has gleaned from publications, of which it required a much more than ordinary familiarity with the literature of the last century, even to know the existence. It is somewhat singular, that no inquiries seem to have been made respecting the history of the descendants of Milton's brother, Sir Christopher; and that it has not been ascertained whether either of his nephews left children. Thomas Milton, the son of Sir Christopher, was, it seems, Secondary to the Crown Office in Chancery; and it could not be very difficult for a resident in London to ascertain the period of his death, and perhaps to discover his residence and the state of his family.

Milton's direct descendants can only exist, if they exist at all, among the posterity of his youngest and favourite daughter Deborah, afterwards Mrs. Clarke, a woman of cultivated understanding, and not unpleasing manners, who was known to Richardson and Professor Ward, and was patronized by Addison.* Her affecting exclamation is well known, on seeing her father's portrait for the first time more than thirty years after his death:—"Oh my father, my dear father!" "She spoke of him," says Richardson, "with great tenderness; she said he was delightful company, the life of the conversation, not only by a flow of subject, but by unaffected cheerfulness and civility." This is the character of one whom Dr. Johnson represents as a morose tyrant, drawn by a supposed victim of his domestic oppression. Her daughter, Mrs. Foster, for whose benefit Dr. Newton and Dr. Birch procured Comus to be acted, survived all her children. The only child of Deborah Milton, of whom we have any accounts besides Mrs. Foster, was Caleb Clarke, who went to Madras in the first years of the eighteenth century, and who then vanishes from the view of the biographers of Milton. We have been enabled, by accident, to enlarge a very little this appendage to his history. It appears from an examination of the parish register of Fort St. George, that Caleb Clarke, who seems to have been parish-clerk of that place from 1717 to 1719, was buried there on the 26th of October of the latter year. By his wife Mary, whose original surname does not appear, he had three children born at Madras; —Abraham, baptized on the 2d of June, 1703; Mary, baptized on the 17th of March, 1706, and buried on December 15th of the same year; and Isaac, baptized 13th of February, 1711. Of Isaac no farther account appears. Abraham, the great-grandson of Milton, in September, 1725, married Anna Clarke; and the baptism of their daughter Mary is registered on the 2d of April, 1727. With this all notices of this family cease. But as neither Abraham, nor any of his family, nor his brother Isaac, died at Madras, and as he was only twenty-four years of age at the baptism of his daughter, it is probable that the family migrated to some other part of India, and that some trace of them might yet be discovered by examination of the parish registers of Calcutta and Bombay. If they had returned to England, they could not have escaped the curiosity of the admirers and historians of Milton. We cannot apologize for the minuteness of this genealogy, or for the eagerness of our desire that it should be enlarged. We profess that superstitious veneration for the memory of the greatest of poets, which would regard the slightest relic of him as sacred; and we cannot conceive either true poetical sensibility, or a just sense of the glory of England, to belong to that Englishman, who would not feel the strongest emotions at the sight of a descendant of Milton, discovered in the person even of the most humble and unlettered of human beings.

While the grandson of Milton resided at Madras, in a condition so humble as to make the office of parish-clerk an object of ambition, it is somewhat remarkable that the elder brother of Addison should have been the Governor of that settlement. The honourable Galston Addison died there in the year 1709. Thomas Pitt, grandfather to Lord Chatham, had been his immediate predecessor in the government.

It was in the same year that Mr. Addison began those contributions to periodical essays, which, as long as any sensibility to the beauties of English style remains, must be considered as its purest and most perfect models. But it was not until eighteen months afterwards,—when, influenced by fidelity to his friends, and attachment to the cause of liberty, he had retired from office, and when, with his usual judgment, he resolved to resume the more active cultivation of literature, as the elegant employment of his leisure,—that he undertook the series of essays on Paradise Lost;—not, as has been weakly supposed, with the presumptuous hope of exalting Milton, but with the more reasonable intention of cultivating the public taste, and instructing the nation in the principles of just criticism, by observations on a work already acknowledged to be the first of English poems. If any doubt could be entertained respecting the purpose of this excellent writer, it must be silenced by the language in which he announces his criticism:—"As the first place among our English poets is due to

* Who intended to have procured a permanent provision for her. She was presented with fifty guineas by Queen Caroline.

W

Milton," says he, "I shall enter into a regular criticism upon his Paradise Lost," &c. It is clear that he takes for granted the paramount greatness of Milton; and that his object was not to disinter a poet who had been buried in unjust oblivion, but to illustrate the rules of criticism by observations on the writings of him whom all his readers revered as the greatest poet of their country. This passage might have been added by Mr. Godwin to the numerous proofs by which he has demonstrated the ignorance and negligence, if not the malice, of those who would persuade us that the English nation could have suspended their admiration of a poem, —the glory of their country, and the boast of human genius,—till they were taught its excellences by critics, and enabled by political revolutions to indulge their feelings with safety. It was indeed worthy of Lord Somers to have been one of its earliest admirers; and to his influence and conversation it is not improbable that we owe, though indirectly, the essays of Addison. The latter's criticism manifests and inspires a more genuine sense of poetical beauty than others of more ambitious pretensions, and now of greater name. But it must not be forgotten that Milton had subdued the adverse prejudices of Dryden and Atterbury, long before he had extorted from a more acrimonious hostility, that unwilling but noble tribute of justice to the poet, for which Dr. Johnson seems to have made satisfaction to his hatred by a virulent libel on the man.*

It is an excellence of Mr. Godwin's narrative, that he thinks and feels about the men and events of the age of Milton, in some measure as Milton himself felt and thought. Exact conformity of sentiment is neither possible nor desirable: but a Life of Milton, written by a zealous opponent of his principles, in the relation of events which so much exasperate the passions, almost inevitably degenerates into a libel. The constant hostility of a biographer to the subject of his narrative, whether it be just or not, is teazing and vexatious: the natural frailty of over-partiality is a thousand times more agreeable.

* The strange misrepresentations, long prevalent among ourselves respecting the slow progress of Milton's reputation, sanctioned as they were both by Johnson and by Thomas Warton, have produced ridiculous effects abroad. On the 16th of November, 1814, a Parisian poet named Campenon was, in the present unhappy state of French literature, received at the Academy as the successor of the Abbé Delille. In his Discours de Réception, he speaks of the Abbé's translation "de ce Paradis Perdu, dont l'Agleterre est si fière depuis qu'elle a cessé d'en ignorer le mérite." The president M. Regnault de St. Jean d'Angely said that M. Delille repaid our hospitality by translating Milton,—" en doublant ainsi la célébrité du Poëte; dont le génie a inspiré à l'Angleterre un si tardif mais si légitime orgueil."

REVIEW

OF

ROGERS' POEMS.

It seems very doubtful, whether the progress and the vicissitudes of the elegant arts can be referred to the operation of general laws, with the same plausibility as the exertions of the more robust faculties of the human mind, in the severer forms of science and of useful art. The action of fancy and of taste seems to be affected by causes too various and minute to be enumerated with sufficient completeness for the purposes of philosophical theory. To explain them, may appear to be as hopeless an attempt, as to account for one summer being more warm and genial than another. The difficulty would be insurmountable, even in framing the most general outline of a theory, if the various forms assumed by imagination, in the fine arts, did not depend on some of the most conspicuous, as well as powerful agents in the moral world. But these arise from revolutions of popular sentiments, and are connected with the opinions of the age, and with the manners of the refined class, as certainly, though not in so great a degree, as with the passions of the multitude. The comedy of a polished monarchy never can be of the same character with that of a bold and tumultuous democracy. Changes of religion and of government, civil or foreign wars, conquests which derive splendour from distance, or extent, or difficulty, long tranquillity,—all these, and indeed every conceivable modification of the state of a community, show themselves in the tone of its poetry, and leave long and deep traces on every part of its literature. Geometry is the same, not only at London and Paris, but in the extremes of Athens and Samarcand: but the state of the general feeling in England, at this moment, requires a different poetry from that which delighted our ancestors in the time of Luther or Alfred.

During the greater part of the eighteenth century, the connection of the character of

English poetry with the state of the country, was very easily traced. The period which extended from the English to the French Revolution, was the golden age of authentic history. Governments were secure, nations tranquil, improvements rapid, manners mild beyond the example of any former age. The English nation which possessed the greatest of all human blessings,—a wisely constructed popular government, necessarily enjoyed the largest share of every other benefit. The tranquillity of that fortunate period was not disturbed by any of those calamitous, or even extraordinary events, which excite the imagination and inflame the passions. No age was more exempt from the prevalence of any species of popular enthusiasm. Poetry, in this state of things, partook of that calm, argumentative, moral, and directly useful character into which it naturally subsides, when there are no events to call up the higher passions,—when every talent is allured into the immediate service of a prosperous and improving society,—and when wit, taste, diffused literature, and fastidious criticism, combine to deter the young writer from the more arduons enterprises of poetical genius. In such an age, every art becomes rational. Reason is the power which presides in a calm. But reason guides, rather than impels; and, though it must regulate every exertion of genius, it never can rouse it to vigorous action.

The school of Dryden and Pope, which prevailed till a very late period of the last century, is neither the most poetical nor the most national part of our literary annals. These great poets sometimes indeed ventured into the regions of pure poetry: but their general character is, that "not in fancy's maze they wandered long;" and that they rather approached the elegant correctness of our Continental neighbours, than supported the daring flight, which, in the former age, had borne English poetry to a sublimer elevation than that of any other modern people of the West.

Towards the middle of the century, great, though quiet changes, began to manifest themselves in the republic of letters in every European nation which retained any portion of mental activity. About that time, the exclusive authority of our great rhyming poets began to be weakened; while new tastes and fashions began to show themselves in the political world. A school of poetry must have prevailed long enough, to be probably on the verge of downfal, before its practice is embodied in a correspondent system of criticism.

Johnson was the critic of our second poetical school. As far as his prejudices of a political or religious kind did not disqualify him for all criticism, he was admirably fitted by nature to be the critic of this species of poetry. Without more imagination, sensibility, or delicacy than it required,—not always with perhaps quite enough for its higher parts,—he possessed sagacity, shrewdness, experience, knowledge of mankind, a taste for rational and orderly compositions, and a disposition to accept, instead of poetry, that lofty and vigorous declamation in harmonious verse, of which he himself was capable, and to which his great master sometimes descended. His spontaneous admiration scarcely soared above Dryden. "Merit of a loftier class he rather saw than felt." Shakespeare has transcendent excellence of every sort, and for every critic, except those who are repelled by the faults which usually attend sublime virtues,—character and manners, morality and prudence, as well as imagery and passion. Johnson did indeed perform a vigorous act of reluctant justice towards Milton; but it was a proof, to use his own words, that

"At length our mighty Bard's victorious lays
Fill the loud voice of universal praise;
And baffled Spite, with hopeless anguish dumb,
Yields to renown the centuries to come!"*

The deformities of the Life of Gray ought not to be ascribed to jealousy,—for Johnson's mind, though coarse, was not mean,—but to the prejudices of his university, his political faction, and his poetical sect: and this last bigotry is the more remarkable, because it is exerted against the most skilful and tasteful of innovators, who, in reviving more poetical subjects and a more splendid diction, has employed more care and finish than those who aimed only at correctness.

The interval which elapsed between the death of Goldsmith and the rise of Cowper, is perhaps more barren than any other twelve years in the history of our poetry since the accession of Elizabeth. It seemed as if the fertile soil was at length exhausted. But it had in fact only ceased to exhibit its accustomed produce. The established poetry had worn out either its own resources, or the constancy of its readers. Former attempts to introduce novelty had been either too weak or too early. Neither the beautiful fancy of Collins, nor the learned and ingenious industry of Warton, nor even the union of sublime genius with consummate art in Gray, had produced a general change in poetical composition. But the fulness of time was approaching; and a revolution has been accomplished, of which the commencement nearly coincides—not, as we conceive, accidentally—with that of the political revolution which has changed the character as well as the condition of Europe. It has been a thousand times observed, that nations become weary even of excellence, and seek a new way of writing, though it should be a worse. But besides the operation of satiety—the general cause of literary revolutions—several particular circumstances seem to have affected the late changes of our poetical taste; of which, two are more conspicuous than the rest.

In the natural progress of society, the songs which are the effusion of the feelings of a

* Prologue to Comus.—Ed.

rude tribe, are gradually polished into a form of poetry still retaining the marks of the national opinions, sentiments, and manners, from which it originally sprung. The plants are improved by cultivation; but they are still the native produce of the soil. The only perfect example which we know, of this sort, is Greece. Knowledge and useful art, and perhaps in a great measure religion, the Greeks received from the East: but as they studied no foreign language, it was impossible that any foreign literature should influence the progress of theirs. Not even the name of a Persian, Assyrian, Phenician, or Egyptian poet is alluded to by any Greek writer: The Greek poetry was, therefore, wholly national. The Pelasgic ballads were insensibly formed into Epic, and Tragic, and Lyric poems: but the heroes, the opinions, and the customs, continued as exclusively Grecian, as they had been when the Hellenic minstrels knew little beyond the Adriatic and the Ægean. The literature of Rome was a copy from that of Greece. When the classical studies revived amid the chivalrous manners and feudal institutions of Gothic Europe, the imitation of ancient poets struggled against the power of modern sentiments, with various event, in different times and countries,—but every where in such a manner, as to give somewhat of an artificial and exotic character to poetry. Jupiter and the Muses appeared in the poems of Christian nations. The feelings and principles of democracies were copied by the gentlemen of Teutonic monarchies or aristocracies. The sentiments of the poet in his verse, were not those which actuated him in his conduct. The forms and rules of composition were borrowed from antiquity, instead of spontaneously arising from the manner of thinking of modern communities. In Italy, when letters first revived, the chivalrous principle was too near the period of its full vigour, to be oppressed by his foreign learning. Ancient ornaments were borrowed; but the romantic form was prevalent: and where the forms were classical, the spirit continued to be romantic. The structure of Tasso's poem was that of the Grecian epic; but his heroes were Christian knights. French poetry having been somewhat unaccountably late in its rise, and slow in its progress, reached its most brilliant period, when all Europe had considerably lost its ancient characteristic principles, and was fully imbued with classical ideas. Hence it acquired faultless elegance:—hence also it became less natural,—more timid and more imitative,—more like a feeble translation of Roman poetry. The first age of English poetry, in the reign of Elizabeth, displayed a combination,—fantastic enough,—of chivalrous fancy and feeling with classical pedantry; but, upon the whole, its native genius was unsubdued. The poems of that age, with all their faults, and partly perhaps from their faults, are the most national part of our poetry, as they undoubtedly contain its highest beauties. From the accession of James, to the Civil War, the glory of Shakespeare turned the whole national genius to the drama; and, after the Restoration, a new and classical school arose, under whom our old and peculiar literature was abandoned, and almost forgotten. But all imported tastes in literature must be in some measure superficial. The poetry which once grew in the bosoms of a people, is always capable of being revived by a skilful hand. When the brilliant and poignant lines of Pope began to pall on the public ear, it was natural that we should revert to the cultivation of our indigenous poetry.

Nor was this the sole, or perhaps the chief agent which was working a poetical change. As the condition and character of the former age had produced an argumentative, didactic, sententious, prudential, and satirical poetry; so the approaches to a new order (or rather at first disorder) in political society, were attended by correspondent movements in the poetical world. Bolder speculations began to prevail. A combination of the science and art of the tranquil period, with the hardy enterprises of that which succeeded, gave rise to scientific poems, in which a bold attempt was made, by the mere force of diction, to give a political interest and elevation to the coldest parts of knowledge, and to those arts which have been hitherto considered as the meanest. Having been forced above their natural place by the wonder at first elicited, they have not yet recovered from the subsequent depression. Nor will a similar attempt be successful, without a more temperate use of power over style, till the diffusion of physical knowledge renders it familiar to the popular imagination, and till the prodigies worked by the mechanical arts shall have bestowed on them a character of grandeur.

As the agitation of men's minds approached the period of an explosion, its effects on literature became more visible. The desire of strong emotion succeeded to the solicitude to avoid disgust. Fictions, both dramatic and narrative, were formed according to the school of Rousseau and Goethe. The mixture of comic and tragic pictures once more displayed itself, as in the ancient and national drama. The sublime and energetic feelings of devotion began to be more frequently associated with poetry. The tendency of political speculation concurred in directing the mind of the poet to the intense and undisguised passions of the uneducated; which fastidious politeness had excluded from the subjects of poetical imitation. The history of nations unlike ourselves, the fantastic mythology and ferocious superstition of distant times and countries, or the legends of our own antique faith, and the romances of our fabulous and heroic ages, became themes of poetry. Traces of a higher order of feeling appeared in the contemplations in which the poet indulged, and in the events and scenes which he delighted to describe. The fire with which a chivalrous tale was told, made the reader inattentive to negligences in the story or the style. Poetry became more devout, more contemplative, more mystical, more visionary,—more alien from the taste of those whose poetry is only a polished prosaic verse,—more full of antique superstition, and more prone to daring innovation,—painting both coarser realities and purer imaginations, than she had before hazarded,—sometimes buried in the profound quiet required by the dreams of fancy,—sometimes turbulent and martial,—seeking "fierce wars and faithful loves" in those times long past, when the frequency of the most dreadful dangers produced heroic energy and the ardour of faithful affection.

Even the direction given to the traveller by the accidents of war has not been without its influence. Greece, the mother of freedom and of poetry in the West, which had long employed only the antiquary, the artist, and the philologist, was at length destined, after an interval of many silent and inglorious ages, to awaken the genius of a poet. Full of enthusiasm for those perfect forms of heroism and liberty, which his imagination had placed in the recesses of antiquity, he gave vent to his impatience of the imperfections of living men and real institutions, in an original strain of sublime satire, which clothes moral anger in imagery of an almost horrible grandeur; and which, though it cannot coincide with the estimate of reason, yet could only flow from that worship of perfection, which is the soul of all true poetry.

The tendency of poetry to become national, was in more than one case remarkable. While the Scottish middle age inspired the most popular poet perhaps of the eighteenth century, the national genius of Ireland at length found a poetical representative, whose exquisite ear, and flexible fancy, wantoned in all the varieties of poetical luxury, from the levities to the fondness of love, from polished pleasantry to ardent passion, and from the social joys of private life to a tender and mournful patriotism, taught by the melancholy fortunes of an illustrious country,—with a range adapted to every nerve in the composition of a people susceptible of all feelings which have the colour of generosity, and more exempt probably than any other from degrading and unpoetical vices.

The failure of innumerable adventurers is inevitable, in literary, as well as in political, revolutions. The inventor seldom perfects his invention. The uncouthness of the novelty, the clumsiness with which it is managed by an unpractised hand, and the dogmatical contempt of criticism natural to the pride and enthusiasm of the innovator, combine to expose him to ridicule, and generally terminate in his being admired (though warmly) by a few of his contemporaries,—remembered only occasionally in after times,—and supplanted in general estimation by more cautious and skilful imitators. With the very reverse of unfriendly feelings, we observe that erroneous theories respecting poetical diction,—exclusive and proscriptive notions in criticism, which in adding new provinces to poetry would deprive her of ancient dominions and lawful instruments of rule,—and a neglect of that extreme regard to general sympathy, and even accidental prejudice, which is necessary to guard poetical novelties against their natural enemy the satirist,—have powerfully counteracted an attempt, equally moral and philosophical, made by a writer of undisputed poetical genius, to enlarge the territories of art, by unfolding the poetical interest which lies latent in the common acts of the humblest men, and in the most ordinary modes of feeling, as well as in the most familiar scenes of nature.

The various opinions which may naturally be formed of the merit of individual writers, form no necessary part of our consideration. We consider the present as one of the most flourishing periods of English poetry: but those who condemn all contemporary poets, need not on that account dissent from our speculations. It is sufficient to have proved the reality, and in part perhaps to have explained the origin, of a literary revolution. At no time does the success of writers bear so uncertain a proportion to their genius, as when the rules of judging and the habits of feeling are unsettled.

It is not uninteresting, even as a matter of speculation, to observe the fortune of a poem which, like the Pleasures of Memory, appeared at the commencement of this literary revolution, without paying court to the revolutionary tastes, or seeking distinction by resistance to them. It borrowed no aid either from prejudice or innovation. It neither copied the fashion of the age which was passing away, nor offered any homage to the rising novelties. It resembles, only in measure, the poems of the eighteenth century, which were written in heroic rhyme. Neither the brilliant sententiousness of Pope, nor the frequent languor and negligence perhaps inseparable from the exquisite nature of Goldsmith, could be traced in a poem, from which taste and labour equally banished mannerism and inequality. It was patronized by no sect or faction. It was neither imposed on the public by any literary cabal, nor forced into notice by the noisy anger of conspicuous enemies. Yet, destitute as it was of every foreign help, it acquired a popularity originally very great; and which has not only continued amidst extraordinary fluctuation of general taste, but has increased amid a succession of formidable competitors. No production, so popular, was probably ever so little censured by criticism: and thus is combined the applause of contemporaries with the suffrage of the representatives of posterity.

It is needless to make extracts from a poem which is familiar to every reader. In selection, indeed, no two readers would probably agree: but the description of the Gipsies,—of the Boy quitting his Father's house,—and of the Savoyard recalling the mountainous scenery of his country,—and the descriptive commencement of the tale in Cumberland, have remained most deeply impressed on our minds. We should be disposed to quote the following verses, as not surpassed, in pure and chaste elegance, by any English lines:–

"When Joy's bright sun has shed his evening ray,
And Hope's delusive meteors cease to play;
When clouds on clouds the smiling prospect close,
Still through the gloom thy star serenely glows:
Like yon fair orb she gilds the brow of Night
With the mild magic of reflected light."

The conclusion of the fine passage on the Veterans at Greenwich and Chelsea, has a pensive dignity which beautifully corresponds with the scene:—

"Long have ye known Reflection's genial ray
Gild the calm close of Valour's various day."

And we cannot resist the pleasure of quoting the moral, tender, and elegant lines which close the Poem:—

"Lighter than air, Hope's summer-visions fly,
If but a fleeting cloud obscure the sky;
If but a beam of sober Reason play,
Lo, Fancy's fairy frost-work melts away!
But can the wiles of Art, the grasp of Power,
Snatch the rich relics of a well-spent hour?
These, when the trembling spirit wings her flight,
Pour round her path a stream of living light;
And gild those pure and perfect realms of rest,
Where Virtue triumphs, and her sons are blest!"

The descriptive passages require indeed a closer inspection, and a more exercised eye, than those of some celebrated contemporaries who sacrifice elegance to effect, and whose figures stand out in bold relief, from the general roughness of their more unfinished compositions: and in the moral parts, there is often discoverable a Virgilian art, which suggests, rather than displays, the various and contrasted scenes of human life, and adds to the power of language by a certain air of reflection and modesty, in the preference of measured terms to those of more apparent energy.

In the View from the House,* the scene is neither delightful from very superior beauty, nor striking by singularity, nor powerful from reminding us of terrible passions or memorable deeds It consists of the more ordinary of the beautiful features of nature, neither exaggerated nor represented with curious minuteness, but exhibited with picturesque elegance, in connection with those tranquil emotions which they call up in the calm order of a virtuous mind, in every condition of society and of life. The verses on the Torso, are in a more severe style. The Fragment of a divine artist, which awakened the genius of Michael Angelo, seems to disdain ornament. It would be difficult to name two small poems, by the same writer, in which he has attained such high degrees of kinds of excellence so dissimilar, as are seen in the Sick Chamber and the Butterfly. The first has a truth of detail, which, considered merely as painting, is admirable; but assumes a higher character, when it is felt to be that minute remembrance, with which affection recollects every circumstance that could have affected a beloved sufferer. Though the morality which concludes the second, be in itself very beautiful, it may be doubted whether the verses would not have left a more unmixed delight, if the address had remained as a mere sport of fancy, without the seriousness of an object, or an application. The verses written in Westminster Abbey are surrounded by dangerous recollections; they aspire to commemorate Fox, and to copy some of the grandest thoughts in the most sublime work of Bossuet. Nothing can satisfy the expectation awakened by such names: yet we are assured that there are some of them which would be envied by the best writers of this age. The scenery of Loch Long is among the grandest in Scotland; and the description of it shows the power of feeling and painting. In this island, the taste for nature has grown with the progress of refinement. It is most alive in those who are most brilliantly distinguished in social and active life. It elevates the mind above the meanness which it might contract in the rivalship for praise; and preserves those habits of reflection and sensibility, which receive so many rude shocks in the coarse contests of the world. Not many summer hours can be passed in the most mountainous solitudes of Scotland, without meeting some who are worthy to be remembered with the sublime objects of nature, which they had travelled so far to admire.

The most conspicuous of the novelties of this volume is the poem or poems, entitled "Fragments of the Voyage of Columbus." The subject of this poem is, politically or philosophically considered, among the most important in the annals of mankind. The introduction of Christianity (humanly viewed), the irruption of the Northern barbarians, the contest between the Christian and Mussulman nations in Syria, the two inventions of gunpowder and printing, the emancipation of the human understanding by the Reformation, the discovery of America, and of a maritime passage to Asia in the last ten years of the fifteenth century, are the events which have produced the greatest and most durable effects, since the establishment of civilization, and the consequent commencement of authentic history. But the poetical capabilities of an event bear no proportion to historical importance. None of the consequences that do not strike the senses or the fancy can interest the poet. The greatest of the transactions above enumerated is obviously incapable of entering into poetry. The Crusades were not without permanent effects on the state of men: but their poeti-

* In the Epistle to a Friend.—Ed.

cal interest does not arise from these effects; and it immeasurably surpasses them.

Whether the voyage of Columbus be destined to be for ever incapable of becoming the subject of an epic poem, is a question which we have scarcely the means of answering. The success of great writers has often so little corresponded with the promise of their subject, that we might be almost tempted to think the choice of a subject indifferent. The story of Hamlet, or of Paradise Lost, would beforehand have been pronounced to be unmanageable. Perhaps the genius of Shakespeare and of Milton has rather compensated for the incorrigible defects of ungrateful subjects, than conquered them. The course of ages may produce the poetical genius, the historical materials and the national feelings, for an American epic poem. There is yet but one state in America, and that state is hardly become a nation. At some future period, when every part of the continent has been the scene of memorable events, when the discovery and conquest have receded into that legendary dimness which allows fancy to mould them at her pleasure, the early history of America may afford scope for the genius of a thousand national poets; and while some may soften the cruelty which darkens the daring energy of Cortez and Pizarro,—while others may, in perhaps new forms of poetry, ennoble the pacific conquests of Penn,—and while the genius, the exploits, and the fate of Raleigh, may render his establishments probably the most alluring of American subjects, every inhabitant of the new world will turn his eyes with filial reverence towards Columbus, and regard, with equal enthusiasm, the voyage which laid the foundation of so many states, and peopled a continent with civilized men. Most epic subjects, but especially such a subject as Columbus, require either the fire of an actor in the scene, or the religious reverence of a very distant posterity. Homer, as well as Erçilla and Camoens, show what may be done by an epic poet who himself feels the passions of his heroes. It must not be denied that Virgil has borrowed a colour of refinement from the court of Augustus, in painting the age of Priam and of Dido. Evander is a solitary and exquisite model of primitive manners, divested of grossness, without losing their simplicity. But to an European poet, in this ag of the world, the Voyage of Columbus is too naked and too exactly defined by history. It has no variety,—scarcely any succession of events. It consists of one scene, during which two or three simple passions continue in a state of the highest excitement. It is a voyage with intense anxiety in every bosom, controlled by magnanimous fortitude in the leader, and producing among his followers a fear,—sometimes submissive, sometimes mutinous, always ignoble. It admits of no variety of character,—no unexpected revolutions. And even the issue, though of unspeakable importance, and admirably adapted to some kinds of poetry, is not an event of such outward dignity and splendour as ought naturally to close the active and brilliant course of an epic poem.

It is natural that the Fragments should give a specimen of the marvellous as well as of the other constituents of epic fiction. We may observe, that it is neither the intention nor the tendency of poetical machinery to supersede secondary causes, to fetter the will, and to make human creatures appear as the mere instruments of destiny. It is introduced to satisfy that insatiable demand for a nature more exalted than that which we know by experience, which creates all poetry, and which is most active in its highest species, and in its most perfect productions. It is not to account for thoughts and feelings, that superhuman agents are brought down upon earth: it is rather for the contrary purpose, of lifting them into a mysterious dignity beyond the cognizance of reason. There is a material difference between the acts which superior beings perform, and the sentiments which they inspire. It is true, that when a god fights against men, there can be no uncertainty or anxiety, and consequently no interest about the event,—unless indeed in the rude theology of Homer, where Minerva may animate the Greeks, while Mars excites the Trojans: but it is quite otherwise with these divine persons inspiring passion, or represented as agents in the great phenomena of nature. Venus and Mars inspire love or valour; they give a noble origin and a dignified character to these sentiments: but the sentiments themselves act according to the laws of our nature; and their celestial source has no tendency to impair their power over human sympathy. No event, which has not too much modern vulgarity to be susceptible of alliance with poetry, can be incapable of being ennobled by that eminently poetical art which ascribes it either to the Supreme Will, or to the agency of beings who are greater than human. The wisdom of Columbus is neither less venerable, nor less his own, because it is supposed to flow more directly than that of other wise men, from the inspiration of heaven. The mutiny of his seamen is not less interesting or formidable because the poet traces it to the suggestion of those malignant spirits, in whom the imagination, independent of all theological doctrines, is naturally prone to personify and embody the causes of evil.

Unless, indeed, the marvellous be a part of the popular creed at the period of the action, the reader of a subsequent age will refuse to sympathize with it. His poetical faith is founded in sympathy with that of the poetical personages. Still more objectionable is a marvellous influence, neither believed in by the reader nor by the hero;—like a great part of the machinery of the Henriade and the Lusiad, which indeed is not only absolutely ineffective, but rather disennobles heroic fiction, by association with light and frivolous ideas. Allegorical persons (if the expression may be allowed) are only in the way to become agents. The abstraction has received a faint outline of form; but it has not yet acquired those individual marks and characteristic peculiarities, which render it a really existing being. On the other hand, the more sublime parts of our own religion, and more especially those which are common to all religion, are too awful and too philosophical for poetical effect. If we except Paradise Lost, where all is supernatural, and where the ancestors of the human race are not strictly human beings, it must be owned that no successful attempt has been made to ally a human action with the sublimer principles of the Christian theology. Some opinions, which may perhaps, without irreverence, be said to be rather appendages to the Christian system, than essential parts of it, are in that sort of intermediate state which fits them for the purposes of poetry;—sufficiently exalted to ennoble the human actions with which they are blended, but not so exactly defined, nor so deeply revered, as to be inconsistent with the liberty of imagination. The guardian angels, in the project of Dryden, had the inconvenience of having never taken any deep root in popular belief: the agency of evil spirits was firmly believed in the age of Columbus. With the truth of facts poetry can have no concern; but the truth of manners is necessary to its persons. If the minute investigations of the Notes to this poem had related to historical details, they would have been insignificant; but they are intended to justify the human and the supernatural parts of it, by an appeal to the manners and to the opinions of the age.

Perhaps there is no volume in our language of which it can be so truly said, as of the present, that it is equally exempt from the frailties of negligence and the vices of affectation. Exquisite polish of style is indeed more admired by the artist than by the people. The gentle and elegant pleasure which it imparts, can only be felt by a calm reason, an exercised taste, and a mind free from turbulent passions. But these beauties of execution can exist only in combination with much of the primary beauties of thought and feeling; and poets of the first rank depend on them for no small part of the perpetuity of their fame. In poetry, though not in eloquence, it is less to rouse the passions of a moment, than to satisfy the taste of all ages.

In estimating the poetical rank of Mr. Rogers, it must not be forgotten that popularity never can arise from elegance alone. The vices of a poem may render it popular; and virtues of a faint character may be sufficient to preserve a languishing and cold reputation. But to be both popular poets and classical writers, is the rare lot of those few who are released from all solicitude about their literary fame. It often happens to successful writers, that the lustre of their first productions throws a temporary cloud over some of those which follow. Of all literary misfortunes, this is the most easily endured, and the most speedily repaired. It is generally no more than a momentary illusion produced by disappointed admiration, which expected more from the talents of the admired writer than any talents could perform. Mr. Rogers has long passed that period of probation, during which it may be excusable to feel some painful solicitude about the reception of every new work. Whatever may be the rank assigned hereafter to his writings, when compared with each other, the writer has most certainly taken his place among the classical poets of his country.

REVIEW

OF

MADAME DE STAËL'S 'DE L'ALLEMAGNE.'*

Till the middle of the eighteenth century, Germany was, in one important respect, singular among the great nations of Christendom. She had attained a high rank in Europe by discoveries and inventions, by science, by abstract speculation as well as positive knowledge, by the genius and the art of war, and above all, by the theological revolution, which unfettered the understanding in one part of Europe, and loosened its chains in the other; but she was without a national literature. The country of Guttenberg, of Copernicus, of Luther, of Kepler, and of Leibnitz, had no writer in her own language, whose name was known to the neighbouring nations. German captains and statesmen, philosophers and scholars, were celebrated; but German writers were unknown. The nations of the Spanish peninsula formed the exact contrast to Germany. She had every mark of mental cultivation but a vernacular

* From the Edinburgh Review, vol. xxii. p. 168.—Ed.

literature: they, since the Reformation, had ceased to exercise their reason; and they retained only their poets, whom they were content to admire, without daring any longer to emulate. In Italy, Metastasio was the only renowned poet; and sensibility to the arts of design had survived genius: but the monuments of ancient times still kept alive the pursuits of antiquities and philology; and the rivalship of small states, and the glory of former ages, preserved an interest in literary history. The national mind retained that tendency towards experimental science, which it perhaps principally owed to the fame of Galileo; and began also to take some part in those attempts to discover the means of bettering the human condition, by inquiries into the principles of legislation and political economy, which form the most honourable distinction of the eighteenth century. France and England abated nothing of their activity. Whatever may be thought of the purity of taste, or of the soundness of opinion of Montesquieu and Voltaire, Buffon and Rousseau, no man will dispute the vigour of their genius. The same period among us was not marked by the loss of any of our ancient titles to fame; and it was splendidly distinguished by the rise of the arts, of history, of oratory, and (shall we not add?) of painting. But Germany remained a solitary example of a civilized, learned, and scientific nation, without a literature. The chivalrous ballads of the middle age, and the efforts of the Silesian poets in the beginning of the seventeenth century, were just sufficient to render the general defect more striking. French was the language of every court; and the number of courts in Germany rendered this circumstance almost equivalent to the exclusion of German from every society of rank. Philosophers employed a barbarous Latin,—as they had throughout all Europe, till the Reformation had given dignity to the vernacular tongues, by employing them in the service of Religion, and till Montaigne, Galileo, and Bacon, broke down the barrier between the learned and the people, by philosophizing in a popular language; and the German language continued to be the mere instrument of the most vulgar intercourse of life. Germany had, therefore, no exclusive mental possession: for poetry and eloquence may, and in some measure must be national; but knowledge, which is the common patrimony of civilized men, can be appropriated by no people.

A great revolution, however, at length began, which in the course of half a century terminated in bestowing on Germany a literature, perhaps the most characteristic possessed by any European nation. It had the important peculiarity of being the first which had its birth in an enlightened age. The imagination and sensibility of an infant poetry were in it singularly blended with the refinements of philosophy. A studious and learned people, familiar with the poets of other nations, with the first simplicity of nature and feeling, were too often tempted to pursue the singular, the excessive, and the monstrous. Their fancy was attracted towards the deformities and diseases of moral nature;—the wildness of an infant literature, combined with the eccentric and fearless speculations of a philosophical age. Some of the qualities of the childhood of art were united to others which usually attend its decline. German literature, various, rich, bold, and at length, by an inversion of the usual progress, working itself into originality, was tainted with the exaggeration natural to the imitator, and to all those who know the passions rather by study than by feeling.

Another cause concurred to widen the chasm which separated the German writers from the most polite nations of Europe. While England and France had almost relinquished those more abstruse speculations which had employed them in the age of Gassendi and Hobbes, and, with a confused mixture of contempt and despair, had tacitly abandoned questions which seemed alike inscrutable and unprofitable, a metaphysical passion arose in Germany, stronger and more extensive than had been known in Europe since the downfall of the Scholastic philosophy. A system of metaphysics appeared, which, with the ambition natural to that science, aspired to dictate principles to every part of human knowledge. It was for a long time universally adopted. Other systems, derived from it, succeeded each other with the rapidity of fashions in dress. Metaphysical publications were multiplied almost to the same degree, as political tracts in the most factious period of a popular government. The subject was soon exhausted, and the metaphysical passion seems to be nearly extinguished: for the small circle of dispute respecting first principles, must be always rapidly described; and the speculator, who thought his course infinite, finds himself almost instantaneously returned to the point from which he began. But the language of abstruse research spread over the whole German style. Allusions to the most subtile speculations were common in popular writings. Bold metaphors, derived from their peculiar philosophy, became familiar in observations on literature and manners. The style of Germany at length differed from that of France, and even of England, more as the literature of the East differs from that of the West, than as that of one European people from that of their neighbours.

Hence it partly arose, that while physical and political Germany was so familiar to foreigners, intellectual and literary Germany continued almost unknown. Thirty years ago,* there were probably in London as many Persian as German scholars. Neither Goëthe nor Schiller conquered the repugnance. Political confusions, a timid and exclusive taste, and the habitual neglect of foreign languages, excluded German litera-

* Written in 1813.—Ed.

ture from France. Temporary and permanent causes contributed to banish it, after a short period of success, from England. Dramas, more remarkable for theatrical effect, than dramatical genius, exhibited scenes and characters of a paradoxical morality (on which no writer has animadverted with more philosophical and moral eloquence than Mad. de Staël),—unsafe even in the quiet of the schools, but peculiarly dangerous in the theatre, where it comes into contact with the inflammable passions of ignorant multitudes,—and justly alarming to those who, with great reason, considered domestic virtue as one of the privileges and safeguards of the English nation. These moral paradoxes, which were chiefly found among the inferior poets of Germany, appeared at the same time with the political novelties of the French Revolution, and underwent the same fate. German literature was branded as the accomplice of freethinking philosophy and revolutionary politics. It happened rather whimsically, that we now began to throw out the same reproaches against other nations, which the French had directed against us in the beginning of the eighteenth century. We were then charged by our polite neighbours with the vulgarity and turbulence of rebellious upstarts, who held nothing sacred in religion, or stable in government; whom—

> "No king could govern, and no God could please;"*

and whose coarse and barbarous literature could excite only the ridicule of cultivated nations. The political part of these charges we applied to America, which had retained as much as she could of our government and laws; and the literary part to Germany, where literature had either been formed on our models, or moved by a kindred impulse, even where it assumed somewhat of a different form. The same persons who applauded wit, and pardoned the shocking licentiousness of English comedy, were loudest in their clamours against the immorality of the German theatre. In our zeal against a few scenes, dangerous only by over-refinement, we seemed to have forgotten the vulgar grossness which tainted the whole brilliant period from Fletcher to Congreve. Nor did we sufficiently remember, that the most daring and fantastical combinations of the German stage, did not approach to that union of taste and sense in the thought and expression, with wildness and extravagance in the invention of monstrous character and horrible incident, to be found in some of our earlier dramas, which, for their energy and beauty, the public taste has lately called from oblivion.

The more permanent causes of the slow and small progress of German literature in France and England, are philosophically developed in two beautiful chapters of the present work.† A translation from German into a language so different in its structure and origin as French, fails, as a piece of music composed for one sort of instrument when performed on another. In Germany, style, and even language, are not yet fixed. In France, rules are despotic: "the reader will not be amused at the expense of his literary conscience; there alone he is scrupulous." A German writer is above his public, and forms it: a French writer dreads a public already enlightened and severe; he constantly thinks of immediate effect; he is in society, even while he is composing; and never loses sight of the effect of his writings on those whose opinions and pleasantries he is accustomed to fear. The German writers have, in a higher degree, the first requisite for writing—the power of feeling with vivacity and force. In France, a book is read to be spoken of, and must therefore catch the spirit of society: in Germany, it is read by solitary students, who seek instruction or emotion; and, "in the silence of retirement, nothing seems more melancholy than the spirit of the world." The French require a clearness which may sometimes render their writers superficial: and the Germans, in the pursuit of originality and depth, often convey obvious thoughts in an obscure style. In the dramatic art, the most national part of literature, the French are distinguished in whatever relates to the action, the intrigue, and the interest of events: but the Germans surpass them in representing the impressions of the heart, and the secret storms of the strong passions.

This work will make known to future ages the state of Germany in the highest degree of its philosophical and poetical activity, at the moment before the pride of genius was humbled by foreign conquest, or the national mind turned from literary enthusiasm by struggles for the restoration of independence. The fleeting opportunity of observation at so extraordinary a moment, has happily been seized by one of those very few persons, who are capable at once of observing and painting manners,—of estimating and expounding philosophical systems,—of feeling the beauties of the most dissimilar forms of literature,—of tracing the peculiarities of usages, arts, and even speculations, to their common principle in national character,—and of disposing them in their natural place as features in the great portrait of a people.

The attainments of a respectable traveller of the second class, are, in the present age, not uncommon. Many persons are perfectly well qualified to convey exact information, wherever the subject can be exactly known. But the most important objects in a country can neither be numbered nor measured. The naturalist gives no picture of scenery by the most accurate catalogue of mineral and vegetable produce; and, after all that the political arithmetician can tell us of wealth and population, we continue ignorant of the spirit which actuates them, and of the character which modifies their appli-

* Absalom and Achitophel.—Ed.
† Part ii., chap. 1, 2.

cation. The genius of the philosophical and poetical traveller is of a higher order. It is founded in the power of catching, at a rapid glance, the physiognomy of man and of nature. It is, in one of its parts, an expansion of that sagacity which seizes the character of an individual, in his features, in his expression, in his gestures, in his tones,—in every outward sign of his thoughts and feelings. The application of this intuitive power to the varied mass called a "nation," is one of the most rare efforts of the human intellect. The mind and the eye must co-operate, with electrical rapidity, to recall what a nation has been, to sympathize with their present sentiments and passions, and to trace the workings of national character in amusements, in habits, in institutions and opinions. There appears to be an extemporaneous facility of theorizing, necessary to catch the first aspect of a new country,—the features of which would enter the mind in absolute confusion, if they were not immediately referred to some principle, and reduced to some system. To embody this conception, there must exist the power of painting both scenery and character,—of combining the vivacity of first impression with the accuracy of minute examination,—of placing a nation, strongly individualized by every mark of its mind and disposition, in the midst of ancient monuments, clothed in its own apparel, engaged in its ordinary occupations and pastimes amidst its native scenes, like a grand historical painting, with appropriate drapery, and with the accompaniments of architecture and landscape, which illustrate and characterize, as well as adorn.

The voice of Europe has already applauded the genius of a national painter in the author of Corinne. But it was there aided by the power of a pathetic fiction, by the variety and opposition of national character, and by the charm of a country which unites beauty to renown. In the work before us, she has thrown off the aid of fiction; she delineates a less poetical character, and a country more interesting by expectation than by recollection. But it is not the less certain that it is the most vigorous effort of her genius, and probably the most elaborate and masculine production of the faculties of woman. What other woman, indeed, (and we may add how many men,) could have preserved all the grace and brilliancy of Parisian society in analyzing its nature,—explained the most abstruse metaphysical theories of Germany precisely, yet perspicuously and agreeably,—and combined the eloquence which inspires exalted sentiments of virtue, with the enviable talent of gently indicating the defects of men or of nations, by the skilfully softened touches of a polite and merciful pleasantry?

In a short introduction, the principal nations of Europe are derived from three races, —the Sclavonic, the Latin, and the Teutonic. The imitative and feeble literature,—the recent precipitate and superficial civilization of the Sclavonic nations, sufficiently distinguish them from the two great races. The Latin nations, who inhabit the south of Europe, are the most anciently civilized: social institutions, blended with Paganism, preceded their reception of Christianity. They have less disposition than their northern neighbours to abstract reflection; they understand better the business and pleasures of the world; they inherit the sagacity of the Romans in civil affairs; and "they alone, like those ancient masters, know how to practice the art of domination." The Germanic nations, who inhabit the north of Europe and the British islands, received their civilization with Christianity: chivalry and the middle ages are the subjects of their traditions and legends; their natural genius is more Gothic than classical; they are distinguished by independence and good faith, —by seriousness both in their talents and character, rather than by address or vivacity. "The social dignity which the English owe to their political constitution, places them at the head of Teutonic nations, but does not exempt them from the character of the race." The literature of the Latin nations is copied from the ancients, and retains the original colour of their polytheism: that of the nations of Germanic origin has a chivalrous basis, and is modified by a spiritual religion. The French and Germans are at the two extremities of the chain; the French considering outward objects, and the Germans thought and feeling, as the prime movers of the moral world. "The French, the most cultivated of Latin nations, inclines to a classical poetry: the English, the most illustrious of Germanic ones, delights in a poetry more romantic and chivalrous."

The theory which we have thus abridged is most ingenious, and exhibits in the liveliest form the distinction between different systems of literature and manners. It is partly true; for the principle of race is doubtless one of the most important in the history of mankind; and the first impressions on the susceptible character of rude tribes may be traced in the qualities of their most civilized descendants. But, considered as an exclusive and universal theory, it is not secure against the attacks of sceptical ingenuity. The facts do not seem entirely to correspond with it. It was among the Latin nations of the South, that chivalry and romance first flourished. Provence was the earliest seat of romantic poetry. A chivalrous literature predominated in Italy during the most brilliant period of Italian genius. The poetry of the Spanish peninsula seems to have been more romantic and less subjected to classical bondage than that of any other part of Europe. On the contrary, chivalry, which was the refinement of the middle age, penetrated more slowly into the countries of the North. In general, the character of the literature of each European nation seems extremely to depend upon the period at which it had reached its highest point of cultivation. Spanish and Italian poetry flourished while Europe was still chivalrous. French literature attained its highest splendour after the Grecian and Roman writers had become the object of universal reverence. The Germans cultivated their poetry a hundred years later, when the study of antiquity had revived the knowledge of the Gothic sentiments and principles. Nature produced a chivalrous poetry in the sixteenth century;—learning in the eighteenth. Perhaps the history of English poetry reflects the revolution of European taste more distinctly than that of any other nation. We have successively cultivated a Gothic poetry from nature, a classical poetry from imitation, and a second Gothic from the study of our own ancient poets.

To this consideration it must be added, that Catholic and Protestant nations must differ in their poetical system. The festal shows and legendary polytheism of the Catholics had the effect of a sort of Christian Paganism. The Protestant poetry was spiritualized by the genius of their worship, and was undoubtedly exalted by the daily perusal of translations of the sublime poems of the Hebrews,—a discipline, without which it is probable that the nations of the West never could have been prepared to endure Oriental poetry. In justice, however, to the ingenious theory of Mad. de Staël, it ought to be observed, that the original character ascribed by her to the Northern nations, must have disposed them to the adoption of a Protestant faith and worship; while the Popery of the South was naturally preserved by an early disposition to a splendid ceremonial, and a various and flexible mythology.

The work is divided into four parts:—on Germany and German Manners; on Literature and the Arts; on Philosophy and Morals; on Religion and Enthusiasm.

The first is the most perfect in its kind, belongs the most entirely to the genius of the writer, and affords the best example of the talent for painting nations which we have attempted to describe. It seems also, as far as foreign critics can presume to decide, to be in the most finished style of any composition of the author, and more securely to bid defiance to that minute criticism, which, in other works, her genius rather disdained than propitiated. The Germans are a just, constant, and sincere people; with great power of imagination and reflection; without brilliancy in society, or address in affairs; slow, and easily intimidated in action; adventurous and fearless in speculation; often uniting enthusiasm for the elegant arts with little progress in the manners and refinements of life; more capable of being inflamed by opinions than by interests; obedient to authority, rather from an orderly and mechanical character than from servility; having learned to value liberty neither by the enjoyment of it, nor by severe oppression; divested by the nature of their governments, and the division of their territories, of patriotic pride; too prone in the relations of domestic life, to substitute fancy and feeling for positive duty; not unfrequently combining a natural character with artificial manners, and much real feeling with affected enthusiasm; divided by the sternness of feudal demarcation into an unlettered nobility, unpolished scholar, and a depressed commonalty; and exposing themselves to derision, when, with their grave and clumsy honesty, they attempt to copy the lively and dexterous profligacy of their Southern neighbours.

In the plentiful provinces of Southern Germany, where religion, as well as government, shackle the activity of speculation, the people have sunk into a sort of lethargic comfort and stupid enjoyment. It is a heavy and monotonous country, with no arts, except the national art of instrumental music,—no literature,—a rude utterance,—no society, or only crowded assemblies, which seemed to be brought together for ceremonial, more than for pleasure,—"an obsequious politeness towards an aristocracy without elegance." In Austria, more especially, are seen a calm and languid mediocrity in sensations and desires,—a people mechanical in their very sports, "whose existence is neither disturbed nor exalted by guilt or genius, by intolerance or enthusiasm,"—a phlegmatic administration, inflexibly adhering to its ancient course, and repelling knowledge, on which the vigour of states must now depend, —great societies of amiable and respectable persons—which suggest the reflection, that "in retirement monotony composes the soul, but in the world it wearies the mind."

In the rigorous climate and gloomy towns of Protestant Germany only, the national mind is displayed. There the whole literature and philosophy are assembled. Berlin is slowly rising to be the capital of enlightened Germany. The Duchess of Weimar, who compelled Napoleon to respect her in the intoxication of victory, has changed her little capital into a seat of knowledge and elegance, under the auspices of Goethe, Wieland, and Schiller. No European palace has assembled so refined a society since some of the small Italian courts of the sixteenth century. It is only by the Protestant provinces of the North that Germany is known as a lettered and philosophical country.

Moralists and philosophers have often remarked, that licentious gallantry is fatal to love, and destructive of the importance of women. "I will venture to assert," says Mad. de Staël, "against the received opinion, that France was perhaps, of all the countries of the world, that in which women had the least happiness in love. It was called the 'paradise' of women, because they enjoyed the greatest liberty; but that liberty arose from the negligent profligacy of the other sex." The observations* which follow this remarkable testimony are so beautiful and

* Part i. chap. 4.

forcible, that they ought to be engraven on the mind of every woman disposed to murmur at those restraints which maintain the dignity of womanhood.

Some enthusiasm, says Mad. de Staël, or, in other words, some high passion, capable of actuating multitudes, has been felt by every people, at those epochs of their national existence, which are distinguished by great acts. Four periods are very remarkable in the progress of the European world: the heroic ages which founded civilization; republican patriotism, which was the glory of antiquity; chivalry, the martial religion of Europe; and the love of liberty, of which the history began about the period of the Reformation. The chivalrous impression is worn out in Germany; and, in future, says this generous and enlightened writer, "nothing great will be accomplished in that country, but by the liberal impulse which has in Europe succeeded to chivalry."

The society and manners of Germany are continually illustrated by comparison or contrast with those of France. Some passages and chapters on this subject, together with the author's brilliant preface to the thoughts of the Prince de Ligne, may be considered as the first contributions towards a theory of the talent—if we must not say of the art—of conversation, which affords so considerable a part of the most liberal enjoyments of refined life. Those, indeed, who affect a Spartan or monastic severity in their estimate of the society of capitals, may almost condemn a talent, which in their opinion only adorns vice. But that must have a moral tendency which raises society from slander or intoxication, to any contest and rivalship of mental power. Wit and grace are perhaps the only means which could allure the thoughtless into the neighbourhood of reflection, and inspire them with some admiration for superiority of mind. Society is the only school in which the indolence of the great will submit to learn. Refined conversation is at least sprinkled with literature, and directed, more often than the talk of the vulgar, to objects of general interest. That talent cannot really be frivolous which affords the channel through which some knowledge, or even some respect for knowledge, may be insinuated into minds incapable of labour, and whose tastes so materially influence the community. Satirical pictures of the vices of a great society create a vulgar prejudice against their most blameless and virtuous pleasures. But, whatever may be the vice of London or Paris, it is lessened, not increased, by the cultivation of every liberal talent which innocently fills their time, and tends, in some measure, to raise them above malice and sensuality. And there is a considerable illusion in the provincial estimate of the immoralities of the capital. These immoralities are public, from the rank of the parties; and they are rendered more conspicuous by the celebrity, or perhaps by the talents, of some of them. Men of letters, and women of wit, describe their own sufferings with eloquence,—the faults of others, and sometimes their own, with energy: their descriptions interest every reader, and are circulated throughout Europe. But it does not follow that the miseries or the faults are greater or more frequent than those of obscure and vulgar persons, whose sufferings and vices are known to nobody, and would be uninteresting if they were known.

The second, and most generally amusing, as well as the largest part of this work, is an animated sketch of the literary history of Germany, with criticisms on the most celebrated German poets and poems, interspersed with reflections equally original and beautiful, tending to cultivate a comprehensive taste in the fine arts, and to ingraft the love of virtue on the sense of beauty. Of the poems criticised, some are well known to most of our readers. The earlier pieces of Schiller are generally read in translations of various merit, though, except the Robbers, they are not by the present taste of Germany placed in the first class of his works. The versions of Leonora, of Oberon, of Wallenstein, of Nathan, and of Iphigenia in Tauris, are among those which do the most honour to English literature. Göetz of Berlichingen has been vigorously rendered by a writer, whose chivalrous genius, exerted upon somewhat similar scenes of British history, has since rendered him the most popular poet of his age.

An epic poem, or a poetical romance, has lately been discovered in Germany, entitled 'Niebelungen,' on the Destruction of the Burgundians by Attila; and it is believed, that at least some parts of it were composed not long after the event, though the whole did not assume its present shape till the completion of the vernacular languages about the beginning of the thirteenth century. Luther's version of the Scriptures was an epoch in German literature. One of the innumerable blessings of the Reformation was to make reading popular by such translations, and to accustom the people to weekly attempts at some sort of argument or declamation in their native tongue. The vigorous mind of the great Reformer gave to his translation an energy and conciseness, which made it a model in style, as well as an authority in language. Hagedorn, Weiss, and Gellert, copied the French without vivacity; and Bodmer imitated the English without genius.

At length Klopstock, an imitator of Milton, formed a German poetry, and Wieland improved the language and versification; though this last accomplished writer has somewhat suffered in his reputation, by the recent zeal of the Germans against the imitation of any foreign, but especially of the French school. "The genius of Klopstock was inflamed by the perusal of Milton and Young." This combination of names is astonishing to an English ear. It creates a presumption against the poetical sensibility of Klopstock, to find that he combined two poets, placed at an immeasurable distance from each other; and whose whole superficial resemblance arises from some part of Milton's subject, and from the doctrines of their theology, rather than the spirit of their religion. Through all the works of Young, written with such a variety of temper and manner, there predominates one talent,—inexhaustible wit, with little soundness of reason or depth of sensibility. His melancholy is artificial; and his combinations are as grotesque and fantastic in his Night Thoughts as in his Satires. How exactly does a poet characterise his own talent, who opens a series of poetical meditations on death and immortality, by a satirical epigram against the selfishness of the world? Wit and ingenuity are the only talents which Milton disdained. He is simple in his conceptions, even when his diction is overloaded with gorgeous learning. He is never gloomy but when he is grand. He is the painter of love, as well as of terror. He did not aim at mirth; but he is cheerful whenever he descends from higher feelings: and nothing tends more to inspire a calm and constant delight, than the contemplation of that ideal purity and grandeur which he, above all poets, had the faculty of bestowing on every form of moral nature. Klopstock's ode on the rivalship of the muse of Germany with the muse of Albion, is elegantly translated by Mad. de Staël; and we applaud her taste for preferring prose to verse in French translations of German poems.

After having spoken of Winkelmann and Lessing, the most perspicuous, concise, and lively of German prose-writers, she proceeds to Schiller and Goëthe, the greatest of German poets. Schiller presents only the genius of a great poet, and the character of a virtuous man. The original, singular, and rather admirable than amiable mind of Goëthe,—his dictatorial power over national literature,—his inequality, caprice, originality, and fire in conversation,—his union of a youthful imagination with exhausted sensibility, and the impartiality of a stern sagacity, neither influenced by opinions nor predilections, are painted with extraordinary skill.

Among the tragedies of Schiller which have appeared since we have ceased to translate German dramas, the most celebrated are, Mary Stuart, Joan of Arc, and William Tell. Such subjects as Mary Stuart generally excite an expectation which cannot be gratified. We agree with Madame de Staël in admiring many scenes of Schiller's Mary, and especially her noble farewell to Leicester. But the tragedy would probably displease English readers, to say nothing of spectators. Our political disputes have given a more inflexible reality to the events of Elizabeth's reign, than history would otherwise have bestowed on facts equally modern. Neither of our parties could endure a Mary who confesses the murder of her husband, or an Elizabeth who instigates the assassination of her prisoner. In William Tell, Schiller has avoided the commonplaces of a republican conspiracy, and faithfully represented the indignation of an oppressed Helvetian Highlander.

Egmont is considered by Mad. de Staël as the finest of Goëthe's tragedies, written, like Werther, in the enthusiasm of his youth. It is rather singular that poets have availed themselves so little of the chivalrous character, the illustrious love, and the awful malady of Tasso. The Torquato Tasso of Goëthe is the only attempt to convert this subject to the purposes of the drama. Two men of genius, of very modern times, have suffered in a somewhat similar manner: but the habits of Rousseau's life were vulgar, and the sufferings of Cowper are both recent and sacred. The scenes translated from Faust well represent the terrible energy of that most odious of the works of genius, in which the whole power of imagination is employed to dispel the charms which poetry bestows on human life,—where the punishment of vice proceeds from cruelty without justice, and "where the remorse seems as infernal as the guilt."

Since the death of Schiller, and the desertion of the drama by Goëthe, several tragic writers have appeared, the most celebrated of whom are Werner, the author of Luther and of Attila, Gerstenberg, Klinger, Tieck, Collin, and Oëhlenschläger, a Dane, who has introduced into his poetry the terrible mythology of Scandinavia.

The result of the chapter on Comedy seems to be, that the comic genius has not yet arisen in Germany. German novels have been more translated into English than other works of literature; and a novel by Tieck, entitled 'Sternbald,' seems to deserve translation. Jean Paul Richter, a popular novelist, but too national to bear translation, said, "that the French had the empire of the land, the English that of the sea, and the Germans that of the air."

Though Schiller wrote the History of the Belgic Revolt, and of the Thirty Years' War, with eloquence and the spirit of liberty, the only classical writer in this department is J. de Müller, the historian of Switzerland. Though born in a speculative age, he has chosen the picturesque and dramatic manner of ancient historians; and his minute erudition in the annals of the Middle Ages supplies his imagination with the particulars which characterise persons and actions. He abuses his extent of knowledge and power of detail; he sometimes affects the sententiousness of Tacitus; and his pursuit of antique phraseology occasionally degenerates into affectation. But his diction is in general grave and severe; and in his posthumous Abridgment of Universal History, he has shown great talents for that difficult sort of composition,—the power of comprehensive outline, of compression without obscurity, of painting characters by few and grand strokes, and of disposing events so skilfully, that their causes and effects are seen without being pointed out. Like Sallust, another affecter of archaism, and declaimer against his age, his private and political life is said to have been repugnant to his historical morality. "The reader of Müller is desirous of believing that of all the virtues which he strongly felt in the composition of his works, there were at least some which he permanently possessed."

The estimate of literary Germany would not be complete, without the observation that it possesses a greater number of laborious scholars, and of useful books, than any other country. The possession of other languages may open more literary enjoyment: the German is assuredly the key to most knowledge. The works of Fulleborn, Buhle, Tiedemann, and Tennemann, are the first attempts to form a philosophical history of philosophy, of which the learned compiler Brucker had no more conception than a monkish annalist of rivalling Hume. The philosophy of literary history is one of the most recently opened fields of speculation. A few beautiful fragments of it are among the happiest parts of Hume's Essays. The great work of Madame de Staël On Literature, was the first attempt on a bold and extensive scale. In the neighbourhood of her late residence,* and perhaps not uninfluenced by her spirit, two writers of great merit, though of dissimilar character, have very recently treated various parts of this wide subject; M. de Sismondi, in his History of the Literature of the South, and M. de Barante, in his Picture of French Literature during the Eighteenth Century. Sismondi, guided by Bouterweck and Schlegel, hazards larger views, indulges his talent for speculation, and seems with difficulty to suppress that bolder spirit, and those more liberal principles, which breathe in his History of the Italian Republics. Barante, more thoroughly imbued with the elegancies and the prejudices of his national literature, feels more delicately the peculiarities of great writers, and traces with a more refined sagacity the immediate effects of their writings. But his work, under a very ingenious disguise of literary criticism, is an attack on the opinions of the eighteenth century; and it will assuredly never be honoured by the displeasure either of Napoleon, or of any of his successors in absolute power.

One of our authoress' chapters is chiefly employed on the works and system of William and Frederic Schlegel;—of whom William is celebrated for his Lectures on Dramatic Poetry, for his admirable translation of Shakespeare, and for versions, said to be of equal excellence, of the Spanish dramatic poets; and Frederic, besides his other merits, has the very singular distinction of having acquired the Sanscrit language, and studied the Indian learning and science in Europe, chiefly by the aid of a British Orientalist, long detained as a prisoner at Paris. The general tendency of the literary system of these critics, is towards the manners, poetry, and religion of the Middle Ages. They have reached the extreme point towards which the general sentiment of Europe has been impelled by the calamities of a philosophical revolution, and the various fortunes of a twenty years' universal war. They are peculiarly adverse to French literature, which, since the age of Louis XIV., has, in their opinion, weakened the primitive principles common to all Christendom, as well as divested the poetry of each people of its originality and character. Their system is exaggerated and exclusive: in pursuit of national originality, they lose sight of the primary and universal beauties of art. The imitation of our own antiquities may be as artificial as the copy of a foreign literature. Nothing is less natural than a modern antique. In a comprehensive system of literature, there is sufficient place for the irregular works of sublime genius, and for the faultless models of classical taste. From age to age, the multitude fluctuates between various and sometimes opposite fashions of literary activity. These are not all of equal value; but the philosophical critic discovers and admires the common principles of beauty, from which they all derive their power over human nature.

The Third Part of this work is the most singular. An account of metaphysical systems by a woman, is a novelty in the history of the human mind; and whatever may be thought of its success in some of its parts, it must be regarded on the whole as the boldest effort of the female intellect. It must, however, not be forgotten, that it is a contribution rather to the history of human nature, than to that of speculation; and that it considers the source, spirit, and moral influence of metaphysical opinions, more than their truth or falsehood. "Metaphysics are at least the gymnastics of the understanding." The common-place clamour of mediocrity will naturally be excited by the sex, and even by the genius of the author. Every example of vivacity and grace, every exertion of fancy, every display of eloquence, every effusion of sensibility, will be cited as a presumption against the depth of her researches, and the accuracy of her statements. On such principles, the evidence against her would doubtless be conclusive. But dulness is not accuracy; nor are ingenious and elegant writers therefore superficial: and those who are best acquainted with the philosophical revolutions of Germany, will be most astonished at the general correctness of this short, clear, and agreeable exposition.

The character of Lord Bacon is a just and noble tribute to his genius. Several eminent writers of the Continent have, however, lately fallen into the mistake of ascribing to him a system of opinions respecting the origin and first principles of human knowledge. What distinguishes him among great philosophers is, that he taught no peculiar opinions, but wholly devoted himself to the improvement of the method of philosophising. He belongs neither to the English nor any

* Coppet, near Geneva.

other school of metaphysics; for he was not a metaphysician. Mr. Locke was not a moralist; and his collateral discussions of ethical subjects are not among the valuable parts of his great work. "The works of Dugald Stewart contain so perfect a theory of the intellectual faculties, that it may be considered as the natural history of a moral being." The French metaphysicians of the eighteenth century, since Condillac, deserve the contempt expressed for them, by their shallow, precipitate, and degrading misapplications of the Lockian philosophy. It is impossible to abridge the abridgment here given of the Kantian philosophy, or of those systems which have arisen from it, and which continue to dispute the supremacy of the speculative world. The opinions of Kant are more fully stated, because he has changed the general manner of thinking, and has given a new direction to the national mind. Those of Fichte, Schelling, and his other successors, it is of less importance to the proper purpose of this work to detail; because, though their doctrines be new, they continue and produce the same effect on national character, and the same influence on sciences and arts. The manner of philosophising remains the same in the Idealism of Fichte, and in the Pantheism of Schelling. Under various names and forms, it is the general tendency of the German philosophy to consider thought not as the produce of objects, or as one of the classes of phenomena, but as the agent which exhibits the appearance of the outward world, and which regulates those operations which it seems only to represent. The philosophy of the human understanding is, in all countries, acknowledged to contain the principles of all sciences; but in Germany, metaphysical speculation pervades their application to particulars.

The subject of the Fourth Part is the state of religion, and the nature of all those disinterested and exalted sentiments which are here comprehended under the name of 'enthusiasm.' A contemplative people like the Germans have in their character the principle which disposes men to religion. The Reformation, which was their Revolution, arose from ideas. "Of all the great men whom Germany has produced, Luther has the most German character. His firmness had something rude; his conviction made him opinionated; intellectual boldness was the source of his courage; in action, the ardour of his passions did not divert him from abstract studies; and though he attacked certain dogmas and practices, he was not urged to the attack by incredulity, but by enthusiasm."

"The right of examining what we ought to believe, is the foundation of Protestanism." Though each of the first Reformers established a practical Popery in his own church, opinions were gradually liberalised, and the temper of sects was softened. Little open incredulity had appeared in Germany; and even Lessing speculated with far more circumspection than had been observed by a series of English writers from Hobbes to Bolingbroke. Secret unbelievers were friendly to Christianity and Protestantism, as institutions beneficial to mankind, and far removed from that anti-religious fanaticism which was more naturally provoked in France by the intolerant spirit and invidious splendour of a Catholic hierarchy.

The reaction of the French Revolution has been felt throughout Europe, in religion as well as in politics. Many of the higher classes adopted some portion of those religious sentiments of which they at first assumed the exterior, as a badge of their hostility to the fashions of France. The sensibility of the multitude, impatient of cold dogmatism and morality, eagerly sought to be once more roused by a religion which employed popular eloquence, and spoke to imagination and emotion. The gloom of general convulsions and calamities created a disposition to seriousness, and to the consolations of piety; and the disasters of a revolution allied to incredulity, threw a more than usual discredit and odium on irreligious opinions. In Great Britain, these causes have acted most conspicuously on the inferior classes; though they have also powerfully affected many enlightened and accomplished individuals of a higher condition. In France, they have produced in some men of letters the play of a sort of poetical religion round the fancy: but the general effect seems to have been a disposition to establish a double doctrine,—a system of infidelity for the initiated, with a contemptuous indulgence and even active encouragement of superstition among the vulgar, like that which prevailed among the ancients before the rise of Christianity. This sentiment (from the revival of which the Lutheran Reformation seems to have preserved Europe), though not so furious and frantic as the atheistical fanaticism of the Reign of Terror, is, beyond any permanent condition of human society, destructive of ingenuousness, good faith, and probity,—of intellectual courage, and manly character,—and of that respect for all human beings, without which there can be no justice or humanity from the powerful towards the humble.

In Germany the effects have been also very remarkable. Some men of eminence in literature have become Catholics. In general, their tendency is towards a pious mysticism, which almost equally loves every sect where a devotional spirit prevails. They have returned rather to sentiment than to dogma,—more to religion than to theology. Their disposition to religious feeling, which they call 'religiosity,' is, to use the words of a strictly orthodox English theologian, "a love of divine things for the beauty of their moral qualities." It is the love of the good and fair, wherever it exists, but chiefly when absolute and boundless excellence is contemplated in "the first good, first perfect, first fair." This moral enthusiasm easily adapts itself to the various ceremonies of worship, and even systems of opinion prevalent among mankind. The devotional spirit, contemplating different parts of the order of nature, or influenced by a different temper of mind, may give rise to very different and apparently repugnant theological doctrines. These doctrines are considered as modifications of human nature, under the influence of the religious principle,—not as propositions which argument can either establish or confute, or reconcile with each other. The Ideal philosophy favours this singular manner of considering the subject. As it leaves no reality but in the mind, it lessens the distance between belief and imagination; and disposes its adherents to regard opinions as the mere play of the understanding,—incapable of being measured by any outward standard, and important chiefly from reference to the sentiment, from which they spring, and on which they powerfully react. The union of a mystical piety, with a philosophy verging towards idealism, has accordingly been observed in periods of the history of the human understanding, very distant from each other, and, in most of their other circumstances, extremely dissimilar. The same language, respecting the annihilation of self, and of the world, may be used by the sceptic and by the enthusiast. Among the Hindu philosophers in the most ancient times,—among the Sufis in modern Persia,—during the ferment of Eastern and Western opinions, which produced the latter Platonism,—in Malebranche and his English disciple Norris,—and in Berkeley himself, though in a tempered and mitigated state,—the tendency to this union may be distinctly traced. It seems, however, to be fitted only for few men; and for them not long. Sentiments so sublime, and so distant from the vulgar affairs and boisterous passions of men, may be preserved for a time, in the calm solitude of a contemplative visionary; but in the bustle of the world they are likely soon to evaporate, when they are neither embodied in opinions, nor adorned by ceremonies, nor animated by the attack and defence of controversy. When the ardour of a short-lived enthusiasm has subsided, the poetical philosophy which exalted fancy to the level of belief, may probably leave the same ultimate result with the argumentative scepticism which lowered belief to the level of fancy.

An ardent susceptibility of every disinterested sentiment,—more especially of every social affection,—blended by the power of imagination with a passionate love of the beautiful, the grand, and the good, is, under the name of 'enthusiasm,' the subject of the conclusion,—the most eloquent part (if we perhaps except the incomparable chapter on 'Conjugal Love,) of a work which, for variety of knowledge, flexibility of power, elevation of view, and comprehension of mind, is unequal among the works of women; and which, in the union of the graces of society and literature with the genius of philosophy, is not surpassed by many among those of men. To affect any tenderness in pointing out its defects or faults, would be an absurd assumption of superiority: it has no need of mercy. The most obvious and general objection will be, that the Germans are too much praised. But every writer must be allowed to value his subject somewhat higher than the spectator: unless the German feelings had been adopted, they could not have been forcibly represented. It will also be found, that the objection is more apparent than real. Mad. de Staël is indeed the most generous of critics; but she almost always speaks the whole truth to intelligent ears; though she often hints the unfavourable parts of it so gently and politely, that they may escape the notice of a hasty reader, and be scarcely perceived by a gross understanding. A careful reader, who brings together all the observations intentionally scattered over various parts of the book, will find sufficient justice (though administered in mercy) in whatever respects manners or literature. It is on subjects of philosophy that the admiration will perhaps justly be considered as more undistinguishing. Something of the wonder excited by novelty in language and opinion still influences her mind. Many writers have acquired philosophical celebrity in Germany, who, if they had written with equal power, would have been unnoticed or soon forgotten in England. Our theosophists, the Hutchinsonians, had as many men of talent among them, as those whom M. de Staël has honoured by her mention among the Germans: but they have long since irrecoverably sunk into oblivion. There is a writer now alive in England,* who has published doctrines not dissimilar to those which Mad. de Staël ascribes to Schelling. Notwithstanding the allurements of a singular character, and an unintelligible style, his paradoxes are probably not known to a dozen persons in this busy country of industry and ambition. In a bigoted age, he might have suffered the martyrdom of Vanini or Bruno: in a metaphysical country, where a new publication was the most interesting event, and where twenty universities, unfettered by Church or State, were hotbeds of speculation, he might have acquired celebrity as the founder of a sect.

In this as in the other writings of Mad. de Staël, the reader (or at least the lazy English reader) is apt to be wearied by too constant a demand upon his admiration. It seems to be part of her literary system, that the pauses of eloquence must be filled up by ingenuity. Nothing plain and unornamented is left in composition. But we desire a plain groundwork, from which wit or eloquence is to arise, when the occasion calls them forth. The effect would be often greater if the talent were less. The natural power of interesting scenes or events over the heart, is somewhat disturbed by too uniform a colour

* Probably Mr. William Taylor, of Norwich. —Ed

of sentiment, and by the constant pursuit of uncommon reflections or ingenious turns. The eye is dazzled by unvaried brilliancy. We long for the grateful vicissitude of repose.

In the statement of facts and reasonings, no style is more clear than that of Mad. de Staël;—what is so lively must indeed be clear: but in the expression of sentiment she has been often thought to use vague language. In expressing either intense degrees, or delicate shades, or intricate combinations of feeling, the common reader will seldom understand that of which he has never been conscious; and the writer placed on the extreme frontiers of human nature, is in danger of mistaking chimeras for realities, or of failing in a struggle to express what language does not afford the means of describing. There is also a vagueness incident to the language of feeling, which is not so properly a defect, as a quality which distinguishes it from the language of thought. Very often in poetry, and sometimes in eloquence, it is the office of words, not so much to denote a succession of separate ideas, as, like musical sounds, to inspire a series of emotions, or to produce a durable tone of sentiment. The terms 'perspicuity' and 'precision,' which denote the relations of language to intellectual discernment, are inapplicable to it when employed as the mere vehicle of a succession of feelings. A series of words may, in this manner, be very expressive, where few of them singly convey a precise meaning: and men of greater intellect than susceptibility, in such passages as those of Mad. de Staël,—where eloquence is employed chiefly to inspire feeling,—unjustly charge their own defects to that deep, moral, and poetical sensibility with which they are unable to sympathise.

The few persons in Great Britain who continue to take an interest in speculative philosophy, will certainly complain of some injustice in her estimate of German metaphysical systems. The moral painter of nations is indeed more authorised than the speculative philosopher to try these opinions by their tendencies and results. When the logical consequences of an opinion are false, the opinion itself must also be false: but whether the supposed pernicious influence of the adoption, or habitual contemplation of an opinion, be a legitimate objection to the opinion itself, is a question which has not yet been decided to the general satisfaction, nor perhaps even stated with sufficient precision.

There are certain facts in human nature, derived either from immediate consciousness or unvarying observation, which are more certain than the conclusions of any abstract reasoning, and which metaphysical theories are destined only to explain. That a theory is at variance with such facts, and logically leads to the denial of their existence, is a strictly philosophical objection to the theory: —that there is a real distinction between right and wrong, in some measure apprehended and felt by all men,—that moral sentiments and disinterested affections, however originating, are actually a part of our nature,—that praise and blame, reward and punishment, may be properly bestowed on actions according to their moral character,—are principles as much more indubitable as they are more important than any theoretical conclusions. Whether they be demonstrated by reason, or perceived by intuition, or revealed by a primitive sentiment, they are equally indispensable parts of every sound mind. But the mere inconvenience or danger of an opinion can never be allowed as an argument against its truth. It is indeed the duty of every good man to present to the public what he believes to be truth, in such a manner as may least wound the feelings, or disturb the principles of the simple and the ignorant: and that duty is not always easily reconcilable with the duties of sincerity and free inquiry. The collision of such conflicting duties is the painful and inevitable consequence of the ignorance of the multitude, and of the immature state, even in the highest minds, of the great talent for presenting truth under all its aspects, and adapting it to all the degrees of capacity or varieties of prejudice which distinguish men. That talent must one day be formed; and we may be perfectly assured that the whole of truth can never be injurious to the whole of virtue. In the mean time philosophers would act more magnanimously, and therefore, perhaps, more wisely, if they were to suspend, during discussion,* their moral anger against doctrines which they deem pernicious; and, while they estimate actions, habits, and institutions, by their tendency, to weigh opinions in the mere balance of reason. Virtue in action may require the impulse of sentiment, and even of enthusiasm: but in theoretical researches, her champions must not appear to decline the combat on any ground chosen by their adversaries, and least of all on that of intellect. To call in the aid of popular feelings in philosophical contests, is some avowal of weakness. It seems a more magnanimous wisdom to defy attack from every quarter, and by every weapon; and to use no topics which can be thought to imply an unworthy doubt whether the principles of virtue be impregnable by argument, or to betray an irreverent distrust of the final and perfect harmony between morality and truth.

* The observation may be applied to Cicero and Stewart, as well as to Mad. de. Staël.

REVIEW OF THE CAUSES

OF

THE REVOLUTION OF 1688.

CHAPTER I.

General state of affairs at home—Abroad.—Characters of the Ministry.—Sunderland.—Rochester.—Halifax.—Godolphin.—Jeffreys.—Feversham.—His conduct after the victory of Sedgemoor.—Kirke.—Judicial proceedings in the West.—Trials of Mrs. Lisle.—Behaviour of the King.—Trial of Mrs. Gaunt and others.—Case of Hampden.—Prideaux.—Lord Brandon.—Delamere.

Though a struggle with calamity strengthens and elevates the mind, the necessity of passive submission to long adversity is rather likely to weaken and subdue it: great misfortunes disturb the understanding perhaps as much as great success; and extraordinary vicissitudes often produce the opposite vices of rashness and fearfulness by inspiring a disposition to trust too much to fortune, and to yield to it too soon. Few men experienced more sudden changes of fortune than James II.; but it was unfortunate for his character that he never owed his prosperity, and not always his adversity, to himself. The affairs of his family seemed to be at the lowest ebb a few months before their triumphant restoration. Four years before the death of his brother, it appeared probable that he would be excluded from the succession to the crown; and his friends seemed to have no other means of averting that doom, than by proposing such limitations of the royal prerogative as would have reduced the government to a merely nominal monarchy. But the dissolution by which Charles had safely and successfully punished the independence of his last Parliament, the destruction of some of his most formidable opponents, and the general discouragement of their adherents, paved the way for his peaceable, and even popular succession; the defeat of the revolts of Monmouth and Argyle appeared to have fixed his throne on immovable foundations; and he was then placed in circumstances more favourable than those of any of his predecessors to the extension of his power, or, if such had been his purpose, to the undisturbed exercise of his constitutional authority. The friends of liberty, dispirited by events which all, in a greater or less degree, brought discredit upon their cause, were confounded with unsuccessful conspirators and defeated rebels: they seemed to be at the mercy of a prince, who, with reason, considered them as the irreconcilable enemies of his designs. The zealous partisans of monarchy believed themselves on the eve of reaping the fruits of a contest of fifty years' duration, under a monarch of mature experience, of tried personal courage, who possessed a knowledge of men, and a capacity as well as an inclination for business; whose constancy, intrepidity, and sternness were likely to establish their political principles; and from whose prudence, as well as gratitude and good faith, they were willing to hope that he would not disturb the security of their religion. The turbulence of the preceding times had more than usually disposed men of pacific temper to support an established government. The multitude, pleased with a new reign, generally disposed to admire vigour and to look with complacency on success, showed many symptoms of that propensity which is natural to them, or rather to mankind, — to carry their applauses to the side of fortune, and to imbibe the warmest passions of a victorious party. The strength of the Tories in a Parliament assembled in such a temper of the nation, was aided by a numerous reinforcement of members of low condition and subservient character, whom the forfeiture of the charters of towns enabled the Court to pour into the House of Commons.* In Scotland the prevalent party had ruled with such barbarity that the absolute power of the King seemed to be their only shield against the resentment of their countrymen. The Irish nation, devotedly attached to a sovereign of their own oppressed religion, offered inexhaustible means of forming a brave and enthusiastic army, ready to quell revolts in every part of his dominions. His revenue was ampler than that of any former King of England: a disciplined army of about twenty thousand men was, for the first time, esta-

---

* "Clerks and gentlemen's servants." Evelyn, Memoirs, vol. i. p. 558. The Earl of Bath carried fifteen of the new charters with him into Cornwall, from which he was called the "Prince Elector." "There are not 135 in this House who sat in the last," p. 562. By the lists in the Parliamentary History they appear to be only 128.

blished during peace in this island; and a formidable fleet was a more than ordinarily powerful weapon in the hands of a prince whose skill and valour in maritime war had endeared him to the seamen, and recommended him to the people.

The condition of foreign affairs was equally favourable to the King. Louis XIV. had, at that moment, reached the zenith of his greatness; his army was larger and better than any which had been known in Europe since the vigorous age of the Roman empire; his marine enabled him soon after to cope with the combined forces of the only two maritime powers; he had enlarged his dominions, strengthened his frontiers, and daily meditated new conquests: men of genius applauded his munificence, and even some men of virtue contributed to the glory of his reign. This potent monarch was bound to James by closer ties than those of treaty,—by kindred, by religion, by similar principles of government, by the importance of each to the success of the designs of the other; and he was ready to supply the pecuniary aid required by the English monarch, on condition that James should not subject himself to the control of his Parliament, but should acquiesce in the schemes of France against her neighbours. On the other hand, the feeble Government of Spain was no longer able to defend her unwieldy empire; while the German branch of the Austrian family had, by their intolerance, driven Hungary into revolt, and thus opened the way for the Ottoman armies twice to besiege Vienna. Venice, the last of the Italian states which retained a national character, took no longer any part in the contests of Europe, content with the feeble lustre which conquests from Turkey shed over the evening of her greatness. The kingdoms of the North were confined within their own subordinate system: Russia was not numbered among civilized nations: and the Germanic states were still divided between their fears from the ambition of France, and their attachment to her for having preserved them from the yoke of Austria. Though a powerful party in Holland was still attached to France, there remained, on the Continent, no security against the ambition of Louis,—no hope for the liberties of mankind but the power of that great republic, animated by the unconquerable soul of the Prince of Orange. All those nations, of both religions, who trembled at the progress of France, turned their eyes towards James, and courted his alliance, in hopes that he might still be detached from his connection with Louis, and that England might resume her ancient and noble station, as the guardian of the independence of nations. Could he have varied his policy, that bright career was still open to him: he, or rather a man of genius and magnanimity in his situation, might have rivalled the renown of Elizabeth, and anticipated the glories of Marlborough. He was courted or dreaded by all Europe. Who could, then, have presumed to foretell that this great monarch, in the short space of four years, would be compelled to relinquish his throne, and to fly from his country, without struggle and almost without disturbance, by the mere result of his own system of measures, which, unwise and unrighteous as it was, seemed in every instance to be crowned with success till the very moment of its overthrow.

The ability of his ministers might have been considered as among the happy parts of his fortune. It was a little before this time that the meetings of such ministers began to be generally known by the modern name of the "Cabinet Council."* The Privy Council had been originally a selection of a similar nature; but when seats in that body began to be given or left to those who did not enjoy the King's confidence, and it became too numerous for secrecy or despatch, a committee of its number, which is now called the "Cabinet Council," was intrusted with the direction of confidential affairs; leaving to the body at large business of a judicial or formal nature,—to the greater part of its members an honourable distinction instead of an office of trust. The members of the Cabinet Council were then, as they still are, chosen from the Privy Council by the King, without any legal nomination, and generally consisted of the ministers at the head of the principal departments of public affairs. A short account of the character of the members of the Cabinet will illustrate the events of the reign of James II.

Robert Spencer, Earl of Sunderland, who soon acquired the chief ascendancy in this administration, entered on public life with all the external advantages of birth and fortune. His father had fallen in the royal army at the battle of Newbury, with those melancholy forebodings of danger from the victory of his own party which filled the breasts of the more generous royalists, and which, on the same occasion, saddened the dying moments of Lord Falkland. His mother was Lady Dorothy Sidney, celebrated by Waller under the name of Sacharissa. He was early employed in diplomatic missions, where he acquired the political knowledge, insinuating address, and polished manners, which are learnt in that school, together with the subtilty, dissimulation, flexibility of principle, indifference on questions of constitutional policy, and impatience of the restraints of popular government, which have been sometimes contracted by English ambassadors in the course of a long intercourse with the ministers of absolute princes. A faint and superficial preference of the general principles of civil liberty was blended in a manner not altogether unusual with his diplomatic vices. He seems to have secured the support of the Duchess of Portsmouth to the administration formed by the advice of Sir William Temple, and to have then also

* North, Life of Lord Keeper Guildford, p. 218.

gained for himself the confidence of that incomparable person, who possessed all the honest arts of a negotiator.* He gave an early earnest of the inconstancy of an over-refined character by fluctuating between the exclusion of the Duke of York and the limitations of the royal prerogative. He was removed from his administration for his vote on the Exclusion Bill; but the love of office soon prevailed over his feeble spirit of independence, and he made his peace with the Court through the Duke of York, who had long been well disposed to him,† and of the Duchess of Portsmouth, who found no difficulty in reconciling to a polished as well as pliant courtier, an accomplished negotiator, and a minister more versed in foreign affairs than any of his colleagues.‡ Negligence and profusion bound him to office by stronger though coarser ties than those of ambition: he lived in an age when a delicate purity in pecuniary matters had not begun to have a general influence on statesmen, and when a sense of personal honour, growing out of long habits of co-operation and friendship, had not yet contributed to secure them against political inconstancy. He was one of the most distinguished of a species of men who perform a part more important than noble in great events; who, by powerful talents, captivating manners, and accommodating opinions, —by a quick discernment of critical moments in the rise and fall of parties,—by not deserting a cause till the instant before it is universally discovered to be desperate, and by a command of expedients and connections which render them valuable to every new possessor of power, find means to cling to office or to recover it, and who, though they are the natural offspring of quiet and refinement, often creep through stormy revolutions without being crushed. Like the best and most prudent of his class, he appears not to have betrayed the secrets of the friends whom he abandoned, and never to have complied with more evil than was necessary to keep his power. His temper was without rancour; and he must be acquitted of prompting, or even preferring the cruel acts which were perpetrated under his administration. Deep designs and premeditated treachery were irreconcilable both with his indolence and his impetuosity; and there is some reason to believe, that in the midst of total indifference about religious opinions, he retained to the end some degree of that preference for civil liberty which he might have derived from the example of his ancestors, and the sentiments of some of his early connections.

* Temple, Memoirs, &c. part iii.

† "Lord Sunderland knows I have always been very kind to him."—Duke of York to Mr. Legge, 23d July, 1679. Legge MSS.

‡ Some of Lord Sunderland's competitors in this province were not formidable. His successor, Lord Conway, when a foreign minister spoke to him of the Circles of the Empire, said, "he wondered what circles should have to do with politics."

Lawrence Hyde, Earl of Rochester, the younger son of the Earl of Clarendon, was Lord Sunderland's most formidable competitor for the chief direction of public affairs. He owed this importance rather to his position and connections than to his abilities, which, however, were by no means contemptible. He was the undisputed leader of the Tory party, to whose highest principles in Church and State he showed a constant, and probably a conscientious attachment. He had adhered to James in every variety of fortune, and was the uncle of the Princesses Mary and Anne, who seemed likely in succession to inherit the crown. He was a fluent speaker, and appears to have possessed some part of his father's talents as a writer. He was deemed sincere and upright; and his private life was not stained by any vice, except violent paroxysms of anger, and an excessive indulgence in wine, then scarcely deemed a fault. "His infirmities," says one of the most zealous adherents of his party, "were passion, in which he would swear like a cutter, and the indulging himself in wine. But his party was that of the Church of England, of whom he had the honour, for many years, to be accounted the head."* The impetuosity of his temper concurred with his opinions on government in prompting him to rigorous measures. He disdained the forms and details of business; and it was his maxim to prefer only Tories, without regard to their qualifications for office. "Do you not think," said he to Lord Keeper Guildford, "that I could understand any business in England in a month?" "Yes, my lord," answered the Lord Keeper, "but I believe you would understand it better in two months." Even his personal defects and unreasonable maxims were calculated to attach adherents to him as a chief; and he was well qualified to be the leader of a party ready to support all the pretensions of any king who spared the Protestant establishment.

Sir George Saville, created Marquis of Halifax by Charles II., claims the attention of the historian rather by his brilliant genius, by the singularity of his character, and by the great part which he acted in the events which preceded and followed, than by his political importance during the short period in which he held office under James. In his youth he appears to have combined the opinions of a republican† with the most refined talents of a polished courtier. The fragments of his writings which remain show such poignant and easy wit, such lively sense, so much insight into character, and so delicate an observation of manners, as could hardly have been surpassed by any of his contemporaries at Versailles. His political speculations being soon found incapable

* North, p. 230.

† "I have long looked upon Lord Halifax and Lord Essex as men who did not love monarchy, such as it is in England."—Duke of York to Mr. Legge, suprà.

of being reduced to practice, melted away in the royal favour: the disappointment of visionary hopes led him to despair of great improvements, to despise the moderate services which an individual may render to the community, and to turn with disgust from public principles to the indulgence of his own vanity and ambition. The dread of his powers of ridicule contributed to force him into office,* and the attractions of his lively and somewhat libertine conversation were among the means by which he maintained his ground with Charles II.; of whom it was said by Dryden, that "whatever his favourites of state might be, yet those of his affection were men of wit."† Though we have no remains of his speeches, we cannot doubt the eloquence of him who, on the Exclusion Bill, fought the battle of the Court against so great an orator as Shaftesbury.‡ Of these various means of advancement, he availed himself for a time with little scruple and with some success. But he never obtained an importance which bore any proportion to his great abilities;—a failure which, in the time of Charles II., may be in part ascribed to the remains of his opinions, but which, from its subsequent recurrence, must be still more imputed to the defects of his character. He had a stronger passion for praise than for power, and loved the display of talent more than the possession of authority. The unbridled exercise of wit exposed him to lasting animosities, and threw a shade of levity over his character. He was too acute in discovering difficulties,—too ingenious in devising objections He had too keen a perception of human weakness and folly not to find many pretexts and temptations for changing his measures, and deserting his connections. The subtilty of his genius tempted him to projects too refined to be understood or supported by numerous bodies of men. His appetite for praise, when sated by the admiration of his friends, was too apt to seek a new and more stimulating gratification in the applauses of his opponents. His weaknesses and even his talents contributed to betray him into inconsistency; which, if not the worst quality of a statesman, is the most fatal to his permanent importance. For one short period, indeed, the circumstances of his situation suited the peculiarities of his genius. In the last years of Charles his refined policy had found full scope in the arts of balancing factions, of occasionally leaning to the vanquished, and always tempering the triumph of the victorious party, by which that monarch then consulted the repose of his declining years. Perhaps he satisfied himself with the reflection, that his compliance with all the evil which was then done was necessary to enable him to save his country from the arbitrary and bigoted faction which was eager to rule it. We know from the evidence of the excellent Tillotson,* that Lord Halifax "showed a compassionate concern for Lord Russell, and all the readiness to save him that could be wished;" and that Lord Russell desired Tillotson "to give thanks to Lord Halifax for his humanity and kindness:" and there is some reason to think that his intercession might have been successful, if the delicate honour of Lord Russell had not refused to second their exertions, by softening his language, on the lawfulness of resistance, a shade more than scrupulous sincerity would warrant.† He seems unintentionally to have contributed to the death of Sidney,‡ by having procured a sort of confession from Monmouth, in order to reconcile him to his father, and to balance the influence of the Duke of York, by Charles' partiality for his son. The compliances and refinements of that period pursued him with, perhaps, too just a retribution during the remainder of his life. James was impatient to be rid of him who had checked his influence during the last years of his brother; and the friends of liberty could never place any lasting trust in the man who remained a member of the Government which put to death Russell and Sidney.

The part performed by Lord Godolphin at this time was not so considerable as to require a full account of his character. He was a gentleman of ancient family in Cornwall, distinguished by the accomplishments of some of its members, and by their sufferings in the royal cause during the civil war. He held offices at Court before he was employed in the service of the State, and he always retained the wary and conciliating manners, as well as the profuse dissipation of his original school. Though a royalist and a courtier he voted for the Exclusion Bill. At the accession of James, he was not considered as favourable to absolute dependence on France, nor to the system of governing without Parliaments. But though a member of the Cabinet, he was, during the whole of this reign, rather a public officer, who confined himself to his own department, than a minister who took a part in the direction of the State.§ The habit of continuing

* Temple, Memoirs, part iii.

† Dedication to King Arthur.

‡ Jotham. of piercing wit and pregnant thought,
Endued by nature and by learning taught
To move assemblies; who but only tried
The worse awhile, then chose the better side;
Nor chose alone, but turned the balance too.
Absalom and Achitophel.

Lord Halifax says, "Mr. Dryden told me that he was offered money to write against me."—Fox MSS.

* Lords' Journals. 20th Dec. 1689. The Duchess of Portsmouth said to Lord Montague, "that if others had been as earnest as my Lord Halifax with the King, Lord Russell might have been saved."—Fox MSS. Other allusions in these MSS., which I ascribe to Lord Halifax, show that his whole fault was a continuance in office after the failure of his efforts to save Lord Russell.

† Life of Lord Russell, by Lord John Russell, p. 215.

‡ Evidence of Mr. Hampden and Sir James Forbes—Lords' Journals, 20th Dec. 1689.

§ "Milord Godolphin, quoiqu'il est du secret

some officers in place under successive administrations, for the convenience of business, then extended to higher persons than it has usually comprehended in more recent times.

James had, soon after his accession, introduced into the Cabinet Sir George Jeffreys, Lord Chief Justice of England,* a person whose office did not usually lead to that station, and whose elevation to unusual honour and trust is characteristic of the Government which he served. His origin was obscure, his education scanty, his acquirements no more than what his vigorous understanding gathered in the course of business, his professional practice low, and chiefly obtained from the companions of his vulgar excesses, whom he captivated by that gross buffoonery which accompanied him to the most exalted stations. But his powers of mind were extraordinary; his elocution was flowing and spirited; and, after his highest preferment, in the few instances where he preserved temper and decency, the native vigour of his intellect shone forth in his judgments, and threw a transient dignity over the coarseness of his deportment. He first attracted notice by turbulence in the petty contests of the Corporation of London; and having found a way to Court through some of those who ministered to the pleasures of the King, as well as to the more ignominious of his political intrigues, he made his value known by contributing to destroy the charter of the capital of which he had been the chief law officer. His services as a counsel in the trial of Russell, and as a judge in that of Sidney, proved still more acceptable to his masters. On the former occasion, he caused a person who had collected evidence for the defence to be turned out of court, for making private suggestions,—probably important to the ends of justice,—to Lady Russell, while she was engaged in her affecting duty.† The same brutal insolence shown in the trial of Sidney, was, perhaps, thought the more worthy of reward, because it was foiled by the calm heroism of that great man. The union of a powerful understanding with boisterous violence and the basest subserviency singularly fitted him to be the tool of a tyrant. He wanted, indeed, the aid of hypocrisy, but he was free from its restraints. He had that reputation for boldness which many men preserve, as long as they are personally safe, by violence in their counsels and in their language. If he at last feared danger, he never feared shame, which much more frequently restrains the powerful. Perhaps the unbridled fury of his temper enabled him to threaten and intimidate with more effect than a man of equal wickedness, with a cooler character. His religion, which seems to have consisted in hatred to Nonconformists, did not hinder him from profaneness. His native fierceness was daily inflamed by debauchery; his excesses were too gross and outrageous for the decency of historical relation;* and his court was a continual scene of scurrilous invective, from which none were exempted but his superiors. A contemporary, of amiable disposition and Tory principles, who knew him well, sums up his character in few words,—"he was by nature cruel, and a slave of the Court."†

It was after the defeat of Monmouth that James gave full scope to his policy, and began that system of measures which characterises his reign. Though Feversham was, in the common intercourse of life, a good-natured man, his victory at Sedgemoor was immediately followed by some of those acts of military license which usually disgrace the suppression of a revolt, when there is no longer any dread of retaliation,—when the conqueror sees a rebel in every inhabitant, and considers destruction by the sword as only anticipating legal execution, and when he is generally well assured, if not positively instructed, that he can do nothing more acceptable to his superiors than to spread a deep impression of terror through a disaffected province. A thousand were slain in a pursuit of a small body of insurgents for a few miles. Feversham marched into Bridgewater on the morning after the battle (July 7th), with a considerable number tied together like slaves; of whom twenty-two were hanged by his orders on a sign-post by the road-side, and on gibbets which he caused to be erected for the occasion. One of them was a wounded officer, named Adlam, who was already in the agonies of death. Four were hanged in chains, with a deliberate imitation of the barbarities of regular law. One miserable wretch, to whom life had been promised on condition of his keeping pace for half a mile with a horse at full speed (to which he was fastened by a rope which went round his neck), was executed in spite of his performance of the feat. Feversham was proceeding thus towards disarmed enemies, to whom he had granted quarter, when Ken, the bishop of the diocese, a zealous royalist, had the courage to rush into the midst of this military execution, calling out, "My Lord, this is murder in law.

n'a pas grand credit, et songe seulement à se conserver par une conduite sage et moderée. Je ne pense pas que s'il en étoit cru, on prit des liaisons avec V. M. qui pussent aller à se passer entièrement de parlement, et à rompre nettement avec le Prince d'Orange."—Barillon to the King, 16th April, 1685. Fox, History of James II., app. lx.

* North, p. 234. (After the Northern Circuit, 1684,—in our computation. 1685.)

† Examination of John Tisard.—Lords' Journals, 20th Dec. 1690.

* See the account of his behaviour at a ball in the city, soon after Sidney's condemnation; Evelyn, vol. i. p. 531; and at the dinner at Duncombe's, a rich citizen, where the Lord Chancellor (Jeffreys) and the Lord Treasurer (Rochester) were with difficulty prevented from appearing naked in a balcony, to drink loyal toasts, Reresby, Memoirs, p. 231, and of his "flaming" drunkenness at the Privy Council, when the King was present.—North, p. 250.

† Evelyn, vol. i. p. 579.

These poor wretches, now the battle is over, must be tried before they can be put to death."* The interposition of this excellent prelate, however, only suspended the cruelties of the conquerors. Feversham was called to court to receive the thanks and honours due to his services.

Kirke, whom he was directed to leave with detachments at Bridgewater and Taunton,† imitated, if he did not surpass, the lawless violence of his commander. When he entered the latter town, on the third day after the battle, he put to death at least nine of his prisoners, with so little sense of impropriety or dread of disapprobation, that they were entered by name as executed for high treason in the parish register of their interment.‡ Of the other excesses of Kirke we have no satisfactory account. The experience of like cases, however, renders the tradition not improbable, that these acts of lawless violence were accompanied by the insults and mockeries of military debauchery. The nature of the service in which the detachment was principally engaged, required more than common virtue in a commander to contain the passions of the soldiery. It was his principal duty to search for rebels. He was urged to the performance of this odious task by malicious or mercenary informers. The friendship, or compassion, or political zeal of the inhabitants, was active in favouring escapes, so that a constant and cruel struggle subsisted between the soldiers and the people abetting the fugitives.§ Kirke's regiment, when in garrison at Tangier, had had the figure of a lamb painted on their colours as a badge of their warfare against the enemies of the Christian name. The people of Somersetshire, when they saw those who thus bore the symbols of meekness and benevolence engaged in the performance of such a task, vented the bitterness of their hearts against the soldiers, by giving them the ironical name of Kirke's "lambs." The unspeakable atrocity imputed to him, of putting to death a person whose life he had promised to a young woman, as the price of compliance with his desires, it is due to the honour of human nature to disbelieve, until more satisfactory evidence be produced than that on which it has hitherto rested.* He followed the example of ministers and magistrates in selling pardons to the prisoners in his district; which, though as illegal as his executions, enabled many to escape from the barbarities which were to come. Base as this traffic was, it would naturally lead him to threaten more evil than he inflicted. It deserves to be remarked, that, five years after his command at Taunton, the inhabitants of that place gave an entertainment, at the public expense, to celebrate his success. This fact seems to countenance a suspicion that we ought to attribute more to the nature of the service in which he was engaged than to any pre-eminence in criminality, the peculiar odium which has fallen on his name, to the exclusion of other officers, whose excesses appear to have been greater, and are certainly more satisfactorily attested. But whatever opinion may be formed of the degree of Kirke's guilt, it is certain that he was rather countenanced than discouraged by the Government. His illegal executions were early notorious in London.† The good Bishop Ken, who then corresponded with the King himself, on the sufferings of his diocese,‡ could not fail to remonstrate against those excesses, which he had so generously interposed to prevent; and if the accounts of the remonstrances of Lord Keeper Guildford, against the excesses of the West, have any foundation,§ they must have related exclusively to the enormities of the soldiery, for the Lord Keeper died at the very opening of Jeffreys' circuit. Yet, with this knowledge, Lord Sunderland instructed Kirke "to secure such of his prisoners as had not been

* For the principal part of the enormities of Feversham, we have the singular advantage of the testimony of two eye-witnesses,—an officer in the royal army, Kennet, History of England, vol. iii. p. 432, and Oldmixon, History of England, vol. i. p. 704. See also Locke's Western Rebellion.

† Lord Sunderland's letter to Lord Feversham, 8th July.—State Paper Office.

‡ Toulmin's Taunton, by Savage, p. 522, where, after a period of near one hundred and forty years, the authentic evidence of this fact is for the first time published, together with other important particulars of Monmouth's revolt, and of the military and judicial cruelties which followed it. These nine are by some writers swelled to nineteen, probably from confounding them with that number executed at Taunton by virtue of Jeffreys' judgments. The number of ninety mentioned on this occasion by others seems to be altogether an exaggeration.

§ Kirke to Lord Sunderland. Taunton, 12th Aug.—State Paper Office.

* This story is told neither by Oldmixon nor Burnet, nor by the humble writers of the Bloody Assizes or the Quadriennium Jacobi. Echard and Kennet, who wrote long after, mentioned it only as a report. It first appeared in print in 1699, in Pomfret's poem of Cruelty and Lust. The next mention is in the anonymous Life of William III., published in 1702. A story very similar is told by St. Augustine of a Roman officer, and in the Spectator, No. 491, of a governor of Zealand, probably from a Dutch chronicle or legend. The scene is laid by some at Taunton, by others at Exeter. The person executed is said by some to be the father, by others to be the husband, and by others again to be the brother of the unhappy young woman, whose name it has been found impossible to ascertain, or even plausibly to conjecture. The tradition, which is still said to prevail at Taunton, may well have originated in a publication of one hundred and twenty years old.

† Narcissus Luttrell, MS. Diary, 15th July, six days after their occurrence.

‡ Ken's examination before the Privy Council, in 1696.—Biographia Britannica, Article Ken.

§ North, p. 260. This inaccurate writer refers the complaint to Jeffreys' proceedings, which is impossible, since Lord Guildford died in Oxfordshire, on the 5th September, after a long illness. Lady Lisle was executed on the 3d; and her execution, the only one which preceded the death of the Lord Keeper, could scarcely have reached him in his dying moments.

executed, in order to trial,"* at a time when there had been no legal proceedings, and when all the executions to which he adverts, without disapprobation, must have been contrary to law. Seven days after, Sunderland informed Kirke that his letter had been communicated to the King, "who was very well satisfied with the proceedings."† In subsequent despatches,‡ he censures Kirke for setting some rebels at liberty (alluding, doubtless, to those who had purchased their lives); but he does not censure that officer for having put others to death. Were it not for these proofs that the King knew the acts of Kirke, and that his Government officially sanctioned them, no credit would be due to the declarations afterwards made by such a man, that his severities fell short of the orders which he had received.§ Nor is this the only circumstance which connects the Government with these enormities. On the 10th of August, Kirke was ordered to come to court to give information on the state of the West. His regiment was soon afterwards removed; and he does not appear to have been employed there during the remainder of that season.‖

Colonel Trelawney succeeded; but so little was Kirke's conduct thought to be blamable, that on the 1st of September three persons were executed illegally at Taunton for rebellion, the nature and reason of their death openly avowed in the register of their interment.¶ In military executions, however atrocious, some allowance must be made for the passions of an exasperated soldiery, and for the habits of officers accustomed to summary and irregular acts, who have not been taught by experience that the ends of justice cannot be attained otherwise than by the observance of the rules of law.** The lawless violence of an army forms no precedent for the ordinary administration of public affairs; and the historian is bound to relate with diffidence events which are generally attended with confusion and obscurity, which are exaggerated by the just resentment of an oppressed party, and where we can seldom be guided by the authentic evidence of records. Neither the conduct of a Government which approves these excesses, however, nor that of judges who imitate or surpass them, allows of such extenuations or requires such caution in relating and characterising facts. The judicial proceedings which immediately followed these military atrocities may be related with more confidence, and must be treated with the utmost rigour of historical justice.

The commencement of proceedings on the Western Circuit, which comprehends the whole scene of Monmouth's operations, was postponed till the other assizes were concluded, in order that four judges, who were joined with Jeffreys in the commission, might be at liberty to attend him.* An order was also issued to all officers in the West, "to furnish such parties of horse and foot, as might be required by the Lord Chief Justice on his circuit, for securing prisoners, and to perform that service in such manner as he should direct."† After these unusual and alarming preparations, Jeffreys began his circuit at Winchester, on the 27th of August, by the trial of Mrs. Alicia Lisle, who was charged with having sheltered in her house, for one night, two fugitives from Monmouth's routed army,—an office of humanity which then was and still is treated as high treason by the law of England. This lady, though unaided by counsel, so deaf that she could very imperfectly hear the evidence, and occasionally overpowerrd by those lethargic slumbers which are incident to advanced age, defended herself with a coolness which formed a striking contrast to the deportment of her judge.‡ The principal witness, a man who had been sent to her to implore shelter for one Hickes, and who guided him and Nelthrope to her house, betrayed a natural repugnance to disclose facts likely to affect a life which he had innocently contributed to endanger. Jeffreys, at the suggestion of the counsel for the crown, took upon himself the examination of this unwilling witness, and conducted it with a union of artifice, menace, and invective, which no well-regulated tribunal would suffer in the advocate of a prisoner, when examining the witness produced by the accuser. With solemn appeals to Heaven for his own pure intentions, he began in the language of candour and gentleness to adjure the witness to discover all that he knew. His nature, however, often threw off this disguise, and broke out into the ribaldry and scurrility of his accustomed style. The Judge and three counsel poured in questions upon the poor rustic in rapid succession. Jeffreys said that he treasured up vengeance for such men, and added, "It is infinite mercy that for those falsehoods

* 14th July.—State Paper Office.

† 21st July.—Ibid.

‡ 25th and 28th July, and 3d August.—State Paper Office.

§ Oldmixon, vol. i. p. 705.

‖ Papers in the War Office. MS.

¶ Savage, p. 525.

** Two years after the suppression of the Western revolt, we find Kirke treated with favour by the King.—"Colonel Kirke is made housekeeper of Whitehall, in the room of his *kinsman*, deceased."—Narcissus Luttrell, Sept. 1687. He was nearly related to, or perhaps the son of George Kirke, groom of the bedchamber to Charles I., one of whose beautiful daughters, Mary, a maid of honour, was the Warmestré of Count Hamilton, (Notes to Mémoires de Grammont), and the other, Diana, was the wife of the last Earl of Oxford, of the house of De Vere.—Dugdale's Baronage, tit. Oxford.

* Lord Chief Baron Montague, Levison, Watkins, and Wright, of whom the three former sat on the subsequent trials of Mr. Cornish and Mrs. Gaunt.

† This order was dated on the 24th August, 1685.—Papers in the War Office. From this circumstance originated the story, that Jeffreys had a commission as Commander-in-Chief.

‡ State Trials, vol. xi. p. 298.

of thine, God does not immediately strike thee into hell." Wearied, overawed, and overwhelmed by such an examination, the witness at length admitted some facts which afforded reason to suspect, rather than to believe, that the unfortunate lady knew the men whom she succoured to be fugitives from Monmouth's army. She said in her defence, that she knew Mr. Hickes to be a Presbyterian minister, and thought he absconded because there were warrants out against him on that account. All the precautions for concealment which were urged as proofs of her intentional breach of law were reconcilable with this defence. Orders had been issued at the beginning of the revolt to seize all "disaffected and suspicious persons, especially all Nonconformist ministers;"* and Jeffreys himself unwittingly strengthened her case by declaring his conviction, that all Presbyterians had a hand in the rebellion. He did not go through the formality of repeating so probable a defence to the jury. They however hesitated: they asked the Chief Justice, whether it were as much treason to receive Hickes before as after conviction? He told them that it was, which was literally true; but he wilfully concealed from them that by the law, such as it was, the receiver of a traitor could not be brought to trial till the principal traitor had been convicted or outlawed;—a provision, indeed, so manifestly necessary to justice, that without the observance of it Hickes might be acquitted of treason after Mrs. Lisle had been executed for harbouring him as a traitor.† Four judges looked silently on this suppression of truth, which produced the same effect with positive falsehood, and allowed the limits of a barbarous law to be overpassed, in order to destroy an aged woman for an act of charity. The jury retired, and remained so long in deliberation, as to provoke the wrath of the Chief Justice. When they returned into court, they expressed their doubt, whether the prisoner knew that Hickes had been in Monmouth's army: the Chief Justice assured them that the proof was complete. Three times they repeated their doubt: the Chief Justice as often reiterated his declaration with growing impatience and rage. At this critical moment of the last appeal of the jury to the Court, the defenceless female at the bar made an effort to speak. Jeffreys, taking advantage of formalities, instantly silenced her, and the jury were at length overawed into a verdict of "guilty." He then broke out into a needless insult to the strongest affections of nature, saying to the jury, "Gentlemen, had I been among you, and if she had been my own mother, I should have found her guilty." On the next morning, when he had to pronounce sentence of death, he could not even then abstain from invectives against Presbyterians, of whom he supposed Mrs. Lisle to be one; yet mixing artifice with his fury, he tried to lure her into discoveries, by ambiguous phrases, which might excite her hopes of life without pledging him to obtain pardon. He directed that she should be burnt alive in the afternoon of the same day; but the clergy of the cathedral of Winchester successfully interceded for an interval of three days. This interval gave time for an application to the King; and that application was made by persons, and with circumstances, which must have strongly called his attention to the case. Mrs. Lisle was the widow of Mr. Lisle, who was one of the judges of Charles the First; and this circumstance, which excited a prejudice against her, served in its consequences to show that she had powerful claims on the lenity of the King. Lady St. John and Lady Abergavenny wrote a letter to Lord Clarendon, then Privy Seal, which he read to the King, bearing testimony, "that she had been a favourer of the King's friends in their greatest extremities during the late civil war," and among others, of these ladies themselves; and on these grounds, as well as for her general loyalty, earnestly recommending her to pardon. Her son had served in the King's army against Monmouth; she often had declared that she shed more tears than any woman in England on the day of the death of Charles the First; and after the attainder of Mr. Lisle, his estate was granted to her at the intercession of Lord Chancellor Clarendon, for her excellent conduct during the prevalence of her husband's party. Lord Feversham, also, who had been promised a thousand pounds for her pardon, used his influence to obtain it. But the King declared that he would not reprieve her for one day. It is said, that he endeavoured to justify himself, by alleging a promise to Jeffreys that Mrs. Lisle should not be spared;—a fact which, if true, shows the conduct of James to have been as deliberate as it seems to be, and that the severities of the circuit arose from a previous concert between him and Jeffreys. On the following day the case was again brought before him by a petition from Mrs. Lisle, praying that her punishment might be changed into beheading, in consideration of her ancient and honourable descent. After a careful search for precedents, the mind of James was once more called to the fate of the prisoner by the signature of a warrant to authorise the infliction of the mitigated punishment. This venerable matron accordingly suffered death on the 2d of September, supported by that piety which had been the guide of her life. Her understanding was so undisturbed, that she clearly instanced the points in which she had been wronged. No resentment troubled the composure of her dying moments; and she carried her religious principles of allegiance and forgiveness so far, as to pray on

---

* Despatch from Lord Sunderland to Lord-Lieutenants of Counties. 20th June, 1685.

† Hale, Pleas of the Crown, part i. c. 22. Foster, Discourse on Accomplices, chap. 1.

the scaffold for the prosperity of a prince from whom she had experienced neither mercy, gratitude, nor justice. The trial of Mrs. Lisle is a sufficient specimen of the proceedings of this circuit. When such was the conduct of the judges in a single trial of a lady of distinction for such an offence, with a jury not regardless of justice, where there was full leisure for the consideration of every question of fact and law, and where every circumstance was made known to the Government and the public, it is easy to imagine what the demeanour of the same tribunal must have been in the trials of several hundred insurgents of humble condition, crowded into so short a time that the wisest and most upright judges could hardly have distinguished the innocent from the guilty.*

As the movements of Monmouth's army had been confined to Dorset and Somerset, the acts of high treason were almost entirely committed there, and the prisoners apprehended elsewhere were therefore removed for trial to these counties.† That unfortunate district was already filled with dismay and horror by the barbarities of the troops; the roads leading to its principal towns were covered with prisoners under military guards; and the display and menace of warlike power were most conspicuous in the retinue of insolent soldiers and trembling culprits who followed the march of the judges, forming a melancholy contrast to the parental confidence which was wont to pervade the administration of the unarmed laws of a free people. Three hundred and twenty prisoners were arraigned at Dorchester, of whom thirty-five pleaded "not guilty;" and on their trial five were acquitted and thirty were convicted. The Chief Justice caused some intimation to be conveyed to the prisoners that confession was the only road to mercy; and to strengthen the effect of this hint, he sent twenty-nine of the persons convicted to immediate execution,—though one of them at least was so innocent that had there been time to examine his case, he might even then have been pardoned.* The intimation illustrated by such a commentary produced the intended effect: two hundred and eight at once confessed.† Eighty persons were, according to contemporary accounts, executed at Dorchester; and though the records state only the execution of fifty, yet as they contain no entry of judgment in two hundred and fifty cases, their silence affords no presumption against the common accounts.

The correspondence of Jeffreys with the King and the minister appears to have begun at Dorchester. From that place he wrote on the 8th of September, in terms of enthusiastic gratitude to Sunderland, to return thanks for the Great Seal.‡ Two days afterwards he informed Sunderland, that though "tortured by the stone," he had that day "despatched ninety-eight rebels."§ Sunderland assured him in answer, that the King approved all his proceedings, of which very minute accounts appear to have been constantly transmitted by Jeffreys directly to the King himself.‖ In the county of Somerset more than a thousand prisoners were arraigned for treason at Taunton and Wells, of whom only six ventured to put themselves on their trial by pleading "not guilty." A thousand and forty confessed themselves to be guilty;—a proportion of confessions so little corresponding to the common chances of precipitate arrests, of malicious or mistaken charges, and of escapes on trial,—all which were multiplied in such violent and hurried proceedings,—as clearly to show that the measures of the circuit had already extinguished all expectation that the judges would observe the rules of justice. Submission afforded some chance of escape: from trial the most innocent could no longer have any hope. Only six days were allowed in this county to find indictments against a thousand prisoners, to arraign them, to try the few who still ventured to appeal to law, to record the confessions of the rest, and to examine the circumstances which ought, in each case, to aggravate or extenuate the punishment. The names of two hundred and thirty-nine persons executed there are preserved:¶ but as no judgments are entered,** we do not know how many more may have suffered. In order to diffuse terror more widely, these executions were directed to take place in thirty-six towns and villages. Three were executed in the village of Wrington, the birthplace of Mr. Locke, whose writings were one

* By the favour of the clerk of assize, I have before me many of the original records of this circuit. The account of it by Lord Lonsdale was written in 1688. The Bloody Assizes, and the Life of Jeffreys, were published in 1689. They were written by one Shirley, a compiler, and by Pitts, a surgeon in Monmouth's army. Six thousand copies of the latter were sold.—Life of John Dunton, vol. i. p. 184. Roger Coke, a contemporary, and Oldmixon, almost an eye-witness, vouch for their general fairness; and I have found an unexpected degree of coincidence between them and the circuit records. Burnet came to reside at Salisbury in 1689, and he and Kennet began to relate the facts about seventeen years after they occurred. Father Orleans, and the writer of James' Life, admit the cruelties, while they vainly strive to exculpate the King from any share in them. From a comparison of those original authorities, and from the correspondence, hitherto unknown, in the State Paper Office, the narrative of the text has been formed.

† There were removed to Dorchester ninety-four from Somerset, eighty-nine from Devon, fifty-five from Wilts, and twenty-three from London.—Circuit Records.

* Bragg, an attorney. Bloody Assizes. Western Rebellion.

† Calendar for Dorsetshire summer assizes, 1685.

‡ The Great Seal had only been vacant three days, as Lord Keeper Guildford died at his seat at Wroxton, on the 5th.

§ 8th and 10th Sept.—State Paper Office.

‖ Windsor, 14th Sept.—Ibid.

¶ Life and Death of George Lord Jeffreys. (London, 1689.)

** Circuit Records.

day to lessen the misery suffered by mankind from cruel laws and unjust judges. The general consternation spread by these proceedings has prevented a particular account of many of the cases from reaching us. In some of those more conspicuous instances which have been preserved, we see what so great a body of obnoxious culprits must have suffered in narrow and noisome prisons, where they were often destitute of the common necessaries of life, before a judge whose native rage and insolence were stimulated by daily intoxication, and inflamed by the agonies of an excruciating distemper, from the brutality of soldiers, and the cruelty of slavish or bigoted magistrates; while one part of their neighbours were hardened against them by faction, and the other deterred from relieving them by fear. The ordinary executioners, unequal to so extensive a slaughter, were aided by novices, whose unskilfulness aggravated the horrors of that death of torture which was then the legal punishment of high treason. Their lifeless remains were treated with those indignities and outrages which still* continue to disgrace the laws of a civilized age. They were beheaded and quartered, and the heads and limbs of the dead were directed to be placed on court-houses, and in all conspicuous elevations in streets, high roads, and churches. The country was filled with the dreadful preparations necessary to fit these inanimate members for such an exhibition; and the roads were covered by vehicles conveying them to great distances in every direction.† There was not a hamlet in which the poor inhabitants were not doomed hourly to look on the mangled remains of a neighbour or a relation. "All the high roads of the country were no longer to be travelled, while the horrors of so many quarters of men and the offensive stench of them lasted."‡

While one of the most fertile and cheerful provinces of England was thus turned into a scene of horror by the mangled remains of the dead, the towns resounded with the cries, and the streets streamed with the blood of men, and even women and children, who were cruelly whipped for real or pretended sedition. The case of John Tutchin, afterwards a noted political writer, is a specimen of these minor cruelties. He was tried at Dorchester, under the assumed name of Thomas Pitts, for having said that Hampshire was up in arms for the Duke of Monmouth, and, on his conviction, was sentenced to be whipped through every market town in the county for seven years. The females in court burst into tears; and even one of the officers of the court ventured to observe to the Chief Justice, that the culprit was very young, and that the sentence would reach to once a fortnight for seven years. These symptoms of pity exposed the prisoner to new brutality from his judge. Tutchin is said to have petitioned the King for the more lenient punishment of the gallows. He was seized with the small-pox in prison; and, whether from unwonted compassion, or from the misnomer in the indictment, he appears to have escaped the greater part of the barbarous punishment to which he was doomed.*

These dreadful scenes are relieved by some examples of generous virtue in individuals of the victorious party. Harte, a clergyman of Taunton, following the excellent example of the Bishop, interceded for some of the prisoners with Jeffreys in the full career of his cruelty. The intercession was not successful; but it compelled him to honour the humanity to which he did not yield, for he soon after preferred Harte to be a prebendary of Bristol. Both Ken and Harte, who were probably at the moment charged with disaffection, sacrificed at a subsequent period their preferments, rather than violate the allegiance which they thought still to be due to the King; while Mew, Bishop of Winchester, who was on the field of battle at Sedgemoor, and who ordered that his coach horses should drag forward the artillery of the royal army, preserved his rich bishopric by compliance with the government of King William. The army of Monmouth also afforded instructive proofs, that the most furious zealots are not always the most consistent adherents. Ferguson and Hooke, two Presbyterian clergymen in that army, passed most of their subsequent lives in Jacobite intrigues, either from incorrigible habits of conspiracy, or from resentment at the supposed ingratitude of their own party, or from the inconstancy natural to men of unbridled passions and distempered minds. Daniel De Foe, one of the most original writers of the English nation, served in the army of Monmouth; but we do not know the particulars of his escape. A great satirist had afterwards the baseness to reproach both Tutchin and De Foe with sufferings, which were dishonourable only to those who inflicted them.†

In the mean time, peculiar circumstances rendered the correspondence of Jeffreys in Somersetshire with the King and his minister more specific and confidential than it had been in the preceding parts of the circuit. Lord Sunderland had apprised Jeffreys of the King's pleasure to bestow a thousand con-

* 1822.—Ed.

† "Nothing could be liker hell than these parts: cauldrons hissing, carcasses boiling, pitch and tar sparkling and glowing, bloody limbs boiling, and tearing, and mangling."—Bloody Assizes. "England is now an Aceldama. The country for sixty miles, from Bristol to Exeter, had a new terrible sort of sign-posts, gibbets, heads and quarters of its slaughtered inhabitants."—Oldmixon, vol. i. p. 707.

‡ Lord Lonsdale, (Memoirs of the Reign of James II., p. 13,) confirms the testimony of the two former more ardent partisans, both of whom, however, were eye-witnesses.

* Savage, p. 509. Western Rebellion. Dorchester Calendar, summer assizes, 1685.

† "Earless on high stood unabashed De Foe,
And Tutchin flagrant from the scourge below." Dunciad, book ii.

victs on several courtiers, and one hundred on a favourite of the Queen,* on these persons finding security that the prisoners should be enslaved for ten years in some West India island;—a limitation intended, perhaps, only to deprive the convicts of the sympathy of the Puritan colonists of New England, but which, in effect, doomed them to a miserable and lingering death in a climate where field-labour is fatal to Europeans. Jeffreys, in his answer to the King, remonstrates against this disposal of the prisoners, who, he says, would be worth ten or fifteen pounds a-piece;† and, at the same time, returns thanks for his Majesty's gracious acceptance of his services. In a subsequent letter from Bristol,‡ he yields to the distribution of the convicts; boasts of his victory over that most factious city, where he had committed the mayor and an alderman, under pretence of their having sold to the plantations men whom they had unjustly convicted with a view to such a sale; and pledges himself "that Taunton, and Bristol, and the county of Somerset, should know their duty both to God and their King before he leaves them." He entreats the King not to be surprised into pardons.

James, being thus regularly apprised of the most minute particulars of Jeffreys' proceedings, was accustomed to speak of them to the foreign ministers under the name of "Jeffreys' campaign."§ He amused himself with horse-races at Winchester, the scene of the recent execution of Mrs. Lisle, during the hottest part of Jeffreys' operations.‖ He was so fond of the phrase of "Jeffreys' campaign," as to use it twice in his correspondence with the Prince of Orange; and, on the latter occasion, in a tone of exultation approaching to defiance.¶ The excellent Ken had written to him a letter of expostulation on the subject. On the 30th of September, on Jeffreys' return to court, his promotion to the office of Lord Chancellor was announced in the Gazette, with a panegyric on his services very unusual in the cold formalities of official appointment. Had James been dissatisfied with the conduct of Jeffreys, he had the means of repairing some part of its consequences, for the executions in Somersetshire were not concluded before the latter part of November; and among the persons who suffered in October was Mr. Hickes, a Nonconformist clergyman, for whom his brother, the learned Dr. Hickes, afterwards a sufferer in the cause of James, sued in vain for pardon.* Some months after, when Jeffreys had brought on a fit of dangerous illness by one of his furious debauches, the King expressed great concern, and declared that his loss could not be easily repaired.†

The public acts and personal demeanour of the King himself agreed too well with the general character of these judicial severities. An old officer, named Holmes, who was taken in Monmouth's army, being brought up to London, was admitted to an interview with the King, who offered to spare his life if he would promise to live quietly. He answered, that his principles had been and still were "republican," believing that form of government to be the best; and that he was an old man, whose life was as little worth asking as it was worth giving,—an answer which so displeased the King, that Holmes was removed to Dorchester, where he suffered death with fortitude and piety.‡ The proceedings on the circuit seem, indeed, to have been so exclusively directed by the King and the Chief Justice, that even Lord Sunderland, powerful as he was, could not obtain the pardon of one delinquent. Yet the case was favourable, and deserves to be shortly related, as characteristic of the times. Lord Sunderland interceded repeatedly§ with Jeffreys for a youth named William Jenkins, who was executed‖ in spite of such powerful solicitations. He was the son of an eminent Nonconformist clergyman, who had recently died in Newgate after a long imprisonment, inflicted on him for the performance of his clerical duties. Young Jenkins had distributed mourning rings, on which was inscribed "William Jenkins, murdered in Newgate." He was in consequence imprisoned in the jail of Ilchester, and, being released by Monmouth's army, he joined his deliverers against his oppressors.

* 14th and 15th Sept.—State Paper Office. 200 to Sir Robert White, 200 to Sir William Booth, 100 to Sir C. Musgrave, 100 to Sir W. Stapleton, 100 to J. Kendall, 100 to —— Triphol, 100 to a merchant. "The Queen has asked 100 more of the rebels."

† Taunton, 19th Sept.—Ibid.

‡ 22d Sept.—Ibid.

§ Burnet, History of his Own Time. (fol.) vol. i. p. 648.

‖ 14th to 18th Sept.—London Gazettes.

¶ 10th and 24th Sept.—Dalrymple, Memoirs of Great Britain, appendix to part i. book ii.

* The Père d'Orleans, who wrote under the eye of James, in 1695, mentions the displeasure of the King at the sale of pardons, and seems to refer to Lord Sunderland's letter to Kirke, who, we know from Oldmixon, was guilty of that practice; and, in other respects, rather attempts to account for, than to deny, the acquiescence of the King in the cruelties.—Révolutions d'Angleterre, liv. xi. The testimony of Roger North, if it has any foundation, cannot be applied to this part of the subject. The part of the Life of James II. which relates to it is the work only of the anonymous biographer, Mr. Dicconson of Lancashire, and abounds with the grossest mistakes. The assertion of Sheffield, Duke of Buckingham in the Account of the Revolution, that Jeffreys disobeyed James' orders, is disproved by the correspondence already quoted. There is, on the whole, no colour for the assertion of Macpherson, (History of Great Britain, vol. i. p. 453), or for the doubts of Dalrymple.

† Barillon, 4th Feb. 1686.—Fox MSS.

‡ Lord Lonsdale, p. 12. Calendar for Dorsetshire. Bloody Assizes. The account of Colonel Holmes by the anonymous biographer (Life of James II. vol. ii. p. 43,) is contradicted by all these authorities. It is utterly improbable, and is not more honourable to James than that here adopted.

§ Lord Sunderland to Lord Jeffreys, 12th Sept.—State Paper Office.

‖ At Taunton, 30th Sept.—Western Rebellion.

Vain attempts have been made to exculpate James, by throwing part of the blame of these atrocities upon Pollexfen, an eminent Whig lawyer, who was leading counsel in the prosecutions;*—a wretched employment, which he probably owed, as a matter of course, to his rank as senior King's counsel on the circuit. His silent acquiescence in the illegal proceedings against Mrs. Lisle must, indeed, brand his memory with indelible infamy; but, from the King's perfect knowledge of the circumstances of that case, it seems to be evident that Pollexfen's interposition would have been unavailing: and the subsequent proceedings were carried on with such utter disregard of the forms, as well as the substance of justice, that counsel had probably no duty to perform, and no opportunity to interfere. To these facts may be added, what, without such preliminary evidence, would have been of little weight, the dying declaration of Jeffreys himself, who, a few moments before he expired, said to Dr. Scott, an eminent divine who attended him in the Tower, "Whatever I did then I did by express orders; and I have this farther to say for myself, that I was not half bloody enough for him who sent me thither."†

Other trials occurred under the eye of James in London, where, according to an ancient and humane usage, no sentence of death is executed till the case is laid before the King in person, that he may determine whether there be any room for mercy. Mr. Cornish, an eminent merchant, charged with a share in the Rye House Plot, was apprehended, tried, and executed within the space of ten days, the court having refused him the time which he alleged to be necessary to bring up a material witness.‡ Colonel Rumsey, the principal witness for the Crown, owned that on the trial of Lord Russell he had given evidence which directly contradicted his testimony against Cornish. This avowal of perjury did not hinder his conviction and execution; but the scandal was so great, that James was obliged, in a few days, to make a tardy reparation for the precipitate injustice of his judges. The mutilated limbs of Cornish were restored to his relations, and Rumsey was confined for life to St. Nicholas' Island, at Plymouth,§ a place of illegal imprisonment, still kept up in defiance of the Habeas Corpus Act. This virtual acknowledgment by the King of the falsehood of Rumsey's testimony assumes an importance in history, when it is considered as a proof of the perjury of one of the two witnesses against Lord Russell,—the man of most unspotted virtue who ever suffered on an English scaffold. Ring, Fernley, and Elizabeth Gaunt, persons of humble condition in life, were tried on the same day with Cornish, for harbouring some fugitives from Monmouth's army. One of the persons to whom Ring afforded shelter was his near kinsman. Fernley was convicted on the sole evidence of Burton, whom he had concealed from the search of the public officers. When a witness was about to be examined for Fernley, the Court allowed one of their own officers to cry out that the witness was a Whig; while one of the judges, still more conversant with the shades of party, sneered at another of his witnesses as a Trimmer. When Burton was charged with being an accomplice in the Rye House Plot, Mrs. Gaunt received him, supplied him with money, and procured him a passage to Holland. After the defeat of Monmouth, with whom he returned, he took refuge in the house of Fernley, where Mrs. Gaunt visited him, again supplied him with money, and undertook a second time to save his life, by procuring the means of his again escaping into Holland. When Burton was apprehended, the prosecutors had their choice, if a victim was necessary, either of proceeding against him, whom they charged with open rebellion and intended assassination, or against Mrs. Gaunt, whom they could accuse only of acts of humanity and charity forbidden by their laws. They chose to spare the wretched Burton, in order that he might swear away the lives of others for having preserved his own. Eight judges, of whom Jeffreys was no longer one, sat on these deplorable trials. Roger North, known as a contributor to our history, was an active counsel against the benevolent and courageous Mrs. Gaunt. William Penn was present when she was burnt alive,* and having familiar access to James, is likely to have related to him the particulars of that and of the other executions at the same time. At the stake, she disposed the straw around her, so as to shorten her agony by a strong and quick fire, with a composure which melted the spectators into tears. She thanked God that he had enabled her to succour the desolate; that "the blessing of those who were ready to perish" came upon her; and that, in the act for which she was doomed by men to destruction, she had obeyed the sacred precepts which commanded her "to hide the outcast, and not to betray him that wandereth." Thus was this poor and uninstructed woman supported under a death of cruel torture, by the lofty consciousness of suffering for righteousness, and by that steadfast faith in the final triumph of justice which can never visit the last moments of the oppressor. The dying speeches of the prisoners executed in London were suppressed, and the outrages offered to the remains of the

* Life of James II., vol. ii. p. 44.

† Burnet (Oxford, 1823), vol. iii. p. 61. Speaker Onslow's Note. Onslow received this information from Sir J. Jekyll, who heard it from Lord Somers, to whom it was communicated by Dr. Scott. The account of Tutchin, who stated that Jeffreys had made the same declaration to him in the Tower, is thus confirmed by indisputable evidence.

‡ State Trials, vol. xi. p. 382.

§ Narcissus Luttrell, 19th April, 1686.

* Clarkson, Life of Penn, vol. i. p. 448.

dead were carried to an unusual degree.* The body of Richard Rumbold, who had been convicted and executed at Edinburgh, under a Scotch law, was brought up to London. The sheriffs of London were commanded, by a royal warrant, to set up one of the quarters on one of the gates of the city, and to deliver the remaining three to the sheriff of Hertford, who was directed by another warrant to place them at or near Rumbold's late residence at the Rye House;†—impotent but studied outrages, which often manifest more barbarity of nature than do acts of violence to the living.

The chief restraint on the severity of Jeffreys seems to have arisen from his rapacity. Contemporaries of all parties agree that there were few gratuitous pardons, and that wealthy convicts seldom sued to him in vain. Kiffin, a Nonconformist merchant, had agreed to give 3000*l.* to a courtier for the pardon of two youths of the name of Luson, his grandsons, who had been in Monmouth's army. But Jeffreys guarded his privilege of selling pardons, by unrelenting rigour towards those prisoners from whom mercy had thus been sought through another channel.‡ He was attended on his circuit by a buffoon, to whom, as a reward for his merriment in one of his hours of revelry, he tossed the pardon of a rich culprit, expressing his hope that it might turn to good account. But this traffic in mercy was not confined to the Chief Justice: the King pardoned Lord Grey to increase the value of the grant of his life-estate, which had been made to Lord Rochester. The young women of Taunton, who had presented colours and a Bible to Monmouth, were excepted by name from the general pardon, in order that they might purchase separate ones. To aggravate this indecency, the money to be thus extorted from them was granted to persons of their own sex,—the Queen's maids of honour; and it must be added with regret, that William Penn, sacrificing other objects to the hope of obtaining the toleration of his religion from the King's favour, was appointed an agent for the maids of honour, and submitted to receive instructions "to make the most advantageous composition he could in their behalf."§ The Duke of Somerset in vain attempted to persuade Sir Francis Warre, a neighbouring gentleman, to obtain 7000*l.* from the young women, without which, he said, the maids of honour were determined to prosecute them to outlawry. Roger Hoare, an eminent trader of Bridgewater, saved his life by the payment to them of 1000*l.*; but he was kept in suspense respecting his pardon till he came to the foot of the gallows, for no other conceivable purpose than that of extorting the largest possible sum. This delay caused the insertion of his execution in the first narratives of these events: but he lived to take the most just revenge on tyrants, by contributing, as representative in several Parliaments for his native town, to support that free government which prevented the restoration of tyranny.

The same disposition was shown by the King and his ministers in the case of Mr. Hampden, the grandson of him who, forty years before, had fallen in battle for the liberties of his country. Though this gentleman had been engaged in the consultations of Lord Russell and Mr. Sidney, yet there being only one witness against him, he was not tried for treason, but was convicted of a misdemeanor, and on the evidence of Lord Howard condemned to pay a fine of 40,000*l.* His father being in possession of the family estate, he remained in prison till after Monmouth's defeat, when he was again brought to trial for the same act as high treason, under pretence that a second witness had been discovered.* It had been secretly arranged, that if he pleaded guilty he should be pardoned on paying a large sum of money to two of the King's favourites. At the arraignment, both the judges and Mr. Hampden performed the respective parts which the secret agreement required; he humbly entreating their intercession to obtain the pardon which he had already secured by more effectual means, and they extolling the royal mercy, and declaring that the prisoner, by his humble confession, had taken the best means of qualifying himself to receive it. The result of this profanation of the forms of justice and mercy was, that Mr. Hampden was in a few months allowed to reverse his attainder, on payment of a bribe of 6000*l.* to be divided between Jeffreys and Father Petre, the two guides of the King in the performance of his duty to God and his people.†

Another proceeding, of a nature still more culpable, showed the same union of mercenary with sanguinary purposes in the King and his ministers. Prideaux, a gentleman of fortune in the West of England, was apprehended on the landing of Monmouth, for no other reason than that his father had been attorney-general under the Commonwealth and the Protectorate. Jeffreys, actuated here by personal motives, employed agents through the prisons to discover evidence against Prideaux. The lowest prisoners were offered their lives, and a sum of 500*l.* if they would give evidence against him. Such, however, was the inflexible morality of the Nonconformists, who formed the bulk of Monmouth's adherents, that they remained unshaken by these offers, amidst the military

* Narcissus Luttrell, 16th Nov., 1685.

† Warrants, 27th and 28th October, 1685.—State Paper Office. One quarter was to be put up at Aldgate; the remaining three at Hoddesdon, the Rye, and Bishop's Stortford.

‡ Kiffin's Memoirs, p. 54. See answer of Kiffin to James, ibid. p. 159.

§ Lord Sunderland to William Penn, 13th Feb. 1686.—State Paper Office.

* State Trials, vol. xi. p. 479.

† Lords' Journals, 20th Dec. 1689. This document has been overlooked by all historians, who, in consequence, have misrepresented the conduct of Mr. Hampden.

violence which surrounded them, and in spite of the judicial rigours which were to follow. Prideaux was enlarged. Jeffreys himself, however, was able to obtain some information, though not upon oath, from two convicts under the influence of the terrible proceedings at Dorchester;* and Prideaux was again apprehended. The convicts were brought to London; and one of them was conducted to a private interview with the Lord Chancellor, by Sir Roger L'Estrange, the most noted writer in the pay of the Court. Prideaux, alarmed at these attempts to tamper with witnesses, employed the influence of his friends to obtain his pardon. The motive for Jeffreys' unusual activity was then discovered. Prideaux's friends were told that nothing could be done for him, as "the King had given him" (the familiar phrase for a grant of an estate either forfeited or about to be forfeited) to the Chancellor, as a reward for his services. On application to one Jennings, the avowed agent of the Chancellor for the sale of pardons, it was found that Jeffreys, unable to procure evidence on which he could obtain the whole of Prideaux's large estates by a conviction, had now resolved to content himself with a bribe of 10,000*l.* for the deliverance of a man so innocent, that by the formalities of law, perverted as they then were, the Lord Chancellor could not effect his destruction. Payment of so large a sum was at first resisted; but to subdue this contumacy, Prideaux's friends were forbidden to have access to him in prison, and his ransom was raised to 15,000*l.* The money was then publicly paid by a banker to the Lord Chancellor of England by name. Even in the administration of the iniquitous laws of confiscation, there are probably few instances where, with so much premeditation and effrontery, the spoils of an accused man were promised first to the judge, who might have tried him, and afterwards to the Chancellor who was to advise the King in the exercise of mercy.†

Notwithstanding the perjury of Rumsey in the case of Cornish, a second experiment was made on the effect of his testimony by producing him, together with Lord Grey and one Saxton, as a witness against Lord Brandon on a charge of treason.‡ The accused was convicted, and Rumsey was still allowed to correspond confidentially with the Prime Minister,§ to whom he even applied for money. But when the infamy of Rumsey became notorious, and when Saxton had perjured himself on the subsequent trial of Lord Delamere, it was thought proper to pardon Lord Brandon, against whom no testimony remained but that of Lord Grey, who, when he made his confession, is said to have stipulated that no man should be put to death on his evidence. But Brandon was not enlarged on bail till fourteen months, nor was his pardon completed till two years after his trial.*

The only considerable trial which remained was that of Lord Delamere, before the Lord Steward (Jeffreys) and thirty peers. Though this nobleman was obnoxious and formidable to the Court, the proof of the falsehood and infamy of Saxton, the principal witness against him, was so complete, that he was unanimously acquitted;—a remarkable and almost solitary exception to the prevalent proceedings of courts of law at that time, arising partly from a proof of the falsehood of the charge more clear than can often be expected, and partly perhaps from the fellow-feeling of the judges with the prisoner, and from the greater reproach to which an unjust judgment exposes its authors, when in a conspicuous station.

The administration of justice in state prosecutions is one of the surest tests of good government. The judicial proceedings which have been thus carefully and circumstantially related afford a specimen of those evils from which England was delivered by the Revolution. As these acts were done with the aid of juries, and without the censure of Parliament, they also afford a fatal proof that judicial forms and constitutional establishments may be rendered unavailing by the subserviency or the prejudices of those who are appointed to carry them into effect. The wisest institutions may become a dead letter, and may even, for a time, be converted into a shelter and an instrument of tyranny, when the sense of justice and the love of liberty are weakened in the minds of a people.

CHAPTER II.

Dismissal of Halifax.—Meeting of Parliament.—Debates on the Address.—Prorogation of Parliament.—Habeas Corpus Act.—State of the Catholic Party.—Character of the Queen.—Of Catherine Sedley.—Attempt to Support the Dispensing Power by a Judgment of a Court of Law.—Godden V. Hales.—Consideration of the Arguments.—Attack on the Church.—Establishment of the Court of Commissioners for Ecclesiastical Causes.—Advancement of Catholics to Offices.—Intercourse with Rome.

THE general appearance of submission which followed the suppression of the revolt, and the punishment of the revolters, encouraged the King to remove from office the Marquis of Halifax, with whose liberal opinions he had recently as well as early been dissatisfied, and whom he suffered to remain in place at his accession, only as an example that old opponents might atone for their of-

* Sunderland to Jeffreys, 14th Sept. 1685.—State Paper Office.

† Commons' Journals, 1st May, 1689.

‡ Narcissus Luttrell, 25th Nov., 1685; which, though very short, is more full than any published account of Lord Brandon's trial.

§ Rumsey to Lord Sunderland, Oct. 1685, and Jan. 1686.—State Paper Office.

* Narcissus Luttrell, Jan. and Oct. 1687.

fences by compliance.* A different policy was adopted in a situation of more strength. As the King found that Halifax would not comply with his projects, he determined to dismiss him before the meeting of Parliament;—an act of vigour which it was thought would put an end to division in his councils, and prevent discontented ministers from countenancing a resistance to his measures. When he announced this resolution to Barillon, he added, that "his design was to obtain a repeal of the Test and Habeas Corpus Acts, of which the former was destructive of the Catholic religion, and the other of the royal authority; that Halifax had not the firmness to support the good cause, and that he would have less power of doing harm if he were disgraced."† James had been advised to delay the dismissal till after the session, that the opposition of Halifax might be moderated, if not silenced, by the restraints of high office; but he thought that his authority would be more strengthened, by an example of a determination to keep no terms with any one who did not show an unlimited compliance with his wishes. "I do not suppose," said the King to Barillon with a smile, "that the King your master will be sorry for the removal of Halifax. I know that it will mortify the ministers of the allies." Nor was he deceived in either of these respects. The news was received with satisfaction by Louis, and with dismay by the ministers of the Empire, of Spain, and of Holland, who lost their only advocate in the councils of England.‡ It excited wonder and alarm among those Englishmen who were zealously attached to their religion and liberty.§ Though Lord Halifax had no share in the direction of public affairs since the King's accession, his removal was an important event in the eye of the public, and gave him a popularity which he preserved by independent and steady conduct during the sequel of James' reign.

It is remarkable that, on the meeting of Parliament (9th November) little notice was taken of the military and judicial excesses in the West. Sir Edward Seymour applauded the punishment of the rebels; and Waller alone, a celebrated wit, an ingenious poet; the father of parliamentary oratory, and one of the refiners of the English language, though now in his eightieth year, arraigned the violence of the soldiers with a spirit still unextinguished. He probably intended to excite a discussion which might gradually have reached the more deliberate and inexcusable faults of the judges. But the opinions and policy of his audience defeated his generous purpose. The prevalent party looked with little disapprobation on severities which fell on Nonconformists and supposed Republicans. Many might be base enough to feel little compassion for sufferers in the humbler classes of society; some were probably silenced by a pusillanimous dread of being said to be the abbettors of rebels; and all must have been, in some measure, influenced by an undue and excessive degree of that wholesome respect for judicial proceedings, which is one of the characteristic virtues of a free country. This disgraceful silence is, perhaps, somewhat extenuated by the slow circulation of intelligence at that period; by the censorship which imposed silence on the press, or enabled the ruling party to circulate falsehood through its means; and by the eagerness of all parties for a discussion of the alarming tone and principles of the speech from the throne.

The King began his speech by observing that the late events must convince every one that the militia was not sufficient, and that nothing but a good force of well-disciplined troops, in constant pay, could secure the government against enemies abroad and at home; and that for this purpose he had increased their number, and now asked a supply for the great charge of maintaining them. "Let no man take exception," he continued, "that there are some officers in the army not qualified, according to the late tests, for their employments; the gentlemen are, I must tell you, most of them well known to me; they have approved the loyalty of their principles by their practice: and I will deal plainly with you, that after having had the benefit of their services in such a time of need and danger, I will neither expose them to disgrace, nor myself to the want of them, if there should be another rebellion to make them necessary to me." Nothing but the firmest reliance on the submissive disposition of the Parliament could have induced James to announce to them his determination to bid defiance to the laws. He probably imagined that the boldness with which he asserted the power of the crown would be applauded by many, and endured by most of the members of such a Parliament. But never was there a more remarkable example of the use of a popular assembly, however ill composed, in extracting from the disunion, jealousy, and ambitition of the victorious enemies of liberty, a new opposition to the dangerous projects of the Crown. The vices of politicians were converted into an imperfect substitute for virtue; and though the friends of the constitution were few and feeble, the inevitable divisions of their opponents in some degree supplied their place.

The disgrace of Lord Halifax disheartened and even offended some supporters of Government. Sir Thomas Clarges, a determined Tory, was displeased at the merited removal of his nephew, the Duke of Albemarle, from the command of the army against Monmouth. Nottingham, a man of talent and ambition, more a Tory than a courtier, was dissatisfied with his own exclusion from office, and jealous of Rochester's ascendency

* Barillon, 5th March, 1685.—Fox, app. p. xlvii. [In these dates the new style only is observed.—Ed.]

† Barillon, 20th October.—Ibid. p. cxxvii.

‡ Barillon, 5th November.—Ibid. p. cxxx.

§ Barillon, 1st March.—Ibid. p. xxxviii.

over the Church party. His relation Finch, though solicitor-general, took a part against the Court. The projects of the Crown were thwarted by the friends of Lord Danby, who had forfeited all hopes of the King's favour by communicating the Popish Plot to the House of Commons, and by his share in the marriage of the Princess Mary with the Prince of Orange. Had the King's first attack been made on civil liberty, the Opposition might have been too weak to embolden all these secret and dispersed discontents to display themselves, and to combine together. But the attack on the exclusive privileges of the Church of England, while it alienated the main force of the Crown, touched a point on which all the subdivisions of discontented Tories professed to agree, and afforded them a specious pretext for opposing the King, without seeming to deviate from their ancient principles. They were gradually disposed to seek or accept the assistance of the defeated Whigs, and the names of Sir Richard Temple, Sir John Lowther, Sergeant Maynard, and Mr. Hampden, appear at last more and more often in the proceedings. Thus admirably does a free constitution not only command the constant support of the wise and virtuous, but often compel the low jealousies and mean intrigues of disappointed ambition to contend for its preservation. The consideration of the King's speech was postponed for three days, in spite of a motion for its immediate consideration by Lord Preston, a secretary of state.

In the committee of the whole House on the speech, which occurred on the 12th, two resolutions were adopted, of which the first was friendly, and the second was adverse, to the Government. It was resolved "that a supply be granted to his Majesty," and "that a bill be brought in to render the militia more useful." The first of these propositions has seldom been opposed since the government has become altogether dependent on the annual grants of Parliament; it was more open to debate on a proposal for extraordinary aid, and it gave rise to some important observations. Clarges declared he had voted against the Exclusion, because he did not believe its supporters when they foretold that a Popish king would have a Popish army. "I am afflicted greatly at this breach of our liberties; what is struck at here is our all." Sir Edward Seymour observed, with truth, that to dispense with the Test was to release the King from all law. Encouraged by the bold language of these Tories, old Serjeant Maynard said, that the supply was asked for the maintenance of an army which was to be officered against a law made, not for the punishment of Papists, but for the defence of Protestants. The accounts of these important debates are so scanty, that we may, without much presumption, suppose the venerable lawyer to have at least alluded to the recent origin of the Test (to which the King had disparagingly adverted in his speech), as the strongest reason for its strict observance. Had it been an ancient law, founded on general considerations of policy, it might have been excusable to relax its rigour from a regard to the circumstances and feelings of the King. But having been recently provided as a security against the specific dangers apprehended from his accession to the throne, it was to the last degree unreasonable to remove or suspend it at the moment when those very dangers had reached their highest pitch. Sir Richard Temple spoke warmly against standing armies, and of the necessity of keeping the Crown dependent on parliamentary grants. He proposed the resolution for the improvement of the militia, with which the courtiers concurred. Clarges moved as an amendment on the vote of supply, the words, for the additional forces,"—to throw odium on the ministerial vote; but this adverse amendment was negatived by a majority of seventy in a house of three hundred and eighty-one. On the 13th, the ministers proposed to instruct the committee of the whole House on the King's speech, to consider, first, the paragraph of the speech which contained the demand of supply. They were defeated by a majority of a hundred and eighty-three to a hundred and eighty-two; and the committee resolved to take into consideration, first, the succeeding paragraph, which related to the officers illegally employed.* On the 16th, an address was brought up from the committee, setting forth the legal incapacity of the Catholic officers, which could only be removed by an Act of Parliament, offering to indemnify them from the penalties they had incurred, but, as their continuance would be taken to be a dispensing with the law, praying that the King would be pleased not to continue them in their employments. The House, having substituted the milder words, "that he would give such directions therein as that no apprehensions or jealousies might remain in the hearts of his subjects," unanimously adopted the address. A supply of seven hundred thousand pounds was voted;—a medium between twelve hundred thousand required by ministers, and two hundred thousand proposed by the most rigid of their opponents. The danger of standing armies to liberty, and the wisdom of such limited grants as should compel the Crown to recur soon and often to the House of Commons, were the general arguments used for the smaller sum. The courtiers urged the ex-

* "The Earl of Middleton, then a secretary of state, seeing many go out upon the division against the Court who were in the service of Government, went down to the bar and reproached them to their faces for voting as they did. He said to a Captain Kendal, 'Sir, have you not a troop of horse in his Majesty's service?' 'Yes, sir,' said the other: 'but my brother died last night, and has left me seven hundred pounds a year.' This I had from my uncle, the first Lord Onslow, who was then a member of the House, and present. This incident upon one vote very likely saved the nation.—Burnet (Oxford, 1823), vol. iii. p. 86. Note by Speaker Onslow.

ample of the late revolt, the superiority of disciplined troops over an inexperienced militia, the necessity arising from the like practice of all other states, and the revolution in the art of war, which had rendered proficiency in it unattainable, except by those who studied and practised it as the profession of their lives. The most practical observation was that of Sir William Trumbull, who suggested that the grant should be annual, to make the existence of the army annually dependent on the pleasure of Parliament. The ministers, taking advantage of the secrecy of foreign negotiations, ventured to assert that a formidable army in the hands of the King was the only check on the ambition of France; though they knew that their master was devoted to Louis XIV., to whom he had been recently suing for a secret subsidy in the most abject language of supplication.* When the address was presented, the King answered, with a warmth and anger very unusual on such occasions,† that "he did not expect such an address; that he hoped his reputation would have inspired such a confidence in him; but that, whatever they might do, he should adhere to all his promises." The reading of this answer in the House the next day produced a profound silence for some minutes. A motion was made by Mr. Wharton to take it into consideration, on which Mr. John Cooke said, "We are Englishmen, and ought not to be frightened from our duty by a few hard words."‡ Both these gentlemen were Whigs, who were encouraged to speak freely by the symptoms of vigour which the House had shown; but they soon discovered that they had mistaken the temper of their colleagues; for the majority, still faithful to the highest pretensions of the Crown whenever the Established Church was not averse to them, committed Mr. Cooke to the Tower, though he disavowed all disrespectful intention, and begged pardon of the King and the House. Notwithstanding the King's answer, they proceeded to provide means of raising the supply, and they resumed the consideration of a bill for the naturalisation of French Protestants,—a tolerant measure, the introduction of which the zealous partisans of the Church had, at first, resisted, as they afterwards destroyed the greater part of its benefit by confining it to those who should conform to the Establishment.§ The motion for considering the King's speech was not pursued, which, together with the proceeding on supply, seemed to imply a submission to the menacing answer of James; arising principally from the subservient character of the majority, but, probably, in some, from a knowledge of the vigorous measures about to be proposed in the House of Lords.

At the opening of the Session, that House had contented themselves with general thanks to the King for his speech, without any allusion to its contents. Jeffreys, in delivering the King's answer, affected to treat this parliamentary courtesy as an approval of the substance of the speech. Either on that or on the preceding occasion, it was said by Lord Halifax or Lord Devonshire (for it is ascribed to both), "that they had now more reason than ever to give thanks to his Majesty for having dealt so plainly with them." The House, not called upon to proceed as the other House was by the demand of supply, continued inactive for a few days, till they were roused by the imperious answer of the King to the Commons. On the 19th, the day of that answer, Lord Devonshire moved to take into consideration the dangerous consequences of an army kept up against law. He was supported by Halifax, by Nottingham, and by Anglesea, who, in a very advanced age, still retained that horror of the yoke of Rome, which he had found means to reconcile with frequent acquiescence in the civil policy of Charles and James. Lord Mordaunt, more known as Earl of Peterborough, signalised himself by the youthful spirit of his speech. "Let us not," he said, "like the House of Commons, speak of jealousy and distrust: ambiguous measures inspire these feelings. What we now see is not ambiguous. A standing army is on foot, filled with officers, who cannot be allowed to serve without overthrowing the laws. To keep up a standing army when there is neither civil nor foreign war, is to establish that arbitrary government which Englishmen hold in such just abhorrence." Compton, Bishop of London, a prelate of noble birth and military spirit, who had been originally an officer in the Guards, spoke for the motion in the name of all his brethren on the episcopal bench, who considered the security of the Church as involved in the issue of the question. He was influenced not only by the feelings of his order, but by his having been the preceptor of the Princesses Mary and Anne, who were deeply interested in the maintenance of the Protestant Church, as well as conscientiously attached to it. Jeffreys was the principal speaker on the side of the Court. He urged the thanks already voted as an approval of the speech. His scurrilous invectives, and the tones and gestures of menace with which he was accustomed to overawe juries, roused the indignation, instead of commanding the acquiescence, of the Lords. As this is a deportment which cuts off all honourable retreat, the contemporary accounts are very probable which represent him as sinking at once from insolence to meanness. His defeat must have been signal; for, in an unusually full House of

* Barillon, 16th July, 1685.—Fox, app p. cix. "Le Roi me dit que si V. M. avoit quelque chose à désirer de lui, il iroit au devant de tout ce qui peut plaire à V. M.; qu'il avoit été élevé en France, et mangé le pain de V. M.; *que son cœur étoit François.*" Only six weeks before (30th May), James had told his parliament that "he had a *true English heart.*"

† Reresby, p. 218. Sir John Reresby, being a member of the House, was probably present.

‡ Commons' Journals, 18th Nov.

§ Ibid., 16th June, 1st July.

Lords,* after so violent an opposition by the Chancellor of England, the motion for taking the address into consideration was, on the 23d, carried without a division.†

On the next day the King prorogued the Parliament; which never again was assembled but for the formalities of successive prorogations, by which its legal existence was prolonged for two years. By this act he lost the subsidy of seven hundred thousand pounds: but his situation had become difficult. Though money was employed to corrupt some of the opponents of his measures, the Opposition was daily gaining strength.‡ By rigorous economy, by diverting parliamentary aids from the purposes for which they were granted, the King had the means of maintaining the army, though his ministers had solemnly affirmed that he had not.§ He was full of maxims for the necessity of firmness and the dangers of concession, which were mistaken by others, and perhaps by himself, for proofs of a vigorous character. He had advanced too far to recede with tolerable dignity. The energy manifested by the House of Lords would have compelled even the submissive Commons to co-operate with them, which might have given rise to a more permanent coalition of the High Church party with the friends of liberty. A suggestion had been thrown out in the Lords to desire the opinion of the judges on the right of the King to commission the Catholic officers;‖ and it was feared that the terrors of impeachment might, during the sitting of Parliament, draw an opinion from these magistrates against the prerogative, which might afterwards prove irrevocable. To reconcile Parliament to the officers became daily more hopeless: to sacrifice those who had adhered to the King in a time of need appeared to be an example dangerous to all his projects, whether of enlarging his prerogative, or of securing, and, perhaps, finally establishing, his religion.

Thus ended the active proceedings of a Parliament which, in all that did not concern the Church, justified the most sanguine hopes that James could have formed of their submission to the Court, as well as their attachment to the monarchy. A body of men so subservient as that House of Commons could hardly be brought together by any mode of election or appointment; and James was aware that, by this angry prorogation, he had rendered it difficult for himself for a long time to meet another Parliament. The Session had lasted only eleven days; during which the eyes of Europe had been anxiously turned towards their proceedings. Louis XIV., not entirely relying on the sincerity or steadiness of James, was fearful that he might yield to the Allies or to his people, and instructed Barillon in that case to open a negotiation with leading members of the Commons, that they might embarrass the policy of the King, if it became adverse to France.* Spain and Holland, on the other hand, hoped, that any compromise between the King and Parliament would loosen the ties that bound the former to France. It was even hoped that he might form a triple alliance with Spain and Sweden, and large sums of money were secretly offered to him to obtain his accession to such an alliance.† Three days before the meeting of Parliament, had arrived in London Monsignor D'Adda, a Lombard prelate of distinction, as the known, though then unavowed, minister of the See of Rome,‡ which was divided between the interest of the Catholic Church of England and the animosity of Innocent XI. against Louis XIV. All these solicitudes, and precautions, and expectations, were suddenly dispelled by the unexpected rupture between James and his Parliament.

From the temper and opinions of that Parliament it is reasonable to conclude, that the King would have been more successful if he had chosen to make his first attack on the Habeas Corpus Act, instead of directing it against the Test. Both these laws were then only of a few years' standing; and he, as well as his brother, held them both in abhorrence. The Test gave exclusive privileges to the Established Church, and was, therefore, dear to the adherents of that powerful body. The Habeas Corpus Act was not then the object of that attachment and veneration which experience of its unspeakable benefits for a hundred and fifty years has since inspired. The most ancient of our fundamental laws had declared the princi-

* The attendance was partly caused by a call of the House, ordered for the trials of Lords Stamford and Delamere. There were present on the 19th November, seventy-five temporal and twenty spiritual lords. On the call, two days before, it appeared that forty were either minors, abroad, or confined by sickness; six had sent proxies; two were prisoners for treason; and thirty absent without any special reason, of whom the great majority were disabled as Catholics: so that very few peers, legally and physically capable of attendance, were absent.

† Barillon, 3d Dec.—Fox MSS. This is the only distinct narrative of the proceedings of this important and decisive day. Burnet was then on the Continent, but I have endeavoured to combine his account with that of Barillon.

‡ Barillon, 26th Nov.—Fox, app. p. cxxxix.

§ Barillon, 13th Dec.—Fox MSS. The expenses of the army of Charles had been 280,000*l.*; that of James was 600,000*l.* The difference of 320,000*l.* was, according to Barillon, thus provided for: 100,000*l.*, the income of James as Duke of York, which he still preserved; 800,000*l.* granted to pay the debts of Charles, which, *as the King was to pay the debts as he thought fit*, would yield for some years 100,000*l.*; 800,000*l.* granted for the navy and the arsenals, on which the King *might proceed slowly, or even do nothing;* 400,000*l.* for the suppression of the rebellion. As these last funds were not to come into the Exchequer for some years, they were estimated as producing annually more than sufficient to cover the deficiency.

‖ Barillon, 10th Dec.—Fox MSS.

* Louis to Barillon, 19th Nov.—Fox, app. p. cxxxvi.

† Barillon, 26th Nov.—Fox, app. p. cxxxix.

‡ D'Adda to the Pope 19th Nov.—D'Adda MSS.

ple that no freeman could be imprisoned without legal authority.* The immemorial antiquity of the writ of Habeas Corpus,—an order of a court of justice to a jailer to bring the body of a prisoner before them, that there might be an opportunity of examining whether his apprehension and detention were legal,—seems to prove that this principal was coeval with the law of England. In irregular times, however, it had been often violated; and the judges under Charles I. pronounced a judgment,† which, if it had not been condemned by the Petition of Right,‡ would have vested in the Crown a legal power of arbitrary imprisonment. By the statute which abolished the Star Chamber, the Parliament of 1641§ made some important provisions to facilitate deliverance from illegal imprisonment. For eleven years Lord Shaftesbury struggled to obtain a law which should complete the securities of personal liberty; and at length that great though not blameless man obtained the object of his labours, and bestowed on his country the most perfect security against arbitrary imprisonment which has ever been enjoyed by any society of men.‖ It has banished that most dangerous of all modes of oppression from England. It has effected that great object as quietly as irresistibly; it has never in a single instance been resisted or evaded; and it must be the model of all nations who aim at securing that personal liberty without which no other liberty can subsist. But in the year 1685, it appeared to the predominant party an odious novelty, an experiment untried in any other nation,—carried through, in a period of popular frenzy, during the short triumph of a faction hostile to Church and State, and by him who was the most obnoxious of all the demagogues of the age. There were then, doubtless, many,—perhaps the majority,—of the partisans of authority who believed, with Charles and James, that to deprive a government of all power to imprison the suspected and the dangerous, unless there was legal ground of charge against them, was incompatible with the peace of society; and this opinion was the more dangerous because it was probably conscientious.¶ In this state of things it may seem singular that James did not first propose the repeal of the Habeas Corpus Act, by which he would have gained the means of silencing opposition to all his other projects. What the fortunate circumstances were which pointed his attack against the Test, we are not enabled by contemporary evidence to ascertain. He contemplated that measure with peculiar resentment, as a personal insult to himself, and as chiefly, if not solely, intended as a safeguard against the dangers apprehended from his succession. He considered it as the most urgent object of his policy to obtain a repeal of it; which would enable him to put the administration, and especially the army, into the hands of those who were devoted by the strongest of all ties to his service, and whose power, honour, and even safety, were involved in his success. An army composed of Catholics must have seemed the most effectual of all the instruments of power in his hands; and it is no wonder that he should hasten to obtain it. Had he been a lukewarm or only a professed Catholic, an armed force, whose interests were the same with his own, might reasonably have been considered as that which it was in the first place necessary to secure. Charles II., with a loose belief in Popery, and no zeal for it, was desirous of strengthening its interests, in order to enlarge his own power. As James was a conscientious and zealous Catholic, it is probable that he was influenced in every measure of his government by religion, as well as ambition. Both these motives coincided in their object: his absolute power was the only security for his religion, and a Catholic army was the most effectual instrument for the establishment of absolute power. In such a case of combined motives, it might have been difficult for himself to determine which predominated on any single occasion. Sunderland, whose sagacity and religious indifference are alike unquestionable, observed to Barillon, that on mere principles of policy James could have no object more at heart than to strengthen the Catholic religion;*—an observation which, as long as the King himself continued to be a Catholic, seems, in the hostile temper which then prevailed among all sects, to have had great weight.

The best reasons for human actions are often not their true motives: but, in spite of the event, it does not seem difficult to defend the determination of the King on those grounds, merely political, which, doubtless, had a considerable share in producing it. It is not easy to ascertain how far his plans in favour of his religion at that time extended. A great division of opinion prevailed among the Catholics themselves on this subject. The most considerable and opulent laymen of that communion, willing to secure moderate advantages, and desirous to employ their superiority with such forbearance as might provoke no new severities under a Protestant successor, would have been content with a repeal of the penal laws, without insisting on an abrogation of the Test. The friends

* Magna Charta, c. 29.

† The famous case of commitments "by the special command of the King," which last words the Court of King's Bench determined to be a sufficient cause for detaining a prisoner in custody, without any specification of an offence.—State Trials, vol. iii. p. 1.

‡ 3 Car. I. c. i.

§ 16 Car. I. c. 10.

‖ 31 C. II. c. 2.

¶ James retained this opinion till his death.—"It was a great misfortune to the people, as well as to the Crown, the passing of the Habeas Corpus Act, since it obliges the Crown to keep a greater force on foot to preserve the government, and encourages disaffected, turbulent, and unquiet spirits to carry on their wicked designs: it was contrived and carried on by the Earl of Shaftesbury to that intent."—Life, vol. ii. p. 621.

* Barillon, 16th July.—Fox, app. p. ciii.

of Spain and Austria, with all the enemies of the French connection, inclined strongly to a policy which, by preventing a rupture between the King and Parliament, might enable, and, perhaps, dispose him to espouse the cause of European independence. The Sovereign Pontiff himself was of this party; and the wary politicians of the court of Rome advised their English friends to calm and slow proceedings: though the Papal minister, with a circumspection and reserve required by the combination of a theological with a diplomatic character, abstained from taking any open part in the division, where it would have been hard for him to escape the imputation of being either a lukewarm Catholic or an imprudent counsellor. The Catholic lords who were ambitious of office, the Jesuits, and especially the King's confessor, together with all the partisans of France, supported extreme counsels better suited to the temper of James, whose choice of political means was guided by a single maxim,—that violence (which he confounded with vigour) was the only safe policy for an English monarch. Their most specious argument was the necessity of taking such decisive measures to strengthen the Catholics during the King's life as would effectually secure them against the hostility of his successor.*

The victory gained by this party over the moderate Catholics, as well as the Protestant Tories, was rendered more speedy and decisive by some intrigues of the Court, which have not hitherto been fully known to historians. Mary of Este, the consort of James, was married at the age of fifteen, and had been educated in such gross ignorance, that she never had heard of the name of England until it was made known to her on that occasion. She had been trained to a rigorous observance of all the practices of her religion, which sunk more deeply into her heart, and more constantly influenced her conduct, than was usual among the Italian princesses. On her arrival in England, she betrayed a childish aversion to James, which was quickly converted into passionate fondness. But neither her attachment nor her beauty could fix the heart of that inconstant prince, who reconciled a warm zeal for his religion with an habitual indulgence in those pleasures which it most forbids. Her life was embittered by the triumph of mistresses, and by the frequency of her own perilous and unfruitful pregnancies. Her most formidable rival, at the period of the accession, was Catherine Sedley, a woman of few personal attractions,† who inherited the wit and vivacity of her father, Sir Charles Sedley, which she unsparingly exercised on the priests and opinions of her royal lover. Her character was frank, her deportment bold, and her pleasantries more amusing than refined.* Soon after his accession, James was persuaded to relinquish his intercourse with her; and, though she retained her lodgings in the palace, he did not see her for several months. The connection was then secretly renewed, and, in the first fervour of a revived passion, the King offered to give her the title of Countess of Dorchester. She declined this invidious distinction, assuring him that, by provoking the anger of the Queen and of the Catholics, it would prove her ruin. He, however, insisted; and she yielded, upon condition that, if he was ever again prevailed upon to dissolve their connection, he should come to her to announce his determination in person.† The title produced the effects she had foreseen. Mary, proud of her beauty, still enamoured of her husband, and full of religious horror at the vices of Mrs. Sedley, gave way to the most clamorous excesses of sorrow and anger at the promotion of her competitor. She spoke to the King with a violence for which she long afterwards reproached herself as a grievous fault. At one time she said to him, "Is it possible that you are ready to sacrifice a crown for your faith, and cannot discard a mistress for it? Will you for such a passion lose the merit of your sacrifices?" On another occasion she exclaimed, "Give me my dowry, make her Queen of England, and let me never see her more."‡ Her transports of grief sometimes betrayed her to foreign ministers; and she neither ate nor spoke with the King at the public dinners of the Court.§ The zeal of the Queen for the Catholic religion, and the profane jests of Lady Dorchester against its doctrines and ministers, had rendered them the leaders of the Popish and Protestant parties at Court. The Queen was supported by the Catholic clergy, who, with whatever indulgence their order had sometimes treated regal frailty, could not remain neuter in a contest between an orthodox Queen and an heretical mistress. These intrigues early mingled with the designs of the two ministers, who still appeared

* Barillon, 12th Nov.—Fox. app. p. cxxxiv.—Barillon, 31st Dec.—Fox MSS. Burnet, vol. i. p. 661. The coincidence of Burnet with the more ample account of Barillon is an additional confirmation of the substantial accuracy of the honest prelate.

† "Elle a beaucoup d'esprit et de la vivacité, mais elle n'a plus aucune beauté, et est d'une extrême maigreur." Barillon, 7th Feb. 1686.—Fox MSS. The insinuation of decline is somewhat singular, as her father was then only forty-six.

* These defects are probably magnified in the verses of Lord Dorset:

"Dorinda's sparkling wit and eyes
United, cast too fierce a light,
Which blazes high, but quickly dies,
Pains not the heart, but hurts the sight.

"Love is a calmer, gentler joy;
Smooth are his looks, and soft his pace:
Her Cupid is a blackguard boy,
That runs his link full in your face."

† D'Adda to Cardinal Cybo, 1st Feb.—D'Adda MSS.

‡ Mémoires Historiques de la Reine d'Angleterre, a MS. formerly in possession of the nuns of Chaillot, since in the Archives Générales de France.

§ Bonrepaux, 7th Feb. 1686, MSS. Evelyn, vol. i. p. 584.

to have equal influence in the royal counsels. Lord Rochester, who had felt the decline of the King's confidence from the day of Monmouth's defeat, formed the project of supplanting Lord Sunderland, and of recovering his ascendant in public affairs through the favour of the mistress. Having lived in a court of mistresses, and maintained himself in office by compliance with them,* he thought it unlikely that wherever a favourite mistress existed she could fail to triumph over a queen. As the brother of the first Duchess of York, Mary did not regard him with cordiality: as the leader of the Church party, he was still more obnoxious to her. He and his lady were the principal counsellors of the mistress. They had secretly advised the King to confer on her the title of honour,—probably to excite the Queen to such violence as might widen the rupture between her and the King; and they declared so openly for her as to abstain for several days, during the heat of the contest, from paying their respects to the Queen;—a circumstance much remarked at a time when the custom was still observed, which had been introduced by the companionable humour of Charles, for the principal nobility to appear almost daily at Court. Sunderland, already connected with the Catholic favourites, was now more than ever compelled to make common cause with the Queen. His great strength lay in the priests; but he also called in the aid of Madame Mazarin, a beautiful woman, of weak understanding, but practised in intrigue, who had been sought in marriage by Charles II. during his exile, refused by him after his Restoration, and who, on her arrival in England, ten years after, failed in the more humble attempt to become his mistress.

The exhortations of the clergy, seconded by the beauty, the affection, and the tears of the Queen, prevailed, after a severe struggle, over the ascendant of Lady Dorchester. James sent Lord Middleton, one of his secretaries of state, to desire that she would leave Whitehall, and go to Holland, to which country a yacht was in readiness to convey her. In a letter written by his own hand, he acknowledged that he violated his promise; but excused himself by saying, that he was conscious of not possessing firmness enough to stand the test of an interview. She immediately retired to her house in St. James' Square, and offered to go to Scotland or Ireland, or to her father's estate in Kent; but protested against going to the Continent, where means might be found of immuring her in a convent for life. When threatened with being forcibly carried abroad, she appealed to the Great Charter against such an invasion of the liberty of the subject. The contest continued for some time; and the King's advisers consented that she should go to Ireland, where Rochester's brother was Lord Lieutenant. She warned the King of his danger, and freely told him, that, if he followed the advice of Catholic zealots, he would lose his crown. She represented herself as the Protestant martyr; and boasted, many years afterwards, that she had neither changed her religion, like Lord Sunderland, nor even agreed to be present at a disputation concerning its truth, like Lord Rochester.* After the complete victory of the Queen, Rochester still preserved his place, and affected to represent himself as wholly unconcerned in the affair. Sunderland kept on decent terms with his rival, and dissembled his resentment at the abortive intrigue for his removal. But the effects of it were decisive: it secured the power of Sunderland, rendered the ascendency of the Catholic counsellors irresistible, gave them a stronger impulse towards violent measures, and struck a blow at the declining credit of Rochester, from which it never recovered. The removal of Halifax was the first step towards the new system of administration, the defeat of Rochester was the second. In the course of these contests, the Bishop of London was removed from the Privy Council for his conduct in the House of Peers; several members of the House of Commons were dismissed from military as well as civil offices for their votes in Parliament; and the place of Lord President of the Council was bestowed on Sunderland, to add a dignity which was then thought wanting to his efficient office of Secretary of State.†

The Government now attempted to obtain, by the judgments of courts of law, that power of appointing Catholic officers which Parliament had refused to sanction. Instances had occurred in which the Crown had dispensed with the penalties of certain laws; and the recognition of this dispensing power, in the case of the Catholic officers, by the judges, appeared to be an easy mode of establishing the legality of their appointments. The King was to grant to every Catholic officer a dispensation from the penalties of the statutes which, when adjudged to be agreeable to law by a competent tribunal, might supply the place of a repeal of the Test Act. To obtain the judgment, it was agreed that an action for the penalties should be collusively brought against one of these officers, which would afford an opportunity to the judges to determine that the dispensation was legal. The plan had been conceived at an earlier period, since (as has been mentioned) one of the reasons of the prorogation was an

* Carte, Life of Ormonde, vol. ii. p. 553. The old duke, high-minded as he was, commended the prudent accommodation of Rochester.

* Halifax MSS.

† These intrigues are very fully related by Bonrepaux, a French minister of talent, at that time sent on a secret mission to London, and by Barillon in his ordinary communications to the King. The despatches of the French ministers afford a new proof of the good information of Burnet; but neither he nor Reresby was aware of the connection of the intrigue with the triumph of Sunderland over Rochester.

apprehension lest the terrors of Parliament might obtain from the judges an irrevocable opinion against the prerogative. No doubt seems to have been entertained of the compliance of magistrates, who owed their station to the King, who had recently incurred so much odium in his service, and who were removable at his pleasure.* He thought it necessary, however, to ascertain their sentiments. His expectations of their unanimity were disappointed. Sir John Jones, who had presided at the trial of Mrs. Gaunt, Montague, who had accompanied Jeffreys in his circuit, Sir Job Charlton, a veteran royalist of approved zeal for the prerogative, together with Neville, a baron of the Exchequer, declared their inability to comply with the desires of the King. Jones answered him with dignity worthy of more spotless conduct:—"I am not sorry to be removed. It is a relief to a man old and worn out as I am. But I am sorry that your Majesty should have expected a judgment from me which none but indigent, ignorant, or ambitious men could give." James, displeased at this freedom, answered, that he would find twelve judges of his opinion. "Twelve judges, Sir," replied Jones, "you may find; but hardly twelve lawyers." However justly these judges are to be condemned for their former disregard to justice and humanity, they deserve great commendation for having, on this critical occasion, retained their respect for law. James possessed that power of dismissing his judges which Louis XIV. did not enjoy; and he immediately exercised it by removing the uncomplying magistrates, together with two others who held the same obnoxious principles. On the 21st of April, the day before the courts were to assemble in Westminster for their ordinary term, the new judges were appointed; among whom, by a singular hazard, was a brother of the immortal John Milton, named Christopher, then in the seventieth year of his age, who is not known to have had any other pretension except that of having secretly conformed to the Church of Rome.†

Sir Edward Hales, a Kentish gentleman who had been secretly converted to Popery at Oxford by his tutor, Obadiah Walker, of University College (himself a celebrated convert), was selected to be the principal actor in the legal pageant for which the Bench had been thus prepared. He was publicly reconciled to the Church of Rome on the 11th of November, 1685;* he was appointed to the command of a regiment on the 28th of the same month; and a dispensation passed the Great Seal on the 9th of January following, to enable him to hold his commission without either complying with the conditions or incurring the penalties of the statute. On the 16th of June, the case was tried in the Court of King's Bench in the form of an action brought against him by Godden, his coachman, to recover the penalty granted by the statute to a common informer, for holding a military commission without having taken the oaths or the sacrament. The facts were admitted; the defence rested on the dispensation, and the case turned on its validity. Northey, the counsel for Godden, argued the case so faintly and coldly, that he scarcely dissembled his desire and expectation of a judgment against his pretended client. Sir Edward Herbert, the Chief Justice, a man of virtue, but without legal experience or knowledge, who had adopted the highest monarchical principles, had been one of the secret advisers of the exercise of the dispensing power: in his court he accordingly treated the validity of the dispensation as a point of no difficulty, but of such importance that it was proper for him to consult all the other judges respecting it. On the 21st of June, after only five days of seeming deliberation had been allowed to a question on the decision of which the liberties of the kingdom at that moment depended, he delivered the opinion of all the judges except Street,—who finally dissented from his brethren,—in favour of the dispensation. At a subsequent period, indeed, two other judges, Powell and Atkyns, affirmed that they had dissented, and another, named Lutwych, declared that he had only assented with limitations.† But as these magistrates did not protest at the time against Herbert's statement,—as they delayed their public dissent until it had become dishonourable, and perhaps unsafe, to have agreed with the majority, no respect is due to their conduct, even if their assertion should be believed. Street, who gained great popularity by his strenuous resistance,‡ remained a judge during the whole reign of James; he was not admitted to the presence of King William,§ nor re-appointed after the Revolution:—circumstances which, combined with some intimations unfavourable to his general character, suggest a painful suspicion, that the only judge who appeared faithful to his trust was, in truth, the basest of all, and that his dissent was prompted or tolerated by the Court,

* "Les juges *declareront* qu'il est la prérogative du Roi de dispenser des peines portées par la loi." Barillon, 3d Dec.—Fox MSS.

† The conversion of Sir Christopher is, indeed, denied by Dodd, the very accurate historian of the English Catholics.—Church History, vol. iii. p. 416. To the former concurrence of all contemporaries we may now add that of Evelyn (vol. i. p. 590,) and Narcissus Luttrell. "All the judges," says the latter, "except Mr. Baron Milton, took the oaths in the Court of Chancery. But he, it said, owns himself a Roman Catholic."—MSS. Diary, 8th June.

* Dodd, vol. iii. p. 451.

† Commons' Journals, 18th June, 1689.

‡ "Mr. Justice Street has lately married a wife, with a good fortune, since his opinion on the dispensing power."—Narcissus Luttrell, Oct. 1686.

§ "The Prince of Orange refused to see Mr. Justice Street. Lord Coote said he was a very ill man."—Clarendon, Diary, 27th December, 1688.

in order to give a false appearance of independence to the acts of the degraded judges.

In shortly stating the arguments which were employed on both sides of this question, it is not within the province of the historian to imitate the laborious minuteness of a lawyer: nor is it consistent with the faith of history to ascribe reasons to the parties more refined and philosophical than could probably have occurred to them, or influenced the judgment of those whom they addressed. The only specious argument of the advocates of prerogative arose from certain cases in which the dispensing power had been exercised by the Crown and apparently sanctioned by courts of justice. The case chiefly relied on was a dispensation from the ancient laws respecting the annual nomination of sheriffs; the last of which, passed in the reign of Henry VI.,* subjected sheriffs, who continued in office longer than a year, to certain penalties, and declared all patents of a contrary tenor, even though they should contain an express dispensation, to be void. Henry VII., in defiance of this statute, had granted a patent to the Earl of Northumberland to be sheriff of that county for life; and the judges in the second year of his reign declared that the Earl's appointment was valid. It has been doubted whether there was any such determination in that case; and it has been urged, with great appearance of reason, that, if made, it proceeded on some exceptions in the statute, and not on the unreasonable doctrine, that an Act of Parliament, to which the King was a party, could not restrain his prerogative. These are, however, considerations which are rather important to the character of those ancient judges than to the authority of the precedent. If they did determine that the King had a right to dispense with a statute, which had by express words deprived him of such a right, so egregiously absurd a judgment, probably proceeding from base subserviency, was more fit to be considered as a warning, than as a precedent by the judges of succeeding times. Two or three subsequent cases were cited in aid of this early precedent. But they either related to the remission of penalties in offences against the revenue, which stood on a peculiar ground, or they were founded on the supposed authority of the first case, and must fall with that unreasonable determination. Neither the unguarded expressions of Sir Edward Coke, nor the admissions incidentally made by Serjeant Glanville, in the debates on the Petition of Right, on a point not material to his argument, could deserve to be seriously discussed as authorities on so momentous a question. Had the precedents been more numerous, and less unreasonable,—had the opinions been more deliberate, and more uniform, they never could be allowed to decide such a case. Though the constitution of England had been from the earliest times founded on the principles of civil and political liberty, the practice of the government, and even the administration of the law had often departed very widely from these sacred principles. In the best times, and under the most regular governments, we find practices to prevail which cannot be reconciled with the principles of a free constitution. During the dark and tumultuous periods of English history, kings had been allowed to do many acts, which, if they were drawn into precedents, would be subversive of public liberty. It is by an appeal to such precedents, that the claim to dangerous prerogatives has been usually justified. The partisans of Charles I. could not deny that the Great Charter had forbidden arbitrary imprisonment, and levy of money without the consent of Parliament. But in the famous cases of imprisonment by the personal command of the King, and of levying a revenue by writs of Ship-money, they thought that they had discovered a means, without denying either of these principles, of universally superseding their application. Neither in these great cases, nor in the equally memorable instance of the dispensing power, were the precedents such as justified the conclusion. If law could ever be allowed to destroy liberty, it would at least be necessary that it should be sanctioned by clear, frequent, and weighty determinations, by general concurrence of opinion after free and full discussion, and by the long usage of good times. But, as in all doubtful cases relating to the construction of the most unimportant statute, we consider its spirit and object; so, when the like questions arise on the most important part of law, called the constitution, we must try obscure and contradictory usage by constitutional principles, instead of sacrificing these principles to such usage. The advocates of prerogative, indeed, betrayed a consciousness, that they were bound to reconcile their precedents with reason; for they, too, appealed to principles which they called "constitutional." A dispensing power, they said, must exist somewhere, to obviate the inconvenience and oppression which might arise from the infallible operation of law; and where can it exist but in the Crown, which exercises the analogous power of pardon? It was answered, that the difficulty never can exist in the English Constitution, where all necessary or convenient powers may be either exercised or conferred by the supreme authority of Parliament. The judgment in favour of the dispensing power was finally rested by the judges on still more general propositions, which, if they had any meaning, were far more alarming than the judgment itself. They declared, that "the Kings of England are sovereign princes; that the laws of England are the King's laws; that, therefore, it is an inseparable prerogative in the King of England to dispense with penal laws in particular cases, and on particular necessary reasons, of which reasons and necessities he

* 23 Hen. VI. c. 7.

is the sole judge; that this is not a trust vested in the King, but the ancient remains of the sovereign power of the Kings of England, which never yet was taken from them, nor can be."* These propositions had either no meaning pertinent to the case, or they led to the establishment of absolute monarchy. The laws were, indeed, said to be the King's, inasmuch as he was the chief and representative of the commonwealth—as they were contradistinguished from those of any other State,—and as he had a principal part in their enactment, and the whole trust of their execution. These expressions were justifiable and innocent, as long as they were employed to denote that decorum and courtesy which are due to the regal magistracy: but if they are considered in any other light, they proved much more than the judges dared to avow. If the King might dispense with the laws, because they were *his* laws, he might for the same reason suspend, repeal, or enact them. The application of these dangerous principles to the Test Act was attended with the peculiar absurdity of attributing to the King a power to dispense with provisions of a law, which had been framed for the avowed and sole purpose of limiting his authority. The law had not hitherto disabled a Catholic from filling the throne. As soon, therefore, as the next person in succession to the Crown was discovered to be a Catholic, it was deemed essential to the safety of the Established religion to take away from the Crown the means of being served by Catholic ministers. The Test Act was passed to prevent a Catholic successor from availing himself of the aid of a party, whose outward badge was adherence to the Roman Catholic religion, and who were seconded by powerful allies in other parts of Europe, in overthrowing the Constitution, the Protestant Church, and at last even the liberty of Protestants to perform their worship and profess their faith. To ascribe to that very Catholic successor the right of dispensing with all the securities provided against such dangers arising from himself, was to impute the most extravagant absurdity to the laws. It might be perfectly consistent with the principle of the Test Act, which was intended to provide against temporary dangers, to propose its repeal under a Protestant prince: but it is altogether impossible that its framers could have considered a power of dispensing with its conditions as being vested in the Catholic successor whom it was meant to bind. Had these objections been weaker, the means employed by the King to obtain a judgment in his favour rendered the whole of this judicial proceeding a gross fraud, in which judges professing impartiality had been named by one of the parties to a question before them, after he had previously ascertained their partiality to him, and effectually secured it by the example of the removal of more independent ones. The character of Sir Edward Herbert makes it painful to disbelieve his assertion, that he was unacquainted with these undue practices; but the notoriety of the facts seem to render it quite incredible. In the same defence of his conduct which contains this assertion, there is another unfortunate departure from fairness. He rests his defence entirely on precedents, and studiously keeps out of view the dangerous principles which he had laid down from the bench as the foundation of his judgment. Public and selemn declarations, which ought to be the most sincere, are, unhappily, among the most disingenuous of human professions. This circumstance, which so much weakens the bonds of faith between men, is not so much to be imputed to any peculiar depravity in those who conduct public affairs, as to the circumstances in which official declarations are usually made. They are generally resorted to in times of difficulty, if not of danger, and are often sure of being countenanced for the time by a numerous body of adherents. Public advantage covers falsehood with a more decent disguise than mere private interest can supply; and the vagueness of official language always affords the utmost facilities for reserve and equivocation. But these considerations, though they may, in some small degree, extenuate the disingenuousness of politicians, must, in the same proportion, lessen the credit which is due to their affirmations.*

After this determination, the judges on their circuit were not received with the accustomed honours.† Agreeably to the memorable observations of Lord Clarendon in the case of Ship-money, they brought disgrace upon themselves, and weakness upon the whole government, by that base compliance which was intended to arm the monarch with undue and irresistible strength. The people of England, peculiarly distinguished by that reverence for the law, and its upright ministers, which is inspired by the love of liberty, have always felt the most cruel disappointment, and manifested the warmest indignation, at seeing the judges converted into instruments of oppression or usurpation. These proceedings were viewed in a very different light by the ministers of absolute princes. D'Adda only informed the Papal Court that the King had removed from office some contumacious judges, who had refused to conform to justice and reason on the subject of the King's dispensing power;‡ and so completely was the spirit of France then subdued, that Barillon, the son of the President of the Parliament of Paris,—the

* State Trials, vol. xi. p. 1199.

* The arguments on this question are contained in the tracts of Sir Edward Herbert, Sir Robert Atkyns, and Mr. Attwood, published after the Revolution.—State Trials, vol. xi. p. 1200. That of Attwood is the most distinguished for acuteness and research. Sir Edward Herbert's is feebly reasoned, though elegantly written.

† Narcissus Luttrell, 16th August, 1686.

‡ D'Adda, 3d May.—MS.

native of a country where the independence of the great tribunals had survived every other remnant of ancient liberty,—describes the removal of judges for their legal opinions as coolly as if he were speaking of the dismissal of an exciseman.*

The King, having, by the decision of the judges, obtained the power of placing the military and civil authority in the hands of his own devoted adherents, now resolved to exercise that power, by nominating Catholics to stations of high trust, and to reduce the Church of England to implicit obedience by virtue of his ecclesiastical supremacy. Both these measures were agreed to at Hampton Court on the 4th of July; at which result he showed the utmost complacency.† It is necessary to give some explanation of the nature of the second, which formed one of the most effectual and formidable measures of his reign.

When Henry VIII. was declared at the Reformation to be the supreme head of the Church of England, no attempt was made to define, with any tolerable precision, the authority to be exercised by him in that character. The object of the lawgiver was to shake off the authority of the See of Rome, and to make effectual provision that all ecclesiastical power and jurisdiction should be administered, like every other part of the public justice of the kingdom, in the name and by the authority of the King. That object scarcely required more than a declaration that the realm was as independent of foreign power in matters relating to the Church as in any other branch of its legislation.‡ That simple principle is distinctly intimated in several of the statutes passed on that occasion, though not consistently pursued in any of them. The true principles of ecclesiastical polity were then nowhere acknowledged. The Court of Rome was far from admitting the self-evident truth, that all coercive and penal jurisdiction exercised by the clergy was, in its nature, a branch of the civil power delegated to them by the State, and that the Church as such could exercise only that influence (metaphorically called "authority") over the understanding and conscience which depended on the spontaneous submission of its members: the Protestant sects were not willing to submit their pretensions to the control of the magistrate: and even the Reformed Church of England, though the creature of statute, showed, at various times, a disposition to claim some rights under a higher title. All religious communities were at that time alike intolerant, and there was, perhaps, no man in Europe who dared to think that the State neither possessed, nor could delegate, nor could recognise as inherent in another body any authority over religious opinions. Neither was any distinction made in the laws to which we have adverted, between the ecclesiastical authority which the King might separately exercise and that which required the concurrence of Parliament. From ignorance, inattention, and timidity, in regard to these important parts of the subject, arose the greater part of the obscurity which still hangs over the limits of the King's ecclesiastical prerogative and the means of carrying it into execution. The statute of the first of Elizabeth, which established the Protestant Church of England, enacted that the Crown should have power, by virtue of that act, to exercise its supremacy by Commissioners for Ecclesiastical Causes, nominated by the sovereign, and vested with uncertain and questionable, but very dangerous powers, for the execution of a prerogative of which neither law nor experience had defined the limits. Under the reigns of James and Charles this court had become the auxiliary and rival of the Star Chamber; and its abolition was one of the wisest of those measures of reformation by which the Parliament of 1641 had signalised the first and happiest period of their proceedings.* At the Restoration, when the Church of England was re-established, a part of the Act for the Abolition of the Court of High Commission, taking away coercive power from all ecclesiastical judges and persons, was repealed; but the clauses for the abolition of the obnoxious court, and for prohibiting the erection of any similar court, were expressly re-affirmed.† Such was the state of the law on this subject when James conceived the design of employing his authority as head of the Church of England, as a means of subjecting that Church to his pleasure, if not of finally destroying it. It is hard to conceive how he could reconcile to his religion the exercise of supremacy in a heretical sect, and thus sanction by his example the usurpations of the Tudors on the rights of the Catholic Church. It is equally difficult to conceive how he reconciled to his morality the employment, for the destruction of a community, of a power with which he was intrusted by that community for its preservation. But the fatal error of believing it to be lawful to use bad means for good ends was not peculiar to James, nor to the zealots of his communion. He, indeed, considered the ecclesiastical supremacy as placed in his hands by Providence to enable him to betray the Protestant establishment. "God," said he to Barillon, "has permitted that all the laws made to establish Protestantism now serve as a foundation for my measures to re-establish true religion, and give me a right to exercise a more extensive power than other Catholic princes possess in the ecclesiastical affairs of their dominions."‡ He found legal advisers ready with paltry expedients for evading the two statutes of 1641 and 1660,

* Barillon, 29th April.—Fox MSS.

† D'Adda, 20th July.—MS.

‡ 24 Hen. VIII. c. 12. 25 Hen. VIII. c. 21. See especially the preambles to these two statutes.

* 17 Car. I. c. 11. † 13 Car. II. c. 12.

‡ Barillon, 22d July, 1686.—Fox MSS.

under the futile pretext that they forbad only a court vested with such powers of corporal punishment as had been exercised by the old Court of High Commission; and in conformity to their pernicious counsel, he issued, in July, a commission to certain ministers, prelates, and judges, to act as a Court of Commissioners in Ecclesiastical Causes. The first purpose of this court was to enforce directions to preachers, issued by the King, enjoining them to abstain from preaching on controverted questions. It must be owned that an enemy of the Protestant religion, placed at the head of the Church, could not adopt a more perfidious measure. He well knew that the Protestant clergy alone could consider his orders as of any authority: those of his own persuasion, totally exempt from his supremacy, would pursue their course, secure of protection from him against the dangers of penal law. The Protestant clergy were forbidden by their enemy to maintain their religion by argument, when they justly regarded it as being in the greatest danger: they disregarded the injunction, and carried on the controversy against Popery with equal ability and success.

Among many others, Sharpe, Dean of Norwich, had distinguished himself; and he was selected for punishment, on pretence that he had aggravated his disobedience by intemperate language, and by having spoken contemptuously of the understanding of all who could be seduced by the arguments for Popery, including of necessity the King himself,—as if it were possible for a man of sincerity to speak on subjects of the deepest importance without a correspondent zeal and warmth. The mode of proceeding to punishment was altogether summary and arbitrary. Lord Sunderland communicated to the Bishop of London the King's commands, to suspend Sharpe from preaching. The Bishop answered that he could proceed only in a judicial manner,—that he must hear Sharpe in his defence before such a suspension, but that Sharpe was ready to give every proof of deference to the King. The Court, incensed at the parliamentary conduct of the Bishop, saw, with great delight, that he had given them an opportunity to humble and mortify him. Sunderland boasted to the Papal minister, that the case of that Bishop would be a great example.* He was summoned before the Ecclesiastical Commission, and required to answer why he had not obeyed his Majesty's commands to suspend Sharpe for seditious preaching.† The Bishop conducted himself with considerable address. After several adjournments he tendered a plea to the jurisdiction, founded on the illegality of their commission; and he was heard by his counsel in vindication of his refusal to suspend an accused clergyman until he had been heard in his own defence. The King took a warm interest in the proceedings, and openly showed his joy at being in a condition to strike bold strokes of authority. He received congratulations on that subject with visible pleasure, and assured the French minister that the same vigorous system should be inflexibly pursued.* He did not conceal his resolution to remove any of the commissioners who should not do "his duty."† The princess of Orange interceded in vain with the King for her preceptor, Compton. The influence of the Church party was also strenuously exerted for that prelate. They were not, indeed, aided by the Primate Sancroft, who, instead of either attending as a commissioner to support the Bishop of London, or openly protesting against the illegality of the court, petitioned for and obtained from the King leave to be excused from attendance on the ground of age and infirmities.‡ By this irresolute and equivocal conduct the Archbishop deserted the Church in a moment of danger, and yet incurred the displeasure of the King. Lord Rochester resisted the suspension, and was supported by Spratt, Bishop of Rochester, and Sir Edward Herbert. Even Jeffreys, for the first time, inclined towards the milder opinion; for neither his dissolute life, nor his judicial cruelty, however much at variance with the principles of religion, were, it seems, incompatible with that fidelity to the Church, which on this and some subsequent occasions prevailed over his zeal for prerogative. A majority of the commissioners were for some time favourable to Compton: Sunderland, and Crew, Bishop of Durham, were the only members of the commission who seconded the projects of the King.§ The presence or protest of the Primate might have produced the most decisive effects. Sunderland represented the authority of Government as interested in the judgment, which, if it were not rigorous, would secure a triumph to a disobedient prelate, who had openly espoused the cause of faction. Rochester at length yielded, in the presence of the King, to whatever his Majesty might determine, giving it to be understood that he acted against his own convic-

* "Il Rè, sommaménte inténto a levare gli ostácoli, che possono impedire l'avanzaménto della religióne Cattólica, a trovato il mezzo più atto a mortificàre il maltalénto di Vescovo di Londra. Sarà un gran buóno e un gran esémpio, come mi ha detto Milord Sunderland." D'Adda, 12th July.—MSS.

† State Trials, vol. xi. p. 1158.

* Barillon, 29th July.—Fox MSS.

† Barillon, 1st August.—Fox MSS.

‡ This petition (in the appendix to Clarendon's Diary) is without a date; but it is a formal one, which seems to imply a regular summons. No such summons could have issued before the 14th July, on which day Evelyn, as one of the Commissioners of the Privy Seal, affixed it to the Ecclesiastical Commission. Sancroft's ambigious petition was therefore subsequent to his knowledge of Compton's danger, so that the excuse of Dr. D'Oyley (Life of Sancroft, vol. i. p. 225,) cannot be allowed.

§ "L'Archevesque de Canterbury s'étoit excusé de se trouver à la Commission Ecclésiastique sur sa mauvaise santé et son grand âge. On a pris aussi ce prétexte pour l'exclure de la séance de conseil." Barillon, 21st Oct.—Fox MSS.

tion.* His followers made no longer any stand, after seeing the leader of their party, and the Lord High Treasurer of England, set the example of sacrificing his opinion as a judge, in favour of lenity, to the pleasure of the King; and the court finally pronounced sentence of suspension on the Bishop against the declared opinion of three fourths of its members.

The attempts of James to bestow toleration on his Catholic subjects would, doubtless, in themselves, deserve high commendation, if we could consider them apart from the intentions which they manifested, and from the laws of which they were a continued breach. But zealous Protestants, in the peculiar circumstances of the time, were, with reason, disposed to regard them as measures of hostility against their religion; and some of them must always be considered as daring or ostentatious manifestations of a determined purpose to exalt prerogative above law. A few days after the resolution of the Council for the admission of Catholics to high civil trust, the first step was made to its execution by the appointment of the Lords Powys, Arundel, Bellasis, and Dover to be Privy Councillors. In a short time afterwards the same honour was conferred on Talbot, who was created Earl of Tyrconnel, and destined to be the Catholic Lord Lieutenant of Ireland. Sheffield, Earl of Mulgrave, a man who professed indifference in religion, but who acquiesced in all the worst measures of this reign, was appointed a member of the Ecclesiastical Commission.† Cartwright, Dean of Ripon, whose talents were disgraced by peculiarly infamous vices, was raised to the vacant bishopric of Chester, in spite of the recommendation of Sancroft, who, when consulted by James, proposed Jeffreys, the Chancellor's brother, for that See.‡ But the merit of Cartwright, which prevailed even over that connection, consisted in having preached a sermon, in which he inculcated the courtly doctrine, that the promises of kings were declarations of a favourable intention, not to be considered as morally binding. A resolution was taken to employ Catholic ministers at the two important stations of Paris and the Hague;—"it being," said James to Barillon, "almost impossible to find an English Protestant who had not too great a consideration for the Prince of Orange."§ White, an Irish Catholic of considerable ability, who had received the foreign title of Marquis D'Abbeville, was sent to the Hague, partly, perhaps, with a view to mortify the Prince of Orange. It was foreseen that the known character of this adventurer would induce the Prince to make attempts to gain him; but Barillon advised his master to make liberal presents to the new minister, who would prefer the bribes of Louis, because the views of that monarch agreed with those of his own sovereign and the interests of the Catholic religion.* James even proposed to the Prince of Orange to appoint a Catholic nobleman of Ireland, Lord Carlingford, to the command of the British regiments;—a proposition, which, if accepted, would embroil that Prince with all his friends in England, and if rejected, as it must have been known that it would be, gave the King a new pretext for displeasure, to be avowed at a convenient season.

But no part of the foreign policy of the King is so much connected with our present subject as the renewal of that open intercourse with the See of Rome which was prohibited by the unrepealed laws passed in the reigns of Henry VIII. and Elizabeth. D'Adda had arrived in England before the meeting of Parliament, as the minister of the Pope, but appeared at court, at first, only as a private gentleman. In a short time, James informed him that he might assume the public character of his Holiness' minister, with the privilege of a chapel in his house, and the other honours and immunities of that character, without going through the formalities of a public audience. The assumption of this character James represented as the more proper, because he was about to send a solemn embassy to Rome as his Holiness' most obedient son.† D'Adda professed great admiration for the pious zeal and filial obedience of the King, and for his determination, as far as possible, to restore religion to her ancient splendour;‡ but he dreaded the precipitate measures to which James was prompted by his own disposition and by the party of zealots who surrounded him. He did not assume the public character till two months afterwards, when he received instructions to that effect from Rome. Hitherto the King had coloured his interchange of ministers with the Roman Court under the plausible pretext of maintaining diplomatic intercourse with the government of the Ecclesiastical State as much as with the other princes of Europe. But his zeal soon became impatient of this slight disguise. In a few days after D'Adda had announced his intention to assume the public character of a minister, Sunderland came to him to convey his Majesty's desire that he might take the title of Nuncio, which would, in

* Barillon, 16th Sept. and 23d Sept.—Fox MSS.; a full and apparently accurate account of these divisions among the commissioners.

† D'Adda, in his letter, 1st Nov. represents Mulgrave as favourable to the Catholics.—MS.

‡ D'Oyley, Life of Sancroft, vol. i. p. 235, where the Archbishop's letter to the King (dated 29th July, 1685.) is printed.

§ Barillon, 22d July.—Fox MSS.

* "M. le Prince d'Orange fera ce qu'il pourra pour la gager; mais je suis persuadé qu'il aimera mieux être dans les intérêts de votre Majesté, sachant bien qu'ils sont conformés à ceux du Roi son maître, et que c'est l'avantage de la religion Catholique." Four thousand livres, which Barillon calculates as then equivalent to three hundred pounds sterling, were given to D'Abbeville in London. Two thousand more were to be advanced to him at the Hague. Barillon, 2d Sept. —Fox MSS.

† D'Adda 14th Dec. 1685.—MS.

‡ Ibid. 31st. Dec.

a more formal and solemn manner, distinguish him from other ministers as the representative of the Apostolic See. D'Adda was surprised at this rash proposal;* about which the Court of Rome long hesitated, from aversion to the foreign policy of James, from a wish to moderate rather than encourage the precipitation of his domestic counsels, and from apprehension of the insults which might be offered to the Holy See, in the sacred person of his Nuncio, by the turbulent and heretical populace of London.

The King had sent the Earl of Castlemaine, the husband of the Duchess of Cleveland, as his ambassador to Rome. "It seemed singular," said Barillon, "that he should have chosen for such a mission a man so little known on his own account, and too well known on that of his wife."† The ambassador, who had been a polemical writer in the defence of the Catholics,‡ and who was almost the only innocent man acquitted on the prosecutions for the Popish Plot, seems to have listened more to zeal and resentment than to discretion in the conduct of his delicate negotiation. He probably expected to find nothing but religious zeal prevalent in the Papal councils: but Innocent XI. was influenced by his character as a temporal sovereign. He considered James not solely as an obedient son of the Church, but rather as the devoted or subservient ally of Louis XIV. As Prince of the Roman state, he resented the outrages offered to him by that monarch, and partook with all other states the dread justly inspired by his ambition and his power. Even as head of the Church, the merits of Louis as the persecutor of the Protestants§ did not, in the eye of Innocent, atone for his encouraging the Gallican Church in their recent resistance to the unlimited authority of the Roman Pontiff. These discordant feelings and embroiled interests, which it would have required the utmost address and temper to reconcile, were treated by Castlemaine with the rude hand of an inexperienced zealot. Hoping, probably, to be received with open arms as the forerunner of the reconciliation of a great kingdom, he was displeased at the reserve and coldness with which the Pontiff treated him; and instead of patiently labouring to overcome obstacles which he ought to have foreseen, he resented them with a violence more than commonly foreign to the decorum of the Papal court. He was instructed to solicit a cardinal's hat for Prince Rinaldo of Este, the Queen's brother;—a moderate suit, the consent to which was for a considerable time retarded by an apprehension of strengthening the French interest in the Sacred College. The second request was that the Pope would confer a titular bishopric* on Edward Petre, an English Jesuit of noble family, who, though not formally the King's confessor,† had more influence on his mind than any other ecclesiastic. This honour was desired in order to qualify this gentleman for performing with more dignity the duties of Dean of the Chapel Royal. Innocent declined, on the ground that the Jesuits were prohibited by their institution from accepting bishopricks, and that he would sooner make a Jesuit a cardinal than a bishop. But as the Popes had often dispensed with this prohibition, Petre himself rightly conjectured that the ascendant of the Austrian party at Rome,—who looked on him with an evil eye as a partisan of France,—was the true cause of the refusal.‡ The King afterwards solicited for his favourite the higher dignity of cardinal: but he was finally refused, though with profuse civility,§ from the same motive, but under the pretence that there had been no Jesuit cardinal since Bellarmine, the great controversialist of the Roman Catholic Church.‖ Besides these personal objects, Castlemaine laboured to reconcile the Pope to Louis XIV., and to procure the interposition of Innocent for the preservation of the general peace. But of these objects, specious as they were, the attainment of the first would strengthen France, and that of the second imported a general acquiescence in her unjust aggrandizement. Even the triumph of monarchy and Popery in England, together with the projects already entertained for the suppression of the "Northern heresy," as the Reformation was then called, and for the conquest of Holland, which was considered as a nest of heretics, could not fail to alarm the most zealous of those Catholic powers who dreaded the power of Louis, and who were averse to strengthen his allies. It was impossible that intelligence of such suggestions at Rome should not immediately reach the courts of Vienna and Madrid, or should not be communicated by them to the Prince of Orange. Castlemaine suffered himself to be engaged in contests for precedency with the Spanish minister, which served, and were perhaps intended, to embroil him more deeply with the Pope. James at first resented the refusal to promote Petre,¶ and for a time seemed to espouse the quarrel of his ambassador. D'Adda was obliged, by his station, and by his intercourse with Lord Sun-

* D'Adda, 22d Feb. 1686. "Io resto alquánto sorpréso da questa ambasciata."

† Barillon, 29th Oct. 1685.—Fox, app. p. cxxii.

‡ Dodd, vol. iii. p. 450.

§ It appears by the copy of a letter in my possession from Don Pedro Ronquillo, the Spanish ambassador in London, to Don Francesco Bernado de Quixos, (dated 5th April, 1686,) that Innocent, though he publicly applauded the zeal of Louis, did not in truth approve the revocation of the Edict of Nantes.

* In partibus infidelium," as it is called. Barillon, 27th June.—Fox MSS.

† This office was held by a learned Jesuit, named Warner.—Dodd, vol. iii. p. 491.

‡ Barillon, 20th Dec. 1686 —Fox MSS.

§ Dodd, vol. iii. p. 511, where the official correspondence in 1687 is published.

‖ D'Adda, 8th August, 1687.—MS.

¶ Barillon, 2d Dec. 1686.—Fox MSS.

derland, to keep up friendly appearances with Petre; but Barillon easily discovered that the Papal minister disliked that Jesuit and his order, whom he considered as devoted to France.* The Pope instructed his minister to complain of the conduct of Castlemaine, as very ill becoming the representative of so pious and so prudent a king; and D'Adda made the representation to James at a private audience where the Queen and Lord Sunderland were present. That zealous princess, with more fervour than dignity, often interrupted his narrative by exclamations of horror at the liberty with which a Catholic minister had spoken to the successor of St. Peter. Lord Sunderland said to him, "The King will do whatever you please." James professed the most unbounded devotion to the Holy See, and assured D'Adda that he would write a letter to his Holiness, to express his regret for the unbecoming conduct of his ambassador.† When this submission was made, Innocent formally forgave Castlemaine for his indiscreet zeal in promoting the wishes of his sovereign;‡ and James publicly announced the admission of his ambassador at Rome into the Privy Council, both to console the unfortunate minister, and to show the more how much he set at defiance the laws which forbade both the embassy and the preferment.§

CHAPTER III.

State of the Army.—Attempts of the King to Convert it.—The Princess Anne.—Dryden.—Lord Middleton and others.—Revocation of the Edict of Nantes.—Attempt to convert Rochester.—Conduct of the Queen.—Religious Conference.—Failure of the attempt.—His Dismissal.

During the summer of 1686, the King had assembled a body of 15,000 troops, who were encamped on Hounslow Heath;—a spectacle new to the people of England, who, though full of martial spirit, have never regarded with favour the separate profession of arms.‖ He viewed this encampment with a complacency natural to princes, and he expressed his feelings to the Prince of Orange in a tone of no friendly boast.* He caressed the officers, and he openly declared that he should keep none but those on whom he could rely.† A Catholic chapel was opened in the camp, and missionaries were distributed among the soldiers. The numbers of the army rendered it an object of very serious consideration. Supposing them to be only 32,000 in England and Scotland alone, they were twice as many as were kept up in Great Britain in the year 1792, when the population of the island had certainly more than doubled. As this force was kept on foot without the consent of Parliament, there was no limit to its numbers, but the means of supporting it possessed by the King; which might be derived from the misapplication of funds granted for other purposes, or be supplied by foreign powers interested in destroying the liberties of the kingdom. The means of governing it were at first a source of perplexity to the King, but, in the sequel, a new object of apprehension to the people. The Petition of Right,‡ in affirmance of the ancient laws, had forbidden the exercise of martial law within the kingdom; and the ancient mode of establishing those summary jurisdictions and punishments which seem to be necessary to secure the obedience of armies was, in a great measure, wanting. The servile ingenuity of aspiring lawyers was, therefore, set at work to devise some new expedient for more easily destroying the constitution, according to the forms of law. For this purpose they revived the provisions of some ancient statutes,§ which had made desertion a capital felony; though these were, in the opinion of the best lawyers, either repealed, or confined to soldiers serving in the case of actual or immediately impending hostilities. Even this device did not provide the means of punishing the other military offences, which are so dangerous to the order of armies, that there can be little doubt of their having been actually punished by other means, however confessedly illegal. Several soldiers were tried, convicted, and executed for the felony of desertion; and the scruples of judges on the legality of these proceedings induced the King more than once to recur to his ordinary measure for the purification of tribunals by the removal of the judges. Sir John Holt, who was destined, in better times, to be one of the most inflexible guardians of the laws, was also then dismissed from the recordership of London.

* Barillon, 17th June, 1686,—10th March, 1687.—Fox MSS.

† D'Adda, 30th May,—6th June, 1687.—MS.

‡ Letter of Innocent to James, 16th Aug.—Dodd, vol. iii. p. 511.

§ London Gazette, 26th Sept.

‖ The army, on the 1st of January, 1685, amounted to 19,979.—Accounts in the War Office. The number of the army in Great Britain in 1824 is 22.019 (Army Estimates), the population being 14,391,681 (Population Returns); which gives a proportion of nearly one out of every 654 persons, or of one soldier out of every 160 men of the fighting age. The population of England and Wales, in 1685, not exceeding five millions, the proportion of the army to it was one soldier to every 250 persons, or of one soldier to every sixty-five men of the fighting age. Scotland, in 1685, had a separate establishment. The army of James, at his accession, therefore, was more than twice and a half greater in comparison with the population than the present force (1822). The comparative wealth, if it could be estimated, would probably afford similar results.

* James to the Prince of Orange, 29th June.—Dalrymple, app. to books iii. & iv.

† Barillon, 8th July. Ibid.

‡ 3 Car. I. c. 1.

§ 7 Hen. VII. c. 1. 3 Hen. VIII. c. 5; & 2 & 3 Edw. VI. c. 2. See Hale, Pleas of the Crown, book i. c. 63.

The only person who ventured to express the general feeling respecting the army was Mr. Samuel Johnson, who had been chaplain to Lord Russell, and who was then in prison for a work which he had published some years before against the succession of James, under the title of "Julian the Apostate."* He now wrote, and sent to an agent to be dispersed (for there was no proof of actual dispersion or sale†), an address to the army, expostulating with them on the danger of serving under illegally commissioned officers, and for objects inconsistent with the safety of their country. He also wrote another paper, in which he asserted that "resistance may be used in case our religion or our rights should be invaded." For these acts he was tried, convicted, and sentenced to pay a small fine, to be thrice pilloried, and to be whipped by the common hangman from Newgate to Tyburn. For both these publications, his spirit was, doubtless, deserving of the highest applause. The prosecution in the first case can hardly be condemned, and the conviction still less: but the cruelty of the punishment reflects the highest dishonour on the judges, more especially on Sir Edward Herbert, whose high pretensions to morality and humanity deeply aggravate the guilt of his concurrence in this atrocious judgment. Previous to its infliction, he was degraded from his sacred character by Crew, Sprat, and White, three bishops authorised to exercise ecclesiastical jurisdiction in the diocese of London during the suspension of Compton. When, as part of the formality, the Bible was taken out of his hands, he struggled to preserve it, and bursting into tears, cried out, "You cannot take from me the consolation contained in the sacred volume." The barbarous judgment was "executed with great rigour and cruelty."‡ In the course of a painful and ignominious progress of two miles through crowded streets, he received three hundred and seventeen stripes, inflicted with a whip of nine cords knotted. It will be a consolation to the reader, as soon as he has perused the narrative of these enormities, to learn, though with some disturbance of the order of time, that amends were in some measure made to Mr. Johnson, and that his persecutors were reduced to the bitter mortification of humbling themselves before their victim. After the Revolution, the judgment pronounced on him was voted by the House of Commons to be illegal and cruel.§ Crew, Bishop of Durham, one of the commissioners who deprived him, made him a considerable compensation in money;‖ and Withins, the Judge who delivered the sentence, counterfeited a dangerous illness, and pretended that his dying hours were disturbed by the remembrance of what he had done, in order to betray Johnson, through his humane and Christian feelings, into such a declaration of forgiveness as might contribute to shelter the cruel judge from further animadversion.

* State Trials, vol. xi. p. 1339.

† In fact, however, many were dispersed.—Kennet, History, vol. iii. p. 450.

‡ Commons' Journals, 24th June, 1690. These are the words of the Report of a Committee who examined evidence on the case, and whose resolutions were adopted by the House. They sufficiently show that Echard's extenuating statements are false.

§ Ibid.

‖ Narcissus Luttrell, February, 1690.

The desire of the King to propagate his religion was a natural consequence of zealous attachment to it. But it was a very dangerous quality in a monarch, especially when the principles of religious liberty were not adopted by any European government. The royal apostle is seldom convinced of the good faith of the opponent whom he has failed to convert: he soon persuades himself that the pertinacity of the heretic arises more from the depravity of his nature than from the errors of his judgment. He first shows displeasure to his perverse antagonists; he then withdraws advantages from them; he, in many cases, may think it reasonable to bring them to reflection by some degree of hardship; and the disappointed disputant may at last degenerate into the furious persecutor. The attempt to convert the army was peculiarly dangerous to the King's own object. He boasted of the number of converts in one of his regiments of Guards, without considering the consequences of teaching controversy to an army. The political canvass carried on among the officers, and the controversial sermons preached to the soldiers, probably contributed to awaken that spirit of inquiry and discussion in his camp which he ought to have dreaded as his most formidable enemy. He early destined the revenue of the Archbishop of York to be a provision for converts,†—being probably sincere in his professions, that he meant only to make it one for those who had sacrificed interest to religion. But experience shows how easily such a provision swells into a reward, and how naturally it at length becomes a premium for hypocrisy. It was natural that his passion for making proselytes should show itself towards his own children. The Pope, in his conversations with Lord Castlemaine, said, that without the conversion of the Princess Anne, no advantage obtained for the Catholic religion could be permanently secured.‡ The King assented to this opinion, and had, indeed, before attempted to dispose his daughter favourably to his religion, influenced probably by the parental kindness, which was one of his best qualities.§ He must have considered as hopeless the case of his eldest daughter, early removed from her father, and the submissive as well as affectionate wife of a husband of decisive character, who was also the leader of the Protestant cause. To Anne, therefore, his attention was turned: but with her he found

* State Trials, vol. xi. p. 1354.

† D'Adda, 10th May, 1686.—MS.

‡ Barillon, 27th June.—Fox MSS.

§ D'Adda, suprà.

insurmountable difficulties. Both these princesses, after their father had become a Catholic, were considered as the hope of the Protestant religion, and accordingly trained in the utmost horror of Popery. Their partialities and resentments were regulated by difference of religion; their political importance and their splendid prospects were dependent on the Protestant Church. Anne was surrounded by zealous Churchmen; she was animated by her preceptor Compton; her favourites Lord and Lady Churchill had become determined partisans of Protestantism; and the King found in the obstinacy of his daughter's character, a resistance hardly to be apprehended from a young princess of slight understanding.* Some of the reasons of this zeal for converting her clearly show that, whether the succession was actually held out to her as a lure or not, at least there was an intention, if she became a Catholic, to prefer her to the Princess of Orange. Bonrepos, a minister of ability, had indeed, at a somewhat earlier period, tried the effect of that temptation on her husband, Prince George.† He ventured to ask his friend the Danish envoy, "whether the Prince had any ambition to raise his consort to the throne at the expense of the Princess Mary, which seemed to be practicable if he became a Catholic." The envoy hinted this bold suggestion to the Prince, who appeared to receive it well, and even showed a willingness to be instructed on the controverted questions. Bonrepos found means to supply the Princess Anne with Catholic books, which, for a moment, she showed some willingness to consider. He represented her to his Court as timid and silent, but ambitious and of some talent, with a violent hatred for the Queen. He reported his attempts to the King, who listened to him with the utmost pleasure; and the subtile diplomatist observes, that, though he might fail in the conversion, he should certainly gain the good graces of James by the effort, which his knowledge of that monarch's hatred of the Prince of Orange had been his chief inducement to hazard.

The success of the King himself, in his attempts to make proselytes, was less than might have been expected from his zeal and influence. Parker, originally a zealous Nonconformist, aftewards a slanderous buffoon, and an Episcopalian of persecuting principles, earned the bishopric of Oxford by showing a strong disposition to favour, if not to be reconciled to, the Church of Rome. Two bishops publicly visited Mr. Leyburn the Catholic prelate, at his apartments in St. James' Palace, on his being made almoner to the King, when it was, unhappily, impossible to impute their conduct to liberality or charity.‡ Walker, the Master of University College in Oxford, and three of the fellows of that society, were the earliest and most noted of the few open converts among the clergy. L'Estrange, though he had for five-and-twenty years written all the scurrilous libels of the Court, refused to abandon the Protestant Church. Dryden, indeed, conformed to the doctrines of his master;* and neither the critical time, nor his general character, have been sufficient to deter some of the admirers of that great poet from seriously maintaining that his conversion was real. The same persons who make this stand for the conscientious character of the poet of a profligate Court, have laboured with all their might to discover and exaggerate those human frailties from which fervid piety and intrepid integrity did not altogether preserve Milton, in the evil days of his age, and poverty, and blindness.† The King failed in a personal attempt to convert Lord Dartmouth, whom he considered as his most faithful servant for having advised him to bring Irish troops into England, such being more worthy of trust than others;‡—a remarkable instance of a man of honour adhering inflexibly to the Church of England, though his counsels relating to civil affairs were the most fatal to public liberty. Middleton, one of the secretaries of state, a man of ability, supposed to have no strong principles of religion, was equally inflexible. The Catholic divine who was sent to him began by attempting to reconcile his understanding to the mysterious doctrine of transubstantiation. "Your Lordship," said he, "believes the Trinity."—"Who told you so?" answered Middleton; "you are come here to prove your own opinions, not to ask about mine." The astonished priest is said to have immediately retired. Sheffield, Earl of Mulgrave, is also said to have sent away a monk who came to convert him by a jest upon the same doctrine:—"I have convinced myself," said he, "by much reflection that God made man; but I cannot believe that man can make God." But though there is no reason to doubt

* Barillon, suprà.

† Bonrepos, 28th March.—Fox MSS.

‡ D'Adda, 21st January, 1686,—MS. The King and Queen took the sacrament at St. James' Chapel "Monsig^re^ Vescovo Leyburn, passato da alcuni giorni nell' apartamento de St. James destinato al gran Elimosiniere de S. M. in habito lungo nero portando la croce nera, si fa vedere in publico visitando i ministri del Principe e altri: furono un giorno per fargli una visita due vescovi Protestanti." As this occurred before the promotion of the two profligate prelates, Parker and Cartwright, one of these visitors must have been Crew, and the other was, too probably, Spratt. The former had been appointed Clerk of the Closet, and Dean of the Chapel Royal, a few days before.

* "Dryden, the famous play-writer, and his two sons, and Mrs. Nelly, were said to go to mass. Such proselytes were no great loss to the Church." Evelyn, vol. i. p. 594. The rumour, as far as it related to Mrs. Gwynne, was calumnious.

† Compare Dr. Johnson's biography of Milton with his generally excellent life of Dryden.

‡ D'Adda, 10th May.—MS. "Diceva il Re che il detto Milord veramente gli aveva dato con sigli molto fedeli, uno di quelli era stato di far venire truppi Irlandesi in Inghilterra, nelli quali poteva S. M. meglio fidarsi che negli altri."

2 A

his pleasantry or profaneness, his integrity is more questionable.* Colonel Kirke, from whom strong scruples were hardly to be expected, is said to have answered the King's desire, that he would listen to Catholic divines, by declaring, that when he was at Tangier he had engaged himself to the Emperor of Morocco, if ever he changed his religion, to become a Mahometan. Lord Churchill, though neither insensible to the kindness of James, nor distinguished by a strict conformity to the precepts of Religion, withstood the attempts of his generous benefactor to bring him over to the Church of Rome. He said of himself, "that though he could not lead the life of a saint, he was resolved, if there was ever occasion for it, to show the resolution of a martyr."† So much constancy in religious opinion may seem singular among courtiers and soldiers: but it must be considered, that the inconsistency of men's actions with their opinions is more often due to infirmity than to insincerity; that the members of the Protestant party were restrained from deserting it by principles of honour; and that the disgrace of desertion was much aggravated by the general unpopularity of the adverse cause, and by the violent animosity then raging between the two parties who divided England and Europe.

Nothing so much excited the abhorrence of all Protestant nations against Louis XIV., as the measures which he adopted against his subjects of that religion. As his policy on that subject contributed to the downfall of James, it seems proper to state it more fully than the internal occurrences of a foreign country ought generally to be treated in English history. The opinions of the Reformers, which triumphed in some countries of Europe, and were wholly banished from others, had very early divided France and Germany into two powerful but unequal parties. The wars between the princes of the Empire which sprung from this source, after a period of one hundred and fifty years, were finally composed by the treaty of Westphalia. In France, where religious enthusiasm was exasperated by the lawless character and mortal animosities of civil war, these hostilities raged for nearly forty years with a violence unparalleled in any civilized age or country. As soon as Henry IV. had established his authority by conformity to the worship of the majority of his people, the first object of his paternal policy was to secure the liberty of the Protestants, and to restore the quiet of the kingdom by a general law on this equally arduous and important subject. The contending opinions in their nature admitted no negotiation or concession. The simple and effectual expedient of permitting them all to be professed with equal freedom was then untried in practice, and almost unknown in speculation. The toleration of error, according to the received principles of that age, differed little from the permission of crimes. Amidst such opinions it was extremely difficult to frame a specific law for the government of hostile sects; and the Edict of Nantes, passed by Henry for that purpose in the year 1598, must be considered as honourable to the wisdom and virtue of his Catholic counsellors. This Edict,* said to be composed by the great historian De Thou, was based on the principle of a treaty of peace between belligerent parties, sanctioned and enforced by the royal authority. Though the transaction was founded merely in humanity and prudence, without any reference to religious liberty, some of its provisions were conformable to the legitimate results of that great principle. All Frenchmen of the reformed religion were declared to be admissible to every office, civil and military, in the kingdom; and they were received into all schools and colleges without distinction. Dissent from the Established Church was exempted from all penalty or civil inconvenience. The public exercise of the Protestant religion was confined to those cities and towns where it had been formerly granted, and to the mansions of the gentry who had seignorial jurisdiction over capital crimes. It might, however, be practised in other places by the permission of the Catholics, who were lords of the respective manors. Wherever the worship of the Protestants was lawful, their religious books might freely be bought and sold. They might inhabit any part of the kingdom without molestation for their opinion; and private worship was everywhere protected by the exemption of their houses from all legal search on account of religion. These restrictions, though they show the Edict to have been a pacification between parties, with little regard to the conscience of individuals, yet do not seem in practice to have much limited the religious liberty of French Protestants. To secure an impartial administration of justice, Chambers, into which Protestants and Catholics were admitted in equal numbers, were established in the principal parliaments.† The Edict was declared to be

* He had been made Lord Chamberlain immediately after Jeffreys' circuit, and had been appointed a member of the Ecclesiastical Commission, in November, 1685, when Sancroft refused to act, in which last office he continued to the last. He held out hopes that he might be converted to a very late period of the reign, (Barillon, 30th August, 1687,) and he was employed by James to persuade Sir George Mackenzie to consent to the removal of the Test.—(Halifax MSS.) He brought a patent for a marquisate to the King half-an-hour before King James went away.—(Ibid.) In October, 1688, he thought it necessary to provide against the approaching storm by obtaining a general pardon. Had not Lord Mulgrave written some memoirs of his own time, his importance as a statesman would not have deserved so full an exposure of his political character.

† Coxe, Memoirs of the Duke of Marlborough, vol. i. p. 27.

* The original is to be found in Benoit, Histoire de l'Edit de Nantes, vol. i. app. pp. 62—85.

† Paris, Toulouse, Grenoble, and Bordeaux. The Chamber of the Edict at Paris took cogni-

a perpetual and irrevocable law. By a separate grant executed at Nantes, the King authorised the Protestants, for eight years, to garrison the towns and places of which they were at that time in military possession, and to hold them under his authority and obedience. The possession of these places of security was afterwards continued from time to time, and the expense of their garrisons defrayed by the Crown. Some cities also, where the majority of the inhabitants were Protestants, and where the magistrates, by the ancient constitution, regulated the armed force, with little dependence on the Crown, such as Nismes, Rochelle, and Montauban,* though not formerly garrisoned by the Reformed, still constituted a part of their military security for the observance of the Edict. An armed sect of dissenters must have afforded many plausible pretexts for attack; and Cardinal Richelieu had justifiable reasons of policy for depriving the Protestants of those important fortresses, the possession of which gave them the character of an independent republic, and naturally led them into dangerous connection with Protestant and rival states. His success in accomplishing that important enterprise is one of the most splendid parts of his administration; though he owed the reduction of Rochelle to the feebleness and lukewarmness, if not to the treachery, of the Court of England. Richelieu discontinued the practice of granting the royal licence to the Protestant body to hold political assemblies; and he adopted it as a maxim of permanent policy, that the highest dignities of the army and the state should be granted to Protestants only in cases of extraordinary merit. In other respects that haughty minister treated them as a mild conqueror. When they were reduced to entire submission, in 1629, an edict of pardon was issued at Nismes, confirming all the civil and religious principles which had been granted by the Edict of Nantes.† At the moment that they were reduced to the situation of private subjects, they disappear from the history of France. They are not mentioned in the dissensions which disturbed the minority of Louis XIV., nor are they named by that Prince in the enumeration which he gives of objects of public anxiety at the period which preceded his assumption of the reins of government, in 1660. The great families attached to them by birth and honour during the civil wars were gradually allured to the religion of the Court; while those of inferior condition, like the members of other sects excluded from power, applied themselves to the pursuit of wealth, and were patronised by Colbert as the most ingenious manufacturers in France. A declaration, prohibiting the relapse of converted Protestants under pain of confiscation, indicated a disposition to persecute, which that prudent minister had the good fortune to check. An edict punishing emigration with death, though long after turned into the sharpest instrument of intolerance, seems originally to have flowed solely from the general prejudices on that subject, which have infected the laws and policy of most states. Till the peace of Nimeguen, when Louis had reached the zenith of his power, the French Protestants experienced only those minute vexations from which sectaries, discouraged by a government, are seldom secure.

The immediate cause of a general and open departure from the moderate system, under which France had enjoyed undisturbed quiet for half a century, is to be discerned only in the character of the King, and the inconsistency of his conduct with his opinions. Those conflicts between his disorderly passions and his unenlightened devotion, which had long agitated his mind, were at last composed under the ascendant of Madame de Maintenon; and in this situation he was seized with a desire of signalizing his penitence, and atoning for his sins, by the conversion of his heretical subjects. Her prudence as well as moderation prevented her from counselling the employment of violence against the members of her former religion; nor do such means appear to have been distinctly contemplated by the King;—still she dared not moderate the zeal on which her greatness was founded. But the passion for conversion, armed with absolute power, fortified by the sanction of mistaken conscience, intoxicated by success, exasperated by resistance, anticipated and carried beyond its purpose by the zeal of subaltern agents, deceived by their false representations, often irrevocably engaged by their rash acts, and too warm to be considerate in choosing means or weighing consequences, led the government of France, under a prince of no cruel nature, by an almost unconscious progress, in the short space of six years, from a successful system of toleration to the most unprovoked and furious persecution ever carried on against so great, so innocent, and so meritorious a body of men. The Chambers of the Edict were suppressed on general grounds of judicial reformation, and because the concord between the two religions rendered them no longer necessary. By a series of edicts the Protestants were excluded from all public offices, and from all professions which were said to give them a dangerous influence over opinion. They were successively rendered incapable of

zance of all causes where Protestants were parties in Normandy and Brittany.

* Cautionary Towns.—"La Rochelle surtout avait des traités avec les Rois de France qui la rendoient presque indépendante."—Benoit, vol. i. p. 251.

† Benoit, vol ii. app. 92. Madame de Duras, the sister of Turenne, was so zealous a Protestant that she wished to educate as a minister, her son, who afterwards went to England, and became Lord Feversham.—Vol. iv. p. 129.

* "Le Roi pense sérieusement à la conversion des hérétiques, et dans peu on y travaillera tout de bon."—Mad. de Maintenon, Oct. 28th, 1679.

being judges, advocates, attorneys, notaries, clerks, officers, or even attendants of courts of law. They were banished in multitudes from places in the revenue, to which their habit of method and calculation had directed their pursuits. They were forbidden to exercise the occupations of printers and booksellers.* Even the pacific and neutral profession of medicine, down to its humblest branches, was closed to their industry. They were prohibited from intermarriage with Catholics, and from hiring Catholic domestics, without exception of convenience or necessity. Multitudes of men were thus driven from their employments, without any regard to the habits, expectations, and plans, which they had formed on the faith of the laws. Besides the misery which immediately flowed from these acts of injustice, they roused and stimulated the bigotry of those, who need only the slightest mark of the temper of government to inflict on their dissenting countrymen those minute but ceaseless vexations which embitter the daily course of human life.

As the Edict of Nantes had only permitted the public worship of Protestants in certain places, it had often been a question whether particular churches were erected conformably to that law. The renewal and multiplication of suits on this subject furnished the means of striking a dangerous blow against the Reformed religion. Prejudice and servile tribunals adjudged multitudes of churches to be demolished by decrees which were often illegal, and always unjust. By these judgments a hundred thousand Protestants were, in fact, prohibited from the exercise of their religion. They were deprived of the means of educating their clergy by the suppression of their flourishing colleges at Sedan, Saumur, and Montauban, which had long been numbered among the chief ornaments of Protestant Europe. Other expedients were devised to pursue them into their families, and harass them in those situations where the disturbance of quiet inflicts the deepest wounds on human nature. The local judges were authorised and directed to visit the death-beds of Protestants, and to interrogate them whether they determined to die in obstinate heresy. Their children were declared competent to abjure their errors at the age of seven; and by such mockery of conversion they might escape, at that age, from the affectionate care of their parents. Every childish sport was received as evidence of abjuration; and every parent dreaded the presence of a Catholic neighbour, as the means of ensnaring a child into irrevocable alienation. Each of these disabilities or severities was inflicted by a separate edict; and each was founded on the allegation of some special grounds, which seemed to guard against any general conclusion at variance with the privileges of Protestants.

* It is singular that they were not excluded from the military service by sea or land.

On the other hand, a third of the King's savings on his privy purse was set apart to recompense converts to the Established religion. The new converts were allowed a delay of three years for the payment of their debts; and they were exempted for the same period from the obligation of affording quarters to soldiers. This last privilege seems to have suggested to Louvois, a minister of great talent but of tyrannical character, a new and more terrible instrument of conversion. He despatched regiments of dragoons into the Protestant provinces, with instructions that they should be almost entirely quartered on the richer Protestants. This practice, which afterwards, under the name of "*Dragonnades*," became so infamous throughout Europe, was attended by all the outrages and barbarities to be expected from a licentious soldiery let loose on those whom they considered as the enemies of their King, and the blasphemers of their religion. Its effects became soon conspicuous in the feigned conversion of great cities and extensive provinces; which, instead of opening the eyes of the Government to the atrocity of the policy adopted under its sanction, served only to create a deplorable expectation of easy, immediate, and complete success. At Nismes, 60,000 Protestants abjured their religion in three days. The King was informed by one despatch that all Poitou was converted, and that in some parts of Dauphiné the same change had been produced by the terror of the dragoons without their actual presence.*

All these expedients of disfranchisement, chicane, vexation, seduction, and military license, almost amounting to military execution, were combined with declarations of respect for the Edict of Nantes, and of resolutions to maintain the religious rights of the new churches. Every successive edict spoke the language of toleration and liberality: every separate exclusion was justified on a distinct ground of specious policy. The most severe hardships were plausibly represented as necessarily arising from a just interpretation and administration of the law. Many of the restrictions were in themselves small; many tried in one province, and slowly extended to all; some apparently excused by the impatience of the sufferers under preceding restraints. In the end, however, the unhappy Protestants saw themselves surrounded by a persecution which, in its full extent, had probably never been contemplated by the author; and, after all the privileges were destroyed, nothing remained but the formality of repealing the law by which these privileges had been conferred.

At length, on the 18th of October, 1685, the Government of France, not unwillingly

* Lémontey. Nouveaux Mémoires de Dangeau, p. 19. The fate of the province of Bearn was peculiarly dreadful. It may be seen in Rulhière (Eclaircissemens, &c. chap. xv.), and Benoît, liv xxii.

deceived by feigned conversions, and, as it now appears, actuated more by sudden impulse than long-premeditated design, revoked the Edict of Nantes. In the preamble of the edict of revocation it was alleged, that, as the better and greater part of those who professed the pretended Reformed religion had embraced the Catholic faith, the Edict of Nantes had become unnecessary. The ministers of the Reformed faith were banished from France in fifteen days, under pain of the galleys. All Protestant schools were shut up; and the unconverted children, at first allowed to remain in France without annoyance on account of their religion, were soon afterwards ordered to be taken from their parents, and committed to the care of their nearest Catholic relations, or, in default of such relations, to the magistrates. The return of the exiled ministers, and the attendance on a Protestant church for religious worship, were made punishable with death. Carrying vengeance beyond the grave, another edict enjoined, that if any new converts should refuse the Catholic sacraments on their death-bed, when required to receive them by a magistrate, their bodies should be drawn on a hurdle along the public way, and then cast into the common sewers.

The conversion sought by James with most apparent eagerness was that of Lord Rochester. Though he had lost all favour, and even confidence, James long hesitated to remove him from office. The latter was willing, but afraid to take a measure which would involve a final rupture with the Church of England. Rochester's connection with the family of Hyde, and some remains perhaps of gratitude for past services, and a dread of increasing the numbers of his enemies, together with the powerful influence of old habits of intimacy, kept his mind for some time in a state of irresolution and fluctuation. His dissatisfaction with the Lord Treasurer became generally known in the summer, and appears to have been considerably increased by the supposed connection of that nobleman with the episcopalian administration in Scotland; of whose removal it will become our duty presently to speak.* The sudden return of Lady Dorchester revived the spirits of his adherents.† But the Queen, a person of great importance in these affairs, was, on this occasion, persuaded to repress her anger, and to profess a reliance on the promise made by the King not to see his mistress."‡ Formerly, indeed, the violence of the Queen's temper is said to have been one source of her influence over the King; and her ascendency was observed to be always greatest after those paroxysms of rage to which she was excited by the detection of his infidelities. But, in circumstances so critical, her experienced advisers dissuaded her from repeating hazardous experiments; and the amours of her husband are said, at this time, to have become so vulgar and obscure as to elude her vigilance. She was mild and submissive to him; but she showed her suspicion of the motive of Lady Dorchester's journey by violent resentment against Clarendon, the Lord Lieutenant of Ireland, whom she believed to be privy to it, and who in vain attempted to appease her anger by the most humble—not to say abject—submissions.† She at this moment seemed to have had more than ordinary influence, and was admitted into the secret of all affairs.‡ Supported, if not instigated by her, Sunderland and Petre, with the more ambitious and turbulent part of the Catholics, represented to the King that nothing favourable to the Catholics was to be hoped from Parliament as long as his Court and Council were divided, and as long as he was surrounded by a Protestant cabal, at the head of which was the Lord Treasurer, professing the most extravagant zeal for the English Church; that, notwithstanding the pious zeal of his Majesty, nothing important had yet been done for religion; that not one considerable person had declared himself a Catholic; that no secret believer would avow himself, and no well-disposed Protestant would be reconciled to the Church, till the King's administration was uniform, and the principles of government more decisive; and that the time was now come when it was necessary for his Majesty to execute the intention which he had long entertained, either to bring the Treasurer to more just sentiments, or to remove him from the important office which he filled, and thus prove to the public that there was no means of preserving power or credit but by supporting the King's measures for the Catholic religion.§ They reminded him of the necessity of taking means to perpetuate the benefits which he designed for the Catholics, and of the alarming facility with which the Tudor princes had made and subverted religious revolutions. Even the delicate question of the succession was agitated, and some had the boldness of throwing out suggestions to James on the most effectual means of insuring a Catholic successor. These extraordinary suggestions appear to have been in some measure known to Van Citters, the Dutch minister, who ex-

* Barillon, 18th July.—Fox MSS.

† Id. 2d Sept.—Ibid.

‡ Report of an agent of Louis XIV. in London, in 1686, of which a copy is in my possession.

* In a MS. among the Stuart papers in possession of his Majesty, which was written by Sheridan, Secretary for Ireland under Tyrconnel, we are told that Petre and Sunderland agreed to dismiss Mrs. Sedley, under pretence of morality, but really because she was thought the support of Rochester; and that it was effected by Lady Powis and Bishop Giffard, to the Queen's great joy.—See farther Barillon, 5th Sept.—Fox MSS.

† Letters of Henry, Earl of Clarendon.

‡ Barillon, 23d Sept.—Fox MSS.

§ The words of Barillon, "pour l'établissement de la religion Catholique," being capable of two senses, have been translated in the text in a manner which admits of a double interpretation. The context removes all ambiguity in this case.

pressed his fears that projects were forming against the rights of the Princess of Orange. The more affluent and considerable Catholics themselves became alarmed, seeing, as clearly as their brethren, the dangers to which they might be exposed under a Protestant successor. But they thought it wiser to entitle themselves to his favour by a moderate exercise of their influence, than to provoke his hostility by precautions so unlikely to be effectual against his succession or his religion. Moderation had its usual fate: the faction of zealots, animated by the superstition, the jealousy, and the violence of the Queen, became the most powerful. Even at this time, however, the Treasurer was thought likely to have maintained his ground for some time longer, if he had entirely conformed to the King's wishes. His friends Ormonde, Middleton, Feversham, Dartmouth, and Preston were not without hope that he might retain office. At last, in the end of October, James declared that Rochester must either go to mass, or go out of office.* His advisers represented to him that it was dangerous to leave this alternative to the Treasurer, which gave him the means of saving his place by a pretended conformity. The King replied that he hazarded nothing by the proposal, for he knew that Rochester would never conform. If this observation was sincere, it seems to have been rash; for some of Rochester's friends still believed he would do whatever was necessary, and advised him to keep his office at any price.† The Spanish and Dutch ambassadors expressed their fear of the fall of their last friend in the Cabinet;‡ and Louis XIV. considered the measure as certainly favourable to religion and to his policy, whether it ended in the conversion of Rochester or in his dismissal; in acquiring a friend, or in disabling an enemy.§

It was agreed that a conference on the questions in dispute should be held in the presence of Rochester, by Dr. Jane and Dr. Patrick on behalf of the Church of England, and by Dr. Giffard and Dr. Tilden‖ on the part of the Church of Rome. It is not easy to believe that the King or his minister should have considered a real change of opinion as a possible result of such a dispute. Even if the influence of attachment, of antipathy, of honour, and of habit on the human mind were suspended, the conviction of a man of understanding on questions of great importance, then the general object of study and discussion, could hardly be conceived to depend on the accidental superiority in skill and knowledge exhibited by the disputants of either party in the course of a single debate. But the proposal, if made by one party, was too specious and popular to be prudently rejected by the other: they were alike interested in avoiding the imputation of shrinking from an argumentative examination of their faith. The King was desirous of being relieved from his own indecision by a signal proof of Rochester's obstinacy; and in the midst of his fluctuations he may sometimes have indulged a lingering hope that the disputation might supply a decent excuse for the apparent conformity of his old friend and servant. In all prolonged agitations of the mind, it is in succession affected by motives not very consistent with each other. Rochester foresaw that his popularity among Protestants would be enhanced by his triumphant resistance to the sophistry of their adversaries; and he gave the King, by consenting to the conference, a pledge of his wish to carry compliance to the utmost boundaries of integrity. He hoped to gain time; he retained the means of profiting by fortunate accidents; at least he postponed the fatal hour of removal; and there were probably moments in which his fainting virtue looked for some honourable pretence for deserting a vanquished party.

The conference took place on the 30th of November.* Each of the contending parties, as usual, claimed the victory. The Protestant writers, though they agree that the Catholics were defeated, vary from each other. Some ascribe the victory to the two divines; others to the arguments of Rochester himself; and one of the disputants of the English Church said that it was unnecessary for them to do much. One writer tells us that the King said he never saw a good cause so ill defended; and all agree that Rochester closed the conference with the most determined declaration that he was confirmed in his religion.† Giffard, afterwards a Catholic prelate of exemplary character, published an account of the particulars of the controversy, which gives a directly opposite account of it. In the only part of it which can in any degree be tried by historical evidence, the Catholic account of the dispute is more probable. Rochester, if we may believe Giffard, at the end of the conference, said—"The disputants have discoursed learnedly, and I desire time to consider."‡ Agreeably to this statement, Barillon, after mentioning the dispute, told his Court that Rochester still

* Barillon, 4th Nov.—Fox MSS. It is curious that the report of Rochester's dismissal is mentioned by Narcissus Luttrell on the same day on which Barillon's despatch is dated.

† Id. 9th Dec.—Ibid.

‡ Id. 18th Nov.—Ibid.

§ The King to Barillon. Versailles, 19th Oct.—Ibid.

‖ This peculiarly respectable divine assumed the name of Godden;—a practice to which Catholic clergymen were then sometimes reduced to elude persecution.

* Dodd, vol. iii. p. 419. Barillon's short account of the conference is dated on the 12th December, which, after making allowance for the difference of calendars, makes the despatch to be written two days after the conference, which deserves to be mentioned as a proof of Dodd's singular exactness.

† Burnet, Echard, and Kennet. There are other contradictions in the testimony of these historians, and it is evident that Burnet did not implicitly believe Rochester's own story.

‡ Dodd, vol. iii. p. 420.

showed a disposition to be instructed with respect to the difficulties which prevented him from declaring himself a Catholic, and added that some even then expected that he would determine for conformity.* This despatch was written two days after the disputation by a minister who could neither be misinformed, nor have any motive to deceive. Some time afterwards, indeed, Rochester made great efforts to preserve his place, and laboured to persuade the moderate party among the Catholics that it was their interest to support him.† He did not, indeed, offer to sacrifice his opinions; but a man who, after the loss of all confidence and real power, clung with such tenacity to mere office, under a system of which he disapproved every principle, could hardly be supposed to be unassailable. The violent or decisive politicians of the Catholic party dreaded that Rochester might still take the King at his word, and defeat all their plans by a feigned compliance. James distrusted his sincerity, suspected that his object was to amuse and temporise, and at length, weary of his own irresolution, took the decisive measure of removing the only minister by whom the Protestant party had a hold on his councils.

The place of Lord Rochester was accordingly supplied on the 5th of January, 1687, by commissioners, of whom two were Catholics, Lord Bellasis of the cautious, and Lord Dover of the zealous party; and the remaining three, Lord Godolphin, Sir John Ernley, and Sir Stephen Fox, were probably chosen for their capacity and experience in the affairs of finance. Two days afterwards Parliament, in which the Protestant Tories, the followers of Rochester, predominated, was prorogued. James endeavoured to soften the removal of his minister by a pension of 4000*l.* a year on the Post Office for a term of years, together with the polluted grant of a perpetual annuity of 1700*l.* a year out of the forfeited estate of Lord Gray,‡ for the sake of which the King, under a false show of mercy, had spared the life of that nobleman. The King was no longer, however, at pains to conceal his displeasure. He told Barillon that Rochester favoured the French Protestants, whom, as a term of reproach, he called "Calvinists," and added that this was one of many instances in which the sentiments of the minister were opposite to those of his master.§ He informed D'Adda that the Treasurer's obstinate perseverance in error had at length rendered his removal inevitable; but that wary minister adds, that they who had the most sanguine hopes of the final success of the Catholic cause were obliged to own that, at that moment, the public temper was inflamed and exasperated, and that the cry of the people was, that since Rochester was dismissed because he would not become a Catholic, there must be a design to expel all Protestants from office.*

The fall of Rochester was preceded, and probably quickened, by an important change in the administration of Scotland, and it was also connected with a revolution in the government of Ireland, of both which events it is now necessary to relate the most important particulars.

* Barillon, 12th Dec.—Fox MSS.
† Id. 30th Dec.—Ibid.
‡ Evelyn, vol. i. p. 595.
§ Barillon, 13th Jan. 1687.—Fox MSS.

CHAPTER IV.

Scotland.—Administration of Queensberry.—Conversion of Perth.—Measures contemplated by the King.—Debates in Parliament on the King's letter.—Proposed bill of toleration—unsatisfactory to James.—Adjournment of Parliament.—Exercise of prerogative.

Ireland.—Character of Tyrconnel.—Review of the state of Ireland.—Arrival of Tyrconnel.—His appointment as Lord Deputy.—Advancement of Catholics to offices.—Tyrconnel aims at the sovereign power in Ireland.—Intrigues with France.

The government of Scotland, under the Episcopal ministers of Charles II., was such, that, to the Presbyterians, who formed the majority of the people, "their native country had, by the prevalence of persecution and violence, become as insecure as a den of robbers."† The chief place in the administration had been filled for some years by Queensberry, a man of ability, the leader of the Episcopal party, who, in that character as well as from a matrimonial connection between their families, was disposed to an union of councils with Rochester.‡ Adopting the principles of his English friends, he seemed ready to sacrifice the remaining liberties of his country, but resolved to adhere to the Established Church. The acts of the first session in the reign of James are such as to have extorted from a great historian of calm temper, and friendly to the house of Stuart, the reflection that "nothing could exceed the abject servility of the Scotch nation during this period but the arbitrary severity of the administration."§ Not content with servility and cruelty for the moment, they laid down principles which would render slavery universal and perpetual, by assuring the King "that they abhor and detest all principles and positions which are contrary or derogatory to the King's sacred, supreme, absolute power and authority, which none, whether persons or collective bodies, can participate of, in any manner or on any pretext, but in dependence on him and by commission from him."||

* D'Adda, 10th Jan. 1687.—MS.
† Hume, History of England, chap. lxix.
‡ His son had married the niece of Lady Rochester.
§ Hume, chap. lxx.
|| Acts of Parliament, vol. viii. p. 459.

But the jealousies between the King's party and that of the Church among the Scotch ministers were sooner visible than those between the corresponding factions in the English council; and they seem, in some degree, to have limited the severities which followed the revolt of Argyle. The Privy Council, at the intercession of some ladies of distinction, prevented the Marquis of Athol from hanging Mr. Charles Campbell, then confined by a fever, at the gates of his father's castle of Inverary:* and it was probably by their representations that James was induced to recall instructions which he had issued to the Duke of Queensberry for the suppression of the name of Campbell;† which would have amounted to a proscription of several noblemen, a considerable body of gentry, and the most numerous and powerful tribe in the kingdom. They did not, however, hesitate in the execution of the King's orders to dispense with the Test in the case of four peers and twenty-two gentlemen, who were required by law to take it before they exercised the office of commissioners to assess the supply in their respective counties.‡

The Earl of Perth, the Chancellor of Scotland, began now to attack Queensberry by means somewhat similar to those employed by Sunderland against Rochester. Queensberry had two years before procured the appointment of Perth, as it was believed, by a present of a sum of 27,000*l.* of public money to the Duchess of Portsmouth. Under a new reign, when that lady was by no means a favourite, both Queensberry and Perth apprehended a severe inquisition into this misapplication of public money;§ Perth, whether actuated by fear or ambition, made haste to consult his security and advancement by conforming to the religion of the Court, on which Lord Halifax observed, that "his faith had made him whole." Queensberry adhered to the Established Church.

The Chancellor soon began to exercise that ascendency which he acquired by his conversion, in such a manner as to provoke immediate demonstrations of the zeal against the Church of Rome, which the Scotch Presbyterians carried farther than any other Reformed community. He issued an order against the sale of any books without license, which was universally understood as intended to prevent the circulation of controversial writings against the King's religion. Glen, a bookseller in Edinburgh, when he received this warning, said, that he had one book which strongly condemned Popery, and desired to know whether he might continue to sell it. Being asked what the book was, he answered, "The Bible."‖ Shortly afterwards the populace manifested their indignation at the public celebration of mass by riots, in the suppression of which several persons were killed. A law to inflict adequate penalties on such offences against the security of religious worship would have been perfectly just. But as the laws of Scotland had, however unjustly, made it a crime to be present at the celebration of mass, it was said, with some plausibility, that the rioters had only dispersed an unlawful assembly. The lawyers evaded this difficulty by the ingenious expedient of keeping out of view the origin and object of the tumults, and prosecuted the offenders, merely for *rioting* in violation of certain ancient statutes, some of which rendered that offence capital. They were pursued with such singular barbarity, that one Keith, who was not present at the tumult, was executed for having said, that he would have helped the rioters, and for having drank confusion to all Papists; though he at the same time drank the health of the King, and though in both cases he only followed the example of the witnesses on whose evidence he was convicted. Attempts were vainly made to persuade this poor man to charge Queensberry with being accessory to the riots, which he had freely ridiculed in private. That nobleman was immediately after removed from the office of Treasurer, but he was at the same time appointed Lord President of the Council with a pension, that the Court might retain some hold on him during the important discussions at the approaching session of Parliament.

The King communicated to the secret committee of the Scotch Privy Council his intended instructions to the Commissioners relative to the measures to be proposed to Parliament. They comprehended the repeal of the Test, the abrogation of the sanguinary laws as far as they related to Papists, the admission of these last to all civil and military employments, and the confirmation of all the King's dispensations, even in the reigns of his successors, unless they were recalled by Parliament. On these terms he declared his willingness to assent to any law (not repugnant to these things) for securing the Protestant religion, and the personal dignities, offices, and possessions of the clergy, and for continuing all laws against fanaticism.* The Privy Council manifested some unwonted scruples about these propositions: James answered them angrily.† Perplexed by this unexpected resistance, as well as by the divisions in the Scottish councils, and the repugnance shown by the Episcopalian party to any measure which might bring the privileges of Catholics more near to a level with their own, he commanded the Duke of Hamilton and Sir George Lockhart, President of the Court of Session, to come to London, with a view to ascertain their inclinations, and to dispose them favourably to his objects, but under colour of consulting them on the nature of the relief which it might be

* Fountainhall, Chronicle, vol. i. p. 366.
† Warrant, 1st June, 1685.—State Paper Office.
‡ Warrant, 7th Dec.—Ibid.
§ Fountainhall, vol. i. p. 189.
‖ Ibid. p. 390.

* 4th March, 1686.—State Paper Office.
† 18th March.—Ibid.

prudent to propose for the members of his own communion.* The Scotch negotiators (for as such they seem to have acted) conducted the discussion with no small discretion and dexterity. They professed their readiness to concur in the repeal of the penal and sanguinary laws against Catholics; observing, however, the difficulty of proposing to confine such an indulgence to one class of dissidents, and the policy of moving for a general toleration, which it would be as much the interests of Presbyterians as of Catholics to promote. They added, that it might be more politic not to propose the repeal of the Test as a measure of government, but either to leave it to the spontaneous disposition of Parliament, which would very probably repeal a law aimed in Scotland against Presbyterians as exclusively as it had in England been intended to exclude Catholics, or to trust to the King's dispensing power, which was there undisputed;—as indeed every part of the prerogative was in that country held to be above question, and without limits.† These propositions embarrassed James and his more zealous counsellors. The King struggled obstinately against the extension of the liberty to the Presbyterians. The Scotch councillors required, that if the Test was repealed, the King should bind himself by the most solemn promise to attempt no farther alteration or abridgment of the privileges of the Protestant clergy. James did not conceal from them his repugnance thus to confirm and to secure the establishment of a heretical Church. He imputed the pertinacity of Hamilton to the insinuations of Rochester, and that of Lockhart to the still more obnoxious influence of his father-in-law, Lord Wharton.‡

The Earl of Moray, a recent convert to the Catholic religion, opened Parliament on the 29th of April, and laid before it a royal letter, exhibiting traces of the indecision and ambiguity which were the natural consequence of the unsuccessful issue of the conferences in London. The King begins with holding out the temptation of a free trade with England, and after tendering an ample amnesty, proceeds to state, that while he shows these acts of mercy to the enemies of his crown and royal dignity, he cannot be unmindful of his Roman Catholic subjects, who had adhered to the Crown in rebellions and usurpations, though they lay under discouragements hardly to be named. He recommends them to the care of Parliament, and desires that they may have the protection of the laws and the same security with other subjects, without being laid under obligations which their religion will not admit of. "This love," he says, "we expect ye will show to your brethren, as you see we are an indulgent father to you all."§

At the next sitting an answer was voted, thanking the King for his endeavours to procure a free trade with England; expressing the utmost admiration of the offer of amnesty to such desperate rebels against so merciful a prince; declaring, "as to that part of your Majesty's letter which relates to your subjects of the Roman Catholic persuasion, we shall, in obedience to your Majesty's commands, and in tenderness to their persons, take the same into our serious and dutiful consideration, and go as great lengths therein as our consciences will allow;" and concluding with these words, which were the more significant because they were not called for by any correspondent paragraph in the King's letter:—"Not doubting that your Majesty will be careful to secure the Protestant religion established by law." Even this answer, cold and guarded as it was, did not pass without some debate, important only as indicating the temper of the assembly. The words, "subjects of the Roman Catholic religion," were objected to, "as not to be given by Parliament to individuals, whom the law treated as criminals, and to a Church which Protestants could not, without inconsistency, regard as entitled to the appellation of Catholic." Lord Fountainhall proposed as an amendment, the substitution of "those commonly called Roman Catholics." The Earl of Perth called this nicknaming the King, and proposed, "those subjects your Majesty has recommended." The Archbishop of Glasgow supported the original answer, upon condition of an entry in the Journals, declaring that the words were used only out of courtesy to the King, as a repetition of the language of his letter. A minority of fifty-six in a house of one hundred and eighty-two voted against the original words, even though they were to be thus explained.* Some members doubted whether they could sincerely profess a disposition to go any farther lengths in favour of the Romanists, being convinced that all the laws against the members of that communion ought to continue in force. The Parliament having been elected under the administration of Queensberry, the Episcopal party was very powerful both in that assembly and in the committee called the "Lords of the Articles," with whom alone a bill could originate. The Scottish Catholics were an inconsiderable body; and the Presbyterians, though comprehending the most intelligent, moral, and religious part of the people, so far from having any influence in the legislature, were proscribed as criminals, and subject to a more cruel and sanguinary persecution at the hands of their Protestant brethren than either of these communions had ever experienced from Catholic rulers.† Those of the prelates who preferred the interest of their order to their

* Fountainhall, vol. i. p. 410.

† Barillon, 22d April.—Fox MSS.

‡ Id. 29th April.—Ibid.

§ Acts of Parliament, vol. viii. p. 580.

* Fountainhall, vol. i. p. 413.

† Wodrow, History of the Church of Scotland, &c., vol. ii. p. 498:—an avowed partisan, but a most sincere and honest writer, to whom great thanks are due for having preserved that collection of facts and documents which will for ever render

own were dissatisfied even with the very limited measure of toleration laid before the Lords of the Articles, which only proposed to exempt Catholics from punishment on account of the private exercise of their religious worship.* The Primate was alarmed by a hint thrown out by the Duke of Hamilton, that a toleration so limited might be granted to dissenting Protestants;† nor, on the other hand, was the resistance of the prelates softened by the lure held out by the King in his first instructions, that if they would remove the Test against Catholics they should be indulged in the persecution of their fellow Protestants. The Lords of the Articles were forced to introduce into the bill two clauses;—one declaring their determination to adhere to the established religion, the other expressly providing, that the immunity and forbearance contemplated should not derogate from the laws which required the oath of allegiance and the test to be taken by all persons in offices of public trust.‡

The arguments on both sides are to be found in pamphlets then printed at Edinburgh; those for the Government publicly and actively circulated, those of the opposite party disseminated clandestinely.§ The principal part, as in all such controversies, consists in personalities, recriminations, charges of inconsistency, and addresses to prejudice, which scarcely any ability can render interesting after the passions from which they spring have subsided and are forgotten. It happened, also, that temporary circumstances required or occasioned the best arguments not to be urged by the disputants. Considered on general principles, the bill, like every other measure of toleration, was justly liable to no permanent objection but its incompleteness and partiality. But no Protestant sect was then so tolerant as to object to the imperfection of the relief to be granted to Catholics; and the ruling party were neither entitled nor disposed to complain, that the Protestant Non-conformists, whom they had so long persecuted, were not to be comprehended in the toleration. The only objection which could reasonably be made to the tolerant principles, now for the first time inculcated by the advocates of the Court, was, that they were not proposed with good faith, or for the relief of the Catholics but for the subversion of the Protestant Church, and the ultimate establishment of Popery, with all the horrors which were to follow in its train. The present effects of the bill were a subject of more urgent consideration than its general character. It was more necessary to ascertain the purpose which it was intended and calculated to promote at the instant, than to examine the principles on which such a measure, in other circumstances and in common times, might be perfectly wise and just. Even then, had any man been liberal and bold enough to propose universal and perfect liberty of worship, the adoption of such a measure would probably have afforded the most effectual security against the designs of the Crown. But very few entertained so generous a principle: and of these, some might doubt the wisdom of its application in that hour of peril, while no one could have proposed it with any hope that it could be adopted by the majority of such a Parliament. It can hardly be a subject of wonder, that the Established clergy, without any root in the opinions and affections of the people, on whom they were imposed by law, and against whom they were maintained by persecution, should not in the midst of conscious weakness have had calmness and fortitude enough to consider the policy of concession, but trembling for their unpopular dignities and invidious revenues, should recoil from the surrender of the most distant outpost which seemed to guard them, and struggle with all their might to keep those who threatened to become their most formidable rivals under the brand at least,—if not the scourge,—of penal laws. It must be owned, that the language of the Court writers was not calculated either to calm the apprehensions of the Church, or to satisfy the solicitude of the friends of liberty. They told Parliament, "that if the King were exasperated by the rejection of the bill, he might, without the violation of any law, alone remove all Protestant officers and judges from the government of the State, and all Protestant bishops and ministers from the government of the Church;"*—a threat the more alarming, because the dispensing power seemed sufficient to carry it into effect in civil offices, and the Scotch Act of Supremacy, passed in one of the paroxysms of servility which were frequent in the first years of the Restoration,† appeared to afford the means of fully accomplishing it against the Church.

The unexpected obstinacy of the Scottish Parliament alarmed and offended the Court. Their answer did not receive the usual compliment of publication in the Gazette.—Orders were sent to Edinburgh to remove two Privy Councillors,‡ to displace Seton, a judge, and to deprive the Bishop of Dunkeld of a pension, for their conduct. Sir George Mackenzie, himself, the most eloquent and accomplished Scotchman of his age, was for

it impossible to extenuate the tyranny exercised over Scotland from the Restoration to the Revolution.

* Wodrow, vol. ii. p. 594.

† Fountainhall, vol. i. p 415.

‡ Wodrow, vol. ii. app.

§ Ibid. Wodrow ascribes the Court pamphlet to Sir Roger L'Estrange, in which he is followed by Mr. Laing, though, in answer to it, it is said to have been written by a clergyman who had preached before the Parliament. L'Estrange was then in Edinburgh, probably engaged in some more popular controversy. The tract in question seems more likely to have been written by Paterson, Bishop of Edinburgh.

* Wodrow, vol. ii. app. † 1669.

‡ The Earl of Glencairn and Sir W. Bruce.

the same reason dismissed from the office of Lord Advocate.* It was in vain that he had dishonoured his genius by being for ten years the advocate of tyranny and the minister of persecution: all his ignominious claims were cancelled by the independence of one day. It was hoped that such examples might strike terror.* Several noblemen, who held commissions in the army, were ordered to repair to their posts. Some members were threatened with the avoidance of their elections.† A prosecution was commenced against the Bishop of Ross, and the proceedings were studiously protracted, to weary out the poorer part of those who refused to comply with the Court. The ministers scrupled at no expedient for seducing, or intimidating, or harassing. But these expedients proved ineffectual. The majority of the Parliament adhered to their principles; and the session lingered for about a month in the midst of ordinary or unimportant affairs.‡ The Bill for Toleration was not brought up by the Lords of the Articles. The commissioners, doubting whether it would be carried, and probably instructed by the Court that it would neither satisfy the expectations nor promote the purposes of the King, in the middle of June adjourned the Parliament, which was never again to assemble.

It was no wonder that the King should have been painfully disappointed by the failure of his attempt; for after the conclusion of the session, it was said by zealous and pious Protestants, that nothing less than a special interposition of Providence could have infused into such an assembly a steadfast resolution to withstand the Court.§ The royal displeasure was manifested by measures of a very violent sort. The despotic supremacy of the King over the Church was exercised by depriving Bruce of his bishopric of Dunkeld;‖—a severity which, not long after, was repeated in the deprivation of Cairncross, Archbishop of Glasgow, for some sup-

* "Sir George Mackenzie was the grandson of Kenneth, first Lord Mackenzie of Kintail, and the nephew of Colin and George, first and second Earls of Seaforth. He was born at Dundee in 1636, and after passing through the usual course of education in his own country, he was sent for three years to the University of Bourges, at that time, as he tells us, called the 'Athens of Lawyers;'—as in later times the Scotch lawyers usually repaired to Utrecht and Leyden. He was called to the Bar, and began to practise before the Restoration; immediately after which he was appointed one of the justices-depute—criminal judges, who exercised that jurisdiction which was soon after vested in five lords of session under the denomination of 'commissioners of justiciary.' His name appears in the Parliamentary proceedings as counsel in almost every important cause. He represented the county of Ross for the four sessions of the Parliament which was called in 1669. In 1677 he was appointed Lord Advocate; and was involved by that preferment, most unhappily for his character, in the worst acts of the Scotch administration of Charles II. At the Revolution he adhered to the fortunes of his master. Being elected a member of the Convention, he maintained the pretensions of James with courage and ability against Sir John Dalrymple and Sir James Montgomery, who were the most considerable of the Revolutionary party; and remaining in his place after the imprisonment of Balcarras and the escape of Dundee, he was one of the minority of five in the memorable division on the forfeiture of the crown. When the death of Dundee destroyed the hopes of his party in Scotland, he took refuge at Oxford,—the natural asylum of so learned and inveterate a Tory. Under the tolerant government of William he appears to have enjoyed his ample fortune,—the fruit of his professional labours,—with perfect comfort as well as security. He died in St. James' Street in May, 1691; and his death is mentioned as that of an extraordinary person by several of those who recorded the events of their time, before the necrology of this country was so undistinguishing as it has now become. The pomp and splendour of his interment at Edinburgh affords farther evidence how little the administration of William was disposed to discourage the funeral honours paid to his most inflexible opponents. The writings of Sir George Mackenzie are literary, legal, and political. His Miscellaneous Essays, both in prose and verse, may now be dispensed with, or laid aside, without difficulty. They have not vigour enough for long life. But if they be considered as the elegant amusements of a statesman and lawyer, who had little leisure for the cultivation of letters, they afford a striking proof of the variety of his accomplishments, and of the refinement of his taste. In several of his Moral Essays, both the subject and the manner betray an imitation of Cowley, who was at that moment beginning the reformation of English style. Sir George Mackenzie was probably tempted by the example of this great master, to write in praise of Solitude: and Evelyn answered by a panegyric on Active life. It seems singular that Mackenzie, plunged in the harshest labours of ambition, should be the advocate of retirement; and that Evelyn, comparatively a recluse, should have commended that mode of life which he did not choose. Both works were, however, rhetorical exercises, in which a puerile ingenuity was employed on questions which admitted no answer, and were not therefore the subject of sincere opinion. Before we can decide whether a retired or a public life be best, we must ask,—best for whom? The absurdity of these childish generalities, which exercised the wit of our forefathers, has indeed been long acknowledged. Perhaps posterity may discover, that many political questions which agitate our times are precisely of the same nature; and that it would be almost as absurd to attempt the establishment of a democracy in China as the foundation of a nobility in Connecticut."—Abridged from the "Edinburgh Review," vol. xxxvi. p. 1. ED.

* Fountainhall, vol. i. p. 414.

† Ibid. p. 419.

‡ Among the frivolous but characteristic transactions of this session was the "Bore Brieve," or authenticated pedigree granted to the Marquis de Seignelai, as a supposed descendant of the ancient family of Cuthbert of Castlehill, in Inverness-shire. His father, the great Colbert, who appears to have been the son of a reputable woollen-draper of Troyes, had attempted to obtain the same certificate of genealogy, but such was the pride of birth at that time in Scotland, that his attempts were vain. It now required all the influence of the Court, set in motion by the solicitations of Barillon, to obtain it for Seignelai. By an elaborate display of all the collateral relations of the Cuthberts, the "Bore Brieve" connects Seignelai with the Royal Family, and with all the nobility and gentry of the kingdom.—Acts of Parliament, vol. iii. p. 611.

§ Fountainhall, vol. i. p. 419. ‖ Ibid. p. 416.

posed countenance to an obnoxious preacher, though that prelate laboured to avert it by promises of support to all measures favourable to the King's religion.* A few days after the prorogation, Queensberry was dismissed from all his offices, and required not to leave Edinburgh until he had rendered an account of his administration of the treasury.† Some part of the royal displeasure fell upon Sir George Mackenzie, the Lord Register, lately created Lord Cromarty, the most submissive servant of every government, for having flattered the King, by too confident assurances of a majority as obsequious as himself. The connection of Rochester with Queensberry now aggravated the offence of the latter, and prepared the way for the downfall of the former. Moray, the commissioner, promised positive proofs, but produced at last only such circumstances as were sufficient to confirm the previous jealousies of James, that the Scotch Opposition were in secret correspondence with Pensionary Fagel, and even with the Prince of Orange.‡ Sir George Mackenzie, whose unwonted independence seems to have speedily faltered, was refused an audience of the King, when he visited London with the too probable purpose of making his peace. The most zealous Protestants being soon afterwards removed from the Privy Council, and the principal noblemen of the Catholic communion being introduced in their stead, James addressed a letter to the Council, informing them that his application to Parliament had not arisen from any doubt of his own power to stop the severities against Catholics; declaring his intention to allow the exercise of the Catholic worship, and to establish a chapel for that purpose in his own palace of Holyrood House; and intimating to the judges, that they were to receive the allegation of this allowance as a valid defence, any law to the contrary notwithstanding.§ The warm royalists, in their proposed answer, expressly acknowledge the King's prerogative to be a legal security: but the Council, in consequence of an objection of the Duke of Hamilton, faintly asserted their independence, by substituting "sufficient" instead of "legal."‖

The determination was thus avowed of pursuing the objects of the King's policy in Scotland by the exercise of prerogative, at least until a more compliant Parliament could be obtained, which would not only remove all doubt for the present, but protect the Catholics against the recall of the dispensations by James' successors. The means principally relied on for the accomplishment of that object was the power now assumed by the King to stop the annual elections in burghs, to nominate the chief magistrates, and through them to command the election by more summary proceedings than those of the English courts. The choice of ministers corresponded with the principles of administration. The disgrace of the Duke of Hamilton, a few months later,* completed the transfer of power to the party which professed an unbounded devotion to the principles of their master in the government both of Church and State. The measures of the Government did not belie their professions. Sums of money, considerable when compared with the scanty revenue of Scotland, were employed in support of establishments for the maintenance and propagation of the Roman Catholic religion. A sum of 1400*l.* a year was granted, in equal portions, to the Catholic missionaries, to the Jesuit missionaries, to the mission in the Highlands, to the Chapel Royal, and to each of the Scotch colleges at Paris, Douay, and Rome.† The Duke of Hamilton, Keeper of the Palace, was commanded to surrender the Chancellor's apartments in Holyrood House to a college of Jesuits.‡ By a manifest act of partiality, two-thirds of the allowance made by Charles the Second to indigent royalists were directed to be paid to Catholics; and all pensions and allowances to persons of that religion were required to be paid in the first place, in preference to all other pensions.§ Some of these grants, it is true, if they had been made by a liberal sovereign in a tolerant age, were in themselves justifiable; but neither the character of the King, nor the situation of the country, nor the opinions of the times, left any reasonable man at liberty then to doubt their purpose; and some of them were attended by circumstances which would be remarkable as proofs of the infatuated imprudence of the King and his counsellors, if they were not more worthy of observation as symptoms of that insolent contempt with which they trampled on the provisions of law, and on the strongest feelings of the people.

The government of Ireland, as well as that of England and Scotland, was, at the accession of James, allowed to remain in the hands of Protestant Tories. The Lord-lieutenancy was, indeed, taken from the Duke of Ormonde, then far advanced in years, but it was bestowed on a nobleman of the same party, Lord Clarendon, whose moderate understanding added little to those claims on high office, which he derived from his birth, connections, and opinions. But the feeble and timid Lord Lieutenant was soon held in check by Richard Talbot, then created Earl

* Fountainhall, vol i. p. 441. Skinner, Ecclesiastical History, vol. ii. p. 503.

† Ibid. p. 420.

‡ Barillon, 1st—22d July, 1686.—Fox MSS. It will appear in the sequel, that these suspicions are at variance with probability, and unsupported by evidence.

§ Wodrow, vol. ii. p. 598.

‖ Fountainhall, vol. i. p. 424.

* Fountainhall, vol. i. p. 449—451. Letter (in State Paper Office,) 1st March, 1687, expressing the King's displeasure at the conduct of Hamilton, and directing the names of his sons-in-law, Panmure and Dunmore, to be struck out of the list of the Council.

† Warrants in the State Paper Office, dated 19th May, 1687.

‡ Ibid. 15th August. § Ibid. 7th January, 1688.

of Tyrconnel, a Catholic gentleman of ancient English extraction, who joined talents and spirit to violent passions, boisterous manners, unbounded indulgence in every excess, and a furious zeal for his religious party.* His character was tainted by that disposition to falsehood and artifice, which, however seemingly inconsistent with violent passions, is often combined with them; and he possessed more of the beauty and bravery than of the wit or eloquence of his unhappy nation. He had been first introduced to Charles II. and his brother before the Restoration, as one who was willing to assassinate Cromwell, and had made a journey into England with that resolution. He soon after received an appointment in the household of the Duke of York, and retained the favour of that prince during the remainder of his life. In the year 1666, he was imprisoned for a few days by Charles II., for having resolved to assassinate the Duke of Ormonde, with whose Irish administration he was dissatisfied.† He did not, however, even by the last of these criminal projects, forfeit the patronage of either of the royal brothers, and at the accession of James held a high place among his personal favourites. He was induced, both by zeal for the Catholic party, and by animosity against the family of Hyde, to give effectual aid to Sunderland in the overthrow of Rochester, and required in return that the conduct of Irish affairs should be left to him.‡ Sunderland dreaded the temper of Tyrconnel, and was desirous of performing his part of the bargain with as little risk as possible to the quiet of Ireland. The latter at first contented himself with the rank of senior General Officer on the Irish staff; in which character he returned to Dublin in June, 1686, as the avowed favourite of the King, and with powers to new-model the army. His arrival, however, had been preceded by reports of extensive changes in the government of the kingdom.* The State, the Church, the administration, and the property of that unhappy island, were bound together by such unnatural ties, and placed on such weak foundations, that every rumour of alteration in one of them spread the deepest alarm for the safety of the whole.

From the colonization of a small part of the eastern coast under Henry II., till the last years of the reign of Elizabeth, an unceasing and cruel warfare was waged by the English governors against the princes and chiefs of the Irish tribes, with little other effect than that of preventing the progress of civilization among the Irish, of replunging many of the English into barbarism, and of generating that deadly animosity between the natives and the invaders, under the names of Irishry and Englishry, which, assuming various forms, and exasperated by a fatal succession of causes, has continued even to our days the source of innumerable woes. During that dreadful period of four hundred years, the laws of the English colony did not punish the murder of a man of Irish blood as a crime.† Even so late as the year 1547, the Colonial Assembly, called a "Parliament," confirmed the insolent laws which prohibited the English "of the pale" from marrying persons of Irish blood.‡ Religious hostility inflamed the hatred of these mortal foes. The Irish, attached to their ancient opinions as well as usages, and little addicted to doubt or inquiry, rejected the reformation of religion offered to them by their enemies. The Protestant worship became soon to be considered by them as the odious badge of conquest and oppression;§ while the ancient religion was endeared by persecution, and by its association with the name, the language, and the manners of their country. The island had long been represented as a fief of the See of Rome; the Catholic clergy, and even laity, had no unchangeable friend but the Sovereign Pontiff; and their chief hope of deliverance from a hostile yoke was long confined to Spain, the

* The means by which Talbot obtained the favour of James, if we may believe the accounts of his enemies, were somewhat singular. "Clarendon's daughter had been got with child in Flanders, on a pretended promise of marriage, by the Duke of York, who was forced by the King, at her father's importunity, to marry her, after he had resolved the contrary, and got her reputation blasted by Lord Fitzharding and Colonel Talbot, who impudently affirmed that they had received the last favours from her."—Sheridan MS. Stuart Papers. "5th July 1694. Sir E. Harley told us, that when the Duke of York resolved on putting away his first wife, particularly on discovery of her commerce with ———, she by her father's advice turned Roman Catholic, and thereby secured herself from reproach, and that the pretence of her father's opposition to it was only to act a part, and secure himself from blame."—MSS. in the handwriting of Lord Treasurer Oxford, in the possession of the Duke of Portland. The latter of these passages from the concluding part must refer to the time of the marriage. But it must not be forgotten that both the reporters were the enemies of Clarendon, and that Sheridan was the bitter enemy of Tyrconnel.

† Clarendon, Continuation of History (Oxford, 1759), p. 362.

‡ Sheridan MS. Stuart Papers.

* Clarendon's Letters, *passim*.

† Sir J. Davies, Discoverie, &c., pp. 102—112. "They were so far out of the protection of the laws that it was often adjudged no felony to kill a mere Irishman in time of peace,"—except he were of the five privileged tribes of the O'Neils of Ulster, the O'Malaghlins of Meath, the O'Connors of Connaught, the O'Briens of Thomond, and the MacMurroughs of Leinster; to whom are to be added the Oastmen of the city of Waterford.—See also Leland, History of Ireland, book i. chap. 3.

‡ 28 Hen. VIII. c. 13. "The English," says Sir W. Petty, "before Henry VII.'s time, lived in Ireland as the Europeans do in America."—Political Anatomy of Ireland, p. 112.

§ That the hostility of religion was, however, a secondary prejudice superinduced on hostility between nations, appears very clearly from the laws of Catholic sovereigns against the Irish, even after the Reformation, particularly the Irish statute of 3 & 4 Phil. & Mar. c. 2, against the O'Mores, and O'Dempsies, and O'Connors, "and others of the Irishry."

leader of the Catholic party in the European commonwealth. The old enmity of Irishry and Englishry thus appeared with redoubled force under the new names of Catholic and Protestant. The necessity of self-defence compelled Elizabeth to attempt the complete reduction of Ireland, which, since she had assumed her station at the head of Protestants, became the only vulnerable part of her dominions, and a weapon in the hands of her most formidable enemies. But few of the benefits which sometimes atone for conquest were felt by Ireland. Neither the success with which Elizabeth broke the barbaric power of the Irish chieftains, nor the real benevolence and seeming policy of introducing industrious colonies under her successor, counterbalanced the dreadful evil which was then for the first time added to her hereditary sufferings. The extensive forfeiture of the lands of the Catholic Irish, and the grant of these lands to Protestant natives of Great Britain, became a new source of hatred between these irreconcilable factions. Forty years of quiet, however, followed, in which a Parliament of all districts, and of both religions, was assembled. The administration of the Earl of Strafford bore the stamp of the political vices which tarnished his genius, and which often prevailed over those generous affections of which he was not incapable towards those who neither rivalled nor resisted him. The state of Ireland abounded with temptations,—to a man of daring and haughty spirit, intent on taming a turbulent people, and impatient of slow discipline of law and justice,—to adopt those violent and summary measures, the necessity of which his nature prompted him too easily to believe.* When his vigorous arm was withdrawn, the Irish were once more excited to revolt by the memory of the provocations which they had received from him and from his predecessors, by the feebleness of their government, and by the confusion and distraction which announced the approach of civil war in Great Britain. This insurrection, which broke out in 1641, and of which the atrocities appear to have been extravagantly exaggerated† by the writers of the victorious party, was only finally subdued by the genius of Cromwell, who, urged by the general antipathy against the Irish,‡ and the peculiar animosity of his own followers towards Catholics, exercised more than once in his Irish campaigns the most odious rights or practices of war, departing from the clemency which usually distinguished him above most men who have obtained supreme power by violence. The confiscation which followed Cromwell's victories, added to the forfeitures under Elizabeth and James, transferred more than two-thirds of the land of the kingdom to British adventurers.* "Not only all the Irish nation (with very few exceptions) were found guilty of the rebellion, and forfeited all their estates, but all the English Catholics of Ireland were declared to be under the same guilt."† The ancient proprietors conceived sanguine hopes, that confiscations by usurpers would not be ratified by the restored government. But their agents were inexperienced, indiscreet, and sometimes mercenary; while their opponents, who were in possession of power and property, chose the Irish House of Commons, and secured the needy and rapacious courtiers of Charles II. by large bribes.‡ The Court became a mart at which much of the property of Ireland was sold to the highest bidder;—the inevitable result of measures not governed by rules of law, but loaded with exceptions and conditions, where the artful use of a single word might affect the possession of considerable fortunes, and where so many minute particulars relating to unknown and uninteresting subjects were necessarily introduced, that none but parties deeply concerned had the patience to examine them. Charles was desirous of an arrangement which should give him the largest means of quieting, by profuse grants, the importunity of his favourites. He began to speak of the necessity of strengthening the English interest in Ireland, and he represented the "settlement" rather as a matter of policy than of justice. The usual and legitimate policy of statesmen and lawgivers is, doubtless, to favour every measure which quiets present possession, and to discourage all retrospective inquisition into the tenure of property. But the Irish Government professed to adopt a principle of compromise, and the general object of the statute called the "Act of Settlement," was to secure the land in the hands of its possessors, on condition of their making a certain compensation to those classes of expelled proprietors who were considered as innocent of the rebellion. Those, however, were declared not to be innocent who had accepted the terms of peace granted by the King in 1648, who had paid contributions to support the insurgent administration, or who enjoyed any real or personal property in the districts occupied by the rebel army. The first of these con-

* See Carte's Life of Ormonde, and the confessions of Clarendon, together with the evidence on the Trial of Strafford.

† Evidence of this exaggeration is to be found in Carte and Leland, in the Political Anatomy of Ireland, by Sir W. Petty, — to say nothing of Curry's Civil Wars, which, though the work of an Irish Catholic, deserves the serious consideration of every historical inquirer. Sir W. Petty limits the number of Protestants *killed* throughout the island, in the first year of the war, to thirty-seven thousand. The massacres were confined to Ulster, and in that province were imputed only to the detachment of insurgents under Sir Phelim O'Neal.

‡ Even Milton calls the Irish Catholics, or, in other words, the Irish nation, "Conscelerata et barbara colluvies."

* Petty, pp. 1—3.

† Life of Clarendon (Oxford, 1759), vol. ii. p. 115.

‡ Carte, Life of Ormonde, vol. ii. p. 295. Talbot, afterwards Earl of Tyrconnel, returned to Ireland with 18,000*l*.

ditions was singularly unjust; the two latter must have comprehended many who were entirely innocent; and all of them were inconsistent with those principles of compromise and provision for the interest of all on which the act was professedly founded. Ormonde, however, restored to his own great estates, and gratified by a grant of 30,000*l.* from the Irish Commons, acquiesced in this measure, and it was not opposed by his friend Clarendon;—circumstances which naturally, though perhaps not justly, have rendered the memory of these celebrated men odious to the Irish Catholics. During the whole reign of Charles II. they struggled to obtain a repeal of the Act of Settlement. But Time opposed his mighty power to their labours. Every new year strengthened the rights of the possessors, and furnished additional objections against the claims of the old owners. It is far easier to do mischief than to repair it; and it is one of the most malignant properties of extensive confiscation that it is commonly irreparable. The land is shortly sold to honest purchasers; it is inherited by innocent children; it becomes the security of creditors; its safety becomes interwoven, by the complicated transactions of life, with all the interests of the community. One act of injustice is not atoned for by the commission of another against parties who may be equally unoffending. In such cases the most specious plans for the investigation of conflicting claims lead either to endless delay, attended by the entire suspension of the enjoyment of the disputed property, if not by a final extinction of its value, or to precipitate injustice, arising from caprice, from favour, from enmity, or from venality. The resumption of forfeited property, and the restoration of it to the heirs of the ancient owners, may be attended by all the mischievous consequences of the original confiscation; by the disturbance of habits, and by the disappointment of expectations; and by an abatement of that reliance on the inviolability of legal possession, which is the mainspring of industry, and the chief source of comfort.

The arrival of Tyrconnel revived the hopes of the Catholics. They were at that time estimated to amount to eight hundred thousand souls; the English Episcopalians, the English Nonconformists, and the Scotch Presbyterians, each to one hundred thousand.* There was an army of three thousand men, which in the sequel of this reign was raised to eight thousand. The net revenue afforded a yearly average of 300,000*l.*† Before the civil war of 1641, the disproportion of numbers of Catholics to Protestants had been much greater; and by the consequences of that event, the balance of property had been entirely reversed.* "In playing of this game or match" (the war of 1641) "upon so great odds, the English," says Sir William Petty, "won, and have a gamester's right at least to their estates."† On the arrival of Tyrconnel, too, were redoubled the fears of the Protestants for possessions always invidious, and now, as it seemed, about to be precarious. The attempt to give both parties a sort of representation in the government, and to balance the Protestant Lord Lieutenant by a Catholic commander of the army, unsettled the minds of the two communions. The Protestants, though they saw that the rising ascendant of Tyrconnel would speedily become irresistible, were betrayed into occasional indiscretion by the declarations of the Lord Lieutenant; and the Catholics, aware of their growing force, were only exasperated by Clarendon's faint and fearful show of zeal for the established laws. The contemptuous disregard, or rather indecent insolence manifested by Tyrconnel in his conversations with Lord Clarendon, betrayed a consciousness of the superiority of a royal favourite over a Lord Lieutenant, who had to execute a system to which he was disinclined, and was to remain in office a little longer only as a pageant of state. He indulged all his habitual indecencies and excesses; he gave loose to every passion, and threw off every restraint of good manners in those conversations. It is difficult to represent them in a manner compatible with the decorum of history: yet they are too characteristic to be passed over. "You must know, my Lord," said Tyrconnel, "that the King is a Roman Catholic, and resolved to employ his subjects of that religion, and that he will not keep one man in his service who ever served under the usurpers. The sheriffs you have made are generally rogues and old Cromwellians. There has not been an honest man sheriff in Ireland these twenty years." Such language, intermingled with oaths, and uttered in the boisterous tone of a braggart youth, somewhat intoxicated, in a military guard-house, are specimens of the manner in which Tyrconnel delivered his opinions to his superior on the gravest affairs of state. It was no wonder that Clarendon told his brother Rochester,—"If this Lord continue in the temper he is in, he will gain here the reputation of a madman; for his treatment of people is scarce to be described."‡ The more moderate of his own communion, comprehending almost all laymen of education or fortune, he reviled as trimmers. He divided the Catholics, and embroiled the King's affairs still farther by a violent prejudice against the native Irish, whom he contemptuously called the "O's

* Petty, p. 8.—As Sir William Petty exaggerates the population of England, which he rates at six millions, considerably more than its amount in 1700 (Population Returns, 1821, Introduction), it is probable he may have overrated that of Ireland; but there is no reason to suspect a mistake in the proportions.

† Supposing the taxes then paid by England and Wales to have been about three millions, each inhabitant contributed ten shillings, while each Irishman paid somewhat more than five.

* Petty, p. 24. † Ibid.

‡ Correspondence of Clarendon and Rochester, vol. ii. Clarendon, Diary, 5th—14th June, 1686.

and Macs."* To the letter of the King's public declarations, or even positive instructions to the Lord Lieutenant, he paid very little regard. He was sent by James "to do the rough work" of remodelling the army and the corporations. With respect to the army, the King professed only to admit all his subjects on an equal footing without regard to religion; but Tyrconnel's language, and, when he had the power, his measures, led to the formation of an exclusively Catholic force.† The Lord Lieutenant reasonably understood the royal intentions to be no more than that the Catholic religion should be no bar to the admission of persons otherwise qualified into corporations: Tyrconnel disregarded such distinctions, and declared, with one of his usual oaths, "I do not know what to say to that; I would have all the Catholics in."‡ Three unexceptionable judges of the Protestant persuasion were, by the King's command, removed from the bench to make way for three Catholics,—Daly, Rice, and Nugent,—also, it ought to be added, of unobjectionable character and competent learning in their profession.§ Officious sycophants hastened to prosecute those incautious Protestants who, in the late times of zeal against Popery, had spoken with freedom against the succession of the Duke of York; though it is due to justice to remark, that the Catholic council, judges, and juries, discouraged these vexatious prosecutions, and prevented them from producing any very grievous effects. The King had in the beginning solemnly declared his determination to adhere to the Act of Settlement; but Tyrconnel, with his usual imprecations, said to the Lord Lieutenant, "These Acts of Settlement, and this new interest, are cursed things."‖ The coarseness and insolence of Tyrconnel could not fail to offend the Lord Lieutenant: but it is apparent, from the latter's own description, that he was still more frightened than provoked; and perhaps more decorous language would not have so suddenly and completely subdued the little spirit of the demure lord. Certain it is that these scenes of violence were immediately followed by the most profuse professions of his readiness to do whatever the King required, without any reservation even of the interest of the Established Church. These professions were not merely formularies of that ignoble obsequiousness which degrades the inferior too much to exalt the superior: they were explicit and precise declarations relating to the particulars of the most momentous measures then in agitation. In speaking of the reformation of the army he repeated his assurance to Sunderland, "that the King may have every thing done here which he has a mind to: and it is more easy to do things quietly than in a storm."* He descended to declare even to Tyrconnel himself, that "it was not material how many Roman Catholics were in the army, if the King would have it so; for whatever his Majesty would have should be made easy as far as lay in me."†

In the mean time Clarendon had incurred the displeasure of the Queen by his supposed civilities to Lady Dorchester during her residence in Ireland. The King was also displeased at the disposition which he imputed to the Lord Lieutenant rather to traverse than to forward the designs of Tyrconnel in favour of the Catholics.‡ It was in vain that the submissive viceroy attempted to disarm these resentments by abject declarations of deep regret and unbounded devotedness. The daily decline of the credit of Rochester deprived his brother of his best support; and Tyrconnel, who returned to Court in August 1686, found it easy to effect a change in the government of Ireland. But he found more difficulty in obtaining that important government for himself. Sunderland tried every means but the resignation of his own office to avert so impolitic an appointment. He urged the declaration of the King, on the removal of Ormonde, that he would not bestow the lieutenancy on a native Irishman: he represented the danger of alarming all Protestants, by appointing to that office an acknowledged enemy of the Act of Settlement, and of exciting the apprehensions of all Englishmen, by intrusting Ireland to a man so devoted to the service of Louis XIV: he offered to make Tyrconnel a Major General on the English staff, with a pension of 5000*l.* a year and with as absolute though as secret authority in the affairs of Ireland, as Lauderdale had possessed in those of Scotland: he promised that after the abrogation of the penal laws in England, Tyrconnel, if he pleased, might be appointed Lord Lieutenant in the room of Lord Powis, who was destined for the present to succeed Clarendon. Tyrconnel turned a deaf ear to these proposals, and threatened to make disclosures to the King and Queen which might overthrow the policy and power of Sunderland. The latter, when he was led by his contest with Rochester to throw himself into the arms of the Roman Catholics, had formed a more particular connection with Jermyn and Talbot, as the King's favourites, and as the enemies of the family of Hyde: Tyrconnel now threatened to disclose the terms and objects of that league, the real purpose of removing Lady Dorchester, and the declaration of Sunderland, when this alliance was formed, "that the King could only be governed by a woman or a priest, and that they must therefore

* Sheridan MS.

† Sheridan MS. It should be observed, that the passages relating to Ireland in the Life of James II., vol. ii. pp. 59—63, were not written by the King, and do not even profess to be founded on the authority of his MSS. They are merely a statement made by Mr. Dicconson, the compiler of that work.

‡ Clarendon, 20th—31st July.

§ Ibid. 19th June.

‖ Ibid. 8th June.

* Clarendon, 20th July.

† Ibid. 30th July.

‡ Ibid. 6th Oct.

§ Clarendon to the King, 6th Oct.; to L[ord] Rochester, 23d Oct.

combine the influence of the Queen with that of Father Petre." Sunderland appears to have made some resistance even after this formidable threat; and Tyrconnel proposed that the young Duke of Berwick should marry his daughter, and be created Lord Lieutenant, while he himself should enjoy the power under the more modest title of "Lord Deputy."* A council, consisting of Sunderland, Tyrconnel, and the Catholic ministers, was held on the affairs of Ireland in the month of October. The members who gave their opinions before Tyrconnel maintained the necessity of conforming to the Act of Settlement; but Tyrconnel exclaimed against them for advising the King to an act of injustice ruinous to the interests of religion. The conscience of James was alarmed, and he appointed the next day to hear the reasons of state which Sunderland had to urge on the opposite side. Tyrconnel renewed his vehement invectives against the iniquity and impiety of the counsels which he opposed; and Sunderland, who began as he often did with useful advice, ended, as usual, with a hesitating and ambiguous submission to his master's pleasure, trusting to accident and his own address to prevent or mitigate the execution of violent measures.† These proceedings decided the contest for office; and Tyrconnel received the sword of state as Lord Deputy on the 12th February, 1687.

The King's professions of equality and impartiality in the distribution of office between the two adverse communions were speedily and totally disregarded. The Lord Deputy and the greater part of the Privy Council, the Lord Chancellor with three fourths of the judges, all the King's counsel but one, almost all the sheriffs, and a majority of corporators and justices, were, in less than a year, Catholics;—numbers so disproportioned to the relative property, education, and ability for business, to be found in the two religions, that even if the appointments had not been tainted with the inexcusable blame of defiance to the laws, they must still have been regarded by the Protestants with the utmost apprehension, as indications of sinister designs. Fitten, the Chancellor, was promoted from the King's Bench prison, where he had been long a prisoner for debt; and he was charged, though probably without reason, by his opponents, with forgery, said to have been committed in a long suit with Lord Macclesfield. His real faults were ignorance and subserviency. Neither of these vices could be imputed to Sir Richard Nagle, the Catholic Attorney General, who seems chargeable only with the inevitable fault of being actuated by a dangerous zeal for his own suffering party. It does not appear that the Catholic judges actually abused their power. We have already seen that, instead of seeking to retaliate for the murders of the Popish Plot, they discountenanced prosecutions against their adversaries with a moderation and forbearance very rarely to be discovered in the policy of parties in the first moments of victory over long oppression. It is true that these Catholic judges gave judgment against the charters of towns; but in these judgments they only followed the example of the most eminent of their Protestant brethren in England.* The evils of insecurity and alarm were those which were chiefly experienced by the Irish Protestants. These mischiefs, very great in themselves, depended so much on the character, temper, and manner, of the Lord Deputy, on the triumphant or sometimes threatening conversation of their Catholic neighbours, on the recollection of bloody civil wars, and on the painful consciousness which haunts the possessors of recently confiscated property, that it may be thought unreasonable to require any other or more positive proof of their prevalence. Some visible fruits of the alarm are pointed out. The Protestants, who were the wealthiest traders as well as the most ingenious artisans of the kingdom, began to emigrate: the revenue is said to have declined: the greater part of the Protestant officers of the army, alarmed by the removal of their brethren, sold their commissions for inadequate prices, and obtained military appointments in Holland, then the home of the exile and the refuge of the oppressed.† But that which Tyrconnel most pursued, and the Protestants most dreaded, was the repeal of the Act of Settlement. The new proprietors were not, indeed, aware how much cause there was for their alarms. Tyrconnel boasted that he had secured the support of the Queen by the present of a pearl necklace worth 10,000*l.*, which Prince Rupert had bequeathed to his mistress. In all extensive transfers of property not governed by rules of law, where both parties to a corrupt transaction have a great interest in concealment, and where there can seldom be any effective responsi-

* London Gazette. All these particulars are to found in Sheridan's MS. It is but fair to add at, in a few months after Sheridan accompanied yrconnel to Ireland, they became violent ene-es.

† D'Adda, 15th Nov. 1687.—MS.

* Our accounts of Tyrconnel's Irish administration before the Revolution are peculiarly imperfect and suspicious. King, afterwards Archbishop of Dublin, whose State of the Protestants has been usually quoted as authority, was the most zealous of Irish Protestants, and his ingenious antagonist, Leslie, was the most inflexible of Jacobites. Though both were men of great abilities, their attention was so much occupied in personalities and in the discussion of controverted opinions, that they have done little to elucidate matters of fact. Clarendon and Sheridan's MS. agree so exactly in their picture of Tyrconnel, and have such an air of truth in their accounts of him, that it is not easy to refuse them credit, though they were both his enemies.

† "The Earl of Donegal," says Sheridan, "sold for 600 guineas a troop of horse which, two years before, cost him 1800 guineas."—Sheridan MS.

bility either judicial or moral, the suspicion of bribery must be incurred, and the temptation itself must often prevail. Tyrconnel asked Sheridan, his secretary, whether he did not think the Irish would give 50,000*l.* for the repeal of the Act of Settlement:—"Certainly," said Sheridan, "since the new interest paid three times that sum to the Duke of Ormonde for passing it." Tyrconnel then authorised Sheridan to offer to Lord Sunderland 50,000*l.* in money, or 5000*l.* a-year in land for the repeal. Sunderland preferred the 50,000*l.*; but with what seriousness of purpose cannot be ascertained, for the repeal was not adopted, and the money was never paid;* and he seems to have continued to thwart and traverse a measure which he did not dare openly to resist. The absolute abrogation of laws under which so much property was held seemed to be beset with such difficulty, that in the autumn of the following year Tyrconnel, on his visit to England, proposed a more modified measure, aimed only at affording a partial relief to the ancient proprietors. In the temper which then prevailed, a partial measure produced almost as much alarm as one more comprehensive, and was thought to be intended to pave the way for total resumption. The danger consisted in inquiry: the object of apprehension was any proceeding which brought this species of legal possession into question; and the proprietors dreaded the approach even of discussion to their invidious and originally iniquitous titles. It would be hard to expect that James should abstain from relieving his friends lest he might disturb the secure enjoyment of his enemies. Motives of policy, however, and some apprehensions of too sudden a shock to the feelings of Protestants in Great Britain, retarded the final adoption of this measure. It could only be carried into effect by the Parliament of Ireland; and it was not thought wise to call it together till every part of the internal policy of the kingdom which could influence the elections of that assembly should be completed. Probably, however, the delay principally arose from daring projects of separation and independence, which were entertained by Tyrconnel; and of which a short statement (in its most important parts hitherto unknown to the public) will conclude the account of his administration.

In the year 1666, towards the close of the first Dutch war, Louis XIV. had made preparations for invading Ireland with an army of twenty thousand men, under the Duc de Beaufort,—assured by the Irish ecclesiastics, that he would be joined by the Catholics, then more than usually incensed by the confirmation of the Act of Settlement, and by the English statutes against the importation of the produce of Ireland. To this plot, (which was discovered by the Queen-Mother at Paris, and by her disclosed to Charles II.,) it is not probable that so active a leader as Tyrconnel could have been a stranger.* We are informed by his secretary, that, during his visits to England in 1686, he made no scruple to avow projects of the like nature, when, after some remarks on the King's declining age, and on the improbability that the Queen's children, if ever she had any, should live beyond infancy, he declared, "that the Irish would be fools or madmen if they submitted to be governed by the Prince of Orange, or by Hyde's grand-daughters; that they ought rather to take that opportunity of resolving no longer to be the slaves of England, but to set up a king of their own under the protection of France, which he was sure would be readily granted;" and added that "nothing could be more advantageous to Ireland or ruinous to England." † His reliance on French support was probably founded on the general policy of Louis XIV., on his conduct towards Ireland in 1666, and, perhaps, on information from Catholic ecclesiastics in France; but he was not long content with these grounds of assurance. During his residence in England in the autumn of 1687, he had recourse to decisive and audacious measures for ascertaining how far he might rely on foreign aid in the execution of his ambitious schemes. A friend of his at Court (whose name is concealed, but who probably was either Henry Jermyn or Father Petre) applied on his behalf to Bonrepos (then employed by the Court of Versailles in London, on a special mission,)‡ expressing his desire, in case of the death of James II., to take measures to prevent Ireland from falling under the domination of the Prince of Orange, and to place that country under the protection of the Most Christian King. Tyrconnel expressed his desire that Bonrepos would go to Chester for the sake of a full discussion of this important proposition; but the wary minister declined a step which should have amounted to the opening of a negotiation, until he had authority from his Government. He promised however, to keep the secret, especially from Barillon, who it was feared would betray it to Sunderland, then avowedly distrusted by the Lord Deputy. Bonrepos, in communicating this proposition to his Court, adds that he very certainly knew the King of Eng

* Sheridan MS.

* There are obscure intimations of this intended invasion in Carte, Life of Ormonde, vol. ii. p. 328 The resolutions of the Parliament of Ireland concerning it are to be found in the Gazette, 25th–28th December, 1665. Louis XIV. himself tell us, that he had a correspondence with those whom he calls the "remains of Cromwell" in England and "with the Irish Catholics, who, always discontented with their condition, seem ever read to join any enterprise which may render it mor supportable."—Oeuvres de Louis XIV., vol. i p. 203. Sheridan's MS. contains more particu lars. It is supported by the printed authorities a far as they go; and being written at St. Germains probably differed little in matters of fact from th received statements of the Jacobite exiles.

† Sheridan MS.

‡ Bonrepos to Seignelai, 4th Sept. 1687.—Fo MSS.

land's intention to be to deprive his presumptive heir of Ireland, to make that country an asylum for all his Catholic subjects, and to complete his measures on that subject in the course of five years,—a time which Tyrconnel thought much too long, and earnestly besought the King to abridge; and that the Prince of Orange certainly apprehended such designs. James himself told the Nuncio that one of the objects of the extraordinary mission of Dykveldt was the affair of Ireland, happily begun by Tyrconnel;* and the same prelate was afterwards informed by Sunderland, that Dykveldt had expressed a fear of some general designs against the succession of the Prince and Princess of Orange.† Bonrepos was speedily instructed to inform Tyrconnel, that if on the death of James he could maintain himself in Ireland, he might rely on effectual aid from Louis to preserve the Catholic religion, and to separate that country from England, when under the dominion of a Protestant sovereign.‡ Tyrconnel is said to have agreed, without the knowledge of his own master, to put four Irish sea-ports, Kinsale, Waterford, Limerick, and either Galway or Coleraine, into the hands of France.§ The remaining particulars of this bold and hazardous negotiation were reserved by Bonrepos till his return to Paris; but he closes his last despatch with the singular intimation that several Scotch lords had sounded him on the succour they might expect from France, on the death of James, to exclude the Prince and Princess of Orange from the throne of Scotland. Objects so far beyond the usual aim of ambition, and means so much at variance with prudence as well as duty, could hardly have presented themselves to any mind whose native violence had not been inflamed by an education in the school of conspiracy and insurrection;—nor even to such but in a country which, from the division of its inhabitants, and the impolicy of its administration, had constantly stood on the brink of the most violent revolutions; where quiet seldom subsisted long but as the bitter fruit of terrible examples of cruelty and rapine; and where the majority of the people easily listened to offers of foreign aid against a government which they considered as the most hostile of foreigners.

* D'Adda, 7th Feb. 1687.—MS.
† Id. 20th June.
‡ Seignelai to Bonrepos, 29th Sept.—Fox MSS.
§ Sheridan MS.

CHAPTER V.

Rupture with the Protestant Tories.—Increased decision of the King's designs.—Encroachments on the Church establishment.—Charter-House.—Oxford, University College.—Christ Church.—Exeter College, Cambridge.—Oxford, Magdalen College.—Declaration of liberty of conscience.—Similar attempts of Charles.—Proclamation at Edinburgh.—Resistance of the Church.—Attempt to conciliate the Nonconformists.—Review of their sufferings.—Baxter.—Bunyan.—Presbyterians.—Independents.—Baptists.—Quakers.—Addresses of thanks for the declaration.

In the beginning of the year 1687 the rupture of James with the powerful party who were ready to sacrifice all but the Church to his pleasure appeared to be irreparable. He had apparently destined Scotland to set the example of unbounded submission, under the forms of the constitution; and he undoubtedly hoped that the revolution in Ireland would supply him with the means of securing the obedience of his English subjects by intimidation or force. The failure of his project in the most Protestant part of his dominions, and its alarming success in the most Catholic, alike tended to widen the breach between parties in England. The Tories were alienated from the Crown by the example of their friends in Scotland, as well as by their dread of the Irish. An unreserved compliance with the King's designs became notoriously the condition by which office was to be obtained or preserved; and, except a very few instances of personal friendship, the public profession of the Catholic faith was required as the only security for that compliance. The royal confidence and the direction of public affairs were transferred from the Protestant Tories, in spite of their services and sufferings during half a century, into the hands of a faction, who, as their title to power was zeal for the advancement of Popery, must be called "Papists;" though some of them professed the Protestant religion, and though their maxims of policy, both in Church and State, were dreaded and resisted by the most considerable of the English Catholics.

It is hard to determine,—perhaps it might have been impossible for James himself to say,—how far his designs for the advancement of the Roman Catholic Church extended at the period of his accession to the throne. It is agreeable to the nature of such projects that he should not, at first, have dared to avow to himself any intention beyond that of obtaining relief for his religion, and of placing it in a condition of safety and honour; but it is altogether improbable that he had even then steadily fixed on a secure toleration as the utmost limit of his endeavours. His schemes were probably vague and fluctuating, assuming a greater distinctness with respect to the removal of grievous penalties and disabilities, but always ready to seek as much advantage for his Church as the progress of circumstances should render attainable;—sometimes drawn back to toleration by prudence or fear, and on other occasions impelled to more daring counsels by the pride of success, or by anger at resistance. In this state of fluctuation it is not altogether irreconcilable with the irregularities of human nature that he might have sometimes yielded a faint and transient assent to those principles of religious liberty which he professed in his public acts; though even this superficial sincerity is hard to be reconciled with his share in the secret treaty of 1670,—with his administration of Scotland, where he carried his passion for intolerance so far as to be the leader of one sect of heretics in the bloody persecution of another,—and with his language to Barillon, to whom, at the very moment of his professed toleration, he declared his approbation of the cruelties of Louis XIV. against his own Protestant subjects.* It would be extravagant to expect that the liberal maxims which adorned his public declarations had taken such a hold on his mind as to withhold him from endeavouring to establish his own religion as soon as his sanguine zeal should lead him to think it practicable; or that he should not in process of time go on to guard it by that code of disabilities and penalties which was then enforced by every state in Europe except Holland, and deemed indispensable security for their religion by every Christian community, except the obnoxious sects of the Socinians, Independents, Anabaptists, and Quakers. Whether he meditated a violent change of the Established religion from the beginning, or only entered on a course of measures which must terminate in its subversion, is rather a philosophical than a political question. In both cases, apprehension and resistance were alike reasonable; and in neither could an appeal to arms be warranted until every other means of self-defence had proved manifestly hopeless.

Whatever opinions may be formed of his intentions at an earlier period, it is evident that in the year 1687 his resolution was taken; though still no doubt influenced by the misgivings and fluctuations incident to vast and perilous projects, especially when they are entertained by those whose character is not so daring as their designs. All the measures of his internal government, during the eighteen months which ensued, were directed to the overthrow of the Established Church,—an object which was to be attained by assuming a power above law, and could only be preserved by a force sufficient to bid defiance to the repugnance of the nation. An absolute monarchy, if not the first instrument of his purpose, must have been the last result of that series of victories over the people which the success of his design required. Such, indeed, were his conscientious opinions of the constitution, that he thought the Habeas Corpus Act inconsistent with it; and so strong was his conviction of the necessity of military force to his designs at that time, that in his dying advice to his son, written long afterwards, in secrecy and solitude, after a review of his own government, his injunction to the Prince is,—"Keep up a considerable body of Catholic troops, without which you cannot be safe."* The liberty of the people, and even the civil constitution, were as much the objects of his hostility as the religion of the great majority, and were their best security against ultimate persecution.

The measures of the King's domestic policy, indeed, consisted rather in encroachments on the Church than in measures of relief to the Catholics. He had, in May, 1686, granted dispensations to the curate of Putney, a convert to the Church of Rome, enabling him to hold his benefices, and relieving him from the performance of all the acts inconsistent with his new religion, which a long series of statutes had required clergymen of the Church of England to perform.† By following this precedent, the King might have silently transferred to ecclesiastics of his own communion many benefices in every diocese in which the bishop had not the courage to resist the dispensing power. The converted incumbents would preserve their livings under the protection of that prerogative, and Catholic priests might be presented to benefices without any new ordination; for the Church of England,—although she treats the ministers of any other Protestant communion as being only in pretended holy orders,—recognises the ordination of the Church of Rome, which she sometimes calls "idolatrous," in order to maintain, even through such idolatrous predecessors, that unbroken connection with the apostles which she deems essential to the power of conferring the sacerdotal character. This obscure encroachment, however, escaped general observation.

The first attack on the laws to which resistance was made was a royal recommendation of Andrew Popham, a Catholic, to the Governors of the Charter House (a hospital school, founded by a merchant of London, named Sutton, on the site of a Carthusian monastery), to be received by them as a pensioner on their opulent establishment, without taking the oaths required both by the general law and by a private statute passed for the government of that foundation.‡ Among the

* "J'ai dit au Roi que V. M. n'avoit plus au cœur que de voir prospérer les soins qu'il prends ici pour y établir la religion Catholique. S. M. B. me dit en me quittant, 'Vous voyez que je n'omêts rien de ce qui est en mon pouvoir. J'espère que le Roi votre maître m'aidera, et que *nous ferons* de concert des grandes choses pour la religion.'" Barillon, 12th May, 1687.—Fox MSS.

* Life of James II., vol. ii. p. 621.

† Gutch, Collectanea Curiosa, vol. i. p. 290, and Reresby, p. 233. Sclater publicly recanted the Romish religion on the 5th of May, 1689,—a pretty rapid retreat.—Account of E. Sclater's Return to the Church of England, by Dr. Horneck. London, 1689. It is remarkable that Sancroft so far exercised his archiepiscopal jurisdiction as to authorise Sclater's admission to the Protestant communion on condition of public recantation, at which Burnet preached: yet the pious Horneck owns that the juncture of time tempted him to smile.

‡ Relation of the Proceedings at the Charter House, London, 1689.—Carte, Life of Ormonde, vol. ii. p. 246.

Governors were persons of the highest distinction in Church and State. The Chancellor, at their first meeting, intimated the necessity of immediate compliance with the King's mandate. Thomas Burnet, the Master, a man justly celebrated for genius, eloquence, and learning, had the courage to maintain the authority of the laws against an opponent so formidable. He was supported by the aged Duke of Ormonde, and Jeffreys' motion was negatived. A second letter to the same effect was addressed to the Governors, which they persevered in resisting; assigning their reasons in an answer to one of the Secretaries of State, which was subscribed by the Archbishop of Canterbury, the Bishop of London, Ormonde, Halifax, Nottingham, and Danby. This courageous resistance by a single clergyman, countenanced by such weighty names, induced the Court to pause till experiments were tried in other places, where politicians so important could not directly interfere. The attack on the Charter House was suspended and never afterwards resumed. To Burnet, who thus threw himself alone into the breach, much of the merit of the stand which followed justly belongs. He was requited like other public benefactors; his friends forgot the service, and his enemies were excited by the remembrance of it to defeat his promotion, on the pretext of his free exercise of reason in the interpretation of the Scriptures,—which the Established Clergy zealously maintained in vindication of their own separation from the Roman Church, but treated with little tenderness in those who dissented from their own creed.

Measures of a bolder nature were resorted to on a more conspicuous stage. The two great Universities of Oxford and Cambridge, the most opulent and splendid literary institutions of Europe, were from their foundation under the government of the clergy,—the only body of men who then possessed sufficient learning to conduct education. Their constitution had not been much altered at the Reformation: the same reverence which spared their monastic regulations happily preserved their rich endowments from rapine; and though many of their members suffered at the close of the Civil War from their adherence to the vanquished party, the corporate property was undisturbed, and their studies flourished both under the Commonwealth and the Protectorate. Their fame as seats of learning, their station as the ecclesiastical capitals of the kingdom, and their ascendant over the susceptible minds of all youth of family and fortune, now rendered them the chief scene of the decisive contest between James and the Established Church. Obadiah Walker, Master of University College, Oxford, a man of no small note for ability and learning, and long a concealed Catholic, now obtained for himself, and two of his fellows, a dispensation from all those acts of participation in the Protestant worship which the laws since the Reformation required, together with a license for the publication of books of Catholic theology.* He established a printing press, and a Catholic chapel in his college, which was henceforth regarded as having fallen into the hands of the Catholics. Both these exertions of the prerogative had preceded the determination of the judges, which was supposed by the King to establish its legality.

Animated by that determination, he (contrary to the advice of Sunderland, who thought it safer to choose a well-affected Protestant,) proceeded to appoint one Massey, a Catholic, who appears to have been a layman, to the high station of Dean of Christ Church, by which he became a dignitary of the Church as well as the ruler of the greatest college in the University. A dispensation and pardon had been granted to him on the 16th of December, 1686, dispensing with the numerous statutes standing in the way of his promotion, one of which was the Act of Uniformity,—the only foundation of the legal establishment of the Church.† His refusal of the oath of supremacy was recorded; but he was, notwithstanding, installed in the deanery without resistance or even remonstrance, by Aldrich, the Sub-Dean, an eminent divine of the High Church party, who, on the part of the College, accepted the dispensation as a substitute for the oaths required by law. Massey appears to have attended the chapter officially on several occasions, and to have presided at the election of a Bishop of Oxford near two years afterwards. Thus did that celebrated society, overawed by power, or still misled by their extravagant principle of unlimited obedience, or, perhaps, not yet aware of the extent of the King's designs, recognise the legality of his usurped power by the surrender of an academical office of ecclesiastical dignity into hands which the laws had disabled from holding it. It was no wonder, that the unprecedented vacancy of the archbishopric of York for two years and a half was generally imputed to the King's intending it for Father Petre;—a supposition countenanced by his frequent application to Rome to obtain a bishopric and a cardinal's hat for that Jesuit:‡ for if he had been a Catholic bishop, and if the chapter of York were as submissive as that of Christ Church, the royal dispensation would have seated him on the archiepiscopal throne. The Jesuits were bound by a vow§ not to accept bishoprics unless compelled by a pre-

* Gutch, Collectanea Curiosa, vol. i. p. 287. Athenæ Oxonienses, vol. iv. p. 438. Dodd, Church History, vol. iii. p. 454.

† Gutch, vol. ii. p. 294. The dispensation to Massey contained an ostentatious enumeration of the laws which it sets at defiance.

‡ Dodd, vol. iii. p. 511. D'Adda MSS.

§ Imposed by Ignatius, at the suggestion of Claude Le Jay, an original member of the order, who wished to avoid a bishopric, probably from humility; but the regulation afterwards prevented the Jesuits from looking for advancement anywhere but to Rome.

cept from the Pope, so that his interference was necessary to open the gates of the English Church to Petre.

An attempt was made on specious grounds to take possession of another college by a suit before the Ecclesiastical Commissioners, in which private individuals were the apparent parties. The noble family of Petre (of whom Father Edward Petre was one), in January, 1687, claimed the right of nomination to seven fellowships in Exeter College, which had been founded there by Sir William Petre, in the reign of Elizabeth. It was acknowledged on the part of the College, that Sir William and his son had exercised that power, though the latter, as they contended, had nominated only by sufferance. The Bishop of Exeter, the Visitor, had, in the reign of James I., pronounced an opinion against the founder's descendants; and a judgment had been obtained against them in the Court of Common Pleas about the same time. Under the sanction of these authorities, the College had for seventy years nominated without disturbance to these fellowships. Allibone, the Catholic lawyer, contended, that this long usage, which would otherwise have been conclusive, deserved little consideration in a period of such iniquity towards Catholics that they were deterred from asserting their civil rights. Lord Chief Justice Herbert observed, that the question turned upon the agreement between Sir William Petre and Exeter College, under which that body received the fellows on his foundation. Jeffreys, perhaps, fearful of violent measures at so early a stage, and taking advantage of the non-appearance of the Crown as an ostensible party, declared his concurrence with the Chief Justice; and the Court determined that the suit was a civil case, dependent on the interpretation of a contract, and therefore not within their jurisdiction as Commissioners of Ecclesiastical Causes. Sprat afterwards took some merit to himself for having contributed to save Exeter College from the hands of the enemy: but the concurrence of the Chancellor and Chief Justice, and the technical ground of the determination, render the vigour and value of his resistance very doubtful.*

The honour of opposing the illegal power of the Crown devolved on Cambridge, second to Oxford in rank and magnificence, but then more distinguished by zeal for liberty;—a distinction probably originating in the long residence of Charles I. at Oxford, and in the prevalence of the Parliamentary party at the same period, in the country around Cambridge. The experiment was made now on the whole University; but it was of a cautious and timid nature, and related to a case important in nothing but the principle which it would have established. Early in February, of this year, the King had recommended Alban Francis, a Benedictine monk (said to have been a missionary employed to convert the young scholars to the Church of Rome, on whom an academical honour could hardly have been conferred without some appearance of countenancing his mission) to be admitted a master of arts,—which was a common act of kingly authority; and had granted him a dispensation from the oaths appointed by law to be taken on such an admission.* Peachell, the Vice-Chancellor, declared, that he could not tell what to do,—to decline his Majesty's letter or his laws. Men of more wisdom and courage persuaded him to choose the better part: and he refused the degree without the legal condition.† On the complaint of Francis he was summoned before the Ecclesiastical Commissioners to answer for his disobedience, and (though vigorously supported by the University, who appointed deputies to attend him to the bar of the hostile tribunal), after several hearings was deprived of his Vice-Chancellorship, and suspended from his office of Master of Magdalen College. Among those deputies at the bar, and probably undistinguished from the rest by the ignorant and arrogant Chancellor, who looked down upon them all with the like scorn, stood Isaac Newton, Professor of Mathematics in the University, then employed in the publication of a work which will perish only with the world, but who showed on that, as on every other fit opportunity in his life, that the most sublime contemplations and the most glorious discoveries could not withdraw him from the defence of the liberties of his country.

But the attack on Oxford, which immediately ensued, was the most memorable of all. The Presidency of Magdalen College, one of the most richly endowed communities of the English Universities, had become vacant at the end of March, which gave occasion to immediate attempts to obtain from the King a nomination to that desirable office. Smith, one of the fellows, paid his court, with this view, to Parker, the treacherous Bishop of Oxford, who, after having sounded his friends at Court, warned him "that the King expected the person to be recommended should be favourable to his religion." Smith answered by general expressions of loyalty, which Parker assured him "would not do." A few days afterwards, Sancroft anxiously asked Smith who was to be the President; to which he answered, "Not I; I never will comply with the conditions." Some rumours of the pro-

* Sprat's Letter to Lord Dorset, p. 12. This case is now published from the Records of Exeter College, for the first time, through the kind permission of Dr. Jones, the present [1826] Rector of that society.

* State Trials, vol. xi. p. 1350. Narcissus Luttrell, April and May, 1687.—MS.

† Pepys, Memoirs, vol. ii. Correspondence, p. 79. He consistently pursued the doctrine of passive obedience. "If," says he, "his Majesty, in his wisdom, and according to his supreme power, contrive other methods to satisfy himself, I shall be no murmurer or complainer, but can be no abettor."—Ibid., p. 81.

jects of James having probably induced the fellows to appoint the election for the 13th of April, on the 5th of that month the King issued his letter mandatory, commanding them to make choice of Anthony Farmer,* —not a member of the College, and a recent convert to the Church of Rome, "any statute or custom to the contrary notwithstanding." On the 9th, the fellows agreed to a petition to the King, which was delivered the next day to Lord Sunderland, to be laid before his Majesty, in which they alleged that Farmer was legally incapable of holding the office, and prayed either that they might be left to make a free election, or that the King would recommend some person fit to be preferred. On the 11th, the mandate arrived, and on the 13th the election was postponed to the 15th,—the last day on which it could by the statutes be held,—to allow time for receiving an answer to the petition. On that day they were informed that the King "expected to be obeyed." A small number of the senior fellows proposed a second petition; but the larger and younger part rejected the proposal with indignation, and proceeded to the election of Mr. Hough, after a discussion more agreeable to the natural feelings of injured men than to the principles of passive obedience recently promulgated by the University.† The fellows were summoned, in June, before the Ecclesiastical Commission, to answer for their contempt of his Majesty's commands. On their appearance, Fairfax, one of their body, having desired to know the commission by which the Court sat, Jeffreys said to him, "What commission have you to be so impudent in court? This man ought to be kept in a dark room. Why do you suffer him without a guardian?"‡ On the 22d of the same month, Hough's election was pronounced to be void, and the Vice-President, with two of the fellows, were suspended. But proofs of such notorious and vulgar profligacy had been produced against Farmer, that it was thought necessary to withdraw him in August; and the fellows were directed by a new mandate to admit Parker, Bishop of Oxford, to the presidency. This man was as much disabled by the statutes of the College as Farmer; but as servility and treachery, though immoralities often of a deeper dye than debauchery, are neither so capable of proof nor so easily stripped of their disguises, the fellows were by this recommendation driven to the necessity of denying the dispensing power. Their inducements, however, to resist him, were strengthened by the impossibility of representing them to the King. Parker, originally a fanatical Puritan, became a bigoted Churchman at the Restoration, and disgraced abilities not inconsiderable by the zeal with which he defended the persecution of his late brethren, and by the unbridled ribaldry with which he reviled the most virtuous men among them. His labours for the Church of England were no sooner rewarded by the bishopric of Oxford, than he transferred his services, if not his faith, to the Church of Rome, which then began to be openly patronised by the Court, and seems to have retained his station in the Protestant hierarchy in order to contribute more effectually to its destruction. The zeal of those who are more anxious to recommend themselves than to promote their cause is often too eager: and the convivial enjoyments of Parker often betrayed him into very imprudent and unseemly language.* Against such an intruder the College had the most powerful motives to make a vigorous resistance. They were summoned into the presence of the King, when he arrived at Oxford in September, and was received by the body of the University with such demonstrations of loyalty as to be boasted of in the Gazette. "The King chid them very much for their disobedience," says one of his attendants, "and with a much greater appearance of anger than ever I perceived in his Majesty; who bade them go away and choose the Bishop of Oxford, or else they should certainly feel the weight of their Sovereign's displeasure."† They answered respectfully, but persevered. They further received private warnings, that it was better to acquiesce in the choice of a head of suspected religion, such as the Bishop, than to expose themselves to be destroyed by the subservient judges, in proceedings of *quo warranto* (for which the inevitable breaches of their innumerable statutes would supply a fairer pretext than was sufficient in the other corporations), or to subject themselves to innovations in their religious worship which might be imposed by the King in virtue of his undefined supremacy over the Church.‡

These insinuations proving vain, the King issued a commission to Cartwright, Bishop of Chester, Chief Justice Wright, and Baron Jenner, to examine the state of the College, with full power to alter the statutes and frame new ones, in execution of the authority which the King claimed as supreme visitor of cathedrals and colleges, and which was held to supersede the powers of their ordinary visitors. The commissioners accordingly arrived at Oxford on the 20th of October, for the purpose of this royal visita-

* State Trials, vol. xii. p. 1.

† "Hot debates arose about the King's letter, and horrible rude reflections were made upon his authority, that he had nothing to do in our affair, *and things of a far worse nature and consequence.* I told one of them that the spirit of Ferguson had got into him."—Smith's Diary, State Trials, vol. xii. p. 58.

‡ In Narcissus Luttrell's Diary, Jeffreys is made to say of Fairfax, "He is fitter to be in a madhouse."

* Athenæ Oxonienses, vol. ii. p. 814. It appears that he refused on his death-bed to declare himself a Catholic, which Evelyn justly thinks strange.—Memoirs, vol. i. p. 605.

† Blathwayt, Secretary of War, Pepys, vol. ii Correspondence, p. 86.

‡ State Trials, vol. xii. p. 19.

tion; and the object of it was opened by Cartwright in a speech full of anger and menace. Hough maintained his own rights and those of his College with equal decorum and firmness. On being asked whether he submitted to the visitation, he answered, "We submit to it as far as it is consistent with the laws of the land and the statutes of the College, but no farther. There neither is nor can be a President as long as I live and obey the statutes." The Court cited five cases of nomination to the Presidency by the Crown since the Reformation, of which he appears to have disputed only one. But he was unshaken: he refused to give up possession of his house to Parker; and when, on the second day they deprived him of the Presidency, and struck his name off the books, he came into the hall, and protested "against all they had done in prejudice of his right, as illegal, unjust, and null." The strangers and young scholars loudly applauded his courage, which so incensed the Court, that the Chief Justice bound him to appear in the King's Bench in a thousand pounds. Parker having been put into possession by force, a majority of the fellows were prevailed on to submit, "as far as was lawful and agreeable to the statutes of the College." The appearance of compromise, to which every man feared that his companion might be tempted to yield, shook their firmness for a moment. Fortunately the imprudence of the King set them again at liberty. The answer with which the commissioners were willing to be content did not satisfy him. He required a written submission, in which the fellows should acknowledge their disobedience, and express their sorrow for it. On this proposition they withdrew their former submission, and gave in a writing in which they finally declared "that they could not acknowledge themselves to have done any thing amiss." The Bishop of Chester, on the 16th of November, pronounced the judgment of the Court; by which, on their refusal to subscribe a humble acknowledgment of their errors, they were deprived and expelled from their fellowships. Cartwright, like Parker, had originally been a Puritan, and was made a Churchman by the Restoration; and running the same race, though with less vigorous powers, he had been made Bishop of Chester for a sermon, inculcating the doctrine, that the promises of kings were not binding.* Within a few months after these services at Oxford, he was rebuked by the King, for saying in his cups that Jeffreys and Sunderland would deceive him.† Suspected as he was of more opprobious vices, the merit of being useful in an odious project was sufficient to cancel all private guilt: and a design was even entertained of promoting him to the see of London, as soon as the contemplated deprivation of Compton should be carried into execution.*

Early in December, the recusant fellows were incapacitated from holding any benefice or preferment in the Church by a decree of the Ecclesiastical Commissioners, which passed that body, however, only by a majority of one;—the minority consisting of Lord Mulgrave, Lord Chief Justice Herbert, Baron Jenner, and Sprat, Bishop of Rochester, who boasts, that he laboured to make the Commission, which he countenanced by his presence, as little mischievous as he could.† This rigorous measure was probably adopted from the knowledge, that many of the nobility and gentry intended to bestow livings on many of the ejected fellows.‡ The King told Sir Edward Seymour, that he had heard that he and others intended to take some of them into their houses, and added that he should look on it as a combination against himself.§ But in spite of these threats considerable collections were made for them; and when the particulars of the transaction were made known in Holland, the Princess of Orange contributed two hundred pounds to their relief.‖ It was probably by these same threats that a person so prudent as well as mild was so transported beyond her usual meekness as to say to D'Abbeville, James' minister at the Hague, that if she ever became Queen, she would signalise her zeal for the Church more than Elizabeth.

The King represented to Barillon the apparently triumphant progress which he had just made through the South and West of England, as a satisfactory proof of the popularity of his person and government.¶ But that experienced statesman, not deceived by these outward shows, began from that moment to see more clearly the dangers which James had to encounter. An attack on the most opulent establishment for education of the kingdom, the expulsion of a body of learned men from their private property without any trial known to the laws, and for no other offence than obstinate adherence to their oaths, and the transfer of their great endowments to the clergy of the King's persuasion, who were legally unable to hold them, even if he had justly acquired the power of bestowing them, were measures of bigotry and rapine,—odious and alarming without being terrible,—by which the King lost the attachment of many friends, without

* The King hath, indeed, promised to govern by law; but the safety of the people (of which he is judge) is an exception implied in every monarchial promise."—Sermon at Ripon, 6th February, 1686. See also his sermon on the 30th January, 1682, at Holyrood House, before the Lady Anne.

† Narcissus Luttrell, February, 1688.—MS.

* Johnstone (son of Warriston) to Burnet, 8th December, 1687.—Welbeck MS. Sprat, in his Letter to Lord Dorset, speaks of "farther proceedings" as being meditated against Compton.

† Johnstone, ibid. He does not name the majority: they, probably, were Jeffreys, Sunderland, the Bishops of Chester and Durham, and Lord Chief Justice Wright.

‡ Johnstone, 17th November.—MS.

§ Id. 8th December.—MS.

‖ Smith's Diary, State Trials, vol. xii. p. 73.

¶ Barillon, 23d—29th Sept.—Fox MSS.

inspiring his opponents with much fear. The members of Magdalen College were so much the objects of general sympathy and respect, that though they justly obtained the honours of martyrdom, they experienced little of its sufferings. It is hard to imagine a more unskilful attempt to persecute, than that which thus inflicted sufferings most easily relieved on men who were most generally respected. In corporations so great as the University the wrongs of every member were quickly felt and resented by the whole body; and the prevalent feeling was speedily spread over the kingdom, every part of which received from thence preceptors in learning and teachers of religion,—a circumstance of peculiar importance at a period when publication still continued to be slow and imperfect. A contest for a corporate right has the advantage of seeming more generous than that for individual interest; and corporate spirit itself is one of the most steady and inflexible principles of human action. An invasion of the legal possessions of the Universities was an attack on the strong holds as well as palaces of the Church, where she was guarded by the magnificence of art, and the dignity and antiquity of learning, as well as by respect for religion. It was made on principles which tended directly to subject the whole property of the Church to the pleasure of the Crown; and as soon as, in a conspicuous and extensive instance, the sacredness of legal possession is intentionally violated, the security of all property is endangered. Whether such proceedings were reconcilable to law, and could be justified by the ordinary authorities and arguments of lawyers, was a question of very subordinate importance.

At an early stage of the proceedings against the Universities, the King, not content with releasing individuals from obedience to the law by dispensations in particular cases, must have resolved on altogether suspending the operation of penal laws relating to religion by one general measure. He had accordingly issued, on the 4th of April, "A Declaration for Liberty of Conscience;" which, after the statement of those principles of equity and policy on which religious liberty is founded, proceeds to make provisions in their own natures so wise and just that they want nothing but lawful authority and pure intention to render them worthy of admiration. It suspends the execution of all penal laws for nonconformity, and of all laws which require certain acts of conformity, as qualifications for civil or military office; it gives leave to all men to meet and serve God after their own manner, publicly and privately; it denounces the royal displeasure and the vengeance of the land against all who should disturb any religious worship; and, finally, "in order that his loving subjects may be discharged from all penalties, forfeitures, and disabilities, which they may have incurred, it grants them a free pardon for all crimes by them committed against the said penal laws." This Declaration, founded on the supposed power of suspending laws, was, in several respects, of more extensive operation than the exercise of the power to dispense with them. The laws of disqualification only became penal when the Nonconformist was a candidate for office, and not necessarily implying immorality in the person disqualified, might, according to the doctrine then received, be the proper object of a dispensation. But some acts of nonconformity, which might be committed by all men, and which did not of necessity involve a conscientious dissent, were regarded as in themselves immoral, and to them it was acknowledged that the dispensing power did not extend. Dispensations, however multiplied, are presumed to be grounded on the special circumstances of each case. But every exercise of the power of indefinitely suspending a whole class of laws which must be grounded on general reasons of policy, without any consideration of the circumstances of particular individuals, is evidently a more undisguised assumption of legislative authority. There were practical differences of considerable importance. No dispensation could prevent a legal proceeding from being commenced and carried on as far as the point where it was regular to appeal to the dispensation as a defence. But the declaration which suspended the laws stopped the prosecutor on the threshold; and in the case of disqualification it seemed to preclude the necessity of all subsequent dispensations to individuals. The dispensing power might remove disabilities, and protect from punishment; but the exemption from expense, and the security against vexation, were completed only by this exercise of the suspending power.

Acts of a similar nature had been twice attempted by Charles II. The first was the Declaration in Ecclesiastical Affairs, in the year of his restoration; in which, after many concessions to Dissenters, which might be considered as provisional, and binding only till the negotiation for a general union in religion should be closed, he adds, "We hereby renew what we promised in our Declaration from Breda, that no man should be disquieted for difference of opinion in matters of religion, which do not disturb the peace of the kingdom."* On the faith of that promise the English Nonconformists had concurred in the Restoration; yet the Convention Parliament itself, in which the Presbyterians were powerful, if not predominant, refused, though by a small majority, to pass a bill to render this tolerant Declaration effectual.† But the next Parliament, elected under the prevalence of a different spirit, broke the public faith by the Act of Uniformity, which prohibited all public worship and religious instruction, except such as were conformable to

* Kennet, History, vol. iii. p. 242.

† Commons' Journals, 28th November, 1660. On the second reading the numbers were, ayes, 157; noes, 183. Sir G. Booth, a teller for the ayes, was a Presbyterian leader.

the Established Church.* The zeal of that assembly had, indeed, at its opening, been stimulated by Clarendon, the deepest stain on whose administration was the renewal of intolerance.† Charles, whether most actuated by love of quiet, or by indifference to religion, or by a desire to open the gates to Dissenters, that Catholics might enter, made an attempt to preserve the public faith, which he had himself pledged, by the exercise of his dispensing power. In the end of 1662 he had published another Declaration,‡ in which he assured peaceable Dissenters, who were only desirous modestly to perform their devotions in their own way, that he would make it his special care to incline the wisdom of Parliament to concur with him in making some act which, he adds, "may enable us to exercise, with a more universal satisfaction, the dispensing power which we conceive to be inherent in us." In the speech with which he opened the next session, he only ventured to say, "I could heartily wish I had such a power of indulgence." The Commons, however, better royalists or more zealous Churchmen than the King, resolved "that it be represented to his Majesty, as the humble advice of this House, that no indulgence be granted to Dissenters from the Act of Uniformity;"§ and an address to that effect was presented to him, which had been drawn up by Sir Heneage Finch, his own Solicitor-General. The King, counteracted by his ministers, almost silently acquiesced; and the Parliament proceeded, in the years which immediately followed, to enact that series of persecuting laws which disgrace their memory, and dishonour an administration otherwise not without claims on our praise. It was not till the beginning of the second Dutch war, that "a Declaration for indulging Nonconformists in matters ecclesiastical" was advised by Sir Thomas Clifford, for the sake of Catholics, and embraced by Shaftesbury for the general interests of religious liberty.‖ A considerable debate on this Declaration took place in the House of Commons, in which Waller alone had the boldness and liberality to contend for the toleration of the Catholics; but the principle of freedom of conscience, and the desire to gratify the King, yielded to the dread of prerogative and the enmity to the Church of Rome. An address was presented to the King, "to inform him that penal statutes in matters ecclesiastical cannot be suspended but by Act of Parliament;" to which the King returned an evasive answer. The House presented another address, declaring "that the King was very much misinformed, no such power having been claimed or recognised by any of his predecessors, and if admitted, might tend to altering the legislature, which has always been acknowledged to be in your Majesty and your two Houses of Parliament;"—in answer to which the King said, "If any scruple remains concerning the suspension of the penal laws, I hereby faithfully promise that what hath been done in that particular shall not be drawn either into consequence or example." The Chancellor and Secretary Coventry, by command of the King, acquainted both Houses separately, on the same day, that he had caused the Declaration to be cancelled in his presence; on which both Houses immediately voted, and presented in a body, an unanimous address of thanks to his Majesty, "for his gracious, full, and satisfactory answer."* The whole of this transaction undoubtedly amounted to a solemn and final condemnation of the pretension to a suspending power by the King in Parliament: it was in substance not distinguishable from a declaratory law; and the forms of a statute seem to have been dispensed with only to avoid the appearance of distrust or discourtesy towards Charles. We can discover, in the very imperfect accounts which are preserved of the debates of 1673, that the advocates of the Crown had laid main stress on the King's ecclesiastical supremacy; it being, as they reasoned, evident that the head of the Church should be left to judge when it was wise to execute or suspend the laws intended for its protection. They relied also on the undisputed right of the Crown to stop the progress of each single prosecution which seemed to justify, by analogy, a more general exertion of the same power.

James, in his Declaration of Indulgence, disdaining any appeals to analogy or to supremacy, chose to take a wider and higher ground, and concluded the preamble in the tone of a master:—"We have thought fit, by virtue of our royal prerogative, to issue

* 14 Car. II. c. iv.

† Speeches, 8th May, 1661, and 19th May, 1662. "The Lords Clarendon and Southampton, together with the Bishops, were the great opposers of the King's intention to grant toleration to Dissenters, according to the promise at Breda."—Life of James II. vol. i. p. 391. These, indeed, are not the words of the King; but for more than twelve years on this part of his Life, the compiler, Mr. Dicconson, does not quote James' MSS.

‡ Kennet, Register, p. 850.—The concluding paragraph, relating to Catholics, is a model of that stately ambiguity under which the style of Clarendon gave him peculiar facilities of cloaking an unpopular proposal.

§ Journals, 25th Feb., 1663.

‖ "We think ourselves obliged to make use of that supreme power in ecclesiastical matters which is inherent in us. We declare our will and pleasure, that the execution of all penal laws in matters ecclesiastical be suspended; and we shall allow a sufficient number of places of worship as they shall be desired, for the use of those who do not conform to the Church of England:—without allowing public worship to Roman Catholics." Most English historians tell us that Sir Orlando Bridgman refused to put the Great Seal to this Declaration, and that Lord Shaftesbury was made Chancellor to seal it. The falsehood of this statement is proved by the mere inspection of the London Gazette, by which we see that the Declaration was issued on the 15th of March, 1672, when Lord Shaftesbury was not yet appointed. —See Locke's Letter from a Person of Quality, and the Life of Shaftesbury (unpublished), p. 247.

* Journals, 8th March, 1673.

forth this our Declaration of Indulgence, making no doubt of the concurrence of our two Houses of Parliament, when we shall think it convenient for them to meet." His Declaration was issued in manifest defiance of the parliamentary condemnation pronounced on that of his brother, and it was introduced in language of more undefined and alarming extent. On the other hand, his measure was countenanced by the determination of the judges, and seemed to be only a more compendious and convenient manner of effecting what these perfidious magistrates had declared he might lawfully do. Their iniquitous decision might excuse many of those who were ignorant of the means by which it was obtained; but the King himself, who had removed judges too honest to concur in it, and had neither continued nor appointed any whose subserviency he had not first ascertained, could plead no such authority in mitigation. He had dictated the oracle which he affected to obey. It is very observable that he himself, or rather his biographer (for it is not just to impute this base excuse to himself), while he claims the protecting authority of the adjudication, is prudently silent on the unrighteous practices by which that show of authority was purchased.*

The way had been paved for the English Declaration by a Proclamation† issued at Edinburgh, on the 12th of February, couched in loftier language than was about to be hazarded in England:—"We, by our sovereign authority, prerogative royal, and absolute power, do hereby give and grant our royal toleration. We allow and tolerate the moderate Presbyterians to meet in their private houses, and to hear such ministers as have been or are willing to accept of our indulgence; but they are not to build meeting-houses, but to exercise in houses. We tolerate Quakers to meet in their form in any place or places appointed for their worship. We, by our sovereign authority, &c. suspend, stop, and disable, all laws or Acts of Parliament made or executed against any of our Roman Catholic subjects, so that they shall be free to exercise their religion and to enjoy all; but they are to exercise in houses or chapels. And we cass, annul, and discharge all oaths by which our subjects are disabled from holding offices." He concludes by confirming the proprietors of Church lands in their possession, which seemed to be wholly unnecessary while the Protestant establishment endured; and adds an assurance more likely to disquiet than to satisfy, "that he will not use force against any man for the Protestant religion." In a short time afterwards he had extended this indulgence to those Presbyterians who scrupled to take the Test or any other oath; and in a few months more, on the 5th of July, all restrictions on toleration had been removed, by the permission granted to all to serve God in their own manner, whether in private houses or chapels, or houses built or hired for the purpose;* or, in other words, he had established, by his own sole authority, the most unbounded liberty of worship and religious instruction in a country where the laws treated every act of dissent as one of the most heinous crimes. There is no other example, perhaps, of so excellent an object being pursued by means so culpable, or for purposes in which evil was so much blended with good.

James was equally astonished and incensed at the resistance of the Church of England. Their warm professions of loyalty, their acquiescence in measures directed only against civil liberty, their solemn condemnation of forcible resistance to oppression (the lawfulness of which constitutes the main strength of every opposition to misgovernment), had persuaded him that they would look patiently on the demolition of all the bulwarks of their own wealth, and greatness, and power, and submit in silence to measures which, after stripping the Protestant religion of all its temporal aid, might at length leave it exposed to persecution. He did not distinguish between legal opposition and violent resistance. He believed in the adherence of multitudes to professions poured forth in a moment of enthusiasm; and he was so ignorant of human nature as to imagine, that speculative opinions of a very extravagant sort, even if they could be stable, were sufficient to supersede interest and habits, to bend the pride of high establishments, and to stem the passions of a nation in a state of intense excitement. Yet James had been admonished by the highest authority to beware of this delusion. Morley, Bishop of Winchester, a veteran royalist and Episcopalian, whose fidelity had been tried, but whose judgment had been informed in the Civil War, almost with his dying breath desired Lord Dartmouth to warn the King, that if ever he depended on the doctrine of Nonresistance he would find himself deceived; for that most of the Church would contradict it in their practice, though not in terms. It was to no purpose that Dartmouth frequently reminded James of Morley's last message; for he answered, "that the Bishop was a good man, but grown old and timid."†

It must be owned, on the other hand, that there were not wanting considerations which excuse the expectation and explain the disappointment of James. Wiser men than he have been the dupes of that natural prejudice, which leads us to look for the same consistency between the different parts of conduct which is in some degree found to prevail among the different reasonings and opinions of every man of sound mind. It cannot be denied that the Church had done

* Life of James II., vol. ii. p. 81. "He," says the biographer, "had no other oracle to apply to for exposition of difficult and intricate points."

† Wodrow, vol. ii. app.

* Wodrow, vol. ii. app. Fountainhall, vol. i. p. 463.

† Burnet, (Oxford, 1823), vol. ii. p. 428. Lord Dartmouth's note.

much to delude him. For they did not content themselves with never controverting, nor even confine themselves to calmly preaching the doctrine of Nonresistance (which might be justified and perhaps commended); but it was constantly and vehemently inculcated. The more furious preachers treated all who doubted it with the fiercest scurrility,* and the most pure and gentle were ready to introduce it harshly and unreasonably;† and they all boasted of it, perhaps with reason, as a peculiar characteristic which distinguished the Church of England from other Christian communities. Nay, if a solemn declaration from an authority second only to the Church, assembled in a national council, could have been a security for their conduct, the judgment of the University of Oxford, in their Convocation in 1683, may seem to warrant the utmost expectations of the King. For among other positions condemned by that learned body, one was, "that if lawful governors become tyrants, or govern otherwise than by the laws of God or man they ought to do, they forfeit the right they had unto their government.‡ Now, it is manifest, that, according to this determination, if the King had abolished Parliaments, shut the courts of justice, and changed the laws according to his pleasure, he would nevertheless retain the same rights as before over all his subjects; that any part of them who resisted him would still contract the full guilt of rebellion; and that the co-operation of the sounder portion to repress the revolt would be a moral duty and a lawful service. How, then, could it be reasonable to withstand him in far less important assaults on his subjects, and to turn against him laws which owed their continuance solely to his good pleasure? Whether this last mode of reasoning be proof against all objections or not, it was at least specious enough to satisfy the King, when it agreed with his passions and supposed interest. Under the influence of these natural delusions, we find him filled with astonishment at the prevalence of the ordinary motives of human conduct over an extravagant dogma, and beyond measure amazed that the Church should oppose the Crown after the King had become the enemy of the Church. "Is this your Church of England loyalty?" he cried to the fellows of Magdalen College; while in his confidential conversations he now spoke with the utmost indignation of this inconsistent and mutinous Church. Against it, he told the Nuncio, that he had by his Declaration struck a blow which would resound through the country;—ascribing their unexpected resistance to a consciousness that, in a general liberty of conscience, "the Anglican religion would be the first to decline."* Sunderland, in speaking of the Church to the same minister, exclaimed, "Where is now their boasted fidelity? The Declaration has mortified those who have resisted the King's pious and benevolent designs. The Anglicans are a ridiculous sect, who affect a sort of moderation in heresy, by a compound and jumble of all other persuasions; and who, notwithstanding the attachment which they boast of having maintained to the monarchy and the royal family, have proved on this occasion the most insolent and contumacious of men."† After the refusal to comply with his designs, on the ground of conscience, by Admiral Herbert, a man of loose life, loaded with the favours of the Crown, and supposed to be as sensible of the obligations of honour as he was negligent of those of religion and morality, James declared to Barillon, that he never could put confidence in any man, however attached to him, who affected the character of a zealous Protestant.‡

The Declaration of Indulgence, however, had one important purpose beyond the assertion of prerogative, the advancement of the Catholic religion, or the gratification of anger against the unexpected resistance of the Church: it was intended to divide Protestants, and to obtain the support of the Nonconformists. The same policy had, indeed, failed in the preceding reign; but it was not unreasonably hoped by the Court, that the sufferings of twenty years had irreconcilably inflamed the dissenting sects against the Establishment, and had at length taught them to prefer their own personal and religious liberty to vague and speculative opposition to the Papacy,—the only bond of union between the discordant communities who were called Protestants. It was natural enough to suppose, that they would show no warm interest in universities from which they were excluded, or for prelates who had excited persecution against them; and that they would thankfully accept the blessings of safety and repose, without anxiously examining whether the grant of these advantages was consistent with the principles of a constitution which treated them as unworthy of all trust or employment. Certainly the penal law from which the Declaration ten-

* South, *passim*.

† Tillotson, On the Death of Lord Russell. About a year before the time to which the text alludes, in a visitation sermon preached before Sancroft by Kettlewell, an excellent man, in whom nothing was stern but this doctrine, it is inculcated to such an extent as, according to the usual interpretation of the passage in Paul's Epistle to the Romans (xiii. 2.), to prohibit resistance to Nero; "who," says nevertheless the preacher, "invaded honest men's estates to supply his own profusion, and embrued his hands in the blood of any he had a pique against, without any regard to law or justice." The Homily, or exhortation to obedience, composed under Edward VI., in 1547, by Cranmer, and sanctioned by authority of the Church, asserts it to be "the calling of God's people to render obedience to governors, although they be wicked or wrong-doers, and *in no case to resist*."

‡ Collier, Ecclesiastical History, vol. ii. p. 902.

* D'Adda, 21st March, 1687; "un colpo strepitoso." "Perche la religióne Anglicana sarebbe stata la prima a declinare in questa mutazióne."

† D'Adda, 4th—18th April.

‡ Barillon, 24th March.—Fox MSS.

dered relief, was not such as to dispose them to be very jealous of the mode of its removal.

An Act in the latter years of Elizabeth* had made refusal to attend the established worship, or presence at that of Dissenters, punishable by imprisonment, and, unless atoned for by conformity within three months, by perpetual banishment,† enforced by death if the offender should return. Within three years after the solemn promise of liberty of conscience from Breda, this barbarous law, which had been supposed to be dormant, was declared to be in force, by an Act which subjected every one attending any but the established worship, where more than five were present, on the third offence, to transportation for seven years to any of the colonies (except New England and Virginia,—the only ones where they might have been consoled by their fellow-religionists, and where labour in the fields was not fatal to an European); and which doomed them in case of their return,—an event not very probable, after having laboured for seven years as the slaves of their enemies under the sun of Barbadoes,—to death. Almost every officer, civil or military, was empowered and encouraged to disperse their congregations as unlawful assemblies, and to arrest their ringleaders. A conviction before two magistrates, and in some cases before one, without any right of appeal or publicity of proceeding, was sufficient to expose a helpless or obnoxious Nonconformist to these tremendous consequences. By a refinement in persecution, the jailer was instigated to disturb the devotions of his prisoners; being subject to a fine if he allowed any one who was at large to join them in their religious worship. The pretext for this statute, which was however only temporary, consisted in some riots and tumults in Ireland and in Yorkshire, evidently viewed by the ministers themselves with more scorn than fear.§ A permanent law, equally tyrannical, was passed in the next session.‖ By it every dissenting clergyman was forbidden from coming within five miles of his former congregation, or of any corporate town or parliamentary borough, under a penalty of forty pounds, unless he should take the following oath:—"I swear that it is not lawful, upon any pretence whatsoever, to take up arms against the King, or those commissioned by him, and that I will not at any time endeavour any alteration of government in Church or State." In vain did Lord Southampton raise his dying voice against this tyrannical act, though it was almost the last exercise of the ministerial power of his friend and colleague Clarendon;—vehemently condemning the oath, which, royalist as he was, he declared that neither he nor any honest man could take.* A faint and transient gleam of indulgence followed the downfall of Clarendon. But, in the year 1670, another Act was passed, reviving that of 1664, with some mitigations of punishment, and with amendments in the form of proceeding;† but with several provisions of a most unusual nature, which, by their manifest tendency to stimulate the bigotry of magistrates, rendered it a sharper instrument of persecution. Of this nature was the declaration, that the statute was to be construed most favourably for the suppression of conventicles, and for the encouragement of those engaged in carrying it into effect; the malignity of which must be measured by its effect in exciting all public officers, especially the lowest, to constant vexation and frequent cruelty towards the poorer Nonconformists, marked by such language as the objects of the fear and hatred of the legislature.

After the defeat of Charles' attempt to relieve all Dissenters by his usurped prerogative, the alarms of the House of Commons had begun to be confined to the Catholics; and they had conceived designs of union with the more moderate of their Protestant brethren, as well as of indulgence towards those whose dissent was irreconcilable. But these designs proved abortive: the Court resumed its animosity against the Dissenters, when it became no longer possible to employ them as a shelter for the Catholics. The laws were already sufficient for all practical purposes of intolerance, and their execution was in the hands of bitter enemies, from the Lord Chief Justice to the pettiest constable. The temper of the Established clergy was such, that even the more liberal of them gravely reproved the victims of such laws for complaining of persecution.‡ The inferior gentry, who constituted the magistracy,—ignorant, intemperate, and tyrannical,—treated dissent as rebellion, and in their conduct to Puritans were actuated by no principles but a furious hatred of those whom they thought the enemies of the monarchy. The whole jurisdiction, in cases of Nonconformity, was so vested in that body, as to release them in its exercise from the greater part of the restraints of fear and shame. With the sanction of the legislature, and the countenance of the Government, what indeed could they fear from a proscribed party, consisting chiefly of the humblest and poorest men? From shame they were effectually secured, since that which is not public cannot be made shameful. The particulars of the conviction of a Dissenter might be unknown beyond his village; the evidence against

* 35 Eliz. c. 1, (1593.)

† A sort of exile, called, in our old law, "abjuring the realm," in which the offender was to banish himself.

‡ 16 Car. II. c. 4.

§ Ralph, History of England, vol. ii. p. 97. "As these plots," says that writer, "were contemptible or formidable, we must acquit or condemn this reign."

‖ 17 Car. II. c. 2.

* Locke, Letter from a Person of Quality.

† 22 Car. II. c. 1.

‡ Stillingfleet, Sermon on the Mischief of Separation.

him, if any, might be confined to the room where he was convicted: and in that age of slow communication, few men would incur the trouble or obloquy of conveying to their correspondents the hardships inflicted, with the apparent sanction of law, in remote and ignorant districts, on men at once obscure and odious, and often provoked by their sufferings into intemperance and extravagance.

Imprisonment is, of all punishments, the most quiet and convenient mode of persecution. The prisoner is silently hid from the public eye; his sufferings, being unseen, speedily cease to excite pity or indignation: he is soon doomed to oblivion. As it is always the safest punishment for an oppressor to inflict, so it was in that age, in England, perhaps the most cruel. Some estimate of the suffering from cold, hunger, and nakedness, in the dark and noisome dungeons, then called prisons, may be formed from the remains of such buildings, which industrious benevolence has not yet every where demolished. Being subject to no regulation, and without means for the regular sustenance of the prisoners, they were at once the scene of debauchery and famine. The Puritans, the most severely moral men of any age, were crowded in cells with the profligate and ferocious criminals with whom the kingdom then abounded. We learn from the testimony of the legislature itself, that "needy persons committed to jail many times perished before their trial."* We are told by Thomas Ellwood, the Quaker, a friend of Milton, that when a prisoner in Newgate for his religion, he saw the heads and quarters of men who had been executed for treason kept for some time close to the cells, and the heads tossed about in sport by the hangman and the more hardened malefactors;† and the description given by George Fox, the founder of the Quakers, of his own treatment when a prisoner at Launceston, too clearly exhibits the unbounded power of his jailers, and its most cruel exercise.‡ It was no wonder that, when prisoners were brought to trial at the assizes, the contagion of jail fever should often rush forth with them from these abodes of all that was loathsome and hideous, and sweep away judges, and jurors, and advocates, with its pestilential blast. The mortality of such prisons must have surpassed the imaginations of more civilized times; and death, if it could be separated from the long sufferings which led to it, might perhaps be considered as the most merciful part of the prison discipline of that age. It would be exceedingly hard to estimate the amount of this mortality, even if the difficulty were not enhanced by the prejudices which led either to its extenuation or aggravation. Prisoners were then so forgotten, that a record of it was not to be expected; and the very nature of the atrocious wickedness which employs imprisonment as the instrument of murder, would, in many cases, render it impossible distinctly and palpably to show the process by which cold and hunger beget mortal disease. But computations have been attempted, and, as was natural, chiefly by the sufferers. William Penn, a man of such virtue as to make his testimony weighty, even when borne to the sufferings of his own party, publicly affirmed at the time, that since the Restoration "more than five thousand persons had died in bonds for matters of mere conscience to God."* Twelve hundred Quakers were enlarged by James.† The calculations of Neale, the historian of the Nonconformists, would carry the numbers still farther; and he does not appear, on this point, to be contradicted by his zealous and unwearied antagonist.‡ But if we reduce the number of deaths to one half of Penn's estimate, and suppose that number to be the tenth of the prisoners, it will afford a dreadful measure of the sufferings of twenty-five thousand prisoners; and the misery within the jails will too plainly indicate the beggary,§ banishment, disquiet, vexation, fear, and horror, which were spread among the whole body of Dissenters.

The sufferings of two memorable men among them, differing from each other still more widely in opinions and disposition than in station and acquirement, may be selected as proofs that no character was too high to be beyond the reach of this persecution, and no condition too humble to be beneath its notice. Richard Baxter, one of the most acute and learned as well as pious and exemplary men of his age, was the most celebrated divine of the Presbyterian persuasion. He had been so well known for his moderation as well as his general merit, that at the Restoration he had been made chaplain to the King, and a bishopric had been offered to him, which he declined, not because he deemed it unlawful, but because it might engage him in severities against the conscientious, and because he was unwilling to give scandal to his brethren by accepting preferment in the hour of their affliction.‖ He joined in the public worship of the

* 18 & 19 Car. II. c. 9. Evidence more conclusive, from its being undesignedly dropped, of the frequency of such horrible occurrences in the jail of Newgate, transpires in a controversy between a Catholic and Protestant clergyman, about the religious sentiments of a dying criminal, and is preserved in a curious pamphlet, called "The Pharisee Unmasked," published in 1687.

† "This prison, where are so many, suffocateth the spirits of aged ministers."—Life of Baxter (Calamy's Abridgment), part iii. p. 200.

‡ Journal, p. 186, where the description of the dungeon called "*Doomsdale*" surpasses all imagination.

* Good Advice to the Church of England.

† Address of the Quakers to James II.—Clarkson, Life of William Penn, vol. i. p. 492. London Gazette, 23d and 26th May, 1687.

‡ Grey, Examination of Neale.

§ "Fifteen thousand families ruined."—Good Advice, &c. In this tract, very little is said of the dispensing power; the far greater part consisting of a noble defence of religious liberty, applicable to all ages and communions

‖ Life of Baxter, part iii. p. 281.

Church of England, but himself preached to a small congregation at Acton, where he soon became the friend of his neighbour, Sir Matthew Hale, who, though then a magistrate of great dignity, avoided the society of those who might be supposed to influence him, and from his jealous regard to independence, chose a privacy as simple and frugal as that of the pastor of a persecuted flock. Their retired leisure was often employed in high reasoning on those sublime subjects of metaphysical philosophy to which both had been conducted by their theological studies, and which, indeed, few contemplative men of elevated thought have been deterred by the fate of their forerunners from aspiring to comprehend. Honoured as he was by such a friendship, esteemed by the most distinguished persons of all persuasions, and consulted by the civil and ecclesiastical authorities in every project of reconciliation and harmony, Baxter was five times in fifteen years dragged from his retirement, and thrown into prison as a malefacter. In 1669 two subservient magistrates, one of whom was the steward of the Archbishop of Canterbury, summoned him before them for preaching at a conventicle; at hearing of which, Hale, too surely foreknowing the event, could scarcely refrain from tears. He was committed to prison for six months; but, after the unavailing intercession of his friends with the King, was at length enlarged in consequence of informalities in the commitment.* Twice afterwards he escaped by irregularities into which the precipitate zeal of ignorant persecutors had betrayed them; and once, when his physician made oath that imprisonment would be dangerous to his life, he owed his enlargement to the pity or prudence of Charles II. At last, in the year 1685, he was brought to trial for some supposed libels, before Jeffreys, in the Court of King's Bench, in which his venerable friend had once presided,—where two Chief Justices, within ten years, had exemplified the extremities of human excellence and depravity, and where he, whose misfortunes had almost drawn tears down the aged cheeks of Hale was doomed to undergo the most brutal indignities from Jeffreys.

The history and genius of Bunyan were as much more extraordinary than those of Baxter as his station and attainments were inferior. He is probably at the head of unlettered men of genius; and perhaps there is no other instance of any man reaching fame from so abject an origin. For other extraordinary men who have become famous without education, though they were without what is called "learning," have had much reading and knowledge; and though they were repressed by poverty, were not, like him, sullied by a vagrant and disreputable occupation. By his trade of a travelling tinker, he had been from his earliest years placed in the midst of profligacy, and on the verge of dishonesty. He was for a time a private in the parliamentary army,—the only military service which was likely to elevate his sentiments and amend his life. Having embraced the opinions of the Baptists, he was soon admitted to preach in a community which did not recognise the distinction between the clergy and the laity.* Even under the Protectorate he had been harassed by some busy magistrates, who took advantage of a parliamentary ordinance, excluding from toleration those who maintained the unlawfulness of infant baptism.† But this officiousness was checked by the spirit of the government; and it was not till the return of intolerance with Charles II. that the sufferings of Bunyan began. Within five months after the Restoration, he was apprehended under the statute 35th of Elizabeth, and was thrown into a prison, or rather dungeon, at Bedford, where he remained for twelve years. The narratives of his life exhibit remarkable specimens of the acuteness and fortitude with which he withstood the threats and snares of the magistrates, and clergymen, and attorneys, who beset him,—foiling them in every contest of argument, especially in that which relates to the independence of religion on civil authority, which he expounded with clearness and exactness; for it was a subject on which his naturally vigorous mind was better educated by his habitual meditations than it could have been by the most skilful instructor. In the year after his apprehension, he had made some informal applications for release to the judges of assize, in a petition presented by his wife, who was treated by one of them, Twisden, with brutal insolence. His colleague, Sir Mathew Hale, listened to her with patience and goodness, and with consolatory compassion pointed out to her the only legal means of obtaining redress. It is a singular gratification thus to find a human character, which, if it be met in the most obscure recess of the history of a bad time, is sure to display some new excellence. The conduct of Hale on this occasion can be ascribed only to strong and pure benevolence; for he was unconscious of Bunyan's genius, he disliked preaching mechanics, and he partook the general prejudice against Anabaptists. In the long years which followed, the time of Bunyan was divided between the manufacture of lace, which he learned in order to support his family, and the composition of those works which have given celebrity to his sufferings. He was at length released, in 1672, by Barlow, Bishop of Lincoln;

* Life of Baxter, part iii. pp. 47—51.

* See Grace Abounding.

† Scobell's Ordinances, chap. 114. This exception is omitted in a subsequent Ordinance against blasphemous opinions, (9th August, 1650), directed chiefly against the Antinomians, who were charged with denying the obligation of morality, —the single case where the danger of nice distinction is the chief objection to the use of punishment against the promulgation of opinions. Religious liberty was afterwards carried much nearer to its just limits by the letter of Cromwells' constitution, and probably to its full extent by its spirit.—See Humble Petition and Advice, sect. xi.

but not till the timid prelate had received an injunction from the Lord Chancellor* to that effect. He availed himself of the Indulgence of James II. without trusting it, and died unmolested in the last year of that prince's government. His Pilgrim's Progress, an allegorical representation of the Calvinistic theology, at first found readers only among those of that persuasion, but, gradually emerging from this narrow circle, by the natural power of imagination over the uncorrupted feelings of the majority of mankind, has at length rivalled Robinson Crusoe in popularity. The bigots and persecutors have sank into oblivion; the scoffs of wits† and worldlings have been unavailing; while, after the lapse of a century, the object of their cruelty and scorn has touched the poetical sympathy, as well as the piety, of Cowper; his genius has subdued the opposite prejudices of Johnson and of Franklin; and his name has been uttered in the same breath with those of Spenser and Dante. It should seem, from this statement, that Lord Castlemaine, himself a zealous Catholic, had some colour for asserting, that the persecution of Protestants by Protestants, after the Restoration, was more violent than that of Protestants by Catholics under Mary; and that the persecution then raging against the Presbyterians in Scotland was not so much more cruel, as it was more bloody, than that which silently consumed the bowels of Eugland.

Since the differences between Churchmen and Dissenters, as such, have given way to other Controversies, a recital of them can have no other tendency than that of disposing men to pardon each other's intolerance, and to abhor the fatal error itself, which all communions have practised, and of which some malignant roots still lurk among all. Without it, the policy of the King, in his attempt to form an alliance with the latter, could not be understood. The general body of Nonconformists were divided into four parties, on whom the Court acted through different channels, and who were variously affected by its advances.

The Presbyterians, the more wealthy and educated sect, were the descendants of the ancient Puritans, who had been rather desirous of reforming the Church of England than of separating from it; and though the breach was widened by the Civil War, they might have been reunited at the Restoration by moderate concession in the form of worship, and by limiting the episcopal authority agreeably to the project of the learned Usher, and to the system of superintendency established among the Lutherans. Gradually, indeed, they learned to prefer the perfect equality of the Calvinistic clergy; but they did not profess that exclusive zeal for it which actuated their Scottish brethren, who had received their Reformation from Geneva. Like men of other communions, they had originally deemed it the duty of the magistrate to establish true religion, and to punish the crime of rejecting it. In Scotland they continued to be sternly intolerant; while in England they reluctantly acquiesced in imperfect toleration. Their object was now what was called a "comprehension," or such an enlargement of the terms of communion as might enable them to unite with the Church;—a measure which would have broken the strength of the Dissenters, as a body, to the eminent hazard of civil liberty. From them the King had the least hopes. They were undoubtedly much more hostile to the Establishment after twenty-five years' persecution; but they were still connected with the tolerant clergy; and as they continued to aim at something besides mere toleration, they considered the royal Declaration, even if honestly meant, as only a temporary advantage.

The Independents, or Congregationalists, were so called from their adoption of the opinion, that every congregation or assembly for worship was a church perfectly independent of all others, choosing and changing their own ministers, maintaining with others a fraternal intercourse, but acknowledging no authority in all the other churches of Christendom to interfere with its internal concerns. Their churches were merely voluntary associations, in which the office of teacher might be conferred and withdrawn by the suffrages of the members. These members were equal, and the government was perfectly democratical; if the term "government" may be applied to assemblies which endured only as long as the members agreed in judgment, and which, leaving all coercive power to the civil magistrate, exercised no authority but that of admonition, censure, and exclusion. They disclaimed the qualification of "national" as repugnant to the nature of a "church."* The religion of the Independents, therefore, could not, without destroying its nature, be established by law. They never could aspire to more than religious liberty; and they accordingly have the honour of having been the first, and long the only, Christian community who collectively adopted that sacred principle.† It is true,

---

* Probably Lord Shaftesbury, who received the Great Seal in November, 1672. The exact date of Bunyan's complete liberation is not ascertained; but he was twelve years a prisoner, and had been apprehended in November, 1660. Ivimey (Life of Bunyan, p. 289) makes his enlargement to be about the close of 1672.

† Hudibras, part i. canto ii. Grey's notes.

* "There is no true visible Church of Christ but a particular ordinary congregation only. Every ordinary assembly of the faithful hath power to elect and ordain, deprive and depose, their ministers. The pastor must have others joined with him by the congregation, to exercise ecclesiastical jurisdiction; neither ought he and they to perform any material act without the free consent of the congregation."—Christian Offer of a Conference tendered to Archbishops, Bishops, &c. London, 1606.)

† An Humble Supplication for Toleration and Liberty to James I. (London, 1609):—a tract which affords a conspicuous specimen of the ability

that in the beginning they adopted the pernicious and inconsistent doctrine of limited toleration; excluding Catholics, as idolaters, and in New England (where the great majority were of their persuasion), punishing, even capitally, dissenters from what they accounted as fundamental opinions.* But, as intolerance could promote no interest of theirs, real or imaginary, their true principles finally worked out the stain of these dishonourable exceptions. The government of Cromwell, more influenced by them than by any other persuasion, made as near approaches to general toleration as public prejudice would endure; and Sir Henry Vane, an Independent, was probably the first who laid down, with perfect precision, the inviolable rights of conscience, and the exemption of religion from all civil authority. Actuated by these principles, and preferring the freedom of their worship even to political liberty, it is not wonderful that many of this persuasion gratefully accepted the deliverance from persecution which was proffered by the King.

Similar causes produced the like dispositions among the Baptists,—a simple and pious body of men, generally unlettered, obnoxious to all other sects for their rejection of infant baptism, as neither enjoined by the New Testament nor consonant to reason, and in some degree, also, from being called by the same name with the fierce fanatics who had convulsed Lower Germany in the first age of the Reformation. Under Edward VI. and Elizabeth many had suffered death for their religion. At the Restoration they had been distinguished from other Nonconformists by a brand in the provision of a statute,† which excluded every clergyman who had opposed infant baptism from re-establishment in his benefice; and they had during Charles' reign suffered more than any other persuasion. Publicly professing the principles of religious liberty,‡ and, like the Independents, espousing the cause of republicanism, they appear to have adopted also the congregational system of ecclesiastical polity. More incapable of union with the Established Church, and having less reason to hope for toleration from its adherents than the Independents themselves, — many, perhaps at first most of them, eagerly embraced the Indulgence. Thus, the sects who maintained the purest principles of religious liberty, and had supported the most popular systems of government, were the most disposed to favour a measure which would have finally buried toleration under the ruins of political freedom.

But of all sects, those who needed the royal Indulgence most, and who could accept it most consistently with their religious principles, were the Quakers. Seeking perfection, by renouncing pleasures, of which the social nature promotes kindness, and by converting self-denial, a means of moral discipline, into one of the ends of life,—it was their more peculiar and honourable error, that by a literal interpretation of that affectionate and ardent language in which the Christian religion inculcates the pursuit of peace and the practice of beneficence, they struggled to extend the sphere of these most admirable virtues beyond the boundaries of nature. They adopted a peculiarity of language, and a uniformity of dress, indicative of humility and equality, of brotherly love—the sole bond of their pacific union, and of the serious minds of men who lived only for the performance of duty,—taking no part in strife, renouncing even defensive arms, and utterly condemning the punishment of death.

George Fox had, during the Civil War, founded this extraordinary community. At a time when personal revelation was generally believed, it was a pardonable self-delusion that he should imagine himself to be commissioned by the Deity to preach a system which could only be objected to as too pure to be practised by man.* This belief, and an ardent temperament, led him and some of his followers into unseasonable attempts to convert their neighbours, and into unseemly intrusions into places of worship for that purpose, which excited general hostility against them, and exposed them to frequent and severe punishments. One or two of them, in the general fermentation of men's minds at that time, had uttered what all other sects considered as blasphemous opinions; and these peaceable men became the objects of general abhorrence. Their rejection of most religious rites, their refusal to sanction testimony by a judicial oath, or to defend their country in the utmost danger, gave plausible pretexts for representing them as alike enemies to religion and the commonwealth; and the fantastic peculiarities of their language and dress seemed to be the badge of a sullen and morose secession from human society. Proscribed as they were by law and prejudice, the Quakers gladly received the boon held out by the King. They indeed were the only consistent professors of passive obedience: as they resisted no wrong, and never sought to disarm hostility otherwise than by benevolence, they naturally yielded with unresisting submission to the injustice of tyrants. Another circumstance also contributed, still more perhaps than these general causes, to throw them into the arms of James. Although their sect, like most other sects, had sprung from among the humbler classes of society,—who, from their

and learning of the ancient Independents, often described as unlettered fanatics.

* The Way of the Churches in New England, by Mr. J. Cotton (London, 1645); and the Way of Congregational Churches, by Mr. J. Cotton (London, 1648);—in answer to Principal Baillie.

† 12 Car. II. c. 17.

‡ Crosby, History of English Baptists, &c., vol. ii. pp. 100—144.

* Journal of the Life of George Fox, by himself:—one of the most extraordinary and instructive narratives in the world, which no reader of competent judgment can peruse without revering the virtue of the writer, pardoning his self-delusion, and ceasing to smile at his peculiarities.

numbers and simplicity, are alone susceptible of those sudden and simultaneous emotions which change opinions and institutions,—they had early been joined by a few persons of superior rank and education, who, in a period of mutation in government and religion, had long contemplated their benevolent visions with indulgent complacency, and had at length persuaded themselves that this pure system of peace and charity might be realised, if not among all, at least among a few of the wisest and best of men. Such a hope would gradually teach the latter to tolerate, and in time to adopt, the peculiarities of their simpler brethren, and to give the most rational interpretation to the language and pretensions of their founders;—consulting reason in their doctrines, and indulging enthusiasm only in their hopes and affections.* Of the first who thus systematised, and perhaps insensibly softened, their creed, was Barclay; whose Apology for the Quakers—a masterpiece of ingenious reasoning, and a model of argumentative composition—extorted praise from Bayle, one of the most acute and least fanatical of men.†

But the most distinguished of their converts was William Penn, whose father, Admiral Sir William Penn, had been a personal friend of the King, and one of his instructors in naval affairs. This admirable person had employed his great abilities in support of civil as well as religious liberty, and had both acted and suffered for them under Charles II. Even if he had not founded the commonwealth of Pennsylvania as an everlasting memorial of his love of freedom, his actions and writings in England would have been enough to absolve him from the charge of intending to betray the rights of his countrymen. But though, as the friend of Algernon Sidney, he had never ceased to intercede, through his friends at Court, for the persecuted,‡ still an absence of two years in America, and the consequent distraction of his mind, had probably loosened his connection with English politicians, and rendered him less acquainted with the principles of the government. On the accession of James he was received by that prince with favour; and hopes of indulgence to his suffering brethren were early held out to him. He was soon admitted to terms of apparent intimacy, and was believed to possess such influence that two hundred suppliants were often seen at his gates, imploring his intercession with the King. That it really was great, appears from his obtaining a promise of pardon for his friend Mr. Locke, which that illustrious man declined, because he thought that the acceptance of it would have been a confession of criminality.§ Penn appears in 1679, through his influence with James when in Scotland, to have obtained the release of all the Quakers who were imprisoned there;* and he subsequently obtained the release of many hundred English ones,† as well as procured letters to be addressed by Lord Sunderland to the various Lord Lieutenants in England in favour of his persuasion,‡ several months before the Declaration of Indulgence. It was no wonder that he should have been gained over by this power of doing good. The very occupations in which he was engaged brought daily before his mind the general evils of intolerance, and the sufferings of his own unfortunate brethren. Though well stored with useful and ornamental knowledge, he was unpractised in the wiles of courts; and his education had not trained him to dread the violation of principle so much as to pity the infliction of suffering. It cannot be doubted that he believed the King's object to be universal liberty in religion, and nothing further: and as his own sincere piety taught him to consider religious liberty as unspeakably the highest of human privileges, he was too just not to be desirous of bestowing on all other men that which he most earnestly sought for himself. One who refused to employ force in the most just defence, must have felt a singular abhorrence of its exertion to prevent good men from following the dictates of their conscience. Such seem to have been the motives which induced this excellent man to lend himself to the measures of the King. Compassion, friendship, liberality, and toleration, led him to support a system the success of which would have undone his country; and he afforded a remarkable proof that, in the complicated combinations of political morality, a virtue misplaced may produce as much immediate mischief as a vice. The Dutch minister represents "the arch-quaker" as travelling over the kingdom to gain proselytes to the dispensing power;§ while Duncombe, a banker in London, and (it must in justice, though in sorrow, be added) Penn, are stated to have been the two Protestant counsellors of Lord Sunderland.‖ Henceforward, it be-

* Mr. Swinton, a Scotch judge during the Protectorate, was one of the earliest of these converts.

† Nouvelles de la République des Lettres, Avril, 1684.

‡ Clarkson, Life of William Penn, vol. i. p. 248.

§ Clarkson, vol. i. pp. 433, 438. Mr. Clarkson is among the few writers from whom I should venture to adopt a fact for which the original authority is not mentioned. By his own extraordinary services to mankind he has deserved to be the biographer of William Penn.

* Address of Scotch Quakers, 1687.

† George Fox, Journal, p. 550.

‡ State Paper Office, November and December, 1686.

§ Van Citters to the States General, 14th Oct. 1687.

‖ Johnstone, 25th Nov. 1687.—MS. Johnstone's connections afforded him considerable means of information. Mrs. Dawson, an attendant of the Queen, was an intimate friend of his sister, Mrs. Baillie of Jerviswood: another of his sisters was the wife of General Drummond, who was deeply engaged in the persecution of the Scotch Presbyterians, and the Earl of Melfort's son had married his niece. His letters were to or for Burnet, his cousin, and intended to be read by the Prince of Orange, to both of whom he had

came necessary for the friends of liberty to deal with him as with an enemy, — to be resisted when his associates possessed, and watched after they had lost power.

Among the Presbyterians, the King's chief agent was Alsop, a preacher at Westminster, who was grateful to him for having spared the life of a son convicted of treason. Baxter, their venerable patriarch, and Howe, one of their most eminent divines, refused any active concurrence in the King's projects. But Lobb, one of the most able of the Independent divines, warmly supported the measures of James: he was favourably received at Court, and is said to have been an adviser as well as an advocate of the King.* An elaborate defence of the dispensing power, by Philip Nye, a still more eminent teacher of the same persuasion, who had been disabled from accepting office at the Restoration, written on occasion of Charles' Declaration of Indulgence in 1672, was now republished by his son, with a dedication to James.† Kiffin, the pastor of the chief congregation of the Baptists, and at the same time an opulent merchant in London, who, with his pastoral office, had held civil and military stations under the Parliament, withstood the prevalent disposition of his communion towards compliance. The few fragments of his life that have reached us illustrate the character of the calamitous times in which he lived. Soon after the Restoration, he had obtained a pardon for twelve persons of his persuasion, who were condemned to death at the same assize at Aylesbury, under the atrocious statute of the 35th of Elizabeth, for refusing either to abjure the realm or to conform to the Church of England.‡ Attempts were made to ensnare him into treason by anonymous letters, inviting him to take a share in plots which had no existence; and he was harassed by false accusations, some of which made him personally known to Charles II. and also to Clarendon. The King applied to him personally for the loan of 40,000*l.*: this he declined, offering the gift of 10,000*l.*, and on its being accepted, congratulated himself on having saved 30,000*l.* Two of his grandsons, although he had offered 3000*l.* for their preservation, suffered death for being engaged in Monmouth's revolt; and Jeffreys, on the trial of one of them, had declared, that had their grandfather been also at the bar, he would have equally deserved death. James, at one of their interviews, persuaded him, partly through his fear of incurring a ruinous fine in case of refusal, in spite of his pleading his inability through age (he was then seventy years old, and could not speak of his grandsons without tears) to accept the office of an alderman under the protection of the dispensing and suspending power.

Every means were employed to excite the Nonconformists to thank the King for his Indulgence. He himself assured D'Adda that it would be of the utmost service to trade and population, by recalling the numerous emigrants "who had been driven from their country by the persecution of the Anglicans;"* and his common conversation now turned on the cruelty of the Church of England towards the Dissenters, which he declared that he would have closed sooner, had he not been restrained by those who promised favour to his own religion, if they were still suffered to vex the latter.† This last declaration was contradicted by the parties whom he named; and their denial might be credited with less reserve, had not one of the principal leaders of the Episcopal party in Scotland owned that his friends would have been contented if they could have been assured of retaining the power to persecute Presbyterians.‡ The King even ordered an inquiry to be instituted into the suits against Dissenters in ecclesiastical courts, and the compositions which they paid, in order to make a scandalous disclosure of the extortion and venality practised under cover of the penal laws,§—assuring (as did also Lord Sunderland) the Nuncio, that the Established clergy traded in such compositions.‖ The most just principles of unbounded freedom in religion were now the received creed at St. James'. Even Sir Roger L'Estrange endeavoured to save his consistency by declaring, that though he had for twenty years resisted religious liberty as a right of the people, he acquiesced in it as a boon from the King.

On the other hand, exertions were made to warn the Dissenters of the snare which was laid for them; while the Church began to make tardy efforts to conciliate them, especially the Presbyterians. The King was agitated by this canvass, and frequently trusted the Nuncio¶ with his alternate hopes and fears about it. Burnet, then at the Hague, published a letter of warning, in which he owns and deplores "the persecution," acknowledging "the temptation under which the Nonconformists are to receive every thing which gives them present ease with a little too much kindness," blaming more severely the members of the Church who applauded the Declaration, but entreat-

the strongest inducements to give accurate information. He had frequent and confidential intercourse with Halifax, Tillotson, and Stillingfleet.

* Wilson, History and Antiquities of Dissenting Churches, &c.—(London, 1808), vol. iii. p. 436.

† Wilson, vol. iii. p. 71. The Lawfulness of the Oath of Supremacy asserted, &c., by Philip Nye. (London, 1687.)

‡ Orme, Life of Kiffin, p. 120. Crosby, vol. ii. p. 181, &c.

* D'Adda, 11th April, 1687.—MS.

† Burnet, (Oxford, 1823), vol. iii. p. 175.

‡ "If it had not been for the fears of encouraging by such a liberty the fanatics, then almost entirely ruined, few would have refused to comply with all your Majesty's demands."—Balcarras, Account of the Affairs of Scotland, p. 8.

§ Burnet, suprà.

‖ D'Adda, 18th April.—MS.—Ministri Anglicani che facevano mercanzia sopra le leggi fatti contro le Nonconformisti.

¶ D'Adda, 2d May, 4th April.—MS

ing the former not to promote the designs of the common enemy.* The residence and connections of the writer bestowed on this publication the important character of an admonition from the Prince of Orange. He had been employed by some leaders of the Church party to procure the Prince's interference with the Dissenting body;† and Dykveldt, the Dutch minister, assured both of his master's resolution to promote union between them, and to maintain the common interest of Protestants. Lord Halifax also published, on the same occasion, a Letter to a Dissenter,—the most perfect model, perhaps, of a political tract,—which, although its whole argument, unbroken by diversion to general topics, is brought exclusively to bear with concentrated force upon the question, the parties, and the moment, cannot be read, after an interval of a century and a half, without admiration at its acuteness, address, terseness, and poignancy.‡

The Nonconformists were thus acted upon by powerful inducements and dissuasives. The preservation of civil liberty, the interest of the Protestant religion, the secure enjoyment of freedom in their own worship, were irresistible reasons against compliance. Gratitude for present relief, remembrance of recent wrongs, and a strong sense of the obligation to prefer the exercise of religion to every other consideration, were very strong temptations to a different conduct. Many of them owed their lives to the King, and the lives of others were still in his hands. The remembrance of Jeffreys' campaign was so fresh as perhaps still rather to produce fear than the indignation and distrust which appear in a more advanced stage of recovery from the wounds inflicted by tyranny. The private relief granted to some of their ministers by the Court on former occasions afforded a facility for exercising adverse influence through these persons,—the more dangerous because it might be partly concealed from themselves under the disguise of gratitude. The result of the action of these conflicting motives seems to have been, that the far greater part of all denominations of Dissenters availed themselves of the Declaration so far as to resume their public worship;§ that the most distinguished of their clergy, and the majority of the Presbyterians, resisted the solicitations of the Court to sanction the dispensing power by addresses of thanks for this exertion of it; and that all the Quakers, the greater part of the Baptists, and perhaps also of the Independents, did not scruple to give this perilous token of their misguided gratitude, though many of them confined themselves to thanks for toleration, and solemn assurances that they would not abuse it.

About a hundred and eighty of these addresses were presented within a period of ten months, of which there are only seventy-seven exclusively and avowedly from Nonconformists. If to these be added a fair proportion of such as were at first secretly and at last openly corporators and grand jurors, and a larger share of those who addressed under very general descriptions, it seems probable that the numbers were almost equally divided between the Dissenting communions and the Established Church.* We have a specimen of these last mentioned by Evelyn, in the address of the Churchmen and dissenters of Coventry,† and of a small congregation in the Isle of Ely, called the "Family of Love." His complaint‡ that the Declaration had thinned his own parish church of Deptford, and had sent a great concourse of people to the meeting-house, throws light on the extent of the previous persecution, and the joyful eagerness to profit by their deliverance.

The Dissenters were led astray not only by the lights of the Church, but by the pretended guardians of the laws. Five bishops, Crew, of Durham, with his chapter, Cartwright of Chester, with his chapter, Barlow, of Lincoln, Wood, of Lichfield, and Watson, of St. David's, with the clergy of their dioceses, together with the Dean and Chapter of Ripon, addressed the King, in terms which were indeed limited to his assurance of continued protection to the Church, but at a time which rendered their addresses a sanction of the dispensing power; Croft, of Hereford, though not an addresser, was a zealous partisan of the measures of the Court; while the profligate Parker was unable to prevail on the Chapter or clergy of Oxford to join him, and the accomplished Sprat was still a member of the Ecclesiasti-

* State Tracts from Restoration to Revolution (London, 1689), vol. ii. p. 289.

† Burnet, Reflections on a Book called "Rights, &c. of a Convocation," p. 16.

‡ Halifax, Miscellanies, p. 233.

§ Bates' Life of Philip Henry, in Wordsworth's Ecclesiastical Biography, vol. vi. p. 290. "*They rejoiced with trembling.*" Henry refused to give in a return of the money levied on him in his sufferings, having, as he said, "long since from his heart forgiven all the agents in that matter." "Mr. Bunyan clearly saw through the designs of the Court, though he accepted the Indulgence with a holy fear."—Ivimey, Life of Bunyan, p. 297.

* The addresses from bishops and their clergy were seven; those from corporations and grand juries seventy-five; those from inhabitants, &c., fourteen; two from Catholics, and two from the Middle and Inner Temple. If six addresses from Presbyterians and Quakers in Scotland, Ireland, and New England be deducted, as it seems that they ought to be, the proportion of Dissenting addresses was certainly less than one half. Some of them, we know, were the produce of a sort of personal canvass, when the King made his progress in the autumn of 1687, "to court the compliments of the people;" and one of them, in which Philip Henry joined, "was not to offer lives and fortunes to him, but to thank him for the liberty, and to promise to demean themselves quietly in the use of it."—Wordsworth, vol. vi. p. 292. Address of Dissenters of Nantwich, Wem, and Whitchurch. London Gazette, 29th August.

† Evelyn, vol. i. Diary, 16th June.

‡ Ibid. 10th April.

cal Commission, in which character he held a high command in the adverse ranks:—so that a third of the episcopal order refused to concur in the coalition which the Church was about to form with public liberty. A bold attempt was made to obtain the appearance of a general concurrence of lawyers also in approving the usurpations of the Crown. From two of the four societies, called "Inns of Court," who have the exclusive privilege of admitting advocates to practise at the bar, the Middle and Inner Temple, addresses of approbation were published; though, from recent examination of the records of these bodies, they do not appear to have been ever voted by either. That of the former, eminent above the others for fulsome servility, is traditionally said to have been the clandestine production of three of the benchers, of whom Chauncy, the historian of Hertfordshire, was one. That of the Inner-Temple purports to have been the act of certain students and the "comptroller,"—an office of whose existence no traces are discoverable. As Roger North had been Treasurer of the Middle Temple three years before, and as the crown lawyers were members of these societies, it is scarcely possible that the Government should not have been apprised of the imposture which they countenanced by their official publication of these addresses.* The necessity of recurring to such a fraud, and the silence of the other law societies, may be allowed to afford some proof that the independence of the Bar was not yet utterly extinguished. The subserviency of the Bench was so abject as to tempt the Government to interfere with private suits, which is one of the last and rarest errors of statesmen under absolute monarchies. An official letter is still extant† from Lord Sunderland, as Secretary of State, to Sir Francis Watkins, a judge of assize, recommending him to show all the favour to Lady Shaftesbury, in the despatch of her suit, to be tried at Salisbury, which the justice of her cause should deserve:—so deeply degraded were the judges in the eyes of the ministers themselves.

* London Gazette, June 9th.

† 24th February.—State Paper Office.

CHAPTER VI.

D'Adda publicly received as the Nuncio.—Dissolution of Parliament.—Final breach.—Preparations for a new Parliament.—New charters.—Removal of Lord Lieutenants.—Patronage of the Crown.—Moderate views of Sunderland.—House of Lords.—Royal progress.—Pregnancy of the Queen.—London has the appearance of a Catholic city.

The war between Religious parties had not yet so far subsided as to allow the avowed intercourse of Princes of Protestant communions with the See of Rome. In the first violence of hostility, indeed, laws were passed in England forbidding, under pain of death, the indispensable correspondence of Catholics with the head of their Church, and even the bare residence of their priests within the realm.* These laws, never to be palliated except as measures of retaliation in a warfare of extermination, had been often executed without necessity and with slight provocation. It was most desirable to prevent their execution and to procure their repeal. But the object of the King in his embassy to Rome was to select these odious enactments, as the most specious case, in which he might set an example of the ostentatious contempt with which he was resolved to trample on every law which stood in the way of his designs. A nearer and more signal instance than that embassy was required by his zeal or his political projects. D'Adda was accordingly obliged to undergo a public introduction to the King at Windsor as Apostolic Nuncio from the Pope; and his reception,—being an overt act of high treason,—was conducted with more than ordinary state, and announced to the public like that of any other foreign minister.† The Bishops of Durham and Chester were perhaps the most remarkable attendants at the ceremonial. The Duke of Somerset, the second Peer of the kingdom, was chosen from the Lords of the Bedchamber as the introducer; and his attendance in that character had been previously notified to the Nuncio by the Earl of Mulgrave, Lord Chamberlain: but, on the morning of the ceremony, the Duke besought his Majesty to excuse him from the performance of an act which might expose him to the most severe animadversion of the law.‡ The King answered, that he intended to confer an honour upon him, by appointing him to introduce the representative of so venerable a potentate; and that the royal power of dispensation had been solemnly determined to be a sufficient warrant for such acts.—The King is said to have angrily asked, "Do you not know that I am above the law?"§ to which the Duke is represented by the same authorities to have replied, "Your Majesty is so, but I am not;"—an answer which was perfectly correct, if it be understood as above punishment by the law. The Duke of Grafton introduced the Nuncio; and it was observed, that while the ambassadors of the Emperor, and of the crowns of France and Spain, were presented by Earls, persons of superior dignity were appointed to do the same office to the Papal minister;—a singularity rather rendered alarming than acceptable by the example of the Court of France, which was appealed to by the courtiers on this occasion. The same cere-

* 13 Eliz. c. 2.—35 Eliz. c. 1.

† D'Adda, 11th July.—MS. London Gazette, 4th to 7th July.

‡ Van Citters, 15th July.—MS.

§ Perhaps saying, or meaning to say, "in this respect."

monious introduction to the Queen Dowager immediately followed. The King was very desirous of the like presentation being made to the Princess Anne, to whom it was customary to present foreign ministers; but the Nuncio declined a public audience of an heretical princess:* and though we learn that, a few days after, he was admitted by her to what is called "a public audience,"† yet, as it was neither published in the Gazette, nor adverted to in his own letter, it seems probable that she only received him openly as a Roman prelate, who was to be treated with the respect due to his rank, and with whom it was equally politic to avoid the appearance of clandestine intercourse and of formal recognition. The King said to the Duke of Somerset, "As you have not chosen to obey my commands in this case, I shall not trouble you with any other;" and immediately removed him from his place in the Household, from his regiment of dragoons, and the Lord-lieutenancy of his county,—continuing for some time to speak with indignation of this act of contumacy, and telling the Nuncio, that the Duke's nearest relations had thrown themselves at his feet, and assured him, that they detested the disobedience of their kinsman.‡ The importance of the transaction consisted in its being a decisive proof of how little estimation were the judicial decisions in favour of the dispensing power in the eyes of the most loyal and opulent of the nobility.§

The most petty incidents in the treatment of the Nuncio were at this time jealously watched by the public. By the influence of the new members placed by James in the corporation, he had been invited to a festival annually given by the city of London, at which the diplomatic body were then, as now, accustomed to be present. Fearful of insult, and jealous of his precedence, he consulted Lord Sunderland, and afterwards the King, on the prudence of accepting the invitation.‖ The King pressed him to go, also signifying to all the other foreign ministers that their attendance at the festival would be agreeable to him. The Dutch¶ and Swedish ministers were absent. The Nuncio was received unexpectedly well by the populace, and treated with becoming courtesy by the magistrates. But though the King honoured the festival with his presence, he could not prevail even on the aldermen of his own nomination to forbear from the thanksgiving, on the 5th of November, for deliverance from the Gunpowder Plot.** On the contrary, Sir John Shorter, the Presbyterian mayor, made haste to atone for the invitation of D'Adda, by publicly receiving

* D'Adda, 16th July.—MS.
† Van Citters, 22d July.—MS.
‡ D'Adda, suprà.
§ Barillon, 21st July.—Fox MSS.
‖ D'Adda, 7th—14th Nov.—MS.
¶ According to the previous instructions of the States General, and the practice of their ministers at the Congresses of Munster and Nimeguen.
** Narcissus Luttrell, Nov. 1687.—MS.

the communion according to the rites of the Church of England;*—a strong mark of distrust in the dispensing power, and of the determination of the Presbyterians to adhere to the common cause of Protestants.†

Another occasion offered itself, then esteemed a solemn one, for the King, in his royal capacity, to declare publicly against the Established Church. The kings of England had, from very ancient times, pretended to a power of curing scrofula by touching those who were afflicted by that malady; and the Church had retained, after the Reformation, a service for the occasion, in which her ministers officiated. James, naturally enough, employed the mass book, and the aid of the Roman Catholic clergy, in the exercise of this pretended power of his crown, according to the precedents in the reign of Mary.‡ As we find no complaint from the Established clergy of the perversion of this miraculous prerogative, we are compelled to suspect that they had no firm faith in the efficacy of a ceremony which they solemnly sanctioned by their prayers.§

On the day before the public reception of the Nuncio, the dissolution of Parliament had announced a final breach between the Crown and the Church. All means had been tried to gain a majority in the House of Commons: persuasion, influence, corruption, were inadequate; the example of dismissal failed to intimidate,—the hope of preferment to allure. Neither the command obtained by the Crown over the corporations, nor the division among Protestants excited by the Toleration, had sufficiently weakened the opposition to the measures of the Court. It was useless to attempt the execution of projects to subdue the resistance of the Peers by new creations, till the other House was either gained or removed. The unyielding temper manifested by an assembly formerly so submissive, seems, at first sight, unaccountable. It must, however, be borne in mind, that the elections had taken place under the influence of the Church party; that the interest of the Church had defeated the ecclesiastical measures of the King in the two former sessions; and that the im-

* Van Citters, 24th Nov.—MS.
† Catharine Shorter, the daughter and heiress of this Presbyterian mayor, became, long after, the wife of Sir Robert Walpole.
‡ Van Citters, 7th June, 1686.—MS.
§ It is well known that Dr. Samuel Johnson was, when a child, touched for the scrofula by Queen Anne. The princes of the House of Brunswick relinquished the practice. Carte, the historian, was so blinded by his zeal for the House of Stuart as to assure the public that one Lovel, a native of Bristol, who had gone to Avignon to be touched by the son of James II. in 1716, was really cured by that prince. A small piece of gold was tied round the patient's neck, which explains the number of applications. The gold sometimes amounted to 3000*l.* a year. Louis XIV. touched sixteen hundred patients on Easter Sunday, 1686. —See Barrington's Observations on Ancient Statutes, pp. 108, 109. Lovel relapsed after Carte had seen him.—General Biographical Dictionary, article "Carte."

mense influence of the clergy over general opinion, now seconded by the zealous exertions of the friends of liberty, was little weakened by the servile ambition of a few of their number, who, being within the reach of preferment, and intensely acted upon by its attraction, too eagerly sought their own advancement to regard the dishonour of deserting their body. England was then fast approaching to that state in which an opinion is so widely spread, and the feelings arising from it are so ardent, that dissent is accounted infamous, and considered by many as unsafe. It is happy when such opinions (however inevitably alloyed by base ingredients, and productive of partial injustice) are not founded in delusion, but on principles, on the whole, beneficial to the community. The mere influence of shame, of fear, of imitation, or of sympathy, is, at such moments, sufficient to give to many men the appearance of an integrity and courage little to be hoped from their ordinary conduct.

The King had, early in the summer, ascertained the impossibility of obtaining the consent of a majority of the House of Commons to a repeal of the Test and penal laws, and appears to have shown a disposition to try a new Parliament.* His more moderate counsellors,† however, headed, as it appears, by the Earl of Sunderland,‡ did not fail to represent to him the mischiefs and dangers of that irrevocable measure. "It was," they said, "a perilous experiment to dissolve the union of the Crown with the Church, and to convert into enemies an order which had hitherto supported unlimited authority, and inculcated unbounded submission. The submission of the Parliament had no bounds except the rights or interests of the Church. The expense of an increasing army would speedily require parliamentary aid; the possible event of the death of the King of Spain without issue might involve all Europe in war:§ for these purposes, and for every other that concerned the honour of the Crown, this loyal Parliament were ready to grant the most liberal supplies. Even in ecclesiastical matters, though they would not at once yield all, they would in time grant much: when the King had quieted the alarm and irritation of the moment, they would, without difficulty, repeal all the laws commonly called "penal." The King's dispensations, sanctioned by the decisions of the highest authority of the law, obviated the evil of the laws of disability; and it would be wiser for the Catholics to leave the rest to time and circumstances, than to provoke severe retaliation by the support of measures which the immense majority of the people dreaded as subversive of their religion and liberty. What hope of ample supply or steady support could the King entertain from a Parliament of Nonconformists, the natural enemies of kingly power? What faith could the Catholics place in these sectaries, the most Protestant of Protestant communions, of whom the larger part looked on relief from persecution, when tendered by Catholic hands, with distrust and fear; and who believed that the friendship of the Church of Rome for them would last no longer than her inability to destroy them?" To this it was answered, "that it was now too late to inquire whether a more wary policy might not have been at first more advisable; that the King could not stand where he was; that he would soon be compelled to assemble a Parliament; and that, if he preserved the present, their first act would be to impeach the judges, who had determined in favour of the dispensing power. To call them together, would be to abandon to their rage all the Catholics who had accepted office on the faith of the royal prerogative. If the Parliament were not to be assembled, they were at least useless; and their known disposition would, as long as they existed, keep up the spirit of audacious disaffection: if they were assembled, they would, even during the King's life, tear away the shield of the dispensing power, which, at all events, never would be stretched out to cover Catholics by the hand of the Protestant successor. All the power gained by the monarchy over corporations having been used in the last election by Protestant Tories, was now acting against the Crown: by extensive changes in the government of counties and corporations, a more favourable House of Commons, and if an entire abrogation should prove impracticable, a better compromise, might be obtained."

Sunderland informed the Nuncio that the King closed these discussions by a declaration that, having ascertained the determination of the present Parliament not to concur in his holy designs, and having weighed all the advantages of preserving it, he considered them as far inferior to his great object, which was the advancement of the Catholic religion. Perhaps, indeed, this determination, thus apparently dictated by religious zeal, was conformable to the maxims of civil

---

* Van Citters, 13th June.—MS.

† Barillon, 12th June.—Fox MSS.

‡ D'Adda, 7th—22d August.—MS.

§ The exact coincidence, in this respect, of Sunderland's public defence, nearly two years afterwards, with the Nuncio's secret despatches of the moment, is worthy of consideration:—

"I hindered the dissolution several weeks, by telling the King that the Parliament would do every thing he could desire but the taking off the tests; that another Parliament would probably not repeal these laws: and, if they did, would do nothing else for the support of government. I said often, if the King of Spain died, his Majesty could not preserve the peace of Europe; that he might be sure of all the help and service he could wish from the present Parliament, but if he dissolved it he must give up all thoughts of foreign affairs, for no other would ever assist him but on such terms as would ruin the monarchy." — Lord Sunderland's Letter, licensed 23d March, 1689.

"Dall' altra parte si poteva promettere S. M. del medesimo parlamento ogni assistenza maggiore de denaro, si S. M. fosse obligato di entrare in una guerra straniera, ponderando il caso possibile della morte del Re di Spagna senza successione. Questi e simili vantaggi non doverse attendere d'un nuovo parlamento composto di Nonconformisti, nutrendo, per li principi, sentimenti totalmente contrarii alla monarchia. "D'Adda."

prudence, unless the King was prepared to renounce his encroachments, and content himself with that measure of toleration for his religion which the most tolerant states then dealt out to their dissenting subjects.

The next object was so to influence the elections as to obtain a more yielding majority. At an early period Sunderland had represented two hundred members of the late House "as necessarily dependent on the Crown;"*—probably not so much a sanguine hope as a political exaggeration, which, if believed, might realise itself. He was soon either undeceived or contradicted: the King desired all bound to him, either by interest or attachment, to come singly to private audiences in his closet,† that he might ask their support to his measures; and the answers which he received were regarded by bystanders as equivalent to a general refusal.‡ This practice, then called "*closeting*," was, it must be owned, a very unskilful species of canvass, where the dignity of the King left little room for more than a single question and answer, and where other parties were necessarily forewarned of the subject of the interview, which must have soon become so generally known as to expose the more yielding part of them to the admonitions of their more courageous friends. It was easy for an eager monarch, on an occasion which allowed so little explanation, to mistake evasion, delay, and mere courtesy, for an assent to his proposal. But the new influence, and, indeed, power, which had been already gained by the Crown over the elective body seemed to be so great as to afford the strongest motives for assembling a new Parliament.

In the six years which followed the first judgments of forfeiture, two hundred and forty-two new charters of incorporation had passed the seals to replace those which had been thus judicially annulled or voluntarily resigned.§ From this number, however, must be deducted those of the plantations on the continent and islands of America, some new incorporations on grounds of general policy,‖ and several subordinate corporations in cities and towns,—though these last materially affected parliamentary elections. The House then consisted of five hundred and five members, of whom two hundred and forty-four were returned on rights of election altogether or in part corporate; this required only a hundred and twenty-two new charters. But to many corporations more than one charter had been issued, after the extorted surrenders of others, to rivet them more firmly in their dependency; and if any were spared, it can only have been because they were considered as sufficiently enslaved, and some show of discrimination was considered as politic. In six years, therefore, it is evident, that by a few determinations of servile judges, the Crown had acquired the direct, uncontrolled, and perpetual nomination of nearly one half of the House of Commons: and when we recollect the independent and ungovernable spirit manifested by that assembly in the last fifteen years of Charles II., we may be disposed to conclude that there is no other instance in history of so great a revolution effected in so short a time by the mere exercise of judicial authority. These charters, originally contrived so as to vest the utmost power in the Crown, might, in any instance where experience showed them to be inadequate, be rendered still more effectual, as a power of substituting others was expressly reserved in each.* In order to facilitate the effective exercise of this power, commissioners were appointed to be "regulators" of corporations, with full authority to remove and appoint freemen and corporate officers at their discretion. The Chancellor, the Lords Powis, Sunderland, Arundel, and Castlemaine, with Sir Nicholas Butler and Father Petre, were regulators of the first class, who superintended the whole operation.† Sir Nicholas Butler and Duncombe, a banker, "regulated" the corporation of London, from which they removed nineteen hundred freemen; and yet Jeffreys incurred a reprimand, from his impatient master, for want of vigour in changing the corporate bodies, and humbly promised to repair his fault: for "every Englishman who becomes rich," said Barillon, "is more disposed to favour the popular party than the designs of the King."‡ These regulators were sent to every part of the country, and were furnished with letters from the Secretary of State, recommending them to the aid of the Lord lieutenants of counties.§

When the election was supposed to be near, circular letters were sent to the Lord lieutenants, and other men of influence, including even the Chief Justice of the King's Bench, recommending them to procure the election of persons mentioned therein by name, to the number of more than a hundred. Among them were eighteen members for counties, and many for those towns which, as their rights of election were not corporate, were not yet subjected to the Crown by legal judgments.‖ In this list we find the unexpected name of John Somers, probably selected from a hope that his zeal for religious liberty might induce him to support a Go-

* D'Adda, 10th Oct. 1686.—7th Feb. 1687.—MS.

† Id. 24th Jan.—MS.

‡ Van Citters, 24th Jan.—MS.

§ Lords' Journals, 20th Dec. 1689.

‖ Of these, those of the College of Physicians and the town of Bombay, are mentioned by Narcissus Luttrell.

* Reign of James II. p. 21.—Parliamentum Pacificum, (London, 1688,) p. 29. The latter pamphlet boasts of these provisions. The Protestant Tories, says the writer, cannot question a power by which many of themselves were brought into the House.

† Lords' Journals, suprà.

‡ Barillon, 8th Sept.—MS.

§ Dated 21st July.—State Paper Office.

‖ Lord Sunderland's Letters, Sept.—Ibid.

vernment which professed so comprehensive a toleration: but it was quickly discovered that he was too wise to be ensnared, and the clerk of the Privy Council was six days after judiciously substituted in his stead. It is due to James and his minister to remark, that these letters are conceived in that official form which appears to indicate established practice: and, indeed, most of these practices were not only avowed, but somewhat ostentatiously displayed as proofs of the King's confidence in the legitimacy and success of his measures. Official letters* had also been sent to the Lord lieutenants, directing them to obtain answers from the deputy-lieutenants and justices of the peace of their respective counties, to the questions,—Whether, if any of them were chosen to serve in Parliament, they would vote for the repeal of the penal laws and the Test? and Whether they would contribute to the election of other members of the like disposition? and also to ascertain what corporations in each county were well affected, what individuals had influence enough to be elected, and what Catholics and Dissenters were qualified to be deputy-lieutenants or justices of the peace.

Several refused to obey so unconstitutional a command: their refusal had been foreseen; and so specious a pretext as that of disobedience was thus found for their removal from office.† Sixteen Lieutenancies,‡ held by fourteen Lieutenants, were immediately changed; the majority of whom were among the principal noblemen of the kingdom, to whom the government of the most important provinces had, according to ancient usage, been intrusted. The removal of Lord Scarsdale§ from his Lieutenancy of Derbyshire displayed the disposition of the Princess Anne, and furnished some scope for political dexterity on her part and on that of her father. Lord Scarsdale holding an office in the household of Prince George, the Princess sent Lord Churchill to the King from herself and her husband, humbly desiring to know his Majesty's pleasure how they should deal with one of the Prince's servants who had incurred the King's disfavour. The King, perceiving that it was intended to throw Scarsdale's removal from their household upon him, and extremely solicitous that it should appear to be his daughter's spontaneous act, and thus seem a proof of her hearty concurrence in his measures, declared his reluctance to prescribe to them in the appointment or dismissal of their officers. The Princess (for Prince George was a cipher) contented herself with this superficial show of respect, and resolved that the sacrifice of Scarsdale, if ever made, should appear to be no more than the bare obedience of a subject and a daughter. James was soon worsted in this conflict of address, and was obliged to notify his pleasure that Scarsdale should be removed, to avoid the humiliation of seeing his daughter's court become the refuge of those whom he had displaced.* The vacant Lieutenancies were bestowed on Catholics, with the exception of Mulgrave, (who had promised to embrace the King's faith, but whose delays begot suspicions of his sincerity,) and of Jeffreys, Sunderland, and Preston; who, though they continued to profess the Protestant religion, were no longer members of the Protestant party. Five colonels of cavalry, two of infantry, and four governors of fortresses, (some of whom were also Lord lieutenants, and most of them of the same class of persons,) were removed from their commands. Of thirty-nine new sheriffs, thirteen were said to be Roman Catholics.† Although the proportion of gentry among the Nonconformists was less, yet their numbers being much greater, it cannot be doubted that a considerable majority of these magistrates were such as the King thought likely to serve his designs.

Even the most obedient and zealous Lord lieutenants appear to have been generally unsuccessful: the Duke of Beaufort made an unfavourable report of the principality of Wales; and neither the vehemence of Jeffreys, nor the extreme eagerness of Rochester, made any considerable impression in their respective counties. Lord Waldegrave, a Catholic, the King's son-in-law, found insurmountable obstacles in Somersetshire;‡ Lord Molyneux, also a Catholic, appointed to the Lieutenancy of Lancashire, made an unfavourable report even of that county, then the secluded abode of an ancient Catholic gentry; and Dr. Leyburn, who had visited every part of England in the discharge of his episcopal duty, found little to encourage the hopes and prospects of the King. The most general answer appears to have been, that if chosen to serve in Parliament, the individuals to whom the questions were put would vote according to their consciences, after hearing the reasons on both sides; that they could not promise to vote in a manner which their own judgment after discussion might condemn; that if they entered into so unbecoming an engagement, they might incur the displeasure of the House of Commons for betraying its privileges; and that they would justly merit condemnation from all good men for disabling themselves from performing the duty of

* Dated 5th Oct.—State Paper Office. Van Citters' account exactly corresponds with the original document.

† Barillon, 8th Dec.—MS. "Il alloit faire cette tentative pour avoir un prétexte de les changer."

‡ Id. 18th Dec. § Id. 15th Dec.

* Barillon, 30th August.—Fox MSS.

† The names are marked in a handwriting apparently contemporary, on the margin of the list, in a copy of the London Gazette now before me. Van Citters (14th Nov.) makes the sheriffs almost all either Roman Catholics or Dissenters,—probably an exaggeration. In his despatch of 16th Dec., he states the sheriffs to be thirteen Catholics, thirteen Dissenters, and thirteen submissive Churchmen.

‡ D'Adda, 12th Dec.—MS.

faithful subjects by the honest declaration of their judgment on those arduous affairs on which they were to advise and aid the King. The Court was incensed by these answers; but to cover their defeat, and make their resolution more known, it was formally notified in the London Gazette,* that "His Majesty, being resolved to maintain the Declaration of Liberty of Conscience, and to use the utmost endeavours that it may pass into a law, and become an established security for after ages, has thought fit to review the lists of deputy-lieutenants and justices of the peace; that those may continue who are willing to contribute to so good and necessary a work, and such others be added from whom he may reasonably expect the like concurrence."

It is very difficult to determine in what degree the patronage of the Crown, military, civil and ecclesiastical, at that period, influenced parliamentary elections. The colonies then scarcely contributed to it.† No offices in Scotland and few in Ireland, were bestowed for English purposes. The revenue was small compared with that of after times, even after due allowance is made for the subsequent change in the value of money: but it was collected at such a needless expense as to become, from the mere ignorance and negligence of the Government, a source of influence much more than proportioned to its amount. The Church was probably guarded for the moment by the zeal and honour of its members, against the usual effects of royal patronage; and even the mitre lost much of its attractions, while the see of York was believed to be kept vacant for a Jesuit. A standing army of thirty thousand men presented new means of provision, and objects of ambition to the young gentry, who then monopolized military appointments. The revenue, small as it now seems, had increased in proportion to the national wealth, more in the preceding half century than in any equal time since; and the army had within that period come into existence. It is not easy to decide whether the novelty and rapid increase of these means of bestowing gratification increased at the same time their power over the mind, or whether it was not necessarily more feeble, until long experience had directed the eyes of the community habitually towards the Crown as the source of income and advancement. It seems reasonable to suppose that it might at first produce more violent movements, and in the sequel more uniform support. All the offices of provincial administration were then more coveted than they are now. Modern legislation and practice had not yet withdrawn any part of that administration from lieutenants, deputy-lieutents, sheriffs, coroners, which had been placed in their hands by the ancient laws. A justice of the peace exercised a power over his inferior never controlled by public opinion, and for the exercise of which he could hardly be said to be practically amenable to law. The influence of Government has abated as the powers of these officers have been contracted, or their exercise more jealously watched. Its patronage cannot be justly estimated, unless it be compared with the advantage to be expected from other objects of pursuit. The professions called "learned" had then fewer stations and smaller incomes than in subsequent periods: in commerce, the disproportion was immense; there could hardly be said to be any manufactures; and agriculture was unskilful, and opulent farmers unheard of. Perhaps the whole amount of income and benefits at the disposal of the Crown bore a larger proportion to that which might be earned in all the other pursuits raised above mere manual labour than might at first sight be supposed: how far the proportion was less than at present it is hard to say. But patronage in the hands of James was the auxiliary of great legal power through the Lord lieutenants, and of the direct nomination of the members for the corporate towns. The grossest species of corruption had been practised among members;* and the complaints which were at that time prevalent of the expense of elections, render it very probable that bribery was spreading among the electors. Expensive elections have, indeed, no other necessary effect than that of throwing the choice into the hands of wealthy candidates; but they afford too specious pretexts for the purchase of votes, not to be employed in eager contests, as a disguise of that practice.

The rival, though sometimes auxiliary, influence of great proprietors, seems to have been at that time, at least, as considerable as at any succeeding moment. The direct power of nominating members must have been vested in many of them by the same state of suffrage and property which confer it on them at present,† while they were not rivalled in more popular elections by a monied interest. The power of landholders over their tenants was not circumscribed; and in all country towns they were the only rich customers of tradesmen who had then only begun to emerge from indigence and dependence. The majority of these landholders were Tories, and now adhered to the Church; the minority, consisting of the most opulent and noble, were the friends of liberty, who received with open arms their unwonted allies.

From the naturally antagonist force of popular opinion little was probably dreaded by the Court. The Papal, the French, and the Dutch ministers, as well as the King and Lord Sunderland, in their unreserved conferences with the first two, seem to have pointed all their expectations and solicitudes towards the uncertain conduct of powerful in-

* Of the 11th Dec.

† Chamberlayne, Present State of England. London, 1674.

* Pension Parliament. † 1826.—Ed.

dividuals. The body of the people could not read: one portion of them had little knowledge of the sentiments of another; no publication was tolerated, on a level with the information then possessed even by the middle classes; and the only channel through which they could be acted upon was the pulpit, which the King had vainly, though perfidiously, endeavoured to shut up. Considerable impediments stood in the way of the King's direct power over elections, in the difficulty of finding candidates for Parliament not altogether disreputable, and corporators whose fidelity might be relied on. The moderate Catholics reluctantly concurred in the precipitate measures of the Court. They were disqualified, by long exclusion from business, for those offices to which their rank and fortune gave them a natural claim; and their whole number was so small, that they could contribute no adequate supply of fit persons for inferior stations.* The number of the Nonconformists were, on the other hand, considerable; amounting, probably, to a sixteenth of the whole people, without including the compulsory and occasional Conformists, whom the Declaration of Indulgence had now encouraged to avow their real sentiments.† Many of them had acquired wealth by trade, which under the Republic and the Protectorate began to be generally adopted as a liberal pursuit; but they were confined to the great towns, and were chiefly of the Presbyterian persuasion, who were ill affected to the Court. Concerning the greater number, who were to form the corporations throughout the country, it was difficult to obtain accurate information, and hard to believe that in the hour of contest, they could forget their enthusiastic animosity against the Church of Rome. As the project of introducing Catholics into the House of Commons by an exercise of the dispensing power had been abandoned, nothing could be expected from them but aid in elections; and if one eighth—a number so far surpassing their natural share—should be Nonconformists, they would still bear a small proportion to the whole body. These intractable difficulties, founded in the situation, habits, and opinions of men, over which measures of policy or legislation have no direct or sudden power, early suggested to the more wary of the King's counsellors the propriety of attempting some compromise, by which he might immediately gain more advantage and security for the Catholics than could have been obtained from the Episcopalian Parliament, and open the way for further advances in a more favourable season.

Shortly after the dissolution, Lord Sunderland communicated to the Nuncio his opinions on the various expedients by which the jealousies of the Nonconformists might be satisfied.* "As we have wounded the Anglican party," said he, "we must destroy it, and use every means to strengthen as well as conciliate the other, that the whole nation may not be alienated, and that the army may not discover the dangerous secret of the exclusive reliance of the Government upon its fidelity." "Among the Nonconformists were," he added, "three opinions relating to the Catholics: that of those who would repeal all the penal laws against religious worship, but maintain the disabilities for office and Parliament; that of those who would admit the Catholics to office, but continue their exclusion from both Houses of Parliament; and that of a still more indulgent party, who would consent to remove the recent exclusion of the Catholic peers, trusting to the oath of supremacy in the reign of Elizabeth, as a legal, though it had not proved in practice a constant, bar against their entrance into the House of Commons:—to say nothing of a fourth project, entertained by zealous Catholics and thorough courtiers, that Catholic peers and commoners should claim their seats in both Houses by virtue of royal dispensations, which would relieve them from the oaths and declarations against their religion required by law,—an attempt which the King himself had felt to be too hazardous, as being likely to excite a general commotion on the first day of the session, to produce an immediate rupture with the new Parliament, and to forfeit all the advantage which had been already gained by a determination of both Houses against the validity of the dispensations." He further added, that "he had not hitherto conferred on these weighty matters with any but the King, that he wished the Nuncio to consider them, and was desirous to govern his own conduct by that prelate's decision." At the same time he gave D'Adda to understand, that he was inclined to some of the above conciliatory expedients, observing, "that it was better to go on step by step, than obstinately to aim at all with the risk of gaining nothing;" and hinting, that this pertinacity was peculiarly dangerous, where all depended on the life of James. Sunderland's purpose was to insinuate his own opinions into the mind of the Nuncio, who was the person most likely to reconcile the King and his priests to only partial advantages. But a prelate of the Roman Court, however inferior to Sunderland in other respects, was more than his match in the art of evading the responsibility which attends advice in perilous conjunctures. With many commendations of his zeal, D'Adda professed "his incapacity

* By Sir William Petty's computation, which was the largest, the number of Catholics in England and Wales, about the accession of James, was thirty-two thousand. The survey of bishops in 1676, by order of Charles II., made it twenty-seven thousand. Barlow (Bishop of Lincoln,) Genuine Remains, (London, 1693,) p. 312. "George Fox," said Petty, "made five times more Quakers in forty-four years than the Pope, with all his greatness, has made Papists."

† Barlow, suprà.—About two hundred and fifty thousand, when the population was little more than four millions.

* D'Adda, 7th August.—MS.

of judging in a case which involved the opinions and interests of so many individuals and classes; but he declared, that the fervent prayers of his Holiness, and his own feeble supplications, would be offered to God, for light and guidance to his Majesty and his ministers in the prosecution of their wise and pious designs."

William Penn proposed a plan different from any of the *temperaments* mentioned above; which consisted in the exclusion of Catholics from the House of Commons, and the division of all the public offices into three equal parts, one of which should belong to the Church, another should be open to the Nonconformists, and a third to the Catholics;*—an extremely unequal distribution, if it implied the exclusion of the members of the Church from two thirds of the stations in the public service; and not very moderate, if it should be understood only as providing against the admission of the dissidents to more than two thirds of these offices. Eligibility to one third would have been a more equitable proposition, and perhaps better than any but that which alone is perfectly reasonable,—that the appointment to office should be altogether independent of religious opinion. An equivalent for the Test was held out at the same time, which had a very specious and alluring appearance. It was proposed that an Act for the establishment of religious liberty should be passed; that all men should be sworn to its observance; that it should be made a part of the coronation oath, and rank among the fundamental laws, as the *Magna Charta* of Conscience; and that any attempt to repeal it should be declared to be a capital crime.†

The principal objections to all these mitigated or attractive proposals arose from distrust in the King's intention. It did not depend on the conditions offered, and was as fatal to moderate compromise as to undistinguishing surrender. The nation were now in a temper to consider every concession made to the King as an advantage gained by an enemy, which mortified their pride, as well as lessened their safety: they regarded negotiation as an expedient of their adversaries to circumvent, disunite, and dishearten them.

The state of the House of Lords was a very formidable obstacle. Two lists of the probable votes in that assembly on the Test and penal laws were sent to Holland, and one to France, which are still extant.‡ These vary in some respects from each other, according to the information of the writers, and probably according to the fluctuating disposition of some Peers. The greatest division adverse to the Court which they present, is ninety-two against the repeal of the penal and disabling laws to thirty-five for it, besides twenty whose votes are called "doubtful," and twenty-three disabled as Catholics: the least is eighty-six to thirty-three, besides ten doubtful and twenty-one Catholic. Singular as it may seem, Rochester, the leader of the Church party, is represented in all the lists as being for the repeal. From this agreement, and from his officious zeal as Lord Lieutenant of Hertfordshire, it cannot be doubted that he had promised his vote to the King; and though it is hard to say whether his promise was sincere, or whether treachery to his party or insincerity to his old master would be most deserving of blame, he cannot be acquitted of a grave offence either against political or personal morality. His brother Clarendon, a man of less understanding and courage, is numbered in one list as doubtful, and represented by another as a supporter of the Court. Lord Churchill is stated to be for the repeal,—probably from the confidence of the writers that gratitude would in him prevail over every other motive; for it appears that on this subject he had the merit of not having dissembled his sentiments to his royal benefactor.* Lord Godolphin, engaged rather in ordinary business than in political councils, was numbered in the ranks of official supporters. As Lord Dartmouth, Lord Preston, and Lord Feversham never fluctuated on religion, they deserve the credit of being rather blinded by personal attachment, than tempted by interest or ambition, in their support of the repeal.† Howard of Escrick and Grey de Werke, who had saved their own lives by contributing to take away those of their friends, appear in the minority as slaves of the Court. Of the bishops only four had gone so far as to be counted in all the lists as voters for the King.‡ Wood of Lichfield appears to be with the four in one list, and doubtful in another. The compliancy of Sprat had been such as to place him perhaps unjustly in the like situation. Old Barlow of Lincoln was thought doubtful. The other aged prelate, Crofts of Hereford, though he deemed himself bound to obey the King as a bishop, claimed the exercise of his own judgment as a lord of Parliament. Sunderland, who is marked as a disabled Catholic in one of the lists, and as a doubtful voter in another, appears to have obtained

* Johnstone, 13th Jan. 1688.—MS.

† "Good Advice." "Parliamentum Pacificum."

‡ The reports sent to Holland were communicated to me by the Duke of Portland. One of them purports to be drawn by Lord Willoughby. That sent by Barillon is from the Depôt des Affaires Etrangères at Paris.

* Coxe, Memoirs, &c. vol. i. pp. 23—29, where the authorities are collected, to which may be added the testimony of Johnstone:—"Lord Churchill swears he will not do what the King requires from him."—Letter 12th Jan. 1688.—MS.

† Johnstone, however, who knew them, did not ascribe their conduct to frailties so generous: "Lord Feversham and Lord Dartmouth are desirous of acting honourably: but the first is mean-spirited; and the second has an empty purse, yet aims at living grandly. Lord Preston desires to be an honest man; but if he were not your friend and my relation, I should say that he is both Feversham and Dartmouth."—Ibid.

‡ Durham (Crew), Oxford (Parker), Chester (Cartwright), and St. David's (Watson).

the royal consent to a delay of his public profession of the Catholic religion, that he might retain his ability to serve it by his vote in Parliament.* Mulgrave was probably in the same predicament. If such a majority was to continue immovable, the counsels of the King must have become desperate, or he must have had recourse to open force: but this perseverance was improbable. Among the doubtful there might have been some who concealed a determined resolution under the exterior of silence or of hesitation. Such, though under a somewhat different disguise, was the Marquis of Winchester, who indulged and magnified the eccentricities of an extravagant character; counterfeited, or rather affected a disordered mind, as a security in dangerous times, like the elder Brutus in the legendary history of Rome; and travelling through England in the summer of 1687, with a retinue of four coaches and a hundred horsemen, slept during the day, gave splendid entertainments in the night, and by torch-light, or early dawn, pursued the sports of hunting and hawking.† But the majority of the doubtful must have been persons who assumed that character to enhance their price, or who lay in wait for the turns of fortune, or watched for the safe moment of somewhat anticipating her determination: of such men the powerful never despair. The example of a very few would be soon followed by the rest, and if they or many of them were gained, the accession of strength could not fail to affect the timid and mercenary who are to be found in all bodies, and whose long adherence to the Opposition was already wonderful.

But the subtile genius of Lord Sunderland, not content with ordinary means of seduction and with the natural progress of desertion, had long meditated an expedient for quickening the latter, and for supplying in some measure the place of both. He had long before communicated to the Nuncio a plan for subduing the obstinacy of the Upper House by the creation of the requisite number of new Peers‡ devoted to his Majesty's measures. He proposed to call up by writ the elder sons of friendly Lords; which would increase his present strength, without the incumbrance of new peerages, whose future holders might be independent. Some of the Irish,§ and probably of the Scotch nobility, whose rank made their elevation to the English peerage specious, and whose fortunes disposed them to dependency on royal bounty, attracted his attention, as they did that of those ministers who carried his project into execution twenty-five years afterwards. He was so enamoured of this plan, that in a numerous company, where the resistance of the Upper House was said to be formidable, he cried out to Lord Churchill, "O silly! why, your troop of guards shall be called to the House of Lords!"* On another occasion (if it be not a different version of the same anecdote) he declared, that sooner than not gain a majority in the House of Lords, he would make all Lord Feversham's troop Peers.† The power of the Crown was in this case unquestionable. The constitutional purpose for which the prerogative of creating Peers exists, is, indeed, either to reward public service, or to give dignity to important offices, or to add ability and knowledge to a part of the legislature, or to repair the injuries of time, by the addition of new wealth to an aristocracy which may have decayed. But no law limits its exercise.‡ By the bold exercise of the prerogative of creating Peers, and of the then equally undisputed right of granting to towns the privilege of sending members to Parliament, it is evident that the King possessed the fullest means of subverting the constitution by law. The obstacles to the establishment of despotism consisted in his own irresolution or unskilfulness, in the difficulty of finding a sufficient number of trustworthy agents, and in such a determined hostility of the body of the people as led sagacious observers to forbode an armed resistance.§ The firmness of the Lords has been ascribed to their fears of a resumption of the Church property confiscated at the Reformation: but at the distance of a century and a half, and after the dispersion of much of that property by successive sales, such fears were too groundless to have had a considerable influence. But though they ceased to be distinctly felt, and to act separately, it cannot be doubted that the remains of apprehensions once so strong, still contributed to fortify that dread of Popery, which was an hereditary point of honour among the great families aggrandized and enriched under the Tudors.

At the same time the edge of religious animosity among the people at large was

* "Ministers and others about the King, who have given him grounds to expect that they will turn Papists, say, that if they change before the Parliament they cannot be useful to H. M. in Parliament, as the Test will exclude them."—Johnstone, 8th Dec. 1687.—MS.

† Reresby, p. 247.

‡ D'Adda, 11th October, 1686.—MS.

§ Johnstone, 27th Feb. 1688.—MS.

* Burnet, (Oxford, 1823), vol. iii. p. 249; Lord Dartmouth's note.

† Halifax MSS. The turn of expression would seem to indicate different conversations. At all events, Halifax affords a strong corroboration.

‡ It is, perhaps, not easy to devise such a limitation, unless it should be provided that no newly created Peer should vote till a certain period after his creation; which, in cases of signal service, would be ungracious, and in those of official dignity inconvenient.

§ On suivra ici le projet d'avoir un parliament tant qu'il ne paroitra pas impraticable; mais s'il ne réussit pas, le Roi d'Angleterre pretendra faire par son autorité ce qu'il n'aura pas obtenu par la voie d'un parliament. C'est en ce cas là qu'il aura besoin de ses amis au dedans et au dehors, et il recevra alors des oppositions qui approcheront fort d'une rebellion ouverte. On ne doit pas douter qu'elle ne soit soutenue par M. le Prince d'Orange, et que beaucoup de gens qui paroissent attachés au Roi d'Angleterre ne lui manquent au besoin; cette épreuve sera fort perilleuse."—Barillon, Windsor, 9th October, 1687.—MS.

sharpened by the controversy then revived between the divines of the two Churches. A dispute about the truth of their religion was insensibly blended with contests concerning the safety of the Establishment; and complete toleration brought with it that hatred which is often fiercer, and always more irreconcilable, against the opponents of our religious opinions than against the destroyers of our most important interests. The Protestant Establishment and the cause of liberty owed much, it must be owned, to this dangerous and odious auxiliary; while the fear, jealousy, and indignation of the people were more legitimately excited against a Roman Catholic Government by he barbarous persecution of the Protestants in France, and by the unprovoked invasion of the valleys of Piedmont;—both acts of a monarch of whom their own sovereign was then believed to be, as he is now known to have been, the creature.

The King had, in the preceding year, tried the efficacy of a progress through a part of the kingdom, to conciliate the nobility by personal intercourse, and to gratify the people by a royal visit to their remote abodes; which had also afforded an opportunity of rewarding compliance by smiles, and of marking the contumacious. With these views he had again this autumn meditated a journey to Scotland, and a coronation in that kingdom: but he confined himself to an excursion through some southern and western counties, beginning at Portsmouth, and proceeding through Bath (at which place the Queen remained during his journey) to Chester, where he had that important interview with Tyrconnel, of which we have already spoken. James was easily led to consider the courtesies of the nobility due to his station, and the acclamations of the multitude naturally excited by his presence, as symptoms of an inflexible attachment to his person, and of a general acquiescence in his designs. These appearances, however, were not considered as of serious importance, either by the Dutch minister, who dreaded the King's popularity, or by the French ambassador, who desired its increase, or by the Papal Nuncio, who was so friendly to the ecclesiastical policy of the Court, and so adverse to its foreign connections as to render him in some measure an impartial observer. The journey was attended by no consequences more important than a few addresses extorted from Dissenters by the importunity of personal canvass, and the unseemly explosion of royal anger at Oxford against the fellows of Magdalen College.* Scarcely any of the King's measures seem to have had less effect on general opinion, and appear less likely to have influenced the election for which he was preparing.

But the Royal Progress was speedily followed by an occurrence which strongly excited the hopes and fears of the public, and at length drove the opponents of the King to decisive resolutions. Soon after the return of the Court to Whitehall,* it began to be whispered that the Queen was pregnant. This event in the case of a young princess, and of a husband still in the vigour of life, might seem too natural to have excited surprise. But five years had elapsed since her last childbirth, and out of eleven children who were born to James by both his wives, only two had outlived the years of infancy. Of these, the Princess of Orange was childless, and the Princess Anne, who had had six children, lost five within the first year of their lives, while the survivor only reached the age of eleven. Such an apparent peculiarity of constitution, already transmitted from parent to child, seemed to the credulous passions of the majority, unacquainted as they were with the latitude and varieties of nature, to be a sufficient security against such an accession to the royal progeny as should disturb the order of succession to the crown. The rumour of the Queen's condition suddenly dispelled this security. The Catholics had long and fervently prayed for the birth of a child, who being educated in their communion, might prolong the blessings which they were beginning to enjoy. As devotion, like other warm emotions, is apt to convert wishes into hopes, they betrayed a confidence in the efficacy of their prayers, which early excited suspicions among their opponents that less pure means might be employed for the attainment of the object. Though the whole importance of the pregnancy depended upon a contingency so utterly beyond the reach of human foresight as the sex of the child, the passions of both parties were too much excited to calculate probabilities; and the fears of the Protestants as well as the hopes of the Catholics anticipated the birth of a male heir. The animosity of the former imputed to the Roman Catholic religion, that unscrupulous use of any means for the attainment of an object earnestly desired, which might more justly be ascribed to inflamed zeal for any religious system, or with still greater reason to all those ardent passions of human nature, which, when shared by multitudes, are released from the restraints of fear or shame. In the latter end of November a rumour that the Queen had

* "The King has returned from his progress so far as Oxford, on his way to the Bath, and we do not hear that his observations or his journey can give him any great encouragement. Besides the considerations of conscience and the public interest, it is grown into a point of honour universally received by the nation not to change their opinions, which will make all attempts to the contrary ineffectual."—Halifax to the Prince of Orange, 1st Sept. Dalrymple, app. to book v.

* James rejoined the Queen at Bath on the 6th September. On the 16th he returned to Windsor, where the Queen came on the 6th October. On the 11th of that month they went to Whitehall.—London Gazettes.

been pregnant for two months became generally prevalent;* and early in December, surmises of imposture began to circulate at Court.† Time did not produce its usual effect of removing uncertainty, for, in the middle of the same month, the Queen's symptoms were represented by physicians as still ambiguous, in letters, which the careful balance of facts on both sides, and the cautious abstinence from a decisive opinion, seem to exempt from the suspicion of bad faith.‡ On the 23d of December, a general thanksgiving for the hope of increasing the royal family was ordered; but on the 15th of the next month, when that thanksgiving was observed in London, Lord Clarendon remarked with wonder, "that not above two or three in the church brought the form of prayer with them; and that it was strange to see how the Queen's pregnancy was every where ridiculed, as if scarce any body believed it to be true." The Nuncio early expressed his satisfaction at the pregnancy, as likely to contribute "to the re-establishment of the Catholic religion in these kingdoms;"§ and in the following month, he pronounced to her Majesty the solemn benediction of the Sovereign Pontiff, on a pregnancy so auspicious to the Church.‖ Of the other ministers most interested in this event, Barillon, a veteran diplomatist, too cool and experienced to be deluded by his wishes, informed his master, "that the pregnancy was not believed to be true in London; and that in the country, those who spread the intelligence were laughed at;"¶ while the Republican minister, Van Citters, coldly communicated the report, with some of the grounds of it, to the States-General, without hazarding an opinion on a matter so delicate. The Princess Anne, in confidential letters** to her sister at the Hague, when she had no motive to dissemble, signified her unbelief, which continued even after the birth of the child, and was neither subdued by her father's solemn declarations, nor by the testimony which he produced.†† On the whole, the suspicion, though groundless and cruel, was too general to be dishonest: there is no evidence that the rumour originated in the contrivance of any indivi uals; and it is for that reason more just, as well as perhaps in itself more probable, to conclude that it arose spontaneously in the minds of many, influenced by the circumstances and prejudices of the time. The currency of the like rumours, on a similar occasion, five years before, favours the opinion that they arose from the obstinate prejudices of the people rather than from the invention of designing politicians.* The imprudent confidence of the Catholics materially contributed to strengthen suspicion. When the King and his friends ascribed the pregnancy to his own late prayers at St. Winifred's well,† or to the vows while living, and intercession after death of the Duchess of Modena, the Protestants suspected that effectual measures would be taken to prevent the interposition of Heaven from being of no avail to the Catholic cause; and their jealous apprehensions were countenanced by the expectation of a son, which was indicated in the proclamation for thanksgiving,‡ and unreservedly avowed in private conversation. As straws shows the direction of the wind, the writings of the lowest scribblers may sometimes indicate the temper of a party; and one such writing, preserved by chance, may probably be a sample of the multitudes which have perished. Mrs. Behn, a loose and paltry poetastress of that age, was bold enough in the title page of what she calls "A Poem to their Majesties," to add, "on the hopes of all loyal persons for a Prince of Wales," and ventures in her miserable verses already to hail the child of unknown sex, as "Royal Boy."§ The lampooners of the opposite party, in verses equally contemptible, showered down derision on the Romish imposture, and pointed the general abhorrence and alarm towards the new Perkin Warbeck whom the Jesuits were preparing to be the instrument of their designs.

While these hopes and fears agitated the multitude of both parties, the ultimate objects of the King became gradually more definite, while he at the same time deliberated, or perhaps, rather decided, about the choice of his means. His open policy assumed a more decisive tone: Castlemaine, who in his embassy had acted with the most ostentatious defiance of the laws, and Petre, the most obnoxious clergyman of the Church of Rome, were sworn of the Privy

* Narcissus Luttrell, 28th Nov.—MS.
† Johnstone, 8th Dec.—MS.
‡ Johnstone, 16th Dec.—MS.,—containing a statement of the symptoms by Sir Charles Scarborough, and another physician whose name I have been unable to decipher.
§ D'Adda, 2d Dec.—MS.
‖ Id. 20th Feb. 1688.—MS.
¶ Barillon, 11th Dec.—MS.
** March 14th—20th, 1688.—Dalrymple, app. to book v. "Her being so positive it will be a son, and the principles of that religion being such that they will stick at nothing, be it ever so wicked, if it will promote their interest, gave some cause to fear that there is foul play intended." On the 18th June, she says, "Except they give very plain demonstration, which seems almost impossible now, I shall ever be of the number of unbelievers." Even the candid and loyal Evelyn (Diary, 10th and 17th of June) very intelligibly intimates his suspicions.
†† Clarendon, Diary, 31st Oct.

* "If it had pleased God to have given his Highness the blessing of a son, as it proved a daughter, you were prepared to make a Perkin of him."—L'Estrange, Observator, 23d August, 1682.
† Life of James II., vol. ii. p. 129.
‡ The object of the thanksgiving was indicated more plainly in the Catholic form of prayer on that occasion:—"Concede propitius ut famula tua regina nostra Maria partu felici prolem edat tibi fideliter servituram."
§ State Poems, vol. iii. and iv.; a collection at once the most indecent and unpoetical probably extant in any language.

Council.* The latter was even promoted to an ecclesiastical office in the household of a prince, who still exercised all the powers of the supreme head of a Protestant Church. Corker, an English Benedictine, the superior of a monastery of that order in London, had an audience of the King in his ecclesiastical habits, as envoy from the Elector of Cologne,† doubtless by a secret understanding between James and that prince;—an act, which Louis XIV. himself condemned as unexampled in Catholic countries, and as likely to provoke heretics, whose prejudices ought not to be wantonly irritated.‡ As the animosity of the people towards the Catholic religion increased, the designs of James for its re-establishment became bolder and more open. The monastic orders, clad in garments long strange and now alarming to the people, filled the streets; and the King prematurely exulted that his capital had the appearance of a Catholic city,§—little aware of the indignation with which that obnoxious appearance inspired the body of his Protestant subjects. He must now have felt that his contest had reached that point in which neither party would submit without a total defeat.

The language used or acquiesced in by him in the most confidential intercourse, does not leave his intention to be gathered by inference. For though the words, "to establish the Catholic religion," may denote no more than to secure its free exercise, another expression is employed on this subject for a long time, and by different persons, in correspondence with him, which has no equivocal sense, and allows no such limitation. On the 12th of May, 1687, Barillon had assured him, that the most Christian King "had nothing so much at heart as to see the success of his exertions to re-establish the Catholic religion." Far from limiting this important term, James adopted it in its full extent, answering, "You see that I omit nothing in my power;" and not content with thus accepting the congratulation in its utmost latitude, he continued, "I hope the King your master will aid me; and that we shall, in concert, do great things for religion." In a few months afterwards, when imitating another part of the policy of Louis XIV., he had established a fund for rewarding converts to his religion, he solicited pecuniary aid from the Pope for that very ambiguous purpose. The Nuncio, in answer, declared the sorrow of his Holiness, at being disabled by the impoverished state of his treasury from contributing money, notwithstanding "his paternal zeal for the promoting, in every way, the re-establishment of the Catholic religion in these kingdoms;"‖ as he had shortly before expressed his hope, that the Queen's pregnancy would insure "the re-establishment of the true religion in these kingdoms."* Another term in familiar use at Court for the final object of the royal pursuit was "the great work,"—a phrase borrowed from the supposed transmutation of metals by the alchemists, which naturally signified a total change, and which never could have been applied to mere toleration by those who were in system, if not in practice, the most intolerant of an intolerant age. The King told the Nuncio, that Holland was the main obstacle to the establishment of the Catholic religion in these kingdoms; and D'Abbeville declared, that without humbling the pride of that republic, there could be no hope of the success "of the great work."† Two years afterwards, James, after reviewing his whole policy and its consequences, deliberately and decisively avows the extent of his own designs:—"Our subjects opposed our government, from the fear that we should introduce the orthodox faith, which we were, indeed, labouring to accomplish when the storm began, and which we have done in our kingdom of Ireland."‡ Mary of Este, during the absence of her husband in Ireland, exhorts the Papal minister, "to earn the glorious title of restorer of the faith in the British kingdoms," and declares, that she "hopes much from his administration for the re-establishment both of religion and the royal family."§ Finally, the term "re-establish," which can refer to no time subsequent to the accession of Elizabeth, had so much become the appropriate term, that Louis XIV., assured the Pope of his determination to aid "the King of England, and to re-establish the Catholic religion in that island."‖

None of the most discerning friends or opponents of the King seem at this time to have doubted that he meditated no less than to transfer to his own religion the privileges of an Established Church. Gourville, one of the most sagacious men of his age, being asked by the Duchess of Tyrconnel, when about to make a journey to London, what she should say to the King if he inquired about the opinion of his old friend Gourville, of his measures for the "re-establishment" of the Catholic religion in England, begged her to answer,—"If I were Pope, I should have excommunicated him for exposing all the English Catholics to the risk of being hanged. I have no doubt, that what he sees done in France is his model; but the circumstances are very different. In my opinion, he ought to be content with favouring the Catholics on every occasion, in order to augment their number, and he should leave to his successors the care of gradually subjecting England altogether to the authority of

* London Gazette, 25th Sept. and 11th Nov. 1687; in the last Petre is styled "Clerk of the Closet."

† Narcissus Luttrell, Jan. 1688.—MS.

‡ The King to Barillon, 26th Feb.—MS.

§ D'Adda, 9th March.—MS.

‖ Ibid. 2d Jan. 1688.—MS.

* D'Adda, 2d Dec. 1687.—MS.

† Ibid. 22d August, 1687.—MS.

‡ James II. to Cardinal Ottoboni. Dublin, 15th Feb. 1690.—Papal MSS.

§ Mary to Ottoboni, St. Germains, 4th—15th Dec. 1689.—Papal MSS.

‖ Louis to the Pope, 17th Feb. 1689.—MS.

the Pope."* Bossuet, the most learned, vigorous, and eloquent of controversialists, ventured at this critical time to foretel, that the pious efforts of James would speedily be rewarded by the reconciliation of the British islands to the Universal Church, and their filial submission to the Apostolic See.†

If Gourville considered James an injudicious imitator of Louis XIV., it is easy to imagine what was thought on the subject in England, at a time when one of the mildest, not to say most courtly, writers, in the quietness and familiarity of his private diary, speaks of "the persecution raging in France," and so far forgets his own temper, and the style suitable to such writings, as to call Louis "the French tyrant."‡ Lord Halifax, Lord Nottingham, and Lord Danby, the three most important opponents of the King's measures, disagreeing as they did very considerably in opinion and character, evidently agreed in their apprehension of the extent of his designs.§ They advert to them as too familiar to themselves and their correspondent to require proof, or even development; they speak of them as being far more extensive than the purposes avowed; and they apply terms to them which might be reasonable in the present times, when many are willing to grant and to be contented with religious liberty, but which are entirely foreign to the conceptions of an age when toleration (a term then synonomous with connivance) was the ultimate object of no great party in religion, but was sometimes sought by Dissenters as a step towards establishment, and sometimes yielded by the followers of an Established Church under the pressure of a stern necessity. Some even of those who, having been gained over by the King, were most interested in maintaining his sincerity, were compelled at length to yield to the general conviction. Colonel Titus, a veteran politician, who had been persuaded to concur in the repeal of the penal laws (a measure agreeable to his general principles), declared "that he would have no more to do with him; that his object was only the repeal of the penal laws; that his design was to bring in his religion right or wrong,—to model the army in order to effect that purpose; and, if that was not sufficient, to obtain assistance from France."‖

The converts to the religious or political party of the King were few and discreditable. Lord Lorn, whose predecessors and successors were the firmest supporters of the religion and liberty of his country, is said to have been reduced by the confiscation of his patrimony to the sad necessity of professing a religion which he must have regarded with feelings more hostile than those of mere unbelief.* Lord Salisbury, whose father had been engaged with Russell and Sydney in the consultation called the "Rye-house Plot," and whose grandfather had sat in the House of Commons after the abolition of the monarchy and the peerage, embraced the Catholic religion, and adhered to it during his life. The offices of Attorney and Solicitor-general, which acquire a fatal importance in this country under Governments hostile to liberty, were newly filled. Sawyer, who had been engaged in the worst prosecutions of the preceding ten years, began to tremble for his wealth, and retired from a post of dishonourable danger. He was succeeded by Sir Thomas Powis, a lawyer of no known opinions or connections in politics, who acted on the unprincipled maxim, that, having had too little concern for his country to show any preference for public men or measures, he might as lawfully accept office under any Government, as undertake the defence of any client. Sir William Williams, the confidential adviser of Lord Russell, on whom a fine of 10,000*l.* had been inflicted, for having authorised, as Speaker of the House of Commons, a publication, though solemnly pledged both to men and measures in the face of the public, now accepted the office of Solicitor-general, without the sorry excuse of any of those maxims of professional ethics by which a powerful body countenance each other in their disregard of public duty. A project was also in agitation for depriving the Bishop of London by a sentence of the Ecclesiastical Commissioners for perseverance in his contumacy;† but Cartwright, of Chester, his intended successor, having, in one of his drunken moments, declared the Chancellor and Lord Sunderland to be scoundrels who would betray the King (which he first denied by his sacred order, but was at last reduced to beg pardon for in tears‡), the plan of raising him to the see was abandoned. Crew, Bishop of Durham, was expected to become a Catholic, and Parker of Oxford,—the only prelate whose talents and learning, seconded by a disregard of danger and disgrace, qualified him for breaking the spirit of the clergy of the capital,—though he had supported the Catholic party during his life, refused to conform to their religion on his death-bed;§ leaving it doubtful, by his habitual alienation from religion and honour, to the linger-

* Mémoires de Gourville, vol. ii. p. 254.

† Histoire des Variations des Eglises Protestants, liv. vii.

‡ Evelyn, vol. i. Diary, 3d Sept. 1687.—23d Feb. 1688.

§ Lord Halifax to the Prince of Orange, 7th Dec. 1686—18th Jan.—31st May, 1687. "Though there appears the utmost vigour to pursue the object which has been so long laid, there seemeth to be no less firmness in the nation and aversion to change."—"Every day will give more light to what is intended; though it is already no more a mystery."—Lord Nottingham to the Prince, 2d Sept. 1687. "For though the end at which they aim is very plain and visible, the methods of arriving at that end have been variable and uncertain."—Dalrymple, app. to book v.

‖ Johnstone 16th Feb.—MS.

* Narcissus Luttrell, 1st April.—MS.:—"arrested for 3000*l.* declares himself a Catholic."

† Johnstone, 8th Dec. 1687.—MS.

‡ Johnstone, 27th Feb.—MS. Narcissus Luttrell, 11th Feb.—MS.

§ Evelyn, vol. i. Diary, 23d March.

ing remains or the faint revival of which of these principles the unwonted delicacy of his dying moments may be most probably ascribed.

CHAPTER VII.

Remarkable quiet.—Its peculiar causes.—Coalition of Nottingham and Halifax.—Fluctuating counsels of the Court.—"Parliamentum Pacificum."—Bill for liberty of conscience.—Conduct of Sunderland.—Jesuits.

ENGLAND perhaps never exhibited an external appearance of more undisturbed and profound tranquillity than in the momentous seven months which elapsed from the end of the autumn of 1687 to the beginning of the following summer. Not a speck in the heavens seemed to the common eye to forebode a storm. None of the riots now occurred which were the forerunners of the civil war under Charles I.: nor were there any of those numerous assemblies of the people which affright by their force, when they do not disturb by their violence, and are sometimes as terrific in disciplined inaction, as in tumultuous outrage. Even the ordinary marks of national disapprobation, which prepare and announce a legal resistance to power, were wanting. There is no trace of any public meetings having been held in counties or great towns where such demonstrations of public opinion could have been made. The current of flattering addresses continued to flow towards the throne, uninterrupted by a single warning remonstrance of a more independent spirit, or even of a mere decent servility. It does not appear that in the pulpit, where alone the people could be freely addressed, political topics were discussed; though it must be acknowledged that the controversial sermons against the opinions of the Church of Rome, which then abounded, proved in effect the most formidable obstacle to the progress of her ambition.

Various considerations will serve to lessen our wonder at this singular state of silence and inactivity. Though it would be idle to speak gravely of the calm which precedes the storm, and thus to substitute a trite illustration for a reason, it is nevertheless true, that there are natural causes which commonly produce an interval, sometimes, indeed, a very short one, of more than ordinary quiet between the complete operation of the measures which alienate a people, and the final resolution which precedes a great change. Amidst the hopes and fears which succeed each other in such a state, every man has much to conceal; and it requires some time to acquire the boldness to disclose it. Distrust and suspicion, the parents of silence, which easily yield to sympathy in ordinary and legal opposition, are called into full activity by the first secret consciousness of a disposition to more daring designs. It is natural for men in such circumstances to employ time in watching their opponents, as well as in ascertaining the integrity and courage of their friends. When human nature is stirred by such mighty agents, the understanding, indeed, rarely deliberates; but the conflict and alternation of strong emotions, which assume the appearance and receive the name of deliberation, produce naturally a disposition to pause before irrevocable action. The boldest must occasionally contemplate their own danger with apprehension; the most sanguine must often doubt their success; those who are alive to honour must be visited by the sad reflection, that if they be unfortunate they may be insulted by the multitude for whom they sacrifice themselves; and good men will be frequently appalled by the inevitable calamities to which they expose their country for the uncertain chance of deliverance. When the fluctuation of mind has terminated in bold resolution, a farther period of reserve must be employed in preparing the means of cooperation and maturing the plans of action.

But there were some circumstances peculiar to the events now under consideration, which strengthened and determined the operation of general causes. In 1640, the gentry and the clergy had been devoted to the Court, while the higher nobility and the great towns adhered to the Parliament. The people distrusted their divided superiors, and the tumultuous display of their force (the natural result of their angry suspicions) served to manifest their own inclinations, while it called forth their friends and intimidated their enemies among the higher orders. In 1688, the state of the country was reversed. The clergy and gentry were for the first time discontented with the Crown; and the majority of the nobility, and the growing strength of the commercial classes, reinforced by these unusual auxiliaries, and by all who either hated Popery or loved liberty, were fully as much disaffected to the King as the great body of the people. The nation trusted their natural leaders, who, perhaps, gave, more than they received, the impulse on this occasion. No popular chiefs were necessary, and none arose to supply the place of their authority with the people, who reposed in quiet and confidence till the signal for action was made. This important circumstance produced another effect: the whole guidance of the opposition fell gradually into fewer and fewer hands; it became every day easier to carry it on more calmly; popular commotion could only have disturbed councils where the people did not suspect their chiefs of lukewarmness, and the chiefs were assured of the prompt and zealous support of the people. It was as important now to restrain the impetuosity of the multitude, as it might be necessary in other circumstances to indulge it. Hence arose the facility of caution and secrecy at one time, of energy and speed at another, of concert and co-operation throughout, which are indispensable in enterprises so perilous. It must not be forgotten that a coalition of parties was necessary on this occasion. It was long before the Tories could be persuaded to oppose the monarch; and there was always some reason to apprehend, that he might by timely concessions recal them to their ancient standard: it was still longer before they could so far relinquish their avowed principles as to contemplate, without horror, any resistance by force, however strictly defensive. Two parties, who had waged war against each other in the contest between monarchy and popular government, during half a century, even when common danger taught them the necessity of sacrificing their differences, had still more than common reason to examine each other's purposes before they at last determined on resolutely and heartily acting together; and it required some time after a mutual belief in sincerity, before habitual distrust could be so much subdued as to allow reciprocal communication of opinion. In these moments of hesitation, the friends of liberty must have been peculiarly desirous not to alarm the new-born zeal of their important and unwonted confederates by turbulent scenes or violent councils. The state of the succession to the crown had also a considerable influence, as will afterwards more fully appear. Suffice it for the present to observe, that the expectation of a Protestant successor restrained the impetuosity of the more impatient Catholics, and disposed the more moderate Protestants to an acquiescence, however sullen, in evils which could only be temporary. The rumour of the Queen's pregnancy had roused the passions of both parties; but as soon as the first shock had passed, the uncertain result produced an armistice, distinguished by the silence of anxious expectation, during which each eagerly but resolutely waited for the event, which might extinguish the hopes of one, and release the other from the restraint of fear.

It must be added, that to fix the precise moment when a wary policy is to be exchanged for bolder measures, is a problem so important, that a slight mistake in the attempt to solve it may be fatal, and yet so difficult, that its solution must generally depend more on a just balance of firmness and caution in the composition of character, than on a superiority of any intellectual faculties. The two eminent persons who were now at the head of the coalition against the Court, afforded remarkable examples of this truth. Lord Nottingham, who occupied that leading station among the Tories, which the timidity if not treachery of Rochester had left vacant, was a man of firm and constant character, but solicitous to excess for the maintenance of that uniformity of measures and language which, indeed, is essential to the authority of a decorous and grave statesman. Lord Halifax, sufficiently pliant, or perhaps fickle, though the boldest of politicians in speculation, became refined, sceptical, and irresolute, at the moment of action. Both hesitated on the brink of a great enterprise: Lord Nottingham pleaded conscientious scruples, and recoiled from the avowal of the principles of resistance which he had long reprobated; Lord Halifax saw difficulty too clearly, and continued too long to advise delay. Those who knew the state of the latter's mind, observed "the war between his constitution and his judgment;"* in which, as usual, the former gained the ascendant for a longer period than, in the midst of the rapid progress of great events, was conducive to his reputation.

Some of the same causes which restrained the manifestation of popular discontent, contributed also to render the counsels of the Government inconstant. The main subject of deliberation, regarding the internal affairs of the kingdom, continued to be the possibility of obtaining the objects sought for by a compliant Parliament, or the pursuit of them by means of the prerogative and the army. On these questions a more than ordinary fluctuation prevailed. Early in the preceding September, Bonrepos, who, on landing, met the King at Portsmouth, had been surprised at the frankness with which he owned, that the repairs and enlargements of that important fortress were intended to strengthen it against his subjects;† and at several periods the King and his most zealous advisers had spoken of the like projects with as little reserve. In October it was said, "that if nothing could be done by parlimentary means, the King would do all by his prerogative;"—an attempt from which Barillon expected that insurrection would ensue.‡ Three months after, the bigoted Romanists, whether more despairing of a Parliament or more confident in their own strength, and incensed at resistance, no longer concealed their contempt for the Protestants of the Royal Family, and the necessity of recurring to arms.§ The same temper showed itself at the eve of the birth of a Prince. The King then declared, that, rather than desert, he should pursue his objects without a Parliament, in spite of any laws which might stand in his way;—a project which Louis XIV., less bigoted and more politic, considered "as equally difficult and dangerous."‖ But the sea might as well cease

* Johnstone, 4th April,—MS.

† Bonrepos to Seignelai, 4th Sept.—Fox MSS.

‡ Barillon, 10th Oct. Bonrepos to Seignelai same date.—Fox MSS.

§ Johnstone, 29th Jan.—MS. Lady Melfort overheard the priests speak to her husband of "blood," probably with reference to foreign war, as well as to the suppression of the disaffected at home.—"Sidney vous fera savoir qu'après des grandes contestations on est enfin résolu de faire leurs affaires sans un parlement."

‖ Barillon, 6th May. The King to Barillon, 14th May.—Fox MSS.—"Le projet que fait la cour ou vous êtes de renverser toutes les lois d'Angleterre pour parvenir au but qu'elle se propose, me paroît d'une difficile et périlleuse exécution."

to ebb and flow, as a council to remain for so many months at precisely the same point in regard to such hazardous designs. In the interval between these plans of violence, hopes were sometimes harboured of obtaining from the daring fraud of returning officers, such a House of Commons as could not be hoped for from the suffrages of any electors; but the prudence of the Catholic gentry, who were named sheriffs, appears to have speedily disappointed this expectation.* Neither do the Court appear to have even adhered for a considerable time to the bold project of accomplishing their purposes without a Parliament. In moments of secret misgiving, when they shrunk from these desperate counsels, they seem frequently to have sought refuge in the flattering hope, that their measures to fill a House of Commons with their adherents, though hitherto so obstinately resisted, would in due time prove successful. The meeting of a Parliament was always held out to the public, and was still sometimes regarded as a promising expedient:† while a considerable time for sounding and moulding the public temper yet remained before the three years within which the Triennial Act required that assembly to be called together, would elapse; and it seemed needless to cut off all retreat to legal means till that time should expire. The Queen's pregnancy affected these consultations in various modes. The boldest considered it as likely to intimidate their enemies, and to afford the happiest opportunity for immediate action. A Parliament might, they said, be assembled, that would either yield to the general joy at the approaching birth of a prince, or by their sullen and mutinous spirit justify the employment of more decisive measures. The more moderate, on the other hand, thought, that if the birth of a prince was followed by a more cautious policy, and if the long duration of a Catholic government were secured by the parliamentary establishment of a regency, there was a better chance than before of gaining all important objects in no very long time by the forms of law and without hazard to the public quiet. Penn desired a Parliament, as the only mode of establishing toleration without subverting the laws, and laboured to persuade the King to spare the Tests, or to offer an equivalent for such parts of them as he wished to take away.‡ Halifax said to a friend, who argued for the equivalent, "Look at my nose; it is a very ugly one, but I would not take one five hundred times better as an equivalent, because my own is fast to my face;"§ and made a more serious attack on these dangerous and seductive experiments, in his masterly tract, entitled "The Anatomy of an Equivalent." Another tract was published to prepare the way for what was called "A Healing Parliament," which, in the midst of tolerant professions and conciliatory language, chiefly attracted notice by insult and menace. In this publication, which, being licensed by Lord Sunderland,* was treated as the act of the Government, the United Provinces were reminded, that "their commonwealth was the result of an absolute rebellion, revolt, and defection, from their prince;" and they were apprised of the respect of the King for the inviolability of their territory, by a menace thrown out to Burnet, that he "might be taken out of their country, and cut up alive in England," in imitation of a supposed example in the reign of Elizabeth;†—a threat the more alarming because it was well known that the first part of such a project had been long entertained, and that attempts had already been made for its execution. Van Citters complained of this libel in vain: the King expressed wonder and indignation, that a complaint should be made of the publication of an universally acknowledged truth,—confounding the fact of resistance with the condemnation pronounced upon it by the opprobrious terms, which naturally imported and were intended to affirm that the resistance was criminal.‡ Another pamphlet, called "A New Test of the Church of England's Loyalty,"§ exposed with scurrility the inconsistency of the Church's recent independence with her long professions and solemn decrees of non-resistance, and hinted that "His Majesty would withdraw his royal protection, which was promised upon the account of her constant fidelity." Such menaces were very serious, at a moment when D'Abbeville, James' minister at the Hague, told the Prince of Orange, that "upon some occasions princes must forget their promises;" and being "reminded by William, that the King ought to have more regard to the Church of England, which was the main body of the nation," answered, "that the body called the 'Church of England' would not have a being in two years."||

The great charter of conscience was now drawn up, in the form of a bill, and prepared to be laid before Parliament. It was entitled "An Act for granting of Liberty of Conscience, without imposing of Oaths and Tests." The preamble thanks the King for the exercise of his dispensing power, and recognises it as legally warranting his subjects to enjoy their religion and their offices during his reign: but, in order to perpetuate his pious and Christian bounty to his people, the bill proceeds to enact, that all persons professing Christ may assemble publicly or privately, without any licence, for the exercise of their religious worship, and that all laws against nonconformity and recusancy,

* Johnstone, 8th Dec.—MS. "Many of the Popish sheriffs have estates, and declare that whoever expects false returns from them will be deceived."

† Ibid. 21st Feb.—MS.

‡ Ibid. 6th Feb.—MS.

§ Ibid. 12th March.—MS.

* Johnstone, 15th Feb.

† Parliamentum Pacificum, p. 57.

‡ Barillon, 19th April.—MS.

§ Somers' Tracts, vol. ix. p. 195.

|| Burnet, vol. iii. p. 207.

or exacting oaths, declarations, or tests, or imposing disabilities or penalties on religion, shall be repealed; and more especially in order "that his Majesty may not be debarred of the service of his subjects, which by the law of nature is inseparably annexed to his person, and over which no Act of Parliament can have any control, any further than he is pleased to allow of the same,"* it takes away the oaths of allegiance and supremacy, and the tests and declarations required by the 25th and 30th of the late king, as qualifications to hold office, or to sit in either House of Parliament. It was, moreover, provided that meetings for religious worship should be open and peaceable; that notice of the place of assembly should be given to a justice of the peace; that no seditious sermons should be preached in them; and that in cathedral and collegiate churches, parish churches, and chapels, no persons shall officiate but such as are duly authorised according to the Act of Uniformity, and no worship be used but what is conformable to the Book of Common Prayer therein established; for the observance of which provision,—the only concession made by the bill to the fears of the Establishment,—it was further enacted, that the penalties of the Act of Uniformity should be maintained against the contravention of that statute in the above respects. Had this bill passed into a law, and had such a law been permanently and honestly executed, Great Britain would have enjoyed the blessings of religious liberty in a degree unimagined by the statesmen of that age, and far surpassing all that she has herself gained during the century and a half of the subsequent progress of almost all Europe towards tolerant principles. But such projects were examined by the nation with a view to the intention of their authors, and to the tendency of their provisions in the actual circumstances of the time and country; and the practical question was, whether such intention and tendency were not to relieve the minority from intolerance, but to lessen the security of the great majority against it. The speciousness of the language, and the liberality of the enactments, in which it rivalled the boldest speculations at that time hazarded by philosophers, were so contrary to the opinions, and so far beyond the sympathy, of the multitude, that none of the great divisions of Christians could heartily themselves adopt, or could prudently trust each other's sincerity in holding them forth: they were regarded not as a boon, but as a snare. From the ally of Louis XIV., three years after the persecution of the Protestants, they had the appearance of an insulting mockery; even though it was not then known that James had during his whole reign secretly congratulated that monarch on his barbarous measures.

The general distrust of the King's designs arose from many circumstances, separately too small to reach posterity, but, taken together, sufficient to entitle near observers to form an estimate of his character. When, about 1679, he had visited Amsterdam, he declared to the magistrates of that liberal and tolerant city, that he "never was for oppressing tender consciences."* The sincerity of these tolerant professions was soon after tried when holding a Parliament as Lord High Commissioner at Edinburgh, in 1681, he exhorted that assembly to suppress the conventicles, or, in other words, the religious worship of the majority of the Scottish people.† It being difficult for the fiercest zealots to devise any new mode of persecution which the Parliament had not already tried, he was content to give the royal assent to an act confirmatory of all those edicts of blood already in force against the proscribed Presbyterians.‡ But very shortly after, when the Earl of Argyle, acting evidently from the mere dictates of conscience, added a modest and reasonable explanation to an oath required of him, which without it would have been contradictory, the Lord Commissioner caused that nobleman to be prosecuted for high treason, and to be condemned to death on account of his conscientious scruples.§ To complete the evidence of his tolerant spirit, it is only necessary to quote one passage which he himself has fortunately preserved. He assures us that, in his confidential communication with his brother, he represented it as an act of "imprudence to have proposed in Parliament the repeal of the 35th of Elizabeth,"‖—a statute almost as sanguinary as those Scottish acts which he had sanctioned. The folly of believing his assurances of equal toleration was at the time evinced by his appeal to those solemn declarations of a resolution to maintain the Edict of Nantz, with which Louis XIV. had accompanied each of his encroachments on it.

* This language seems to have been intentionally equivocal. The words "allow of the same," may in themselves mean till he gives his royal assent to the Act. But in this construction the paragraph would be an unmeaning boast, since no bill can become an Act of Parliament till it receives the royal assent; and, secondly, it would be inconsistent with the previous recognition of the legality of the King's exercise of the dispensing power; Charles II. having given his assent to the Acts dispensed with. It must therefore be understood to declare, that Acts of Parliament disabling individuals from serving the public, restrain the King only till he dispenses with them.

* Account of James II.'s visit to Amsterdam, by William Carr, then English consul (said by mistake to be in 1681).—Gentleman's Magazine, vol. lix. part 2. p. 659.

† Life of James II., vol. i. p. 694. The words of his speech are copied from his own MS. Memoirs.

‡ Acts of Parliament, vol. viii. p. 242.

§ State Trials, vol. viii. p. 843. Wodrow, vol. i. pp. 205—217,—a narrative full of interest, and obviously written with a careful regard to truth. Laing, vol. iv. p. 125,—where the moral feelings of that upright and sagacious historian are conspicuous.

‖ Life of James II., vol. ii. p. 656, verbatim from the King's Memoirs.

Where a belief prevailed that a law was passed without an intention to observe it, all scrutiny of its specific provisions became needless:—yet it ought to be remarked, that though it might be fair to indemnify those who acted under the dispensing power, the recognition of its legality was at least a wanton insult to the Constitution, and appeared to betray a wish to reserve that power for further and more fatal measures. The dispensation which had been granted to the incumbent of Putney showed the facility with which such a prerogative might be employed to elude the whole proviso of the proposed bill in favour of the Established Church. It contained no confirmation of the King's promises to protect the endowments of the Protestant clergy; and instead of comprehending, as all wise laws should do, the means of its own execution, it would have facilitated the breach of its own most important enactments. If it had been adopted by the next Parliament, another still more compliant would have found it easier, instead of more difficult, to establish the Catholic religion, and to abolish toleration. This essential defect was confessed rather than obviated by the impracticable remedies recommended in a tract,* which, for the security of the great charter of religious liberty about to be passed, proposed "that every man in the kingdom should, on obtaining the age of twenty-one, swear to observe it; that no Peer or Commoner should take his seat in either House of Parliament till he had taken the like oath; and that all sheriffs, or others, making false returns, or Peers or Commoners, presuming to sit in either House without taking the oath, or who should move or mention any thing in or out of Parliament that might tend to the violating or altering the liberty of conscience, should be hanged on a gallows made out of the timber of his own house, which was for that purpose to be demolished."† It seems not to have occurred to this writer that the Parliament whom he thus proposes to restrain, might have begun their operations by repealing his penal laws.

Notwithstanding the preparations for convening a Parliament, it was not believed, by the most discerning and well-informed, that any determination was yet adopted on the subject. Lord Nottingham early thought that, in case of a general election, "few Dissenters would be chosen, and that such as were, would not, *in present circumstances*, concur in the repeal of so much as the penal laws; because to do it might encourage the Papists to greater attempts."‡ Lord Halifax, at a later period, observes, "that the moderate Catholics acted reluctantly; that the Court, finding their expectations not answered by the Dissenters, had thoughts of returning to their old friends the High Churchmen; and that he thought a meeting of Parliament impracticable, and continued as much an unbeliever for October, as he had before been for April."* In private, he mentioned, as one of the reasons of his opinion, that some of the courtiers had declined to take up a bet for five hundred pounds, which he had offered, that the Parliament would not meet in October; and that, though they liked him very little, they liked his money as well as any other man's.†

The perplexities and variations of the Court were multiplied by the subtile and crooked policy of Sunderland, who, though willing to purchase his continuance in office by unbounded compliance, was yet extremely solicitous, by a succession of various projects and reasonings adapted to the circumstances of each moment, to divert the mind of James as long as possible from assembling Parliament, or entering on a foreign war, or committing any acts of unusual severity or needless insult to the Constitution, or undertaking any of those bold or even decisive measures, the consequences of which to his own power, or to the throne of his sovereign, no man could foresee. Sunderland had gained every object of ambition: he could only lose by change, and instead of betraying James by violent counsels, he appears to have better consulted his own interest, by offering as prudent advice to him as he could venture without the risk of incurring the royal displeasure. He might lose his greatness by hazarding too good counsel, and he must lose it if his master was ruined. Thus placed between two precipices, and winding his course between them, he could find safety only by sometimes approaching one, and sometimes the other. Another circumstance contributed to augment the seeming inconsistencies of the minister:—he was sometimes tempted to deviate from his own path by the pecuniary gratifications which, after the example of Charles and James, he clandestinely received from France;—an infamous practice, in that age very prevalent among European statesmen, and regarded by many of them as little more than forming part of the perquisites of office.‡ It will appear in the sequel that, like his master, he received French money only for doing what he otherwise desired to do; and that it rather induced him to quicken or retard, to enlarge or contract, than substantially to alter his measures. But though he was too prudent to hazard the power which produced all his emolument for a single gratuity, yet this dangerous practice must have multiplied the

* A New Test instead of the Old One. By G. S. Licensed 24th March, 1688.

† The precedent alleged for this provision is the decree of Darius, for rebuilding the temple of Jerusalem:—"And I have made a decree that whoever shall alter this word, let timber be pulled down from his house, and being set up, let him be hanged thereon."—Ezra, chap. vi. v. 11.

‡ Lord Nottingham to the Prince of Orange, 2d Sept. 1687.—Dalrymple, app. to book v.

* Lord Halifax to the Prince of Orange, 12th April, 1688.—Dalrymple, app. to book v.

† Johnstone, 27th Feb.—MS.

‡ D'Avaux, passim. See Lettres de De Witt, vol. iv., and Ellis, History of the Iron Mask.

windings of his course; and from these deviations arose, in some measure, the fluctuating counsels and varying language of the Government of which he was the chief. The divisions of the Court, and the variety of tempers and opinions by which he was surrounded, added new difficulties to the game which he played. This was a more simple one at first, while he coalesced with the Queen and the then united Catholic party, and professed moderation as his sole defence against Rochester and the Protestant Tories; but after the defeat of the latter, and the dismissal of their chief, divisions began to show themselves among the victorious Catholics, which gradually widened as the moment of decisive action seemed to approach. It was then* that he made an effort to strengthen himself by the revival of the office of Lord Treasurer in his own person;—a project in which he endeavoured to engage Father Petre by proposing that Jesuit to be his successor as Secretary of State, and in which he obtained the co-operation of Sir Nicholas Butler, a new convert, by suggesting that he should be Chancellor of the Exchequer. The King, however, adhered to his determination that the treasury should be in commission notwithstanding the advice of Butler, and the Queen declined to interfere in a matter where her husband appeared to be resolute. It should seem, from the account of this intrigue by James himself, that Petre neither discouraged Sunderland in his plan, nor supported it by the exercise of his own ascendency over the mind of the King.

In the spring of 1688, the Catholics formed three separate and unfriendly parties, whose favour it was not easy for a minister to preserve at the same time. The nobility and gentry of England were, as they continued to the last, adverse to those rash courses which honour obliged them apparently to support, but which they had always dreaded as dangerous to their sovereign and their religion. Lords Powis, Bellasis, and Arundel, vainly laboured to inculcate their wise maxims on the mind of James; while the remains of the Spanish influence, formerly so powerful among British Catholics, were employed by the ambassador, Don Pedro Ronquillo, in support of this respectable party. Sunderland, though he began, soon after his victory over Rochester, to moderate and temper the royal measures, was afraid of displeasing his impatient master by openly supporting them. The second party, which may be called the Papal, was that of the Nuncio, who had at first considered the Catholic aristocracy as lukewarm in the cause of their religion, but who, though he continued outwardly to countenance all domestic efforts for the advancement of the faith, became at length more hostile to the connection of James with France, than zealous for the speedy accomplishment of that Prince's ecclesiastical policy in England. To him the Queen seems to have adhered, both from devotion to Rome, and from that habitual apprehension of the displeasure of the House of Austria which an Italian princess naturally entertained towards the masters of Lombardy and Naples.* When hostility towards Holland was more openly avowed, and when Louis XIV., no longer content with acquiescence, began to require from England the aid of armaments and threats, if not co-operation in war, Sunderland and the Nuncio became more closely united, and both drew nearer to the more moderate party. The third, known by the name of the French or Jesuit party, supported by Ireland and the clergy, and possessing the personal favour and confidence of the King, considered all delay in the advancement of their religion as dangerous, and were devoted to France as the only ally able and willing to insure the success of their designs. Emboldened by the pregnancy of the Queen, and by so signal a mark of favour as the introduction of Father Petre into the Council,—an act of folly which the moderate Catholics would have resisted, if the secret had not been kept from them till the appointment,†—they became impatient of Sunderland's evasion and procrastination, especially of his disinclination to all hostile demonstrations against Holland. Their agent, Skelton, the British minister at Paris, represented the minister's policy to the French Government, as "a secret opposition to all measures against the interest of the Prince of Orange;"‡ and though Barillon acquits him of such treachery,§ it would seem that from that moment he ceased to enjoy the full confidence of the French party.

It was with difficulty that at the beginning of the year Sunderland had prevailed on the majority of the Council to postpone the calling a Parliament till they should be strengthened by the recall of the English troops from the Dutch service:‖ and when, two months later, just before the delivery of the Queen, (in which they would have the advantage of the expectation of a Prince of Wales,) the King and the majority of the Council declared for this measure, conformably to his policy of delaying decisive, and perhaps irretrievable

---

* "A little before Christmas."—Life of James II. vol. ii. p. 131; passages quoted from James' Memoirs. The King's own Memoirs are always deserving of great consideration, and in unmixed cases of fact are, I am willing to hope, generally conclusive.

* The King to Barillon, 2d June.—MS. Louis heard of this partiality from his ministers at Madrid and Vienna, and desired Barillon to insinuate to her that neither she nor her husband had any thing to hope from Spain.

† The account of Petre's advancement by Dodd is a specimen of the opinion entertained by the secular clergy of the regulars, but especially of the Jesuits.

‡ The King to Barillon, 11th Dec. 1687.—MS.

§ Barillon to the King, 5th Jan. 1688.—MS.

‖ Johnstone, 16th Jan.—MS. "Sidney believes that Sunderland has prevailed, after a great struggle, to dissuade the Council from a war or a Parliament."

steps, he again resisted it with success, on the ground that matters were not ripe, that it required much longer time to prepare the corporations, and that, if the Nonconformists in the Parliament should prove mutinous, an opposition so national would render the employment of any other means more hazardous.* Sunderland owed his support to the Queen, who, together with the Nuncio, protected him from the attack of Father Petre, who, after a considerable period of increasing estrangement, had now declared against him with violence.† In the meantime the French Government, which had hitherto affected impartiality in the divisions of the British Catholics, had made advances to Petre as he receded from Sunderland; while the former had, as long ago as January, declared in Council, that the King ought to be solicitous only for the friendship of France.‡ James now desired Barillon to convey the assurances of his high esteem for the Jesuit;§ and the ambassador undertook to consider of some more efficacious proof of respect to him, agreeably to the King's commands.||

Henceforward the power of Sunderland was seen to totter. It was thought that he himself saw that it could not, even with the friendship of the Queen, stand long, since the French ambassador had begun to trim, and the whole French party leant against him.¶ Petre, through whom Sunderland formerly had a hold on the Jesuit party, became now himself a formidable rival for power, and was believed to be so infatuated by ambition as to pursue the dignity of a cardinal, that he might more easily become prime minister of England.** At a later period, Barclay, the celebrated Quaker, boasted of having reconciled Sunderland to Melfort, trusting that it would be the ruin of Petre;†† and Sunderland then told the Nuncio that he considered it as the first principle of the King's policy to frame all his measures with a view to their reception by Parliament;‡‡—a strong proof of the aversion to extreme measures, to which he afterwards adhered. A fitter opportunity will present itself hereafter for relating the circumstances in which he demanded a secret gratuity from France, in addition to his pension from that Court of 60,000 livres yearly (2500*l.*); of the skill with which Barillon beat down his demands, and made a bargain less expensive to his Government; and of the address with which Sunderland claimed the bribe for measures on which he had before determined,—so that he might seem rather to have obtained it under false pretences, than to have been diverted by it from his own policy. It is impossible to trace clearly the serpentine course of an intriguing minister, whose opinions were at variance with his language, and whose craving passions often led him astray from his interest; but an attempt to discover it is necessary to the illustration of the government of James. In general, then, it seems to be clear that, from the beginning of 1687, Sunderland had struggled in secret to moderate the measures of the Government; and that it was not till the spring of 1688, when he carried that system to the utmost, that the decay of his power became apparent. As Halifax had lost his office by liberal principles, and Sunderland had outbidden Rochester for the King's favour, so Sunderland himself was now on the eve of being overthrown by the influence of Petre, at a time when no successor of specious pretensions presented himself. He seems to have made one attempt to recover strength, by remodelling the Cabinet Council. For a considerable time the Catholic counsellors had been summoned separately, together with Sunderland himself, on all confidential affairs, while the more ordinary business only was discussed in the presence of the Protestants:—thus forming two Cabinets; one ostensible, the other secret. He now proposed to form them into one, in order to remove the jealousy of the Protestant counsellors, and to encourage them to promote the King's designs. To this united Cabinet the affairs of Scotland and Ireland were to be committed, which had been separately administered before, with manifest disadvantage to uniformity and good order. Foreign affairs, and others requiring the greatest secrecy, were still to be reserved to a smaller number. The public pretences for this change were specious: but the object was to curb the power of Petre, who now ruled without control in a secret cabal of his own communion and selection.*

The party which had now the undisputed ascendant were denominated "Jesuits," as a term of reproach, by the enemies of that famous society in the Church of Rome, as well as by those among the Protestant communions. A short account of their origin and character may facilitate a faint conception of the admiration, jealousy, fear, and hatred,—the profound submission or fierce resistance,—which that formidable name once inspired. Their institution originated in pure zeal for religion, glowing in the breast of Loyola, a Spanish soldier,—a man full of imagination and sensibility,—in a country where wars, rather civil than foreign, waged against unbelievers for ages, had rendered a

* D'Adda, 12th March.—MS. "Il y avaient beaucoup d'intrigues et de cabales de cour sur cela dirigées contre mi Lord Sunderland: la reine le soutient, et il a emporté."—Barillon, Mazure, Histoire de la Revolution, vol. ii. p. 399. Shrewsbury to the Prince of Orange (communicating the disunion), 14th March, 1688. Dalrymple, app. to books v. and vi.

† Van Citters, 9th April.—MS.

‡ Barillon, 2d Feb.—MS.

§ The King to Barillon, 19th March.—MS.

|| Barillon, 29th March.—MS.

¶ Johnstone, 12th March and 2d April.—MS.

** Lettre au Roi, 1 Août, 1687, in the Depôt des Affaires Etrangères at Paris, not signed, but probably from Bonrepos.

†† Clarendon, Diary, 23d June.

‡‡ D'Adda, 4th June.—MS.

* D'Adda, 23d April.—MS.

passion for spreading the Catholic faith a national point of honour, and blended it with the pursuit of glory as well as with the memory of past renown. The legislative forethought of his successors gave form and order to the product of enthusiasm, and bestowed laws and institutions on their society which were admirably fitted to its various ends.* Having arisen in the age of the Reformation, they naturally became the champions of the Church against her new enemies,—and in that also of the revival of letters, instead of following the example of the unlettered monks, who decried knowledge as the mother of heresy, they joined in the general movement of mankind; they cultivated polite literature with splendid success; they were the earliest and, perhaps, most extensive reformers of European education, which, in their schools, made a larger stride than it has done at any succeeding moment;† and, by the just reputation of their learning, as well as by the weapons with which it armed them, they were enabled to carry on a vigorous contest against the most learned impugners of the authority of the Church. Peculiarly subjected to the See of Rome by their constitution, they became ardently devoted to its highest pretensions, in order to maintain a monarchical power, the necessity of which they felt for concert, discipline, and energy in their theological warfare.

While the nations of the Peninsula hastened with barbaric chivalry to spread religion by the sword in the newly explored regions of the East and West, the Jesuits alone, the missionaries of that age, either repaired or atoned for the evils caused by the misguided zeal of their countrymen. In India, they suffered martyrdom with heroic constancy.‡ They penetrated through the barrier which Chinese policy opposed to the entrance of strangers,—cultivating the most difficult of languages with such success as to compose hundreds of volumes in it; and, by the public utility of their scientific acquirements, obtained toleration, patronage, and personal honours, from that jealous government. The natives of America, who generally felt the comparative superiority of the European race only in a more rapid or a more gradual destruction, and to whom even the excellent Quakers dealt out little more than penurious justice, were, under the paternal rule of the Jesuits, reclaimed from savage manners, and instructed in the arts and duties of civilized life. At the opposite point of society, they were fitted by their release from conventual life, and their allowed intercourse with the world, for the perilous office of secretly guiding the conscience of princes. They maintained the highest station as a religious body in the literature of Catholic countries. No other association ever sent forth so many disciples who reached such eminence in departments so various and unlike. While some of their number ruled the royal penitents at Versailles or the Escurial, others were teaching the use of the spade and the shuttle to the naked savages of Paraguay; a third body daily endangered their lives in an attempt to convert the Hindûs to Christianity; a fourth carried on the controversy against the Reformers; a portion were at liberty to cultivate polite literature; while the greater part continued to be employed either in carrying on the education of Catholic Europe, or in the government of their society, and in ascertaining the ability and disposition of the junior members, so that well-qualified men might be selected for the extraordinary variety of offices in their immense commonwealth. The most famous constitutionalists, the most skilful casuists, the ablest schoolmasters, the most celebrated professors, the best teachers of the humblest mechanical arts, the missionaries who could most bravely encounter martyrdom, or who with most patient skill could infuse the rudiments of religion into the minds of ignorant tribes or prejudiced nations, were the growth of their fertile schools. The prosperous administration of such a society for two centuries, is probably the strongest proof afforded from authentic history that an artificially-formed system of government and education is capable, under some circumstances, of accomplishing greater things than the general experience of it would warrant us in expecting.

Even here, however, the materials were supplied, and the first impulse given by enthusiasm; and in this memorable instance the defects of such a system are discoverable. The whole ability of the members being constantly, exclusively, and intensely directed to the various purposes of their Order, their minds had not the leisure, or liberty, necessary for works of genius, or even for discoveries in science,—to say no-

* Originally consisting of seven men, the society possessed, at the end of the sixteenth century, one thousand five hundred colleges, and contained twenty-two thousand avowed members. Parts of their constitution were allowed (by Paul III.) to be kept and to be altered, without the privity of the Pope himself. The simple institution of lay brethren, combined with the privilege of secrecy, afforded the means of enlisting powerful individuals, among whom Louis XIV. and James II. are generally numbered.

† "For education," says Bacon, within fifty years of the institution of the Order, "consult the schools of the Jesuits. Nothing hitherto tried in practice surpasses them."—De Augment. Scient. lib. vi. cap. 4. "Education, that excellent part of ancient discipline, has been, in some sorts, revived of late times in the colleges of the Jesuits, of whom, in regard of this and of some other points of human learning and moral matters, I may say, "Talis cum sis utinam noster esses."—Advancement of Learning, book i. Such is the disinterested testimony of the wisest of men to the merit of the Jesuits, to the unspeakable importance of reforming education, and to the infatuation of those who, in civilized nations, attempt to resist new opinions by mere power, without calling in aid such a show of reason, if not the whole substance of reason, as cannot be maintained without a part of the substance.

‡ See the Lettres Edifiantes, &c.

thing of the original speculations in philosophy which are interdicted by implicit faith. That great society, which covered the world for two hundred years, has no names which can be opposed to those of Pascal and Racine, produced by the single community of Port Royal, persecuted as it was during the greater part of its short existence. But this remarkable peculiarity amounts perhaps to little more than that they were more eminent in active than in contemplative life. A far more serious objection is the manifest tendency of such a system, while it produces the precise excellences aimed at by its mode of cultivation, to raise up all the neighbouring evils with a certainty and abundance,—a size and malignity,—unknown to the freer growth of nature. The mind is narrowed by the constant concentration of the understanding; and those who are habitually intent on one object learn at last to pursue it at the expense of others equally or more important. The Jesuits, the reformers of education, sought to engross it, as well as to stop it at their own point. Placed in the front of the battle against the Protestants, they caught a more than ordinary portion of that theological hatred against their opponents which so naturally springs up where the greatness of the community, the fame of the controversialist, and the salvation of mankind seem to be at stake. Affecting more independence in their missions than other religious orders, they were the formidable enemies of episcopal jurisdiction, and thus armed against themselves the secular clergy, especially in Great Britain, where they were the chief missionaries. Intrusted with the irresponsible guidance of Kings, they were too often betrayed into a compliant morality,—excused probably to themselves, by the great public benefits which they might thus obtain, by the numerous temptations which seemed to palliate royal vices, and by the real difficulties of determining, in many instances, whether there was more danger of deterring such persons from virtue by unreasonable austerity, or of alluring them into vice by unbecoming relaxation. This difficulty is indeed so great, that casuistry has, in general, vibrated between these extremes, rather than rested near the centre. To exalt the Papal power they revived the scholastic doctrine of the popular origin of government,—that rulers might be subject to the people, while the people themselves, on all questions so difficult as those which relate to the limits of obedience, were to listen with reverential submission to the judgment of the Sovereign Pontiff, the common pastor of sovereigns and subjects, and the unerring oracle of humble Christians in all cases of perplexed conscience.* The ancient practice of excommunication, which, in its original principle, was no more than the expulsion from a community of an individual who did not observe its rules, being stretched so far as to interdict intercourse with offenders, and, by consequence, to suspend duty towards them, became, in the middle age, the means of absolving nations from obedience to excommunicated sovereigns.* Under these specious colours both Popes and Councils had been guilty of alarming encroachments on the civil authority. The Church had, indeed, never solemnly adopted the principle of these usurpations into her rule of faith or of life, though many famous doctors gave them a dangerous countenance; but she had not condemned or even disavowed those equally celebrated divines who resisted them: and though the Court of Rome undoubtedly patronised opinions so favourable to its power, the Catholic Church, which had never pronounced a collective judgment on them, was still at liberty to disclaim them, without abandoning her haughty claim of exemption from fundamental error.†

On the Jesuits, as the most staunch of the polemics who struggled to exalt the Church above the State, and who ascribed to the Supreme Pontiff an absolute power over the Church, the odium of these doctrines principally fell.‡ Among Reformed nations, and especially in Great Britain, the greatest of them, the whole Order were regarded as incendiaries who were perpetually plotting the overthrow of all Protestant governments, and as immoral sophists who employed their subtle casuistry to silence the remains of conscience in tyrants of their own persuasion. Nor was the detestation of Protestants rewarded by general popularity in Catholic countries: all other regulars envied their greatness; the universities dreaded their acquiring a monopoly of education; while monarchs the most zealously Catholic, though they often favoured individual Jesuits, looked with fear and hatred on a society which would reduce them to the condition of vassals of the priesthood. In France, the magistrates, who preserved their integrity and dignity in the midst of general servility, maintained a more constant conflict with these formidable adversaries of the independence of the State and the Church. The Kings of Spain and Portugal envied their well-earned authority, in the missions of

* It is true that Mariana (De Rege et Regis Institutione) only contends for the right of the people to depose sovereigns, without building the authority of the Pope on that principle, as the schoolmen have expressly done; but his manifest approbation of the assassination of Henry III. by Clement, a fanatical partisan of the League, sufficiently discloses his purpose. See La Mennais, La Religion considérée dans ses Rapports avec l'Ordre politique. (Paris, 1826.)

* Fleury, Discours sur l'Histoire Ecclésiastique, No. iii. sect. 18.

† "Il est vrai que Gregoire VII. n'a jamais fait aucune décision sur ce point. *Dieu ne l'a pas permis.*"—Ibid. It is evident that if such a determination had, in Fleury's opinion, subsequently been pronounced by the Church, the last words of this passage would have been unreasonable.

‡ Bayle, Dictionnaire Historique, &c., article "Bellarmine,"—who is said by that unsuspected judge to have had the best pen for controversy of any man of that age.

Paraguay and California, over districts which they had conquered from the wilderness. The impenetrable mystery in which a part of their constitution was enveloped, though it strengthened their association, and secured the obedience of its members, was an irresistible temptation to abuse power, and justified the apprehensions of temporal sovereigns, while it opened an unbounded scope for heinous accusations. Even in the eighteenth century, when many of their peculiarities had become faint, and when they were perhaps little more than the most accomplished, opulent, and powerful of religious orders, they were charged with spreading secret confraternities over France.* The greatness of the body became early so invidious as to be an obstacle to the advancement of their members; and it was generally believed that if Bellarmine had belonged to any other than the most powerful Order in Christendom, he would have been raised to the chair of Peter.† The Court of Rome itself, for whom they had sacrificed all, dreaded auxiliaries so potent that they might easily become masters; and these champions of the Papal monarchy were regarded with jealousy by Popes whose policy they aspired to dictate or control. But temporary circumstances at this time created a more than ordinary alienation between them.

In their original character of a force raised for the defence of the Church against the Lutherans, the Jesuits always devoted themselves to the temporal sovereign who was at the head of the Catholic party. They were attached to Philip II., at the time when Sextus V. dreaded his success; and they now placed their hopes on Louis XIV., in spite of his patronage, for a time, of the independent maxims of the Gallican Church.‡ On the other hand, Odeschalchi, who governed the Church under the name of Innocent XI., feared the growing power of France, resented the independence of the Gallican Church, and was, to the last degree, exasperated by the insults offered to him in his capital by the command of Louis. He was born in the Spanish province of Lombardy, and, as an Italian sovereign, he could not be indifferent to the bombardment of Genoa, and to the humiliation of that respectable republic, in the required public submission of the Doge at Versailles. As soon then as James became the pensioner and creature of Louis, the resentments of Odeschalchi prevailed over his zeal for the extension of the Church. The Jesuits had treated him and those of his predecessors who hesitated between them and their opponents with offensive liberty;* but while they bore sway at Versailles and St. James', they were, on that account, less obnoxious to the Roman Court. Men of wit remarked at Paris, that things would never go on well till the Pope became a Catholic, and King James a Huguenot.† Such were the intricate and dark combinations of opinions, passions, and interests which placed the Nuncio in opposition to the most potent Order of the Church, and completed the alienation of the British nation from James, by bringing on the party which now ruled his councils, the odious and terrible name of Jesuits.

CHAPTER VIII.

Declaration of Indulgence renewed.—Order that it should be read in Churches.—Deliberations of the Clergy.—Petition of the Bishops to the King.—Their examination before the Privy Council, Committal, Trial, and Acquittal.—Reflections.—Conversion of Sunderland.—Birth of the Prince of Wales.—State of Affairs.

When the changes in the secret councils of the King had rendered them most irreconcilable to the national sentiments, and when the general discontent produced by progressive encroachment had quietly grown into disaffection, nothing was wanting to the least unfortunate result of such an alienation, but that an infatuated Government should exhibit to the public thus disposed one of those tragic spectacles of justice violated, of religion menaced, of innocence oppressed, of unarmed dignity outraged, with all the conspicuous solemnities of abused law, in the persons of men of exalted rank and venerated functions who encounter wrongs and indignities with mild intrepidity. Such scenes, performed before a whole nation, revealed to each man the hidden thoughts of his fellow citizens, added the warmth of personal feeling to the strength of public principle, animated patriotism by the pity and indignation which the sufferings of good men call forth, and warmed every heart by the reflection of the same passions from the hearts of thousands; until at length the enthusiasm of a nation, springing up in the bosoms of the generous and brave, breathed a momentary spirit into the most vulgar souls, and dragged

* Montlosier Mémoire à consulter (Paris, 1826), pp. 20, 22,—quoted only to prove that such accusations were made.

† Bayle, article "Bellarmine."

‡ Bayle, Nouvelles de la République des Lettres, April, 1686. "Aujourd'hui plus attachés à la France qu'à l'Espagne."—Ibid. Nov. They were charged with giving secret intelligence to Louis XIV. of the state of the Spanish Netherlands. The French Jesuits suspended for a year the execution of the Pope's order to remove Father Maimbourg from their society, in consequence of a direction from the King.

* Ibid., Oct. and Nov.

† "Le chevalier de Silleri,
En parlant de ce Pape-ci,
Souhaitoit, pour la paix publique,
Qu'il se fût rendu Catholique,
Et le roi Jacques Huguenot."
La Fontaine to the Duc de Vendome.

Racine (Prologue to Esther) expresses the same sentiments in a milder form :—

"Et l'enfer, couvrant tout de ses vapeurs funèbres,
Sur les yeux les plus saints a jeté les ténèbres."

into its service the herd of the selfish, the cold, the mean, and the cowardly. The combustibles were accumulated; a spark was only wanting to kindle the flame. Accidents in themselves trivial, seem on this occasion, as in other times and countries, to have filled up the measure of provocation. In such a government as that of James, formed of adverse parties, more intent on weakening or supplanting each other than on securing their common foundation, every measure was too much estimated by its bearing on these unavowed objects, to allow a calm consideration of its effect on the interest or even on the temper of the public.

On the 27th of April, the King republished his Declaration of the former year for Liberty of Conscience;—a measure, apparently insignificant,* which was probably proposed by Sunderland, to indulge his master in a harmless show of firmness, which might divert him from rasher councils.† To this Declaration a supplement was annexed, declaring, that the King was confirmed in his purpose by the numerous addresses which had assured him of the national concurrence; that he had removed all civil and military officers who had refused to co-operate with him; and that he trusted that the people would do their part, by the choice of fit members to serve in Parliament, which he was resolved to assemble in November "at farthest." This last, and only important part of the Proclamation, was promoted by the contending parties in the Cabinet with opposite intentions. The moderate Catholics, and Penn, whose fault was only an unseasonable zeal for a noble principle, desired a Parliament from a hope, that if its convocation were not too long delayed, it might produce a compromise, in which the King might for the time be contented with an universal toleration of worship. The Jesuitical party also desired a Parliament; but it was because they hoped that it would produce a final rupture, and a recurrence to those more vigorous means which the age of the King now required, and the safety of which the expected birth of a Prince of Wales appeared to warrant.‡ Sunderland acquiesced in the insertion of this pledge, because he hoped to keep the violent in check by the fear of the Parliament, and partly, also, because he by no means had determined to redeem the pledge. "This language is held," said he to Barillon (who was alarmed at the sound of a Parliament), "rather to show, that Parliament will not meet for six months, than that it will be then assembled, which must depend on the public temper at that time."§ For so far, it seems, did this ingenious statesman carry his system of liberal interpretation, that he employed words in the directly opposite sense to that in which they were understood. So jarring were the motives from which this Declaration proceeded, and so opposite the constructions of which its authors represented it to be capable. Had no other step, however, been taken but the publication, it is not probable that it would have been attended by serious consequences.

But in a week afterwards, an Order was made by the King in Council, commanding the Declaration to be read at the usual time of divine service, in all the churches in London on the 20th and 27th of May, and in all those in the country on the 3d and 10th of June.* Who was the adviser of this Order, which has acquired such importance from its immediate effects, has not yet been ascertained. It was publicly disclaimed by Sunderland,† but at a time which would have left no value to his declaration, but what it might derive from being uncontradicted; and it was agreeable to the general tenor of his policy. It now appears, however, that he and other counsellors disavowed it at the time; and they seem to have been believed by keen and watchful observers. Though it was then rumoured that Petre had also disavowed this fatal advice, the concurrent testimony of all contemporary historians ascribe it to him; and it accords well with the policy of that party, which received in some degree from his ascendant over them the unpopular appellation of Jesuits. It must be owned, indeed, that it was one of the numerous cases in which the evil effects of an imprudent measure proved far greater than any foresight could have apprehended. There was considerable reason for expecting submission from the Church.

The clergy had very recently obeyed a similar order in two obnoxious instances. In compliance with an Order made in Council by Charles II. (officiously suggested to him, it is said, by Sancroft himself),‡ they had read from their pulpits that Prince's apology for the dissolution of his two last Parliaments, severally arraigning various Parliamentary proceedings, and among others a Resolution of the House of Commons against the persecution of the Protestant Dissenters.§ The compliance of the clergy on this occasion was cheerful, though they gave offence by it to many of the people.‖ Now, this seemed to be an open interference of the ecclesiastical order in the fiercest contests of political

* "The Declaration, so long spoken of, is published. As nothing is said more than last year, politicians cannot understand the reason of so ill-timed a measure."—Van Citters, 11th May. (Secret Despatch.) MS.

† Barillon, 6th May.—MS.

‡ Burnett, vol. iii. p. 211.

§ Barillon 13th May.—MS.

* Letter from the Hague, 28th March, 1689.—MS.

† Johnstone, 23d May.—MS. "Sunderland, Melfont, Penn, and, *they say*, Petre, deny having advised this Declaration." But Van Citters, (25th May), says that Petre is believed to have advised the order.

‡ Burnet, vol. iii. p. 212.

§ London Gazette, 7th—11th April, 1681.

‖ Kennet, History, vol. iii. p. 388. Echard, History of England, vol. iii. p. 625

parties, which the duty of undistinguishing obedience alone could warrant.* The same principle appears still more necessary to justify their reading the Declaration of Charles on the Rye House Plot,† published within a week of the death of Lord Russell; when it was indecent for the ministers of religion to promulgate their approval of bloodshed, and unjust to inflame prejudice against those who remained to be tried. This Declaration had been immediately preceded by the famous decree of the University of Oxford, and had been followed by a persecution of the Nonconformists, on whom it reflected as the authors of the supposed conspiracy.‡ These examples of compliance appeared to be grounded on the undefined authority claimed by the King, as supreme ordinary, on the judicial determinations, which recognised his right in that character to make ordinaries for the outward rule of the Church,§ and on the rubric of the Book of Common Prayer (declared, by the Act of Uniformity,‖ to be a part of that statute), which directs, "that nothing shall be published in church by the minister, but what is prescribed by this book, or enjoined by the King." These reasonings and examples were at least sufficient to excuse the confidence with which some of the Royal advisers anticipated the obedience either of the whole Church, or of so large a majority as to make it safe and easy to punish the disobedient.

A variation from the precedents of a seemingly slight and formal nature seems to have had some effect on the success of the measure. The bishops were now, for the first time, commanded by the Order published in the Gazette to distribute the Declaration in their dioceses, in order to its being read by the clergy. Whether the insertion of this unusual clause was casual, or intended to humble the bishops, it is now difficult to conjecture: it was naturally received and represented in the most offensive sense.¶ It fixed the eyes of the whole nation on the prelates, rendering the conduct of their clergy visibly dependent solely on their determination, and thus concentrating, on a small number, the dishonour of submission which would have been lost by dispersion among the whole body. So strongly did the belief that insult was intended prevail, that Petre, to whom it was chiefly ascribed, was said to have declared it in the gross and contumelious language used of old, by a barbarous invader, to the deputies of a besieged city.* But though the menace be imputed to him by most of his contemporaries,† yet, as they were all his enemies, and as no ear-witness is quoted, we must be content to be doubtful whether he actually uttered the offensive words, or was only so generally imprudent as to make it easily so believed.

The first effect of this Order was to place the prelates who were then in the capital or its neighbourhood in a situation of no small perplexity. They must have been still more taken by surprise than the more moderate ministers; and, in that age of slow conveyance and rare publication, they were allowed only sixteen days from the Order, and thirteen from its official publication,‡ to ascertain the sentiments of their brethren and of their clergy, without the knowledge of which their determination, whatever it was, might promote that division which it was one of the main objects of their enemies, by this measure, to excite. Resistance could be formidable only if it were general. It is one of the severest tests of human sagacity to call for instantaneous judgment from a few leaders when they have not support enough to be assured of the majority of their adherents. Had the bishops taken a single step without concert, they would have been assailed by charges of a pretension to dictatorship,—equally likely to provoke the proud to desertion, and to furnish the cowardly with a pretext for it. Their difficulties were increased by the character of the most distinguished laymen whom it was fit to consult. Rochester was no longer trusted: Clarendon was zealous, but of small judgment: and both Nottingham, the chief of their party, and Halifax, with whom they were now compelled to coalesce, hesitated at the moment of decision.§

The first body whose judgment was to be ascertained was the clergy of London, among whom were, at that time, the lights and ornaments of the Church. They at first ventured only to converse and correspond privately with each other.‖ A meeting be-

* It was accompanied by a letter from the King to Sancroft, which seems to imply a previous usage in such cases. "Our will is, that you give such directions as have been usual in such cases for the reading of our said Declaration."—Kennet, suprà. Note from Lambeth MSS. D'Oyley, Life of Sancroft, vol. i. p. 253. "Now," says Ralph, (vol. i. p. 590), "the cry of Church and King was echoed from one side of the kingdom to the other." Immediately after began the periodical libels of L'Estrange, and the invectives against Parliament, under the form of loyal addresses.

† London Gazette, 2d—6th August, 1683. Kennet, vol. iii. p. 408. Echard, vol. iii. p. 695.

‡ This fact is reluctantly admitted by Roger North. Examen, p. 369.

§ Cro. Jac. p. 87.

‖ 14 Car. II. chap. 4.

¶ Van Citters, 15th—25th May. MS. One of the objections was, that the Order was not transmitted in the usual and less ostentatious manner, through the Primate, as in 1681.

* Rabshekah, the Assyrian general, to the officers of Hezekiah, 2 Kings, xviii. 27.

† Burnet, Echard, Oldmixon, Ralph. The earliest printed statement of this threat is probably in a pamphlet, called, "An Answer from a Country Clergyman to the Letter of his Brother in the City" (Dr. Sherlock), which must have been published in June, 1668.—Baldwin's Farther State Tracts, p. 314. (London, 1692.)

‡ London Gazette, 7th April.

§ "Halifax and Nottingham wavered at first, which had almost ruined the business."—Johnstone, 27th May. MS.

‖ Van Citters, 28th May. (Secret Despatch.)—MS.

came necessary, and was hazarded. A diversity of opinions prevailed. It was urged on one side that a refusal was inconsistent with the professions and practice of the Church; that it would provoke the King to desperate extremities, expose the country to civil confusions, and be represented to the Dissenters as a proof of the incorrigible intolerance of the Establishment; that the reading of a Proclamation implied no assent to its contents; and that it would be presumption in the clergy to pronounce a judgment against the legality of the Dispensing Power, which the competent tribunal had already adjudged to be lawful. Those of better spirit answered, or might have answered, that the danger of former examples of obsequiousness was now so visible that they were to be considered as warnings rather than precedents; that compliance would bring on them command after command, till at last another religion would be established; that the reading, unnecessary for the purpose of publication, would be understood as an approval of the Declaration by the contrivers of the Order, and by the body of the people; that the Parliamentary condemnations of the Dispensing Power were a sufficient reason to excuse them from a doubtful and hazardous act; that neither conscience nor the more worldly principle of honour would suffer them to dig the grave of the Protestant Church, and to desert the cause of the nobility, the gentry, and the whole nation; and finally, that in the most unfavourable event, it was better to fall then under the King's displeasure, when supported by the consolation of having fearlessly performed their duty, than to fall a little later unpitied and despised, amid the curses of that people whom their compliance had ruined. From such a fall they would rise no more.* One of those middle courses was suggested which is very apt to captivate a perplexed assembly:—it was proposed to gain time, and smooth a way to a compromise, by entreating the King to revert to the ancient methods of communicating his commands to the Church. The majority appeared at first to lean towards submission, or evasion, which was only disguised and deferred submission; when, happily, a decisive answer was produced to the most plausible argument of the compliant party. Some of the chief ministers and laymen among the Nonconformists earnestly besought the clergy not to judge them by a handful of their number who had been gained by the Court, but to be assured that, instead of being alienated from the Church, they would be drawn closer to her, by her making a stand for religion and liberty.† A clergyman present read a note of these generous declarations, which he was authorized by the Nonconformists to exhibit to the meeting. The independent portion of the clergy made up, by zeal and activity, for their inferiority in numbers. Fatal concession, however, seemed to be at hand, when the spirit of an individual, manifested at a critical moment, contributed to rescue his order from disgrace, and his country from slavery. This person, whose fortunate virtue has hitherto remained unknown, was Dr. Edward Fowler, then incumbent of a parish in London, who, originally bred a Dissenter, had been slow to conform at the Restoration, was accused of the crime of Whiggism* at so dangerous a period as that of Monmouth's riot, and, having been promoted to the See of Gloucester, combined so much charity with his unsuspected orthodoxy as to receive the last breath of Firmin, the most celebrated Unitarian of that period.† When Fowler perceived that the courage of his brethren faltered, he addressed them shortly:—"I must be plain. There has been argument enough: more only will heat us. Let every man now say 'Yea' or 'Nay.' I shall be sorry to give occasion to schism, but I cannot in conscience read the Declaration; for that reading would be an exhortation to my people to obey commands which I deem unlawful." Stillingfleet declared, on the authority of lawyers, that reading the Declaration would be an offence, as the publication of an unlawful document; but excused himself from being the first subscriber to an agreement not to comply, on the ground that he was already proscribed for the prominent part which he had taken in the controversy against the Romanists. Patrick offered to be the first, if any man would second him; and Fowler answered to the appeal which his own generosity had called forth.‡ They were supported by Tillotson, though only recovering from an attack of apoplexy, and by Sherlock, who then atoned for the slavish doctrines of former times. The opposite party were subdued by this firmness, declaring that they would not divide the Church:§ and the sentiments of more than fourscore of the London clergy‖ were made known to the Metropolitan.

At a meeting at Lambeth, on Saturday, the 12th of May, where there were present, besides Sancroft himself, only the Earl of Clarendon, three bishops, Compton, Turner, and White, together with Tenison, it was resolved not to read the Declaration, to petition the King that he would dispense with that act of obedience, and to entreat all the prelates within reach of London, to repair thither to the aid of their brethren.¶ It was fit to wait a short time for the concurrence of these absent bishops. Lloyd of St. Asaph, late of Chichester, Ken of Bath and Wells, and Trelawney, quickly complied with the

* Sherlock's "Letter from a Gentleman in the City to a Friend in the Country."-Baldwin, p. 309.

† Johnstone, 18th May.—MS.

* Athenæ Oxonienses, vol. ii. p. 1029.

† Birch, Life of Tillotson, p. 320.

‡ Kennet, vol. iii. p. 570, note. This narrative reconciles Johnstone, Van Citters, and Kennet.

§ Johnstone, 23d May.—MS.

‖ This victory was early communicated to the Dutch ambassador. Van Citters, 25th May.—MS.

¶ Clarendon, 12th May.

summons; and were present at another and more decisive meeting at the archiepiscopal palace on Friday, the 18th, where, with the assent of Tillotson, Stillingfleet, Patrick, Tenison, Grove, and Sherlock, it was resolved, that a Petition, prepared and written by Sancroft, should be forthwith presented to His Majesty. It is a calumny against the memory of these prelates to assert, that they postponed their determination till within two days of the Sunday appointed for reading the Declaration, in order to deprive the King of time to retire from his purpose with dignity or decency: for we have seen that the period since the publication of the Order was fully occupied by measures for concert and cooperation; and it would have been treachery to the Church and the kingdom to have sacrificed any portion of time so employed to relieve their most formidable enemy.* The Petition, after setting forth that "their averseness to read the King's Declaration arose neither from want of the duty and obedience which the Church of England had always practised, nor from want of tenderness to Dissenters, to whom they were willing to come to such a temper as might be thought fit in Parliament and Convocation, but because it was founded in a Dispensing Power declared illegal in Parliament; and that they could not in prudence or conscience make themselves so far parties to it as the publication of it in the church at the time of divine service must amount to in common and reasonable construction," concludes, by "humbly and earnestly beseeching His Majesty not to insist on their distributing and reading the said Declaration." It is easy to observe the skill with which the Petition distinguished the case from the two recent examples of submission, in which the Royal declarations, however objectionable, contained no matter of questionable legality. Compton, being suspended, did not subscribe the Petition; and Sancroft, having had the honour to be forbidden the Court nearly two years, took no part in presenting it. Nor was it thought proper that the private divines, who were the most distinguished members of the meeting, should attend the presentation.

With no needless delay, six Bishops proceeded to Whitehall about ten o'clock in the evening,—no unusual hour of audience at the accessible courts of Charles and James. They were remarked, as they came from the landing-place, by the watchful eyes of the Dutch ambassador,* who was not uninformed of their errand. They had remained at the house of Lord Dartmouth, till Lloyd of St. Asaph, the boldest of their number, should ascertain when and where the King would receive them. He requested Lord Sunderland to read the Petition, and to acquaint the King with its contents, that His Majesty might not be surprised at it. The wary minister declined, but informed the King of the attendance of the Bishops, who were then introduced into the bedchamber.† When they had knelt down before the monarch, St. Asaph presented the Petition, purporting to be that "of the Archbishop of Canterbury, with divers suffragan bishops of his province, in behalf of themselves and several of their absent brethren, and of the clergy of their respective dioceses." The King, having been told by the Bishop of Chester, that they would desire no more than a recurrence to the former practice of sending Declarations to chancellors and archdeacons,‡ desired them to rise, and received them at first graciously, saying, on opening the Petition, "This is my Lord of Canterbury's handwriting;" but when he read it over, and after he had folded it up, he spoke to them in another tone:§—"This is a great surprise to me. Here are strange words. I did not expect this from you. This is a standard of rebellion." St. Asaph replied, "We have adventured our lives for Your Majesty, and would lose the last drop of our blood rather than lift up a finger against you." The King continued:—"I tell you this is a standard of rebellion. I never saw such an address." Trelawney of Bristol, falling again on his knees, said, "Rebellion, Sir! I beseech your Majesty not to say any thing so hard of us. For God's sake, do not believe we are or can be guilty of rebellion." It deserves remark, that the two who uttered these loud and vehement protestations were the only prelates present who were conscious of having harboured projects of more decisive resistance. The Bishops of Chichester and Ely made professions of unshaken loy-

* Life of James II., vol. ii. p. 158. But this is the statement, not of the King, but of Mr. Dicconson the compiler, who might have been misled by the angry traditions of his exiled friends. A week is added to the delay, by referring the commencement of it to the Declaration of the 27th of April, instead of the Order of the 4th of May, which alone called on the bishops to deliberate. The same suppression is practised, and the same calumny insinuated, in "An Answer to the Bishops' Petition," published at the time.—Somers' Tracts, vol. ix. p. 119. In the extract made, either by Carte or Macpherson, an insinuation against the bishops is substituted for the bold charge made by Dicconson. "The bishops' petition on the 18th of May, against what they are to read on the 20th"—(Macpherson, Original Papers, vol. i. p. 151.) But as throughout that inaccurate publication no distinction is made between what was written by James, and what was added by his biographer, the disgrace of the calumnious insinuation is unjustly thrown on the Kings' memory.

* Van Citters, 28th May.—MS.

† Gutch, Collectanea Curiosa, vol. i. p. 335. Clarendon, State Papers, vol. i. p. 287, and D'Oyley, vol. i. p. 263.

‡ Burnet, iii. 216.

§ "S. M. rispose loro con ardezza."—D'Adda, 30th May; or, as the same circumstance was viewed by another through a different medium,—"The King answered very disdainfully, and with the utmost anger."—Van Citters, 1st June. The mild Evelyn (Diary, 18th May) says, "the King was so incensed, that, with threatening language, he commanded them to obey at their peril."

alty, which they afterwards exemplified. The Bishop of Bath and Wells pathetically and justly said, "Sir, I hope you will give that liberty to us, which you allow to all mankind." He piously added, "We will honour the King, but fear God." James answered at various times, "It tends to rebellion. Is this what I have deserved from the Church of England? I will remember you who have signed this paper. I will keep this paper: I will not part with it. I did not expect this from you, especially from some of you. I will be obeyed." Ken, in the spirit of a martyr, answered only with a humble voice, "God's will be done." The angry monarch called out, "What's that?" The Bishop, and one of his brethren, repeated what had been said. James dismissed them with the same unseemly, unprovoked, and incoherent language:—"If I think fit to alter my mind, I will send to you. God has given me this Dispensing Power, and I will maintain it. I tell you, there are seven thousand men, and of the Church of England too, that have not bowed the knee to Baal." Next morning, when on his way to chapel, he said to the Bishop of St. David's, "My Lord, your brethren presented to me, yesterday, the most seditious paper that ever was penned. It is a trumpet of rebellion." He frequently repeated what Lord Halifax said to him,—"Your father suffered for the Church, not the Church for him."*

The Petition was printed and circulated during the night, certainly not by the Bishops, who delivered to the King their only copy, written in the hand of Sancroft, for the express purpose of preventing publication,—probably, therefore, by some attendant of the Court, for lucre or from disaffection. In a few days, six other prelates† had declared their concurrence in the Petition; and the Bishop of Carlisle agreed to its contents, lamenting that he could not subscribe it, because his diocese was not in the province of Canterbury:‡ two others agreed to the measure of not reading.§ The archbishopric of York had now been kept vacant for Petre more than two years; and the vacancy which delivered Oxford from Parker had not yet been filled up. Lloyd of Bangor, who died a few months afterwards, was probably prevented by age and infirmities from taking any part in this transaction. The see of Lichfield, though not vacant, was deserted by Wood, who (having been appointed by the Duchess of Cleveland, in consequence of his bestowing his neice, a rich heiress, of whom he was guardian, on one of her sons,)‖ had openly and perpetually abandoned his diocese: for this he had been suspended by Sancroft, and though restored on submission, had continued to reside at Hackney, without professing to discharge any duty, till his death. Sprat, who would have honoured the episcopal dignity by his talents, if he had not earned it by a prostitution of them,* Cartwright, who had already approved himself the ready instrument of lawless power against his brethren, Crewe, whose servility was rendered more conspicuously disgraceful by birth and wealth, Watson, who, after a long train of offences, was at length deprived of his see, together with Croft, in extreme old age, and Barlow, who had fallen into second childhood, were, since the death of Parker, the only faithless members of an episcopal body, which in its then incomplete state amounted to twenty-two.

On Sunday, the 20th, the first day appointed for reading the Declaration in London, the Order was generally disobeyed; though the administration of the diocese during the suspension of the bishop, was placed in the perfidious hands of Sprat and Crewe. Out of a hundred, the supposed number of the London clergy at that time, seven were the utmost who are, by the largest account, charged with submission.† Sprat himself chose to officiate as Dean in Westminster Abbey, where, as soon as he gave orders for the reading, so great a murmur arose that nobody could hear it; and, before it was finished, no one was left in the church but a few prebendaries, the choristers, and the Westminster scholars. He, himself, could hardly hold the Proclamation in his hands for trembling.‡ Even in the chapel at Whitehall, it was read by a chorister.§ At Serjeant's Inn, on the Chief Justice desiring that it should be read, the clerk said that he had forgotten it.‖ The names of four complying clergymen only are preserved,—Elliott, Martin, Thomson, and Hall,—who, obscure as they were, may be enumerated as specimens of so rare a vice as the sinister courage which, for base ends, can brave the most generous feelings of all the spectators of their conduct. The temptation on this occasion seems to have been the bishopric of Oxford; in the pursuit of which, Hall, who had been engaged in negotiations with the Duchess of Portsmouth for the purchase of Hampden's pardon,¶ by such connections and services prevailed over his competitors. On the following Sunday the disobedience was equally general; and the new reader at the Chapel Royal was so agitated as to be unable to read the Declara-

* Van Citters, 1st June.—MS.

† London, Norwich, Gloucester, Salisbury, Winchester, and Exeter.—D'Oyley, vol. i. p. 269.

‡ Gutch, vol. i. p. 334.

§ Llandaff and Worcester.—Gutch, vol. i. p. 331.

‖ Kennet in Lansdowne MSS. in the British Museum.—D'Oyley, vol. i. p. 193.

* Narrative of the Rye House Plot.

† "La lettura non se essequì che in pochissimi luoghi." D'Adda, 30th May.—MS. Clarendon states the number to be four; Kennet and Burnet, seven. Perhaps the smaller number refers to parochial clergy, and the larger to those of every denomination.

‡ Burnet, vol. iii. p. 218, note by Lord Dartmouth, then present as a Westminster scholar.

§ Evelyn, 20th May.

‖ Van Citters, suprà.—MS.

¶ Lords' Journals, 19th Dec. 1689

tion audibly.* In general, the clergy of the country displayed the same spirit. In the dioceses of the faithful bishops, the example of the diocesan was almost universally followed; in that of Norwich, which contains twelve hundred parishes, the Declaration was not read by more than three or four.† In Durham, on the other side, Crewe found so great a number of his poor clergy more independent than a vast revenue could render himself, that he suspended many for disobedience. The other deserters were disobeyed by nineteen twentieths of their clergy; and not more than two hundred in all are said to have complied out of a body of ten thousand.‡ "The whole Church," says the Nuncio, "espouses the cause of the Bishops. There is no reasonable expectation of a division among the Anglicans, and our hopes from the Nonconformists are vanished."§ Well, indeed, might he despair of the Dissenters, since, on the 20th of May, the venerable Baxter, above sectarian interests, and unmindful of ancient wrongs, from his tolerated pulpit extolled the Bishops for their resistance to the very Declaration to which he now owed the liberty of commending them.‖

It was no wonder that such an appearance of determined resistance should disconcert the Government. No prospect now remained of seducing some, and of punishing other Protestants, and, by this double example, of gaining the greater part of the rest. The King, after so many previous acts of violence, seemed to be reduced to the alternative of either surrendering to exasperated antagonists, or engaging in a mortal combat with all his Protestant subjects. In the most united and vigorous government, the choice would have been among the most difficult which human wisdom is required to make. In the distracted councils of James, where secret advisers thwarted responsible ministers, and fear began to disturb the judgment of some, while anger inflamed the minds of others, a still greater fluctuation and contradiction prevailed, than would have naturally arisen from the great difficulty of the situation. Pride impelled the King to advance; Caution counselled him to retreat; Calm Reason, even at this day, discovers nearly equal dangers in either movement. It is one of the most unfortunate circumstances in human affairs, that the most important questions of practice either perplex the mind so much by their difficulty, as to be always really decided by temper, or excite passions too strong for such an undisturbed exercise of the understanding as alone affords a probability of right judgment. The nearer approach of perils, both political and personal, rendered the counsels of Sunderland more decisively moderate;* in which he was supported by the Catholic lords in office, conformably to their uniform principles,† and by Jeffreys, who, since he had gained the prize of ambition, began more and more to think of safety.‡ It appears, also, that those who recoiled from an irreparable breach with the Church, the nation, and the Protestants of the Royal Family, were now not unwilling that their moderation should be known. Jeffreys spoke to Lord Clarendon of "moderate counsels," declared, that "some men would drive the King to destruction," and made professions of "service to the Bishops," which he went so far as to desire him to communicate to them. William Penn, on a visit, after a very long interval, to Clarendon, betrayed an inquietude, which sometimes prompts men almost instinctively to acquire or renew friendships.§ Sunderland disclosed the nature and grounds of his own counsels, very fully, both to the Nuncio and to the French ambassador.‖ "The great question," he said, "was how the punishment of the Bishops would affect the probability of accomplishing the King's purpose through a Parliament. Now, it was not to be expected, that any adequate penalty could be inflicted on them in the ordinary course of law. Recourse must be had to the Ecclesiastical Commission, which was already sufficiently obnoxious. Any legal proceeding would be long enough, in the present temper of men, to agitate all England. The suspension or deprivation by the Ecclesiastical Commissioners, which might not exclude the Bishops from their Parliamentary seats, would, in a case of so extensive delinquency, raise such a fear and cry of arbitrary power, as to render all prospect of a Parliament desperate, and to drive the King to a reliance on arms alone;—a fearful resolution, not to be entertained without fuller assurance that the army was and would remain untainted." He therefore advised, that "His Majesty should content himself with publishing a declaration, expressing his high and just resentment at the hardihood of the Bishops, in disobeying the supreme head of their Church, and disputing a Royal prerogative recently recognised by all the judges of England; but stating that, in consideration of the fidelity of the Church of England in past times, from which these prelates had been the first to depart, his Majesty was desirous of treating their offence with clemency, and would refer their conduct to the consideration of the next Parliament, in the hope that their intermediate conduct might warrant entire for-

* Van Citters.—MS.
† D'Oyley, vol. i. p. 270.
‡ Van Citters, 25th June.—MS.
§ D'Adda, 11th June.—MS.
‖ Johnstone, 23d May.—MS.

* D'Adda and Barillon, 3d June.—MS.
† "Lords Powis, Arundel, Dover, and Bellasis, are very zealous for moderation."—Van Citters, 11th June.—MS.
‡ Clarendon, 14th and 27th June, 5th July, 13th August.
§ Clarendon, 21st May. "The first time I had seen him for a long time. He professed great kindness."
‖ D'Adda and Barillon, suprà.

giveness." It was said, on the other hand, "that the safety of the government depended on an immediate blow; that the impunity of such audacious contumacy would embolden every enemy at home and abroad; that all lenity would be regarded as the effect of weakness and fear; and that the opportunity must now or never be seized, of employing the Ecclesiastical Commission to strike down a Church, which supported the Crown only as long as she dictated to it, and became rebellious at the moment when she was forbidden to be intolerant." To strengthen these topics, it was urged "that the factions had already boasted that the Court would not dare to proceed juridically against the Bishops."

Both the prudent ministers, to whom these discussions were imparted, influenced probably by their wishes, expected that moderation would prevail.* But, after a week of discussion, Jeffreys, fearing that the King could not be reconciled to absolute forbearance, and desirous of removing the odium from the Ecclesiastical Commission, of which he was the head,† proposed that the Bishops should be prosecuted in the Court of King's Bench, and the consideration of mercy or rigour postponed till after judgment;—a compromise probably more impolitic than either of the extremes, inasmuch as it united a conspicuous and solemn mode of proceeding, and a form of trial partly popular, with room for the utmost boldness of defence, some probability of acquittal, and the least punishment in case of conviction. On the evening of the 27th, the second Sunday appointed for reading the Declaration, it was accordingly determined to prosecute them; and they were summoned to appear before the Privy Council on the 8th of June, to answer a charge of misdemeanour.

In obedience to this summons, the Bishops attended at Whitehall on the day appointed, about five o'clock in the afternoon, and being called into the Council Chamber, were graciously received by the King. The Chancellor asked the Archbishop, whether a paper now shown to him was the Petition written by him, and presented by the other Bishops to his Majesty. The Archbishop, addressing himself to the King, answered, "Sir, I am called hither as a criminal, which I never was before: since I have that unhappiness, I hope your Majesty will not be offended that I am cautious of answering questions which may tend to accuse myself." The King called this chicanery; adding, "I hope you will not deny your own hand." The Archbishop said, "The only reason for the question is to draw an answer which may be ground of accusation;" and Lloyd, of St. Asaph, added, "All divines of all Christian churches are agreed that no man in our situation is obliged to answer such questions:" but the King impatiently pressing for an answer, the Archbishop said, "Sir, though not obliged to answer, yet, if Your Majesty commands it, we are willing to obey, trusting to your justice and generosity that we shall not suffer for our obedience." The King said he should not command them, and Jeffreys directed them to withdraw. On their return, being commanded by the King to answer, they owned the Petition. There is some doubt whether they repeated the condition on which they made their first offer of obedience;* but, if they did not, their forbearance must have arisen from a respectful confidence, which disposed them, with reason, to consider the silence of the King as a virtual assent to their unretracted condition. A tacit acceptance of conditional obedience is indeed as distinct a promise to perform the condition as the most express words. They were then again commanded to withdraw; and on their return a third time, they were told by Jeffreys that they would be proceeded against, "but," he added (alluding to the obnoxious Commission), "with all fairness, in Westminister Hall." He desired them to enter into a recognisance (or legal engagement) to appear. They declared their readiness to answer, whenever they were called upon, without it, and, after some conversation, insisted on their privilege as Peers not to be bound by a recognisance in misdemeanour. After several ineffectual attempts to prevail on them to accept the offer of being discharged on their own recognisances, as a favour, they were committed to the Tower by a warrant, which all the Privy Councillors present (except Lord Berkeley and Father Petre) subscribed; of whom it is observable, that nine only were avowed Catholics, and nine professed members of the English Church, besides Sunderland, whose renunciation of that religion was not yet made public.† The Order for the prosecution was, however, sanctioned in the usual manner, by placing the names of all Privy Councillors present at its head.

The people who saw the Bishops as they walked to the barges which were to conduct

* D'Adda and Barillon, 11th June.—MS.

† Van Citters, 11th June.—MS. The biographer of James II. (Life, vol. ii. p. 158,) tells us that the Chancellor advised the King to prosecute the Bishops for tumultuous petitioning, ignorantly supposing the statute passed at the Restoration against such petitioning to be applicable to their case. The passage in the same page, which quotes the King's own MSS., is more naturally referable to the secret advisers of the Order in Council. The account of Van Citters, adopted in the text, reconciles the Jacobite tradition followed by Dicconson with the language of Jeffreys to Clarendon, and with the former complaints of Catholics against his lukewarmness mentioned by Barillon.

* D'Oyley, (vol. i. p. 278,) seems on this point to vary from the narrative in Gutch (vol. i. p. 351.) It seems to me more probable that the condition was repeated after the second entrance; for Dr. D'Oyley is certainly right in thinking that the statement of the Archbishop's words, as having been spoken "after the third or fourth coming in," must be a mistake. It is evidently at variance with the whole course of the examination.

† Gutch, vol. i. p. 353.

them to the Tower, were deeply affected by the spectacle, and, for the first time, manifested their emotions in a manner which would have still served as a wholesome admonition to a wise Government. The demeanour of the Prelates is described by eye-witnesses as meek, composed, cheerful, betraying no fear, and untainted by ostentation or defiance, but endowed with a greater power over the fellow-feeling of the beholders by the exhortations to loyalty, which were doubtless uttered with undesigning sincerity by the greater number of the venerable sufferers.* The mode of conveyance, though probably selected for mere convenience, contributed to deepen and prolong the interest of the scene. The soldiers who escorted them to the shore had no need to make any demonstrations of violence; for the people were too much subdued by pity and reverence to vent their feelings otherwise than by tears and prayers. Having never before seen prelates in opposition to the King, and accustomed to look at them only in a state of pacific and inviolate dignity, the spectators regarded their fall to the condition of prisoners and the appearance of culprits with amazement, awe, and compassion. The scene seemed to be a procession of martyrs. "Thousands," says Van Citters, probably an eye-witness, "begged their blessing."† Some ran into the water to implore it. Both banks of the Thames were lined with multitudes, who, when they were too distant to be heard, manifested their feelings by falling down on their knees, and raising up their hands, beseeching Heaven to guard the sufferers for religion and liberty. On landing at the Tower, several of the guards knelt down to receive their blessing; while some even of the officers yielded to the general impulse. As the Bishops chanced to land at the accustomed hour of evening prayer, they immediately repaired to the chapel; where they heard, in the ordinary lesson of the day, a remarkable exhortation to the primitive teachers of Christianity, "to approve themselves the ministers of God, in much patience, in afflictions, in imprisonments."‡ The Court ordered the guard to be doubled.

On the following days multitudes crowded to the Tower,§ of whom the majority gazed on the prison with distant awe, while a few entered to offer homage and counsel to the venerable prisoners. "If it be a crime to lament," said a learned contemporary, in a confidential letter, "innumerable are the transgressors. The nobles of both sexes, as it were, keep their court at the Tower, whither a vast concourse daily go to beg the holy men's blessing. The very soldiers act as mourners."|| The soldiers on guard, indeed, drank their healths, and though reprimanded by Sir Edward Hales, now Lieutenant of the Tower, declared that they would persevere. The amiable Evelyn did not fail to visit them on the day previous to that on which he was to dine with the Chancellor, appearing to distribute his courtesies with the neutrality of Atticus;* but we now know that Jeffreys himself, on the latter of these days, had sent a secret message by Clarendon, assuring the Bishops that he was much troubled at the prosecution, and offering his services to them.† None of their visiters were more remarkable than a deputation of ten Nonconformist ministers, which so incensed the King that he personally reprimanded them; but they answered, that they could not but adhere to the Bishops, as men constant to the Protestant religion,—an example of magnanimity rare in the conflicts of religious animosities. The Dissenting clergy seem, indeed, to have been nearly unanimous in preferring the general interest of religious liberty to the enlargement of their peculiar privileges.‡ Alsop was full of sorrow for his compliances in the former year. Lobb, who was seized with so enthusiastic an attachment to James, that he was long after known by the singular name of the "Jacobite Independent," alone persevered in devotedness to the Court; and when the King asked his advice respecting the treatment of the Bishops, advised that they should be sent to the Tower.§

No exertion of friendship or of public zeal was wanting to prepare the means of their defence, and to provide for their dignity, in every part of the proceeding. The Bishop of London, Dr. Tennyson, and Johnstone, the secret agent of the Prince of Orange, appear to have been the most active of their friends. Pemberton and Pollexfen, accounted the most learned among the elder lawyers, were engaged in their cause. Sir John Holt, destined to be the chief ornament of a bench purified by liberty, contributed his valuable advice. John Somers, then in the thirty-eight year of his age, was objected to at one of their consultations, as too young and obscure to be one of their counsel; and, if we may believe Johnstone, it was owing to him that this memorable cause afforded the earliest opportunity of making known the superior intellect of that great man. Twenty-eight peers were prepared to bail them, if bail should be required.|| Stanley, chaplain to the Princess of Orange, had already assured Sancroft that the Prince and Princess approved their firmness, and were deeply interested in their fate.¶ One of them, probably Trelawney, a prelate who had served in the Civil War, had early told Johnstone that if they were sent to the Tower, he hoped the Prince of

* Reresby, p. 261. † 18th June.—MS.
‡ 2 Corinthians, vi. 4, 5.
§ Clarendon, 9th, 10th, 12th June.
|| Dr. Nelson, Gutch, vol. i. p. 360.

* Diary, 13th—14th June.
† Clarendon, 14th June.
‡ Johnstone, 13th June.—MS.
§ Johnstone, 13th June.—MS. "I told the Archbishop of Canterbury," says Johnstone, "that their fate depended on very mean persons."—Burnet, vol. iii. p. 217.
|| Gutch, vol. i. p. 357, where their names appear.
¶ Ibid. p. 307.

Orange would take them out, which two regiments and his authority would do;* and, a little later, the Bishop of St. Asaph assured the same trusty agent, who was then collecting the opinions of several eminent persons on the seasonableness of resistance, that "the matter would be easily done."† This bold Prelate had familiarised himself with extraordinary events, and was probably tempted to daring counsels by an overweening confidence in his own interpretation of mysterious prophecies, which he had long laboured to illustrate by vain efforts of ability and learning. He made no secret of his expectations; but, at his first interview with a chaplain of the Archbishop, exhorted him to be of good courage, and declared that the happiest results were now to be hoped; for that the people, incensed by tyranny, were ready to take up arms to expel the Papists from the kingdom, and to punish the King himself, which was to be deprecated, by banishment or death; adding, that if the Bishops escaped from their present danger, they would reform the Church from the corruptions which had crept into her frame, throw open her gates for the joyful entrance of the sober and pious among Protestant Dissenters, and relieve even those who should continue to be pertinacious in their Nonconformity from the grievous yoke of penal laws.‡ During the imprisonment, Sunderland and the Catholic lords, now supported by Jeffreys, used every means of art and argument to persuade James that the birth of the Prince of Wales (which will presently be related) afforded a most becoming opportunity for signalising that moment of national joy by a general pardon, which would comprehend the Bishops, without involving any apparent concession to them.§ The King, as usual, fluctuated. A Proclamation, couched in the most angry and haughty language, commanding all clergymen, under pain of immediate suspension, to read the Declaration, was several times sent to the press, and as often withdrawn.‖ "The King," said Jeffreys, "had once resolved to let the proceedings fall; but some men would hurry him to destruction."¶ The obstinacy of James, inflamed by bigoted advisers, and supported by commendation, with proffered aid from France, prevailed over sober counsels.

On the 15th of June, the prisoners were brought before the Court of King's Bench by a writ of Habeas Corpus. On leaving the Tower they refused to pay the fees required by Sir Edward Hales as lieutenant, whom they charged with discourtesy. He so far forgot himself as to say that the fees were a compensation for the irons with which he might have loaded them, and the bare walls and floor to which he might have confined their accommodation.* They answered, "We lament the King's displeasure; but every other man loses his breath who attempts to intimidate us." On landing from their barge, they were received with increased reverence by a great multitude, who made a lane for them, and followed them into Westminster Hall.† The Nuncio, unused to the slightest breath of popular feeling, was subdued by these manifestations of enthusiasm, which he relates with more warmth than any other contemporary. "Of the immense concourse of people," says he, "who received them on the bank of the river, the majority in their immediate neighbourhood were on their knees: the Archbishop laid his hands on the heads of such as he could reach, exhorting them to continue stedfast in their faith; they cried aloud that all should kneel, while tears flowed from the eyes of many.‡ In the court they were attended by the twenty-nine Peers who offered to be their sureties; and it was instantly filled by a crowd of gentlemen attached to their cause.

The return of the lieutenant of the Tower to the writ set forth that the Bishops were committed under a warrant signed by certain Privy Councillors for a seditious libel. The Attorney General moved, that the information should be read, and that the Bishops should be called on to plead, or, in common language, either to admit the fact, deny it, or allege some legal justification of it. The counsel for the Bishops objected to reading the information, on the ground that they were not legally before the court, because the warrant, though signed by Privy Councillors, was not stated to be issued by them in that capacity, and because the Bishops, being Peers of Parliament, could not lawfully be committed for a libel. The Court over-ruled these objections;—the first with evident justice, because the warrant of commitment set forth its execution at the Council Chamber, and in the presence of the King, which sufficiently showed it to be the act of the subscribing Privy Councillors acting as such,—the second, with much doubt touching the extent of privilege of Parliament, acknowledged on both sides to exempt from apprehension in all cases but treason, felony, and breach of the peace, which last term was said by the counsel for the Crown to comprehend all such constructive offences

* Johnstone, 27th May.—MS.

† Johnstone, 18th June.—MS. The Bishop's observation is placed between the opinions of Mr. Hampden and Sir J. Lee, both zealous for immediate action.

‡ Diary of Henry Wharton, 25th June, 1686. D'Oyley, vol. ii. p. 134. The term "ponteficious," which is rendered in the text by Papists, may perhaps be limited, by a charitable construction, to the more devoted partisans of Papal authority. "The Bishop of St. Asaph was a secret favourer of a foreign interest."—Life of Kettlewell, p. 175, compiled (London, 1718) from the papers of Hicks and Nelson.

§ Johnstone, 13th June.—MS.

‖ Van Citters, 8th June.—MS.

¶ Clarendon, 14th June.

* Johnstone, 18th June.—MS. See a more general statement to the same effect, in Evelyn's Diary, 29th June.

† Clarendon, 15th June.

‡ D'Adda, 22d June.—MS.

against the peace as libels, and argued on behalf of the Bishops, to be confined to those acts or threats of violence which, in common language, are termed "breaches of the peace." The greatest judicial authority on constitutional law since the accession of the House of Brunswick has pronounced the determination of the Judges in 1688 to be erroneous.* The question depends too much upon irregular usage and technical subtilties to be brought under the cognisance of the historian, who must be content with observing, that the error was not so manifest as to warrant an imputation of bad faith in the Judges. A delay of pleading till the next term, which is called an "imparlance," was then claimed. The officers usually referred to for the practice of the Court declared such for the last twelve years to have been that the defendants should immediately plead. Sir Robert Sawyer, Mr. Finch, Sir Francis Pemberton, and Mr. Pollexfen, bore a weighty testimony, from their long experience, to the more indulgent practice of the better times which preceded; but Sawyer, covered with the guilt of so many odious proceedings, Finch, who was by no means free from participation in them, and even Pemberton, who had the misfortune to be Chief Justice in evil days, seemed to contend against the practice of their own administration with a bad grace: the veteran Pollexfen alone, without fear of retaliation, appealed to the pure age of Sir Matthew Hale. The Court decided that the Bishops should plead; but their counsel considered themselves as having gained their legitimate object by showing that the Government employed means at least disputable against them.† The Bishops then pleaded "Not guilty," and were enlarged, on their own undertaking to appear on the trial, which was appointed for the 29th of June.

As they left the court they were surrounded by crowds, who begged their blessing. The Bishop of St. Asaph, detained in Palace Yard by a multitude, who kissed his hands and garments, was delivered from their importunate kindness by Lord Clarendon, who, taking him into his carriage, found it necessary to make a circuit through the Park to escape from the bodies of people by whom the streets were obstructed.‡ Shouts and huzzas broke out in the court, and were repeated all around at the moment of the enlargement. The bells of the Abbey Church of Westminster had begun to ring a joyful peal, when they were stopped by Sprat amidst the execrations of the people.* "No one knew," said the Dutch minister, "what to do for joy." When the Archbishop landed at Lambeth, the grenadiers of Lord Lichfield's regiment, though posted there by his enemies, received him with military honours, made a lane for his passage from the river to his palace, and fell on their knees to ask his blessing.† In the evening the premature joy at this temporary liberation displayed itself in bonfires, and in some outrages to Roman Catholics, as the supposed instigators of the prosecution.‡

No doubt was entertained at Court of the result of the trial, which the King himself took measures to secure by a private interview with Sir Samuel Astry, the officer whose province it was to form the jury.§ It was openly said that the Bishops would be condemned to pay large fines, to be imprisoned till payment, and to be suspended from their functions and revenues.|| A fund would thus be ready for the King's liberality to Catholic colleges and chapels; while the punishment of the Archbishop would remove the only licenser of the press¶ who was independent of the Crown. Sunderland still contended for the policy of being generous after victory, and of not seeking to destroy those who would be sufficiently degraded; and he believed that he had made a favourable impression on the King.** But the latter spoke of the feebleness which had disturbed the reign of his brother, and brought his father to the scaffold; and Barillon represents him as inflexibly resolved on rigour,†† which opinion seems to have been justified by the uniform result of every previous deliberation. Men of common understanding are much disposed to consider the contrary of the last unfortunate error as being always the sound policy; they are incapable of estimating the various circumstances which may render vigour or caution applicable at different times and in different stages of the same proceedings; and pursue their single maxim, often founded on shallow views, even of one case, with headlong obstinacy. If they be men also of irresolute nature, they are unable to resist the impetuosity of violent counsellors, they are prone to rid themselves of the pain

* Lord Camden in Wilkes' case, 1763.

† State Trials, vol. xii. p. 183. The general reader may be referred with confidence to the excellent abridgment of the State Trials, by Mr. Phillipps,—a work probably not to be paralleled by the union of discernment, knowledge, impartiality, calmness, clearness, and precision, it exhibits on questions the most angrily contested. It is, indeed, far superior to the huge and most unequal compilation of which it is an abridgment,—to say nothing of the instructive observations on legal questions in which Mr. Phillipps rejudges the determinations of past times.

‡ Clarendon, 15th June.

* Van Citters, 25th June.—MS.

† Johnstone, 18th June.—MS.

‡ Narcissus Luttrell, MS.; and the two last-mentioned authorities.

§ Clarendon, 21st—27th June, where an agent of the Court is said to have busied himself in striking the jury.

|| Barillon, 1st July.—MS. Van Citters, 2d July.—MS.

¶ It appears from Wharton's Diary, that the chaplains at Lambeth discharged this duty with more regard even then to the feelings of the King than to the rights of Protestant controversialists.

** D'Adda, 9th July.—MS.

†† Barillon, 1st July.—MS.

of fluctuation by a sudden determination to appear decisive, and they often take refuge from past fears, and seek security from danger to come, by a rash and violent blow. "Lord Sunderland," says Barillon, "like a good courtier and an able politician, every where vindicates, with warmth and vigour, the measures which he disapproved and had opposed."*

The Bishops, on the appointed day, entered the court, surrounded by the lords† and gentlemen who, on this solemn occasion, chose that mode of once more testifying their adherence to the public cause. Some previous incidents inspired courage. Levinz, one of the counsel retained, having endeavoured to excuse himself from an obnoxious duty, was compelled, by the threats of attorneys, to perform it. The venerable Serjeant Maynard, urged to appear for the Crown, in the discharge of his duty as King's Serjeant, boldly answered, that if he did he was bound also to declare his conscientious opinion of the case to the King's Judges.‡ The appearance of the bench was not consolatory to the accused. Powell was the only impartial and upright Judge. Allibone, as a Roman Catholic, was, in reality, about to try the question whether he was himself legally qualified for his office. Wright and Holloway were placed there to betray the law. Jeffreys himself, who had appointed the Judges, now loaded them with the coarsest reproaches,§—more, perhaps, from distrust of their boldness than from apprehension of their independence. Symptoms of the overawing power of national opinion are indeed perceptible in the speech of the Attorney-General, which was not so much the statement of an accusation as an apology for a prosecution. He disclaimed all attack on the Bishops in their episcopal character, and did not now complain of their refusal to read the King's Declaration; but only charged them with the temporal offence of composing and publishing a seditious libel, under pretence of presenting a humble petition to His Majesty. His doctrine on this head was, indeed, subversive of liberty; but it has often been repeated in better times, though in milder terms, and with some reservations. "The Bishops," said he, "are accused of censuring the government, and giving their opinion about affairs of State. No man may say of the great officers of the kingdom, far less of the King, that they act unreasonably, for that may beget a desire of reformation, and the last age will abundantly satisfy us whither such a thing does tend."

The first difficulty arose as to the proof of the handwriting, which seems to have been decisive against Sancroft, sufficient against some others, and altogether wanting in the cases of Ken and Lake. All the witnesses on this subject gave their testimony with the most evident reluctance. The Court was equally divided on the question whether there was sufficient proof of it to warrant the reading of the Petition in evidence against the accused. The objection to its being so read was groundless; but the answers to it were so feeble as to betray a general irresolution and embarrassment. The counsel for the Crown were then driven to the necessity of calling the clerk of the Privy Council to prove the confessions before that body, in obedience to the commands of the King. When they were proved, Pemberton, with considerable dexterity, desired the witness to relate all the circumstances which attended these confessions. Blathwaite, the clerk, long resisted, and evaded the question, of which he evidently felt the importance; but he was at length compelled to acknowledge that the Bishops had accompanied their offer to submit to the Royal command, with an expression of their hope that no advantage would be taken of their confession against them. He could not pretend that they had been previously warned against such a hope; but he eagerly added, that no promise to such an effect had been made,—as if chicanery could be listened to in a matter which concerned the personal honour of a sovereign. Williams, the only one of the counsel for the Crown who was more provoked than intimidated by the public voice, drew the attention of the audience to this breach of faith by the vehemence with which he resisted the admission of the evidence which proved it.

Another subtile question sprung from the principle of English law, that crimes are triable only in the county where they are committed. It was said that the alleged libel was written at Lambeth in Surrey, and not proved to have been published in Middlesex; so that neither of the offences charged could be tried in the latter county. That it could not have been written in Middlesex was proved by the Archbishop, who was the writer, having been confined by illness to his palace for some months. The prosecutor then endeavoured to show by the clerks of the Privy Council,* that the Bishops had owned the delivery of the Petition to the King, which would have been a publication in Middlesex: but the witnesses proved only an admission of the signatures. On every failure, the audience showed their feelings by a triumphant laugh or a shout of joy. The Chief Justice, who at first feebly repri-

* Barillon, 1st July.—MS.

† "Thirty-five lords."—(Johnstone, 2d July. MS.); probably about one half of the legally qualified peers then in England and able to attend. There were eighty-nine temporal lords who were Protestants. Minority, absence from the kingdom, and sickness, may account for nineteen.

‡ Johnstone, 2d July.—MS.

§ "Rogues," "Knaves," "Fools."—Clarendon, 27th June—5th July. He called Wright "a beast;" but this, it must be observed, was after his defeat.

* Pepys, the noted Secretary to the Admiralty, was one of the witnesses examined. He was probably a Privy Councillor.

manded them, soon abandoned the attempt to check them. In a long and irregular altercation, the advocates of the accused spoke with increasing boldness, and those for the prosecution with more palpable depression,—except Williams, who vented the painful consciousness of inconsistency, unvarnished by success, in transports of rage which descended to the coarsest railing. The Court had already, before the examination of the latter witnesses, determined that there was no evidence of publication; notwithstanding which, and the failure of these last, the Attorney and Solicitor General proceeded to argue that the case was sufficient,—chiefly, it would seem, to prolong the brawl till the arrival of Lord Sunderland, by whose testimony they expected to prove the delivery of the Petition to the King. But the Chief Justice, who could no longer endure such wearisome confusion, began to sum up the evidence to the Jury, whom, if he had adhered to his previous declarations, he must have instructed to acquit the accused. Finch, either distrusting the Jury, or excused, if not justified, by the Judge's character, by the suspicious solemnity of his professions of impartiality, and by his own too long familiarity with the darkest mysteries of state trials, suspected some secret design, and respectfully interrupted Wright, in order to ascertain whether he still thought that there was no sufficient proof of writing in Middlesex, or of publication any where. Wright, who seemed to be piqued, said, "he was sorry Mr. Finch should think him capable of not leaving it fairly to the Jury,"—scarcely containing his exultation over his supposed indiscretion.* Pollexfen requested the Judge to proceed; and Finch pressed his interruption no farther. But Williams, who, when Wright had began to sum up, countermanded his request for the attendance of Lord Sunderland as too late, seized the opportunity of this interruption to despatch a second message, urging him to come without delay, and begged the Court to suspend the summing up, as a person of great quality was about to appear who would supply the defects in the evidence,—triumphantly adding, that there was a fatality in this case. Wright then said to the accused's counsel, "You see what comes of the interruption; now we must stay." All the bystanders condemned Finch as much as he soon afterwards compelled them to applaud him. An hour was spent in waiting for Sunderland. It appears to have been during this fortunate delay that the Bishops' counsel determined on a defence founded on the illegality of the Dispensing Power, from which they had before been either deterred from an apprehension that they would not be suffered to question an adjudged point, or diverted at the moment by the prospect that the Chief Justice would sum up for an acquittal.* By this resolution, the verdict, instead of only insuring the escape of the Bishops, became a triumph of the constitution. At length Sunderland was carried through Westminster in a chair, the head of which was down;—no one saluting him, and the multitude hooting and hissing and crying out "Popish dog!" He was so disordered by this reception that when he came into court he trembled, changed colour, and looked down, as if fearful of the countenances of ancient friends, and unable to bear the contrast between his own disgraceful greatness and the honourable calamity of the Bishops. He only proved that the Bishops came to him with a petition, which he declined to read; and that he introduced them immediately to the King, to whom he had communicated the purpose for which they prayed an audience.

The general defence then began, and the counsel for the Bishops, without relinquishing their minor objections, arraigned the Dispensing Power, and maintained the right of petition with a vigour and boldness which entitles such of them as were only mere advocates to great approbation, and those among them who were actuated by higher principles to the everlasting gratitude of their country. When Sawyer began to question the legality of the Declaration, Wright, speaking aside, said, "I must not suffer them to dispute the King's power of suspending laws." Powell answered, "They must touch that point; for if the King had no such power (as clearly he hath not,) the Petition is no attack on the King's legal power, and therefore no libel." Wright peevishly replied, "I know you are full of that doctrine, but the Bishops shall have no reason to say I did not hear them. Brother, you shall have your way for once. I will hear them. Let them talk till they are weary." The substance of the argument was, that a Dispensing Power was unknown to the ancient constitution; that the Commons, in the reign of Richard II., had formally consented that the King should, with the assent of the Lords, exercise such a power respecting a single law till the next Parlia-

* "The C. J. said, 'Gentlemen, you do not know your own business; but since you will be heard, you shall be heard.'" Johnstone, 2d July.—MS. He seems to have been present, and, as a Scotchman, was not very likely to have invented so good an illustration of the future tense. It is difficult not to suspect that Wright, after admitting that there was no positive evidence of publication in Middlesex, did not intend to tell the Jury that there were circumstances proved from which they might reasonably infer the fact. The only circumstance, indeed, which could render it doubtful that he would lay down a doctrine so well founded, and so suitable to his purpose, at a time when he could no longer be contradicted, is the confusion which, on this trial, seems to have more than usually clouded his weak understanding.

† "They waited about an hour for Sunderland, which luckily fell out, for in this time the Bishops' lawyers recollected themselves, in order to what followed." A minute examination of the trial explains these words of Johnstone, and remarkably proves his accuracy. From the eagerness of Pollexfen that Wright should proceed with his address to the Jury, it is evident that they did not then intend to make the defence which was afterwards made.

ment;* that the acceptance of such a trust was a Parliamentary declaration against the existence of such a prerogative; that though there were many cases of dispensations from penalties granted to individuals, there never was an instance of a pretension to dispense with laws before the Restoration; that it was in the reign of Charles II. twice condemned by Parliament, twice relinquished, and once disclaimed by the Crown; that it was declared to be illegal by the House of Commons in their very last session; and finally, that the power to suspend was in effect a power to abrogate; that it was an assumption of the whole legislative authority, and laid the laws and liberties of the kingdom at the mercy of the King. Mr. Somers, whose research had supplied the ancient authorities quoted by his seniors, closed the defence in a speech admirable for a perspicuous brevity well adapted to the stage of the trial at which he spoke; in which, with a mind so unruffled by the passions which raged around him as even to preserve a beautiful simplicity of expression, — rarely reconcilable with anxious condensation, — he conveyed in a few luminous sentences the substance of all that had been dispersed over a rugged, prolix, and disorderly controversy. "My Lord, I would only mention the case respecting a dispensation from a statute of Edward VI., wherein all the judges determined that there never could be an abrogation or suspension (which is a temporary abrogation) of an Act of Parliament but by the legislative power. It was, indeed, disputed how far the King might dispense with the penalties of such a particular law, as to particular persons; but it was agreed by all that the King had no power to suspend any law. Nay, I dare venture to appeal to Mr. Attorney-General, whether, in the late case of Sir Edward Hales, he did not admit that the King could not suspend a law, but only grant a dispensation from its observance to a particular person. My Lord, by the law of all civilized nations, if the prince requires something to be done, which the person who is to do it takes to be unlawful, it is not only lawful, but his duty, *rescribere principi*,† — to petition the sovereign. This is all that is done here; and that in the most humble manner that could be thought of. Your Lordships will please to observe how far that humble caution went; how careful they were that they might not in any way justly offend the King: they did not interpose by giving advice as peers; they never stirred till it was brought home to themselves as bishops. When they made this Petition, all they asked was, that it might not be so far insisted on by his Majesty as to oblige them to read it. Whatever they thought of it, they do not take it upon them to desire the Declaration to be revoked. My Lord, as to the matters of fact alleged in the Petition, that they are perfectly true we have shown by the Journals of both Houses. In every one of those years which are mentioned in the Petition, this power was considered by Parliament, and upon debate declared to be contrary to law. There could then be no design to diminish the prerogative, for the King has no such prerogative. Seditious, my Lord, it could not be, nor could it possibly stir up sedition in the minds of the people, because it was presented to the King in private and alone; false it could not be, for the matter of it was true; there could be nothing of malice, for the occasion was not sought, but the thing was pressed upon them; and a libel it could not be, because the intent was innocent, and they kept within the bounds set up by the law that gives the subject leave to apply to his prince by petition when he is aggrieved."

The Crown lawyers, by whom this extensive and bold defence seems to have been unforeseen, manifested in their reply their characteristic faults. Powis was feebly technical, and Williams was offensively violent.* Both evaded the great question of the prerogative by professional common-places of no avail with the Jury or the public. They both relied on the usual topics employed by their predecessors and successors, that the truth of a libel could not be the subject of inquiry; and that the falsehood, as well as the malice and sedition charged by the information, were not matters of fact to be tried by the Jury, but qualifications applied by the law to every writing derogatory to the government. Both triumphantly urged that the Parliamentary proceedings of the last and present reign, being neither acts nor judgments of Parliament, were no proof of the illegality of what they condemned,— without adverting to the very obvious consideration that the Bishops appealed to them only as such manifestations of the sense of Parliament as it would be imprudent in them to disregard. Williams, in illustration of this argument, asked "Whether the name of 'a declaration in Parliament' could be given to the Bill of Exclusion, because it had passed the Commons (where he himself had been very active in promoting it)?" This indiscreet allusion was received with a general hiss.† He was driven to the untenable position, that a petition from these prelates was warrantable only to Parliament; and that they were bound to delay it till Parliament should be assembled.

---

* 15 Ric. II.

† This phrase of the Roman law, which at first sight seems mere pedantry, conveys a delicate and happy allusion to the liberty of petition, which was allowed even under the despotism of the Emperors of Rome.

* "Pollexfen and Finch took no small pains to inveigh against the King's Dispensing power. The counsel for the Crown waived that point, though Mr. Solicitor was fiercely earnest against the Bishops, and took the management upon himself; Mr. Attorney's province being to put a smooth question now and then."—Mr. (afterwards Baron) Price to the Duke of Beaufort.—Macpherson, Original Papers, vol. i. p. 266.

† Van Citters, 9th July.—MS.

Wright, waiving the question of the Dispensing Power,* instructed the Jury that a delivery to the King was a publication; and that any writing which was adapted to disturb the government, or make a stir among the people, was a libel;—language of fearful import, but not peculiar to him, nor confined to his time. Holloway thought, that if the intention of the Bishops was only to make an innocent provision for their own security, the writing could not be a libel. Powell declared that they were innocent of sedition, or of any other crime, saying, "If such a Dispensing Power be allowed, there will need no Parliament; all the legislature will be in the King. I leave the issue to God and to your consciences." Allibone overleaped all the fences of decency or prudence so far as to affirm, "that no man can take upon himself to write against the actual exercise of the government, unless he have leave from the government, but he makes a libel, be what he writes true or false. The government ought not to be impeached by argument. This is a libel. No private man can write concerning the government at all, unless his own interest be stirred, and then he must redress himself by law. Every man may petition in what relates to his private interest; but neither the Bishops, nor any other man, has a right to intermeddle in affairs of government."

After a trial which lasted ten hours, the Jury retired at seven o'clock in the evening to consider their verdict. The friends of the Bishops watched at the door of the jury-room, and heard loud voices at midnight and at three o'clock; so anxious were they about the issue, though delay be in such cases a sure symptom of acquittal. The opposition of one Arnold, the brewer of the King's house, being at length subdued by the steadiness of the others, the Chief Justice was informed, at six o'clock in the morning, that the Jury were agreed in their verdict.† The Court met at nine o'clock. The nobility and gentry covered the benches; and an immense concourse of people filled the Hall, and blocked up the adjoining streets. Sir Robert Langley, the foreman of the Jury, being, according to established form, asked whether the accused were guilty or not guilty, pronounced the verdict, "Not guilty." No sooner were these words uttered than a loud huzza arose from the audience in the court. It was instantly echoed from without by a shout of joy, which sounded like a crack of the ancient and massy roof of Westminster Hall.* It passed with electrical rapidity from voice to voice along the infinite multitude who waited in the streets, reaching the Temple in a few minutes. For a short time no man seemed to know where he was. No business was done for hours. The Solicitor-General informed Lord Sunderland, in the presence of the Nuncio, that never within the remembrance of man had there been heard such cries of applause mingled with tears of joy.† "The acclamations," says Sir John Reresby, "were a very rebellion in noise." In no long time they ran to the camp at Hounslow, and were repeated with an ominous voice by the soldiers in the hearing of the King, who, on being told that they were for the acquittal of the Bishops, said, with an ambiguity probably arising from confusion, "So much the worse for them." The Jury were every where received with the loudest acclamations: hundreds, with tears in their eyes, embraced them as deliverers.‡ The Bishops, almost alarmed at their own success, escaped from the huzzas of the people as privately as possible, exhorting them to "fear God and honour the King." Cartwright, Bishop of Chester, had remained in court during the trial unnoticed by any of the crowd of nobility and gentry, and Sprat met with little more regard.§ The former, in going to his carriage, was called a "wolf in sheep's clothing;" and as he was very corpulent, the mob cried out, "Room for the man with a pope in his belly!" They bestowed also on Sir William Williams very mortifying proofs of disrespect.‖

Money having been thrown among the populace for that purpose, they in the evening drank the healths of the King, the Bishops, and the Jury together with confusion to the Papists, amidst the ringing of bells, and around bonfires blazing before the windows of the King's palace;¶ where the Pope was burnt in effigy** by those who were not aware of his lukewarm friendship for their enemies. Bonfires were also kindled before the doors of the most distinguished Roman Catholics, who were required to defray the expense of this annoyance. Lord Arundel, and others, submitted: Lord Salisbury, with the zeal of a new convert, sent his servants to disperse the rabble; but after having fired upon and

* "The Dispensing Power is more effectually knocked on the head than if an Act of Parliament had been made against it. The Judges said nothing about it, except Powell, who declared against it: so it is given up in Westminster Hall. My Lord Chief Justice is much blamed at Court for allowing it to be debated."—Johnstone, 2d July.—MS.

† Letter of Ince, the solicitor for the Bishops, to Sancroft. Gutch, vol. i. p. 374. From this letter we learn that the perilous practice then prevailed of successful parties giving a dinner and money to the jury. The solicitor proposed that the dinner should be omitted, but that 150 or 200 guineas should be distributed among twenty-two of the panel who attended. "Most of them (*i. e.* the panel of the Jury) are Church of England men; several are employed by the King in the navy and revenue; and some are or once were of the Dissenters' party."—Ellis, Original Letters, 2d series, vol. iv. p. 105. Of this last class we are told by Johnstone, that, "on being sounded by the Court agents," they declared that if they were jurors, they should act according to their conscience."

* Clarendon. 30th June.

† D'Adda, 16th July.—MS.

‡ Van Citters, 13th July.—MS.

§ Gutch, vol. i. p. 382.

‖ Van Citters, 13th July.—MS. ¶ Ibid.

** Johnstone, 2d July.—MS. Gerard, News Letter, 4th July.

killed only the parish beadle, who came to quench the bonfire, they were driven back into the house. All parties, Dissenters as well as Churchmen, rejoiced in the acquittal: the Bishops and their friends vainly laboured to temper the extravagance with which their joy was expressed.* The Nuncio, at first touched by the effusion of popular feeling, but now shocked by this boisterous triumph, declared, "that the fires over the whole city, the drinking in every street, accompanied by cries to the health of the Bishops and confusion to the Catholics, with the play of fireworks, and the discharge of fire-arms, and the other demonstrations of furious gladness, mixed with impious outrage against religion, which were continued during the night, formed a scene of unspeakable horror, displaying, in all its rancour, the malignity of this heretical people against the Church."† The bonfires were kept up during the whole of Saturday; and the disorderly rejoicings of the multitude did not cease till the dawn of Sunday reminded them of the duties of their religion.‡ These same rejoicings spread through the principal towns. The Grand Jury of Middlesex refused to find indictments for a riot against some parties who had tumultuously kindled bonfires, though four times sent out with instructions to do so.§

The Court also manifested its deep feelings on this occasion. In two days after the acquittal, the rank of a baronet was conferred upon Williams; while Powell for his honesty, and Holloway for his hesitation, were removed from the bench. The King betrayed the disturbance of his mind even in his camp;‖ and, though accustomed to unreserved conversation with Barillon, observed a silence on the acquittal which that minister was too prudent to interrupt.¶

In order to form a just estimate of this memorable trial, it is necessary to distinguish its peculiar grievances from the evils which always attend the strict administration of the laws against political libels. The doctrine that every writing which indisposes the people towards the administration of the government, however subversive of all political discussion, is not one of these peculiar grievances, for it has often been held in other cases, and perhaps never distinctly disclaimed; and the position that a libel may be conveyed in the form of a petition is true, though the case must be evident and flagrant which would warrant its application. The extravagances of Williams and Allibone might in strictness be laid out of the case, as peculiar to themselves, and not necessary to support the prosecution, were it not that they pointed out the threatening positions which success in it might encourage and enable the enemy to occupy. It was absolutely necessary for the Crown to contend that the matter of the writing was so inflammatory as to change its character from that of a petition to that of a libel; that the intention in composing it was not to obtain relief, but to excite discontent; and that it was presented to the King to insult him, and to make its contents known to others. But the attempt to extract such conclusions from the evidence against the Bishops was an excess beyond the furthest limits of the law of libel, as it was even then received. The generous feelings of mankind did not, however, so scrupulously weigh the demerits of the prosecution. The effect of this attempt was to throw a strong light on all the odious qualities (hid from the mind in their common state by familiarity) of a jealous and restrictive legislation, directed against the free exercise of reason and the fair examination of the interests of the community. All the vices of that distempered state in which a Government cannot endure a fearless discussion of its principles and measures, appeared in the peculiar evils of a single conspicuous prosecution. The feelings of mankind, in this respect more provident than their judgment, saw, in the loss of every post, the danger to the last entrenchments of public liberty. A multitude of contemporary circumstances, wholly foreign to its character as a judicial proceeding, gave the trial the strongest hold on the hearts of the people. Unused to popular meetings, and little accustomed to political writings, the whole nation looked on this first public discussion of their rights in a high place, surrounded by the majesty of public justice, with that new and intense interest which it is not easy for those who are familiar with such scenes to imagine. It was a prosecution of men of the most venerable character and of manifestly innocent intention, after the success of which no good man could have been secure. It was an experiment, in some measure, to ascertain the means and probabilities of general deliverance. The Government was on its trial; and by the verdict of acquittal, the King was justly convicted of a conspiracy to maintain usurpation by oppression.

The solicitude of Sunderland for moderation in these proceedings had exposed him to such charges of lukewarmness, that he deemed it necessary no longer to delay the long-promised and decisive proof of his identifying his interest with that of his master.

---

* News Letter, 4th July.

† D'Adda, 16th July.—MS.

‡ Ellis, vol. iv. p. 110.

§ Reresby, p. 265. Gerard, News Letter, 7th July.

‖ Reresby, suprà.

¶ "His Majesty has been pleased to remove Sir Richard Holloway and Sir John Powell from being justices of the King's Bench." London Gazette, 6th July. In the Life of James II., (vol. ii. p. 163,) it is said, that "the King gave no marks of his displeasure to the Judges Holloway and Powell." It is due to the character of James, to say that this falsehood does not proceed from him; and justice requires it to be added, that as Dicconson, the compiler, thus evidently neglected the most accessible means of ascertaining the truth, very little credit is due to those portions of his narrative for which, as in the present case, he cites no authority.

Sacrifices of a purely religious nature cost him little.* Some time before, he had compounded for his own delay by causing his eldest son to abjure Protestantism; "choosing rather," says Barillon, "to expose his son than himself to future hazard." The specious excuse of preserving his vote in Parliament had hitherto been deemed sufficient; while the shame of apostasy, and an anxiety not to embroil himself irreparably with a Protestant successor, were the real motives for delay. But nothing less than a public avowal of his conversion would now suffice to shut the mouths of his enemies, who imputed his advice of lenity towards the Bishops to a desire of keeping measures with the adherents of the Prince of Orange.† It was accordingly in the week of the Bishops' trial that he made public his renunciation of the Protestant religion, but without any solemn abjuration, because he had the year before secretly performed that ceremony to Father Petre.‡ By this measure he completely succeeded in preserving or recovering the favour of the King, who announced it with the warmest commendations to his Catholic counsellors, and told the Nuncio that a resolution so generous and holy would very much contribute to the service of God. "I have, indeed, been informed," says that minister, "that some of the most fanatical merchants of the city have observed that the Royal party must certainly be the strongest, since, in the midst of the universal exasperation of men's minds, it is thus embraced by a man so wise, prudent, rich, and well informed."§ The Catholic courtiers also considered the conversion as an indication of the superior strength and approaching triumph of their religion. Perhaps, indeed, the birth of the Prince of Wales might have somewhat encouraged him to the step; but it chiefly arose from the prevalence of the present fear for his place over the apprehension of remote consequences. Ashamed of his conduct, he employed a friend to communicate his change to his excellent wife, who bitterly deplored it.‖ His uncle, Henry Sidney, the most confidential agent of the Prince of Orange, was incensed at his apostasy, and only expressed the warmest wishes for his downfall.*

Two days after the imprisonment of the Bishops,—as if all the events which were to hasten the catastrophe of this reign, however various in their causes or unlike in their nature, were to be crowded into the same scene,—the Queen had been delivered in the palace of St. James', of a son, whose birth had been the object of more hopes and fears, and was now the hinge on which greater events turned, than that of any other Royal infant since human affairs have been recorded in authentic history. Never did the dependence of a monarchical government on physical accident more strikingly appear. On Trinity Sunday, the 10th of June, between nine and ten in the morning, the Prince of Wales was born, in the presence of the Queen Dowager, of most of the Privy Council, and of several ladies of quality,—of all, in short, who were the natural witnesses on such an occasion, except the Princess Anne, who was at Bath, and the Archbishop of Canterbury, who was a prisoner in the Tower. The cannons of the Tower were fired; a general thanksgiving was ordered; and the Lord Mayor was enjoined to give directions for bonfires and public rejoicing. Some addresses of congratulation followed; and compliments were received on so happy an occasion from foreign powers. The British ministers abroad, in due time, celebrated the auspicious birth,—with undisturbed magnificence, at Rome,—amidst the loudest manifestations of dissatisfaction and apprehension at Amsterdam. From Jamaica to Madras, the distant dependencies, with which an unfrequent intercourse was then maintained by tedious voyages, continued their prescribed rejoicings long after other feelings openly prevailed in the mother country. The genius of Dryden, which often struggled with the difficulty of a task imposed, commemorated the birth of the "son of prayer" in no ignoble verse, but with prophecies of glory which were speedily clouded, and in the end most signally disappointed.†

The universal belief that the child was supposititious is a fact which illustrates

* "On ne scait pas de quelle religion il est."—Lettre d'un Anonyme (peut-être Bonrepos) sur la Cour de Londres, 1688, MSS. in the Dépôt des Affaires Etrangères, at Paris.

† "Il a voulu fermer la bouche à ses ennemis, et leur ôter toute prétexte de dire qu'il peut entrer dans sa conduite quelque ménagement pour la partie de M. le Prince d'Orange."—Barillon, 8th July.—MS.

‡ Ibid. suprà. "Father Petre, though it was irregular, was forced to say two masses in one morning, because Lord Sunderland and Lord Mulgrave were not to know of each other's conversion."—Halifax MSS. The French ambassador at Constantinople informed Sir William Trumbull of the secret abjuration.—Ibid. "It is now necessary," says Van Citters (6th July), "to secure the King's favour; the Queen's, if she be regent; and his own place in the Council of Regency, if there be one."

§ D'Adda, 9th July.—MS.

‖ Evelyn, who visited Althorp a fortnight afterwards, thus alludes to it: "I wish from my soul that the Lord her husband, whose parts are otherwise conspicuous, were as worthy of her, *as by a fatal apostasy* and court ambition he has made himself unworthy."—Diary, 18th July.

* Johnstone, 2d July.—MS.

† "Born in broad daylight, that the ungrateful rout
May find no room for a remaining doubt:
Truth, which itself is light, does darkness shun,
And the true eaglet safely dares the sun.
Fain would the fiends have made a dubious birth.
* * * *
No future ills, nor accidents, appear,
To sully or pollute the sacred infant's year.
* * * *
But kings too tame are despicably good.
Be this the mixture of the regal child,
By nature manly, but by virtue mild."
Britannia Rediviva.

several principles of human nature, and affords a needful and wholesome lesson of scepticism, even in cases where many testimonies seem to combine, and all judgments for a time agree. The historians who wrote while the dispute was still pending enlarge on the particulars: in our age, the only circumstances deserving preservation are those which throw light on the origin and reception of a false opinion which must be owned to have contributed to subsequent events. Few births are so well attested as that of the unfortunate Prince whom almost all English Protestants then believed to be spurious. The Queen had, for months before, alluded to her pregnancy, in the most unaffected manner, to the Princess of Orange.* The delivery took place in the presence of many persons of unsuspected veracity, a considerable number of whom were Protestants. Messengers were early sent to fetch Dr. Chamberlain, an eminent obstetrical practitioner, and a noted Whig, who had been oppressed by the King, and who would have been the last person summoned to be present at a pretended delivery.† But as not one in a thousand had credited the pregnancy, the public now looked at the birth with a strong predisposition to unbelief, which a very natural neglect suffered for some time to grow stronger from being uncontradicted. This prejudice was provoked to greater violence by the triumph of the Catholics; as suspicion had before been awakened by their bold predictions. The importance of the event had, at the earlier period of the pregnancy, produced mystery and reserve,—the frequent attendants of fearful anxiety,—which were eagerly seized on as presumptions of sinister purpose. When a passionate and inexperienced Queen disdained to take any measures to silence malicious rumours, her inaction was imputed to inability; and when she submitted to the use of prudent precautions, they were represented as betraying the fears of conscious guilt. Every act of the Royal Family had some handle by which ingenious hostility could turn it against them. Reason was employed only to discover argument in support of the judgment which passion had pronounced. In spite of the strongest evidence, the Princess Anne honestly persevered in her incredulity.‡ Johnstone, who received minute information of all the particulars of the delivery from one of the Queen's attendants,§ could not divest himself of suspicions, the good faith of which seems to be proved by his not hazarding a positive judgment on the subject. By these the slightest incidents of a lying-in room were darkly coloured. No incidents in human life could have stood the test of a trial by minds so prejudiced,—especially as long as adverse scrutiny had the advantages of the partial selection and skilful insinuation of facts, undisturbed by that full discussion in which all circumstances are equally sifted. When the before-mentioned attendant of the Queen declared to a large company of gainsayers that "she would swear," (as she afterwards did "that the Queen had a child," it was immediately said, "How ambiguous is her expression! the child might have been born dead." At one moment Johnstone boasts of the universal unbelief: at another he is content with saying that even wise men see no evidence of the birth; that, at all events, there is doubt enough to require a Parliamentary inquiry; and that the general doubt may be lawfully employed as an argument by those who, even if they do not share it, did nothing to produce it. He sometimes endeavours to stifle his own scepticism with the public opinion, and on other occasions has recourse to these very ambiguous maxims of factious casuistry; but the whole tenour of his confidential letters shows the groundless unbelief in the Prince's legitimacy to have been as spontaneous as it was general. Various, and even contradictory, accounts of the supposed imposture were circulated: it was said that the Queen was never pregnant; that she had miscarried at Easter; that one child, and by some accounts two children in succession, had been substituted in the room of the abortion. That these tales contradicted each other, was a very slight objection in the eye of a national prejudice: the people were very slow in seeing the contradiction; some had heard only one story, and some jumbled parts of more together. The zealous, when beat out of one version, retired upon another: the skilful chose that which, like the abortion (of which there had actually been a danger), had some apparent support from facts. When driven successively from every post, they took refuge in the general remark, that so many stories must have a foundation; that they all coincided in the essential circumstance of a supposititious birth, though they differed in facts of inferior moment; that the King deserved, by his other breaches of faith, the humiliation which he now underwent; and that the natural punishment of those who have often deceived is to be disbelieved when they speak truth. It is the policy of most parties not to discourage zealous partisans. The multitude considered every man who hesitated in thinking the worst of an enemy, as his abettor; and the loudness of the popular cry subdued the remains of candid doubt in those who had at first, from policy, countenanced, though they did not contrive, the delusion. In subsequent times, it was not thought the part of a good citizen to aid in detecting a prevalent error, which enabled the partisans

* Ellis, Original Letters, 1st series, vol. iii. p. 348. 21st Feb. 15th May, 6th—13th July. The last is decisive.

† Dr. Chamberlain's Letter to the Princess Sophia. Dalrymple, app. to book v.

‡ Princess Anne to the Princess of Orange. Ibid.

§ Mrs. Dawson, one of the gentlewomen of the Queen's bedchamber, a Protestant, afterwards examined before the Privy Council, who communicated all the circumstances to her friend, Mrs. Baillie, of Jerviswood, Johnstone's sister.

of inviolable succession to adhere to the principles of the Revolution without inconsistency during the reign of Anne,* and through which the House of Hanover itself were brought at least nearer to an hereditary right. Johnstone on the spot, and at the moment, almost worked himself into a belief of it; while Lloyd, Bishop of St. Asaph, honestly adhered to it many years afterwards.† The collection of inconsistent rumours on this subject by Burnet reflects more on his judgment than any other passage of his history; yet, zealous as he was, his conscience would not allow him to profess his own belief in what was still a fundamental article of the creed of his party. Echard, writing under George I., intimates his disbelief, for which he is almost rebuked by Kennet. The upright and judicious Rapin, though a French Protestant, and an officer in the army led by the Prince of Orange into England, yet, in the liberty of his foreign retirement, gave an honest judgment against his prejudices. Both parties, on this subject, so exactly believed what they wished, that perhaps scarcely any individual before him examined it on grounds of reason. The Catholics were right by chance, and by chance the Protestants were wrong. Had it been a case of the temporary success of artful impostures, so common an occurrence would have deserved no notice: but the growth of a general delusion from the prejudice and passion of a nation, and the deep root which enabled it to keep a place in history for half a century, render this transaction worthy to be remembered by posterity.

The triumph of the Bishops did not terminate all proceedings of the Ecclesiastical Commissioners against the disobedient clergy. They issued an order‡ requiring the proper officers in each diocese to make a return of the names of those who had not read the Royal Declaration. On the day before that which was fixed for the giving in the return, a meeting of chancellors and archdeacons was held; of whom eight agreed to return that they had no means of procuring the information but at their regular visitation, which did not fall within the appointed time; six declined to make any return at all, and five excused themselves on the plea that the order had not been legally served upon them.§ The Commissioners, now content to shut their eyes on lukewarmness, resistance, or evasion, affected a belief in the reasons assigned for non-compliance, and directed another return to be made on the 6th of December, appointing a previous day for a visitation.* On the day when the Board exhibited these symptoms of debility and decay, it received a letter from Sprat, tendering the resignation of his seat, which was universally regarded as foreboding its speedy dissolution;† and the last dying effort of its usurped authority was to adjourn to a day on which it was destined never to meet. Such, indeed, was the discredit into which these proceedings had fallen, that the Bishop of Chichester had the spirit to suspend one of his clergy for obedience to the King's order in reading the Declaration.‡

The Court and the Church now contended with each other for the alliance of the Dissenters, but with very unequal success. The last attempt of the King to gain them, was the admission into the Privy Council of three gentlemen, who were either Nonconformists, or well disposed towards that body,—Sir John Trevor, Colonel Titus, and Mr. Vane, the posthumous son of the celebrated Sir Henry Vane.§ The Church took better means to unite all Protestants against a usurpation which clothed itself in the garb of religious liberty; and several consultations were held on the mode of coming to a better understanding with the Dissenters.‖ The Archbishop and clergy of London had several conferences with the principal Dissenting ministers on the measures fit to be proposed about religion in the next Parliament.¶ The Primate himself issued admonitions to his clergy, in which he exhorted them to have a very tender regard towards their Dissenting brethren, and to entreat them to join in prayer for the union of all Reformed churches "at home and abroad, against the common enemy,"** conformably to the late Petition of himself and his brethren, in which they had declared their willingness to come into such a temper as should be thought fit with the Dissenters, whenever that matter should be considered in Parliament and Convocation. He even carried this new-born tenderness so far as to renew those projects for uniting the more moderate to the Church by some concessions in the terms of worship, and for exempting those whose scruples were insurmountable from the severity of penal laws, which had been foiled by his friends, when they were negotiated by Hale and Baxter in the preceding reign, and which

* Caveat Against the Whigs, part ii. p. 50,—where the question is left in doubt at the critical period of 1712.

† See his account, adverted to by Burnet and others, published by Oldmixon, vol. i. p. 734. "The Bishop whom your friends know, bids me tell them that he had met with neither man nor woman who were so good as to believe the Prince of Wales to be a lawful child."—Johnstone, 2d July.—MS. This bold bishop was probably Compton.

‡ London Gazette, 12th July.

§ Sayers' News-Letter, 18th August.

* London Gazette, 16th August.

† Sayers' News-Letter, 22d August. "The secretary gave this letter to the Chancellor, who swore that the Bishop was mad. He gave it to the Lord President, but it was never read to the Board." Such was then the disorder in their minds and in their proceedings.

‡ Ibid. 19th Sept., Kennet, vol. iii. p. 515, note; in both which, the date of Sprat's letter is 15th August, the day before the last meeting of the Commissioners.

§ London Gazette, 6th July.

‖ Sayers' News-Letter, 7th July.

¶ Ibid. 21st July. Ellis, vol. iv. p. 117.

** D'Oyley, vol. i. p. 324.

were again within a few months afterwards to be resisted, by the same party, and with too much success. Among the instances of the disaffection of the Church the University of Oxford refused so small a compliance as that of conferring the degree of doctor of divinity on their Bishop, according to the royal mandamus,* and hastened to elect the young Duke of Ormonde to be their Chancellor on the death of his grandfather, in order to escape the imposition of Jeffreys, in whose favour they apprehended a recommendation from the Court.

Several symptoms now indicated that the national discontent had infected the armed force. The seamen of the squadron at the Nore received some monks who were sent to officiate among them with boisterous marks of derision and aversion; and, though the tumult was composed by the presence of the King, it left behind dispositions favourable to the purposes of disaffected officers. James' proceedings respecting the army were uniformly impolitic. He had, very early, boasted of the number of his guards who were converted to his religion; thus disclosing to them the dangerous secret of their importance to his designs.† The sensibility evinced at the Tower and at Lambeth, betokened a proneness to fellow-feeling with the people, which Sunderland had before intimated to the Nuncio, and of which he had probably forewarned his master. After the triumph of the prelates, on which occasion the feelings of the army declared themselves still more loudly, the King had recourse to the very doubtful expedient of paying open court to it. He dined twice a week in the camp,‡ and showed an anxiety to ingratiate himself by a display of affability, of precautions for the comfort, and pride in the discipline and appearance of the troops. Without the boldness which quells a mutinous spirit, or the firmness which, where activity would be injurious, can quietly look at a danger till it disappears or may be surmounted, he yielded to the restless fearfulness which seeks a momentary relief in rash and mischievous efforts, that rouse many rebellious tempers and subdue none. A written test was prepared, which even the privates were required to subscribe, by which they bound themselves to contribute to the repeal of the penal laws.§ It was first to be tendered to the regiments who were most confidentially expected to set a good example to the others. The experiment was first tried on Lord Lichfield's, and all who hesitated to comply with the King's commands were ordered to lay down their arms:—the whole regiment, except two captains and a few catholic privates, actually did lay down their arms. The King was thunderstruck; and, after a gloomy moment of silence, ordered them to take up their muskets, saying, "that he should not again do them the honour to consult them."* When the troops returned from the encampment to their quarters, another plan was attempted for securing their fidelity, by the introduction of trustworthy recruits. With this view, fifty Irish Catholics were ordered to be equally distributed among the ten companies of the Duke of Berwick's regiment at Portsmouth, which, having already a colonel incapacitated by law, was expected to be better disposed to the reception of recruits liable to the same objection. But the experiment was too late, and was also conducted with a slow formality alien to the genius of soldiers. The officers were now actuated by the same sentiments with their own class in society. Beaumont, the lieutenant-colonel, and the five captains who were present, positively refused to comply. They were brought to Windsor under an escort of cavalry, tried by a council of war, and sentenced to be cashiered. The King now relented, or rather faltered, offering pardon, on condition of obedience,—a fault as great as the original attempt: they all refused. The greater part of the other officers of the regiment threw up their commissions; and, instead of intimidation, a great and general discontent was spread throughout the army. Thus, to the odium incurred by an attempt to recruit it from those who were deemed the most hostile of foreign enemies, was superadded the contempt which feebleness in the execution of obnoxious designs never fails to inspire.†

Thus, in the short space of three years from the death of Monmouth and the destruction of his adherents, when all who were not zealously attached to the Crown seemed to be dependent on its mercy, were all ranks and parties of the English nation, without any previous show of turbulence, and with not much of that cruel oppression of individuals which is usually necessary to awaken the passions of a people, slowly and almost imperceptibly conducted to the brink of a great revolution. The appearance of the Prince of Wales filled the minds of those who believed his legitimacy with terror; while it roused the warmest indignation of those who considered his supposed birth as a flagitious imposture. Instead of the government of a Protestant successor, it presented, after the death of James, both during the regency of the Queen, and the reign of a prince educated under her superintendence, no prospect but an administration certainly not more favourable than his to religion and liberty. These apprehensions had been

* Sayers' News-Letter, 25th July.

† D'Adda, 5th Dec. 1687, MS.

‡ Ellis, vol. iv. p. 111.

§ Johnstone, 2d July, MS. Oldmixon, vol. i. p. 739.

* Kennet, vol. iii. p. 516. Ralph speaks doubtfully of this scene, of which, indeed, no writer has mentioned the place or time. The written test is confirmed by Johnstone, and Kennet could hardly have been deceived about the sequel. The place must have been the camp at Hounslow, and the time was probably about the middle of July.

† Reresby, p. 270, who seems to have been a captain in this regiment. Burnet, vol. iii. p. 272.

brought home to the feelings of the people by the trial of the Bishops, and had at last affected even the army, the last resource of power,—a tremendous weapon, which cannot burst without threatening destruction to all around, and which, if it were not sometimes happily so overcharged as to recoil on him who wields it, would rob all the slaves in the world of hope, and all the freemen of safety.

The state of the other British kingdoms was not such as to abate the alarms of England. In Ireland the government of Tyrconnel was always sufficiently in advance of the English minister to keep the eyes of the nation fixed on the course which their rulers were steering.* Its influence in spreading alarm and disaffection through the other dominions of the King, was confessed by the ablest and most zealous of his apologists.

Scotland was also a mirror in which the English nation might behold their approaching doom. The natural tendency of the Dispensing and Suspending Powers to terminate in the assumption of the whole authority of legislation, was visible in the Declarations of Indulgence issued in that kingdom. They did not, as in England, profess to be founded on limited and peculiar prerogatives of the King, either as the head of the Church or as the fountain of justice, nor on usages and determinations which, if they sanctioned such acts of power, at least confined them within fixed boundaries, but upon what the King himself displayed, in all its amplitude and with all its terrors, as "our sovereign authority, prerogative royal, and absolute power, which all our subjects are bound to obey without reservation."† In the exercise of this alarming power, not only were all the old oaths taken away, but a new one, professing passive obedience, was proposed as the condition of toleration. A like Declaration in 1688, besides the repetition of so high an act of legislative power as that of "annulling" oaths which the legislature had prescribed, proceeds to dissolve all the courts of justice and bodies of magistracy in that kingdom, in order that by their acceptance of new commissions conformably to the royal pleasure, they might renounce all former oaths;—so that every member of them would hold his office under the Suspending and even Annulling Powers, on the legitimacy of which the whole judicature and administration of the realm would thus exclusively rest.* Blood had now ceased to flow for religion; and the execution of Renwick,† a pious and intrepid minister, who, according to the principles of the Cameronians, openly denied James II. to be his rightful sovereign, is rather an apparent than a real exception: for the offence imputed to him was not of a religious nature, and must have been punished by every established authority; though an impartial observer would rather regret the imprudence than question the justice of such a declaration from the mouths of these persecuted men. Books against the King's religion were reprehended or repressed by the Privy Council.‡ Barclay, the celebrated Quaker, was at this time in such favour, that he not only received a liberal pension, but had influence enough to procure an indecent, but successful, letter from the King to the Court of Session, in effect annulling a judgment for a large sum of money which had been obtained against Sir Ewen Cameron, a bold and fierce chieftain, the brother-in-law of the accomplished and pacific apologist.§ Though the clergy of the Established Church had two years before resisted an unlimited toleration by prerogative, yet we are assured by a competent witness, that their opposition arose chiefly from the fear that it would encourage the unhappy Presbyterians, then almost entirely ruined and scattered through the world.‖ The deprivation of two prelates, Bruce, Bishop of Dunkeld, for his conduct in Parliament, and Cairncross, Archbishop of Glasgow, in spite of subsequent submission, for not censuring a preacher against the Church of Rome,¶ showed the English clergy that suspensions like that of Compton might be followed by more decisive measures; but seems to have silenced the

* "I do not vindicate all that Lord Tyrconnel, and others, did in Ireland before the Revolution; which, most of any thing, brought it on. I am sensible that their carriage gave greater occasion to King James' enemies than all the other mal-administrations charged upon his government."—Leslie, Answer to King's State of the Protestants, p. 73. Leslie is the ablest of James' apologists. He skilfully avoids all the particulars of Tyrconnel's government before the Revolution. That silence, and this general admission, may be considered as conclusive evidence against it.

† Proclamation, 12th Feb. 1687. Wodrow, vol. ii. app. no. cxxix. "We here in England see what we must look to. A Parliament in Scotland proved a little stubborn; now *absolute power* comes to set all right: so when the closeting has gone round, we may perhaps see a Parliament here: but if it chance to be untoward, then our reverend judges will copy from Scotland, and will discover to us this new mystery of absolute power, which we are all obliged to obey without reserve."—Burnet, Reflections on Proclamation for Toleration.

* Proclamation, 15th May. Wodrow, vol. ii. app. no. cxxxviii. Fountainhall, vol. i. p. 504. The latter writer informs us, that "this occasioned several sheriffs to forbear awhile." Perth, the Scotch Chancellor, who carried this Declaration to Scotland, assured the Nuncio, before leaving London, "that the royal prerogative was then so extensive as not to require the concurrence of Parliament, which was only an useful corroboration."—D'Adda, 21st May, MS.

† On the 17th Feb. 1688.

‡ A bookseller in Edinburgh was "threatened for publishing an account of the persecution in France."—Fountainhall, 8th Feb. 1688. Cockburn, a minister, was forbidden to continue a Review, taken chiefly from Le Clerc's Bibliothèque Universelle, containing some extracts from Mabillon's Iter Italicum, which were supposed to reflect on the Church of Rome.

§ Fountainhall, 2d June.

‖ Balcarras, Affairs of Scotland, (London, 1714), p. 8.

¶ Skinner, Ecclesiastical History of Scotland, vol. ii. pp. 500—504.

complaints of the Scottish Church. From that time, at least, their resistance to the Court entirely ceased. It was followed by symptoms of an opposite disposition; among which may probably be reckoned the otherwise inexplicable return, to the office of Lord Advocate, of the eloquent Sir George Mackenzie, their principal instrument in the cruel persecution of the Presbyterians,—who now accepted that station at the moment of the triumph of those principles by opposing which he had forfeited it two years before.* The Primate prevailed on the University of St. Andrews to declare, by an address to the King, their opinion that he might take away the penal laws without the consent of Parliament.† No manifestation of sympathy appears to have been made towards the English Bishops, at the moment of their danger, or of their triumph, by their brethren in Scotland. At a subsequent period, when the prelates of England offered wholesome and honest counsel to their Sovereign, those of Scotland presented an address to him, in which they prayed that "God might give him the hearts of his subjects and the necks of his enemies."‡ In the awful struggle in which the English nation and Church were about to engage, they had to number the Established Church of Scotland among their enemies.

CHAPTER IX.

Doctrine of obedience.—Right of resistance.—Comparison of foreign and civil war.—Right of calling auxiliaries.—Relations of the people of England and of Holland.

The time was now come when the people of England were called upon to determine, whether they should by longer submission sanction the usurpations and encourage the further encroachments of the Crown, or take up arms against the established authority of their Sovereign for the defence of their legal rights, as well as of those safeguards which the constitution had placed around them. Though the solution of this tremendous problem requires the calmest exercise of reason, the circumstances which bring it forward commonly call forth mightier agents, which disturb and overpower the action of the understanding. In conjunctures so awful, where men feel more than they reason, their conduct is chiefly governed by the boldness or wariness of their nature, by their love of liberty or their attachment to quiet, by their proneness or slowness to fellow-feeling with their countrymen. The generous virtues and turbulent passions rouse the brave and aspiring to resistance; some gentle virtues and useful principles second the qualities of human nature in disposing many to submission. The duty of legal obedience seems to forbid that appeal to arms which the necessity of preserving law and liberty allows, or rather demands. In such a conflict there is little quiet left for moral deliberation. Yet by the immutable principles of morality, and by them alone, must the historian try the conduct of all men, before he allows himself to consider all the circumstances of time, place, opinion, example, temptation, and obstacle, which, though they never authorise a removal of the everlasting landmarks of right and wrong, ought to be well weighed, in allotting a due degree of commendation or censure to human actions.

The English law, like that of most other countries, lays down no limits of obedience. The clergy of the Established Church, the authorised teachers of public morality, carried their principles much farther than was required by a mere concurrence with this cautious silence of the law. Not content with inculcating, in common with all other moralists, religious or philosophical obedience to civil government as one of the most essential duties of human life, the English Church perhaps alone had solemnly pronounced that in the conflict of obligations no other rule of duty could, under any circumstances, become more binding than that of allegiance. Even the duty which seems paramount to every other,—that which requires every citizen to contribute to the preservation of the community,—ceased, according to their moral system, to have any binding force, whenever it could not be performed without resistance to established government. Regarding the power of a monarch as more sacred than the paternal authority from which they vainly laboured to derive it, they refused to nations oppressed by the most cruel tyrants* those rights of self-defence which no moralist or lawgiver had ever denied to children against unnatural parents. To palliate the extravagance of thus representing obedience as the only duty without an exception, an appeal was made to the divine origin of government;—as if every other moral rule were not, in the opinion of all theists, equally enjoined and sanctioned by the Deity. To denote these singular doctrines, it was thought necessary to devise the terms of "passive obedience" and "non-resistance,"—uncouth and jarring forms of speech, not unfitly representing a violent departure from the general judgment of mankind. This attempt to exalt submission so high as to be always the highest duty, constituted the undistinguishing loyalty of which the Church of England boasted as her exclusive attribute, in contradistinction to the other Reformed communions, as well as to the Church of Rome. At the dawn of the Reformation it had been promulgated in the Homilies or discourses appointed by the Church to be read from the pulpit to the

* Fountainhall, 23d February.
† Id. 29th March.
‡ Skinner, vol. ii. p. 513.

* Interpretation of Romans, xiii. 1—7, written under Nero. See, among many others, South, Sermon on the 5th November, 1663.

people;* and all deviations from it had been recently condemned by the University of Oxford with the solemnity of a decree from Rome or from Trent.† The Seven Bishops themselves, in the very Petition which brought the contest with the Crown to a crisis, boasted of the inviolable obedience of their Church, and of the honour conferred on them by the King's repeated acknowledgments of it. Nay, all the ecclesiastics and the principal laymen of the Church had recorded their adherence to the same principles, in a still more solemn and authoritative mode. By the Act of Uniformity,‡ which restored the legal establishment of the Episcopal Church, it was enacted that every clergyman, schoolmaster, and private tutor should subscribe a declaration, affirming that "it was not lawful on any pretext to take up arms against the King," which members of corporations§ and officers of militia‖ were by other statutes of the same period also compelled to swear;—to say nothing of the still more comprehensive oath which the High-Church leaders, thirteen years before the trial of the Bishops, had laboured to impose on all public officers, magistrates, ecclesiastics, and members of both Houses of Parliament.

That no man can lawfully promise what he cannot lawfully do is a self-evident proposition. That there are some duties superior to others, will be denied by no one; and that when a contest arises the superior ought to prevail, is implied in the terms by which the duties are described. It can hardly be doubted that the highest obligation of a citizen is that of contributing to preserve the community; and that every other political duty, even that of obedience to the magistrates, is derived from and must be subordinate to it. It is a necessary consequence of these simple truths, that no man who deems self-defence lawful in his own case, can, by any engagement, bind himself not to defend his country against foreign or domestic enemies. Though the opposite propositions really involve a contradiction in terms, yet declarations of their truth were imposed by law, and oaths to renounce the defence of our country were considered as binding, till the violent collision of such pretended obligations with the security of all rights and institutions awakened the national mind to a sense of their repugnance to the first principles of morality. Maxims, so artificial and over-strained, which have no more root in nature than they have warrant from reason, must always fail in a contest against the affections, sentiments, habits, and interests which are the motives of human conduct,—leaving little more than compassionate indulgence to the small number who conscientiously cling to them, and fixing the injurious imputation of inconsistency on the great body who forsake them for better guides.

The war of a people against a tyrannical government may be tried by the same tests which ascertain the morality of a war between independent nations. The employment of force in the intercourse of reasonable beings is never lawful, but for the purpose of repelling or averting wrongful force. Human life cannot lawfully be destroyed, or assailed, or endangered, for any other object than that of just defence. Such is the nature and such the boundary of legitimate self-defence in the case of individuals. Hence the right of the lawgiver to protect unoffending citizens by the adequate punishment of crimes: hence, also, the right of an independent state to take all measures necessary to her safety, if it be attacked or threatened from without; provided always that reparation cannot otherwise be obtained, that there is a reasonable prospect of obtaining it by arms, and that the evils of the contest are not probably greater than the mischiefs of acquiescence in the wrong; including, on both sides of the deliberation, the ordinary consequences of the example, as well as the immediate effects of the act. If reparation can otherwise be obtained, a nation has no necessary, and therefore no just cause of war; if there be no probability of obtaining it by arms, a government cannot, with justice to their own nation, embark it in war; and if the evils of resistance should appear, on the whole, greater than those of submission, wise rulers will consider an abstinence from a pernicious exercise of right as a sacred duty to their own subjects, and a debt which every people owes to the great commonwealth of mankind, of which they and their enemies are alike members. A war is just against the wrongdoer when reparation for wrong cannot otherwise be obtained; but it is then only conformable to all the principles of morality, when it is not likely to expose the nation by whom it is levied to greater evils than it professes to avert, and when it does not inflict on the nation which has done the wrong sufferings altogether disproportioned to the extent of the injury. When the rulers of a nation are required to determine a question of peace or war, the bare justice of their case against the wrongdoer never can be the sole, and is not always the chief matter on which they are morally bound to exercise a conscientious deliberation. Prudence in conducting the affairs of their subjects is, in them, a part of justice.

On the same principles the justice of a war made by a people against their own government must be examined. A government is entitled to obedience from the people, because without obedience it cannot perform the duty, for which alone it exists, of protecting them from each other's injustice. But when a government is engaged in systematically oppressing a people, or in destroying their securities against future oppression, it commits the same species of

* Homilies of Edward VI. and Elizabeth.

† Parliamentary History, 20th July, 1683.

‡ 14 Ch. II. c. 4.

§ 13 Ch. II. stat. ii. c. 1.

‖ 14 Ch. II. c. 3.

wrong towards them which warrants an appeal to arms against a foreign enemy. A magistrate who degenerates into a sytematic oppressor shuts the gates of justice, and thereby restores them to the original right of defending them by force. As he withholds the protection of law from them, he forfeits his moral claim to enforce their obedience by the authority of law. Thus far civil and foreign war stand on the same moral foundation: the principles which determine the justice of both against the wrong-doer are, indeed, throughout the same.

But there are certain peculiarities, of great importance in point of fact, which in other respects permanently distinguish them from each other. The evils of failure are greater in civil than in foreign war. A state generally incurs no more than loss in war: a body of insurgents is exposed to ruin. The probabilities of success are more difficult to calculate in cases of internal contest than in a war between states, where it is easy to compare those merely material means of attack and defence which may be measured or numbered. An unsuccessful revolt strengthens the power and sharpens the cruelty of the tyrannical ruler; while an unfortunate war may produce little of the former evil and of the latter nothing. It is almost peculiar to intestine war that success may be as mischievous as defeat. The victorious leaders may be borne along by the current of events far beyond their destination; a goverment may be overthrown which ought to have been only repaired; and a new, perhaps a more formidable, tyranny may spring out of victory. A regular government may stop before its fall becomes precipitate, or check a career of conquest when it threatens destruction to itself: but the feeble authority of the chiefs of insurgents is rarely able, in the one case, to maintain the courage, in the other to repress the impetuosity, of their voluntary adherents. Finally, the cruelty and misery incident to all warfare are greater in domestic dissension than in contests with foreign enemies. Foreign wars have little effect on the feelings, habits, or condition of the majority of a great nation, to most of whom the worst particulars of them may be unknown. But civil war brings the same or worse evils into the heart of a country and into the bosom of many families: it eradicates all habits of recourse to justice and reverence for law; its hostilities are not mitigated by the usages which soften wars between nations; it is carried on with the ferocity of parties who apprehend destruction from each other; and it may leave behind it feuds still more deadly, which may render a country depraved and wretched through a long succession of ages. As it involves a wider waste of virtue and happiness than any other species of war, it can only be warranted by the sternest and most dire necessity. The chiefs of a justly disaffected party are unjust to their fellows and their followers, as well as to all the rest of their countrymen, if they take up arms in a case where the evils of submission are not more intolerable, the impossibility of reparation by pacific means more apparent, and the chances of obtaining it by arms greater than are necessary to justify the rulers of a nation in undertaking a foreign war. A wanton rebellion, when considered with the aggravation of its ordinary consequences, is one of the greatest of crimes. The chiefs of an inconsiderable and ill-concerted revolt, however provoked, incur the most formidable responsibility to their followers and their country. An insurrection rendered necessary by oppression, and warranted by a reasonable probability of a happy termination, is an act of public virtue, always environed with so much peril as to merit admiration.

In proportion to the degree in which a revolt spreads over a large body till it approaches unanimity, the fatal peculiarities of civil war are lessened. In the insurrection of provinces, either distant or separated by natural boundaries,—more especially if the inhabitants, differing in religion and language, are rather subjects of the same government than portions of the same people,—hostilities which are waged only to sever a legal tie may assume the regularity, and in some measure the mildness, of foreign war. Free men, carrying into insurrection those habits of voluntary obedience to which they have been trained, are more easily restrained from excess by the leaders in whom they have placed their confidence. Thus far it may be affirmed, happily for mankind, that insurgents are most humane where they are likely to be most successful. But it is one of the most deplorable circumstances in the lot of man, that the subjects of despotic governments, and still more those who are doomed to personal slavery, though their condition be the worst, and their revolt the most just, are disabled from conducting it to a beneficial result by the very magnitude of the evils under which they groan: for the most fatal effect of the yoke is, that it darkens the understanding and debases the soul: and that the victims of long oppression, who have never imbibed any noble principle of obedience, throw off every curb when they are released from the chain and the lash. In such wretched conditions of society, the rulers may, indeed, retain unlimited power as the moral guardians of the community, while they are conducting the arduous process of gradually transforming slaves into men; but they cannot justly retain it without that purpose, or longer than its accomplishment requires: and the extreme difficulty of such a reformation, as well as the dire effects of any other emancipation, ought to be deeply considered, as proofs of the enormous guilt of those who introduce any kind or degree of unlimited power, as well as of those who increase, by their obstinate resistance, the natural obstacles to the pacific amendment of evils so tremendous.

The frame of the human mind, and the structure of civilized society, have adapted themselves to these important differences between civil and foreign war. Such is the force of the considerations which have been above enumerated; so tender is the regard of good men for the peace of their native country,—so numerous are the links of interest and habit which bind those of a more common sort to an establishment,—so difficult and dangerous is it for the bad and bold to conspire against a tolerably vigilant administration,—the evils which exist in moderate governments appear so tolerable, and those of absolute despotism so incorrigible, that the number of unjust wars between states unspeakably surpasses those of wanton rebellions against the just exercise of authority. Though the maxim, that there are no unprovoked revolts, ascribed to the Duc de Sully, and adopted by Mr. Burke,* cannot be received without exceptions, it must be owned that in civilized times mankind have suffered less from a mutinous spirit than from a patient endurance of bad government.

Neither can it be denied that the objects for which revolted subjects take up arms do, in most cases, concern their safety and well-being more deeply than the interests of states are in general affected by the legitimate causes of regular war. A nation may justly make war for the honour of her flag, or for dominion over a rock, if the one be insulted, and the other be unjustly invaded; because acquiescence in the outrage or the wrong may lower her reputation, and thereby lessen her safety. But if these sometimes faint and remote dangers justify an appeal to arms, shall it be blamed in a people who have no other chance of vindicating the right to worship God according to their consciences,—to be exempt from imprisonment and exaction at the mere will and pleasure of one or a few, and to enjoy as perfect a security for their persons, for the free exercise of their industry, and for the undisturbed enjoyment of its fruits, as can be devised by human wisdom under equal laws and a pure administration of justice? What foreign enemy could do a greater wrong to a community than the ruler who would reduce them to hold these interests by no higher tenure than the duration of his pleasure? What war can be more necessary than that which is waged in defence of ancient laws and venerable institutions, which, as far as they are suffered to act, have for ages approved themselves to be the guard of all these sacred privileges,—the shield which protects Reason in her fearless search of truth, and Conscience in the performance of her humble duty towards God,—the nursery of genius and valour,—the spur of probity, humanity, and generosity,—of every faculty of man.

As James was unquestionably an aggressor, and the people of England drew their swords only to prevent him from accomplishing a revolution which would have changed a legal and limited power into a lawless despotism, it is needless, on this occasion, to moot the question, whether arms may be as justly wielded to obtain as to defend liberty. It may, however, be observed, that the rulers who obstinately persist in withholding from their subjects securities for good government, obviously necessary for the permanence of that blessing, generally desired by competently informed men, and capable of being introduced without danger to public tranquillity, appear thereby to place themselves in a state of hostility against the nation whom they govern. Wantonly to prolong a state of insecurity seems to be as much an act of aggression as to plunge a nation into it. When a people discover their danger, they have a moral claim on their governors for security against it. As soon as a distemper is discovered to be dangerous, and a safe and effectual remedy has been found, those who withhold the remedy are as much morally answerable for the deaths which may ensue as if they had administered poison. But though a reformatory revolt may in these circumstances become perfectly just, it has not the same likelihood of a prosperous issue with those insurrections which are more strictly and directly defensive. A defensive revolution, the sole purpose of which is to preserve and secure the laws, has a fixed boundary, conspicuously marked out by the well-defined object which it pursues, and which it seldom permanently over-reaches, and it is thus exempt from that succession of changes which disturbs all habits of peaceable obedience, and weakens every authority not resting on mere force.

Whenever war is justifiable, it is lawful to call in auxiliaries. But though always legitimate against a foreign or domestic enemy, it is often in civil contentions peculiarly dangerous to the wronged people themselves. It must always hazard national independence, and will therefore be the last resource of those who love their country. Good men, more especially if they are happy enough to be the natives of a civilized, and still more of a free country, religiously cultivate their natural repugnance to a remedy of which despair alone can warrant the employment. Yet the dangers of seeking foreign aid vary extremely in different circumstances, and these variations are chiefly regulated by the power, the interest, and the probable disposition of the auxiliary to become an oppressor. The perils are the least where the inferiority of national strength in the foreign ally is such as to forbid all projects of conquest, and where the independence and greatness of the nation to be succoured are the main or sole bulwarks of his own.

These fortunate peculiarities were all to be found in the relations between the people

* Thoughts on the Present Discontents.

of England and the republic of the United Provinces; and the two nations were farther united by their common apprehensions from France, by no obscure resemblance of national character, by the strong sympathies of religion and liberty, by the remembrance of the renowned reign in which the glory of England was founded on her aid to Holland, and, perhaps, also by the esteem for each other which both these maritime nations had learnt in the fiercest and most memorable combats, which had been then celebrated in the annals of naval warfare. The British people derived a new security from the dangers of foreign interposition from the situation of him who was to be the chief of the enterprise to be attempted for their deliverance, who had as deep an interest in their safety and well-being as in those of the nation whose forces he was to lead to their aid. William of Nassau, Prince of Orange, Stadtholder of the republic of the United Provinces, had been, before the birth of the Prince of Wales, first Prince of the Blood Royal of England; and his consort the Lady Mary, the eldest daughter of the King, was at that period presumptive heiress to the crown.

MEMOIR

OF THE AFFAIRS OF HOLLAND.

A. D. 1667—1686.

The Seven United Provinces which established their independence made little change in their internal institutions. The revolt against Philip's personal commands was long carried on under colour of his own legal authority, conjointly exercised by his lieutenant, the Prince of Orange, and by the States,—composed of the nobility and of the deputies of towns,—who had before shared a great portion of it. But, being bound to each other in an indissoluble confederacy, established at Utrecht in 1579, the care of their foreign relations and of all their common affairs was intrusted to delegates, sent from each, who gradually assumed that name of "States-General," which had been originally bestowed only on the occasional assemblies of the whole States of all the Belgic provinces. These arrangements, hastily adopted in times of confusion, drew no distinct lines of demarcation between the provincial and federal authorities. Hostilities had been for many years carried on before the authority of Philip was finally abrogated; and after that decisive measure the States showed considerable disposition to the revival of a monarchical power in the person of an Austrian or French prince, or of the Queen of England. William I., seems about to have been invested with the ancient legal character of Earl of Holland at the moment of his murder.* He and his successors were Stadtholders of the greater provinces, and sometimes of all: they exercised in that character a powerful influence on the election of the magistrates of towns; they commanded the forces of the confederacy by sea and land; they combined the prerogatives of their ancient magistracy with the new powers, the assumption of which the necessities of war seemed to justify; and they became engaged in constant disputes with the great political bodies, whose pretensions to an undivided sovereignty were as recent and as little defined as their own rights. While Holland formed the main strength of the confederacy, the city of Amsterdam predominated in the councils of that province. The provincial States of Holland, and the patricians in the towns from whom their magistrates were selected, were the aristocratical antagonists of the stadtholderian power, which chiefly rested on official patronage, on military command, on the favour of the populace, and on the influence of the minor provinces in the States-General.

The House of Nassau stood conspicuous, at the dawn of modern history, among the noblest of the ruling families of Germany. In the thirteenth century, Adolphus of Nassau succeeded Rodolph of Hapsburg in the imperial crown,—the highest dignity of the Christian world. A branch of this ancient house had acquired ample possessions in the Netherlands, together with the principality of Orange in Provence; and under Charles V., William of Nassau was the most potent lord of the Burgundian provinces. Educated in the palace and almost in the chamber of the Emperor, he was nominated in the earliest years of manhood to the government of Holland,* and to the command of the imperial army, by that sagacious monarch, who, in the memo-

* Commentarii de Republicâ Bataviensi (Ludg. Bat. 1795), vol. ii. pp. 42, 43.

* By the ancient name of "Stadthouder" (lieutenant). Kluit, Vetus Jus Pub. Belg. p. 364.

rable solemnity of abdication, leant upon his shoulder as the first of his Belgic subjects. The same eminent qualities which recommended him to the confidence of Charles awakened the jealousy of Philip, whose anger, breaking through all the restraints of his wonted simulation, burst into furious reproaches against the Prince of Orange as the fomenter of the resistance of the Flemings to the destruction of their privileges. Among the three rulers who, perhaps unconsciously, were stirred up at the same moment to preserve the civil and religious liberties of mankind, William I. must be owned to have wanted the brilliant and attractive qualities of Henry IV., and to have yielded to the commanding genius of Elizabeth; but his principles were more inflexible than those of the amiable hero, and his mind was undisturbed by the infirmities and passions which lowered the illustrious queen. Though he performed great actions with weaker means than theirs, his course was more unspotted. Faithful to the King of Spain as long as the preservation of the commonwealth allowed, he counselled the Duchess of Parma against all the iniquities by which the Netherlands were lost; but faithful also to his county, in his dying instructions he enjoined his son to beware of insiduous offers of compromise from the Spaniard, to adhere to his alliance with France and England, to observe the privileges of the provinces and towns, and to conduct himself in all things as became the chief magistrate of the republic.* Advancing a century beyond his contemporaries in civil wisdom, he braved the prejudices of the Calvinistic clergy, by contending for the toleration of Catholics, the chiefs of whom had sworn his destruction.† Thoughtful, of unconquerable spirit, persuasive though taciturn, of simple character, yet maintaining due dignity and becoming magnificence in his public character, an able commander and a wise statesman, he is perhaps the purest of those who have risen by arms from private station to supreme authority, and the greatest of the happy few who have enjoyed the glorious fortune of bestowing liberty upon a people.‡ The whole struggle of this illustrious prince was against foreign oppression. His posterity, less happy, were engaged in domestic broils, in part arising from their undefined authority, and from the very complicated constitution of the commonwealth.

Maurice, the eldest Protestant son of William, surpassed his father in military genius, but fell far short of him in that moderation of temper and principle which is the most indispensable virtue of the leader of a free state. The blood of Barneveldt and the dungeon of Grotius have left an indelible stain on his memory; nor is it without apparent reason that the aristocratical party have charged him with projects of usurpation,—natural to a family of republican magistrates allied by blood to all the kings of Europe, and distinguished by many approaches and pretensions to the kingly power.* Henry Frederic, his successor, was the son of William I. by Louise de Coligny,—a woman singular in her character as well as in her destiny, who, having seen her father and the husband of her youth murdered at the massacre of Saint Bartholomew, was doomed to witness the fall of a more illustrious husband by the hand of an assassin of the same faction, and who in her last widowhood won the affection of William's children by former wives, for her own virtuous son. Having maintained the fame of his family in war, he was happier than his more celebrated brother in a domestic administration, which was moderate, tolerant, and unsuspected.† He lived to see the final recognition of Dutch independence by the treaty of Munster, and was succeeded by his son, William II., who, after a short and turbulent rule, died in 1650, leaving his widow, the Princess Royal of England, pregnant.

William III., born on the 14th of November, 1650, eight days after the death of his father, an orphan of feeble frame, with early indications of disease, seemed to be involved in the cloud of misfortune which then covered the deposed and exiled family of his mother. The patricians of the commercial cities, who had gathered strength with their rapidly increasing wealth, were incensed at the late attack of William II. on Amsterdam; they were equally emboldened by the establishment of a republic in England, and prejudiced, not without reason, against the Stuart family, whose absurd principle of the divine right of kings had always disposed James I. to regard the Dutch as no better than successful rebels,‡ and had led his son, in 1631, a period of profound peace and professed friendship, to conclude a secret treaty with Spain for the partition of the Republic, in which England was to be rewarded for her treachery and rapine by the sovereignty of Zealand.§ They found no difficulty in persuading the States to assume all the authority hitherto exercised by the Stadtholder, without fixing any period for conferring on the infant Prince those dignities which had been enjoyed by three generations of his

* D'Estrades, MSS. in the hands of his youngest son.

† Burnet, History of his own time (Oxford, 1823), vol. i. p. 547.

‡ Even Strada himself bears one testimony to this great man, which outweighs all his vain reproaches. "Nec postea mutavere (Hollandi) qui videbant et gloriabantur ab *unius hominis* conatu, cæptisque illi utcunque infelicibus, assurgere in dies Hollandicum nomen imperiumque."—Strada, De Bello Belgico, dec. ii. lib. v.

* Du Maurier, Mémoires de la Hollande, p. 293. Vandervynkt, Troubles des Pays Bas, vol. iii. p. 27.

† D'Estrades, Lettres (Lond. 1743), vol. i. p. 55.

‡ "In his table discourse he pronounced the Dutch to be rebels, and condemned their cause, and said that Ostend *belonged* to the Archduke."—Carte, History of England, vol. iii. p. 714.

§ Clarendon, State Papers, vol. i. p. 49, and vol. ii. app. xxvii.

family. At the peace of 1654, the States of Holland bound themselves by a secret article, yielded with no great reluctance to the demands of Cromwell, never to choose the Prince of Orange to be their Stadtholder, nor to consent to his being appointed Captain-General of the forces of the confederacy;—a separate stipulation, at variance with the spirit of the union of Utrecht, and disrespectful to the judgment, if not injurious to the rights, of the weaker confederates.* After the Restoration this engagement lost its power. But when the Prince of Orange had nearly reached years of discretion, and the brilliant operations of a military campaign against England had given new vigour to the republican administration, John De Witt, who, under the modest title of "Pensionary" of Holland, had long directed the affairs of the confederacy with a success and reputation due to his matchless honesty and prudence, prevailed on the States of that province to pass a "Perpetual Edict for the Maintenance of Liberty." By this law they abolished the Stadtholdership in their own province, and agreed to take effectual means to obtain from their confederates edicts excluding all those who might be Captain-Generals from the Stadtholdership of any of the provinces,—binding themselves and their successors by oath to observe these provisions, and imposing the like oath on all who might be appointed to the chief command by land or sea.† Guelderland, Utrecht, and Overyssell acceded. Friesland and Groningen, then governed by a Stadtholder of another branch of the family of Nassau, were considered as not immediately interested in the question. Zealand alone, devoted to the House of Orange, resisted the separation of the supreme military and civil officers. On this footing De Witt professed his readiness to confer the office of Captain-General on the Prince, as soon as he should be of fit age. He was allowed meanwhile to take his seat in the Council of State, and took an oath to observe the Perpetual Edict. His opponents struggled to retard his military appointment, to shorten its duration, and to limit its powers. His partisans, on the other hand, supported by England, and led by Amelia of Solms, the widow of Prince Henry,—a woman of extraordinary ability, who had trained the young Prince with parental tenderness,—seized every opportunity of pressing forward his nomination, and of preparing the way for the enlargement of his authority.

This contest might have been longer protracted, if the Conspiracy of Louis and Charles, and the occupation of the greater part of the country by the former, had not brought undeserved reproach on the administration of De Witt. Fear and distrust became universal; every man suspected his neighbour; accusations were heard with greedy credulity; misfortunes were imputed to treachery; and the multitude cried aloud for victims. The corporate officers of the great towns, originally chosen by the burghers, had, on the usual plea of avoiding tumult, obtained the right of filling up all vacancies in their own number. They thus strengthened their power, but destroyed their security. No longer connected with the people by election, the aristocratical families received no fresh infusion of strength, and had no hold on the attachment of the community; though they still formed, indeed, the better part of the people. They had raised the fishermen of a few marshy districts to be one of the greatest nations of Europe; but the misfortunes of a moment banished the remembrance of their services. Their grave and harsh virtues were more unpopular than so many vices; while the needs and disasters of war served to heighten the plebeian clamour, and to strengthen the military power, which together formed the combined force of the Stadtholderian party. It was then in vain that the Republicans endeavoured to satisfy that party, and to gain over the King of England by the nomination of the Prince of Orange to be Captain-General: Charles was engaged in deeper designs. The progress of the French arms still farther exasperated the populace, and the Republicans incurred the reproach of treachery by a disposition,—perhaps carried to excess,—to negotiate with Louis XIV. at a moment when all negotiation wore the appearance of submission. So it had formerly happened:—Barneveldt was friendly to peace with Spain, when Maurice saw no safety but in arms. Men equally wise and honest may differ on the difficult and constantly varying question, whether uncompromising resistance, or a reservation of active effort for a more favourable season, be the best mode of dealing with a formidable conqueror. Though the war policy of Demosthenes terminated in the destruction of Athens, we dare not affirm that the pacific system of Phocion would have saved it. In the contest of Maurice with Barneveldt, and of De Witt with the adherents of the House of Orange, both parties had an interest distinct from that of the commonwealth; for the influence of the States grew in peace, and the authority of the Captain-General was strengthened by war. The populace now revolted against their magistrates in all the towns, and the States of Holland were compelled to repeal the Edict, which they—called "Perpetual,"—to release themselves and all the officers from the oath which they had taken to observe it, and to confer, on the 4th of July, 1672, on the Prince the office of Stadtholder,—which, then only elective for life, was,

* Cromwell was prevailed upon to content himself with this separate stipulation, very imperfect in form, but which the strength of the ruling province rendered in substance sufficient. Whitelock, Memorials, 12th May, 1684.

† 3d August 1667. The immediate occasion of this edict seems to have been a conspiracy, for which one Buat, a spy employed by Lord Arlington, was executed. Histoire de J. D. De Witt (Utrecht, 1709), liv. ii. chap. 2.

after two years more, made hereditary to his descendants.

The commotions which accompanied this revolution were stained by the murder of John and Cornelius De Witt,—a crime perpetrated with such brutal ferocity, and encountered with such heroic serenity, that it may almost seem to be doubtful whether the glory of having produced such pure sufferers may not in some degree console a country for having given birth to assassins so atrocious. These excesses are singularly at variance with the calm and orderly character of the Dutch,—than whom perhaps no free state has, in proportion to its magnitude, contributed more amply to the amendment of mankind by examples of public virtue. The Prince of Orange, thus hurried to the supreme authority at the age of twenty-two, was ignorant of these crimes, and avowed his abhorrence of them. They were perpetrated more than a month after his highest advancement, when they could produce no effect but that of bringing odium upon his party. But it must be for ever deplored that the extreme danger of his position should have prevented him from punishing the offences of his partisans, till it seemed too late to violate that species of tacit amnesty which time insensibly establishes. It would be impossible ever to excuse this unhappy impunity, if we did not call to mind that Louis XIV. was at Utrecht; that it was the populace of the Hague that had imbrued their hands in the blood of the De Witts; and that the magistrates of Amsterdam might be disposed to avenge on their country the cause of their virtuous chiefs. Henceforward William directed the counsels and arms of Holland, gradually forming and leading a confederacy to set bounds to the ambition of Louis XIV., and became, by his abilities and dispositions, as much as by his position, the second person in Europe.

We possess unsuspected descriptions of his character from observers of more than ordinary sagacity, who had an interest in watching its development, before it was surrounded by the dazzling illusions of power and fame. Among the most valuable of these witnesses were some of the subjects and servants of Louis XIV. At the age of eighteen the Prince's good sense, knowledge of affairs, and seasonable concealment of his thoughts, attracted the attention of Gourville, a man of experience and discernment. St. Evremond, though himself distinguished chiefly by vivacity and accomplishments, saw the superiority of William's powers through his silence and coldness. After long intimacy, Sir William Temple describes his great endowments and excellent qualities, his—then almost singular—combination of "charity and religious zeal," "his desire—rare in every age—to grow great rather by the service than the servitude of his country;"—language so manifestly considerate, discriminating, and unexaggerated, as to bear on it the inimitable stamp of truth, in addition to the weight which it derives from the probity of the writer. But there is no testimony so important as that of Charles II., who, in the early part of his reign, had been desirous of gaining an ascendant in Holland by the restoration of the House of Orange, and of subverting the government of De Witt, whom he never forgave for his share in the treaty with the English Republic. Some retrospect is necessary, to explain the experiment by which that monarch both ascertained and made known the ruling principles of his nephew's mind.

The mean negotiations about the sale of Dunkirk first betrayed to Louis XIV. the passion of Charles for French money. The latter had, at the same time, offered to aid Louis in the conquest of Flanders, on condition of receiving French succour against the revolt of his own subjects,* and had strongly expressed his desire of an offensive and defensive alliance to Ruvigni, one of the most estimable of that monarch's agents.† But the most pernicious of Charles' vices, never bridled by any virtue, were often mitigated by the minor vices of indolence and irresolution. Even the love of pleasure, which made him needy and rapacious, unfitted him for undertakings full of toil and peril. Projects for circumventing each other in Holland, which Charles aimed at influencing through the House of Orange, and Louis hoped to master through the Republican party, retarded their secret advances to an entire union. De Witt was compelled to consent to some aggrandisement of France, rather than expose his country to a war without the co-operation of the King of England, who was ready to betray a hated ally. The first Dutch war appears to have arisen from the passions of both nations, and their pride of maritime supremacy,—employed as instruments by Charles wherewith to obtain booty at sea, and supply from his Parliament,—and by Louis wherewith to seize the Spanish Netherlands. At the peace of Breda (July, 1667,) the Court of England seemed for a moment to have changed its policy, by the conclusion of the Triple Alliance, which prescribed some limits to the ambition of France,—a system which De Witt, as soon as he met so honest a negotiator as Sir William Temple, joyfully hastened to embrace.

Temple was, however, duped by his master. It is probable that the Triple Alliance was the result of a fraudulent project, suggested originally by Gourville to ruin De Witt, by embroiling him irreconcilably with France.‡ Charles made haste to disavow the intentions professed in it;§ and a nego-

* D'Estrades, vol. v. p. 450.

† Mémoire de Ruvigni au Roi. Dalrymple, Memoirs of Great Britain, &c. vol. ii. p. 11. D'Estrades, vol. v., 20th Dec. 1663. 18th Dec. 1664.

‡ Mémoires de Gourville (Paris, 1724), vol. ii p. 14—18, 160.

§ Charles II. to the Duchess of Orleans, 13th Jan. 1668.—Dalrymple, vol. ii. p. 5. [The old style is used throughout these references.—Ed.]

tiation with France was immediately opened, partly by the personal intercourse of Charles with the French ministers at his court, but chiefly through his sister, the Duchess of Orleans,—an amiable princess, probably the only person whom he ever loved. This correspondence, which was concealed from those of his ministers who were not either Catholics or well affected to the Catholic religion, lingered on till May, 1670, when (on the 22d) a secret treaty was concluded under cover of a visit made by the Duchess to her brother.*

The essential stipulations of this unparalleled compact were three: that Louis should advance money to Charles, to enable him the more safely to execute what is called "a declaration of his adherence to the Catholic religion," and should support him with men and money, if that measure should be resisted by his subjects; that both powers should join their arms against Holland, the islands of Walcheren and Cadsand being alloted to England as her share of the prey (which clearly left the other territories of the Republic at the disposal of Louis); and that England should aid Louis in any new pretensions to the crown of Spain, or, in other and plainer language, enable him, on the very probable event of Charles II. of Spain dying without issue,* to incorporate with a monarchy already the greatest in Europe the long-coveted inheritance of the House of Burgundy, and the two vast peninsulas of Italy and Spain. The strength of Louis would thus have been doubled at one blow, and all limitations to his farther progress on the Continent must have been left to his own moderation. It is hard to imagine what should have hindered him from rendering his monarchy universal over the civilized world. The port of Ostend, the island of Minorca, and the permission to conquer Spanish America, with a very vague promise of assistance of France, were assigned to England as the wages of her share of this conspiracy against mankind. The fearful stipulations for rendering the King of England independent of Parliament, by a secret supply of foreign money, and for putting into his hands a foreign military force, to be employed against his subjects, were, indeed, to take effect only in case of the avowal of his reconciliation with the Church of Rome. But as he himself considered a re-establishment of that Church as essential to the consolidation of his authority,—which the mere avowal of his religion would rather have weakened, and the bare toleration of it could little, if at all, have promoted; as he confessedly meditated measures for quieting the alarms of the possessors of Church lands, whom the simple letter of the treaty could not have much disturbed; as he proposed a treaty with the Pope to obtain the cup for the laity, and the mass in English,—concessions which are scarcely intelligible without the supposition that the Church of Rome was to be established; as he concealed this article from Shaftesbury, who must have known his religion, and was then friendly to a toleration of it; and as other articles were framed for the destruction of the only powerful Protestant state on the Continent, there cannot be the slightest doubt that the real object of this atrocious compact, however disguised under the smooth and crafty language of diplomacy, was the forcible imposition of a hated religion upon the British nation, and that the conspirators foresaw a national resistance, which must be stifled or quelled by a foreign army.† It was evident that the most tyrannical measures would have been necessary for the accomplishment of such purposes, and that the transfer of all civil, military, and ecclesiastical power to the members of a communion, who had no barrier against public hatred but the throne, must have tended to render the power of Charles absolute, and must have afforded

* It was signed by Lords Arlington and Arundel, Sir Thomas Clifford, and Sir Richard Bealing, on the part of England, and by Colbert de Croissy, the brother of the celebrated financier, on the part of France. Rose, Observations on Fox's History, p. 51. Summary collated with the original, in the hands of the present Lord Clifford. The draft of the same treaty, sent to Paris by Arundel, does not materially differ. Dalrymple, vol. i. p. 44. "The Life of James II. (vol. i. pp. 440—450,) agrees, in most circumstances, with these copies of the treaties, and with the correspondence. There is one important variation. In the treaty it is stipulated that Charles' measures in favour of the Catholic religion should precede the war against Holland, according to the plan which he had always supported. 'The Life' says, that the resolution was taken at Dover to begin with the war against Holland, and the despatch of Colbert from Dover, 20th May (Dalrymple, vol. ii. p. 57), almost justifies the statement, which may refer to a verbal acquiescence of Charles, probably deemed sufficient in these clandestine transactions, where that prince desired nothing but such assurances as satisfy gentlemen in private life. It is true that the narrative of the Life is not here supported by those quotations from the King's original Memoirs, on which the credit of the compilation essentially depends. But as in the eighteen years, 1660—1678, which exhibit no such quotations, there are internal proofs that some passages, at least, of the Life are taken from the Memoirs, the absence of quotation does not derogate so much from the credit of this part of the work as it would from that of any other." See Edinburgh Review, vol. xxvi. pp. 402—430. This treaty has been laid to the charge of the Cabinet called the "Cabal," unjustly; for, of the five members of that administration, two only, Clifford and Arlington, were privy to the designs of the King and the Duke of York. Ashley and Lauderdale were too zealous Protestants to be trusted with it. Buckingham (whatever might be his indifference in religion) had too much levity to be trusted with such secrets; but he was so penetrating that it was thought prudent to divert his attention from the real negotiation, by engaging him in negotiating a simulated treaty, in which the articles favourable to the Catholic religion were left out. On the other hand, Lord Arundel and Sir Richard Bealing, Catholics not of the "Cabal," were negotiators.

* Charles II., King of Spain, was then a feeble and diseased child of nine years old.

† Dalrymple, vol. ii. p. 84.

him the most probable means of effectually promoting the plans of his ally for the subjugation of Europe.* If the foreign and domestic objects of this treaty be considered, together with the means by which they were to have been accomplished, and the dire consequences which must have flowed from their attainment, it seems probable that so much falsehood, treachery, and mercenary meanness were never before combined, in the decent formalities of a solemn compact between sovereigns, with such premeditated bloodshed and unbridled cruelty. The only semblance of virtue in the dark plot was the anxiety shown to conceal it; which, however, arose more from the fears than the shame of the conspirators. In spite of all their precautions it transpired: the secret was extorted from Turenne, in a moment of weakness, by a young mistress.† He also disclosed some of the correspondence to Puffendorf, the Swedish minister at Paris, to detach the Swedes from the Triple Alliance;‡ and it was made known by that minister, as well as by De Groot, the Dutch ambassador at Paris, to De Witt, who had never ceased to distrust the sincerity of the Stuarts towards Holland.§ The suspicions of Temple himself had been early awakened; and he seems to have in some measure played the part of a willing dupe, in the hope of entangling his master in honest alliances. The substance of the secret treaty was the subject of general conversation at the Court of England at the time of Puffendorf's discovery.‖ A pamphlet published, or at least printed, in 1673, intelligibly hints at its existence "about four years before."¶ Not long after, Louis XIV., in a moment of dissatisfaction with Charles II., permitted or commanded the Abbate Primi to print a History of the Dutch War at Paris, which derived credit from being soon suppressed at the instance of the English minister, and which gave an almost verbally exact summary of the secret treaty, with respect to three of its objects,—the partition of Holland, the re-establishment of the Catholic religion in the British Islands, and the absolute authority of the King.** The project for the dismemberment of Holland, adopted by Charles I. in 1631 appears to have been entertained by his eldest son till the last years of his reign.*

As one of the articles of the secret treaty had provided a petty sovereignty for the Prince of Orange out of the ruins of his country, Charles took the opportunity of his nephew's visit to England, in October 1670, to sound him on a project which was thus baited for his concurrence. "All the Protestants," said the King, "are a factious body, broken among themselves since they have been broken from the main stock. Look into these things better; do not be misled by your Dutch blockheads."† The King immediately imparted the failure of this attempt to the French ambassador: "I am satisfied with the Prince's abilities, but I find him too zealous a Dutchman and a Protestant to be trusted with the secret."‡ But enough had escaped to disclose to the sagacious youth the purposes of his uncle, and to throw a strong light on the motives of all his subsequent measures. The inclination of Charles towards the Church of Rome could never have rendered a man so regardless of religion solicitous for a conversion, if he had not considered it as subservient to projects for the civil establishment of that Church,—which, as it could subsist only by his favour, must have been the instrument of his absolute power. Astonished as William was by the discovery, he had the fortitude, during the life of Charles, to conceal it from all but one, or, at most, two friends. It was reserved for later times to discover that Charles had the inconceivable baseness to propose the detention of his nephew in England, where the temptation of a sovereignty being aided by the prospect of the recovery of his freedom, might act more powerfully on his mind; and that this proposal was refused by Louis, either from magnanimity, or from regard to decency, or, perhaps, from reluctance to trust his ally with the sole disposal of so important a prisoner.

Though—to return,—in 1672 the French army had advanced into the heart of Holland, the fortitude of the Prince was unshaken. Louis offered to make him sovereign of the remains of the country, under the protection of France and England:§ but at that moment of extreme peril, he answered with his usual calmness, "I never will betray a trust, nor sell the liberties of my country, which my ancestors have so long defended." All around him despaired.—One of his very few confidential friends, after having long expostulated with him on his fruitless obstinacy, at length asked him, if he had considered how and where he should live after Holland was lost. "I have thought of that;" he replied; "I am resolved

* It is but just to mention, that Burnet calls it only the "*toleration* of popery."—vol. i. p. 522. He had seen only Primi's history, and he seems to speak of the negotiation carried on through Buckingham, from whom we know that the full extent of the plan was concealed.

† Ramsay, Histoire de Turenne (Paris, 1735), vol. i. p. 429.

‡ Sir W. Temple to Sir Orlando Bridgman, 24th April, 1669.

§ De Witt observed to Temple, even in the days of the Triple Alliance:—"A change of councils in England would be our ruin. Since the reign of Elizabeth there has been such a fluctuation in the English councils that it has been impossible to concert measures with them for two years."

‖ Pepys' Memoirs, vol. ii. p. 336.

¶ England's Appeal from the Private Cabal at Whitehall.

** State Trials in the reign of Wm. III. (Lond. 1705), Introd. p. 10.

* Preston Papers in the possession of Sir James Graham, of Netherby.

† Burnet, vol. i. p. 475.

‡ Dalrymple, vol. ii. p. 70. § Ibid, p. 79.

to live on the lands I have left in Germany. I had rather pass my life in hunting there, than sell my country or my liberty to France at any price."* Buckingham and Arlington were sent from England to try, whether, beset by peril, the lure of sovereignty might not seduce him. The former often said, "Do you not see that the country is lost?" The answer of the Prince to the profligate buffoon spoke the same unmoved resolution with that which he had made to Zulestein or Fagel; but it naturally rose a few degrees towards animation:—"I see it is in great danger, but there is a sure way of never seeing it lost; and that is, to die in the last ditch."† The perfect simplicity of these declarations may authorise us to rank them among the most genuine specimens of true magnanimity. Perhaps the history of the world does not hold out a better example, how high above the reach of fortune the pure principle of obedience to the dictates of conscience, unalloyed by interest, passion, or ostentation, can raise the mind of a virtuous man. To set such an example is an unspeakably more signal service to mankind, than all the outward benefits which flow to them from the most successful virtue. It is a principle independent of events, and one that burns most brightly in adversity,—the only agent, perhaps, of sufficient power to call forth the native greatness of soul which lay hid under the cold and unattractive deportment of the Prince of Orange.

His present situation was calculated to ascertain whether his actions would correspond with his declarations. Beyond the important country extending from Amsterdam to Rotterdam,—a district of about forty miles in length, the narrow seat of the government, wealth, and force of the commonwealth, which had been preserved from invasion by the bold expedient of inundation, and out of which the cities and fortresses arose like islands,—little remained of the republican territory except the fortress of Maestricht, the marshy islands of Zealand, and the secluded province of Friesland. A French army of a hundred and ten thousand men, encouraged by the presence of Louis, and commanded by Condé and Turenne, had their head-quarters at Utrecht, within twenty miles of Amsterdam, and impatiently looked forward to the moment when the ice should form a road to the spoils of that capital of the commercial world. On the other side, the hostile flag of England was seen from the coast. The Prince of Orange, a sickly youth of twenty-two, without fame or experience, had to contend against such enemies at the head of a new government, of a divided people, and of a little army of twenty thousand men,—either raw recruits or foreign mercenaries,—whom the exclusively maritime policy of the late administration had left without officers of skill or name. His immortal ancestor, when he founded the republic about a century before, saw at the lowest ebb of his fortune the hope of aid from England and France: far darker were the prospects of William III. The degenerate successor of Elizabeth, abusing the ascendant of a parental relation, sought to tempt him to become a traitor to his country for a share in her spoils. The successor of Henry IV. offered him only the choice of being bribed or crushed. Such was their fear of France, that the Court of Spain did not dare to aid him, though their only hope was from his success. The German branch of the House of Austria was then entangled in a secret treaty with Louis, by which the Low Countries were ceded to him, on condition of his guaranteeing to the Emperor the reversion of the Spanish monarchy on the death of Charles II. without issue. No great statesman, no illustrious commander but Montecucculi, no able prince but the great Elector of Brandenburgh, was to be found among the avowed friends or even secret well-wishers of William. The territories of Cologne and Liege, which presented all the means of military intercourse between the French and Dutch frontiers, were ruled by the creatures of Louis. The final destruction of a rebellious and heretical confederacy was foretold with great, but not apparently unreasonable confidence, by the zealots of absolute authority in Church and State; and the inhabitants of Holland began seriously to entertain the heroic project of abandoning an enslaved country, and transporting the commonwealth to their dominions in the Indian islands.

At this awful moment Fortune seemed to pause. The unwieldly magnificence of a royal retinue encumbered the advance of the French army. Though masters of Naerden, which was esteemed the bulwark of Amsterdam, they were too late to hinder the opening of the sluices at Murden, which drowned the country to the gates of that city. Louis, more intoxicated with triumph than intent on conquest, lost in surveying the honours of victory the time which should have been spent in seizing its fruits. Impatient of so long an interruption of his pleasures, he hastened to display at Versailles the trophies of a campaign of two months, in which the conquest of three provinces, the capture of fifty fortified places, and of twenty-four thousand prisoners, were ascribed to him by his flatterers. The cumbrous and tedious formalities of the Dutch constitution enabled the Stadtholder to gain some time without suspicion. Even the perfidious embassy of Buckingham and Arlington contributed somewhat to prolong negotiations. He amused them for a moment by appearing to examine the treaties they had brought from London, by which France was to gain all the fortresses which commanded the country, leaving Zealand to England, and the rest of the

* Temple, Works (Lond. 1721), vol. i. p. 381. This friend was probably his uncle Zulestein, for the conversation passed before his intimacy with Bentinck.

† Burnet, vol. i. p. 569.

country as a principality to himself.* Submission seemed inevitable and speedy; still the inundation rendered military movements inconvenient and perhaps hazardous; and the Prince thus obtained a little leisure for the execution of his measures. The people, unable to believe the baseness of the Court of London, were animated by the appearance of the ministers who came to seal their ruin: the Government, surrounded by the waters, had time to negotiate at Madrid, Vienna, and Berlin. The Marquis de Monterey, governor of the Catholic Netherlands, without instructions from the Escurial, had the boldness to throw troops into the important fortresses of Dutch Brabant,—Breda, Bergen-op-Zoom, and Bois-le-Duc,—under pretence of a virtual guarantee of that territory by Spain.

In England, the continuance of prorogations—relieving the King from parliamentary opposition, but depriving him of sufficient supply,—had driven him to resources alike inadequate and infamous,† and had foreboded that general indignation which, after the combined fleets of England and France had been worsted by the marine of Holland‡ alone, at the very moment when the remnant of the Republic seemed about to be swallowed up, compelled him to desist from the open prosecution of the odious conspiracy against her.§ The Emperor Leopold, roused to a just sense of the imminent danger of Europe, also concluded a defensive alliance with the States-General;‖ as did the Germanic body generally, including Frederic William of Brandenburgh, called the "Great Elector."

Turenne had been meanwhile compelled to march from the Dutch territory to observe, and, in case of need, to oppose, the Austrian and Brandenburgh troops; and the young Prince ceased to incur the risk and to enjoy the glory of being opposed to that great commander, who was the grandson of William I.,¶ and had been trained to arms under Maurice. The winter of 1672 was unusually late and short. As soon as the ice seemed sufficiently solid, Luxemburgh, who was left in command at Utrecht, advanced, in the hope of surprising the Hague; when a providential thaw obliged him to retire. His operations were limited to the destruction of two petty towns; and it seems doubtful whether he did not owe his own escape to the irresolution or treachery of a Dutch officer intrusted with a post which commanded the line of retreat. At the perilous moment of Luxemburgh's advance, took place William's long march through Brabant to the attack of Charleroi,—undertaken probably more with a view of raising the drooping spirits of his troops than in the hope of ultimate success. The deliverance of Holland in 1672 was the most signal triumph of a free people over mighty invaders, since the defeat of Xerxes.

In the ensuing year, William's offensive operations had more outward and lasting consequences. Having deceived Luxemburgh, he recovered Naerden, and shortly hazarding another considerable march beyond the frontier, he captured the city of Bonn, and thus compelled Turenne to provide for the safety of his army by recrossing the Rhine. The Spanish governor of the Low Countries then declared war against France; and Louis was compelled to recall his troops from Holland. Europe now rose on all sides against the monarch who not many months before appeared to be her undisputed lord. So mighty were the effects of a gallant stand by a small people, under an inexperienced chief, without a council or minister but the Pensionary Fagel,—the pupil and adherent of De Witt, who, actuated by the true spirit of his great master, continued faithfully to serve his country, in spite of the saddest examples of the ingratitude of his countrymen. In the six years of war which followed, the Prince commanded in three battles against the greatest generals of France. At Senef,* it was a sufficient honour that he was not defeated by Condé; and that the veteran declared, on reviewing the events of the day,—"The young Prince has shown all the qualities of the most experienced commander, except that he exposed his own person too much." He was defeated without dishonour at Cassel,† by Luxemburgh, under the nominal command of the Duke of Orleans. He gained an advantage over the same great general, after an obstinate and bloody action, at St. Denis, near Mons. This last proceeding was of more doubful morality than any other of his military life, the battle being fought four days after the signature of a separate treaty of peace by the Dutch plenipotentiaries at Nimeguen.‡ It was not, indeed, a breach of faith, for there was no armistice, and the ratifications were not executed. It is uncertain, even, whether he had information of what had passed at Nimeguen; the official despatches from the States-General reaching him only the next morning. The treaty had been suddenly and unexpectedly brought to a favourable conclusion by the French ministers; and the Prince, who condemned it as

* The official despatches of these ambassadors are contained in a MS. volume, probably the property of Sir W. Trumbull, now in the hands of his descendant, the Marquis of Downshire. These despatches show that the worst surmises circulated at the time of the purposes of this embassy were scarcely so bad as the truth.

† Shutting up of the Exchequer, 2d January, 1672.

‡ Battle of Southwold Bay, 28th and 29th May, 1672. In these memorable actions even the biographer of James II. in effect acknowledges that De Ruyter had the advantage.—Life, vol. i. pp. 457—476.

§ Peace concluded at Westminster, Feb. 19th, 1674.

‖ 25th July, 1672.

¶ By Elizabeth of Nassau, Duchess of Bouillon.

* 11th August, 1674.

† 11 April, 1677.

‡ 10th August, 1678.

alike offensive to good faith and sound policy, had reasonable hopes of obtaining a victory, which, if gained before the final signature, might have determined the fluctuating counsels of the States to the side of vigour and honour. The morality of soldiers, even in our own age, is not severe in requiring proof of the necessity of bloodshed, if the combat be fair, the event brilliant, and, more particularly, if the commander freely exposes his own life. His gallant enemies warmly applauded this attack, distinguished, as it seems eminently to have been, for the daring valour, which was brightened by the gravity and modesty of his character; and they declared it to be "the only heroic action of a six years' war between all the great nations of Europe." If the official despatches had not hindered him from prosecuting the attack on the next day with the English auxiliaries, who must then have joined him, he was likely to have changed the fortune of the war.

The object of the Prince and the hope of his confederates had been to restore Europe to the condition in which it had been placed by the treaty of the Pyrenees.* The result of the negotiations at Nimeguen was to add the province of Franche Comté, and the most important fortresses of the Flemish frontier, to the cessions which Louis at Aix-la-Chapelle† had extorted from Spain. The Spanish Netherlands were thus farther stripped of their defence, the barrier of Holland weakened, and the way opened for the reduction of all the posts which face the most defenceless parts of the English coast. The acquisition of Franche Comté broke the military connection between Lombardy and Flanders, secured the ascendant of France in Switzerland, and, together with the usurpation of Lorraine, exposed the German empire to new aggression. The ambition of the French monarch was inflamed, and the spirit of neighbouring nations broken, by the ineffectual resistance as much as by the long submission of Europe.

The ten years which followed the peace of Nimeguen were the period of his highest elevation. The first exercise of his power was the erection of three courts, composed of his own subjects, and sitting by his authority, at Brissac, Mentz, and Besançon, to determine whether certain territories ought not to be annexed to France, which he claimed as fiefs of the provinces ceded to him by the Empire by the treaty of Westphalia. These courts, called "Chambers of Union," summoned the possessors of these supposed fiefs to answer the King's complaints. The justice of the claim and the competence of the tribunals were disputed with equal reason. The Chamber at Metz decreed the confiscation of eighty fiefs, for default of appearance by the feudatories, among whom were the Kings of Spain and Sweden, and the Elector Palatine. Some petty spiritless princes actually did homage to Louis for territories, said to have been anciently fiefs of the see of Verdun;* and, under colour of a pretended judgment of the Chamber at Brissac,† the city of Strasburgh, a flourishing Protestant republic, which commanded an important pass on the Rhine, was surrounded at midnight, in a time of profound peace, by a body of French soldiers, who compelled those magistrates who had not been previously corrupted to surrender the city to the crown of France,‡ amidst the consternation and affliction of the people. Almost at the same hour, a body of troops entered Casal, in consequence of a secret treaty with the Duke of Mantua, a dissolute and needy youth, who for a bribe of a hundred thousand pounds, betrayed into the hands of Louis that fortress, then esteemed the bulwark of Lombardy.§ Both these usurpations were in contempt of a notice from the Imperial minister at Paris, against the occupation of Strasburgh, an Imperial city, or Casal, the capital of Montferrat, a fief of the Empire.‖

On the Belgic frontier, means were employed more summary and open than pretended judgments or clandestine treaties. Taking it upon himself to determine the extent of territory ceded to him at Nimeguen, Louis required from the Court of Madrid the possession of such districts as he thought fit. Much was immediately yielded. Some hesitation was shown in surrendering the town and district of Alost. Louis sent his troops into the Netherlands, there to stay till his demands were absolutely complied with; and he notified to the governor, that the slightest resistance would be the signal of war. Hostilities soon broke out, which after having made him master of Luxemburg, one of the strongest fortresses of Europe, were terminated in the summer of 1684, by a truce for twenty years, leaving him in pos-

* 7th Nov. 1659. † 2d May, 1668.

* Dumont, Corps Diplomatique, vol. vii. part ii. p. 13.

† Flassan, Histoire de la Diplomatie Française, vol. iv. pp. 59, 63.

‡ Œuvres de Louis XIV., vol. iv. p. 194, where the original correspondence is published. The pretended capitulation is dated on the 30th September, 1681. The design against Strasburg had been known in July.—MS. letters of Sir Henry Saville (minister at Paris) to Sir Leoline Jenkins. Downshire Papers.

§ Œuvres de Louis XIV., vol. iv. pp. 216, 217. The mutinous conscience of Catinat astonished and displeased the haughty Louvois. Casal had been ceded in 1678 by Matthioli, the Duke's minister, who, either moved by remorse or by higher bribes from the House of Austria, advised his master not to ratify the treaty; for which he was carried prisoner into France, and detained there in close and harsh custody. He was the famous man with the Iron Mask, who died in the Bastile. The bargain for Casal was disguised in the diplomatic forms of a convention between the King and the Duke.—Dumont, vol. vii. part ii. p. 14. An army of one thousand five hundred men was collected in Dauphiny, at the desire of the Duke, to give his sale the appearance of necessity.—Letter of Sir Henry Saville.

‖ Sir Henry Saville to Sir Leoline Jenkins. Fontainbleau, 12th Sept. 1681.

session of, and giving the sanction of Europe to, his usurpations.

To a reader of the nineteenth century, familiar with the present divisions of territory in Christendom, and accustomed to regard the greatness of France as well adapted to the whole state of the European system, the conquests of Louis XIV. may seem to have inspired an alarm disproportioned to their magnitude. Their real danger, however, will be speedily perceived by those who more accurately consider the state of surrounding countries, and the subdivision of dominion in that age. Two monarchies only of the first class existed on the continent, as the appellation of "the two Crowns," then commonly used in speaking of France and Spain, sufficiently indicate. But Spain, which, under the last Austrian king, had perhaps reached the lowest point of her extraordinary fall, was in truth no longer able to defend herself. The revenue of somewhat more than two millions sterling was inadequate to the annual expense.* Ronquillo, the minister of this vast empire in London, was reduced to the necessity of dismissing his servants without payment.† An invader who had the boldness to encounter the shadow of a great name had little to dread, except from the poverty of the country, which rendered it incapable of feeding an army. Naples, Lombardy, and the Catholic Netherlands, though the finest provinces of Europe, were a drain and a burden in the hands of a government sunk into imbecile dotage, and alike incapable of ruling and of maintaining these envied possessions. While Spain, a lifeless and gigantic body, covered the South of Europe, the manly spirit and military skill of Germany were rendered of almost as little avail by the minute subdivisions of its territory. From the Rhine to the Vistula, a hundred princes, jealous of each other, fearful of offending the conqueror, and often competitors for his disgraceful bounty, broke into fragments the strength of the Germanic race. The houses of Saxony and Bavaria, Brandenburg and Brunswick, Wurtemburg, Baden, and Hesse, though among the most ancient and noble of the ruling families of Europe, were but secondary states. Even the genius of the late Elector of Brandenburg did not exempt him from the necessity or the temptation of occasional compliance with Louis. From the French frontier to the Baltic, no one firm mass stood in the way of his arms. Prussia was not yet a monarchy, nor Russia an European state. In the south-eastern provinces of Germany, where Rodolph of Hapsburg had laid the foundations of his family, the younger branch had, from the death of Charles V. formed a monarchy which, aided by the Spanish alliance, the imperial dignity, and a military position on the central frontier of Christendom, rendering it the bulwark of the Empire against the irruptions of the Turkish barbarians, rose during the thirty years' war to such a power, that it was prevented only by Gustavus Adolphus from enslaving the whole of Germany. France, which under Richelieu had excited and aided that great prince and his followers, was for that reason regarded for a time as the protector of the German States against the Emperor. Bavaria, the Palatinate, and the three ecclesiastical Electorates, partly from remaining jealousy of Austria, and partly from growing fear of Louis, were disposed to seek his protection and acquiesce in many of his encroachments.* This numerous, weak, timid, and mercenary body of German princes, supplied the chief materials out of which it was possible that an alliance against the conqueror might one day be formed. On the other hand, the military power of the Austrian monarchy was crippled by the bigotry and tyranny of its princes. The persecution of the Protestants, and the attempt to establish an absolute government, had spread disaffection through Hungary and its vast dependencies. In a contest between one tyrant and many, where the people in a state of personal slavery are equally disregarded by both, reason and humanity might be neutral, if reflection did not remind us, that even the contests and factions of a turbulent aristocracy call forth an energy, and magnanimity, and ability, which are extinguished under the quieter and more fatally lasting domination of a single master. The Emperor Leopold I., instigated by the Jesuits, of which order he was a lay member, rivalled and anticipated Louis XIV.† in his cruel prosecution of the Hungarian Protestants, and thereby drove the nation to such despair that they sought refuge in the aid of the common enemy of the Christian name. Encouraged by their revolt, and stimulated by the continued intrigues of the Court of Versailles,‡ the Turks at length invaded Austria with a

* Mémoires de Gourville, vol. ii. p. 82. An account apparently prepared with care. I adopt the proportion of thirteen livres to the pound sterling, which is the rate of exchange given by Barillon, in 1679.

† Ronquillo, MS. letter.

* The Palatine, together with Bavaria, Mentz and Cologne, promised to vote for Louis XIV. as emperor in 1658.—Pfeffel, Abrégé Chronologique, &c. (Paris, 1776), vol. ii. p. 360. A more authentic and very curious account of this extraordinary negotiation, extracted from the French archives, is published by Lemontey, (Monarchie de Louis XIV. Pièces Justificatives, No. 2,) by which it appears that the Elector of Metz betrayed Mazarin, who had distributed immense bribes to him and his fellows.

† He banished the Protestant clergy, of whom two hundred and fifty, originally condemned to be stoned or burnt to death, but having under pretence, probably, of humanity, been sold to the Spaniards, were redeemed from the condition of galley slaves by the illustrious De Ruyter after his victory over the French, on the coast of Sicily.—Coxe, House of Austria, chap. 66.

‡ Sir William Trumbull, ambassador at Constantinople from August, 1687, to July, 1691, names French agents employed in fomenting the Hungarian rebellion, and negotiating with the Vizier.—Downshire MSS.

mighty army, and would have mastered the capital of the most noble of Christian sovereigns, had not the seige of Vienna been raised, after a duration of two months, by John Sobieski, King of Poland,—the heroic chief of a people, whom in less than a century the House of Austria contributed to blot out of the map of nations. While these dangers impended over the Austrian monarchy, Louis had been preparing to deprive it of the Imperial sceptre, which in his own hands would have proved no bauble. By secret treaties, to which the Elector of Bavaria had been tempted to agree, in 1670, by the prospect of matrimonial alliance with the House of France, and which were imposed on the Electors of Brandenburg and Saxony in 1679, after the humiliation of Europe at Nimeguen, these princes had agreed to vote for Louis in case of the death of the Emperor Leopold,—an event which his infirm health had given frequent occasion to expect. The four Rhenish electors, especially after the usurpation of Strasburg and Luxemburg, were already in his net.

At home the vanquished party, whose antipathy to the House of Orange had been exasperated by the cruel fate of De Witt, sacrificed the care of the national independence to jealousy of the Stadtholderian princes, and carried their devotedness to France to an excess which there was nothing in the example of their justly revered leader to warrant.* They had obliged the Prince of Orange to accede to the unequal conditions of Nimeguen; they had prevented him from making military preparations absolutely required by safety; and they had compelled him to submit to that truce for twenty years, which left the entrances of Flanders, Germany, and Italy, in the hands of France. They had concerted all measures of domestic opposition with the French minister at the Hague; and, though there is no reason to believe that the opulent and creditable chiefs of the party, if they had received French money at all, would have deigned to employ it for any other than what they had unhappily been misled to regard as a public purpose, there is the fullest evidence of the employment of bribes to make known at Versailles the most secret counsels of the commonwealth.† Amsterdam had raised troops for her own defence, declaring her determination not to contribute towards the hostilities which the measures of the general government might occasion, and had entered into a secret correspondence with France. Friesland and Croningen had recalled their troops from the common defence, and bound themselves, by a secret convention with Amsterdam, to act in concert with that potent and mutinous city. The provinces of Guelderland, Overyssell, Utrecht, and Zealand, adhered, indeed, to the Prince, and he still preserved a majority in the States of Holland; but this majority consisted only of the order of nobles and of the deputies of inconsiderable towns. Fagel, his wise and faithful minister, appeared to be in danger of destruction at the hands of the Republicans, who abhorred him as a deserter. But Heinsius, Pensionary of Delft, probably the ablest man of that party, having, on a mission to Versailles, seen the effects of the civil and religious policy of Louis XIV., and considering consistency as dependent, not on names, but on principles, thought it the duty of a friend of liberty also to join the party most opposed to that monarch's designs. So trembling was the ascendant of the Prince in Holland, that the accession of individuals was, from their situation or ability, of great importance to him. His cousin, the Stadtholder of Friesland, was gradually gained over; and Conrad Van Benningen, one of the chiefs of Amsterdam, an able, accomplished, and disinterested Republican, fickle from over-refinement, and betrayed into French councils by jealousy of the House of Orange, as soon as he caught a glimpse of the abyss into which his country was about to fall, recoiled from the brink. Thus did the very country where the Prince of Orange held sway, fluctuate between him and Louis; insomuch, indeed, that if that monarch had observed any measure in his cruelty towards French Protestants, it might have been impossible, till it was too late, to turn the force of Holland against him.

But the weakest point in the defences of European independence was England. It was not, indeed, like the continental states, either attacked by other enemies, or weakened by foreign influence, or dwindling from inward decay. The throne was filled by a traitor; a creature of the common enemy commanded this important post: for a quarter of a century Charles had connived at the conquests of Louis. During the last ten years of his reign he received a secret pension; but when Louis became desirous of possessing Luxemburg, Charles extorted an additional bribe for connivance at that new act of rapine.* After he had sold the fortress, he proposed himself to Spain as arbitrator in the dispute regarding it;† and so notorious was his perfidy, that the Spanish ministers at Paris did not scruple to justify their re-

* The speed and joy with which he and Temple concluded the Triple Alliance seem, indeed, to prove the contrary. That treaty, so quickly concluded by two wise, accomplished, and, above all, honest men, is perhaps unparalleled in diplomatic transactions. "*Nulla dies unquam memori vos eximet ævo.*"

† D'Avaux, Négociations en Hollande (Paris, 1754), vol. i. pp. 13, 23, 25, &c.—examples of treachery, in some of which the secret was known only to three persons. Sometimes, copies of orders were obtained from the Prince's private repositories, vol. ii. p. 53.

* "My Lord Hyde (Rochester) ne m'a pas caché que si son avis est suivi le Roi s'en entrera dans un concert secret pour avoir à V. M. la ville de Luxemburg."—Barillon to Louis, 7th Nov. 1681.

† The same to the same, 15th Dec.

fusal to his ambassador, by telling him, "that they refused because they had no mind to part with Luxemburg, which they knew was to be sacrificed if they accepted the offer."*

William's connection with the House of Stuart was sometimes employed by France to strengthen the jealous antipathy of the Republicans against him; while on other occasions he was himself obliged to profess a reliance on that connection which he did not feel, in order to gain an appearance of strength. As the Dutch Republicans were prompted to thwart his measures by a misapplied zeal for liberty, so the English Whigs were for a moment compelled to enter into a correspondence with the common enemy by the like motives. But in his peculiar relations with England the imprudent violence of the latter party was as much an obstacle in his way as their alienation or opposition. The interest of Europe required that he should never relinquish the attempt to detach the English government from the conqueror. The same principle, together with legitimate ambition, prescribed that he should do nothing, either by exciting enemies, or estranging friends, which could endanger his own and the Princess' right of succession to the crown. It was his obvious policy, therefore, to keep up a good understanding with the popular party, on whom alone he could permanently rely; to give a cautious countenance to their measures of constitutional opposition, and especially to the Bill of Exclusion,*—a more effectual mode of cutting asunder the chains which bound England to the car of Louis, than the proposed limitations on a Catholic successor, which might permanently weaken the defensive force of the monarchy;† and to discourage and stand aloof from all violent counsels,—likely either to embroil the country in such lasting confusion as would altogether disable it for aiding the sinking fortunes of Europe, or, by their immediate suppression, to subject all national interests and feelings to Charles and his brother. As his open declaration against the King or the popular party would have been perhaps equally dangerous to English liberty and European independence, he was averse from those projects which reduced him to so injurious an alternative. Hence his conduct in the case of what is called the "Rye House Plot," in which his confidential correspondence‡ manifests indifference and even dislike to those who were charged with projects of revolt; all which might seem unnatural if we did not bear in mind that at the moment of the siege of Vienna, he must have looked at England almost solely, as the only counterpoise of France. His abstinence from English intrigues was at this juncture strengthened by lingering hopes that it was still possible to lure Charles into those unions which he had begun to form against farther encroachment, under the modest and inoffensive name of "Associations to maintain the Treaty of Nimeguen," which were in three

* Lord Preston to Secretary Jenkins, Paris, 16th Dec. 1682. Admitted within the domestic differences of England, Louis had not scrupled to make advances to the enemies of the court; and they, desirous of detaching their own sovereign from France, and of thus depriving him of the most effectual ally in his project for rendering himself absolute, had reprehensibly accepted the aid of Louis in counteracting a policy which they had good reason to dread. They considered this dangerous understanding as allowable for the purpose of satisfying their party, that in opposing Charles they would not have to apprehend the power of Louis, and disposing the King of France to spare the English constitution, as some curb on the irresolution and inconstancy of his royal dependent. To destroy confidence between the Courts seemed to be an object so important, as to warrant the use of ambiguous means; and the usual sophistry, by which men who are not depraved excuse to themselves great breaches of morality, could not be wanting. They could easily persuade themselves that they could stop when they pleased, and that the example could not be dangerous in a case where the danger was too great not to be of very rare occurrence. Some of them are said by Barillon to have so far copied their prince as to have received French money, though they are not charged with being, like him, induced by it to adopt any measures at variance with their avowed principles. If we must believe, that in an age of little pecuniary delicacy, when large presents from sovereigns were scarcely deemed dishonourable, and when many princes, and almost all ministers, were in the pay of Louis XIV., the statement may be true, it is due to the haughty temper, not to say to the high principles of Sidney,—it is due, though in a very inferior degree, to the ample fortunes of others of the persons named, also to believe, that the polluted gifts were applied by them to elections and other public interests of the popular party, which there might be a fantastic gratification in promoting by treasures diverted from the use of the Court. These unhappy transactions, which in their full extent require a more critical scrutiny of the original documents than that to which they have been subjected, are not pretended to originate till ten years after the concert of the two Courts, and were relinquished as soon as that concert was resumed. Yet the reproach brought upon the cause of liberty by the infirmity of some men of great soul, and of others of the purest virtue, is, perhaps, the most wholesome admonition pronounced by the warning voice of history against the employment of sinister and equivocal means for the attainment of the best ends.

* Burnet, vol. ii. p. 245. Temple, vol. i. p. 355. "My friendship with the Prince (says Temple) I could think no crime, considering how little he had ever meddled, to my knowledge, in our domestic concerns since the first heats in Parliament, though sensible of their influence on all his nearest concerns at home; the preservation of Flanders from French conquests, and thereby of Holland from absolute dependence on that Crown."

† Letters of the Prince to Sir Leoline Jenkins, July, 1680.—February, 1681. Dalrymple, Appendix to Review.

‡ MS. letters from the Prince to Mr. Bentinck, in England, July and August, 1683. By the favour of the Duke of Portland, I possess copies of the whole of the Prince's correspondence with his friend, from 1677 to 1700; written with the unreserved frankness of warm and pure friendship, in which it is quite manifest that there is nothing concealed.

years afterwards completed by the League of Augsburgh, and which, in 1689, brought all Europe into the field to check the career of Louis XIV.

The death of Charles II. gave William some hope of an advantageous change in English policy. Many worse men and more tyrannical kings than that prince, few persons of more agreeable qualities and brilliant talents have been seated on a throne. But his transactions with France probably afford the most remarkable instance of a king with no sense of national honour or of legal independence,—the last vestiges which departing virtue might be expected to leave behind in a royal bosom. More jealousy of dependence on a foreign prince was hoped from the sterner temper of his successor. William accordingly made great efforts and sacrifices to obtain the accession of England to the European cause. He declared his readiness to sacrifice his resentments, and even his personal interests, and to conform his conduct to the pleasure of the King in all things compatible with his religion and with his duty to the republic;*—limitations which must have been considered as pledges of sincerity by him to whom they were otherwise unacceptable. He declared his regret at the appearance of opposition to both his uncles, which had arisen only from the necessity of resisting Louis, and he sent M. D'Auverquerque to England to lay his submission before the King. James desired that he should relinquish communication with the Duke of Monmouth,† dismiss the malcontent English Officers in the Dutch army, and adapt his policy to such engagements as

---

* Davaux, 13th—26th Feb., 1685. The last contains an account of a conversation of William with Fagel, overheard by a person who reported it to Davaux. A passage in which Davaux shows his belief that the policy of the Prince now aimed at gaining James, is suppressed in the printed collection.

† During these unexpected advances to a renewal of friendship, an incident occurred, which has ever since, in the eyes of many, thrown some shade over the sincerity of William. This was the landing in England of the Duke of Monmouth, with a small number of adherents who had embarked with him at Amsterdam. He had taken refuge in the Spanish Netherlands, and afterwards in Holland, during the preceding year, in consequence of a misunderstanding between him and the ministers of Charles respecting the nature and extent of the confession concerning the reality of the Rye House Plot, published by them in language which he resented as conveying unauthorised imputations on his friends. The Prince and Princess of Orange received him with kindness, from personal friendship, from compassion for his sufferings, and from his connection with the popular and Protestant party in England. The transient shadow of a pretension to the crown did not awaken their jealousy. They were well aware that whatever complaints might be made by his ministers, Charles himself would not be displeased by kindness shown towards his favourite son. There is, indeed, little doubt, that in the last year of his life, Charles had been prevailed on by Halifax to consult his ease, as well as his inclination, by the recall of his son, as a counterpoise to the Duke of York, and thus to produce the balance of parties at court, which was one of the darling refinements of that too ingenious statesman.¶ Reports were prevalent that Monmouth had privately visited England, and that he was well pleased with his journey. He was assured by confidential letters, evidently sanctioned by his father, that he should be recalled in February. It appears also, that Charles had written with his own hand a letter to the Prince of Orange, beseeching him to treat Monmouth kindly, which D'Auverquerque was directed to lay before James as a satisfactory explanation of whatever might seem suspicious in the unusual honours paid to him. Before he left the Hague the Prince and Princess approved the draft of a submissive letter to James, which he had laid before them; and they exacted from him a promise that he would engage in no violent enterprises inconsistent with this submission. Despairing of clemency from his uncle, he then appears to have entertained designs of retiring into Sweden, or of serving in the Imperial army against the Turks; and he listened for a moment to the projects of some French Protestants, who proposed that he should put himself at the head of their unfortunate brethren. He himself thought the difficulties of an enterprise against England insuperable; but the importunity of the English and Scotch refugees in Holland induced him to return privately there to be present at their consultations. He found the Scotch exiles, who were proportionately more numerous and of greater distinction, and who felt more bitterly from the bloody tyranny under which their countrymen suffered, impatiently desirous to make an immediate attempt for the delivery of their country. Ferguson, the Nonconformist preacher, either from treachery, or from rashness, seconded the impetuosity of his countrymen. Andrew Fletcher of Saltoun, a man of heroic spirit, and a lover of liberty even to enthusiasm, who had just returned from serving in Hungary, dissuaded his friends from an enterprise which his political sagacity and military experience taught him to consider as hopeless. In assemblies of suffering and angry exiles it was to be expected that rash counsels should prevail; yet Monmouth appears to have resisted them longer than could have been hoped from his judgment or temper. It was not till two months after the death of Charles II. (9th April, 1685,) that the vigilant Davaux intimated his suspicion of a design to land in England. Nor was it till three weeks that he was able to transmit to his Court the particulars of the equipment. It was only then that Skelton, the minister of James, complained of these petty armaments to the President of the States-General and the magistrates of Amsterdam, neither of whom had any authority in the case. They referred him to the Admiralty of Amsterdam, the competent authority in such cases, who, as soon as they were authorised by an order from the States-General, proceeded to arrest the vessels freighted by Argyle. But in consequence of a mistake in Skelton's description of their station, their exertions were too late to prevent the sailing of the unfortunate expedition on the 5th of May. The natural delays of a slow and formal government, the jealousy of rival authorities, exasperated by the spirit of party, and the license shown in such a country to navigation and traffic, are sufficient to account for this short delay. If there was in this case a more than usual indisposition to overstep the formalities of the constitution, or to quicken the slow pace of the administration, it may be well imputed to natural compassion towards the exiles, and to the strong fellow-feeling which arose from agreement in religious opinion, especially with the Scotch. If there were proof even of absolute connivance, it must be ascribed solely to the magistrates and inhabitants of Am-

the King should see fit to contract with his neighbours. To the former conditions the Prince submitted without reserve: the last, couched in strong language by James to Barillon, hid under more general expressions by the English minister to Davaux, but implying in its mildest form an acquiescence in the projects of the conqueror, was probably conveyed to the Prince himself in terms capable of being understood as amounting only to an engagement to avoid an interruption of the general peace. In that inoffensive sense it seems to have been accepted by the Prince; since the King declared to him that his concessions, which could have reached no farther, were perfectly satisfactory.*

Sidney was sent to Holland—a choice which seemed to indicate an extraordinary deference for the wishes of the Prince, and which was considered in Holland as a decisive mark of good understanding between the two governments. The proud and hostile city of Amsterdam presented an address of congratulation to William on the defeat of Monmouth; and the Republican party began to despair of effectual resistance to the power of the Stadtholder, now about to be strengthened by the alliance with England. The Dutch ambassadors in London, in spite of the remonstrances of Barillon, succeeded in concluding a treaty for the renewal of the defensive alliance between England and Holland, which, though represented to Louis as a mere formality, was certainly a step which required little more than that liberal construction to which a defensive treaty is always entitled, to convert it into an accession by England to the concert of the other states of Europe, for the preservation of their rights and dominions. The connection between the Dutch and English governments answered alike the immediate purposes of both parties. It overawed the malcontents of Holland, as well as those of England; and James commanded his ministers to signify to the magistrates of Amsterdam, that their support of the Stadtholder would be acceptable to his Majesty.

William, who, from the peace of Nimeguen, had been the acknowledged chief of the confederacy gradually forming to protect the remains of Europe, had now slowly and silently removed all the obstacles to its formation, except those which arose from the unhappy jealousies of the friends of liberty at home, and the fatal progress towards absolute monarchy in England. Good sense, which, in so high a degree as his, is one of the rarest of human endowments, had full scope for its exercise in a mind seldom invaded by the disturbing passions of fear and anger. With all his determined firmness, no man was ever more solicitous not to provoke or keep up needless enmity. It is no wonder that he should have been influenced by this principle in his dealings with Charles and James, for there are traces of it even in his rare and transient intercourse with Louis XIV. He caused it to be intimated to him "that he was ambitious of being restored to his Majesty's favour;"* to which it was haughtily answered, "that when *such a disposition was shown in his conduct*, the King would see what was to be done." Yet Davaux believed that the Prince really desired to avoid the enmity of Louis, as far as was compatible with his duties to Holland, and his interests in England. In a conversation with Gourville,† which affords one of the most characteristic specimens of intercourse between a practised courtier and a man of plain inoffensive temper, when the minister had spoken to him in more soothing language, he professed his warm wish to please the King, and proved his sincerity by adding that he never could neglect the safety of Holland, and that the decrees of re-union, together with other marks of projects of universal monarchy, were formidable obstacles to good understanding. It was probably after one of these attempts that he made the remarkable declaration,—"Since I cannot earn his Majesty's favour, I must endeavour to earn his esteem." Nothing but an extraordinary union of wariness with perseverance—two qualities which he possessed in a higher degree, and united in juster proportions, perhaps, than any other man—could have fitted him for that incessant, unwearied, noiseless exertion which alone suited his difficult situation. His mind, naturally dispassionate, became, by degrees, steadfastly and intensely fixed upon the single object of his high calling. Brilliant only on the field of battle; loved by none but a few intimate connections; considerate and circumspect in council; in the execution of his designs bold even to rashness, and inflexible to the verge of obstinacy, he held his onward way with a quiet and even course, which wore down opposition, outlasted the sallies of enthusiasm, and disappointed the subtle contrivances of a refined policy.

sterdam,—the ancient enemies of the House of Orange,—who might look with favour on an expedition which might prevent the Stadtholder from being strengthened by his connection with the King of England, and who, as we are told by Davaux himself, were afterwards filled with consternation when they learned the defeat of Monmouth. We know little with certainty of the particulars of his intercourse with his inexorable uncle, from his capture till his execution, except the compassionate interference of the Queen Dowager in his behalf; but whatever it was, from the King's conduct immediately after, it tended rather to strengthen than to shake his confidence in the Prince.

* James to the Prince of Orange, 6th, 16th, and 17th March.—Dalrymple, app. to part i.

* Davaux, vol. i. p. 5.

† Gourville, vol. ii. p. 204.

DISCOURSE

READ AT THE OPENING OF

THE LITERARY SOCIETY OF BOMBAY.

[26th Nov. 1804.]

Gentlemen,—The smallest society, brought together by the love of knowledge, is respectable in the eye of Reason; and the feeblest efforts of infant Literature in barren and inhospitable regions are in some respects more interesting than the most elaborate works and the most successful exertions of the human mind. They prove the diffusion, at least, if not the advancement of science; and they afford some sanction to the hope, that Knowledge is destined one day to visit the whole earth, and, in her beneficial progress, to illuminate and humanise the whole race of man. It is, therefore, with singular pleasure that I see a small but respectable body of men assembled here by such a principle. I hope that we agree in considering all Europeans who visit remote countries, whatever their separate pursuits may be, as detachments of the main body of civilized men, sent out to levy contributions of knowledge, as well as to gain victories over barbarism.

When a large portion of a country so interesting as India fell into the hands of one of the most intelligent and inquisitive nations of the world, it was natural to expect that its ancient and present state should at last be fully disclosed. These expectations were, indeed, for a time disappointed: during the tumult of revolution and war it would have been unreasonable to have entertained them; and when tranquillity was established in that country, which continues to be the centre of the British power in Asia,* it ought not to have been forgotten that every Englishman was fully occupied by commerce, by military service, or by administration; that we had among us no idle public of readers, and, consequently, no separate profession of writers; and that every hour bestowed on study was to be stolen from the leisure of men often harassed by business, enervated by the climate, and more disposed to seek amusement than new occupation, in the intervals of their appointed toils.

It is, besides, a part of our national character, that we are seldom eager to display, and not always ready to communicate, what we have acquired. In this respect we differ considerably from other lettered nations. Our ingenious and polite neighbours on the continent of Europe,—to whose enjoyment the applause of others seems more indispensable, and whose faculties are more nimble and restless, if not more vigorous than ours,—are neither so patient of repose, nor so likely to be contented with a secret hoard of knowledge. They carry even into their literature a spirit of bustle and parade;—a bustle, indeed, which springs from activity, and a parade which animates enterprise, but which are incompatible with our sluggish and sullen dignity. Pride disdains ostentation, scorns false pretensions, despises even petty merit, refuses to obtain the objects of pursuit by flattery or importunity, and scarcely values any praise but that which she has the right to command. Pride, with which foreigners charge us, and which under the name of a 'sense of dignity' we claim for ourselves, is a lazy and unsocial quality; and is in these respects, as in most others, the very reverse of the sociable and good-humoured vice of vanity. It is not, therefore, to be wondered at, if in India our national character, co-operating with local circumstances, should have produced some real and perhaps more apparent inactivity in working the mine of knowledge of which we had become the masters.

Yet some of the earliest exertions of private Englishmen are too important to be passed over in silence. The compilation of laws by Mr. Halhed, and the Ayeen Akbaree, translated by Mr. Gladwin, deserve honourable mention. Mr. Wilkins gained the memorable distinction of having opened the treasures of a new learned language to Europe.

But, notwithstanding the merit of these individual exertions, it cannot be denied that the era of a general direction of the mind of Englishmen in this country towards learned inquiries, was the foundation of the Asiatic Society by Sir William Jones. To give such an impulse to the public understanding is one of the greatest benefits that a man can confer on his fellow men. On such an occasion as the present, it is impossible to pronounce the name of Sir William Jones without feelings of gratitude and reverence. He was among the distinguished persons who adorned one of the brightest periods of English literature. It was no mean distinction to be conspicuous in the age of Burke and

---

* Bengal.—Ed.

Johnson, of Hume and Smith, of Gray and Goldsmith, of Gibbon and Robertson, of Reynolds and Garrick. It was the fortune of Sir William Jones to have been the friend of the greater part of these illustrious men. Without him, the age in which he lived would have been inferior to past times in one kind of literary glory: he surpassed all his contemporaries, and perhaps even the most laborious scholars of the two former centuries, in extent and variety of attainment. His facility in acquiring was almost prodigious; and he possessed that faculty of arranging and communicating his knowledge which these laborious scholars very generally wanted. Erudition, which in them was often disorderly and rugged, and had something of an illiberal and almost barbarous air, was by him presented to the world with all the elegance and amenity of polite literature. Though he seldom directed his mind to those subjects the successful investigation of which confers the name of a "philosopher," yet he possessed in a very eminent degree that habit of disposing his knowledge in regular and analytical order, which is one of the properties of a philosophical understanding. His talents as an elegant writer in verse were among his instruments for attaining knowledge, and a new example of the variety of his accomplishments. In his easy and flowing prose we justly admire that order of exposition and transparency of language, which are the most indispensable qualities of style, and the chief excellencies of which it is capable, when it is employed solely to instruct. His writings everywhere breathe pure taste in morals as well as in literature; and it may be said with truth, that not a single sentiment has escaped him which does not indicate the real elegance and dignity which pervaded the most secret recesses of his mind. He had lived, perhaps, too exclusively in the world of learning for the cultivation of his practical understanding. Other men have meditated more deeply on the constitution of society, and have taken more comprehensive views of its complicated relations and infinitely varied interests. Others have, therefore, often taught sounder principles of political science; but no man more warmly felt, and no author is better calculated to inspire, those generous sentiments of liberty, without which the most just principles are useless and lifeless, and which will, I trust, continue to flow through the channels of eloquence and poetry into the minds of British youth. It has, indeed, been somewhat lamented that he should have exclusively directed inquiry towards antiquities. But every man must be allowed to recommend most strongly his own favourite pursuits; and the chief difficulty as well as the chief merit is his, who first raises the minds of men to the love of any part of knowledge. When mental activity is once roused, its direction is easily changed; and the excesses of one writer, if they are not checked by public reason, are compensated by the opposite ones of his successor. "Whatever withdraws us from the dominion of the senses—whatever makes the past, the distant, and the future, predominate over the present, advances us in the dignity of thinking beings."*

It is not for me to attempt an estimate of those exertions for the advancement of knowledge which have arisen from the example and exhortations of Sir William Jones. In all judgments pronounced on our contemporaries it is so certain that we shall be accused, and so probable that we may be justly accused, of either partially bestowing, or invidiously withholding praise, that it is in general better to attempt no encroachment on the jurisdiction of Time, which alone impartially and justly estimates the works of men. But it would be unpardonable not to speak of the College at Calcutta, the original plan of which was doubtless the most magnificent attempt ever made for the promotion of learning in the East. I am not conscious that I am biassed either by personal feelings, or literary prejudices when I say, that I consider that original plan as a wise and noble proposition, the adoption of which in its full extent would have had the happiest tendency in securing the good government of India, as well as in promoting the interest of science. Even in its present mutilated state we have seen, at the last public exhibition, Sanscrit declamation by English youth;†—a circumstance so extraordinary, that, if it be followed by suitable advances, it will mark an epoch in the history of learning.

Among the humblest fruits of this spirit I take the liberty to mention the project of forming this Society, which occurred to me before I left England, but which never could have advanced even to its present state without your hearty concurrence, and which must depend on your active co-operation for all hopes of future success.

You will not suspect me of presuming to dictate the nature and object of our common exertions. To be valuable they must be spontaneous; and no literary society can subsist on any other principle than that of equality. In the observations which I shall make on the plan and subject of our inquiries, I shall offer myself to you only as the representative of the curiosity of Europe. I am ambitious of no higher office than that of faithfully conveying to India the desires and wants of the learned at home, and of stating the subjects on which they wish and expect satisfaction, from inquiries which can be pursued only in India.

In fulfilling the duties of this mission, I shall not be expected to exhaust so vast a subject; nor is it necessary that I should attempt an exact distribution of science. A very general sketch is all that I can pro-

---

* Dr. Johnson at Iona.—Ed.

† It must be remembered that this was written in 1804.—Ed.

mise; in which I shall pass over many subjects rapidly, and dwell only on those parts on which from my own habits of study I may think myself least disqualified to offer useful suggestions.

The objects of these inquiries, as of all human knowledge, are reducible to two classes, which, for want of more significant and precise terms, we must be content to call "Physical" and "Moral,"—aware of the laxity and ambiguity of these words, but not affecting a greater degree of exactness than is necessary for our immediate purpose.

The physical sciences afford so easy and pleasing an amusement; they are so directly subservient to the useful arts; and in their higher forms they so much delight our imagination and flatter our pride, by the display of the authority of man over nature, that there can be no need of arguments to prove their utility, and no want of powerful and obvious motives to dispose men to their cultivation. The whole extensive and beautiful science of Natural History, which is the foundation of all physical knowledge, has many additional charms in a country where so many treasures must still be unexplored.

The science of Mineralogy, which has been of late years cultivated with great activity in Europe, has such a palpable connection with the useful arts of life, that it cannot be necessary to recommend it to the attention of the intelligent and curious. India is a country which I believe no mineralogist has yet examined, and which would doubtless amply repay the labour of the first scientific adventurers who explore it. The discovery of new sources of wealth would probably be the result of such an investigation; and something might perhaps be contributed towards the accomplishment of the ambitious projects of those philosophers, who from the arrangement of earths and minerals have been bold enough to form conjectures respecting the general laws which have governed the past revolutions of our planet, and which preserve its parts in their present order.

The Botany of India has been less neglected, but it cannot be exhausted. The higher parts of the science, the structure, the functions, the habits of vegetables,—all subjects intimately connected with the first of physical sciences, though, unfortunately, the most dark and difficult, the philosophy of life,—have in general been too much sacrificed to objects of value, indeed, but of a value far inferior: and professed botanists have usually contented themselves with observing enough of plants to give them a name in their scientific language, and a place in their artificial arrangement.

Much information also remains to be gleaned on that part of natural history which regards Animals. The manners of many tropical races must have been imperfectly observed in a few individuals separated from their fellows, and imprisoned in the unfriendly climate of Europe.

The variations of temperature, the state of the atmosphere, all the appearances that are comprehended under the words "weather" and "climate," are the conceivable subject of a science of which no rudiments yet exist. It will probably require the observations of centuries to lay the foundations of theory on this subject. There can scarce be any region of the world more favourably circumstanced for observation than India; for there is none in which the operation of these causes is more regular, more powerful, or more immediately discoverable in their effect on vegetable and animal nature. Those philosophers who have denied the influence of climate on the human character were not inhabitants of a tropical country.

To the members of the learned profession of medicine, who are necessarily spread over every part of India, all the above inquiries peculiarly, though not exclusively, belong. Some of them are eminent for science; many must be well-informed; and their professional education must have given to all some tincture of physical knowledge. With even moderate preliminary acquirements they may be very useful, if they will but consider themselves as philosophical collectors, whose duty it is never to neglect a favourable opportunity for observations on weather and climate, to keep exact journals of whatever they observe, and to transmit, through their immediate superiors, to the scientific depositories of Great Britain, specimens of every mineral, vegetable, or animal production which they conceive to be singular, or with respect to which they suppose themselves to have observed any new and important facts. If their previous studies have been imperfect, they will, no doubt, be sometimes mistaken: but these mistakes are perfectly harmless. It is better that ten useless specimens should be sent to London, than that one curious one should be neglected.

But it is on another and still more important subject that we expect the most valuable assistance from our medical associates:—this is, the science of Medicine itself. It must be allowed not to be quite so certain as it is important. But though every man ventures to scoff at its uncertainty as long as he is in vigorous health, yet the hardiest sceptic becomes credulous as soon as his head is fixed to the pillow. Those who examine the history of medicine without either scepticism or blind admiration, will find that every civilized age, after all the fluctuations of systems, opinions, and modes of practice, has at length left some balance, however small, of new truth to the succeeding generation; and that the stock of human knowledge in this as well as in other departments is constantly, though, it must be owned, very slowly, increasing. Since my arrival here, I have had sufficient reason to believe that the practitioners of medicine in India are not unworthy of their enlightened and benevolent profession.—

From them, therefore, I hope the public may derive, through the medium of this Society, information of the highest value. Diseases and modes of cure unknown to European physicians may be disclosed to them; and if the causes of disease are more active in this country than in England, remedies are employed and diseases subdued, at least in some cases, with a certainty which might excite the wonder of the most successful practitioners in Europe. By full and faithful narratives of their modes of treatment they will conquer that distrust of new plans of cure, and that incredulity respecting whatever is uncommon, which sometimes prevail among our English physicians; which are the natural result of much experience and many disappointments; and which, though individuals have often just reason to complain of their indiscriminate application, are not ultimately injurious to the progress of the medical art. They never finally prevent the adoption of just theory or of useful practice: they retard it no longer than is necessary for such a severe trial as precludes all future doubt. Even in their excess, they are wholesome correctives of the opposite excesses of credulity and dogmatism; they are safeguards against exaggeration and quackery; they are tests of utility and truth. A philosophical physician, who is a real lover of his art, ought not, therefore, to desire the extinction of these dispositions, though he may suffer temporary injustice from their influence.

Those objects of our inquiries which I have called "Moral" (employing that term in the sense in which it is contradistinguished from "Physical") will chiefly comprehend the past and present condition of the inhabitants of the vast country which surrounds us.

To begin with their present condition:—I take the liberty of very earnestly recommending a kind of research, which has hitherto been either neglected or only carried on for the information of Government,—I mean the investigation of those facts which are the subjects of political arithmetic and statistics, and which are a part of the foundation of the science of Political Economy. The numbers of the people; the number of births, marriages, and deaths; the proportion of children who are reared to maturity; the distribution of the people according to their occupations and castes, and especially according to the great division of agricultural and manufacturing; and the relative state of these circumstances at different periods, which can only be ascertained by permanent tables,—are the basis of this important part of knowledge. No tables of political arithmetic have yet been made public from any tropical country. I need not expatiate on the importance of the information which such tables would be likely to afford. I shall mention only as an example of their value, that they must lead to a decisive solution of the problems with respect to the influence of polygamy on population, and the supposed origin of that practice in the disproportioned number of the sexes. But in a country where every part of the system of manners and institutions differs from those of Europe, it is impossible to foresee the extent and variety of the new results which an accurate survey might present to us.

These inquiries are naturally followed by those which regard the subsistence of the people; the origin and distribution of public wealth; the wages of every kind of labour, from the rudest to the most refined; the price of commodities, and especially of provisions, which necessarily regulates that of all others; the modes of the tenure and occupation of land; the profits of trade; the usual and extraordinary rates of interest, which is the price paid for the hire of money; the nature and extent of domestic commerce, everywhere the greatest and most profitable, though the most difficult to be ascertained; those of foreign traffic, more easy to be determined by the accounts of exports and imports; the contributions by which the expenses of government, of charitable, learned, and religious foundations are defrayed; the laws and customs which regulate all these great objects, and the fluctuation which has been observed in all or any of them at different times and under different circumstances. These are some of the points towards which I should very earnestly wish to direct the curiosity of our intelligent countrymen in India.

These inquiries have the advantage of being easy and open to all men of good sense. They do not, like antiquarian and philological researches, require great previous erudition and constant reference to extensive libraries. They require nothing but a resolution to observe facts attentively, and to relate them accurately; and whoever feels a disposition to ascend from facts to principles will, in general, find sufficient aid to his understanding in the great work of Dr. Smith,—the most permanent monument of philosophical genius which our nation has produced in the present age.

They have the further advantage of being closely and intimately connected with the professional pursuits and public duties of every Englishman who fills a civil office in this country: they form the very science of administration. One of the first requisites to the right administration of a district is the knowledge of its population, industry, and wealth. A magistrate ought to know the condition of the country which he superintends; a collector ought to understand its revenue; a commercial resident ought to be thoroughly acquainted with its commerce. We only desire that part of the knowledge which they ought to possess should be communicated to the world.*

[* "The English in India are too familiar with that country to feel much wonder in most parts

I will not pretend to affirm that no part of this knowledge ought to be confined to Government. I am not so intoxicated by philosophical prejudice as to maintain that the safety of a state is to be endangered for the gratification of scientific curiosity. Though I am far from thinking that this is the department in which secrecy is most useful, yet I do not presume to exclude it. But let it be remembered, that whatever information is thus confined to a Government may, for all purposes of science, be supposed not to exist. As long as the secrecy is thought important, it is of course shut up from most of those who could turn it to best account; and when it ceases to be guarded with jealousy, it is as effectually secured from all useful examination by the mass of official lumber under which it is usually buried: for this reason, after a very short time, it is as much lost to the Government itself as it is to the public. A transient curiosity, or the necessity of illustrating some temporary matter, may induce a public officer to dig for knowledge under the heaps of rubbish that encumber his office; but I have myself known intelligent public officers content themselves with the very inferior information contained in printed books, while their shelves groaned under the weight of MSS., which would be more instructive if they could be read. Further, it must be observed, that publication is always the best security to a Government that they are not deceived by the reports of their servants; and where these servants act at a distance the importance of such a security for their veracity is very great. For the truth of a manuscript report they never can have a better warrant than the honesty of one servant who prepares it, and of another who examines it; but for the truth of all long-uncontested narrations of important facts in printed accounts, published in countries where they may be contradicted, we have the silent testimony of every man who might be prompted by interest, prejudice, or humour, to dispute them if they were not true.

I have already said that all communications merely made to Government are lost to science; while, on the other hand, perhaps, the knowledge communicated to the public is that of which a Government may most easily avail itself, and on which it may most securely rely. This loss to science is very great; for the principles of political economy have been investigated in Europe, and the application of them to such a country as India must be one of the most curious tests which could be contrived of their truth and universal operation. Every thing here is new; and if they are found here also to be the true principles of natural subsistence and wealth, it will be no longer possible to dispute that they are the general laws which

---

of it, and are too transiently connected with it to take a national interest in its minute description. To these obstacles must be opposed both a sense of duty and a prospect of reputation. The servants of the Company would qualify themselves for the performance of their public duties, by collecting the most minute accounts of the districts which they administer. The publication of such accounts must often distinguish the individuals, and always do credit to the meritorious body of which they are a part. Even the most diffident magistrate or collector might enlarge or correct the articles relating to his district and neighbourhood, in the lately published Gazetteer of India; and, by the communication of such materials, the very laudable and valuable essay of Mr. Hamilton might, in successive editions, grow into a complete system of Indian topography. . . . Meritorious publications by servants of the East India Company, have, in our opinion, peculiar claims to liberal commendation. The price which Great Britain pays to the inhabitants of India for her dominion, is the security that their government shall be administered by a class of respectable men. In fact, they are governed by a greater proportion of sensible and honest men, than could fall to their lot under the government of their own or of any other nation. Without this superiority, and the securities which exist for its continuance, in the condition of the persons, in their now excellent education, in their general respect for the public opinion of a free country, in the protection afforded, and the restraint imposed by the press and by Parliament, all regulations for the administration of India would be nugatory, and the wisest system of laws would be no more than waste paper. The means of executing the laws, are in the character of the administrators. To keep that character pure, they must be taught to respect themselves; and they ought to feel, that distant as they are, they will be applauded and protected by their country, when they deserve commendation, or require defence. Their public is remote, and ought to make some compensation for distance by promptitude and zeal. The principal object for which the East India Company exists in the newly modified system [of 1813,—ED.] is to provide a safe body of electors to Indian officers. Both in the original appointments, and in subsequent preferment, it was thought that there was no medium between preserving their power, or transferring the patronage to the Crown. Upon the whole, it cannot be denied that they are tolerably well adapted to perform these functions. They are sufficiently numerous and connected with the more respectable classes of the community, to exempt their patronage from the direct influence of the Crown, and to spread their choice so widely, as to afford a reasonable probability of sufficient personal merit. Much—perhaps enough—has been done by legal regulations, to guard preferment from great abuse. Perhaps, indeed, the spirit of activity and emulation may have been weakened by precautions against the operation of personal favour. But this is, no doubt, the safe error. The Company, and indeed any branch of the Indian administration in Europe, can do little directly for India: they are far too distant for much direct administration. The great duty which they have to perform, is to control their servants and to punish delinquency in deeds; but as the chief principle of their administration—to guard the privileges of these servants, to maintain their dignity, to encourage their merits, to animate those principles of self-respect and honourable ambition, which are the true securities of honest and effectual service to the public. In every government, the character of the subordinate officers is of great moment: but the privileges, the character and the importance of the civil and military establishments, are, in the last result, the only conceivable security for the preservation and good government of India."—*Edinburgh Review*, vol. xxv. p. 435.—ED.]

every where govern this important part of the movements of the social machine.

It has been lately observed, that "if the various states of Europe kept and published annually an exact account of their population, noting carefully in a second column the exact age at which the children die, this second column would show the relative merit of the governments and the comparative happiness of their subjects. A simple arithmetical statement would then, perhaps, be more conclusive than all the arguments which could be produced." I agree with the ingenious writers who have suggested this idea, and I think it must appear perfectly evident that the number of children reared to maturity must be among the tests of the happiness of a society, though the number of children born cannot be so considered, and is often the companion and one of the causes of public misery. It may be affirmed, without the risk of exaggeration, that every accurate comparison of the state of different countries at the same time, or of the same country at different times, is an approach to that state of things in which the manifest palpable interest of every Government will be the prosperity of its subjects, which never has been, and which never will be, advanced by any other means than those of humanity and justice. The prevalence of justice would not indeed be universally insured by such a conviction; for bad governments, as well as bad men, as often act against their own obvious interest as against that of others: but the chances of tyranny must be diminished when tyrants are compelled to see that it is folly. In the mean time, the ascertainment of every new fact, the discovery of every new principle, and even the diffusion of principles known before, add to that great body of slowly and reasonably formed public opinion, which, however weak at first, must at last, with a gentle and scarcely sensible coercion, compel every Government to pursue its own real interest. This knowledge is a control on subordinate agents for Government, as well as a control on Government for their subjects: and it is one of those which has not the slightest tendency to produce tumult or convulsion. On the contrary, nothing more clearly evinces the necessity of that firm protecting power by which alone order can be secured. The security of the governed cannot exist without the security of the governors.

Lastly, of all kinds of knowledge, Political Economy has the greatest tendency to promote quiet and safe improvement in the general condition of mankind; because it shows that improvement is the interest of the government, and that stability is the interest of the people. The extraordinary and unfortunate events of our times have indeed damped the sanguine hopes of good men, and filled them with doubt and fear: but in all possible cases the counsels of this science are at least safe. They are adapted to all forms of government: they require only a wise and just administration. They require, as the first principle of all prosperity, that perfect security of persons and property which can only exist where the supreme authority is stable.

On these principles, nothing can be a means of improvement which is not also a means of preservation. It is not only absurd, but contradictory, to speak of sacrificing the present generation for the sake of posterity. The moral order of the world is not so disposed. It is impossible to promote the interest of future generations by any measures injurious to the present; and he who labours industriously to promote the honour, the safety, and the prosperity of his own country, by innocent and lawful means, may be assured that he is contributing, probably as much as the order of nature will permit a private individual, towards the welfare of all mankind.

These hopes of improvement have survived in my breast all the calamities of our European world, and are not extinguished by that general condition of national insecurity which is the most formidable enemy of improvement. Founded on such principles, they are at least perfectly innocent: they are such as, even if they were visionary, an admirer or cultivator of letters ought to be pardoned for cherishing. Without them, literature and philosophy can claim no more than the highest rank among the amusements and ornaments of human life. With these hopes, they assume the dignity of being part of that discipline under which the race of man is destined to proceed to the highest degree of civilization, virtue, and happiness, of which our nature is capable.

On a future occasion I may have the honour to lay before you my thoughts on the principal objects of inquiry in the geography, ancient and modern, the languages, the literature, the necessary and elegant arts, the religion, the authentic history and the antiquities of India; and on the mode in which such inquiries appear to me most likely to be conducted with success.

Vindiciae Gallicae.

A DEFENCE OF THE FRENCH REVOLUTION

AND ITS

ENGLISH ADMIRERS,

AGAINST THE ACCUSATIONS OF THE RIGHT HON. EDMUND BURKE, INCLUDING SOME STRICTURES ON THE LATE PRODUCTION OF MONS. DE CALONNE.

INTRODUCTION.

THE late opinions of Mr. Burke furnished more matter of astonishment to those who had distantly observed, than to those who had correctly examined, the system of his former political life. An abhorrence for abstract politics, a predilection for aristocracy, and a dread of innovation, have ever been among the most sacred articles of his public creed: and it was not likely that at his age he should abandon, to the invasion of audacious novelties, opinions which he had received so early, and maintained so long,—which had been fortified by the applause of the great, and the assent of the wise,—which he had dictated to so many illustrious pupils, and supported against so many distinguished opponents. Men who early attain eminence, repose in their first creed, to the neglect of the progress of the human mind subsequent to its adoption; and when, as in the present case, it has burst forth into action, they regard it as a transient madness, worthy only of pity or derision. They mistake it for a mountain torrent that will pass away with the storm that gave it birth: they know not that it is the stream of human opinion *in omne volubilis ævum*, which the accession of every day will swell, and which is destined to sweep into the same oblivion the resistance of learned sophistry, and of powerful oppression.

But there still remained ample matter of astonishment in the Philippic of Mr. Burke.* He might deplore the sanguinary excesses,—he might deride the visionary policy, that seemed to him to tarnish the lustre of the Revolution; but it was hard to suppose that he would exhaust against it every epithet of contumely and opprobrium that language can furnish to indignation; that the rage of his declamation would not for one moment be suspended, and that his heart would not betray one faint glow of triumph, at the splendid and glorious delivery of so great a people. All was invective: the authors and admirers of the Revolution,—every man who did not execrate it, even his own most enlightened and accomplished friends,—were devoted to odium and ignominy. The speech did not stoop to argument; the whole was dogmatical and authoritative: the cause seemed decided without discussion,—the anathema fulminated before trial.

But the ground of the opinions of this famous speech, which, if we may believe a foreign journalist, will form an epoch in the history of the eccentricities of the human mind, was impatiently expected in a work soon after announced. The name of the author, the importance of the subject, and the singularity of his opinions, all contributed to inflame the public curiosity, which, though it languished in a subsequent delay, has been revived by the appearance, and will be rewarded by the perusal of the work.*

It is certainly in every respect a performance, of which to form a correct estimate would prove one of the most arduous efforts of critical skill

"We scarcely can praise it, or blame it too much."†

Argument, every where dexterous and specious, sometimes grave and profound, clothed in the most rich and various imagery, and aided by the most pathetic and picturesque description, speaks the opulence and the powers of that mind, of which age has neither dimmed the discernment, nor en-

* The speech on the Army Estimates, 9th Feb. 1790.—ED.

* The Reflections on the Revolution in France, published in 1790.—ED.

† Retaliation.—ED.

feebled the fancy—neither repressed the ardour, nor narrowed the range. Virulent encomiums on urbanity and inflammatory harangues against violence, homilies of moral and religious mysticism, better adapted to the amusement than to the conviction of an incredulous age, though they may rouse the languor of attention, can never be dignified by the approbation of the understanding.

Of the senate and people of France, Mr. Burke's language is such as might have been expected towards a country which his fancy has peopled only with plots, assassinations, and massacres, and all the brood of dire chimeras which are the offspring of a prolific imagination, goaded by an ardent and deluded sensibility. The glimpses of benevolence, which irradiate this gloom of invective, arise only from generous illusion,—from misguided and misplaced compassion. His eloquence is not at leisure to deplore the fate of beggared artisans, and famished peasants, —the victims of suspended industry, and languishing commerce. The sensibility which seems scared by the homely miseries of the vulgar, is attracted only by the splendid sorrows of royalty, and agonises at the slenderest pang that assails the heart of sottishness or prostitution, if they are placed by fortune on a throne.* To the English friends of French freedom, his language is contemptuous, illiberal, and scurrilous. In one of the ebbings of his fervour, he is disposed not to dispute "their good intentions:" but he abounds in intemperate sallies and ungenerous insinuations, which wisdom ought to have checked, as ebullitions of passion,—which genius ought to have disdained, as weapons of controversy.

The arrangement of his work is as singular as the matter. Availing himself of all the privileges of epistolary effusion, in their utmost latitude and laxity, he interrupts, dismisses, and resumes argument at pleasure. His subject is as extensive as political science: his allusions and excursions reach almost every region of human knowledge. It must be confessed that in this miscellaneous and desultory warfare, the superiority of a man of genius over common men is infinite. He can cover the most ignominious retreat by a brilliant allusion; he can parade his arguments with masterly generalship, where they are strong; he can escape from an untenable position into a splendid declamation; he can sap the most impregnable conviction by pathos, and put to flight a host of syllogisms with a sneer; absolved from the laws of vulgar method, he can advance a group of magnificent horrors to make a breach in our hearts, through which the most undisciplined rabble of arguments may enter in triumph.

Analysis and method, like the discipline and armour of modern nations, correct in some measure the inequalities of controversial dexterity, and level on the intellectual field the giant and the dwarf. Let us then analyse the production of Mr. Burke, and, dismissing what is extraneous and ornamental, we shall discover certain leading questions, of which the decision is indispensable to the point at issue. The natural order of these topics will dictate the method of reply. Mr. Burke, availing himself of the indefinite and equivocal term 'Revolution,' has altogether reprobated that transaction. The first question, therefore, that arises, regards the general expediency and necessity of a Revolution in France. This is followed by the discussion of the composition and conduct of the National Assembly, of the popular excesses which attended the Revolution, and of the new Constitution that is to result from it. The conduct of its English admirers forms the last topic, though it is with rhetorical inversion first treated by Mr. Burke; as if the propriety of approbation should be determined before the discussion of the merit or demerit of what was approved. In pursuance of this analysis, the following sections will comprise the substance of our refutation.

SECT. I. *The General Expediency and Necessity of a Revolution in France.*

SECT. II. *The Composition and Character of the National Assembly considered.*

SECT. III. *The Popular Excesses which attended, or followed the Revolution.*

SECT. IV. *The new Constitution of France.*

SECT. V. *The Conduct of its English Admirers justified.*

With this reply to Mr. Burke will be mingled some strictures on the late publication of M. de Calonne.* That minister, who has for some time exhibited to the eyes of indignant Europe the spectacle of an exiled robber living in the most splendid impunity, has, with an effrontery that beggars invective, assumed in his work the tone of afflicted patriotism, and delivers his polluted Philippics as the oracles of persecuted virtue. His work is more methodical than that of his

* "The vulgar clamour which has been raised with such malignant art against the friends of freedom, as the apostles of turbulence and sedition, has not even spared the obscurity of my name. To strangers I can only vindicate myself by defying the authors of such clamours to discover one passage in this volume not in the highest degree favourable to peace and stable government: those to whom I am known would, I believe, be slow to impute any sentiments of violence to a temper which the partiality of my friends must confess to be indolent, and the hostility of enemies will not deny to be mild. I have been accused, by valuable friends, of treating with ungenerous levity the misfortunes of the Royal Family of France. They will not however suppose me capable of deliberately violating the sacredness of misery in a palace or a cottage; and I sincerely lament that I should have been betrayed into expressions which admitted that construction."—(*Advertisement to the third edition.*)—ED.

* De l'Etat de la France. London, 1790.—ED.

coadjutor.* Of his financial calculations it may be remarked, that in a work professedly popular they afford the strongest presumption of fraud. Their extent and intricacy seem contrived to extort assent from public indolence; for men will rather believe than examine them. His inferences are so outrageously incredible, that most men of sense will think it more safe to trust their own plain conclusions than to enter such a labyrinth of financial sophistry.. The only part of his production that here demands reply, is that which relates to general political questions. Remarks on what he has offered concerning them will naturally find a place under the corresponding sections of the reply to Mr. Burke. Its most important view is neither literary nor argumentative: it appeals to judgments more decisive than those of criticism, and aims at wielding weapons more formidable than those of logic. It is the manifesto of a Counter-Revolution, and its obvious object is to inflame every passion and interest, real or supposed, that has received any shock in the establishment of freedom. He probes the bleeding wounds of the princes, the nobility, the priesthood, and the great judicial aristocracy: he adjures one body by its dignity degraded, another by its inheritance plundered, and a third by its authority destroyed, to repair to the holy banner of his philanthropic crusade. Confident in the protection of all the monarchs of Europe, whom he alarms for the security of their thrones, and, having insured the moderation of a fanatical rabble, by giving out among them the savage *war-whoop* of atheism, he already fancies himself in full march to Paris, not to re-instate the deposed despotism (for he disclaims the purpose, and who would not trust such virtuous disavowals!) but at the head of this army of priests, mercenaries, and fanatics, to dictate, as the tutelary genius of France, the establishment of a just and temperate freedom, obtained without commotion and without carnage, and equally hostile to the interested ambition of demagogues and the lawless authority of kings. Crusades were an effervescence of chivalry, and the modern St. Francis has a knight for the conduct of these crusaders, who will convince Mr. Burke, that the age of chivalry is not past, nor the glory of Europe gone for ever. The Compte d' Artois,† that scion worthy of Henry the Great, the rival of the Bayards and Sidneys, the new model of French knighthood, is to issue from Turin with ten thousand cavaliers, to deliver the peerless and immaculate Antoinetta of Austria from the durance vile in which she has so long been immured in the Tuilleries, from the swords of the discourteous knights of Paris, and the spells of the sable wizards of democracy.

* It cannot be denied that the production of M. de Calonne is 'eloquent, able,' and certainly very 'instructive' in what regards his own character and designs. But it contains one instance of historical ignorance so egregious, that I cannot resist quoting it. In his long discussion of the pretensions of the Assembly to the title of a 'National Convention,' he deduces the origin of that word from Scotland, where he informs us (p. 328), "On lui donna le nom de Convention Ecossoise; le résultat de ses délibérations fut appellé '*Covenant*,' *et* ceux qui l'avoient souscrit ou qui y adheroient '*Covenanters!*'"

† 'Ce digne rejeton du grand Henri.'—Calonne. 'Un nouveau modèle de la Chevalerie Françoise.' Ibid. pp. 413—114.

SECTION I.

The General Expediency and Necessity of a Revolution in France.

It is asserted in many passages of Mr. Burke's work, though no where with that precision which the importance of the assertion demanded, that the French Revolution was not only in its parts reprehensible, but in the whole was absurd, inexpedient, and unjust; yet he has nowhere exactly informed us what he understands by the term. The 'French Revolution,' in its most popular sense, perhaps, would be understood in England to consist of those splendid events that formed the prominent portion of its exterior,—the Parisian revolt, the capture of the Bastile, and the submission of the King. But these memorable events, though they strengthened and accelerated, could not constitute a political revolution, which must include a change of government. But the term, even when limited to that meaning, is equivocal and wide. It is capable of three senses. The King's recognition of the rights of the States-General to a share in the legislation, was a change in the actual government of France, where the whole legislative and executive power had, without the shadow of an interruption, for nearly two centuries been enjoyed by the crown; in that sense the meeting of the States-General was the Revolution, and the 5th of May was its æra. The union of the three Orders in one assembly was a most important change in the forms and spirit of the legislature; this too may be called the Revolution, and the 23d of June will be its æra. This body, thus united, are forming a new Constitution;* this may be also called a Revolution, because it is of all the political changes the most important, and its epoch will be determined by the conclusion of the labours of the National Assembly. Thus equivocal is the import of Mr. Burke's expressions. To extricate them from this ambiguity, a rapid survey of these events will be necessary. It will prove, too, the fairest and most forcible confutation of his arguments. It will best demonstrate the necessity and justice of all the successive changes in the state of France, which formed what is called the 'Revolution.' It will discriminate legislative acts from popular excesses, and distinguish transient confusion

* The Vindiciæ Galicæ was published in April, 1791.—Ed.

from permanent establishment. It will evince the futility and fallacy of attributing to the conspiracy of individuals, or bodies, a Revolution which, whether it be beneficial or injurious, was produced only by general causes, and in which the most conspicuous individual produced little real effect.

The Constitution of France resembled in the earlier stages of its progress the Gothic governments of Europe. The history of its decline and the causes of its extinction are abundantly known. Its infancy and youth were like these of the English government. The *Champ de Mars*, and the *Wittenagemot*,—the tumultuous assemblies of rude conquerors,—were in both countries melted down into representative bodies. But the downfall of the feudal aristocracy happening in France before commerce had elevated any other class of citizens into importance, its power devolved on the crown. From the conclusion of the fifteenth century the powers of the States-General had almost dwindled into formalities. Their momentary re-appearance under Henry III. and Louis XIII. served only to illustrate their insignificance: their total disuse speedily succeeded.

The intrusion of any popular voice was not likely to be tolerated in the reign of Louis XIV.—a reign which has been so often celebrated as the zenith of warlike and literary splendour, but which has always appeared to me to be the consummation of whatever is afflicting and degrading in the history of the human race. Talent seemed, in that reign, robbed of the conscious elevation,—of the erect and manly port, which is its noblest associate and its surest indication. The mild purity of Fenelon,—the lofty spirit of Bossuet,—the masculine mind of Boileau, the sublime fervour of Corneille,—were confounded by the contagion of ignominious and indiscriminate servility. It seemed as if the 'representative majesty' of the genius and intellect of man were prostrated before the shrine of a sanguinary and dissolute tyrant, who practised the corruption of courts without their mildness, and incurred the guilt of wars without their glory. His highest praise is to have supported the stage trick of Royalty with effect: and it is surely difficult to conceive any character more odious and despicable, than that of a puny libertine, who, under the frown of a strumpet, or a monk, issues the mandate that is to murder virtuous citizens,—to desolate happy and peaceful hamlets,—to wring agonising tears from widows and orphans. Heroism has a splendour that almost atones for its excesses: but what shall we think of him, who, from the luxurious and dastardly security in which he wallows at Versailles, issues with calm and cruel apathy his orders to butcher the Protestants of Languedoc, or to lay in ashes the villages of the Palatinate? On the recollection of such scenes, as a scholar, I blush for the prostitution of letters,—as a man, I blush for the patience of humanity.

But the despotism of this reign was pregnant with the great events which have signalised our age: it fostered that literature which was one day destined to destroy it. The profligate conquests of Louis have eventually proved the acquisitions of humanity; and his usurpations have served only to add a larger portion to the great body of freemen. The spirit of his policy was inherited by his successor: the rage of conquest, repressed for a while by the torpid despotism of Fleury, burst forth with renovated violence in the latter part of the reign of Louis XV. France, exhausted alike by the misfortunes of one war, and the victories of another, groaned under a weight of impost and debt, which it was equally difficult to remedy or to endure. But the profligate expedients were exhausted by which successive ministers had attempted to avert the great crisis, in which the credit and power of the government must perish.

The wise and benevolent administration of M. Turgot,* though long enough for his

* "Louis XVI. called to his councils the two most virtuous men in his dominions, M. Turgot and M. de Lamoignon Malesherbes. Few things could have been more unexpected than that such a promotion should have been made; and still fewer have more discredited the sagacity and humbled the wisdom of man than that so little good should ultimately have sprung from so glorious an occurrence. M. Turgot appears beyond most other men to have been guided in the exertion of his original genius and comprehensive intellect by impartial and indefatigable benevolence. He preferred nothing to the discovery of truth but the interest of mankind; and he was ignorant of nothing of which he did not forego the attainment, that he might gain time for the practice of his duty. Co-operating with the illustrious men who laid the foundation of the science of political economy, his writings were distinguished from theirs by the simplicity, the geometrical order, and precision of a mind without passion, intent only on the progress of reason towards truth. The character of M. Turgot considered as a private philosopher, or as an inferior magistrate, seems to have approached more near the ideal model of a perfect sage, than that of any other man of the modern world. But he was destined rather to instruct than to reform mankind. Like Bacon (whom he so much resembled in the vast range of his intellect) he came into a court, and like Bacon,—though from far nobler causes,—he fell. The noble error of supposing men to be more disinterested and enlightened than they are, betrayed him. Though he had deeply studied human nature, he disdained that discretion and dexterity without which wisdom must return to her cell, and leave the dominion of the world to cunning. The instruments of his benevolence depended on others: but the sources of his own happiness were independent, and he left behind him in the minds of his friends that enthusiastic attachment and profound reverence with which, when superior attainments were more rare, the sages of antiquity inspired their disciples. The virtue of M. de Lamoignon was of a less perfect but of a softer and more natural kind. Descended from one of the most illustrious families of the French magistracy, he was early called to high offices. He employed his influence chiefly in lightening the fetters which impeded the free exercise of reason; and he exerted his courage and his eloquence in defending the people against oppressive taxation. While he was a minister, he had prepared the means of abolishing arbitrary imprisonment. No part of science or art was

own glory, was too short, and perhaps too early, for those salutary and grand reforms which his genius had conceived, and his virtue would have effected. The aspect of purity and talent spread a natural alarm among the minions of a court; and they easily succeeded in the expulsion of such rare and obnoxious intruders. The magnificent ambition of M. de Vergennes, the brilliant, profuse, and rapacious career of M. de Calonne, the feeble and irresolute violence of M. de Brienne,—all contributed their share to swell this financial embarrassment. The *deficit*, or inferiority of the revenue to the expenditure, at length rose to the enormous sum of 115 millions of livres, or about 4,750,000*l.* annually.* This was a disproportion between income and expense with which no government, and no individual, could long continue to exist.

In this exigency there was no expedient left, but to guarantee the ruined credit of bankrupt despotism by the sanction of the national voice. The States-General were a dangerous mode of collecting it: recourse was, therefore, had to the Assembly of the Notables; a mode well known in the History of France, in which the King summoned a number of individuals, selected, at *his* discretion, from the mass, to advise him in great emergencies. They were little better than a popular Privy Council. They were neither recognised nor protected by law: their precarious and subordinate existence hung on the nod of despotism.

The Notables were accordingly called together by M. de Calonne, who has now the inconsistent arrogance to boast of the schemes which he laid before them, as the model of the Assembly whom he traduces. He proposed, it is true, the equalisation of imposts and the abolition of the pecuniary exemptions of the Nobility and Clergy; and the difference between his system and that of the Assembly, is only in what makes the sole distinction in human actions—its end. *He* would have destroyed the privileged Orders, as obstacles to despotism: *they* have destroyed them, as derogations from freedom. The object of *his* plans was to facilitate fiscal oppression: the motive of *theirs* is to fortify general liberty. *They* have levelled all Frenchmen as men: *he* would have levelled them as slaves. The Assembly of the Notables, however, soon gave a memorable proof, how dangerous are all public meetings of men, even without legal powers of control, to the permanence of despotism. They had been assembled by M. de Calonne to admire the plausibility and splendour of his speculations, and to veil the extent and atrocity of his rapine: but the fallacy of the one and the profligacy of the other were detected with equal ease. Illustrious orators, who have since found a nobler sphere for their talents, in a more free and powerful Assembly, exposed the plunderer. Detested by the Nobles and Clergy, of whose privileges he had suggested the abolition; undermined in the favour of the Queen, by his attack on one of her favourites (Breteuil); exposed to the fury of the people, and dreading the terrors of judicial prosecution, he speedily sought refuge in England, without the recollection of one virtue, or the applause of one party, to console his retreat. Thus did the Notables destroy their creator. Little appeared to be done to a superficial observer: but to a discerning eye, all was done; for the dethroned authority of Public Opinion was restored.

The succeeding Ministers, uninstructed by the example of their predecessors, by the destruction of public credit, and by the fermentation of the popular mind, hazarded measures of a still more preposterous and perilous description. The usurpation of some share in the sovereignty by the Parliament of Paris had become popular and venerable, because its tendency was useful, and its exercise virtuous. That body had, as it is well known, claimed a right, which, in fact, amounted to a negative on all the acts of the King:—they contended, that the registration of his edicts by them was necessary to give them force. They would, in that case, have possessed the same share of legislation as the King of England. It is unnecessary to descant on the historical fallacy, and political inexpediency, of doctrines, which would vest in a narrow aristocracy of lawyers, who had bought their places, such extensive powers. It cannot be denied that their resistance had often proved salutary, and was some feeble check on the capricious wantonness of despotic exaction: but the temerity of the Minister now assigned them a more important part. They refused to register two edicts for the creation of imposts, averring that the power of imposing taxes was vested only in the national representatives, and claiming the immediate convocation of the States-General of the kingdom: the Minister banished them to Troyes. But he soon found how much the French were changed from that abject and frivolous people, which had so often endured the exile of its magistrates: Paris exhibited the tumult and clamour of a London mob. The Cabinet, which could neither advance nor recede with safety, had recourse to the expedient of a compulsory registration. The Duke of Orleans, and the magistrates who protested against this exe-

foreign to his elegant leisure. His virtue was without effort or system, and his benevolence was prone to diffuse itself in a sort of pleasantry and even drollery. In this respect he resembled Sir Thomas More; and it is remarkable that this playfulness—the natural companion of a simple and innocent mind—attended both these illustrious men to the scaffold on which they were judicially murdered."—MS. Ed.

* For this we have the authority of M. de Calonne himself, p. 56. This was the account presented to the Notables in April, 1787. He, indeed, makes some deductions on account of part of this *deficit* being expirable: but this is of no consequence to our purpose, which is to view the influence of the *present* urgency,—the political, not the financial, state of the question.

crable mockery, were exiled or imprisoned. But all these hacknied expedients of despotism were in vain. These struggles, which merit notice only as they illustrate the progressive energy of Public Opinion, were followed by events still less equivocal. *Lettres de Cachet* were issued against MM. d'Espréménil and Goeslard. They took refuge in the sanctuary of justice, and the Parliament pronounced them under the safeguard of the law and the King. A deputation was sent to Versailles, to entreat his Majesty to listen to sage counsels; and Paris expected, with impatient solicitude, the result. When towards midnight, a body of two thousand troops marched to the palace where the Parliament were seated, and their Commander, entering into the Court of Peers, demanded his victims, a loud and unanimous acclamation replied,—"We are all d'Espréménil and Goeslard!" These magistrates surrendered themselves; and the satellite of despotism led them off in triumph, amid the execrations of an aroused and indignant people. These spectacles were not without their effect: the spirit of resistance spread daily over France. The intermediate commission of the States of Bretagne, the States of Dauphiné, and many other public bodies, began to assume a new and menacing tone. The Cabinet was dissolved by its own feebleness, and M. Neckar was recalled.

That Minister, probably upright, and not illiberal, but narrow, pusillanimous, and entangled by the habits of detail* in which he had been reared, possessed not that erect and intrepid spirit,—those enlarged and original views, which adapt themselves to new combinations of circumstances, and sway in the great convulsions of human affairs. Accustomed to the tranquil accuracy of commerce, or the elegant amusements of literature, he was called on to

"Ride in the whirlwind, and direct the storm."†

He seemed superior to his privacy while he was limited to it, and would have been adjudged by history equal to his elevation had he never been elevated.‡ The reputation of few men, it is true, has been exposed to so severe a test; and a generous observer will be disposed to scrutinize less rigidly the claims of a statesman, who has retired with the applause of no party,—who is detested by the aristocracy as the instrument of their ruin, and despised by the democratic leaders for pusillanimous and fluctuating policy. But had the character of M. Neckar possessed more originality or decision, it could have had little influence on the fate of France. The minds of men had received an impulse; and individual aid and individual opposition were equally vain. His views, no doubt, extended only to palliation; but he was involved in a stream of opinions and events, of which no force could resist the current, and no wisdom adequately predict the termination. He is represented by M. de Calonne as the Lord Sunderland of Louis XVI. seducing the King to destroy his own power: but he had neither genius nor boldness for such designs.

To return to our rapid survey:—The autumn of 1788 was peculiarly distinguished by the enlightened and disinterested patriotism of the States of Dauphiné. They furnished, in many respects, a model for the future senate of France. Like them they deliberated amidst the terrors of ministerial vengeance and military execution. They annihilated the absurd and destructive distinction of Orders; the three estates were melted into a Provincial Assembly; they declared, that the right of imposing taxes resided ultimately in the States-General of France; and they voted a deputation to the King to solicit the convocation of that Assembly. Dauphiné was emulously imitated by all the provinces that still retained the shadow of Provincial States. The States of Languedoc, of Velay, and Vivarois, the Tiers Etat of Provence, and all the Municipalities of Bretagne, adopted similar resolutions. In Provence and Bretagne, where the Nobles and Clergy, trembling for their privileges, and the Parliaments for their jurisdiction, attempted a feeble resistance, the fermentation was peculiarly strong. Some estimate of the fervour of public sentiment may be formed from the reception of the Count de Mirabeau in his native province, where the burgesses of Aix assigned him a body-guard, where the citizens of Marseilles crowned him in the theatre, and where, under all the terrors of despotism, he received as numerous and tumultuous proofs of attachment as ever were bestowed on a favourite by the enthusiasm of the most free people. M. Caraman, the Governor of Provence, was even reduced to implore his interposition with the populace, to appease and prevent their excesses. The contest in Bretagne was more violent and sanguinary. She had preserved her independence more than any of those provinces which had been united to the crown of France. The Nobles and Clergy possessed almost the whole power of the States, and their obstinacy was so great, that their deputies did not take their seats in the National Assembly till an advanced period of its proceedings.

The return of M. Neckar, and the recall of the exiled magistrates, restored a momentary calm. The personal reputation of the minister for probity, reanimated the credit of France. But the finances were too

* The late celebrated Dr. Adam Smith, always held this opinion of Neckar, whom he had known intimately when a banker in Paris. He predicted the fall of his fame when his talents should be brought to the test, and always emphatically said, "He is but a man of detail." At a time when the commercial abilities of Mr. Eden, the present Lord Auckland, were the theme of profuse eulogy, Dr. Smith characterized him in the same words.

† Addison, The Campaign.—Ed.

‡ Major privato visus, dum privatus fuit, et omnium consensu capax imperii, nisi imperasset.—Tacitus, Hist. lib. i. cap. 49.

irremediably embarrassed for palliatives; and the fascinating idea of the States-General, presented to the public imagination by the unwary zeal of the Parliament, awakened recollections of ancient freedom, and prospects of future splendour, which the virtue or popularity of no minister could banish. The convocation of that body was resolved on; but many difficulties respecting the mode of electing and constituting it remained, which a second Assembly of Notables was summoned to decide.

The Third Estate demanded representatives equal to those of the other two Orders jointly. They required that the number should be regulated by the population of the districts, and that the three Orders should vote in one Assembly. All the committees into which the Notables were divided, except that of which MONSIEUR was President, decided against the Third Estate in every one of these particulars. They were strenuously supported by the Parliament of Paris, who, too late sensible of the suicide into which they had been betrayed, laboured to render the Assembly impotent, after they were unable to prevent its meeting. But their efforts were in vain: M. Neckar, whether actuated by respect for justice, or desire of popularity, or yielding to the irresistible torrent of public sentiment, advised the King to adopt the propositions of the Third Estate in the two first particulars, and to leave the last to be decided by the States-General themselves.

Letters-Patent were accordingly issued on the 24th of January, 1789, for assembling the States-General, to which were annexed regulations for the detail of their elections. In the constituent assemblies of the several provinces, bailliages, and constabularies of the kingdom, the progress of the public mind became still more evident. The Clergy and Nobility ought not to be denied the praise of having emulously sacrificed their pecuniary privileges. The instructions to the representatives breathed every where a spirit of freedom as ardent, though not so liberal and enlightened, as that which has since presided in the deliberations of the National Assembly. Paris was eminently conspicuous. The union of talent, the rapid communication of thought, and the frequency of those numerous assemblies, where men learn their force, and compare their wrongs, ever make a great capital the heart that circulates emotion and opinion to the extremities of an empire. No sooner had the convocation of the States-General been announced, than the batteries of the press were opened. Pamphlet succeeded pamphlet, surpassing each other in boldness and elevation; and the advance of Paris to light and freedom was greater in three months than it had been in almost as many centuries. Doctrines were universally received in May, which in January would have been deemed treasonable, and which in March had been derided as the visions of a few deluded fanatics.*

It was amid this rapid diffusion of light, and increasing fervour of public sentiment, that the States-General assembled at Versailles on the 5th of May, 1789,—a day which will probably be accounted by posterity one of the most memorable in the annals of the human race. Any detail of the parade and ceremonial of their assembly would be totally foreign to our purpose, which is not to narrate events, but to seize their spirit, and to mark their influence on the political progress from which the Revolution was to arise. The preliminary operation necessary to constitute the Assembly gave rise to the first great question,—the mode of authenticating the commissions of the deputies. It was contended by the Clergy and Nobles, that according to ancient usage, each Order should separately scrutinize and authenticate the commissions of its own deputies. It was argued by the Commons, that, on general principles, all Orders, having an equal interest in the purity of the national representative, had an equal right to take cognizance of the authenticity of the commissions of all the members who composed the body, and therefore to scrutinize them in common. To the authority of precedent it was answered, that it would establish too much; for in the ancient States, their examination of powers was subordinate to the revision of Royal Commissaries,—a subjection too degrading and injurious for the free and vigilant spirit of an enlightened age.

This controversy involved another of more magnitude and importance. If the Orders united in this scrutiny, they were likely to continue in one Assembly; the separate voices of the two first Orders would be annihilated, and the importance of the Nobility and Clergy reduced to that of their individual suffrages. This great revolution was obviously meditated by the leaders of the Commons. They were seconded in the chamber of the Noblesse by a minority eminently distinguished for rank, character, and talent. The obscure and useful portion of the Clergy were, from their situation, accessible to popular sentiment, and naturally coalesced with the Commons. Many who favoured the division of the Legislature in the ordinary arrangements of government, were convinced that the grand and radical reforms, which the situation of France demanded, could only be effected by its union as one Assembly.† So many prejudices were

* The principles of freedom had long been understood, perhaps better than in any country of the world, by the philosophers of France. It was as natural that they should have been more diligently cultivated in that kingdom than in England, as that the science of medicine should be less understood and valued among simple and vigorous, than among luxurious and enfeebled nations. But the progress which we have noticed was among the less instructed part of society.

† "Il n'est pas douteux que pour aujourd'hui,

to be vanquished,—so many difficulties to be surmounted, such obstinate habits to be extirpated, and so formidable a power to be resisted, that there was an obvious necessity to concentrate the force of the reforming body. In a great revolution, every expedient ought to facilitate change: in an established government, every thing ought to render it difficult. Hence the division of a legislature, which in an established government, may give a beneficial stability to the laws, must, in a moment of revolution, be proportionably injurious, by fortifying abuse and unnerving reform. In a revolution, the enemies of freedom are external, and all powers are therefore to be united: under an establishment her enemies are internal, and power is therefore to be divided. But besides this general consideration, the state of France furnished others of more local and temporary cogency. The States-General, acting by separate Orders, were a body from which no substantial reform could be hoped. The two first Orders were interested in the perpetuity of every abuse that was to be reformed: their possession of two equal and independent voices must have rendered the exertions of the Commons impotent and nugatory. And a collusion between the Assembly and the Crown would probably have limited its illusive reforms to some sorry palliatives,—the price of financial disembarrassment. The state of a nation lulled into complacent servitude by such petty concessions, is far more hopeless than that of those who groan under the most galling despotism; and the condition of France would have been more irremediable than ever.

Such reasonings produced an universal conviction, that the question, whether the States-General were to vote individually, or in Orders, was a question, whether they were or were not to produce any important benefit. Guided by these views, and animated by public support, the Commons adhered inflexibily to their principle of incorporation. They adopted a provisory organization, but studiously declined whatever might seem to suppose legal existence, or to arrogate constitutional powers. The Nobles, less politic or timid, declared themselves a legally constituted Order, and proceeded to discuss the great objects of their convocation. The Clergy affected to preserve a mediatorial character, and to conciliate the discordant claims of the two hostile Orders. The Commons, faithful to their system, remained in a wise and masterly inactivity, which tacitly reproached the arrogant assumption of the Nobles, while it left no pretext to calumniate their own conduct, gave time for the increase of the popular fervour, and distressed the Court by the delay of financial aid. Several conciliatory plans were proposed by the Minister, and rejected by the haughtiness of the Nobility and the policy of the Commons.

Thus passed the period between the 5th of May and the 12th of June, when the popular leaders, animated by public support, and conscious of the maturity of their schemes, assumed a more resolute tone. The Third Estate then commenced the scrutiny of commissions, summoned the Nobles and Clergy to repair to the Hall of the States-General, and resolved that the absence of the deputies of some districts and classes of citizens could not preclude them, who formed the representatives of ninety-six hundredths of the nation, from constituting themselves a National Assembly.

These decisive measures betrayed the designs of the Court, and fully illustrate that bounty and liberality for which Louis XVI. has been so idly celebrated. That feeble Prince, whose public character varied with every fluctuation in his Cabinet,—the instrument alike of the ambition of Vergennes, the prodigality of Calonne, and the ostentatious popularity of Neckar,—had hitherto yielded to the embarrassment of the finances, and the clamour of the people. The cabal that retained its ascendant over his mind, permitted concessions which they hoped to make vain, and flattered themselves with frustrating, by the contest of struggling Orders, all idea of substantial reform. But no sooner did the Assembly betray any symptom of activity and vigour, than their alarms became conspicuous in the Royal conduct. The Compte d'Artois, and the other Princes of the Blood, published the boldest manifestoes against the Assembly; the credit of M. Neckar at Court declined every day; the Royalists in the chamber of the Noblesse spoke of nothing less than an impeachment of the Commons for high-treason, and an immediate dissolution of the States; and a vast military force and a tremendous park of artillery were collected from all parts of the kingdom towards Versailles and Paris. Under these menacing and inauspicious circumstances, the meeting of the States-General was prohibited by the King's order till a Royal Session, which was destined for the twenty-second but not held till the twenty-third of June, had taken place. On repairing to their Hall on the twentieth, the Commons found it invested with soldiers, and themselves excluded by the point of the bayonet. They were summoned by their President to a *Tennis-Court*, where they were

que pour cette premiere tenue une Chambre Unique n'ait été préferable et peut-être *nécessaire;* il y avoit tant de difficultés à surmonter, tant de prejugés à vaincre, tant de sacrifices à faire, de si vieilles habitudes à déraciner, une puissance si forte à contenir, en un mot, tant à détruire et *presque tout à créer*."—"Ce nouvel ordre de choses que vous avez fait eclorre, tout cela vous en êtes bien surs n'a jamais pu naître que de la réunion de toutes les personnes, de tous les sentiments, et de tous les cœurs."—Discours de M. Lally-Tollendal à l'Assemblée Nationale, 31 Août, 1789, dans ses Pièces Justificatifs, pp. 105, 106. This passage is in more than one respect remarkable. It fully evinces the conviction of the author, that changes were necessary great enough to deserve the name of a Revolution, and, considering the respect of Mr. Burke for his authority, ought to have weight with him.

reduced to hold their assembly, and which they rendered famous as the scene of their unanimous and memorable oath,—never to separate till they had achieved the regeneration of France.

The Royal Session thus announced, corresponded with the new tone of the Court. Its exterior was marked by the gloomy and ferocious haughtiness of despotism. The Royal Puppet was now evidently moved by different persons from those who had prompted its Speech at the opening of the States. He probably now spoke both with the same spirit and the same heart, and felt as little firmness under the cloak of arrogance, as he had been conscious of sensibility amidst his professions of affection; he was probably as feeble in the one as he had been cold in the other: but his language is some criterion of the system of his prompters. This speech was distinguished by insulting condescension and ostentatious menace. He spoke not as the Chief of a free nation to its sovereign Legislature, but as a Sultan to his Divan. He annulled and prescribed deliberations at pleasure. He affected to represent his will as the rule of their conduct, and his bounty as the source of their freedom. Nor was the matter of his harangue less injurious than its manner was offensive. Instead of containing any concession important to public liberty, it indicated a relapse into a more lofty despotism than had before marked his pretensions. Tithes, feudal and seignorial rights, he consecrated as the most inviolable property; and of *Lettres de Cachet* themselves, by recommending the regulation, he obviously condemned the abolition. The distinction of Orders he considered as essential to the Constitution of the kingdom, and their present union as only legitimate by his permission. He concluded with commanding them to separate, and to assemble on the next day in the Halls of their respective Orders.

The Commons, however, inflexibly adhering to their principles, and conceiving themselves constituted as a National Assembly, treated these threats and injunctions with equal neglect. They remained assembled in the Hall, which the other Orders had quitted in obedience to the Royal command; and when the Marquis de Brézé, the King's Master of the Ceremonies, reminded them of his Majesty's orders, he was answered by M. Bailly, with Spartan energy,—"The Nation assembled has no orders to receive." They proceeded to pass resolutions declaratory of adherence to their former decrees, and of the personal inviolability of the members. The Royal Session, which the Aristocratic party had expected with such triumph and confidence, proved the severest blow to their cause. Forty-nine members of the Nobility, at the head of whom was M. de Clermont-Tonnerre, repaired on the 26th of June to the Assembly.* The popular enthusiasm was inflamed to such a degree, that alarms were either felt or affected, for the safety of the King, if the union of Orders was delayed. The union was accordingly resolved on; and the Duke of Luxembourg, President of the Nobility, was authorised by his Majesty to announce to his Order the request and even command of the King, to unite themselves with the others. He remonstrated with the King on the fatal consequences of this step. "The Nobility," he remarked, "were not fighting their own battles, but those of the Crown. The support of the monarchy was inseparably connected with the division of the States-General: divided, that body was subject to the Crown; united, its authority was sovereign, and its force irresistible."* The King was not, however, shaken by these considerations, and on the following day, notified his pleasure in an official letter to the Presidents of the Nobility and the Clergy. A gloomy and reluctant obedience was yielded to this mandate, and the union of the National Representatives at length promised some hope to France.

But the general system of the Government formed a suspicious and tremendous contrast with this applauded concession. New hordes of foreign mercenaries were summoned to the blockade of Paris and Versailles, from the remotest provinces; an immense train of artillery was disposed in all the avenues of these cities; and seventy thousand men already invested the Capital, when the last blow was hazarded against the public hopes, by the ignominious banishment of M. Neckar. Events followed, the most unexampled and memorable in the annals of mankind, which history will record and immortalize, but, on which, the object of the political reasoner is only to speculate. France was on the brink of civil war. The Provinces were ready to march immense bodies to the rescue of their representatives. The courtiers and their minions, princes and princesses, male and female favourites, crowded to the camps with which they had invested Versailles, and stimulated the ferocious cruelty of their mercenaries, by caresses, by largesses, and by promises. Mean time the people of Paris revolted; the French soldiery felt that they were citizens; and the fabric of Despotism fell to the ground.

These soldiers, whom posterity will celebrate for patriotic heroism, are stigmatized by Mr. Burke as "base hireling deserters," who sold their King for an increase of pay.†

* It deserves remark, that in this number were Noblemen who have ever been considered as of the *moderate* party. Of these may be mentioned MM. Lally, Virieu, and Clermont-Tonnerre, none of whom certainly can be accused of democratic enthusiasm.

* These remarks of M. de Luxembourg are equivalent to a thousand defences of the Revolutionists against Mr. Burke. They unanswerably prove that the division of Orders was supported *only* as necessary to palsy the efforts of the Legislature against the Despotism.

† Mr. Burke is sanctioned in this opinion by an authority not the most respectable, that of his late countryman Count Dalton, Commander of the

This position he every where asserts or insinuates: but nothing seems more false. Had the defection been confined to Paris, there might have been some speciousness in the accusation. The exchequer of a faction might have been equal to the corruption of the guards: the activity of intrigue might have seduced the troops cantoned in the neighbourhood of the capital. But what policy, or fortune, could pervade by their agents, or donatives, an army of one hundred and fifty thousand men, dispersed over so great a monarchy as France. The spirit of resistance to uncivic commands broke forth at once in every part of the empire. The garrisons of the cities of Rennes, Bourdeaux, Lyons, and Grenoble, refused, almost at the same moment, to resist the virtuous insurrection of their fellow-citizens. No largesses could have seduced,—no intrigues could have reached so vast and divided a body. Nothing but sympathy with the national spirit could have produced their noble disobedience. The remark of Mr. Hume is here most applicable, "that what depends on a few may be often attributed to chance (secret circumstances); but that the actions of great bodies must be ever ascribed to general causes." It was the apprehension of Montesquieu, that the spirit of increasing armies would terminate in converting Europe into an immense camp, in changing our artisans and cultivators into military savages, and reviving the age of Attila and Genghis. Events are our preceptors, and France has taught us that this evil contains in itself its own remedy and limit. A domestic army cannot be increased without increasing the number of its ties with the people, and of the channels by which popular sentiment may enter. Every man who is added to the army is a new link that unites it to the nation. If all citizens were compelled to become soldiers, all soldiers must of necessity adopt the feelings of citizens; and despots cannot increase their army without admitting into it a greater number of men interested in destroying them. A small army may have sentiments different from the great body of the people, and no interest in common with them, but a numerous soldiery cannot. This is the barrier which Nature has opposed to the increase of armies. They cannot be numerous enough to enslave the people, without becoming the people itself. The effects of this truth have been hitherto conspicuous only in the military defection of France, because the enlightened sense of general interest has been so much more diffused in that nation than in any other despotic monarchy of Europe: but they must be felt by all. An elaborate discipline may for a while in Germany debase and brutalize soldiers too much to receive any impressions from their fellow men: artificial and local institutions are, however, too feeble to resist the energy of natural causes. The constitution of man survives the transient fashions of despotism; and the history of the next century will probably evince on how frail and tottering a basis the military tyrannies of Europe stand.

The pretended seduction of the troops by the promise of increased pay, is in every view contradicted by facts. This increase of pay did not originate in the Assembly; it was not even any part of their policy: it was prescribed to them by the instructions of their constituents, before the meeting of the States.* It could not therefore be the project of any cabal of demagogues to seduce the army: it was the decisive and unanimous voice of the nation; and if there was any conspiracy, it must have been that of the people. What had demagogues to offer? The soldiery knew that the States must, in obedience to their instructions, increase their pay. This increase could, therefore, have been no temptation to them; for of it they felt themselves already secure, as the national voice had prescribed it. It was in fact a necessary part of the system which was to raise the army to a body of respectable citizens, from a gang of mendicant ruffians. An increase of pay must infallibly operate to limit the increase of armies in the North. This influence has been already felt in the Netherlands, which fortune seems to have restored to Leopold, that they might furnish a school of revolt to German soldiers. The Austrian troops have there murmured at their comparative indigence, and have supported their plea for increase of pay by the example of France. The same example must operate on the other armies of Europe: and the solicitations of armed petitioners must be heard. The indigent despots of Germany and the North will feel a limit to their military rage, in the scantiness of their exchequer. They will be compelled to reduce the number, and increase the pay of their armies: and a new barrier will be opposed to the progress of that depopulation and barbarism, which philosophers have dreaded from the rapid increase of military force. These remarks on the spirit which actuated the French army in their unexampled, misconceived, and calumniated conduct, are peculiarly important, as they serve to illustrate a principle, which cannot too frequently be presented to view,—that in the French Revolution all is to be attributed to general causes influencing the whole body of the people, and almost nothing to the schemes and the ascendant of individuals.

But to return to our rapid sketch:—it was at the moment of the Parisian revolt, and of the defection of the army, that the whole power of France devolved on the National Assembly. It is at that moment, therefore, that the discussion commences, whether that

---

Austrian troops in the Netherlands. In September, 1789, he addressed the Régiment de Ligne, at Brussels, in these terms:—"J'espère que vous n'imiterez jamais ces laches François qui ont abandonné leur Souverain!"

* Calonne, p. 390

body ought to have re-established and reformed the government which events had subverted, or to have proceeded to the establishment of a new constitution, on the general principles of reason and freedom. The arm of the ancient Government had been palsied, and its power reduced to a mere formality, by events over which the Assembly possessed no control. It was theirs to decide, not whether the monarchy was to be subverted, for that had been already effected, but whether, from its ruins, fragments were to be collected for the reconstruction of the political edifice. They had been assembled as an ordinary Legislature under existing laws: they were transformed by these events into a National Convention, and vested with powers to organize a government. It is in vain that their adversaries contest this assertion, by appealing to the deficiency of forms;* it is in vain to demand the legal instrument that changed their constitution, and extended their powers. Accurate forms in the conveyance of power are prescribed by the wisdom of law, in the regular administration of states: but great revolutions are too immense for technical formality. All the sanction that can be hoped for in such events, is the voice of the people, however informally and irregularly expressed. This cannot be pretended to have been wanting in France. Every other species of authority was annihilated by popular acts, but that of the States-General. On them, therefore, devolved the duty of exercising their *unlimited* trust,† according to their best views of general interest. Their enemies have, even in their invectives, confessed the *subsequent adherence* of the people, for they have inveighed against it as the infatuation of a dire fanaticism. The authority of the Assembly was then first conferred on it by public confidence; and its acts have been since ratified by public approbation. Nothing can betray a disposition to indulge in puny and technical sophistry more strongly, than to observe with M. de Calonne, "that this ratification, to be valid, ought to have been made by France, not in her new organization of municipalities, but in her ancient division of bailliages and provinces." The same *individuals* act in both forms; the approbation of the *men* legitimatizes the government: it is of no importance, whether they are assembled in bailliages or in municipalities.

If this latitude of informality, this subjection of laws to their principle, and of government to its source, are not permitted in revolutions, how are we to justify the assumed authority of the English Convention of 1688? "They did not hold the authority they exercised under any constitutional law of the State." They were not even legally elected, as, it must be confessed, was the case with the French Assembly. An evident, though irregular, ratification by the people, alone legitimatized their acts. Yet they possessed, by the confession of Mr. Burke, an authority only limited by prudence and virtue. Had the people of England given instructions to the members of that Convention, its ultimate measures would probably have departed as much from those instructions as the French Assembly have deviated from those of their constituents; and the public acquiescence in the deviation would, in all likelihood, have been the same. It will be confessed by any man who has considered the public temper of England at the landing of William, that the majority of those instructions would not have proceeded to the deposition of James. The first aspect of these great changes perplexes and intimidates men too much for just views and bold resolutions: it is by the progress of events that their hopes are emboldened, and their views enlarged. This influence was felt in France. The people, in an advanced period of the Revolution, virtually recalled the instructions by which the feebleness of their political infancy had limited the power of their representatives; for they sanctioned acts by which those instructions were contradicted. The formality of instructions was indeed wanting in England; but the change of public sentiment, from the opening of the Convention to its ultimate decision, was as remarkable as the contrast which has been so ostentatiously displayed by M. de Calonne, between the decrees of the National Assembly and the first instructions of their constituents.

We now resume the consideration of this exercise of authority by the Assembly, and proceed to inquire, whether they ought to have reformed, or destroyed their government? The general question of innovation

* "This circumstance is thus shortly stated by Mr. Burke, (p. 242):—I can never consider this Assembly as anything else than a voluntary association of men, who have availed themselves of circumstances to seize upon the power of the State. They do not hold the authority they exercise under any constitutional law of the State. They have departed from the instructions of the people that sent them." The same argument is treated by M. de Calonne, in an expanded memorial of forty-four pages, (314—358), against the pretensions of the Assembly to be a Convention, with much unavailing ingenuity and labour.

† A distinction made by Mr. Burke between the *abstract* and *moral* competency of a Legislature (p. 27), has been much extolled by his admirers. To me it seems only a novel and objectionable mode of distinguishing between *a right* and the *expediency* of using it. But the mode of illustrating the distinction is far more pernicious than a mere novelty of phrase. This moral competence is subject, says our author, to "faith, justice, and fixed fundamental policy:" thus illustrated, the distinction appears liable to a double objection. It is false that the *abstract* competence of a Legislature extends to the violation of faith and justice: it is false that its *moral* competence does not extend to the most fundamental policy. Thus to confound fundamental policy with faith and justice, for the sake of stigmatizing innovators, is to stab the vitals of morality. There is only one maxim of policy truly fundamental—the good of the governed; and the stability of that maxim, rightly understood, demonstrates the mutability of all policy that is subordinate to it.

is an exhausted common-place, to which the genius of Mr. Burke has been able to add nothing but splendour of eloquence and felicity of illustration. It has long been so notoriously of this nature, that it is placed by Lord Bacon among the sportive contests which are to exercise rhetorical skill. No man will support the extreme on either side: perpetual change and immutable establishment are equally indefensible. To descend therefore from these barren generalities to a nearer view of the question, let us state it more precisely:—Was the civil order in France corrigible, or was it necessary to destroy it? Not to mention the extirpation of the feudal system, and the abrogation of the civil and criminal code, we have first to consider the destruction of the three great corporations, of the Nobility, the Church, and the Parliaments. These three Aristocracies were the pillars which in fact formed the government of France. The question then of forming or destroying these bodies was fundamental.

There is one general principle applicable to them all adopted by the French legislators,—that the existence of Orders is repugnant to the principles of the social union. An Order is a legal rank, a body of men combined and endowed with privileges by law. There are two kinds of inequality: the one personal, that of talent and virtue, the source of whatever is excellent and admirable in society; the other, that of fortune, which must exist, because property alone can stimulate to labour, and labour, if it were not necessary to the existence, would be indispensable to the happiness of man. But though it be necessary, yet in its excess it is the great malady of civil society. The accumulation of that power which is conferred by wealth in the hands of the few, is the perpetual source of oppression and neglect to the mass of mankind. The power of the wealthy is farther concentrated by their tendency to combination, from which, number, dispersion, indigence, and ignorance equally preclude the poor. The wealthy are formed into bodies by their professions, their different degrees of opulence (called "ranks"), their knowledge, and their small number. They necessarily in all countries administer government, for they alone have skill and leisure for its functions. Thus circumstanced, nothing can be more evident than their inevitable preponderance in the political scale. The preference of partial to general interests is, however, the greatest of all public evils. It should therefore have been the object of all laws to repress this malady; but it has been their perpetual tendency to aggravate it. Not content with the inevitable inequality of fortune, they have superadded to it honorary and political distinctions. Not content with the inevitable tendency of the wealthy to combine, they have embodied them in classes. They have fortified those conspiracies against the general interest, which they ought to have resisted, though they could not disarm. Laws, it is said, cannot equalize men;—No: but ought they for that reason to aggravate the inequality which they cannot cure? Laws cannot inspire unmixed patriotism: but ought they for that reason to foment that *corporation spirit* which is its most fatal enemy? "All professional combinations," said Mr. Burke, in one of his late speeches in Parliament, "are dangerous in a free state." Arguing on the same principle, the National Assembly has proceeded further. They have conceived that the laws ought to create no inequality of combination, to recognise all only in their capacity of citizens, and to offer no assistance to the natural preponderance of partial over general interest.

But, besides the general source of hostility to Orders, the particular circumstances of France presented other objections, which it is necessary to consider more in detail.

It is in the first place to be remarked, that all the bodies and institutions of the kingdom participated in the spirit of the ancient government, and in that view were incapable of alliance with a free constitution. They were tainted by the despotism of which they had been either members or instruments. Absolute monarchies, like every other consistent and permanent government, assimilate every thing with which they are connected to their own genius. The Nobility, the Priesthood, the Judicial Aristocracy, were unfit to be members of a free government, because their corporate character had been formed under arbitrary establishments. To have preserved these great corporations, would be to have retained the seeds of reviving despotism in the bosom of freedom. This remark may merit the attention of Mr. Burke, as illustrating an important difference between the French and English Revolutions. The Clergy, the Peerage, and Judicature of England had imbibed in some degree the sentiments inspired by a government in which freedom had been eclipsed, but not extinguished. They were therefore qualified to partake of a more stable and improved liberty. But the case of France was different. These bodies had there imbibed every sentiment, and adopted every habit under arbitrary power. Their preservation in England, and their destruction in France, may in this view be justified on similar grounds. It is absurd to regard the Orders as remnants of that free constitution which France, in common with the other Gothic nations of Europe, once enjoyed. Nothing remained of these ancient Orders but the name. The Nobility were no longer those haughty and powerful Barons, who enslaved the people, and dictated to the King. The Ecclesiastics were no longer that Priesthood before whom, in a benighted and superstitious age, all civil power was impotent and mute. They had both dwindled into dependents on the Crown. Still less do the opulent and enlightened Commons of France resemble its servile and beggared populace in the sixteenth century. Two hundred years of uninterrupted exercise had legitimatized absolute authority as much as prescription can consecrate usurpation. The ancient French Constitution was therefore no farther a model than that of any foreign nation which was to be judged of alone by its utility, and possessed in no respect the authority of establishment. It had been succeeded by another government; and if France was to recur to a period antecedent to her servitude for legislative models, she might as well ascend to the æra of Clovis or Charlemagne, as be regulated by the precedents of Henry III. or Mary of Medicis. All these forms of government existed only historically.

These observations include all the Orders. Let us consider each of them successively. The devotion of the Nobility of France to the Monarch was inspired equally by their sentiments, their interests, and their habits. "The feudal and chivalrous spirit of fealty," so long the prevailing passion of Europe, was still nourished in their bosoms by the military sentiments from which it first arose. The majority of them had still no profession but war,—no hope but in Royal favour. The youthful and indigent filled the camps; the more opulent and mature partook the splendour and bounty of the Court: but they were equally dependents on the Crown. To the plenitude of the Royal power were attached those immense and magnificent privileges, which divided France into distinct nations; which exhibited a Nobility monopolizing the rewards and offices of the State, and a people degraded to political helotism.* Men do not cordially resign such privileges, nor quickly dismiss the sentiments which they have inspired. The ostentatious sacrifice of pecuniary exemptions in a moment of general fermentation is a wretched criterion of their genuine feelings. They affected to bestow as a gift, what they would have been speedily compelled to abandon as an usurpation; and they hoped by the sacrifice of a part to purchase security for the rest. They have been most justly stated to be a band of political Janissaries,†—far more valuable to a Sultan than mercenaries, because attached to him by unchangeable interest and indelible sentiment. Whether any reform could have extracted from this body an element which might have entered into the new Constitution is a question which we shall consider when that political system comes under our review. Their existence, as a member of the Legislature, is a question distinct from their preservation as a separate Order, or great corporation, in the State. A senate of Nobles might have been established, though the Order of the Nobility had been destroyed; and England would then have been exactly copied. But it is of the Order that we now speak; for we are now considering the destruction of the old, not the formation of the new government. The suppression of the Nobility has been in England most absurdly confounded with the prohibition of titles. The union of the Orders in one Assembly was the first step towards the destruction of a legislative Nobility: the abolition of their feudal rights, in the memorable session of the 4th of August, 1789, may be regarded as the second. They retained after these measures no distinction but what was purely nominal; and it remained to be determined what place they were to occupy in the new Constitution. That question was decided by the decree of the 22d of December, in the same year, which enacted, that the Electoral Assemblies were to be composed without any regard to rank; and that citizens of all Orders were to vote in them indiscriminately. The distinction of Orders was thus destroyed: the Nobility were to form no part of the new Constitution, and were stripped of all that they had enjoyed under the old government, but their titles.

Hitherto all had passed unnoticed, but no sooner did the Assembly, faithful to their principles, proceed to extirpate the external signs of the ranks, which they no longer tolerated, than all Europe resounded with clamours against their Utopian and levelling madness. The "incredible"* decree of the 19th of June, 1790, for the suppression of titles, is the object of all these invectives; yet without that measure the Assembly would certainly have been guilty of the grossest inconsistency and absurdity. An untitled Nobility forming a member of the State, had been exemplified in some commonwealths of antiquity;—such were the Patricians in Rome: but a titled Nobility, without legal privileges, or political existence, would have been a monster new in the annals of legislative absurdity. The power was possessed without the bauble by the Roman aristocracy: the bauble would have been reverenced, while the power was trampled on, if titles had been spared in France. A titled Nobility is the most undisputed progeny of feudal barbarism. Titles had in all nations *denoted offices:* it was reserved for Gothic Europe to attach them to *ranks.* Yet this conduct of our remote ancestors admits explanation; for with them offices were hereditary, and hence the titles denoting them became hereditary too. But we, who have rejected hereditary office, retain an usage to which it gave rise, and which it alone could justify. So egregiously is this recent origin of a titled Nobility misconceived, that it has been even pretended to be necessary to the order and existence of society;—a narrow and arrogant mistake, which would limit all political remark to the Gothic states of Europe, or establish general principles on events that occupy so short a period of history, and manners that have been adopted by so slender a portion of the human race. A titled

* I say *political* in contradistinction to *civil*, for in the latter sense the assertion would have been untrue.

† See Mr. Rous' excellent Thoughts on Government.

* So called by M. de Calonne.

Nobility was equally unknown to the splendid monarchies of Asia, and to the manly simplicity of the ancient commonwealths.* It arose from the peculiar circumstances of modern Europe; and yet its necessity is now erected on the basis of universal experience, as if these other renowned and polished states were effaced from the records of history, and banished from the society of nations. "Nobility is the Corinthian capital of polished states:"—the august fabric of society is deformed and encumbered by such Gothic ornaments. The massy Doric that sustains it is Labour; and the splendid variety of arts and talents that solace and embellish life, form the decorations of its Corinthian and Ionic capitals.

Other motives besides the extirpation of feudality, disposed the French Legislature to the suppression of titles. To give stability to a popular government, a democratic character must be formed, and democratic sentiments inspired. The sentiment of equality which titular distinctions have, perhaps, more than any other cause, extinguished in Europe, and without which democratic forms are impotent and short-lived, was to be revived; and a free government was to be established, by carrying the spirit of equality and freedom into the feelings, the manners, and the most familiar intercourse of men. The badges of inequality, which were perpetually inspiring sentiments adverse to the spirit of the government, were therefore destroyed, as distinctions which only served to unfit the Nobility for obedience, and the people for freedom,—to keep alive the discontent of the one, and to perpetuate the servility of the other,—to deprive the one of the moderation that sinks them into citizens, and to rob the other of the spirit that exalts them into free men. A single example can alone dispel inveterate prejudices. Thus thought our ancestors at the Revolution, when they deviated from the succession, to destroy the prejudice of its sanctity. Thus also did the legislators of France feel, when, by the abolition of titles, they gave a mortal blow to the slavish prejudices which unfitted their country for freedom. It was a practical assertion of that equality which had been consecrated in the Declaration of Rights, but which no abstract assertion could have conveyed into the spirits and the hearts of men. It proceeded on the principle that the security of a revolution of *government* can only arise from a revolution of *character*.

To these reasonings it has been opposed, that hereditary distinctions are the *moral treasure* of a state, by which it excites and rewards public virtue and public service, and which, without national injury or burden, operates with resistless force on generous minds. To this I answer, that of *personal* distinctions this description is most true; but that this moral treasury of honour is in fact impoverished by the improvident profusion that has made them hereditary. The possession of honours by that multitude, who have inherited but not acquired them, engrosses and depreciates these incentives and rewards of virtue. Were they purely personal, their value would be doubly enhanced, as the possessors would be fewer while the distinction was more honourable. Personal distinctions then every wise state will cherish as its surest and noblest resource; but of hereditary title,—at least in the circumstances of France,*—the abolition seems to have been just and politic.

The fate of the Church, the second great corporation that sustained the French despotism, has peculiarly provoked the indignation of Mr. Burke. The dissolution of the Church as a body, the resumption of its territorial revenues, and the new organization of the priesthood, appear to him to be dictated by the union of robbery and irreligion, to glut the rapacity of stockjobbers, and to gratify the hostility of atheists. All the outrages and proscriptions of ancient or modern tyrants vanish, in his opinion, in comparison with this confiscation of the property of the Gallican Church. Principles had, it is true, been on this subject explored, and reasons had been urged by men of genius, which vulgar men deemed irresistible. But with these reasons Mr. Burke will not deign to combat. "You do not imagine, Sir," says he to his correspondent, "that I am going to compliment this *miserable description of persons* with any long discussion?"† What immediately follows this contemptuous passage is so outrageously offensive to candour and urbanity, that an

* Aristocratic bodies did indeed exist in the ancient world, but *titles* were unknown. Though they possessed political privileges, yet as these did not affect the *manners*, they had not the same inevitable tendency to taint the public character as titular distinctions. These bodies too being in general open to *property*, or *office*, they are in no respect to be compared to the Nobles of Europe. They might affect the *forms* of a free government as much, but they did not in the same proportion injure the *spirit* of freedom.

* I have been grossly misunderstood by those who have supposed this qualification an assumed or affected reserve. I believe the principle only as qualified by the circumstances of different nations.

† The Abbé Maury, who is not less remarkable for the fury of eloquent declamation, than for the inept parade of historical erudition, attempted in the debate on this subject to trace the opinion higher. Base lawyers, according to him, had insinuated it to the Roman Emperors, and against it was pointed the maxim of the civil law, "Omnia tenes Cæsar imperio, sed non dominio." Louis XIV. and Louis XV. had, if we may believe him, both been assailed by this Machiavelian doctrine, and both had repulsed it with magnanimous indignation. The learned Abbé committed only one mistake. The despots of Rome and France had indeed been poisoned with the idea that they were the immediate proprietors of their subjects' estates. That opinion is execrable and flagitious; but it is not, as we shall see, the doctrine of the French legislators

honourable adversary will disdain to avail himself of it. The passage itself, however, demands a pause. It alludes to an opinion, of which I trust Mr. Burke did not know the origin. That the Church lands were national property was not first asserted among the Jacobins, or in the Palais Royal. The author of that opinion,—the master of that wretched description of persons, whom Mr. Burke disdains to encounter, was one whom he might have combated with glory,—with confidence of triumph in victory, and without fear or shame in defeat The author of that opinion was Turgot! a name now too high to be exalted by eulogy, or depressed by invective. That benevolent and philosophic statesman delivered it, in the article "Foundation" of the Encyclopédie, as the calm and disinterested opinion of a scholar, at a moment when he could have no object in palliating rapacity, or prompting irreligion. It was no doctrine contrived for the occasion by the agents of tyranny: it was a principle discovered in pure and harmless speculation, by one of the best and wisest of men. I adduce the authority of Turgot, not to oppose the arguments (if there had been any), but to counteract the insinuations of Mr. Burke. The authority of his assertions forms a prejudice, which is thus to be removed before we can hope for a fair audience at the bar of Reason. If he insinuates the flagitiousness of these opinions by the supposed vileness of their origin, it cannot be unfit to pave the way for their reception, by assigning to them a more illustrious pedigree.

But dismissing the genealogy of doctrines, let us examine their intrinsic value, and listen to no voice but that of truth. "Are the lands occupied by the Church the property of its members?" Various considerations present themselves, which may elucidate the subject.

It has not hitherto been supposed that any class of public servants are proprietors.—They are salaried* by the State for the performance of certain duties. Judges are paid for the distribution of justice; kings for the execution of the laws; soldiers, where there is a mercenary army, for public defence; and priests, where there is an established religion, for public instruction. The mode of their payment is indifferent to the question. It is generally in rude ages by land, and in cultivated periods by money. But a territorial pension is no more property than a pecuniary one. The right of the State to regulate the salaries of those servants whom it pays in money has not been disputed: and if it has chosen to provide the revenue of a certain portion of land for the salary of another class of servants, wherefore is its right more disputable, to resume that land, and to establish a new mode of payment? in the early history of Europe, before fiefs became hereditary, great landed estates were bestowed by the sovereign, on condition of military service. By a similar tenure did the Church hold its lands. No man can prove, that because the State has intrusted its ecclesiastical servants with a portion of land, as the source and security of their *pensions*, they are in any respect more the proprietors of it, than the other servants of the State are of that portion of the revenue from which they are paid.

The lands of the Church possess not the most simple and indispensable requisites of property. They are not even pretended to be held for the *benefit* of those who enjoy them. This is the obvious criterion between private property and a pension for public service. The destination of the first is avowedly the comfort and happiness of the individual who enjoys it: as he is conceived to be the sole judge of this happiness, he possesses the most unlimited rights of enjoyment, of alienation, and even of abuse. But the lands of the Church, destined for the support of public servants, exhibited none of these characters of property. They were inalienable, because it would have been not less absurd for the priesthood to have exercised such authority over these lands, than it would be for seamen to claim the property of a fleet which they manned, or soldiers that of a fortress they garrisoned.

It is confessed that no individual priest was a proprietor, and that the utmost claim of any one was limited to a possession for life of his stipend. If all the priests, taken individually, were not proprietors, the priesthood, as a body, cannot claim any such right. For what is a body, but an aggregate of individuals? and what new right can be conveyed by a mere change of name? Nothing can so forcibly illustrate this argument as the case of other corporations. They are voluntary associations of men for their own benefit. Every member of them is an absolute sharer in their property: it is therefore alienated and inherited. Corporate property is here as sacred as individual, because in the ultimate analysis it is the same. But the priesthood is a corporation, endowed by the country, and destined for the benefit of others: hence the members have no separate, nor the body any collective, right of property. They are only intrusted with the administration of the lands from which their salaries are paid.*

It is from this last circumstance that the legal semblance of property arises. In charters, bonds, and all other proceedings of law, these salaries are treated with the same formalities as real property. "They are identified," says Mr. Burke, "with the mass of

* "Ils sont ou *salariés*, ou mendians, ou voleurs,"—was the expression of M. Mirabeau respecting the priesthood.

* This admits a familiar illustration. If a landholder chooses to pay his steward for the collection of his rents, by permitting him to possess a farm *gratis*, is he conceived to have resigned his property in the farm? The case is precisely similar.

private property;" and it must be confessed, that if we are to limit our view to form, this language is correct. But the repugnance of these formalities to legal truth proceeds from a very obvious cause. If estates are vested in the clergy, to them most unquestionably ought to be intrusted the protection of these estates in all contests at law; and actions for that purpose can only be maintained with facility, simplicity, and effect, by the fiction of their being proprietors. Nor is this the only case in which the spirit and the forms of law are at variance respecting property. Scotland, where lands still are held by feudal tenures, will afford us a remarkable example. There, if we extend our views no further than legal forms, the "superior" is to be regarded as the proprietor, while the real proprietor appears to be only a tenant for life. In this case, the vassal is formally stript of the property which he in fact enjoys: in the other, the Church is formally invested with a property, to which in reality it had no claim. The argument of Prescription will appear to be altogether untenable: for prescription implies a certain period during which the rights of property have been exercised; but in the case before us they never were exercised, because they never could be supposed to exist. It must be proved that these possessions were of the nature of property, before it can follow that they are protected by prescription; and to plead the latter is to take for granted the question in dispute.*

When the British Islands, the Dutch Republic, and the German and Scandinavian States, reformed their ecclesiastical establishments, the howl of sacrilege was the only armour by which the Church attempted to protect its pretended property: the age was too tumultuous and unlettered for discussions of abstract jurisprudence. This howl seems, however, to have fallen into early contempt. The Treaty of Westphalia secularised many of the most opulent benefices of Germany, under the mediation and guarantee of the first Catholic powers of Europe. In our own island, on the abolition of episcopacy in Scotland at the Revolution, the revenues of the Church peaceably devolved on the sovereign, and he devoted a portion of them to the support of the new establishment. When, at a still later period, the Jesuits were suppressed in most Catholic monarchies, the wealth of that formidable and opulent body was everywhere seized by the sovereign. In all these memorable examples, no traces are to be discovered of the pretended property of the Church. The salaries of a class of public servants were resumed by the State, when it ceased to deem their service, or the mode of it, useful. That claim, now so forcibly urged by M. de Calonne, was probably little respected by him, when he lent his agency to the destruction of the Jesuits with such peculiar activity and rancour. The sacredness of their property could not have strongly impressed one who was instrumental in degrading the members of that renowned and accomplished society, the glory of Catholic Europe, from their superb endowments to the rank of scanty and beggarly pensioners. The religious horror which the priesthood had attached to spoliation of Church property has long been dispelled; and it was reserved for Mr. Burke to renew that cry of sacrilege, which, in the darkness of the sixteenth century, had resounded in vain. No man can be expected to oppose arguments to epithets. When a definition of sacrilege is given, consistent with good logic and plain English, it will be time enough to discuss it. Till that definition (with the Greek Calends) comes, I should as soon dispute about the meaning of sacrilege as about that of heresy or witchcraft.

The whole subject is indeed so clear that little diversity of opinion could have arisen, if the question of the inviolability of Church property had not been confounded with the claims of the present incumbents. The distinction, though neither stated by Mr. Burke nor M. de Calonne, is extremely simple. The State is the proprietor of the Church revenues; but its faith, it may be said, is pledged to those who have entered into the Church, for the continuance of the incomes, for which they have abandoned all other pursuits. The right of the State to arrange at its pleasure the revenues of any future priests may be confessed; while a doubt may be entertained, whether it is competent to change the fortune of those to whom it has solemnly promised a certain income for life. But these distinct subjects have been confounded, that sympathy with suffering individuals might influence opinion on a general question,—that feeling for the de-

* There are persons who may not relish the mode of reasoning here adopted. They contend that property, being the creature of civil society, may be resumed by that public will which created it; and on this principle they justify the National Assembly of France. But such a justification is adverse to the principles of that Assembly, for they have consecrated it as one of the first maxims of their Declaration of Rights, "that the State cannot violate property, except in cases of urgent necessity, and on condition of previous indemnification." This defence too will not justify their selection of Church property, in preference of all others, for resumption. It certainly ought in this view to have fallen equally on all citizens. The principle is besides false in the extreme to which it is assumed. Property is indeed in some sense created by an act of the public will: but it is by one of those *fundamental* acts which constitute society. Theory proves it to be essential to the social state. Experience proves that it has, in some degree, existed in every age and nation of the world. But those public acts which form and endow corporations are subsequent and subordinate; they are only *ordinary expedients* of legislation. The property of individuals is established on *a general principle*, which seems coeval with civil society itself: but corporate bodies are instruments fabricated by the legislator for a *specific* purpose, which ought to be preserved while they are beneficial, amended when they are impaired, and rejected when they become useless or injurious.

gradation of its hierarchy might supply the place of argument to establish the property of the Church. In considering this subject distinctly, it cannot be denied, that the mildest, the most equitable, and the most usual expedient of civilized states in periods of emergency, is the reduction of the salaries of their servants, and the superfluous places. This and no more has been done regarding the Church of France. Civil, naval, and military servants of the State are subject to such retrenchments in a moment of difficulty. Neither the reform, of a civil office, nor the reduction of a regiment, can be effected without wounding individuals.* But all men who enter into the public service must do so with the implied condition of subjecting their emoluments, and even their official existence, to the exigencies of the State. The great grievance of such derangements is the shock they give to family sentiments. This was precluded in the instance under discussion by the compulsory celibacy of the Romish Church; and when the debts of the clergy are incorporated with those of the State, and their subsistence insured by moderate incomes, though Sensibility may, in the least retrenchment, find somewhat to lament, Justice will, in the whole of these arrangements, discover little to condemn. To the individual members of the Church of France, whose hopes and enjoyments have been abridged by this resumption, no virtuous mind will refuse the tribute of its sympathy and its regrets. Every man of humanity must wish, that public exigencies had permitted the French Legislature to spare the income of the present incumbents, and more especially of those whom they still continue in the discharge of active functions. But these sentiments imply no sorrow at the downfall of a great corporation,—the implacable enemy of freedom,—at the conversion of an immense public property to national use,—or at the reduction of a servile and imperious priesthood to humble utility. The attainment of these great objects console us for the portion of evil that was, perhaps, inseparable from it, and will be justly applauded by a posterity too remote to be moved by comparatively minute afflictions.

The enlightened observer of an age thus distant will contemplate with peculiar astonishment the rise, progress, decay and downfall of spiritual power in Christian Europe.† It will attract his attention as an appearance which stands alone in history. Its connection in all stages of its progress with the civil power will peculiarly occupy his mind. He will remark the unpresuming humility by which it gradually gained the favour, and divided the power, of the magistrate,—the haughty and despotic tone which it afterwards gave law to sovereigns and their subjects, — the zeal with which, in the first desperate moments of decline, it armed the people against the magistrate, and aimed at re-establishing spiritual despotism on the ruins of civil order; and he will point out the asylum which it at last found from the hostilities of Reason in the prerogatives of that temporal despotism, of which it had so long been the implacable foe. The first and last of these periods will prove, that the priesthood are servilely devoted when they are weak: the second and third, that they are dangerously ambitious when strong. In a state of feebleness, they are dangerous to liberty: possessed of power, they are dangerous to civil government itself. But the last period of their progress will be that which will appear to have been peculiarly connected with the state of France.

There can be no protection for the opulence and even existence* of an European priesthood in an enlightened period, but the throne. It forms the only bulwark against the inroads of reason: for the superstition which once formed its power is gone. Around the throne therefore they rally; and to the monarch they transfer the devotion which formerly attached them to the Church; while the fierceness of priestly† zeal has been succeeded by the more peaceful sentiments of a courtly and polished servility. Such is, in a greater or less degree, the present condition of the Church in every nation of Europe. Yet it is for the dissolution of such a body that France has been reproached. It might as well be maintained, that in her conquests over despotism, she ought to have spared the strongest fortresses and most faithful troops of her adversary: — for such in truth were the corporations of the Nobility and the Church. The National Assembly have only insured permanence to their establishments, by dismantling the fortresses, and disbanding the troops of their vanquished foe.

In the few remarks that are here made on the Nobility and Clergy of France, we confine ourselves strictly to their *political* and *collective* character: Mr. Burke, on the contrary, has grounded his eloquent apology purely on their *individual* and *moral* character. The latter, however, is totally irrelevant; for we are not discussing what place they ought to occupy in society as individuals, but as a body. We are not considering the demerit of citizens whom it is fit to punish, but the spirit of a body which it is politic to dissolve.

The Judicial Aristocracy formed by the Parliaments, seems still less susceptible of union with a free government. Their spirit and claims were equally incompatible with liberty. They had imbibed a spirit congenial to the authority under which they had acted, and suitable to the arbitrary genius of the laws which they had dispensed; while

* This is precisely the case of "damnum absque injuriâ."

† Did we not dread the ridicule of political prediction, it would not seem difficult to assign its period. Church power (unless some Revolution, auspicious to priestcraft, should replunge Europe into ignorance) will certainly not survive the nineteenth century.

* I always understand their *corporate* existence.

† *Odium Theologicum.*

they retained those ambiguous and indefinite claims to a share in the legislation, which the fluctuations of power in the kingdom had in some degree countenanced. The spirit of a corporation was from the smallness of their numbers more concentrated and vigorous in them than in the Nobles and Clergy; and whatever aristocratic zeal is laid to the charge of the Nobility, was imputable with tenfold force to the ennobled magistrates, who regarded their recent honours with an enthusias[illegible] of vanity, inspired by that bigoted ver[illegible] rank which is the perpetual cha[illegible] of [illegible]pstarts. A free people could not form its [illegible]ibunals of men who pretended to [illegible]y [illegible]ntrol on the legislature. Courts of justice, in which seats were legally purchased, had too long been endured: judges who regarded the right of dispensing justice as a marketable commodity, could neither be fit organs of equitable laws, nor suitable magistrates for a free state. It is vain to urge with Mr. Burke the past services of these judicial bodies. It is not to be denied that Montesquieu is correct, when he states, that under bad governments one abuse often limits another. The usurped authority of the Parliaments formed, it is true, some bulwark against the caprice of the Court. But when the abuse is destroyed, why preserve the remedial evil? Superstition certainly alleviates the despotism of Turkey: but if a rational government could be erected in that empire, it might with confidence disclaim the aid of the Koran, and despise the remonstrances of the Mufti. To such establishments, let us pay the tribute of gratitude for past benefit; but when their utility no longer exists, let them be canonized by death, that their admirers may be indulged in all the plenitude of posthumous veneration.

The three Aristocracies—Military, Sacerdotal, and Judicial—may be considered as having formed the French Government.—They have appeared, so far as we have considered them, incorrigible. All attempts to improve them would have been little better than (to use the words of Mr. Burke) "mean reparations on mighty ruins." They were not perverted by the accidental depravity of their members; they were not infected by any transient passion, which new circumstances would extirpate: the fault was in the essence of the institutions themselves, which were irreconcilable with a free government.

But, it is objected, these institutions might have been *gradually* reformed:* the spirit of freedom would have silently entered; the progressive wisdom of an enlightened nation would have remedied, in process of time, their defects, without convulsion. To this argument I confidently answer, that these institutions would have destroyed Liberty, before Liberty had corrected their spirit. Power vegetates with more vigour after these gentle prunings. A slender reform amuses and lulls the people: the popular enthusiasm subsides; and the moment of effectual reform is irretrievably lost. No important political improvement was ever obtained in a period of tranquillity. The corrupt interest of the governors is so strong, and the cry of the people so feeble, that it were vain to expect it. If the effervescence of the popular mind is suffered to pass away without effect, it would be absurd to expect from languor what enthusiasm has not obtained. If radical reform is not, at such a moment, procured, all partial changes are evaded and defeated in the tranquillity which succeeds.* The gradual reform that arises from the presiding principle exhibited in the specious theory of Mr. Burke, is belied by the experience of all ages. Whatever excellence, whatever freedom is discoverable in governments, has been infused into them by the shock of a revolution; and their subsequent progress has been only the accumulation of abuse. It is hence that the most enlightened politicians have recognised the necessity of frequently recalling their first principles;—a truth equally suggested to the penetrating intellect of Machiavel, by his experience of the Florentine democracy, and by his research into the history of ancient commonwealths. Whatever is good ought to be pursued at the moment it is attainable. The public voice, irresistible in a period of convulsion, is contemned with impunity, when spoken during the lethargy into which nations are lulled by the tranquil course of their ordinary affairs. The ardour of reform languishes in unsupported tediousness: it perishes in an impotent struggle with adversaries, who receive new strength with the progress of the day. No hope of great political improvement—let us repeat it—is to be entertained from tranquillity;† for its natural operation is to strengthen all those who are interested in perpetuating abuse. The National Assembly seized the moment of eradicating the corruptions and abuses which afflicted their country. Their reform was total, that it might be commensurate with the evil: and no part of it was delayed, because to spare an abuse at such a period was to consecrate it; and as the enthusiasm which carries nations to such enterprises is short-lived, so the opportunity of reform, if once neglected, might be irrevocably fled.

* Burke, pp. 248—252.

* "Ignore-t-on que c'est en attaquant, en renversant tous les abus à la fois, qu'on peut espérer de s'en voir délivré sans retour; que les réformes lentes et partielles ont toujours fini par ne rien reformer; enfin, que l'abus que l'on conserve devient l'appui et bientôt le restaurateur de tous ceux qu'on croioit avoir détruits?"—Adresse aux François, par l'Evêque d'Autun, 11 Février, 1790.

† The only apparent exception to this principle is the case where sovereigns make important concessions to appease discontent, and avert convulsion. This, however, rightly understood, is no exception; for it arises evidently from the same causes, acting at a period less advanced in the progress of popular interposition.

But let us ascend to more general principles, and hazard bolder opinions. Let us grant that the state of France was not so desperately incorrigible. Let us suppose that changes far more gentle,—innovations far less extensive,—would have remedied the grosser evils of her government, and placed it almost on a level with free and celebrated constitutions. These concessions, though too large for truth, will not convict the Assembly. By what principle of reason, or of justice, were they precluded from aspiring to give France a government less imperfect than accident had formed in other states? Who will be hardy enough to assert, that a better constitution is not attainable than any which has hitherto appeared? Is the limit of human wisdom to be estimated in the science of politics alone, by the extent of its present attainments? Is the most sublime and difficult of all arts,—the improvement of the social order,—the alleviation of the miseries of the civil condition of man,—to be alone stationary, amid the rapid progress of every other—liberal and vulgar—to perfection? Where would be the atrocious guilt of a grand experiment, to ascertain the portion of freedom and happiness, that can be created by political institutions?

That guilt (if it be guilt) is imputable to the National Assembly. They are accused of having rejected the guidance of experience,—of having abandoned themselves to the illusion of theory,—and of having sacrificed great and attainable good to the magnificent chimeras of ideal excellence. If this accusation be just,—if they have indeed abandoned experience, the basis of human knowledge, as well as the guide of human action,—their conduct deserves no longer any serious argument: but if (as Mr. Burke more than once insinuates) their contempt of it is avowed and ostentatious, it was surely unworthy of him to have expended so much genius against so preposterous an insanity. But the explanation of *terms* will diminish our wonder. Experience may, both in the arts and in the conduct of human life, be regarded in a double view, either as finishing *models*, or *principles*. An artist who frames his machine in exact imitation of his predecessor, is in the *first sense* said to be guided by experience. In this sense all improvements of human life, have been *deviations* from experience. The first visionary innovator was the savage who built a cabin, or covered himself with a rug. If this be experience, man is degraded to the unimprovable level of the instinctive animals. But in the second acceptation, an artist is said to be guided by experience, when the inspection of a machine discovers to him principles, which teach him to improve it; or when the comparison of many, both with respect to their excellences and defects, enables him to frame one different from any he had examined, and still more perfect. In this latter sense, the National Assembly have perpetually availed themselves of experience. History is an immense collection of experiments on the nature and effect of the various parts of various governments. Some institutions are experimentally ascertained to be beneficial; some to be most indubitably destructive; a third class, which produces partial good, obviously possesses the capacity of improvement. What, on such a survey, was the dictate of enlightened experience? Not surely to follow any model in which these institutions lay indiscriminately mingled; but, like the mechanic, to compare and generalize, and, guided equally by experience, to imitate and reject. The process is in both cases the same: the rights and the nature of man are to the legislator what the general properties of matter are to the mechanic,—the first guide,—because they are founded on the widest experience. In the second class are to be ranked observations on the excellences and defects of all governments which have already existed, that the construction of a more perfect machine may result. But experience is the basis of all:—not the puny and trammelled experience of a *statesman by trade*, who trembles at any change in the *tricks* which he has been taught, or the *routine* in which he has been accustomed to move; but an experience liberal and enlightened, which hears the testimony of ages and nations, and collects from it the general principles which regulate the mechanism of society.

Legislators are under no obligation to retain a constitution, because it has been found "*tolerably* to answer the common purposes of government." It is absurd to *expect*, but it is not absurd to *pursue* perfection. It is absurd to acquiesce in evils, of which the remedy is obvious, because they are less grievous than those which are endured by others. To suppose that social order is not capable of improvement from the progress of the human understanding, is to betray the inconsistent absurdity of an arrogant confidence in our attainments, and an abject distrust of our powers. If, indeed, the sum of evil produced by political institutions, even in the least imperfect governments, were small, there might be some pretence for this dread of innovation—this horror at any remedy,—which has raised such a clamour over Europe. But, on the contrary, in an estimate of the sources of human misery, after granting that one portion is to be attributed to disease, and another to private vices, it might perhaps be found that a third equal part arose from the oppressions and corruptions of government, disguised under various forms. All the governments that now exist in the world (except that of the United States of America) have been fortuitously formed: they are not the work of art. They have been altered, impaired, improved and destroyed by accidental circumstances, beyond the foresight or control of wisdom. Their parts thrown up against present emergencies formed no systematic whole. It was certainly not to have been presumed, that these *fortuitous products* should have surpassed the works of intellect, and precluded all nearer approaches to perfection. Their origin without doubt furnishes a strong presumption of an opposite nature. It might teach us to expect in them many discordant principles, many jarring forms, much unmixed evil, and much imperfect good,—many institutions which had long survived their motive, and many of which reason had never been the author, nor utility the object. Experience, *even in the best of them,* accords with such expectations.

A government of art, the work of legislative intellect, reared on the immutable basis of natural right and general happiness, which should combine the excellences, and exclude the defects of the various constitutions which chance has scattered over the world, instead of being precluded by the perfection of any of those forms, was loudly demanded by the injustice and absurdity of them all. It was time that men should learn to tolerate nothing ancient that reason does not respect, and to shrink from no novelty to which reason may conduct. It was time that the human powers, so long occupied by subordinate objects, and inferior arts, should mark the commencement of a new æra in history, by giving birth to the art of improving government, and increasing the civil happiness of man. It was time, as it has been wisely and eloquently said, that legislators, instead of that narrow and dastardly *coasting* which never ventures to lose sight of usage and precedent, should, guided by the *polarity* of reason, hazard a bolder navigation, and discover, in unexplored regions, the treasure of public felicity.

The task of the French legislators was, however, less hazardous. The philosophers of Europe had for a century discussed all objects of public œconomy. The conviction of a great majority of enlightened men had, after many controversies, become on most questions of general politics, uniform. A degree of certainty, perhaps nearly equal to that which such topics will admit, had been attained. The National Assembly were therefore not called on to make discoveries: it was sufficient if they were not uninfluenced by the opinions, nor exempt from the spirit of their age. They were fortunate enough to live in a period when it was only necessary to affix the stamp of laws to what had been prepared by the research of philosophy. They will here, however, be attacked by a futile common-place. The most specious theory, it will be said, is often impracticable; and any attempt to transfer speculative doctrines into the practice of states is chimerical and frantic. If by "theory" be understood vague conjecture, the objection is not worth discussion: but if by theory be meant inference from the moral nature and political state of man, then I assert, that whatever such theory pronounces to be true, must be practicable; and that whatever on the subject is impracticable, must be false. To resume the illustration from the mechanical arts:—geometry, it may be justly said, bears nearly the same relation to mechanics that abstract reasoning does to politics.* The moral forces which are employed in politics are the passions and interests of men, of which it is the province of metaphysics to teach the nature and calculate the strength, as mathematics do those of the mechanical powers. Now suppose it had been mathematically proved, that by a certain alteration in the structure of a machine, its effect would be increased fourfold, would an instructed mechanic hesitate about the change? Would he be deterred, because he was the first to discover it? Would he thus sacrifice his own advantage to the blindness of his predecessors, and the obstinacy of his contemporaries? Let us suppose a whole nation, of which the artisans thus rejected theoretical improvement: mechanics might there, as a *science,* be most profoundly understood, while as an *art,* it exhibited nothing but rudeness and barbarism. The principles of Newton and Archimedes might be taught in the schools, while the architecture of the people might not have reached beyond the cabins of New Holland, or the ship-building of the Esquimaux. In a state of political science somewhat similar has Europe continued for a great part of the eighteenth century.†

All the great questions of general politics had, as we have remarked, been nearly decided, and almost all the decisions had been hostile to established institutions; yet these institutions still flourished in all their vigour. The same man who cultivated liberal science in his cabinet was compelled to administer a barbarous jurisprudence on the bench. The same Montesquieu, who at Paris reasoned as a philosopher of the eighteenth, was compelled to decide at Bourdeaux as a magistrate of the fourteenth century. The apostles of toleration and the ministers of the Inquisition were cotemporaries. The torture continued to be practised in the age of Beccaria: the Bastile devoured its victims in the country of Turgot. The criminal code, even where it was the mildest, was oppressive and savage. The laws respecting religious opinion, even where there was a pretended toleration,

* I confess my obligation for this parallel to a learned friend, who though so justly admired in the republic of letters for his excellent writings, is still more so by his friends for the rich, original, and masculine turn of thought that animates his conversation. But the Continuator of the History of Philip III. little needs my praise.

† Mechanics, because no passion or interest is concerned in the perpetuity of abuse, always yield to scientific improvement: politics, for the contrary reason, always resist it. It was the remark of Hobbes, "that if any interest or passion were concerned in disputing the theorems of geometry, different opinions would be maintained regarding them." It has actually happened (as if to justify the remark of that great man) that under the administration of Turgot a financial reform, grounded on a mathematical demonstration, has been derided as visionary nonsense! So much for the sage preference of practice to theory.

outraged the most evident deductions of reason. The true principles of commercial policy, though they had been reduced to demonstration, influenced the councils of no states. Such was the fantastic spectacle presented by the European nations, who, philosophers in theory, and barbarians in practice, exhibited to the observing eye two opposite and inconsistent aspects of manners and opinions. But such a state of things carried in itself the seeds of its own destruction. Men will not long dwell in hovels, with the model of a palace before their eyes.

Such was indeed in some measure the position of the ancient world. But the art of printing had not then provided a channel by which the opinions of the learned pass insensibly into the popular mind. A bulwark then existed between the body of mankind and the reflecting few. They were distinct nations, inhabiting the same country; and the opinions of the one (I speak *comparatively* with modern times) had little influence on those of the other. But that bulwark is now levelled with the ground. The convictions of philosophy insinuate themselves by a slow, but certain progress, into popular sentiment. It is vain for the arrogance of learning to condemn the people to ignorance by reprobating superficial knowledge. The people cannot be profound; but the truths which regulate the moral and political relations of man, are at no great distance from the surface. The great works in which discoveries are contained cannot be read by the people; but their substance passes through a variety of minute and circuitous channels to the shop and the hamlet. The conversion of these works of unproductive splendour into latent use and unobserved activity, resembles the process of nature in the external world. The expanse of a noble lake,—the course of a majestic river, imposes on the imagination by every impression of dignity and sublimity: but it is the moisture that insensibly arises from them which, gradually mingling with the soil, nourishes all the luxuriancy of vegetation, and adorns the surface of the earth.

It may then be remarked, that though liberal opinions so long existed with defective establishments, it was not natural that this state of things should be permanent. The philosophers of antiquity did not, like Archimedes, want a spot on which to fix their engines; but they wanted an engine wherewith to move the moral world. The press is that engine, and has subjected the powerful to the wise. The discussion of great truths has prepared a body of laws for the National Assembly: the diffusion of political knowledge has *almost* prepared a people to receive them; and good men are at length permitted to indulge the *hope*, that the miseries of the human race are about to be alleviated. That hope may be illusive, for the grounds of its enemies are strong,—the folly and villany of men: yet they who entertain it will feel no shame in defeat, and no envy of the triumphant prediction of their adversaries;—"Mehercule malim cum Platone errare." Whatever be the ultimate fate of the French Revolutionists, the friends of freedom must ever consider them as the authors of the greatest attempt that has hitherto been made in the cause of man. They never can cease to rejoice, that in the long catalogue of calamities and crimes which blacken human annals, the year 1789 presents one spot on which the eye of humanity may with complacence dwell.

SECTION II.

Of the composition and character of the National Assembly.

Events are rarely separated by the historian from the character of those who are conspicuous in conducting them. From this alone they often receive the tinge which determines their moral colour. What is admired as noble pride in Sully, would be execrated as intolerable arrogance in Richelieu. But the degree of this influence varies with the importance of the events. In the ordinary affairs of state it is great, because in fact they are only of importance to posterity, as they illustrate the characters of those who have acted distinguished parts on the theatre of the world. But in events which themselves are of immense magnitude, the character of those who conduct them becomes of far less relative importance. No ignominy is at the present day reflected on the Revolution of 1688 from the ingratitude of Churchill, or the treachery of Sunderland. The purity of Somers, and the profligacy of Spencer, are equally lost in the splendour of that great transaction,—in the sense of its benefits, and the admiration of its justice. No moral impression remains on our mind, but that whatever voice speaks truth, whatever hand establishes freedom, delivers the oracles and dispenses the gifts of God.

If this be true of the deposition of James II. it is far more so of the French Revolution. Among many circumstances which distinguished that event, as unexampled in history, it was none of the least extraordinary, that it might truly be said to have been a Revolution *without leaders*. It was the effect of general causes operating on the people. It was the revolt of a nation enlightened from a common source. Hence it has derived its peculiar character; and hence the merits of the most conspicuous individuals have had little influence on its progress. The character of the National Assembly is of secondary importance indeed: but as Mr. Burke has expended so much invective against that body, a few strictures on his account of it will not be improper.

The representation of the Third Estate was, as he justly states, composed of lawyers, physicians, merchants, men of letters, tradesmen and farmers. The choice was, indeed, limited by necessity; for except men of these ranks and professions, the people had no objects of election, the army and the Church being engrossed by the Nobility. "No vestige of the landed interest of the country appeared in this representation," for an obvious reason;—because the Nobility of France, like the Gentry of England, formed almost exclusively the landed interest of the kingdom. These professions then could only furnish representatives for the *Tiers Etat*. They form the majority of that middle rank among whom almost all the sense and virtue of society reside. Their pretended incapacity for political affairs is an arrogant fiction of statesmen which the history of revolutions has ever belied. These emergencies have never failed to create politicians. The subtle counsellors of Philip II. were baffled by the Burgomasters of Amsterdam and Leyden. The oppression of England summoned into existence a race of statesmen in her colonies. The lawyers of Boston, and the planters of Virginia, were transformed into ministers and negotiators, who proved themselves inferior neither in wisdom as legislators, nor in dexterity as politicians. These facts evince that the powers of mankind have been unjustly depreciated,—the difficulty of political affairs artfully magnified; and that there exists a quantity of talent *latent* among men, which ever rises to the level of the great occasions that call it forth.

But the predominance of the profession of the law,—that professsion which teaches men "to augur misgovernment at a distance, and snuff the approach of tyranny in every tainted breeze,"*—was the fatal source from which, if we may believe Mr. Burke, have arisen the calamities of France. The majority of the Third Estate was indeed composed of lawyers. Their talents of public speaking, and their professional habits of examining questions analogous to those of politics, rendered them the most probable objects of popular choice, especially in a despotic country, where political speculation was no natural amusement for the leisure of opulence. But it does not appear that the majority of them consisted of the unlearned, mechanical, members of the profession.† From the list of the States-General, it would seem that the majority were *provincial advocates*,—a name of very different import from "*country attorneys*," and whose importance is not to be estimated by purely English ideas.

All forensic talent and eminence is here concentrated in the capital: but in France, the institution of circuits did not exist; the provinces were imperfectly united; their laws various; their judicatures distinct, and almost independent. Twelve or thirteen Parliaments formed as many circles of advocates, who nearly emulated in learning and eloquence the Parisian Bar. This dispersion of talent was in some respect also the necessary effect of the immensity of the kingdom. No liberal man will in England bestow on the Irish and Scottish Bar the epithet "provincial" with a view of disparagement. The Parliaments of many provinces in France, presented as wide a field for talent as the Supreme Courts of Ireland and Scotland. The Parliament of Rennes, for example, dispensed justice to a province which contained two million three hundred thousand inhabitants*—a population equal to that of some respectable kingdoms of Europe. The cities of Bordeaux, Lyons, and Marseilles, surpass in wealth and population Copenhagen, Stockholm, Petersburg, and Berlin. Such were the theatres on which the provincial advocates of France pursued professional fame. A general Convention of the British empire would yield, perhaps, as distinguished a place to Curran and Erskine, and the other eminent and accomplished barristers of Dublin and Edinburg, as to those of the capital: and on the same principles have the Thourets and Chapeliers of Rouen, and Rennes, acquired as great an ascendant in the National Assembly as the Targets and Camus's of the Parisian Bar.

The proof that this "faculty influence," as Mr. Burke chooses to phrase it, was not injuriously predominant, is to be found in the decrees of the Assembly respecting the judicial order. It must on his system have been their object to have established what he calls "a litigious constitution." The contrary has so notoriously been the case,—all their decrees have so obviously tended to lessen the importance of lawyers, by facilitating arbitrations, by the adoption of juries, by diminishing the expense and tediousness of suits, by the destruction of an intricate and barbarous jurisprudence, and by the simplicity introduced into all judicial proceedings, that their system has been accused of a direct tendency to extinguish the profession of the law. It is a system which may be condemned as leading to visionary excess, but which cannot be pretended to bear very strong marks of the supposed ascendant of "chicane."

To the lawyers, besides the parochial clergy, whom Mr. Burke contemptuously styles "Country Curates,"† were added, those Noblemen whom he so severely stigmatizes as deserters from their Order. Yet the deputation of the Nobility who first joined the Commons, and to whom therefore that title best belongs, was not composed of men whom desperate fortunes and profligate ambition prepared for civil confusion. In that number were found the heads of the most ancient and opulent families in France,—the Rochefoucaults, the Richelieus, the Montmorències, the Noailles. Among them was

* Mr. Burke's Speech on American Affairs, 1775.

† See an accurate list of them in the Supplement to the Journal de Paris, 31st of May, 1789.

* See a Report of the Population of France to the National Assembly, by M. Biron de la Tour, Engineer and Geographer to the King, 1790.

† It is hardly necessary to remark that *curé* means *rector*.

M. Lally, who has received such liberal praise from Mr. Burke. It will be difficult to discover in one individual of that body any interest adverse to the preservation of order, and the security of rank and wealth.

Having thus followed Mr. Burke in a very short sketch of the classes of men who compose the Assembly, let us proceed to consider his representation of the spirit and general rules which have guided it, and which, according to him, have presided over all the events of the Revolution. "A cabal of philosophic atheists had conspired the abolition of Christianity. A monied interest, who had grown into opulence from the calamities of France, contemned by the Nobility for their origin, and obnoxious to the people by their exactions, sought the alliance of these philosophers; by whose influence on public opinion they were to avenge themselves on the Nobility, and conciliate the people. The atheists were to be gratified with the extirpation of religion, and the stock-jobbers with the spoils of the Nobles and the Church. The prominent features of the Revolution bear evidence of this league of impiety and rapine. The degraded establishment of the Church is preparatory to the abolition of Christianity; and all the financial operations are designed to fill the coffers of the monied capitalists of Paris." Such is the theory of Mr. Burke respecting the spirit and character of the French Revolution. To separate the portion of truth that gives plausibility to his statement from the falsehood that invests it with all its horrors, will however neither be a tedious nor a difficult task.

The commercial or monied interest has in all nations of Europe (taken as a body) been less prejudiced, more liberal, and more intelligent than the landed gentry. Their views are enlarged by a wider intercourse with mankind; and hence the important influence of commerce in liberalizing the modern world. We cannot wonder then that this enlightened class ever prove the most ardent in the cause of freedom, and the most zealous for political reform. It is not wonderful that philosophy should find in them more docile pupils, and liberty more active friends, than in a haughty and prejudiced aristocracy. The Revolution in 1688 produced the same division in England. The monied interest long formed the strength of Whiggism, while a majority of the landed gentlemen long continued zealous Tories. It is not unworthy of remark, that the pamphleteers of Toryism accused the Whigs of the same hostility to religion of which Mr. Burke now supposes the existence in France. They predicted the destruction of the Church, and even the downfall of Christianity itself from the influx of heretics, infidels, and atheists, which the new Government of England protected. Their pamphlets have perished with the topic which gave them birth; but the talents and fame of Swift have preserved his, which furnish abundant proof of this coincidence in clamour between the enemies of the English, and the detractors of the French Revolution.

That the philosophers, the other party in this unwonted alliance between affluence and literature, in this new union of authors and bankers, did prepare the Revolution by their writings, it is the glory of its admirers to avow.* What the speculative opinions of these philosophers were on remote and mysterious questions is here of no importance. It is not as atheists, or theists, but as political reasoners, that they are to be considered in a political revolution. All their writings, on the subjects of metaphysics and theology, are foreign to the question. If Rousseau has had any influence in promoting the Revolution, it is not by his Letters from the Mountains, but by his Social Contract. If Voltaire contributed to spread liberality in France, it was not by his Philosophical Dictionary, but by his Defences of Toleration. The obloquy of their atheism (if it existed) is personal: it does not belong to the Revolution; for that event could neither have been promoted nor retarded by abstract discussions of theology. The supposition of their conspiracy for the abolition of Christianity, is one of the most extravagant chimeras that ever entered the human imagination. Let us grant their infidelity in the fullest extent: still their philosophy must have taught them that the passions, whether rational or irrational, from which religion arises, could be eradicated by no human power from the heart of man; while their incredulity must have made them indifferent as to what particular mode of religion might prevail. These philosophers were not the apostles of any new revelation that was to supplant the faith of Christ: they knew that the heart can on this subject bear no void, and they had no interest in substituting the Vedam, or the Koran for the Gospel. They could have no reasonable motives to promote any revolution in the popular faith: their purpose was accomplished when the priesthood was disarmed. Whatever might be the freedom of their private speculations, it was not against religion, but against the Church, that their political hostility was directed.

But, says Mr. Burke, the degraded pensionary establishment, and the elective con-

* Mr. Burke's remark on the English Freethinkers is unworthy of him. It more resembles the rant by which priests inflame the languid bigotry of their fanatical adherents, than the calm, ingenuous, and manly criticism of a philosopher and a scholar. Had he made extensive inquiries among his learned friends, he must have found many who have read and admired Collins' incomparable tract on Liberty and Necessity. Had he looked abroad into the world, he would have found many who still read the philosophical works of Bolingbroke, not as philosophy, but as eloquent and splendid declamation. What he means by "their successors," I will not conjecture: I will not suppose that, with Dr. Hurd, he regards David Hume as "a puny dialectician from the north!"—yet it is hard to understand him in any other sense.

stitution of the new clergy of France is sufficient evidence of the design. The clergy are to be made contemptible, that the popular reverence for religion may be destroyed, and the way thus paved for its abolition. It is amusing to examine the different aspects which the same object presents to various minds. Mr. Hume vindicates the policy of an opulent establishment, as a bribe which purchases the useful inactivity of the priesthood. They have no longer, he supposes, any temptation to court a dangerous dominion over the minds of the people, because they are independent of it. Had that philosopher been now alive, he must on the same principle have remarked, that an elective clergy and a scantily endowed Church, had a far greater tendency to produce fanaticism than irreligion. If the priests depend on the people, they can only maintain their influence by cultivating those passions in the popular mind, which gave them an ascendant over it: to inflame these passions is their obvious ambition. Priests would be in a nation of sceptics contemptible,—in a nation of fanatics omnipotent. It has not therefore been more uniformly the habit of a clergy that depends on a court, to practise servility, than it would evidently be the interest of a clergy that depends on the people to cultivate religious enthusiasm. Scanty endowments too would still more dispose them to seek a consolation for the absence of worldly enjoyments, in the exercise of a flattering authority over the minds of men. Such would have been the view of a philosopher who was indifferent to Christianity, on the new constitution of the Gallican Church. He never would have dreamt of rendering Religion unpopular by devoting her ministers to activity,—contemptible by compelling them to purity,—or unamiable by divesting her of invidious splendour. He would have seen in these changes the seeds of enthusiasm and not of laxity. But he would have been consoled by the reflection, that the dissolution of the Church as a corporation had broken the strength of the priesthood; that religious liberty without limit would disarm the animosity of sects; and that the diffusion of knowledge would restrain the extravagances of fanaticism.

I am here only considering the establishment of the Gallican Church as an evidence of the supposed plan for abolishing Christianity: I am not discussing its intrinsic merits. I therefore personate a philosophic infidel, who, it would appear, must have discerned the tendency of this plan to be directly the reverse of that conceived by Mr. Burke.*

It is in truth rather a fanatical than an irreligious spirit which dictates the organization of the Church of France. A Jansenist party had been formed in the old Parliaments through their long hostilities to the Jesuits and the See of Rome; members of which party have in the National Assembly, by the support of the inferior Clergy, acquired the ascendant in ecclesiastical affairs. Of this number is M. Camus. The new constitution of the Church accords exactly with their dogmas.* The clergy are, according to their principles, to notify to the Bishop of Rome their union in doctrine, but to recognise no subordination in discipline. The spirit of a dormant sect thus revived in a new shape at so critical a period,—the unintelligible subtleties of the Bishop of Ypres thus influencing the institutions of the eighteenth century, might present an ample field of reflection to an enlightened observer of human affairs: but it is sufficient for our purpose to observe the fact, and to remark the error of attributing to the hostile designs of atheism what in so great a degree has arisen from the ardour of religious zeal.

The establishment of the Church has not furnished any evidence of that to which Mr. Burke has attributed so much of the system of the National Assembly. Let us examine whether a short review of their financial operations will supply the defect.†

To the gloomy statement of French finance offered by M. de Calonne, let us oppose the report of M. de la Rochefoucault, from the Committee of Finance, on the 9th of December, 1790, which from premises that appear indisputable, infers a considerable *surplus* revenue in the present year. The purity of that distinguished person has hitherto been arraigned by no party. That understanding must be of a singular construction which could hesitate between the statements of the Duc de la Rochefoucault and M. de Calonne. But without using this *argumentum ad verecundiam*, we remark, that there are radical faults, which vitiate the whole calculations of the latter, and the consequent reasonings of Mr. Burke. They are taken from a year of languishing and disturbed industry, and absurdly applied to the future revenue of

* The theory of Mr. Burke on the subject of religious establishments, I am utterly at a loss to comprehend. He will not adopt the impious reasoning of Mr. Hume, nor does he suppose with Warburton any "*alliance* between Church and State;" for he seems to conceive them to be originally the same. When he or his admirers translate his statements (pp. 145, 146,) into a series of propositions expressed in precise and unadorned English, they may become the proper objects of argument and discussion. In their present state they irresistibly remind one of the observations of Lord Bacon:—"Pugnax enim philosophiæ genus et sophisticum illaqueat intellectuam; at illud alterum phantasticum, et tumidum, et quasi poeticum, magis blanditur intellectui. Inest enim homini quædam intellectûs ambitio non minor quam voluntatis, præsertim in ingeniis altis et elevatis."—Novum Organum, sect. xlv.

* See the Speech of M. Sieyes on Religious Liberty, where he reproaches the Ecclesiastical Committee with abusing the Revolution for the purpose of reviving the seminary of Port Royal. See also M. Condorcet, Sur l'Instruction Publique.

† It may be remarked, that on the subject of finance I have declined all details. They were not necessary to my purpose, which was to consider the Assembly's arrangements of revenue, more with a view to their supposed political profligacy, than to their financial talents.

peaceful and flourishing periods;—from a year in which much of the old revenue of the state had been destroyed, and during which the Assembly had scarcely commenced its new scheme of taxation. It is an error to assert that it was the Assembly that destroyed the former oppressive taxes, which formed so important a source of revenue: these taxes perished in the expiring struggle of the ancient government. No authority remaining in France could have maintained them. Calculations cannot fail of being most grossly illusive, which are formed from a period when many taxes had failed before they could be replaced by new impost, and when productive industry itself, the source of all revenue, was struck with a momentary palsy.* Mr. Burke discussed the financial merit of the Assembly before it had begun its system of taxation. It is still premature to examine its general scheme of revenue, or to establish general maxims on the survey of a period which may be considered as an *interregnum* of finance.

The only financial operation which may be regarded as complete is their emission of *assignats*—the paper representative of the national property; which, while it facilitated the sale of that property, should supply the absence of specie in ordinary circulation. On this, as well as most other topics, the predictions of their enemies have been completely falsified. They predicted that no purchasers would be found hardy enough to trust their property on the tenure of a new and insecure establishment: but the national property has in all parts been bought with the greatest avidity. They predicted that the estimate of its value would prove exaggerated: but it has sold uniformly for double and treble that estimate. They predicted that the depreciation of the *assignats* would in effect heighten the price of the necessaries of life, and fall with the most cruel severity on the most indigent class of mankind: the event has however been, that the *assignats*, supported in their credit by the rapid sale of the property which they represented, have kept almost at *par;* that the price of the necessaries of life has lowered; and that the sufferings of the indigent have been considerably alleviated. Many millions of *assignats*, already committed to the flames, form the most unanswerable reply to the objections urged against them.† Many purchasers, not availing themselves of that indulgence for gradual payment, which in so immense a sale was unavoidable, have paid the whole price in advance. This has been peculiarly the case in the northern provinces, where opulent farmers have been the chief purchasers;—a happy circumstance, if it only tended to multiply that most useful and respectable class of men, who are at once proprietors and cultivators of the ground.

The evils of this emission in the circumstances of France were transient;—the beneficial effects permanent. Two great objects were to be obtained by it;—one of policy, and another of finance. The first was to attach a great body of proprietors to the Revolution, on the stability of which must depend the security of their fortunes. This is what Mr. Burke terms, making them accomplices in confiscation; though it was precisely the policy adopted by the English Revolutionists, when they favoured the growth of a national debt, to interest a body of creditors in the permanence of their new establishment. To render the attainment of the other great object,—the liquidation of the public debt,—improbable, M. de Calonne has been reduced to so gross a misrepresentation, as to state the probable value of the national property at only two *milliards*, (about eighty-three millions sterling,) though the best calculations have rated it at more than double that sum. There is every probability that this immense national estate will spedily disburden France of the greatest part of her national debt, remove the load of impost under which her industry has groaned, and open to her that career of prosperity for which she was so evidently destined by the bounty of Nature. With these great benefits, with the acquittal of the public debt, and the stability of freedom, this operation has, it must be confessed, produced some evils. It cannot be denied to have promoted, in some degree, a spirit of gambling; and it may give an undue ascendant in the municipal bodies to the agents of the paper circulation. But these evils are fugitive: the moment that witnesses the extinction of the *assignats*, by the complete sale of the national lands, must terminate them; and that period, our past experience renders probable is not very remote. There was one general view, which to persons conversant with political economy, would, from the commencement of the operation have appeared decisive. Either the *assignats* were to retain their value, or they were not: if they retained their value, none of the apprehended evils could arise: if they were discredited, every fall in their value was a new motive to their holders to exchange them for national lands. No man would retain depreciated paper who could acquire solid property. If a great portion of them should be thus employed, the value of those left in circulation must immediately rise, both because their number was diminished, and their security become more obvious. The failure, as a medium of circulation, must have improved them as an instrument of sale; and their success as an instrument of sale must in return have restored their utility as a medium of circulation. This action and re-action was inevitable, though

* Mr. Burke exults in the deficiency confessed by M. Vernet to amount in August, 1790, to eight millions sterling. He follows it with an invective against the National Assembly, which one simple reflection would have repressed. The suppression of the *gabelle* alone accounted for almost half of that deficiency! Its produce was estimated at sixty millions of livres, or about two millions and a half sterling.

† At this moment nearly *one-third.*

the slight depreciation of the *assignats* had not made its effects very conspicuous in France.

So determined is the opposition of Mr. Burke to those measures of the Assembly which regard the finances of the Church, that even monastic institutions have in him found an advocate. Let us discuss the arguments which he urges for the preservation of these monuments of human madness. In support of an opinion so singular, he produces one *moral* and one *commercial* reason:*—"In monastic institutions was found a great power for the mechanism of politic benevolence; to destroy any power growing wild from the rank productive force of the human mind, is almost tantamount, in the moral world, to the destruction of the apparently active properties of bodies in the material." In one word, the spirit and the institutions of monachism were an instrument in the hand of the legislator, which he ought to have converted to some public use. I confess myself so far to share the blindness of the National Assembly, that I cannot form the most remote conjecture concerning the various uses which "have suggested themselves to a contriving mind." But without expatiating on them, let us attempt to construct an answer to his argument on a broader basis. The moral powers by which a legislator moves the mind of man are his passions; and if the insane fanaticism which first peopled the deserts of Upper Egypt with anchorites, still existed in Europe, he must attempt the direction of a spirit which humanity forbids him to persecute, and wisdom to neglect. But monastic institutions have for ages survived the spirit which gave them birth; and it is not necessary for any legislature to destroy "that power growing wild out of the rank productive force of the human mind," from which monachism arose. Being, like all other furious and unnatural passions, in its nature transient, it languished in the discredit of miracles and the absence of persecution, and was gradually melted in the sunshine of tranquillity and opulence so long enjoyed by the Church. The soul which actuated monachism had fled: the skeleton only remained to deform society. The dens of fanaticism, where they did not become the recesses of sensuality, were converted into the styes of indolence and apathy. The moral power, therefore, no longer existed, for the spirit by which the legislator could alone have moved these bodies was no more. Nor had any new spirit succeeded which might be an instrument in the hands of legislative skill. These short-lived phrenzies leave behind them an inert product, in the same manner as, when the fury and splendour of volcanic eruption is past for ages, there still remains a mass of *lava* to encumber the soil, and deform the aspect of the earth.†

The sale of the monastic estates is also questioned by Mr. Burke on commercial principles. The sum of his reasoning may be thus expressed:—The surplus product of the earth forms the income of the landed proprietor; that surplus the expenditure of some one must disperse; and of what import is it to society, whether it be circulated by the expense of one landholder, or of a society of monks? A very simple statement furnishes an unanswerable reply to this defence. The wealth of society is its stock of productive labour. There must, it is true, be unproductive consumers, but, the fewer their number, the greater (all things else being the same) must be the opulence of a state. The possession of an estate by a society of monks establishes, let us suppose forty, unproductive consumers: the possession of the same estate by a single landholder only necessarily produces one. It is therefore evident that there is forty times the quantity of labour subtracted from the public stock, in the first case, than there is in the second. If it be objected that the domestics of a landholder are unproductive, let it be remarked that a monastery has its servants; and that those of a lay proprietor are not professionally and perpetually unproductive, as many of them become farmers and artisans, and that, above all, many of them are married. Nothing then can appear, on plain commercial views, more evident than the distinction between lay and monkish landholders. It is surely unnecessary to appeal to the motives which have every where produced statutes of mortmain, the neglect in which the land of ecclesiastical corporations is suffered to remain, and the infinite utility which arises from changes of property in land. The face of those countries where the transfers have been most rapid, will sufficiently prove their benefit. Purchasers seldom adventure without fortune; and the novelty of their acquisition inspires them with the ardour of improvement.

No doubt can be entertained that the estates possessed by the Church will increase immensely in their value. It is vain

* Burke, pp. 232—241.

† It is urged by Mr. Burke, as a species of incidental defence of monachism, that there are many modes of industry, from which benevolence would rather rescue men than from monastic quiet. This must be allowed, in one view, to be true. But, though the laws *must permit* the natural progress which produces this species of labour, does it follow, that they ought to *create* monastic seclusion? Is the existence of one source of misery a reason for opening another? Because noxious drudgery must be *tolerated*, are we to *sanction* compulsory inutility? Instances of similar bad reasoning from what society *must suffer* to what she *ought to enact*, occur in other parts of Mr. Burke's production. We in England, he says, do not think ten thousand pounds a year worse in the hands of a bishop than in those of a baronet or a 'squire. Excessive inequality is in both cases an enormous evil. The laws must *permit* property to grow as the course of things effect it: but ought they to add a new factitious evil to this natural and irremediable one? They cannot avoid inequality in the income of *property*, because they must permit property to distribute itself: but they can remedy excessive inequalities in the income of *office*, because the income and the office are their creatures.

to say that they will be transferred to Stock-jobbers. Situations, not names, are to be considered in human affairs. He that has once tasted the indolence and authority of a landholder, will with difficulty return to the comparative servility and drudgery of a monied capitalist. But should the usurious habits of the immediate purchaser be inveterate, his son will imbibe other sentiments from his birth. The heir of the stock-jobbing Alpheus may acquire as perfectly the habits of an active improver of his patrimonial estate, as the children of Cincinnatus or Cato.

To aid the feebleness of these arguments, Mr. Burke has brought forward a panegyrical enumeration of the objects on which monastic revenue is expended. On this masterpiece of fascinating and magnificent eloquence it is impossible to be too lavish of praise. It would have been quoted by Quintilian as a splended model of rhetorical common-place. But criticism is not our object; and all that the display of such powers of oratory can on such a subject suggest, is embodied in a sentiment which might perhaps have served as a characteristic motto to Mr. Burke's production:

Addidit *invalidæ* robur Facundia *causæ*.

SECTION III.

Popular excesses which attended the Revolution.

That no great revolutions can be accomplished without excesses and miseries at which humanity revolts, is a truth which cannot be denied. This unfortunately is true in a peculiar manner of those Revolutions, which, like that of France, are strictly popular. Where the people are led by a faction, its leaders find no difficulty in the re-establishment of that order, which must be the object of their wishes, because it is the sole security of their power. But when a general movement of the popular mind levels a despotism with the ground, it is far less easy to restrain excess. There is more resentment to satiate and less authority to control. The passion which produced an effect so tremendous, is too violent to subside in a moment into serenity and submission.

The attempt to punish the spirit that actuates a people, if it were just, would be vain, and if it were possible, would be cruel. No remedies are therefore left but the progress of instruction,—the force of persuasion,—the mild authority of opinion: and these though infallible are of slow operation. In the interval which elapses before a calm succeeds the boisterous moments of a revolution, it is vain to expect that a people inured to barbarism by their oppressors, and which has ages of oppression to avenge, will be punctiliously generous in their triumph, nicely discriminative in their vengeance, or cautiously mild in their mode of retaliation. "They will break their chains on the heads of their oppressors."*

Such was the state of France; and such were the obvious causes of scenes which the friends of freedom deplore as tarnishing her triumphs. They feel these evils as men of humanity: but they will not bestow this name on that womanish sensibility, towards which, even in the still intercourse of private life, love is not unmingled with indulgence. The only humanity which, in the great affairs of men, claims their respect, is that manly and expanded sentiment, which fixes its steady eye on the means of general happiness. The sensibility which shrinks at present evil, without extending its view to future good, is not a virtue; for it is not a quality beneficial to mankind. It would arrest the arm of a surgeon in amputating a gangrened limb, or the hand of a judge in signing the sentence of a parricide. I do not say (God forbid!) that a crime may be committed for the attainment even of a good end: such a doctrine would shake morals to their centre. The man who would erect freedom on the ruins of morals neither understands nor loves either. But the case of the French Revolutionists is totally different. Has any moralist ever pretended, that we are to decline the pursuit of a good which our duty prescribes to us, because we foresee that some partial and incidental evil would arise from it? But the number of the French leaders against whom such charges have been insinuated is so small, that supposing (what I do not believe) its truth, it only proves that some corrupt and ambitious men will mix with all great bodies. The question with respect to the rest, is reducible to this:—Whether they were to abstain from establishing a free government, because they foresaw that it could not be effected without confusion and temporary distress, or to be consoled for such calamities by the view of that happiness to which their labours were to give ultimate permanence and diffusion? A Minister is not conceived to be guilty of systematic immorality, because he balances the evils of the most just war with the advantages of that national security which is produced by the reputation of spirit and power:—neither ought the patriot, who balancing the evils of transient anarchy against the inestimable good of established liberty, finds the last preponderate in the scale.

Such, in fact, has ever been the reasoning of the leaders in those insurrections which have preserved the remnant of freedom that still exists among mankind. Holland, England, and America, must have reasoned thus; and the different portions of liberty which they enjoy, have been purchased by the endurance of far greater calamities than have been suffered by France. It is unnecessary

* The eloquent expression of Mr. Curran in the Irish House of Commons.

to appeal to the wars which for almost a century afflicted the Low Countries: but it may not be so to remind England of the price she paid for the establishment of the principles of the Revolution. The disputed succession which arose from that event, produced a destructive civil war in Ireland, two rebellions in Scotland, and the consequent slaughter and banishment of thousands of citizens, with the widest confiscation of their properties;—not to mention the continental connections and the foreign wars into which it plunged us, and the necessity thus imposed upon us of maintaining a standing army, and accumulating an enormous public debt.*

The freedom of America was purchased by calamities still more inevitable. The authors of it must have foreseen them; for they were not contingent or remote, but ready in a moment to burst on their heads. Their case is most similar to that of France, and best answers one of Mr. Burke's most triumphant arguments. They enjoyed *some* liberty, which their oppressors did not attack; and the object for which they resisted, was conceded in the progress of the war: but like France, after the concessions of her King, they refused to acquiesce in an imperfect liberty, when a more perfect one was within their reach. They pursued what Mr. Burke,—whatever were then his sentiments,—on his present system, must reprobate as a speculative and ideal good. They sought their beloved independence through new calamities, and the prolonged horrors of civil war. Their resistance, from that moment, "was against concession; and their blows were aimed at a hand holding forth immunity and favours." Events have indeed justified that noble resistance: America has emerged from her struggle into tranquillity and freedom,—into affluence and credit; and the authors of her Constitution have constructed a great permanent experimental answer to the sophisms and declamations of the detractors of liberty.

But what proportion did the price she paid for so great blessing bear to the transient misfortunes which have afflicted France? The extravagance of the comparison shocks every unprejudiced mind. No series of events in history have probably been more widely, malignantly, and systematically exaggerated than the French commotions. An enraged, numerous, and opulent body of exiles, dispersed over Europe, have possessed themselves of every venal press, and filled the public ear with a perpetual buz of the crimes and horrors that were acting in France. Instead of entering on a minute scrutiny, of which the importance would neither expiate the tediousness, nor reward the toil, let us content ourselves with opposing one general fact to this host of falsehoods:—*no commercial house of importance has failed in France since the Revolution!* How is this to be reconciled with the tales that have been circulated? As well might the transfers of the Royal Exchange be quietly executed in the ferocious anarchy of Gondar, and the peaceful opulence of Lombard-street flourish amidst hordes of Galla and Agows.* Commerce, which shrinks from the breath of civil confusion, has resisted this tempest; and a mighty Revolution has been accomplished with less commercial derangement than could arise from the bankruptcy of a second-rate house in London or Amsterdam. The manufacturers of Lyons, the merchants of Bourdeaux and Marseilles, are silent amidst the lamentations of the Abbé Maury, M. de Calonne, and Mr. Burke. Happy is that people whose commerce flourishes in ledgers, while it is bewailed in orations; and remains untouched in calculation, while it expires in the pictures of eloquence. This unquestionable fact is, on such a subject, worth a thousand arguments, and to any mind qualified to judge, must expose in their true light those execrable fabrications, which have sounded such a "senseless yell" through Europe.

But let us admit for a moment their truth, and take as a specimen of the evils of the Revolution, the number of lives which have been lost in its progress. That no possibility of cavil may remain, let us surpass in an exaggerated estimate the utmost audacity of falsehood: let us make a statement, from which the most frontless hireling of M. de Calonne would shrink. Let us for a moment suppose, that in the course of the Revolution twenty thousand lives have been lost. On the comparison of even this loss with parallel events in history, is there anything in it from which a manly and enlightened humanity will recoil? Compare it with the expenditure of blood by which in ordinary wars so many pernicious and ignoble objects are fought. Compare it with the blood spilt by England in the attempt to subjugate America: and if such be the guilt of the Revolutionists of France, for having, at the *hazard* of this evil, sought the establishment of freedom, what new name of obloquy shall be applied to the Min[illegible] of England, who with the *certainty* of a destruction so much greater, attempted the establishment of tyranny?

The illusion which prevents the effects of these comparisons, is not peculiar to Mr. Burke. The massacres of war, and the murders committed by the sword of justice, are disguised by the solemnities which invest them: but the wild [illegible] of the people has a naked and undisguised horror. Its slightest motion awakens all our indignation; while murder and rapine, if arrayed in the gorgeous disguise of acts of state, may with impunity stalk abroad. We forget that the

* Yet this was only the combat of reason and freedom against one prejudice,—that of hereditary right; whereas the French Revolution is, as has been sublimely said by the Bishop of Autun, "Le premier combat qui se soit jamais livré entre tous les Principes et toutes les Erreurs!"

* Abyssinian tribes.—Ed.

evils of anarchy must be short-lived, while those of despotism are fatally permanent.

Another illusion has, particularly in England, favoured the exaggeration of the exiles; —we judge of France by our own situation, instead of comparing her conduct with that of other nations in similar circumstances. With us "the times may be moderate, and therefere ought to be peaceable:"* but in France the times were not moderate, and could not be peaceable. Let us correct these illusions of *moral optics* which make near objects so disproportionately large. Let us place the scene of the French Revolution in a remote age, or in a distant nation, and then let us calmly ask our own minds, whether the most reasonable subject of wonder be not its unexampled mildness, and the small number of individuals crushed in the fall of so vast a pile.

Such are the general reflections suggested by the disorders of the French Revolution. Of these, the first in point of time, as well as of importance, was the Parisian insurrection and the capture of the Bastile. The mode in which that memorable event is treated by Mr. Burke, is worthy of notice. It occupies no conspicuous place in his work; it is only obscurely and contemptuously hinted at as one of those examples of successful revolt, which have fostered a mutinous spirit in the soldiery. "They have not forgot the taking of the King's castles in Paris and Marseilles. That they murdered with impunity in both places the governors, has not escaped their minds."† Such is the courtly circumlocution by which Mr. Burke designates the Bastile—"*the King's castle at Paris!*" such is the ignominious language in which he speaks of the summary justice executed on the titled ruffian who was its governor; and such is the apparent art with which he has thrown into the back-ground invective and asperity, that, had they been prominent, would have provoked the indignation of mankind! "Je sais," says Mounier, in the language of that frigid and scanty approbation that is extorted from an enemy, "qu'il est des circonstances qui legitiment l'insurrection, et je mets dans ce nombre celles qui ont causé le siège de la Bastile."‡

But the admiration of Europe and of posterity, is not to be estimated by the penurious applause of M. Mounier, nor repressed by the insidious hostility of Mr. Burke. It will correspond to the splendour of an insurrection, as much ennobled by heroism as it was justified by necessity, in which the citizens of Paris,—the unwarlike inhabitants of a voluptuous capital,—listening to no voice but that of the danger which menaced their representatives, their families, and their country, and animated, instead of awed, by the host of disciplined mercenaries which invested them on every side, attacked with a gallantry and success equally incredible, fortress formidable from its strength, and tremendous from its destination, and changed the destiny of France. To palliate or excuse such a revolt, would be abject treachery to its principles. It was a case in which revolt was the dictate of virtue, and the path of duty; and in which submission would have been the most dastardly baseness, and the foulest crime. It was an action not to be excused, but applauded,—not to be pardoned, but admired. I shall not therefore descend to vindicate acts of heroism, which history will teach the remotest posterity to revere, and of which the recital is destined to kindle in unborn millions the holy enthusiasm of freedom.

Commotions of another description followed, partly arising from the general causes before stated, and partly from others of more limited and local operation. The peasantry of the provinces, buried for so many ages in the darkness of servitude, saw but indistinctly and confusedly, in the first dawn of liberty, the boundaries of their duties and their rights. It was no wonder that they should little understand that freedom which so long had been remote from their views. The name conveyed to their ear a right to reject all restraint, to gratify every resentment, and to attack all property. Ruffians, mingling with the deluded peasants, in hopes of booty, inflamed their ignorance and prejudices, by forged authorities from the King and the Assembly for their licentiousness. Many country houses were burnt; and some obnoxious persons were assassinated: but one may without excessive scepticism doubt, whether they had been the mildest masters whose *chateaux* had undergone that fate; and the peasants had to avenge those silent grinding oppressions which formed almost the only intercourse of the rich with the indigent, and which, though less flagrant than those of Government, were perhaps productive of more intolerable and diffused misery.

But whatever was the demerit of these excesses, they can by no process of reasoning be made imputable to the National Assembly, or the leaders of the Revolution. In what manner were they to repress them? If they exerted against them their own authority with rigour, they must have provoked a civil war: if they invigorated the police and tribunals of the deposed government,—besides incurring the hazard of the same calamity,—they put arms into the hands of their enemies. Placed in this dilemma, they were compelled to expect a slow remedy from the returning serenity of the public mind, and from the progress of the new government towards consistence and vigour.*

* Junius. † Burke, p. 307.
‡ Exposé, &c. p. 24.

* If this statement be candid and exact, what shall we think of the language of Mr. Burke, when he speaks of the Assembly as "*authorising* treasons, robberies, rapes, assassinations, slaughters, and burnings, throughout all their harassed land." (p. 58.) In another place (p. 200,) he connects the legislative extinction of the Order of Nobles with the popular excesses committed against individual

That the conduct of the populace of Paris towards them should not have been the most decorous and circumspect,—that it should have been frequently irregular and tumultuous, was, in the nature of things inevitable. But the horrible picture which Mr. Burke has drawn of that "stern necessity" under which this "captive" Assembly votes, is neither justified by this concession, nor by the state of facts. It is the overcharged colouring of a fervid imagination. Those to whom he alludes as driven away by assassins,—M. M. Lally and Mounier,—might, surely, have remained with perfect safety in an Assembly in which such furious invectives are daily bellowed forth with impunity against the popular leaders. No man will deny, that that member of the minority enjoyed liberty of speech in its utmost plenitude, who called M. Mirabeau "*le plus vil de tous les assassins.*" "The terrors of the lamp-post and bayonet" have hitherto been visionary. Popular fury has hitherto spared the most furious declaimers of Aristocracy; and the only "decree," so far as I can discern, which has even been *pretended* to have been materially influenced by the populace, is that respecting the prerogatives of war and peace. That tumult has frequently derogated from the dignity which ought to distinguish the deliberations of a legislative assembly, is not to be denied. But that their debates have been tumultuous, is of little importance, if their decisions have been independent. Even in this question of war and peace, "the highest bidder at the auction of popularity"* did not succeed. The scheme of M. Mirabeau, with few amendments, prevailed, while the more "splendidly popular" propositions, which vested in the legislature alone the prerogative of war and peace, were rejected.

We are now conducted by the course of these strictures to the excesses committed at Versailles on the 5th and 6th of October, 1789. After the most careful perusal of the voluminous evidence before the Châtelet, of the controversial pamphlets of M. M. d'Orleans and Mounier, and of the official report of M. Chabroud to the Assembly, the details of the affair seem to me so much involved in obscurity and contradiction, that they afford little on which a candid mind can with confidence pronounce. They afford, indeed, to frivolous and puerile adversaries the means of convicting Mr. Burke of some minute errors. M. Miomandre, the sentinel at the Queen's gate, it is true, survives; but it is no less true, that he was left for dead by his assassins. On the comparison of evidence it seems probable, that the Queen's chamber was not broken into,—"that the asylum of beauty and Majesty was not profaned."† But these slight corrections palliate little the atrocity, and alter not in the least the general complexion, of these flagitious scenes.

The most important question which the subject presents is, whether the Parisian populace were the instruments of conspirators, or whether their fatal march to Versailles was a spontaneous movement, produced by real or chimerical apprehensions of plots against their freedom. I confess that I incline to the latter opinion. Natural causes seem to me adequate to account for the movement. A scarcity of provision is not denied to have existed in Paris. The dinner of the body-guards might surely have provoked the people of a more tranquil city. The maledictions poured forth against the National Assembly, the insults offered to the patriotic cockade, the obnoxious ardour of loyalty displayed on that occasion, might have awakened even the jealousy of a people whose ardour had been sated by the long enjoyment, and whose alarms had been quieted by the secure possession, of liberty. The escape of the King would be the infallible signal of civil war: the exposed situation of the Royal residence was therefore a source of perpetual alarm. These causes, operating on that credulous jealousy which is the malady of the public mind in times of civil confusion, seeing hostility and conspiracy on every side, would seem sufficient ones. The apprehensions of the people in such a period torture the most innocent and frivolous accidents into proofs of sanguinary plots:—witness the *war of conspiracies* carried on by the contending factions in the reign of Charles the Second. The participation of Queen Mary in Babington's plot against Elizabeth, is still the subject of controversy. We, at the present day, dispute about the nature of the connection which subsisted between Charles the First and the Catholic insurgents of Ireland. It has occupied the labour of a century to separate truth from falsehood in the Rye-house Plot,—the views of the leaders from the schemes of the inferior conspirators,—and to discover that Russell and Sydney had, indeed, conspired a revolt, but that the underlings alone had plotted the assassination of the King.

It may indeed be said, that ambitious leaders availed themselves of the inflamed state of public feeling,—that by false rumours, and exaggerated truths, they stimulated the revenge, and increased the fears of the populace,—that their emissaries, mixing with the mob, and concealed by its confusion, were to execute their flagitious purposes, and fanatics, as usual, were the dupes of hypocrites. Such are the accusations which have been made against M. M. d'Or-

Noblemen, to load the Assembly with the accumulated obloquy;—a mode of proceeding more remarkable for controversial dexterity than for candour.

* Burke, p. 353.

† The expression of M. Chabroud. Five witnesses assert that the ruffians did not break into the Queen's chamber. Two give the account followed by Mr. Burke, and to give this preponderance its due force, let it be recollected, that the whole proceedings before the Châtelet were *ex parte*. See Procédure Criminelle fait au Châtelet de Paris, &c., 1790.

leans and Mirabeau. The defence of profligate ambition is not imposed on the admirers of the French Revolution; and to become the advocate of individuals were to forget the dignity of a discussion that regards the rights and interests of an emancipated nation. Of their guilt, however, I will be bold to say no evidence was collected, by the malignant activity of an avowedly hostile tribunal, which, for a moment, would have suspended their acquittal by an English jury. It will be no mean testimony to the innocence of M. Mirabeau, that an opponent, not the mildest in his enmity, nor the most candid in his judgment, confessed, that he saw no serious ground of accusation against him.*

The project is attributed to them, of intimidating the King into a flight, that there might be a pretext for elevating the Duke of Orleans to the office of Regent. But the King could have had no rational hopes of escaping;† for he must have traversed two hundred miles of a country guarded by a people in arms, before he could reach the nearest frontier of the kingdom. The object was too absurd to be pursued by conspirators, to whom talent and sagacity have not been denied by their enemies. That the popular leaders in France did, indeed, desire to fix the Royal residence at Paris, it is impossible to doubt: the name, the person, and the authority of the King, would have been most formidable weapons in the hands of their adversaries. The peace of their country,—the stability of their freedom, called on them to use every measure that could prevent their enemies from getting possession of that "Royal Figure." The name of the King would have sanctioned foreign powers in supporting the aristocracy. Their interposition, which *now* would be hostility against the King and kingdom, would *then* have been only regarded as aid against rebellion. Against all these dreadful consequences there seemed only one remedy,—the residence of the King at Paris. Whether that residence is to be called a "captivity," or any other harsh name, I will not hesitate to affirm, that the Parliament of England would have merited the gratitude of their country, and of posterity, by a similar prevention of the escape of Charles I. from London. Fortunate would it have been for England if the person of James II. had been retained while his authority was limited. She would then have been circumstanced as France is now. The march to Versailles seems to have been the spontaneous movement of an alarmed populace. Their views, and the suggestions of their leaders, were probably bounded by procuring the King to change his residence to Paris; but the collision of armed multitudes terminated in unforeseen excesses and execrable crimes.

In the eye of Mr. Burke, however, these crimes and excesses assume an aspect far more important than can be communicated to them by their own insulated guilt. They form, in his opinion, the crisis of a revolution,—a far more important one than any mere change of government,—in which the sentiments and opinions that have formed the manners of the European nations are to perish. "The age of chivalry is gone, and the glory of Europe extinguished for ever." He follows this exclamation by an eloquent eulogium on chivalry, and by gloomy predictions of the future state of Europe, when the nation that has been so long accustomed to give her the tone in arts and manners is thus debased and corrupted. A caviller might remark that ages, much more near the meridian fervour of chivalry than ours, have witnessed a treatment of queens as little gallant and generous as that of the Parisian mob. He might remind Mr. Burke, that in the age and country of Sir Philip Sidney, a Queen of France, whom no blindness to accomplishment,—no malignity of detraction, can reduce to the level of Marie Antoinette, was, by "a nation of men of honour and cavaliers," permitted to languish in captivity and expire on a scaffold; and he might add, that the manners of a country are more surely indicated by the systematic cruelty of a sovereign than by the licentious frenzy of a mob. He might remark, that the mild system of modern manners which survived the massacres with which fanaticism had for a century desolated, and almost barbarised Europe, might, perhaps, resist the shock of one day's excesses committed by a delirious populace. He might thus, perhaps, oppose specious and popular topics to the declamation of Mr. Burke.

But the subject itself is, to an enlarged thinker, fertile in reflections of a different nature. That system of manners which arose among the Gothic nations of Europe, and of which chivalry was more properly the effusion than the source, is without doubt one of the most peculiar and interesting appearances in human affairs. The moral causes which formed its character have not, perhaps, been hitherto investigated with the happiest success: but,—to confine ourselves to the subject before us,—chivalry was certainly one of the most prominent of its features and most remarkable of its effects. Candour must confess, that this singular institution was not admirable only as the corrector of the ferocious ages in which it flourished; but that in contributing to polish and soften manners it paved the way for the diffusion of knowledge and the extension of commerce, which afterwards, in some measure, supplanted it. Society is inevitably progressive. Commerce has overthrown the "feudal and chivalrous system" under whose shade it first grew; while learning has subverted the superstition whose opulent endowments had first fostered it. Peculiar circumstances connected with the manners

* Discours de M. l'Abbé Maury dans l'Assemblée Nationale, 1 Octobre, 1790.

† The circumstances of his late attempt [the flight to Varennes—Ed.] sanction this reasoning.

of chivalry favoured this admission of commerce and this growth of knowledge; while the sentiments peculiar to it, already enfeebled in the progress from ferocity and turbulence, were almost obliterated by tranquillity and refinement. Commerce and diffused knowledge have, in fact, so completely assumed the ascendant in polished nations, that it will be difficult to discover any relics of Gothic manners, but in a fantastic exterior, which has survived the generous illusions through which these manners once seemed splendid and seductive. Their *direct* influence has long ceased in Europe; but their *indirect* influence, through the medium of those causes which would not perhaps have existed but for the mildness which chivalry created in the midst of a barbarous age, still operates with increasing vigour. The manners of the middle age were, in the most singular sense, compulsory: enterprising benevolence was produced by general fierceness,—gallant courtesy by ferocious rudeness; and artificial gentleness resisted the torrent of natural barbarism. But a less incongruous system has succeeded, in which commerce, which unites men's interests, and knowledge, which excludes those prejudices that tend to embroil them, present a broader basis for the stability of civilized and beneficent manners.

Mr. Burke, indeed, forbodes the most fatal consequences to literature from events, which he supposes to have given a mortal blow to the spirit of chivalry. I have ever been protected from such apprehensions by my belief in a very simple truth,—"that diffused knowledge immortalizes itself." A literature which is confined to a few, may be destroyed by the massacre of scholars and the conflagration of libraries: but the diffused knowledge of the present day could only be annihilated by the extirpation of the civilized part of mankind.

Far from being hostile to letters, the French Revolution has contributed to serve their cause in a manner hitherto unexampled. The political and literary progress of nations has hitherto been simultaneous; the period of their eminence in arts has also been the era of their historical fame; and no example occurs in which their great political splendour has been subsequent to the Augustan age of a people. But in France, which is destined to refute every abject and arrogant doctrine that would limit the human powers, the ardour of a youthful literature has been infused into a nation tending to decline; and new arts are called forth when all seemed to have passed their zenith. She enjoyed one Augustan age, fostered by the favour of despotism: she seems about to witness another, created by the energy of freedom.

In the opinion of Mr. Burke, however, she is advancing by rapid strides to ignorance and barbarism.* "Already," he informs us, "there appears a poverty of conception, a coarseness and vulgarity in all the proceedings of the Assembly, and of all their instructors. Their liberty is not liberal. Their science is presumptuous ignorance. Their humanity is savage and brutal." To animadvert on this modest and courteous picture belongs not to the present subject: and *impressions* cannot be disputed, more especially when their grounds are not assigned. All that is left to us to do, is to declare opposite impressions with a confidence authorised by his example. The proceedings of the National Assembly of France appear to me to contain models of more splendid eloquence, and examples of more profound political research, than have been exhibited by any public body in modern times. I cannot therefore augur, from these proceedings, the downfall of philosophy, or the extinction of eloquence.

Thus various are the aspects which the French Revolution, not only in its influence on literature, but in its general tenor and spirit, presents to minds occupied by various opinions. To the eye of Mr. Burke, it exhibits nothing but a scene of horror: in his mind it inspires no emotion but abhorrence of its leaders, commiseration for their victims, and alarms at the influence of an event which menaces the subversion of the policy, the arts, and the manners of the civilized world. Minds who view it through another medium are filled by it with every sentiment of admiration and triumph,—of admiration due to splendid exertions of virtue, and of triumph inspired by widening prospects of happiness.

Nor ought it to be denied by the candour of philosophy, that events so great are never so unmixed as not to present a double aspect to the acuteness and exaggeration of contending parties. The same ardour of passion which produces patriotic and legislative heroism becomes the source of ferocious retaliation, of visionary novelties, and of precipitate change. The attempt were hopeless to increase the fertility, without favouring the rank luxuriance of the soil. He that on such occasions expects unmixed good, ought to recollect, that the economy of nature has invariably determined the equal influence of high passions in giving birth to virtues and to crimes. The soil of Attica was observed to produce at once the most delicious fruits and the most virulent poisons. It was thus with the human mind; and to the frequency of convulsions in the ancient commonwealths, they owe those examples of sanguinary tumult and virtuous heroism, which distinguish their history from the monotonous tranquillity of modern states. The passions of a nation cannot be kindled to the degree which renders it capable of great achievements, without involving the commission of violence and crime. The reforming ardour of a senate cannot be inflamed sufficiently to combat and overcome abuses, without hazarding the evils which arise from legislative temerity. Such are the immutable laws, which are more properly to be regarded as libels on our nature than as

* Burke, p. 118.

charges against the French Revolution. The impartial voice of History ought, doubtless, to record the blemishes as well as the glories of that great event: and to contrast the delineation of it which might have been given by the specious and temperate Toryism of Mr. Hume, with that which we have received from the repulsive and fanatical invectives of Mr. Burke, might still be amusing and instructive. Both these great men would be averse to the Revolution; but it would not be difficult to distinguish between the undisguised fury of an eloquent advocate, and the well-dissembled partiality of a philosophical judge. The passion of the latter would only *feel* the excesses which have dishonoured the Revolution: but the philosophy of the former would instruct him, that our sentiments, raised by such events so much above their ordinary level, become the source of guilt and heroism unknown before,—of sublime virtues and splendid crimes.

SECTION IV.

*New Constitution of France.**

A DISSERTATION approaching to completeness on the new Constitution of France, would, in fact, be a vast system of political science. It would include a development of the principles that regulate every portion of government. So immense an attempt is little suited to our present limits. But some remarks on the prominent features of the French system are exacted by the nature of our vindication. They will consist chiefly of a defence of their grand theoretic principle, and their most important practical institution.

The principle which has actuated the legislators of France has been, "that the object of all legitimate government is the assertion and protection of the natural rights of man." They cannot indeed be absolved from some deviations† from it;—few, indeed, compared with those of any other body of whom history has preserved any record; but too many for their own glory, and for the happiness of the human race. This principle, however, is the basis of their edifice, and if it be false, the structure must fall to the ground. Against this principle, therefore, Mr. Burke has, with great judgment, directed his attack. Appeals to natural right are, according to him, inconsistent and preposterous. A complete abdication and surrender of all natural right is made by man in entering into society; and the only rights which he retains are created by the compact which holds together the society of which he is member. This doctrine he thus explicitly asserts:—"The moment," says he, "you abate any thing from the full rights of men each to govern himself, and suffer any artificial positive limitation on those rights, from that moment the whole organization of society becomes a consideration of convenience." "How can any man claim under the conventions of civil society rights which do not so much as suppose its existence,—which are absolutely repugnant to it?"* To examine this doctrine, therefore, is of fundamental importance. To this effect it is not necessary to enter into any elaborate research into the metaphysical principles of politics and ethics. A full discussion of the subject would indeed demand such an investigation:†—the origin of natural rights must have been illustrated, and even their existence proved against some theorists. But such an inquiry would have been inconsistent with the nature of a publication, the object of which is to enforce conviction on the people. We are besides absolved from the necessity of it in a controversy with Mr. Burke, who himself recognises, in the most ample form, the existence of those natural rights.

Granting their existence, the discussion is short. The only criterion by which we can estimate the portion of natural right surrendered by man on entering into society is the *object* of the surrender. If more is claimed than that object exacts, what was an *object* becomes a *pretext*. Now the object for which a man resigns any portion of his natural sovereignty over his own actions is, that he may be protected from the abuse of the same dominion in other men. Nothing, therefore, can be more fallacious than to pretend, that we are precluded in the social state from *any* appeal to natural right.‡ It remains in

* I cannot help exhorting those who desire to have accurate notions on the subject of this section, to peruse and study the delineation of the French constitution which with a correctness so admirable has been given by Mr. Christie.—(Letters on the Revolution in France, London, 1791. ED.)

† I particularly allude to their colonial policy; but I think it candid to say, that I see in their full force the difficulties of that embarrassing business.

* Burke, pp. 88—89. To the same purpose is his whole reasoning from p. 86, to p. 92.

† It might, perhaps, not be difficult to prove, that far from a *surrender*, there is not even a *diminution* of the natural rights of men by their entrance into society. The existence of some union, with greater or less permanence and perfection of public force for public protection (the essence of government), might be demonstrated to be coeval and co-extensive with man. All theories, therefore, which suppose the actual existence of any state antecedent to the social, might be convicted of futility and falsehood.

‡ "Trouver une forme d'association qui défende et protège de toute la force commune la personne et les biens de chaque associé, et par laquelle chacun, s'unissant à tous, n'obéisse pourtant qu'à lui-même et reste aussi libre qu'auparavant?" —Rousseau, Contrat Social, livre i. chap. vi. I am not intimidated from quoting Rousseau by the derision of Mr. Burke. Mr. Hume's report of his literary secrets seems most unfaithful. The sensibility, the pride, the fervour of his character, are pledges of his sincerity; and had he even commenced with the fabrication of paradoxes, for attracting attention, it would betray great ignorance of human nature to suppose, that in the ar-

its full integrity and vigour, if we except that portion of it which men have thus mutually agreed to sacrifice. Whatever, under *pretence* of that surrender, is assumed beyond what that object rigorously prescribes, is an usurpation supported by sophistry,—a despotism varnished by illusion. It follows that the surrender of right must be equal in all the members of society, as the object is to all precisely the same. In effect, society, instead of destroying, realizes and substantiates equality. In a state of nature, the equality of right is an impotant theory, which inequalities of strength and skill every moment violate. As neither natural equality nor the equality of the sum of right surrendered by every individual is contested, it cannot be denied that the remnant spared by the social compact must be equal also. Civil inequalities, or, more correctly, civil distinction, must exist in the social body, because it must possess organs destined for different functions: but political inequality is equally inconsistent with the principles of natural right and the object of civil institution.*

Men, therefore, only retain a right to a share in their own government, because the exercise of the right by one man is not inconsistent with its possession by another. This doctrine is not more abstractedly evident than it is practically important. The slightest deviation from it legitimatizes every tyranny. If the only criterion of governments be the supposed convention which forms them, all are equally legitimate; for the only interpreter of the convention is the usage of the government, which is thus preposterously made its own standard. Governors must, indeed, abide by the maxims of the constitution they administer; but what that constitution is must be on this system immaterial. The King of France is not permitted to put out the eyes of the Princes of the Blood; nor the Sophi of Persia to have recourse to *lettres de cachet*. They must tyrannize by precedent, and oppress in reverent imitation of the models consecrated by the usage of despotic predecessors. But if they adhere to these, there is no remedy for the oppressed, since an appeal to the rights of nature were treason against the principles of the social union. If, indeed, any offence against precedent, in the kind or degree of oppression, be committed, this theory may (though most inconsistently) permit resistance. But as long as the forms of any government are preserved, it possesses, in the view of justice (whatever be its nature) equal claims to obedience. This inference is irresistible; and it is thus evident, that the doctrines of Mr. Burke are doubly refuted by the fallacy of the logic which supports them, and the absurdity of the conclusions to which they lead.

They are also virtually contradicted by the laws of all nations. Were his opinions true, the language of laws should be *permissive*, not *restrictive*. Had men surrendered all their rights into the hands of the magistrate, the object of laws should have to announce the portion he was pleased to return them, not the part of which he is compelled to deprive them. The criminal code of all nations consists of prohibitions; and whatever is not prohibited by the law, men every where conceive themselves entitled to do with impunity. They act on the principle which this language of law teaches them, that they retain rights which no power can impair or infringe,—which are not the boon of society, but the attribute of their nature. The rights of magistrates and public officers are truly the creatures of society: they, therefore, are guided not by what the law does not prohibit, but by what it authorises or enjoins. Were the rights of citizens equally created by social institution, the language of the civil code would be similar, and the obedience of subjects would have the same limits.

This doctrine, thus false in its principles, absurd in its conclusions, and contradicted by the avowed sense of mankind, is, lastly, even abandoned by Mr. Burke himself. He is betrayed into a confession directly repugnant to his general principle:—"Whatever each man can do without trespassing on others, he has a right to do for himself; and he has a right to a fair portion of all that society, with all its combinations of skill and force, can do for him." Either this right is universal, or it is not:—if it be universal, it cannot be the offspring of a convention; for conventions must be as various as forms of government, and there are many of them which do not recognise this right, nor place man in this condition of just equality. All governments, for example, which tolerate slavery neglect this right; for a slave is neither entitled to the fruits of his own industry, nor to any portion of what the combined force and skill of society produce. If it be not universal it is no right at all; and can only be called a *privilege* accorded by some governments, and withheld by others. I can discern no mode of escaping from this di-

dour of contest, and the glory of success, he must not have become the dupe of his own illusions, and a convert to his own imposture. It is, indeed, not improbable, that when rallied on the eccentricity of his paradoxes, he might, in a moment of gay effusion, have spoken of them as a sport of fancy, and an experiment on the credulity of mankind. The Scottish philosopher, inaccessible to enthusiasm, and little susceptible of those depressions and elevations—those agonies and raptures, so familiar to the warm and wayward heart of Rousseau, neither knew the sport into which he could be relaxed by gaiety, nor the ardour into which he could be exalted by passion. Mr. Burke, whose temperament is so different, might have experimentally known such variation, and learnt better to discriminate between effusion and deliberate opinion.

* "But as to the share of power, authority, and direction which each individual ought to have in the management of a state, that I must deny to be among the direct original rights of man in civil society." This is evidently denying the existence of what has been called *political*, in contradistinction to *civil* liberty.

lemma, but the avowal that these civil claims are the remnant of those "metaphysic rights" which Mr. Burke holds in such abhorrence; but which it seems the more natural object of society to protect than destroy.

But it may be urged, that though all appeals to natural rights be not precluded by the social compact, and though their integrity and perfection in the civil state may *theoretically* be admitted, yet as men unquestionably may refrain from the exercise of their rights, if they think their exertion unwise, and as government is not a scientific subtlety, but a *practical* expedient for general good, all recourse to these elaborate abstractions is frivolous and futile; and that the grand question is not the source, but the tendency of government,—not a question of right, but a consideration of expediency. Political forms, it may be added, are only the *means* of insuring a certain portion of public felicity: if the *end* be confessedly obtained, all discussion of the theoretical aptitude of the *means* to produce it is nugatory and redundant.

To this I answer, first, that such reasoning proves too much, and that, taken in its proper extent, it impeaches the great system of morals, of which political principles form only a part. All morality is, no doubt, founded on a broad and general expediency; and the sentiment—

"Ipsa utilitas justi prope mater et æqui,"*

may be safely adopted, without the reserve dictated by the timid and inconstant philosophy of the poet. Justice is expediency, but it is expediency speaking by general maxims, into which reason has consecrated the experience of mankind. Every general principle of justice is demonstrably expedient; and it is this utility alone that confers on it a moral obligation. But it would be fatal to the existence of morality, if the utility of every particular act were to be the subject of deliberation in the mind of every moral agent. Political principles are only moral ones adapted to the civil union of men. When I assert that a man has a right to life, liberty, &c. I only mean to enunciate a moral maxim founded on the general interest, which prohibits any attack on these possessions. In this primary and radical sense, all rights, natural as well as civil, arise from expediency. But the moment the moral edifice is reared, its basis is hid from the eye for ever. The moment these maxims, which are founded on an utility that is paramount and perpetual, are embodied and consecrated, they cease to yield to partial and subordinate expediency. It then becomes the perfection of virtue to consider, not whether an action be useful, but whether it be right.

The same necessity for the substitution of general maxims exists in politics as in morals. Those precise and inflexibile principles, which yield neither to the seductions of passion, nor to the suggestions of interest, ought to be the guide of public as well as private morals. "Acting according to the natural rights of men," is only another expression for acting according to those general maxims of social morals which prescribe what is right and fit in human intercourse. We have proved that the social compact does not alter these maxims, or destroy these rights; and it incontestably follows, from the same principles which guide all morality, that no expediency can justify their infraction.

The inflexibility of general principles is, indeed, perhaps more necessary in political morals than in any other class of actions. If the consideration of expediency be admitted, the question recurs,—Who are to judge of it? The appeal is never made to the *many* whose interest is at stake, but to the *few*, whose interest is linked to the perpetuity of oppression and abuse. Surely that judge ought to be bound down by the strictest rules, who is undeniably interested in the decision: and he would scarcely be esteemed a wise legislator, who should vest in the next heir to a lunatic a discretionary power to judge of his sanity. Far more necessary, then, is obedience to general principles, and maintenance of natural rights, in politics than in the morality of common life. The moment that the slightest infraction of these rights is permitted through motives of *convenience*, the bulwark of all upright politics is lost. If a small convenience will justify a little infraction, a greater will expiate a bolder violation: the Rubicon is past. Tyrants never seek in vain for sophists: pretences are multiplied without difficulty and without end. Nothing, therefore, but an inflexible adherence to the principles of general right can preserve the purity, consistency, and stability of a free state.

If we have thus successfully vindicated the first theoretical principle of French legislation, the doctrine of an absolute surrender of natural rights by civil and social man, has been shown to be deduced from inadequate premises,—to conduct to absurd conclusions, to sanctify the most atrocious despotism, to outrage the avowed convictions of men, and, finally, to be abandoned, as hopelessly untenable by its own author. The existence and perfection of these rights being proved, the first duty of lawgivers and magistrates is to assert and protect them. Most wisely and auspiciously then did France commence her regenerating labours with a solemn declaration of these sacred, inalienable, and imprescriptible rights,—a declaration which must be to the citizen the monitor of his duties, as well as the oracle of his rights, and by a perpetual recurrence to which the deviations of the magistrate will be checked, the tendency of power to abuse corrected, and every political proposition (being compared with the end of society) correctly and dispassionately estimated. To the juvenile vigour of reason and freedom in the New World,—where the human mind was unincumbered with that vast mass of usage and prejudice, which

* Horace, lib. ii. Sat. 3.—Ed.

so many ages of ignorance had accumulated, to load and deform society in Europe,—France owed this, among other lessons. Perhaps the only expedient that can be devised by human wisdom to keep alive public vigilance against the usurpation of partial interests, is that of perpetually presenting the general right and the general interest to the public eye. Such a principle has been the Polar Star, by which the National Assembly has hitherto navigated the vessel of the state, amid so many tempests howling destruction around it.

There remains a much more extensive and complicated inquiry, in the consideration of their political institutions. As it is impossible to examine all, we must limit our remarks to the most important. To speak then generally of their Constitution, it is a preliminary remark, that the application of the word "democracy" to it is fallacious and illusive. If that word, indeed, be taken in its etymological sense, as the "power of the people," it is a democracy; and so are all legitimate governments. But if it be taken in its historical sense, it is not so; for it does not resemble those governments which have been called democracies in ancient or modern times. In the ancient democracies there was neither representation nor division of powers: *the rabble legislated, judged* and *exercised every political authority*. I do not mean to deny that in Athens, of which history has transmitted to us the most authentic monuments, there did exist some feeble control. But it has been well remarked, that a multitude, if it was composed of Newtons, must be a mob: their will must be equally unwise, unjust, and irresistible. The authority of a corrupt and tumultuous populace has indeed by the best writers of antiquity been regarded rather as an ochlocracy than a democracy,—as the despotism of the rabble, not the dominion of the people. It is a degenerate democracy: it is a febrile paroxysm of the social body which must speedily terminate in convalescence or dissolution. The new Constitution of France is almost directly the reverse of these forms. It vests the legislative authority in the representatives of the people, the executive in an hereditary First Magistrate, and the judicial in judges, periodically elected, and unconnected either with the legislature or with the Executive Magistrate. To confound such a constitution with the democracies of antiquity, for the purpose of quoting historical and experimental evidence against it, is to recur to the most paltry and shallow arts of sophistry.

In discussing it, the first question that arises regards the mode of constituting the legislature; the first division of which, relating to the right of suffrage, is of primary importance. Here I most cordially agree with Mr. Burke* in reprobating the impotent and preposterous qualification by which the Assembly has disfranchised every citizen who does not pay a direct contribution equivalent to the price of three days' labour. Nothing can be more evident than its inefficacy for any purpose but the display of inconsistency, and the violation of justice. These remarks were made at the moment of the discussion; and the plan* was combated in the Assembly with all the force of reason and eloquence by the most conspicuous leaders of the popular party,—MM. Mirabeau, Target, and Petion, more particularly distinguishing themselves by their opposition. But the more timid and prejudiced members of it shrunk from so bold an innovation in political systems as justice. They fluctuated between their principles and their prejudices; and the struggle terminated in an illusive compromise,—the constant resource of feeble and temporizing characters. They were content that little practical evil should in fact be produced; while their views were not sufficiently enlarged to perceive, that the inviolability of principles is the palladium of virtue and of freedom. Such members do not, indeed, form the majority of their own party; but the aristocratic minority, anxious for whatever might dishonour or embarrass the Assembly, eagerly coalesced with them, and stained the infant Constitution with this absurd usurpation.

An enlightened and respectable antagonist of Mr. Burke has attempted the defence of this measure. In a Letter to Earl Stanhope, it is contended, that the spirit of this regulation accords exactly with the principles of natural justice, because, even in an unsocial state, the pauper has a claim only on charity, and he who produces nothing has no right to share in the regulation of what is produced by the industry of others. But whatever be the justice of disfranchising the unproductive poor, the argument is, in point of fact, totally misapplied. Domestic servants are excluded by the decree though they subsist as evidently on the produce of their own labour as any other class; and to them therefore the argument of our acute and ingenious writer is totally inapplicable.† But it is the consolation of the consistent friends of freedom, that this abuse must be short-lived: the spirit of reason and liberty, which has achieved such mighty victories, cannot long be resisted by this puny foe. The number of primary electors is at present so great, and the importance of their single votes so proportionally little, that their interest in resisting the extension of the right of suffrage is insignificantly small. Thus much have I spoken of the usurpation of the rights of suf-

* Burke, p. 257.

* See the Procès Verbaux of the 27th and 29th of October, 1789, and the Journal de Paris, No. 301, and Les Révolutions de Paris, No. 17, p. 73.

† It has been very justly remarked, that even with reference to taxation, all men have equal rights of election. For the man who is too poor to pay a direct contribution, still pays a tax in the increased price of his food and clothes. It is besides to be observed, that life and liberty are more sacred than property, and that the right of suffrage is the only shield that can guard them.

frage, with the ardour of anxious affection, and with the freedom of liberal admiration. The moment is too serious for compliment; and I leave untouched to the partisans of despotism, their monopoly of blind and servile applause.*

I must avow, with the same frankness, equal disapprobation of the admission of territory and contribution as elements entering into the proportion of representation.† The representation of land or money is a monstrous relic of ancient prejudice: men only can be represented; and population alone ought to regulate the number of representatives which any district delegates.

The next consideration that presents itself is, the nature of those bodies into which the citizens of France are to be organized for the performance of their political functions. In this important part of the subject, Mr. Burke has committed some fundamental errors: it is more amply, more dexterously, and more correctly treated by M. de Calonne; of whose work this discussion forms the most interesting part. These assemblies are of four kinds:—Municipal, Primary, Electoral, and Administrative.

To the Municipalities belong the care of preserving the police, and collecting the revenue within their jurisdiction. An accurate idea of their nature and object may be formed by supposing the *country* of England uniformly divided, and governed, like its cities and towns, by magistracies of popular election.

The Primary Assemblies, the first elements of the commonwealth, are formed by all citizens, who pay a direct contribution, equal to the price of three days' labour, which may be averaged at half-a-crown sterling. Their functions are purely electoral. They send representatives, in the proportion of one to every hundred adult citizens, to the Assembly of the *Department* directly, and not through the medium of the District, as was originally proposed by the Constitutional Committee, and has been erroneously stated by Mr. Burke. They send, indeed, representatives to the Assembly of the District; but it is for the purpose of choosing the Administrators of such District, not the Electors of the Department. The Electoral Assemblies of the Departments elect the members of the legislature, the judges, the administrators, and the bishop of the Department. The Administrators are every where the organs and instruments of the executive power.

Against the arrangement of these Assemblies, many subtle and specious objections are urged, both by Mr. Burke and the exiled Minister of France. The first and most formidable is, "the supposed tendency of it to dismember France into a body of confederated republics." To this there are several unanswerable replies. But before I state them, it is necessary to make one distinction:—these several bodies are, in a certain sense, independent, in what regards subordinate and interior regulation; but they are not independent in the sense which the objection supposes,—that of possessing a separate will from that of the nation, or influencing, but by their representatives, the general system of the state. Nay, it may be demonstrated, that the legislators of France have solicitously provided more elaborate precautions against this dismemberment than have been adopted by any recorded government.

The first circumstance which is adverse to it is the minuteness of the divided parts. They are too small to possess a separate force. As elements of the social order, as particles of a great political body, they are something; but, as insulated states, they would be impotent. Had France been separated into great masses, each might have been strong enough to claim a separate will; but, divided as she is, no body of citizens is conscious of sufficient strength to feel their sentiments of any importance, but as constituent parts of the general will. Survey the Primary, the Electoral, and the Administrative Assemblies, and nothing will be more evident than their impotence in individuality. The Municipalities, surely, are not likely to arrogate independence. A forty-eight thousandth part of the kingdom has not energy sufficient for separate existence; nor can a hope arise in it of influencing, in a direct and dictatorial manner, the councils of a great state. Even the Electoral Assemblies of the Departments do not, as we shall afterwards show, possess force enough to become independent confederated republics.

Another circumstance, powerfully hostile to this dismemberment, is the destruction of the ancient Provincial division of the kingdom. In no part of Mr. Burke's work have his arguments been chosen with such infelicity of selection as in what regards this subject. He has not only erred; but his error is the precise reverse of truth. He represents as the harbinger of discord, what is, in fact, the instrument of union. He mistakes the cement of the edifice for a source of instability and a principle of repulsion. France was, under the ancient government, an union of provinces, acquired at various times and on different conditions, and differing in constitution, laws, language, manners, privileges, jurisdiction, and revenue. It had the exterior of a simple monarchy, but it

* "He who freely magnifies what has been nobly done, and fears not to declare as freely what might have been done better, gives you the best covenant of his fidelity. His highest praise is not flattery, and his plainest advice is praise."—Areopagitica.

† Montesquieu, I think, mentions a federative republic in Lycia, where the proportion of representatives deputed by each state was in a *ratio* compounded of its population and its contribution. There might be some plausibility in this institution among confederated independent states; but it is grossly absurd in a commonwealth, which is vitally one. In such a state, the contribution of all being proportioned to their capacity, it is relatively equal; and if it can confer any political claims, they must be derived from equal rights.

was in reality an aggregate of independent states. The monarch was in one place King of Navarre, in another Duke of Brittany, in a third Count of Provence, in a fourth Dauphin of Vienne. Under these various denominations he possessed, at least nominally, different degrees of power, and he certainly exercised it under different forms. The mass composed of these heterogeneous and discordant elements, was held together by the compressing force of despotism. When that compression was withdrawn, the provinces must have resumed their ancient independence,—perhaps in a form more absolute than as members of a federative republic. Every thing tended to inspire *provincial* and to extinguish *national* patriotism. The inhabitants of Brittany, or Guienne, felt themselves linked together by ancient habitudes, by congenial prejudices, by similar manners, by the relics of their constitution, and the common name of their country: but their character as members of the French Empire, could only remind them of long and ignominious subjection to a tyranny, of which they had only felt the strength in exaction, and blessed the lenity in neglect. These causes must have formed the provinces into independent republics; and the destruction of their provincial existence was indispensable to the prevention of this dismemberment. It is impossible to deny, that men united by no previous habitude (whatever may be said of the policy of the union in other respects) are less qualified for that union of will and force, which produces an independent republic, than provincials, who were attracted by every circumstance towards local and partial interests, and from the common centre of the national system. Nothing could have been more inevitable than the independence of those great provinces, which had never been moulded into one empire; and we may boldly pronounce, in direct opposition to Mr. Burke, that the new division of the kingdom was the only expedient that could have prevented its dismemberment into a confederacy of sovereign republics.

The solicitous and elaborate division of powers, is another expedient of infallible operation, to preserve the unity of the body politic. The Municipalities are limited to minute and local administration; the Primary Assemblies solely to election; the Assemblies of the District to objects of administration and control of a superior class; and the Assemblies of the Departments possess functions purely electoral, exerting no authority legislative, administrative, or judicial.

But whatever danger might be apprehended of the assumption of power by these formidable Assemblies, they are biennially renewed; and their fugitive nature makes systematic usurpation hopeless. What power, indeed, can they possess of dictating to the National Assembly?* or what interest can the members of that Assembly have in obeying the mandates of those whose tenure of power is as fugitive and precarious as their own? The provincial Administrators have that amount of independence which the constitution demands; while the judges, who are elected for six years, must feel themselves independent of constituents, whom three elections may so radically and completely change. These circumstances, then, —the minuteness of the divisions, the dissolution of Provincial ties, the elaborate distribution of powers, and the fugitive constitution of the Electoral Assemblies,—seem to form an insuperable barrier against the assumption of such powers by any of the bodies into which France is organized, as would tend to produce the federal form.

The next objection to be considered is peculiar to Mr. Burke. The subordination of elections has been regarded by the admirers of the French lawgivers as a masterpiece of their legislative wisdom. It seemed as great an improvement on representative government, as representation itself was on pure democracy. No extent of territory is too great for a popular government thus organized; and as the Primary Assemblies may be divided to any degree of minuteness, the most perfect order is reconcilable with the widest diffusion of political right. Democracies were supposed by philosophers to be necessarily small, and therefore feeble,—to demand numerous assemblies, and to be therefore venal and tumultuous. Yet this great discovery, which gives force and order in so high a degree to popular governments, is condemned and derided by Mr. Burke. An immediate connection between the representative and the primary constituent, he considers as essential to the idea of representation. As the electors in the Primary Assemblies do not immediately elect their lawgivers, he regards their rights of suffrage as nominal and illusory.*

It will in the first instance be remarked, from the statement which has already been given, that in stating three interposed elections between the Primary Electors and the Legislature, Mr. Burke has committed a most important error, in point of fact. The original plan of the Constitutional Committee was indeed agreeable to the statement of Mr. Burke:—the Primary Assemblies were to elect deputies to the District,—the District to the Department,—and the Department to the National Assembly. But this plan was represented as tending to introduce a vicious complexity into the system, and, by making the channel through which the national will passes into its public acts too circuitous, to

* I do not mean that their voice will not be there respected: that would be to suppose the Legislature as insolently corrupt as that of a neighbouring nation. I only mean to assert, that they cannot possess such a power as will enable them to dictate instructions to their representatives as authoritatively as sovereigns do to their ambassadors; which is the idea of a confederated republic.

* Burke, pp. 270—272.

enfeeble its energy under pretence of breaking its violence; and it was accordingly successfully combated. The series of three elections was still preserved for the choice of Departmental Administrators; but the Electoral Assemblies in the Departments, who are the immediate constituents of the Legislature, are directly chosen by the Primary Assemblies, in the proportion of one elector to every hundred active citizens.*

But,—to return to the general question, which is, perhaps, not much affected by these details,—I profess I see no reason why the right of election is not as susceptible of delegation as any other civil function,—why a citizen may not as well delegate the right of choosing lawgivers, as that of making laws. Such a gradation of elections, says Mr. Burke, excludes responsibility and substantial election, since the primary electors neither can know nor bring to account the members of the Assembly. This argument has (considering the peculiar system of Mr. Burke) appeared to me to be the most singular and inconsistent that he has urged in his work. Representation itself must be confessed to be an infringement on the most perfect liberty; for the best organized system cannot preclude the possibility of a variance between the popular and the representative will. Responsibility, strictly speaking, it can rarely admit; for the secrets of political fraud are so impenetrable, and the line which separates corrupt decision from erroneous judgment so indiscernibly minute, that the cases where the deputies could be made properly responsible are too few to be named as exceptions. Their dismissal is the only punishment that can be inflicted; and all that the best constitution can attain is a high probability of unison between the constituent and his deputy. This seems attained in the arrangements of France. The Electors of the Departments are so numerous, and so popularly elected, that there is the highest probability of their being actuated in their elections, and re-elections, by the sentiments of the Primary Assemblies. They have too many points of contact with the general mass to have an insulated opinion, and too fugitive an existence to have a separate interest. This is true of those cases, where the merits or demerits of candidates may be supposed to have reached the Primary Assemblies: but in those far more numerous cases, where they are too obscure to obtain that notice, but by the polluted medium of a popular canvass, this delegation of the franchise is still more evidently wise. The peasant, or artisan, who is a Primary Elector, knows intimately among his equals, or immediate superiors, many men who have information and honesty enough to choose a good representative, but few who have genius, leisure, and ambition for the situation themselves. Of Departmental Electors he may be a disinterested, deliberate, and competent judge: but were he to be complimented, or rather mocked, with the direct right of electing legislators, he must, in the tumult, venality, and intoxication of an election mob, give his suffrage without any possible just knowledge of the situation, character, and conduct of the candidates. So unfortunately false, indeed, seems the opinion of Mr. Burke, that this arrangement is the only one that substantially, and in good faith, provides for the exercise of deliberate discrimination in the constituent.

This hierarchy of electors was, moreover, obtruded on France by necessity. Had they rejected it, they would have had only the alternative of tumultuous electoral assemblies, or a tumultuous Legislature. If the primary electoral assemblies had been so divided as to avoid tumult, their deputies would have been so numerous as to have made the national assembly a mob. If the number of electoral assemblies had been reduced to the number of deputies constituting the Legislature, each of them would have been too numerous. I cannot perceive that peculiar unfitness which is hinted at by Mr. Burke in the right of *personal* choice to be delegated.* It is in the practice of all states delegated to great officers, who are intrusted with the power of nominating their subordinate agents. It is in the most ordinary affairs of common life delegated, when our *ultimate* representatives are too remote from us to be within the sphere of our observation. It is remarkable that M. de Calonne, addressing his work to a people enlightened by the masterly discussions to which these subjects have given rise, has not, in all the fervour of his zeal to criminate the new institutions, hazarded this objection. This is not the only instance in which the Ex-Minister has shown more respect to the nation whom he addresses, than Mr. Burke has paid to the intellect and information of the English public.†

* For a charge of such fundamental inaccuracy against Mr. Burke, the Public will most justly and naturally expect the highest evidence. See the Décret sur la nouvelle Division du Royaume, Art. 17, and the Procès Verbal of the Assembly for the 22d Dec., 1789. If this evidence should demand any collateral aid, the authority of M. de Calonne (which it is remarkable that Mr. Burke should have overlooked) corroborates it most amply. "On ordonne que chacune de ces Assemblées (Primaires) nommera un électeur à raison de 100 citoyens actifs."... "Ces cinquantes mille électeurs (des Départements) choisis de deux ans en deux ans par les Assemblées Primaires," p. 360. The Ex-Minister, indeed, is rarely to be detected in any departure from the solicitous accuracy of professional detail.

* Burke, p. 271.

† Though it may, perhaps, be foreign to the purpose, I cannot help thinking one remark on this topic interesting. It will illustrate the difference of opinion between even the Aristocratic party in France and the rulers of England. M. de Calonne (p. 383,) rightly states it to be the unanimous instruction of France to her representatives, to enact the equal admissibility of all citi-

Thus much of the elements of the legislative body. Concerning that body, thus constituted, various questions remain. Its unity or division will admit of much dispute. It will be deemed of the greatest moment by the zealous admirers of the English constitution, to determine whether any semblance of its legislative organization could have been attained by France, if good, or ought to have been pursued by her, if attainable. Nothing has been asserted with more confidence by Mr. Burke than the facility with which the fragments of the long subverted liberty of France might have been formed into a British constitution: but of this general position, he has neither explained the mode, nor defined the limitations. Nothing is more favourable to the popularity of a work than these lofty generalities which are light enough to pass into vulgar currency, and to become the maxims of a popular creed. Proclaimed as they are by Mr. Burke, they gratify the pride and indolence of the people, who are thus taught to speak what gains applause, without any effort of intellect, and imposes silence, without any labour of confutation; but touched by definition, they become too simple and precise for eloquence,—too cold and abstract for popularity. It is necessary to inquire with more precision in what manner France could have assimilated the remains of her ancient constitution to that of the English Legislature. Three modes only seem conceivable:—the preservation of the three Orders distinct; the union of the Clergy and Nobility in one upper chamber; or some mode of selecting from these two Orders a body like the House of Lords. Unless the insinuations of Mr. Burke point to one or other of these schemes, I cannot divine their meaning.

The first mode would neither have been congenial in spirit nor similar in form to the constitution of England:—convert the Convocation into an integrant and co-ordinate branch of our Legislature, and some faint semblance of structure might be discovered. But it would then be necessary to arm our Clergy with an immense mass of property, rendered still more formidable by the concentration of great benefices in the hands of a few, and to bestow on this clerico-military aristocracy, in each of its shapes of Priest and Noble, a separate and independent voice. The Monarch would thus possess three negatives,—one avowed and disused, and two latent and in perpetual activity,—on the single voice which impotent and illusive formality had yielded to the Third Estate.

zens to public employ! England adheres to the Test Act! The arrangements of M. Neckar for elections to the States-General, and the scheme of MM. Mounier and Lally-Tollendal for the new constitution, included a representation of the people nearly exact. Yet the idea of it is regarded with horror in England! The highest *Aristocrates* of France approach more nearly to the creed of general liberty than the most popular politicians of England.

Even under the reign of despotism the second plan was proposed by M. de Calonne,*—that the Clergy and Nobility should form an Upper House, to exercise conjointly with the King and the Commons the legislative authority. That such a constitution would have been diametrically opposite in its spirit and principles to that of England, will be evident to those who reflect how different were the Nobility of each country. In England they are a small body, united to the mass by innumerable points of contact, receiving from it perpetually new infusions, and returning to it, undistinguished and unprivileged, the majority of their children. In France they formed an immense caste, insulated by every barrier that prejudice or policy could raise. The Nobles of England are a senate of two hundred: the Noblesse of France were a *tribe* of two hundred thousand. Nobility is in England only hereditary, so far as its professed object—the support of an hereditary senate—demands. Nobility in France was as widely inheritable as its real purpose—the maintenance of a privileged *caste*—prescribed. It was therefore necessarily descendible to all male children. The Noblesse of France were at once formidable from the immense property of their body, and dependent from the indigence of their patrician rabble of cadets, whom honour inspired with servility, and servility excluded from the path to independence. To this formidable property were added the revenues of the Church, monopolized by some of their children; while others had no patrimony but their sword. If these last were generous, the habits of military service devoted them, from loyalty,—if they were prudent, the hope of military promotion devoted them, from interest, to the King. How immense therefore and irresistible would the Royal influence have been over electors, of whom the majority were the servants and creatures of the Crown? What would be thought in England of a House of Lords, which, while it represented or contained the whole landed interest of the kingdom, should necessarily have a majority of its members septennially or triennially nominated by the King? Yet such a one would still yield to the French Upper House of M. de Calonne: for the monied and commercial interests of England, which would continue to be represented by the Commons, are important and formidable, while in France they are comparatively insignificant. The aristocracy could have been strong only against the people,—impotent against the Crown.

There remains only the selection of an

* See his Lettre au Roi, 9th February, 1789. See also Sur l'Etat de France, p. 167. It was also, as we are informed by M. de Calonne, suggested in the *Cahiers* of the Nobility of Metz and Montargis. It is worthy of incidental. The proposition of such radical changes by the Nobility, is incontestable evidence of the general conviction that a total change was necessary, and is an unanswerable reply to Mr. Burke and M. de Calonne.

Upper House from among the Nobility and Clergy: and to this there are insuperable objections. Had the right of thus forming a branch of the Legislature by a single act of prerogative been given to the King, it must have strengthened his influence to a degree terrible at any,—but fatal at this period. Had any mode of election by the provinces, or the Legislature, been adopted, or had any control on the nomination of the Crown been vested in them, the new dignity would have been sought with an activity of corruption and intrigue, of which, in such a national convulsion, it is impossible to estimate the danger. No general principle of selection, such as that of opulence or antiquity, would have remedied the evil; for the excluded and degraded would have felt that nobility was equally the patrimony of all. By the abolition of nobility, no one was degraded; for to "degrade" is to lower from a rank that continues to exist in society.

So evident indeed was the impossibility of what Mr. Burke supposes to have been attainable, that no party in the Assembly suggested the imitation of the English model. The system of his oracles in French politics, —MM. Lally and Mounier,—approached more near to the constitution of the American States. They proposed a Senate to be chosen for life by the King, from candidates offered to his choice by the provinces. This Senate was to enjoy an absolute negative on legislative acts, and to form the great national court for the trial of public delinquents. In effect, such a body would have formed a far more vigorous aristocracy than the English Peerage. The latter body only preserves its dignity by a wise disuse of its power. But the Senate of M. Mounier would have been an aristocracy moderated and legalized, which, because it appeared to have less independence, would in fact have been emboldened to exert more. Deriving their rights equally with the Lower House from the people, and vested with a more dignified and extensive trust, they would neither have shrunk from the conflict with the Commons nor the King. The permanence of their authority must have given them a superiority over the former;—the speciousness of their cause over the latter: and it seems probable, that they would have ended in subjugating both. Let those who suppose that this Senate would not have been infected by the "corporation spirit," consider how keenly the ancient judicatures of France had been actuated by it.

As we quit the details of these systems, a question arises for our consideration of a more general and more difficult nature,—Whether a simple representative legislature, or a constitution of mutual control, be the best form of government?* To examine this question at length is inconsistent with the object and limits of the present publication (which already grows insensibly beyond its intended size); but a few general principles may be hinted, on which the decision of the question chiefly depends.

It will not be controverted, that the object of establishing a representative legislature is to collect the general will. That will is one: it cannot, therefore, without a solecism, be *doubly* represented. Any absolute* negative opposed to the national will, decisively spoken by its representatives, is null, as an usurpation of the popular sovereignty. Thus far does the abstract principle of representation condemn the division of the legislature.

All political bodies, as well as all systems of law, foster the preponderance of partial interests. A controlling senate would be most peculiarly accessible to this contagious spirit: a representative body itself can only be preserved from it by those frequent elections which break combinations, and infuse new portions of popular sentiments. Let us grant that a popular assembly may sometimes be precipitated into unwise decision by the seductions of eloquence, or the rage of faction, and that a controlling senate might remedy this evil: but let us recollect, that it is better the public interest should be occasionally mistaken than systematically opposed.

It is perhaps susceptible of proof, that these governments of balance and control have never existed but in the vision of theorists. The fairest example will be that of England. If the two branches of the Legislature, which it is pretended control each other, are ruled by the same class of men, the control must be granted to be imaginary. The great proprietors, titled and untitled, possess the whole force of both Houses of Parliament that is not immediately dependent on the Crown. The Peers have a great influence in the House of Commons. All political parties are formed by a confederacy of the members of both Houses. The Court party, acting equally in both, is supported by a part of the independent aristocracy;—the Opposition by the remainder of the aristocracy, whether peers or commoners. Here is every symptom of collusion,—no vestige of control. The only case indeed, where control could arise, is where the interest of the Peerage is distinct from that of the other great proprietors. But their separate interests are so few and paltry, that the history of England will not afford one undisputed instance.†

* This question, translated into familiar language, may perhaps be thus expressed,—"Whether the vigilance of the master, or the squabbles of the servants, be the best security for faithful service?"

* The suspensive veto vested in the French King is only an appeal to the people on the conduct of their representatives. The voice of the people clearly spoken, the negative ceases.

† The rejection of the Peerage Bill of George the First is urged with great triumph by De Lolme. There it seems the Commons rejected the Bill, purely actuated by their fears, that the aristocracy would acquire a strength, through a limitation of the number of Peers, destructive of the balance of their respective powers. It is un-

"Through a diversity of members and interests," if we may believe Mr. Burke, "general liberty had as many securities as there were separate views in the several orders." If by "general liberty" be understood the power of the collective body of these orders, the position is undeniable: but if it means,—what it ought to mean,—the liberty of mankind, nothing can be more false. The higher class in society,—whether their names be nobles, bishops, judges, or possessors of landed and commercial wealth, —has ever been united by common views, far more powerful than those petty repugnancies of interest to which this variety of description may give rise. Whatever may be the little conflicts of ecclesiastical with secular, or of commercial with landed opulence, they have the one common interest of preserving their elevated place in the social order. There never was, and never will be, in civilized society, but two grand interests,—that of the rich and that of the poor. The privileges of the several orders among the former will be guarded, and Mr. Burke will decide that general liberty is secure! It is thus that a Polish Palatine and the Assembly of Jamaica profanely appeal to the principles of freedom. It is thus that Antiquity, with all her pretended political philosophy, cannot boast one philosopher who questioned the justice of servitude,—nor with all her pretended public virtue, one philanthropist who deplored the misery of slaves.

One circumstance more concerning the proposed Legislature remains to be noticed,—the exclusion of the King's Ministers from it. This "Self-denying Ordinance" I unequivocally disapprove. I regard all disfranchisement as equally unjust in its principle, destructive in its example, and impotent in its purpose. Their presence would have been of great utility with a view to business, and perhaps, by giving publicity to their opinions, favourable on the whole to public liberty. The fair and open influence of a Government is never formidable. To exclude them from the Legislature, is to devote them to the purposes of the Crown, and thereby to enable them to use their indirect and secret influence with more impunity and success. The exclusion is equivalent to that of all men of superior talent from the Cabinet: for no man of genius will accept an office which banishes him from the supreme assembly, which is the natural sphere of his powers.

Of the plan of the Judicature, I have not yet presumed to form a decided opinion. It certainly approaches to an experiment, whether a code of laws can be formed sufficiently simple and intelligible to supersede the necessity of professional lawyers.* Of all the attempts of the Assembly, the complicated relations of civilized society seem to render this the most problematical. They have not, however, concluded this part of their labours: and the feebleness attributed to the elective judicatures of the Departments may be remedied by the dignity and force with which they will invest the two high national tribunals.†

On the subject of the Executive Magistracy, the Assembly have been accused of violating their own principles by the assumption of executive powers; and their advocates have pleaded guilty to the charge. It has been forgotten that they had a double function to perform: they were not only to erect a new constitution, but they were to guard it from destruction. Had a superstitious tenderness for a principle confined them to theoretical abstractions which the breath of power might destroy, they would indeed have merited the epithets of visionaries and enthusiasts. We must not, as has been justly observed, mistake for the new political edifice what is only the scaffolding necessary to its erection. The powers of the First Magistrate are not to be estimated by the debility to which the convulsions of the moment have reduced them, but by the provisions of the future constitution.

The portion of power with which the King of France is invested is certainly as much as pure theory would demand for an executive magistrate. An organ to collect the public will, and a hand to execute it, are the only necessary constituents of the social union: the popular representative forms the first,—the executive officer the second. To the point where this principle would have conducted them, the French have not ventured to proceed. It has been asserted by Mr. Burke, that the French King is to have no negative on the laws. This, however, is not true. The minority who opposed any species of negative in the Crown was only one hundred out of eight hundred members. The King possesses the power of withholding his assent to a proposed law for two successive Assemblies. This species of suspensive *veto* is with great speciousness and ingenuity contended by M. Neckar to be more efficient than the obsolete negative of the English princes.‡ A mild and limited negative may, he remarked, be exercised without danger or odium; while a prerogative, like the absolute *veto*, must sink into impotence from its invidious magnitude. Is not that negative really efficient, which is only to yield to the national voice, spoken after four years' de-

fortunate that political theorists do not consult the *history* as well as the *letter* of legislative proceedings. The rejection of that Bill was occasioned by the secession of Walpole. The debate was not guided by any general legislative principles. It was simply an experiment on the strength of the two parties contending for power, in a Parliament to which we owe the Septennial Act.

* The sexennial election of the Judges is strongly and ably opposed by M. de Calonne,—chiefly on the principle, that the stability of judicial offices is the only inducement to men to devote their lives to legal study.

† The Cour de Cassation and the Haute Cour Nationale.

‡ Rapport fait au Roi dans son Conseil, 11th Sept., 1789.

liberation? The most absolute *veto* must, if the people persist, prove eventually only suspensive.* "The power of remonstrance," says Mr. Burke, "which was anciently vested in the Parliament of Paris, is now absurdly intrusted to the Executive Magistrate." But the *veto* of the Parliament was directed against the legislative authority; whereas the proposed one of the King is an appeal to the people against their representatives: the latter is the only share in legislation,—whether it be nominally absolute, or nominally limited,—that a free government can intrust to its Supreme Magistrate.†

On the Prerogative of declaring War and Peace, Mr. Burke† has shortly, and M. de Calonne‡ at great length, arraigned the system of the Assembly. In it war is to be declared by a decree of the Legislature, on the proposition of the King, who possesses exclusively the initiative. The difference between it and the theory of the English constitution is purely nominal. That theory supposes an independent House of Commons, a rigorous responsibility of the King's Ministers, and an effective power of impeachment of them. Were these in any respect realized, it is perfectly obvious, that a decision for war must in every case depend on the deliberation of the Legislature. No minister would hazard hostilities without the sanction of a body who held a sword suspended over his head; and no power would remain to the Executive Magistrate but the initiative. The forms indeed, in the majority of cases, aim at a semblance of the theory. A Royal Message announces impending hostilities, and is re-echoed by a Parliamentary Address of promised support. It is this address alone which emboldens and authorizes the Cabinet to proceed. The Royal Message corresponds to the French initiative; and if the purity of our practice bore any proportion to the speciousness of our theory, the address would be a "decree" of the Legislature, adopting the proposition of the King. No man, therefore, who is a sincere and enlightened admirer of the English constitution, as it ought, and is pretended to exist, can consistently reprobate an arrangement, which differs from it only in the most frivolous circumstances. In our practice, indeed, no trace of those discordant powers which are supposed in our theoretical constitution remains: there the most beautiful simplicity prevails. The same influence determines the executive, and legislative power: the same Cabinet makes war in the name of the King, and sanctions it in the name of the Parliament. But France is destitute of the cement which unites these discordant materials:—her exchequer is ruined.

Granted, however, that this formidable prerogative is more curtailed than it is in our theory, the expediency of such limitation remains to be considered. The chief objections to it, are its tendency to favour the growth of foreign factions, and to derogate from the promptitude so necessary to military success. To both these objections there is one general answer:—they proceed on the supposition that France will retain her ancient political system. But if she adheres to her own declarations, war must become to her so rare an occurrence, that the objections become insignificant. Foreign powers have no temptation to purchase factions in a state which does not interpose in foreign politics: and a wise nation will regard victorious war as not less fatally intoxicating to the victors, than widely destructive to the vanquished. France, after having renounced for ever the idea of conquest, can indeed have no source of probable hostilities, but her colonies. Colonial possessions have been so unanswerably demonstrated to be commercially useless, and politically ruinous, that the conviction of philosophers cannot fail of having, in due time, its effect on the minds of enlightened Europe, and delivering the French empire from this cumbrous and destructive appendage.

But even were the exploded villany that has obtained the name of "politics" to be re-adopted in France, the objections would still be feeble. The first, which must be confessed to have a specious and formidable air, seems evidently to be founded on the history of Sweden and Poland, and on some facts in that of the Dutch Republic. It is a remarkable example of those loose and remote analogies by which sophists corrupt and abuse history. Peculiar circumstances in the situation of these states disposed them to be the seat of foreign faction. This did not arise from war being decided upon by public bodies; for if it had, a similar evil must have existed in ancient Rome and Carthage, in modern Venice, and Switzerland, in the Republican Parliament of England, and in the Congress of the United States of America. Holland, too, was perfectly exempt from it, till the age of Charles II. and Louis XIV. when, divided between jealousy of the commerce of England and dread of the conquests of France, she threw herself into the arms of the House of Orange, and forced the partisans of freedom into a reliance on French support. The case of Sweden is with the utmost facility explicable. An indigent and martial people, whether it be governed by one or many despots, will ever be sold to enterprising and opulent ambition: and recent facts have proved, that a change in the government of Sweden has not changed the stipendiary spirit of its mili-

* The negative possessed by the King is precisely double that of the Assembly. He may oppose his will to that of his whole people for four years,—the term of the existence of two Assemblies. The whole of this argument is in some measure *ad hominem*, for I myself am dubious about the utility of any species of *veto*,—absolute or suspensive.

† Burke, p. 301.

‡ Ibid p. 295. § Calonne, pp. 170—200.

tary system. Poland is an example still less relevant:—there a crowd of independent despots naturally league themselves variously with foreign Powers. Yet Russian force has done more than Russian gold; and Poland has suffered still more from feebleness than venality.

No analogy can be supposed to exist between these cases and that of France. All the Powers of Europe could not expend money enough to form and *maintain* a faction in that country. Suppose it possible that its Legislature could *once* be corrupted; yet to purchase in succession a series of assemblies, Potosi itself would be unequal. All the states which have been quoted were poor,—therefore cheaply corrupted: their governments were aristocratic, and were therefore only to be *once* bought; the people were ignorant, and could therefore be sold by their governors with impunity. The reverse of these circumstances will save France, as they have saved England, from this "worst of evils:"—their wealth makes the attempt difficult; their discernment makes it hazardous; their short trust of power renders the object worthless, and its permanence impossible.

That subjecting such a decision to the deliberations of a popular assembly will, in a great measure, unnerve the vigour of hostilities, I am not disposed to deny. France must, however, when her constitution is cemented, be, in a defensive view, invincible: and if her government is unfitted for aggression, it is little wonder that the Assembly should have made no provision for a case which their principles do not suppose.

This is the last important arrangement respecting the executive power which Mr. Burke has treated; and its consideration conducts us to a subject of infinite delicacy and difficulty, which has afforded no small triumph to the enemies of the Revolution, the organization of the army. To reconcile the existence of an army of a hundred and fifty thousand men, of a navy of a hundred ships of the line, and of a frontier guarded by a hundred fortresses, with the existence of a free government, is a tremendous problem. History affords no example in which such a force has not recoiled on the state, and become the ready instrument of military usurpation: and if the state of France were not perfectly unexampled, the inference would be inevitable. An army, with the sentiments and habits which it is the system of modern Europe to inspire, is not only hostile to freedom, but incompatible with it. A body possessed of the whole force of a state, and systematically divested of every civic sentiment, is a monster that no rational polity can tolerate; and every circumstance clearly shows it to be the object of French legislation to destroy it,—not as a body of armed citizens, but as an army. This is wisely and gradually to be effected: two grand operations conduct to it,—arming the people, and unsoldiering the army.

An army of four millions can never be coerced by one of a hundred and fifty thousand; neither can they have a separate sentiment from the body of the nation, for they are the same. Whence the horror of Mr. Burke at thus arming the nation, under the title of "a municipal army," has arisen, it is difficult even to conjecture. Has it ceased to be true, that the defence of a free state is only to be committed to its citizens? Are the long opposition to a standing army in England, its tardy and jealous admission, and the perpetual clamour (at length illusively gratified) for a militia, to be exploded, as the gross and uncourtly sentiments of our unenlightened ancestors? "They must rule," says Mr. Burke, "by an army." If that be the system of the Assembly, their policy is still more wretched than he has represented it: for they systematically strengthen the governed, while they enfeeble their engine of government. A military democracy, if it means a deliberative body of soldiers, is the most execrable of tyrannies; but if it be understood to denote a popular government, under which every citizen is disciplined and armed, it must then be pronounced to be the only free one which retains within itself the means of preservation.

The professional soldiers, rendered harmless by the strength of the municipal army, are in many other ways invited to throw off those abject and murderous habits which form the perfect modern soldier. In other states the soldiery are in general disfranchised by their poverty: but in France a great part may enjoy the full rights of citizens. They are not then likely to sacrifice their superior to their inferior capacity, nor to elevate their military importance by committing political suicide. The diffusion of political knowledge among them, which is ridiculed and reprobated by Mr. Burke, is the only remedy that can fortify them against the seduction of an aspiring commander. They, have, indeed, gigantic strength, and they may crush their fellow-citizens, by dragging down the social edifice; but they must themselves be overwhelmed by its fall. The despotism of armies is the slavery of soldiers: an army cannot be strong enough to tyrannize, that is not itself cemented by the most absolute interior tyranny. The diffusion of these great truths will perpetuate, as they have produced, a revolution in the character of the French soldiery. Military services will be the *duty* of all citizens, and the *trade* of none.* If a separate body of citizens, as an army, is deemed necessary,

* Again I must encounter the derision of Mr. Burke, by quoting the ill-fated citizen of Geneva, whose life was embittered by the cold friendship of a philosopher, and whose memory is proscribed by the alarmed enthusiasm of an orator. I shall presume to recommend to the perusal of every reader his tract entitled, "Considérations sur le Gouvernement de Pologne," &c.—more especially what regards the military system.

it will probably be formed by rotation: a certain period of military service will be exacted from every citizen, and may, as in the ancient republics, be made a necessary qualification for the pursuit of civil honours. "Gallos quoque in bellis floruisse audivimus,"* may again be the sentiment of our children. The glory of heroism, and the splendour of conquest, have long enough been the patrimony of that great nation. It is time that it should seek a new glory, and a new splendour, under the shade of freedom, in cultivating the arts of peace, and extending the happiness of mankind. Happy would it be for us all, if the example of that "manifesto of humanity" which has been adopted by the legislators of France, should make an adequate impression on surrounding nations.

Tunc genus humanum positis sibi consulat armis,
Inque vicem gens omnis amet.†

SECTION V.

English admirers vindicated.

It is thus that Mr. Burke has spoken of the men and measures of a foreign nation, where there was no patriotism to excuse his prepossession or his asperity, and no duty or feeling to preclude him from adopting the feelings of a disinterested posterity, and assuming the dispassionate tone of a philosopher and a historian. What wonder then if he should wanton in all the eloquence and virulence of an advocate against fellow-citizens, to whom he attributes the flagitious purpose of stimulating England to the imitation of such enormities. The Revolution and Constitutional Societies, and Dr. Price, whom he regards as their oracle and guide, are the grand objects of his hostility. For them no contumely is too debasing,—no invective too intemperate,—no imputation too foul. Joy at the downfall of despotism is the indelible crime, for which no virtue can compensate, and no punishment can atone. An inconsistency, however, betrays itself not unfrequently in literary quarrels:—he affects to despise those whom he appears to dread. His anger exalts those whom his ridicule would vilify; and on those whom at one moment he derides as too contemptible for resentment, he at another confers a criminal eminence, as too audacious for contempt. Their voice is now the importunate chirp of the meagre shrivelled insects of the hour,—now the hollow murmur, ominous of convulsions and earthquakes, that are to lay the fabric of society in ruins. To provoke against the doctrines and persons of these unfortunate Societies this storm of execration and derision, it was not sufficient that the French Revolution should be traduced; every record of English policy and law is to be distorted.

The Revolution of 1688 is confessed to have established principles by those who lament that it has not reformed institutions. It has sanctified the theory, if it has not insured the practice of a free government. It declared, by a memorable precedent, the right of the people of England to revoke abused power, to frame the government, and bestow the crown. There was a time, indeed, when some wretched followers of Filmer and Blackwood lifted their heads in opposition: but more than half a century had withdrawn them from public contempt, to the amnesty and oblivion which their innoxious stupidity had purchased.

It was reserved for the latter end of the eighteenth century to construe these innocent and obvious inferences into libels on the constitution and the laws. Dr. Price has asserted (I presume without fear of contradiction) that the House of Hanover owes the crown of England to the choice of their people, and that the Revolution has established our right "to choose our own governors, to cashier them for misconduct, and to frame a government for ourselves."* The first proposition, says Mr. Burke, is either false or nugatory. If it imports that England is an elective monarchy, "it is an unfounded, dangerous, illegal, and unconstitutional position." "If it alludes to the election of his Majesty's ancestors to the throne, it no more legalizes the government of England than that of other nations, where the founders of dynasties have generally founded their claims on some sort of election." The first member of this dilemma merits no reply. The people may certainly, as they have done, choose an hereditary rather than an elective monarchy: they may elect a race instead of an individual. It is vain to compare the pretended elections in which a council of barons, or an army of mercenaries, have imposed usurpers on enslaved and benighted kingdoms, with the solemn, deliberate, national choice of 1688. It is, indeed, often expedient to sanction these deficient titles by subsequent acquiescence in them. It is not among the projected innovations of France to revive the claims of any of the posterity of Pharamond and Clovis, or to arraign the usurpations of Pepin or Hugh Capet. Public tranquillity thus demands a veil to be drawn over the successful crimes through which kings have so often "waded to the throne." But wherefore should we not exult, that the supreme magistracy of England is free from this blot,—that as a direct emanation from the sovereignty of the people, it is as legitimate in its origin as in its administration. Thus under-

* The expression of Tacitus (Agricola), quoted by Mr. Burke in the Speech on the Army Estimates.—Ed.

† Pharsalia, lib. i.

* A Discourse on the Love of our Country, delivered on Nov. 4th, 1789, at the Meeting-house in Old Jewry, to the Society for commemorating the Revolution in Great Britain. London, 1789.

stood, the position of Dr. Price is neither false nor nugatory. It is not nugatory, for it honourably distinguishes the English monarchy among the governments of the world; and if it be false, the whole history of our Revolution must be a legend. The fact was shortly, that the Prince of Orange was elected King of England, in contempt of the claims, not only of the exiled monarch and his son, but of the Princesses Mary and Anne, the undisputed progeny of James. The title of William III. was then clearly not by succession; and the House of Commons ordered Dr. Burnet's tract to be burnt by the hands of the hangman, for maintaining that it was by conquest. There remains only election: for these three claims to royalty are all that are known among men. It is futile to urge, that the Convention deviated only slightly from the order of succession. The deviation was indeed slight, but the principle was destroyed. The principle that justified the elevation of William III. and the preference of the posterity of Sophia of Hanover to those of Henrietta of Orleans, would equally, in point of right, have vindicated the election of Chancellor Jeffreys or Colonel Kirke. The choice was, like every other choice, to be guided by views of policy and prudence; but it was a choice still.

From these views arose that repugnance between the conduct and the language of the Revolutionists, of which Mr. Burke has availed himself. Their conduct was manly and systematic: their language was conciliating and equivocal. They kept measures with a prejudice which they deemed necessary to the order of society. They imposed on the grossness of the popular understanding, by a sort of compromise between the constitution and the abdicated family. "They drew a politic well-wrought veil," to use the expression of Mr. Burke, over the glorious scene which they had acted. They affected to preserve a semblance of succession,—to recur for the objects of their election to the posterity of Charles and James,—that respect and loyalty might with less violence to public sentiment attach to the new Sovereign. Had a Jacobite been permitted freedom of speech in the Parliaments of William III. he might thus have arraigned the Act of Settlement:—"Is the language of your statutes to be at eternal war with truth? Not long ago you profaned the forms of devotion by a thanksgiving, which either means nothing, or insinuates a lie: you thanked Heaven for the preservation of a King and a Queen on the throne of their ancestors,—an expression which either alluded only to their descent, which was frivolous, or insinuated their hereditary right, which was false. With the same contempt for consistency and truth, we are this day called on to settle the crown of England on a princess of Germany, 'because' she is the granddaughter of James the First. If that be, as the phraseology insinuates, the true and sole reason of the choice, consistency demands that the words after 'excellent' should be omitted, and in their place be inserted 'Victor Amadeus, Duke of Savoy, married to the daughter of the most excellent Princess Henrietta, late Duchess of Orleans, daughter of our late Sovereign Lord Charles I. of glorious memory.' Do homage to royalty in your actions, or abjure it in your words: avow the grounds of your conduct, and your manliness will be respected by those who detest your rebellion." What reply Lord Somers, or Mr. Burke, could have devised to this Philippic, I know not, unless they confessed that the authors of the Revolution had one language for novices and another for adepts. Whether this conduct was the fruit of caution and consummate wisdom, or of a narrow, arrogant, and dastardly policy, which regarded the human race as only to be governed by being duped, it is useless to inquire, and might be presumptuous to determine. But it certainly was not to be expected, that any controversy should have arisen by confounding their *principles* with their *pretexts:* with the latter the position of Dr. Price has no connection; from the former, it is an infallible inference.

The next doctrine of this obnoxious Sermon that provokes the indignation of Mr. Burke, is, "that the Revolution has established our right to cashier our governors for misconduct." Here a plain man could have foreseen scarcely any diversity of opinion. To contend that the deposition of a king for the abuse of his powers did not establish a principle in favour of the like deposition, when the like abuse should again occur, is certainly one of the most arduous enterprises that ever the heroism of paradox encountered. He has, however, not neglected the means of retreat. "No government," he tells us, "could stand a moment, if it could be blown down with anything so loose and indefinite as opinion of misconduct." One might suppose, from the dexterous levity with which the word "misconduct" is introduced, that the partisans of democracy had maintained the expediency of deposing a king for every frivolous and venial fault,—of revolting against him for the choice of his titled or untitled valets,—his footmen, or his Lords of the Bedchamber. It would have been candid in Mr. Burke not to have dissembled what he must know, that by "misconduct" was meant that precise species of misconduct for which James II. was dethroned,—a conspiracy against the liberty of his country.

Nothing can be more weak than to urge the constitutional irresponsibility of kings or parliaments. The law can never suppose them responsible, because their responsibility supposes the dissolution of society, which is the annihilation of law. In the governments which have hitherto existed, the power of the magistrate is the only article in the social compact: destroy it, and society is dissolved. It is because they cannot be legally and constitutionally, that they must be morally and rationally responsible. It is because there are no remedies to be found within the pale of society, that we are to seek them in nature, and throw our parchment chains in the face of our oppressors. No man can deduce a precedent of law from the Revolution; for law cannot exist in the dissolution of government: a precedent of reason and justice only can be established in it. And perhaps the friends of freedom merit the misrepresentation with which they have been opposed, for trusting their cause to such frail and frivolous auxiliaries, and for seeking in the profligate practices of men what is to be found in the sacred rights of nature. The system of lawyers is indeed widely different. They can only appeal to usage, precedents, authorities, and statutes. They display their elaborate frivolity, and their perfidious friendship, in disgracing freedom with the fantastic honour of a pedigree. A pleader at the Old Bailey, who would attempt to aggravate the guilt of a robber or a murderer, by proving that King John or King Alfred punished robbery and murder, would only provoke derision. A man who should pretend that the reason why we had right to property is, because our ancestors enjoyed that right four hundred years ago, would be justly contemned. Yet so little is plain sense heard in the mysterious nonsense which is the cloak of political fraud, that the Cokes, the Blackstones, and the Burkes, speak as if our right to freedom depended on its possession by our ancestors. In the common cases of morality we should blush at such an absurdity. No man would justify murder by its antiquity, or stigmatize benevolence for being new. The genealogist who should emblazon the one as coeval with Cain, or stigmatize the other as upstart with Howard, would be disclaimed even by the most frantic partisan of aristocracy. This Gothic transfer of genealogy to truth and justice is peculiar to politics. The existence of robbery in one age makes its vindication in the next; and the champions of freedom have abandoned the stronghold of right for precedent, which, when the most favourable, is, as might be expected from the ages which furnish it, feeble, fluctuating, partial, and equivocal. It is not because we *have been* free, but because we *have a right to be* free, that we ought to demand freedom. Justice and liberty have neither birth nor race, youth nor age. It would be the same absurdity to assert, that we have a right to freedom, because the Englishmen of Alfred's reign were free, as that three and three are six, *because* they were so in the camp of Genghis Khan. Let us hear no more of this ignoble and ignominious pedigree of freedom. Let us hear no more of her Saxon, Danish, or Norman ancestors. Let the immortal daughter of Reason, of Justice, and of God, be no longer confounded with the spurious abortions that have usurped her name.

"But," says Mr. Burke, "we do not contend that right is created by antiquarian research. We are far from contending that possession legitimates tyranny, or that fact ought to be confounded with right. But (to strip his eulogies on English wisdom of their declamatory appendage) the impression of antiquity endears and ennobles freedom, and fortifies it by rendering it august and venerable in the popular mind." The illusion is useful; the expediency of political imposture is the whole force of the argument;—a principle odious to the friends of freedom, as the grand bulwark of secular and spiritual despotism. To pronounce that men are only to be governed by delusion is to libel the human understanding, and to consecrate the frauds that have elevated despots and muftis, pontiffs and sultans, on the ruin of degraded and oppressed humanity. But the doctrine is as false as it is odious. Primary political truths are few and simple. It is easy to make them understood, and to transfer to government the same enlightened self-interest that presides in the other concerns of life. It may be made to be respected, not because it is ancient, or because it is sacred, —not because it has been established by barons, or applauded by priests,—but because it is useful. Men may easily be instructed to maintain rights which it is their interest to maintain, and duties which it is their interest to perform. This is the only principle of authority that does not violate justice and insult humanity: it is also the only one which can possess stability. The various fashions of prejudice and factitious sentiment which have been the basis of governments, are short-lived things. The illusions of chivalry, and the illusions of superstition, which have given to them splendour or sanctity, are in their turn succeeded by new modes of opinion and new systems of manners. Reason alone and natural sentiment are the denizens of every nation, and the contemporaries of every age. A conviction of the utility of government affords the only stable and honourable security for obedience.

Our ancestors at the Revolution, it is true, were far from feeling the full force of these sublime truths: nor was the public mind of Europe, in the seventeenth century, sufficiently enlightened and matured for the grand enterprises of legislation. The science which teaches the rights of man, and the eloquence that kindles the spirit of freedom, had for ages been buried with the other monuments of wisdom and the other relics of the genius of antiquity. The revival of letters first unlocked,—but only to a few,— the sacred fountain. The necessary labours of criticism and lexicography occupied the earlier scholars; and some time elapsed before the spirit of antiquity was transfused into its admirers. The first man of that period who united elegant learning to original and masculine thought was Buchanan;* and he

* It is not a little remarkable, that Buchanan puts into the mouth of his antagonist, Maitland, the same alarms for the downfall of literature that have been excited in the mind of Mr. Burke by the French Revolution. We can smile at such alarms on a retrospect of the literary history of Europe for the seventeenth of eighteen centuries.

too seems to have been the first scholar who caught from the ancients the noble flame of republican enthusiasm. This praise is merited by his neglected, though incomparable tract, De Jure Regni, in which the principles of popular politics, and the maxims of a free government, are delivered with a precision, and enforced with an energy, which no former age had equalled, and no succeeding one has surpassed. The subsequent progress of the human mind was slow. The profound views of Harrington were derided as the ravings of a visionary; and who can wonder, that the frantic loyalty which depressed Paradise Lost, should involve in ignominy the eloquent Apology of Milton for the People of England against a feeble and venal pedant. Sidney,

"By ancient learning to th' enlighten'd love
Of ancient freedom warm'd,"*

taught the principles which he was to seal with his blood; and Locke, whose praise is less that of being bold and original, than of being temperate, sound, lucid, and methodical, deserves the immortal honour of having systematized and rendered popular the doctrines of civil and religious liberty. In Ireland, Molyneux, the friend of Locke, produced The Case of Ireland,—a production of which it is sufficient praise to say, that it was ordered to be burnt by the despotic parliament. In Scotland, Andrew Fletcher, the scholar of Algernon Sidney, maintained the case of his deserted country with the force of ancient eloquence, and the dignity of ancient virtue. Such is a rapid enumeration of those who had before, or near the Revolution, contributed to the diffusion of political light. But their number was small, their writings were unpopular, their dogmas were proscribed. The habits of reading had only then begun to reach the great body of mankind, whom the arrogance of rank and letters has ignominiously confounded under the denomination of the vulgar.

Many causes too contributed to form a powerful Tory interest in England. The remnant of that Gothic sentiment, the extinction of which Mr. Burke so pathetically deplores, which engrafted loyalty on a point of honour in military attachment, formed one part, which may be called the "Toryism of chivalry." Doctrines of a divine right in kings, which are now too much forgotten even for successful ridicule, were then supported and revered;—these may be called the "Toryism of superstition." A third species arose from the great transfer of property to an upstart commercial interest, which drove the ancient gentry of England, for protection against its inroads, behind the throne;—this may be called the "Toryism of landed aristocracy."† Religious prejudices, outrages on natural sentiments, which any artificial system is too feeble to withstand, and the stream of events which bore them along to extremities which no man could have foreseen, involved the Tories in the Revolution, and made it a truly national act: but their repugnance to every shadow of innovation was invincible.

Something the Whigs may be supposed to have conceded for the sake of conciliation; but few even of their leaders, it is probable, had grand and liberal views. What indeed could have been expected from the delegates of a nation, in which, a few years before, the University of Oxford, representing the national learning and wisdom, had, in a solemn decree, offered their congratulations to Sir George Mackenzie (infamous for the abuse of brilliant accomplishments to the most servile and profligate purposes) for having confuted the abominable doctrines of Buchanan and Milton, and for having demonstrated the divine rights of kings to tyrannise and oppress mankind! It must be evident, that a people who could thus, by the organ of its most learned body, prostrate its reason before such execrable absurdities, was too *young* for legislation. Hence the absurd debates in the Convention about the palliative phrases of "abdicate," "desert," &c., which were better cut short by the Parliament of Scotland, when they used the correct and manly expression, that James II. had "forfeited the throne." Hence we find the Revolutionists perpetually belying their political conduct by their legal phraseology: hence their impotent and illusive reforms: hence their neglect of foresight* in not providing bulwarks against the natural tendency of a disputed succession to accelerate most rapidly the progress of Royal influence, by rendering it necessary to strengthen so much

---

and should our controversies reach the enlightened scholars of a future age, they will probably, with the same reason, smile at the alarms of Mr. Burke.

* Thomson's Summer.

† Principle is respectable, even in its mistakes; and these Tories of the last century were a party of principle. There were accordingly among them men of the most elevated and untainted honour. Who will refuse that praise to Clarendon and Southampton, to Ormonde and Montrose? But Toryism, as a party of principle, cannot now exist in England; for the principles on which we have seen it to be founded, exist no more. The Gothic sentiment is effaced; the superstition is exploded; and the landed and commercial interests are completely intermixed. The Toryism of the present day can only arise from an abject spirit, or a corrupt heart.

* This progress of Royal influence from a disputed succession has, in fact, most fatally taken place. The Protestant succession was the supposed means of preserving our liberties; and to that *means* the *end* has been most deplorably sacrificed. The Whigs, the sincere though timid and partial friends of freedom, were forced to cling to the throne as the anchor of liberty. To preserve it from utter shipwreck, they were forced to yield something to its protectors;—hence a national debt, a septennial Parliament, and a standing army. The avowed reason of the two last was Jacobitism;—hence the unnatural coalition between Whiggism and Kings during the reigns of the two first princes of the House of Hanover, which the pupilage of Leicester House so totally broke.

the possessor of the crown against the pretender to it.

But to elucidate the question more fully, "let us listen to the genuine oracles of Revolution policy;"—not to the equivocal and palliative language of their statutes, but to the unrestrained effusion of sentiment in that memorable conference between the Lords and Commons, on Tuesday the 5th of February, 1688, which terminated in establishing the present government of England. The Tories, yielding to the torrent in the personal exclusion of James, resolved to embarrass the Whigs, by urging that the declaration of the abdication and vacancy of the throne, was a change of the government, *pro hâc vice*, into an elective monarchy. The inference is irresistible: and it must be confessed, that though the Whigs were the better citizens, the Tories were the more correct logicians. It is in this conference that we see the Whig leaders compelled to disclose so much of those principles, which tenderness for prejudice, and reverence for usage, had influenced them to dissemble. It is here that we shall discover sparks kindled in the collision of debate sufficient to enlighten the "politic gloom" in which they had enveloped their measures.

If there be any names venerable among the constitutional lawyers of England, they are those of Lord Somers and Serjeant Maynard. They were both conspicuous managers for the Commons in this conference; and the language of both will more than justify the inferences of Dr. Price, and the creed of the Revolution Society. My Lord Nottingham, who conducted the conference on the part of the Tories, in a manner most honourable to his dexterity and acuteness, demanded of the managers for the Commons:—"Whether they mean the throne to be so vacant as to annul the succession in the hereditary line, and so all the heirs to be cut off? which we (the Lords) say, will make the crown *elective*." Maynard, whose argument always breathed much of the old republican spirit, replied with force and plainness:—"It is not that the Commons do say the crown of England is always and perpetually elective; but it is necessary there be a supply where there is a defect." It is impossible to mistake the import of these words. Nothing can be more evident, than that by the mode of denying "that the crown was always and perpetually elective," he confesses that it was for the then exigency elective. In pursuance of his argument, he uses a comparison strongly illustrative of his belief in dogmas anathematised by Mr. Burke:—"If two of us make a mutual agreement to help and defend each other from any one that should assault us in a journey, and he that is with me turns upon me, and breaks my head, he hath undoubtedly abdicated my assistance, and revoked." Sentiments of the kingly office, more irreverent and more correct, are not to be found in the most profane evangelist that disgraces the Democratic canon. It is not unworthy of incidental remark, that there were then persons who felt as great horror at novelties, which have since been universally received, as Mr. Burke now feels at the "rights of men." The Earl of Clarendon, in his strictures on the speech of Mr. Somers, said:—"I may say thus much in general, that this breaking the original contract is a language that has not long been used in this place, nor known in any of our law books, or public records. It is sprung up but as taken from some late authors, and those none of the best received!" This language one might have supposed to be that of Mr. Burke: it is not however his; it is that of a Jacobite lord of the seventeenth century.

The Tories continued to perplex and intimidate the Whigs with the idea of election. Maynard again replies, "The word 'elective' is none of the Commons' word. The provision must be made, and if it be, that will not render the kingdom perpetually elective." If it were necessary to multiply citations to prove, that the Revolution was to all intents and purposes an election, we might hear Lord Nottingham, whose distinction is peculiarly applicable to the case before us. "If," says he, "you do once make it elective, I do not say you are always bound to go to election; but it is enough to make it so, if by that precedent there be a breach in the hereditary succession." The reasoning of Sir Robert Howard, another of the managers for the Commons, is bold and explicit:—"My Lords, you will do well to consider. Have you not yourselves limited the succession, and cut off some that might have a line of right? Have you not concurred with us in our vote, that it is inconsistent with our religion and our laws to have a Papist to reign over us? Must we not then come to an election, if the next heir be a Papist?"—the precise fact which followed. But what tends the most strongly to illustrate that contradiction between the exoteric and esoteric doctrine,—the legal language, and the real principles,—which forms the basis of this whole argument, is the avowal of Sir Richard Temple, another of the managers for the Commons:—"We are in as natural a capacity as any of our predecessors were to provide for a remedy in such exigencies as this." Hence it followed infallibly, that their posterity to all generations would be in the same "natural capacity," to provide a remedy for such exigencies.

But let us hear their statutes:—there "the Lords Spiritual and Temporal, and Commons, do, in the name of all the people of England, most humbly and faithfully submit themselves, their heirs and posterity for ever," &c. Here is the triumph of Mr. Burke;—a solemn abdication and renunciation of right to change the monarch or the constitution! His triumph is increased by this statutory abolition of the rights of men being copied from a similar profession of eternal allegiance made by the Parliament of Elizabeth.

It is difficult to conceive any thing more preposterous. In the very act of exercising a right which their ancestors had abdicated in their name, they abdicate the same right in the name of their posterity. To increase the ridicule of this legislative farce, they impose an irrevocable law on their posterity, in the precise words of that law irrevocably imposed on them by their ancestors, at the moment when they are violating it. The Parliament of Elizabeth submit themselves and their posterity for ever: the Convention of 1688 spurn the submission for themselves, but re-enact it for their posterity. And after such a glaring inconsistency, this language of statutory adulation is seriously and triumphantly brought forward as "the unerring oracles of Revolution policy."

Thus evidently has it appeared, from the conduct and language of the leaders of the Revolution, that it was a deposition and an election; and that all language of a contrary tendency, which is to be found in their acts, arose from the remnant of their own prejudice, or from concession to the prejudice of others, or from the superficial and presumptuous policy of imposing august illusions on mankind. The same spirit regulated,—the same prejudices impeded their progress in every department. "They acted," says Mr. Burke, "by their ancient States:"—they did not. Were the Peers, and the Members of a dissolved House of Commons, with the Lord Mayor of London, &c. convoked by a summons from the Prince of Orange, the Parliament of England?—no: they were neither lawfully elected, nor lawfully assembled. But they affected a semblance of a Parliament in their Convention, and a semblance of hereditary right in their election. The subsequent Act of Parliament is nugatory; for as that Legislature derived its whole existence and authority from the Convention, it could not return more than it had received, and could not, therefore, legalise the acts of the body which created it. If they were not previously legal, the Parliament itself was without legal authority, and could therefore give no legal sanction.

It is, therefore, without any view to a prior, or allusion to a subsequent revolution, that Dr. Price, and the Revolution Society of London, think themselves entitled to conclude, that abused power is revocable, and that corrupt governments ought to be reformed. Of the first of these Revolutions,—that in 1648, —they may, perhaps, entertain different sentiments from Mr. Burke. They will confess that it was debased by the mixture of fanaticism; they may lament that History has so often prostituted her ungenerous suffrage to success; and that the commonwealth was obscured and overwhelmed by the splendid profligacy of military usurpation: but they cannot arrogate to themselves the praise of having been the first to maintain,—nor can Mr. Burke support his claim to have been the first to reprobate,—since that period, the audacious heresy of popular politics.

The prototype of Mr. Burke is not a less notorious personage than the predecessor he has assigned to Dr. Price. History has preserved fewer memorials of Hugh Peters than of Judge Jeffries. It was the fortune of that luminary and model of lawyers to sit in judgment on one of the fanatical apostles of democracy. In the present ignominious obscurity of the sect in England, it may be necessary to mention, that the name of this criminal was Algernon Sidney, who had, it is true, in his own time acquired some renown,—celebrated as the hero, and deplored as the martyr of freedom. But the learned magistrate was above this "epidemical fanaticism:" he inveighed against his pestilential dogmas in a spirit that deprives Mr. Burke's invective against Dr. Price of all pretensions to originality. An unvarnished statement will so evince the harmony both of the culprits and the accusers, that remark is superfluous:—

"And that the aforesaid Algernon Sidney did make, compose and write, or cause to be made, composed and written, a certain false, scandalous and seditious libel, in which is contained the following English words:—'The Power originally in the people is delegated to the Parliament. He (meaning the King) is subject to the laws of God, as he is a man, and to the people that made him a king, inasmuch as he is a king.' And in another place of the said libel he says, 'We may therefore take away kings without breaking any yoke, or that is made a yoke, which ought not to be one; and the injury therefore is making or imposing, and there can be none in breaking it,' &c."—*Indictment of Algernon Sidney, State Trials*, vol. iii. p. 716.	"We have a right to choose our own governors, to cashier them for misconduct, and to frame a government for ourselves."—*Dr. Price's Sermon.*

Thus we see the harmony of the culprits: the one is only a perspicuous and precise abridgment of the other. The harmony of the judges will not be found less remarkable: Mr. Burke, "when he talks as if he had made a discovery, only follows a precedent:"—

"The King, it says, is responsible to them, and he is only their trustee. He has misgoverned, and he is to give it up, that they may be all kings themselves. Gentlemen, I must tell you, I think I ought, more than ordinarily, to press this on you, because I know the misfortunes of the late unhappy rebellion; and the bringing of the late blessed King to the scaffold was first begun by such kind of principles."—*Jeffries' Charge.*	"The Revolution Society chooses to assert, that a king is no more than the first servant of the public, created by it, and responsible to it." "The second claim of the Revolution Society is cashiering the monarch 'for misconduct."—"The Revolution Society, the heroic band of fabricators of governments, electors of sovereigns."—"This sermon is in a strain which has never been heard in this kingdom in any of the pulpits which are tolerated or encouraged in it since 1648."—*Mr. Burke's Reflections.*

Thus does Mr. Burke chant his political song in exact unison with the strains of the venerable magistrate: they indict the same crimes; they impute the same motives; they dread the same consequences.

The Revolution Society felt, from the great event which they professedly commemorated, new motives to exult in the emancipation of France. The Revolution of 1688 deserves more the attention of a philosopher from its indirect influence on the progress of human opinion, than from its immediate effects on the government of England. In the first view, it is perhaps difficult to estimate the magnitude of its effects. It sanctified, as we have seen, the general principles of freedom. It gave the first example in civilized modern Europe of a government which reconciled a semblance of political, and a large portion of civil liberty, with stability and peace. But above all, Europe owes to it the inestimable blessing of an asylum for freedom of thought. Hence England became the preceptress of the world in philosophy and freedom: hence arose the school of sages, who unshackled and emancipated the human mind; from among whom issued the Lockes, the Rousseaus, the Turgots, and the Franklins,—the immortal band of preceptors and benefactors of mankind. They silently operated a grand moral revolution, which was in due time to ameliorate the social order. They had tyrants to dethrone more formidable than kings, and from whom kings held their power. They wrested the sceptre from Superstition, and dragged Prejudice in triumph. They destroyed the arsenal whence Despotism had borrowed her thunders and her chains. These grand enterprises of philosophic heroism must have preceded the reforms of civil government. The Colossus of tyranny was undermined, and a pebble overthrew it.

With this progress of opinion arose the American Revolution; and from this last, most unquestionably, the delivery of France. Nothing, therefore, could be more natural, than that those who, without blind bigotry for the forms, had a rational reverence for the principles of our ancestors, should rejoice in a Revolution, in which these principles, long suffered to repose in impotent abstraction in England, are called forth into energy, expanded, invigorated, and matured. If, as we have presumed to suppose, the Revolution of 1688 may have had no small share in accelerating the progress of light which has dissolved the prejudices that supported despotism, they may be permitted, besides their exultation as friends of humanity, to indulge some pride as Englishmen.

It must be confessed that our ancestors in 1688, confined, in their practical regulations, their views solely to the urgent abuse. They punished the usurper without ameliorating the government; and they proscribed usurpations without correcting their source. They were content to clear the turbid stream, instead of purifying the polluted fountain. They merit, however, veneration for their achievements, and the most ample amnesty for their defects; for the first were their own, and the last are imputable to the age in which they lived. The true admirers of the Revolution will pardon it for having spared useless establishments, only because they revere it for having established grand principles. But the case of Mr. Burke is different; he deifies its defects, and derides its principles: and were Lord Somers to listen to such misplaced eulogy, and tortured inference, he might justly say, "You deny us the only praise we can claim; and the only merit you allow us is in the sacrifices we were compelled to make to prejudice and ignorance. Your glory is our shame." Reverence for the principles, and pardon of the defects of civil changes, which arise in ages but partially enlightened, are the plain dictates of common sense. Admiration of Magna Charta does not infer any respect for villainage; reverence for Roman patriotism is not incompatible with detestation of slavery; nor does veneration for the Revolutionists of 1688 impose any blindness to the gross, radical, and multiplied absurdities and corruptions in their political system. The true admirers of Revolution principles cannot venerate institutions as sage and effectual protections of freedom, which experience has proved to be nerveless and illusive.

"The practical claim of impeachment,"—the vaunted responsibility of ministers,—is the most sorry juggle of political empiricism by which a people were ever attempted to be lulled into servitude. State prosecutions in free states have ever either languished in impotent and despised tediousness, or burst forth in a storm of popular indignation, that has at once overwhelmed its object, without discrimination of innocence or guilt. Nothing but this irresistible fervor can destroy the barriers within which powerful and opulent delinquents are fortified. If it is not with imminent hazard to equity and humanity gratified at the moment, it subsides. The natural influence of the culprit, and of the accomplices interested in his impunity, resumes its place. As these trials are necessarily long, and the facts which produce conviction, and the eloquence which rouses indignation, are effaced from the public mind by time, by ribaldry, and by sophistry, the shame of a corrupt decision is extenuated. Every source of obloquy or odium that can be attached to the obnoxious and invidious character of an accuser is exhausted by the profuse corruption of the delinquent. The tribunal of public opinion, which alone preserves the purity of others, is itself polluted; and a people wearied, disgusted, irritated, and corrupted, suffer the culprit to retire in impunity and splendour.*

"Damnatus inani
Judicio. Quid enim salvis infamia nummis?"†

Such has ever been the state of things, when

* Part of this description is purely historical. Heaven forbid that the sequel should prove prophetic! — When this subject [the late trial of Warren Hastings.—Ed.] presents Mr. Burke to mind, I must say, "Talis cum sis, utinam noster esses."

† Juvenal, Sat. i.

the force of the Government has been sufficient to protect the accused from the first ebullition of popular impetuosity. The democracies of antiquity presented a spectacle directly the reverse; but no history affords any example of a just medium. State trials will always either be impotent or oppressive,—a persecution or a farce.

Thus vain is the security of impeachment: and equally absurd, surely, is our confidence in "the control of parliaments," in their present constitution, and with their remaining powers. To begin with the last:—they possess the nominal power of impeachment. Not to mention its disuse in the case of any minister for more than seventy years, it is always too late to remedy the evil, and probably always too weak to punish the criminal. They possess a pretended power of withholding supplies: but the situation of society has in truth wrested it from them. The supplies they must vote: for the army must have its pay, and the public creditors their interest. A power that cannot be exercised without provoking mutiny, and proclaiming bankruptcy, the blindest bigot cannot deny to be purely nominal. A practical substitute for these theoretical powers existed till our days in the negative exercised by the House of Commons on the choice of the Minister of the Crown. But the elevation of Mr. Pitt has establised a precedent which has extirpated the last shadow of popular control from the government of England:—

> "Olim vera fides, Sulla Marioque receptis,
> Libertatis obit: Pompeio rebus adempto,
> Nunc et ficta perit."*

In truth, the force and the privileges of Parliament are almost indifferent to the people; for it is not the guardian of their rights, nor the organ of their voice. We are said to be "*unequally* represented." This is one of those contradictory phrases that form the political jargon of half-enlightened periods. Unequal freedom is a contradiction in terms. The law is the deliberate reason of all, guiding their occasional will. Representation is an expedient for peacefully, systematically, and unequivocally collecting this universal voice:—so thought and so spoke the Edmund Burke of better times. "To follow, not to force the public inclination, to give a direction, a form, a technical dress, and a specific sanction to the general sense of the community, is the true end of legislature:"†—there spoke the correspondent of Franklin,‡ the champion of America, the enlightened advocate of humanity and freedom! If these principles be true, and they are so true that it seems almost puerile to repeat them, who can without indignation hear the House of Commons of England called a popular representative body? A more insolent and preposterous abuse of language is not to be found in the vocabulary of tyrants. The criterion that distinguishes laws from dictates, freedom from servitude, rightful government from usurpation,—a law being an expression of the general will,—is wanting. This is the grievance which the admirers of the Revolution of 1688 desire to remedy according to its principles. This is that perennial source of corruption which has increased, is increasing, and ought to be diminished. If the general interest is not the object of our government, it is—it must be because the general will does not govern.

We are boldly challenged to produce our proofs; our complaints are asserted to be chimerical; and the excellence of our government is inferred from its beneficial effects. Most unfortunately for us,—most unfortunately for our country, these proofs are too ready and too numerous. We find them in that "monumental debt," the bequest of wasteful and profligate wars, which already wrings from the peasant something of his hard-earned pittance,—which already has punished the industry of the useful and upright manufacturer, by robbing him of the asylum of his house, and the judgment of his peers,*—to which the madness of political Qŭixotism adds a million for every farthing that the pomp of ministerial empiricism pays,—and which menaces our children with convulsions and calamities, of which no age has seen the parallel. We find them in the black and bloody roll of persecuting statutes that are still suffered to stain our code;—a list so execrable, that were no monument to be preserved of what England was in the eighteenth century but her Statute Book, she might be deemed to have been then still plunged in the deepest gloom of superstitious barbarism. We find them in the ignominious exclusion of great bodies of our fellow-citizens from political trusts, by tests which reward falsehood and punish probity,—which profane the rights of the religion they pretend to guard, and usurp the dominion of the God they profess to revere. We find them in the growing corruption of those who administer the government,—in the venality of a House of Commons, which has become only a cumbrous and expensive chamber for registering ministerial edicts,—in the increase of a nobility degraded by the profusion and prostitution of honours, which the most zealous partisans of democracy would have spared them. We find them, above all, in the rapid progress which has been made in silencing the great organ of public opinion,—that Press, which is the true control over the Ministers and Parliaments, who might else, with impunity, trample on the impotent formalities that form the pretended bulwark of our freedom. The mutual control, the well-poised balance of

* Pharsalia, lib. ix.

† Burke's "Two Letters to Gentlemen in the City of Bristol" (1778), p. 52.

‡ Mr. Burke has had the honour of being traduced for corresponding, during the American war, with this great man, because he was a rebel!

* Alluding to the stringent provisions of the "Tobacco Act."—Ed.

the several members of our Legislature, are the visions of theoretical, or the pretext of practical politicians. It is a government, not of check, but of conspiracy,—a conspiracy which can only be repressed by the energy of popular opinion.

These are no visionary ills,—no chimerical apprehensions: they are the sad and sober reflections of as honest and enlightened men as any in the kingdom. Nor are they alleviated by the torpid and listless security into which the people seem to be lulled. "Summum otium forense non quiescentis sed senescentis civitatis." It is in this fatal temper that men become sufficiently debased and embruted to sink into placid and polluted servitude. It is then that it may most truly be said, that the mind of a country is slain. The admirers of Revolution principles naturally call on every aggrieved and enlightened citizen to consider the source of his oppression. If penal statutes hang over our Catholic brethren,*—if Test Acts outrage our Protestant fellow-citizens,—if the remains of feudal tyranny are still suffered to exist in Scotland,—if the press is fettered,—if our right to trial by jury is abridged,—if our manufacturers are proscribed and hunted down by excise,—the reason of all these oppressions is the same:—no branch of the Legislature represents the people. Men are oppressed because they have no share in their own government. Let all these classes of oppressed citizens melt their local and partial grievances into one great mass. Let them cease to be suppliants for their rights, or to sue for them like mendicants, as a precarious boon from the arrogant pity of usurpers. Until the Legislature speaks their voice it will oppress them. Let them unite to procure such a Reform in the representation of the people as will make the House of Commons their representative. If, dismissing all petty views of obtaining their own particular ends, they unite for this great object, they must succeed. The co-operating efforts of so many bodies of citizens must awaken the nation; and its voice will be spoken in a tone that virtuous governors will obey, and tyrannical ones must dread.

This tranquil and legal Reform is the ultimate object of those whom Mr. Burke has so foully branded. In effect, this would be amply sufficient. The powers of the King and the Lords have never been formidable in England, but from discords between the House of Commons and its pretended constituents. Were that House really to become the vehicle of the popular voice, the privileges of other bodies, in opposition to the sense of the people and their representatives, would be but as dust in the balance. From this radical improvement all subaltern reform would naturally and peaceably arise. We dream of no more; and in claiming this, instead of meriting the imputation of being apostles of sedition, we conceive ourselves entitled to be considered as the most sincere friends of tranquil and stable government. We desire to avert revolution by reform,—subversion by correction.* We admonish our governors to reform, while they retain the force to reform with dignity and security; and we conjure them not to await the moment, which will infallibly arrive, when they shall be obliged to supplicate that people, whom they oppress and despise, for the slenderest pittance of their present powers.

The grievances of England do not now, we confess, justify a change by violence: but they are in a rapid progress to that fatal state, in which they will both justify and produce it. It is because we sincerely love tranquil freedom,† that we earnestly deprecate the arrival of the moment when virtue and honour shall compel us to seek her with our swords. Are not they the true friends to authority who desire, that whatever is granted by it "should issue as a gift of her bounty and beneficence, rather than as claims recovered against a struggling litigant? Or, at least, that if her beneficence obtained no credit in her concessions, they should appear the salutary provisions of wisdom and foresight, not as things wrung with blood by the cruel gripe of a rigid necessity."‡ We desire that the political light which is to break in on England should be "through well-contrived and well-disposed windows, not through flaws and breaches,—through the yawning chasms of our ruin."§

Such was the language of Mr. Burke in cases nearly parallel to the present. But of those who now presume to give similar counsels, his alarm and abhorrence are extreme. They deem the "present times" favourable "to all exertions in the cause of liberty." They naturally must: their hopes in that great cause are from the determined and recording voices of enlightened men. The shock that has destroyed the despotism of France has widely dispersed the clouds that intercepted reason from the political and

* No body of men in any state that pretends to freedom have ever been so insolently oppressed as the Catholic majority of Ireland. Their cause has been lately pleaded by an eloquent advocate, whose virtues might have been supposed to have influenced my praise, as the partial dictate of friendship, had not his genius extorted it as a strict tribute to justice. I perceive that he retains much of that admiration which we cherished in common, by his classical quotation respecting Mr. Burke:—

" Uni quippe vacat, studiisque odiisque carenti,
Humanum legere genus." Pharsalia, lib. ii.

See "The Constitutional Interests of Ireland with respect to the Popery Laws," (Dublin, 1791,) part iv.

* Let the governors of all states compare the convulsion which the obstinacy of the Government provoked in France, with the peaceful and dignified reform which its wisdom effected in Poland. The moment is important, the dilemma inevitable, the alternative awful, the lesson most instructive.

† " Manus hæc inimica tyrannis
Ense petit placidam sub libertate quietem."
[The lines inserted by Algernon Sidney in the Album of the University of Copenhagen.—Ed.]

‡ Burke, Speech at Bristol.

§ Ibid.

moral world; and we cannot suppose, that England is the only spot that has not been reached by this "flood of light" that has burst upon the human race. We might suppose, too, that Englishmen would be shamed out of their torpor by the great exertions of nations whom we had long deemed buried in hopeless servitude.

But nothing can be more absurd than to assert, that all who admire wish to imitate the French Revolution. In one view, there is room for diversity of opinion among the warmest and wisest friends of freedom,—as to the amount of democracy infused into the new government. In another, and a more important one, it is to be recollected, that the conduct of nations is apt to vary with the circumstances in which they are placed. Blind admirers of Revolutions take them for implicit models. Thus Mr. Burke admires that of 1688: but we, who conceive that we pay the purest homage to the authors of that Revolution, not in contending for what they then did, but for what they now would do, can feel no inconsistency in looking on France, not to model our conduct, but to invigorate the spirit of freedom. We permit ourselves to imagine how Lord Somers, in the light and knowledge of the eighteenth century,—how the patriots of France, in the tranquillity and opulence of England, would have acted. We are not bound to copy the conduct to which the last were driven by a bankrupt exchequer and a dissolved government, nor to maintain the establishments, which were spared by the first in a prejudiced and benighted age. Exact imitation is not necessary to reverence. We venerate the principles which presided in both events; and we adapt to political admiration a maxim which has long been received in polite letters,—that the only manly and liberal imitation is to speak as a great man would have spoken, had he lived in our times, and had been placed in our circumstances.

But let us hear the charge of Mr. Burke. "Is our monarchy to be annihilated, with all the laws, all the tribunals, all the ancient corporations of the kingdom? Is every landmark of the kingdom to be done away in favour of a geometrical and arithmetical constitution? Is the House of Lords to be useless? Is episcopacy to be abolished?"—and, in a word, is France to be imitated? Yes! if our governors imitate her policy, the state must follow her catastrophe. Man is every where man: imprisoned grievance will at length have vent; and the storm of popular passion will find a feeble obstacle in the solemn imbecility of human institutions. But who are the true friends of order, the prerogative of the monarch, the splendour of the hierarchy, and the dignity of the peerage?—those most certainly who inculcate, that to withhold Reform is to stimulate convulsion,—those who admonish all to whom honour, and rank, and dignity, and wealth are dear, that they can only in the end preserve them by conceding, while the moment of concession remains,—those who aim at draining away the fountains that feed the torrent, instead of opposing puny barriers to its course. "The beginnings of confusion in England are at present feeble enough; but with you we have seen an infancy still more feeble growing by moments into a strength to heap mountains upon mountains, and to wage war with Heaven itself. Whenever our neighbour's house is on fire, it cannot be amiss for the engines to play a little upon our own." This language, taken in its most natural sense, is exactly what the friends of Reform in England would adopt. Every gloomy tint that is added to the horrors of the French Revolution by the tragic pencil of Mr. Burke, is a new argument in support of their claims; and those only are the real enemies of the Nobility, the Priesthood, and other bodies of men that suffer in such convulsions, who stimulate them to unequal and desperate conflicts. Such are the sentiments of those who can admire without servilely copying recent changes, and can venerate the principles without superstitiously defending the corrupt reliques of old revolutions.

"Grand, swelling sentiments of liberty," says Mr. Burke, "I am sure I do not despise. Old as I am, I still read the fine raptures of Lucan and Corneille with pleasure." Long may that virtuous and venerable age enjoy such pleasures! But why should he be indignant that "the glowing sentiment and the lofty speculation should have passed from the schools and the closet to the senate," and no longer only serving

"To point a moral or adorn a tale,"*

should be brought home to the business and the bosoms of men? The sublime genius, whom Mr. Burke admires, and who sung the obsequies of Roman freedom, has one sentiment, which the friends of liberty in England, if they are like him condemned to look abroad for a free government, must adopt:—

"Redituraque nunquam
Libertas ultra Tigrim Rhenumque recessit,
Et toties nobis jugulo quæsita negatur."†

SECTION VI.

Speculations on the probable consequences of the French Revolution in Europe.

THERE is perhaps only one opinion about the French Revolution in which its friends and its enemies agree:—they both conceive that its influence will not be confined to France; they both predict that it will produce important changes in the general state of Europe. This is the theme of the exultation of its admirers; this is the source of the alarms of its detractors. It were indeed difficult to suppose that a Revolution so un-

* Vanity of Human Wishes.—ED.
† Pharsalia, lib. vii.

paralleled should take place in the most renowned of the European nations, without spreading its influence throughout the Christian commonwealth; connected as it is by the multiplied relations of politics, by the common interest of commerce, by the wide intercourse of curiosity and of literature, by similar arts, and by congenial manners. The channels by which the prevailing sentiments of France may enter into the other nations of Europe, are so obvious and so numerous, that it would be unnecessary and tedious to detail them; but I may remark, as among the most conspicuous, a central situation, a predominating language, and an authority almost legislative in the ceremonial of the private intercourse of life. These and many other causes must facilitate the diffusion of French politics among neighbouring nations: but it will be justly remarked, that their effect must in a great measure depend on the stability of the Revolution. The suppression of an honourable revolt would strengthen all the governments of Europe: the view of a splendid revolution would be the signal of insurrection to their subjects. Any reasonings on the influence of the French Revolution may therefore be supposed to be premature until its permanence be ascertained. Of that permanence my conviction is firm: but I am sensible that in the field of political prediction, where veteran sagacity* has so often been deceived, it becomes me to harbour with distrust, and to propose with diffidence, a conviction influenced by partial enthusiasm, and perhaps produced by the inexperienced ardour of youth.

The moment at which I write (August 25th, 1791,) is peculiarly critical. The invasion of France is now spoken of as immediate by the exiles and their partisans; and a confederacy of despots† is announced with new confidence. Notwithstanding these threats, I retain my doubts whether the jarring interests of the European Courts will permit this alliance to have much energy or cordiality; and whether the cautious prudence of despots will send their military slaves to a school of freedom in France. But if there be doubts about the likelihood of the enterprise being undertaken, there be few about the probability of its event. History celebrates many conquests of obscure tribes, whose valour was animated by enthusiasm; but she records no example where a foreign force has subjugated a powerful and gallant people, governed by the most imperious passion that can sway the human breast.*—Whatever wonders fanaticism has performed, may be again effected by a passion as ardent, though not so transitory, because it is sanctioned by virtue and reason. To animate patriotism,—to silence tumult,—to banish division,—would be the only effects of an invasion in the present state of France. A people abandoned to its own inconstancy, have often courted the yoke which they had thrown off: but to oppose foreign hostility to the enthusiasm of a nation, can only have the effect of adding to it ardour, and constancy, and force. These and similar views must offer themselves to the European Cabinets; but perhaps they perceive themselves to be placed in so peculiar a situation, that exertion and inactivity are equally perilous. If they fail in the attempt to crush the infant liberty of France, the ineffectual effort will recoil on their own governments: if they tamely suffer a school† of freedom to be founded in the centre of Europe, they must foresee the hosts of disciples that are to issue from it for the subversion of their despotism.

They cannot be blind to a species of danger which the history of Europe reveals to them in legible characters. They see, indeed, that the negotiations, the wars, and the revolutions of vulgar policy, pass away without leaving behind them any vestige of their transitory and ignominious operation: but they must remark also, that be-

* Witness the memorable example of Harrington, who published a demonstration of the impossibility of re-establishing monarchy in England six months before the restoration of Charles II. Religious prophecies have usually the inestimable convenience of relating to a distant futurity.

† The malignant hostility displayed against French freedom by a perfidious Prince, who occupies and dishonours the throne of Gustavus Vasa, cannot excite our wonder, though it may provoke our indignation. The pensioner of French despotism could not rejoice in its destruction; nor could a monarch, whose boasted talents have hitherto been confined to perjury and usurpation, fail to be wounded by the establishment of freedom: for freedom demands genius, not intrigue,—wisdom, not cunning.

* May I be permitted to state how the ancestors of a nation now stigmatized for servility, felt this powerful sentiment? The Scottish Nobles, contending for their liberty under Robert Bruce, thus spoke to the Pope:—"Non pugnamus propter divitias, honores, aut dignitates, sed propter libertatem tantummodo, quam nemo bonus nisi simul cum vitâ amittit!" Nor was this sentiment confined to the Magnates; for the same letter declares the assent of the Commons:—"Totaque Communitas Regni Scotiæ!" Reflecting on the various fortunes of my country, I cannot exclude from my mind the comparison between its present reputation and our ancient character,—"terrarum et libertatis extremos:" nor can I forget the honourable reproach against the Scottish name in the character of Buchanan by Thuanus, (Hist. lib. lxxvi. cap. 11,) "Libertate genti innatâ in regium fastigium acerbior." This melancholy retrospect is however relieved by the hope that a gallant and enlightened people will not be slow in renewing the era for such reproaches.

† The most important materials for the philosophy of history are collected from remarks on the coincidence of the situations and sentiments of distant periods; and it may be curious as well as instructive, to present to the reader the topics by which the Calonnes of Charles I. were instructed, to awaken the jealousy and solicit the aid of the European courts:—"A dangerous combination of his Majesty's subjects have laid a design to dissolve the monarchy and frame of government, becoming a dangerous precedent to all the monarchies of Christendom, if attended with success in their design."—Charles I.'s Instructions to his Minister in Denmark, Ludlow's Memoirs, vol. iii. p. 257.

sides this monotonous villany, there are cases in which Europe, actuated by a common passion, has appeared as one nation. The religious passion animated and guided the spirit of chivalry:—hence arose the Crusades. "A nerve was touched of exquisite feeling; and the sensation vibrated to the heart of Europe."* In the same manner the Reformation gave rise to religious wars, the duration of which exceeded a century and a half. Both examples prove the existence of that sympathy, by the means of which a great passion, taking its rise in any considerable state of Europe, must circulate through the whole Christian commonwealth. Illusion is, however, transient, while truth is immortal. The epidemical fanaticism of former times was short-lived, for it could only flourish in the eclipse of reason: but the virtuous enthusiasm of liberty, though it be like that fanaticism contagious, is not like it transitory.

But there are other circumstances which entitle us to expect, that the example of France will have a mighty influence on the subjects of despotic governments. The Gothic governments of Europe have lived their time. "Man, and for ever!" is the sage exclamation of Mr. Hume.† Limits are no less rigorously prescribed by Nature to the age of governments than to that of individuals. The Heroic governments of Greece yielded to a body of legislative republics: these were in their turn swallowed up by the conquests of Rome. That great empire itself, under the same forms, passed through various modes of government. The first usurpers concealed it under a republican disguise: their successors threw off the mask, and avowed a military despotism: it expired in the ostentatious feebleness of an Asiatic monarchy.‡ It was overthrown by savages, whose rude institutions and barbarous manners have, until our days, influenced Europe with a permanance refused to wiser and milder laws. But, unless historical analogy be altogether delusive, the decease of the Gothic governments cannot be distant. Their maturity is long past: and symptoms of their decrepitude are rapidly accumulating. Whether they are to be succeeded by more beneficial or more injurious forms may be doubted; but that they are about to perish, we are authorized to suppose, from the usual age to which the governments recorded in history have arrived.

There are also other presumptions furnished by historical analogy, which favour the supposition that legislative governments are about to succeed to the rude usurpations of Gothic Europe. The commonwealths which in the sixth and seventh centuries before the Christian era were erected on the ruins of the heroic monarchies of Greece, are perhaps the only genuine example of governments truly legislative recorded in history. A close inspection will, perhaps, discover some coincidence between the circumstances which formed them and those which now influence the state of Europe. The Phenician and Egyptian colonies were not like our colonies in America, populous enough to subdue or extirpate the native savages of Greece: they were, however, sufficiently so to instruct and civilize them. From that alone could their power be derived: to that therefore were their efforts directed. Imparting the arts and the knowledge of polished nations to rude tribes, they attracted, by avowed superiority of knowledge, a submission necessary to the effect of their legislation,—a submission which impostors acquire through superstition, and conquerors derive from force. An age of legislation supposes great inequality of knowledge between the legislators and those who receive their institutions. The Asiatic colonists, who first scattered the seeds of refinement, possessed this superiority over the Pelasgic hordes; and the legislators who in subsequent periods organised the Grecian commonwealths, acquired from their travels in the polished states of the East, that reputation of superior knowledge, which enabled them to dictate laws to their fellow-citizens. Let us then compare Egypt and Phenicia with the enlightened part of Europe,—separated as widely from the general mass by the moral difference of instruction, as these countries were from Greece by the physical obstacles which impeded a rude navigation,—and we must discern, that philosophers become legislators are colonists from an enlightened country reforming the institutions of rude tribes. The present moment indeed resembles with wonderful exactness the legislative age of Greece. The multitude have attained sufficient knowledge to value the superiority of enlightened men; and they retain a sufficient consciousness of ignorance to preclude rebellion against their dictates. Philosophers have meanwhile long remained a distinct nation in the midst of an unenlightened multitude. It is only now that the conquests of the press are enlarging the dominion of reason; as the vessels of Cadmus and Cecrops spread the arts and the wisdom of the East among the Pelasgic barbarians.

These general causes,—the unity of the European commonwealth, the decrepitude on which its fortuitous governments are verging, and the similarity between our age and the only recorded period when the ascendant of philosophy dictated laws,—entitle us to hope that freedom and reason will be rapidly propagated from their source in France. And there are not wanting symptoms which justify the speculation. The first symptoms which indicate the approach of

* Gibbon, Decline and Fall, &c., chap. lvii.

† Philosophical Works, vol. iii. p. 579.—Ed.

‡ See this progress stated in the concise philosophy of Montesquieu, and illustrated by the copious eloquence of Gibbon. The republican disguise extends from Augustus to Severus; the military despotism from Severus to Diocletian; the Asiatic *Sultanship* from Diocletian to the final extinction of the Roman name.

a contagious disease are the precautions adopted against it: the first marks of the probable progress of French principles are the alarms betrayed by despots. The Courts of Europe seem to look on France, and to exclaim in their despair,—

"Hinc populum late regem, belloque superbum,
Venturum excidio Libyæ."

The King of Spain already seems to tremble for his throne, though it be erected on so firm a basis of general ignorance and triumphant priestcraft. By expelling foreigners, and by subjecting the entrance of travellers to such multiplied restraints, he seeks the preservation of his despotism in a vain attempt to convert his kingdom into a Bastile, and to banish his subjects from the European commonwealth. The Chinese government has indeed thus maintained its permanency; but it is insulated by Nature more effectually than by policy. Let the Court of Madrid recall her ambassadors, shut up her ports, abandon her commerce, sever every tie that unites her to Europe: the effect of such shallow policy must be that of all ineffectual rigour (and all rigour short of extirpation is here ineffectual), to awaken reflection,—to stimulate inquiry,—to aggravate discontent, —and to provoke convulsion. "There are no longer Pyrenees," said Louis XIV., on the accession of his grandson to the Spanish throne: "There are no longer Pyrenees," exclaimed the alarmed statesmen of Aranjuez,—"to protect our despotism from being consumed by the sun of liberty." The alarm of the Pope for the little remnant of his authority naturally increases with the probability of the diffusion of French principles. Even the mild and temperate aristocracies of Switzerland seem to apprehend the arrival of that period, when men will not be content to owe the benefits of government to the fortuitous character of their governors, but to its own intrinsic excellence. Even the unsuccessful struggle of Liege, and the theocratic insurrection of Brabant, have left behind them traces of a patriotic party, whom a more favourable moment may call into more successful action. The despotic Court of the Hague is betraying alarm that the Dutch republic may yet revive, on the destruction of a government odious and intolerable to an immense majority of the people. Every where then are those alarms discernible, which are the most evident symptoms of the approaching downfall of the European despotisms.

But the impression produced by the French Revolution in England,—in an enlightened country, which had long boasted of its freedom,—merits more particular remark. Before the publication of Mr. Burke, the public were not recovered from that astonishment into which they had been plunged by unexampled events, and the general opinion could not have been collected with precision. But that performance has divided the nation into marked parties. It has produced a controversy, which may be regarded as the trial of the French Revolution before the enlightened and independent tribunal of the English public. What its decision has been I shall not presume to decide; for it does not become an advocate to announce the decision of the judge. But this I may be permitted to remark, that the conduct of our enemies has not resembled the usual triumph of those who have been victorious in the war of reason. Instead of the triumphant calmness that is ever inspired by conscious superiority, they have betrayed the bitterness of defeat, and the ferocity of resentment, which are peculiar to the black revenge of detected imposture. Priestcraft and Toryism have been supported only by literary advocates of the most miserable description: but they have been ably aided by auxiliaries of another kind. Of the two great classes of enemies to political reform,—the interested and the prejudiced,—the activity of the first usually supplies what may be wanting in the talents of the last. Judges have forgotten the dignity of their function,—priests the mildness of their religion; the Bench, which should have spoken with the serene temper of justice, the Pulpit, whence only should have issued the healing sounds of charity, have been prostituted to party purposes, and polluted with invectives against freedom. The churches have resounded with language at which Laud would have shuddered, and Sacheverell would have blushed: the most profane comparisons between our duty to the Divinity and to kings, have been unblushingly pronounced: flattery of the Ministers has been mixed with the solemnities of religion, by the servants, and in the temple of God. These profligate proceedings have not been limited to a single spot: they have been general over England. In many churches the French Revolution has been *expressly named*: in a majority it was the constant theme of invective for many weeks before its intended celebration. Yet these are the peaceful pastors, who so sincerely and meekly deprecate political sermons.*

Nor was this sufficient. The grossness of the popular mind, on which political invective made but a faint impression, was to be roused into action by religious fanaticism,—the most intractable and domineering of all destructive passions. A clamour which had for half a century lain dormant has been revived:—the Church was in danger! The spirit of persecution against an unpopular sect has been artfully excited; and the friends of freedom, whom it might be odious and dangerous professedly to attack, are to be overwhelmed as Dissenters. That the ma-

* These are no vague accusations. A sermon was preached in a parish church in Middlesex on the anniversary of the Restoration, in which eternal punishment was denounced against political disaffection! Persons for whose discernment and veracity I can be responsible, were among the indignant auditors of this infernal homily.

jority of the advocates for the French Revolution are not Dissenters is, indeed, sufficiently known to their enemies. They are well known to be philosophers and friends of humanity, superior to the creed of any sect, and indifferent to the dogmas of any popular faith. But it has suited the purpose of their profligate adversaries to confound them with the Dissenters, and to animate against them the fury of prejudices which those very adversaries despised.

The diffusion of these invectives has produced those obvious and inevitable effects, which it may require something more than candour to suppose not foreseen and desired. A banditti, which had been previously stimulated, as it has since been excused and panegyrized by incendiary libellers, have wreaked their vengeance on a philosopher,* illustrious by his talents and his writings, venerable for the spotless purity of his life, and amiable for the unoffending simplicity of his manners. The excesses of this mob of churchmen and loyalists are to be poorly expiated by the few misguided victims who are sacrificed to the vengeance of the law.

We are, however, only concerned with these facts, as they are evidence from our enemies of the probable progress of freedom. The probability of that progress they all conspire to prove. The briefs of the Pope, and the pamphlets of Mr. Burke, the edicts of the Spanish Court, and the mandates of the Spanish inquisition, the Birmingham rioters, and the Oxford graduates, equally render to Liberty the involuntary homage of their alarm.

* Alluding to the destruction of Dr. Priestley's house in the neighbourhood of Birmingham by the mob, on the 14th of July, 1791.—Ed.

REASONS

AGAINST THE FRENCH WAR OF 1793.*

At the commencement of the year 1793 the whole body of the supporters of the war seemed unanimous; yet even then was perceptible the germ of a difference which time and events have since unfolded. The Minister had early and frequent recourse to the high principles of Mr. Burke, in order to adorn his orations,—to assail his antagonists in debate,—to blacken the character of the enemy,—and to arouse the national spirit against them. Amid the fluctuating fortune of the war, he seemed in the moment of victory to deliver opinions scarcely distinguishable from those of Mr. Burke, and to recede from them by imperceptible degrees, as success abandoned the arms of the Allies. When the armies of the French republic were every where triumphant, and the pecuniary embarrassments of Great Britain began to be severely felt, he at length dismissed altogether the consideration of the internal state of France, and professed to view the war as merely defensive against aggressions committed on Great Britain and her allies.

That the war was not just on such principles perhaps a very short argument will be sufficient to demonstrate. War is just only to those by whom it is unavoidable; and every appeal to arms is unrighteous, except that of a nation which has no other resource for the maintenance of its security or the assertion of its honour. Injury and insult do not of themselves make it lawful for a nation to seek redress by war, because they do not make it necessary: another means of redress is still in her power, and it is still her duty to employ it. It is not either injury or insult; but injury for which reparation has been asked and denied, or insult for which satisfaction has been demanded and refused, that places her in a state in which, having in vain employed every other means of vindicating her rights, she may justly assert them by arms. Any commonwealth, therefore, which shuts up the channel of negotiation while disputes are depending, is the author of the war which may follow. As a perfect equality prevails in the society and intercourse of nations, no state is bound to degrade herself by submitting to unavowed and clandestine negotiation; but every government has a perfect right to be admitted to that open, avowed, authorized, honourable negotiation which in the practice of nations is employed for the pacific adjustment of their contested claims. To refuse authorized negotiation is to refuse the only negotiation to which a government is forced to submit: it is, therefore, in effect to refuse negotiation altogether; and it follows, as a necessary consequence, that they who refuse such authorized negotiation are responsible for a war which that refusal makes on their part unjust.

These principles apply with irresistible force to the conduct of the English Government in the commencement of the present war. They complained, perhaps justly, of the opening of the Scheldt,—of the Decree of Fraternity,—of the countenance shown to disaffected Englishmen: but they refused

* From the Monthly Review, vol. xl. p. 435.—Ed.

that authorised intercourse with the French Government through its ambassador, M. Chauvelin, which *might* have amicably terminated these disputes. It is no answer that they were ready to carry on a clandestine correspondence with that government through Noel and Maret, or any other of its secret agents. That Government was not obliged to submit to such an intercourse; and the British Government put itself in the wrong by refusing an intercourse of another sort.

No difficulties arising from a refusal to negotiate embarrass the system of Mr. Burke. It is founded on the principle that the nature of the French Government is a just ground of war for its destruction, and regards the particular acts of that government no farther than as they are proofs of its irreconcilable hostility to all other states and communities.

We are not disposed to deny that so mighty a change in the frame of government and the state of society, of one of the greatest nations of the civilized world, as was effected by the Revolution in France,—attended by such extravagant opinions, and producing such violent passions,—was of a nature to be dangerous to the several governments and to the quiet of the various communities, which compose the great commonwealth of Europe. To affirm the contrary would be in effect to maintain that man is not the creature of sympathy and imitation,—that he is not always disposed, in a greater or less degree, to catch the feelings, to imbibe the opinions, and to copy the conduct of his fellow-men. Most of the revolutions which have laid ancient systems in ruins, and changed the whole face of society, have sprung from these powerful and active principles of human nature. The remote effect of these revolutions has been sometimes beneficial and sometimes pernicious: but the evil which accompanied them has ever been great and terrible; their future tendency was necessarily ambiguous and contingent; and their ultimate consequences were always dependent on circumstances much beyond the control of the agents. With these opinions, the only question that can be at issue between Mr. Burke and ourselves is, whether a war was a just, effectual, and safe mode of averting the danger with which the French Revolution might threaten the established governments of Europe;—just in its principle,—effectual for its proposed end,—and safe from the danger of collateral evil. On all the three branches of this comprehensive question we are obliged to dissent very widely from the opinions of Mr. Burke.

We are not required to affirm universally that there never are cases in which the state of the internal government of a foreign nation may become a just ground of war; and we know too well the danger of universal affirmations to extend our line of posts farther than is absolutely necessary for our own defence. We are not convinced of the fact that the French Government in the year 1791 (when the Royal confederacy originated) was of such a nature as to be incapable of being so ripened and mitigated by a wise moderation in the surrounding Powers, that it might not become perfectly safe and inoffensive to the neighbouring states. Till this fact be proved, the whole reasoning of Mr. Burke appears to us inconclusive. Whatever may be done by prudence and forbearance is not to be attempted by war. Whoever, therefore, proposes war as the means of attaining any public good, or of averting any public evil, must first prove that his object is unattainable by any other means. And peculiarly heavy is the burden of proof on the man who, in such cases as the present, is the author of violent counsels,—which, even when they are most specious in promise, are hard and difficult in trial, as well as most uncertain in their issue,—which usually preclude any subsequent recurrence to milder and more moderate expedients,—and from which a safe retreat is often difficult, and an honourable retreat is generally impossible.

Great and evident indeed must be the necessity which can justify a war that in its nature must impair, and in its effects may subvert, the sacred principle of national independence,—the great master-principle of public morality, from which all the rules of the law of nations flow, and which they are all framed only to defend,—of which the balance of power itself (for which so many wars, in our opinion just, have been carried on) is only a safeguard and an outwork,—and of which the higher respect and the more exact observance have so happily distinguished our western parts of Europe, in these latter times, above all other ages and countries of the world. Under the guard of this venerable principle, our European societies, with the most different forms of government and the greatest inequalities of strength, have subsisted and flourished in almost equal security,—the character of man has been exhibited in all that variety and vigour which are necessary for the expansion and display both of his powers and of his virtues,—the spring and spirit and noble pride and generous emulation, which arise from a division of territory among a number of independent states, have been combined with a large measure of that tranquil security which has been found so rarely reconcilable with such a division,—the opinion of enlightened Europe has furnished a mild but not altogether ineffectual, control over the excesses of despotism itself,—and the victims of tyranny have at least found a safe and hospitable asylum in foreign countries from the rage of their native oppressors. It has alike exempted us from the lethargic quiet of extensive empire,—from the scourge of wide and rapid conquest,—and from the pest of frequent domestic revolutions.

This excellent principle, like every other rule which governs the moral conduct of men, may be productive of occasional evil. It must be owned that the absolute independence of states, and their supreme exclusive jurisdiction over all acts done within their own territory, secure an impunity to the most atrocious crimes either of usurpers or of lawful governments degenerated into tyrannies. There is no tribunal competent to punish such crimes, because it is not for the interest of mankind, to vest in any tribunal an authority adequate to their punishment; and it is better that these crimes should be unpunished, than that nations should not be independent. To admit such an authority would only be to supply fresh incitements to ambition and rapine,—to multiply the grounds of war,—to sharpen the rage of national animosity,—to destroy the confidence of independence and internal quiet,—and to furnish new pretexts for invasion, for conquest, and for partition. When the Roman general Flaminius was accomplishing the conquest of Greece, under pretence of enfranchising the Grecian republics, he partly covered his ambitious designs under colour of punishing the atrocious crimes of the Lacedæmonian tyrant Nabis.* When Catherine II. and her accomplices perpetrated the greatest crime which any modern government has ever committed against another nation, it was easy for them to pretend that the partition of Poland was necessary for the extirpation of Jacobinism in the north of Europe.

We are therefore of opinion that the war proposed by Mr. Burke is unjust, both because it has not been proved that no other means than war could have preserved us from the danger; and because war was an expedient, which it was impossible to employ for such a purpose, without shaking the authority of that great tutelary principle, under the shade of which the nations of Europe have so long flourished in security. There is no case of fact made out to which the principles of the law of vicinage are to apply. If the fact had been proved, we might confess the justice of the war; though even in that case its wisdom and policy would still remain to be considered.

The first question to be discussed in the examination of every measure of policy is, whether it is likely to be effectual for its proposed ends. That the war against France was inadequate to the attainment of its object, is a truth which is now demonstrated by fatal experience; but which, in our opinion, at the time of its commencement, was very evident to men of sagacity and foresight. The nature of the means to be employed was of itself sufficient to prove their inadequacy. The first condition essential to the success of the war was, that the confederacy of ambitious princes who were to carry it on, should become perfectly wise, moderate, and disinterested,—that they should bury in oblivion past animosities and all mutual jealousies—that they should sacrifice every view of ambition and every opportunity of aggrandisement to the great object of securing Europe from general confusion by re-establishing the ancient monarchy of France. No man has proved this more unanswerably than Mr. Burke himself. This moderation and this disinterestedness were not only necessary for the union of the Allies, but for the disunion of France.

But we will venture to affirm, that the supposition of a disinterested confederacy of ambitious princes is as extravagant a chimera as any that can be laid to the charge of the wildest visionaries of democracy. The universal peace of the Abbé St. Pierre was plausible and reasonable, when compared with this supposition. The universal republic of Anacharsis Cloots himself was not much more irreconcilable with the uniform experience and sober judgment of mankind. We are far from confounding two writers,—one of whom was a benevolent visionary and the other a sanguinary madman,—who had nothing in common but the wildness of their predictions and the extravagance of their hopes. The Abbé St. Pierre had the simplicity to mistake an ingenious raillery of the Cardinal Fleuri for a deliberate adoption of his reveries. That minister had told him "that he had forgotten an indispensable preliminary—that of sending a body of missionaries to turn the hearts and minds of the princes of Europe." Mr. Burke, with all his knowledge of human nature, and with all his experience of public affairs, has forgotten a circumstance as important as that which was overlooked by the simple and recluse speculator. He has forgotten that he must have made ambition disinterested,—power moderate,—the selfish generous,—and the short-sighted wise, before he could hope for success in the contest which he recommended.* To say that if the authors of the partition of Poland could be made perfectly wise and honest, they might prevail over the French democracy, is very little more than the most chimerical projector has to offer for his wildest scheme. Such an answer only gives us this new and important information, that impracticable projects will be realised when insurmountable obstacles are overcome. Who are you that presume to frame laws for men without taking human passions into account,—to regulate the actions of mankind

* Livy, lib. xxxiv. cap. 24. The whole narrative is extremely curious, and not without resemblance and application to later events.

* Perhaps something more of flexibility of character and accommodation of temper,—a mind more broken down to the practice of the world,—would have fitted Mr. Burke better for the execution of that art which is the sole instrument of political wisdom, and without which the highest political wisdom is but barren speculation—we mean the art of guiding and managing mankind. How can he have forgotten that these vulgar politicians were the only tools with which he had to work in reducing his schemes to practice? These "creatures of the desk and creatures of favour" unfortunately govern Europe. The ends of generosity were to be compassed alone through the agency of the selfish; and the objects of prospective wisdom were to be attained by the exertions of the short-sighted. — Monthly Review (*N. S.*), vol. xix. p. 317.—Ed.

without regarding the source and principle of those actions? A chemist who in his experiments should forget the power of steam or of electricity, would have no right to be surprised that his apparatus should be shivered to pieces, and his laboratory covered with the fragments.

It must be owned, indeed, that no one could have ventured to predict the extent and extravagance of that monstrous and almost incredible infatuation which has distracted the strength and palsied the arms of the Allied Powers: but it was easy to foresee, and it was in fact predicted, that a sufficient degree of that infatuation must prevail to defeat the attainment of their professed object. We cannot help expressing our surprise, that the immense difference in this respect between the present confederacy and the Grand Alliance of King William III. did not present itself to the great understanding of Mr. Burke. This is a war to avert the danger of the French Revolution, in which it is indispensably necessary to avoid all appearance of a design to aggrandise the Allies at the expense of France. The other was one designed to limit the exorbitant power of Louis, which was chiefly to be effected by diminishing his overgrown dominions. The members of that confederacy gratified their own ambition by the same means which provided for the general safety. In that contest, every conquest promoted the general object:—in this, every conquest retards and tends to defeat it. No romantic moderation—no chimerical disinterestedness—no sacrifice of private aggrandisement to the cause of Europe, was required in that confederacy. Yet, with that great advantage, it is almost the only one recorded in history, which was successful. Still it required, to build it up, and hold it together, all the exalted genius, all the comprehensive wisdom, all the disinterested moderation, and all the unshaken perseverance of William*—other talents than those of petty intrigue and pompous declamation. The bitterest enemies of our present ministers could scarcely imagine so cruel a satire upon them, as any comparison between their talents and policy, and those of the great monarch. The disapprobation of the conduct of the British Cabinet must have arisen to an extraordinary degree of warmth in the mind of Mr. Burke, before he could have prevailed on himself to bring into view the policy of other and better times, and to awaken recollections of past wisdom and glory which must tend so much to embitter our indignation at the present mismanagement of public affairs. In a word, the success of the war required it to be felt by Frenchmen to be a war directed against the Revolution, and not against France; while the ambition of the Allies necessarily made it a war against France, and not against the Revolution. Mr. Burke, M. de Calonne, M. Mallet du Pan, and all the other distinguished writers who have appeared on behalf of the French Royalists—a name which no man should pronounce without pity, and no Englishman ought to utter without shame—have acknowledged, lamented, and condemned the wretched policy of the confederates. We have still to impeach their sagacity, for not having originally foreseen what a brittle instrument such a confederacy must prove; we have still to reproach them, for not having from the first perceived, that to embark the safety of Europe on the success of such an alliance, was a most ambiguous policy,—only to be reluctantly embraced, after every other expedient was exhausted, in a case of the most imminent danger, and in circumstances of the most imperious necessity.

These reflections naturally lead us to the consideration of the safety of the war, or of the collateral evil with which it was pregnant in either alternative, of its failure or success; and we do not hesitate to affirm, that, in our humble opinion, its success was dangerous to the independence of nations, and its failure hostile to the stability of governments. The choice between two such dreadful evils is embarrassing and cruel: yet, with the warmest zeal for the tranquillity of every people,—with the strongest wishes that can arise from personal habits and character for quiet and repose,—with all our heartfelt and deeply-rooted detestation for the crimes, calamities, and horrors of civil confusion, we cannot prevail on ourselves to imagine that a greater evil could befall the human race than the partition of Europe among the spoilers of Poland. All the wild freaks of popular licentiousness,—all the fantastic transformations of government,—all the frantic cruelty of anarchical tyranny, almost vanish before the terrible idea of gathering the whole civilized world under the iron yoke of military despotism. It is—at least, it was—an instinct of the English character, to feel more alarm and horror at despotism than at any other of those evils which afflict human society; and we own our minds to be still under the influence of this old and perhaps exploded national preju-

* "If there be any man in the present age who deserves the honour of being compared with this great prince, it is George Washington. The merit of both is more solid than dazzling. The same plain sense, the same simplicity of character, the same love of their country, the same unaffected heroism, distinguished both these illustrious men; and both were so highly favoured by Providence as to be made its chosen instruments for redeeming nations from bondage. As William had to contend with greater captains, and to struggle with more complicated political difficulties, we are able more decisively to ascertain his martial prowess, and his civil prudence. It has been the fortune of Washington to give a more signal proof of his disinterestedness, as he was placed in a situation in which he could without blame resign the supreme administration of that commonwealth which his valour had guarded in infancy against a foreign force, and which his wisdom has since guided through still more formidable domestic perils."—Monthly Review, vol. xi. p. 308.—Ed.

dice. It is a prejudice, however, which appears to us founded on the most sublime and profound philosophy; and it has been implanted in the minds of Englishmen by their long experience of the mildest and freest government with which the bounty of Divine Providence has been pleased for so many centuries to favour so considerable a portion of the human race. It has been nourished by the blood of our forefathers; it is embodied in our most venerable institutions; it is the spirit of our sacred laws; it is the animating principle of the English character; it is the very life and soul of the British constitution; it is the distinguishing nobility of the meanest Englishman; it is that proud privilege which exalts him, in his own respect, above the most illustrious slave that drags his gilded chain in the court of a tyrant. It has given vigour and lustre to our warlike enterprises, justice and humanity to our laws, and character and energy to our national genius and literature. Of such a prejudice we are not ashamed: and we have no desire to outlive its extinction in the minds of our countrymen:—

> tunc omne Latinum
> Fabula nomen erit.*

To return from what may be thought a digression, but which is inspired by feelings that we hope at least a few of our readers may still be old-fashioned enough to pardon us for indulging,—we proceed to make some remarks on the dangers with which the failure of this war threatened Europe. It is a memorable example of the intoxication of men, and of their governors, that at the commencement of this war, the bare idea of the possibility of its failure would have been rejected with indignation and scorn: yet it became statesmen to consider this event as at least possible; and, in that alternative, what were the consequences which the European governments had to apprehend? With their counsels baffled, their armies defeated, their treasuries exhausted, their subjects groaning under the weight of taxes, their military strength broken, and their reputation for military superiority destroyed, —they have to contend, in their own states, against the progress of opinions, which their own unfortunate policy has surrounded with the dazzling lustre of heroism, and with all the attractions and fascinations of victory. Disgraced in a conflict with democracy abroad, with what vigour and effect can they repress it at home? If they had forborne from entering on the war, the reputation of their power would at least have been whole and entire: the awful question, whether the French Revolution, or the established governments of Europe, are the strongest, would at least have remained undecided; and the people of all countries would not have witnessed the dangerous examples of their sovereigns humbled before the leaders of the new sect. Mr. Burke tells us that the war has at least procured a respite for Europe; but he has forgotten to inform us, that there are respites which aggravate the severity of the punishment, and that there are violent struggles which provoke a fate that might otherwise be avoided.

We purposely forbear to enlarge on this subject, because the display of those evils which, at the commencement of the war, were likely to arise from its failure, is now become, unfortunately, the melancholy picture of the actual situation of Europe. This is a theme more adapted for meditation than discourse. It is as sincere wellwishers to the stability and tranquil improvement of established governments,—as zealous and ardent friends to that admirable constitution of government, and happy order of society, which prevail in our native land, that we originally deprecated, and still condemn, a war which has brought these invaluable blessings into the most imminent peril. All the benevolence and patriotism of the human heart cannot, in our opinion, breathe a prayer more auspicious for Englishmen to the Supreme Ruler of the world, than that they may enjoy to the latest generations the blessings of that constitution which has been bequeathed to them by their forefathers. We desire its improvement, indeed,—we ardently desire its improvement—as a means of its preservation; but, above all things, we desire its preservation.

We cannot close a subject, on which we are serious even to melancholy, without offering the slender but unbiassed tribute of our admiration and thanks to that illustrious statesman,—the friend of what we must call the better days of Mr. Burke,—whose great talents have been devoted to the cause of liberty and of mankind,—who, of all men, most ardently loves, because he most thoroughly understands, the British constitution, —who has made a noble and memorable, though unavailing, struggle to preserve us from the evils and dangers of the present war,—who is requited for the calumnies of his enemies, the desertion of his friends, and the ingratitude of his country, by the approbation of his own conscience, and by a well-grounded expectation of the gratitude and reverence of posterity. We never can reflect on the event of this great man's counsel without calling to mind that beautiful passage of Cicero, in which he deplores the death of his illustrious rival Hortensius: "Si fuit tempus ullum cum extorquere arma posset e manibus iratorum civium boni civis auctoritas et oratio, tum profecto fuit, cum patrocinium pacis exclusum est aut errore hominum aut timore."*

* Pharsalia, lib. vii.

* De Claris Oratoribus.

ON THE STATE OF FRANCE IN 1815.*

To appreciate the effects of the French Revolution on the people of France, is an undertaking for which no man now alive has sufficient materials, or sufficient impartiality, even if he had sufficient ability. It is a task from which Tacitus and Machiavel would have shrunk; and to which the little pamphleteers, who speak on it with dogmatism, prove themselves so unequal by their presumption, that men of sense do not wait for the additional proof which is always amply furnished by their performances. The French Revolution was a destruction of great abuses, executed with much violence, injustice, and inhumanity. The destruction of abuse is, in itself, and for so much, a good: injustice and inhumanity would cease to be vices, if they were not productive of great mischief to society. This is a most perplexing account to balance.

As applied, for instance, to the cultivators and cultivation of France, there seems no reason to doubt the unanimous testimony of all travellers and observers, that agriculture has advanced, and that the condition of the agricultural population has been sensibly improved. M. de la Place calculates agricultural produce to have increased one fifth, during the last twenty-five years. M. Cuvier, an unprejudiced and dispassionate man, rather friendly than adverse to much of what the Revolution destroyed, and who, in his frequent journeys through France, surveyed the country with the eyes of a naturalist and a politician, bears the most decisive testimony to the same general result. M. de Candolle, a very able and enlightened Genevese, who is Professor of Botany at Montpellier, is preparing for the press the fruit of several years devoted to the survey of French cultivation, in which we are promised the detailed proofs of its progress. The apprehensions lately entertained by the landed interest of England, and countenanced by no less an authority than that of Mr. Malthus, that France, as a permanent exporter of corn, would supply our market, and drive our inferior lands out of cultivation,—though we consider them as extremely unreasonable,—must be allowed to be of some weight in this question. No such dread of the rivalship of French corn-growers was ever felt or affected in this country in former times. Lastly, the evidence of Mr. Birkbeck, an independent thinker, a shrewd observer, and an experienced farmer, though his journey was rapid, and though he perhaps wished to find benefits resulting from the Revolution, must be allowed to be of high value.

But whatever may have been the benefits conferred by the Revolution on the cultivators, supposing them to have been more questionable than they appear to have been, it is at all events obvious, that the division of the confiscated lands among the peasantry must have given that body an interest and a pride in the maintenance of the order or disorder which that revolution had produced. All confiscation is unjust. The French confiscation, being the most extensive, is the most abominable example of that species of legal robbery. But we speak only of its political effects on the temper of the peasantry. These effects are by no means confined to those who had become proprietors. The promotion of many inspired all with pride: the whole class was raised in self-importance by the proprietary dignity acquired by numerous individuals. Nor must it be supposed that the apprehensions of such a rabble of ignorant owners, who had acquired their ownerships by means of which their own conscience would distrust the fairness, were to be proportioned to the reasonable probabilities of danger. The alarms of a multitude for objects very valuable to them, are always extravagantly beyond the degree of the risk, especially when they are strengthened by any sense, however faint and indistinct, of injustice, which, by the immutable laws of human nature, stamps every possession which suggests it with a mark of insecurity. It is a panic fear;—one of those fears which are so rapidly spread and so violently exaggerated by sympathy, that the lively fancy of the ancients represented them as inflicted by a superior power.

Exemption from manorial rights and feudal services was not merely, nor perhaps principally, considered by the French farmers as a relief from oppression. They were connected with the exulting recollections of deliverance from a yoke,—of a triumph over superiors, aided even by the remembrance of the licentiousness with which they had exercised their saturnalian privileges in the first moments of their short and ambiguous liberty. They recollected these distinctions as an emancipation of their caste. The interest, the pride, the resentment, and the fear, had a great tendency to make the

---

* From the Edinburgh Review, vol. xxiv. p. 518. These remarks were written during the Hundred Days, the author having spent part of the preceding winter in Paris.—Ed.

maintenance of these changes a point of honour among the whole peasantry of France. On this subject, perhaps, they were likely to acquire that jealousy and susceptibility which the dispersed population of the country rarely exhibit, unless when their religion, or their national pride, or their ancient usages, are violently attacked. The only security for these objects would appear to them to be a government arising, like their own property and privileges, out of the Revolution.

We are far from commending these sentiments, and still farther from confounding them with the spirit of liberty. If the forms of a free constitution could have been preserved under a counter-revolutionary government, perhaps these hostile dispositions of the peasants and new proprietors against such a government, might have been gradually mitigated and subdued into being one of the auxiliaries of freedom. But, in the present state of France, there are unhappily no elements of such combinations. There is no such class as landed gentry,—no great proprietors resident on their estates,—consequently no leaders of this dispersed population, to give them permanent influence on the public counsels, to animate their general sluggishness, or to restrain their occasional violence. In such a state they must, in general, be inert;—in particular matters, which touch their own prejudices and supposed interest, unreasonable and irresistible. The extreme subdivision of landed property might, under some circumstances, be favourable to a democratical government. Under a limited monarchy it is destructive of liberty, because it annihilates the strongest bulwarks against the power of the crown. Having no body of great proprietors, it delivers the monarch from all regular and constant restraint, and from every apprehension but that of an inconstant and often servile populace. And, melancholy as the conclusion is, it seems too probable that the present state of property and prejudice among the larger part of the people of France, rather disposes them towards a despotism deriving its sole title from the Revolution, and interested in maintaining the system of society which it has established, and armed with that tyrannical power which may be necessary for its maintenance.

Observations of a somewhat similar nature are applicable to other classes of the French population. Many of the tradesmen and merchants, as well as of the numerous bodies of commissaries and contractors grown rich by war, had become landed proprietors. These classes in general had participated in the early movements of the Revolution. They had indeed generally shrunk from its horrors; but they had associated their pride, their quiet, almost their moral character, with its success, by extensive purchases of confiscated land. These feelings were not to be satisfied by any assurances, however solemn and repeated, or however sincere, that the sales of national property were to be inviolable. The necessity of such assurance continually reminded them of the odiousness of their acquisitions, and of the light in which the acquirers were considered by the government. Their property was to be spared as an evil, incorrigible from its magnitude. What they must have desired, was a government from whom no such assurances could have been necessary.

The middle classes in cities were precisely those who had been formerly humbled, mortified, and exasperated by the privileges of the nobility,—for whom the Revolution was a triumph over those who, in the daily intercourse of life, treated them with constant disdain,—and whom that Revolution raised to the vacant place of these deposed chiefs. The vanity of that numerous, intelligent, and active part of the community—merchants, bankers, manufacturers, tradesmen, lawyers, attorneys, physicians, surgeons, artists, actors, men of letters—had been humbled by the monarchy, and had triumphed in the Revolution: they rushed into the stations which the gentry—emigrant, beggared, or proscribed—could no longer fill: the whole government fell into their hands.

Buonaparte's nobility was an institution framed to secure the triumph of all these vanities, and to provide against the possibility of a second humiliation. It was a body composed of a Revolutionary aristocracy, with some of the ancient nobility,—either rewarded for their services to the Revolution, by its highest dignities, or compelled to lend lustre to it, by accepting in it secondary ranks, with titles inferior to their own,—and with many lawyers, men of letters, merchants, physicians, &c., who often receive inferior marks of honour in England, but whom the ancient system of the French monarchy had rigorously excluded from such distinctions. The military principle predominated, not only from the nature of the government, but because military distinction was the purest that was earned during the Revolution. The Legion of Honour spread the same principle through the whole army, which probably contained six-and-thirty thousand out of the forty thousand who composed the order. The whole of these institutions was an array of new against old vanities,—of that of the former roturiers against that of the former nobility. The new knights and nobles were daily reminded by their badges, or titles, of their interest to resist the re-establishment of a system which would have perpetuated their humiliation. The real operation of these causes was visible during the short reign of Louis XVIII. Military men, indeed, had the courage to display their decorations, and to avow their titles: but most civilians were ashamed, or afraid, to use their new names of dignity; they were conveyed, if at all, in a subdued voice, almost in a whisper; they were considered as extremely unfashionable and vulgar. Talleyrand renounced his title of Prince of Beneventum; and Massena's resumption of his dignity of Prince was regarded as an act of audacity, if not of intentional defiance.

From these middle classes were chosen another body, who were necessarily attached to the Revolutionary government,—the immense body of civil officers who were placed in all the countries directly or indirectly subject to France,—in Italy, in Germany, in Poland, in Holland, in the Netherlands,—for the purposes of administration of finance, and of late to enforce the vain prohibition of commerce with England. These were all thrown back on France by the peace. They had no hope of employment: their gratitude, their resentment, and their expectations bound them to the fortune of Napoleon.

The number of persons in France interested, directly or indirectly, in the sale of confiscated property—by original purchase, by some part in the successive transfers, by mortgage, or by expectancy,—has been computed to be ten millions. This must be a great exaggeration: but one half of that number would be more than sufficient to give colour to the general sentiment. Though the lands of the Church and the Crown were never regarded in the same invidious light with those of private owners, yet the whole mass of confiscation was held together by its Revolutionary origin: the possessors of the most odious part were considered as the outposts and advanced guards of the rest. The purchasers of small lots were peasants; those of considerable estates were the better classes of the inhabitants of cities. Yet, in spite of the powerful causes which attached these last to the Revolution, it is certain, that among the class called "*La bonne bourgeoisie*" are to be found the greatest number of those who approved the restoration of the Bourbons as the means of security and quiet. They were weary of revolution, and they dreaded confusion: but they are inert and timid, and almost as little qualified to defend a throne as they are disposed to overthrow it. Unfortunately, their voice, of great weight in the administration of regular governments, is scarcely heard in convulsions. They are destined to stoop to the bold;—too often, though with vain sorrow and indignation, to crouch under the yoke of the guilty and the desperate.

The populace of great towns (a most important constituent part of a free community, when the union of liberal institutions, with a vigorous authority, provides both a vent for their sentiments, and a curb on their violence,) have, throughout the French Revolution, showed at once all the varieties and excesses of plebeian passions, and all the peculiarities of the French national character in their most exaggerated state. The love of show, or of change,—the rage for liberty or slavery, for war or for peace, soon wearing itself out into disgust and weariness,—the idolatrous worship of demagogues, soon abandoned, and at last cruelly persecuted,—the envy of wealth, or the servile homage paid to it,—all these, in every age, in every place, from Athens to Paris, have characterised a populace not educated by habits of reverence for the laws, or bound by ties of character and palpable interest to the other classes of a free commonwealth. When the Parisian mob were restrained by a strong government, and compelled to renounce their democratic orgies, they became proud of conquest,—proud of the splendour of their despotism,—proud of the magnificence of its exhibitions and its monuments. Men may be so brutalised as to be proud of their chains. That sort of interest in public concerns, which the poor, in their intervals of idleness, and especially when they are met together, feel perhaps more strongly than other classes more constantly occupied with prudential cares, overflowed into new channels. They applauded a general or a tyrant, as they had applauded Robespierre, and worshipped Marat. They applauded the triumphal entry of a foreign army within their walls as a grand show; and they huzzaed the victorious sovereigns, as they would have celebrated the triumph of a French general. The return of the Bourbons was a novelty, and a sight, which, as such, might amuse them for a day; but the establishment of a pacific and frugal government, with an infirm monarch and a gloomy court, without sights or donatives, and the cessation of the gigantic works constructed to adorn Paris, were sure enough to alienate the Parisian populace. There was neither vigour to overawe them,—nor brilliancy to intoxicate them,—nor foreign enterprise to divert their attention.

Among the separate parties into which every people is divided, the Protestants are to be regarded as a body of no small importance in France. Their numbers were rated at between two and three millions; but their importance was not to be estimated by their numerical strength. Their identity of interest,—their habits of concert,—their common wrongs and resentments,—gave them far more strength than a much larger number of a secure, lazy, and dispirited majority. It was, generally speaking, impossible that French Protestants should wish well to the family of Louis XIV., peculiarly supported as it was by the Catholic party. The lenity with which they had long been treated, was ascribed more to the liberality of the age than that of the Government. Till the year 1788, even their marriages and their inheritances had depended more upon the connivance of the tribunals, than upon the sanction of the law. The petty vexations, and ineffectual persecution of systematic exclusion from public offices, and the consequent degradation of their body in public opinion, long survived the detestable but effectual persecution which had been carried on by missionary dragoons, and which had benevolently left them the choice to be hypocrites, or exiles, or galley-slaves. The Revolution first gave them a secure and effective equality with the Catholics, and a real admission into civil office. It is to be feared that they may have sometimes exulted over the sufferings of the Catholic Church, and thereby contracted some part of the depravity of their ancient persecutors. But it cannot be doubted that they were generally attached to the Revolution, and to governments founded on it.

The same observations may be applied, without repetition, to other sects of Dissidents. Of all the lessons of history, there is none more evident in itself, and more uniformly neglected by governments, than that persecutions, disabilities, exclusions, — all systematic wrong to great bodies of citizens, —are sooner or later punished; though the punishment often falls on individuals, who are not only innocent, but who may have had the merit of labouring to repair the wrong.

The voluntary associations which have led or influenced the people during the Revolution, are a very material object in a review like the present. The very numerous body who, as Jacobins or Terrorists, had participated in the atrocities of 1793 and 1794, had, in the exercise of tyranny, sufficiently unlearned the crude notions of liberty with which they had set out. But they all required a government established on Revolutionary foundations. They all took refuge under Buonaparte's authority. The more base accepted clandestine pensions or insignificant places: Barrere wrote slavish paragraphs at Paris; Tallien was provided for by an obscure or a nominal consulship in Spain. Fouché, who conducted this part of the system, thought the removal of an active Jacobin to a province cheaply purchased by five hundred a year. Fouché himself, one of the most atrocious of the Terrorists, had been gradually formed into a good administrator under a civilized despotism,—regardless indeed of forms, but paying considerable respect to the substance, and especially to the appearance of justice,—never shrinking from what was necessary to crush a formidable enemy, but carefully avoiding wanton cruelty and unnecessary evil. His administration, during the earlier and better part of Napoleon's government, had so much repaired the faults of his former life, that the appointment of Savary to the police was one of the most alarming acts of the internal policy during the violent period which followed the invasion of Spain.

At the head of this sort of persons, not indeed in guilt, but in the conspicuous nature of the act in which they had participated, were the Regicides. The execution of Louis XVI. being both unjust and illegal, was unquestionably an atrocious murder: but it would argue great bigotry and ignorance of human nature, not to be aware, that many who took a share in it must have viewed it in a directly opposite light. Mr. Hume himself, with all his passion for monarchy, admits that Cromwell probably considered his share in the death of Charles I. as one of his most distinguished merits. Some of those who voted for the death of Louis XVI. have proved that they acted only from erroneous judgment, by the decisive evidence of a virtuous life. One of them perished in Guiana, the victim of an attempt to restore the Royal Family. But though among the hundreds who voted for the death of that unfortunate Prince, there might be seen every shade of morality from the blackest depravity to the very confines of purity—at least in sentiment, it was impossible that any of them could be contemplated without horror by the brothers and daughter of the murdered Monarch. Nor would it be less vain to expect that the objects of this hatred should fail to support those Revolutionary authorities, which secured them from punishment,—which covered them from contempt by station and opulence,—and which compelled the monarchs of Europe to receive them into their palaces as ambassadors. They might be—the far greater part of them certainly had become—indifferent to liberty, —perhaps partial to that exercise of unlimited power to which they had been accustomed under what they called a "free" government: but they could not be indifferent in their dislike of a government, under which, their very best condition was that of pardoned criminals, whose criminality was the more odious on account of the sad necessity which made it pardoned. All the Terrorists, and almost all the Regicides, had accordingly accepted emoluments and honours from Napoleon, and were eager to support his authority as a Revolutionary despotism, strong enough to protect them from general unpopularity, and to insure them against the vengeance or the humiliating mercy of a Bourbon government.

Another party of Revolutionists had committed great errors in the beginning, which co-operated with the alternate obstinacy and feebleness of the Counter-revolutionists, to produce all the evils which we feel and fear, and which can only be excused by their own inexperience in legislation, and by the prevalence of erroneous opinions, at that period, throughout the most enlightened part of Europe. These were the best leaders of the Constituent Assembly, who never relinquished the cause of liberty, nor disgraced it by submissions to tyranny, or participation in guilt.

The best representative of this small class, is M. de La Fayette, a man of the purest honour in private life, who has devoted himself to the defence of liberty from his earliest youth. He may have committed some mistakes in opinion; but his heart has always been worthy of the friend of Washington and of Fox. In due time the world will see how victoriously he refutes the charges against him of misconduct towards the Royal Family, when the palace of Versailles was attacked by the mob, and when the King escaped to Varennes. Having hazarded his life to preserve Louis XVI., he was imprisoned in various dungeons, by Powers, who at the same time released Regicides. His wife fell a victim to her conjugal heroism. His liberty was obtained by Buonaparte, who paid court to him during the short period of apparent liberality and moderation which opened his political career. M. de La Fayette repaid him, by faithful counsel; and when he saw his rapid strides towards arbitrary power, he terminated all correspondence with him, by a letter, which breathes the calm dignity of constant and intrepid virtue. In the choice of evils, he considered the prejudices of the Court and the Nobility as more capable of being reconciled with liberty, than the power of an army. After a long absence from courts, he appeared at the levee of Monsieur, on his entry into Paris; and was received with a slight,—not justified by his character, nor by his rank—more important than character in the estimate of palaces. He returned to his retirement, far from courts or conspiracies, with a reputation for purity and firmness, which, if it had been less rare among French leaders, would have secured the liberty of that great nation, and placed her fame on better foundations than those of mere military genius and success.

This party, whose principles are decisively favourable to a limited monarchy, and indeed to the general outlines of the institutions of Great Britain, had some strength among the reasoners of the capital, but represented no interest and no opinion in the country at large. Whatever popularity they latterly appeared to possess, arose but too probably from the momentary concurrence, in opposition to the Court, of those who were really their most irreconcilable enemies,—the discontented Revolutionists and concealed Napoleonists. During the late short pause of restriction on the press, they availed themselves of the half-liberty of publication which then existed, to employ the only arms in which they were formidable,—those of argument and eloquence. The pamphlets of M. Benjamin Constant were by far the most distinguished of those which they produced; and he may be considered as the literary representative of a party, which their enemies, as well as their friends, called the "Liberal," who were hostile to Buonaparte and to military power, friendly to the general principles of the constitution established by Louis XVIII., though disapproving some of its parts, and seriously distrusting the spirit in which it was executed, and the maxims prevalent at Court. M. Constant, who had been expelled from the *Tribunat*, and in effect exiled from France, by Buonaparte, began an attack on him before the Allies had crossed the Rhine, and continued it till after his march from Lyons. He is unquestionably the first political writer of the Continent, and apparently the ablest man in France. His first Essay, that on Conquest, is a most ingenious development of the principle, that a system of war and conquest, suitable to the condition of barbarians, is so much at variance with the habits and pursuits of civilized, commercial, and luxurious nations, that it cannot be long-lived in such an age as ours. If the position be limited to those rapid and extensive conquests which tend towards universal monarchy, and if the tendency in human affairs to resist them be stated only as of great force, and almost sure within no long time of checking their progress, the doctrine of M. Constant will be generally acknowledged to be true. With the comprehensive views, and the brilliant poignancy of Montesquieu, he unites some of the defects of that great writer. Like him, his mind is too systematical for the irregular variety of human affairs; and he sacrifices too many of those exceptions and limitations, which political reasonings require, to the pointed sentences which compose his nervous and brilliant style. His answer to the Abbé Montesquieu's foolish plan of restricting the press, is a model of polemical politics, uniting English solidity and strength with French urbanity. His tract on Ministerial Responsibility, with some errors (though surprisingly few) on English details, is an admirable discussion of one of the most important institutions of a free government, and, though founded on English practice, would convey instruction to most of those who have best studied the English constitution. We have said thus much of these masterly productions, because we consider them as the only specimens of the Parisian press, during its semi-emancipation, which deserve the attention of political philosophers, and of the friends of true liberty, in all countries. In times of more calm, we should have thought a fuller account of their contents, and a free discussion of their faults, due to the eminent abilities of the author. At present we mention them, chiefly because they exhibit, pretty fairly, the opinions of the liberal party in that country.

But, not to dwell longer on this little fraternity (who are too enlightened and conscientious to be of importance in the shocks of faction, and of whom we have spoken more from esteem for their character, than from an opinion of their political influence), it will be already apparent to our readers, that many of the most numerous and guiding classes in the newly-arranged community of France, were bound, by strong ties of interest and pride, to a Revolutionary government, however little they might be qualified or sincerely disposed for a free constitution, —which they struggled to confound with the former; that these dispositions among the civil classes formed one great source of danger to the administration of the Bourbons; and that they now constitute a material part of the strength of Napoleon. To them he appeals in his Proclamations, when he speaks of "a new dynasty founded on the same bases with the new interests and new institutions which owe their rise to the Revolution." To them he appeals, though more covertly, in his professions of zeal for the dignity of the people, and of hostility to feudal nobility, and monarchy by Divine right.

It is natural to inquire how the conscription, and the prodigious expenditure of human life in the campaigns of Spain and Russia, were not of themselves sufficient to make the government of Napoleon detested by the great majority of the French people. But it is a very melancholy truth, that the body of a people may be gradually so habituated to war, that their habits and expectations are at least so adapted to its demand for men, and its waste of life, that they become almost insensible to its evils, and require long discipline to re-inspire them with a relish for the blessings of peace, and a capacity for the virtues of industry. The complaint is least when the evil is greatest: — it is as difficult to teach such a people the value of peace, as it would be to reclaim a drunkard, or to subject a robber to patient labour.

A conscription is, under pretence of equality, the most unequal of all laws; because it assumes that military service is equally easy to all classes and ranks of men. Accordingly, it always produces pecuniary commutation in the sedentary and educated classes. To them in many of the towns of France it was an oppressive and grievous tax. But to the majority of the people, always accustomed to military service, the life of a soldier became perhaps more agreeable than any other. Families even considered it as a means of provision for their children; each parent labouring to persuade himself that his children would be among those who should have the fortune to survive. Long and constant wars created a regular demand for men, to which the principle of population adapted itself. An army which had conquered and plundered Europe, and in which a private soldier might reasonably enough hope to be a marshal or a prince, had more allurements, and not more repulsive qualities, than many of those odious, disgusting, unwholesome, or perilous occupations, which in the common course of society are always amply supplied. The habit of war unfortunately perpetuates itself: and this moral effect is a far greater evil than the more destruction of life. Whatever may be the justness of these speculations, certain it is, that the travellers who lately visited France, neither found the conscription so unpopular, nor the decay of male population so perceptible, as plausible and confident statements had led them to expect.

It is probable that among the majority of the French (excluding the army), the restored Bourbons gained less popularity by abolishing the conscription, than they lost by the cession of all the conquests of France. This fact affords a most important warning of the tremendous dangers to which civilized nations expose their character by long war. To say that liberty cannot survive it, is saying little: — liberty is one of the luxuries which only a few nations seem destined to enjoy; — and they only for a short period. It is not only fatal to the refinements and ornaments of civilized life: — its long continuance must inevitably destroy even that degree (moderate as it is) of order and security which prevails even in the pure monarchies of Europe, and distinguishes them above all other societies ancient or modern. It is vain to inveigh against the people of France for delighting in war, for exulting in conquest, and for being exasperated and mortified by renouncing those vast acquisitions. These deplorable consequences arise from an excess of the noblest and most necessary principles in the character of a nation, acted upon by habits of arms, and "cursed with every granted prayer," during years of victory and conquest. No nation could endure such a trial. Doubtless those nations who have the most liberty, the most intelligence, the most virtue,—who possess in the highest degree all the constituents of the most perfect civilization, will resist it the longest. But, let us not deceive ourselves,—long war renders all these blessings impossible: it dissolves all the civil and pacific virtues; it leaves no calm for the cultivation of reason; and by substituting attachment to leaders, instead of reverence for laws, it destroys liberty, the parent of intelligence and of virtue.

The French Revolution has strongly confirmed the lesson taught by the history of all ages, that while political divisions excite the activity of genius, and teach honour in enmity, as well as fidelity in attachment, the excess of civil confusion and convulsion produces diametrically opposite effects,—subjects society to force, instead of mind,—renders its distinctions the prey of boldness and atrocity, instead of being the prize of talent, — and concentrates the thoughts and feelings of every individual upon himself,—his own sufferings and fears. Whatever beginnings of such an unhappy state may be observed in France,—whatever tendency it may have had to dispose the people to a light transfer of allegiance, and an undistinguishing profession of attachment,—it is more useful to consider them as the results of these general causes, than as vices peculiar to that great nation.

To this we must add, before we conclude our cursory survey, that frequent changes of government, however arising, promote a disposition to acquiesce in change. No people can long preserve the enthusiasm, which first impels them to take an active part in change. Its frequency at least teaches them patiently to bear it. They become indifferent to governments and sovereigns. They are spectators of revolutions, instead of actors in them. They are a prey to be fought for by the hardy and bold, and are generally disposed of by an army. In this state of things, revolutions become bloodless, not from the humanity, but from the indifference of a people. Perhaps it may be true, though it will appear paradoxical to many, that such revolutions, as those of England and America, conducted with such a regard for moderation and humanity, and even with such respect for established authorities and institutions, independently of their necessity for the preservation of liberty, may even have a tendency to strengthen, instead of weakening, the frame of the commonwealth. The example of reverence for justice,—of caution in touching ancient institutions, — of not innovating, beyond the necessities of the case, even in a season of violence and anger, may impress on the minds of men those conservative principles of society, more deeply and strongly, than the most uninterrupted observation of them in the ordinary course of quiet and regular government.

ON

THE RIGHT OF PARLIAMENTARY SUFFRAGE.*

WHAT mode of representation is most likely to secure the liberty, and consequently the happiness, of a community circumstanced like the people of Great Britain? On the elementary part of this great question, it will be sufficient to remind the reader of a few undisputed truths. The object of government, is security against wrong.—Most civilized governments, tolerably secure their subjects against wrong from each other. But to secure them, by laws, against wrong from the government itself, is a problem of a far more difficult sort, which few nations have attempted to solve,—and of which it is not so much as pretended that, since the beginning of history, more than one or two great states have approached the solution. It will be universally acknowledged, that this approximation has never been affected by any other means than that of a legislative assembly, chosen by some considerable portion of the people.

The direct object of a popular representation is, that one, at least, of the bodies exercising the legislative power being dependent on the people by election, should have the strongest inducement to guard their interests, and to maintain their rights. For this purpose, it is not sufficient, that it should have the same general interests with the people; for every government has, in truth, the same interests with its subjects. It is necessary that the more direct and palpable interest, arising from election, should be superadded. In every legislative senate, the modes of appointment ought to be such as to secure the nomination of members the best qualified, and the most disposed, to make laws conducive to the well-being of the whole community. In a representative assembly this condition, though absolutely necessary, is not of itself sufficient.

To understand the principles of its composition thoroughly, we must divide the people into classes, and examine the variety of local and professional interests of which the whole is composed. Each of these classes must be represented by persons who will guard its peculiar interest, whether that interest arises from inhabiting the same district, or pursuing the same occupation,—such as traffic, or husbandry, or the useful or ornamental arts. The fidelity and zeal of such representatives, are to be secured by every provision which, to a sense of common interest, can superadd a fellow-feeling with their constituents. Nor is this all: in a great state, even that part of the public interest which is common to all classes, is composed of a great variety of branches. A statesman should indeed have a comprehensive view of the whole: but no one man can be skilled in all the particulars. The same education, and the same pursuits, which qualify men to understand and regulate some branches, disqualify them for others. The representative assembly must therefore contain, some members peculiarly qualified for discussions of the constitution and the laws,—others for those of foreign policy,—some for those of the respective interests of agriculture, commerce, and manufactures,—some for those of military affairs by sea and land,—and some also who are conversant with the colonies and distant possessions of a great empire. It would be a mistake to suppose that the place of such representatives could be supplied by witnesses examined on each particular subject. Both are not more than sufficient;—skilful witnesses occasionally, for the most minute information,—skilful representatives continally, to discover and conduct evidence, and to enforce and illustrate the matters belonging to their department with the weight of those who speak on a footing of equality.

It is obvious, that as long as this composition is insured, it is for the present purpose a matter of secondary importance whether it be effected by direct or indirect means. To be a faithful representative, it is necessary that such an assembly should be numerous, —that it should learn, from experience, the movements that agitate multitudes,—and that it should be susceptible, in no small degree, of the action of those causes which

* From the Edinburgh Review, vol. xxxi. p. 174.—ED.

sway the thoughts and feelings of assemblies of the people. For the same reason, among others, it is expedient that its proceedings should be public, and the reasonings on which they are founded, submitted to the judgment of mankind. These democratical elements are indeed to be tempered and restrained by such contrivances as may be necessary to maintain the order and independence of deliberation: but, without them, no assembly, however elected, can truly represent a people.

Among the objects of representation, two may, in an especial manner, deserve observation: — the qualifications for making good laws, and those for resisting oppression.

Now, the capacity of an assembly to make good laws, evidently depends on the quantity of skill and information of every kind which it possesses. But it seems to be advantageous that it should contain a large proportion of one body of a more neutral and inactive character,—not indeed to propose much, but to mediate or arbitrate in the differences between the more busy classes, from whom important propositions are to be expected. The suggestions of every man relating to his province, have doubtless a peculiar value: but most men imbibe prejudices with their knowledge; and, in the struggle of various classes for their conflicting interests, the best chance for an approach to right decision, lies in an appeal to the largest body of well-educated men, of leisure, large property, temperate character, and who are impartial on more subjects than any other class of men. An ascendency, therefore, of landed proprietors must be considered, on the whole, as a beneficial circumstance in a representative body.

For resistance to oppression, it is peculiarly necessary that the lower, and, in some places, the lowest classes, should possess the right of suffrage. Their rights would otherwise be less protected than those of any other class; for some individuals of every other class, would generally find admittance into the legislature; or, at least, there is no other class which is not connected with some of its members. But in the uneducated classes, none can either sit in a representative assembly, or be connected on an equal footing with its members. The right of suffrage, therefore, is the only means by which they can make their voice heard in its deliberations. They also often send to a representative assembly, members whose character is an important element in its composition,—men of popular talents, principles, and feelings,—quick in suspecting oppression,—bold in resisting it,—not thinking favourably of the powerful,—listening, almost with credulity to the complaints of the humble and the feeble,—and impelled by ambition, where they are not prompted by generosity, to be the champions of the defenceless.

In all political institutions, it is a fortunate circumstance when legal power is bestowed on those who already possess a natural influence and ascendant over their fellow-citizens. Wherever, indeed, the circumstances of society, and the appointments of law, are in this respect completely at variance, submission can hardly be maintained without the odious and precarious means of force and fear. But in a representative assembly, which exercises directly no power, and of which the members are too numerous to derive much individual consequence from their stations, the security and importance of the body, more than in any other case, depend on the natural influence of those who compose it. In this respect, talent and skill, besides their direct utility, have a secondary value of no small importance. Together with the other circumstances which command respect or attachment among men,—with popularity, with fame, with property, with liberal education and condition,—they form a body of strength, which no law could give or take away. As far as an assembly is deprived of any of these natural principles of authority, so far it is weakened both for the purpose of resisting the usurpations of government and of maintaining the order of society.

An elective system tends also, in other material respects, to secure that free government, of which it is the most essential member. As it calls some of almost every class of men to share in legislative power, and many of all classes to exercise the highest franchises, it engages the pride, the honour, and the private interest as well as the generosity, of every part of the community, in defence of the constitution. Every noble sentiment, every reasonable consideration, every petty vanity, and every contemptible folly, are made to contribute towards its security. The performance of some of its functions becomes part of the ordinary habits of bodies of men numerous enough to spread their feelings over great part of a nation.

Popular representation thus, in various ways, tends to make governments good, and to make good governments secure:—these are its primary advantages. But free, that is just, governments, tend to make men more intelligent, more honest, more brave, more generous. Liberty is the parent of genius,—the nurse of reason,—the inspirer of that valour which makes nations secure and powerful,—the incentive to that activity and enterprise to which they owe wealth and splendour, the school of those principles of humanity and justice which bestow an unspeakably greater happiness, than any of the outward advantages of which they are the chief sources, and the sole guardians.

These effects of free government on the character of a people, may, in one sense, be called indirect and secondary; but they are not the less to be considered as among its greatest blessings: and it is scarcely necessary to observe, how much they tend to enlarge and secure the liberty from which they spring. But their effect will perhaps be better shown by a more particular view of the influence of popular elections on the character of the different classes of the community.

To begin with the higher classes:—the English nobility, who are blended with the gentry by imperceptible shades, are the most opulent and powerful order of men in Europe. They are comparatively a small body, who unite great legal privileges with ample possessions, and names both of recent renown and historical glory. They have attained almost all the objects of human pursuit. They are surrounded by every circumstance which might seem likely to fill them with arrogance,—to teach them to scorn their inferiors, and which might naturally be supposed to extinguish enterprise, and to lull every power of the understanding to sleep. What has preserved their character? What makes them capable of serving or adorning their country as orators and poets, men of letters and men of business, in as great a proportion as in any equal number of the best educated classes of their countrymen? Surely only one solution can be given of these phenomena, peculiar to our own country.* Where all the ordinary incentives to action are withdrawn, a free constitution excites it, by presenting political power as a new object of pursuit. By rendering that power in a great degree dependent on popular favour, it compels the highest to treat their fellow-creatures with decency and courtesy, and disposes the best of them to feel, that inferiors in station may be superiors in worth, as they are equals in right. Hence chiefly arises that useful preference for country life, which distinguishes the English gentry from that of other nations. In despotic countries they flock to the court, where all their hopes are fixed; but here, as they have much to hope from the people, they must cultivate the esteem, and even court the favour of their own natural dependants. They are quickened in the pursuit of ambition, by the rivalship of that enterprising talent, which is stimulated by more urgent motives. These dispositions and manners have become, in some measure, independent of the causes which originally produced them, and extend to many on whom these causes could have little operation. In a great body, we must allow for every variety of form and degree. It is sufficient that a system of extensively popular representation has, in a course of time, produced this general character, and that the English democracy is the true preservative of the talents and virtues of the aristocracy.

The effects of the elective franchise upon the humbler classes, are, if possible, still more obvious and important. By it the peasant is taught to "venerate himself as a man"—to employ his thoughts, at least occasionally, upon high matters,—to meditate on the same subjects with the wise and the great,—to enlarge his feelings beyond the circle of his narrow concerns,—to sympathise, however irregularly, with great bodies of his fellow-creatures, and sometimes to do acts which he may regard as contributing directly to the welfare of his country. Much of this good tendency is doubtless counteracted by other circumstances. The outward form is often ridiculous or odious. The judgments of the multitude are never exact, and their feelings often grossly misapplied: but, after all possible deductions, great benefits must remain. The important object is, that they should think and feel,—that they should contemplate extensive consequences as capable of arising from their own actions, and thus gradually become conscious of the moral dignity of their nature.

Among the very lowest classes, where the disorders of elections are the most offensive, the moral importance of the elective franchise is, in some respects, the greatest. As individuals, they feel themselves of no consequence;—hence, in part, arises their love of numerous assemblies,—the only scenes in which the poor feel their importance. Brought together for elections, their tumultuary disposition, which is little else than a desire to display their short-lived consequence, is gratified at the expense of inconsiderable evils. It is useful that the pride of the highest should be made occasionally to bend before them,—that the greatest objects of ambition should be partly at their disposal; it teaches them to feel that *they* also are men. It is to the exercise of this franchise, by some bodies of our lowest classes, that we are to ascribe that sense of equality,—that jealousy of right,—that grave independence, and calm pride, which has been observed by foreigners as marking the deportment of Englishmen.

By thus laying open some of the particular modes in which representation produces its advantages to the whole community, and to its separate classes, we hope that we have contributed somewhat to the right decision of the practical question which now presents itself to our view. Systems of election may be of very various kinds. The right of suffrage may be limited, or universal; it may be secretly, or openly exercised; the representatives may be directly, or indirectly, chosen by the people; and where a qualification is necessary, it may be uniform, or it may vary in different places. A variety of rights of suffrage is the principle of the English representation. In the reign of Edward the First, as much as at the present moment, the members for counties were chosen by freeholders, and those for cities and towns by freemen, burgage tenants, householders or freeholders. Now, we prefer this general principle of our representation to any uniform

* To be quite correct, we must remind the reader, that we speak of the character of the whole body, composed, as it is, of a small number. In a body like the French noblesse, amounting perhaps to a hundred thousand, many of whom were acted upon by the strongest stimulants of necessity, and, in a country of such diffused intelligence as France, it would have been a miracle if many had not risen to eminence in the state, and in letters, as well as in their natural profession of arms.

right of suffrage; though we think that, in the present state of things, there are many particulars which, according to that principle, ought to be amended.

Our reasons for this preference are shortly these: — every uniform system which seriously differs from universal suffrage, must be founded on such a qualification, as to take away the elective franchise from those portions of the inferior classes who now enjoy it. Even the condition of paying direct taxes would disfranchise many. After what we have already said, on the general subject of representation, it is needless for us to add, that we should consider such a disfranchisement as a most pernicious mutilation of the representative system. It has already been seen, how much, in our opinion, the proper composition of the House of Commons, the justice of the government and the morality of the people, depend upon the elections which would be thus sacrificed.

This tendency of an uniform qualification is visible in the new French system. The qualification for the electors, is the annual payment of direct taxes to the amount of about 12*l*. When the wealth of the two countries is compared, it will be apparent that, in this country, such a system would be thought a mere aristocracy. In France, the result is a body of one hundred thousand electors;* and in the situation and temper of the French nation, such a scheme of representation may be eligible. But we mention it only as an example, that every uniform qualification, which is not altogether illusory, must incline towards independent property, as being the only ground on which it can rest. The reform of Cromwell had the same aristocratical character, though in a far less degree. It nearly excluded what is called the "populace;" and, for that reason, is commended by the most sagacious† of our Tory writers. An uniform qualification, in short, must be so high as to exclude true popular election, or so low, as to be liable to most of the objections which we shall presently offer against universal suffrage. It seems difficult to conceive how it could be so adjusted, as not either to impair the spirit of liberty, or to expose the quiet of society to continual hazard.

Our next objection to uniformity is, that it exposes the difference between the proprietors and the indigent, in a way offensive and degrading to the feelings of the latter. The difference itself is indeed real, and cannot be removed: but in our present system, it is disguised under a great variety of usages; it is far from uniformly regulating the franchise; and, even where it does, this invidious distinction is not held out in its naked form. It is something, also, that the system of various rights does not constantly thrust forward that qualification of property which, in its undisguised state, may be thought to teach the people too exclusive a regard for wealth.

This variety, by giving a very great weight to property in some elections, enables us safely to allow an almost unbounded scope to popular feeling in others. While some have fallen under the influence of a few great proprietors, others border on universal suffrage. All the intermediate varieties, and all their possible combinations, find their place. Let the reader seriously reflect how all the sorts of men, who are necessary component parts of a good House of Commons, could on any other scheme find their way to it. We have already sufficiently animadverted on the mischief of excluding popular leaders. Would there be no mischief in excluding those important classes of men, whose character unfits them for success in a canvass, or whose fortune may be unequal to the expense of a contest? A representative assembly, elected by a low uniform qualification, would fluctuate between country gentlemen and demagogues:—elected on a high qualification, it would probably exhibit an unequal contest between landholders and courtiers. All other interests would, on either system, be unprotected: no other class would contribute its contingent of skill and knowledge to aid the deliberations of the legislature.

The founders of new commonwealths must, we confess, act upon some uniform principle. A builder can seldom imitate, with success, all the fantastic but picturesque and comfortable irregularities, of an old mansion, which through a course of ages has been repaired, enlarged, and altered, according to the pleasure of various owners. This is one of the many disadvantages attendant on the lawgivers of infant states. Something, perhaps, by great skill and caution, they might do; but their wisdom is most shown, after guarding the great principles of liberty, by leaving time to do the rest.

Though we are satisfied, by the above and by many other considerations, that we ought not to exchange our diversified elections for any general qualification, we certainly consider universal suffrage as beyond calculation more mischievous than any other uniform right. The reasons which make it important to liberty, that the elective franchise should be exercised by large bodies of the lower classes, do not in the least degree require that it should be conferred on them all. It is necessary to their security from oppression, that the whole class should have some representatives: but as their interest is every where the same, representatives elected by one body of them are necessarily the guardians of the rights of all. The great object of representation for them, is to be protected against violence and cruelty. Sympathy with suffering, and indignation against cruelty, are easily excited in numerous assemblies, and must either be felt or assumed by all their members. Popular elections generally insure the return of some men, who shrink from no

* The population of France is now [1818, Ed.] estimated at twenty-nine millions and a half.

† Clarendon, Hume, &c.

appeal, however invidious, on behalf of the oppressed. We must again repeat, that we consider such men as invaluable members of a House of Commons;—perhaps their number is at present too small. What we now maintain is, that, though elected by one place, they are in truth the representatives of the same sort of people in other places. Their number must be limited, unless we are willing to exclude other interests, and to sacrifice other most important objects of representation.

The exercise of the elective franchise by some of the labouring classes, betters the character, raises the spirit, and enhances the consequence of all. An English farmer or artisan is more high-spirited and independent than the same classes in despotic countries; but nobody has ever observed that there is in England a like difference between the husbandman and mechanic, who have votes, and who have not. The exclusion of the class degrades the whole: but the admission of a part bestows on the whole a sense of importance, and a hold on the estimation of their superiors. It must be admitted, that a small infusion of popular election would not produce these effects: whatever might seem to be the accidental privilege of a few, would have no influence on the rank of their fellows. It must be considerable, and,—what is perhaps still more necessary,—it must be conspicuous, and forced on the attention by the circumstances which excite the feelings, and strike the imagination of mankind. The value of external dignity is not altogether confined to kings or senates. The people also have their majesty; and they too ought to display their importance in the exercise of their rights.

The question is, whether all interests will be protected, where the representatives are chosen by all men, or where they are elected by considerable portions only, of all classes of men. This question will perhaps be more clearly answered by setting out from examples, than from general reasonings. If we suppose Ireland to be an independent state, governed by its former House of Commons, it will at once be admitted, that no shadow of just government existed, where the legislature were the enemies, instead of being the protectors, of the Catholics, who formed a great class in the community. That this evil was most cruelly aggravated by the numbers of the oppressed, is true. But, will it be contended, that such a government was unjust, only because the Catholics were a majority? We have only then to suppose the case reversed;—that the Catholics were to assume the whole power, and to retaliate upon the Protestants, by excluding them from all political privilege. Would this be a just or equal government? That will hardly be avowed. But what would be the effect of establishing universal suffrage in Ireland? It would be, to do that in substance, which no man would propose in form. The Catholics, forming four-fifths of the population, would, as far as depends on laws, possess the whole authority of the state. Such a government, instead of protecting all interests, would be founded in hostility to that which is the second interest in numbers, and in many respects the first. The oppressors and the oppressed would, indeed, change places;—we should have Catholic tyrants, and Protestant slaves: but our only consolation would be, that the island would contain more tyrants, and fewer slaves. If there be persons who believe that majorities have any power over the eternal principles of justice, or that numbers can in the least degree affect the difference between right and wrong, it would be vain for us to argue against those with whom we have no principles in common. To all others it must be apparent, that a representation of *classes* might possibly be so framed as to secure both interests; but that a representation of *numbers* must enslave the Protestant minority.

That the majority of a people may be a tyrant as much as one or a few, is most apparent in the cases where a state is divided, by conspicuous marks, into a permanent majority and minority. Till the principles of toleration be universally felt, as well as acknowledged, religion will form one of these cases. Till reason and morality be far more widely diffused than they are, the outward distinctions of colour and feature will form another, more pernicious, and less capable of remedy. Does any man doubt, that the establishment of universal suffrage, among emancipated slaves, would be only another word for the oppression, if not the destruction, of their former masters? But is slavery itself really more unjust, where the slaves are a majority, than where they are a minority? or may it not be said, on the contrary, that to hold men in slavery is most inexcusable, where society is not built on that unfortunate foundation,—where the supposed loss of the labour would be an inconsiderable evil, and no danger could be pretended from their manumission? Is it not apparent, that the lower the right of suffrage descends in a country, where the whites are the majority, the more cruel would be the oppression of the enslaved minority? An aristocratical legislature might consider, with some impartiality, the disputes of the free and of the servile labourers; but a body, influenced chiefly by the first of these rival classes, must be the oppressors of the latter.

These, it may be said, are extreme cases;—they are selected for that reason: but the principle which they strikingly illustrate, will, on a very little reflection, be found applicable in some degree to all communities of men.

The labouring classes are in every country a perpetual majority. The diffusion of education will doubtless raise their minds, and throw open prizes for the ambition of a few which will spread both activity and content among the rest: but in the present state of the population and territory of European countries, the majority of men must earn their subsistence by daily labour. Notwithstanding local differences, persons in this situation have a general resemblance of character, and sameness of interest. Their interest, or what they think their interest, may be at variance with the real or supposed interests of the higher orders. If they are considered as forming, in this respect, one class of society, a share in the representation may be allotted to them, sufficient to protect their interest, compatibly with the equal protection of the interests of all other classes, and regulated by a due regard to all the qualities which are required in a well-composed legislative assembly. But if representation be proportioned to numbers alone, every other interest in society is placed at the disposal of the multitude. No other class can be effectually represented; no other class can have a political security for justice; no other can have any weight in the deliberations of the legislature. No talents, no attainments, but such as recommend men to the favour of the multitude, can have any admission into it. A representation so constituted, would produce the same practical effects, as if every man whose income was above a certain amount, were excluded from the right of voting. It is of little moment to the proprietors, whether they be disfranchised, or doomed, in every election, to form a hopeless minority.

Nor is this all. A representation, founded on numbers only, would be productive of gross inequality in that very class to which all others are sacrificed. The difference between the people of the country and those of towns, is attended with consequences which no contrivance of law can obviate. Towns are the nursery of political feeling. The frequency of meeting, the warmth of discussion, the variety of pursuit, the rivalship of interest, the opportunities of information, even the fluctuations and extremes of fortune, direct the minds of their inhabitants to public concerns, and render them the seats of republican governments, or the preservers of liberty in monarchies. But if this difference be considerable among educated men, it seems immeasurable when we contemplate its effects on the more numerous classes. Among them, no strong public sentiment can be kept up without numerous meetings. It is chiefly when they are animated by a view of their own strength and numbers, —when they are stimulated by an eloquence suited to their character,—and when the passions of each are strengthened by the like emotions of the multitude which surround him, that the thoughts of such men are directed to subjects so far from their common callings as the concerns of the commonwealth. All these aids are necessarily wanting to the dispersed inhabitants of the country, whose frequent meetings are rendered impossible by distance and poverty,—who have few opportunities of being excited by discussion or declamation, and very impe[illegible]ct means of correspondence or concert with those at a distance. An agricultural people is generally submissive to the laws, and observant of the ordinary duties of life, but stationary and stagnant, without the enterprise which is the source of improvement, and the public spirit which preserves liberty. If the whole political power of the state, therefore, were thrown into the hands of the lowest classes, it would be really exercised only by the towns. About two-elevenths of the people of England inhabit towns which have a population of ten thousand souls or upwards. A body so large, strengthened by union, discipline, and spirit, would without difficulty domineer over the lifeless and scattered peasants. In towns, the lower part of the middle classes are sometimes tame; while the lowest class are always susceptible of animation. But the small freeholders, and considerable farmers, acquire an independence from their position, which makes them very capable of public spirit. While the classes below them are incapable of being permanently rendered active elements in any political combination, the dead weight of their formal suffrages would only oppress the independent votes of their superiors. All active talent would, in such a case, fly to the towns, where alone its power could be felt. The choice of the country would be dictated by the cry of the towns, wherever it was thought worth while to take it from the quiet influence of the resident proprietors. Perhaps the only contrivance, which can in any considerable degree remedy the political inferiority of the inhabitants of the country to those of towns, has been adopted in the English constitution, which, while it secures an ascendant of landholders in the legislature, places the disposal of its most honoured and envied seats in the hands of the lowest classes among the agricultural population, who are capable of employing the right of suffrage with spirit and effect.

They who think representation chiefly valuable, because whole nations cannot meet to deliberate in one place, have formed a very low notion of this great improvement. It is not a contrivance for conveniently collecting or blindly executing all the pernicious and unjust resolutions of ignorant multitudes. To correct the faults of democratical government, is a still more important object of representation, than to extend the sphere to which that government may be applied. It balances the power of the multitude by the influence of other classes: it substitutes skilful lawgivers for those who are utterly incapable of any legislative function; and it continues the trust long enough to guard the legislature from the temporary delusions of the people. By a system of universal suffrage and annual elections, all these temperaments would be destroyed. The effect of a crowded population, in increasing the intensity and activity of the political passions, is extremely accelerated in cities of the first class. The population of London and its environs is nearly equal to that of all other towns in England of or above ten thousand souls. According to the principle of universal suffrage, it would contain about two hundred and fifty thousand electors; and send fifty-five members to Parliament. This electoral army would be occupied for the whole year in election or canvass, or in the endless animosities in which both would be fertile. A hundred candidates for their suffrages would be daily employed in inflaming their passions. No time for deliberation,—no interval of repose in which inflamed passions might subside, could exist. The representatives would naturally be the most daring, and, for their purposes, the ablest of their body. They must lead or overawe the legislature. Every transient delusion, or momentary phrênsy of which a multitude is susceptible, must rush with unresisted violence into the representative body. Such a representation would differ in no beneficial respect from the wildest democracy. It would be a democracy clothed in a specious disguise, and armed with more effective instruments of oppression,—but not wiser or more just than the democracies of old, which Hobbes called "an *aristocracy* of orators, sometimes interrupted by the *monarchy* of a single orator."

It may be said that such reasonings suppose the absence of those moral restraints of property and opinion which would temper the exercise of this, as well as of every other kind of suffrage. Landholders would still influence their tenants,—farmers their labourers,—artisans and manufacturers those whom they employ;—property would still retain its power over those who depend on the proprietor. To this statement we in some respects accede; and on it we build our last and most conclusive argument against universal suffrage.

It is true, that in very quiet times, a multiplication of dependent voters would only augment the influence of wealth. If votes were bestowed on every private soldier, the effect would be only to give a thousand votes to the commanding officer who marched his battalion to the poll. Whenever the people felt little interest in public affairs, the same power would be exercised by every master through his dependants. The traders who employ many labourers in great cities would possess the highest power; the great consumers and landholders would engross the remainder; the rest of the people would be insignificant. As the multitude is composed of those individuals who are most incapable of fixed opinions, and as they are, in their collective capacity, peculiarly alive to present impulse, there is no vice to which they are so liable as inconstancy. Their passions are quickly worn out by their own violence. They become weary of the excesses into which they have been plunged. Lassitude and indifference succeed to their fury, and are proportioned to its violence. They abandon public affairs to any hand disposed to guide them. They give up their favourite measures to reprobation, and their darling leaders to destruction. Their acclamations are often as loud around the scaffold of the demagogue, as around his triumphal car.

Under the elective system, against which we now argue, the opposite evils of too much strengthening wealth, and too much subjecting property to the multitude, are likely, by turns, to prevail. In either case, in may be observed that the power of the middle classes would be annihilated. Society, on such a system, would exhibit a series of alternate fits of phrensy and lethargy. When the people were naturally disposed to violence, the mode of election would inflame it to madness. When they were too much inclined of themselves to listlessness and apathy, it would lull them to sleep. In these, as in every other respect, it is the reverse of a wisely constituted representation, which is a restraint on the people in times of heat, and a stimulant to their sluggishness when they would otherwise fall into torpor. This even and steady interest in public concerns, is impossible in a scheme which, in every case, would aggravate the predominant excess.

It must never be forgotten, that the whole proprietary body must be in a state of permanent conspiracy against an extreme democracy. They are the natural enemies of a constitution, which grants them no power and no safety. Though property is often borne down by the torrent of popular tyranny, yet it has many chances of prevailing at last. Proprietors have steadiness, vigilance, concert, secrecy, and, if need be, dissimulation. They yield to the storm: they regain their natural ascendant in the calm. Not content with persuading the people to submit to salutary restraints, they usually betray them, by insensible degrees, into absolute submission.

If the commonwealth does not take this road to slavery, there are many paths that lead to that state of perdition. "A demagogue seizes on that despotic power for himself, which he for a long time has exercised in the name of his faction;—a victorious general leads his army to enslave their country: and both these candidates for tyranny too often find auxiliaries in those classes of society which are at length brought to regard absolute monarchy as an asylum. Thus, wherever property is not allowed great weight in a free state, it will destroy liberty. The history of popular clamour, even in England, is enough to show that it is easy sometimes to work the populace into "a sedition for slavery."

These obvious consequences have disposed most advocates of universal suffrage to propose its combination with some other ingredients, by which, they tell us, that the poison will be converted into a remedy. The composition now most in vogue is its union with the Ballot. Before we proceed to the consideration of that proposal, we shall bestow a few words on some other plans which have been adopted or proposed, to render uniform popular election consistent with public quiet. The most remarkable of these are that of Mr. Hume, where the freeholders and the inhabitants assessed to the poor, elect those who are to name the members of the Supreme Council;—that lately proposed in France, where a popular body would propose candidates, from whom a small number of the most considerable proprietors would select the representatives;—and the singular plan of Mr. Horne Tooke, which proposed to give the right of voting to all persons rated to the land-tax or parish-rates at *2l. 2s.* per annum, on condition of their paying to the public *2l. 2s.* at the time of voting; but providing, that if the number of voters in any district fell short of four thousand, every man rated at *20l.* per annum might give a second vote, on again paying the same sum; and making the same provision, in case of the same failure, for third, fourth, fifth, &c. votes for every additional *100l.* at which the voter is rated, till the number of four thousand votes for the district should be completed.

This plan of Mr. Tooke is an ingenious stratagem for augmenting the power of wealth, under pretence of bestowing the suffrage almost universally. To that of Mr. Hume it is a decisive objection, that it leaves to the people only those subordinate elections which would excite no interest in their minds, and would consequently fail in attaining one of the principal objects of popular elections. All schemes for separating the proposition of candidates for public office from the choice of the officers, become in practice a power of nomination in the proposers. It is easy to leave no choice to the electors, by coupling the favoured candidates with none but such as are absolutely ineligible. Yet one reasonable object is common to these projects:—they all aim at subjecting elections to the joint influence of property and popularity. In none of them is overlooked the grand principle of equally securing all orders of men, and interesting all in the maintenance of the constitution. It is possible that any of them might be in some measure effectual; but it would be an act of mere wantonness in us to make the experiment. By that variety of rights of suffrage which seems so fantastic, the English constitution has provided for the union of the principles of property and popularity, in a manner much more effectual than those which the most celebrated theorists have imagined. Of the three, perhaps the least unpromising is that of Mr. Tooke, because it approaches nearest to the forms of public and truly popular elections.

In the system now established in France, where the right of suffrage is confined to those who pay direct taxes amounting to twelve pounds by the year, the object is evidently to vest the whole power in the hands of the middling classes. The Royalists, who are still proprietors of the greatest estates in the kingdom, would have preferred a greater extension of suffrage, in order to multiply the votes of their dependants. But, as the subdivision of forfeited estates has created a numerous body of small land-owners, who are deeply interested in maintaining the new institutions, the law, which gives them almost the whole elective power, may on that account be approved as politic. As a general regulation, it is very objectionable.

If we were compelled to confine all elective influence to one order, we must indeed vest it in the middling classes; both because they possess the largest share of sense and virtue, and because they have the most numerous connections of interest with the other parts of society. It is right that they should have a preponderating influence, because they are likely to make the best choice. But that is not the sole object of representation; and, if it were, there are not wanting circumstances which render it unfit that they should engross the whole influence. Perhaps there never was a time or country in which the middling classes were of a character so respectable and improving as they are at this day in Great Britain: but it unfortunately happens, that this sound and pure body have more to hope from the favour of Government than any other part of the nation. The higher classes may, if they please, be independent of its influence; the lower are almost below its direct action. On the middling classes, it acts with concentrated and unbroken force. Independent of that local consideration, the virtues of that excellent class are generally of a circumspect nature, and apt to degenerate into timidity. They have little of that political boldness which sometimes belongs to commanding fortune, and often, in too great a degree, to thoughtless poverty. They require encouragement and guidance from higher leaders; and they need excitement from the numbers and even turbulence of their inferiors. The end of representation is not a medium between wealth and numbers, but a combination of the influence of both. It is the result of the separate action of great property, of deliberate opinion, and of popular spirit, on different parts of the political system.

"That principle of representation," said Mr. Fox, "is the best which calls into activity the greatest number of independent votes, and excludes those whose condition takes from them the powers of deliberation." But even this principle, true in general, cannot be universally applied. Many who are neither independent nor capable of deliberation, are at present rightly vested with the elective franchise,—not because they are qualified to make a good general choice of members,—but because they indirectly contribute to secure the good composition and right conduct of the legislature.

The question of the Ballot remains. On the Ballot the advocates of universal suffrage seem exclusively to rely for the defence of their schemes: without it, they appear tacitly to admit that universal suffrage would be an impracticable and pernicious proposal.

But all males in the kingdom, it is said, may annually vote at elections with quiet and independence, if the Ballot enables them to give their votes secretly. Whether this expectation be reasonable, is the question on which the decision of the dispute seems now to depend.

The first objection to this proposal is, that the Ballot would not produce secrecy. Even in those classes of men who are most accustomed to keep their own secret, the effect of the Ballot is very unequal and uncertain. The common case of clubs, in which a small minority is generally sufficient to exclude a candidate, may serve as an example. Where the club is numerous, the secret may be kept, as it is difficult to distinguish the few who reject: but in small clubs, where the dissentients may amount to a considerable proportion of the whole, they are almost always ascertained. The practice, it is true, is, in these cases, still useful; but it is only because it is agreed, by a sort of tacit convention, that an exclusion by Ballot is not a just cause of offence: it prevents quarrel, not disclosure. In the House of Commons, Mr. Bentham allows that the Ballot does not secure secrecy or independent choice. The example of the elections at the India House is very unfortunately selected; for every thing which a Ballot is supposed to prevent is to be found in these elections: public and private canvass,—the influence of personal friendship, connexion, gratitude, expectation,—promises almost universally made and observed,—votes generally if not always known,—as much regard, indeed, to public grounds of preference as in most other bodies,—but scarcely any exclusion of private motives, unless it be the apprehension of incurring resentment, which is naturally confined within narrow limits, by the independent condition of the greater part of the electors. In general, indeed, they refuse the secrecy which the legislature seems to tender to them. From kindness, from esteem, from other motives, they are desirious that their votes should be known to candidates whom they favour. And what is disclosed to friends, is speedily discovered by opponents.

If the Ballot should be thought a less offensive mode of voting against an individual than the voice, this slight advantage is altogether confined to those classes of society who have leisure for such fantastic refinements. But are any such influences likely, or rather sure, to act on the two millions of voters who would be given to us by universal suffrage? Let us examine them closely. Will the country labourer ever avail himself of the proffered means of secrecy? To believe this, we must suppose that he performs the most important act of his life,—that which most flatters his pride, and gratifies his inclination,—without speaking of his intention before, or boasting of his vote when he has given it. His life has no secrets. The circle of his village is too small for concealment. His wife, his children, his fellow-labourers, the companions of his recreations, know all that he does, and almost all that he thinks. Can any one believe that he would pass the evening before, or the evening after the day of election, at his alehouse, wrapt up in the secrecy of a Venetian senator, and concealing a suffrage as he would do a murder? If his character disposed him to secrecy, would his situation allow it? His landlord, or his employer, or their agents, or the leaders of a party in the election, could never have any difficulty in discovering him. The simple acts of writing his vote, of delivering it at the poll, or sending it if he could not attend, would betray his secret in spite of the most complicated Ballot ever contrived in Venice. In great towns, the very mention of secret suffrage is ridiculous. By what contrivance are public meetings of the two hundred and fifty thousand London electors to be prevented? There may be quiet and secrecy at the poll; but this does not in the least prevent publicity and tumult at other meetings occasioned by the election. A candidate will not forego the means of success which such meetings afford. The votes of those who attend them must be always known. If the Council of Ten were dispersed among a Westminster mob while candidates were speaking, they would catch its spirit, and betray their votes by huzzas or hisses. Candidates and their partisans, committees in parishes, agents in every street during an active canvass, would quickly learn the secret of almost any man in Westminster. The few who affected mystery would be detected by their neighbours. The evasive answer of the ablest of such dissemblers to his favoured friend or party, would be observably different, at least in tone and manner, from that which he gave to the enemy. The zeal, attachment, and enthusiasm, which must prevail in such elections, as long as they continue really popular, would probably bring all recurrence to means of secrecy into discredit, and very speedily into general disuse. Even the smaller tradesmen, to whom the Ballot might seem desirable, as a shield from the displeasure of their opulent customers, would betray the part they took in the election, by their ambition to be leaders in their parishes. The formality of the Ballot might remain: but the object of secrecy is incompatible with the nature of such elections.

The second objection is, that if secrecy of suffrage could be really adopted, it would, in practice, contract, instead of extending, the elective franchise, by abating, if not extinguishing, the strongest inducements to its exercise. All wise laws contain in themselves effectual means for their own execution: but, where votes are secret, scarcely any motive for voting is left to the majority of electors. In a blind eagerness to free the franchise from influence, nearly all the common motives for its exercise are taken away. The common elector is neither to gain the favour of his superiors, nor the kindness of his fellows, nor the gratitude of the candidate for whom he votes: from all these, secrecy must exclude him. He is forbidden to strengthen his conviction,—to kindle his zeal,—to conquer his fears or selfishness, in numerous meetings of those with whom he agrees; for, if he attends such meetings, he must publish his suffrage, and the Ballot, in his case, becomes altogether illusory. Every blamable motive of interest,—every pardonable inducement of personal impartiality, is, indeed, taken away. But what is left in their place? Nothing but a mere sense of public duty, unaided by the popular discipline which gives fervour and vigour to public sentiments. A wise lawgiver does not trust to a general sense of duty in the most unimportant law. If such a principle could be trusted, laws would be unnecessary. Yet to this cold feeling, stripped of all its natural and most powerful aids, would the system of secret suffrage alone trust for its execution. At the poll it is said to be sufficient, because all temptations to do ill are supposed to be taken away: but the motives by which electors are induced to go to a poll, have been totally overlooked. The inferior classes, for whom this whole system is contrived, would, in its practice, be speedily disfranchised. They would soon relinquish a privilege when it was reduced to a troublesome duty. Their public principles are often generous; but they do not arise from secret meditation, and they do not flourish in solitude.

Lastly, if secret suffrage were to be permanently practised by all voters, it would deprive election of all its popular qualities, and of many of its beneficial effects. The great object of popular elections is, to inspire and strengthen the love of liberty. On the strength of that sentiment freedom wholly depends, not only for its security against the power of time and of enemies, but for its efficiency and reality while it lasts. If we could suppose a people perfectly indifferent to political measures, and without any disposition to take a part in public affairs, the most perfect forms and institutions of liberty would be among them a dead letter. The most elaborate machinery would stand still for want of a moving power. In proportion as a people sinks more near to that slavish apathy, their constitution becomes so far vain, and their best laws impotent. Institutions are carried into effect by men, and men are moved to action by their feelings. A system of liberty can be executed only by men who love liberty. With the spirit of liberty, very unpromising forms grow into an excellent government: without it, the most specious cannot last, and are not worth preserving. The institutions of a free state are safest and most effective, when numerous bodies of men exercise their political rights with pleasure and pride,—consequently with zeal and boldness,—when these rights are endeared to them by tradition and by habit, as well as by conviction and feeling of their inestimable value,—and when the mode of exercising privileges is such as to excite the sympathy of all who view it, and to spread through the whole society a jealous love of popular right, and a proneness to repel with indignation every encroachment on it.

Popular elections contribute to these objects, partly by the character of the majority of the electors, and partly by the mode in which they give their suffrage. Assemblies of the people of great cities, are indeed very ill qualified to exercise authority; but without their occasional use, it can never be strongly curbed. Numbers are nowhere else to be collected. On numbers, alone, much of their power depends. In numerous meetings, every man catches animation from the feelings of his neighbour, and gathers courage from the strength of a multitude. Such assemblies, and they alone, with all their defects and errors, have the privilege of inspiring many human beings with a perfect, however transient, disinterestedness, and of rendering the most ordinary men capable of foregoing interest, and forgetting self, in the enthusiasm of zeal for a common cause. Their vices are a corrective of the deliberating selfishness of their superiors. Their bad, as well as good qualities, render them the portion of society the most susceptible of impressions, and the most accessible to public feelings. They are fitted to produce that democratic spirit which, tempered in its progress through the various classes of the community, becomes the vital principle of liberty. It is very true, that the occasional absurdity and violence of these meetings, often alienate men of timid virtue from the cause of liberty. It is enough for the present purpose, that in those long periods to which political reasonings must always be understood to apply, they contribute far more to excite and to second, than to offend or alarm, the enlightened friends of the rights of the people. But meetings for election are by far the safest and the most effective of all popular assemblies. They are brought together by the constitution; they have a legal character; they display the ensigns of public authority; they assemble men of all ranks and opinions; and, in them, the people publicly and conspicuously bestow some of the highest prizes pursued by a generous ambition. Hence they derive a consequence, and give a sense of self-importance, to their humblest members, which would be vainly sought for in spontaneous meetings. They lend a part of their own seriousness and dignity to other meetings occasioned by the election, and even to those which, at other times are really, or even nominally, composed of electors.

In elections, political principles cease to be mere abstractions. They are embodied in individuals; and the cold conviction of a truth, or the languid approbation of a measure, is animated by attachment for leaders, and hostility to adversaries. Every political passion is warmed in the contest. Even the outward circumstances of the scene strike the imagination, and affect the feelings. The recital of them daily spreads enthusiasm over a country. The various fortunes of the combat excite anxiety and agitation on all sides; and an opportunity is offered of discussing almost every political question, under circumstances in which the hearts of hearers and readers take part in the argument: till the issue of a controversy is regarded by the nation with some degree of the same solicitude as the event of a battle. In this manner is formed democratical ascendency, which is most perfect when the greatest numbers of independent judgments influence the measures of government. Reading may, indeed, increase the number and intelligence of those whose sentiments compose public opinion; but numerous assemblies, and consequently popular elections, can alone generate the courage and zeal which form so large a portion of its power.

With these effects it is apparent that secret suffrage is absolutely incompatible: they cannot exist together. Assemblies to elect, or assemblies during elections, make all suffrages known. The publicity and boldness in which voters give their suffrage are of the very essence of popular elections, and greatly contribute to their animating effect. The advocates of the Ballot tell us, indeed, that it would destroy canvass and tumult. But after the destruction of the canvass, elections would no longer teach humility to the great, nor self-esteem to the humble. Were the causes of tumult destroyed, elections would no longer be nurseries of political zeal, and instruments for rousing national spirit. The friends of liberty ought rather to view the turbulence of the people with indulgence and pardon, as powerfully tending to exercise and invigorate their public spirit. It is not to be extinguished, but to be rendered safe by countervailing institutions of an opposite tendency on other parts of the constitutional system.

The original fallacy, which is the source of all erroneous reasoning in favour of the Ballot, is the assumption that the value of popular elections chiefly depends on the exercise of a deliberate judgment by the electors. The whole anxiety of its advocates is to remove the causes which might disturb a considerate choice. In order to obtain such a choice, which is *not* the great purpose of popular elections, these speculators would deprive them of the power to excite and diffuse public spirit,—the great and inestimable service which a due proportion of such elections renders to a free state. In order to make the forms of democracy universal, their plan would universally extinguish its spirit. In a commonwealth where universal suffrage was already established, the Ballot might perhaps be admissible as an expedient for tempering such an extreme democracy. Even there, it might be objected to, as one of these remedies for licentiousness which are likely to endanger liberty by destroying all democratic spirit;—it would be one of those dexterous frauds by which the people are often weaned from the exertion of their privileges.

The system which we oppose is established in the United States of America; and it is said to be attended with no mischievous effects. To this we answer, that, in America, universal suffrage is not the rule, but the exception. In twelve out of the nineteen states* which compose that immense confederacy, the disgraceful institution of slavery deprives great multitudes not only of political franchises, but of the indefeasible rights of all mankind. The numbers of the representatives of the Slave-states in Congress is proportioned to their population, whether slaves or freemen;—a provision arising, indeed, from the most abominable of all human institutions, but recognising the just principle, that property is one of the elements of every wise representation. In many states, the white complexion is a necessary qualification for suffrage, and the disfranchised are separated from the privileged order by a physical boundary, which no individual can ever pass. In countries of slavery, where to be free is to be noble, the universal distribution of privilege among the ruling caste, is a natural consequence of the aristocratical pride with which each man regards the dignity of the whole order, especially when they are all distinguished from their slaves by the same conspicuous and indelible marks. Yet, in Virginia, which has long been the ruling state of the confederacy, even the citizens of the governing class cannot vote without the possession of a freehold estate. A real or personal estate is required in New England,—the ancient seat of the character and spirit of America,—the parent of those seamen, who, with a courage and skill worthy of our common forefathers, have met the followers of Nelson in war,—the nursery of the intelligent and moral, as well as hardy and laborious race, who now annually colonize the vast regions of the West.

But were the fact otherwise, America contains few large, and no very great towns; the people are dispersed, and agricultural; and, perhaps, a majority of the inhabitants are either land-owners, or have that immediate expectation of becoming proprietors, which produces nearly the same effect on character with the possession of property. Adventurers who, in other countries, disturb society, are there naturally attracted towards the frontier, where they pave the way for industry, and become the pioneers of civilization. There is no part of their people in the situation where democracy is dangerous, or even usually powerful. The dispersion of the inhabitants, and their distance from the

* This was written in 1819. In 1845 the proportion is thirteen Slave to fourteen Free states exclusive of Texas.—Ed.

scene of great affairs, are perhaps likely rather to make the spirit of liberty among them languid, than to rouse it to excess.

In what manner the present elective system of America may act, at the remote period when the progress of society shall have conducted that country to the crowded cities and unequal fortunes of Europe, no man will pretend to foresee, except those whose presumptuous folly disables them from forming probable conjectures on such subjects. If, from the unparalleled situation of America, the present usages should quietly prevail for a very long time, they may insensibly adapt themselves to the gradual changes in the national condition, and at length be found capable of subsisting in a state of things to which, if they had been suddenly introduced, they would have proved irreconcilably adverse. In the thinly peopled states of the West, universal suffrage itself may be so long exercised without the possibility of danger, as to create a national habit which may be strong enough to render its exercise safe in the midst of an indigent populace. In that long tranquillity it may languish into forms, and these forms may soon follow the spirit. For a period far exceeding our foresight, it cannot affect the confederacy further than the effect which may arise from very popular elections in a few of the larger Western towns. The order of the interior country wherever it is adopted, will be aided by the compression of its firmer and more compact confederates. It is even possible that the extremely popular system which prevails in some American elections, may, in future times, be found not more than sufficient to counterbalance the growing influence of wealth in the South, and the tendencies towards Toryism which are of late perceptible in New England.

The operation of different principles on elections, in various parts of the Continent, may even now be discerned. Some remarkable facts have already appeared. In the state of Pennsylvania, we have* a practical proof that the Ballot is not attended with secrecy. We also know,† that committees composed of the leaders of the Federal and Democratic parties, instruct their partisans how they are to vote at every election; and that in this manner the leaders of the Democratic party who now predominate in their Caucus‡ or committee at Washington, do in effect nominate to all the important offices in North America. Thus, we already see combinations formed, and interests arising, on which the future government of the confederacy may depend more than on the forms of election, or the letter of its present laws. Those who condemn the principle of party, may disapprove these associations as unconstitutional. To us who consider parties as inseparable from liberty, they seem remarkable as examples of those undesigned and unforeseen correctives of inconvenient laws which spring out of the circumstances of society. The election of so great a magistrate as the President, by great numbers of electors, scattered over a vast continent, without the power of concert, or the means of personal knowledge, would naturally produce confusion, if it were not tempered by the confidence of the members of both parties in the judgment of their respective leaders. The permanence of these leaders, slowly raised by a sort of insensible election to the conduct of parties, tends to counteract the evil of that system of periodical removal, which is peculiarly inconvenient in its application to important executive offices. The internal discipline of parties may be found to be a principle of subordination of great value in republican institutions. Certain it is, that the affairs of the United States have hitherto been generally administered, in times of great difficulty and under a succession of Presidents, with a forbearance, circumspection, constancy, and vigour, not surpassed by those commonwealths who have been most justly renowned for the wisdom of their councils.

The only disgrace or danger which we perceive impending over America, arises from the execrable institution of slavery,—the unjust disfranchisement of free Blacks,—the trading in slaves carried on from state to state,—and the dissolute and violent character of those adventurers, whose impatience for guilty wealth spreads the horrors of slavery over the new acquisitions in the South. Let the lawgivers of that Imperial Republic deeply consider how powerfully these disgraceful circumstances tend to weaken the love of liberty,—the only bond which can hold together such vast territories, and therefore the only source and guard of the tranquillity and greatness of America.

* Fearon, Travels in North America, p. 138. How could this intelligent writer treat the absence of tumult, in such a city and country, as bearing any resemblance to the like circumstance in Europe?

† Ibid. p. 320.

‡ The following account of this strange term, will show its probable origin, and the long-experienced efficacy of such an expedient for controlling the Ballot:—"About the year 1738, the father of Samuel Adams, and twenty others who lived in the north or shipping part of Boston, used to meet, to make a *Caucus*, and lay their plan for introducing certain persons into places of trust. Each distributed the ballots in his own circle, and they generally carried the election. In this manner Mr. S. Adams first became representative for Boston. *Caucusing* means electioneering."—(Gordon, History of the American Revolution, p. 216, note.) It is conjectured, that as this practice originated in the shipping part of Boston, 'Caucus' was a corruption of Caulkers' Meeting. For this information we are indebted to Pickering's American Vocabulary (Boston, 1816); a modest and sensible book, of which the principal fault is, that the author ascribes too much importance to some English writers, who are not objects of much reverence to a near observer. Mr. Pickering's volume, however, deserves a place in English libraries.

A SPEECH

IN

DEFENCE OF JEAN PELTIER,

ACCUSED OF A LIBEL ON THE FIRST CONSUL OF FRANCE.

DELIVERED IN THE COURT OF KING'S BENCH ON THE 21ST OF FEBRUARY, 1803.*

GENTLEMEN OF THE JURY,

The time is now come for me to address you on behalf of the unfortunate Gentleman who is the defendant on this record.

I must begin with observing, that though I know myself too well to ascribe to any thing but to the kindness and good-nature of my learned friend the Attorney-General † the unmerited praises which he has been pleased to bestow on me, yet I will venture to say, he has done me no more than justice in supposing that in this place, and on this occasion, where I exercise the functions of an inferior minister of justice,—an inferior minister indeed, but a minister of justice still,—I am incapable of lending myself to the passions of any client, and that I will not make the proceedings of this Court subservient to any political purpose. Whatever is respected by the laws and government of my country, shall, in this place, be respected by me. In considering matters that deeply interest the quiet, the safety, and the liberties of all mankind, it is impossible for me not to feel warmly and strongly; but I shall make an effort to control my feelings, however painful that effort may be, and where I cannot speak out at the risk of offending either sincerity or prudence, I shall labour to contain myself and be silent.

I cannot but feel, Gentlemen, how much I stand in need of your favourable attention and indulgence. The charge which I have to defend is surrounded with the most invidious topics of discussion. But they are not of my seeking. The case, and the topics which are inseparable from it, are brought here by the prosecutor. Here I find them, and here it is my duty to deal with them, as the interests of Mr. Peltier seem to me to require. He, by his choice and confidence, has cast on me a very arduous duty, which I could not decline, and which I can still less betray. He has a right to expect from me a faithful, a zealous, and a fearless defence; and this his just expectation, according to the measure of my humble abilities, shall be fulfilled. I have said, a fearless defence:—perhaps that word was unnecessary in the place where I now stand. Intrepidity in the discharge of professional duty is so common a quality at the English Bar, that it has, thank God! long ceased to be a matter of boast or praise. If it had been otherwise, Gentlemen,—if the Bar could have been silenced or overawed by power, I may presume to say, that an English jury would not this day have been met to administer justice. Perhaps I need scarce say that my defence shall be fearless, in a place where fear never entered any heart but that of a criminal. But you will pardon me for having said so much, when you consider who the real parties before you are.

Gentlemen, the real prosecutor is the master of the greatest empire the civilized world ever saw. The Defendant is a defenceless proscribed exile. He is a French Royalist, who fled from his country in the autumn of 1792, at the period of that memorable and awful emigration when all the proprietors and magistrates of the greatest civilized country of Europe were driven from their homes by the daggers of assassins;—when our shores were covered, as with the wreck of a great tempest, with old men, and women, and children, and ministers of religion, who fled from the ferocity of their countrymen as before an army of invading barba-

* The First Consul had for some time previously shown considerable irritability under the fire of the English journalists, when the Peace of Amiens, by permitting a *rapprochement* with the English Ministry, afforded an opening through which his paw could reach the source of annoyance. M. Jean Peltier, on whom it lighted, was an emigrant, who had been conducting for some years various periodical works in the Royalist interest. From one of these,—"L'Ambigu"—three articles, which are alluded to separately in the course of the speech, were selected by the law officers of the Crown for prosecution, as instigating the assassination of the First Consul. Nor perhaps, could such a conclusion have been successfully struggled with by any advocate. The proceeding was one that was accompanied with much excitement in public opinion, as was evidenced by the concourse of persons surrounding the court on the day of trial. It was supposed by some that a verdict of acquittal would have had an unfavourable effect upon the already feverish state of the intercourse between the two Governments. In fact, though found 'guilty,' the Defendant escaped any sentence through the recurrence of hostilities.—ED.

† The Right Honourable Spencer Perceval. —ED.

rians. The greater part of these unfortunate exiles,—of those I mean who have been spared by the sword, or who have survived the effect of pestilential climates or broken hearts,—have been since permitted to revisit their country. Though despoiled of their all, they have eagerly embraced even the sad privilege of being suffered to die in their native land. Even this miserable indulgence was to be purchased by compliances,—by declarations of allegiance to the new government,—which some of these suffering royalists deemed incompatible with their conscience, with their dearest attachments and their most sacred duties. Among these last is Mr. Peltier. I do not presume to blame those who submitted; and I trust you will not judge harshly of those who refused. You will not think unfavourably of a man who stands before you as the voluntary victim of his loyalty and honour. If a revolution (which God avert!) were to drive us into exile, and to cast us on a foreign shore, we should expect, at least, to be pardoned by generous men, for stubborn loyalty, and unseasonable fidelity, to the laws and government of our fathers.

This unfortunate Gentleman had devoted a great part of his life to literature. It was the amusement and ornament of his better days: since his own ruin, and the desolation of his country, he has been compelled to employ it as a means of support. For the last ten years he has been engaged in a variety of publications of considerable importance: but, since the peace, he has desisted from serious political discussion, and confined himself to the obscure journal which is now before you,—the least calculated, surely, of any publication that ever issued from the press, to rouse the alarms of the most jealous government,—which will not be read in England, because it is not written in our language,—which cannot be read in France, because its entry into that country is prohibited by a power whose mandates are not very supinely enforced, nor often evaded with impunity,—which can have no other object than that of amusing the companions of the author's principles and misfortunes, by pleasantries and sarcasms on their victorious enemies. There is, indeed, Gentlemen, one remarkable circumstance in this unfortunate publication: it is the only, or almost the only, journal, which still dares to espouse the cause of that royal and illustrious family, which but fourteen years ago was flattered by every press, and guarded by every tribunal, in Europe. Even the court in which we are met affords an example of the vicissitudes of their fortune. My Learned Friend has reminded you, that the last prosecution tried in this place, at the instance of a French government, was for a libel on that magnanimous princess, who has since been butchered in sight of her palace.

I do not make these observations with any purpose of questioning the general principles which have been laid down by my Learned Friend. I must admit his right to bring before you those who libel any government recognised by His Majesty, and at peace with the British empire. I admit that, whether such a government be of yesterday or a thousand years old,—whether it be a crude and bloody usurpation, or the most ancient, just, and paternal authority upon earth,—we are equally bound by His Majesty's recognition to protect it against libellous attacks. I admit that if, during our Usurpation, Lord Clarendon had published his History at Paris, or the Marquis of Montrose his verses on the murder of his sovereign, or Mr. Cowley his Discourse on Cromwell's Government, and if the English ambassador had complained, the President de Molé, or any other of the great magistrates who then adorned the Parliament of Paris, however reluctantly, painfully, and indignantly, might have been compelled to have condemned these illustrious men to the punishment of libellers. I say this only for the sake of bespeaking a favourable attention from your generosity and compassion to what will be feebly urged in behalf of my unfortunate Client, who has sacrificed his fortune, his hopes, his connections, and his country, to his conscience,—who seems marked out for destruction in this his last asylum.

That he still enjoys the security of this asylum,—that he has not been sacrificed to the resentment of his powerful enemies, is perhaps owing to the firmness of the King's Government. If that be the fact, Gentlemen,—if his Majesty's Ministers have resisted the applications to expel this unfortunate Gentleman from England, I should publicly thank them for their firmness, if it were not unseemly and improper to suppose that they could have acted otherwise,—to thank an English Government for not violating the most sacred duties of hospitality,—for not bringing indelible disgrace on their country. But be that as it may, Gentlemen, he now comes before you perfectly satisfied that an English jury is the most refreshing prospect that the eye of accused innocence ever met in a human tribunal; and he feels with me the most fervent gratitude to the Protector of empires, that, surrounded as we are with the ruins of principalities and powers, we still continue to meet together, after the manner of our fathers, to administer justice in this her ancient sanctuary.

There is another point of view, Gentlemen, in which this case seems to me to merit your most serious attention. I consider it as the first of a long series of conflicts between the greatest power in the world, and the only free press remaining in Europe. No man living is more thoroughly convinced than I am, that my Learned Friend will never degrade his excellent character,—that he will never disgrace his high magistracy by mean compliances,—by an immoderate and unconscientious exercise of power; yet I am convinced by circumstances which I shall now abstain from discussing, that I *am to consider this as the first of a long series of conflicts, between the greatest power in the world, and the only free press now remaining in Europe.* Gentlemen, this distinction of the English press is new: it is a proud and melancholy distinction. Before the great earthquake of the French Revolution had swallowed up all the asylums of free discussion on the Continent, we enjoyed that privilege, indeed, more fully than others, but we did not enjoy it exclusively. In great monarchies the press has always been considered as too formidable an engine to be intrusted to unlicensed individuals. But in other Continental countries, either by the laws of the state, or by long habits of liberality and toleration in magistrates, a liberty of discussion has been enjoyed, perhaps sufficient for the most useful purposes. It existed, in fact, where it was not protected by law: and the wise and generous connivance of governments was daily more and more secured by the growing civilization of their subjects. In Holland, in Switzerland, and in the Imperial towns of Germany, the press was either legally or practically free. Holland and Switzerland are no more: and, since the commencement of this prosecution, fifty Imperial towns have been erased from the list of independent states, by one dash of the pen. Three or four still preserve a precarious and trembling existence. I will not say by what compliances they must purchase its continuance. I will not insult the feebleness of states whose unmerited fall I do most bitterly deplore.

These governments were in many respects one of the most interesting parts of the ancient system of Europe. Unfortunately for the repose of mankind, great states are compelled, by regard to their own safety, to consider the military spirit and martial habits of their people as one of the main objects of their policy. Frequent hostilities seem almost the necessary condition of their greatness: and, without being great, they cannot long remain safe. Smaller states, exempted from this cruel necessity,—a hard condition of greatness, a bitter satire on human nature,—devoted themselves to the arts of peace, to the cultivation of literature, and the improvement of reason. They became places of refuge for free and fearless discussion: they were the impartial spectators and judges of the various contests of ambition, which, from time to time, disturbed the quiet of the world. They thus became peculiarly qualified to be the organs of that public opinion which converted Europe into a great republic, with laws which mitigated, though they could not extinguish, ambition, and with moral tribunals to which even the most despotic sovereigns were amenable. If wars of aggrandisement were undertaken, their authors were arraigned in the face of Europe. If acts of internal tyranny were perpetrated, they resounded from a thousand presses throughout all civilized countries. Princes on whose will there were no legal checks, thus found a moral restraint which the most powerful of them could not brave with absolute impunity. They acted before a vast audience, to whose applause or condemnation they could not be utterly indifferent. The very constitution of human nature,—the unalterable laws of the mind of man, against which all rebellion is fruitless, subjected the proudest tyrants to this control. No elevation of power,—no depravity, however consummate,—no innocence, however spotless, can render man wholly independent of the praise or blame of his fellow-men.

These governments were in other respects one of the most beautiful and interesting parts of our ancient system. The perfect security of such inconsiderable and feeble states,—their undisturbed tranquillity amidst the wars and conquests that surrounded them, attested, beyond any other part of the European system, the moderation, the justice, the civilization to which Christian Europe had reached in modern times. Their weakness was protected only by the habitual reverence for justice, which, during a long series of ages, had grown up in Christendom. This was the only fortification which defended them against those mighty monarchs to whom they offered themselves so easy a prey. And, till the French Revolution, this was sufficient. Consider, for instance, the situation of the republic of Geneva: think of her defenceless position in the very jaws of France; but think also of her undisturbed security,—of her profound quiet,—of the brilliant success with which she applied to industry and literature, while Louis XIV. was pouring his myriads into Italy before her gates. Call to mind, if ages crowded into years have not effaced them from your memory, that happy period when we scarcely dreamt more of the subjugation of the feeblest republic of Europe, than of the conquest of her mightiest empire, and tell me if you can imagine a spectacle more beautiful to the moral eye, or a more striking proof of progress in the noblest principles of true civilization.

These feeble states,—these monuments of the justice of Europe,—the asylums of peace, of industry, and of literature,—the organs of public reason,—the refuge of oppressed innocence and persecuted truth,—have perished with those ancient principles which were their sole guardians and protectors. They have been swallowed up by that fearful convulsion which has shaken the uttermost corners of the earth. They are destroyed and gone for ever. One asylum of free discussion is still inviolate. There is still one spot in Europe where man can freely exercise his reason on the most important concerns of society,—where he can boldly publish his judgment on the acts of the proudest and most powerful tyrants. The press of England is still free. It is guarded by the free constitution of our forefathers;—it is guarded by the hearts and arms of Englishmen; and I trust I may venture to say, that if it be to fall, it will fall only under the ruins of the British empire. It is an awful consideration, Gentlemen:—every other monument of European liberty has perished: that ancient fabric which has been gradually reared by the wisdom and virtue of our fathers still stands. It stands, (thanks be to God!) solid and entire; but it stands alone, and it stands amidst ruins.

In these extraordinary circumstances, I repeat that I must consider this as the first of a long series of conflicts between the greatest power in the world and the only free press remaining in Europe; and I trust that you will consider yourselves as the advanced guard of liberty, as having this day to fight the first battle of free discussion against the most formidable enemy that it ever encountered. You will therefore excuse me, if on so important an occasion I remind you at more length than is usual, of those general principles of law and policy on this subject, which have been handed down to us by our ancestors.

Those who slowly built up the fabric of our laws, never attempted anything so absurd as to define by any precise rule the obscure and shifting boundaries which divide libel from history or discussion. It is a subject which, from its nature, admits neither rules nor definitions. The same words may be perfectly innocent in one case, and most mischievous and libellous in another. A change of circumstances, often apparently slight, is sufficient to make the whole difference. These changes, which may be as numerous as the variety of human intentions and conditions, can never be foreseen or comprehended under any legal definitions; and the framers of our law have never attempted to subject them to such definitions. They left such ridiculous attempts to those who call themselves philosophers, but who have in fact proved themselves most grossly and stupidly ignorant of that philosophy which is conversant with human affairs.

The principles of the law of England on the subject of political libel are few and simple; and they are necessarily so broad, that, without an habitually mild administration of justice, they might encroach materially on the liberty of political discussion. Every publication which is intended to vilify either our own government or the government of any foreign state in amity with this kingdom, is, by the law of England, a libel. To protect political discussion from the danger to which it would be exposed by these wide principles, if they were severely and literally enforced, our ancestors trusted to various securities; some growing out of the law and constitution, and others arising from the character of those public officers whom the constitution had formed, and to whom its administration is committed. They trusted in the first place to the moderation of the legal officers of the Crown, educated in the maxims and imbued with the spirit of a free government, controlled by the superintending power of Parliament, and peculiarly watched in all political prosecutions by the reasonable and wholesome jealousy of their fellow-subjects. And I am bound to admit, that since the glorious era of the Revolution,—making due allowance for the frailties, the faults, and the occasional vices of men,—they have upon the whole not been disappointed. I know that, in the hands of my Learned Friend, that trust will never be abused. But, above all, they confided in the moderation and good sense of juries,—popular in their origin,—popular in their feelings,—popular in their very prejudices,—taken from the mass of the people, and immediately returning to that mass again. By these checks and temperaments they hoped that they should sufficiently repress malignant libels, without endangering that freedom of inquiry which is the first security of a free state. They knew that the offence of a political libel is of a very peculiar nature, and differing in the most important particulars from all other crimes. In all other cases the most severe execution of law can only spread terror among the guilty; but in political libels it inspires even the innocent with fear. This striking peculiarity arises from the same circumstances which make it impossible to define the limits of libel and innocent discussion,—which make it impossible for a man of the purest and most honourable mind to be always perfectly certain, whether he be within the territory of fair argument and honest narrative, or whether he may not have unwittingly overstepped the faint and varying line which bounds them. But, Gentlemen, I will go farther:—this is the only offence where severe and frequent punishments not only intimidate the innocent, but deter men from the most meritorious acts, and from rendering the most important services to their country,—indispose and disqualify men for the discharge of the most sacred duties which they owe to mankind. To inform the public on the conduct of those who administer public affairs, requires courage and conscious security. It is always an invidious and obnoxious office; but it is often the most necessary of all public duties. If it is not done boldly, it cannot be done effectually: and it is not from writers trembling under the uplifted scourge, that we are to hope for it.

There are other matters, Gentlemen, to which I am desirous of particularly calling your attention. These are, the circumstances in the condition of this country, which have induced our ancestors, at all times, to handle with more than ordinary tenderness that branch of the liberty of discussion which is applied to the conduct of foreign states. The relation of this kingdom to the commonwealth of Europe is so peculiar, that no history, I think, furnishes a parallel to it. From the moment in which we abandoned all projects of Continental aggrandisement, we could have no interest respecting the state of the Continent, but the interests of national safety, and of commercial prosperity. The paramount interest of every state, — that which comprehends every other, is security: and the security of Great Britain requires nothing on the Continent but the uniform observance of justice. It requires nothing but the inviolability of ancient boundaries, and the sacredness of ancient possessions, which, on these subjects, is but another form of words for justice.

As to commercial prosperity, it is, indeed, a secondary, but still a very important branch of our national interest; and it requires nothing on the Continent of Europe but the maintenance of peace, as far as the paramount interest of security will allow. Whatever ignorant or prejudiced men may affirm, no war was ever gainful to a commercial nation. Losses may be less in some, and incidental profits may arise in others. But no such profits ever formed an adequate compensation for the waste of capital and industry which all wars must produce. Next to peace, our commercial greatness depends chiefly on the affluence and prosperity of our neighbours. A commercial nation has, indeed, the same interest in the wealth of her neighbours, that a tradesman has in the wealth of his customers. The prosperity of England has been chiefly owing to the general progress of civilized nations in the arts and improvements of social life. Not an acre of land has been brought into cultivation in the wilds of Siberia, or on the shores of the Mississippi, which has not widened the market for English industry. It is nourished by the progressive prosperity of the world; and it amply repays all that it has received. It can only be employed in spreading civilization and enjoyment over the earth; and by the unchangeable laws of nature, in spite of the impotent tricks of governments, it is now partly applied to revive the industry of those very nations who are the loudest in their senseless clamours against its pretended mischiefs. If the blind and barbarous project of destroying English prosperity could be accomplished, it could have no other effect than that of completely beggaring the very countries, which now stupidly ascribe their own poverty to our wealth.

Under these circumstances, Gentlemen, it became the obvious policy of this kingdom, —a policy in unison with the maxims of a free government,—to consider with great indulgence even the boldest animadversions of our political writers on the ambitious projects of foreign states. Bold, and sometimes indiscreet, as these animadversions might be, they had at least the effect of warning the people of their danger, and of rousing the national indignation against those encroachments which England has almost always been compelled in the end to resist by arms. Seldom, indeed, has she been allowed to wait, till a provident regard to her own safety should compel her to take up arms in defence of others. For, as it was said by a great orator of antiquity, "that no man ever was the enemy of the republic who had not first declared war against him,"* so I may say, with truth, that no man ever meditated the subjugation of Europe, who did not consider the destruction, or the corruption, of England as the first condition of his success. If you examine history you will find, that no such project was ever formed in which it was not deemed a necessary preliminary, either to detach England from the common cause, or to destroy her. It seems as if all the conspirators against the independence of nations might have sufficiently taught other states that England is their natural guardian and protector,—that she alone has no interest but their preservation,—that her safety is interwoven with their own. When vast projects of aggrandisement are manifested,—when schemes of criminal ambition are carried into effect, the day of battle is fast approaching for England. Her free government cannot engage in dangerous wars, without the hearty and affectionate support of her people. A state thus situated cannot without the utmost peril silence those public discussions, which are to point the popular indignation against those who must soon be enemies. In domestic dissensions, it may sometimes be the supposed interest of government to overawe the press: but it never can be even their apparent interest when the danger is purely foreign. A King of England who, in such circumstances, should conspire against the free press of this country, would undermine the foundations of his own throne; — he would silence the trumpet which is to call his people round his standard.

Gentlemen, the public spirit of a people (by which I mean the whole body of those affections which unites men's hearts to the commonwealth) is in various countries composed of various elements, and depends on a great variety of causes. In this country, I may venture to say, that it mainly depends on the vigour of the popular parts and principles of our government; and that the spirit of liberty is one of its most important elements. Perhaps it may depend less on those advantages of a free government, which are most highly estimated by calm reason, than upon those parts of it which delight the imagination, and flatter the just and natural pride of mankind. Among these we are certainly not to forget the political rights which are not uniformly withheld from the lowest classes, and the continual appeal made to them, in public discussion, upon the greatest interests of the state. These are undoubtedly among the circumstances which endear to Englishmen their government and their country, and animate their zeal for that glorious institution which confers on the meanest of them a sort of distinction and nobility unknown to the most illustrious slaves who tremble at the frown of a tyrant. Whoever was unwarily and rashly to abolish or narrow these privileges (which it must be

* The reference is probably to Cicero. Orat. in Catilinam, iv. cap. 10.—Ed.

owned are liable to great abuse, and to very specious objections), might perhaps discover, too late, that he had been dismantling the fortifications of his country. Of whatever elements public spirit is composed, it is always and every where the chief defensive principle of a state (it is perfectly distinct from courage:—perhaps no nation—certainly no European nation ever perished from an inferiority of courage); and undoubtedly no considerable nation was ever subdued, in which the public affections were sound and vigorous. It is public spirit which binds together the dispersed courage of individuals, and fastens it to the commonwealth:—it is therefore, as I have said, the chief defensive principle of every country. Of all the stimulants which rouse it into action, the most powerful among us is certainly the press: and the press cannot be restrained or weakened without imminent danger that the national spirit may languish, and that the people may act with less zeal and affection for their country in the hour of its danger.

These principles, Gentlemen, are not new: they are genuine old English principles. And though in our days they have been disgraced and abused by ruffians and fanatics, they are in themselves as just and sound as they are liberal; and they are the only principles on which a free state can be safely governed. These principles I have adopted since I first learnt the use of reason; and I think I shall abandon them only with life.

On these principles I am now to call your attention to the libel with which this unfortunate Gentleman is charged. I heartily rejoice that I concur with the greatest part of what has been said by my Learned Friend, who has done honour even to *his* character by the generous and liberal principles which he has laid down. He has told you that he does not mean to attack historical narrative; —he has told you that he does not mean to attack political discussion;—he has told you also that he does not consider every intemperate word into which a writer, fairly engaged in narration or reasoning, might be betrayed, as a fit subject for prosecution. The essence of the crime of libel consists in the malignant mind which the publication proves, and from which it flows. A jury must be convinced, before they find a man guilty of libel, that his intention was to libel,—not to state facts which he believed to be true, or reasonings which he thought just. My Learned Friend has told you that the liberty of history includes the right of publishing those observations which occur to intelligent men when they consider the affairs of the world; and I think he will not deny that it includes also the right of expressing those sentiments which all good men feel on the contemplation of extraordinary examples of depravity or excellence.

One more privilege of the historian, which the Attorney-General has not named, but to which his principles extend, it is now my duty to claim on behalf of my client:—I mean, the right of republishing, historically, those documents (whatever their original malignity may be) which display the character and unfold the intentions of governments, or factions, or individuals. I think my Learned Friend will not deny, that an historical compiler may innocently republish in England the most insolent and outrageous declaration of war ever published against His Majesty by a foreign government. The intention of the original author was to vilify and degrade his Majesty's government: but the intention of the compiler is only to gratify curiosity, or perhaps to rouse just indignation against the calumniator whose production he republishes; his intention is not libellous,—his republication is therefore not a libel. Suppose this to be the case with Mr. Peltier;—suppose him to have republished libels with a merely historical intention. In that case it cannot be pretended that he is more a libeller than my learned friend Mr. Abbott,* who read these supposed libels to you when he opened the pleadings. Mr. Abbott republished them to you, that you might know and judge of them: Mr. Peltier, on the supposition I have made, also republished them that the public might know and judge of them.

You already know that the general plan of Mr. Peltier's publication was to give a picture of the cabals and intrigues,—of the hopes and projects, of French factions. It is undoubtedly a natural and necessary part of this plan to republish all the serious and ludicrous pieces which these factions circulate against each other. The Ode ascribed to Chenier or Ginguené I do really believe to have been written at Paris,—to have been circulated there,—to have been there attributed to one of these writers,—to have been sent to England as their work,—and as such, to have been republished by Mr. Peltier. But I am not sure that I have evidence to convince you of the truth of this. Suppose that I have not: will my Learned Friend say that my client must necessarily be convicted? I, on the contrary, contend, that it is for my Learned Friend to show that it is not an historical republication:—such it professes to be, and that profession it is for him to disprove. The profession may indeed be a "mask:" but it is for my Friend to pluck off the mask, and expose the libeller, before he calls upon you for a verdict of "guilty."

If the general lawfulness of such republications be denied, then I must ask Mr. Attorney-General to account for the long impunity which English newspapers have enjoyed. I must request him to tell you why they have been suffered to republish all the atrocious, official and unofficial, libels which have been published against His Majesty for the last ten years, by the Brissots, the Marats, the Dantons, the Robespierres, the Barrères, the Talliens, the Reubells, the Merlins, the Barras', and all that long line of bloody ty-

* The junior counsel for the prosecution, afterwards Lord Tenterden.—Ed.

rants who oppressed their own country, and insulted every other which they had not the power to rob. What must be the answer? That the English publishers were either innocent if their motive was to gratify curiosity, or praiseworthy if their intention was to rouse indignation against the calumniators of their country. If any other answer be made, I must remind my Friend of a most sacred part of his duty—the duty of protecting the honest fame of those who are absent in the service of their country. Within these few days, we have seen in every newspaper in England, a publication, called the Report of Col. Sebastiani, in which a gallant British officer (General Stuart) is charged with writing letters to procure assassination. The publishers of that infamous Report are not and will not be prosecuted, because their intention is not to libel General Stuart. On any other principle, why have all our newspapers been suffered to circulate that most atrocious of all libels against the King and the people of England, which purports to be translated from the Moniteur of the 9th of August, 1802; a libel against a Prince, who has passed through a factious and stormy reign of forty-three years without a single imputation on his personal character,—against a people who have passed through the severest trials of national virtue with unimpaired glory, who alone in the world can boast of mutinies without murder, of triumphant mobs without massacre, of bloodless revolutions and of civil wars unstained by a single assassination;—that most impudent and malignant libel, which charges such a King of such a people not only with having hired assassins, but with being so shameless,—so lost to all sense of character, as to have bestowed on these assassins, if their murderous projects had succeeded, the highest badges of public honour,—the rewards reserved for statesmen and heroes,—the Order of the Garter;—the Order which was founded by the heroes of Creçy and Poitiers,—the Garter which was worn by Henry the Great and by Gustavus Adolphus,—which might now be worn by the Hero* who, on the shores of Syria, the ancient theatre of English chivalry, has revived the renown of English valour and of English humanity,—that unsullied Garter, which a detestable libeller dares to say is to be paid as the price of murder.

If I had now to defend an English publisher for the republication of that abominable libel, what must I have said on his defence? I must have told you that it was originally published by the French Government in their official gazette,—that it was republished by the English editor to gratify the natural curiosity, perhaps to rouse the just resentment, of his English readers. I should have contended, and, I trust, with success, that his republication of a libel was not libellous,—that it was lawful,—that it was laudable. All that would be important, at least all that would be essential in such a defence I now state to you on behalf of Mr. Peltier; and if an English newspaper may safely republish the libels of the French Government against His Majesty, I shall leave you to judge whether Mr. Peltier, in similar circumstances, may not, with equal safety, republish the libels of Chenier against the First Consul. On the one hand you have the assurances of Mr. Peltier in the context that this Ode is merely a republication;—you have also the general plan of his work, with which such a republication is perfectly consistent. On the other hand, you have only the suspicions of Mr. Attorney-General that this Ode is an original production of the Defendant.

But supposing that you should think it his production, and that you should also think it a libel,—even in that event, which I cannot anticipate, I am not left without a defence. The question will still be open:—is it a libel on Buonaparte, or is it a libel on Chenier or Ginguené? This is not an information for a libel on Chenier; and if you should think that this Ode was produced by Mr. Peltier, and ascribed by him to Chenier for the sake of covering that writer with the odium of Jacobinism, the Defendant is entitled to your verdict of "not guilty." Or if you should believe that it is ascribed to Jacobinical writers for the sake of satirising a French Jacobinical faction, you must also in that case acquit him. Butler puts seditious and immoral language into the mouths of rebels and fanatics; but Hudibras is not for that reason a libel on morality or government. Swift, in the most exquisite piece of irony in the world (his Argument against the Abolition of Christianity), uses the language of those shallow, atheistical coxcombs whom his satire was intended to scourge. The scheme of his irony required some levity, and even some profaneness of language; but nobody was ever so dull as to doubt whether Swift meant to satirise atheism or religion. In the same manner Mr. Peltier, when he wrote a satire on French Jacobinism, was compelled to ascribe to Jacobins a Jacobinical hatred of government. He was obliged, by dramatic propriety, to put into their mouths those anarchical maxims which are complained of in this Ode. But it will be said, these incitements to insurrection are here directed against the authority of Buonaparte. This proves nothing, because they must have been so directed, if the Ode was a satire on Jacobinism. French Jacobins must inveigh against Buonaparte, because he exercises the powers of government: the satirist who attacks them must transcribe their sentiments, and adopt their language.

I do not mean to say, Gentlemen, that Mr. Peltier feels any affection, or professes any allegiance to Buonaparte. If I were to say so, he would disown me. He would disdain to purchase an acquittal by the profession of sentiments which he disclaims and abhors. Not to love Buonaparte is no crime. The question is not whether Mr. Peltier loves or

* Sir Sydney Smith.—Ed.

hates the First Consul, but whether he has put revolutionary language into the mouth of Jacobins, with a view to paint their incorrigible turbulence, and to exhibit the fruits of Jacobinical revolutions to the detestation of mankind.

Now, Gentlemen, we cannot give a probable answer to this question without previously examining two or three questions on which the answer to the first must very much depend. Is there a faction in France which breathes the spirit, and is likely to employ the language of this Ode? Does it perfectly accord with their character and views? Is it utterly irreconcilable with the feelings, opinions, and wishes of Mr. Peltier? If these questions can be answered in the affirmative, then I think you must agree with me, that Mr. Peltier does not in this Ode speak his own sentiments,—that he does not here vent his own resentment against Buonaparte, but that he personates a Jacobin, and adopts his language for the sake of satirising his principles.

These questions, Gentlemen, lead me to those political discussions, which, generally speaking, are in a court of justice odious and disgusting. Here, however, they are necessary, and I shall consider them only as far as the necessities of this cause require.

Gentlemen, the French Revolution—I must pause, after I have uttered words which present such an overwhelming idea. But I have not now to engage in an enterprise so far beyond my force as that of examining and judging that tremendous revolution. I have only to consider the character of the factions which it must have left behind it. The French Revolution began with great and fatal errors. These errors produced atrocious crimes. A mild and feeble monarchy was succeeded by bloody anarchy, which very shortly gave birth to military despotism. France, in a few years, described the whole circle of human society. All this was in the order of nature. When every principle of authority and civil discipline,—when every principle which enables some men to command, and disposes others to obey, was extirpated from the mind by atrocious theories, and still more atrocious examples,—when every old institution was trampled down with contumely, and every new institution covered in its cradle with blood,—when the principle of property itself, the sheet-anchor of society, was annihilated,—when in the persons of the new possessors, whom the poverty of language obliges us to call proprietors, it was contaminated in its source by robbery and murder, and became separated from the education and the manners, from the general presumption of superior knowledge and more scrupulous probity which form its only liberal titles to respect,—when the people were taught to despise every thing old, and compelled to detest every thing new, there remained only one principle strong enough to hold society together, — a principle utterly incompatible, indeed, with liberty, and unfriendly to civilization itself, — a tyrannical and barbarous principle, but, in that miserable condition of human affairs, a refuge from still more intolerable evils: — I mean the principle of military power, which gains strength from that confusion and bloodshed in which all the other elements of society are dissolved, and which, in these terrible extremities, is the cement that preserves it from total destruction. Under such circumstances, Buonaparte usurped the supreme power in France;—I say *usurped*, because an illegal assumption of power is an usurpation. But usurpation, in its strongest moral sense, is scarcely applicable to a period of lawless and savage anarchy. The guilt of military usurpation, in truth, belongs to the authors of those confusions which sooner or later give birth to such an usurpation. Thus, to use the words of the historian, "by recent as well as all ancient example, it became evident, that illegal violence, with whatever pretences it may be covered, and whatever object it may pursue, must inevitably end at last in the arbitrary and despotic government of a single person."* But though the government of Buonaparte has silenced the Revolutionary factions, it has not and it cannot have extinguished them. No human power could reimpress upon the minds of men all those sentiments and opinions which the sophistry and anarchy of fourteen years had obliterated. A faction must exist, which breathes the spirit of the Ode now before you.

It is, I know, not the spirit of the quiet and submissive majority of the French people. They have always rather suffered, than acted in, the Revolution. Completely exhausted by the calamities through which they have passed, they yield to any power which gives them repose. There is, indeed, a degree of oppression which rouses men to resistance; but there is another and a greater which wholly subdues and unmans them. It is remarkable that Robespierre himself was safe, till he attacked his own accomplices. The spirit of men of virtue was broken, and there was no vigour of character left to destroy him, but in those daring ruffians who were the sharers of his tyranny.

As for the wretched populace who were made the blind and senseless instrument of so many crimes,—whose frenzy can now be reviewed by a good mind with scarce any moral sentiment but that of compassion,—that miserable multitude of beings, scarcely human, have already fallen into a brutish forgetfulness of the very atrocities which they themselves perpetrated: they have already forgotten all the acts of their drunken fury. If you ask one of them, who destroyed that magnificent monument of religion and art? or who perpetrated that massacre? they stupidly answer, "The Jacobins!"—though he who gives the answer was probably one of these Jacobins himself: so that a traveller,

* Hume, History of England, vol. vii. p. 220.

ignorant of French history, might suppose the Jacobins to be the name of some Tartar horde, who, after laying waste France for ten years, were at last expelled by the native inhabitants. They have passed from senseless rage to stupid quiet: their delirium is followed by lethargy.

In a word, Gentlemen, the great body of the people of France have been severely trained in those convulsions and proscriptions which are the school of slavery. They are capable of no mutinous, and even of no bold and manly political sentiments: and if this Ode professed to paint their opinions, it would be a most unfaithful picture. But it is otherwise with those who have been the actors and leaders in the scene of blood: it is otherwise with the numerous agents of the most indefatigable, searching, multiform, and omnipresent tyranny that ever existed, which pervaded every class of society,—which had ministers and victims in every village in France.

Some of them, indeed,—the basest of the race,—the Sophists, the Rhetors, the Poet-laureates of murder,—who were cruel only from cowardice, and calculating selfishness, are perfectly willing to transfer their venal pens to any government that does not disdain their infamous support. These men, republicans from servility, who published rhetorical panegyrics on massacre, and who reduced plunder to a system of ethics, as are ready to preach slavery as anarchy. But the more daring—I had almost said the more respectable—ruffians cannot so easily bend their heads under the yoke. These fierce spirits have not lost

"The unconquerable will, the study of revenge, immortal hate."*

They leave the luxuries of servitude to the mean and dastardly hypocrites,—to the Belials and Mammons of the infernal faction. They pursue their old end of tyranny under their old pretext of liberty. The recollection of their unbounded power renders every inferior condition irksome and vapid: and their former atrocities form, if I may so speak, a sort of moral destiny which irresistibly impels them to the perpetration of new crimes. They have no place left for penitence on earth: they labour under the most awful proscription of opinion that ever was pronounced against human beings: they have cut down every bridge by which they could retreat into the society of men. Awakened from their dreams of democracy,—the noise subsided that deafened their ears to the voice of humanity,—the film fallen from their eyes which hid from them the blackness of their own deeds,—haunted by the memory of their inexpiable guilt,—condemned daily to look on the faces of those whom their hand has made widows and orphans, they are goaded and scourged by these real furies, and hurried into the tumult of new crimes, to drown the cries of remorse, or, if they be too depraved for remorse, to silence the curses of mankind. Tyrannical power is their only refuge from the just vengeance of their fellow creatures: murder is their only means of usurping power. They have no taste, no occupation, no pursuit, but power and blood. If their hands are tied, they must at least have the luxury of murderous projects. They have drunk too deeply of human blood ever to relinquish their cannibal appetite.

Such a faction exists in France: it is numerous; it is powerful; and it has a principle of fidelity stronger than any that ever held together a society. They are banded together by despair of forgiveness,—by the unanimous detestation of mankind. They are now contained by a severe and stern government: but they still meditate the renewal of insurrection and massacre; and they are prepared to renew the worst and most atrocious of their crimes,—that crime against posterity and against human nature itself,—that crime of which the latest generations of mankind may feel the fatal consequences,—the crime of degrading and prostituting the sacred name of liberty. I must own that, however paradoxical it may appear, I should almost think not worse, but more meanly of them if it were otherwise. I must then think them destitute of that—I will not call it courage, because that is the name of a virtue—but of that ferocious energy which alone rescues ruffians from contempt. If they were destitute of that which is the heroism of murderers, they would be the lowest as well as the most abominable of beings. It is impossible to conceive any thing more despicable than wretches who, after hectoring and bullying over their meek and blameless sovereign, and his defenceless family,—whom they kept so long in a dungeon trembling for their existence,—whom they put to death by a slow torture of three years,—after playing the republicans and the tyrannicides to women and children,—become the supple and fawning slaves of the first government that knows how to wield the scourge with a firm hand.

I have used the word "Republican," because it is the name by which this atrocious faction describes itself. The assumption of that name is one of their crimes. They are no more "Republicans" than "Royalists:" they are the common enemies of all human society. God forbid, that by the use of that word, I should be supposed to reflect on the members of those respectable republican communities which did exist in Europe before the French Revolution. That Revolution has spared many monarchies, but it has spared no republic within the sphere of its destructive energy. One republic only now exists in the world—a republic of English blood, which was originally composed of republican societies, under the protection of a monarchy, which had therefore no great and perilous change in their internal constitution to effect, and of which (I speak it with plea-

* Paradise Lost, book ii.—Ed.

sure and pride), the inhabitants, even in the convulsions of a most deplorable separation, displayed the humanity as well as valour, which, I trust, I may say they inherited from their forefathers. Nor do I mean, by the use of the word "Republican," to confound this execrable faction with all those who, in the liberty of private speculation, may prefer a republican form of government. I own, that after much reflection, I am not able to conceive an error more gross than that of those who believe in the possibility of erecting a republic in any of the old monarchical countries of Europe,—who believe that in such countries an elective supreme magistracy can produce any thing but a succession of stern tyrannies and bloody civil wars. It is a supposition which is belied by all experience, and which betrays the greatest ignorance of the first principles of the constitution of society. It is an error which has a false appearance of superiority over vulgar prejudice; it is, therefore, too apt to be attended with the most criminal rashness and presumption, and too easy to be inflamed into the most immoral and anti-social fanaticism. But as long as it remains a mere quiescent error, it is not the proper subject of moral disapprobation.

If then, Gentlemen, such a faction, falsely calling itself "Republican," exists in France, let us consider whether this Ode speaks their sentiments, — describes their character, — agrees with their views. Trying it by the principle I have stated, I think you will have no difficulty in concluding, that it is agreeable to the general plan of this publication to give an historical and satirical view of the Brutus' and brutes of the Republic,—of those who assumed and disgraced the name of Brutus,* and who, under that name, sat as judges in their mock tribunals with pistols in their girdles, to anticipate the office of the executioner on those unfortunate men whom they treated as rebels, for resistance to Robespierre and Couthon.

I now come to show you, that this Ode cannot represent the opinions of Mr. Peltier. He is a French Royalist; he has devoted his talents to the cause of his King; for that cause he has sacrificed his fortune and hazarded his life;—for that cause he is proscribed and exiled from his country. I could easily conceive powerful topics of Royalist invective against Buonaparte: and if Mr. Peltier had called upon Frenchmen by the memory of St. Louis and Henry the Great, —by the memory of that illustrious family which reigned over them for seven centuries, and with whom all their martial renown and literary glory are so closely connected,—if he had adjured them by the spotless name of that Louis XVI., the martyr of his love for his people, which scarce a man in France can now pronounce but in the tone of pity and veneration;—if he had *thus* called upon them to change their useless regret and their barren pity into generous and active indignation,—if he had reproached the conquerors of Europe with the disgrace of being the slaves of an upstart stranger,—if he had brought before their minds the contrast between their country under her ancient monarchs, the source and model of refinement in manners and taste, and since their expulsion the scourge and opprobrium of humanity, —if he had exhorted them to drive out their ignoble tyrants, and to restore their native sovereign, I should then have recognised the voice of a Royalist,—I should have recognised language that must have flowed from the heart of Mr. Peltier, and I should have been compelled to acknowledge that it was pointed against Buonaparte.

But instead of these, or similar topics, what have we in this Ode? On the supposition that it is the invective of a Royalist, how is it to be reconciled to common sense? What purpose is it to serve? To whom is it addressed? To what interests does it appeal? What passions is it to rouse? If it be addressed to Royalists, then I request, Gentlemen, that you will carefully read it, and tell me whether, on that supposition, it can be any thing but the ravings of insanity, and whether a commission of lunacy be not a proceeding more fitted to the author's case, than a conviction for a libel. On that supposition, I ask you whether it does not amount, in substance, to such an address as the following:—"Frenchmen! Royalists! I do not call upon you to avenge the murder of your innocent sovereign, the butchery of your relations and friends, or the disgrace and oppression of your country. I call upon you by the hereditary right of Barras, transmitted through a long series of ages,—by the beneficent government of Merlin and Reubell, those worthy successors of Charlemagne, whose authority was as mild as it was lawful,—I call upon you to revenge on Buonaparte the deposition of that Directory who condemned the far greater part of yourselves to beggary and exile,—who covered France with Bastiles and scaffolds,—who doomed the most respectable remaining members of their community, the Pichegrus, the Barbé-Marbois', the Barthelemis, to a lingering death in the pestilential wilds of Guiana. I call upon you to avenge on Buonaparte the cause of those Councils of Five Hundred, or of Two Hundred, of Elders or of Youngsters,—those disgusting and nauseous mockeries of representative assemblies, —those miserable councils which sycophant sophists had converted into machines for fabricating decrees of proscription and confiscation,—which not only proscribed unborn thousands, but, by a refinement and innovation in rapine, visited the sins of the children upon the fathers and beggared parents, not for the offences but for the misfortunes of their sons. I call upon you to restore this Directory and these Councils, and all this horrible profanation of the name of a repub-

* A Citizen *Brutus* was President of the Military Commission at Marseilles, in January, 1794.

lic, and to punish those who delivered you from them. I exhort you to reverence the den of these banditti as 'the sanctuary of the laws,' and to lament the day in which this intolerable nuisance was abated as 'an unfortunate day.' Last of all, I exhort you once more to follow that deplorable chimera, —the first lure that led you to destruction, —the sovereignty of the people; although I know, and you have bitterly felt, that you never were so much slaves in fact, as since you have been sovereigns in theory!" Let me ask Mr. Attorney-General, whether, upon his supposition, I have not given you a faithful translation of this Ode; and I think I may safely repeat, that, if this be the language of a Royalist addressed to Royalists, it must be the production of a lunatic. But, on my supposition, every thing is natural and consistent. You have the sentiments and language of a Jacobin:—it is therefore probable, if you take it as an historical republication of a Jacobin piece; it is just, if you take it as a satirical representation of Jacobin opinions and projects.

Perhaps it will be said, that this is the production of a Royalist writer, who assumes a Republican disguise to serve Royalist purposes. But if my Learned Friend chooses that supposition, I think an equal absurdity returns upon him in another shape. We must then suppose it to be intended to excite Republican discontent and insurrection against Buonaparte. It must then be taken as addressed to Republicans. Would Mr. Peltier, in that case, have disclosed his name as the publisher? Would he not much rather have circulated the Ode in the name of Chenier, without prefixing his own, which was more than sufficient to warn his Jacobinical readers against all his counsels and exhortations. If he had circulated it under the name of Chenier only, he would indeed have hung out Republican colours; but by prefixing his own, he appears without disguise. You must suppose him then to say: —"Republicans! I, your mortal enemy for fourteen years, whom you have robbed of his all,—whom you have forbidden to revisit his country under pain of death,—who, from the beginning of the Revolution, has unceasingly poured ridicule upon your follies, and exposed your crimes to detestation,—who in the cause of his unhappy sovereign braved your daggers for three years, and who escaped, almost by miracle, from your assassins in September,—who has since been constantly employed in warning other nations by your example, and in collecting the evidence upon which history will pronounce your condemnation,—I who at this moment deliberately choose exile and honourable poverty, rather than give the slightest mark of external compliance with your abominable institutions,—I your most irreconcilable and indefatigable enemy, offer you counsel which you know can only be a snare into which I expect you to fall, though by the mere publication of my name I have sufficiently forewarned you that I can have no aim but that of your destruction." I ask you again, Gentlemen, is this common sense? Is it not as clear, from the name of the author, that it is not addressed to Jacobins, as, from the contents of the publication, that it is not addressed to Royalists? It may be the genuine work of Chenier; for the topics are such as he would employ: it may be a satire on Jacobinism; for the language is well adapted to such a composition: but it cannot be a Royalist's invective against Buonaparte, intended by him to stir up either Royalists or Republicans to the destruction of the First Consul.

I cannot conceive it to be necessary that I should minutely examine this Poem to confirm my construction. There are one or two passages on which I shall make a few observations. The first is the contrast between the state of England and that of France, of which an ingenious friend* has favoured me with a translation, which I shall take the liberty of reading to you:—

"Her glorious fabric England rears
 On law's fix'd base alone;
Law's guardian pow'r while each reveres,
England! thy people's freedom fears
 No danger from the throne.

"For there, before almighty law,
High birth, high place, with pious awe,
 In reverend homage bend:
There's man's free spirit, unconstrain'd,
Exults, in man's best rights maintain'd,—
Rights, which by ancient valour gain'd,
 From age to age descend.

"Britons, by no base fear dismay'd,
 May power's worst acts arraign.
Does tyrant force their rights invade?
They call on law's impartial aid,
 Nor call that aid in vain.

"Hence, of her sacred charter proud,
With every earthly good endow'd,
 O'er subject seas unfurl'd,
Britannia waves her standard wide;—
Hence, sees her freighted navies ride,
Up wealthy Thames' majestic tide,
 The wonder of the world."

Here, at first sight, you may perhaps think that the consistency of the Jacobin character is not supported—that the Republican disguise is thrown off,—that the Royalist stands unmasked before you:—but, on more consideration, you will find that such an inference would be too hasty. The leaders of the Revolution are now reduced to envy that British constitution which, in the infatuation of their presumptuous ignorance, they once rejected with scorn. They are now slaves (as themselves confess) because twelve years ago they did not believe Englishmen to be free. They cannot but see that England is the only popular government in Europe; and they are compelled to pay a reluctant homage to the justice of English principles. The praise of England is too striking a satire on their own government to escape them; and I may accordingly venture to appeal to all

* Mr. Canning.—Ed.

those who know any thing of the political circles of Paris, whether such contrasts between France and England as that which I have read to you be not the most favourite topics of the opponents of Buonaparte. But in the very next stanza:—

> Cependant, encore affligée
> Par l'odieuse hérédité,
> Londres de titres surchargée,
> Londres n'a pas *l'Egalité:*—

you see that though they are forced to render an unwilling tribute to our liberty, they cannot yet renounce all their fantastic and deplorable chimeras. They endeavour to make a compromise between the experience on which they cannot shut their eyes, and the wretched systems to which they still cling. Fanaticism is the most incurable of all mental diseases; because in all its forms,—religious, philosophical, or political,—it is distinguished by a sort of mad contempt for *experience*, which alone can correct the errors of practical judgment. And these democratical fanatics still speak of the odious principle of "hereditary government;" they still complain that we have not "*equality:*" they know not that this odious principle of inheritance is our bulwark against tyranny, —that if we had their pretended equality we should soon cease to be the objects of their envy. These are the sentiments which you would naturally expect from half-cured lunatics: but once more I ask you, whether they can be the sentiments of Mr. Peltier? Would he complain that we have too much monarchy, or too much of what they call "aristocracy?" If he has any prejudices against the English government, must they not be of an entirely opposite kind?

I have only one observation more to make on this Poem. It relates to the passage which is supposed to be an incitement to assassination. In my way of considering the subject, Mr. Peltier is not answerable for that passage, whatever its demerits may be. It is put into the mouth of a Jacobin; and it will not, I think, be affirmed, that if it were an incitement to assassinate, it would be very unsuitable to his character. Experience, and very recent experience, has abundantly proved how widely the French Revolution has blackened men's imaginations, —what a daring and desperate cast it has given to their characters,—how much it has made them regard the most extravagant projects of guilt as easy and ordinary expedients,—and to what a horrible extent it has familiarised their minds to crimes which before were only known among civilized nations by the history of barbarous times, or as the subject of poetical fiction. But, thank God! Gentlemen, we in England have not learned to charge any man with inciting to assassination,—not even a member of that atrocious sect who have revived political assassination in Christendom,—except when we are compelled to do so by irresistible evidence. Where is that evidence here? in general it is immoral,—because it is indecent,—to speak with levity, still more to anticipate with pleasure, the destruction of any human being. But between this immorality and the horrible crime of inciting to assassination, there is a wide interval indeed. The real or supposed author of this Ode gives you to understand that he would hear with no great sorrow of the destruction of the First Consul. But surely the publication of that sentiment is very different from an exhortation to assassinate.

But, says my Learned Friend, why is the example of Brutus celebrated? Why are the French reproached with their baseness in not copying that example? Gentlemen, I have no judgment to give on the act of Marcus Brutus. I rejoice that I have not: I should not dare to condemn the acts of brave and virtuous men in extraordinary and terrible circumstances, and which have been, as it were, consecrated by the veneration of so many ages. Still less should I dare to weaken the authority of the most sacred rules of duty, by praises which would be immoral, even if the acts themselves were in some measure justified by the awful circumstances under which they were done. I am not the panegyrist of "those instances of doubtful public spirit at which morality is perplexed, reason is staggered, and from which affrighted nature recoils."* But whatever we may think of the act of Brutus, surely my Learned Friend will not contend that every allusion to it, every panegyric on it, which has appeared for eighteen centuries, in prose and verse, is an incitement to assassination. From the "*conspicuæ divinæ Philippica famæ,*" down to the last schoolboy declamation, he will find scarce a work of literature without such allusions, and not very many without such panegyrics. I must say that he has construed this Ode more like an Attorney-General than a critic in poetry. According to his construction, almost every fine writer in our language is a preacher of murder.

Having said so much on the first of these supposed libels, I shall be very short on the two that remain:—the Verses ascribed to a Dutch Patriot, and the Parody of the Speech of Lepidus.

In the first of these, the piercing eye of Mr. Attorney-General has again discovered an incitement to assassinate,—the most learned incitement to assassinate that ever was addressed to such ignorant ruffians as are most likely to be employed for such purposes!—in an obscure allusion, to an obscure, and perhaps fabulous, part of Roman history,—to the supposed murder of Romulus, about which none of us know any thing, and of which the Jacobins of Paris and Amsterdam probably never heard.

But the Apotheosis:—here my Learned Friend has a little forgotten himself:—he seems to argue as if Apotheosis always presupposed death. But he must know, that

* Burke, Works, (quarto,) vol. iv. p. 427.

Augustus, and even Tiberius and Nero, were deified during their lives; and he cannot have forgotten the terms in which one of the court-poets of Augustus speaks of his master's divinity:—

> ——Præsens divus habebitur
> Augustus, adjectis Britannis
> Imperio —*

If any modern rival of Augustus should choose that path to Olympus, I think he will find it more steep and rugged than that by which Pollux and Hercules climbed to the etherial towers; and that he must be content with "purpling his lips" with Burgundy on earth, as he has very little chance of doing so with nectar among the gods.

The utmost that can seriously be made of this passage is, that it is a wish for a man's death. I repeat, that I do not contend for the decency of publicly declaring such wishes, or even for the propriety of entertaining them. But the distance between such a wish and a persuasive to murder, is immense. Such a wish for a man's death is very often little more than a strong, though I admit not a very decent, way of expressing detestation of his character.

But without pursuing this argument any farther, I think myself entitled to apply to these Verses the same reasoning which I have already applied to the first supposed libel on Buonaparte. If they be the real composition of a pretended Dutch Patriot, Mr. Peltier may republish them innocently: if they be a satire on such pretended Dutch patriots, they are not a libel on Buonaparte. Granting, for the sake of argument, that they did contain a serious exhortation to assassinate, is there any thing in such an exhortation inconsistent with the character of these pretended patriots? They who were disaffected to the mild and tolerant government of their flourishing country, because it did not exactly square with all their theoretical whimsies,—who revolted from that administration as tyrannical, which made Holland one of the wonders of the world for protected industry, for liberty of action and opinion, and for a prosperity which I may venture to call the greatest victory of man over hostile elements,—who served in the armies of Robespierre, under the impudent pretext of giving liberty to their own country, and who have, finally, buried in the same grave its liberty, its independence, and perhaps its national existence,—such men are not entitled to much tenderness from a political satirist; and he will scarcely violate dramatic propriety if he impute to them any language, however criminal and detestable. They who could not brook the authority of their old, lazy, good-natured government, are not likely to endure with patience the yoke of that stern domination which they have brought upon themselves, and which, as far as relates to them, is only the just punishment of their crimes.

I know nothing more odious than their character, unless it be that of those who invoked the aid of the oppressors of Switzerland to be the deliverers of Ireland! The latter guilt has, indeed, peculiar aggravations. In the name of liberty they were willing to surrender their country into the hands of tyrants, the most lawless, faithless, and merciless that ever scourged Europe,—who, at the very moment of the negotiation, were covered with the blood of the unhappy Swiss, the martyrs of real independence and of real liberty. Their success would have been the destruction of the only free community remaining in Europe,—of England, the only bulwark of the remains of European independence. Their means were the passions of an ignorant and barbarous peasantry, and a civil war, which could not fail to produce all the horrible crimes and horrible retaliations of the last calamity that can befall society,—a servile revolt. They sought the worst of ends by the most abominable of means. They laboured for the subjugation of the world at the expense of crimes and miseries which men of humanity and conscience would have thought too great a price for its deliverance.

The last of these supposed libels, Gentlemen, is the Parody on the Speech of Lepidus, in the Fragments of Sallust. It is certainly a very ingenious and happy parody of an original, attended with some historical obscurity and difficulty, which it is no part of our present business to examine. This Parody is said to have been clandestinely placed among the papers of one of the most amiable and respectable men in France, M. Camille Jourdan, in order to furnish a pretext for involving that excellent person in a charge of conspiracy. This is said to have been done by a spy of Fouché. Now, Gentlemen, I take this to be a satire of Fouché,—on his manufacture of plots,—on his contrivances for the destruction of innocent and virtuous men; and I should admit it to be a libel on Fouché, if it were possible to libel him. I own that I should like to see Fouché appear as a plaintiff, seeking reparation for his injured character, before any tribunal, safe from his fangs,—where he had not the power of sending the judges to Guiana or Madagascar. It happens that we know something of the history of M. Fouché, from a very credible witness against him,—from himself. You will perhaps excuse me for reading to you some passages of his letters in the year 1793, from which you will judge whether any satire can be so severe as the portrait he draws of himself:—"Convinced that there are no innocent men in this infamous city," (the unhappy city of Lyons), "but those who are oppressed and loaded with irons by the assassins of the people," (he means the murderers who were condemned to death for their crimes) "we are on our guard against *the tears of repentance!* nothing can disarm our severity. They have not yet *dared* to solicit the repeal of your first decree for the annihilation of the city

* Horace, lib. iii. ode 5.—Ed.

of Lyons! but scarcely anything has yet been done to carry it into execution." (Pathetic!) "The demolitions are too slow. More rapid means are necessary to republican impatience. The explosion of the mine, and the devouring activity of the flames, can alone adequately represent the omnipotence of the people." (Unhappy populace, always the pretext, the instrument, and the victim of political crimes!) "Their will cannot be checked like that of tyrants—it ought to have the effects of thunder!"* The next specimen of this worthy gentleman which I shall give, is in a speech to the Jacobin Club of Paris, on the 21st of December, 1793, by his worthy colleague in the mission to Lyons, Collot d'Herbois:—"We are accused" (you, Gentlemen, will soon see how unjustly) "of being cannibals, men of blood; but it is in counter-revolutionary petitions, hawked about for signature by aristocrats, that this charge is made against us. They examine with the most scrupulous attention how the counter-revolutionists are put to death, and they affect to say, that they are not killed at one stroke." (He speaks for himself and his colleague Fouché, and one would suppose that he was going to deny the fact,—but nothing like it.) "Ah, Jacobins, did Chalier die at the first stroke?" (This Chalier was the Marat of Lyons.) "A drop of blood poured from generous veins goes to my heart" (humane creature!); "but I have no pity for conspirators." (He however proceeds to state a most undeniable proof of his compassion.) "We caused two hundred to be shot at once, and it is charged upon us as a crime!" (Astonishing! that such an act of humanity should be called a crime!) "They do not know that *it is a proof of our sensibility!* When twenty criminals are guillotined, the last of them dies twenty deaths: but those two hundred conspirators perished at once. They speak of sensibility; *we also are full of sensibility! The Jacobins have all the virtues! They are compassionate, humane, generous!*" (This is somewhat hard to be understood, but it is perfectly explained by what follows;) "but they reserve these sentiments for the patriots who are their brethren, which the aristocrats never will be."†

The only remaining document with which I shall trouble you, is a letter from Fouché to his amiable colleague Collot d'Herbois, which, as might be expected in a confidential communication, breathes all the native tenderness of his soul:—"Let us be terrible, that we may run no risk of being feeble or cruel. Let us annihilate in our wrath, at a single blow, all rebels, all conspirators, all traitors," (comprehensive words in his vocabulary) "to spare ourselves the pain, the long agony, of punishing like kings!" (Nothing but philanthropy in this worthy man's heart.) "Let us exercise justice after the example of nature; let us avenge ourselves like a people; let us strike like the thunderbolt; and let even the ashes of our enemies disappear from the soil of liberty! Let the perfidious and ferocious English be attacked from every side; let the whole republic form a volcano to pour devouring lava upon them; may the infamous island which produced these monsters, who no longer belong to humanity, be for ever buried under the waves of the ocean! Farewell, my friend! Tears of joy stream from my eyes" (we shall soon see for what); "they deluge my soul."* Then follows a little postscript, which explains the cause of this excessive joy, so hyperbolical in its language, and which fully justifies the indignation of the humane writer against the "ferocious English," who are so stupid and so cruel as never to have thought of a benevolent massacre, by way of sparing themselves the pain of punishing individual criminals. "We have only one way of celebrating victory. We send this evening two hundred and thirteen rebels to be shot!"

Such, Gentlemen, is M. Fouché, who is said to have procured this Parody to be mixed with the papers of my excellent friend Camille Jourdan, to serve as a pretext for his destruction. Fabricated plots are among the most usual means of such tyrants for such purposes; and if Mr. Peltier intended to libel—shall I say?—Fouché by this composition, I can easily understand both the Parody and the history of its origin. But if it be directed against Buonaparte to serve Royalist purposes, I must confess myself wholly unable to conceive why Mr. Peltier should have stigmatised his work, and deprived it of all authority and power of persuasion, by prefixing to it the infamous name of Fouché.

On the same principle I think one of the observations of my Learned Friend, on the title of this publication, may be retorted on him. He has called your attention to the title,—"L'Ambigu, ou Variétés atroces et amusantes." Now, Gentlemen, I must ask whether, had these been Mr. Peltier's own invectives against Buonaparte, he would himself have branded them as "atrocious?" But if they be specimens of the opinions and invectives of a French faction, the title is very natural, and the epithets are perfectly intelligible. Indeed I scarce know a more appropriate title for the whole tragi-comedy of the Revolution than that of "atrocious and amusing varieties."

My Learned Friend has made some observations on other parts of this publication, to show the spirit which animates the author; but they do not seem to be very material to the question between us. It is no part of my case that Mr. Peltier has not spoken with some unpoliteness,—with some flippancy,—with more severity than my Learned Friend may approve, of factions and of adminis-

* Moniteur, 24th November, 1793.
† Moniteur, 24th December.

* Moniteur, 25th December.

trations in France. Mr. Peltier cannot love the Revolution, or any government that has grown out of it and maintains it. The Revolutionists have destroyed his family; they have seized his inheritance; they have beggared, exiled, and proscribed himself. If he did not detest them he would be unworthy of living; he would be a base hypocrite if he were to conceal his sentiments. But I must again remind you, that this is not an Information for not sufficiently honouring the French Revolution,—for not showing sufficient reverence for the Consular government. These are no crimes among us. England is not yet reduced to such an ignominious dependence. Our hearts and consciences are not yet in the bonds of so wretched a slavery. This is an Information for a libel on Buonaparte, and if you believe the principal intention of Mr. Peltier to have been to republish the writings or to satirise the character of other individuals, you must acquit him of a libel on the First Consul.

Here, Gentlemen, I think I might stop, if I had only to consider the defence of Mr. Peltier. I trust that you are already convinced of his innocence. I fear I have exhausted your patience, as I am sure I have very nearly exhausted my own strength. But so much seems to me to depend on your verdict, that I cannot forbear from laying before you some considerations of a more general nature.

Believing as I do that we are on the eve of a great struggle,—that this is only the first battle between reason and power,—that you have now in your hands, committed to your trust, the only remains of free discussion in Europe, now confined to this kingdom; addressing you, therefore, as the guardians of the most important interests of mankind; convinced that the unfettered exercise of reason depends more on your present verdict than on any other that was ever delivered by a jury, I cannot conclude without bringing before you the sentiments and examples of our ancestors in some of those awful and perilous situations by which Divine Providence has in former ages tried the virtue of the English nation. We are fallen upon times in which it behoves us to strengthen our spirits by the contemplation of great examples of constancy. Let us seek for them in the annals of our forefathers.

The reign of Queen Elizabeth may be considered as the opening of the modern history of England, especially in its connection with the modern system of Europe, which began about that time to assume the form that it preserved till the French Revolution. It was a very memorable period, the maxims of which ought to be engraven on the head and heart of every Englishman. Philip II., at the head of the greatest empire then in the world, was openly aiming at universal domination; and his project was so far from being thought chimerical by the wisest of his contemporaries, that in the opinion of the great Duc de Sully he must have been successful, "if, by a most singular combination of circumstances, he had not at the same time been resisted by two such strong heads as those of Henry IV. and Queen Elizabeth." To the most extensive and opulent dominions, the most numerous and disciplined armies, the most renowned captains, the greatest revenue, he added also the most formidable power over opinion. He was the chief of a religious faction, animated by the most atrocious fanaticism, and prepared to second his ambition by rebellion, anarchy, and regicide, in every Protestant state. Elizabeth was among the first objects of his hostility. That wise and magnanimous Princess placed herself in the front of the battle for the liberties of Europe. Though she had to contend at home with his fanatical faction, which almost occupied Ireland, which divided Scotland, and was not of contemptible strength in England, she aided the oppressed inhabitants of the Netherlands in their just and glorious resistance to his tyranny; she aided Henry the Great in suppressing the abominable rebellion which anarchical principles had excited and Spanish arms had supported in France; and after a long reign of various fortune, in which she preserved her unconquered spirit through great calamities, and still greater dangers, she at length broke the strength of the enemy, and reduced his power within such limits as to be compatible with the safety of England, and of all Europe. Her only effectual ally was the spirit of her people: and her policy flowed from that magnanimous nature which in the hour of peril teaches better lessons than those of cold reason. Her great heart inspired her with the higher and a nobler wisdom, which disdained to appeal to the low and sordid passions of her people even for the protection of their low and sordid interests; because she knew, or rather she felt, that these are effeminate, creeping, cowardly, short-sighted passions, which shrink from conflict even in defence of their own mean objects. In a righteous cause she roused those generous affections of her people which alone teach boldness, constancy, and foresight, and which are therefore the only safe guardians of the lowest as well as the highest interests of a nation. In her memorable address to her army, when the invasion of the kingdom was threatened by Spain, this woman of heroic spirit disdained to speak to them of their ease and their commerce, and their wealth [illegible] heir safety. No! She touched another chord;—she spoke of their national honour, of their dignity as Englishmen, of "the foul scorn that Parma or Spain should dare to invade the borders of her realms!" She breathed into them those grand and powerful sentiments which exalt vulgar men into heroes,—which led them into the battle of their country armed with holy and irresistible enthusiasm, which even cover with their shield all the ignoble interests that base calculation and cowardly selfishness tremble to hazard, but shrink from defending. A sort of prophetic instinct,—if I may so speak,—seems to have revealed to her the importance of that great instrument for rousing and guiding the minds of men, of the effects of which she had had no experience,—which, since her time, has changed the condition of the world,—but which few modern statesmen have thoroughly understood or wisely employed,—which is no doubt connected with many ridiculous and degrading details,—which has produced, and which may again produce, terrible mischiefs,—but the influence of which must after all be considered as the most certain effect and the most efficacious cause of civilization,—and which, whether it be a blessing or a curse, is the most powerful engine that a politician can move:—I mean the press. It is a curious fact, that, in the year of the Armada, Queen Elizabeth caused to be printed the first Gazettes that ever appeared in England; and I own, when I consider that this mode of rousing a national spirit was then absolutely unexampled,—that she could have no assurance of its efficacy from the precedents of former times,—I am disposed to regard her having recourse to it as one of the most sagacious experiments,—one of the greatest discoveries of political genius,—one of the most striking anticipations of future experience, that we find in history. I mention it to you, to justify the opinion that I have ventured to state, of the close connection of our national spirit with our press, and even our periodical press. I cannot quit the reign of Elizabeth without laying before you the maxims of her policy, in the language of the greatest and wisest of men. Lord Bacon, in one part of his discourse on her reign, speaks thus of her support of Holland:—"But let me rest upon the honourable and continual aid and relief she hath given to the distressed and desolate people of the Low Countries; a people recommended unto her by ancient confederacy and daily intercourse, by their cause so innocent, and their fortune so lamentable!"—In another passage of the same discourse, he thus speaks of the general system of her foreign policy, as the protector of Europe, in words too remarkable to require any commentary:—"Then it is her government, and her government alone, that hath been the sconce and fort of all Europe, which hath lett this proud nation from overrunning all. If any state be yet free from his factions erected in the bowels thereof; if there be any state wherein this faction is erected that is not yet fired with civil troubles; if there be any state under his protection that enjoyeth moderate liberty, upon whom he tyrannizeth not; it is the mercy of this renowned Queen that standeth between them and their misfortunes!"

The next great conspirator against the rights of men and nations, against the security and independence of all European states, against every kind and degree of civil and religious liberty, was Louis XIV. In his time the character of the English nation was the more remarkably displayed, because it was counteracted by an apostate and perfidious government. During great part of his reign, you know that the throne of England was filled by princes who deserted the cause of their country and of Europe,—who were the accomplices and the tools of the oppressor of the world,—who were even so unmanly, so unprincely, so base, as to have sold themselves to his ambition,—who were content that he should enslave the Continent, if he enabled them to enslave Great Britain. These princes, traitors to their own royal dignity and to the feelings of the generous people whom they ruled, preferred the condition of the first slave of Louis XIV. to the dignity of the first freeman of England. Yet, even under these princes, the feelings of the people of this kingdom were displayed on a most memorable occasion towards foreign sufferers and foreign oppressors. The Revocation of the Edict of Nantes, threw fifty thousand French Protestants on our shores. They were received, as I trust the victims of tyranny ever will be in this land, which seems chosen by Providence to be the home of the exile,—the refuge of the oppressed. They were welcomed by a people high-spirited as well as humane, who did not insult them by clandestine charity,—who did not give alms in secret lest their charity should be detected by neighbouring tyrants! No! they were publicly and nationally welcomed and relieved. They were bid to raise their voice against their oppressor, and to proclaim their wrongs to all mankind. They did so. They were joined in the cry of just indignation by every Englishman worthy of the name. It was a fruitful indignation, which soon produced the successful resistance of all Europe to the common enemy. Even then, when Jeffreys disgraced the Bench which his Lordship* now adorns, no refugee was deterred by prosecution for libel from giving vent to his feelings,—from arraigning the oppressor in the face of all Europe.

During this ignominious period of our history, a war arose on the Continent, which cannot but present itself to the mind on such an occasion as this,—the only war that was ever made on the avowed ground of attacking a free press. I speak of the invasion of Holland by Louis XIV. The liberties which the Dutch gazettes had taken in discussing his conduct were the sole cause of this very extraordinary and memorable war, which was of short duration, unprecedented in its avowed principle, and most glorious in its event for the liberties of mankind. That republic, at all times so interesting to Englishmen,—in the worst times of both countries our brave enemies,—in their best times our most faithful and valuable friends,—was then charged with the defence of a free press against the oppressor of Europe, as a sacred trust for the benefit of all generations. They

* Lord Ellenborough.—Ed.

felt the sacredness of the deposit; they felt the dignity of the station in which they were placed: and though deserted by the un-English Government of England, they asserted their own ancient character, and drove out the great armies and great captains of the oppressor with defeat and disgrace. Such was the result of the only war hitherto avowedly undertaken to oppress a free country because she allowed the free and public exercise of reason:—and may the God of Justice and Liberty grant that such may ever be the result of wars made by tyrants against the rights of mankind, especially of those against that right which is the guardian of every other.

This war, Gentlemen, had the effect of raising up from obscurity the great Prince of Orange, afterwards King William III.—the deliverer of Holland, the deliverer of England, the deliverer of Europe,—the only hero who was distinguished by such a happy union of fortune and virtue that the objects of his ambition were always the same with the interests of humanity,—perhaps, the only man who devoted the whole of his life exclusively to the service of mankind. This most illustrious benefactor of Europe,—this "hero without vanity or passion," as he has been justly and beautifully called by a venerable prelate,* who never made a step towards greatness without securing or advancing liberty, who had been made Stadtholder of Holland for the salvation of his own country, was soon after made King of England for the deliverance of ours. When the people of Great Britain had once more a government worthy of them, they returned to the feelings and principles of their ancestors, and resumed their former station and their former duties as protectors of the independence of nations. The people of England, delivered from a government which disgraced, oppressed, and betrayed them, fought under William as their forefathers had fought under Elizabeth, and after an almost uninterrupted struggle of more than twenty years, in which they were often abandoned by fortune, but never by their own constancy and magnanimity, they at length once more defeated those projects of guilty ambition, boundless aggrandisement, and universal domination, which had a second time threatened to overwhelm the whole civilized world. They rescued Europe from being swallowed up in the gulf of extensive empire, which the experience of all times points out as the grave of civilization,—where men are driven by violent conquest and military oppression into lethargy and slavishness of heart,—where, after their arts have perished with the mental vigour from which they spring, they are plunged by the combined power of effeminacy and ferocity into irreclaimable and hopeless barbarism. Our ancestors established the safety of their own country by providing for that of others, and rebuilt the European system upon such firm foundations, that nothing less than the tempest of the French Revolution could have shaken it.

This arduous struggle was suspended for a short time by the Peace of Ryswick. The interval between that Treaty and the War of the Succession enables us to judge how our ancestors acted in a very peculiar situation which requires maxims of policy very different from those which usually govern states. The treaty which they had concluded was in truth and substance only a truce. The ambition and the power of the enemy were such as to render real peace impossible; and it was perfectly obvious that the disputed succession of the Spanish monarchy would soon render it no longer practicable to preserve even the appearance of amity. It was desirable, however, not to provoke the enemy by unseasonable hostility; but it was still more desirable,—it was absolutely necessary, to keep up the national jealousy and indignation against him who was soon to be their open enemy. It might naturally have been apprehended that the press might have driven into premature war a prince who not long before had been violently exasperated by the press of another free country. I have looked over the political publications of that time with some care, and I can venture to say, that at no period were the system and projects of Louis XIV animadverted on with more freedom and boldness than during that interval. Our ancestors, and the heroic Prince who governed them, did not deem it wise policy to disarm the national mind for the sake of prolonging a truce:—they were both too proud and too wise to pay so great a price for so small a benefit.

In the course of the eighteenth century, a great change took place in the state of political discussion in this country:—I speak of the multiplication of newspapers. I know that newspapers are not very popular in this place, which is, indeed, not very surprising, because they are known here only by their faults. Their publishers come here only to receive the chastisement due to their offences. With all their faults, I own, I cannot help feeling some respect for whatever is a proof of the increased curiosity and increased knowledge of mankind; and I cannot help thinking, that if somewhat more indulgence and consideration were shown for the difficulties of their situation, it might prove one of the best correctives of their faults, by teaching them that self-respect which is the best security for liberal conduct towards others. But however that may be, it is very certain that the multiplication of these channels of popular information has produced a great change in the state of our domestic and foreign politics. At home, it has, in truth, produced a gradual revolution in our government. By increasing the number of those who exercise some sort of judgment on public affairs, it has created a substantial democracy, infinitely more important

* Dr. Shipley, Bishop of St. Asaph.

than those democratical forms which have been the subject of so much contest. So that I may venture to say, England has not only in its *forms* the most democratical government that ever existed in a great country, but, in *substance*, has the most democratical government that ever existed in *any* country; —if the most *substantial* democracy be that state in which the greatest number of men feel an interest and express an opinion upon political questions, and in which the greatest number of judgments and wills concur in influencing public measures.

The same circumstance gave great additional importance to our discussion of continental politics. That discussion was no longer, as in the preceding century, confined to a few pamphlets, written and read only by men of education and rank, which reached the multitude very slowly and rarely. In newspapers an almost daily appeal was made, directly or indirectly, to the judgment and passions of almost every individual in the kingdom upon the measures and principles not only of his own country, but of every state in Europe. Under such circumstances, the tone of these publications in speaking of foreign governments became a matter of importance. You will excuse me, therefore, if, before I conclude, I remind you of the general nature of their language on one or two very remarkable occasions, and of the boldness with which they arraigned the crimes of powerful sovereigns, without any check from the laws and magistrates of their own country. This toleration, or rather this protection, was too long and uniform to be accidental. I am, indeed, very much mistaken if it be not founded upon a policy which this country cannot abandon without sacrificing her liberty and endangering her national existence.

The first remarkable instance which I shall choose to state of the unpunished and protected boldness of the English press,—of the freedom with which they animadverted on the policy of powerful sovereigns, is on the Partition of Poland in 1772,—an act not perhaps so horrible in its means, nor so deplorable in its *immediate* effects, as some other atrocious invasions of national independence which have followed it, but the most abominable in its general tendency and ultimate consequences of any political crime recorded in history, because it was the first practical breach in the system of Europe,—the first example of atrocious robbery perpetrated on unoffending countries, which has been since so liberally followed, and which has broken down all the barriers of habit and principle that guarded defenceless states. The perpetrators of this atrocious crime were the most powerful sovereigns of the Continent, whose hostility it certainly was not the interest of Great Britain wantonly to incur. They were the most illustrious princes of their age; and some of them were doubtless entitled to the highest praise for their domestic administration, as well as for the brilliant qualities which distinguished their character. But none of these circumstances,—no dread of their resentment,—no admiration of their talents,—no consideration for their rank,—silenced the animadversion of the English press. Some of you remember,—all of you know, that a loud and unanimous cry of reprobation and execration broke out against them from every part of this kingdom. It was perfectly uninfluenced by any considerations of our own mere national interest, which might perhaps be supposed to be rather favourably affected by that partition. It was not, as in some other countries, the indignation of rival robbers, who were excluded from their share of the prey: it was the moral anger of disinterested spectators against atrocious crimes,—the gravest and the most dignified moral principle which the God of Justice has implanted in the human heart,—that one, the dread of which is the only restraint on the actions of powerful criminals, and the promulgation of which is the only punishment that can be inflicted on them. It is a restraint which ought not to be weakened: it is a punishment which no good man can desire to mitigate. That great crime was spoken of as it deserved in England. Robbery was not described by any courtly circumlocutions: rapine was not called "policy:" nor was the oppression of an innocent people termed a "*mediation*" in their domestic differences. No prosecutions,—no Criminal Informations followed the liberty and the boldness of the language then employed. No complaints even appear to have been made from abroad;—much less any insolent menaces against the free constitution which protected the English press.—The people of England were too long known throughout Europe for the proudest potentate to expect to silence our press by such means.

I pass over the second partition of Poland in 1792 (you all remember what passed on that occasion—the universal abhorrence expressed by every man and every writer of every party,—the succours that were publicly preparing by large bodies of individuals of all parties for the oppressed Poles); I hasten to the final dismemberment of that unhappy kingdom, which seems to me the most striking example in our history of the habitual, principled, and deeply-rooted forbearance of those who administer the law towards political writers. We were engaged in the most extensive, bloody, and dangerous war that this country ever knew; and the parties to the dismemberment of Poland were our allies, and our only powerful and effective allies. We had every motive of policy to court their friendship: every reason of state seemed to require that we should not permit them to be abused and vilified by English writers. What was the fact? Did any Englishman consider himself at liberty, on account of temporary interests, however urgent, to silence those feelings of humanity and justice which guard the certain and permanent interests of all countries? You all remember that every voice, and every pen, and every press in England were unceasingly employed to brand that abominable robbery. You remember that this was not confined to private writers, but that the same abhorrence was expressed by every member of both Houses of Parliament who was not under the restraints of ministerial reserve. No minister dared even to blame the language of honest indignation which might be very inconvenient to his most important political projects; and I hope I may venture to say, that no English assembly would have endured such a sacrifice of eternal justice to any miserable interest of an hour. Did the Law-officers of the Crown venture to come into a court of justice to complain of the boldest of the publications of that time? They did not. I do not say that they felt any disposition to do so;—I believe that they could not. But I do say, that if they had,—if they had spoken of the necessity of confining our political writers to cold narrative and unfeeling argument,—if they had informed a jury, that they did not prosecute history, but invective,—that if private writers be at liberty at all to blame great princes, it must be with moderation and decorum,—the sound heads and honest hearts of an English jury would have confounded such sophistry, and would have declared, by their verdict, that moderation of language is a relative term, which varies with the subject to which it is applied,—that atrocious crimes are not to be related as calmly and coolly as indifferent or trifling events,—that if there be a decorum due to exalted rank and authority, there is also a much more sacred decorum due to virtue and to human nature, which would be outraged and trampled under foot, by speaking of guilt in a lukewarm language, falsely called moderate.

Soon after, Gentlemen, there followed an act, in comparison with which all the deeds of rapine and blood perpetrated in the world are innocence itself,—the invasion and destruction of Switzerland,—that unparalleled scene of guilt and enormity,—that unprovoked aggression against an innocent country, which had been the sanctuary of peace and liberty for three centuries,—respected as a sort of sacred territory by the fiercest ambition,—raised, like its own mountains, beyond the region of the storms which raged around on every side,—the only warlike people that never sent forth armies to disturb their neighbours,—the only government that ever accumulated treasures without imposing taxes,—an innocent treasure, unstained by the tears of the poor, the inviolate patrimony of the commonwealth, which attested the virtue of a long series of magistrates, but which at length caught the eye of the spoiler, and became the fatal occasion of their ruin! Gentlemen, the destruction of such a country,—"its cause so innocent, and its fortune so lamentable!"—made a deep impression on the people of England. I will ask my Learned Friend, if we had then been at peace with the French republic, whether we must have been silent spectators of the foulest crimes that ever blotted the name of humanity?—whether we must, like cowards and slaves, have repressed the compassion and indignation with which that horrible scene of tyranny had filled our hearts? Let me suppose, Gentlemen, that Aloys Reding, who has displayed in our times the simplicity, magnanimity, and piety of ancient heroes, had, after his glorious struggle, honoured this kingdom by choosing it as his refuge,—that, after performiug prodigies of valour at the head of his handful of heroic peasants on the field of Morgarten (where his ancestor, the Landamman Reding, had, five hundred years before, defeated the first oppressors of Switzerland), he had selected this country to be his residence, as the chosen abode of liberty, as the ancient and inviolable asylum of the oppressed, would my Learned Friend have had the boldness to have said to this hero, "that he must hide his tears" (the tears shed by a hero over the ruins of his country!) "lest they might provoke the resentment of Reubell or Rapinat,—that he must smother the sorrow and the anger with which his heart was loaded,—that he must breathe his murmurs low, lest they might be overheard by the oppressor!" Would this have been the language of my Learned Friend? I know that it would not. I know, that by such a supposition, I have done wrong to his honourable feelings—to his honest English heart. I am sure that he knows as well as I do, that a nation which should *thus* receive the oppressed of other countries, would be preparing its own neck for the yoke. He knows the slavery which such a nation would deserve, and must speedily incur. He knows, that sympathy with the unmerited sufferings of others, and disinterested anger against their oppressors, are, if I may so speak, the masters which are appointed by Providence to teach us fortitude in the defence of our own rights,—that selfishness is a dastardly principle, which betrays its charge and flies from its post,—and that those only can defend themselves with valour, who are animated by the moral approbation with which they can survey their sentiments towards others,—who are ennobled in their own eyes by a consciousness that they are fighting for justice as well as interest,—a consciousness which none can feel, but those who have felt for the wrongs of their brethren. These are the sentiments which my Learned Friend would have felt. He would have told the hero:—"Your confidence is not deceived: this is still that England, of which the history may, perhaps, have contributed to fill your heart with the heroism of liberty.—Every other country of Europe is crouching under the bloody tyrants who destroyed your country: we are unchanged. We are still the same people which received with open arms the victims of the tyranny of Philip II. and Louis XIV. We shall not exercise a cowardly and clandestine humanity. Here we are not so dastardly as to rob you of your greatest consolation;—here, protected by a free, brave, and high-minded people, you may give vent to your indignation,—you may proclaim the crimes of your tyrants,—you may devote them to the execration of mankind. There is still one spot upon earth in which they are abhorred, without being dreaded!"

I am aware, Gentlemen, that I have already abused your indulgence; but I must entreat you to bear with me for a short time longer, to allow me to suppose a case which might have occurred, in which you will see the horrible consequences of enforcing rigorously principles of law, which I cannot contest, against political writers. We might have been at peace with France during the whole of that terrible period which elapsed between August 1792 and 1794, which has been usually called the "reign of Robespierre!"—the only series of crimes, perhaps, in history, which, in spite of the common disposition to exaggerate extraordinary facts, has been beyond measure under-rated in public opinion. I say this, Gentlemen, after an investigation, which I think entitles me to affirm it with confidence. Men's minds were oppressed by the atrocity and the multitude of crimes; their humanity and their indolence took refuge in scepticism from such an overwhelming mass of guilt: and the consequence was, that all these unparalleled enormities, though proved, not only with the fullest historical, but with the strictest judicial evidence, were at the time only half-believed, and are now scarcely half-remembered. When these atrocities,—of which the greatest part are as little known to the public in general as the campaigns of Genghis Khan, but are still protected from the scrutiny of men by the immensity of those voluminous records of guilt in which they are related, and under the mass of which they will lie buried, till some historian be found with patience and courage enough to drag them forth into light, for the shame, indeed, but for the instruction of mankind,—which had the peculiar malignity, through the pretexts with which they were covered, of making the noblest objects of human pursuit seem odious and detestable,—which had almost made the names of liberty, reformation, and humanity, synonymous with anarchy, robbery, and murder,—which thus threatened not only to extinguish every principle of improvement, to arrest the progress of civilized society, and to disinherit future generations of that rich succession to be expected from the knowledge and wisdom of the present, but to destroy the civilization of Europe (which never gave such a proof of its vigour and robustness, as in being able to resist their destructive power),—when all these horrors were acting in the greatest empire of the Continent, I will ask my Learned Friend, if we had then been at peace with France, how English writers were to relate them so as to escape the charge of libelling a friendly government?

When Robespierre, in the debates in the National Convention on the mode of murdering their blameless sovereign, objected to the formal and tedious mode of murder called a "trial," and proposed to put him immediately to death without trial, "*on the principles of insurrection*,"—because to doubt the guilt of the King would be to doubt of the innocence of the Convention, and if the King were not a traitor, the Convention must be rebels,—would my Learned Friend have had an English writer state all this with "decorum and moderation?" Would he have had an English writer state, that though this reasoning was not perfectly agreeable to our national laws, or perhaps to our national prejudices, yet it was not for him to make any observations on the judicial proceedings of foreign states? When Marat, in the same Convention, called for two hundred and seventy thousand heads, must our English writers have said, that the remedy did, indeed, seem to their weak judgment rather severe; but that it was not for them to judge the conduct of so illustrious an assembly as the National Convention, or the suggestions of so enlightened a statesman as M. Marat? When that Convention resounded with applause at the news of several hundred aged priests being thrown into the Loire, and particularly at the exclamation of Carrier, who communicated the intelligence:—"*What a revolutionary torrent is the Loire!*"—when these suggestions and narratives of murder, which have hitherto been only hinted and whispered in the most secret cabals, in the darkest caverns of banditti, were triumphantly uttered, patiently endured, and even loudly applauded by an assembly of seven hundred men, acting in the sight of all Europe, would my Learned Friend have wished that there had been found in England a single writer so base as to deliberate upon the most safe, decorous, and polite manner of relating all these things to his countrymen? When Carrier ordered five hundred children under fourteen years to be shot, the greater part of whom escaped the fire from their size,—when the poor victims ran for protection to the soldiers, and were bayoneted clinging round their knees, would my Friend—But I cannot pursue the strain of interrogation; it is too much! It would be a violence which I cannot practise on my own feelings; it would be an outrage to my Friend; it would be an affront to you; it would be an insult to humanity.

No! better,—ten thousand times better, would it be that every press in the world were burnt,—that the very use of letters were abolished,—that we were returned to the honest ignorance of the rudest times, than that the results of civilization should be made subservient to the purposes of barbarism;—than that literature should be employed to teach a toleration for cruelty,—to weaken moral hatred for guilt,—to deprave and brutalise the human mind. I know that I speak my Friend's feelings as well as my own, when I say, God forbid that the dread of any punishment should ever make any Englishman an accomplice in so corrupting his countrymen,—a public teacher of depravity and barbarity!

Mortifying and horrible as the idea is, I must remind you, Gentlemen, that even at that time, even under the reign of Robespierre, my Learned Friend, if he had then been Attorney-General, might have been compelled by some most deplorable necessity, to have come into this Court to ask your verdict against the libellers of Barrère and Collot d'Herbois. Mr. Peltier then employed his talents against the enemies of the human race, as he has uniformly and bravely done. I do not believe that any peace, any political considerations, any fear of punishment, would have silenced him. He has shown too much honour and constancy, and intrepidity, to be shaken by such circumstances as these. My Learned Friend might then have been compelled to have filed a Criminal Information against Mr. Peltier, for "wickedly and maliciously intending to vilify and degrade Maximilian Robespierre, President of the Committee of Public Safety of the French Republic!" He might have been reduced to the sad necessity of appearing before you to belie his own better feelings by prosecuting Mr. Peltier for publishing those sentiments which my Friend himself had a thousand times felt, and a thousand times expressed. He might have been obliged even to call for punishment upon Mr. Peltier, for language which he and all mankind would for ever despise Mr. Peltier, if he were not to employ. Then indeed, Gentlemen, we should have seen the last humiliation fall on England;—the tribunals, the spotless and venerable tribunals of this free country, reduced to be the ministers of the vengeance of Robespierre! What could have rescued us from this last disgrace?—the honesty and courage of a jury. They would have delivered the judges of their country from the dire necessity of inflicting punishment on a brave and virtuous man, because he spoke truth of a monster. They would have despised the threats of a foreign tyrant as their ancestors braved the power of oppressors at home.

In the court where we are now met, Cromwell twice sent a satirist on his tyranny to be convicted and punished as a libeller, and in this court,—almost in sight of the scaffold streaming with the blood of his Sovereign,—within hearing of the clash of his bayonets which drove out Parliaments with scorn and contumely,—a jury twice rescued the intrepid satirist* from his fangs, and sent out with defeat and disgrace the Usurper's Attorney-General from what he had the impudence to call *his* court! Even then, Gentlemen, when all law and liberty were trampled under the feet of a military banditti,—when those great crimes were perpetrated in a high place and with a high hand against those who were the objects of public veneration, which more than any thing else upon earth overwhelm the minds of men, break their spirits, and confound their moral sentiments, obliterate the distinctions between right and wrong in their understanding, and teach the multitude to feel no longer any reverence for that justice which they thus see triumphantly dragged at the chariot wheels of a tyrant,—even then, when this unhappy country, triumphant indeed abroad, but enslaved at home, had no prospect but that of a long succession of tyrants "wading through slaughter to a throne,"—even then, I say, when all seemed lost, the unconquerable spirit of English liberty survived in the hearts of English jurors. That spirit is, I trust in God, not extinct: and if any modern tyrant were, in the plenitude of his insolence, to hope to overawe an English jury, I trust and I believe that they would tell him:—"Our ancestors braved the bayonets of Cromwell;—we bid defiance to yours. Contempsi Catilinæ gladios;—non pertimescam tuos!"

What could be such a tyrant's means of overawing a jury? As long as their country exists, they are girt round with impenetrable armour. Till the destruction of their country, no danger can fall upon them for the performance of their duty. And I do trust that there is no Englishman so unworthy of life as to desire to outlive England. But if any of us are condemned to the cruel punishment of surviving our country,—if in the inscrutable counsels of Providence, this favoured seat of justice and liberty,—this noblest work of human wisdom and virtue, be destined to destruction (which I shall not be charged with national prejudice for saying would be the most dangerous wound ever inflicted on civilization), at least let us carry with us into our sad exile the consolation that we ourselves have not violated the rights of hospitality to exiles,—that we have not torn from the altar the suppliant who claimed protection as the voluntary victim of loyalty and conscience.

Gentlemen, I now leave this unfortunate gentleman in your hands. His character and his situation might interest your humanity: but, on his behalf, I only ask justice from you. I only ask a favourable construction of what cannot be said to be more than ambiguous language; and this you will soon be told from the highest authority is a part of justice.

* Lilburne.

A CHARGE,

DELIVERED

TO THE GRAND JURY OF THE ISLAND OF BOMBAY,

ON THE 20TH OF JULY, 1811.

Gentlemen of the Grand Jury,

The present calendar is unfortunately remarkable for the number and enormity of crimes. To what cause we are to impute the very uncommon depravity which has, in various forms, during the last twelve months, appeared before this Court, it is difficult, and perhaps impossible, to determine. But the length of this calendar may probaby be, in a great measure, ascribed to the late commendable disuse of irregular punishment at the Office of Police: so that there may be not so much an increase of crimes as of regular trials.

To frame and maintain a system of police, warranted by law, vigorous enough for protection, and with sufficient legal restraints to afford a security against oppression, must be owned to be a matter of considerable difficulty in the crowded, mixed, and shifting population of a great Indian sea-port. It is no wonder, then, that there should be defects in our system, both in the efficacy of its regulations and in the legality of its principles. And this may be mentioned with more liberty, because these defects have originated long before the time of any one now in authority; and have rather, indeed, arisen from the operation of time and chance on human institutions, than from the fault of any individual. The subject has of late occupied much of my attention. Government have been pleased to permit me to lay my thoughts before them,—a permission of which I shall in a few days avail myself; and I hope that my diligent inquiry and long reflection may contribute somewhat to aid their judgment in the establishment of a police which may be legal, vigorous, and unoppressive.

In reviewing the administration of law in this place since I have presided here, two circumstances present themselves, which appear to deserve a public explanation.

The first relates to the principles adopted by the Court in cases of commercial insolvency.

In India, no law compels the equal distribution of the goods of an insolvent merchant: we have no system of bankrupt laws. The consequence is too well known. Every mercantile failure has produced a disreputable scramble, in which no individual could be blamed; because, if he were to forego his rights, they would not be sacrificed to equitable division, but to the claims of a competitor no better entitled than himself. A few have recovered all, and the rest have lost all. Nor was this the worst. Opulent commercial houses, either present, or well served by vigilant agents, almost always foresaw insolvency in such time as to secure themselves. But old officers, widows, and orphans in Europe, could know nothing of the decaying credit of their Indian bankers, and they had no agents but those bankers themselves: they, therefore, were the victims of every failure. The rich generally saved what was of little consequence to them, and the poor almost constantly lost their all. These scenes have frequently been witnessed in various parts of India: they have formerly occurred here. On the death of one unfortunate gentleman, since I have been here, the evil was rather dreaded than felt.

Soon after my arrival, I laid before the British merchants of this island a plan for the equal distribution of insolvent estates, of which accident then prevented the adoption. Since that time, the principle of the plan has been adopted in several cases of actual or of apprehended insolvency, by a conveyance of the whole estate to trustees, for the equal benefit of all the creditors. Some disposition to adopt similar arrangements appears of late to manifest itself in Europe. And certainly nothing can be better adapted to the present dark and unquiet condition of the commercial world. Wherever they are adopted early, they are likely to prevent bankruptcy. A very intelligent merchant justly observed to me, that, under such a system, the early disclosure of embarrassment would not be attended with that shame and danger which usually produce concealment and final ruin. In all cases, and at every period, such arrangements would limit the evils of bankruptcy to the least possible amount. It cannot, therefore, be matter of wonder that a court of justice should protect such a system with all the weight of their opinion, and to the utmost extent of their legal power.

I by no means presume to blame those creditors who, on the first proposal of this experiment, withheld their consent, and preferred the assertion of their legal rights.

They had, I dare say, been ill used by their debtors, who might personally be entitled to no indulgence from them. It is too much to require of men, that, under the influence of cruel disappointment and very just resentment, they should estimate a plan of public utility in the same manner with a dispassionate and disinterested spectator. But experience and reflection will in time teach them, that, in seeking to gratify a just resentment against a culpable insolvent, they, in fact, direct their hostility against the unoffending and helpless part of their fellow-creditors.

One defect in this voluntary system of bankrupt laws must be owned to be considerable: it is protected by no penalties against the fraudulent concealment of property.—There is no substitute for such penalties, but the determined and vigilant integrity of trustees. I have, therefore, with pleasure, seen that duty undertaken by European gentlemen of character and station. Besides the great considerations of justice and humanity to the creditors, I will confess that I am gratified by the interference of English gentlemen to prevent the fall of eminent or ancient commercial families among the natives of India.*

The second circumstance which I think myself now bound to explain, relates to the dispensation of penal law.

Since my arrival here, in May, 1804, the punishment of death has not been inflicted by this Court. Now, the population subject to our jurisdiction, either locally or personally, cannot be estimated at less than two hundred thousand persons. Whether any evil consequence has yet arisen from so unusual,—and in the British dominions unexampled,—a circumstance as the disuse of capital punishment, for so long a period as seven years, among a population so considerable, is a question which you are entitled to ask, and to which I have the means of affording you a satisfactory answer.

The criminal records go back to the year 1756. From May, 1756, to May, 1763, the capital convictions amounted to one hundred and forty-one; and the executions were forty-seven. The annual average of persons who suffered death was almost seven; and the annual average of capital crimes ascertained to have been perpetrated was nearly twenty. From May, 1804, to May, 1811, there have been one hundred and nine capital convictions. The annual average, therefore, of capital crimes, legally proved to have been perpetrated during that period, is between fifteen and sixteen. During this period there has been no capital execution. But as the population of this island has much more than doubled during the last fifty years, the annual average of capital convictions during the last seven years ought to have been forty, in order to show the same proportion of criminality with that of the first seven years. Between 1756 and 1763, the military force was comparatively small: a few factories or small ports only depended on this government. Between 1804 and 1811, five hundred European officers, and probably four thousand European soldiers, were scattered over extensive territories. Though honour and morality be powerful aids of law with respect to the first class, and military discipline with respect to the second, yet it might have been expected, as experience has proved, that the more violent enormities would be perpetrated by the European soldiery—uneducated and sometimes depraved as many of them must originally be,—often in a state of mischievous idleness,—commanding, in spite of all care, the means of intoxication, and corrupted by contempt for the feelings and rights of the natives of this country. If these circumstances be considered, it will appear that the capital crimes committed during the last seven years, with no capital execution, have, in proportion to the population, not been much more than a third of those committed in the first seven years, notwithstanding the infliction of death on forty-seven persons. The intermediate periods lead to the same results. The number of capital crimes in any one of these periods does not appear to be diminished either by the capital executions of the same period, or of that immediately preceding: they bear no assignable proportion to each other.

In the seven years immediately preceding the last, which were chiefly in the presidency of my learned predecessor, Sir William Syer, there was a remarkable diminution of capital punishments. The average fell from about four in each year, which was that of the seven years before Sir William Syer, to somewhat less than two in each year. Yet the capital convictions were diminished about one-third.

"The punishment of death is principally intended to prevent the more violent and atrocious crimes. From May, 1797, there were eighteen convictions for murder, of which I omit two, as of a very particular kind. In that period there were twelve capital executions. From May, 1804, to May, 1811, there were six convictions for murder,* omitting one which was considered

* . . . "I am persuaded that your feelings would have entirely accorded with mine; convinced that, both as jurors and as private gentlemen, you will always consider yourselves as intrusted, in this remote region of the earth, with the honour of that beloved country, which, I trust, becomes more dear to you, as I am sure it does to me, during every new moment of absence; that, in your intercourse with each other as well as with the natives of India, you will keep unspotted the ancient character of the British nation,—renowned in every age, and in no age more than the present, for valour, for justice, for humanity, and generosity,—for every virtue which supports, as well as for every talent and accomplishment which adorns human society."—*Charge*, 21st July, 1805.—Ed.

* . . . "The truth seems to be, as I observed to you on a former occasion, that the natives of India, though incapable of the crimes which arise from violent passions, are, beyond every other people of the earth, addicted to those vices which proceed from the weakness of natural feeling, and

by the jury as in substance a case of manslaughter with some aggravation. The murders in the former period were, therefore, very nearly as three to one to those in the latter, in which no capital punishment was inflicted. From the number of convictions, I of course exclude those cases where the prisoner escaped; whether he owed his safety to defective proof of his guilt, or to a legal objection. This cannot affect the justness of a comparative estimate, because the proportion of criminals who escape on legal objections before courts of the same law, must, in any long period, be nearly the same. But if the two cases,—one where a formal verdict of murder, with a recommendation to mercy, was intended to represent an aggravated manslaughter; and the other of a man who escaped by a repugnancy in the indictment, where, however, the facts were more near manslaughter than murder,—be added, then the murders of the last seven years will be eight, while those of the former seven years will be sixteen.

"This small experiment has, therefore, been made without any diminution of the security of the lives and properties of men. Two hundred thousand men have been governed for seven years without a capital punishment, and without any increase of crimes. If any experience has been acquired, it has been safely and innocently gained. It was, indeed, impossible that the trial could ever have done harm. It was made on no avowed principle of impunity or even lenity. It was in its nature gradual, subject to cautious reconsideration in every new instance, and easily capable of being altogether changed on the least appearance of danger. Though the general result be rather remarkable, yet the usual maxims which regulate judicial discretion have in a very great majority of cases been pursued. The instances of deviation from those maxims scarcely amount to a twentieth of the whole convictions.

I have no doubt of the right of society to inflict the punishment of death on enormous crimes, wherever an inferior punishment is not sufficient. I consider it as a mere modification of the right of self-defence, which may as justly be exercised in deterring from attack, as in repelling it. I abstain from the discussions in which benevolent and enlightened men have, on more sober principles, endeavoured to show the wisdom of, at least, confining the punishment of death to the highest class of crimes. I do not even presume in this place to give an opinion regarding the attempt which has been made by one* whom I consider as among the wisest and most virtuous men of the present age, to render the letter of our penal law more conformable to its practice. My only object is to show that no evil has hitherto resulted from the exercise of judicial discretion in this Court. I speak with the less reserve, because the present sessions are likely to afford a test which will determine whether I have been actuated by weakness or by firmness,—by fantastic scruples and irrational feelings, or by a calm and steady view to what appeared to me the highest interests of society.†

I have been induced to make these explanations by the probability of this being the last time of my addressing a grand jury from this place. His Majesty has been graciously pleased to approve of my return to Great Britain, which the state of my health has for some time rendered very desirable. It is therefore probable, though not certain, that I may begin my voyage before the next sessions.

In that case, Gentlemen, I now have the honour to take my leave of you, with those serious thoughts that naturally arise at the close of every great division of human life,—with the most ardent and unmixed wishes for the welfare of the community with which I have been for so many years connected by an honourable tie,—and with thanks to you, Gentlemen, for the assistance which many of you have often afforded me in the discharge of duties, which are necessary, indeed, and sacred, but which, to a single judge, in a recent court, and small society, are peculiarly arduous, invidious, and painful.

---

the almost total absence of moral restraint. This observation may, in a great measure, account for that most aggravated species of child-murder which prevails among them. They are not actively cruel; but they are utterly insensible. They have less ferocity, perhaps, than most other nations; but they have still less compassion. Among them, therefore, infancy has lost its natural shield. The paltry temptation of getting possession of the few gold and silver ornaments, with which parents in this country load their infants, seems sufficient to lead these timid and mild beings to destroy a child without pity, without anger, without fear, without remorse, with little apprehension of punishment, and with no apparent shame on detection."—*Charge*, 19th April, 1806.—Ed.

* Sir Samuel Romilly.—Ed.

† Alluding to the impending trial of a native artillery-man for murder, who was eventually executed.—Ed.

SPEECH

ON

THE ANNEXATION OF GENOA TO THE KINGDOM OF SARDINIA.

DELIVERED IN THE HOUSE OF COMMONS ON THE 27TH OF APRIL, 1815.*

Mr. Speaker,—I now rise, pursuant to my notice, to discharge the most arduous, and certainly the most painful, public duty which I have ever felt myself called upon to perform. I have to bring before the House, probably for its final consideration, the case of Genoa, which, in various forms of proceedings and stages of progress, has already occupied a considerable degree of our attention. All these previous discussions of this great question of faith and justice, have been hitherto of necessity almost confined to one side. When my Honourable Friend† moved for papers on this subject, the reasoning was only on this side of the House. The gentlemen on the opposite side professedly abstained from discussion of the merits of the case, because they alleged that discussion was then premature, and that a disclosure of the documents necessary to form a right judgment, would at that period have been injurious to the public interest. In what that danger consisted, or how such a disclosure would have been more inconvenient on the 22d of February than on the 27th of April, they will doubtless this day explain. I have in vain examined the papers for an explanation of it. It was a serious assertion, made on their Ministerial responsibility, and absolutely requires to be satisfactorily established. After the return of the Noble Lord* from Vienna, the discussion was again confined to one side, by the singular course which he thought fit to adopt. When my Honourable Friend† gave notice of a motion for all papers respecting those arrangements at Vienna, which had been substantially completed, the Noble Lord did not intimate any intention of acceding to the motion. He suffered it to proceed as if it were to be adversely debated, and instead of granting the papers, so that they might be in the possession of every member a sufficient time for careful perusal and attentive consideration, he brought out upon us in the middle of his speech a number of documents, which had been familiar to him for six months, but of which no private member of the House could have known the existence. It was impossible for us to discuss a great mass of papers, of which we had heard extracts once read in the heat and hurry of debate. For the moment we were silenced by this ingenious stratagem: the House was taken by surprise. They were betrayed into premature applause of that of which it was absolutely impossible that they should be competent judges. It might be thought to imply a very unreasonable distrust in the Noble Lord of his own talents, if it were not much more naturally imputable to his well-grounded doubts of the justice of his cause.

I have felt, Sir, great impatience to bring the question to a final hearing, as soon as every member possessed that full information in which alone I well knew that my strength must consist. The production of the papers has occasioned some delay; but it has been attended also with some advantage to me, which I ought to confess. It has given me an opportunity of hearing in another place a most perspicuous and forcible statement of the defence of Ministers,‡—a statement which, without disparagement to the talents of the Noble Lord, I may venture to consider

---

* On the general reverses that befell the arms of France in the spring of 1814, and the consequent withdrawal of her troops from Italy, Lord William Bentinck was instructed to occupy the territories of the republic of Genoa, "without committing his Court or the Allies with respect to their ultimate disposition." Of the proclamation which he issued upon the occasion of carrying these orders into effect, dated March 14th, Lord Castlereagh had himself observed, that "an expression or two, taken separately, might create an impression that his views of Italian liberation went to the form of the government, as well as to the expulsion of the French." On the success of the military movement, the General reported that he had, "in consequence of the unanimous desire of the Genoese to return to their ancient state," proclaimed the old form of government. That this desire was unjustly thwarted, and that these expectations, fairly raised by Lord William Bentinck's proclamation, had been wrongfully disappointed by the final territorial settlement of the Allies at Paris, it was the scope of this speech to prove. For the papers referred to, see Hansard's Parliamentary Debates, vol. xxx. p. 387; and for the Resolutions moved, ibid., p. 932.—Ed.

† Mr. Lambton (afterwards Earl of Durham) had on the 22d of February made a motion for papers connected with the case of Genoa, on which occasion Sir James Mackintosh had supported him.—Ed

* Viscount Castlereagh.—Ed.

† Mr. Whitbread.—Ed.

‡ By Earl Bathurst, in the House of Lords.—Ed.

as containing the whole strength of their case. After listening to that able statement, —after much reflection for two months,—after the most anxious examination of the papers before us, I feel myself compelled to adhere to my original opinion, and to bring before the House the forcible transfer of the Genoese territory to the foreign master whom the Genoese people most hate,—a transfer stipulated for by British ministers, and executed by British troops,—as an act by which the pledged faith of this nation has been forfeited, the rules of justice have been violated, the fundamental principles of European policy have been shaken, and the odious claims of conquest stretched to an extent unwarranted by a single precedent in the good times of Europe. On the examination of these charges, I entreat gentlemen to enter with a disposition which becomes a solemn and judicial determination of a question which affects the honour of their country,—certainly without forgetting that justice which is due to the King's Ministers, whose character it does most deeply import.

I shall not introduce into this discussion any of the practical questions which have arisen out of recent and terrible events.* They may, like other events in history, supply argument or illustration; but I shall in substance argue the case, as if I were again speaking on the 22d of February, without any other change than a tone probably more subdued than would have been natural during that short moment of secure and almost triumphant tranquillity.

For this transaction, and for our share in all the great measures of the Congress of Vienna, the Noble Lord has told that he is "pre-eminently responsible." I know not in what foreign school he may have learnt such principles or phrases; but however much his colleagues may have resigned their discretion to him, I trust that Parliament will not suffer him to relieve them from any part of their responsibility. I shall not now inquire on what principle of constitutional law the whole late conduct of Continental negotiations by the Noble Lord could be justified. A Secretary of State has travelled over Europe with the crown and sceptre of Great Britain, exercising the royal prerogatives without the possibility of access to the Crown, to give advice, and to receive commands, and concluding his country by irrevocable acts, without communication with the other responsible advisers of the King. I shall not now examine into the nature of what our ancestors would have termed an "accroachment" of royal power,—an offence described indeed with dangerous laxity in ancient times, but, as an exercise of supreme power in another mode than by the forms, and under the responsibility prescribed by law, undoubtedly tending to the subversion of the fundamental principles of the British monarchy.

In all the preliminary discussions of this subject, the Noble Lord has naturally laboured to excite prejudice against his opponents. He has made a liberal use of the commonplaces of every Administration, against every Opposition; and he has assailed us chiefly through my Honourable Friend (Mr. Whitbread) with language more acrimonious and contumelious than is very consistent with his recommendations of decorum and moderation. He speaks of our "foul calumnies;" though calumniators do not call out as we did for inquiry and for trial. He tells us "that our discussions inflame nations more than they correct governments;"—a pleasant antithesis, which I have no doubt contains the opinion entertained of all popular discussion by the sovereigns and ministers of absolute monarchies, under whom he has lately studied constitutional principles. Indeed, Sir, I do not wonder that, on his return to this House, he should have been provoked into some forgetfulness of his usual moderation:—after long familiarity with the smooth and soft manners of diplomatists, it is natural that he should recoil from the turbulent freedom of a popular assembly. But let him remember, that to the uncourtly and fearless turbulence of this House Great Britain owes a greatness and power so much above her natural resources, and that rank among nations which gave him ascendency and authority in the deliberations of assembled Europe:—"Sic fortis Etruria crevit!" By that plainness and roughness of speech which wounded the nerves of courtiers, this House has forced kings and ministers to respect public liberty at home and to observe public faith abroad. He complains that this should be the first place where the faith of this country is impugned:—I rejoice that it is. It is because the first approaches towards breach of faith are sure of being attacked here, that there is so little ground for specious attack on our faith in other places. It is the nature and essence of the House of Commons to be jealous and suspicious, even to excess, of the manner in which the conduct of the Executive Government may affect that dearest of national interests—the character of the nation for justice and faith. What is destroyed by the slightest speck of corruption can never be sincerely regarded unless it be watched with jealous vigilance.

In questions of policy, where inconvenience is the worst consequence of error, and where much deference may be reasonably paid to superior information, there is much room for confidence beforehand and for indulgence afterwards: but confidence respecting a point of honour is a disregard of honour. Never, certainly, was there an occasion when these principles became of more urgent application than during the deliberations of the Congress of Vienna. Disposing, as they did, of rights and interests more momentous than were ever before placed at the disposal of a human assembly, is it fit that no channel should be left open by which they may learn the opinion of the public respecting their

* Napoleon's return from Elba.—Ed.

councils, and the feelings which their measures have excited from Norway to Andalusia? Were these princes and ministers really desirous, in a situation of tremendous responsibility, to bereave themselves of the guidance, and release their judgments from the control, which would arise from some knowledge of the general sentiments of mankind? Were they so infatuated by absolute power as to wish they might never hear the public judgments till their system was unalterably established, and the knowledge could no longer be useful? It seems so. There was only one assembly in Europe from whose free discussions they might have learnt the opinions of independent men,—only one in which the grievances of men and nations might have been published with any effect. The House of Commons was the only body which represented in some sort the public opinions of Europe; and the discussions which might have conveyed that opinion to the Sovereigns at Vienna, seem, from the language of the Noble Lord, to have been odious and alarming to them. Even in that case we have one consolation:—those who hate advice most, always need it most. If our language was odious, it must in the very same proportion have been necessary; and notwithstanding all the abuse thrown upon it may have been partly effectual. Denial at least proves nothing;—we are very sure that if we had prevented any evil, we should only have been the more abused.

Sir, I do not regret the obloquy with which we have been loaded during the present session:—it is a proof that we are following, though with unequal steps, the great men who have filled the same benches before us. It was their lot to devote themselves to a life of toilsome, thankless, and often unpopular opposition, with no stronger allurement to ambition than a chance of a few months of office in half a century, and with no other inducement to virtue than the faint hope of limiting and mitigating evil,—always certain that the merit would never be acknowledged, and generally obliged to seek for the best proof of their services in the scurrility with which they were reviled. To represent them as partisans of a foreign nation, for whom they demanded justice, was always one of the most effectual m[illegible]les of exciting a vulgar prejudice against them. When Mr. Burke and Mr. Fox exhorted Great Britain to be wise in relation to America, and just towards Ireland, they were called Americans and Irishmen. But they considered it as the greatest of all human calamities to be unjust;—they thought it worse to inflict than to suffer wrong: and they rightly thought themselves then most truly Englishmen, when they most laboured to dissuade England from tyranny. Afterwards, when Mr. Burke, with equal disinterestedness as I firmly believe, and certainly with sufficient zeal, supported the administration of Mr. Pitt, and the war against the Revolution, he did not restrain the freedom which belonged to his generous character. Speaking of that very alliance on which all his hopes were founded, he spoke of it, as I might speak (if I had his power of language) of the Congress at Vienna:—"There can be no tie of honour in a society for pillage." He was perhaps blamed for indecorum; but no one ever made any other conclusion from his language, than that it proved the ardour of his attachment to that cause which he could not endure to see dishonoured.

The Noble Lord has charged us, Sir, with a more than unusual interference in the functions of the monarchy and with the course of foreign negotiations. He has not indeed denied the right of this House to interfere:—he will not venture to deny "that this House is not only an accuser of competence to criminate, but a council of weight and wisdom to advise."* He incautiously, indeed, "said that there was a necessary collision between the powers of this House and the prerogatives of the Crown." It would have been more constitutional to have said that there was a liability to collision, and that the deference of each for the other has produced mutual concession, compromise, and co-operation, instead of collision. It has been, in fact, by the exercise of the great Parliamentary function of counsel, that in the best times of our history the House of Commons has suspended the exercise of its extreme powers. Respect for its opinion has rendered the exertion of its authority needless. It is not true that the interposition of its advice respecting the conduct of negotiations, the conduct of war, or the terms of peace, has been more frequent of late than in former times:—the contrary is the truth. From the earliest periods, and during the most glorious reigns in our history, its counsel has been proffered and accepted on the highest questions of peace and war. The interposition was necessarily even more frequent and more rough in these early times,—when the boundaries of its authority were undefined,—when its principal occupation was a struggle to assert and fortify its rights, and when it was sometimes as important to establish the legality of a power by exercise as to exercise it well,—than in these more fortunate periods of defined and acknowledged right, when a mild and indirect intimation of its opinion ought to preclude the necessity of resorting to those awful powers with which [illegible]isely armed. But though these interpositions of Parliament were more frequent in ancient times,—partly from the necessity of asserting contested rights,—and more rare in recent periods,—partly from the more submissive character of the House,—they are wanting at no time in number enough to establish the grand principle of the constitution, that Parliament is the first council of the King in war as well as in peace. This great principle has been acted

* Burke, A Representation to His Majesty, &c.—Ed.

on by Parliament in the best times:—it has been reverenced by the Crown in the worst. A short time before the Revolution it marked a struggle for the establishment of liberty:—a short time after the Revolution it proved the secure enjoyment of liberty. The House of Commons did not suffer Charles II. to betray his honour and his country, without constitutional warning to choose a better course;* its first aid to William III. was by counsels relating to war.† When, under the influence of other feelings, the House rather thwarted than aided their great Deliverer, even the party in it most hostile to liberty carried the rights of Parliament as a political council to the utmost constitutional limit, when they censured the treaty of Partition as having been passed under the Great Seal during the session of Parliament, and "without the advice of the same."‡ During the War of the Succession, both Houses repeatedly counselled the Crown on the conduct of the war,§—on negotiation with our allies,—and even on the terms of peace with the enemy. But what needs any further enumerations? Did not the vote of this House put an end to the American War?

Even, Sir, if the right of Parliament to advise had not been as clearly established as the prerogative of the Crown to make war or peace,—if it had not been thus constantly exercised,—if the wisest and best men had not been the first to call it forth into action, we might reasonably have been more forward than our ancestors to exercise this great right, because we contemplate a system of political negotiation, such as our ancestors never saw. All former Congresses were assemblies of the ministers of belligerent Powers to terminate their differences by treaty,—to define the rights and decide on the pretensions which had given rise to war, or to make compensation for the injuries which had been suffered in the course of it. The firm and secure system of Europe admitted no rapid, and few great changes of power and possession. A few fortresses in Flanders, a province on the frontiers of France and Germany, were generally the utmost cessions earned by the most victorious wars, and recovered by the most important treaties. Those who have lately compared the transactions at Vienna with the Treaty of Westphalia,—which formed the code of the Empire, and an era in diplomatic history,—which terminated the civil wars of religion, not only in Germany, but throughout Christendom, and which removed all that danger with which, for more than a century, the power of the House of Austria had threatened the liberties of Europe,—will perhaps feel some surprise when they are reminded that, except secularising a few Ecclesiastical principalities, that renowned and memorable treaty ceded only Alsace to France and part of Pomerania to Sweden,—that its stipulations did not change the political condition of half a million of men,—that it affected no pretension to dispose of any territory but that of those who were parties to it,—and that not an acre of land was ceded without the express and formal consent of its legal sovereign.* Far other were the pretensions, and indeed the performances, of the ministers assembled in congress at Vienna. They met under the modest pretence of carrying into effect the thirty-second article of the Treaty of Paris:† but under colour of this humble language, they arrogated the power of doing that, in comparison with which the whole Treaty of Paris was a trivial convention, and which made the Treaty of Westphalia appear no more than an adjustment of parish boundaries. They claimed the absolute disposal of every territory which had been occupied by France and her vassals, from Flanders to Livonia, and from the Baltic to the Po. Over these, the finest countries in the world, inhabited by twelve millions of mankind,—under pretence of delivering whom from a conqueror they had taken up arms,—they arrogated to themselves the harshest rights of conquest. It is true that of this vast territory they restored, or rather granted, a great part to its ancient sovereigns. But these sovereigns were always reminded by some new title, or by the disposal of some similarly circumstanced neighbouring territory, that they owed their restoration to the generosity, or at most to the prudence of the Congress, and that they were not entitled to require it from its justice. They came in by a new tenure:—they were the feudatories of the new corporation of kings erected at Vienna, exercising joint power in effect over all Europe, consisting in form of eight or ten princes, but in substance of three great military Powers,—the spoilers of Poland, the original invaders of the European constitution,—sanctioned by the support of England, and checked, however feebly, by France alone. On these three Powers, whose reverence for national independence and title to public confidence were so firmly established by the partition of Poland, the dictatorship of Europe has fallen. They agree that Germany shall have a federal constitution,—that Switzerland shall govern herself,—that unhappy Italy shall, as they say, be composed of sovereign states:—

* Commons' Ad[illegible] 15th of March, 1627; 29th of March, 1677; 25th of May, 1677; 30th of December, 1680.

† 24th of April, 1689, (advising a declaration of war).

‡ 21st of March, 1701.

§ 27th of November, 1705; 22d of December, 1707 3d of March, 1709; 18th of February, 1710.

* This is certainly true respecting Pomerania and Alsace: whether the Ecclesiastical principalities were treated with so much ceremony may be more doubtful, and it would require more research to ascertain it than can now be applied to the object.

† "All the Powers engaged on either side in the present war, shall, within the space of two months, send plenipotentiaries to Vienna for the purpose of regulating in general congress the arrangements which are to complete the provisions of the present treaty."

but it is all by grant from these lords paramount. Their will is the sole title to dominion,—the universal tenure of sovereignty. A single acre granted on such a principle is, in truth, the signal of a monstrous revolution in the system of Europe. Is the House of Commons to remain silent, when such a principle is applied in practice to a large part of the Continent, and proclaimed in right over the whole? Is it to remain silent when it has heard the King of Sardinia, at the moment when he received possession of Genoa from a British garrison, and when the British commander stated himself to have made the transfer in consequence of the decision at Vienna, proclaim to the Genoese, that he took possession of their territory "in concurrence with the wishes of the principal Powers of Europe?"

It is to this particular act of the Congress, Sir, that I now desire to call the attention of the House, not only on account of its own atrocity, but because it seems to represent in miniature the whole system of that body,—to be a perfect specimen of their new public law, and to exemplify every principle of that code of partition which they are about to establish on the ruins of that ancient system of national independence and balanced power, which gradually raised the nations of Europe to the first rank of the human race. I contend that all the parties to this violent transfer, and more especially the British Government, have been guilty of perfidy,—have been guilty of injustice; and I shall also contend, that the danger of these violations of faith and justice is much increased, when they are considered as examples of those principles by which the Congress of Vienna arrogate to themselves the right of regulating a considerable portion of Europe.

To establish the breach of faith, I must first ask,—What did Lord William Bentinck promise, as commander-in-chief of His Majesty's troops in Italy, by his Proclamations of the 14th of March and 26th of April, 1814? The first is addressed to the people of Italy. It offers them the assistance of Great Britain to rescue them from the iron yoke of Buonaparte. It holds out the example of Spain, enabled, by the aid of Great Britain, to rescue "her independence,"—of the neighbouring Sicily, "which hastens to resume her ancient splendour among independent nations. . . Holland is about to obtain the same object. . . Warriors of Italy, you are invited to vindicate your own rights, and to be free! Italy, by our united efforts, shall become what she was in her most prosperous periods, and what Spain now is!"

Now, Sir, I do contend that all the powers of human ingenuity cannot give two senses to this Proclamation: I defy the wit of man to explain it away. Whether Lord William Bentinck had the power to promise is an after question:—what he did promise, can be no question at all. He promised the aid of England to obtain Italian independence. He promised to assist the Italians in throwing off a yoke,—in escaping from thraldom,—in establishing liberty,—in asserting rights,—in obtaining independence. Every term of emancipation known in human language is exhausted to impress his purpose on the heart of Italy. I do not now inquire whether the generous warmth of this language may not require in justice some understood limitation:—perhaps it may. But can independence mean a transfer to the yoke of the most hated of foreign masters? Were the Genoese invited to spill their blood, not merely for a choice of tyrants, but to earn the right of wearing the chains of the rival and the enemy of two centuries? Are the references to Spain, to Sicily, and to Holland mere frauds on the Italians,—"words full of sound and fury, signifying nothing?" If not, can they mean less than this,—that those countries of Italy which were independent before the war, shall be independent again? These words, therefore, were at least addressed to the Genoese;—suppose them to be limited, as to any other Italians;—suppose the Lombards, or, at that time, the Neapolitans, to be tacitly excluded. Addressed to the Genoese, they either had no meaning, or they meant their ancient independence.

Did the Genoese act upon these promises? What did they do in consequence of that first Proclamation of the 14th of March, from Leghorn, addressed to all the Italians, but applicable at least to the Genoese, and necessarily understood by that people as comprehending them? I admit that the promises were conditional; and to render them conclusive, it was necessary for the Genoese to fulfil the condition:—I contend that they did. I shall not attempt again to describe the march of Lord William Bentinck from Leghorn to Genoa, which has already been painted by my Honourable and Learned Friend* with all the chaste beauties of his moral and philosophical eloquence: my duty confines me to the dry discussion of mere facts. The force with which Lord William Bentinck left Leghorn consisted of about three thousand English, supported by a motley band of perhaps five thousand Sicilians, Italians, and Greeks, the greater part of whom had scarcely ever seen a shot fired. At the head of this force, he undertook a long march through one of the most defensible countries of Europe, against a city garrisoned or defended by seven thousand French veterans, and which it would have required twenty-five thousand men to invest, according to the common rules of military prudence. Now, Sir, I assert, without fear of contradiction, that such an expedition would have been an act of frenzy, unless Lord William Bentinck had the fullest assurance of the good-will and active aid of the Genoese people. The fact sufficiently speaks for itself. I cannot here name the high military authority on which my assertion rests; but I defy the Right Honourable Gentlemen, with all their

* Mr. Horner.—Ed.

means of commanding military information, to contradict me. I know they will not venture. In the first place, then, I assume, that the British general would not have begun his advance without assurance of the friendship of the Genoese, and that he owes his secure and unmolested march to the influence of the same friendship—supplying his army, and deterring his enemies from attack. He therefore, in truth, owed his being before the walls of Genoa to Genoese co-operation. The city of Genoa, which, in 1799, had been defended by Massena for three months, fell to Lord William Bentinck in two days. In two days seven thousand French veterans laid down their arms to three thousand British soldiers, encumbered rather than aided by the auxiliary rabble whom I have described. Does any man in his senses believe, that the French garrison could have been driven to such a surrender by any cause but their fear of the Genoese people? I have inquired, from the best military authorities accessible to me, what would be the smallest force with which the expedition might probably have been successful, if the population had been—I do not say enthusiastically,—but commonly hostile to the invaders:—I have been assured, that it could not have been less than twenty-five thousand men. Here, again, I venture to challenge contradiction. If none can be given, must I not conclude that the known friendship of the Genoese towards the British, manifested after the issue of the Proclamation, and in no part created by it, was equivalent to an auxiliary force of seventeen thousand men? Were not the known wishes of the people, acting on the hopes of the British, and on the fears of the French, the chief cause of the expulsion of the French from the Genoese territory? Can Lord William Bentinck's little army be considered as more than auxiliaries to the popular sentiment? If a body of four thousand Genoese had joined Lord William, on the declared ground of his Proclamation, all mankind would have exclaimed that the condition was fulfilled, and the contract indissoluble. Is it not the height of absurdity to maintain that a manifestation of public sentiment, which produced as much benefit to him as four times that force, is not to have the same effect. A ship which is in sight of a capture is entitled to her share of the prize, though she neither had nor could have fired a shot, upon the plain principle that apprehension of her approach probably contributed to produce the surrender. If apprehension of Genoese hostility influenced the French garrison,—if assurance of Genoese friendship encouraged the British army, on what principle do you defraud the Genoese of their national independence,—the prize which you promised them, and which they thus helped to wrest from the enemy?

In fact, I am well informed, Sir, that there was a revolt in the city, which produced the surrender,—that Buonaparte's statue had been overthrown with every mark of indignity,—and that the French garrison was on the point of being expelled, even if the besiegers had not appeared. But I am not obliged to risk the case upon the accuracy of that information. Be it that the Genoese complied with Lord Wellesley's wise instruction, to avoid premature revolt: I affirm that Lord William Bentinck's advance is positive evidence of an understanding with the Genoese leaders; that there would have been such evidence in the advance of any judicious officer, but most peculiarly in his, who had been for three years negotiating in Upper Italy, and was well acquainted with the prevalent impatience of the French yoke. I conceive it to be self-evident, that if the Genoese had believed the English army to be advancing in order to sell them to Sardinia, they would not have favoured the advance. I think it demonstrable, that to their favourable disposition the expedition owed its success. And it needs no proof that they favoured the English, because the English promised them the restoration of independence. The English have, therefore, broken faith with them: the English have defrauded them of solemnly-promised independence: the English have requited their co-operation, by forcibly subjecting them to the power of the most odious of foreign masters. On the whole, I shall close this part of the question with challenging all the powers of human ingenuity to interpret the Proclamation as any thing but a promise of independence to such Italian nations as were formerly independent, and would now co-operate for the recovery of their rights. I leave to the Gentlemen on the other side the task of convincing the House that the conduct of the Genoese did not co-operate towards success, though without it success was impossible.

But we have been told that Lord William Bentinck was not authorised to make such a promise. It is needless for me to repeat my assent to a truth so trivial, as that no political negotiation is naturally within the province of a military commander, and that for such negotiations he must have special authority. At the same time I must observe, that Lord William Bentinck was not solely a military commander, and could not be considered by the Italians in that light. In Sicily his political functions had been more important than his military command. From 1811 to 1814 he had, with the approbation of his Government, performed the highest acts of political authority in that island; and he had, during the same period, carried on the secret negotiations of the British Government with all Italians disaffected to France. To the Italians, then, he appeared as a plenipotentiary; and they had a right to expect that his Government would ratify his acts and fulfil his engagements. In fact, his special authority was full and explicit. Lord Wellesley's Instructions of the 21st of October and 27th of December, 1811, speak with the manly firmness which distinguishes that great statesman as much as his commanding character and splendid talents. His meaning is always precisely expressed:—he leaves himself no retreat from his engagements in the ambiguity and perplexity of an unintelligible style. The principal object of these masterly despatches is to instruct Lord William Bentinck respecting his support of any eventual effort of the Italian states to rescue Italy. They remind him of the desire of the Prince Regent to afford every practicable assistance to the people of Italy in any such effort. They convey so large a discretion, that it is thought necessary to say,—"In all arrangements respecting the expulsion of the enemy, your Lordship will not fail to give due consideration to our engagements with the courts of Sicily and Sardinia." Lord William Bentinck had therefore powers which would have extended to Naples and Piedmont, unless they had been specially excepted. On the 19th of May, 1812, Lord Castlereagh virtually confirms the same extensive and confidential powers. On the 4th of March preceding, Lord Liverpool had, indeed, instructed Lord William Bentinck to employ a part of his force in a diversion in favour of Lord Wellington, by a descent on the eastern coast of Spain. This diversion doubtless suspended the negotiations with the patriotic Italians, and precluded for a time the possibility of affording them aid. But so far from withdrawing Lord William Bentinck's political power, in Italy, they expressly contemplate their revival:—"This operation would leave the question respecting Italy open for further consideration, if circumstances should subsequently render the prospect there more inviting." The despatches of Lord Bathurst, from March 1812 to December 1813, treat Lord William Bentinck as still in possession of those extensive powers originally vested in him by the despatch of Lord Wellesley. Every question of policy is discussed in these despatches, not as with a mere general,—not even as with a mere ambassador, but as with a confidential minister for the *Italian Department*. The last despatch is that which closes with the remarkable sentence, which is, in my opinion, decisive of this whole question:—"Provided it be clearly with the entire concurrence of the inhabitants, you may take possession of Genoa in the name of His Sardinian Majesty." Now this is, in effect, tantamount to an instruction not to transfer Genoa to Sardinia without the concurrence of the inhabitants. It is a virtual instruction to consider the wishes of the people of Genoa as the rule and measure of his conduct: it is more—it is a declaration that he had no need of any instruction to re-establish Genoa, if the Genoese desired it. That re-establishment was provided for by his original instructions: only the new project of a transfer to a foreign sovereign required new ones. Under his original instructions, then, thus ratified by a long series of succeeding despatches from a succession of ministers, did Lord William Bentinck issue the Proclamation of the 14th of March.

Limitations there were in the original instructions:—Sicily and Sardinia were excepted. New exceptions undoubtedly arose, in the course of events, so plainly within the principle of the original exceptions as to require no specification. Every Italian province of a sovereign with whom Great Britain had subsequently contracted an alliance was, doubtless, as much to be excepted out of general projects of revolt for Italian independence as those which had been subject to the Allied Sovereigns in 1811. A British minister needed no express instructions to comprehend that he was to aid no revolt against the Austrian Government in their former province of Lombardy. The change of circumstances sufficiently instructed him. But in what respect were circumstances changed respecting Genoa? The circumstances of Genoa were the same as at the time of Lord Wellesley's instructions. The very last despatches (those of Lord Bathurst, of the 28th of December, 1813,) had pointed to the Genoese territory as the scene of military operations, without any intimation that the original project was not still applicable there, unless the Genoese nation should agree to submit to the King of Sardinia. I contend, therefore, that the original instruction of Lord Wellesley, which authorised the promise of independence to every part of the Italian peninsula except Naples and Piedmont, was still in force, wherever it was not manifestly limited by subsequent engagements with the sovereigns of other countries, similar to our engagements with the sovereigns of Naples and Piedmont,—that no such engagement existed respecting the Genoese authority,—and that to the Genoese people the instruction of Lord Wellesley was as applicable as on the day when that instruction was issued.

The Noble Lord may then talk as he pleases of "disentangling from the present question the question of Italy," to which on a former occasion he applied a phraseology so singular. He cannot "disentangle these questions:"—they are inseparably blended. The Instructions of 1811 authorised the promise of independence to all Italians, except the people of Naples and Piedmont. The Proclamation of the 14th of March 1814 promised independence to all Italians, with the manifestly implied exception of those who had been the subjects of Powers who were now become the allies of Great Britain. A British general, fully authorised, promised independence to those Italians who, like the Genoese, had not been previously the subjects of an ally of Britain, and by that promise, so authorised, his Government is inviolably bound.

But these direct instructions were not all. He was indirectly authorised by the acts and language of his own Government and of the other great Powers of Europe. He was authorised to re-establish the republic of Genoa, because the British Government in the Treaty of Amiens had refused to acknowledge its destruction. He was authorised to believe that Austria desired the re-establishment of a republic whose destruction that Government in 1808 had represented as a cause of war. He was surely authorised to consider that re-establishment as conformable to the sentiments of the Emperor Alexander, who at the same time had, on account of the annexation of Genoa to France, refused even at the request of Great Britain to continue his mediation between her and a Power capable of such an outrage on the rights of independent nations. Where was Lord William Bentinck to learn the latest opinions of the Allied Powers? If he read the celebrated Declaration of Frankfort, he there found an alliance announced of which the object was the restoration of Europe. Did restoration mean destruction? Perhaps before the 14th of March,—certainly before the 26th of April,—he had seen the first article of the Treaty of Chaumont, concluded on the 1st of March,—

"Dum curæ ambiguæ, dum spes incerta futuri,"*

in which he found the object of the war declared by the assembled majesty of confederated Europe to be "a general peace under which the rights and liberties of all nations may be secured"—words eternally honourable to their authors if they were to be observed—more memorable still if they were to be openly and perpetually violated! Before the 26th of April he had certainly perused these words, which no time will efface from the records of history; for he evidently adverts to them in the preamble of his Proclamation, and justly considers them as a sufficient authority, if he had no other, to warrant its provisions. "Considering," says he, "that the general desire of the Genoese nation seems to be, to return to their ancient government, and considering that the desire seems to be conformable to the principles recognised by the High Allied Powers of restoring to all their ancient rights and privileges." In the work of my celebrated friend, Mr. Gentz, of whom I can never speak without regard and admiration, On the Balance of Power, he would have found the incorporation of Genoa justly reprobated as one of the most unprincipled acts of French tyranny; and he would have most reasonably believed the sentiments of the Allied Powers to have been spoken by that eminent person—now, if I am not misinformed, the Secretary of that Congress, on whose measures his writings are the most severe censure.

But that Lord William Bentinck did believe himself to have offered independence to the Genoese,—that he thought himself directly and indirectly authorised to make such an offer,—and that he was satisfied that the Genoese had by their co-operation performed their part of the compact, are facts which rest upon the positive and precise testimony of Lord William Bentinck himself. I call upon him as the best interpreter of his own language, and the most unexceptionable witness to prove the co-operation of the Genoese. Let this Proclamation of the 26th of April be examined:—it is the clearest commentary on that of the 14th of March. It is the most decisive testimony to the active aid of the Genoese people. On the 26th of April he bestows on the people of Genoa that independence which he had promised to all the nations of Italy (with the implied exception, already often enough mentioned), on condition of their aiding to expel the oppressor. He, therefore, understood his own Proclamation to be such a promise of independence: he could not doubt but that he was authorised to make it: and he believed that the Genoese were entitled to claim the benefit of it by their performance of its condition.

This brings me to the consideration of this Proclamation, on which I should have thought all observation unnecessary, unless I had heard some attempts made by the Noble Lord to explain it away, and to represent it as nothing but the establishment of a provisional government. I call on any member of the House to read that Proclamation, and to say whether he can in common honour assent to such an interpretation. The Proclamation, beyond all doubt, provides for two perfectly distinct objects:—the establishment of a provisional government till the 1st of January 1815, and the re-establishment of the ancient constitution of the republic, with certain reforms and modifications, from and after that period. Three-fourths of the Proclamation have no reference whatever to a provisional government;—the first sentence of the preamble, and the third and fourth articles only, refer to that object: but the larger paragraph of the preamble, and four articles of the enacting part, relate to the re-establishment of the ancient constitution alone. "The desire of the Genoese nation was to return to their ancient government, under which they had enjoyed independence:"—was this relating to a provisional government? Did "the principles recognised by the High Allied Powers" contemplate only the establishment of provisional governments? Did provisional governments imply "restoring to all their ancient rights and privileges?" Why should the ancient constitution be re-established—the very constitution given by Andrew Doria when he delivered his country from a foreign yoke,—if nothing was meant but a provisional government, preparatory to foreign slavery? Why was the government to be modified according to the general wish, the public good, and the spirit of Doria's constitution, if nothing was meant beyond a temporary administration, till the Allied Powers could decide on what vassal they were to bestow Genoa? But I may have been at first mistaken, and time

* Æneid. lib. viii.—Ed.

may have rendered my mistake incorrigible. Let every gentleman, before he votes on this question, calmly peruse the Proclamation of the 26th of April, and determine for himself whether it admits of any but one construction. Does it not provide for a provisional government immediately, and for the establishment of the ancient constitution hereafter;—the provisional government till the 1st of January, 1815, the constitution from the 1st of January, 1815? The provisional government is in its nature temporary, and a limit is fixed to it. The constitution of the republic is permanent, and no term or limit is prescribed beyond which it is not to endure. It is not the object of the Proclamation to establish the ancient constitution as a provisional government. On the contrary, the ancient constitution is not to be established till the provisional government ceases to exist. So distinct are they, that the mode of appointment to the supreme powers most materially differs. Lord William Bentinck nominates the two colleges, who compose the provisional government. The two colleges who are afterwards to compose the permanent government of the republic, are to be nominated agreeably to the ancient constitution. Can it be maintained that the intention was to establish two successive provisional governments? For what conceivable reason? Even in that case, why engage in the laborious and arduous task of reforming an ancient constitution for the sake of a second provisional government which might not last three weeks? And what constitution was more unfit for a provisional government,—what was more likely to indispose the people to all farther change, and above all, to a sacrifice of their independence, than the ancient constitution of the republic, which revived all their feelings of national dignity, and seemed to be a pledge that they were once more to be Genoese? In short, Sir, I am rather fearful that I shall be thought to have overlaboured a point so extremely clear. But if I have dwelt too long upon this Proclamation, and examined it too minutely, it is not because I think it difficult, but because I consider it is decisive of the whole question. If Lord William Bentinck in that Proclamation bestowed on the people of Genoa their place among nations, and the government of their forefathers, it must have been because he deemed himself authorised to make that establishment by the repeated instructions of the British Government, and by the avowed principles and solemn acts of the Allied Powers, and because he felt bound to make it by his own Proclamation of the 14th of March, combined with the acts done by the Genoese nation, in consequence of that Proclamation. I think I have proved that he did so,—that he believed himself to have done so, and that the people of Genoa believed it likewise.

Perhaps, however, if Lord William Bentinck had mistaken his instructions, and had acted without authority, he might have been disavowed, and his acts might have been annulled? I doubt whether, in such a case, any disavowal would have been sufficient. Wherever another people, in consequence of the acts of our agent whom they had good reason to trust, have done acts which they cannot recall, I do not conceive the possibility of a just disavowal of such an agent's acts. Where one party has innocently and reasonably advanced too far to recede, justice cuts off the other also from retreat. But, at all events, the disavowal, to be effectual, must have been prompt, clear, and public. Where is the disavowal here? Where is the public notice to the Genoese, that they were deceived? Did their mistake deserve no correction, even on the ground of compassion? I look in vain through these Papers for any such act. The Noble Lord's letter of the 30th of March was the first intimation which Lord William Bentinck received of any change of system beyond Lombardy. It contains only a caution as to future conduct; and it does not hint an intention to cancel any act done on the faith of the Proclamation of the 14th of March. The allusion to the same subject in the letter of the 3d of April, is liable to the very same observation, and being inserted at the instance of the Duke of Campochiaro, was evidently intended only to prevent the prevalence of such ideas of Italian liberty as were inconsistent with the accession then proposed to the territory of Naples. It certainly could not have been supposed by Lord William Bentinck to apply to Genoa; for Genoa was in his possession on the 26th, when he issued the Proclamation, which he never could have published if he had understood the despatch in that sense.

The Noble Lord's despatch of the 6th of May is, Sir, in my opinion, fatal to his argument. It evidently betrays a feeling that acts had been done, to create in the Genoese a hope of independence: yet it does not direct these acts to be disavowed;—it contains no order speedily to undeceive the people. It implies that a deception had been practised; and instead of an attempt to repair it, there is only an injunction not to repeat the fault. No expressions are to be used which may prejudge the fate of Genoa. Even then that fate remained doubtful. So far from disavowal, the Noble Lord proposes the re-establishment of Genoa, though with some curtailment of territory, to M. Pareto, who maintained the interests of his country with an ability and dignity worthy of happier success.

And the Treaty of Paris itself, far from a disavowal, is, on every principle of rational construction, a ratification and adoption of the act of Lord William Bentinck. The 6th article of that Treaty provides that "Italy, beyond the limits of the country which is to revert to Austria, shall be composed of sovereign states." Now, Sir, I desire to know the meaning of this provision. I can conceive only three possible constructions. Either that every country shall have some sovereign, or, in other words, some government:—it will not be said that so trivial a proposition required a solemn stipulation. Or that there is to be more than one sovereign:—that was absolutely unnecessary: Naples, the States of the Church, and Tuscany, already existed. Or, thirdly, that the ancient sovereign states shall be re-established, except the country which reverts to Austria:—this, and this only, was an intelligible and important object of stipulation. It is the most reasonable of the only three possible constructions of these words. The phrase "sovereign states" seems to have been preferred to that of "sovereigns," because it comprehended republics as well as monarchies. According to this article, thus understood, the Powers of Europe had by the Treaty of Paris (to speak cautiously) given new hopes to the Genoese that they were again to be a nation.

But, according to every principle of justice, it is unnecessary to carry the argument so far. The act of an agent, if not disavowed in reasonable time, becomes the act of the principal. When a pledge is made to a people—such as was contained in the Proclamations of the 14th of March and 26th of April—it can be recalled only by a disavowal equally public.

On the policy of annexing Genoa to Piedmont, Sir, I have very little to say. That it was a compulsory, and therefore an unjust union, is, in my view of the subject, the circumstance which renders it most impolitic. It seems a bad means of securing Italy against France, to render a considerable part of the garrison of the Alps so dissatisfied with their condition, that they must consider every invader as a deliverer. But even if the annexation had been just, I should have doubted whether it was desirable. In former times, the House of Savoy might have been the guardians of the Alps:—at present, to treat them as such, seems to be putting the keys of Italy into hands too weak to hold them. Formerly, the conquest of Genoa and Piedmont were two distinct operations:—Genoa did not necessarily follow the fate of Turin. In the state of things created by the Congress, a French army has no need of separately acting against the Genoese territory:—it must fall with Piedmont. And, what is still more strange, it is bound to the destinies of Piedmont by the same Congress which has wantonly stripped Piedmont of its natural defences. The House of Sardinia is stripped of great part of its ancient patrimony:—a part of Savoy is, for no conceivable reason, given to France. The French are put in possession of the approaches and outposts of the passes of Mont Cenis: they are brought a campaign nearer to Italy. At this very moment they have assembled an army at Chambery, which, unless Savoy had been wantonly thrown to them, they must have assembled at Lyons. You impose on the House of Savoy the defence of a longer line of Alps with one hand, and you weaken the defence of that part of the line which covers their capital with the other. But it is perfectly sufficient for me, in the present case, if the policy is only doubtful, or the interests only slight. The laxest moralist will not, publicly at least, deny, that more advantage is lost by the loss of a character for good faith than can be gained by a small improvement in the distribution of territory. Perhaps, indeed, this annexation of Genoa is the only instance recorded in history of great Powers having (to say no more) brought their faith and honour into question without any of the higher temptations of ambition,—with no better inducement than a doubtful advantage in distributing territory more conveniently,—unless, indeed, it can be supposed that they are allured by the pleasures of a triumph over the ancient principles of justice, and of a parade of the new maxims of convenience which are to regulate Europe in their stead.

I have hitherto argued this case as if the immorality of the annexation had arisen solely from the pledge made to the Genoese nation. I have argued it as if the Proclamation of Lord William Bentinck had been addressed to a French province, on which there could be no obligation to confer independence, if there were no promise to do so. For the sake of distinctness, I have hitherto kept out of view that important circumstance, which would, as I contend, without any promise, have of itself rendered a compulsory annexation unjust. Anterior to all promise, independent of all pledged faith, I conceive that Great Britain could not morally treat the Genoese territory as a mere conquest, which she might hold as a province, or cede to another power, at her pleasure. In the year 1797, when Genoa was conquered by France (then at war with England), under pretence of being revolutionised, the Genoese republic was at peace with Great Britain; and consequently, in the language of the law of nations, they were "friendly states." Neither the substantial conquest in 1797, nor the formal union of 1805, had ever been recognised by this kingdom. When the British commander, therefore, entered the Genoese territory in 1814, he entered the territory of a friend in the possession of an enemy. Supposing him, by his own unaided force, to have conquered it from the enemy, can it be inferred that he conquered it from the Genoese people? He had rights of conquest against the French:—but what right of conquest would accrue from their expulsion, against the Genoese? How could we be at war with the Genoese?—not as with the ancient republic of Genoa, which fell when in a state of amity with us,—not as subjects of France, because we had never legally and formally acknowledged their subjection to that Power. There could be no right of conquest against them, because there was neither the state of war, nor the right of war. Perhaps the Powers of the Continent, which had either expressly or tacitly recognised the annexation of Genoa in their treaties with France, might consistently treat these Genoese people as mere French subjects, and consequently the Genoese territory as a French province, conquered from the French government, which as regarded them had become the sovereign of Genoa. But England stood in no such position:—in her eye the republic of Genoa still of right subsisted. She had done no act which implied the legal destruction of a commonwealth, with which she had had no war, nor cause of war. Genoa ought to have been regarded by England as a friendly state, oppressed for a time by the common enemy, and entitled to re-assume the exercise of her sovereign rights as soon as that enemy was driven from her territory by a friendly force. Voluntary, much more cheerful, union,—zealous co-operation,—even long submission,—might have altered the state of belligerent rights:—none of these are here pretended. In such a case, I contend, that, according to the law of nations, anterior to all promises, and independent of all pledged faith, the republic of Genoa was restored to the exercise of her sovereignty, which, in our eyes, she had never lost, by the expulsion of the French from her soil.

These, Sir, are no reasonings of mine: I read them in the most accredited works on public law, delivered long before any events of our time were in contemplation, and yet as applicable to this transaction, as if they had been contrived for it. Vattel, in the thirteenth and fourteenth chapters of his third book, has stated fully and clearly those principles respecting the application of the *jus postliminii* to the case of states, which he had taken from his eminent predecessors, or rather which they and he had discovered to be agreeable to the plainest dictates of reason, and which they have transcribed from the usage of civilized nations. I shall not trouble the House with the passages,* unless I see some attempt to reconcile them with the annexation of Genoa. I venture to predict no such attempts will be hazarded. It is not my disposition to overrate the authority of this class of writers, or to consider authority in any case as a substitute for reason. But these eminent writers were at least necessarily impartial. Their weight, as bearing testimony to general sentiment and civilized usage, receives a new accession from every statesman who appeals to their writings, and from every year in which no contrary practice is established or hostile principles avowed. Their works are thus attested by successive generations to be records of the customs of the best times, and depositories of the deliberate and permanent judgments of the more enlightened part of mankind. Add to this, that their authority is usually invoked by the feeble, and despised by those who are strong enough to need no aid from moral sentiment, and to bid defiance to justice. I have never heard their principles questioned, but by those whose flagitious policy they had by anticipation condemned.

Here, Sir, let me for a moment lower the claims of my argument, and abandon some part of the ground which I think it practicable to maintain. If I were to admit that the pledge here is not so strong, nor the duty of re-establishing a rescued friend so imperious as I have represented, still it must be admitted to me, that it was a promise, though perhaps not unequivocal, to perform that which was moral and right, whether within the sphere of strict duty or not. Either the doubtful promise, or the imperfect duty, might singly have been insufficient: but, combined, they reciprocally strengthen each other. The slightest promise to do what was before a duty, becomes as binding as much stronger words to do an indifferent act:—strong assurances that a man will do what it is right for him to do are not required. A slight declaration to such an effect is believed by those to whom it is addressed, and therefore obligatory on those by whom it is uttered. Was it not natural and reasonable for the people of Genoa to believe, on the slenderest pledges, that such a country as England, with which they had never had a difference, would avail herself of a victory, due at least in part to their friendly sentiments, in order to restore them to that independence of which they had been robbed by her enemy and theirs,—by the general oppressor of Europe.

I shall not presume to define on invariable principles the limits of the right of conquest.

* "When a nation, a people, a state, has been entirely subjugated, whether a revolution can give it the right of Postliminium? To which we answer, that if the conquered state has not assented to the new subjection, if it did not yield voluntarily, if it only ceased to resist from inability, if the conqueror has not yet sheathed the sword to wield the sceptre of a pacific sovereign,—such a state is only conquered and oppressed, and when the arms of an ally deliver it, returns without doubt to its first state. Its ally cannot become its conqueror; he is a deliverer, who can have a right only to compensation for his services." . . . . "If the last conqueror, not being an ally of the state, claims a right to retain it under his authority as the prize of victory, he puts himself in the place of the conqueror, and becomes the enemy of the oppressed state. That state may legitimately resist him, and avail herself of a favourable occasion to recover her liberty. A state unjustly oppressed ought to be re-established in her rights by the conqueror who delivers her from the oppressor." Whoever carefully considers the above passage will observe, that it is intended to be applicable to two very distinct cases;—that of deliverance by an ally, where the duty of restoration is strict and precise,—and that of deliverance by a state unallied, but not hostile, where in the opinion of the writer the re-establishment of the oppressed nation is at least the moral duty of the conqueror, though arising only from our common humanity, and from the amicable relation which subsists between all men and all communities, till dissolved by wrongful oppression. It is to the latter case that the strong language in the second part of the above quotation is applied. It seems very difficult, and it has not hitherto been attempted, to resist the application to the case of Genoa.

It is founded, like every right of war, on a regard to security,—the object of all just war. The modes in which national safety may be provided for,—by reparation for insult,—by compensation for injury,—by cessions and by indemnifications,—vary in such important respects, according to the circumstances of various cases, that it is perhaps impossible to limit them by an universal principle. In the case of Norway,* I did not pretend to argue the question upon grounds so high as those which were taken by some writers on public law. These writers, who for two centuries have been quoted as authorities in all the controversies of Europe, with the moderate and pacific Grotius at their head, have all concurred in treating it as a fundamental principle, that a defeated sovereign may indeed cede part of his dominions to the conqueror, but that he thereby only abdicates his own sovereignty over the ceded dominion,—that the consent of the people is necessary to make them morally subject to the authority of the conqueror. Without renouncing this limitation of the rights of conquest, founded on principles so generous, and so agreeable to the dignity of human nature, I was content to argue the cession of Norway,—as I am content to argue the cession of Genoa,—on lower and humbler, but perhaps safer grounds. Let me waive the odious term "rights,"—let me waive the necessity of any consent of a people, express or implied, to legitimate the cession of their territory: at least this will not be denied,—that to unite a people by force to a nation against whom they entertain a strong antipathy, is the most probable means of rendering the community unhappy, —of making the people discontented, and the sovereign tyrannical. But there can be no right in any governor, whether he derives his power from conquest, or from any other source, to make the governed unhappy:—all the rights of all governors exist only to make the governed happy. It may be disputed among some, whether the rights of government be *from* the people; but no man can doubt that they are *for* the people. Such a forcible union is an immoral and cruel exercise of the conqueror's power; and as soon as that concession is made, it is not worth while to discuss whether it be within his right,—in other words, whether he be forbidden by any law to make it.

But if every cession of a territory against the deliberate and manifest sense of its inhabitants be a harsh and reprehensible abuse of conquest, it is most of all culpable,—it becomes altogether atrocious and inhuman, where the antipathy was not the feeling of the moment, or the prejudice of the day, but a profound sentiment of hereditary repugnance and aversion, which has descended from generation to generation,—has mingled with every part of thought and action,—and has become part of patriotism itself. Such is the repugnance of the Genoese to a union with Piedmont: and such is commonly the peculiar horror which high-minded nations feel of the yoke of their immediate neighbours. The feelings of Norway towards Sweden,—of Portugal towards Spain,—and in former and less happy times of Scotland towards England,—are a few out of innumerable examples. There is nothing either unreasonable or unnatural in this state of national feelings. With neighbours there are most occasions of quarrel; with them there have been most wars; from them there has been most suffering:—of them there is most fear. The resentment of wrongs, and the remembrance of victory, strengthen our repugnance to those who are most usually our enemies. It is not from illiberal prejudice, but from the constitution of human nature, that an Englishman animates his patriotic affections, and supports his national pride, by now looking back on victories over Frenchmen,—on Cressy and Agincourt, on Blenheim and Minden,—as our posterity will one day look back on Salamanca and Vittoria. The defensive principle ought to be the strongest where the danger is likely most frequently to arise. What, then, will the House decide concerning the morality of compelling Genoa to submit to the yoke of Piedmont,—a state which the Genoese have constantly dreaded and hated, and against which their hatred was sharpened by continual apprehensions for their independence? Whatever construction may be attempted of Lord William Bentinck's Proclamations,—whatever sophistry may be used successfully, to persuade you that Genoa was disposable as a conquered territory, will you affirm that the disposal of it to Piedmont was a just and humane exercise of your power as a conqueror?

It is for this reason, among others, that I detest and execrate the modern doctrine of rounding territory, and following natural boundaries, and melting down small states into masses, and substituting lines of defence, and right and left flanks, instead of justice and the law of nations, and ancient possession and national feeling,—the system of Louis XIV. and Napoleon, of the spoilers of Poland, and of the spoilers of Norway and Genoa,—the system which the Noble Lord, when newly arrived from the Congress, and deeply imbued with its doctrines, in the course of his ample and elaborate invective against the memory and principles of ancient Europe, defined in two phrases so characteristic of his reverence for the rights of nations, and his tenderness for their feelings, that they ought not easily to be forgotten,—when he told us, speaking of this very antipathy of Genoa to Piedmont, "that great questions are not to be influenced by popular impressions," and "that a people may be happy without independence." The principal feature of this new system is the incorporation

* On Mr. Charles Wynn's motion (May 12th, 1814,) condemnatory of its forced annexation to Sweden.—Ed.

of neighbouring, and therefore hostile communities. The system of justice reverenced the union of men who had long been members of the same commonwealth, because they had all the attachments and antipathies which grow out of that fellowship:—the system of rapine tears asunder those whom nature has joined, and compels those to unite whom the contests of ages have rendered irreconcilable.

And if all this had been less evident, would no aggravation of this act have arisen from the peculiar nature of the general war of Europe against France? It was a war in which not only the Italians, but every people in Europe, were called by their sovereigns to rise for the recovery of their independence. It was a revolt of the people against Napoleon. It owed its success to the spirit of popular insurrection. The principle of a war for the restoration of independence, was a pledge that each people was to be restored to its ancient territory. The nations of Europe accepted the pledge, and shook off the French yoke. But was it for a change of masters? Was it that three Foreign Ministers at Paris might dispose of the Genoese territory?—was it for this that the youth of Europe had risen in arms from Moscow to the Rhine?

> Ergo pari voto gessisti bella juventus?
> Tu quoque pro dominis et Pompeiana fuisti
> Non Romana manus!*

The people of Europe were, it seems, roused to war, not to overthrow tyranny, but to shift it into new hands,—not to re-establish the independence and restore the ancient institutions of nations, but to strengthen the right flank of one great military power, and to cover the left flank of another. This, at least, was not the war for the success of which I offered my most ardent prayers. I prayed for the deliverance of Europe, not for its transfer to other lords,—for the restoration of Europe, by which all men must have understood at least the re-establishment of that ancient system, and of those wise principles, under which it had become great and prosperous. I expected the re-establishment of every people in those territories, of which the sovereignty had been lost by recent usurpation,—of every people who had been an ancient member of the family of Europe,—of every people who had preserved the spirit and feelings which constitute a nation,—and, above all, of every people who had lost their territory or their independence under the tyranny which the Allies had taken up arms to overthrow. I expected a reverence for ancient boundaries,—a respect for ancient institutions,—certainly without excluding a prudent regard to the new interests and opinions which had taken so deep a root that they could not be torn up without incurring the guilt and the mischief of the most violent innovation.

* Pharsalia, lib. ix.—Ed.

The very same reasons, indeed, both of morality and policy (since I must comply so far with vulgar usage as to distinguish what cannot be separated) bound the Allied Sovereigns to respect the ancient institutions, and to regard the new opinions and interests of nations. The art of all government, not tyrannical, whatever may be its form, is to conduct mankind by their feelings. It is immoral to disregard the feelings of the governed, because it renders them miserable. It is, and it ought to be, dangerous to disregard these feelings, because bold and intelligent men will always consider it as a mere question of prudence, whether they ought to obey governments which counteract the only purpose for which they all exist. The feelings of men are most generally wounded by any violence to those ancient institutions under which these feelings have been formed, the national character has been moulded, and to which all the habits and expectations of life are adapted. It was well said by Mr. Fox, that as ancient institutions have been sanctioned by a far greater concurrence of human judgments than modern laws can be, they are, upon democratic principles, more respectable. But new opinions and new interests, and a new arrangement of society, which has given rise to other habits and hopes, also excite the strongest feelings, which, in proportion to their force and extent, claim the regard of all moral policy.

As it was doubtless the policy of the Allies to consider the claims of ancient possession as sacred, as far as the irrevocable changes of the political system would allow, the considerate part of mankind did, I believe, hope that they would hail the long-continued and recently-lost sovereignty of a territory as generally an inviolable right, and that, as they could not be supposed wanting in zeal for restoring the sovereignty of ancient reigning families, so they would guard that re-establishment, and render it respectable in the eyes of the world, by the impartiality with which they re-established also those ancient and legitimate governments of a republican form, which had fallen in the general slavery of nations. We remembered that republics and monarchies were alike called to join in the war against the French Revolution, not for forms of government, but for the existence of social order. We hoped that Austria—to select a striking example—would not pollute her title to her ancient dominion of Lombardy, by blending it with the faithless and lawless seizure of Venice. So little republican territory was to be restored, that the act of justice was to be performed, and the character of impartiality gained, at little expense;—even if such expense be measured by the meanest calculations of the most vulgar politics. Other vacant territory remained at the disposal of the Congress to satisfy the demands of policy. The sovereignity of the Ecclesiastical territories might be fairly considered as lapsed: no reigning family could have any interest in it;—no people could be attached to such a rule of nomination to supreme power. And in fact, these Principalities had lost all pride of independence and all consciousness of national existence. Several other territories of Europe had been reduced to a like condition. Ceded, perhaps, at first questionably, they had been transferred so often from master to master,—they had been so long in a state of provincial degradation, that no violence could be offered to their feelings by any new transfer or partition. They were, as it were, a sort of splinters thrown off from nations in the shocks of warfare during two centuries; and they lay like stakes on the board, to be played for at the terrible game which had detached them, and to satisfy the exchanges and cessions by which it is usually closed.

Perhaps the existence of such detached members is necessary to the European system; but they are in themselves great evils. They are amputated and lifeless members, which, as soon as they lose the vital principle of national spirit, no longer contribute aught to the vigour and safety of the whole living system. From them is to be expected no struggle against invasion,—no resistance to the designs of ambition,—no defence of their country. Individuals, but no longer a nation, they are the ready prey of every candidate for universal monarchy, who soon compels their passive inhabitants to fight for his ambition, as they would not fight against it, and to employ in enslaving other nations, that courage which they had no noble interest to exert in defence of their own.— Why should I seek examples of this truth in former times? What opened Europe to the first inroads of the French armies?—not, I will venture to say, the mere smallness of the neighbouring states; for if every one of them had displayed as much national spirit in 1794, as the smallest states of Switzerland did in 1798, no French army could ever have left the territory of France,—but the unhappy course of events, which had deprived Flanders, and the Electorates, and Lombardy, of all national spirit. Extinguished as this spirit was by the form of government in some of these countries, and crushed by a foreign yoke in others,—without the pride of liberty, which bestows the highest national spirit on the smallest nations, or the pride of power, which sometimes supplies its place in mighty empires, or the consciousness of self-dependence, without which there is no nationality, —they first became the prey of France, and afterwards supplied the arms with which she almost conquered the world. To enlarge this dead part of Europe,—to enrich it by the accession of countries renowned for their public feelings,—to throw Genoa into the same grave with Poland, with Venice, with Finland, and with Norway,—is not the policy of those who would be the preservers or restorers of the European commonwealth.

It is not the principle of the Balance of Power, but one precisely opposite. The system of preserving some equilibrium of power,—of preventing any state from becoming too great for her neighbours, is a system purely defensive, and directed towards the object of universal preservation. It is a system which provides for the security of all states by balancing the force and opposing the interests of great ones. The independence of nations is the end, the balance of power is only the means. To destroy independent nations, in order to strengthen the balance of power, is a most extravagant sacrifice of the end to the means. This inversion of all the principles of the ancient and beautiful system of Europe, is the fundamental maxim of what the Noble Lord, enriching our language with foreign phrases as well as doctrines, calls "a repartition of power." In the new system, small states are annihilated by a combination of great ones:—in the old, small states were secured by the mutual jealousy of the great.

The Noble Lord very consistently treats the re-establishment of small states as an absurdity. This single tenet betrays the school in which he has studied. Undoubtedly, small communities are an absurdity, or rather their permanent existence is an impossibility, on his new system. They could have had no existence in the continual conquests of Asia;—they were soon destroyed amidst the turbulence of the Grecian confederacy:—they must be sacrificed on the system of rapine established at Vienna.— Nations powerful enough to defend themselves, may subsist securely in most tolerable conditions of society: but states too small to be safe by their own strength, can exist only where they are guarded by the equilibrium of force, and the vigilance which watches over its preservation. When the Noble Lord represents small states as incapable of self-defence, he in truth avows that he is returned in triumph from the destruction of that system of the Balance of Power, of which indeed great empires were the guardians, but of which the perfect action was indicated by the security of feebler commonwealths. Under this system, no great violation of national independence had occurred from the first civilization of the European states till the partition of Poland. The safety of the feeblest states, under the authority of justice, was so great, that there seemed little exaggeration in calling such a society the "commonwealth" of Europe. Principles, which stood in the stead of laws and magistrates, provided for the security of defenceless communities, as perfectly as the safety of the humblest individual is maintained in a well-ordered commonwealth. Europe can no longer be called a commonwealth, when her members have no safety but in their strength.

In truth, the Balancing system is itself only a secondary guard of national independence. The paramount principle—the moving power, without which all such machinery would be perfectly inert, is national spirit. The love of country, the attachment to laws and government, and even to soil and scenery, the feelings of national glory in arms and arts, the remembrances of common triumph and common suffering, with the mitigated but not obliterated recollection of common enmity, and the jealousy of dangerous neighbours,—all are instruments employed by nature to draw more closely the bands of affection that bind us to our country and to each other. This is the only principle by which sovereigns can, in the hour of danger, rouse the minds of their subjects:—without it the policy of the Balancing system would be impotent.

The Congress of Vienna seems, indeed, to have adopted every part of the French system, except that they have transferred the dictatorship of Europe from an individual to a triumvirate. One of the grand and parent errors of the French Revolution was the fatal opinion that it was possible for human skill to make a government. It was an error too generally prevalent, not to be excusable.—The American Revolution had given it a fallacious semblance of support; though no event in history more clearly showed its falsehood. The system of laws, and the frame of society in North America, remained after the Revolution, and remain to this day, fundamentally the same as they ever were. The change in America, like the change in 1688, was made in defence of legal right, not in pursuit of political improvement; and it was limited by the necessity of self-defence which produced it. The whole internal order remained, which had always been essentially republican. The somewhat slender tie which loosely joined these republics to a monarchy, was easily and without violence divided. But the error of the French Revolutionists was, in 1789, the error of Europe. From that error we have been long reclaimed by fatal experience. We know, or rather we have seen and felt, that a government is not, like a machine or a building, the work of man; that it is the work of nature, like the nobler productions of the vegetable and animal world, which man may improve, and damage, and even destroy, but which he cannot create. We have long learned to despise the ignorance or the hypocrisy of those who speak of giving a free constitution to a people, and to exclaim with a great living poet—

"A gift of that which never can be given
By all the blended powers of earth and heaven!"

We have, perhaps,—as usual,—gone too near to the opposite error, and we do not make sufficient allowances for those dreadful cases—though we must not call them desperate,—where, in long enslaved countries, we must either humbly and cautiously labour to lay some foundations from which the fabric of liberty may slowly rise, or acquiesce in the doom of perpetual bondage.

But though we no longer dream of making governments, the confederacy of kings seem to feel no doubt of their own power to make nations. Yet the only reason why it is impossible to make a government is, because it is impossible to make a nation. A government cannot be made, because its whole spirit and principles arise from the character of the nation. There would be no difficulty in framing a government, if the habits of a people could be changed by a lawgiver;—if he could obliterate their recollections, transfer their attachment and reverence, extinguish their animosities, and correct those sentiments which, being at variance with his opinions of public interest, he calls prejudices. Now, this is precisely the power which our statesmen at Vienna have arrogated to themselves. They not only form nations, but they compose them of elements apparently the most irreconcilable. They made one nation out of Norway and Sweden: they tried to make another out of Prussia and Saxony. They have, in the present case, forced together Piedmont and Genoa to form a nation which is to guard the avenues of Italy, and to be one of the main securities of Europe against universal monarchy.

It was not the pretension of the ancient system to form states,—to divide territory according to speculations of military convenience,—and to unite and dissolve nations better than the course of events had done before. It was owned to be still more difficult to give a new constitution to Europe, than to form a new constitution for a single state. The great statesmen of former times did not speak of their measures as the Noble Lord did about the incorporation of Belgium with Holland (against which I say nothing), "as a great improvement in the system of Europe." That is the language only of those who revolutionise that system by a partition like that of Poland, by the establishment of the Federation of the Rhine at Paris, or by the creation of new states at Vienna. The ancient principle was to preserve all those states which had been founded by time and nature,—which were animated by national spirit, and distinguished by the diversity of character which gave scope to every variety of talent and virtue,—whose character had been often preserved, and whose nationality had been even created, by those very irregularities of frontier and inequalities of strength, of which a shallow policy complains;—to preserve all those states, down to the smallest, first, by their own national spirit, and, secondly, by that mutual jealousy which made every great power the opponent of the dangerous ambition of every other. Its object was to preserve nations, as living bodies produced by the hand of nature—not to form artificial dead machines, called "states," by the words and parchment of a diplomatic act. Under this ancient system, which secured the weak by the jealousy of the strong, provision was made alike for the permanency of civil institutions, the stability of governments, the progressive reformation of laws and constitutions,—for combining the general quiet with the highest activity and energy of the human mind, —for uniting the benefits both of rivalship and of friendship between nations,—for cultivating the moral sentiments of men, by the noble spectacle of the long triumph of justice in the security of the defenceless,—and, finally, for maintaining uniform civilization by the struggle as well as union of all the moral and intellectual combinations which compose that vast and various mass. It effected these noble purposes, not merely by securing Europe against one master, but by securing her against any union or conspiracy of sovereignty, which, as long as it lasts, is in no respect better than the domination of an individual. The object of the new system is to crush the weak by the combination of the strong,—to subject Europe, in the first place, to an oligarchy of sovereigns, and ultimately to swallow it up in the gulf of universal monarchy, in which civilization has always perished, with freedom of thought, with controlled power, with national character and spirit, with patriotism and emulation,—in a word, with all its characteristic attributes, and with all its guardian principles.

I am content, Sir, that these observations should be thought wholly unreasonable by those new masters of civil wisdom, who tell us that the whole policy of Europe consists in strengthening the right flank of Prussia, and the left flank of Austria,—who see in that wise and venerable system, long the boast and the safeguard of Europe, only the millions of souls to be given to one Power, or the thousands of square miles to be given to another,—who consider the frontier of a river as a better protection for a country than the love of its inhabitants,—and who provide for the safety of their states by wounding the pride and mortifying the patriotic affection of a people, in order to fortify a line of military posts. To such statesmen I will apply the words of the great philosophical orator, who so long vainly laboured to inculcate wisdom in this House:—"All this, I know well enough, will sound wild and chimerical to the profane herd of those vulgar and mechanical politicians who have no place among us; a sort of people who think that nothing exists but what is gross and material; and who, therefore, far from being qualified to be directors of the great movement of empire, are not fit to turn a wheel in the machine. But to men truly initiated and rightly taught, these ruling and master principles, which, in the opinion of such men as I have mentioned, have no substantial existence, are in truth every thing, and all in all." This great man, in the latter part of his life, and when his opinions were less popular, was often justly celebrated for that spirit of philosophical prophecy which enabled him early to discern in their causes all the misfortunes which the leaders of the French Revolution were to bring on the world by their erroneous principles of reformation,—"quod ille pene solus Romanorum animo vidit, ingenio complexus est, eloquentia illuminavit:" but it has been remembered, that his foresight was not limited to one party or to one source of evil. In one of his immortal writings,*—of which he has somewhat concealed the durable instruction by the temporary title,—he clearly enough points out the first scene of partition and rapine—the indemnifications granted out of the spoils of Germany in 1802:—"I see, indeed, a fund from whence equivalents will be proposed. It opens another Iliad of woes to Europe."

The policy of a conqueror is to demolish, to erect on new foundations, to bestow new names on authority, and to render every power around him as new as his own. The policy of a restorer is to re-establish, to strengthen, cautiously to improve, and to seem to recognise and confirm even that which necessity compels him to establish anew. But, in our times, the policy of the avowed conqueror has been adopted by the pretended restorers. The most minute particulars of the system of Napoleon are revived in the acts of those who overthrew his power. Even English officers, when they are compelled to carry such orders into execution, become infected by the spirit of the system of which they are doomed to be the ministers. I cannot read without pain and shame the language of Sir John Dalrymple's Despatch,—language which I lament as inconsistent with the feelings of a British officer, and with the natural prejudices of a Scotch gentleman. I wish that he had not adopted the very technical language of Jacobin conquest,—"the downfall of the aristocracy," and "the irritation of the priests." I do not think it very decent to talk with levity of the destruction of a sovereignty exercised for six centuries by one of the most ancient and illustrious bodies of nobility in Europe.

Italy is, perhaps, of all civilized countries, that which affords the most signal example of the debasing power of provincial dependence, and of a foreign yoke. With independence, and with national spirit, they have lost, if not talent, at least the moral and dignified use of talent, which constitutes its only worth. Italy alone seemed to derive some hope of independence from those convulsions which had destroyed that of other nations. The restoration of Europe annihilated the hopes of Italy:—the emancipation of other countries announced her bondage. Stern necessity compelled us to suffer the re-establishment of foreign masters in the greater part of that renowned and humiliated country. But as to Genoa, our hands were unfettered; we were at liberty to be just, or, if you will, to be generous. We had in our hands the destiny of the last of that great body of republics which united the ancien

* Second Letter on a Regicide Peace.—Ed.

and the modern world,—the children and heirs of Roman civilisation, who spread commerce, and with it refinement, liberty, and humanity over Western Europe, and whose history has lately been rescued from oblivion, and disclosed to our times, by the greatest of living historians.* I hope I shall not be thought fanciful when I say that Genoa, whose greatness was founded on naval power, and which, in the earliest ages, gave the almost solitary example of a commercial gentry,—Genoa, the remnant of Italian liberty, and the only remaining hope of Italian independence, had peculiar claims —to say no more—on the generosity of the British nation. How have these claims been satisfied? She has been sacrificed to a frivolous, a doubtful, perhaps an imaginary, speculation of convenience. The most odious of foreign yokes has been imposed upon her by a free state,—by a people whom she never injured,—after she had been mocked by the re-appearance of her ancient government, and by all the ensigns and badges of her past glory. And after all this, she has been told to be grateful for the interest which the Government of England has taken in her fate. By this confiscation of the only Italian territory which was at the disposal of justice, the doors of hope have been barred on Italy for ever. No English general can ever again deceive Italians.

Will the House decide that all this is right? —That is the question which you have now to decide. To vote with me, it is not necessary to adopt my opinions in their full extent. All who think that the national faith has been brought into question,—all who think that there has been an unprecedented extension, or an ungenerous exercise of the rights of conquest,—are, I humbly conceive, bound to express their disapprobation by their votes. We are on the eve of a new war,—perhaps only the first of a long series, —in which there must be conquests and cessions, and there may be hard and doubtful exertions of rights in their best state sufficiently odious:—I call upon the House to interpose their council for the future in the form of an opinion regarding the past. I hope that I do not yield to any illusive feelings of national vanity, when I say that this House is qualified to speak the sentiments of mankind, and to convey them with authority to cabinets and thrones. Single among representative assemblies, this House is now in the seventh century of its recorded existence. It appeared with the first dawn of legal government. It exercised its highest powers under the most glorious princes. It survived the change of a religion, and the extinction of a nobility,—the fall of Royal Houses, and an age of civil war. Depressed for a moment by the tyrannical power which is the usual growth of civil confusions, it revived with the first glimpse of tranquillity, —gathered strength from the intrepidity of religious reformation,—grew with the knowledge, and flourished with the progressive wealth of the people. After having experienced the excesses of the spirit of liberty during the Civil War, and of the spirit of loyalty at the Restoration, it was at length finally established at the glorious era of the Revolution; and although since that immortal event it has experienced little change in its formal constitution, and perhaps no accession of legal power, it has gradually cast its roots deep and wide, blending itself with every branch of the government, and every institution of society, and has, at length, become the grandest example ever seen among men of a solid and durable representation of the people of a mighty empire.

* Sismondi.

SPEECH

ON MOVING FOR A COMMITTEE TO INQUIRE INTO

THE STATE OF THE CRIMINAL LAW,

DELIVERED IN THE HOUSE OF COMMONS, ON THE 2D MARCH, 1819.*

Mr. Speaker,—I now rise, in pursuance of the notice which I gave, to bring before the House a motion for the appointment of a Select Committee "to consider of so much of the Criminal Laws as relates to Capital Punishment in Felonies, and to report their observations and opinions thereon to the House." And I should have immediately proceeded to explain the grounds and objects of such a motion, which is almost *verbatim* the same as a resolution entered on the Journals in the year 1770, when authority was delegated to

* This speech marks an epoch in the progress of the reformation of the Criminal Law, inasmuch as the motion with which it concluded, though opposed by Lord Castlereagh, with all the force of the Government, under cover of a professed enlargement of its principle, was carried by a majority of nineteen in a House of two hundred and seventy-five members.—Ed.

a committee for the same purpose,—I should have proceeded, I say, to state at once why I think such an inquiry necessary, had it not been for some concessions made by the Noble Lord* last night, which tend much to narrow the grounds of difference between us, and to simplify the question before the House. If I considered the only subject of discussion to be that which exists between the Noble Lord and myself, it would be reduced to this narrow compass;—namely, whether the Noble Lord's proposal or mine be the more convenient for the conduct of the same inquiry; but as every member in this House is a party to the question, I must make an observation or two on the Noble Lord's statements.

If I understood him rightly, he confesses that the growth of crime, and the state of the Criminal Law in this country, call for investigation, and proposes that these subjects shall be investigated by a Select Committee;—this I also admit to be the most expedient course. He expressly asserts also his disposition to make the inquiry as extensive as I wish it to be. As far, therefore, as he is concerned, I am relieved from the necessity of proving that an inquiry is necessary, that the appointment of a Select Committee is the proper course of proceeding in it, and that such inquiry ought to be extensive. I am thus brought to the narrower question, Whether the committee of the Noble Lord, or that which I propose, be the more convenient instrument for conducting an inquiry into the special subject to which my motion refers? I shall endeavour briefly to show, that the mode of proceeding proposed by him, although embracing another and very fit subject of inquiry, must be considered as precluding an inquiry into that part of the Criminal Law which forms the subject of my motion, for two reasons.

In the first place, Sir, it is physically impossible; and, having stated that, I may perhaps dispense with the necessity of adding more. We have heard from an Honourable Friend of mine,† whose authority is the highest that can be resorted to on this subject, that an inquiry into the state of two or three jails occupied a committee during a whole session. My Honourable Friend,‡ a magistrate of the city, has stated that an inquiry into the state of the prisons of the Metropolis, occupied during a whole session the assiduous committee over which he presided. When, therefore, the Noble Lord refers to one committee not only the state of the Criminal Law, but that of the jails, of transportation, and of that little adjunct the hulks, he refers to it an inquiry which it can never conduct to an end;—he proposes, as my Honourable Friend§ has said, to institute an investigation which must outlive a Parliament. The Noble Lord has in fact acknowledged, by his proposed subdivision, that it would be impossible for one committee to inquire into all the subjects which he would refer to it. And this impossibility he would evade by an unconstitutional violation of the usages of the House; as you, Sir, with the authority due to your opinions, have declared the proposition for subdividing a committee to be. I, on the other hand, in accordance with ancient usage, propose that the House shall itself nominate these separate committees.

My second objection is, Sir, that the Noble Lord's notice, and the order made by the House yesterday upon it, do not embrace the purpose which I have in view. To prove this, I might content myself with a reference to the very words of the instruction under which his proposed committee is to proceed. It is directed "to inquire into the state and description of jails, and other places of confinement, and into the best method of providing for the reformation, as well as for the safe custody and punishment of offenders." Now, what is the plain meaning of those expressions? Are they not the same offenders, whose punishment as well as whose reformation and safe custody is contemplated? And does not the instruction thus directly exclude the subject of Capital Punishment. The matter is too plain to be insisted on; but must not the meaning, in any fair and liberal construction, be taken to be that the committee is to consider the reformation and safe custody of those offenders of whom imprisonment forms the whole or the greatest part of the punishment? It would be absurd to suppose that the question of Capital Punishment should be made an inferior branch of the secondary question of imprisonments, and that the great subject of Criminal Law should skulk into the committee under the cover of one vague and equivocal word. On these grounds, Sir, I have a right to say that there is no comparison as to the convenience or the efficacy of the two modes of proceeding.

Let us now see whether my proposition casts a greater censure on the existing laws than his. Every motion for inquiry assumes that inquiry is necessary,—that some evil exists, which may be remedied. The motion of the Noble Lord assumes thus much; mine assumes no more; it casts no reflection on the law, or on the magistrates by whom it is administered.

With respect to the question whether Secondary Punishments should be inquired into before we dispose of the Primary, I have to say, that in proposing the Present investigation, I have not been guided by my own feelings, nor have I trusted entirely to my own judgment. My steps have been directed and assured by former examples.

The first of these is the notable one in 1750, when, in consequence of the alarm created by the increase of some species of crimes, a committee was appointed "to examine into and consider the state of the laws

* Viscount Castlereagh.—Ed.

† The Honourable Henry Grey Bennet.—Ed.

‡ Alderman Waithman.—Ed.

§ Mr. Bennet.—Ed.

relating to felonies, and to report to the House their opinion as to the defects of those laws, and as to the propriety of amending or repealing them." What does the Noble Lord say to this large reference,—this ample delegation,—this attack on the laws of our ancestors? Was it made in bad times, by men of no note, and of indifferent principles? I will mention the persons of whom the committee was composed:—they were, Mr. Pelham, then Chancellor of the Exchequer; Mr. Pitt, afterwards Lord Chatham; Mr. George Grenville, afterwards Lord Grenville; Mr. Lyttleton and Mr. Charles Townsend, afterwards Secretaries of State; and Sir Dudley Ryder, the Attorney-General, afterwards Chief Justice of England. Those great lawyers and statesmen will, at least, not be accused of having been rash theorists, or, according to the new word, 'ultra-philosophers." But it will be thought remarkable that those great men, who were, in liberality, as superior to some statesmen of the present day, as in practical wisdom they were not inferior to them, found two sessions necessary for the inquiry into which they had entered. The first resolution to which those eminent and enlightened individuals agreed, was, "that it was reasonable to exchange the punishment of death for some other adequate punishment." Such a resolution is a little more general and extensive than that which I shall venture to propose;—such a resolution, however, did that committee, vested with the powers which I have already described, recommend to the adoption of the House. One circumstance, not necessarily connected with my present motion, I will take the liberty of mentioning:—to that committee the credit is due of having first denounced the Poor-laws as the nursery of crime. In this country pauperism and crime have always advanced in parallel lines, and with equal steps. That committee imputed much evil to the divisions among parishes on account of the maintenance of the poor. That committee too, composed of practical men as it was, made a statement which some practical statesmen of the present day will no doubt condemn as too large;—namely, "that the increase of crime was in a great measure to be attributed to the neglect of the education of the children of the poor." A bill was brought in, founded on the resolutions of the committee and passed this House. It was however negatived in the House of Lords, although not opposed by any of the great names of that day,—by any of the luminaries of that House. Lord Hardwicke, for instance, did not oppose a bill, the principal object of which was the substitution of hard labour and imprisonment for the punishment of death.

In 1770, another alarm, occasioned by the increase of a certain species of crime, led to the appointment, on the 27th of November in that year, of another committee of the same kind, of which Sir Charles Saville, Sir William Meredith, Mr. Fox, Mr. Serjeant Glynn, Sir Charles Bunbury, and others, were members. To that committee the reference was nearly the same as that which I am now proposing; though mine be the more contracted one. That committee was occupied for two years with the branch of the general inquiry which the Noble Lord proposes to add to the already excessive labours of an existing committee. In the second session they brought their report to maturity; and, on that report, a bill was introduced for the repeal of eight or ten statutes, which bill passed the House of Commons without opposition. I do not mean to enter into the minute history of that bill, which was thrown out in the House of Lords. It met with no hostility from the great ornaments of the House of Lords of that day, Lord Camden and Lord Mansfield; but it was necessarily opposed by others, whom I will not name, and whose names will be unknown to posterity.

Sir, it is upon these precedents that I have formed, and that I bring forward my motion. I have shown, that the step I proposed to take accords with the usage of Parliament in the best of times, but that if we follow the plan recommended by the Noble Lord, we cannot effect the purpose which we have in view without evading or violating the usage of Parliament. Accepting, therefore, his concession, that a committee ought to be appointed for this investigation, here I might take my stand, and challenge him to drive me from this ground, which, with all his talents, he would find some difficulty in doing. But I feel that there is a great difference between our respective situations; and that, although he last night contented himself with stating the evils which exist, without adverting to the other essential part of my proposal for a Parliamentary inquiry,—namely, the probability of a remedy,—I must take a different course. Although I cannot say that I agree with my Honourable Friend, who says that a Select Committee is not the proper mode of investigating this subject, yet I agree with him that there are two things necessary to justify an investigation, whether by a committee, or in any other manner:—the first is, the existence of an evil; the second is, the probability of a remedy. Far, therefore, from treating the sacred fabric reared by our ancestors more lightly, I approach it more reverently than does the Noble Lord. I should not have dared, merely on account of the number of offences, to institute an inquiry into the state of the Criminal Law, unless, while I saw the defects, I had also within view, not the certainty of a remedy (for that would be too much to assert), but some strong probability, that the law may be rendered more efficient, and a check be given to that which has alarmed all good men,—the increase of crime. While I do what I think it was the bounden duty of the Noble Lord to have done, I trust I shall not be told that I am a rash speculator,—that I am holding out impunity to criminals, or foreshadowing what he is pleased to call "a golden age for crime." Sir Dudley Ryder, at the head of the criminal jurisprudence of the country, and Serjeant Glynn, the Recorder of London, —an office that unhappily has the most extensive experience of the administration of Criminal Law in the world,—both believed a remedy to the evil in question to be practicable, and recommended it as necessary; and under any general reprobation which the Noble Lord may apply to such men, I shall not be ashamed to be included.

I must now, Sir, mention what my object is not, in order to obviate the misapprehensions of over-zealous supporters, and the misrepresentations of desperate opponents. I do not propose to form a new criminal code. Altogether to abolish a system of law, admirable in its principle, interwoven with the habits of the English people, and under which they have long and happily lived, is a proposition very remote from my notions of legislation, and would be too extravagant and ridiculous to be for a moment listened to. Neither is it my intention to propose the abolition of the punishment of death. I hold the right of inflicting that punishment to be a part of the rights of self-defence, with which society as well as individuals are endowed. I hold it to be, like all other punishments, an evil when unnecessary, but, like any other evil employed to remedy a greater evil, capable of becoming a good. Nor do I wish to take away the right of pardon from the Crown. On the contrary, my object is, to restore to the Crown the practical use of that right, of which the usage of modern times has nearly deprived it.

The declaration may appear singular, but I do not aim at realising any universal principle. My object is, to bring the letter of the law more near to its practice,—to make the execution of the law form the rule, and the remission of its penalties the exception. Although I do not expect that a system of law can be so graduated, that it can be applied to every case without the intervention of a discretionary power, I hope to see an effect produced on the vicious, by the steady manner in which the law shall be enforced. The main part of the reform which I should propose would be, to transfer to the statute book the improvements which the wisdom of modern times has introduced into the practice of the law. But I must add, that even in the case of some of that practice with which the feelings of good men are not in unison, I should propose such a reform as would correct that anomaly. It is one of the greatest evils which can befall a country when the Criminal Law and the virtuous feeling of the community are in hostility to each other. They cannot be long at variance without injury to one,—perhaps to both. One of my objects is to approximate them;—to make good men the anxious supporters of the Criminal Law, and to restore, if it has been injured, that zealous attachment to the law in general, which, even in the most tempestuous times of our history, has distinguished the people of England among the nations of the world.

Having made these few general remarks, I will now, Sir, enter into a few illustrative details. It is not my intention to follow the Noble Lord in his inquiry into the causes of the increase of crimes. I think that his statement last night was in the main just and candid. I agree with him, that it is consolatory to remark, that the crimes in which so rapid an increase has been observable, are not those of the blackest die, or of the most ferocious character; that they are not those which would the most deeply stain and dishonour the ancient moral character of Englishmen; that they are crimes against property alone, and are to be viewed as the result of the distresses, rather than of the depravity of the community. I also firmly believe, that some of the causes of increased crime are temporary. But the Noble Lord and I, while we agree in this proposition, are thus whimsically situated: — he does not think that some of these causes are temporary which I conceive to be so; while, on the other hand, he sets down some as temporary, which I believe to be permanent. As to the increase of forgery, for example (which I mention only by way of illustration), I had hoped that when cash payments should be restored, that crime would be diminished. But the Noble Lord has taken pains to dissipate that delusion, by asserting that the withdrawal of such a mass of paper from circulation would be attended with no such beneficial consequences. According to him, the progress of the country in manufactures and wealth, is one of the principal causes of crime. But is our progress in manufactures and wealth to be arrested? Does the Noble Lord imagine, that there exists a permanent and augmenting cause of crime, —at once increasing with our prosperity, and undermining it through its effects on the morals of the people. According to him, the increase of great cities would form another cause of crime. This cause, at least, cannot diminish, for great cities are the natural consequences of manufacturing and commercial greatness. In speaking, however, of the population of London, he has fallen into an error. Although London is positively larger now than it was in 1700, it is relatively smaller:—although it has since that time become the greatest commercial city in Europe,—the capital of an empire whose colonies extend over every quarter of the world,—London is not so populous now, with reference to the population of the whole kingdom, as it was in the reign of William III.

It is principally to those causes of crime, which arise out of errors in policy or legislation, that I wish to draw the attention of Parliament. Among other subjects, it may be a question whether the laws for the protection of the property called "game," have not created a clandestine traffic highly injurious to the morals of the labouring classes. I am happy to find that that subject is to be taken up by my Honourable Friend the Member for Hertfordshire,* who will draw to it the attention which every proposition of his deserves. A smuggling traffic of another species, although attended with nearly the same effects, has been fostered by some of the existing laws relating to the revenue. I would propose no diminution of revenue, for unfortunately we can spare none: but there are some taxes which produce no revenue, and which were never intended to produce any, but which are, nevertheless, very detrimental. The cumbrous system of drawbacks, and protecting duties, is only a bounty on smuggling. Poachers and smugglers are the two bodies from which malefactors are principally recruited. The state which does not seek to remedy these diseases, is guilty of its own destruction.

Another subject I must mention: for, viewing it as I do, it would be unpardonable to omit it. On examining the summary of crimes which has been laid on the table, it appears that it was in 1808 that the great increase of crime took place. The number of crimes since that time has never fallen below the number of that year; although subsequent years have varied among one another. But it is extremely remarkable, and is, indeed, a most serious and alarming fact, that the year 1808 was precisely the period when the great issues of the Bank of England began. As it has been observed in the "Letter to the Right Honourable Member for the University of Oxford,"† a work which has been already mentioned in this House (the author‡ of which, although he has concealed his name, cannot conceal his talents, and his singular union of ancient learning with modern science), it was at that time that pauperism and poor rates increased. Pauperism and crime, as I have before said, go hand in hand. Both were propelled by the immense issues of Bank paper in 1808. By those issues the value of the one-pound note was reduced to fourteen shillings. Every labourer, by he knew not what mysterious power,—by causes which he could not discover or comprehend,—found his wages diminished at least in the proportion of a third. No enemy had ravaged the country; no inclement season had blasted the produce of the soil; but his comforts were curtailed, and his enjoyments destroyed by the operation of the paper system, which was to him like the workings of a malignant fiend, that could be traced only in their effects. Can any one doubt that this diminution of the income of so many individuals, from the highest to the lowest classes of society, was one of the chief sources of the increase of crime?

There is one other secondary cause of crime, which I hope we have at length seriously determined to remove;—I mean the state of our prisons. They never were fitted for reformation by a wise system of discipline: but that is now become an inferior subject of complaint. Since the number of criminals have out-grown the size of our prisons, comparatively small offenders have been trained in them to the contemplation of atrocious crime. Happily this terrible source of evil is more than any other within our reach. Prison discipline may fail in reforming offenders: but it is our own fault if it further corrupts them.

But the main ground which I take is this,—that the Criminal Law is not so efficacious as it might be, if temperate and prudent alterations in it were made. It is well known that there are two hundred capital felonies on the statute book; but it may not be so familiar to the House, that by the Returns for London and Middlesex, it appears that from 1749 to 1819, a term of seventy years, there are only twenty-five sorts of felonies for which any individuals have been executed. So that there are a hundred and seventy-five capital felonies respecting which the punishment ordained by various statutes has not been inflicted. In the thirteen years since 1805, it appears that there are only thirty descriptions of felonies on which there have been any capital convictions throughout England and Wales. So that there are a hundred and seventy felonies created by law, on which not one capital conviction has taken place. This rapidly increasing discordance between the letter and the practice of the Criminal Law, arose in the best times of our history, and, in my opinion, out of one of its most glorious and happy events. As I take it, the most important consequence of the Revolution of 1688, was the establishment in this country of a Parliamentary government. That event, however, has been attended by one inconvenience—the unhappy facility afforded to legislation. Every Member of Parliament has had it in his power to indulge his whims and caprices on that subject; and if he could not do any thing else, he could create a capital felony! The anecdotes which I have heard of this shameful and injurious facility, I am almost ashamed to repeat. Mr. Burke once told me, that on a certain occasion, when he was leaving the House, one of the messengers called him back, and on his saying that he was going on urgent business, replied, "Oh! it will not keep you a single moment, it is only a felony without benefit of clergy!" He also assured me, that although, as may be imagined, from his political career, he was not often entitled to ask favour from the ministry of the day, he was persuaded that his interest was at any time good enough to obtain their assent to the creation of a felony without benefit of clergy. This facility of granting an increase of the severity of the law to every proposer, with the most impartial disregard of political considerations,—this unfortunate facility, arose at a time when the humane

* The Honourable Thomas Brand.—Ed.
† The Right Honourable Robert Peel.—Ed.
‡ The Rev. Edward Copleston (now Bishop of Llandaff).—Ed.

feelings of the country were only yet ripening amidst the diffusion of knowledge. Hence originated the final separation between the letter and the practice of the law; for both the government and the nation revolted from the execution of laws which were regarded, not as the results of calm deliberation or consummate wisdom, but rather as the fruit of a series of perverse and malignant accidents, impelling the adoption of temporary and short-sighted expedients. The reverence, therefore, generally due to old establishments, cannot belong to such laws.

This most singular, and most injurious opposition of the legislative enactments, and their judicial enforcement, has repeatedly attracted the attention of a distinguished individual, who unites in himself every quality that could render him one of the greatest ornaments of this House, and whom, as he is no longer a member, I may be permitted to name,—I mean Sir William Grant,—a man who can never be mentioned by those who know him without the expression of their admiration — a man who is an honour, not merely to the profession which he has adorned but to the age in which he lives—a man who is at once the greatest master of reason and of the power of enforcing it, — whose sound judgment is accompanied by the most perspicuous comprehension,—whose views, especially on all subjects connected with legislation, or the administration of the law, are directed by the profoundest wisdom,—whom no one ever approaches without feeling his superiority,—who only wants the two vices of ostentation and ambition (vices contemned by the retiring simplicity and noble modesty of his nature) to render his high talents and attainments more popularly attractive. We have his authority for the assertion, that the principle of the Criminal Law is diametrically opposite to its practice. On one occasion particularly, when his attention was called to the subject, he declared it to be impossible "that both the law and the practice could be right; that the toleration of such discord was an anomaly that ought to be removed; and that, as the law might be brought to an accordance with the practice, but the practice could never be brought to an accordance with the law, the law ought to be altered for a wiser and more humane system." At another time, the same eminent individual used the remarkable expression, "that during the last century, there had been a general confederacy of prosecutors, witnesses, counsel, juries, judges, and the advisers of the Crown, to prevent the execution of the Criminal Law." Is it fitting that a system should continue which the whole body of the intelligent community combine to resist, as a disgrace to our nature and nation?

Sir, I feel that I already owe much to the indulgence of the House, and I assure you that I shall be as concise as the circumstances of the case, important as it confessedly is, will allow; and more especially in the details attendant upon it. The Noble Lord last night dwelt much upon the consequences of a transition from war to peace in the multiplication of crimes; but, upon consulting experience, I do not find that his position is borne out. It is not true that crime always diminishes during a state of war, or that it always increases after its conclusion. In the Seven-Years' War, indeed, the number of crimes was augmented,—decreasing after its termination. They were more numerous in the seven years preceding the American War, and continued to advance, not only during those hostilities, but, I am ready to admit, after the restoration of peace. It is, however, quite correct to state, that there was no augmentation of crime which much outran the progress of population until within about the last twenty, and more especially within the last ten years; and that the augmentation which has taken place is capable of being accounted for, without any disparagement to the ancient and peculiar probity of the British character.

As to the variations which have taken place in the administration of the law, with respect to the proportion of the executions to the convictions, some of them have certainly been remarkable. Under the various administrations of the supreme office of the law, down to the time of Lord Thurlow, the proportion of executions to convictions was for the most part uniform. Lord Rosslyn was the first Chancellor under whose administration a great diminution of executions, as compared with convictions, is to be remarked; and this I must impute, not only to the gentle disposition of that distinguished lawyer, but to the liberality of those principles which, however unfashionable they may now have become, were entertained by his early connexions. Under Lord Rosslyn's administration of the law, the proportion of executions was diminished to one in eight, one in nine, and finally as low as one in eleven.

But, Sir, to the Noble Lord's argument, grounded on the diminution in the number of executions, I wish to say a few words. If we divide crimes into various sorts, separating the higher from the inferior offences, we shall find, that with respect to the smaller felonies, the proportion of executions to convictions has been one in twenty, one in thirty, and in one year, only one in sixty. In the higher felonies (with the exception of burglary and robbery, which are peculiarly circumstanced) the law has been uniformly executed. The Noble Lord's statement, therefore, is applicable only to the first-mentioned class; and a delusion would be the result of its being applied unqualifiedly to the whole criminal code.

For the sake of clearness, I will divide the crimes against which our penal code denounces capital punishments into three classes. In the first of these I include murder, and murderous offences, or such offences as are likely to lead to murder, such as shooting or stabbing, with a view to the malicious destruction of human life:—in these cases the law is invariably executed. In the second class appear arson, highway-robbery, piracy, and other offences, to the number of nine or ten, which it is not necessary, and which it would be painful, to specify:—on these, at present, the law is carried into effect in a great many instances. In these two first divisions I will admit, for the present, that it would be unsafe to propose any alteration. Many of the crimes comprehended in them ought to be punished with death. Whatever attacks the life or the dwelling of man deserves such a punishment; and I am persuaded that a patient and calm investigation would remove the objections of a number of well-meaning persons who are of a contrary opinion.*

But looking from these offences at the head of the criminal code to the other extremity of it, I there find a third class of offences,—some connected with frauds of various kinds, but others of the most frivolous and fantastic description,—amounting in number to about one hundred and fifty, against which the punishment of death is still denounced by the law, although never carried into effect. Indeed, it would be most absurd to suppose that an execution would in such cases be now tolerated, when one or two instances even in former times excited the disgust and horror of all good men. There can be no doubt—even the Noble Lord, I apprehend, will not dispute—that such capital felonies should be expunged from our Statute Book as a disgrace to it. Can any man think, for instance, that such an offence as that of cutting down a hop vine or a young tree in a gentleman's pleasure ground should remain punishable with death? The "Black Act," as it is called, alone created about twenty-one capital felonies,—some of them of the most absurd description. Bearing particular weapons, — having the face blackened at night,—and being found disguised upon the high road,—were some of them. So that if a gentleman is going to a masquerade, and is obliged to pass along a highway, he is liable, if detected, to be hanged without benefit of clergy! Who, again, can endure the idea that a man is exposed to the punishment of death for such an offence as cutting the head of a fish-pond? Sir, there are many more capital felonies of a similar nature, which are the relics of barbarous times, and which are disgraceful to the character of a thinking and enlightened people. For such offences punishments quite adequate and sufficiently numerous would remain. It is undoubtedly true, that for the last seventy years no capital punishment has been inflicted for such offences; the statutes denouncing them are therefore needless. And I trust I shall never live to see the day when any member of this House will rise and maintain that a punishment avowedly needless ought to be continued.

The debatable ground on this subject is afforded by a sort of middle class of offences, consisting of larcenies and frauds of a heinous kind, although not accompanied with violence and terror. It is no part of my proposal to take away the discretion which is reposed in the judicial authorities respecting these offences. Nothing in my mind would be more imprudent than to establish an undeviating rule of law,—a rule that in many cases would have a more injurious and unjust operation than can easily be imagined. I do not, therefore, propose in any degree to interfere with the discretion of the judges, in cases in which the punishment of death ought, under certain aggravated circumstances, to attach, but only to examine whether or not it is fit that death should remain as the punishment expressly directed by the law for offences, which in its administration are never, even under circumstances of the greatest aggravation, more severely punished than with various periods of transportation.

It is impossible to advert to the necessity of reforming this part of the law, without calling to mind the efforts of that highly distinguished and universally lamented individual, by whom the attention of Parliament was so often roused to the subject of our penal code. Towards that excellent man I felt all the regard which a friendship of twenty years' duration naturally inspired, combined with the respect which his eminently superior understanding irresistibly claimed. But I need not describe his merits; to them ample justice has been already done by the unanimous voice of the Empire, seconded by the opinion of all the good men of all nations,—and especially by the eulogium of the Honourable Member for Bramber,* whose kindred virtues and kindred eloquence enable him justly to appreciate the qualities of active philanthropy and profound wisdom. I trust the House will bear with me if, while touching on this subject, I cannot restrain myself from feebly expressing my admiration for the individual by whose benevolent exertions it has been consecrated. There was, it is well known, an extraordinary degree of original sensibility belonging to the character of my lamented Friend, combined with the greatest moral purity, and inflexibility of public principle; but yet, with these elements, it is indisputably true, that his conduct as a statesman was always controlled by a sound judgment, duly and deliberately weighing every consideration of legislative expediency and practical policy. This was remarkably shown in his exertions respecting the criminal code. In his endeavours to rescue his country from the disgrace arising out of the character of that code, he never indulged in any visionary views;—he

* This passage is left intact on account of the momentous nature of its subject-matter, but the speaker has evidently been here too loosely reported.—Ed.

* Mr. Wilberforce.—Ed.

was at once humane and just,—generous and wise. With all that ardour of temperament with which he unceasingly pursued the public good, never was there a reformer more circumspect in his means,—more prudent in his end;—and yet all his propositions were opposed. In one thing, however, he succeeded,—he redeemed his country from a great disgrace, by putting a stop to that career of improvident and cruel legislation, which, from session to session was multiplying capital felonies. Sir, while private virtue and public worth are distinguished among men, the memory of Sir Samuel Romilly will remain consecrated in the history of humanity. According to the views of my lamented Friend, the punishment of death ought not to attach by law to any of those offences for which transportation is a sufficient punishment, and for which, in the ordinary administration of the law by the judges, transportation alone is inflicted. In that view I entirely concur.

I will not now enter into any discussion of the doctrine of Dr. Paley with respect to the expediency of investing judges with the power of inflicting death even for minor offences, where, in consequence of the character of the offence and of the offender, some particular good may appear to be promised from the example of such a punishment on a mischievous individual. The question is, whether the general good derived by society from the existence of such a state of the law is so great as to exceed the evil. And I may venture to express my conviction, that the result of such an inquiry as that which I propose will be to show, that the balance of advantage is decidedly against the continuance of the existing system. The late Lord Chief Justice of the Common Pleas,* whose authority is undoubtedly entitled to great consideration in discussing this question, expressed an opinion, that if the punishment of death for certain crimes were inflicted only in one case out of sixty, yet that the chance of having to undergo such a punishment must serve to impose an additional terror on the ill-disposed, and so operate to prevent the commission of crime. But I, on the contrary, maintain that such a terror is not likely to arise out of this mode of administering the law. I am persuaded that a different result must ensue; because this difference in the punishment of the same offence must naturally encourage a calculation in the mind of a person disposed to commit crime, of the manifold chances of escaping its penalties. It must also operate on a malefactor's mind in diminution of the terrors of transportation. Exulting at his escape from the more dreadful infliction, joy and triumph must absorb his faculties, eclipsing and obscuring those apprehensions and regrets with which he would otherwise have contemplated the lesser penalty, and inducing him, like Cicero, to consider exile as a refuge rather than as a punishment. In support of this opinion I will quote the authority of one who, if I cannot describe him as an eminent lawyer, all will agree was a man deeply skilled in human nature, as well as a most active and experienced magistrate,—I allude to the celebrated Henry Fielding. In a work of his, published at the period when the first Parliamentary inquiry of this nature was in progress, entituled "A Treatise on the Causes of Crime," there is this observation:—"A single pardon excites a greater degree of hope in the minds of criminals than twenty executions excite of fear." Now this argument I consider to be quite analagous to that which I have just used with reference to the opinion of the late Chief Justice of the Common Pleas, because the chance of escape from death, in either case, is but too apt to dislodge all thought of the inferior punishments.

But, Sir, another most important consideration is, the effect which the existing system of law has in deterring injured persons from commencing prosecutions, and witnesses from coming forward in support of them. The chances of escape are thus multiplied by a system which, while it discourages the prosecutor, increases the temptations of the offender. The better part of mankind, in those grave and reflecting moments which the prosecution for a capital offence must always bring with it, frequently shrink from the task imposed on them. The indisposition to prosecute while the laws continue so severe is matter of public notoriety. This has been evinced in various cases. It is not long since an act of George II., for preserving bleaching-grounds from depredation, was repealed on the proposition of Sir Samuel Romilly, backed by a petition from the proprietors of those grounds, who expressed their unwillingness to prosecute while the law continued so severe, and who represented that by the impunity thus given to offenders, their property was left comparatively unprotected. An eminent city banker has also been very recently heard to declare in this House, that bankers frequently declined to prosecute for the forgery of their notes in consequence of the law which denounced the punishment of death against such an offence. It is notorious that the concealment of a bankrupt's effects is very seldom prosecuted, because the law pronounces that to be a capital offence: it is undoubtedly, however, a great crime, and would not be allowed to enjoy such comparative impunity were the law less severe.

There is another strong fact on this subject, to which I may refer, as illustrating the general impression respecting the Criminal Law;—I mean the Act which was passed in 1812, by which all previous enactments of capital punishments for offences against the revenue not specified in it were repealed. That Act I understand was introduced at the instance of certain officers of the revenue. And why?—but because from the excessive

* Sir Vicary Gibbs.—Ed.

severity of the then existing revenue laws, the collectors of the revenue themselves found that they were utterly inefficient. But I have the highest official authority to sustain my view of the criminal code. I have the authority of the late Chief Baron of the Exchequer, Sir Archibald Macdonald, who, when he held the office of Attorney-General, which he discharged with so much honour to himself, and advantage to the country, distinctly expressed his concurrence in the opinion of Lord Bacon that great penalties deadened the force of the laws.

The House will still bear in mind, that I do not call for the entire abolition of the punishment of death, but only for its abolition in those cases in which it is very rarely, and ought never to be, carried into effect. In those cases I propose to institute other, milder, but more invariable punishments. The courts of law should, in some cases, be armed with the awful authority of taking away life: but in order to render that authority fully impressive, I am convinced that the punishment of death should be abolished where inferior punishments are not only applicable, but are usually applied. Nothing indeed can, in my opinion, be more injurious than the frequency with which the sentence of death is at the present time pronounced from the judgment-seat, with all the solemnities prescribed on such an occasion, when it is evident, even to those against whom it is denounced, that it will never be carried into effect. Whenever that awful authority,—the jurisdiction over life and death, is disarmed of its terrors by such a formality, the law is deprived of its beneficent energy, and society of its needful defence.

Sir William Grant, in a report of one of his speeches which I have seen, observes, "that the great utility of the punishment of death consists in the horror which it is naturally calculated to excite against the criminal; and that all penal laws ought to be in unison with the public feeling; for that when they are not so, and especially when they are too severe, the influence of example is lost, sympathy being excited towards the criminal, while horror prevails against the law." Such indeed was also the impression of Sir William Blackstone, of Mr. Fox, and of Mr. Pitt. It is also the opinion of Lord Grenville, expressed in a speech* as distinguished for forcible reasoning, profound wisdom, and magnificent eloquence, as any that I have ever heard.

It must undoubtedly happen, even in the best regulated conditions of society, that the laws will be sometimes at variance with the opinions and feelings of good men. But that, in a country like Great Britain, they should remain permanently in a state not less inconsistent with obvious policy than with the sentiments of all the enlightened and respectable classes of the community, is indeed scarcely credible. I should not be an advocate for the repeal of any law because it happened to be in opposition to temporary prejudices: but I object to the laws to which I have alluded, because they are inconsistent with the deliberate and permanent opinion of the public. In all nations an agreement between the laws and the general feeling of those who are subject to them is essential to their efficacy: but this agreement becomes of unspeakable importance in a country in which the charge of executing the laws is committed in a great measure to the people themselves.

I know not how to contemplate, without serious apprehension, the consequences that may attend the prolongation of a system like the present. It is my anxious desire to remove, before they become insuperable, the impediments that are already in the way of our civil government. My object is to make the laws popular,—to reconcile them with public opinion, and thus to redeem their character. It is to render the execution of them easy,—the terror of them overwhelming,—the efficacy of them complete,—that I implore the House to give to this subject their most grave consideration. I beg leave to remind them, that Sir William Blackstone has already pointed out the indispensable necessity under which juries frequently labour of committing, in estimating the value of stolen property, what he calls "pious perjuries." The resort to this practice in one of the wisest institutions of the country, so clearly indicates the public feeling, that to every wise statesman it must afford an instructive lesson. The just and faithful administration of the law in all its branches is the great bond of society,—the point at which authority and obedience meet most nearly. If those who hold the reins of government, instead of attempting a remedy, content themselves with vain lamentations at the growth of crime,—if they refuse to conform the laws to the opinions and dispositions of the public mind, that growth must continue to spread among us a just alarm.

With respect to petitions upon this subject, I have reason to believe that, in a few days, many will be presented from a body of men intimately connected with the administration of the Criminal Law,—I mean the magistracy of the country,—praying for its revision. Among that body I understand that but little difference of opinion prevails, and that when their petitions shall be presented, they will be found subscribed by many of the most respectable individuals in the empire as to moral character, enlightened talent, and general consideration. I did not, however, think it right to postpone my motion for an inquiry so important until those petitions should be actually laid on the table. I should, indeed, have felt extreme regret if the consideration of this question had been preceded by petitions drawn up and agreed to at popular and tumultuary

* Since published by Mr. Basil Montagu, in his Collections On the Punishment of Death.—Ed.

assemblies. No one can be more unwilling than myself to see any proceeding that can in the slightest degree interfere with the calm, deliberate, and dignified consideration of. Parliament, more especially on a subject of this nature.

The Petition from the City of London, however, ought to be considered in another light, and is entitled to peculiar attention. It proceeds from magistrates accustomed to administer justice in a populous metropolis, and who necessarily possess very great experience. It proceeds from a body of most respectable traders—men peculiarly exposed to those depredations against which Capital Punishment is denounced. An assembly so composed, is one of weight and dignity; and its representations on this subject are entitled to the greater deference, inasmuch as the results of its experience appear to be in direct opposition to its strongest prejudices. The first impulse of men whose property is attacked, is to destroy those by whom the attack is made: but the enlightened traders of London perceive, that the weapon of destruction which our penal code affords, is ineffective for its purpose; they therefore, disabusing themselves of vulgar prejudice, call for the revision of that code.

Another Petition has been presented to the House which I cannot pass over without notice: I allude to one from that highly meritorious and exemplary body of men—the Quakers. It has, I think, been rather hardly dealt by; and has been described as containing very extravagant recommendations; although the prayer with which it concludes is merely for such a change in the Criminal Law as may be consistent with the ends of justice. The body of the Petition certainly deviates into a speculation as to the future existence of some happier condition of society, in which mutual goodwill may render severe punishments unnecessary. But this is a speculation in which, however unsanctioned by experience, virtuous and philosophical men have in all ages indulged themselves, and by it have felt consoled for the evils by which they have been surrounded. The hope thus expressed, has exposed these respectable Petitioners to be treated with levity: but they are much too enlightened not to know that with such questions statesmen and lawyers, whose arrangements and regulations must be limited by the actual state and the necessary wants of a community, have no concern. And while I make these remarks, I cannot but request the House to recollect what description of people it is to whom I apply them,—a people who alone of all the population of the kingdom send neither paupers to your parishes, nor criminals to your jails,—a people who think a spirit of benevolence an adequate security to mankind (a spirit which certainly wants but the possibility of its being universal to constitute the perfection of our nature)—a people who have ever been foremost in undertaking and promoting every great and good work,—who were among the first to engage in the abolition of the slave trade, and who, by their firm yet modest perseverance, paved the way for the accomplishment of that incalculable benefit to humanity. Recollecting all this, and recollecting the channel through which this Petition was presented to the House,* I consider it to be entitled to anything but disrespect. The aid of such a body must always be a source of encouragement to those who are aiming at any amelioration of the condition of human beings; and on this occasion it inspires me, not only with perfect confidence in the goodness of my cause, but with the greatest hopes of its success.

* It had been presented by Mr. Wilberforce.—Ed.

SPEECH

ON MR. BROUGHAM'S MOTION FOR AN ADDRESS TO THE CROWN,

WITH REFERENCE TO THE TRIAL AND CONDEMNATION OF

THE REV. JOHN SMITH, OF DEMERARA,

DELIVERED IN THE HOUSE OF COMMONS, ON THE 1st OF JUNE, 1824.*

Mr. Speaker,—Even if I had not been loudly called upon, and directly challenged by the Honourable Gentleman,†—even if his accusations, now repeated after full consideration, did not make it my duty to vindicate the Petition which I had the honour to present from unjust reproach, I own that I should have been anxious to address the House on this occasion; not to strengthen a case already invincible, but to bear my solemn testimony against the most unjust and cruel abuse of power, under a false pretence of law, that has in our times dishonoured any portion of the British empire. I am sorry that the Honourable Gentleman, after so long an interval for reflection, should have this night repeated those charges against the London Missionary Society, which when he first made them I thought rash, and which I am now entitled to treat as utterly groundless. I should regret to be detained by them for a moment, from the great question of humanity and justice before us, if I did not feel that they excite a prejudice against the case of Mr. Smith, and that the short discussion sufficient to put them aside, leads directly to the vindication of the memory of that oppressed man.

The Honourable Gentleman calls the London Missionary Society "bad philosophers,"—by which, I presume, he means bad reasoners,—because they ascribe the insurrection partly "to the long and inexplicable delay of the government of Demerara in promulgating the instructions favourable to the slave population;" and because he, adopting one of the arguments of that speech by which the deputy judge-advocate disgraced his office, contends that a partial revolt cannot have arisen from a general cause of discontent,—a position belied by the whole course of history, and which is founded upon the absurd assumption, that one part of a people, from circumstances sometimes easy, sometimes very hard to be discovered, may not be more provoked than others by grievances common to all. So inconsistent, indeed, is the defence of the rulers of Demerara with itself, that in another part of the case they represent a project for an universal insurrection as having been formed, and ascribe its being, in fact, confined to the east coast, to unaccountable accidents. Paris, the ringleader, in what is called his "confession," (to be found in the Demerara Papers, No. II., p. 21,) says, "The whole colony was to have risen on Monday; and I cannot account for the reasons why only the east rose at the time appointed." So that, according to this part of their own evidence, they must abandon their argument, and own the discontent to have been as general as the grievance.

Another argument against the Society's

* The Rev. John Smith, an Independent minister, had been sent out to Demerara in the year 1816 by the London Missionary Society. The exemplary discharge of his sacred functions on the eastern shore of that colony for six years, amid difficulties which are said to have distinguished Demerara even among all her sister slave colonies, had so far impaired his health, that he was, by medical advice, on the point of leaving the country for a more salubrious climate, when, in the month of August, 1823, a partial insurrection of the negroes in his neighbourhood proved the means of putting a period alike to his labours and his life. The rising was not of an extensive or organised character, and was, in fact, suppressed immediately, with little loss of life or property. Its suppression was, however, immediately followed by the establishment of martial law, and the arrest of Mr. Smith as privy beforehand to the plot. As the evidence in support of this charge had necessarily to be extracted for the most part from prisoners trembling for their own lives, incurable suspicion would seem to attach to the whole of it; though candour must admit, on a careful consideration of the whole circumstances, including the sensitive feelings and ardent temperament of the accused, that it was not impossible that he had been made the involuntary depositary of the confidence of his flock. It was not till he had been in prison for nearly two months that Mr. Smith, on the 14th of October, was brought to trial before a court-martial. After proceedings abounding in irregularities, which lasted for six weeks, he was found guilty, and sentenced to death, but was recommended to the mercy of the Crown. He died in prison on the 6th of February following, awaiting the result. Sir James Mackintosh had presented, at an earlier period of the session, the appeal of the London Missionary Society on behalf of his memory and his widow. The present speech was delivered in support of Mr. Brougham's motion for an Address to the Crown on the subject.—Ed.

† Mr. Wilmot Horton, who conducted the defence of the authorities at Demerara.—Ed.

Petition, is transplanted from the same nursery of weeds. It is said, that cruelty cannot have contributed to this insurrection, because the leaders of the revolt were persons little likely to have been cruelly used, being among the most trusted of the slaves. Those who employ so gross a fallacy, must be content to be called worse reasoners than the London Missionary Society. It is, indeed, one of the usual common-places in all cases of discontent and tumult; but it is one of the most futile. The moving cause of most insurrections, and in the opinion of two great men (Sully and Burke) of all, is the distress of the great body of insurgents; but the ringleaders are generally, and almost necessarily, individuals who, being more highly endowed or more happily situated, are raised above the distress which is suffered by those of whom they take the command.

But the Honourable Gentleman's principal charge against the Petition, is the allegation contained in it, "that the life of no white man was voluntarily taken away by the slaves." When I heard the confidence with which a confutation of this averment was announced, I own I trembled for the accuracy of the Petition. But what was my astonishment, when I heard the attempt at confutation made! In the Demerara Papers, No. II., there is an elaborate narrative of an attack on the house of Mrs. Walrand, by the insurgents, made by that lady, or for her—a caution in statements which the subsequent parts of these proceedings prove to be necessary in Demerara. The Honourable Gentleman has read the narrative, to show that two lives were unhappily lost in this skirmish; and this he seriously quotes as proving the inaccuracy of the Petition. Does he believe, —can he hope to persuade the House, that the Petitioners meant to say, that there was an insurrection without fighting, or skirmishes without death? The attack and defence of houses and posts are a necessary part of all revolts; and deaths are the natural consequences of that, as well as of every species of warfare. The revolt in this case was, doubtless, an offence; the attack on the house was a part of that offence: the defence was brave and praiseworthy. The loss of lives is deeply to be deplored; but it was inseparable from all such unhappy scenes: it could not be the "voluntary killing," intended to be denied in the Petition. The Governor of Demerara, in a despatch to Lord Bathurst, makes the same statement with the Petition:—"I have not," he says, "heard of one white who was deliberately murdered:" yet he was perfectly aware of the fact which has been so triumphantly displayed to the House. "At plantation Nabaclis, where the whites were on their guard, two out of three were killed in the defence of their habitations." The defence was legitimate, and the deaths lamentable: but as the Governor distinguishes them from murder, so do the Society. They deny that there was any killing in cold blood. They did not mean to deny,—any more than to affirm—(for the Papers which mention the fact were printed since their Petition was drawn up), that there was killing in battle, when each party were openly struggling to destroy their antagonists and to preserve themselves. The Society only denies that this insurrection was dishonoured by those murders of the unoffending or of the vanquished, which too frequently attend the revolts of slaves. The Governor of Demerara agrees with them; the whole facts of the case support them; and the quotation of the Honourable Gentleman leaves their denial untouched. The revolt was absolutely unstained by excess. The killing of whites, even in action, was so small as not to appear in the trial of Mr. Smith, or in the first accounts laid before us. I will not stop to inquire whether "killing in action" may not, in a strictly philosophical sense, be called "voluntary." It is enough for me, that no man will call it calm, needless, or deliberate.

This is quite sufficient to justify even the words of the Petition. The substance of it is now more than abundantly justified by the general spirit of humanity which pervaded the unhappy insurgents,—by the unparalleled forbearance and moderation which characterised the insurrection. On this part of the subject, so important to the general question, as well as to the character of the Petition for accuracy, the London Missionary Society appeal to the highest authority, that of the Reverend Mr. Austin, not a missionary or a Methodist, but the chaplain of the colony, a minister of the Church of England, who has done honour even to that Church, so illustrious through the genius and learning and virtue of many of her clergy, by his Christian charity,—by his inflexible principles of justice,—by his intrepid defence of innocence against all the power of a government, and against the still more formidable prejudices of an alarmed and incensed community. No man ever did himself more honour by the admirable combination of strength of character with sense of duty; which needed nothing but a larger and more elevated theatre to place him among those who will be in all ages regarded by mankind as models for imitation and objects of reverence. That excellent person,—speaking of Mr. Smith, a person with whom he was previously unacquainted, a minister of a different persuasion, a missionary, considered by many of the established clergy as a rival, if not an enemy, a man then odious to the body of the colonists, whose good-will must have been so important to Mr. Austin's comfort,—after declaring his conviction of the perfect innocence and extraordinary merit of the persecuted missionary, proceeds to bear testimony to the moderation of the insurgents, and to the beneficent influence of Mr. Smith, in producing that moderation, in language, far warmer and bolder than that of the Petition. "I feel no hesitation in declaring," says he, "from the intimate knowledge which my most anxious inquiries have obtained, that in the late scourge which the hand of an all-wise Creator has inflicted on this ill-fated country, nothing but those religious impressions which, under Providence, Mr. Smith has been instrumental in fixing,—nothing but those principles of the Gospel of Peace, which he had been proclaiming, could have prevented a dreadful effusion of blood here, and saved the lives of those very persons who are now, I shudder to write it, seeking his life."

And here I beg the House to weigh this testimony. It is not only valuable from the integrity, impartiality, and understanding of the witness, but from his opportunities of acquiring that intimate knowledge of facts on which he rests his opinion. He was a member of the Secret Commission of Inquiry established on this occasion, which was armed with all the authority of government, and which received much evidence relating to this insurrection not produced on the trial of Mr. Smith.

This circumstance immediately brings me to the consideration of the hearsay evidence illegally received against Mr. Smith. I do not merely or chiefly object to it on grounds purely technical, or as being inadmissible by the law of England. I abstain from taking any part in the discussions of lawyers or philosophers, with respect to the wisdom of our rules of evidence; though I think that there is more to be said for them than the ingenious objectors are aware of. What I complain of is, the admission of hearsay, of the vaguest sort, under circumstances where such an admission was utterly abominable. In what I am about to say, I shall not quote from the Society's edition of the Trial, but from that which is officially before the House: so that I may lay aside all that has been said on the superior authority of the latter. Mr. Austin, when examined in chief, stated, that though originally prepossessed against Mr. Smith, yet, in the course of numerous inquiries, he could not see any circumstances which led to a belief that Mr. Smith had been, in any degree, instrumental in the insurrection; but that, on the contrary, when he (Mr. Austin) said to the slaves, that bloodshed had not marked the progress of their insurrection, their answer was:—"It is contrary to the religion we profess" (which had been taught to them by Mr. Smith);—"we cannot give life, and therefore we will not take it." This evidence of the innocence of Mr. Smith, and of the humanity of the slaves, appears to have alarmed the impartial judge-advocate; and he proceeded, in his cross-examination, to ask Mr. Austin whether any of the negroes had ever insinuated, that their misfortunes were occasioned by the prisoner's influence over them, or by the doctrines he taught them? Mr. Austin, understanding this question to refer to what passed before the Committee, appears to have respectfully hesitated about the propriety of disclosing these proceedings; upon which the Court, in a tone of discourtesy and displeasure, which a reputable advocate for a prisoner would not have used towards such a witness in this country, addressed the following illegal and indecent question to Mr. Austin:—"Can you take it upon yourself to swear that you do not recollect any insinuations of that sort at the Board of Evidence?" How that question came to be waived, does not appear in the official copy. It is almost certain, however, from the purport of the next question, that the Society's Report is correct in supplying this defect, and that Mr. Austin still doubted its substantial propriety, and continued to resent its insolent form. He was actually asked, "whether he *heard*, before the Board of Evidence, any negro imputing the cause of revolt to the prisoner?" He answered, "Yes:"—and the inquiry is pursued no further. I again request the House to bear in mind, that this question and answer rest on the authority of the official copy; and I repeat, that I disdain to press the legal objection of its being hearsay evidence, and to contend, that to put such a question and receive such an answer, were acts of mere usurpation in any English tribunal.

Much higher matter arises on this part of the evidence. Fortunately for the interests of truth, we are now in possession of the testimony of the negroes before the Board of Inquiry which is adverted to in this question, and which, be it observed, was wholly unknown to the unfortunate Mr. Smith. We naturally ask, why these negroes themselves were not produced as witnesses, if they were alive; or, if they were executed, how it happened that none of the men who gave such important evidence before the Board of Inquiry were preserved to bear testimony against him before the Court-martial? Why were they content with the much weaker evidence actually produced? Why were they driven to the necessity of illegally obtaining, through Mr. Austin, what they might have obtained from his informants? The reason is plain:—they disbelieved the evidence of the negroes, who threw out the "insinuations," or "imputations." That might have been nothing; but they knew that all mankind would have rejected that pretended evidence with horror. They knew that the negroes, to whom their question adverted, had told a tale to the Board of Evidence, in comparison with which the story of Titus Oates was a model of probability, candour, and truth. One of them (Sandy) said, that Mr. Smith told him, though not a member of his congregation, nor even a Christian, "that a good thing was come for the negroes, and that if they did not seek for it now, the whites would trample upon them, and upon their sons and daughters, to eternity."* Another (Paris) says, "that all the male whites (except the doctors and missionaries) were to be murdered, and all

* Demerara Papers. No. II. p. 26.

the females distributed among the insurgents; that one of their leaders was to be a king, another to be a governor, and Mr. Smith to be emperor;* that on Sunday, the 17th of August, Mr. Smith administered the sacrament to several leading negroes, and to Mr. Hamilton, the European overseer of the estate Le Ressouvenir; that he swore the former on the Bible to do him no harm when they had conquered the country, and afterwards blessed their revolt, saying, "Go; as you have begun in Christ, you must end in Christ!"† All this the prosecutor concealed, with the knowledge of the Court. While they asked, whether Mr. Austin had heard statements made against Mr. Smith before the Board of Evidence, they studiously concealed all those incredible, monstrous, impossible fictions which accompanied these statements, and which would have annihilated their credit. Whether the question was intended to discredit Mr. Austin, or to prejudice Mr. Smith, it was, in either case, an atrocious attempt to take advantage of the stories told by the negroes, and at the same time to screen them from scrutiny, contradiction, disbelief, and abhorrence. If these men could have been believed, would they not have been produced on the trial? Paris, indeed, the author of this horrible fabrication, charges Bristol, Manuel, and Azor, three of the witnesses afterwards examined on the trial of Mr. Smith, with having been parties to the dire and execrable oath: not one of them alludes to such horrors; all virtually contradict them. Yet this Court-martial sought to injure Mr. Austin, or to contribute to the destruction of Mr. Smith, by receiving as evidence a general statement of what was said by those whom they could not believe, whom they durst not produce, and who were contradicted by their own principal witnesses, — who, if their whole tale had been brought into view, would have been driven out of any court with shouts of execration.

I cannot yet leave this part of the subject. It deeply affects the character of the whole transaction. It shows the general terror, which was so powerful as to stimulate the slaves to the invention of such monstrous falsehoods. It throws light on that species of skill with which the prosecutors kept back the absolutely incredible witnesses, and brought forward only those who were discreet enough to tell a more plausible story, and on the effect which the circulation of the fictions, which were too absurd to be avowed, must have had in exciting the body of the colonists to the most relentless animosity against the unfortunate Mr. Smith. It teaches us to view with the utmost jealousy the more guarded testimony actually produced against him, which could not be exempt from the influence of the same fears and prejudices. It authorises me to lay a much more than ordinary stress on every defect of the evidence; because, in such circumstances, I am warranted in affirming that whatever was not proved, could not have been proved.

But in answer to all this, we are asked by the Honourable Gentleman, "Would President Wray have been a party to the admission of improper evidence?" Now, Sir, I wish to say nothing disrespectful of Mr. Wray; and the rather, because he is well spoken of by those whose good opinion is to be respected. We do not know that he may not have dissented from every act of this Court-martial. I should heartily rejoice to hear that it was so: but I am aware we can never know whether he did or not. The Honourable Gentleman unwarily asks, — "Would not Mr. Wray have publicly protested against illegal questions?" Does he not know, or has he forgotten, that every member of a court-martial is bound by oath not to disclose its proceedings? But really, Sir, I must say that the character of no man can avail against facts:—"Tolle e causâ nomen Catonis." Let character protect accused men, when there is any defect in the evidence of their guilt: let it continue to yield to them that protection which Mr. Smith, in his hour of danger, did not receive from the tenor of his blameless and virtuous life: let it be used for mercy, not for severity. Let it never be allowed to aid a prosecutor, or to strengthen the case of an accuser. Let it be a shield to cover the accused: but let it never be converted into a dagger, by which he is to be stabbed to the heart. Above all, let it not be used to destroy his good name, after his life has been taken away.

The question is, as has been stated by the Honourable Gentleman, whether, on a review of the whole evidence, Mr. Smith can be pronounced to be guilty of the crimes charged against him, and for which he was condemned to death. That is the fact on which issue is to be joined. In trying it, I can lay my hand on my heart, and solemnly declare, upon my honour, or whatever more sacred sanction there be, that I believe him to have been an innocent and virtuous man,—illegally tried, unjustly condemned to death, and treated in a manner which would be disgraceful to a civilized government in the case of the worst criminal. I heartily rejoice that the Honourable Gentleman has been manly enough directly to dissent from my Honourable Friend's motion,—that the case is to be fairly brought to a decision,—and that no attempt is to be made to evade a determination, by moving the previous question. That, of all modes of proceeding, I should most lament. Some may think Mr. Smith guilty; others will agree with me in thinking him innocent; but no one can doubt that it would be dishonourable to the Grand Jury of the Empire, to declare that they will not decide, when a grave case is brought before them, whether a British subject has been

* Demarara Papers, No. II. p. 30.
† Ibid. p. 41.

lawfully or unlawfully condemned to death. We still observe that usage of our forefathers, according to which the House of Commons, at the commencement of every session of Parliament, nominates a grand committee of justice; and if, in ordinary cases, other modes of proceeding have been substituted in practice for this ancient institution, we may at least respect it as a remembrancer of our duty, which points out one of the chief objects of the original establishment. All evasion is here refusal; and a denial of justice in Parliament, more especially in an inquest for blood, would be a fatal and irreparable breach in the English constitution.

The question before us resolves itself into several questions, relating to every branch and stage of the proceedings against Mr. Smith: — Whether the Court-martial had jurisdiction? whether the evidence against him was warranted by law, or sufficient in fact? whether the sentence was just, or the punishment legal? These questions are so extensive and important, that I cannot help wishing they had not been still further enlarged and embroiled by the introduction of matter wholly impertinent to any of them.

To what purpose has the Honourable Gentleman so often told us that Mr. Smith was an "enthusiast?" It would have been well if he had given us some explanation of the sense in which he uses so vague a term. If he meant by it to denote the prevalence of those disorderly passions, which, whatever be their source or their object, always disturb the understanding, and often pervert the moral sentiments, we have clear proof that it did not exist in Mr. Smith, so far as to produce the first of these unfortunate effects: and it is begging the whole question in dispute, to assert that it manifested itself in him by the second and still more fatal symptom. There is, indeed, another temper of mind called enthusiasm, which, though rejecting the authority neither of reason nor of virtue, triumphs over all the vulgar infirmities of men, contemns their ordinary pursuits, braves danger, and despises obloquy,—which is the parent of heroic acts and apostolical sacrifices,—which devotes the ease, the pleasure, the interest, the ambition, the life of the generous enthusiast, to the service of his fellow-men. If Mr. Smith had not been supported by an ardent zeal for the cause of God and man, he would have been ill qualified for a task so surrounded by disgust, by calumny, by peril, as that of attempting to pour instruction into the minds of unhappy slaves. Much of this excellent quality was doubtless necessary for so long enduring the climate and the government of Demerara.

I am sorry that the Honourable Gentleman should have deigned to notice any part of the impertinent absurdities with which the Court have suffered their minutes to be encumbered, and which have no more to do with this insurrection than with the Popish Plot. What is it to us that a misunderstanding occurred, three or four years ago, between Mr. Smith and a person called Captain or Doctor Macturk, whom he had the misfortune to have for a neighbour,—a misunderstanding long antecedent to this revolt, and utterly unconnected with any part of it! It was inadmissible evidence; and if it had been otherwise, it proved nothing but the character of the witness,—of the generous Macturk; who, having had a trifling difference with his neighbour five years ago, called it to mind at the moment when that neighbour's life was in danger. Such is the chivalrous magnanimity of Dr. Macturk! If I were infected by classical superstition, I should forbid such a man to embark in the same vessel with me. I leave him to those from whom, if we may trust his name or his manners, he may be descended; and I cannot help thinking that he deserves, as well as they, to be excluded from the territory of Christians.

I very sincerely regret, Sir, that the Honourable Gentleman, by quotations from Mr. Smith's manuscript journal, should appear to give any countenance or sanction to the detestable violation of all law, humanity, and decency, by which that manuscript was produced in evidence against the writer. I am sure that, when his official zeal has somewhat subsided, he will himself regret that he appealed to such a document. That which is unlawfully obtained cannot be fairly quoted. The production of a paper in evidence, containing general reflections and reasonings, or narratives of fact, not relating to any design, or composed to compass any end, is precisely the iniquity perpetrated by Jeffreys, in the case of Sidney, which has since been reprobated by all lawyers, and which has been solemnly condemned by the legislature itself. I deny, without fear of contradiction from any one of the learned lawyers who differ from me in this debate, that such a paper has been received in evidence, since that abominable trial, by any body of men calling themselves a court of justice. Is there a single line in the extracts produced which could have been written to forward the insurrection? I defy any man to point it out? Could it be admissible evidence on any other ground? I defy any lawyer to maintain it; for, if it were to be said that it manifests opinions and feelings favourable to negro insurrection, and which rendered probable the participation of Mr. Smith in this revolt, (having first denied the fact,) I should point to the statute reversing the attainder of Sidney, against whom the like evidence was produced precisely under the same pretence. Nothing can be more decisive on this point than the authority of a great judge and an excellent writer. "Had the papers found in Sidney's closets," says Mr. Justice Foster, "been plainly relative to the other treasonable practices charged in the indictment, they might have been read in evidence against him, though not published. The papers found on Lord Preston were written in prosecution of certain determined purposes which were treasonable, and then (namely, at the time of writing) in the contemplation of the offenders." But the iniquity in the case of Sidney vanishes, in comparison with that of this trial. Sidney's manuscript was intended for publication: it could not be said that its tendency, when published, was not to excite dispositions hostile to the bad government which then existed; it was perhaps in strictness indictable as a seditious libel. The journal of Mr. Smith was meant for no human eyes: it was seen by none; only extracts of it had been sent to his employers in England,—as inoffensive, doubtless, as their excellent instructions required. In the midst of conjugal affection and confidence, it was withheld even from his wife. It consisted of his communings with his own mind, or the breathings of his thoughts towards his Creator; it was neither addressed nor communicated to any created being. That such a journal should have been dragged from its sacred secrecy is an atrocity—I repeat it—to which I know no parallel in the annals of any court that has professed to observe a semblance of justice.

I dwell on this circumstance, because the Honourable Gentleman, by his quotation, has compelled me to do so, and because the admission of this evidence shows the temper of the Court. For I think the extracts produced are, in truth, favourable to Mr. Smith; and I am entitled to presume that the whole journal, withheld as it is from us,—withheld from the Colonial Office, though circulated through tho Court to excite West Indian prejudices against Mr. Smith,—would, in the eyes of impartial men, have been still more decisively advantageous to his cause. How, indeed, can I think otherwise? What, in the opinion of the judge-advocate, is the capital crime of this journal? It is, that in it the prisoner "avows he feels an aversion to slavery!!" He was so depraved, as to be an enemy of that admirable institution! He was so lost to all sense of morality, as to be dissatisfied with the perpetual and unlimited subjection of millions of reasonable creatures to the will, and caprice, and passions of other men! This opinion, it is true, Mr. Smith shared with the King, Parliament, and people of Great Britain,—with all wise and good men, in all ages and nations: still, it is stated by the judge-advocate as if it were some immoral paradox, which it required the utmost effrontery to "avow." One of the passages produced in evidence, and therefore thought either to be criminal in itself, or a proof of criminal intention, well deserves attention:—"While writing this, my very heart flutters at the almost incessant cracking of the whip!" As the date of this part of the journal is the 22d of March 1819, more than four years before the insurrection, it cannot be so distorted by human ingenuity as to be brought to bear on the specific charges which the Court had to try. What, therefore, is the purpose for which it is produced? They overheard, as it were, a man secretly complaining to himself of the agitation produced in his bodily frame by the horrible noise of a whip constantly resounding on the torn and bloody backs of his fellow-creatures. As he does not dare to utter them to any other, they must have been unaffected, undesigning almost involuntary ejaculations of feeling The discovery of them might have recalled unhardened men from practices of which they had thus casually perceived the impression upon an uncorrupted heart. It could hardly have been supposed that the most practised negro-driver could have blamed them more severely than by calling them effusions of weak and womanish feelings. But it seemed good to the prosecutors of Mr. Smith to view these complaints in another light. They regard "the fluttering of his heart at the incessant cracking of the whip," as an overt act of the treason of "abhorring slavery." They treat natural compassion, and even its involuntary effects on the bodily frame, as an offence. Such is the system of their society, that they consider every man who feels pity for sufferings, or indignation against cruelty, as their irreconcilable enemy. Nay, they receive a secret expression of those feelings as evidence against a man on trial for his life, in what they call a court of justice. My Right Honourable Friend* has, on a former occasion, happily characterised the resistance, which has not been obscurely threatened, against all measures for mitigating the evils of slavery, as a "rebellion for the whip." In the present instance we see how sacred that instrument is held,—how the right to use it is prized as one of the dearest of privileges,—and in what manner the most private murmur against its severest inflictions is brought forward as a proof, that he who breathes it must be prepared to plunge into violence and blood.

In the same spirit, conversations are given in evidence, long before the revolt, wholly unconnected with it, and held with ignorant men, who might easily misunderstand or misremember them; in which Mr. Smith is supposed to have expressed a general and speculative opinion, that slavery never could be mitigated, and that it must die a violent death. These opinions the Honourable Gentleman calls "fanatical." Does he think Dr. Johnson a fanatic, or a sectary, or a Methodist, or an enemy of established authority? But he must know from the most amusing of books, that Johnson, when on a visit to Oxford, perhaps when enjoying lettered hospitality at the table of the Master of University College,† proposed as a toast, "Success to the first revolt of negroes in the West Indies!" He neither meant to make a jest of such matters, nor to express a deliberate wish for an event so full of horror, but merely to express in the strongest manner his honest hatred of slavery. For no man ever more detested actual oppression; though his Tory

* Mr. Canning.—Ed.

† Dr. Wetherell, father of the Solicitor-General.

prejudices hindered him from seeing the value of those liberal institutions which alone secure society from oppression. This justice will be universally done to the aged moralist, who knew slavery only as a distant evil,—whose ears were never wounded by the cracking of the whip. Yet all the casual expressions of the unfortunate Mr. Smith, in the midst of dispute, or when he was fresh from the sight of suffering, rise up against him as legal proof of settled purposes and deliberate designs.

On the legality of the trial, Sir, the impregnable speech of my Learned Friend* has left me little if any thing to say. The only principle on which the law of England tolerates what is called "martial law," is necessity; its introduction can be justified only by necessity; its continuance requires precisely the same justification of necessity; and if it survives the necessity, in which alone it rests, for a single minute, it becomes instantly a mere exercise of lawless violence. When foreign invasion or civil war renders it impossible for courts of law to sit, or to enforce the execution of their judgments, it becomes necessary to find some rude substitute for them, and to employ for that purpose the military, which is the only remaining force in the community. While the laws are silenced by the noise of arms, the rulers of the armed force must punish, as equitably as they can, those crimes which threaten their own safety and that of society; but no longer;—every moment beyond is usurpation. As soon as the laws can act, every other mode of punishing supposed crimes is itself an enormous crime. If argument be not enough on this subject,—if, indeed, the mere statement be not the evidence of its own truth, I appeal to the highest and most venerable authority known to our law. "Martial law," says Sir Matthew Hale, "is not a law, but something indulged rather than allowed, as a law. The necessity of government, order, and discipline in an army, is that only which can give it countenance. 'Necessitas enim, quod cogit, defendit.' Secondly, this indulged law is only to extend to members of the army, or to those of the opposite army, and never may be so much indulged as to be exercised or executed upon others. Thirdly, the exercise of martial law may not be permitted in time of peace, when the king's courts are" (or may be) "open."† The illustrious Judge on this occasion appeals to the Petition of Right, which, fifty years before, had declared all proceedings by martial law, in time of peace, to be illegal. He carries the principle back to the cradle of English liberty, and quotes the famous reversal of the attainder of the Earl of Kent, in the first year of Edward III., as decisive of the principle, that nothing but the necessity arising from the absolute interruption of civil judicature by arms, can warrant the exercise of what is called martial law. Wherever, and whenever, they are so interrupted, and as long as the interruption continues, necessity justifies it.

No other doctrine has ever been maintained in this country, since the solemn Parliamentary condemnation of the usurpations of Charles I., which he was himself compelled to sanction in the Petition of Right. In none of the revolutions or rebellions which have since occurred has martial law been exercised, however much, in some of them, the necessity might seem to exist. Even in those most deplorable of all commotions, which tore Ireland in pieces, in the last years of the eighteenth century,—in the midst of ferocious revolt and cruel punishment,—at the very moment of legalising these martial jurisdictions in 1799, the very Irish statute, which was passed for that purpose, did homage to the ancient and fundamental principles of the law, in the very act of departing from them. The Irish statute 39 Geo. III. c. 2, after reciting "that martial law had been successfully exercised to the restoration of peace, so far as to permit the course of the common law partially to take place, but that the rebellion continued to rage in considerable parts of the kingdom, whereby it has become necessary for Parliament to interpose," goes on to enable the Lord Lieutenant "to punish rebels by courts-martial." This statute is the most positive declaration, that where the common law can be exercised in some parts of the country, martial law cannot be established in others, though rebellion actually prevails in those others, without an extraordinary interposition of the supreme legislative authority itself.

I have already quoted from Sir Matthew Hale his position respecting the two-fold operation of martial law;—as it affects the army of the power which exercises it, and as it acts against the army of the enemy. That great Judge, happily unused to standing armies, and reasonably prejudiced against military jurisdiction, does not pursue his distinction through all its consequences, and assigns a ground for the whole, which will support only one of its parts. "The necessity of order and discipline in an army," is, according to him, the reason why the law tolerates this departure from its most valuable rules; but this necessity only justifies the exercise of martial law over the army of our own state. One part of it has since been annually taken out of the common law, and provided for by the Mutiny Act, which subjects the military offences of soldiers only to punishment by military courts, even in time of peace. Hence we may now be said annually to legalise military law; which, however, differs essentially from martial law, in being confined to offences against military discipline, and in not extending to any persons but those who are members of the army.

Martial law exercised against enemies or rebels cannot depend on the same principle;

* Mr. Brougham.—Ed.

† History of the Common Law, chap. xi.

for it is certainly not intended to enforce or preserve discipline among them. It seems to me to be only a more regular and convenient mode of exercising the right to kill in war,—a right originating in self-defence, and limited to those cases where such killing is necessary, as the means of insuring that end. Martial law put in force against rebels, can only be excused as a mode of more deliberately and equitably selecting the persons from whom quarter ought to be withheld, in a case where all have forfeited their claim to it. It is nothing more than a sort of better regulated decimation, founded upon choice, instead of chance, in order to provide for the safety of the conquerors, without the horrors of undistinguished slaughter: it is justifiable only where it is an act of mercy. Thus the matter stands by the law of nations. But by the law of England, it cannot be exercised except where the jurisdiction of courts of justice is interrupted by violence. Did this necessity exist at Demerara on the 13th of October, 1823. Was it on that day impossible for the courts of law to try offences? It is clear that, if the case be tried by the law of England, and unless an affirmative answer can be given to these questions of fact, the Court-martial had no legal power to try Mr. Smith.

Now, Sir, I must in the first place remark, that General Murray has himself expressly waived the plea of necessity, and takes merit to himself for having brought Mr. Smith to trial before a court-martial, as the most probable mode of securing impartial justice,—a statement which would be clearly an attempt to obtain commendation under false pretences, if he had no choice, and was compelled by absolute necessity to recur to martial law:—"In bringing *this man* (Mr. Smith) to trial, under present circumstances, I have endeavoured to secure to him the advantage of the most cool and dispassionate consideration, by framing a court entirely of officers of the army, who, having no interests in the country, are without the bias of public opinion, which is at present so violent against Mr. Smith."* This paragraph I conceive to be an admission, and almost a boast, that the trial by court-martial was a matter of choice, and therefore not of necessity; and I shall at present say nothing more on it, than earnestly to beseech the House to remark the evidence which it affords of the temper of the colonists, and to bear in mind the inevitable influence of that furious temper on the prosecutors who conducted the accusation,—on the witnesses who supported it by their testimony,—on the officers of the Court-martial, who could have no other associates or friends but among these prejudiced and exasperated colonists. With what suspicion and jealousy ought we not to regard such proceedings? What deductions ought to be made from the evidence? How little can we trust the fairness of the prosecutors, or the impartiality of the judges? What hope of acquittal could the most innocent prisoner entertain? Such, says in substance Governor Murray, was the rage of the inhabitants of Demerara against the unfortunate Mr. Smith, that his only chance of impartial trial required him to be deprived of all the safeguards which are the birthright of British subjects, and to be tried by a judicature which the laws and feelings of his country alike abhor.

But the admission of Governor Murray, though conclusive against him, is not necessary to the argument; for my Learned Friend has already demonstrated that, in fact, there was no necessity for a court-martial on the 13th of October. From the 31st of August, it appears by General Murray's letters, that no impediment existed to the ordinary course of law; "no negroes were in arms; no war or battle's sound was heard" through the colony. There remained, indeed, a few runaways in the forests behind; but we know, from the best authorities,* that the forests were never free from bodies of these wretched and desperate men in those unhappy settlements in Guiana,—where, under every government, rebellion has as uniformly sprung from cruelty, as pestilence has arisen from the marshes. Before the 4th of September, even the detachment which pursued the deserters into the forest had returned into the colony. For six weeks, then, before the Court-martial was assembled, and for twelve weeks before that Court pronounced sentence of death on Mr. Smith, all hostility had ceased, no necessity for their existence can be pretended, and every act which they did was an open and deliberate defiance of the law of England.

Where, then, are we to look for any colour of law in these proceedings? Do they derive it from the Dutch law? I have diligently examined the Roman law, which is the foundation of that system, and the writings of those most eminent jurists who have contributed so much to the reputation of Holland:—I can find in them no trace of any such principle as martial law. Military law, indeed, is clearly defined; and provision is made for the punishment by military judges of the purely military offences of soldiers. But to any power of extending military jurisdiction over those who are not soldiers, there is not an allusion. I will not furnish a subject for the pleasantries of my Right Honourable Friend, or tempt him into a repetition of his former innumerable blunders, by naming the greatest of these jurists;† lest his date, his occupation, and his rank might be again mistaken; and the venerable President of the Supreme Court of Holland might be once more called a "clerk of the States-

* General Murray (Governor of Demerara) to Earl Bathurst, 21st of October, 1823.

* See Stedman, Bolingbroke, &c.

† Bynkershoek,—of whose professional rank Mr. Canning had professed ignorance.—Ed.

General." "Persecutio militis," says that learned person, "pertinet ad judicem militarem quando delictum sit militare, et ad judicem communem quando delictum sit commune." Far from supposing it to be possible, that those who were not soldiers could ever be triable by military courts for crimes not military, he expressly declares the law and practice of the United Provinces to be, that even soldiers are amenable, for ordinary offences against society, to the court of Holland and Friesland, of which he was long the chief. The law of Holland, therefore, does not justify this trial by martial law.

Nothing remains but some law of the colony itself. Where is it? It is not alleged or alluded to in any part of this trial. We have heard nothing of it this evening. So unwilling was I to believe that this Court-martial would dare to act without some pretence of legal authority, that I suspected an authority for martial law would be dug out of some dark corner of a Guiana ordinance. I knew it was neither in the law of England, nor in that of Holland; and I now believe that it does not exist even in the law of Demerara. The silence of those who are interested in producing it, is not my only reason for this belief. I happen to have seen the instructions of the States-General to their Governor of Demerara, in November, 1792,—probably the last ever issued to such an officer by that illustrious and memorable assembly. They speak at large of councils of war, both for consultation and for judicature. They authorise these councils to try the military offences of soldiers; and therefore, by an inference which is stronger than silence, authorise us to conclude that the governor had no power to subject those who were not soldiers to their authority.

The result, then, is, that the law of Holland does not allow what is called "martial law" in any case; and that the law of England does not allow it without a necessity, which did not exist in the case of Mr. Smith. If, then, martial law is not to be justified by the law of England, or by the law of Holland, or by the law of Demerara, what is there to hinder me from affirming, that the members of this pretended court had no more right to try Mr. Smith than any other fifteen men on the face of the earth,—that their acts were nullities, and their meeting a conspiracy,—that their sentence was a direction to commit a crime,—that, if it had been obeyed, it would not have been an execution, but a murder,—and that they, and all other parties engaged in it, must have answered for it with their lives.

I hope, Sir, no man will, in this House, undervalue that part of the case which relates to the illegality of the trial. I should be sorry to hear any man represent it as an inferior question, whether we are to be governed by law or by will. Every breach of law, under pretence of attaining what is called "substantial justice," is a step towards reducing society under the authority of arbitrary caprice and lawless force. As in many other cases of evil-doing, it is not the immediate effect, but the example (which is the larger part of the consequences of every act), which is most mischievous. If we listen to any language of this sort, we shall do our utmost to encourage governors of colonies to discover some specious pretexts of present convenience for relieving themselves altogether, and as often as they wish, from the restraints of law. In spite of every legal check, colonial administrators are already daring enough, from the physical impediments which render it nearly impossible to reduce their responsibility to practice. If we encourage them to proclaim martial law without necessity, we shall take away all limitations from their power in this department; for pretences of convenience can seldom be wanting in a state of society which presents any temptation to abuse of power.

But I am aware, Sir, that I have undertaken to maintain the innocence of Mr. Smith, as well as to show the unlawfulness and nullity of the proceedings against him. I am relieved from the necessity of entering at large into the facts of his conduct, by the admirable and irresistible speech of my Learned Friend, who has already demonstrated the virtue and innocence of this unfortunate Gentleman, who died the martyr of his zeal for the diffusion of religion, humanity, and civilization, among the slaves of Demerara. The Honourable Gentleman charges him with a want of discretion. Perhaps it may be so. That useful quality, which Swift somewhere calls "an alderman-like virtue," is deservedly much in esteem among those who are "wise in their generation," and to whom the prosperity of this world belongs; but it is rarely the attribute of heroes and of martyrs,—of those who voluntarily suffer for faith or freedom,—who perish on the scaffold in attestation of their principles;—it does not animate men to encounter that honourable death which the colonists of Demerara were so eager to bestow on Mr. Smith.

On the question of actual innocence, the Honourable Gentleman has either bewildered himself, or found it necessary to attempt to bewilder his audience, by involving the case in a labyrinth of words, from which I shall be able to extricate it by a very few and short remarks. The question is, not whether Mr. Smith was wanting in the highest vigilance and foresight, but whether he was guilty of certain crimes laid to his charge? The first charge is, that he promoted discontent and dissatisfaction among the slaves, "intending thereby to excite revolt." The Court-martial found him guilty of the fact, but not of the intention; thereby, in common sense and justice, acquitting him. The second charge is, that, on the 17th of August, he consulted with Quamina concerning the intended rebellion; and, on the 19th and 20th, during its progress, he aided and assisted it by consulting and corresponding with Quamina, an insurgent. The Court-martial found him guilty of the acts charged on the 17th and 20th, but acquitted him of that charged on the 19th. But this charge is abandoned by the Honourable Gentleman, and, as far as I can learn, will not be supported by any one likely to take a part in this debate. On the fourth charge, which, in substance, is, that Mr. Smith did not endeavour to make Quamina prisoner on the the 20th of August,—the Court-martial have found him guilty. But I will not waste the time of the House, by throwing away a single word upon an accusation which I am persuaded no man here will so insult his own reputation as to vindicate.

The third charge, therefore, is the only one which requires a moment's discussion. It imputes to Mr. Smith, that he previously knew of the intended revolt, and did not communicate his knowledge to the proper authorities. It depends entirely on the same evidence which was produced in support of the second. It is an offence analogous to what, in our law, is denominated "misprision" of treason; and it bears the same relation to an intended revolt of slaves against their owners, which misprision in England bears to high treason. To support this charge, there should be sufficient evidence of such a concealment as would have amounted to misprision, if a revolt of slaves against their private masters had been high treason. Now, it had been positively laid down by all the judges of England, that "one who is told only, in general, that there will be a rising, without persons or particulars, is not bound to disclose."* Concealment of the avowal of an intention is not misprision, because such an avowal is not an overt act of high treason. Misprision of treason is a concealment of an overt act of treason. A consultation about the means of revolt is undoubtedly an overt act, because it is one of the ordinary and necessary means of accomplishing the object: but it is perfectly otherwise with a conversation, even though in the course of it improper declarations of a general nature should be made. I need not quote Hale or Foster in support of positions which I believe will not be controverted. Contenting myself with having laid them down, I proceed to apply them to the evidence on this charge.

I think myself entitled to lay aside—and, indeed, in that I only follow the example of the Honourable Gentleman—the testimony of the coachman and the groom, which, if understood in one sense is incredible, and in the other is insignificant. It evidently amounts to no more than a remark by Mr. Smith, after the insurrection broke out, that he had long foreseen danger. The concealment of such a general misapprehension, if he had concealed it, was no crime; for it would be indeed most inconvenient to magistrates and rulers, and most destructive of the quiet of society, if men were bound to communicate to the public authorities every alarm that might seize the minds of any of them.

But he did not conceal that general apprehension: on the contrary, he did much more than strict legal duty required. Divide the facts into two parts, those which preceded Sunday the 17th of August, and those which occurred then and afterwards. I fix on this day, because it will not be said, by any one whose arguments I should be at the trouble of answering, that there is any evidence of the existence of a specific plan of revolt previous to the 17th of August. What did not exist could neither be concealed nor disclosed. But the conduct of Mr. Smith respecting the general apprehensions which he entertained before that day is evidence of great importance as to what would have been his probable conduct, if any specific plan had afterwards been communicated to him. If he made every effort to disclose a general apprehension, it is not likely that he should have deliberately concealed a specific plan. It is in that light that I desire the attention of the House to it.

It is quite clear that considerable agitation had prevailed among the negroes from the arrival of Lord Bathurst's Dispatch in the beginning of July. They had heard from seamen arrived from England, and by servants in the Governor's house, and by the angry conversations of their masters, that some projects for improving their condition had been favourably received in this country. They naturally entertained sanguine and exaggerated hopes of the extent of the reformation. The delay in making the Instructions known naturally led the slaves to greater exaggerations of the plan, and gradually filled their minds with angry suspicions that it was concealed on account of the extensive benefits it was to confer. Liberty seemed to be offered from England, and pushed aside by their masters and rulers at Demerara. This irritation could not escape the observation of Mr. Smith, and instead of concealing it, he early imparted it to a neighbouring manager and attorney. How comes the Honourable Gentleman to have entirely omitted the evidence of Mr. Stewart?* It appears from his testimony, that Mr. Smith, several weeks before the revolt, communicated to him, (Stewart) the manager of plantation Success, that alarming rumours about the Instructions prevailed among the negroes. It appears that Mr. Smith went publicly with his friend Mr. Elliott, another missionary, to Mr. Stewart, to repeat the information at a subsequent period; and that, in consequence, Mr. Stewart, with Mr. Cort, the attorney of plantation Success, went on the 8th of August to Mr. Smith, who confirmed his previous statements,—said that Quamina and other negroes had asked whether their freedom had come out,—and mentioned that he had some thoughts of disabusing them, by telling them from the pulpit that their expectations of freedom were erroneous. Mr. Cort dis-

* Kelynge, p. 22.

* Trial, &c., p. 47.

suaded him from taking so much upon himself. Is it not evident from this testimony, that Mr. Smith had the reverse of an intention to conceal the dangerous agitation on or before the 8th of August? It is certain that all evidence of his privity or participation before that day must be false. He then told all that he knew, and offered to do much more than he was bound to do. His disclosures were of a nature to defeat a project of revolt, or to prevent it from being formed;—he enabled Cort or Stewart to put the Government on their guard. He told no particulars, because he knew none; but he put it into the power of others to discover them if they existed. He made these discoveries on the 8th of August: what could have changed his previous system of conduct in the remaining ten days? Nay, more, he put it out of his own power to change his conduct effectually: it no longer depended on himself whether what he knew should not be so perfectly made known to the Government as to render all subsequent concealment ineffectual. He could not even know on the 17th whether his conversations with Stewart and Cort had not been communicated to the Governor, and whether measures had not been taken, which had either ascertained that the agitation no longer generally prevailed, or had led to such precautions as could not fail to end in the destruction of those who should deliberately and criminally conceal the designs of the insurgents. The crime of misprision consists in a design to deceive,—which, after such a disclosure, it was impossible to harbour. If this had related to the communication of a formed plan, it might be said, that the disclosure to private persons was not sufficient, and that he was bound to make it to the higher authorities. I believe Mr. Cort was a member of the Court of Policy. [Here Mr. Gladstone intimated by a shake of his head that Mr. Cort was not.] I yield to the local knowledge of my Honourable Friend—if I may venture to call him so in our present belligerent relations. If Mr. Cort be not a member of the Court of Policy, he must have had access to its members:—he stated to Mr. Smith the reason of their delay to promulgate the Instructions; and in a communication which related merely to general agitation, Mr. Smith could not have chosen two persons more likely to be on the alert about a revolt of slaves than the manager and attorney of a neighbouring plantation. Stewart and Cort were also officers of militia.

A very extraordinary part of this case appears in the Demerara Papers (No. II.) to which I have already adverted. Hamilton, the manager of plantation Ressouvenir, had, it seems, a negro mistress, from whom few of his secrets were hid. This lady had the singularly inappropriate name of Susannah. I am now told that she had been the wife of Jack, one of the leaders of the revolt—I have no wish to penetrate into his domestic misfortunes;—at all events, Jack kept up a constant and confidential intercourse with his former friend, even in the elevated station which she had attained. She told him (if we may believe both him and her) of all Hamilton's conversations. By the account of Paris, it seems that Hamilton had instructed them to destroy the bridges. Susannah said that he entreated them to delay the revolt for two weeks, till he could remove his things. They told Hamilton not only of the intention to rise three weeks before, but of the particular time. On Monday morning Hamilton told her, that it was useless for him to manumit her and her children, as she wished, for that all would soon be free; and that the Governor kept back the Instructions because he was himself a slave-owner. Paris and Jack agree in laying to Hamilton's charge the deepest participation in their criminal designs. If this evidence was believed, why was not Hamilton brought to trial rather than Smith? If it was disbelieved, as the far greater part of it must have been, why was it concealed from Smith that such wicked falsehoods had been contrived against another man,—a circumstance which so deeply affects the credit of all the negro accomplices, who swore to save their own lives. If, as I am inclined to believe, some communications were made through Susannah, how hard was the fate of Mr. Smith, who suffers for not promulgating some general notions of danger, which, from this instance, must have entered through many channels into the minds of the greater number of whites. But, up to the 17th of August, it appears that Mr. Smith did not content himself with bare disclosure, but proffered his services to allay discontent, and showed more solicitude than any other person known to us, to preserve the peace of the community.

The question now presents itself, which I allow constitutes the vital part of this case,—Whether any communication was made to Mr. Smith on the evening of Sunday the 17th, of which the concealment from his superiors was equivalent to what we call misprision of treason? No man can conscientiously vote against the motion who does not consider the affirmative as proved. I do not say that this would be of itself sufficient to negative the motion; I only say, that it is indispensably necessary. There would still remain behind the illegality of the jurisdiction, as well as the injustice of the punishment. And on this latter most important part of the case I must here remark, that it would not be sufficient to tell us, that the Roman and Dutch law ranked misprision as a species of treason, and made it punishable by death. It must be shown, not only that the Court were by this law entitled to condemn Mr. Smith to death, but that they were also bound to pronounce such a sentence. For if they had any discretion, it will not be said that an English court-martial ought not to regulate the exercise of it by the more humane and reasonable principles of their own law, which does not treat misprision as a capital offence.

. . . I am sorry to see that the Honourable Agent for Demerara* has quitted his usual place, and has taken a very important position. I feel no ill-will; but I dread the sight of him when pouring poison into the ears of the powerful. He is but too formidable in his ordinary station, at the head of those troops whom his magical wand brings into battle in such numbers as no eloquence can match, and no influence but his own can command. . . . .

Let us now consider the evidence of what passed on the 17th of August. And here, once more, let me conjure the House to consider the condition of the witnesses who gave that evidence. They were accomplices in the revolt, who had no chance of life but what acceptable testimony might afford.—They knew the fierce, furious hatred, which the ruling party had vowed against Mr. Smith. They were surrounded by the skeletons of their brethren: — they could perhaps hear the lash resounding on the bloody backs of others, who were condemned to suffer a thousand lashes, and to work for life in irons under the burning sun of Guiana. They lived in a colony where such unexampled barbarities were inflicted as a mitigated punishment, and held out as acts of mercy. Such were the dreadful terrors which acted on their minds, and under the mental torture of which every syllable of their testimony was uttered. There was still another deduction to be made from their evidence:—they spoke to no palpable facts; they gave evidence only of conversation. "Words," says Mr. Justice Foster, "are transient and fleeting as the wind; frequently the effects of a sudden transport easily misunderstood, and often misreported." If he spoke thus of words used in the presence of witnesses intelligent, enlightened, and accustomed to appreciate the force and distinctions of terms, what would he have said of the evidence of negro slaves, accomplices in the crime, trembling for their lives, reporting conversations of which the whole effect might depend on the shades and gradations of words in a language very grossly known to them,—of English words, uttered in a few hurried moments, and in the presence of no other witnesses from whom they could dread an exposure of their falsehood? It may be safely affirmed, that it is difficult for imagination to conceive admissible evidence of lower credit, and more near the verge of utter rejection.

But what, after all, is the sum of the evidence? It is, that the negroes who followed Mr. Smith from church on Sunday the 17th, spoke to him of some design which they entertained for the next day. It is not pretended that time, or place, or persons, were mentioned: — the contrary is sworn. Mr. Smith, who was accustomed for six weeks to their murmurs, and had before been successful in dissuading them from violence, contents himself with repeating the same dissuasives,—believes he has again succeeded in persuading them to remain quiet,—and abstains for twenty-four hours from any new communication of designs altogether vague and undigested, which he hoped would evaporate, as others of the same kind had done, without any serious effects. The very utmost that he seems to have apprehended was, a plan for obliging, or "driving," as they called it, their managers to join in an application to the Governor on the subject of the new law, —a kind of proceeding which had more than once occurred, both under the Dutch and English governments. It appears from the witnesses for the prosecution, that they had more than once gone to Mr. Smith before on the same subject, and that his answer was always the same; and that some of the more exasperated negroes were so dissatisfied with his exhortations to submission, that they cried out, "Mr. Smith was making them fools,—that he would not deny his own colour for the sake of black people." Quamina appears to have shown at all times a more than ordinary deference towards his pastor. He renewed these conversations on the evening of Sunday the 17th, and told Mr. Smith, who again exhorted them to patience, that two of the more violent negroes, Jack and Joseph, spoke of taking their liberty by force. I desire it to be particularly observed, that this intention, or even violent language, appears to have been attributed only to two, and that in such a manner as naturally to exclude the rest. Mr. Smith again repeated the advice which had hitherto proved efficacious. "He told them to wait, and not to be so foolish. How do you mean that they should take it by force? You cannot do any thing with the white people, because the soldiers will be more strong than you; therefore you had better wait. You had better go and tell the people, and Christians particularly, that they had better have nothing to do with it." When Mr. Smith spoke of the resistance of the soldiers, Quamina, with an evident view to persuade Mr. Smith that nothing was intended which would induce the military to proceed to the last extremity, observed, that they would drive the managers to town; which, by means of the expedient of a general "strike" or refusal to work, appears to have been the project spoken of by most of the slaves. To this observation Mr. Smith justly answered, that even if they did "drive" the managers to town, they "would not be able to go against the soldiers," who would very properly resist such tumultuary and dangerous movements. Be it again observed, that Bristol, the chief witness for the prosecution, clearly distinguishes this plan from that of Jack and Joseph, "who intended to fight with the white people." I do not undertake to determine whether the more desperate measure was at that time

* Mr. William Holmes, who was also the Treasury "whipper-in," was for the moment seated next, and whispering to, Mr. Canning.—Ed.

confined to these two men: it is sufficient for me that such was the representation made to Mr. Smith. Whoever fairly compares the evidence of Bristol with that of Seaton will, I think, find the general result to be such as I have now stated. It is true, that there are contradictions between them, which, in the case of witnesses of another caste, might be considered as altogether subversive of their credit. But I make allowance for their fears, —for their confusion,—for their habitual inaccuracy, — for their ignorance of the language,—for their own incorrectness, if they gave evidence in English,—for that of the interpreters, if they employed any other language. In return, I expect that no fair opponent will rely on minute circumstances,—that he will also allow the benefit of all chances of inaccuracy to the accused,—and that he will not rely on the manner, where a single word, mistaken or misremembered, might make the whole difference between the most earnest and the faintest dissuasive.

I do not know what other topics Mr. Smith could have used. He appeals to their prudence: "the soldiers," says he, "will overcome your vain revolt." He appeals to their sense of religion:—"as Christians you ought not to use violence." What argument remained, if both these failed? What part of human nature could he have addressed, where neither danger could deter, nor duty restrain? He spoke to their conscience and to their fears:—surely admonition could go no further. There is not the least appearance that these topics were not urged with as perfect good faith, as they must have been in those former instances where he demonstrated his sincerity by the communications which he made to Stewart and Cort. His temper of mind on this subject continued, then, to be the same on the evening of the 17th that it had been before. And, if so, how absolutely incredible it is, that he should, on that night, and on the succeeding morning, advisedly, coolly, and malignantly, form the design of hiding a treasonable plot confidentially imparted to him by the conspirators, in order to lull the vigilance of the Government, and commit himself and his countrymen to the mercy of exasperated and triumphant slaves!

I have already stated the reasons which might have induced him to believe that he had once more succeeded in dissuading the negroes from violence. Was he inexcusable in overrating his own ascendant,—in overestimating the docility of his converts,—in relying more on the efficacy of his religious instructions than men of more experience and colder temper would deem reasonable? I entreat the House to consider whether this self-deception be improbable; for if he believed that he had been successful, and that the plan of tumult or revolt was abandoned, would it not have been the basest and most atrocious treachery to have given such information as might have exposed the defenceless slaves to punishments of unparalleled cruelty, for offences which they had meditated, but from which he believed that he had reclaimed them? Let me for a moment again remind the House of the facts which give such weight to this consideration. He lived in a colony where, for an insurrection in which no white man was wantonly or deliberately put to death, and no property was intentionally destroyed or even damaged, I know not how many negroes perished on the gibbet, and others,—under the insolent, atrocious, detestable pretext of mercy!—suffered a thousand lashes, and were doomed to hard labour in irons for life, under the burning sun, and among the pestilential marshes of Guiana? These dreadful cruelties, miscalled punishments, did indeed occur after the 17th of August. But he, whose "heart had fluttered from the incessant cracking of the whip," must have strongly felt the horrors to which he was exposing his unhappy flock by a hasty or needless disclosure of projects excited by the impolitic delay of their rulers. Every good man must have wished to find the information unnecessary. Would not Mr. Smith have been the most unworthy of pastors, if he had not desired that such a cup might pass from him? And if he felt these benevolent desires,—if he recoiled with horror from putting these poor men into the hands of what in Demerara is called justice, there was nothing in the circumstances which might not have seemed to him to accord with his wishes. Even without the influence of warm feeling, I do not think that it would have been unreasonable for any man to believe that the negroes had fully agreed to wait. Nay, I am convinced that with Quamina Mr. Smith was successful. Quamina, I believe, used his influence to prevent the revolt; and it was not till after he was apprehended on Monday, on unjust suspicions, and was rescued, that he took refuge among the revolters, and was at last shot by the soldiery when he was a runaway in the forest,—a fact which was accepted by the Court-martial as the sufficient, though sole, evidence of his being a ringleader in the rebellion.

The whole period during which it is necessary to account for Mr. Smith's not communicating to the Government an immature project, of which he knew no particulars, and which he might well believe to be abandoned, is a few hours in the morning of Monday; for it is proved by the evidence of Hamilton, that he was informed of the intended revolt by a Captain Simson, at one o'clock of that day, in George-Town, the seat of government, at some miles distant from the scene of action. It was then so notorious, that Hamilton never dreamt of troubling the Governor with such needless intelligence; yet this was only four or five hours later than the time when Mr. Smith was held to be bound, under pain of death, to make such a communication! The Governor himself, in his dispatches, said that he had received the information, but did not believe it.* This disbelief, however, could not have been of long duration; for active measures were taken, and Mr. Stewart apprehended Quamina and his son Jack a little after three o'clock on Monday; which, considering the distance, necessarily implies that some general order of that nature had been issued by the Government at George-Town not long after noon on that day.† As all these proceedings occurred before Mr. Smith received the note from Jack of Dochfour about half an hour before the revolt, I lay that fact out of the case, as wholly immaterial. The interview of Mr. Smith with Quamina, on the 19th of August, is negatived by the finding of the Court-martial:—that on the 20th will be relied on by no man in this House, because there is not the slightest proof, nor, indeed, probability, that the conversation at that interview was not perfectly innocent. Nothing, then, called for explanation but the conversation of Sunday evening, and the silence of Monday morning, which I think I have satisfactorily explained, as fully as my present strength will allow, and much more so than the speech of my Learned Friend left it necessary to do.

There is one other circumstance which occurred on Sunday, and which I cannot pass over in silence:—it is the cruel perversion of the beautiful text from the Gospel on which Mr. Smith preached his last sermon. That circumstance alone evinces the incurable prejudice against this unfortunate man, which so far blinded his prosecutors, that they actually represent him as choosing that most affecting lamentation over the fall of Jerusalem, in order to excite the slaves to accomplish the destruction of Demerara. The lamentation of one who loved a country was by them thought to be selected to stimulate those who were to destroy a country;—as if tragical reprehensions of the horrors of an assault were likely to be exhibited in the camp of the assailants the night before they were to storm a city. It is wonderful that these prosecutors should not have perceived that such a choice of a text would have been very natural for Mr. Smith, only on the supposition that he had been full of love and compassion and alarm for the European inhabitants of Demerara. The simple truth was, that the estate was about to be sold, the negroes to be scattered over the colony by auction, and that,—by one of those somewhat forced analogies, which may appear to me unreasonable, but which men of the most sublime genius as well as fervent piety have often applied to the interpretation of Scripture,—he likened their sad dispersion, in connection with their past neglect of the means of improvement, and the chance of their now losing all religious consolation and instruction, to the punishment inflicted on the Jews by the conquest and destruction of Jerusalem.

In what I have now addressed to the House, I have studiously abstained from all discussions of those awful questions which relate to the general structure of colonial society. I am as adverse as any one to the sudden emancipation of slaves,—much out of regard to the masters, but still more, as affecting a far larger portion of mankind, out of regard to the unhappy slaves themselves. Emancipation by violence and revolt I consider as the greatest calamity that can visit a community, except perpetual slavery. I should not have so deep an abhorrence of that wretched state, if I did not regard it as unfitting slaves for the safe exercise of the common rights of mankind. I should be grossly inconsistent with myself, if, believing this corrupt and degrading power of slavery over the mind to be the worst of all its evils, I were not very fearful of changes which would set free those beings, whom a cruel yoke had transformed into wild beasts, only that they might tear and devour each other. I acknowledge that the pacific emancipation of great multitudes thus wretchedly circumstanced is a problem so arduous as to perplex and almost silence the reason of man. Time is undoubtedly necessary; and I shall never object to time if it be asked in good faith. If I be convinced of the sincerity of the reformer, I will not object to the reformation merely on account of the time which it requires. But I have a right to be jealous of every attempt which, under pretence of asking time for reformation, may only aim at evading urgent demands, and indefinitely procrastinating the deliverance of men from bondage.

And here, Sir, I should naturally close; but I must be permitted to relate the subsequent treatment of Mr. Smith, because it reflects back the strongest light on the intentions and dispositions of those who prosecuted him, and of those who ratified the sentence of death. They who can cruelly treat the condemned, are not in general scrupulous about convicting the innocent. I have seen the widow of this unhappy sufferer,—a pious and amiable woman, worthy to be the helpmate of her martyred husband, distinguished by a calm and clear understanding, and, as far as I could discover, of great accuracy, anxious rather to understate facts, and to counteract every lurking disposition to exaggerate, of which her judgment and humility might lead her to suspect herself. She told me her story with temper and simplicity; and, though I ventured more near to cross examination in my inquiries than delicacy would, perhaps, in any less important case have warranted, I saw not the least rea son to distrust the exactness, any more than the honesty, of her narrative. Within a few days of his apprehension, Mr. Smith and his wife were closely confined in two small rooms at the top of a building, with only the outward roof between them and the sun, when the thermometer in the shade at their residence in the country stood at an average of

* Demerara Papers, No. II. p. 1. † Ibid., p. 70.

eighty-three degrees of Fahrenheit. There they were confined from August to October, with two sentries at the door, which was kept open day and night. These sentries, who were relieved every two hours, had orders at every relief to call on the prisoner, to ascertain by his answer that he had not escaped. The generality, of course, executed their orders: "a few, more humane," said Mrs. Smith, "contented themselves during the night with quietly looking into the bed." Thus was he, under a mortal disease, and his wife, with all the delicacy of her sex, confined for two months, without seeing a human face except those of the sentries, and of the absolutely necessary attendants:—no physician, no friends to console, no legal adviser to guide the prisoner to the means of proving his innocence, no mitigation, no solace! The first human face which she saw, was that of the man who came to bear tidings of accusation, and trial, and death, to her husband. I asked her, "whether it was possible that the Governor knew that they were in this state of desolation?" She answered, "that she did not know, for nobody came to inquire after them!" He was afterwards removed to apartments on the ground floor, the damp of which seems to have hastened his fate. Mrs. Smith was set at large, but obliged to ask a daily permission to see her husband for a limited time, and if I remember right, before witnesses! After the packet had sailed, and when there was no longer cause to dread their communication with England, she was permitted to have unrestricted access to him, as long as his intercourse with earthly things endured. At length he was mercifully released from his woes. The funeral was ordered to take place at two o'clock in the morning, that no sorrowing negroes might follow the good man's corpse. The widow desired to accompany the remains of her husband to the grave:—even this sad luxury was prohibited. The officer declared that his instructions were peremptory: Mrs. Smith bowed with the silent submission of a broken heart. Mrs. Elliot, her friend and companion, not so borne down by sorrow, remonstrated. "Is it possible," she said, "That General Murray can have forbidden a poor widow from following the coffin of her husband." The officer again answered that his orders were peremptory. "At all events," said Mrs. Elliot, "he cannot hinder us from meeting the coffin at the grave." Two negroes bore the coffin, with a single lantern going before; and at four o'clock in the morning, the two women met it in silent anguish at the grave, and poured over the remains of the persecuted man that tribute which nature pays to the memory of those whom we love. Two negro workmen, a carpenter and a bricklayer,—who had been members of his congregation,—were desirous of being permitted to protect and distinguish the spot where their benefactor reposed:—

"That ev'n his bones from insult to protect,
Some frail memorial, still erected nigh,
With uncouth rhymes and shapeless sculpture deckt,
Might claim the passing tribute of a sigh."*

They began to rail in and to brick over the grave: but as soon as this intelligence reached the First Fiscal, his Honour was pleased to forbid the work; he ordered the bricks to be taken up, the railing to be torn down, and the whole frail memorial of gratitude and piety to be destroyed!

"English vengeance wars not with the dead:"—it is not so in Guiana. As they began, so they concluded; and at least it must be owned that they were consistent in their treatment of the living and of the dead. They did not stop here: a few days after the death of Mr. Smith, they passed a vote of thanks to Mr. President Wray, for his services during the insurrection, which, I fear, consisted entirely in his judicial acts as a member of the Court-martial. It is the single instance, I believe, in the history of the world, where a popular meeting thanked a judge for his share in a trial which closed with a sentence of death! I must add, with sincere regret, that Mr. Wray, in an unadvised moment, accepted these tainted thanks, and expressed his gratitude for them. Shortly after they did their utmost to make him repent, and be ashamed of his rashness. I hold in my hand a Demerara newspaper, containing an account of a meeting, which must have been held with the knowledge of the Governor, and among whom I see nine names, which from the prefix "Honourable," belong, I presume, to persons who were members either of the Court of Justice or of the Court of Policy. It was an assembly which must be taken to represent the colony. Their first proceeding was a Declaration of Independence:—they resolved, that the King and Parliament of Great Britain had no right to change their laws without the consent of their Court of Policy. They founded this pretension,—which would be so extravagant and insolent, if it were not so ridiculous,—on the first article of the Capitulation now lying before me, bearing date on the 19th of September, 1803, by which it was stipulated that no new establishments should be introduced without the consent of the Court of Policy,—as if a military commander had any power to perpetuate the civil constitution of a conquered country, and as if the subsequent treaty had not ceded Demerara in full sovereignty to his Majesty. I should have disdained to notice such a declaration if it were not for what followed. This meeting took place eighteen days after the death of Mr. Smith. It might be hoped, that, if their hearts were not touched by his fate, at least their hatred might have been buried in his grave; but they showed how little chance of justice he had when living

* Gray's Elegy.—Ed.

within the sphere of their influence, by their rancorous persecution of his memory after death. Eighteen days after he had expired in a dungeon, they passed a resolution of strong condemnation against two names not often joined,—the London Missionary Society and Lord Bathurst;—the Society, because they petitioned for mercy (for that is a crime in their eyes),—Lord Bathurst, because he advised His Majesty to dispense it to Mr. Smith. With an ignorance suitable to their other qualities, they consider the exercise of mercy as a violation of justice. They are not content with persecuting their victim to death; —they arraign nature, which released him, and justice, in the form of mercy, which would have delivered him out of their hands. Not satisfied with his life, they are incensed at not being able to brand his memory,—to put an ignominious end to his miseries, and to hang up his skeleton on a gibbet, which, as often as it waved in the winds, should warn every future missionary to fly from such a shore, and not dare to enter that colony to preach the doctrines of peace, of justice, and of mercy!

SPEECH

ON PRESENTING A PETITION FROM THE MERCHANTS OF LONDON FOR THE RECOGNITION OF

THE INDEPENDENT STATES

ESTABLISHED IN THE COUNTRIES OF AMERICA FORMERLY SUBJECT TO SPAIN.

DELIVERED IN THE HOUSE OF COMMONS, ON THE 15TH OF JUNE, 1824.

Scit . . . . . .
Unde petat Romam, libertas ultima mundi
Quo steterit ferienda loco.—*Pharsalia*, lib. vii. 579.

"As for the wars anciently made on behalf of a parity or tacit conformity of estate,—to set up or pull down democracies and oligarchies,—I do not see how they may be well justified."—Bacon, Essay on the True Greatness of Kingdoms.

Mr. Speaker,—I hold in my hand a Petition from the Merchants of the City of London who are engaged in trade with the countries of America formerly subject to the crown of Spain, praying that the House would adopt such measures as to them may seem meet to induce His Majesty's Government to recognise the independence of the states in those countries which have, in fact, established independent governments.

In presenting this Petition, I think it right to give the House such information as I possess relating to the number and character of the Petitioners, that it may be seen how far they are what they profess to be,—what are their means of knowledge,—what are likely to be the motives of their application,—what faith is due to their testimony, and what weight ought to be allowed to their judgment. Their number is one hundred and seventeen. Each of them is a member of a considerable commercial house interested in the trade to America; the Petition, therefore, conveys the sentiments of three or four hundred merchants. The signatures were collected in two days, without a public meeting, or even an advertisement. It was confined to the American merchants, but the Petitioners have no reason to believe that any merchant in London would have declined to put his name to it. I am but imperfectly qualified to estimate the importance and station of the Petitioners. Judging from common information, I should consider many of them as in the first rank of the mercantile community. I see among them the firm of Baring and Company, which, without disparagement to any others, may be placed at the head of the commercial establishments of the world. I see also the firms of Herring, Powles, and Company; of Richardson and Company; Goldsmid and Company; Montefiore and Company; of Mr. Benjamin Shaw, who, as Chairman of Lloyd's Coffee-house, represents the most numerous and diversified interests of traffic; together with many others not equally known to me, but whom, if I did know, I have no doubt that I might with truth describe as persons of the highest mercantile respectability. I perceive among them the name of Ricardo, which I shall ever honour, and which I cannot now pronounce without emotion.* In a word, the Petitioners are the City of London. They contain individuals of all political parties; they are deeply interested in the subject,—perfectly conversant with all its commercial

* Mr. Ricardo had died on the 11th of September preceding.—Ed.

bearings; and they could not fill the high place where they stand, if they were not as much distinguished by intelligence and probity, as by those inferior advantages of wealth which with them are not fortunate accidents, but proofs of personal worth and professional merit.

If, Sir, it had been my intention to enter fully on this subject, and especially to discuss it adversely to the King's Government, I might have chosen a different form of presenting it to the House. But though I am and ever shall be a member of a party associated, as I conceive, for preserving the liberties of the kingdom, I present this Petition in the spirit of those by whom it is subscribed, in the hope of relieving that anxious desire which pervades the commercial world, —and which is also shared by the people of England,—that the present session may not close without some discussion or some explanation on this important subject, as far as that explanation can be given without inconvenience to the public service. For such a purpose, the presentation of a petition affords a convenient opportunity, both because it implies the absence of any intention to blame the past measures of Government as foreign from the wishes of the Petitioners, and because it does not naturally require to be followed by any motion which might be represented as an invasion of the prerogative of the Crown, or as a restraint on the discretion of its constitutional advisers.

At the same time I must add, that in whatever form or at whatever period of the session I had brought this subject forward, I do not think that I should have felt myself called upon to discuss it in a tone very different from that which the nature of the present occasion appears to me to require. On a question of policy, where various opinions may be formed about the past, and where the only important part is necessarily prospective, I should naturally have wished to speak in a deliberative temper. However much I might lament the delays which had occurred in the recognition of the American States, I could hardly have gone further than strongly to urge that the time was now at least come for more decisive measures.

With respect, indeed, to the State Papers laid before us, I see nothing in them to blame or to regret, unless it be that excess of tenderness and forbearance towards the feelings and pretensions of European Spain which the Despatches themselves acknowledge. In all other respects, I can only describe them as containing a body of liberal maxims of policy and just principles of public law, expressed with a precision, a circumspection, and a dignity which will always render them models and master-pieces of diplomatic composition.* Far from assailing these valuable documents, it is my object to uphold their doctrines, to reason from their principles, and to contend for nothing more than that the future policy of England on this subject may be governed by them. On them I rest: from them seems to me to flow every consequence respecting the future, which I think most desirable. I should naturally have had no other task than that of quoting them, of showing the stage to which they had conducted the question, of unfolding their import where they are too short for the generality of readers, and of enforcing their application to all that yet remains undone. But something more is made necessary by the confusion and misconception which prevail on one part of this subject. I have observed with astonishment, that persons otherwise well informed should here betray a forgetfulness of the most celebrated events in history, and an unacquaintance with the plainest principles of international law, which I should not have thought possible if I had not known it to be real. I am therefore obliged to justify these State Papers before I appeal to them. I must go back for a moment to those elementary principles which are so grossly misunderstood.

And first, Sir, with respect to the term "recognition," the introduction of which into these discussions has proved the principal occasion of darkness and error. It is a term which is used in two senses so different from each other as to have nothing very important in common. The first, which is the true and legitimate sense of the word "recognition," as a technical term of international law, is that in which it denotes the explicit acknowledgment of the independence of a country by a state which formerly exercised sovereignty over it. Spain has been doomed to exhibit more examples of this species of recognition than any other European state; of which the most memorable cases are her acknowledgment of the independence of Portugal and Holland. This country also paid the penalty of evil councils in that hour of folly and infatuation which led to a hostile separation between the American Colonies and their mother country. Such recognitions are renunciations of sovereignty,—surrenders of the power or of the claim to govern.

But we, who are as foreign to the Spanish states in America as we are to Spain herself, —who never had any more authority over them than over her,—have in this case no claims to renounce, no power to abdicate, no sovereignty to resign, no legal rights to confer. What we have to do is therefore not recognition in its first and most strictly proper sense. It is not by formal stipulations or solemn declarations that we are to recognise the American states, but by measures of practical policy, which imply that we acknowledge their independence. Our recognition is virtual. The most conspicuous part of such a recognition, is the act of sending and receiving diplomatic agents. It implies

* They were among the first papers issued from the Foreign Office, after the accession to office of Mr. Canning, and represented the spirit of *his*—as distinguished from the preceding Castlereagh policy.—Ed.

no guarantee, no alliance, no aid, no approbation of the successful revolt,—no intimation of an opinion concerning the justice or injustice of the means by which it has been accomplished. These are matters beyond our jurisdiction. It would be an usurpation in us to sit in judgment upon them. As a state, we can neither condemn nor justify revolutions which do not affect our safety, and are not amenable to our laws. We deal with the authorities of new states on the same principles and for the same object as with those of old. We consider them as governments actually exercising authority over the people of a country, with whom we are called upon to maintain a regular intercourse by diplomatic agents for the interests of Great Britain, and for the security of British subjects. Antiquity affords a presumption of stability, which, like all other presumptions, may and does fail in particular instances; but in itself it is nothing, and when it ceases to indicate stability, it ought to be regarded by a foreign country as of no account. The tacit recognition of a new state, with which alone I am now concerned, not being a judgment for the new government, or against the old, is not a deviation from perfect neutrality, or a cause of just offence to the dispossessed ruler.* When Great Britain recognised the United States, it was a concession by the recognising Power, the object of which was the advantage and security of the government recognised. But when Great Britain (I hope very soon) recognises the states of Spanish America, it will not be as a concession to them, for they need no such recognition; but it will be for her own sake,—to promote her own interest,—to protect the trade and navigation of her subjects,—to acquire the best means of cultivating friendly relations with important countries, and of composing by immediate negotiation those differences which might otherwise terminate in war. Are these new doctrines?—quite the contrary. They are founded on the ancient practice of Europe. They have been acted upon for more than two centuries by England as well as other nations.

I have already generally alluded, Sir, to the memorable and glorious revolt by which the United Provinces of the Netherlands threw off the yoke of Spain. Nearly fourscore years passed from the beginning of that just insurrection to the time when a recognition of independence was at last extorted from Castilian pride and obstinacy. The people of the Netherlands first took up arms to obtain the redress of intolerable grievances; and for many years they forbore from proceeding to the last extremity against their tyrannical king.* It was not till Philip had formally proscribed the Prince of Orange,—the purest and most perfect model of a patriotic hero,—putting a price on his head, and promising not only pardon for every crime, but the honours of nobility to any one who should assassinate him,† that the States-General declared the King of Spain to have forfeited, by a long course of merciless tyranny, his rights of sovereignty over the Netherlands.‡ Several assassins attempted the life of the good and great Prince of Orange: one wounded him dangerously; another consummated the murder,—a zealot of what was then, as it is now, called "legitimacy." He suffered the punishment due to his crime; but the King of Spain bestowed

* These doctrines are so indisputable, that they are not controverted even by the jurists of the Holy Alliance, whose writings in every other respect bear the most ignominious marks of the servitude of the human understanding under the empire of that confederacy. Martens, who in the last edition of his Summary of International Law has sacrificed even the principle of national independence (liv. iii. c. ii. s. 74), without which no such law could be conceived, yet speaks as follows on recognitions:—" Quant à la simple reconnaissance, il semble qu'une nation etrangère, n'étant pas obligée à juger de la légitimité, peut toutes les fois qu'elle est douteuse se permettre de s'attacher au seul fait de la possession, et traiter comme indépendant de son ancien gouvernement, l'état ou la province qui jouit dans le fait de l'indépendance, sans blesser par là les devoirs d'une rigoureuse neutralité."—Précis du Droit des Gens, liv. iii. c. ii. s. 80. Göttingen, 1821. Yet a comparison of the above sentence with the parallel passage of the same book in the edition of 1789 is a mortifying specimen of the decline of liberty of opinion in Europe. Even Kluber, the publisher of the proceedings of the Congress of Vienna, assents to the same doctrine, though he insidiously contrives the means of evading it by the insertion of one or two ambiguous words:—" La souveraineté est acquise par un état, ou lors de sa fondation ou bien lorsqu'il se dégage légitimement de la dépendance dans laquelle il se trouvait. Pour être valide, elle n'a pas besoin d'être reconnue ou garantie par une puissance quelconque: pourvu que la possession ne soit pas *vicieuse*."—Droit des Gens, part i. c. i. s. 23. Mr. Kluber would find it difficult to answer the question, " Who is to judge whether the acquisition of independence be *legitimate*, or its possession *vicious*?" And it is evident that the latter qualification is utterly unmeaning; for if there be an original fault, which vitiates the possession of independence, it cannot be removed by foreign recognition, which, according to this writer himself, is needless where the independence is lawful, and must therefore be useless in those cases where he insinuates rather than asserts that foreign states are bound or entitled to treat it as unlawful.

* The following are the words of their illustrious historian:—" Post longam dubitationem, ab ordinibus Belgarum Philippo, ob violatas leges, imperium abrogatum est; lataque in illum sententia cum quo, si verum fatemur, novem jam per annos bellatum erat; sed tunc primum desitum nomen ejus et insignia usurpari, mutataque verba solennis jurisjurandi, ut qui princeps hactenus erat: hostis vocaretur. Hoc consilium *vicinas apud gentes necessitate et tot irritis ante precibus excusatum*, haud desiere Hispani ut scelus insectari, parum memores, pulsum a majoribus suis regno invisæ crudelitatis regem, eique prælatam stirpem non ex legibus genitam; ut jam taceantur vetera apud Francos, minus vetera apud Anglos, recentiora apud Danos et Sueonas dejectorum regum exempla."—Grotii Annales, lib. iii.

† Dumont, Corps Diplomatique, vol. v. p. 368.

‡ Ibid. p. 413.

on his family the infamous nobility which had been earned by the assassin,—an example which has also disgraced our age. Before and after that murder, the greatest vicissitudes of fortune had attended the arms of those who fought for the liberties of their country. Their chiefs were driven into exile; their armies were dispersed. The greatest and most opulent of the Belgic Provinces, misled by priests, had made their peace with the tyrant. The greatest captains of the age commanded against them. The Duke of Alva employed his valour and experience to quell the revolts which had been produced by his cruelty. The genius of the Prince of Parma long threatened the infant liberty of Holland. Spinola balanced the consummate ability of Prince Maurice, and kept up an equal contest, till Gustavus Adolphus rescued Europe from the Holy Allies of that age. The insurgents had seen with dread the armament called "Invincible," which was designed, by the conquest of England, to destroy the last hopes of the Netherlands. Their independence appeared more than once to be annihilated; it was often endangered; it was to the last fiercely contested. The fortune of war was as often adverse as favourable to their arms.

It was not till the 30th of January, 1648,* nearly eight years after the revolt, nearly seventy after the declaration of independence, that the Crown of Spain, by the Treaty of Munster, recognised the Republic of the United Provinces, and renounced all pretensions to sovereignty over their territory. What, during that long period, was the policy of the European states? Did they wait for eighty years, till the obstinate punctilio or lazy pedantry of the Escurial was subdued? Did they forego all the advantages of friendly intercourse with a powerful and flourishing republic? Did they withhold from that republic the ordinary courtesy of keeping up a regular and open correspondence with her through avowed and honourable ministers? Did they refuse to their own subjects that protection for their lives and properties, which such a correspondence alone could afford?

All this they ought to have done, according to the principles of those who would resist the prayer of the Petition in my hand. But nothing of this was then done or dreamt of. Every state in Europe, except the German branch of the House of Austria, sent ministers to the Hague, and received those of the States-General. Their friendship was prized,—their alliance courted; and defensive treaties were formed with them by Powers at peace with Spain, from the heroic Gustavus Adolphus to the barbarians of Persia and Muscovy. I say nothing of Elizabeth herself,—proscribed as she was as an usurper,—the stay of Holland, and the leader of the liberal party throughout Europe. But no one can question the authority on this point of her successor,—the great professor of legitimacy,—the founder of that doctrine of the divine right of kings, which led his family to destruction. As king of Scotland, in 1594, forty-four years before the recognition by Spain, James recognised the States-General as the successors of the Houses of Austria and Burgundy, by stipulating with them the renewal of a treaty concluded between his mother Queen Mary and the Emperor Charles V.* In 1604, when he made peace with Spain, eager as he was by that transaction to be admitted into the fraternity of legitimate kings, he was so far curbed by the counsellors of Elizabeth, that he adhered to his own and to her recognition of the independence of Holland: the Court of Madrid virtually acknowledging, by several articles of the treaty,† that such perseverance in the recognition was no breach of neutrality, and no obstacle to friendship with Spain. At the very moment of the negotiation, Winwood was despatched with new instructions as minister to the States-General. It is needless to add that England, at peace with Spain, continued to treat Holland as an independent state for the forty-four years which passed from that treaty to the recognition of Munster.

The policy of England towards Portugal, though in itself far less memorable, is still more strikingly pertinent to the purpose of this argument. On the 1st of December 1640, the people of Portugal rose in arms against the tyranny of Spain, under which they had groaned about sixty years. They seated the Duke of Braganza on the throne. In January 1641, the Cortes of the kingdom were assembled to legalize his authority, though seldom convoked by his successors after their power was consolidated. Did England then wait the pleasure of Spain? Did she desist from connection with Portugal, till it appeared from long experience that the attempts of Spain to recover that country must be unavailing? Did she even require that the Braganza Government should stand the test of time before she recognised its independent authority? No: within a year of the proclamation of the Duke of Braganza by the Cortes, a treaty of peace and alliance was signed at Windsor between Charles I. and John IV., which not only treats with the latter as an independent sovereign, but expressly speaks of the King of Castile as a dispossessed ruler; and alleges on the part of the King of England, that he was moved to conclude this treaty *"by his solicitude to preserve the tranquillity of his kingdoms, and to secure the liberty of trade of his beloved subjects."*‡ The contest was carried on: the Spaniards obtained victories; they excited conspiracies; they created divisions.

* Dumont, vol. vi. p. 429.

* Dumont, vol. v. p. 507.

† See particularly Art. xii. and xiv. in Rymer, vol. xvi. The extreme anxiety of the English to adhere to their connection with Holland, appears from the Instructions and Despatches in Winwood.

‡ Dumont, vol. vi. p. 238.

The palace of the King of Portugal was the scene of domestic discord, court intrigue, and meditated usurpation. There is no trace of any complaint or remonstrance, or even murmur, against the early recognition by England, though it was not till twenty-six years afterwards that Spain herself acknowledged the independence of Portugal, and (what is remarkable) made that acknowledgment in a treaty concluded under the mediation of England.*

To these examples let me add an observation upon a part of the practice of nations, strongly illustrative of the principles which ought to decide this question. All the Powers of Europe treated England, under the Commonwealth and the Protectorate, as retaining her rights of sovereignty. They recognised these governments as much as they had recognised the Monarchy. The friends of Charles II. did not complain of this policy. That monarch, when restored, did not disallow the treaties of foreign Powers with the Republic or with Cromwell. Why? Because these Powers were obliged, for the interest of their own subjects, to negotiate with the government which, whatever might be its character, was actually obeyed by the British nation. They pronounced no opinion on the legitimacy of that government,—no judgment unfavourable to the claims of the exiled prince; they consulted only the security of the commerce and intercourse of their own subjects with the British Islands.

It was quite otherwise with the recognition by Louis XIV. of the son of James II., when his father died, as King of Great Britain. As that prince was not acknowledged and obeyed in England, no interest of France required that Louis should maintain an intercourse, or take any notice of his pretensions. That recognition was therefore justly resented by England as a wanton insult,—as a direct interference in her internal affairs,—as an assumption of authority to pronounce against the lawfulness of her government.†

I am aware, Sir, that our complaints of the interference of France in the American war may be quoted against my argument. Those who glance over the surface of history may see some likeness between that case and the present: but the resemblance is merely superficial; it disappears on the slightest examination. It was not of the establishment of diplomatic relations with America by France in 1778, that Great Britain complained. We now know from the last edition of the Memoirs of the Marquis de Bouillé, that from the first appearance of discontent in 1765, the Duc de Choiseul employed secret agents to excite commotion in North America. That gallant and accomplished officer himself was no stranger to these intrigues after the year 1768, when he became governor of Guadaloupe.* It is well known that the same clandestine and treacherous machinations were continued to the last, in a time of profound peace, and in spite of professions of amity so repeated and so solemn, that the breach of them produced a more than political resentment in the mind of King George III. against the House of Bourbon. We also learn, from no contemptible authority, that at the very time that the preliminaries of peace were signed at Fontainbleau in 1762 by the Duc de Choiseul and the Duke of Bedford, the former of these ministers concluded a secret treaty with Spain, by which it was stipulated, that in eight years both Powers should attack England;—a design of which the removal of Choiseul defeated the execution.† The recognition of the United States was no more than the consummation and avowal of these dark designs. So conscious was the Court of Versailles of their own perfidy, that they expected war to be the immediate consequence of it. On the same day with the treaty of commerce they signed another secret treaty,‡ by which it was stipulated, that in case of hostilities between France and England, America should make common cause with the former. The division of the territories to be conquered was even provided for. Negligent and supine as were the English Ministers, they can hardly be supposed to have been altogether ignorant of these secret treaties. The cause of war, then, was not a mere recognition after a long warning to the mother country,—after a more than generous forbearance shown to her dignity and claims (as it would be now in the case with Spanish America): it was that France, in defiance of the most solemn assurances of her Ministers, and also as it is said of her Sovereign, at length openly avowed those machinations to destroy the union between the British nation and the people of America,—Englishmen by blood, and freemen by principle, dear to us by both ties, but most dear by the last,—which they had carried on during so many years of peace and pretended friendship.

I now proceed to review the progress which we have already made towards the

* Treaty of Lisbon, February 23d, 1688. Dumont, vol. vii. p. 70.

† "Le Comte de Manchester, ambassadeur d'Angleterre, ne parut plus à Versailles après la reconnaissance du Prince de Galles, et partit, sans prendre congé, quelques jours après l'arrivée du Roi à Fontainbleau. Le Roi Guillaume reçut en sa maison de Loo en Hollande la nouvelle de la mort du Roi Jacques et de cette reconnaissance. Il était alors à table avec quelques autres seigneurs. Il ne proféra pas une seule parole outre la nouvelle; mais il rougit, enfonça son chapeau, et ne put contenir son visage. Il envoya ordre à Londres d'en chasser sur le champ Poussin, et de lui faire repasser la mer aussi-tôt après. Il faisait les affaires du Roi en l'absence d'un ambassadeur et d'un envoyé. Cet éclat fut suivi de près de la signature de la Grande Alliance défensive et offensive contre la France et l'Espagne, entre l'Empereur et l'Empire, l'Angleterre et la Hollande."—Mémoires de St. Simon, vol. iii. p. 228.

* Mémoires de Bouillé, p. 15. Choiseul, Relation du Voyage de Louis XVI. à Varennes, p. 14.

† Ferrand, Trois Démembremens de la Pologne, vol. i. p. 76.

‡ Martens, Recueil de Traités, vol. i. p. 701.

recognition of the states of Spanish America, as it appears in the Papers before the House. I will not dwell on the statute 3 Geo. IV. c. 43, which provides, "that the merchandize of countries in America or the West Indies, *being or having been a part of the dominions of the King of Spain*, may be imported into Great Britain in ships which are the build of these countries;" though that clause must be allowed to be an acknowledgment of independence, unless it could be said that the provinces separated from Spain were either countries without inhabitants, or inhabited by men without a government. Neither will I say any thing of the declaration made to Spain, that consuls must be immediately sent to South America; though I shall hereafter argue, that the appointment of consuls is as much an act of recognition as the appointment of higher ministers. Lord Liverpool indeed said, that by doing so we were "treating South America as independent,"—which is the only species of recognition which we have a right to make. I should be the last to blame the suspension of such a purpose during the lawless and faithless invasion of Spain, then threatened, and soon after executed. So strongly was I convinced that this was a sacred duty, that I at that time declined to present a petition of a nature similar to that which I now offer to your consideration. Nothing under heaven could have induced me to give the slightest aid to the unrighteous violence which then menaced the independence of Spain.

The Despatch of Mr. Secretary Canning to Sir Charles Stuart, of the 31st of March, 1823, is the first paper which I wish to recall to the remembrance, and recommend to the serious attention of the House. It declares that time and events have decided the separation of Spanish America,—that various circumstances in their internal condition may *accelerate or retard* the recognition of their independence; and it concludes with intelligibly intimating that Great Britain would resist the conquest of any part of these provinces by France. The most explicit warning was thus given to Spain, to France, and to all Europe, as well as to the states of Spanish America, that Great Britain considered their independence as certain,—that she regarded the time of recognising it as a question only of policy,—and that she would not suffer foreign Powers to interfere for preventing its establishment. France, indeed, is the only Power named; but the reason of the case applied to every other, and extended as much to conquest *under the name of Spain* as if it were made avowedly for France herself.

The next document to which I shall refer is the Memorandum of a Conference between M. de Polignac and Mr. Secretary Canning, on the 9th of October, 1823; and I cannot help earnestly recommending to all persons who have any doubt with respect to the present state of this question, or to the footing on which it has stood for many months,—who do not see or do not own that our determination has long been made and announced,—to observe with care the force and extent of the language of the British Government on this important occasion.—"The British Government," it is there said, "were of opinion that any attempt to bring Spanish America under its ancient submission must be utterly hopeless; that all negotiation for that purpose would be unsuccessful; and that the prolongation or renewal of war for the same object could be only a waste of human life and an infliction of calamities on both parties to no end." Language cannot more strongly declare the conviction of Great Britain that the issue of the contest was even then no longer doubtful,—that there was indeed no longer any such contest as could affect the policy of foreign states towards America. As soon as we had made known our opinion in terms so positive to Europe and America, the pretensions of Spain could not in point of justice be any reason for a delay. After declaring that we should remain, however, "strictly neutral if war should be unhappily prolonged," we go on to state more explicitly than before, "that the junction of any Power in an enterprise of Spain against the colonies would be viewed as an entirely new question, upon which they must take such decision as the interest of Great Britain might require;"—language which, however cautious and moderate in its forms, is in substance too clear to be misunderstood. After this paragraph, no state in Europe would have had a right to affect surprise at the recognition, if it had been proclaimed on the following day. Still more clearly, if possible, is the same principle avowed in a subsequent paragraph:—"That the British Government had no desire to precipitate the recognition, so long as there was any reasonable chance of an accommodation with the mother country, by which such a recognition might come first from Spain:" but that it could not wait indefinitely for that result; that it could not consent to make its recognition of the new states dependent on that of Spain; "and that it would consider any foreign interference, either by force or by menace, in the dispute between Spain and the colonies, as a motive for recognising the latter without delay." And here in a matter less important I should be willing to stop, and to rest my case on this passage alone. Words cannot be more explicit: it is needless to comment on them, and impossible to evade them. We declare, that the only accommodation which we contemplate, is one which is to terminate in recognition by Spain; and that we cannot indefinitely wait even for that result. We assert our right to recognise, whether Spain does so or not; and we state a case in which we should immediately recognise, independently of the consent of the Spanish Government, and without regard to the internal state of the American provinces. As a natural consequence of these positions, we decline any part in a proposed congress of European Powers for regulating the affairs of America.

Sir, I cannot quit this document without paying a just tribute to that part which relates to commerce,—to the firmness with which it asserts the right of this country to continue her important trade with America, as well as the necessity of the appointment of consuls for the protection of that trade,—and to the distinct annunciation, "that an attempt to renew the obsolete interdictions would be best cut short by a speedy and unqualified recognition of the independence of the South American states." Still more do I applaud the declaration, "that Great Britain had no desire to set up any separate right to the free enjoyment of this trade; that she considered the force of circumstances and the irreversible progress of events to have already determined the question of the existence of that freedom for all the world." These are declarations equally wise and admirable. They coincide indeed so evidently with the well-understood interest of every state, that it is mortifying to be compelled to speak of them as generous; but they are so much at variance with the base and short-sighted policy of Governments, that it is refreshing and consolatory to meet them in Acts of State;—at least when, as here, they must be sincere, because the circumstances of their promulgation secure their observance, and indeed render deviation from them impossible. I read them over and over with the utmost pleasure. They breathe the spirit of that just policy and sound philosophy, which teaches us to regard the interest of our country as best promoted by an increase of the industry, wealth, and happiness of other nations.

Although the attention of the House is chiefly directed to the acts of our own Government, it is not foreign from the purpose of my argument to solicit them for a few minutes to consider the admirable Message sent on the 2d of December, 1823, by the President of the United States* to the Congress of that great republic. I heartily rejoice in the perfect agreement of that message with the principles professed by us to the French Minister, and afterwards to all the great Powers of Europe, whether military or maritime, and to the great English State beyond the Atlantic. I am not anxious to ascertain whether the Message was influenced by our communication, or was the mere result of similarity of principle and coincidence of interest. The United States had at all events long preceded us in the recognition. They sent consuls and commissioners two years before us, who found the greater part of South America quiet and secure, and in the agitations of the remainder, met with no obstacles to friendly intercourse. This recognition neither interrupted amicable relations with Spain, nor occasioned remonstrances from any Power in Europe. They declared their neutrality at the moment of recognition: they solemnly renew that declaration in the Message before me. That wise Government, in grave but determined language, and with that reasonable and deliberate tone which becomes true courage, proclaims the principles of her policy, and makes known the cases in which the care of her own safety will compel her to take up arms for the defence of other states. I have already observed its coincidence with the declarations of England; which indeed is perfect, if allowance be made for the deeper, or at least more immediate, interest in the independence of South America, which near neighbourhood gives to the United States. This coincidence of the two great English Commonwealths (for so I delight to call them, and I heartily pray that they may be for ever united in the cause of justice and liberty) cannot be contemplated without the utmost pleasure by every enlightened citizen of either. Above all, Sir, there is one coincidence between them, which is, I trust, of happy augury to the whole civilized world:—they have both declared their neutrality in the American contest as long as it shall be confined to Spain and her former colonies, or as long as no foreign Power shall interfere.

On the 25th of December 1823, M. Ofalia, the Spanish Minister for Foreign Affairs, proposed to the principal Powers of Europe a conference at Paris on the best means of enabling his Catholic Majesty to re-establish his legitimate authority, and to spread the blessings of his paternal government over the vast provinces of America which once acknowledged the supremacy of Spain. To this communication, which was made also to this government, an answer was given on the 30th of January following, which cannot be read by Englishmen without approbation and pleasure. In this answer, the proposition of a congress is once more rejected; the British Government adheres to its original declaration, that it would wait for a time,—but a limited time only,—and would rejoice to see his Catholic Majesty have the grace and advantage of taking the lead among the Powers of Europe in the recognition of the American states, as well for the greater benefit and security of these states themselves, as from the generous disposition felt by Great Britain to spare the remains of dignity and grandeur, however infinitesimally small, which may still be fancied to belong to the thing called the crown of Spain. Even the shadow of long-departed greatness was treated with compassionate forbearance. But all these courtesies and decorums were to have their limit. The interests of Europe and America imposed higher duties, which were not to be violated for the sake of leaving undisturbed the precedents copied by public offices at Madrid, from the power of Charles V. or the arrogance of Philip II. The principal circumstance in which this Despatch added to the preceding, was, that

* Mr. Monroe.—Ed.

it both laid a wider foundation for the policy of recognition, and made a much nearer approach to exactness in fixing the time beyond which it could not be delayed.

I have no subsequent official information. I have heard, and I believe, that Spain has answered this Despatch,—that she repeats her invitation to England to send a minister to the proposed congress, and that she has notified the assent of Russia, Austria, France, and Prussia. I have heard, and I also believe, that England on this occasion has proved true to herself,—that, in conformity to her ancient character, and in consistency with her repeated declarations, she has declined all discussion of this question with the Holy (or *un*-Holy) Alliance. Would to God that we had from the beginning kept aloof from these Congresses, in which we have made shipwreck of our ancient honour! If that were not possible, would to God that we had protested, at least by silence and absence against that conspiracy at Verona, which has annihilated the liberties of continental Europe!

In confirmation of the review which I have taken of the documents, I may also here mention the declaration made in this House, that during the occupation of Spain by a French army, every armament against the Spanish ports must be considered as having a French character, and being therefore within the principle repeatedly laid down in the Papers. Spain indeed, as a belligerent, can be now considered only as a fang of the Holy Alliance, powerless in itself, but which that monster has the power to arm with thrice-distilled venom.

As the case now stands, Sir, I conceive it to be declared by Great Britain, that the acknowledgment of the independence of Spanish America is no breach of faith or neutrality towards Spain,—that such an acknowledgment might long ago have been made without any violation of her rights or interposition in her affairs,—that we have been for at least two years entitled to make it by all the rules of international law,—that we have delayed it, from friendly consideration for the feelings and claims of the Spanish Government,—that we have now carried our forbearance to the utmost verge of reasonable generosity,—and, having exhausted all the offices of friendship and good neighbourhood, are at perfect liberty to consult only the interest of our own subjects, and the just pretensions of the American states.

In adopting this recognition now, we shall give just offence to no other Power. But if we did, and once suffer ourselves to be influenced by the apprehension of danger in resisting unjust pretensions, we destroy the only bulwark, — that of principle, — that guards a nation. There never was a time when it would be more perilous to make concessions, or to show feebleness and fear. We live in an age of the most extravagant and monstrous pretensions, supported by tremendous force. A confederacy of absolute monarchs claim the right of controlling the internal government of all nations. In the exercise of that usurped power they have already taken military possession of the whole continent of Europe. Continental governments either obey their laws or tremble at their displeasure. England alone has condemned their principles, and is independent of their power. They ascribe all the misfortunes of the present age to the example of her institutions. On England, therefore, they must look with irreconcilable hatred. As long as she is free and powerful, their system is incomplete, all the precautions of their tyrannical policy are imperfect, and their oppressed subjects may turn their eyes to her, indulging the hope that circumstances will one day compel us to exchange the alliance of kings for the friendship of nations.

I will not say that such a state of the world does not require a considerate and circumspect policy. I acknowledge, and should earnestly contend, that there never was a moment at which the continuance of peace was more desirable. After passing through all the sufferings of twenty years universal war, and feeling its internal evils perhaps more severely since its close than when it raged most widely and fiercely, we are only now beginning to taste the natural and genuine fruits of peace. The robust constitution of a free community is just showing its power to heal the deepest wounds,—to compose obstinate convulsions,—and to restore health and vigour to every disordered function or disabled member. I deprecate the occurrence of what must disturb this noble process,—one of the miracles of Liberty. But I am also firmly convinced, that prudence in the present circumstances of Europe forbids every measure that can be represented as having the appearance of fear. If we carry our caution further than strict abstinence from injustice, we cannot doubt to what motive our forbearance will be imputed. Every delay is liable to that interpretation. The least scrupulous politicians condemn falsehood when it wears the appearance of fear. It may be sometimes unsafe to fire at the royal tiger who suddenly crosses your path in an eastern forest; but it is thought fully as dangerous to betray your fear by running away: prudent men quietly pursue their road without altering their pace,—without provoking or tempting the ferocious animal.

Having thus traced the progress of measures which have lead us to the very verge of recognition, the question naturally presents itself, Why do we not now recognize? It is not so much my duty as it is that of the Government, to tell us why they do not complete their own system. Every preparation is made; every adverse claim is rejected; ample notice is given to all parties. Why is the determination delayed? We are irrevocably pledged to maintain our principles, and to act on them towards America. We have cut off all honourable retreat. Why should we seem to hesitate? America expects from

as the common marks of amity and respect. Spain cannot complain at their being granted. No other state can intimate an opinion on the subject, without an open attack on the independence of Great Britain. What then hinders the decisive word from being spoken?

We have already indeed taken one step more, in addition to those on which I have too long dwelt. We have sent consuls to all the ports of Spanish America to which we trade, as well as to the seats of the new government in that country. We have seen in the public papers, that the consul at Buenos Ayres has presented a letter from the Secretary of State for Foreign Affairs in this country to the Secretary of that Government, desiring that they would grant the permission to the consul, without which he cannot exercise his powers. Does not this act acknowledge the independence of the State of Buenos Ayres? An independent state alone can appoint consuls:—an independent state only can receive consuls. We have not only sent consuls, but commissioners. What is their character? Can it be any other than that of an envoy with a new title? Every agent publicly accredited to a foreign government, and not limited by his commission to commercial affairs, must in reality be a diplomatic minister, whatever may be his official name. We read of the public and joyful reception of these commissioners, of presents made by them to the American administrators, and of speeches in which they announce the good-will of the Government and people of England towards the infant republics. I allude to the speech of Colonel Hamilton at Bogota, on which, as I have seen it only in a translation, I can only venture to conjecture (after making some allowance for the overflow of courtesy and kindness which is apt to occur on such occasions) that it expressed the anxious wishes and earnest hopes of this country, that he might find Columbia in a state capable of maintaining those relations of amity which we were sincerely desirous to establish. Where should we apply for redress, if a Columbian privateer were to capture an English merchantman? Not at Madrid, but at Bogota. Does not this answer decide the whole question?

But British subjects, Sir, have a right to expect, not merely that their Government shall provide some means of redress, but that they should provide adequate and effectual means,—those which universal experience has proved to be the best. They are not bound to be content with the unavowed agency and precarious good offices of naval officers, nor even with the inferior and imperfect protection of an agent whose commission is limited to the security of trade. The power of a consul is confined to commercial affairs; and there are many of the severest wrongs which the merchant suffers, which, as they may not directly affect him in his trading concerns, are not within the proper province of the consul. The English trader at Buenos Ayres ought not to feel his safety less perfect than that of other foreign merchants. The habit of trusting to an ambassador for security has a tendency to reconcile the spirit of adventurous industry with a constant affection for the place of a man's birth. If these advantages are not inconsiderable to any European nation, they must be important to the most commercial and maritime people of the world.

The American Governments at present rate our friendship too high, to be jealous and punctilious in their intercourse with us. But a little longer delay may give rise to an unfavourable judgment of our conduct. They may even doubt our neutrality itself. Instead of admitting that the acknowledgment of their independence would be a breach of neutrality towards Spain, they may much more naturally conceive that the delay to acknowledge it is a breach of neutrality towards themselves. Do we in truth deal equally by both the contending parties? We do not content ourselves with consuls at Cadiz and Barcelona. If we expect justice to our subjects from the Government of Ferdinand VII., we in return pay every honour to that Government as a Power of the first class. We lend it every aid that it can desire from the presence of a British minister of the highest rank. We do not inquire whether he *legitimately* deposed his father, or *legally* dispersed the Cortes who preserved his throne. The inequality becomes the more strikingly offensive, when it is considered that the number of English in the American States is far greater, and our commerce with them much more important.

We have long since advised Spain to acknowledge the independence of her late provinces in America: we have told her that it is the only basis on which negotiations can be carried on, and that it affords her the only chance of preserving some of the advantages of friendship and commerce with these vast territories. Whatever rendered it right for Spain to recognise them, must also render it right for us. If we now delay, Spain may very speciously charge us with insincerity "It now," she may say, "appears from your own conduct, that under pretence of friendship you advised us to do that from which you yourselves recoil."

We have declared that we should immediately proceed to recognition, either if Spain were to invade the liberty of trade which we now possess, or if any other Power were to take a part in the contest between her and the American states. But do not these declarations necessarily imply that they are in fact independent? Surely no injustice of Spain, or France, or Russia could authorize England to acknowledge that to be a fact which we do not know to be so. Either therefore we have threatened to do what ought not to be done, or these states are now in a condition to be treated as independent.

It is now many months since it was declared to M. de Polignac, that we should consider "any foreign interference, by force or *menace*, in the dispute between Spain and her colonies, as a motive for recognising the latter without delay." I ask whether the interference "by menace" has not now occurred? M. Ofalia, on the 26th of December, proposed a congress on the affairs of America, in hopes that the allies of King Ferdinand "will assist him in accomplishing the worthy object of upholding the principles of order and legitimacy, the subversion of which, once commenced in America, would speedily communicate." Now I have already said, that, if I am rightly informed, this proposition, happily rejected by Great Britain, has been acceded to by the Allied Powers. Preparations for the congress are said to be already made. Can there be a more distinct case of interference by menace in the American contest, than the agreement to assemble a congress for the purpose described in the despatch of M. Ofalia?

But it is said, Sir, that we ought not to recognise independence where a contest is still maintained, or where governments of some apparent stability do not exist. Both these ideas seem to be comprehended in the proposition,—"that we ought to recognise only where independence is actually enjoyed;" though that proposition properly only affirms the former. But it is said that we are called upon only to acknowledge the fact of independence, and before we make the acknowledgment we ought to have evidence of the fact. To this single point the discussion is now confined. All considerations of European policy are (I cannot repeat it too often) excluded: the policy of Spain, or France, or Russia, is no longer an element in the problem. The fact of independence is now the sole object of consideration. If there be no independence, we cannot acknowledge it: if there be, we must.

To understand the matter rightly, we must consider separately—what are often confounded—the two questions,—Whether there is a contest with Spain still pending? and Whether internal tranquillity be securely established? As to the first, we must mean such a contest as exhibits some equality of force, and of which, if the combatants were left to themselves, the issue would be in some degree doubtful. It never can be understood so as to include a bare chance, that Spain might recover her ancient dominions at some distant and absolutely uncertain period.

In this inquiry, do you consider Spanish America as one mass, or do you apply your inquiry to the peculiar situation of each individual state? For the purposes of the present argument you may view them in either light:—in the latter, because they are sovereign commonwealths, as independent of each other as they all are of Europe; or in the former, because they are united by a treaty of alliance offensive and defensive, which binds them to make common cause in this contest, and to conclude no separate peace with Spain.

If I look on Spanish America as one vast unit, the question of the existence of any serious contest is too simple to admit the slightest doubt. What proportion does the contest bear to the country in which it prevails? My geograghy, or at least my recollection, does not serve me so far, that I could enumerate the degrees of latitude and longitude over which that vast country extends. On the western coast, however, it reaches from the northern point of New California to the utmost limit of cultivation towards Cape Horn. On the eastern it extends from the mouth of the Mississippi to that of the Orinoco; and, after the immense exception of Guiana and Brazil, from the Rio de la Plata to the southern footsteps of civilized man. The prodigious varieties of its elevation exhibit in the same parallel of latitude all the climates and products of the globe. It is the only abundant source of the metals justly called "precious,"—the most generally and permanently useful of all commodities, except those which are necessary to the preservation of human life. It is unequally and scantily peopled by sixteen or eighteen millions,—whose numbers, freedom of industry, and security of property must be quadrupled in a century. Its length on the Pacific coast is equal to that of the whole continent of Africa from the Cape of Good Hope to the Straits of Gibraltar. It is more extensive than the vast possessions of Russia or of Great Britain in Asia. The Spanish language is spoken over a line of nearly six thousand miles. The State of Mexico alone is five times larger that European Spain. A single communication cut through these territories between the Atlantic and Pacific would bring China six thousand miles nearer to Europe;* and the Republic of Columbia or that of Mexico may open and command that new road for the commerce of the world.

What is the Spanish strength? A single castle in Mexico, an island on the coast of Chili, and a small army in Upper Peru! Is this a contest approaching to equality? Is it sufficient to render the independence of such a country doubtful? Does it deserve the name of a contest? It is very little more than what in some of the wretched governments of the East is thought desirable to keep alive the vigilance of the rulers, and to exercise the martial spirit of the people. There is no present appearance that the country can be reduced by the power of Spain alone; and if any other Power were to interfere, it is acknowledged that such an interference would impose new duties on Great Britain.

If, on the other hand, we consider the American states as separate, the fact of independence is undisputed, with respect at least to some of them. What doubts can be entertained of the independence of the immense provinces of Caraccas, New Grenada,

* See Humboldt's admirable Essay on New Spain.

and Quito, which now form the Republic of Columbia? There, a considerable Spanish army has been defeated: all have been either destroyed, or expelled from the territory of the Republic: not a Royalist soldier remains. Three Congresses have successively been assembled: they have formed a reasonable and promising Constitution; and they have endeavoured to establish a wise system and a just administration of law. In the midst of their difficulties the Columbians have ventured (and hitherto with perfect success) to encounter the arduous and perilous, but noble problem of a pacific emancipation of their slaves. They have been able to observe good faith with their creditors, and thus to preserve the greatest of all resources for times of danger. Their tranquillity has stood the test of the long absence of Bolivar in Peru. Englishmen who have lately traversed their territories in various directions, are unanimous in stating that their journeys were made in the most undisturbed security. Every where they saw the laws obeyed, justice administered, armies disciplined, and the revenue peaceably collected. Many British subjects have indeed given practical proofs of their faith in the power and will of the Columbian Government to protect industry and property:—they have established houses of trade; they have undertaken to work mines; and they are establishing steam-boats on the Orinoco and the Magdalena. Where is the state which can give better proofs of secure independence?

The Republic of Buenos Ayres has an equally undisputed enjoyment of independence. There no Spanish soldier has set his foot for fourteen years. It would be as difficult to find a Royalist there, as it would be a Jacobite in England (I mean only a personal adherent of the House of Stuart, for as to Jacobites in principle, I fear they never were more abundant). Its rulers are so conscious of internal security, that they have crossed the Andes, and interposed with vigour and effect in the revolutions of Chili and Peru. Whoever wishes to know the state of Chili, will find it in a very valuable book lately published by Mrs. Graham,* a lady whom I have the happiness to call my friend, who, by the faithful and picturesque minuteness of her descriptions, places her reader in the midst of the country, and introduces him to the familiar acquaintance of the inhabitants. Whatever seeds of internal discord may be perceived, we do not discover the vestige of any party friendly to the dominion of Spain. Even in Peru, where the spirit of independence has most recently appeared, and appears most to fluctuate, no formidable body of Spanish partisans has been observed by the most intelligent observers; and it is very doubtful whether even the army which keeps the field in that province against the American cause be devoted to the restored despotism of Spain. Mexico, the greatest, doubtless, and most populous, but not perhaps the most enlightened, portion of Spanish America, has passed through severe trials, and seems hitherto far from showing a disposition again to fall under the authority of Spain. Even the party who long bore the name of Spain on their banners, imbibed in that very contest the spirit of independence, and at length ceased to look abroad for a sovereign. The last Viceroy who was sent from Spain* was compelled to acknowledge the independence of Mexico; and the Royalist officer,† who appeared for a time so fortunate, could not win his way to a transient power without declaring against the pretensions of the mother country.

If, then, we consider these states as one nation, there cannot be said to be any remaining contest. If, on the other hand, we consider them separately, why do we not immediately comply with the prayer of this Petition, by recognising the independence of those which we must allow to be in fact independent? Where is the objection to the instantaneous recognition at least of Columbia and Buenos Ayres?

But here, Sir, I shall be reminded of the second condition (as applicable to Mexico and Peru),—the necessity of a stable government and of internal tranquillity. Independence and good government are unfortunately very different things. Most countries have enjoyed the former: hot above three or four since the beginning of history have had any pretensions to the latter. Still, many grossly misgoverned countries have performed the common duties of justice and good-will to their neighbours,—I do not say so well as more wisely ordered commonwealths, but still tolerably, and always much better than if they had not been controlled by the influence of opinion acting through a regular intercourse with other nations.

We really do not deal with Spain and America by the same weight and measure. We exact proofs of independence and tranquillity from America: we dispense both with independence and tranquillity in Old Spain. We have an ambassador at Madrid, though the whole kingdom be in the hands of France. We treat Spain with all the honours due to a civilized state of the first rank, though we have been told in this House, that the continuance of the French army there is an act of humanity, necessary to prevent the faction of frantic Royalists from destroying not only the friends of liberty, but every Spaniard who hesitates to carry on a war of persecution and extirpation against all who are not the zealous supporters of unbounded tyranny. On the other hand, we require of the new-born states of America to solve the awful problem of reconciling liberty with order. We expect that all the efforts incident to a fearful struggle shall at once subside into the most perfect and undisturbed tran-

* Journal of a Residence in Chili.—Ed.

* Admiral Apodaca.—Ed.

† Don Augustin Iturbide.—Ed.

quillity,—that every visionary or ambitious hope which it has kindled shall submit without a murmur to the counsels of wisdom and the authority of the laws. Who are we who exact the performance of such hard conditions? Are we the English nation, to look thus coldly on rising liberty? We have indulgence enough for tyrants; we make ample allowance for the difficulties of their situation; we are ready enough to deprecate the censure of their worst acts. And are we, who spent ages of bloodshed in struggling for freedom, to treat with such severity others now following our example? Are we to refuse that indulgence to the errors and faults of other nations, which was so long needed by our own ancestors? We who have passed through every form of civil and religious tyranny,—who persecuted Protestants under Mary,—who—I blush to add—persecuted Catholics under Elizabeth,—shall we now inconsistently,—unreasonably,—basely hold, that distractions so much fewer and milder and shorter, endured in the same glorious cause, will unfit other nations for its attainment, and preclude them from the enjoyment of that rank and those privileges which we at the same moment recognise as belonging to slaves and barbarians?

I call upon my Right Honourable Friend* distinctly to tell us, on what principle he considers the perfect enjoyment of internal quiet as a condition necessary for the acknowledgment of an independence which cannot be denied to exist. I can discover none, unless the confusions of a country were such as to endanger the personal safety of a foreign minister. Yet the European Powers have always had ministers at Constantinople, though it was well known that the barbarians who ruled there would, on the approach of a quarrel, send these unfortunate gentlemen to a prison in which they might remain during a long war. But if there is any such insecurity in these states, how do the ministers of the United States of North America reside in their capitals? or why do we trust our own consuls and commissioners among them? Is there any physical pecularity in a consul, which renders him invulnerable where an ambassador or an envoy would be in danger? Is he bullet-proof or bayonet-proof? or does he wear a coat of mail? The same Government, one would think, which redresses an individual grievance on the application of a consul, may remove a cause of national difference after listening to the remonstrance of an envoy.

I will venture even to contend, that internal distractions, instead of being an impediment to diplomatic intercourse, are rather an additional reason for it. An ambassador is more necessary in a disturbed than in a tranquil country, inasmuch as the evils against which his presence is intended to guard are more likely to occur in the former than in the latter. It is in the midst of civil commotions that the foreign trader is the most likely to be wronged; and it is then that he therefore requires not only the good offices of a consul, but the weightier interposition of a higher minister. In a perfectly well-ordered country the laws and the tribunals might be sufficient. In the same manner it is obvious, that if an ambassador be an important security for the preservation of good understanding between the best regulated governments, his presence must be far more requisite to prevent the angry passions of exasperated factions from breaking out into war. Whether therefore we consider the individual or the public interests which are secured by embassies, it seems no paradox to maintain, that if they could be dispensed with at all, it would rather be in quiet than in disturbed countries.

The interests here at stake may be said to be rather individual than national. But a wrong done to the humblest British subject, an insult offered to the British flag flying on the slightest skiff, is, if unrepaired, a dishonour to the British nation.

Then the amount of private interests engaged in our trade with Spanish America is so great as to render them a large part of the national interest. There are already at least a hundred English houses of trade established in various parts of that immense country. A great body of skilful miners have lately left this country, to restore and increase the working of the mines of Mexico. Botanists, and geologists, and zoologists, are preparing to explore regions too vast to be exhausted by the Condamines and Humboldts. These missionaries of civilization, who are about to spread European, and especially English opinions and habits, and to teach industry and the arts, with their natural consequences —the love of order and the desire of quiet,— are at the same time opening new markets for the produce of British labour, and new sources of improvement as well as enjoyment to the people of America.

The excellent petition from Liverpool to the King sets forth the value of our South American commerce very clearly, with respect to its present extent, its rapid increase, and its probable permanence. In 1819, the official returns represent the value of British exports at thirty-five millions sterling,—in 1822, at forty-six millions; and, in the opinion of the Petitioners, who are witnesses of the highest authority, a great part of this prodigious increase is to be ascribed to the progress of the South American trade. On this point, however, they are not content with probabilities. In 1822, they tell us that the British exports to the late Spanish colonies amounted in value to three millions eight hundred thousand pounds sterling; and in 1823, to five millions six hundred thousand;—an increase of near two millions in one year. As both the years compared are subsequent to the opening of the American ports, we may lay out of the account the indirect trade formerly carried on with the

* Mr. Canning.—Ed.

Spanish Main through the West Indies, the far greater part of which must now be transferred to a cheaper, shorter, and more convenient channel. In the year 1820 and the three following years, the annual average number of ships which sailed from the port of Liverpool to Spanish America, was one hundred and eighty-nine; and the number of those who have so sailed in five months of the present year, is already one hundred and twenty-four; being an increase in the proportion of thirty to nineteen. Another criterion of the importance of this trade, on which the traders of Liverpool are peculiarly well qualified to judge, is the export of cotton goods from their own port. The result of the comparison of that export to the United States of America, and to certain parts* of Spanish and Portuguese America, is peculiarly instructive and striking:—

ACTUAL VALUE OF COTTON GOODS EXPORTED FROM LIVERPOOL.

Year ending Jan. 5, 1820.	
To United States - - -	£882,029
To Spanish and Portuguese America	852,651
Year ending Jan. 5, 1821.	
To United States - - -	£1,033,206
To Spanish and Portuguese America	1,111,574

It is to be observed, that this last extraordinary statement relates to the comparative infancy of this trade; that it comprehends neither Vera Cruz nor the ports of Columbia; and that the striking disproportion in the rate of increase does not arise from the abatement of the North American demand (for that has increased), but from the rapid progress of that in the South American market. Already, then, this new commerce surpasses in amount, and still more in progress, that trade with the United States which is one of the oldest and most extensive, as well as most progressive branches of our traffic.

If I consult another respectable authority, and look at the subject in a somewhat different light, I find the annual value of our whole exports estimated in Lord Liverpool's speech† on this subject at forty-three millions sterling, of which about twenty millions' worth goes to Europe, and about the value of seventeen millions to North and South America; leaving between four and five millions to Africa and Asia. According to this statement, I may reckon the trade to the new independent states as one eighth of the trade of the whole British Empire. It is more than our trade to all our possessions on the continent and islands of America was, before the beginning of the fatal American war in 1774:—for fatal I call it, not because I lament the independence of America, but because I deeply deplore the hostile separation of the two great nations of English race.

The official accounts of exports and imports laid before this House on the 3d of May, 1824, present another view of this subject, in which the Spanish colonies are carefully separated from Brazil. By these accounts it appears that the exports to the Spanish colonies were as follows:—

1818,	£735,344.	1821,	£917,916.
1819,	£850,943.	1822,	£1,210,825.
1820,	£431,615.	1823,	£2,016,276.

I quote all these statements of this commerce, though they do not entirely agree with each other, because I well know the difficulty of attaining exactness on such subjects,—because the least of them is perfectly sufficient for my purpose,—and because the last, though not so large as others in amount, shows more clearly than any other its rapid progress, and the proportion which its increase bears to the extension of American independence.

If it were important to swell this account, I might follow the example of the Liverpoo Petitioners (who are to be heard with more respect, because on this subject they have no interest), by adding to the general amount of commerce the supply of money to the American states of about twelve millions sterling. For though I of course allow that such contracts cannot be enforced by the arms of this country against a foreign state, yet I consider the commerce in money as equally legitimate and honourable with any other sort of commercial dealing, and equally advantageous to the country of the lenders, wherever it is profitable to the lenders themselves. I see no difference in principle between a loan on the security of public revenue, and a loan on a mortgage of private property; and the protection of such dealings is in my opinion a perfectly good additional reason for hastening to do that which is previously determined to be politic and just.

If, Sir, I were further called to illustrate the value of a free intercourse with South America, I should refer the House to a valuable work, which I hope all who hear me have read, and which I know they ought to read,—I mean Captain Basil Hall's Travels in that country. The whole book is one continued proof of the importance of a Free Trade to England, to America, and to mankind. No man knows better how to extract information from the most seemingly trifling conversations, and to make them the means of conveying the most just conception of the opinions, interests, and feelings of a people. Though he can weigh interests in the scales of Smith, he also seizes with the skill of Plutarch on those small circumstances and expressions which characterize not only individuals but nations. "While we were admiring the scenery," says he, "our people had established themselves in a hut, and were preparing supper under the direction of a peasant,—a tall copper-coloured semi-barbarous native of the forest,—but who, notwithstanding his uncivilized appearance, turned out to be a very shrewd fellow, and

* Viz., Brazil, Buenos Ayres, Monte Video, Chili, and the West Coast of America.

† Delivered in the House of Lords on the 15th of March.—Ed.

gave us sufficiently pertinent answers to most of our queries. A young Spaniard of our party, a Royalist by birth, and half a patriot in sentiment, asked the mountaineer what harm the King had done. 'Why,' answered he, 'as for the King, his only fault, at least that I know of, was his living too far off. If a king be really good for a country, it appears to me that he ought to live in that country, not two thousand leagues away from it.' On asking him what was his opinion of free trade, 'My opinion,' said he, 'is this:—formerly I paid nine dollars for the piece of cloth of which this shirt is made; I now pay two:—that is my opinion of free trade.'"* This simple story illustrates better than a thousand arguments the sense which the American *consumer* has of the consequences of free trade to him.

If we ask how it affects the American *producer*, we shall find a decisive answer in the same admirable work. His interest is to produce his commodities at less expense, and to sell them at a higher price, as well as in greater quantity:—all these objects he has obtained. Before the Revolution, he sold his copper at seven dollars a quintal: in 1821, he sold it at thirteen. The articles which he uses in the mines are, on the other hand, reduced;—steel from fifty dollars a quintal to sixteen dollars; iron from twenty-five to eight; the provisions of his labourers in the proportion of twenty-one to fourteen; the fine cloth which he himself wears, from twenty-three dollars a yard to twelve; his crockery from three hundred and fifty reals per crate to forty; his hardware from three hundred to one hundred reals; and his glass from two hundred to one hundred.†

It is justly observed by Captain Hall, that however incompetent a Peruvian might be to appreciate the benefits of political liberty, he can have no difficulty in estimating such sensible and palpable improvements in the condition of himself and his countrymen. With Spanish authority he connects the remembrance of restriction, monopoly, degradation, poverty, discomfort, privation. In those who struggle to restore it, we may be assured that the majority of Americans can see only enemies who come to rob them of private enjoyments and personal accommodations.

It will perhaps be said, that Spain is willing to abandon her monopolies. But if she does now, might she not by the same authority restore them? If her sovereignty be restored, she must possess abundant means of evading the execution of any concessions now made in the hour of her distress. The faith of a Ferdinand is the only security she offers. On the other hand, if America continues independent, our security is the strong sense of a most palpable interest already spread among the people,—the interest of the miner of Chili in selling his copper, and of the peasant of Mexico in buying his shirt. I prefer it to the royal word of Ferdinand. But do we not know that the Royalist General Canterac, in the summer of 1823, declared the old prohibitory laws to be still in force in Peru, and announced his intention of accordingly confiscating all English merchandise which he had before generously spared? Do we not know that English commerce every where flies from the Royalists, and hails with security and joy the appearance of the American flag?* But it is needless to reason on this subject, or to refer to the conduct of local agents. We have a decree of Ferdinand himself to appeal to, bearing date at Madrid on the 9th February, 1824. It is a very curious document, and very agreeable to the general character of his most important edicts;—in it there is more than the usual repugnance between the title and the purport. As he published a table of proscription under the name of a decree of amnesty, so his professed grant of free trade is in truth an establishment of monopoly. The first article does indeed promise a free trade to Spanish America. The second, however, hastens to declare, that this free trade is to be "regulated" by a future law,—that it is to be confined to certain ports,—and that it shall be subjected to duties, which are to be regulated by the same law. The third also declares, that the preference to be granted to Spain shall be "regulated" in like manner. As if the duties, limitations, and preferences thus announced had not provided such means of evasion as were equivalent to a repeal of the first article, the Royal lawgiver proceeds in the fourth article to enact, that "till the two foregoing articles can receive their perfect execution, there shall be nothing innovated in the state of America." As the Court of Madrid does not recognise the legality of what has been done in America since the revolt, must not this be reasonably interpreted to import a re-establishment of the Spanish laws of absolute monopoly, till the Government of Spain shall be disposed to promulgate that code of restriction, of preference, and of duties,—perhaps prohibitory ones,—which, according to them, constitutes free trade.

But, Sir, it will be said elsewhere, though not here, that I now argue on the selfish and sordid principle of exclusive regard to British interest,—that I would sacrifice every higher consideration to the extension of our traffic, and to the increase of our profits. For this is the insolent language, in which those who gratify their ambition by plundering and destroying their fellow-creatures, have in all ages dared to speak of those who better their own condition by multiplying the enjoyments of mankind. In answer, I might content myself with saying, that having

* Vol. ii. p. 188.

† Vol. ii. p. 47. This curious table relates to Chili,—the anecdote to Mexico.

* As in the evacuation of Lima in the spring of 1824.

proved the recognition of the independence of these states to be conformable to justice, I have a perfect right to recommend it as conducive to the welfare of this nation. But I deny altogether the doctrine, that commerce has a selfish character,—that it can benefit one party without being advantageous to the other. It is twice blessed: it blesses the giver as well as the receiver. It consists in the interchange of the means of enjoyment; and its very essence is to employ one part of mankind in contributing to the happiness of others. What is the instrument by which a savage is to be raised from a state in which he has nothing human but the form, but commerce,—exciting in his mind the desire of accommodation and enjoyment, and presenting to him the means of obtaining these advantages? It is thus only that he is gradually raised to industry,—to foresight,—to a respect for property,—to a sense of justice,—to a perception of the necessity of laws. What corrects his prejudices against foreign nations and dissimilar races?—commercial intercourse. What slowly teaches him that the quiet and well-being of the most distant regions have some tendency to promote the prosperity of his own? What at length disposes him even to tolerate those religious differences which led him to regard the greater part of the species with abhorrence? Nothing but the intercourse and familiarity into which commerce alone could have tempted him. What diffuses wealth, and therefore increases the leisure which calls into existence the works of genius, the discoveries of science, and the inventions of art? What transports just opinions of government into enslaved countries,—raises the importance of the middle and lower classes of society, and thus reforms social institutions, and establishes equal liberty? What but Commerce—the real civilizer and emancipator of mankind?

A delay of recognition would be an important breach of justice to the American states. We send consuls to their territory, in the confidence that their Government and their judges will do justice to British subjects; but we receive no authorised agents from them in return. Until they shall be recognised by the King, our courts of law will not acknowledge their existence. Our statutes allow certain privileges to ships coming from the "provinces in America lately subject to Spain;" but our courts will not acknowledge that these provinces are subject to any government. If the maritime war which has lately commenced should long continue, many questions of international law may arise out of our anomalous situation, which it will be impossible to determine by any established principles. If we escape this difficulty by recognising the actual governments in courts of Prize, how absurd, inconsistent, and inconvenient it is not to extend the same recognition to all our tribunals!

The reception of a new state into the society of civilized nations by those acts which amount to recognition, is a proceeding which, as it has no legal character, and is purely of a moral nature, must vary very much in its value, according to the authority of the nations who, upon such occasions, act as the representatives of civilized men. I will say nothing of England, but that she is the only anciently free state in the world. For her to refuse her moral aid to communities struggling for liberty, is an act of unnatural harshness, which, if it does not recoil on herself, must injure America in the estimation of mankind.

This is not all. The delay of recognition tends to prolong and exasperate the disorders which are the reason alleged for it. It encourages Spain to waste herself in desperate efforts; it encourages the Holy Alliance to sow division,—to employ intrigue and corruption,—to threaten, perhaps to equip and despatch, armaments. Then it encourages every incendiary to excite revolt, and every ambitious adventurer to embark in projects of usurpation. It is a cruel policy, which has the strongest tendency to continue for a time, of which we cannot foresee the limits, rapine and blood, commotions and civil wars, throughout the larger portion of the New World. By maintaining an outlawry against them, we shall give them the character of outlaws. The long continuance of confusion,—in part arising from our refusing to countenance their governments, to impose on them the mild yoke of civilized opinion, and to teach them respect for themselves by associating them with other free communities, —may at length really unfit them for liberty or order, and destroy in America that capacity to maintain the usual relations of peace and amity with us which undoubtedly exists there at present.

It is vain to expect that Spain, even if she were to reconquer America, could establish in that country a vigorous government, capable of securing a peaceful intercourse with other countries. America is too determined, and Spain is too feeble. The only possible result of so unhappy an event would be, to exhibit the wretched spectacle of beggary, plunder, bloodshed, and alternate anarchy and despotism in a country almost depopulated. It may require time to give firmness to native governments; but it is impossible that a Spanish one should ever again acquire it.

Sir, I am far from foretelling that the American nations will not speedily and completely subdue the agitations which are in some degree, perhaps, inseparable from a struggle for independence. I have no such gloomy forebodings; though even if I were to yield to them, I should not speak the language once grateful to the ears of this House, if I were not to say that the chance of liberty is worth the agitations of centuries. If any Englishman were to speak opposite doctrines to these rising communities, the present power and prosperity and glory of England would enable them to detect his slavish sophistry. As a man, I trust that the virtue and fortune of these American states will spare them many of the sufferings which appear to be the price set on liberty; but as a Briton, I am desirous that we should aid them by early treating them with that honour and kindness which the justice, humanity, valour, and magnanimity which they have displayed in the prosecution of the noblest object of human pursuit, have so well deserved.

To conclude:—the delay of the recognition is not due to Spain: it is injurious to America: it is inconvenient to all European nations,—and only most inconvenient to Great Britain, because she has a greater intercourse with America than any other nation. I would not endanger the safety of my own country for the advantage of others; I would not violate the rules of duty to promote its interest; I would not take unlawful means even for the purpose of diffusing liberty among men; I would not violate neutrality to serve America, nor commit injustice to extend the commerce of England: but I would do an act, consistent with neutrality, and warranted by impartial justice, tending to mature the liberty and to consolidate the internal quiet of a vast continent,—to increase the probability of the benefits of free and just government being attained by a great portion of mankind,—to procure for England the honour of a becoming share in contributing to so unspeakable a blessing,—to prevent the dictators of Europe from becoming the masters of the New World,—to re-establish some balance of opinions and force, by placing the republics of America, with the wealth and maritime power of the world, in the scale opposite to that of the European Allies,—to establish beyond the Atlantic an asylum which may preserve, till happier times, the remains of the Spanish name,—to save nations, who have already proved their generous spirit, from becoming the slaves of the Holy Alliance,—and to rescue sixteen millions of American Spaniards from sharing with their European brethren that sort of law and justice,—of peace and order,—which now prevails from the Pyrenees to the Rock of Gibraltar.

SPEECH

ON THE CIVIL GOVERNMENT OF CANADA.

DELIVERED IN THE HOUSE OF COMMONS ON THE 2D OF MAY, 1828.

Mr. Speaker,—I think I may interpret fairly the general feeling of the House, when I express my congratulations upon the great extent of talent and information which the Honourable Member for St. Michael's* has just displayed, and that I may venture to assert he has given us full assurance, in his future progress, of proving a useful and valuable member of the Parliament of this country. I cannot, also, avoid observing, that the laudable curiosity which carried him to visit that country whose situation is now the subject of discussion, and still more the curiosity which led him to visit that Imperial Republic which occupies the other best portion of the American continent, gave evidence of a mind actuated by enlarged and liberal views.

After having presented a petition signed by eighty-seven thousand of the inhabitants of Lower Canada—comprehending in that number nine-tenths of the heads of families in the province, and more than two-thirds of its landed proprietors, and after having shown that the Petitioners had the greatest causes of complaint against the administration of the government in that colony, it would be an act of inconsistency on my part to attempt to throw any obstacle in the way of that inquiry which the Right Honourable Gentleman* proposes. It might seem, indeed, a more natural course on my part, if I had seconded such a proposition. Perhaps I might have been contented to give a silent acquiescence in the appointment of a committee, and to reserve any observations I may have to offer until some specific measure is proposed, or until the House is in possession of the information which may be procured through the labours of the committee,—perhaps, I say, I might have been disposed to adopt this course if I had not been intrusted with the presentation of that Petition. But I feel bound by a sense of the trust reposed in me to allow no opportunity to pass over of calling the attention of the House to the grievances of the Petitioners,

* Mr. [now the Right Honourable] Henry Labouchere.—Ed.

* Mr. Huskisson, Secretary for the Colonial Department, had moved to refer the whole question of the already embroiled affairs of the Canadian provinces to a Select Committee of the House of Commons, which was eventually agreed to.—Ed.

and to their claims for redress and for the maintenance of their legitimate rights. This duty I hold myself bound to execute, according to the best of my ability, without sacrificing my judgment, or rendering it subordinate to any sense of duty;—but feeling only that the confidence of the Petitioners binds me to act on their behalf, and as their advocate, in precisely the same manner, and to the same extent, as if I had been invested with another character, and authorised to state their complaints in a different situation.*

To begin then with the speech of the Right Honourable Gentleman, I may take leave to observe, that in all that was contained in the latter part of it he has my fullest and most cordial assent. In 1822, when the Canadians were last before the House, I stated the principles which ought to be maintained with respect to what the Right Honourable Gentleman has very properly and very eloquently called the "Great British Confederacy." I hold now, as I did then, that all the different portions of that Confederacy are integral parts of the British Empire, and as such entitled to the fullest protection. I hold that they are all bound together as one great class, by an alliance prior in importance to every other,—more binding upon us than any treaty ever entered into with any state,—the fulfilment of which we can never desert without the sacrifice of a great moral duty. I hold that it can be a matter of no moment, in this bond of alliance, whether the parties be divided by oceans or be neighbours:—I hold that the moral bond of duty and protection is the same. My maxims of Colonial Policy are few and simple:—a full and efficient protection from all foreign influence; full permission to conduct the whole of their own internal affairs; compelling them to pay all the reasonable expenses of their own government, and giving them at the same time a perfect control over the expenditures of the money; and imposing no restrictions of any kind upon the industry or traffic of the people. These are the only means by which the hitherto almost incurable evil of distant government can be either mitigated or removed. And it may be a matter of doubt, whether in such circumstances the colonists would not be under a more gentle control, and in a happier state, than if they were to be admitted to a full participation in the rule, and brought under the immediate and full protection, of the parent government. I agree most fully with the Honourable Gentleman who spoke last, when he expressed a wish that we should leave the regulation of the internal affairs of the colonies to the colonists, except in cases of the most urgent and manifest necessity. The most urgent and manifest necessity, I say; and few and rare ought to be the exceptions to the rule even upon the strength of those necessities.

Under these circumstances of right I contend it is prudent to regard all our colonies; and peculiarly the population of these two great provinces;—provinces placed in one of those rare and happy states of society in which the progress of population must be regarded as a blessing to mankind,—exempt from the curse of fostering slavery,—exempt from the evils produced by the contentions of jarring systems of religion,—enjoying the blessings of universal toleration,—and presenting a state of society the most unlike that can possibly be imagined to the fastidious distinctions of Europe. Exempt at once from the slavery of the West, and the castes of the East,—exempt, too, from the embarrassments of that other great continent which we have chosen as a penal settlement, and in which the prejudices of society have been fostered, I regret to find, in a most unreasonable degree,—exempt from all the artificial distinctions of the Old World, and many of the evils of the New, we see a great population rapidly growing up to be a great nation. None of the claims of such a population ought to be cast aside; and none of their complaints can receive any but the most serious consideration.

In the first part of his speech the Right Honourable Gentleman declared, that the excesses and complaints of the colonists arose from the defect of their constitution, and next from certain contentions into which they had fallen with Lord Dalhousie. In any thing I may say on this occasion, I beg to be understood as not casting any imputation upon the character of that Noble Lord: I speak merely of the acts of his Government; and I wish solely to be understood as saying, that my opinion of the acts of that Government are different from those which I believe to have been conscientiously his.

I, however, must say, that I thought the Right Honourable Gentleman in one part of his address had indulged himself in some pleasantries which seemed ill suited to the subject to which he claimed our attention;—I allude to the three essential grievances which he seemed to imagine led to many, if not all, of the discontents and complaints of the colonists. There was the perplexed system of real-property-law, creating such a vexatious delay, and such enormous costs to the suitor as to amount very nearly to a denial of justice: this, he said, arose from adhering to the Custom of Paris. The next cause of discontent is the inadequate representation of the people in Parliament: that he recommended to the immediate attention of the committee, for the purpose of revision. Lastly, the members of the Legislature were so absurdly ignorant of the first principles of political economy, as to have attempted to exclude all the industry and capital of other countries from flowing in to enrich and fertilise their shores. These were the three grounds upon which he formally impeached

* This alludes to his nomination some time previously by the House of Assembly of Lower Canada as the Agent of the Province, which nomination had not however taken effect.—Ed.

the people of Canada before the Knights, Citizens, and Burgesses of Great Britain and Ireland in Parliament assembled.

Did the Right Honourable Gentleman never hear of any other system of law, in any other country than Canada, in which a jumble of obsolete usages were mixed up and confounded with modern subtleties, until the mind of the most acute men of the age and nation—men who had, in a service of forty years, passed through every stage of its gradations—were driven to declare that they felt totally unable to find their way through its labyrinths, and were compelled, by their doubts of what was law and what was not, to add in a most ruinous degree to the expenses of the suitor? This system has been called the "Common Law,"—"the wisdom of our ancestors,"—and various other venerable names. Did he never hear of a system of representation in any other country totally irreconcilable either with the state of the population or with any rule or principle under heaven? Have I not heard over and over again from the lips of the Right Honourable Gentleman, and from one* whom, alas! I shall hear no more, that this inadequate system of representation possessed extraordinary advantages over those more systematic contrivances which resulted from the studies of the "constitution makers" of other countries? And yet it is for this very irregularity in their mode of representation that the Canadians are now to be brought before the judgment of the Right Honourable Gentleman's committee. I felt still greater wonder, however, when I heard him mention his third ground of objection to the proceedings of the colonists, and his third cause of their discontent—their ignorance of political economy. Too surely the laws for the exclusion of the capital and industry of other countries did display the grossest ignorance of that science! I should not much wonder if I heard of the Canadians devising plans to prevent the entrance of a single grain of foreign corn into the provinces. I should not wonder to hear the members of their Legislature and their great land-owners contending that it was absolutely necessary that the people should be able to raise all their own food; and consequently (although, perhaps, they do not see the consequences) to make every other nation completely independent of their products and their industry. It is perhaps barely possible that some such nonsense as this might be uttered in the legislative assembly of the Canadians.

Then again, Sir, the Right Honourable Gentleman has alluded to the Seigneurs and their vassals. Some of these "most potent, grave, and reverend" Seigneurs may happen to be jealous of their manorial rights: for seigneuralty means manor, and a seigneur is only, therefore, a lord of the manor. How harmless this lofty word seems to be when translated! Some of these seigneurs might happen, I say, to be jealous of their manorial privileges, and anxious for the preservation of their game. I am a very bad sportsman myself, and not well acquainted with the various objects of anxiety to such persons; but there may be, too, in these colonies also, persons who may take upon themselves to institute a rigorous inquiry into the state of their game, and into the best methods of preserving red game and black game, and pheasants and partridges; and who might be disposed to make it a question whether any evils arise from the preservation of these things for their sport, or whether the safety, the liberty, and the life of their fellow-subjects ought not to be sacrificed for their personal gratification.

With regard to the observance of the Custom of Paris, I beg the House to consider that no change was effected from 1760 to 1789; and (although I admit with the Right Honourable Gentleman that it may be bad as a system of conveyance, and may be expensive on account of the difficulties produced by mortgages) that the Canadians cannot be very ill off under a code of laws which grew up under the auspices of the Parliament of Paris—a body comprising the greatest learning and talent ever brought to the study of the law, and boasting the names of L'Hôpital and Montesquieu.

Neither can it be said, that the Assembly of Canada was so entirely indifferent to its system of representation: for it ought to be recollected, that they passed a bill to amend it, which was thrown out by the Council,—that is, in fact, by the Government. At all events, this shows that there was no want of a disposition to amend the state of their representation; although Government might differ from them as to the best method of accomplishing it. A bill for establishing the independence of the judges was another remedial measure thrown out by the Upper House.

As at present informed, however, without going further into these questions, I see enough stated in the Petition upon the table of the House, to justify the appointment of a committee of inquiry.

In every country, Sir, the wishes of the greater number of the inhabitants, and of those in possession of the great mass of the property, ought to have great influence in the government;—they ought to possess the power of the government. If this be true generally, the rule ought, *à multò fortiori*, to be followed in the government of distant colonies, from which the information that is to guide the Government at home is sent by a few, and is never correct or complete. A Government on the spot, though with the means of obtaining correct information, is exposed to the delusions of prejudice:—for a Government at a distance, the only safe course to pursue is to follow public opinion. In making the practical application of this principle, if I find the Government of any country engaged in squabbles with the great

* Mr. Canning.—Ed.

mass of the people,—if I find it engaged in vexatious controversies and ill-timed disputes,—especially if that Government be the Government of a colony,—I say, that there is a reasonable presumption against that Government. I do not charge it with injustice, but I charge it with imprudence and indiscretion; and I say that it is unfit to hold the authority intrusted to it. The ten years of squabbles and hostility which have existed in this instance, are a sufficient charge against this Government.

I was surprised to hear the Right Honourable Gentleman put the People and the Government on the same footing in this respect. What is government good for, if not to temper passion with wisdom? The People are said to be deficient in certain qualities, and a government are said to possess them. If the People are not deficient in them, it is a fallacy to talk of the danger of intrusting them with political power: if they are deficient, where is the common sense of exacting from them that moderation which government is instituted for the very purpose of supplying?

Taking this to be true as a general principle, it cannot be false in its application to the question before the House. As I understand it, the House of Assembly has a right to appropriate the supplies which itself has granted. The House of Commons knows well how to appreciate that right, and should not quarrel with the House of Assembly for indulging in a similar feeling. The Right Honourable Gentleman himself admits the existence of this right. The Governor-General has, however, infringed it, by appropriating a sum of one hundred and forty thousand pounds without the authority of the Assembly. That House does not claim to appropriate the revenue raised under the Act of 1774: they only claim a right to examine the items of the appropriation in order to ascertain if the Government need any fresh supplies. The Petitioners state it as one of their not unimaginary grievances, that they have lost one hundred thousand pounds by the neglect of the Receiver-General. This is not one of those grievances which are said to arise from the Assembly's claim of political rights. Another dispute arises from the Governor-General claiming, in imitation of the power of the King, a right to confirm the Speaker of the House of Assembly. This right,—a very ancient one, and venerable from its antiquity and from being an established fact of an excellent constitution at home,—is a most absurd adjunct to a colonial government. But I will not investigate the question, nor enter into any legal argument with regard to it; for no discussion can in any case, as I feel, be put in competition with the feelings of a whole people. It is a fatal error in the rulers of a country to despise the people: its safety, honour, and strength, are best preserved by consulting their wishes and feelings. The Government at Quebec, despising such considerations, has been long engaged in a scuffle with the people, and has thought hard words and hard blows not inconsistent with its dignity.

I observe, Sir, that twenty-one bills were passed by the House of Assembly in 1827, —most of them reformatory,—of which not one was approved of by the Legislative Council. Is the Governor responsible for this? I answer, he is. The Council is nothing else but his tool: it is not, as at present constituted, a fair and just constitutional check between the popular assembly and the Governor. Of the twenty-seven Councillors, seventeen hold places under the Government at pleasure, dividing among themselves yearly fifteen thousand pounds, which is not a small sum in a country in which a thousand a-year is a large income for a country gentleman. I omit the Bishop, who is perhaps rather too much inclined to authority, but is of a pacific character. The minority, worn out in their fruitless resistance, have withdrawn from attendance on the Council. Two of them, being the most considerable landholders in the province, were amongst the subscribers to the Petition. I appeal to the House, if the Canadians are not justified in considering the very existence of this Council as a constitutional grievance?

It has been said that there is no aristocracy formed in the province. It is not possible that this part of Mr. Pitt's plan could ever have been carried into execution: an aristocracy—the creature of time and opinion—cannot be created. But men of great merit and superior qualifications get an influence over the people; and they form a species of aristocracy, differing, indeed, from one of birth and descent, but supplying the materials out of which a constitutional senate may be constituted. Such an aristocracy there is in Canada; but it is excluded from the Council.

There are then, Sir, two specific classes of grievances complained of by the Lower-Canadians: the first is, the continued hostility to all the projected measures of the Assembly by the Governor; the second is, the use he makes of the Council to oppose them. These are the grounds on which inquiry and change are demanded. I, however, do not look upon these circumstances alone as peremptorily requiring a change in the constitution of the province. These are wrongs which the Government might have remedied. It might have selected a better Council; and it might have sent out instructions to the Governor to consult the feelings of the people. It might have pointed out to him the example of a Government which gave way to the wishes of a people,—of a majority of the people, expressed by a majority of their representatives,—on a question, too, of religious liberty,* and instead of weakening themselves, had thereby more firmly seated themselves in the hearts of the people. On reviewing the whole question, the only practical remedy which I see, is to

* Alluding to the repeal of the Test Act.—Ed.

introduce more prudence and discretion into the counsels of the Administration of the Province.

The Right Honourable Gentleman has made allusion to the English settlers in Lower-Canada, as if they were oppressed by the natives. But I ask what law has been passed by the Assembly that is unjust to them? Is it a remedy for this that it is proposed to change the scheme of representation? The English inhabitants of Lower-Canada, with some few exceptions, collected in towns as merchants or the agents of merchants,—very respectable persons, I have no doubt,—amount to about eighty thousand: would it not be the height of injustice to give them the same influence which the four hundred thousand Canadians, from their numbers and property, ought to possess? Sir, when I hear of an inquiry on account of measures necessary to protect English settlers, I greatly lament that any such language should have been used. Are we to have an English colony in Canada separated from the rest of the inhabitants,—a favoured body, with peculiar privileges? Shall they have a sympathy with English sympathies and English interests? And shall we deal out to Canada six hundred years of such miseries as we have to Ireland? Let us not, in God's name, introduce such curses into another region. Let our policy be to give all the King's subjects in Canada equal law and equal justice. I cannot listen to unwise distinctions, generating alarm, and leading to nothing but evil, without adverting to them; and I shall be glad if my observations supply the Gentlemen opposite with the opportunity of disavowing,—knowing, as I do, that the disavowal will be sincere—that any such distinction is to be kept up.

As to Upper Canada, the statement of the Right Honourable Gentleman appears to be scanty in information: it does not point out,—as is usual in proposing such a Committee,—what is to be the termination of the change proposed. He has thrown out two or three plans; but he has also himself supplied objections to them. The Assembly there appears to be as independent as the one in the Lower province. I have heard of some of their measures—an Alien bill, a Catholic bill, and a bill for regulating the Press: and these discussions were managed with as much spirit as those of an assembly which I will not say is better, but which has the good fortune to be their superiors. The people have been much disappointed by the immense grants of land which have been reserved for the Church of England,—which faith is not that of the majority of the people. Such endowments are to be held sacred where they have been long made; but I do not see the propriety of creating them anew,—and for a Church, too, to which the majority of the people do not belong. Then, with regard to the regulations which have been made for the new college, I see with astonishment that, in a country where the majority of the people do not belong to the Church of England, the professors are all to subscribe to the Thirty-nine Articles: so that, if Dr. Adam Smith were alive, he could not fill the chair of political economy, and Dr. Black would be excluded from that of chemistry. Another thing should be considered:—a large portion of the population consists of American settlers, who can least of all men bear the intrusion of law into the domains of conscience and religion. It is a bad augury for the welfare of the province, that opinions prevalent at the distance of thousands of miles, are to be the foundations of the college-charter: it is still worse, if they be only the opinions of a faction, that we cannot interfere to correct the injustice.

To the proposed plan for the union of the two provinces there are so many and such powerful objections, that I scarcely think that such a measure can soon be successfully concluded. The Bill proposed in 1822, whereby the bitterness of the Lower-Canada Assembly was to be mitigated by an infusion of mildness from the Upper province,—failing as it did,—has excited general alarm and mistrust among all your colonies. Except that measure, which ought to be looked upon as a warning rather than a precedent, I think the grounds upon which we have now been called upon to interfere the scantiest that ever were exhibited.

I do not know, Sir, what other plans are to be produced, but I think the wisest measure would be to send out a temperate Governor, with instructions to be candid, and to supply him with such a Council as will put an end to the present disputes, and infuse a better spirit into the administration than it has known for the last ten years. I wish, however, to state, that I have not come to a final judgment, but have merely described what the bearing of my mind is on those general maxims of colonial policy, any deviation from which is as inconsistent with national policy as it is with national justice.

SPEECH

ON MOVING FOR

PAPERS RELATIVE TO THE AFFAIRS OF PORTUGAL.

DELIVERED IN THE HOUSE OF COMMONS, ON THE 1ST OF JUNE, 1829.

MR. SPEAKER,—I think it will be scarcely necessary for any man who addresses the House from that part of it where I generally sit, to disclaim any spirit of party opposition to His Majesty's Ministers during the present session. My own conduct in dealing with the motion which I regret that it is now my painful duty to bring forward, affords, I believe I may say, a pretty fair sample of the principle and feeling which have guided all my friends in the course they have adopted since the very first day of this Session, when I intimated my intention to call public attention to the present subject. For the first two months of the session, I considered myself and my political friends as acting under a sacred and irresistible obligation not to do any thing which might appear even to ruffle the surface of that hearty and complete co-operation which experience has proved to have been not more than necessary to the success of that grand healing measure* brought forward by His Majesty's Ministers,—that measure which I trust and believe will be found the most beneficent ever adopted by Parliament since the period when the happy settlement of a Parliamentary and constitutional crown on the House of Brunswick, not only preserved the constitution of England, but struck a death-blow against all pretensions to unbounded power and indefeasible title throughout the world. I cannot now throw off the feelings that actuated me in the course of the contest by means of which this great measure has been effected. I cannot so soon forget that I have fought by the side of the Gentlemen opposite for the attainment of that end. Such are my feelings upon the present occasion, that while I will endeavour to discharge my duty, as I feel no hostility, so I shall assume no appearance of acrimony. At the same time, I trust my conduct will be found to be at an immeasurable distance from that lukewarmness, which, on a question of national honour, and in the cause of the defenceless, I should hold to be aggravated treachery. I am influenced by a solicitude that the councils of England should be and should seem unspotted, not only at home, but in the eye of the people as well as the rulers of Europe,—by a desire for an explanation of measures which have ended in plunging our most ancient ally into the lowest depths of degradation,—by a warm and therefore jealous regard to national honour, which, in my judgment, consists still more in not doing or abetting, or approaching, or conniving at wrong to others, than in the spirit never tamely to brook wrong done to ourselves.

I hold it, Sir, as a general principle to be exceedingly beneficial and wholesome, that the attention of the House should be sometimes drawn to the state of our foreign relations: and this for the satisfaction of the people of England;—in the first place, in order to assure them that proper care is taken for the maintenance of peace and security;—above all, to convince them that care is taken of the national honour, the best, and indeed only sufficient guard of that peace and security. I regard such discussions as acts of courtesy due to our fellow-members of the great commonwealth of European states; more particularly now that some of them are bound to us by kindred ties of liberty, and by the possession of institutions similar to our own. Two of our neighbouring states,—one our closest and most congenial ally,—the other, in times less happy, our most illustrious antagonist, but in times to come our most illustrious rival—have adopted our English institutions of limited monarchy and representative assemblies: may they consolidate and perpetuate their wise alliance between authority and freedom! The occasional discussions of Foreign Policy in such assemblies will, I believe, in spite of cross accidents and intemperate individuals, prove on the whole, and in the long-run, favourable to good-will and good understanding between nations, by gradually softening prejudices, by leading to public and satisfactory explanations of ambiguous acts, and even by affording a timely vent to jealousies and resentments. They will, I am persuaded, root more deeply that strong and growing passion for peace, which, whatever may be the projects or intrigues of Cabinets, is daily spreading in the hearts of European nations, and which, let me add, is the best legacy bequeathed to us by the fierce wars which have desolated Europe from Copenhagen to Cadiz. They will foster this useful disposition, through the most generous sentiments

---

* The Bill for removing the Roman Catholic disabilities.

of human nature, instead of attempting to attain the same end by under-rating the resources or magnifying the difficulties of any single country, at a moment when distress is felt by all:—attempts more likely to rouse and provoke the just sense of national dignity which belongs to great and gallant nations, than to check their boldness or to damp their spirit.

If any thing was wanting to strengthen my passion for peace, it would draw new vigour from the dissuasive against war which I heard fall with such weight from the lips of him,* of whom alone in the two thousand years that have passed since Scipio defeated Hannibal at Zama, it can be said, that in a single battle he overthrew the greatest of commanders. I thought, at the moment, of verses written and sometimes quoted for other purposes, but characteristic of a dissuasive, which derived its weight from so many victories, and of the awful lesson taught by the fate of his mighty antagonist:—

> " Si admoveris ora,
> Cannas et Trebiam ante oculos, Thrasymenaque busta, .
> Et Pauli stare ingentem miraberis umbram."†

Actuated by a passion for peace, I own that I am as jealous of new guarantees of foreign political arrangements, as I should be resolute in observing the old. I object to them as multiplying the chances of war. And I deprecate virtual, as well as express ones: for such engagements may be as much contracted by acts as by words. To proclaim by our measures, or our language, that the preservation of the integrity of a particular state is to be introduced as a principle into the public policy of Europe, is in truth to form a new, and, perhaps, universal, even if only a virtual, guarantee. I will not affect to conceal that I allude to our peculiarly objectionable guarantee of the Ottoman empire.‡ I cannot see the justice of a policy, which would doom to perpetual barbarism and barrenness the eastern and southern shores of the Mediterranean,—the fair and famous lands which wind from the Euxine to the Atlantic. I recoil from thus riveting the Turkish yoke on the neck of the Christian nations of Asia Minor, of Mesopotamia, of Syria, and of Egypt; encouraged as they are on the one hand to hope for deliverance by the example of Greece, and sure that the barbarians will be provoked, by the same example, to maltreat them with tenfold cruelty. It is in vain to distinguish in this case between a guarantee against foreign enemies, and one against internal revolt. If all the Powers of Europe be pledged by their acts to protect the Turkish territory from invasion, the unhappy Christians of the East must look on all as enemies; while the Turk, relieved from all foreign fear, is at perfect liberty to tyrannize over his slaves. The Christians must despair not only of aid, but even of good-will, from states whose interest it will become, that a Government which they are bound to shield from abroad should be undisturbed at home. Such a guarantee cannot be long enforced; it will shortly give rise to the very dangers against which it is intended to guard. The issue will assuredly, in no long time, be, that the great military Powers of the neighbourhood, when they come to the brink of war with each other, will recur to their ancient secret of avoiding a quarrel, by fairly cutting up the prey that lies at their feet. They will smile at the credulity of those most distant states, whose strength, however great, is neither of the kind, nor within the distance, which would enable them to prevent the partition. But of this, perhaps, too much.

The case of Portugal touches us most nearly. It is that of a country connected with England by treaty for four hundred and fifty years, without the interruption of a single day's coldness,—with which we have been connected by a treaty of guarantee for more than a century, without ever having been drawn into war, or exposed to the danger of it,—which, on the other hand, for her steadfast faith to England, has been three times invaded—in 1760, in 1801, and in 1807,—and the soldiers of which have fought for European independence, when it was maintained by our most renowned captains against Louis XIV. and Napoleon. It is a connection which in length and intimacy the history of mankind cannot match. All other nations have learnt to regard our ascendant, and their attachment, as two of the elements of the European system. May I venture to add, that Portugal preceded us, though but for a short period, in the command of the sea, and that it is the country of the greatest poet who has employed his genius in celebrating nautical enterprise?

Such is the country which has fallen under the yoke of an usurper, whose private crimes rather remind us of the age of Commodus and Caracalla, than of the level mediocrity of civilized vice,—who appears before the whole world with the deep brand on his brow of a pardon from his king and father for a parricide rebellion,—who has waded to the throne through a succession of frauds, falsehoods, and perjuries, for which any man amenable to the law would have suffered the most disgraceful,—if not the last punishment. Meanwhile the lawful sovereign, Donna Maria II., received by His Majesty with parental kindness,—by the British nation with the interest due to her age, and sex, and royal dignity,—solemnly recognised by the British Government as Queen of Portugal,—whom all the great Powers of Europe once co-operated to place on her throne, continues still to be an exile; though the very acts by which she is unlawfully dispossessed

* Alluding to a passage contained in a speech of the Duke of Wellington on the Catholic Relief Bill.—Ed.

† Pharsalia, lib. vii.—Ed.

‡ Which formed part of the basis of the arrangements for liberating Greece.—Ed.

are outrages and indignities of the highest nature against these Powers themselves.

His Majesty has twice told his Parliament that he has been compelled, by this alike perfidious and insolent usurpation, to break off all diplomatic intercourse with Portugal. Europe has tried the Usurper. Europe is determined that under his sway the usual relations of amity and courtesy cannot be kept up with a once illustrious and still respectable nation. So strong a mark of the displeasure of all European rulers has never yet been set on any country in time of peace. It would be a reflection on them, to doubt that they have been in some measure influenced by those unconfuted—I might say, uncontradicted—charges of monstrous crimes which hang over the head of the Usurper. His crimes, public and private, have brought on her this unparalleled dishonour. Never before were the crimes of a ruler the avowed and sufficient ground of so severe a visitation on a people. It is, therefore, my public duty to state them here; and I cannot do so in soft words, without injustice to Portugal and disgrace to myself. In a case touching our national honour, in relation to our conduct towards a feeble ally, and to the unmatched ignominy which has now befallen her, I must use the utmost frankness of speech.

I must inquire what are the causes of this fatal issue? Has the fluctuation of British policy had any part in it? Can we safely say that we have acted not merely with literal fidelity to engagements, but with generous support to those who risked all in reliance on us,—with consistent friendship towards a people who put their trust in us,—with liberal good faith to a monarch whom we acknowledge as lawful, and who has taken irretrievable steps in consequence of our apparent encouragement? The motion with which I shall conclude, will be for an address to obtain answers to these important questions, by the production of the principal despatches and documents relating to Portuguese affairs, from the summer of 1826 to to the present moment; whether originating at London, at Lisbon, at Vienna, at Rio Janeiro, or at Terceira.

As a ground for such a motion, I am obliged, Sir, to state at some length, though as shortly as I can, the events on which these documents may throw the needful light. In this statement I shall first lighten my burden by throwing overboard the pretended claim of Miguel to the crown, under I know not what ancient laws: not that I have not examined it,* and found it to be altogether absurd; but because he renounced it by repeated oaths,—because all the Powers of Europe recognised another settlement of the Portuguese crown, and took measures, though inadequate ones, to carry it into effect,—because His Majesty has withdrawn his minister from Lisbon, in acknowledgment of Donna Maria's right. I content myself with these authorities, as, in this place, indisputable. In the performance of my duty, I shall have to relate facts which I have heard from high authority, and to quote copies which I consider as accurate, of various despatches and minutes. I believe the truth of what I shall relate, and the correctness of what I shall quote. I shall be corrected wheresoever I may chance to be misinformed. I owe no part of my intelligence to any breach of duty. The House will not wonder that many copies of documents interesting to multitudes of men, in the disastrous situation of some of the parties, should have been scattered over Europe.

I pass over the revolution of 1820, when a democratical monarchy was adopted. The principles of its best adherents have been modified by the reform of 1826: its basest leaders are now among the tools of the Usurper, while he proscribes the loyal sufferers of that period. I mention only in passing the Treaty of Rio Janeiro, completed in August, 1825, by which Brazil was separated from Portugal, under the mediation of England and Austria;—the result of negotiations in which Sir Charles Stuart (now Lord Stuart de Rothesay), one of the most distinguished of British diplomatists, acted as the plenipotentiary of Portugal. In the following spring, John VI., the late King of Portugal, died, after having, in the ratification of the treaty, acknowledged Dom Pedro as his heir. It was a necessary interpretation of that treaty that the latter was not to continue King of Portugal in his own right, but only for the purpose of separating and settling the two kingdoms. He held Portugal in trust, and only till he had discharged this trust: for that purpose some time was necessary; the duration could not be precisely defined; but it was sufficient that there should appear no symptom of bad faith,—no appearance of an intention to hold it longer than the purposes of the trust absolutely required. For these purposes, and for that time, he was as much King of Portugal as his forefathers; and as such was recognised by all Europe, with the exception of Spain, which did not throw the discredit of her recognition on his title.

To effect the separation safely and beneficially for both countries, Dom Pedro abdicated the crown of Portugal in favour of his daughter Donna Maria, who was to be affianced to Dom Miguel, on condition of his swearing to observe the Constitution at the same time bestowed by Dom Pedro on the Portuguese nation. With whatever pangs he thus sacrificed his daughter, it must be owned that no arrangement seemed more likely to secure peace between the parties who divided Portugal, than the union of the chief of the Absolutists with a princess who became the hope of the Constitutionalists. Various opinions may be formed of the fitness of Portugal for a free constitution: but no one can doubt that the foundations of tranquillity could be laid no otherwise than in the security of each party from being oppressed by the other,—that a fair distribu-

* See the Case of Donna Maria.—Ed.

tion of political power between them was the only means of shielding either,—and that no such distribution could be effected without a constitution comprehending all classes and parties.

In the month of June, 1826, this Constitution was brought to Lisbon by the same eminent English minister who had gone from that city to Brazil as the plenipotentiary of John VI., and who now returned from Rio to the Tagus, as the bearer of the Constitutional Charter granted by Dom Pedro. I do not meddle with the rumours of dissatisfaction then produced by that Minister's visit to Lisbon. It is easier to censure at a distance, than to decide on a pressing emergency. It doubtless appeared of the utmost importance to Sir Charles Stuart, that the uncertainty of the Portuguese nation as to their form of government should not be continued; and that he, a messenger of peace, should hasten with its tidings. No one can doubt that the people of Portugal received such a boon, by such a bearer, as a mark of the favourable disposition of the British Government towards the Constitution. It is matter of notoriety that many of the Nobility were encouraged by this seeming approbation of Great Britain publicly to espouse it in a manner which they might and would otherwise have considered as an useless sacrifice of their own safety. Their constitutional principles, however sincere, required no such devotion, without these reasonable hopes of success, which every mark of the favour of England strongly tended to inspire. No diplomatic disavowal (a proceeding so apt to be considered as merely formal) could, even if it were public, which it was not, undo the impression made by this act of Sir Charles Stuart. No avowal, however public, made six months after, of an intention to abstain from all interference in intestine divisions, could replace the Portuguese in their first situation: they had taken irrevocable steps, and cut themselves off from all retreat.

But this is not all. Unless I be misinformed by those who cannot deceive, and are most unlikely to be deceived, the promulgation of the Constitution was suspended at Lisbon till the Regency could receive advice from His Majesty. The delay lasted at least a fortnight. The advice given was, to put the Charter in force. I do not know the terms of this opinion, or the limitations and conditions which might accompany it; nor does it import to my reasoning that I should. The great practical fact that it was asked for, was sure to be published, as it instantly was, through all the societies of Lisbon.—The small accessories were either likely to be concealed, or sure to be disregarded, by eager and ardent reporters. In the rapid succession of governments which then appeared at Lisbon, it could not fail to be known to every man of information, and spread with the usual exaggerations among the multitude, that Great Britain had declared for the Constitution. Let it not be thought that I mention these acts to blame them. They were the good offices of an ally. Friendly advice is not undue interference: it involves no encroachment on independence,—no departure from neutrality. "Strict neutrality consists merely, first, in abstaining from all part in the operations of war; and, secondly, in equally allowing or forbidding the supply of instruments of war to both parties."* Neutrality does not imply indifference. It requires no detestable impartiality between right or wrong. It consists in an abstinence from certain outward acts, well defined by international law,—leaving the heart entirely free, and the hands at liberty, where they are not visibly bound. We violated no neutrality in execrating the sale of Corsica,—in loudly crying out against the partition of Poland. Neutrality did not prevent Mr. Canning from almost praying in this House for the defeat of the French invasion of Spain. No war with France, or Austria, or Prussia, or Russia, ensued. Neutrality is not a point, but a line extending from the camp of one party to the camp of his opponent. It comprehends a great variety of shades and degrees of good and ill opinion: so that there is scope within its technical limits for a change from the most friendly to the most adverse policy, as long as arms are not taken up.

Soon after, another encouragement of an extraordinary nature presented itself to this unfortunate people, the atrocious peculiarities of which throw into shade its connection, through subsequent occurrences, with the acts of Great Britain. On the 30th October following, Dom Miguel, at Vienna, first swore to the Constitution, and was consequently affianced by the Pope's Nuncio, in the presence of the Imperial Ministers, to Donna Maria, whom he then solemnly acknowledged as Queen of Portugal. This was the first of his perjuries. It was a deliberate one, for it depended on the issue of a Papal dispensation, which required time and many formalities. The falsehood had every aggravation that can arise from the quality of the witnesses, the importance of the object which it secured to him, and the reliance which he desired should be placed on it by this country. At the same moment, a rebellion, abetted by Spain, broke out in his name, which still he publicly disavowed. Two months more, and the perfidy of Spain became apparent: the English troops were landed in Portugal; the rebels were driven from the territory of our ancient friends, by one of the most wise, honourable, vigorous, and brilliant strokes of policy ever struck by England. Mr. Canning delivered Portugal, and thus paid the debt which we owed for four centuries of constant faith and friendship,—for three invasions and a conquest endured in our cause. Still we were neutral: but what Portuguese could doubt that the nation which had scattered the Absolutists

* Martens, Précis du Droit des Gens, p. 524.

was friendly to the Constitution? No technical rule was broken; but new encouragement was unavoidably held out. These repeated incentives to a nation's hopes,—these informal but most effective, and therefore most binding acts, are those on which I lay the stress of this argument, still more than on federal and diplomatic proceedings.

There occurred in the following year a transaction between the Governments, more nearly approaching the nature of a treaty, and which, in my humble judgment, partakes much of its nature, and imposes its equitable and honourable duties. I now come to the conferences of Vienna in autumn, 1827. On the 3d of July in that year, Dom Pedro had issued an edict by which he approached more nearly to an abdication of the crown, and nominated Dom Miguel lieutenant of the kingdom. This decree had been enforced by letters of the same date,—one to Dom Miguel, commanding and requiring him to execute the office in conformity with the Constitution, and others to his allies, the Emperor of Austria and the King of Great Britain, committing to them as it were the execution of his decree, and beseeching them to take such measures as should render the Constitutional Charter the fundamental law of the Portuguese monarchy.* On these conditions, for this purpose, he prayed for aid in the establishment of Miguel. In consequence of this decree, measures had been immediately taken for a ministerial conference at Vienna, to concert the means of its execution.

And here, Sir, I must mention one of them, as of the utmost importance to both branches of my argument;—as an encouragement to the Portuguese, and as a virtual engagement with Dom Pedro: and I entreat the House to bear in mind the character of the transactions of which I am now to speak, as it affects both these important points. Count Villa Real, at that time in London, was appointed, I know not by whom, to act as a Portuguese minister at Vienna. Under colour of want of time to consult the Princess Regent at Lisbon, unsigned papers of advice, amounting in effect to instructions, were put into his hands by an Austrian and an English minister. In these papers he was instructed to assure Miguel, that by observing the Constitutional Charter, he would insure the support of England. The tone and temper fit to be adopted by Miguel in conversations at Paris were pointed out. Count Villa Real was more especially instructed to urge the necessity of Miguel's return by England. "His return," it was said, "is itself an immense guarantee to the Royalists; his return through this country will be a security to the other party." Could the Nobility and people of Portugal fail to consider so active a part in the settlement of their government, as an encouragement from their ancient and powerful ally to adhere to the Constitution? Is it possible that language so remarkable should not speedily have spread among them? May not some of those before whose eyes now rises a scaffold have been emboldened to act on their opinions by encouragement which seemed so flattering?

In the month of September, 1827, when Europe and America were bewailing the death of Mr. Canning, a note was given in at Vienna by the Marquess de Rezendé, the Brazilian minister at that court, containing the edict and letters of the 3d of July. The ministers of Austria, England, Portugal, and Brazil, assembled there on the 18th of October. They began by taking the Brazilian note and the documents which accompanied it, as the basis of their proceedings. It was thus acknowledged, solemnly, that Dom Pedro's title was unimpaired, and his settlement of the constitutional crown legitimate. They thus also accepted the execution of the trust on the conditions under which he committed it to them.

It appears from a despatch of Prince Metternich to Prince Esterhazy (the copy of which was entered on the minutes of the conference), that Prince Metternich immediately proceeded to dispose Dom Miguel towards a prudent and obedient course. He represented to him that Dom Pedro had required "the effectual aid of Austria to engage the Infant to submit with entire deference to the orders of his brother;" and he added, that "the Emperor of Austria could, in no case, consent to his return through Spain, which would be contrary to the wishes of Dom Pedro, and to the opinion of all the Governments of Europe." These representations were vain: the good offices of an August Person were interposed:—Miguel continued inflexible. But in an interview, where, if there had been any truth in him, he must have uttered it, he spontaneously added, that "he was determined to maintain in Portugal the Charter to which he had sworn, and that His Majesty might be at ease in that respect." This voluntary falsehood,—this daring allusion to his oath, amounting, virtually, to a repetition of it,—this promise, made at a moment when obstinacy in other respects gave it a fraudulent credit, deserves to be numbered among the most signal of the perjuries by which he deluded his subjects, and insulted all European sovereigns.

Prince Metternich, after having consulted Sir Henry Wellesley (now Lord Cowley) and the other Ministers, "on the means of conquering the resistance of the Infant," determined, conformably, (be it remembered) with the concurrence of all, to have a last and categorical explanation with that Prince. "I declared to him," says Prince Metternich, "without reserve, that, in his position, he had only to choose between immediately going to England on his way to Portugal, or

* "Je supplie V. M. de m'aider non seulement à faire que cette régence entre promptement en fonctions, mais encore à effectuer que la Charte Constitutionelle octroyée par moi devienne la loi fondamentale du Royaume."—Dom Pedro to the King of Great Britain, 3d July, 1827.

waiting at Vienna the further determination of Dom Pedro, to whom the Courts of London (be it not forgotten) and Vienna would communicate the motives which had induced the Infant not immediately to obey his brother's orders." Prince Metternich describes the instantaneous effect of this menace of further imprisonment with the elaborate softness of a courtier and a diplomatist. "I was not slow in perceiving that I had the happiness to make a profound impression on the mind of the Infant. After some moments of reflection, he at last yielded to the counsels of friendship and of reason." He owned "that he dreaded a return through England, because he knew that there were strong prejudices against him in that country, and he feared a bad reception there." He did justice to the people of England;—his conscious guilt foresaw their just indignation: but he could not be expected to comprehend those higher and more generous qualities which disposed them to forget his former crimes, in the hope that he was about to atone for them by the establishment of liberty. Nothing in their own nature taught them that it was possible for a being in human shape to employ the solemn promises which deluded them as the means of perpetrating new and more atrocious crimes.

Here, Sir, I must pause. Prince Metternich, with the concurrence of the English Minister, announced to Miguel, that if he did not immediately return to Portugal by way of England, he must remain at Vienna until Dom Pedro's further pleasure should be known. Reflections here crowd on the mind. Miguel had before agreed to maintain the Charter: had he hesitated on that subject, it is evident that the language used to him must have been still more categorical. No doubt is hinted on either side of his brother's sovereign authority: the whole proceeding implies it; and in many of its parts it is expressly affirmed. He is to be detained at Vienna, if he does not consent to go through England, in order to persuade the whole Portuguese nation of his sincerity, and to hold out—in the already quoted words of the English Minister—"a security to the Constitutional party," or, in other language, the strongest practical assurance to them, that he was sent by Austria, and more especially by England, to exercise the Regency, on condition of adhering to the Constitution. Whence did this right of imprisonment arise? I cannot question it without charging a threat of false imprisonment on all the great Powers. It may, perhaps, be thought, if not said, that it was founded on the original commitment by John VI. for rebellion and meditated parricide, and on the, perhaps, too lenient commutation of it into a sentence of transportation to Vienna. The pardon and enlargement granted by Dom Pedro were, on that supposition, conditional, and could not be earned without the fulfilment of all the conditions. Miguel's escape from custody must, then, be regarded as effected by fraud; and those to whom his person was intrusted by Dom Pedro, seem to me to have been bound, by their trust, to do all that was necessary to repair the evil consequences of his enlargement to the King and people of Portugal. But the more natural supposition is, that they undertook the trust, the custody, and the conditional liberation, in consequence of the application of their ally, the lawful Sovereign of Portugal, and for the public object of preserving the quiet of that kingdom, and with it the peace of Europe and the secure tranquillity of their own dominions. Did they not thereby contract a federal obligation with Dom Pedro to complete their work, and, more especially, to take care that Miguel should not immediately employ the liberty, the sanction, the moral aid, which they had given him, for the overthrow of the fundamental laws which they too easily trusted that he would observe his promises and oaths to uphold? When did this duty cease? Was it not fully as binding on the banks of the Tagus as on those of the Danube? If, in the fulfilment of this obligation, they had a right to imprison him at Vienna, because he would not allay the suspicions of the Constitutional party, by returning through England, is it possible to contend that they were not bound to require and demand at Lisbon, that he should instantly desist from his open overthrow of the Charter?

I do not enter into any technical distinctions between a protocol and a treaty. I consider the protocol as the minutes of conferences, in which the parties verbally agreed on certain important measures, which, being afterwards acted upon by others, became conclusively binding, in faith, honour, and conscience, on themselves. In consequence of these conferences, Dom Miguel, on the 19th of October, wrote letters to his brother, His Britannic Majesty, and Her Royal Highness the Regent of Portugal. In the two former, he solemnly re-affirmed his determination to maintain the charter "granted by Dom Pedro;" and, in the last, he more fully assures his sister his unshaken purpose "to maintain, and cause to be observed, the laws and institutions legally granted by our august brother, and which we have all sworn to maintain; and I desire that you should give to this solemn declaration the necessary publicity." On the faith of these declarations, he was suffered to leave Vienna. The Powers who thus enlarged him taught the world, by this act, that they believed him. They lent him their credit, and became vouchers for his fidelity. On the faith of these declations, the King and people of England received him with kindness, and forgot the criminal, to hail the first Constitutional King of emancipated Portugal. On the same faith, the English ambassadors attended him; and the English flag, which sanctioned his return, proclaimed to the Constitutionalists, that they might lay aside their fears for liberty and their reasonable apprehensions for themselves. The British ministers, in their instructions to Count Villa Real, had expressly declared, that his return through England was a great security to the Constitutional party. Facts had loudly spoken the same language; but the very words of the British Minister must inevitably have resounded through Portugal—lulling vigilance, seeming to dispense with caution, and tending to extinguish the blackest suspicions. This is not all: Count Villa Flor, then a minister, who knew his man, on the first rumours of Miguel's return obtained the appointment of Ambassador to Paris, that he might not be caught by the wolf in his den. It was apprehended that such a step would give general alarm:—he was prevailed upon to remain, by letters from Vienna, with assurances of Miguel's good dispositions, which were not unknown to the British Ministers at Vienna; and he continued in office a living pledge from the two Powers to the whole Portuguese people, that their Constitution was to be preserved. How many irrevocable acts were done,—how many dungeons were crowded,—how many deaths were braved,—how many were suffered—from faith in perfidious assurances, accredited by the apparent sanction of two deluded and abused Courts! How can these Courts be released from the duty of repairing the evil which their credulity has caused!

I shall say nothing of the Protocol of London of the 12th of January, 1828, except that it adopted and ratified the conferences of Vienna,—that it provided for a loan to Miguel to assist his re-establishment,—and that it was immediately transmitted to Dom Pedro, together with the Protocol of Vienna. Dom Pedro had originally besought the aid of the Powers to secure the Constitution. They did not refuse it;—they did not make any reservations or limitations respecting it: on the contrary, they took the most decisive measures on the principle of his proposition. So implicitly did Dom Pedro rely on them that, in spite of all threatening symptoms of danger, he has sent his daughter to Europe;—a step from which he cannot recede, without betraying his own dignity, and seeming to weaken her claims; and which has proved a fruitful source of embarrassment, vexation, and humiliation, to himself and his most faithful councillors. By this decisive measure, he has placed his loyal subjects in a more lasting and irreconcilable state of hostility with those who have mastered their country, and has rendered compromise under better rulers more difficult.

Under all these circumstances, Sir, I cannot doubt that the Mediating Powers have acquired a right imperatively to require that Miguel shall renounce that authority which by fraud and falsehood he has obtained from them the means of usurping. They are bound to exercise that right by a sacred duty towards Dom Pedro, who has intrusted them with the conditional establishment of the Regency, and the people of Portugal, with whom their obligation of honour is the more inviolable, because it must be informal. I shall be sorry to hear that such duties are to be distinguished, by the first Powers of Christendom, from the most strictly literal obligations of a treaty.

On the 28th of February, Miguel landed at Lisbon, accompanied by an English ambassador, who showed as much sagacity and firmness as were perhaps ever combined in such circumstances. The Cortes met to receive the oaths of the Regent to the Emperor and the Constitution. A scene then passed which is the most dastardly of all his perjuries,—the basest evasion that could be devised by a cowardly and immoral superstition. He acted as if he were taking the oaths, slurring them over in apparent hurry, and muttering inarticulately, instead of uttering their words. A Prince of one of the most illustrious of Royal Houses, at the moment of undertaking the sacred duties of supreme magistracy, in the presence of the representatives of the nation, and of the ministers of all civilized states, had recourse to the lowest of the knavish tricks formerly said (but I hope calumniously) to have been practised by miscreants at the Old Bailey, who by bringing their lips so near the book without kissing it as to deceive the spectator, satisfied their own base superstition, and dared to hope that they could deceive the Searcher of Hearts.

I shall not follow him through the steps of his usurpation. His designs were soon perceived: they were so evident that Sir Frederick Lamb, with equal sense and spirit, refused to land the money raised by loan, and sent it back to this country. They might have been then defeated by the Loyalists: but an insurmountable obstacle presented itself. The British troops were instructed to abstain from interference in domestic dissensions:—there was one exception, and it was in favour of the basest man in Portugal. The Loyalists had the means of sending Miguel to his too merciful brother in Brazil: they were bound by their allegiance to prevent his rebellion; and loyalty and liberty alike required it. The right was not doubted by the British authorities: but they were compelled to say that the general instruction to protect the Royal Family would oblige them to protect Miguel against attack. Our troops remained long enough to give him time to displace all faithful officers, and to fill the garrison with rebels; while by the help of monks and bribes, he stirred up the vilest rabble to a "sedition for slavery." When his designs were ripe for execution, we delivered him from all shadow of restraint by recalling our troops to England. I do not mention this circumstance as matter of blame, but of the deepest regret. It is too certain, that if they had left Lisbon three months sooner, or remained there three months longer, in either case Portugal would have been saved. This consequence, however unintended, surely imposes on us the duty of showing much more than ordinary consideration towards those who were destroyed by the effect of our measures. The form in which the blockade of Oporto was announced did not repair this misfortune. I have never yet heard why we did not speak of "the persons exercising the power of government," instead of calling Miguel "Prince Regent,"—a title which he had forfeited, and indeed had himself rejected. Nor do I see why in the singular case of two parties,—one falsely, the other truly,—professing to act on behalf of Dom Pedro, both might not have been impartially forbidden to exercise belligerent rights at sea until his pleasure was made known. The fatal events which have followed are, I have serious reasons to believe, no proof of the state of general opinion in Portugal. A majority of the higher nobility, with almost all the considerable inhabitants of towns, were and are still well affected. The clergy, the lower gentry, and the rabble, were, but I believe are not now, adverse. The enemies of the Constitution were the same classes who opposed our own Revolution for fourscore years. Accidents, unusually unfortunate, deprived the Oporto army of its commanders. Had they disregarded this obstacle, and immediately advanced from Coimbra, it is the opinion of the most impartial and intelligent persons, then at Lisbon, that they would have succeeded without a blow. It is certain that the Usurper and his mother had prepared for a flight to Madrid, and, after the fatal delay at Coimbra, were with difficulty persuaded to adopt measures of courage. As soon as Miguel assumed the title of King, all the Foreign Ministers fled from Lisbon: a nation which ceased to resist such a tyrant was deemed unworthy of remaining a member of the European community. The brand of exclusion was fixed, which is not yet withdrawn. But, in the mean time, the delay at Coimbra, the strength thence gained by the Usurper, and the discouragement spread by the retreat of the Loyalists, led to the fall of Oporto, and compelled its loyal garrison, with many other faithful subjects, to leave their dishonoured country. They were doubly honoured by the barbarous inhospitality of Spain on the one hand, and on the other by the sympathy of France and of England.

At this point, Sir, I must deviate a moment from my line, to consider the very peculiar state of our diplomatic intercourse with Dom Pedro and Donna Maria, in relation to the crown of Portugal. All diplomatic intercourse with the Usurper in possession of it was broken off. There were three ministers from the legitimate sovereigns of the House of Braganza in London:—the Marquess Palmella, ambassador from Portugal, who considered himself in that character as the minister of Donna Maria, the Queen acknowledged by us,—the Marquess Barbacena, the confidential adviser appointed by Dom Pedro to guide the infant Queen,—and the Viscount Itabayana, the recognised minister from that monarch as Emperor of Brazil. They all negotiated, or attempted to negotiate, with us. The Marquess Palmella was told that the success of the usurpation left him no Portuguese interests to protect,—that his occupation was gone. The Viscount Itabayana was repelled as being merely the minister from Brazil, a country finally separated from Portugal. The Marquess Barbacena was positively apprised that we did not recognise the right of Dom Pedro to interfere as head of the House of Brazil, or as international guardian of his daughter. By some ingenious stratagem each was excluded, or driven to negotiate in an inferior and unacknowledged character. This policy seems to me very like what used to be called in the courts, "sharp practice." It is not free from all appearance of international special pleading, which seems to me the less commendable, because the Government were neither guided nor hampered by precedent. It is a câse, I will venture to say, without parallel. The result was, that an infant Queen, recognised as legitimate, treated with personal honour and kindness, is left without a guardian to guide her, or a minister to act for her. Such was the result of our international subtleties and diplomatic punctilios!

To avoid such a practical absurdity, nothing seemed more simple than to hold that nature and necessity, with the entire absence of any other qualified person, had vested in Dom Pedro the guardianship of his Royal daughter, for the purpose of executing the separation of the two countries, and the abdication of the Portuguese crown. His character would have had some analogy to that of the guardian named in a court of justice to a minor party in a law-suit. Ingenuity would, I think, have been better employed in discovering the legal analogies, or political reasons, which are favourable to this natural and convenient doctrine. Even the rejection of the minister of a deposed sovereign has not always been rigidly enforced. Queen Elizabeth's virtues were not indulgent; nor did her treatment of the Queen of Scots do honour to her character: yet she continued for years after the deposition of Mary to treat with Bishop Leslie; and he was not pronounced to have forfeited the privileges of an ambassador till he was detected in a treasonable conspiracy.

A negotiation under the disadvantage of an unacknowledged character was, however, carried on by the Marquess Palmella, and the Marquess Barbacena, between the months of November and February last, in which they claimed the aid of Great Britain against the Usurper, by virtue of the ancient treaties, and of the conferences at Vienna. Perhaps I must allow that the first claim could not in strictness be maintained:—perhaps this case was not in the bond. But I have already stated my reasons for considering the conferences at Vienna, the measures concerted there, and the acts done on their faith. as equivalent to an engagement on the part of Austria and England with Dom Pedro. At all events, this series of treaties for four hundred and fifty years, from Edward III. to George IV.—longer and more uninterrupted than any other in history,—containing many articles closely approaching the nature of a guarantee, followed, as it has been by the strong marks of favour showed by England to the Constitution, and by the principles and plan adopted by England and Austria (with the approbation of France, Russia, and Prussia), at Vienna, altogether hold out the strongest virtual encouragement to the Constitutionalists. How could Portugal believe that those who threatened to imprison Miguel at Vienna, would hesitate about hurling him from an usurped throne at Lisbon? How could the Portuguese nation suppose that, in a case where Austria and England had the concurrence of all the great Powers, they should be deterred from doing justice by a fear of war? How could they imagine that the rule of non-interference,—violated against Spain,—violated against Naples,—violated against Piedmont,—more honourably violated for Greece but against Turkey,—should be held sacred, only when it served to screen the armies and guard the usurpation of Miguel? Perhaps their confidence might have been strengthened by what they must think the obvious policy of the two Courts. It does seem to me that they might have commanded Miguel to quit his prey (for war is ridiculous) as a mere act of self-defence. Ferdinand VII. is doubtless an able preacher of republicanism; but he is surpassed in this particular by Miguel. I cannot think it a safe policy to allow the performance of an experiment to determine how low the kingly character may sink in the Pyrenean Peninsula, without abating its estimation in the rest of Europe. Kings are sometimes the most formidable of all enemies to royalty.

The issue of our conduct towards Portugal for the last eighteen months is, in point of policy, astonishing. We are now bound to defend a country of which we have made all the inhabitants our enemies. It is needless to speak of former divisions: there are now only two parties there. The Absolutists hate us: they detest the country of juries and of Parliaments,—the native land of Canning,—the source from which their Constitution seemed to come,—the model which has excited the love of liberty throughout the world. No half-measures, however cruel to their opponents, can allay their hatred. If you doubt, look at their treatment of British subjects, which I consider chiefly important, as indicating their deep-rooted and irreconcilable malignity to us. The very name of an Englishman is with them that of a jacobin and an atheist. Look at their treatment of the city of Oporto and of the island of Madeira, which may be almost considered as English colonies. If this hatred was in any degree excited by the feelings of the English inhabitants towards them, from what could such feelings spring but from a knowledge of the execrable character of the ruling faction? Can they ever forgive us for degrading their Government and disgracing their minion, by an exclusion from international intercourse more rigorous than any incurred under a Papal interdict of the fourteenth century? Their trust alone is in the Spanish Apostolicals. The Constitutionalists, who had absorbed and softened all the more popular parties of the former period, no longer trust us. They consider us as having incited them to resistance, and as having afterwards abandoned them to their fate. They do not distinguish between treaties and protocols,—between one sort of guarantee and another. They view us, more simply, as friends who have ruined them. Their trust alone is in Constitutional France. Even those who think, perhaps justly, that the political value of Portugal to us is unspeakably diminished by the measures which we have happily taken for the security of Ireland, cannot reasonably expect that any nation of the second order, which sees the fate of Portugal, will feel assurance of safety from the protection of England.

If we persist in an unfriendly neutrality, it is absurd voluntarily to continue to submit to obligations from which we may justly release ourselves. For undoubtedly a government so covered with crimes, so disgraced by Europe as that of Miguel, is a new source of danger, not contemplated in the treaties of alliance and guarantee. If Mr. Canning, with reason, held that an alliance of Portugal with the Spanish Revolutionists would, on that principle, release us from our obligations, it cannot be doubted that by the standing infamy of submission to the present Government, she well deserves to forfeit all remaining claims to our protection.

Notwithstanding the failure of the negotiations to obtain our aid as an ally, I believe that others have been carried on, and probably are not yet closed, in London and at Rio Janeiro. It has been proposed, by the Mediating Powers, to Dom Pedro, to complete the marriage, to be silent on the Constitution,—but to obtain an universal amnesty. I cannot wonder at Dom Pedro's rejection of conditions, one of which only can be effectual,—that which imposes on his daughter the worst husband in Europe. What wonder that he should reject a proposal to put the life of a Royal infant under the care of murderers,—to join her youthful hand, at the altar, with one embrued in the blood of her most faithful friends! As for the other conditions, what amnesty can be expected from the wolf of Oporto? What imaginable security can be devised for an amnesty, unless the vanquished party be shielded by some political privileges? Yet I rejoice that these negotiations have not closed,—that the two Powers have adopted the decisive principle of stipulating what Miguel must do, without consulting him; and that, whether from the generous feelings of a Royal mind at home, or from the spirit of constitutional liberty in the greatest of foreign countries, or from both these causes, the negotiations have assumed a more amicable tone. I do not wonder that Dom Pedro, after having protested against the rebellion of his brother, and the coldness of his friends, should indignantly give orders for the return of the young Queen, while he provides for the assertion of her rights, by the establishment of a regency in Europe. I am well pleased however to learn, that the Mediating Powers have advised his ministers to suspend the execution of his commands till he shall be acquainted with the present state of affairs. The monstrous marriage is, at all events, I trust, for ever abandoned. As long as a negotiation is on foot respecting the general question, I shall not despair of our ancient Ally.

Sir, I must own, that there is no circumstance in this case, which, taken singly, I so deeply regret as the late unhappy affair of Terceira. The Portuguese troops and Royalists who landed in England, had been stationed, after some time, at Plymouth, where their exemplary conduct gained the most public and general marks of the esteem of the inhabitants. In the month of November, a proposition to disperse them in the towns and villages of the adjacent counties, without their officers, was made by the British Government. Far be it from me to question the right of His Majesty to disperse all military bodies in his dominions, and to prevent this country from being used as an arsenal or port of equipment by one belligerent against another,—even in cases where, as in the present, it cannot be said that the assemblage was dangerous to the peace of this kingdom, or menacing to the safety of any other. I admit, in their fullest extent, the rights and duties of neutral states. Yet the dispersion of these troops, without their officers, could scarcely fail to discourage them, to deprive them of military spirits and habits, and to end in the utter disbanding of the feeble remains of a faithful army. The ministers of Donna Maria considered this as fatal to their hopes. An unofficial correspondence was carried on from the end of November to the beginning of January on the subject, between the Duke of Wellington and the Marquess Palmella,—a man of whom I cannot help saying, that he is perhaps the individual by whom his country is most favourably known to foreign nations,—that, highly esteemed as he is among statesmen for his share in the greatest affairs of Europe for the last sixteen years, he is not less valued by his friends for his amiable character and various accomplishments,—and that there is no one living more incapable of forgetting the severest dictates of delicacy and honour. The Marquess chose rather to send the faithful remnant of Donna Maria's troops to Brazil, than to subject them to utter annihilation. Various letters passed on the reasonableness of this dispersion, and the mode of removal, from the 20th of November to the 20th of December, in which Brazil was considered as the destination of the troops. In a letter of the 20th of December, the Marquess Palmella, for the first time, mentioned the Island of Terceira. It had been twice before mentioned, in negotiations, by two ministers of the House of Braganza, with totally different views, which, if the course of debate should call for it, I trust I shall explain: but it was first substituted for Brazil by the Marquess Palmella on the 20th of December. I anxiously particularize the date, because it is alone sufficient to vindicate his scrupulous honour. In the month of May, some partisans of Miguel had shaken the loyalty of a part of the inhabitants: Dom Pedro and the Constitution were proclaimed on the 22d of June; the ringleaders of the rebellion were arrested; and the lawful government was re-established. Some disturbances, however, continued, which enabled the priests to stir up a revolt in the end of September. The insurgents were again suppressed in a few days; but it was not till the 4th of December that Donna Maria was proclaimed as Queen of Portugal in conformity to the treaty of separation, to the Constitutional Charter, and to the Act of Abdication. Since that time I have now before me documents which demonstrate that her authority has been regularly exercised and acknowledged in that island, with no other disturbance than that occasioned by one or two bands of Guerillas, quickly dispersed, and without any pretence for alleging that there was in that island a disputed title, or an armed contest.

On the 20th of December, then, the Marquess Palmella informed the Duke of Wellington, that though he (the Marquess) had hitherto chosen Brazil as being the only safe, though distant, refuge for the troops, "yet, from the information which he had just received of the entire and peaceable submission of Terceira to the young Queen, and of the disappearance of the squadron sent by the actual Government of Portugal to blockade the Azores, he now intended to send her troops to that part of her dominions where she was not only the rightful but the actual Sovereign, and for which he conceived that they might embark at Plymouth, without any infringement of the neutrality of the British territories." This letter contains the explanation of the change of destination. Unarmed troops could not have been safely sent to Terceira, nor merchant vessels either, while there were intestine divisions, or apprehensions of a blockade, or indeed till there was full and authentic information of the establishment of quiet and legitimate authority. The Marquess Palmella thought that the transportation of the troops had now become as lawful as it was obviously desirable. To remove the Queen's troops to a part of her own actual dominions, seemed to him, as I own it still seems to me, an act consistent even with the cold and stern neutrality assumed by England. Had not a Queen, acknowledged in England, and obeyed in Terceira, a perfect right to send her own soldiers home from a neutral country? If the fact of the actual return of Terceira to its allegiance be not denied and disproved, I shall be anxious to hear the reasons, to me unknown, which authorise a neutral power to forbid such a movement. It is vain to say, that Great Britain, as mediator in the Treaty of 1825, was entitled to prevent the separation of the Azores from Portugal, and their subjection to Brazil; for, on the 4th of December, Donna Maria had been proclaimed at Terceira as Queen of Portugal, in virtue of the possession of the Portuguese crown. It is vain to say that the embarcation had a hostile character; since it was immediately destined for the territory of the friendly sovereign. Beyond this point the neutral is neither bound nor entitled to inquire. It was not, as has been inconsiderately said, an expedition against the Azores. It was the movement of Portuguese troops from neutral England to obedient and loyal Terceira,—where surely the Sovereign might employ her troops in such manner as she judged right. How far is the contrary proposition to go? Should we,—could we, as a neutral Power, have hindered Miguel from transporting those of his followers, who might be in England, to Lisbon, because they might be sent thence against the Azores. It is true, the group of islands have the generic name of the Azores: but so,—though the American islands are called the West Indies,—I presume it will not be contended that a rebellion in Barbadoes could authorise a foreign Sovereign in preventing British troops which happened to be on his territory from being despatched by His Majesty to strengthen his garrison of Jamaica. Supposing the facts which I have stated to be true, I can see no mode of impugning the inferences which I have made from them. Until I receive a satisfactory answer, I am bound to say, that I consider the prohibition of this embarcation as a breach of neutrality in favour of the Usurper.

And even, Sir, if these arguments are successfully controverted, another proposition remains, to which it is still more difficult for me to conceive the possibility of an answer. Granting that the permission of the embarcation was a breach of neutrality, which might be, and must be, prevented on British land, or in British waters, where is the proof from reason, from usage,—even from example or authority, that England was bound, or entitled, to pursue the expedition over the ocean, —to use force against them on the high seas, —most of all to levy war against them within the waters of Terceira? Where are the proofs of the existence of any such right or duty? I have searched for them in vain. Even if an example or two could be dug up, they would not affect my judgment. I desire to know where the series of examples from good times can be found which might amount to general usage, and thus constitute a part of international law. I never can consider mere general reasoning as a sufficient justification of such an act. There are many instances in which international law rejects such reasonings. For example, to allow a passage to a belligerent through a neutral territory, is not in itself a departure from neutrality. But to fire on a friendly ship within the waters of a friendly state, for a wrong done in an English harbour, is an act which appears to me a most alarming innovation in the law of civilized war. The attack on the Spanish frigates in 1805 is probably reconcilable with the stern and odious rights of war: yet I am sure that every cool-headed and true-hearted Englishman would desire to blot the scene from the annals of Europe. Every approach towards rigour, beyond the common and well-known usage of war, is an innovation: and it must ever be deplored that we have made the first experiment of its extension beyond former usage in the case of the most ancient of our allies, in the season of her utmost need.

I shrink from enlarging on the scene which closed,—I fear for ever,—a friendship of four hundred and fifty years. On the 16th of January last, three English vessels and a Russian brig, having aboard five hundred unarmed Portuguese, attempted to enter the port of Praya, in the island of Terceira. Captain Walpole, of His Majesty's ship "Ranger," fired on two of these vessels, which had got under the guns of the forts protecting the harbour: the blood of Her Most Faithful Majesty's subjects was spilt; one soldier was killed; a peaceable passenger was dangerously wounded. I forbear to state further particulars. I hope and confidently trust that Captain Walpole will acquit himself of all negligence,—of all want of the most anxious endeavours to spare blood, and to be frugal of violence, in a proceeding where such defects would be crimes. Warmly as I rejoice in the prevalence of that spirit of liberty, and, as a consequence, of humanity, of which the triumph in France is so happy for Europe, I must own that I cannot contemplate without mortification the spectacle of the loyal Portuguese exhibiting in a French port wounds inflicted by the arms of their ancient ally, protector, and friend. The friendship of four centuries and a half should have had a more becoming close: it should not have been extinguished in fire and blood.

I will now conclude, Sir, with the latest, and perhaps the saddest incident in this tragic story of a nation's "hopes too fondly raised," perhaps, but surely "too rudely crossed." I shall not quote it as a proof of the Usurper's inhumanity;—there is no man in this House who would not say that such proofs are needless: I produce it, only as a sample of the boldness with which he now throws down the gauntlet to the governments and nations of Christendom. On Thursday the 7th of May, little more than three weeks ago, in the city of Oporto, ten gentlemen were openly murdered on the avowed ground, that on the 16th of May, 1828, while Miguel himself still pretended to be the lieutenant of Dom Pedro, they followed the example of Austria and England, in treating Dom Pedro as their lawful sovereign, and in endeavouring to carry into execution the laws established by him. Two were reserved for longer suffering by a pretended pardon:—the tender mercies of the wicked are cruel. One of these two was condemned to a lingering yet agonizing death in the galleys of Angola; the other, the brother of the Ambassador at Brussels, was condemned to hard labour for life, but adjudged first to witness the execution of his friends; —an aggravation light to the hard-hearted, heart-breaking to the generous, which, by a hateful contrivance, draws the whole force of the infliction from the virtues of the sufferer. The city of Oporto felt this scene with a horror not lessened by the sentiments which generations of Englishmen have, I would fain hope, left behind them. The rich fled to their villas; the poor shut up their doors and windows; the peasants of the neighbourhood withheld their wonted supplies from the markets of the tainted city; the deserted streets were left to the executioner, his guards, and his victims,—with no more beholders than were needful to bear witness, that those "faithful found among the faithless" left the world with the feelings of men who die for their country.

On the 16th of May, 1828, the day on which the pretended treasons were charged to have been committed, the state of Portugal was, in the light most indulgent to Miguel, that of a contest for the crown. It was not a rebellion: it was a civil war. At the close of these wars without triumph, civilized victors hasten to throw the pall of amnesty over the wounds of their country. Not so Miguel: ten months after submission, he sheds blood for acts done before the war. He has not the excuses of Robespierre and Marat:—no army is marching on Lisbon; no squadron is entering the Tagus with the flag of deliverance. The season of fulness and safety, which stills the tiger, rouses the coward's thirst for blood. Is this the blind instinct of ferocity? Is it only to carry despair into the thousands of loyal Portuguese whom he has scattered over the earth? No! acts of later date might have served that purpose: his choice of time is a defiance to Europe. The offence here was resisting an usurpation, the consummation of which a few weeks after made the representatives of Europe fly from Lisbon, as from a city of the plague. The indignity is chiefly pointed at the two Mediating Powers, who have not yet relinquished all hopes of compromise. But it is not confined to them: though he is aware that a breath would blow him away without blood or cost, he makes a daring experiment on the patience of all Europe. He will draw out for slaughter handful after handful of those, whose sole crime was to trust the words and follow the example of all civilized nations. He believes that an attempt will at length be made to stop his crimes by a recognition of his authority,—that by dint of murders he may force his way into the number of the dispensers of justice and mercy. He holds up the bleeding heads of Oporto to tell sovereigns and nations alike how he scorns their judgment and defies their power.

SPEECH

ON THE SECOND READING OF

THE BILL TO AMEND THE REPRESENTATION

OF THE PEOPLE OF ENGLAND AND WALES.

DELIVERED IN THE HOUSE OF COMMONS, ON THE 4TH OF JULY, 1831.

Mr. Speaker,—I feel no surprise, and certainly no regret, at the applause which followed the speech of the Honourable and Learned Gentleman,* whose speeches never leave any unpleasant impression, but the reflection that he speaks so seldom. Much of that excellent speech so immediately bears on the whole question of Parliamentary Reform, that it will naturally lead me to the consideration of the general principle of the Bill before us.

I must, Sir, however, premise a very few remarks on the speech of the Honourable

* Mr. Fynes Clinton, M. P. for Aldborough. —Ed.

Baronet;* though I shall not follow him through his account of the squabble between the labourers and their employers at Merthyr Tidvil, which I leave to the justice of the law, or, what is better, to the prudence and principle of both parties. Neither can I seriously handle his objection to this Bill, that it has produced a strong interest, and divided opinions throughout the kingdom. Such objections prove too much: they would exclude most important questions, and, certainly, all reformatory measures. It is one of the chief advantages of free governments, that they excite,—sometimes to an inconvenient degree, but, upon the whole, with the utmost benefit,—all the generous feelings, all the efforts for a public cause, of which human nature is capable. But there is one point in the ingenious speech of the Honourable Baronet, which, as it touches the great doctrines of the Constitution, and involves a reflection on the conduct of many Members of this House, cannot be passed over, without an exposition of the fallacy which shuts his eyes to very plain truths.—Mr. Burke, in the famous speech at Bristol, told, indeed, his constituents, that as soon as he should be elected, however much he might respect their opinions, his votes must be governed by his own conscience. This doctrine was indisputably true. But did he not, by his elaborate justification of his public conduct, admit their jurisdiction over it, and acknowledge, that if he failed in converting them, they had an undoubted right to reject him? Then, if they could justly reject him, for differing from what they thought right, it follows, most evidently, that they might, with equal justice, refuse their suffrages to him, if they thought his future votes likely to differ from those which they deemed indispensable to the public weal. If they doubted what that future conduct might be, they were entitled, and bound, to require a satisfactory explanation, either in public or in private; and in case of unsatisfactory, or of no explanation, to refuse their support to the candidate. This duty the people may exercise in whatever form they deem most effectual. They impose no restriction on the conscience of the candidate; they only satisfy their own conscience, by rejecting a candidate, of whose conduct, on the most momentous question, they have reason to doubt. Far less could constituents be absolved, on the present occasion, from the absolute duty of ascertaining the determination of candidates on the subject of Parliamentary Reform. His Majesty, in his speech from the throne, on the 22d of April, was pleased to declare, "I have come to meet you, for the purpose of proroguing Parliament, with a view to its immediate dissolution. I have been induced to resort to this measure, for the purpose of ascertaining the sense of my people, in the way in which it can be most constitutionally and authentically expressed, on the expediency of making such changes in the representation as circumstances may appear to require; and which, founded upon the acknowledged principles of the Constitution, may tend at once to uphold the just rights and prerogatives of the Crown, and to give security to the liberties of the subject." What answer could the people have made to the appeal thus generously made to them, without taking all necessary means to be assured that the votes of those, whom they chose, would sufficiently manifest to him the sense of his people, on the changes necessary to be made in the representation.

On subjects of foreign policy, Sir, a long silence has been observed on this side of the House,—undisturbed, I am bound to add, by the opposite side, for reasons which are very obvious. We are silent, and we are allowed to be silent; because, a word spoken awry, might occasion fatal explosions. The affairs of the Continent are so embroiled, that we have forborne to express those feelings, which must agitate the breast of every human being, at the sight of that admirable and afflicting struggle* on which the eyes of Europe are constantly, however silently, fixed. As it is admitted by the Honourable Baronet, that the resistance of the French to an usurpation of their rights last year was glorious to all who were concerned in it, it follows that, being just, it has no need of being sanctioned by the approbation of fortune. Who then are morally answerable for the unfortunate confusions which followed, and for the further commotion, which, if heaven avert it not, may convulse France and Europe? Who opened the floodgates of discord on mankind? Not the friends of liberty,—not the advocates of popular principles: their hands are clean;—they took up arms only to defend themselves against wrong. I hold sacred every retreat of misfortune, and desire not to disturb fallen greatness; but justice compels me to say, that the hands of the late King of France were made to unlock these gates by his usurping ordinances,—

"To open; but to shut surpassed his power."

The dangers of Europe do not originate in democratical principles, or democratical power, but in a conspiracy for the subversion of all popular rights, however sanctioned by oaths, by constitution, and by laws.

I shall now, Sir, directly proceed to the latter part of the speech of the Honourable and Learned Member for Boroughbridge, which regards the general principle and character of this Bill. In so doing, I shall endeavour, as far as may be, not to displease the fastidious ears of the Honourable Baronet, by frequently repeating the barbarous names of the Tudors and Plantagenets. I

* Sir John Walsh, who had moved the amendment that the Bill be read that day six months, which Mr. Clinton had seconded.—Ed.

* The insurrection in Poland.—Ed.

must, however, follow the Honourable and Learned Member to the fountains of our government and laws, whither, indeed, he calls upon me with no unfriendly voice to accompany him.

That no example can be found from the time of Simon de Montfort to the present year, either in the practice of ancient legislation, or in the improvements proposed by modern Reformers, which sanctions the general principle of this Bill, is an assertion, which I am sure the Honourable Gentleman will discover to be unadvisedly hazarded.

I shall begin with one of the latest examples of a Reformer of great weight and authority,—that which is afforded by the speech and the plan of Mr. Pitt, in 1785, because it does not only itself exhibit the principle of the schedules of this Bill, but because it proves, beyond all possibility of dispute, his thorough conviction that this principle is conformable to the ancient laws and practice of the constitution. The principle of Schedules A. and B. is the abolition, partial or total, of the elective rights of petty and dependent boroughs. The principle of Schedules C. D. and E. is the transfer of that resumed right to great towns, and to other bodies of constituents deemed likely to use it better. Let me now state Mr. Pitt's opinion, in his own words, on the expediency of acting on both these principles, and on the agreement of both with the ancient course and order of the constitution. His plan, it is well known, was to take away seventy-two members from thirty-six small boroughs, and to add them to the county representation, with a permanent provision for such other transfers of similar rights to great towns, as should from time to time seem necessary. His object, in this disfranchisement and enfranchisement, was, according to his own words, "to make the House of Commons an assembly which should have the closest union, and the most perfect sympathy with the mass of the people." To effect this object, he proposed to buy up these boroughs by the establishment of a fund, (*cheers from the Opposition,*) of which the first effect was expected to be considerable, and the accumulation would prove an irresistible temptation. Gentlemen would do well to hear the whole words of Mr. Pitt, before they so loudly exult:—"It is an indisputable doctrine of antiquity, that the state of the representation is to be changed with the change of circumstances. Change in the borough representation was frequent. A great number of the boroughs, originally Parliamentary, had been disfranchised,—that is, the Crown had ceased to summon them to send burgesses. Some of these had been restored on their petitions: the rest had not recovered their lost franchise. Considering the restoration of the former, and the deprivation of the latter, *the constitution had been grossly violated, if it was true* (*which he denied,*) that the extension of the elective franchise to one set of boroughs, and the resumption of it from others, was a violation of the constitution. The alterations were not made from principle; but they were founded on the general notion which gave the discretionary power to the Crown,—viz., that the principal places, and not the decayed boroughs, should exercise the right of election."* I know full well that these boroughs were to be bought. I also know, that the late Member for Dorset (Mr. Bankes), the college-friend, the zealous but independent supporter of Mr. Pitt, exclaimed against the purchase, though he applauded the Reform. How did Mr. Pitt answer? Did he say, I cannot deprive men of inviolable privileges without compensation; I cannot promote Reform by injustice? Must he not have so answered, if he had considered the resumption of the franchise as "corporation robbery?" No! he excuses himself to his friend: he declares the purchase to be "the tender part of the subject," and apologizes for it, as "having become a necessary evil, if any Reform was to take place." Would this great master of language, who so thoroughly understood and practised precision and propriety of words, have called that a necessary evil which he thought an obligation of justice,—the payment of a sacred debt? It is clear from the very words that follow,—"if any Reform were to take place," that he regarded the price of the boroughs merely as a boon to so many borough-holders to become proselytes to it. It is material also to observe, that as compensation was no part of his plans or suggestions in 1782 and 1783, he could not have consistently represented it as of right due. Another decisive reason renders it impossible to annex any other meaning to his language:—he justifies his system of transferring the franchise by analogy to the ancient practice of ceasing to summon some boroughs to send members, while the prerogative of summoning others at pleasure was acknowledged. But the analogy would have failed, if he thought compensation was due; for it is certain that no compensation was dreamt of, till his own plan. Would he have so strenuously maintained the constitutional authority to disfranchise and enfranchise different places, if he had entertained the least suspicion that it could not be exercised without being justly characterised as an act of rapine? Another circumstance is conclusive:—his plan, as may be seen in his speech, was to make the compensation to the borough-holders,—not to the poor freemen, the scot and lot voters, the pot-wallopers,—whose spoliation has been so much deprecated on this occasion,—who alone could have had any pretence of justice or colour of law to claim it. They at least had legal privileges: the compensation to the borough-holders was to be for the loss of their profits by breaches of law. One passage only in Mr. Pitt's speech, may be

* Parl. Hist. vol. xxv. p. 435.—Ed.

thought favourable to another sense :—"To a Reform by violence he had an insurmountable objection." Now these words might mean only an objection to effect his purpose by an act of the supreme power, when he could introduce the same good by milder means. The reports of that period were far less accurate than they now are: the general tenor of the speech must determine the meaning of a single word. It seems to me impossible to believe, that he could have intended more than that he preferred a pacific accommodation of almost any sort to formidable resistance, and the chance of lasting discontent. This preference, founded either on personal feelings, or on supposed expediency, is nothing against my present purpose. What an imputation would be thrown on his memory, by supposing that he who answered the objection of Reform being *unconstitutional*, could pass over the more serious objection that it was *unjust*.

That I may not be obliged to return to this case, I shall add one other observation, which more strictly belongs to another part of the argument. Mr. Pitt never once hints, that the dependent boroughs were thought necessary to the security of property. It never occurred to him that any one could think them intrinsically good. It was impossible that he could propose to employ a million sterling in demolishing the safeguards of the British constitution. Be it observed, that this remark must be considered by all who respect the authority of Mr. Pitt as of great weight, even if they believe compensation and voluntary surrender to be essential to the justice of transferring the elective franchise. It must, then, I think, be acknowledged by the Honourable and Learned Member for Aldborough himself, that there was a Reformer of great name before my Noble Friend, who maintained the transfer of the elective franchise, by disfranchisement and enfranchisement, to be conformable to ancient rights or usages, and for that reason, among others, fit to be employed as parts of a plan of Parliamentary Reform.*

The two plans of Reform, Sir, that have been proposed, during the last seventy years, may be divided into the Simultaneous and the Progressive. Of the first it is manifest, that the two expedients of resuming the franchise from those who cannot use it for the public good, and bestowing it where it will probably be better employed, are indispensable, or rather essential parts. I shall presently show that it is impossible to execute the most slowly Progressive scheme of Reformation, without some application, however limited, of these now altogether proscribed principles.

I do not wish to displease the Honourable Baronet by frequent or extensive excursions into the Middle Ages; but the Honourable and Learned Gentleman will admit that the right of the Crown to summon new boroughs, was never disputed until its last exercise by Charles II. in the well-known instance of Newark. In the Tudor reigns, this prerogative had added one hundred and fifty members to this House. In the forty-five years of Elizabeth, more than sixty were received into it. From the accession of Henry VII. to the disuse of the prerogative, the representation received an accession of about two hundred, if we include the cases where representation was established by Parliament, and those where, after a disuse of centuries, it was so restored. Let me add, without enlarging on it, that forty-four boroughs, and a city, which anciently sent burgesses to this House, are unrepresented at this day. I know no Parliamentary mode of restoring their franchises, but by a statute, which would be in effect a new grant. I believe, that if such matters were cognizable by courts of law, the judges would presume, or, for greater security, advise a jury to presume, after a disuse of so many centuries, that it had originated either in a surrender, or in some other legal mode of terminating the privilege. According to the common maxim, that there is no right without a remedy, we may infer the absence of right from the absence of remedy. In that case, the disuse of granting summonses by the King, or his officers, must be taken to have been legal, in spite of the authority of Serjeant Glanville and his Committee, who, in the reign of James I., held the contrary doctrine. But I waive this question, because the answer to it is needless to the purpose of my argument. It is enough for me that the disuse had been practically maintained, without being questioned, till the end of James' reign; and that it still shuts our doors on ninety persons who might otherwise be chosen to sit in this House. The practice *of resuming the franchise*, therefore, prevailed as certainly in ancient times, as the exercise of the prerogative of conferring it. The effect of both combined, was to take from the representation the character of immutability, and to bestow on it that flexibility which, if it had been then properly applied, might have easily fitted it for every change of circumstances. These powers were never exercised on any fixed principle. The prerogative was often grievously abused; but the abuse chiefly consisted in granting the privilege to beggarly villages, or to the manor or demesne of a favoured lord: there are few examples of withholding the franchise from considerable towns. On a rapid review of the class of towns next in importance to London, such as York, Bristol, Exeter, Norwich, Lincoln, &c., it appears to me, that they all sent Members to the House of Commons of Edward I. Boston did not occur to me; but, admitting the statement respecting that place to be accurate, the Honourable and Learned Gentleman must allow this instance to be at variance with the general spirit and tendency of the ancient constitution, in the dis-

* The Reforms proposed by Mr. Flood in 1790, and by Lord Grey in 1797, might have been added to those of Mr. Pitt in 1782, 1783 and 1785.

tribution of elective privileges. I do not call it an exception to a rule; for there were no rules: it was no departure from principle; for no general principle was professed, or, perhaps, thought of: but it was at variance with that disposition not to leave grant towns unrepresented, which, though not reduced to system, yet practically influenced the coarse good sense of our ancestors, and, what is remarkable, is most discernible in the earliest part of their legislation.*

It was not the Union with Scotland that stopped the exercise of the prerogative. With the exception of Newark, there was no instance of its exertion for nearly seventy years before that date. We know that the Stuart Kings dreaded an increase of members in this House, as likely to bestow a more democratical character on its proceedings: but still the true cause of the extinction of the prerogative, was the jealousy of a people become more enlightened, and suspicious of a power which had already been abused, and which might be made the means of enslaving the kingdom. The discussions in this House respecting the admission of the members for Newark, though they ended favourably to the Crown in that instance, afforded such a specimen of the general sentiments and temper respecting the prerogative, that no man was bold enough to advise its subsequent exercise.

The course of true wisdom would have been to regulate the employment of the prerogative by a law, which, acting quietly, calmly, but constantly, would have removed or prevented all gross inequality in the representation. It would have then been necessary only to enact that every town, which grew to a certain number of houses, should be summoned to send members to Parliament, and that every town which fell below a certain number, should cease to be so summoned. The consequence of this neglect became apparent as the want of some remedial power was felt. The regulator of the representation, which had been injuriously active in stationary times, was suffered to drop from the machine at a moment when it was much needed to adapt the elective system to the rapid and prodigious changes which have occurred in the state of society, —when vast cities have sprung up in every province, and the manufacturing world may be said to have been created. There was no longer any renovating principle in the frame of the constitution. All the marvellous works of industry and science are unnoticed in our system of representation. The changes of a century and a half since the case of Newark,—the social revolution of the last sixty years, have altered the whole condition of mankind more than did the three centuries which passed before:—the representation alone has stood still. It is to this interruption of the *vis medicatrix et conservatrix* of the commonwealth that we owe the necessity of now recurring to the extensive plan of Simultaneous Reform, of which I do not dispute the inconveniences. We are now called on to pay the arrears of a hundred and sixty years of an unreformed representation. The immediate settlement of this constitutional balance is now difficult;—it may not be without danger: but it is become necessary that we may avoid ruin. It may soon be impossible to save us by that, or by any other means.

But, Sir, we are here met by a serious question, which, being founded on a principle generally true, acquires a great effect by specious application. We are reminded by the Honourable and Learned Gentleman, that governments are to be valued for their beneficial effects,—not for their beauty as ingenious pieces of machinery. We are asked, what is the practical evil which we propose to remove, or even to lesson, by Reform? We are told, that the representative system "works well," and that the excellence of the English constitution is attested by the admirable fruits, which for at least a century and a half it has produced. I dare not take the high ground of denying the truth of the facts thus alleged. God forbid that I should ever derogate from the transcendent merits of the English constitution, which it has been the chief occupation of my life to study, and which I now seek, because I love it, to reform!

Much as I love and revere this constitution, I must say, that, during the last century, the representative system has not worked well. I do not mean to undervalue its general results; but it has not worked well for one grand purpose, without which, no other benefit can be safe:—the means employed in elections, has worked all respect for the constitution out of the hearts of the people. The foulness and shamefulness, or the fraud and mockery of borough elections, have slowly weaned the people from their ancient attachments. With less competence, perhaps, than others, to draw up the general comparison between the good and evil results, they were shocked by the barefaced corruption which the increasing frequency of contests constantly brought home to them. These disgusting scenes could not but uproot attachment to the government to which they seemed to pertain. The people could see nothing venerable in venality,—in bribery,—in the sale of some, and in the gift of other seats,—in nominal elections carried on by individuals, under the disguise of popular forms.

It is true, that the vile machinery of openly marketable votes, was the most powerful cause which alienated them. But half the nomination-boroughs were so marketable. Though I know one nomination borough*

* For a more detailed reference to the earlier statutory regulations affecting the franchise, see Appendix A.—Ed.

* Knaresborough, the property of the Duke of Devonshire, which he had represented since 1818.—Ed.

where no seat was ever sold,—where no Member ever heard a whisper of the wishes of a patron,—where One Member at least was under no restraint beyond the ties of political opinion and friendship, which he voluntarily imposed upon himself. It does not become me to say how the Member to whom I advert would have acted in other circumstances; but I am firmly convinced that the generous nature of the other Party would as much recoil from imposing dependency, as any other could recoil from submitting to it. I do not pretend to say that this is a solitary instance: but I believe it to be too favourable a one to be a fair sample of the general practice.

Even in the best cases, the pretended election was an eye-sore to all that witnessed it. A lie was solemnly acted before their eyes. While the popular principles of the constitution had taught them that popular elections belonged to the people, all the acts that the letter of the law had expressly forbidden were now become the ordinary means of obtaining a Parliamentary seat. These odious and loathsome means became more general as the country increased in wealth, and as the people grew better informed,—more jealous of encroachment on their rights, and more impatient of exclusion from power. In the times of the Stuarts and Tudors, the burgesses, as we see from the lists, had been very generally the sons of neighbouring gentlemen, chosen with little contest and noise, and so seldom open to the charge of bribery, that when it occurred, we find it mentioned as a singular event. It was not till after the Revolution that monied candidates came from the Capital to invade a tranquillity very closly allied to blind submission. At length, the worst of all practical effects was produced:—the constitution sunk in popular estimation; the mass of the people were estranged from the objects of their hereditary reverence. An election is the part of our constitution with which the multitude come into most frequent contact. Seeing in many of them nothing but debauchery,—riot,—the sale of a right to concur in making law,—the purchase in open market of a share in the choice of lawgivers,—absolute nomination under the forms of election, they were conscious that many immoral, many illegal practices became habitual, and were even justified. Was it not natural for the majority of honest men to form their judgments rather by means of their moral feelings, than as the results of refined arguments, fcunded on a calm comparison of evils? Such at least was the effect of this most mischievous practice, that when any misfortune of the country, any error of the Government, any commotion abroad, or any disorder at home arose, they were all ascribed, with exaggeration, but naturally, to the corruption, which the humblest of the people saw had tainted the vital organs of the commonwealth.

My Honourable and Excellent Friend, the Member for the University of Oxford,* indeed told the last Parliament, that the clamours about the state of the representation were only momentary cries, which, however magnified at the moment, always quickly yielded to a vigorous and politic government. He might have looked back somewhat farther. What were the Place Bills and Triennial Bills of Sir Robert Walpole's time? Were they not, in truth, demands of Parliamentary Reform? The cry is therefore one of the symptoms of a distemper, which has lasted for a century. But to come to his more recent examples:—in 1770, Lord Chatham was the agitator; Mr. Burke was the incendiary pamphleteer, who exaggerated the importance of a momentary delusion, which was to subside as quickly as it had risen. Unfortunately for this reasoning, though the delusion subsided after 1770, it revived again in 1780, under Sir George Saville; under Mr. Pitt in 1782, 1783, and 1784: it was felt at the time of Mr. Flood's motion in 1790. Lord Grey's motion in 1797 was supported by respectable Tories, such as Sir William Dolben, Sir Rowland Hill, and by conscientious men, more friendly to Mr. Pitt than to his opponents, of whom it is enough to name Mr. Henry Thornton, then Member for Surrey. Instead of being the expressions of a transient delusion, these constantly recurring complaints are the symptoms of a deep-rooted malady, sometimes breaking out, sometimes dying away, sometimes repelled, but always sure to return,—re-appearing with resistless force in the elections of 1830, and still more decisively in those of 1831. If we seek for proof of an occasional provocation, which roused the people to a louder declaration of their opinions, where shall we find a more unexceptionable witness, than in one of the ablest and most unsparing opponents of the Ministers and of their Bill. Mr. Henry Drummond, in his very able Address to the Freeholders of Surrey, explicitly ascribes the irritation which now prevails to the unwise language of the late Ministers. The declaration of the late Ministers against Reform, says he, "proved their gross ignorance of the national feeling, and drove the people of England to despair."

Many allege, Sir, that the people have gained so much strength and influence through the press, that they need no formal privileges or legal franchises to reinforce it. If it be so, I consider it to be a decisive reason for a reformation of the scheme of the representation. A country in which the masses are become powerful by their intelligence and by their wealth, while they are exasperated by exclusion from political rights, never can be in a safe condition. I hold it to be one of the most invariable maxims of legislation, to bind to the constitution, by the participation of legal privilege, all persons who have risen in wealth,—in intelligence,—in any of the legitimate sources

* Sir Robert Harry Inglis, Bart.—Ed.

of ascendancy. I would do now what our forefathers, though rudely, aimed at doing, by calling into the national councils every rising element in the body politic.

The grand objection to this Bill, Sir, is what ought to be fatal to any Bill, if the objection had any foundation but loud and bold assertion,—that it is unjust. This argument was never, indeed, urged by the Right Honourable Baronet, and it seems to be on the eve of being abandoned. But the walls of the House still seem to resound with the vociferations of my Honourable and Learned Friend, the Member for Boroughbridge,* against what he called "corporation robbery." Now many of these boroughs have no corporations at all; while none who have will be deprived of their corporate rights. But if all these corporations had been about to be divested of their character,—divested of rights which have been, or are likely to be abused, the term "robbery" would have been ridiculously inapplicable. Examples are more striking than general reasonings. Was the disuse of issuing Writs of Summons, as a consequence of which near a hundred Members are excluded from this House, an act of "robbery?" Was the Union with Scotland, which reduced the borough representation from sixty-five to fifteen, an act of "robbery?" Yes, surely it was, if the term can be properly applied to this Bill. The Scotch boroughs were thrown into clusters of four and five, each of which sent a burgess. But if it be "robbery" to take away the whole of a franchise, is it not in principle as violent an invasion of property to take away four-fifths or three-fourths of it. What will be said of the Union with Ireland? Was it "robbery" to reduce her representation from three hundred to one hundred Members? Was it "robbery" to disfranchise, as they did then, one hundred boroughs, on the very principle of the present Bill,—because they were decayed, dependent, and so unfit to exercise the franchise? Was it "robbery" to deprive the Peers of Scotland of their birthright, and compel them to be contented with a bare possibility of being occasionally elected? Was it "robbery" to mutilate the legislative rights of the Irish Peerage? No! because in all these cases, the powers taken away or limited were trusts resumable by Parliament for the general well-being.

Further, I contend that if this be "robbery," every borough disfranchised for corruption has been "robbed" of its rights. Talk not to me of the *guilt* of these boroughs: individuals are innocent or guilty, —bodies politic can be neither. If disfranchisement be considered as a punishment, where is the trial,—where are the witnesses on oath,—where are the precautions against partiality,—where are the responsible judges?—who, indeed, are the judges? men who have avowedly committed and have justified as constitutional the very offence. Why, in such cases, are the unborn punished for the offences of the present generation? Why should the innocent minority suffer for the sins of a venal majority? If the rights of unoffending parties are reserved, of what importance is the reservation, if they are to be merged in those of hundreds or thousands of fellow-voters? Would not the opening of the suffrage in the city of Bath be as destructive to the close Corporation as if they were to be by name disfranchised? Viewed in that light, every Bill of Disfranchisement is a Bill of Pains and Penalties, and in the nature of a Bill of Attainder. How are these absurdities avoided?—only by the principle of this Bill,—that political trust may be justly resumed by the supreme power, whenever it is deemed injurious to the commonwealth.

The test, Sir, which distinguishes property from trust, is simple, and easily applied:—property exists for the benefit of the proprietor; political power exists only for the service of the state. Property is, indeed, the most useful of all human institutions: it is so, because the power of every man to do what he will with his own, is beneficial and even essential to the existence of society. A trustee is legally answerable for the abuse of his power: a proprietor is not amenable to human law for any misuse of his property, unless it should involve a direct violation of the rights of others. It is said, that property is a trust; and so it may, in figurative language, be called: but it is a moral, not a legal one. In the present argument, we have to deal only with the latter. The confusion of the ideas misled the Stuarts so far, that they thought the kingdom their property, till they were undeceived by the Revolution, which taught us, that man cannot have a property in his fellows. As all government is a trust, the share which each voter has in the nomination of lawgivers is one also. Otherwise, if the voter, as such, were a proprietor, he must have a property in his fellow citizens, who are governed by laws, of which he has a share in naming the makers. If the doctrine of the franchise being property be admitted, all Reform is for ever precluded. Even the enfranchisement of new boroughs, or districts, must be renounced; for every addition diminishes the value of the previous suffrage: and it is no more lawful to lessen the value of property, than to take it away.

Of all doctrines which threaten the principle of property, none more dangerous was ever promulgated, than that which confounds it with political privileges. None of the disciples of St. Simon, or of the followers of the ingenious and benevolent Owen, have struck so deadly a blow at it, as those who would reduce it to the level of the elective rights of Gatton and Old Sarum. Property, the nourisher of mankind,—the incentive to industry,—the cement of human society,—will be in a perilous condition, if the people be taught to identify it with political abuse, and to deal with it as being involved in its im-

* Sir Charles Wetherell.—Ed.

pending fate. Let us not teach the spoilers of future times to represent our resumption of a right of suffrage as a precedent for their seizure of lands and possessions.

Much is said in praise of the practice of nomination, which is now called "the most unexceptionable part of our representation." To nomination, it seems, we owe the talents of our young Members,—the prudence and experience of the more aged. It supplies the colonies and dependencies of this great empire with virtual representation in this House. By it commercial and funded property finds skilful advocates and intrepid defenders. All these happy consequences are ascribed to that flagrant system of breaches of the law, which is now called "the practice of the English constitution."

Sir, I never had, and have not now, any objection to the admission of representatives of the colonies into this House, on fair and just conditions. But I cannot conceive that a Bill which is objected to, as raising the commercial interest at the expense of the landed, will also lessen the safeguards of their property. Considering the well-known and most remarkable subdivision of funded income,—the most minutely divided of any mass of property,—I do not believe that any representatives, or even any constituents, could be ultimately disposed to do themselves so great an injury as to invade it. Men of genius, and men of experience, and men of opulence, have found their way into this House through nomination, or worse means, —through any channel that was open: the same classes of candidates will now direct their ambition and their efforts to the new channels opened by the present Bill; they will attain their end by only varying their means.

A list has been read to us of illustrious men who found an introduction to Parliament, or a refuge from unmerited loss of popularity, by means of decayed boroughs. What does such a catalogue prove, but that England, for the last sixty years, has been a country full of ability,—of knowledge,—of intellectual activity,—of honourable ambition, and that a large portion of these qualities has flowed into the House of Commons? Might not the same dazzling common-places have been opposed to the abolition of the court of the Star Chamber? "What," it might have been said, "will you, in your frantic rage of innovation, demolish the tribunal in which Sir Thomas More, the best of men, and Lord Bacon, the greatest of philosophers, presided,—where Sir Edward Coke, the oracle of law,—where Burleigh and Walsingham, the most revered of English statesmen, sat as judges,—which Bacon, enlightened by philosophy and experience, called the peculiar glory of our legislation, as being 'a court of criminal equity?' Will you, in your paroxysms of audacious frenzy, abolish this Prætorian tribunal,—this sole instrument for bridling popular incendiaries? Will you dare to persevere in your wild purpose, at a moment when Scotland is agitated by a rebellious League and Covenant,—when Ireland is threatened with insurrection and massacre? Will you surrender the shield of the crown,—the only formidable arm of prerogative,—at a time when his Majesty's authority is openly defied in the capital where we are assembled?"

I cannot, indeed, Sir, recollect a single instance in that long course of reformation, which constitutes the history of the English constitution, where the same plausible arguments, and the same exciting topics, might not have been employed as are now pointed against the present measure. The Honourable and Learned Gentleman has alluded to Simon de Montfort,—the first and most extensive Parliamentary Reformer,—who placed the representatives of the burgesses in Parliament. The haughty and unlettered Barons disdained argument; but their murmurs were doubtless loud and vehement. Even they could exclaim that the new constitution was an "untried scheme,"—that it was a "daring experiment,"—that it "would level all the distinctions of society,"—that it would throw the power of the state into the hands of traffickers and burgesses. Were men but yesterday slaves, now to be seated by the side of Plantagenets engaged in the arduous duty of making laws? Are these not the topics which are substantially used against Parliamentary Reform? They are now belied by experience, which has taught us that the adoption of the lower classes into the constitution, the concessions made to them, and the widening of the foundation of the legislature, have been the source of peace, of order, of harmony,—of all that is excellent in our government, and of all that secures the frame of our society. The Habeas Corpus Act, in the reign of Charles the Second, was obtained only by repeated, persevering, unwearied exertions of the Earl of Shaftesbury, after a meritorious struggle of many years. I mention the facts with pleasure in the presence of his descendant.* It is now well known, from the confidential correspondence of Charles and his brother James, that they both believed sincerely that a government without the power of arbitrary imprisonment would not long exist; and that Shaftesbury had forced this Act upon them, in order either to expose them unarmed to the populace, or to drive them to have recourse to the odious and precarious protection of a standing army. The belief of the Royal Brothers was the more incorrigible, because it was sincere. It is the fatal effect of absolute power to corrupt the judgment of its possessors, and to insinuate into their minds the false and pernicious opinion, that power is always weakened by limitation.

Shall I be told, that the sale of seats is not in itself an evil? The same most ingenious person† who hazarded this paradox,

* Viscount Ashley.—Ed.

† It would not seem easy to specify the person alluded to.—Ed.

quoted the example of the sale of the judicial office in Old France, with a near approach to approbation. That practice has been vindicated by French writers of great note; and it had, in fact, many guards and limitations not to be found in our system of marketable boroughs: but it has been swept away by the Revolution; and there is now no man disposed to palliate its shameless enormity. The grossest abuses, as long as they prevail, never want advocates to find out specious mitigations of their effects: their downfall discovers their deformity to every eye. For my part, I do not see, why the sale of a power to make laws should not be as immoral as the sale of a power to administer them.

We have heard it said, Sir, that the Peerage, and even the Monarchy, cannot survive the loss of these boroughs; and we are referred to the period that has elapsed since the Revolution, as that during which this influence has been their main guard against popular assault and dictation. I respectfully lay aside the Crown in this debate; and in the few words that I am now about to utter, I am desirous to express myself in cautious and constitutional language. Since the Revolution,—since the defeat of the attempts to establish absolute monarchy, the English government has undoubtedly become Parliamentary. But during that time, also, the hereditary elements of the constitution have been uniformly respected as wholesome temperaments of the rashness of popular assemblies. I can discover nothing in this proposed change which will disable the Peers from usefully continuing to perform this duty. If some inconvenient diminution of the influence of great property should follow, we must encounter the risk; for nothing can, in my judgment, be more certain, than that the constitution can no longer bear the weight of the obloquy thrown upon it by our present mode of conducting elections. The community cannot afford to purchase any advantage at such an expense of private character. But so great is the natural influence of property, especially in a country where the various ranks of society have been so long bound together by friendly ties as in ours, that I can scarcely conceive any laws or institutions which could much diminish the influence of well-spent wealth, whether honourably inherited, or honestly earned.

The benefits of any reformation might indeed be hazarded, if the great proprietors were to set themselves in battle array against the permanent desires of the people. If they treat their countrymen as adversaries, they may, in their turn, excite a hostile spirit. Distrust will beget distrust: jealousy will awaken an adverse jealousy. I trust these evil consequences may not arise. The Nobility of England, in former times, have led their countrymen in the battles of liberty. those among them who are most distinguished by ample possessions, by historical names, or by hereditary fame, interwoven with the glory of their country, have, on this occasion, been the foremost to show their confidence in the people,—their unsuspecting liberality in the enlargement of popular privilege,—their reliance on the sense and honesty of their fellow-citizens, as the best safeguard of property and of order, as well as of all other interests of society. Already, this measure has exhibited a disinterestedness which has united all classes, from the highest borough-holder to the humblest non-resident freeman, in the sacrifice of their own exclusive advantages to what they think a great public good. There must be something good in what produces so noble a sacrifice.

This, Sir, is not solely a reformatory measure; it is also conciliatory. If it were proposed exclusively for the amendment of institutions, I might join in the prevalent cry "that it goes too far," or at least "travels too fast,"—farther and faster than the maxims of wise reformation would warrant. But as it is a means of regaining national confidence, it must be guided by other maxims. In that important view of the subject, I consider the terms of this plan as of less consequence than the temper which it breathes, and the spirit by which it is animated. A conciliatory measure deserves the name only, when it is seen and felt by the simplest of men, to flow from the desire and determination to conciliate. At this moment, when, amidst many causes of discord, there is a general sympathy in favour of reformation, the superior classes of society, by opening their arms to receive the people,—by giving to the people a signal and conspicuous proof of confidence,—may reasonably expect to be trusted in return. But to reach this end, they must not only be, but appear to be, liberally just and equitably generous. Confidence can be purchased by confidence alone. If the leading classes follow the example of many of their own number,—if they show, by gracious and cheerful concessions,—by striking acts, not merely by specious language or cold formalities of law,—that they are willing to rest on the fidelity and conscience of the people, I do not believe that they will lean on a broken reed. As for those wise saws which teach us that there is always danger in trust, and that policy and generosity are at perpetual variance, I hold them in little respect. Every unbending maxim of policy is hollow and unsafe. Base principles are often not the more prudent because they are pusillanimous. I rather agree with the beautiful peroration of Mr. Burke's second speech on North America:—"Magnanimity in politics is not seldom the truest wisdom: a great empire and little minds go ill together. If we are conscious of our situation, and glow with zeal to fill our place, as becomes our station and ourselves, we ought to auspicate our proceedings respecting America, with the old warning of the Church,—'*Sursum Corda.*' We ought to elevate our minds to the dignity of that trust, to which the order of Providence has called us."

Whether we consider this measure, either as a scheme of reformation, or an attempt to form an alliance with the people, it must be always remembered, that it is a question of the comparative safety or danger of the only systems now before us for our option;—that of undistinguishing adherence to present institutions,—that of ample redress and bold reformation,—and that of niggardly, evasive, and unwilling Reform. I say "comparative" safety or danger; for not one of those who have argued this question seem to have remembered that it has two sides. They have thrown all the danger of the times upon the Reform. They load it with as much odium as if the age were otherwise altogether exempt from turbulence and agitation, and first provoked from its serene quiet by this wanton attempt. They make it answerable for mischiefs which it may not have the power to prevent, and which might have occurred if no such measure had ever been attempted. They, at least, tacitly assume that it must aggravate every evil arising from other sources. In short, they beg the whole question in dispute. They ask us, Whether there be not danger in Reform? I answer by asking them, Is there no danger in not reforming? To this question, to which they have never yet attempted to answer, I expect no answer now; because a negative one would seem to me impossible, while an affirmative would reduce the whole discussion to a cool computation and calm comparison of the different degrees of danger opening upon us.

A niggardly Reform, Sir, seems to me the most unsafe step of all systems. It cannot conciliate; for it is founded in distrust. It practically admits an evil, of which dissatisfaction is a large part; and yet it has been already proved by experience that it yet satisfied nobody. Other systems may be unsatisfactory: this scheme is so already. In the present temper of the people, and circumstances of the world, I can see no one good purpose to be answered by an evasive and delusive Reform. To what extent will they trust the determined enemies of the smallest step towards reformation,—who, to avoid the grant of the franchise to Birmingham, have broken up one Administration, and who, if they be sincere, must try every expedient to render impotent a measure which they can no longer venture avowedly to oppose.

On the other hand, Sir, the effect of the Bill before us has hitherto confirmed the opinion of those who thought that a measure of a conciliatory temper, and of large and liberal concession, would satisfy the people. The tone and scope of their petitions, which were at first extravagant, became moderate and pacific, as soon as the Bill was known. As soon as they saw so unexpected a project of substantial amendment, proceeding from sincere Reformers, they at once sacrificed all vague projects of indefinite perfection. Nothing can be more ludicrously absurd, than the supposition which has been hazarded among us, that several millions of men are such deep dissemblers,—such dark conspirators,—as to be able to conceal all their farther projects, till this Bill arms them with the means of carrying them into execution. The body of a people cannot fail to be sincere. I do not expect any measure of legislation to work miracles. Discontent may and will continue; but I believe that it will be by this measure permanently abated. Others there doubtless are, who foretell far other effects: it seems to me, that the favourers of the Bill rest their predictions on more probable foundations.

Among the numerous assumptions of our opponents, there is none which appears to me more remarkable, than their taking for granted that concession is always, or even generally, more dangerous to the stability of government than resistance. As the Right Honourable Baronet introduced several happy quotations from Cicero on this subject, which he seemed to address more particularly to me, I hope I shall not be charged with pedantry, if I begin my proofs of the contrary, with the testimony of that great writer. In the third book of his work, "De Legibus," after having put an excellent aristocratical speech, against the tribunitian power, into the mouth of his brother Quintus, he proceeds to answer him as follows:—"Concessâ Plebi a Patribus istâ potestate, arma ceciderunt, restincta seditio est, inventum est temperamentum quo tenuiores cum principibus æquari se putarint; in quo uno fuit civitatis salus." It will not be said, that Cicero was a radical or a demagogue, or that he had any personal cause to be favourable to the tribunitian power. It will not be said, that to grant to a few, a right to stop the progress of every public measure, was a slender, or likely to be a safe concession. The ancients had more experience of democracy, and a better knowledge of the character of demagogues, than the frame of modern society allows us the means of attaining. This great man, in spite of his natural prejudices, and just resentments, ascribes to this apparently monstrous power, not merely the spirit and energy which may be expected even from the excess of popular institutions, but whatever safety and tranquillity the commonwealth enjoyed through a series of ages. He would not, therefore, have argued as has been argued on this occasion, that if the multitude appeal to violence, before legal privileges are conferred on them, they will be guilty of tenfold excesses when they become sharers in legitimate authority. On the contrary, he lays it down in the context of the passage quoted, that their violence is abated, by allowing a legal vent to their feelings.

But it appears, Sir, to be taken for granted, that concession to a people is always more dangerous to public quiet than resistance. Is there any pretence for such a doctrine? I appeal to history, as a vast magazine of facts, all leading to the very opposite conclusion,—

teaching that this fatal principle has overthrown more thrones and dismembered more empires than any other—proving that late reformation,—dilatory reformation,—reformation refused at the critical moment,—which may pass for ever,—in the twinkling of an eye, has been the most frequent of all causes of the convulsions which have shaken states, and for a time burst asunder the bonds of society. Allow me very briefly to advert to the earliest revolution of modern times:—was it by concession that Philip II. lost the Netherlands? Had he granted timely and equitable concessions,—had he not plotted the destruction of the ancient privileges of these flourishing provinces, under pretence that all popular privilege was repugnant to just authority, would he not have continued to his death the master of that fair portion of Europe? Did Charles I. lose his throne and his life by concession? Is it not notorious, that if, before losing the confidence of the Parliament and the people (after that loss all his expedients of policy were vain, as in such a case all policy is unavailing), he had adhered to the principles of the Petition of Right, to which he had given his Royal Assent,—if he had forborne from the persecution of the Puritans,—if he had refrained from levying money without a grant from Parliament, he would, in all human probability, have reigned prosperously to the last day of his life. If there be any man who doubts it, his doubts will be easily removed without pursuing his studies farther than the first volume of Lord Clarendon's History. Did the British Parliament lose North America by concession? Is not the loss of that great empire solely to be ascribed to the obstinate resistance of this House to every conciliatory proposition, although supported by their own greatest men, tendered in the loyal petitions of the Colonies, until they were driven into the arms of France, and the door was for ever closed against all hopes of re-union? Had we yielded to the latest prayers of the Americans, it is hard to say how long the two British nations might have been held together: the separation, at all events, if absolutely necessary, might have been effected on quiet and friendly terms.' Whatever may be thought of recent events (of which it is yet too early to firm a final judgment), the history of their origin and progress would of itself be enough to show the wisdom of those early reformations, which, as Mr. Burke says, "are accommodations with a friend in power."

I feel, Sir, some curiosity to know how many of the high-principled, consistent, inflexible, and hitherto unyielding opponents of this Bill, will continue to refuse to make a declaration in favour of any Reform, till the last moment of this discussion. Although I differ from them very widely in opinion, I know how to estimate their fidelity towards each other, and their general fairness to others, as well as their firmness under circumstances of a discouraging and disheartening nature, calculated to sow distrust and disunion in any political party. What I dread and deprecate in their system is, that they offer no option but Reform or coercion. Let any man seriously consider what is the full import of this last tremendous word. Restrictions will be first laid on the people, which will be assuredly productive of new discontents, provoking in turn an incensed Government to measures still more rigorous. Discontent will rankle into disaffection: disaffection will break out into revolt, which, supposing the most favourable termination, will not be quelled without spilling the blood of our countrymen, and will leave them in the end full of hatred for their rulers, and watching for the favourable opportunity of renewing their attack. It is needless to consider the consequences of a still more disastrous and irreparable termination of the contest. It is enough for me to say, that the long continuance of such wretched scuffles between the Government and the people is absolutely incompatible with the very existence of the English constitution. But although a darkness hangs over the event, is there nothing in the present temper,—in the opinions,—in the circumstances of all European nations, which renders the success of popular principles probable? The mode in which this matter has been argued, will excuse me for once more reminding the House that the question is one of comparative danger. I vote for the present Bill, not only because I approve of it as a measure of Reform, but because I consider it as affording the greatest probability of preserving the integrity of our fundamental laws. Those who shut their eyes on the tempests which are abroad,—on the gloomy silence with which the extreme parties look at each other, may obstinately persist in ascribing the present agitation of mind in Great Britain to a new Cabinet in November, or to a Reform Bill in March.

Our opponents, Sir, deal much in prophecy: they foretell all the evils which will spring from Reform. They do right: such anticipations are not only legitimate arguments; but they form the hinge on which the whole case turns. But they have two sets of weights and measures:—they use the probability of future evil resulting from Reform as their main stay; but when we employ the probability of future evil from No-Reform, in support of our opinion, they call it menace, and charge us with intimidation.

In this, and indeed in every other branch of the case, the arguments of our opponents have so singular a resemblance to those employed by them on the Catholic Question, that we might quote as answers to them their own language. Then, as now, Ministers were charged with yielding to clamour and menace, and with attempting to frighten other men from their independence. As a brief, but conclusive answer, I have only to say, that all policy consists in such considerations as to whether a measure be safe and beneficial,—that every statesman or lawgiver *ought* to fear what he considers as dangerous to the public,—and that I avow myself a coward at the prospect of the civil disorders which I think impending over my country.

Then, Sir, we are told,—as we were told in the case of the Catholics,—that this measure is not final, and that it is sought only as a vantage ground from which it will be more easy to effect other innovations. I denied the disposition to encroach, with which the Catholics were charged; and however afflicting the condition of Ireland may now be, I appeal to every dispassionate man, whether the relief granted to them has not, on the whole, bettered the situation, and strengthened the security of the country. I was then taught by the Right Honourable Baronet,* that concession would divide loyal from disaffected opponents, and unite all friends of their country against those whose demands were manifestly insatiable. Is it not reasonable to expect some degree of the same benefits on the present occasion?

Nothing human is, in one sense of the word, final. Of a distant futurity I know nothing; and I am, therefore, altogether unfitted to make laws for it. Posterity may rightly measure their own wants, and their capacity,—we cannot; the utmost that we can aspire to, is to remove elements of discord from their path. But within the very limited horizon to which the view of politicians can reach, I have pointed out some reasons why I expect that a measure of concession, made in a spirit of unsuspecting confidence, may inspire the like sentiments, and why I believe that the people will acquiesce in a grant of these extensive privileges to those whose interests must be always the same as their own. After all, is it not obvious that the people already possess that power through their numbers, of which the exercise is dreaded? It is ours, indeed, to decide, whether they are to exert their force in the market-place, in the street, in the field, or in discussion, and debate in this House. If we somewhat increase their legal privileges, we must, also, in the same measure, abate their supposed disposition to use it ill.

On the great proprietors, much of the grace,—of the generous character,—of the conciliatory effect of this measure, must certainly depend. But its success cannot ultimately depend upon a single class. If they be deluded or enraged by tales of intimidation and of riot,—if they can be brought to doubt that there is in the public mind on the necessity of Reform any more doubt than is necessary to show the liberty of publishing opinion,—whenever or wherever they act on these great errors, they may abate the healing efficacy of a great measure of conciliation and improvement; but they cannot prevent its final adoption. Above all other considerations, I advise these great proprietors to cast from them those reasonings which would involve property in the approaching downfall of political abuse. If they assent to the doctrine that political privilege is property, they must be prepared for the inevitable consequence,—that it is no more unlawful to violate their possessions, than to resume a delegated trust. The suppression of dependent boroughs is at hand: it will be the truest wisdom of the natural guardians of the principle of property, to maintain, to inculcate, to enforce the essential distinction between it and political trust,—if they be not desirous to arm the spoilers, whom they dread, with arguments which they can never consistently answer.

* Sir Robert Peel.—Ed.

APPENDIX.

A.

The first article in a wise plan of reformation, would, in our opinion, be the immediate addition of twenty Members to the House of Commons, to be chosen by the most opulent and populous of the communities which are at present without direct representation; with such varieties in the right of suffrage as the local circumstances of each community might suggest, but in all of them on the principle of a widely diffused franchise. In Scotland, Glasgow ought to be included: in Ireland we think there are no unrepresented communities to which the principle could be applied.

In endeavouring to show that this proposal is strictly constitutional, according to the narrowest and most cautious use of that term,—that it requires only the exercise of an acknowledged right, and the revival of a practice observed for several ages, we shall abstain from those controverted questions which relate to the obscure and legendary part of our Parliamentary history. A very cursory review of the authentic annals of the House of Commons, is sufficient for the present purpose. In the writs of summons of the 11th of Edward I., the Sheriffs were directed (as they are by the present writ) to send two Members from *each* city and borough within their respective bailiwicks. The letter of this injunction appears, from the beginning, to have been disobeyed, The Crown was, indeed, desirous of a full attendance of citizens and burgesses, a class of men then subservient to the Royal pleasure, and who, it was expected, would reconcile their neighbours in the provinces to the burthen of Parliamentary grants; but to many boroughs, the wages of burgesses in Parliament were a heavy and sometimes an insupportable burthen: and this struggle between the policy of the Crown and the poverty of the boroughs, occasioned great fluctuation in the towns who sent Members to the House of Commons, in-the course of the fourteenth century. Small boroughs were often excused by the Sheriff on account of their poverty, and at other times neglected or disobeyed his order. When he persisted, petitions were presented to the King in Parliament, and perpetual or temporary charters of exemption were obtained by the petitioning boroughs. In the 1st of Edward III. the county of Northumberland, and the town of Newcastle, were exempted, on account of the devastations of the Scotch war. The boroughs in Lancashire sent no Members from the reign of Edward III. to that of Henry VI.; the Sheriff stating, in his returns, that there was no borough in his bailiwick able to bear the expense. Of one hundred and eighty-four cities and boroughs, summoned to Parliament in the reigns of the three first Edwards, only ninety-one continued to send Members in the reign of Richard II. In the midst of this great irregularity in the composition of the House of Commons, we still see a manifest, though irregular, tendency to the establishment of a constitutional principle,—viz. that deputies from all the most important communities, with palpably distinct interests, should form part of a national assembly. The separate and sometimes clashing interests of the town and the country, were not intrusted to the same guardians. The Knights of the Shire were not considered as sufficient representatives even of the rude industry and infant commerce of that age.

The dangerous discretion of the Sheriffs was taken away by the statutes for the regulation of elections, passed under the princes of the House of Lancaster. A seat in the House of Commons had now begun to be an object of general ambition. Landed gentlemen, lawyers, even courtiers, served as burgesses, instead of those traders,—sometimes, if we may judge from their names, of humble occupation,—who filled that station in former times. Boroughs had already fallen under the influence of neighbouring proprietors: and, from a curious passage in the Paston Letters, (vol. i. p. 96,) we find, that in the middle of the fifteenth century, the nomination of a young gentleman to serve for a borough, by the proprietor, or by a great man of the Court, was spoken of as not an unusual transaction. From this time the power of the Crown, of granting representation to new boroughs, formed a part of the regular practice of the government, and was exercised without interruption for two hundred years.

In the cases of Wales, Chester, and long after of Durham, representation was bestowed by statute, probably because it was thought that no inferior authority could have admitted Members from those territories, long subject to a distinct government, into the Parliament of England. In these ancient grants of representation, whether made by the King or by Parliament, we discover a great uniformity of principle, and an approach to the maxims of our present constitution. In Wales and Chester, as well as in England, the counties were distinguished from the towns; and the protection of their separate interests was committed to different representatives: the rights of election were diversified, according to the local interests and municipal constitution of the several towns. In the preamble of the Chester Act, representation is stated to be the means of securing the county from the wrong which it had suffered while it was unrepresented. It was bestowed on Wales with the other parts of the laws of England, of which it was thought the necessary companion: and the exercise of popular privileges is distinctly held out as one of the means which were to quiet and civilize that principality. In the cases of Calais and Berwick, the frontier fortresses against France and Scotland,—where modern politicians would have been fearful of introducing the disorders of elections,—Henry the VIIIth granted the elective franchise, apparently for the purpose of strengthening the attachment, and securing the fidelity of their inhabitants. The Knights of the Shire for Northumberland were not then thought to represent Berwick sufficiently.

While we thus find in these ancient examples so much solicitude for an adequate representation of the separate interests of classes and districts, it is particularly worthy of remark, that we find no trace in any of them of a representation founded merely on numbers. The statute that gave representatives to Wales, was within a century of the act of Henry VI. for regulating the qualifications for the voters in counties; and on that subject, as well as others, may be regarded as no inconsiderable evidence on the ancient state of the constitution. Had universal suffrage prevailed till the fifteenth century, it seems wholly incredible, that no trace of it should be found in the numerous Royal and Parliamentary grants of representation, which occur in the early part of the sixteenth. Mere accident must have revived it in some instances; for it certainly had not *then* become an argument of jealousy or apprehension.

In the reigns of Edward the VIth, Mary, and Elizabeth, the struggles between the Catholic and Protestant parties occasioned a great and sudden increase of the House of Commons. Fourteen boroughs were thus privileged by the first of these Sovereigns, ten by the second, and twenty-four by Elizabeth. The choice, in the reign of Edward and Elizabeth, was chiefly in the western and southern counties, where the adherents of the Reformation were most numerous, and the towns were most under the influence of the Crown. By this extraordinary exertion of prerogative, a permanent addition of ninety-four Members was made to the House in little more than fifty years. James and Charles, perhaps, dreading the accession of strength which a more numerous House might give to the popular cause, made a more sparing use of this power. But the popular party in the House, imitating the policy of the ministers of Elizabeth, began to strengthen their Parliamentary influence by a similar expedient. That House had, indeed, no pretensions to the power of making new Parliamentary boroughs; but the same purpose was answered, by the revival of those which had long disused their privilege. Petitions were obtained from many towns well effected to the popular cause, alleging that they had, in ancient times, sent Members to Parliament, and had not legally lost the right. These petitions were referred to the Committee of Privileges; and, on a favourable report, the Speaker was directed to issue his warrant for new writs. Six towns (of which Mr. Hampden's borough of Wendover was one) were in this manner empowered to send Members to Parliament in the reign of James. Two were added in 1628 by like means, and six more by the Long Parliament on the very eve of the civil war.

No further addition was made to the representation of England except the borough of Newark, on which Charles II., in 1672, bestowed the privilege of sending burgesses to the House of Commons, as a reward for the fidelity of the inhabitants to his father. The right of the first burgesses returned by this borough in 1673 was questioned,—though on what ground our scanty and confused accounts of the Parliamentary transactions of that period do not enable us to determine. The question was suspended for about three years; and at last, on the 26th of March, 1676, it was determined by a majority of one hundred and twenty-five against seventy-three, that the town *had* a right to send burgesses. But on a second division, it was resolved, by a majority of one, that the Members returned were not duly elected. And thus suddenly, and somewhat unaccountably, ceased the exercise of a prerogative which, for several centu ries, had continued to augment, and, in some measure, to regulate the English representation.

Neither this, nor any other constitutional power, originated in foresight and contrivance. Occasional convenience gave rise to its first exercise: the course of time gave it a sanction of law. It was more often exercised for purposes of temporary policy, or of personal favour, than with any regard to the interest of the constitution. Its entire cessation is, however, to be considered as forming an epoch in the progress of our government. However its exercise might have been abused, its existence might be defended, on the ground that it was the constitutional means of remedying the defects of the representation. It was a tacit acknowledgment that a representative system must, from time to time, require amendment. Every constitutional reasoner must have admitted, that it was rightly exercised only in those cases where it contributed to the ends for the sake of which alone it could be justified. Its abuse consisted much more in granting the suffrage to insignificant villages, than from withholding it from large towns. The cases of the latter sort are very few, and may be imputed to accident and negligence, which would probably have been corrected in process of time. No such instance occurs with respect to any town of the first, or even of the second class. And, indeed, it cannot be supposed, that, before the disuse of that prerogative, four or five of the principal towns in the kingdom should have continued without representatives for more than a century. Whatever the *motive* might have been for granting representatives to Westminster by Edward VI., no *reason* could have been assigned for the grant, but the growing importance of that city. Lord Clarendon's commendation of the constitution of Cromwell's Parliament, to which Manchester, Leeds, and Halifax, then towns of moderate size, sent representatives, may be considered as an indication of the general opinion on this subject.

In confirmation of these remarks, we shall close this short review of the progress of the representation before the Revolution, by an appeal to two legislative declarations of the principles by which it ought to be governed.

The first is the Chester Act, (34 & 35 Hen. 8. c. 13,) the preamble of which is so well known as the basis of Mr. Burke's plan for conciliation with America. It was used against him, to show that Parliament might legislate for unrepresented counties; but it was retorted by him, with much greater force, as a proof from experience, and an acknowledgment from the Legislature, that counties in that situation had no security against misrule. The Petition of the inhabitants of Cheshire, which was adopted as the preamble of the Act, complained that they had neither knight nor burgess in Parliament for the said county-palatine; and that the said inhabitants, "for lack thereof, have been oftentimes touched and grieved with acts and statutes made within the said court." On this recital the Statute proceeds:—"For remedy thereof may it please your Highness, that it may be enacted, that from the end of this present session, the said county-palatine shall have two knights for the said county-palatine, and likewise two citizens to be burgesses for the city of Chester."

The Statute enabling Durham to send knights and burgesses to Parliament, which has been less frequently quoted, is still more explicit on the purposes of the present argument:—

"Whereas the inhabitants of the said county-palatine of Durham have not hitherto had the liberty and privilege of electing and sending any knights and burgesses to the High Court of Parliament, although the inhabitants of the said county-palatine are liable to all payments, rates, and subsidies granted by Parliament, equally with the inhabitants of other counties, cities, and boroughs in this kingdom, who have their knights and burgesses in the Parliament, and are therefore concerned equally with others the inhabitants of this kingdom to have knights and burgesses in the said High Court of Parliament, of their own election, to represent the condition of their county, as the inhabitants of other counties, cities, and boroughs of this kingdom have.... Wherefore, be it enacted, that the said county-palatine of Durham may have two knights for the same county, and the city of Durham two citizens to be burgesses for the same city, for ever hereafter, to serve in the High Court of Parliament... The elections of the knights to serve for the said county, from time to time hereafter, to be made by the greater number of freeholders of the said county-palatine, which from time to time shall be present at such elections, accordingly as is used in other counties in this your Majesty's kingdom; and the election of the said burgesses for the city of Durham, to be made from time to time by the major part of the mayor, aldermen, and freemen of the said city of Durham, which from time to time shall be present at such elections." This Statute does not, like the Chester Act, allege that any specific evil had arisen from the previous want of representatives; but it recognises, as a general principle of the English constitution, that the interests of every unrepresented district are in danger of being overlooked or sacrificed, and that the inhabitants of such districts are therefore interested to have knights and burgesses in Parliament, "of their own election, to represent the condition of their country."

The principle is, in effect, as applicable to towns as to counties. The town of Newcastle had then as evident an interest in the welfare of the county of Durham, as the county of Warwick can now have in the prosperity of the town of Birmingham; but the members for Newcastle were not considered, by this statute, as sufficient guardians of the prosperity of the county of Durham. Even the knights who were to serve for the county, were not thought to dispense with the burgesses to serve for the city. As we have before observed, the distinct interests of country and town were always, on such occasions, provided for by our ancestors; and *a principle* was thereby established, that every great community, with distinct interest, ought to have separate representatives.

It is also observable, that the right of suffrage is not given to all the inhabitants, nor even to all the taxable inhabitants, but to the freeholders of the county, and freemen of the city,—who have a common interest and fellow-feeling with the whole. As these electors were likely to partake the sentiments of the rest of the inhabitants, and as every public measure must affect both classes alike, the members chosen by such a part of the people were considered as virtually representing all.—The claim to representation is acknowledged as belonging to all districts and communities, to all classes and interests,—but not to all men. Some degree of actual election was held necessary to virtual representation. The guardians of the interest of the country were to be, to use the language of the preamble, "of their own election;" though it evidently appears from the enactments, that these words imported only an election by a considerable portion of them. It is also to be observed, that there is no trace in this Act of a care to proportion the number of the new representatives to the population of the district, though a very gross deviation on either side would probably have been avoided.

When we speak of *principles* on this subject, we are not to be understood as ascribing to them the character of rules of law, or of axioms of science. They were maxims of constitutional policy, to which there is a visible, though not a uniform, reference in the acts of our forefathers. They were more or less regarded, according to the character of those who directed the public councils: the wisest and most generous men made the nearest approaches to their observance. But in the application of these, as well as of all other political maxims, it was often necessary to yield to circumstances,—to watch for opportunities,—to consult the temper of the people, the condition of the country, and the dispositions of powerful leaders. It is from want of due regard to considerations like these, that the theory of the English representation has, of late years, been disfigured by various and opposite kinds of reasoners. Some refuse to acknowledge any principles on this subject, but those most general considerations of expediency and abstract justice, which are applicable to all governments, and to every situation of mankind. But these remote principles shed too faint a light to guide us on our path; and can seldom be directly applied with any advantage to human affairs. Others represent the whole constitution, as contained in the written laws; and treat every principle as vague or visionary, which is not sanctioned by some legal authority. A third class, considering (rightly) the representation as originating only in usage, and incessantly though insensibly altered in the course of time, erroneously infer, that it is altogether a matter of coarse and confused practice, incapable of being reduced to any theory. The truth is, however, that out of the best parts of that practice have gradually arisen a body of maxims, which guide our judgment in each particular case; and which, though beyond the letter of the law, are better defined, and more near the course of business, than general notions of expediency or justice. Often disregarded, and never rigorously adhered to, they have no support but a general conviction, growing with experience, of their fitness and value. The mere speculator disdains them as beggarly details: the mere lawyer asks for the statute or case on which they rest: the mere practical politician scorns them as airy visions. But these intermediate maxims constitute the principles of the British constitution, as distinguished, on the one hand, from abstract notions of government, and, on the other, from the provisions of law, or the course of practice. "Civil knowledge," says Lord Bacon, "is of all others the most immersed in matter, and the hardliest reduced to axioms." Politics, therefore, if they should ever be reduced to a science, will require the greatest number of intermediate laws, to connect its most general principles with the variety and intricacy of the public concerns. But in every branch of knowledge, we are told by the same great Master, (Novum Organum,) "that while generalities are barren, and the multiplicity of single facts present nothing but confusion, the middle principles alone are solid, orderly, and fruitful."

The nature of virtual representation may be illustrated by the original controversy between Great Britain and America. The Americans alleged, perhaps untruly, that being unrepresented they could not legally be taxed. They, added, with truth, that being unrepresented, they ought not constitutionally to be taxed. But they defended this true position, on a ground untenable in argument. They sought for the constitution in the works of abstract reasoners, instead of searching for it in its own ancient and uniform practice. They were told that virtual, not actual, representation, was the principle of the constitution; and that they were as much virtually represented as the majority of the people of England. In answer to this, they denied that virtual representation was a constitutional principle, instead of denying the fact, that they were virtually represented. Had they chosen the latter ground, their case would have been unanswerable. The unrepresented part of England could not be taxed, without taxing the represented: the laws affected alike the members who passed them, their constituents, and the rest of the people. On the contrary, separate laws might be, and were, made for America: separate taxes might be, and were, laid on her. The case of that country, therefore, was the very reverse of virtual representation. Instead of identity, there was a contrariety of apparent interest. The English land-holder was to be relieved by an American revenue. The prosperity of the English manufacturer was supposed to depend on a monopoly of the American market. Such a system of governing a great nation was repugnant to the principles of a constitution which had solemnly pronounced, that the people of the small territories of Chester and Durham could not be virtually represented without some share of actual representation.—*Edinburgh Review*, vol. xxxiv. p. 477.

B.

The principle of short Parliaments was solemnly declared at the Revolution. On the 29th of January 1689, seven days after the Convention was assembled, the following resolution was adopted by the House of Commons:—"That a committee be appointed to bring in general heads of such things as are absolutely necessary to be considered, for the better securing our Religion, Laws, and Liberties." Of this Committee Mr. Somers was one. On the 2d of February, Sir George Treby, from the Committee thus appointed, reported the general heads on which they had agreed. The 11th article of these general heads was as follows:—"That the too long continuance of the same Parliament be prevented." On the 4th of February it was ordered, "That it be referred to the Committee to distinguish such general heads as are introductive of new laws, from those that are declaratory of ancient rights." On the 7th of the same month, the Committee made their Second Report; and, after going through the declaratory part, which constitutes the Bill of Rights as it now stands, proposed the following, among other clauses, relating to the introduction of new laws:—"And towards the making a more firm and perfect settlement of the said Religion, Laws, and Liberties, and for remedying several defects and inconveniences, it is proposed and advised by [blank left for 'Lords'] and Commons, that there be provision, by new laws, made in such manner, and with such limitations, as by the wisdom and justice of Parliament shall be considered and ordained in the particulars; and in particular, and to the purposes following, viz. for preventing the too long continuance of the same Parliament." The articles which required new laws being thus distinguished, it was resolved on the following day, on the motion of Mr. Somers, "that it be an instruction to the said Committee, to connect, to the vote of the Lords, such parts of the heads passed this House yesterday as are declaratory of ancient rights; leaving out such parts as are introductory of new laws." The declaratory articles were accordingly formed into the Declaration of Rights; and in that state were, by both Houses, presented to the Prince and Princess of Orange, and accepted by them, with the crown of England. But the articles introductive of new laws, though necessarily omitted in a Declaration of Rights, had been adopted without a division by the House of Commons; who thus, at the very moment of the Revolution, determined, "that a firm and perfect settlement of the Religion, Laws, and Liberties," required provision for a new law, "for preventing the too long continuance of the same Parliament."

But though the principle of short Parliaments was thus solemnly recognised at the Revolution, the time of introducing the new law, the means by which its object was to be attained, and the precise term to be fixed for their duration, were reserved for subsequent deliberation. Attempts were made to give effect to the principle in 1692 and 1693, by a Triennial Bill. In the former year, it passed both Houses, but did not receive the Royal Assent: in the latter, it was rejected by the House of Commons. In 1694, after Sir John Somers was raised to the office of Lord Keeper, the Triennial Bill passed into a law.* It was not confined, like the bills under the same title, in the reigns of Charles I. and Charles II., (and with which it is too frequently confounded,) to provisions for securing the frequent sitting of Parliament: it for the first time limited its duration. Till the passing of this bill, Parliament, unless dissolved by the King, might legally have continued till the demise of the Crown,—its only natural and necessary termination.

The Preamble is deserving of serious consideration: — "Whereas, by the ancient laws and statutes of this kingdom, frequent Parliaments ought to be held; and whereas frequent and new Parliaments tend very much to the happy union and good agreement of the King and People." The Act then proceeds, in the first section, to provide for the frequent holding of Parliaments, according to the former laws; and in the second and third sections, by enactments which were before unknown to our laws, to direct, that there shall be *a new Parliament every three years*, and that no Parliament shall have continuance longer than *three years at the farthest*. Here, as at the time of the Declaration of Rights, the holding of Parliaments is carefully distinguished from their election. The two parts of the Preamble refer separately to each of these objects: the frequent holding of Parliaments is declared to be conformable to the ancient laws; but the frequent election of Parliament is considered only as a measure highly expedient on account of its tendency to preserve harmony between the Government and the People.

The principle of the Triennial Act, therefore, seems to be of as high constitutional authority as if it had been inserted in the Bill of Rights itself, from which it was separated only that it might be afterwards carried into effect in a more convenient manner. The particular term of three years is an arrangement of expediency, to which it would be folly to ascribe any great importance. This Act continued in force only for twenty years. Its opponents have often expatiated on the corruption and disorder in elections, and the instability in the national councils which prevailed during that period: but the country was then so much disturbed by the weakness of a new government, and the agitation of a disputed succession, that it is impossible to ascertain whether more frequent elections had any share in augmenting the disorder. At the accession of George I. the duration of Parliament was extended to seven years, by the famous statute called the "Septennial Act," 1 Geo. I. st. 2. c. 38, the preamble of which asserts, that the last provision of the Triennial Act, "if it should continue, may probably at this juncture, when a restless and Popish faction are designing and endeavouring to renew the rebellion within this kingdom, and an invasion from abroad, be destructive to the peace and security of the government." This allegation is now ascertained to have been perfectly true. There is the most complete historical evidence that all the Tories of the kingdom were then engaged in a conspiracy to effect a counter-revolution, — to wrest from the people all the securities which they had obtained for liberty,—to brand them as rebels, and to stigmatise their rulers as usurpers,—and to re-establish the principles of slavery, by the restoration of a family, whose claim to power was founded on their pretended authority. It is beyond all doubt, that a general election at that period would have endangered all these objects. In these circumstances the Septennial Act was passed, because it was necessary to secure liberty. But it was undoubtedly one of the highest exertions of the legislative authority. It was a deviation from the course of the constitution too extensive in its effects, and too dangerous in its example, to be warranted by motives of political expediency: it could be justified only by the necessity of preserving liberty. The Revolution itself was a breach of the laws; and it was as great a deviation from the principles of monarchy, as the Septennial Act could be from the constitution of the House of Commons:—and the latter can only be justified by the same ground of necessity, with that glorious Revolution of which it probably contributed to preserve—would to God we could say perpetuate—the inestimable blessings.

It has been said by some, that as the danger was temporary, the law ought to have been passed only for a time, and that it should have been delayed till the approach of a general election should ascertain, whether a change in the temper of the people had not rendered it unnecessary. But it was necessary, at the *instant*, to confound the hopes of conspirators, who were then supported and animated by the prospect of a general election: and if any period had been fixed for its duration, it might have weakened its effects, as a declaration of the determined resolution of Parliament to stand or fall with the Revolution.

It is now certain, that the conspiracy of the Tories against the House of Hanover, continued till the last years of the reign of George II. The Whigs, who had preserved the fruits of the Revolution, and upheld the tottering throne of the Hanoverian Family during half a century, were, in this state of things, unwilling to repeal a law, for which the reasons had not entirely ceased. The hostility of the Tories to the Protestant succession was not extinguished, till the appearance of their leaders at the court of King George III. proclaimed to the world their hope, that Jacobite principles might re-ascend the throne of England with a monarch of the House of Brunswick.

The effects of the Septennial Act on the constitution were materially altered in the late reign, by an innovation in the exercise of the prerogative of dissolution. This important prerogative is the buckler of the monarchy: it is intended for great emergencies, when its exercise may be the only means of averting immediate danger from the throne: it is strictly a defensive right. As no necessity arose, under the two first Georges, for its defensive exercise, it lay, during that period, in a state of almost total inactivity. Only one Parliament, under these two Princes, was dissolved till its seventh year. The same inoffensive maxims were pursued during the early part of the reign of George III. In the year 1784, the power of dissolution, hitherto reserved for the defence of the monarchy, was, for the first time, employed to support the power of an Administration. The majority of the House of Commons had, in 1782, driven one Administration from office, and compelled another to retire. Its right to interpose, with decisive weight, in the choice of ministers, as well as the adoption of measures, seemed by these vigorous exertions to be finally established. George II. had, indeed, often been compelled to receive ministers whom he hated: but his successor, more tenacious of his prerogative, and more inflexible in his resentment, did not so easily brook the subjection to which he thought himself about to be reduced. When the latter, in 1784, again

* 6 W. & M. c. 2.

saw his Ministers threatened with expulsion by a majority of the House of Commons, he found a Prime Minister who, trusting to his popularity, ventured to make common cause with him, and to brave that Parliamentary disapprobation to which the prudence or principle of both his predecessors had induced them to yield. Not content with this great victory, he proceeded, by a dissolution of Parliament, to inflict such an exemplary punishment on the majority, as might deter all future ones from following their dangerous example.

The ministers of 1806 gave some countenance to Mr. Pitt's precedent, by a very reprehensible dissolution: and in 1807, its full consequences were unfolded. The House of Commons was then openly threatened with a dissolution, if a majority should vote against Ministers; and in pursuance of this threat, the Parliament was actually dissolved. From that moment, the new prerogative of penal dissolution was added to all the other means of ministerial influence.

Of all the silent revolutions which have materially changed the English government, without any alteration in the latter of the law, there is, perhaps, none more fatal to the constitution than the power thus introduced by Mr. Pitt, and strengthened by his followers. And it is the more dangerous, because it is hardly capable of being counteracted by direct laws. The prerogative of dissolution, being a means of defence on sudden emergencies, is scarcely to be limited by law. There is, however, an indirect, but effectual mode of meeting its abuse:—by shortening the duration of Parliaments, the punishment of dissolution will be divested of its terrors. While its defensive power will be unimpaired, its efficacy, as a means of influence, will be nearly destroyed. The attempt to reduce Parliament to a greater degree of dependence, will thus be defeated; due reparation be made to the constitution; and future ministers taught, by a useful example of just retaliation, that the Crown is not likely to be finally the gainer, in struggles to convert a necessary prerogative into a means of unconstitutional influence.—*Ibid.* p. 494.

THE END.

www.ingramcontent.com/pod-product-compliance
Lightning Source LLC
LaVergne TN
LVHW021225110826
845150LV00002B/248

* 9 7 8 1 4 2 5 5 6 4 1 0 0 *